ARMSTRONG'S HANDBOOK OF HUMAN RESOURCE MANAGEMENT PRACTICE

ALSO AVAILABLE BY MICHAEL ARMSTRONG

Armstrong's Handbook of Management and Leadership

Armstrong's Essential Human Resource Management Practice

Armstrong's Handbook of Strategic Human Resource Management

Armstrong's Handbook of Performance Management

Armstrong's Handbook of Reward Management Practice

How to Manage People

How to be an Even Better Manager

Human Capital Management (with Angela Baron)

The Reward Management Toolkit (with Ann Cummings)

Evidence-based Reward Management (with Duncan Brown and Peter Reilly)

MICHAEL ARMSTRONG
AND STEPHEN TAYLOR

13TH EDITION

ARMSTRONG'S HANDBOOK OF HUMAN RESOURCE MANAGEMENT PRACTICE

KoganPage

Publisher's note

Every possible effort has been made to ensure that the information contained in this book is accurate at the time of going to press, and the publishers and authors cannot accept responsibility for any errors or omissions, however caused. No responsibility for loss or damage occasioned to any person acting, or refraining from action, as a result of the material in this publication can be accepted by the editor, the publisher or any of the authors.

First edition published in 1977 as *A Handbook of Personnel Management Practice* by Kogan Page Limited
Seventh edition published in 1999 as *A Handbook of Human Resource Management Practice*
Eleventh edition published in 2009 as *Armstrong's Handbook of Human Resource Management Practice*
Twelfth edition 2012
Thirteenth edition 2014
Reprinted 2014, 2015

2nd Floor, 45 Gee Street
London EC1V 3RS
United Kingdom
www.koganpage.com

1518 Walnut Street, Suite 1100
Philadelphia PA 19102
USA

4737/23 Ansari Road
Daryaganj
New Delhi 110002
India

ISBN 978 0 7494 6964 1
E-ISBN 978 0 7494 6965 8

British Library Cataloguing-in-Publication Data

A CIP record for this book is available from the British Library.

Library of Congress Cataloging-in-Publication Data

Armstrong, Michael, 1928-
Armstrong's handbook of human resource management practice / Michael Armstrong. – 13th Edition.
pages cm
ISBN 978-0-7494-6964-1 – ISBN 978-0-7494-6965-8 (ebk) 1. Personnel management–Handbooks, manuals, etc. I. Title. II. Title: Handbook of human resource management practice.
HF5549.17.A76 2013
658.3–dc23

2013038558

Typeset by Graphicraft Limited, Hong Kong
Print production managed by Jellyfish
Printed and bound in the UK by Ashford Colour press Ltd

CONTENTS IN BRIEF

CONTENTS

LIST OF FIGURES

LIST OF TABLES

LIST OF EXHIBITS

PREFACE TO THE 13TH EDITION

The 13th edition of the *Handbook of Human Resource Management Practice* includes an entirely new part containing three chapters covering the increasingly important subject of international human resource management. Other new chapters have been added on rewarding special groups and employment law. The chapters on HRM, motivation and engagement have been completely revised. Apart from these substantial changes, the handbook has been brought up-to-date by reference to the findings of a number of significant research projects and other investigations of how HRM operates in practice. The plan of the book is illustrated in the 'route map' shown in Figure 0.1.

The companion website at **www.koganpage.com/armstrong/HRMPresources** provides extensive additional resources for lecturers and students. These comprise:

- A lecturers' manual containing notes on how teaching could be organized by reference to the chapters in the main text and the supplementary material in the manual. Suggestions are made on various kinds of semesters and guidance is provided on the links between the handbook text and CIPD programmes. The manual includes sections for each of the first 43 general HRM chapters containing a summary of the main learning points, an outline of the subject matter, discussion points and questions with comments on the points to be considered. There are 136 multiple choice questions, 78 case studies and four role playing exercises. Most of the chapters contain supplementary abstracts from relevant HRM literature – a total of 150.
- Additional material is provided for lecturers in the shape of 613 PowerPoint slides with notes covering all the chapters except the toolkits.
- A students' manual consisting of material which can be used to reinforce the contents of the main book. Summaries of each chapter are provided and in addition most of the chapters include supplementary abstracts from relevant HRM literature (150 in all). To assist in revision, the extra material includes 135 multiple choice questions and 420 'flash' cards containing questions and answers about key aspects of the subject matter. There are also 43 case studies.
- A glossary of HRM terms (988 entries).
- An HRM bibliography (832 entries).

FIGURE 0.1 *Handbook of Human Resource Management Practice* route map

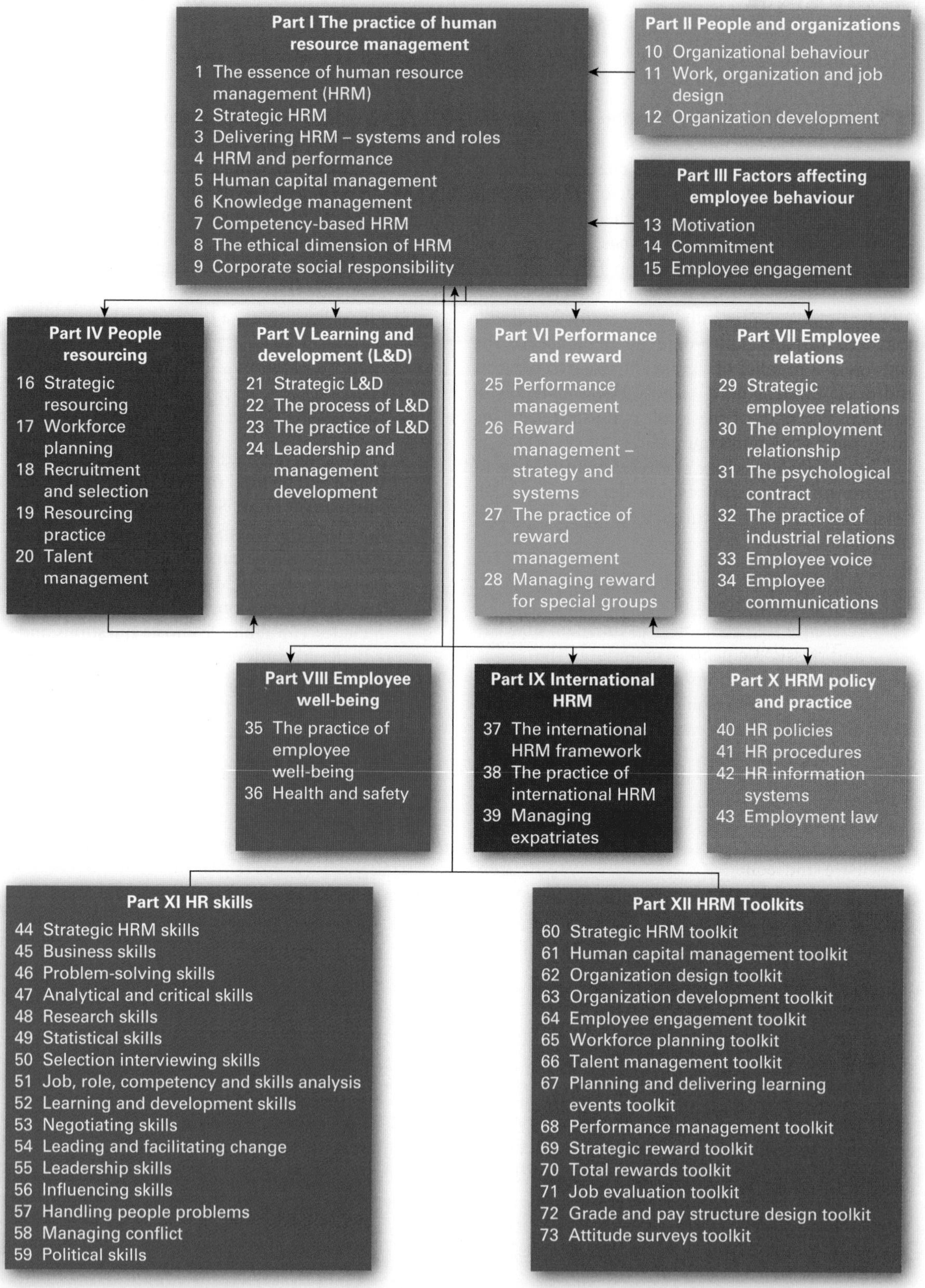
Part I The practice of human resource management
1 The essence of human resource management (HRM)
2 Strategic HRM
3 Delivering HRM – systems and roles
4 HRM and performance
5 Human capital management
6 Knowledge management
7 Competency-based HRM
8 The ethical dimension of HRM
9 Corporate social responsibility
Part II People and organizations
10 Organizational behaviour
11 Work, organization and job design
12 Organization development
Part III Factors affecting employee behaviour
13 Motivation
14 Commitment
15 Employee engagement
Part IV People resourcing
16 Strategic resourcing
17 Workforce planning
18 Recruitment and selection
19 Resourcing practice
20 Talent management
Part V Learning and development (L&D)
21 Strategic L&D
22 The process of L&D
23 The practice of L&D
24 Leadership and management development
Part VI Performance and reward
25 Performance management
26 Reward management – strategy and systems
27 The practice of reward management
28 Managing reward for special groups
Part VII Employee relations
29 Strategic employee relations
30 The employment relationship
31 The psychological contract
32 The practice of industrial relations
33 Employee voice
34 Employee communications
Part VIII Employee well-being
35 The practice of employee well-being
36 Health and safety
Part IX International HRM
37 The international HRM framework
38 The practice of international HRM
39 Managing expatriates
Part X HRM policy and practice
40 HR policies
41 HR procedures
42 HR information systems
43 Employment law
Part XI HR skills
44 Strategic HRM skills
45 Business skills
46 Problem-solving skills
47 Analytical and critical skills
48 Research skills
49 Statistical skills
50 Selection interviewing skills
51 Job, role, competency and skills analysis
52 Learning and development skills
53 Negotiating skills
54 Leading and facilitating change
55 Leadership skills
56 Influencing skills
57 Handling people problems
58 Managing conflict
59 Political skills
Part XII HRM Toolkits
60 Strategic HRM toolkit
61 Human capital management toolkit
62 Organization design toolkit
63 Organization development toolkit
64 Employee engagement toolkit
65 Workforce planning toolkit
66 Talent management toolkit
67 Planning and delivering learning events toolkit
68 Performance management toolkit
69 Strategic reward toolkit
70 Total rewards toolkit
71 Job evaluation toolkit
72 Grade and pay structure design toolkit
73 Attitude surveys toolkit

PART I

The practice of human resource management

PART I CONTENTS

Introduction

Human resource management (HRM) is a comprehensive and coherent approach to the employment and development of people. HRM can be regarded as a philosophy about how people should be managed, which is underpinned by a number of theories relating to the behaviour of people and organizations. It is concerned with the contribution it can make to improving organizational effectiveness through people but it is, or should be, equally concerned with the ethical dimension – how people should be treated in accordance with a set of moral values. HRM involves the application of policies and practices in the fields of organization design and development, employee resourcing, learning and development, performance and reward and the provision of services that enhance the well-being of employees. These are based on human resource (HR) strategies that are integrated with one another and aligned to the business strategy.

Some people object to the term 'human resources' because it implies that people can be manipulated like any other factor of production. Instead they favour 'people management'. But HRM is the most commonly used term.

Whatever term is adopted the approach should be based on the principle laid down by Schneider (1987: 450): 'Organizations are the people in them; that people make the place.' He went on to explain that: 'Positive job attitudes for workers in an organization can be expected when the natural inclinations of the persons there are allowed to be reflected in their behaviours by the kinds of processes and structures that have evolved there.'

As Keegan and Francis (2010: 873) noted: HR work is now 'largely framed as a business issue'. The emphasis is on business alignment and strategic fit. These are important requirements but focusing on them can lead HR professionals to place correspondingly less emphasis on employee needs and motivations when developing their new and altered arrangements. A simplistic view of the business imperative permits little room for considering how HR strategy should impact on individual employees. HRM indeed aims to support the achievement of business goals but, equally, it should aim to build a relationship based on trust, openness and personal fulfilment.

This first part of the handbook deals with the broad areas and concerns of the practice of HRM covering its conceptual basis, the strategic framework within which HRM activities take place and the various factors that affect it, including the impact of HRM on performance, the specific functions of human capital management, knowledge management and competency-based HRM and, importantly, the ethical and social responsible considerations that need to be taken into account when practising HRM. International HRM is dealt with in Part IX.

References

Keegan, A and Francis, H (2010) Practitioner talk: the changing textscape of HRM and emergence of HR business partnership, *The International Journal of Human Resource Management*, 21 (6), pp 873–98

Schneider, B (1987) The people make the place, *Personnel Psychology*, 40 (3), pp 437–53

01
The essence of human resource management (HRM)

KEY CONCEPTS AND TERMS

Added value
Agency theory
AMO theory
Commitment
Contextual model of HRM
Contingency theory
European model of HRM
5-P model of HRM
Hard HRM
Harvard framework
HR philosophy
Human capital theory
Human relations
Human resource management (HRM)
Humanism
Institutional theory
Matching model of HRM
Motivation
Organizational behaviour theory
Organizational capability
Resource-based theory
Resource dependence theory
Soft HRM
Strategic alignment
Strategic human resource management (SHRM)
Transaction costs theory
Unitarist

LEARNING OUTCOMES

On completing this chapter you should be able to define these key concepts. You should also know about:

- The fundamental concept of HRM and how it developed
- The meaning of HRM
- The goals of HRM
- The philosophy of HRM
- The underpinning theories
- The reservations made about HRM
- Models of HRM
- The position of HRM today

Introduction – the HRM concept

Human resource management (HRM) is concerned with all aspects of how people are employed and managed in organizations. It covers the activities of strategic HRM, human capital management, knowledge management, corporate social responsibility, organization development, resourcing (workforce planning, recruitment and selection and talent management), learning and development, performance and reward management, employee relations, employee well-being and the provision of employee services. It also has an international dimension. As described in Chapter 3, HRM is delivered through the HR architecture of systems and structures, the HR function and, importantly, line management.

The practice of referring to people as resources as if they were any other factor of production is often criticised. Osterby and Coster (1992: 31) argued that: 'The term "human resources" reduces people to the same category of value as materials, money and technology – all resources, and resources are only valuable to the extent they can be exploited or leveraged into economic value.' People management is sometimes preferred as an alternative, but in spite of its connotations, HRM is most commonly used.

The development of the HRM concept

The term HRM has largely taken over that of 'personnel management', which took over that of 'labour management' in the 1940s, which took over that of 'welfare' in the 1920s (the latter process emerged in the munitions factories of the First World War). HRM largely replaced the human relations approach to managing people founded by Elton Mayo (1933) who based his beliefs on the outcome of the research project conducted in the 1920s known as the Hawthorne studies. Members of this school believed that productivity was directly related to job satisfaction and that the output of people would be high if someone they respected took an interest in them. HRM also shifted the emphasis away from humanism – the belief held by writers such as Likert (1961) and McGregor (1960) that human factors are paramount in the study of organizational behaviour and that people should be treated as responsible and progressive beings.

An early reference to human resources was made by Bakke (1966). Later, Armstrong (1977: 13) observed that in an enterprise 'the key resource is people'. But HRM did not emerge in a fully fledged form until the 1980s through what might be called its founding fathers. These were the US academics Charles Fombrun and his colleagues in the 'matching model', and Michael Beer and his colleagues in the 'Harvard framework' as described on page 9.

In the UK they were followed by a number of commentators who developed, explained and frequently criticized the concept of human resource management. Legge (2005: 101) commented that: 'The term [HRM] was taken up by both UK managers (for example, Armstrong, 1987; Fowler, 1987) and UK academics'. Hendry and Pettigrew (1990: 18) stated that HRM was 'heavily normative from the start: it provided a diagnosis and proposed solutions'. They also mentioned that: 'What HRM did at this point was to provide a label to wrap around some of the observable changes, while providing a focus for challenging deficiencies – in attitudes, scope, coherence, and direction – of existing personnel management' (ibid: 20). Armstrong (1987: 31) argued that:

> HRM is regarded by some personnel managers as just a set of initials or old wine in new bottles. It could indeed be no more and no less than another name for personnel management, but as usually perceived, at least it has the virtue of emphasising the virtue of treating people as a key resource, the management of which is the direct concern of top management as part of the strategic planning processes of the enterprise. Although there is nothing new in the idea, insufficient attention has been paid to it in many organizations.

However, commentators such as Guest (1987) and Storey (1995) regarded HRM as a substantially different model built on unitarism (employees share the same interests as employers), individualism, high commitment and strategic alignment (integrating HR strategy with the business strategy). It was also claimed that HRM was more holistic than traditional personnel management and that, importantly, it emphasized the notion that people should be regarded as assets rather than variable costs.

The conceptual framework of HRM

HRM as conceived in the 1980s had a conceptual framework consisting of a philosophy underpinned by a number of theories drawn from the behavioural sciences and from the fields of strategic management, human capital and industrial relations. The HRM philosophy has been heavily criticized by academics as being managerialist and manipulative but this criticism has subsided, perhaps because it became increasingly evident that the term HRM had been adopted as a synonym for what used to be called personnel management. As noted by Storey (2007: 6): 'In its generic broad and popular sense it [HRM] simply refers to any system of people management.'

HRM practice today

HRM practice is no longer governed by the original philosophy – if it ever was. It is simply what HR people and line managers do. Few references are made to the HRM conceptual framework. This is a pity – an appreciation of the goals, philosophy and underpinning theories of HRM and the various HRM models provides a sound basis for understanding and developing HR practice. But account needs to be taken of the limitations of that philosophy as expressed by the critics of HRM set out later in this chapter.

Aim of this chapter

The aim of this chapter is to remedy this situation. It starts with a selection of definitions (there have been many) and elaborates on these by examining HRM goals. Because the original concept of HRM is best understood in terms of its philosophy and underpinning theories these are dealt with in the next two sections. Reference is then made to the reservations made about HRM but it is noted that while these need to be understood, much of what HRM originally set out to do is still valid. However, as explained in the next section of the chapter, HRM is more diverse than interpretations of the original concept can lead us to believe. This is illustrated by the various models summarized in this section which provide further insights into the nature of HRM. The chapter ends with an assessment of where the concept of HRM has got to now. Following this analysis the next two chapters explain how in general terms HRM is planned through the processes of strategic HRM and delivered through the HR architecture and system, the HR function and its members, and, importantly, line managers.

HRM defined

Human resource management can be defined as a strategic, integrated and coherent approach to the employment, development and well-being of the people working in organizations. It was defined by Boxall and Purcell (2003: 1) as 'all those activities associated with the management of employment relationships in the firm'. A later comprehensive definition was offered by Watson (2010: 919):

> HRM is the managerial utilisation of the efforts, knowledge, capabilities and committed behaviours which people contribute to an authoritatively co-ordinated human enterprise as part of an employment exchange (or more temporary contractual arrangement) to carry out work tasks in a way which enables the enterprise to continue into the future.

The goals of HRM

The goals of HRM are to:

- support the organization in achieving its objectives by developing and implementing human resource (HR) strategies that are integrated with the business strategy (strategic HRM);
- contribute to the development of a high-performance culture;
- ensure that the organization has the talented, skilled and engaged people it needs;
- create a positive employment relationship between management and employees and a climate of mutual trust;

- encourage the application of an ethical approach to people management.

An earlier list of HR goals was made by Dyer and Holder (1988: 22–28) who analysed them under the headings of contribution (what kind of employee behaviour is expected?), composition (what headcount, staffing ratio and skill mix?), competence (what general level of ability is desired?) and commitment (what level of employee attachment and identification?). Guest (1987) suggested that the four goals of HRM were strategic integration, high commitment, high quality and flexibility. And Boxall (2007: 63) proposed that 'the mission of HRM is to support the viability of the firm through stabilizing a cost-effective and socially legitimate system of labour management'.

The philosophy of human resource management

Doubts were expressed by Noon (1992) as to whether HRM was a map, a model or a theory. But it is evident that the original concept could be interpreted as a philosophy for managing people in that it contained a number of general principles and beliefs as to how that should be done. The following explanation of HRM philosophy was made by Legge (1989: 25) whose analysis of a number of HRM models identified the following common themes:

> That human resource policies should be integrated with strategic business planning and used to reinforce an appropriate (or change an inappropriate) organizational culture, that human resources are valuable and a source of competitive advantage, that they may be tapped most effectively by mutually consistent policies that promote commitment and which, as a consequence, foster a willingness in employees to act flexibly in the interests of the 'adaptive organization's' pursuit of excellence.

Storey (2001: 7) noted that the beliefs of HRM included the assumptions that it is the human resource that gives competitive edge, that the aim should be to enhance employee commitment, that HR decisions are of strategic importance and that therefore HR policies should be integrated into the business strategy.

Underpinning theories of HRM

The original notion of HRM had a strong theoretical base. Guest (1987: 505) commented that: 'Human resource management appears to lean heavily on theories of commitment and motivation and other ideas derived from the field of organizational behaviour.' A number of other theories, especially the resource-based view, have contributed to the understanding of purpose and meaning of HRM. These theories are summarized below.

Commitment

The significance in HRM theory of organizational commitment (the strength of an individual's identification with, and involvement in, a particular organization) was highlighted in a seminal *Harvard Business Review* article by Richard Walton (1985).

Source review

From control to commitment – Walton (1985: 77)

Workers respond best – and most creatively – not when they are tightly controlled by management, placed in narrowly defined jobs and treated as an unwelcome necessity, but, instead, when they are given broader responsibilities, encouraged to contribute and helped to take satisfaction in their work. It should come as no surprise that eliciting commitment – and providing the environment in which it can flourish – pays tangible dividends for the individual and for the company.

The traditional concept of organizational commitment resembles the more recent notion of organizational engagement (see Chapter 15).

Motivation

Motivation theory explains the factors that affect goal-directed behaviour and therefore influences the approaches used in HRM to enhance engagement (the situation in which people are committed to their work and the organization and are motivated to achieve high levels of performance).

The resource-based view

Resource-based theory expressed as 'the resource-based view' states that competitive advantage is achieved if a firm's resources are valuable, rare and costly to imitate. It is claimed that HRM can play a major part in ensuring that the firm's human resources meet these criteria.

Organizational behaviour theory

Organizational behaviour theory describes how people within their organizations act individually or in groups and how organizations function in terms of their structure, processes and culture. It therefore influences HRM approaches to organization design and development and enhancing organizational capability (the capacity of an organization to function effectively in order to achieve desired results).

Contingency theory

Contingency theory states that HRM practices are dependent on the organization's environment and circumstances. This means that, as Paauwe (2004: 36) explained: 'The relationship between the relevant independent variables (eg HRM policies and practices) and the dependent variable (performance) will vary according to the influences such as company size, age and technology, capital intensity, degree of unionization, industry/sector ownership and location.'

Contingency theory is associated with the notion of fit – the need to achieve congruence between an organization's HR strategies, policies and practices and its business strategies within the context of its external and internal environment. This is a key concept in strategic HRM.

Institutional theory

Organizations conform to internal and external environmental pressures in order to gain legitimacy and acceptance.

Human capital theory

Human capital theory is concerned with how people in an organization contribute their knowledge, skills and abilities to enhancing organizational capability and the significance of that contribution.

Resource dependence theory

Resource dependence theory states that groups and organizations gain power over each other by controlling valued resources. HRM activities are assumed to reflect the distribution of power in the system.

AMO theory

The 'AMO' formula as set out by Boxall and Purcell (2003) states that performance is a function of Ability + Motivation + Opportunity to Participate. HRM practices therefore impact on individual performance if they encourage discretionary effort, develop skills and provide people with the opportunity to perform. The formula provides the basis for developing HR systems that attend to employees' interests, namely their skill requirements, motivations and the quality of their job.

Social exchange theory

Employees will reciprocate their contribution to the organization if they perceive that the organization has treated them well.

Transaction costs theory

Transaction costs economics assumes that businesses develop organizational structures and systems that economize the costs of the transactions (interrelated exchange activities) that take place during the course of their operations.

Agency theory

Agency theory states that the role of the managers of a business is to act on behalf of the owners of the business as their agents. But there is a separation between the owners (the principals) and the agents (the managers) and the principals may not have complete control over their agents. The latter may therefore act in ways that are against the interests of those principals. Agency theory indicates that it is desirable to operate a system of incentives for agents, ie directors or managers, to motivate and reward acceptable behaviour.

Reservations about the original concept of HRM

On the face of it, the original concept of HRM as described above had much to offer, at least to management. But for some time, HRM was a controversial topic, especially in academic circles. The main reservations as set out below have been that HRM promises more than it delivers and that its morality is suspect:

- Guest (1991: 149) referred to the 'optimistic but ambiguous label of human resource management'.
- HRM 'remains an uncertain and imprecise notion' Noon (1992: 16).
- 'The HRM rhetoric presents it as an all or nothing process which is ideal for any organization, despite the evidence that different business environments require different approaches'. (Armstrong, 2000: 577)
- HRM is simplistic – as Fowler (1987: 3) wrote: 'The HRM message to top management tends to be beguilingly simple. Don't bother too much about the content or techniques of personnel management, it says. Just manage the context. Get out from behind your desk, bypass the hierarchy, and go and talk to people. That way you will unlock an enormous potential for improved performance.'
- The unitarist approach to industrial relations implicit in HRM (the belief that management and employees share the same concerns and it is therefore in both their interests to work together) is questionable. Fowler (1987: 3) commented that: 'At the heart of the concept is the complete identification of employees with the aims and values of the business – employee involvement but on the company's terms. Power in the HRM system remains very firmly in the hands of the employer. Is it really possible to claim full mutuality when at the end of the day the employer can decide unilaterally to close the company or sell it to someone else?' Later, Ramsey *et al* (2000: 521) questioned the unitarist assumption underlying much mainstream management theory that claims that everyone benefits from managerial innovation.
- HRM is 'macho-management dressed up as benevolent paternalism' Legge (1998: 42).
- HRM is manipulative. Willmott (1993: 534) asserted that: 'any (corporate) practice/value is as good as any other so long as it secures the compliance of employees'. HRM was dubbed by the Labour Research Department (1989: 8) as 'human resource manipulation'. John Storey (2007: 4) referred to 'the potential manipulative nature of seeking to shape human behaviour at work'.
- HRM is managerialist. 'The analysis of employment management has become increasingly myopic and progressively more irrelevant to the daily experience of being employed. While the reasons for this development are immensely complex... it is primarily a consequence of the adoption of the managerialist conception of the discourse of HRM' (Delbridge and Keenoy, 2010: 813).
- HRM overemphasizes business needs. Keegan and Francis (2010) have rightly criticized the increasing focus on the business partnership role of HR at the expense of its function as an employee champion. An illustration of this is provided by the Professional Map produced by the British Chartered Institute of Personnel and Development (CIPD), which as stated by the CIPD (2013: 2): 'Sets out standards for HR professionals around the world: the activities, knowledge and behaviours needed for success.' The map refers to 'business' 82 times but to 'ethics' only once and 'ethical' only twice.

These concerns merit attention, but the more important messages conveyed by the original notion of HRM such as the need for strategic integration, the treatment of employees as assets rather than costs, the desirability of gaining commitment, the virtues of partnership and participation and the key role of line managers are still valid and are now generally accepted, and the underpinning theories are as relevant today as they ever were.

And it should be remembered that these objections, with the exception of the last one, mainly apply to the original concept of HRM. But today, as explained in the final section of this chapter, HRM in action does not necessarily conform to this concept as a whole. The practice of HRM is diverse. Dyer and Holder (1988) pointed out that HRM goals vary according to competitive choices, technologies, characteristics of employees (eg could be different for managers) and the state of the labour market. Boxall (2007: 48) referred to 'the profound diversity' of HRM and observed that: 'Human resource management covers a vast array of activities and shows a huge range of variations across occupations, organizational levels, business units, firms, industries and societies.' There are in fact a number of different models of HRM as described below.

Models of HRM

The most familiar models defining what HRM is and how it operates are as follows.

The matching model of HRM

Fombrun *et al* (1984) proposed the 'matching model', which indicated that HR systems and the organization structure should be managed in a way that is congruent with organizational strategy. This point was made in their classic statement that: 'The critical management task is to align the formal structure and human resource systems so that they drive the strategic objectives of the organization' (ibid: 37). Thus they took the first steps towards the concept of strategic HRM.

The Harvard model of HRM

Beer *et al* (1984) produced what has become known as the 'Harvard framework'. They started with the proposition that: 'Human resource management (HRM) involves all management decisions and actions that affect the nature of the relationship between the organization and employees – its human resources' (ibid: 1). They believed that: 'Today... many pressures are demanding a broader, more comprehensive and more strategic perspective with regard to the organization's human resources' (ibid: 4). They also stressed that it was necessary to adopt 'a longer-term perspective in managing people and consideration of people as a potential asset rather than merely a variable cost' (ibid: 6). Beer and his colleagues were the first to underline the HRM tenet that it belongs to line managers. They suggested that HRM had two characteristic features: 1) line managers accept more responsibility for ensuring the alignment of competitive strategy and HR policies; 2) HR has the mission of setting policies that govern how HR activities are developed and implemented in ways that make them more mutually reinforcing.

Contextual model of HRM

The contextual model of HRM emphasizes the importance of environmental factors by including variables such as the influence of social, institutional and political forces that have been underestimated in other models. The latter, at best, consider the context as a contingency variable. The contextual approach is broader, integrating the human resource management system in the environment in which it is developed. According to Martin-Alcázar *et al* (2005: 638): 'Context both conditions and is conditioned by the HRM strategy.' A broader set of stakeholders is involved in the formulation and implementation of human resource strategies that is referred to by Schuler and Jackson (2000: 229) as a 'multiple stakeholder framework'. These stakeholders may be external as well as internal and both influence and are influenced by strategic decisions

The 5-P model of HRM

As formulated by Schuler (1992) the 5-P model of HRM describes how HRM operates under the five headings of:

1. HR philosophy – a statement of how the organization regards its human resources,

the role they play in the overall success of the business, and how they should be treated and managed.

2 HR policies – these provide guidelines for action on people-related business issues and for the development of HR programmes and practices based on strategic needs.

3 HR programmes – these are shaped by HR policies and consist of coordinated HR efforts intended to initiate and manage organizational change efforts prompted by strategic business needs.

4 HR practices – these are the activities carried out in implementing HR policies and programmes. They include resourcing, learning and development, performance and reward management, employee relations and administration.

5 HR processes – these are the formal procedures and methods used to put HR strategic plans and policies into effect.

European model of HRM

Brewster (1993) described a European model of HRM as follows:

- *environment* – established legal framework;
- *objectives* – organizational objectives and social concern – people as a key resource;
- *focus* – cost/benefits analysis, also environment;
- *relationship with employees* – union and non-union;
- *relationship with line managers* – specialist/line liaison;
- *role of HR specialist* – specialist managers – ambiguity, tolerance, flexibility.

The main distinction between this model and what Brewster referred to as 'the prescribed model' was that the latter involves deregulation (no legal framework), no trade unions and a focus on organizational objectives but not on social concern.

As set out by Mabey *et al* (1998: 107) the characteristics of the European model are:

- dialogue between social partners;
- emphasis on social responsibility;
- multicultural organizations;
- participation in decision-making;
- continuous learning.

The hard and soft HRM models

Storey (1989: 8) distinguished between the 'hard' and 'soft' versions of HRM. He wrote that: 'The hard one emphasises the quantitative, calculative and business-strategic aspects of managing human resources in as "rational" a way as for any other economic factor. By contrast, the soft version traces its roots to the human-relations school; it emphasizes communication, motivation and leadership.'

However, it was pointed out by Keenoy (1997: 838) that 'hard and soft HRM are complementary rather than mutually exclusive practices'. Research in eight UK organizations by Truss *et al* (1997) indicated that the distinction between hard and soft HRM was not as precise as some commentators have implied. Their conclusions were as follows.

Source review

Conclusions on hard and soft models of HRM – Truss *et al* (1997: 70)

Even if the rhetoric of HRM is 'soft', the reality is almost always 'hard', with the interests of the organization prevailing over those of the individual. In all the organizations, we found a mixture of both hard and soft approaches. The precise ingredients of this mixture were unique to each organization, which implies that factors such as the external and internal environment of the organization, its strategy, culture and structure all have a vital role to play in the way in which HRM operates.

HRM today

As a description of people management activities in organizations the term HRM is here to stay, even if it is applied diversely or only used as a label to describe traditional personnel management practices. Emphasis is now placed on the need for HR to be strategic and businesslike and to add value, ie to generate extra value (benefit to the business) by the expenditure of effort, time and money on HRM activities. There have been plenty of new interests, concepts and developments, including human capital management, engagement, talent management, competency-based HRM, e-HRM, high performance work systems, and performance and reward management. But these have not been introduced under the banner of the HRM concept as originally defined.

HRM has largely become something that organizations do rather than an aspiration or a philosophy and the term is generally in use as a way of describing the process of managing people. A convincing summary of what HRM means today, which focuses on what HRM is rather than on its philosophy, was provided by Peter Boxall, John Purcell and Patrick Wright (2007), representing the new generation of commentators.

Source review

The meaning of HRM – Boxall *et al* (2007: 1)

Human resource management (HRM), the management of work and people towards desired ends, is a fundamental activity in any organization in which human beings are employed. It is not something whose existence needs to be radically justified: HRM is an inevitable consequence of starting and growing an organization. While there are a myriad of variations in the ideologies, styles, and managerial resources engaged, HRM happens in some form or other. It is one thing to question the *relative* performance of particular models of HRM in particular contexts... It is quite another thing to question the necessity of the HRM process itself, as if organizations cannot survive or grow without making a reasonable attempt at organizing work and managing people.

Key learning points: The essence of human resource management

HRM defined

Human resource management (HRM) is concerned with all aspects of how people are employed and managed in organizations.

Goals of HRM

The goals of HRM are to:

- support the organization in achieving its objectives by developing and implementing human resource (HR) strategies that are integrated with the business strategy (strategic HRM);
- contribute to the development of a high-performance culture;
- ensure that the organization has the talented, skilled and engaged people it needs; create a positive employment relationship between management and employees and a climate of mutual trust;
- encourage the application of an ethical approach to people management.

Philosophy of HRM

The beliefs of HRM included the assumptions that it is the human resource that gives competitive edge, that the aim should be to enhance employee commitment, that HR decisions are of strategic importance and that therefore HR policies should be integrated into the business strategy (Storey, 2001: 7).

Underpinning theories

'Human resource management appears to lean heavily on theories of commitment and motivation and other ideas derived from the field of organizational behaviour' (Guest, 1987: 505).

The diversity of HRM

Many HRM models exist, and practices within different organizations are diverse, often only corresponding to the conceptual version of HRM in a few respects.

Reservations about HRM

On the face of it, the concept of HRM has much to offer, at least to management. But reservations have been expressed about it. There may be something in these criticisms, but the fact remains that as a description of people management activities in organizations HRM is here to stay, even if it is applied diversely or only used as a label to describe traditional personnel management practices.

Questions

1. What is HRM?
2. What was the main message of the Harvard framework?
3. What was the main message of the matching model?
4. What are the goals of HRM?
5. What is the difference between hard and soft HRM?
6. What is the essence of the philosophy of HRM?
7. What is resource-based theory?
8. What is the significance of contingency theory?
9. What are the key reservations made by commentators about the early version of HRM?
10. What is the position of HRM today?

References

Armstrong, M (1977) *A Handbook of Personnel Management Practice*, 1st edn, London, Kogan Page

Armstrong, M (1987) Human resource management: a case of the emperor's new clothes, *Personnel Management*, August, pp 30–35

Armstrong, M (2000) The name has changed but has the game remained the same? *Employee Relations*, 22 (6), pp 576–89

Bakke, E W (1966) *Bonds of Organization: An appraisal of corporate human relations*, Archon, Hamden

Beer, M, Spector, B, Lawrence, P, Quinn Mills, D and Walton, R (1984) *Managing Human Assets*, New York, The Free Press

Boxall, P F (2007) The goals of HRM, in (eds) P Boxall, J Purcell and P Wright, *Oxford Handbook of Human Resource Management*, Oxford, Oxford University Press, pp 48–67

Boxall, P F and Purcell, J (2003) *Strategy and Human Resource Management*, Basingstoke, Palgrave Macmillan

Boxall, P F, Purcell, J and Wright, P (2007) Human resource management: scope, analysis and significance, in (eds) P Boxall, J Purcell and P Wright, *Oxford Handbook of Human Resource Management*, Oxford, Oxford University Press, pp 1–16

Brewster, C (1993) Developing a 'European' model of human resource management, *The International Journal of Human Resource Management*, 4 (4), pp 765–84

Chartered Institute of Personnel and Development (2013) *HR Profession Map*, http://www.cipd.co.uk/hr-profession-map-download.aspx [accessed 25 January 2013]

Delbridge, R and Keenoy, T (2010) Beyond managerialism? *The International Journal of Human Resource Management*, 21 (6), pp 799–817

Dyer, L and Holder, G W (1988) Strategic human resource management and planning, in (ed) L Dyer, *Human Resource Management: Evolving roles and responsibilities*, Washington DC, Bureau of National Affairs, pp 1–46

Fombrun, C J, Tichy, N M and Devanna, M A (1984) *Strategic Human Resource Management*, New York, Wiley
Fowler, A (1987) When chief executives discover HRM, *Personnel Management*, January, p 3
Guest, D E (1987) Human resource management and industrial relations, *Journal of Management Studies*, 24 (5), pp 503–21
Guest, D E (1991) Personnel management: the end of orthodoxy, *British Journal of Industrial Relations*, 29 (2), pp 149–76
Hendry, C and Pettigrew, A (1990) Human resource management: an agenda for the 1990s, *International Journal of Human Resource Management*, 1 (1), pp 17–44
Keegan, A and Francis, H (2010) Practitioner talk: the changing textscape of HRM and emergence of HR business partnership, *The International Journal of Human Resource Management*, 21 (6), pp 873–98
Keenoy, T (1997) HRMism and the images of re-presentation. *Journal of Management Studies*, 34 (5), pp 825–41
Labour Research Department (1989) HRM – human resource manipulation? *Labour Research*, August, pp 8–9
Legge, K (1989) Human resource management: a critical analysis, in (ed) J Storey, *New Perspectives in Human Resource Management*, London, Routledge, pp 19–40
Legge, K (1998) The morality of HRM, in (eds) C Mabey, D Skinner and T Clark, *Experiencing Human Resource Management*, Sage, London, pp 14–32
Legge, K (2005) *Human Resource Management – Rhetorics and realities*, Macmillan, Basingstoke
Likert, R (1961) *New Patterns of Management*, New York, Harper & Row
Mabey, C, Salaman, G and Storey, J (1998) *Human resource management: A strategic introduction*, 2nd edition, Oxford, Blackwell
Martin-Alcázar, F, Romero-Fernandez, P M and Sánchez-Gardey, G (2005) Strategic human resource management: integrating the universalistic, contingent, configurational and contextual perspectives, *International Journal of Human Resource Management*, 16 (5), pp 633–59
Mayo, E (1933) *The Human Problems of an Industrial Civilisation*, London, Macmillan
McGregor, D (1960) *The Human Side of Enterprise*, New York, McGraw-Hill
Noon, M (1992) HRM: a map, model or theory? in (eds) P Blyton and P Turnbull, *Reassessing Human Resource Management*, London, Sage, pp 16–32
Osterby, B and Coster, C (1992) Human resource development – a sticky label, *Training and Development*, April, pp 31–32
Paauwe, J (2004) *HRM and Performance: Achieving long term viability*, Oxford, Oxford University Press
Ramsay, H, Scholarios, D and Harley, B (2000) Employees and high-performance work systems: testing inside the black box, *British Journal of Industrial Relations*, 38 (4), pp 501–31
Schuler, R S (1992) Strategic HRM: linking people with the needs of the business, *Organizational Dynamics*, 21, pp 19–32
Schuler, R S and Jackson, S E (2000) *Strategic Human Resource Management*, Oxford, Blackwell
Storey, J (1989) From personnel management to human resource management, in (ed) J Storey, *New Perspectives on Human Resource Management*, London, Routledge, pp 1–18
Storey, J (1995) Human resource management: still marching on or marching out? in (ed) J Storey, *Human Resource Management: A critical text*, 1st edn, London, Routledge
Storey, J (2001) Human resource management today: an assessment, in (ed) J Storey, *Human Resource Management: A critical text*, 2nd edn, London, Thompson Learning, pp 3–20
Storey, J (2007) What is human resource management? in (ed), J Storey, *Human Resource Management: A critical text*, 3rd edn, London, Thompson Learning, pp 3–19
Truss, C, Gratton, L, Hope-Hailey, V, McGovern, P and Stiles, P (1997) *Soft and hard models of human resource management: a re-appraisal*, *Journal of Management Studies*, 34 (1), pp 53–73
Walton, R E (1985) From control to commitment in the workplace, *Harvard Business Review*, March–April, pp 77–84
Watson, T J (2010) Critical social science, pragmatism and the realities of HRM, *The International Journal of Human Resource Management*, 21 (6), pp 915–31
Willmott, H (1993) Strength is ignorance, slavery is freedom: managing culture in modern organizations, *Journal of Management Studies*, 30 (4), pp 515–52

02 Strategic HRM

KEY CONCEPTS AND TERMS

- Best fit
- Best practice
- Bundling
- Business model
- Business model innovation
- Competency framework
- Competitive advantage
- Configuration
- Contingent determinism
- High-commitment management
- High-involvement management
- High-performance management
- High-performance work system
- Human resource advantage
- Life cycle model
- Resource-based view
- Resource dependence theory
- Strategic configuration
- Strategic fit
- Strategic HRM
- Strategic management
- Strategy

LEARNING OUTCOMES

On completing this chapter you should be able to define these key concepts. You should also understand:

- The conceptual basis of strategic HRM
- The fundamental characteristics of strategy
- How strategy is formulated
- The aims of strategic HRM
- The resource-based view and its implications
- The meaning of strategic fit
- The three HRM 'perspectives' of Delery and Doty
- The significance of bundling
- The significance of the concepts of 'best practice' and 'best fit'
- The significant features of strategic HRM
- The content and formulation of HR strategies

Introduction

Strategic human resource management (strategic HRM or SHRM) is an approach to the development and implementation of HR strategies that are integrated with business strategies and support their achievement. SHRM has been described by Boxall (1996) as the interface between HRM and strategic management. Schuler and Jackson (2007: 5) stated that SHRM is fundamentally about 'systematically linking people with the firm'.

Baird and Meshoulam (1988: 116) pointed out that: 'Business objectives are accomplished when human resource practices, procedures and systems are developed and implemented based on organizational needs, that is, when a strategic perspective to human resource management is adopted.' Wright and McMahan (1992: 295) explained that the field of HRM has 'sought to become integrated with the strategic management process through the development of a new discipline referred to as strategic human resource management'.

In essence, strategic HRM is conceptual; it is a general notion of how integration or 'fit' between HR and business strategies is achieved, the benefits of taking a longer-term view of where HR should be going and how to get there, and how coherent and mutually supporting HR strategies should be developed and implemented. Importantly, it is also about how members of the HR function should adopt a strategic approach on a day-to-day basis. This means that they operate as part of the management team, ensure that HR activities support the achievement of business strategies on a continuous basis and add value.

The aim of this chapter is to explore what this involves. It starts with an analysis of the meaning of SHRM. It then covers: an examination of its nature and its aims; an analysis of its underpinning concepts – the resource-based view and strategic fit. This is followed by a description of how strategic HRM works, namely the universalistic, contingency and configurational perspectives defined by Delery and Doty (1996) and the three approaches associated with those perspectives – best practice, best fit and bundling. The chapter continues with a summary of the distinctive features of strategic HRM and ends with an examination of how HR strategies are developed and implemented when an SHRM approach is adopted.

The conceptual basis of strategic HRM

Strategic HRM takes the notion of HRM as a strategic, integrated and coherent process and associates it with an approach to management that involves adopting a broad and long-term view of where the business is going and managing it in ways that ensure that this strategic thrust is maintained. It is influenced by the concepts of strategic management and strategy.

Strategic management

According to Boxall and Purcell (2003: 44): 'Strategic management is best defined as a process. It is a process of strategy making, of forming and, if the firm survives, reforming its strategy over time.' Strategic management was described by Johnson *et al* (2005: 6) as 'understanding the strategic position of an organization, making strategic choices for the future, and turning strategy into action'. The purpose of strategic management has been expressed by Kanter (1984: 288) as being to 'elicit the present actions for the future' and become 'action vehicles – integrating and institutionalizing mechanisms for change' (ibid: 301).

The key strategic management activity identified by Thompson and Strickland (1996: 3) is 'deciding what business the company will be in and forming a strategic vision of where the organization needs to be headed – in effect, infusing the organization with a sense of purpose, providing long-term direction, and establishing a clear mission to be accomplished.'

The focus is on identifying the organization's mission and strategies, but attention is also given to the resource base required to make it succeed. Managers who think strategically will have a broad and long-term view of where they are going. But they will also be aware that they are responsible, first, for planning how to allocate resources to opportunities that contribute to the implementation of strategy, and second, for managing these opportunities in ways that will add value to the results achieved by the firm.

The concept of strategy

Strategy is the approach selected to achieve specified goals in the future. As defined by Chandler (1962:

13) it is: 'The determination of the long-term goals and objectives of an enterprise, and the adoption of courses of action and the allocation of resources necessary for carrying out those goals.' The formulation and implementation of corporate strategy is a process for developing a sense of direction, making the best use of resources and ensuring strategic fit.

Strategy has three fundamental characteristics. First, it is forward looking. It is about deciding where you want to go and how you mean to get there. It is concerned with both ends and means. In this sense a strategy is a declaration of intent: 'This is what we want to do and this is how we intend to do it.' Strategies define longer-term goals but they also cover how those goals will be attained. They guide purposeful action to deliver the required result. A good strategy is one that works, one that in Abell's (1993: 1) phrase enables organizations to adapt by 'mastering the present and pre-empting the future'. As Boxall (1996: 70) explained: 'Strategy should be understood as a framework of critical ends and means.'

The second characteristic of strategy is the recognition that the organizational capability of a firm (its capacity to function effectively) depends on its resource capability (the quality and quantity of its resources and their potential to deliver results). This is the resource-based view as described later in this chapter.

The third characteristic of strategy is that it aims to achieve strategic fit – the need when developing functional strategies such as HR to achieve congruence between them and the organization's business strategies within the context of its external and internal environment.

Implementation of strategy

'Implementation entails converting the strategic plan into action and then into results' (Thompson and Strickland, 1996: 20). Dreaming up a strategy is fairly easy; getting it to work is hard. Kanter (1984: 305) noted that: 'Many companies, even very sophisticated ones, are much better at generating impressive plans on paper than they are at getting "ownership" of the plans so that they actually guide operational decisions.'

Critical evaluation of the concept of strategy

The development of corporate strategy is often assumed to be a logical, step-by-step affair, the outcome of which is a formal written statement that provides a definitive guide to the organization's intentions. Many people still believe and act as if this were the case, but it is a misrepresentation of reality. In practice, the formulation of strategy may not be as rational and linear a process as some writers describe it or as some managers attempt to make it. There are limitations to the totally logical model of management that underpins the concept of strategic human resource management. In the words of Mabey *et al* (1998: 74): 'The reality is... that strategies may not always be easy to discern, that the processes of decision-making may be implicit, incremental, negotiated and compromised.'

Sparrow *et al* (2010: 4) asserted succinctly that: 'Strategy is not rational and never has been.' Strategy formulation can best be described as 'problem solving in unstructured situations' (Digman, 1990: 53) and strategies will always be formed under conditions of partial ignorance. Quinn (1980: 9) stated that a strategy may simply be 'a widely held understanding resulting from a stream of decisions'. He believed that strategy formulation takes place by means of 'logical incrementalism', ie it evolves in several steps rather than being conceived as a whole. Pettigrew and Whipp (1991: 26) observed that: 'strategy does not move forward in a direct linear way, nor through easily discernable sequential phases. Quite the reverse; the pattern is much more appropriately seen as continuous, iterative and uncertain.'

Another difficulty is that strategies are often based on the questionable assumption that the future will resemble the past. Some years ago, Heller (1972: 150) had a go at the cult of long-range planning: 'What goes wrong' he wrote, 'is that sensible anticipation gets converted into foolish numbers: and their validity always hinges on large loose assumptions.' Faulkner and Johnson (1992: 17–18) said of long-term planning that it:

> was inclined to take a definitive view of the future, and to extrapolate trend lines for the key business variables in order to arrive at this view. Economic turbulence was insufficiently considered, and the reality that much strategy is formulated and

> implemented in the act of managing the enterprise was ignored. Precise forecasts ending with derived financials were constructed, the only weakness of which was that the future almost invariably turned out differently.

Strategy formulation is not necessarily a deterministic, rational and continuous process, as was emphasized by Mintzberg (1987). He noted that, rather than being consciously and systematically developed, strategy reorientation happens in what he calls brief 'quantum loops'. A strategy, according to Mintzberg, can be deliberate – it can realize the intentions of senior management, for example to attack and conquer a new market. But this is not always the case. In theory, he says, strategy is a systematic process: first we think, then we act; we formulate then we implement. But we also 'act in order to think'. In practice, 'a realized strategy can emerge in response to an evolving situation' (ibid: 68) and the strategic planner is often 'a pattern organizer, a learner if you like, who manages a process in which strategies and visions can emerge as well as be deliberately conceived' (ibid: 73). This concept of 'emergent strategy' conveys the essence of how in practice organizations develop their business and HR strategies.

Boxall and Purcell (2003: 34) suggested that 'it is better if we understand the strategies of firms as sets of strategic choices some of which may stem from planning exercises and set-piece debates in senior management, and some of which may emerge in a stream of action'. Research conducted by Tyson (1997: 280) confirmed that, realistically, strategy:

- has always been emergent and flexible – it is always 'about to be', it never exists at the present time;
- is not only realized by formal statements but also comes about by actions and reactions;
- is a description of a future-oriented action that is always directed towards change;
- is conditioned by the management process itself.

The nature of strategic HRM

Strategic HRM is an approach that defines how the organization's goals will be achieved through people by means of HR strategies and integrated HR policies and practices. It was defined by Mabey *et al* (1998: 25) as the process of 'developing corporate capability to deliver new organizational strategies'. It is based on two key ideas, namely the resource-based view and the need for strategic fit, as discussed later in this chapter.

SHRM can be regarded as a mindset underpinned by certain concepts rather than a set of techniques. It provides the foundation for strategic reviews in which analyses of the organizational context and existing HR practices lead to decisions on strategic plans for the development of overall or specific HR strategies. SHRM involves the exercise of strategic choice (which is always there) and the establishment of strategic priorities. It is essentially about the integration of business and HR strategies so that the latter contribute to the achievement of the former.

Strategic HRM is not just about strategic planning, nor does it only deal with the formulation of individual HR strategies. Its main concern is with integrating what HR does and plans to do with what the business does and plans to do. As modelled in Figure 2.1, SHRM is about both HR strategies and the strategic management activities of HR professionals.

Aims of SHRM

The fundamental aim of strategic HRM is to generate organizational capability by ensuring that the organization has the skilled, engaged, committed and well-motivated employees it needs to achieve sustained competitive advantage. Alvesson (2009: 52) wrote that strategic HRM is about 'how the employment relationships for all employees can be managed in such a way as to contribute optimally to the organization's goal achievement'.

SHRM has three main objectives: first to achieve integration – the vertical alignment of HR strategies with business strategies and the horizontal integration of HR strategies. The second objective is to provide a sense of direction in an often turbulent environment so that the business needs of the organization and the individual and the collective needs of its employees can be met by the development and implementation of coherent and practical HR policies and programmes. The third objective

FIGURE 2.1 Strategic HRM model

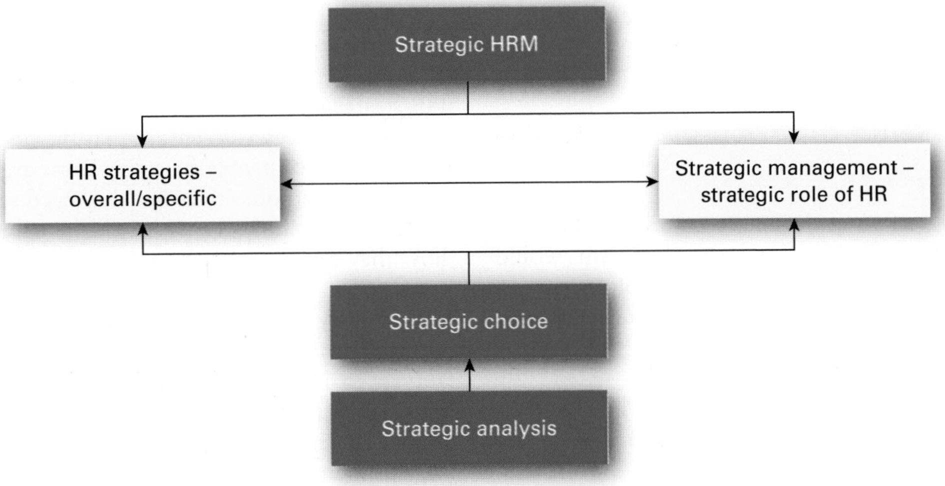

is to contribute to the formulation of business strategy by drawing attention to ways in which the business can capitalize on the advantages provided by the strengths of its human resources.

Critical evaluation of the concept of SHRM

The whole concept of SHRM is predicated on the belief that HR strategies should be integrated with corporate or business strategies. Vertical integration (strategic fit between business and HR strategies) may be desirable but it is not easy to achieve for the following reasons.

Diversity of strategic processes, levels and styles

The different levels at which strategy is formulated and the different styles adopted by organizations may make it difficult to develop a coherent view of what sort of HR strategies will fit the overall strategies and what type of HR contributions are required during the process of formulation.

The complexity of the strategy formulation process

Business strategy formulation and implementation is a complex, interactive process heavily influenced by a variety of contextual and historical factors. In these circumstances, as Guest (1991) has asked, how can there be a straightforward flow from the business strategy to the HR strategy? It has been pointed out by Truss (1999: 44) that the assumption of some matching models of strategic HRM is that there is a simple linear relationship between business strategy and human resource strategy, but this assumption 'fails to acknowledge the complexities both between and within notions of strategy and human resource management... [It] is based on a rational model of organizations and individuals which takes no account of the significance of power, politics and culture.'

The evolutionary nature of business strategy

The evolutionary and incremental nature of strategy making may make it difficult to pin down the HR issues that are likely to be relevant. Hendry and Pettigrew (1990) suggest that there are limits to the extent to which rational HR strategies can be drawn up if the process of business strategic planning is itself irrational.

The absence of articulated business strategies

If, because of its evolutionary nature, the business strategy has not been clearly articulated, this would add to the problems of clarifying the business strategic issues that human resource strategies should address.

The qualitative nature of HR issues

Business strategies tend, or at least aim, to be expressed in the common currency of figures and hard data on portfolio management, growth, competitive position, market share, profitability, etc. HR strategies may deal with quantifiable issues such as resourcing and skill acquisition but are equally likely to refer to qualitative factors such as engagement, commitment, motivation, good employee relations and high employment standards. The relationship between the pursuit of policies in these areas and individual and organizational performance may be difficult to establish.

Integration with what?

The concept of SHRM implies that HR strategies must be totally integrated with corporate/business strategies in the sense that they both flow from and contribute to such strategies. But as Brewster (2004) argued, HR strategy will be subjected to considerable external pressure; for example, in Europe, legislation about involvement. These may mean that HR strategies cannot be entirely governed by the corporate/business strategy.

The question: 'To what extent should HR strategy take into account the interests of all the stakeholders in the organization, employees in general as well as owners and management?' also needs to be answered.

Conclusions

The difficulties mentioned above are real, but they are frequently glossed over in rhetorical statements about the need for integration. Too often the outcome is a platitudinous statement such as: 'Our HR strategy is to develop a performance culture' or: 'Our HR strategy is to ensure that the organization has the talented people it needs'. These are perfectly laudable broad objectives but they need to be more specific about how the aims will be achieved and how they will support the achievement of business goals.

Matching HR and business strategies is a problematic process but this doesn't mean that the attempt to do so should be abandoned. HR strategists must make every effort to understand the business model of their organization (ie a picture of an organization that explains how it achieves competitive advantage and makes money) and the plans for business model innovation (the process followed by an organization to develop a new business model or change an existing one). They have to take into account the difficulties mentioned above but they need to overcome these by persistent efforts designed to obtain insight into the real issues facing the organization, leading to plans for practical interventions that address those issues.

The resource-based view of SHRM

To a very large extent, the philosophy of SHRM is underpinned by the resource-based view. This states that it is the range of resources in an organization, including its human resources, that produces its unique character and creates competitive advantage. The resource-based view is founded on the ideas of Penrose (1959: 24–25), who wrote that the firm is 'an administrative organization and a collection of productive resources' and saw resources as 'a bundle of potential services'. It was expanded by Wernerfelt (1984: 172), who explained that strategy 'is a balance between the exploitation of existing resources and the development of new ones'. Resources were defined by Hunt (1991: 322) as 'anything that has an enabling capacity'.

The concept was developed by Barney (1991: 102), who stated that 'a firm is said to have a competitive advantage when it is implementing a value-creating strategy not simultaneously being implemented by any current or potential competitors and when these other firms are unable to duplicate the benefits of this strategy'. This will happen if their resources are valuable, rare, inimitable and non-substitutable. He noted later (Barney 1995: 49) that an environmental analysis of strengths, weaknesses, opportunities and threats (SWOT analysis) was only half the story: 'A complete understanding of sources of a firm's competitive advantage requires the analysis of a firm's internal strengths and weaknesses as well.' He emphasized that:

> Creating sustained competitive advantage depends on the unique resources and capabilities that a firm brings to competition in its environment. To discover these resources and capabilities, managers must look inside their firm for valuable, rare and costly-to-imitate resources, and then exploit these resources through their organization. (ibid: 60)

The following rationale for resource-based strategy was produced by Grant (1991: 13):

> The resources and capabilities of a firm are the central considerations in formulating its strategy: they are the primary constants upon which a firm can establish its identity and frame its strategy, and they are the primary sources of the firm's profitability. The key to a resource-based approach to strategy formulation is understanding the relationships between resources, capabilities, competitive advantage and profitability – in particular, an understanding of the mechanisms through which competitive advantage can be sustained over time. This requires the design of strategies which exploit to maximum effect each firm's unique characteristics.

Resource-based SHRM can produce what Boxall and Purcell (2003) referred to as 'human resource advantage'. The aim is to develop strategic capability. This means strategic fit between resources and opportunities, obtaining added value from the effective deployment of resources, and developing managers who can think and plan strategically in the sense that they understand the key strategic issues and ensure that what they do enables the strategic goals of the business to be achieved. In line with human capital theory, the resource-based view emphasizes that investment in people increases their value to the firm. It proposes that sustainable competitive advantage is attained when the firm has a human resource pool that cannot be imitated or substituted by its rivals.

Boxall (1996: 66) suggested that 'the resource-based view of the firm provides a conceptual basis, if we needed one, for asserting that key human resources are sources of competitive advantage'. He noted that human resource advantage is achieved by a combination of 'human capital advantage', which results from employing people with competitively valuable knowledge and skills, and 'human process advantage', which follows from the establishment of 'difficult to imitate, highly evolved processes within the firm, such as cross-departmental cooperation and executive development'. Accordingly, 'human resource advantage', the superiority of one firm's labour management over another's, can be thought of as the product of its human capital and human process advantages. He also observed (ibid: 66) that the strategic goal emerging from the resource-based view was to 'create firms which are more intelligent and flexible than their competitors' by hiring and developing more talented staff and by extending their skills base. Resource-based strategy is therefore concerned with the enhancement of the human or intellectual capital of the firm. As Ulrich (1998: 126) commented: 'Knowledge has become a direct competitive advantage for companies selling ideas and relationships. The challenge to organizations is to ensure that they have the capability to find, assimilate, compensate and retain the talented individuals they need.'

The strategic goal emerging from the resource-based view is to create firms that are more intelligent and flexible than their competitors (Boxall, 1996) by hiring and developing more talented staff and by extending their skills base. Resource-based strategy is therefore concerned with the enhancement of the human or intellectual capital of the firm. Resource dependence theory (Pfeffer and Davis-Blake, 1992) suggests that HR strategies such as those concerned with reward are strongly influenced by the need to attract, retain and energize high-quality people.

Critical evaluation of the resource-based view

The resource-based view has had considerable influence on thinking about human resource management. It provides a justification for attaching importance to resourcing activities, especially those concerned with talent management. It can also be used to enhance the value of the HR contribution in achieving competitive advantage. But it has the following limitations:

- it may be difficult to find resources that satisfy all the criteria;
- external factors such as product market pressures are ignored;
- it provides only generalized guidance on what resources are suitable;
- different resource configurations can provide the same value for firms;
- as Priem and Butler (2001) pointed out, the theory is tautological because valuable resources and competitive advantage are defined in the same terms.

Strategic fit

The concept of strategic fit stresses that when developing HR strategies it is necessary to achieve congruence between them and the organization's business strategies within the context of its external and internal environment. This notion is fundamental to SHRM, as was stressed by Wright and Snell (1998: 758) who wrote: 'The primary role of strategic HRM should be to promote a fit with the demands of the competitive environment.' In more detail, Schuler (1992: 18) stated that:

> Strategic human resource management is largely about integration and adaptation. Its concern is to ensure that: (1) human resources (HR) management is fully integrated with the strategy and strategic needs of the firm (vertical fit); (2) HR policies cohere both across policy areas and across hierarchies (horizontal fit); and (3) HR practices are adjusted, accepted and used by line managers and employees as part of their everyday work.

Perspectives on SHRM

Taking into account the concepts of the resource-based view and strategic fit, Delery and Doty (1996: 802) contended that 'organizations adopting a particular strategy require HR practices that are different from those required by organizations adopting different strategies' and that organizations with 'greater congruence between their HR strategies and their (business) strategies should enjoy superior performance' (ibid: 803). They identified three HRM perspectives:

1. *The universalistic perspective* – some HR practices are better than others and all organizations should adopt these best practices. There is a universal relationship between individual 'best' practices and firm performance.
2. *The contingency perspective* – to be effective an organization's HR policies must be consistent with other aspects of the organization. The primary contingency factor is the organization's strategy. This can be described as 'vertical fit'.
3. *The configurational perspective* – this is a holistic approach that emphasizes the importance of the pattern of HR practices and is concerned with how this pattern of independent variables is related to the dependent variable of organizational performance.

This typology provided the basis for what has become the most commonly used classification of approaches, which is to adopt the terms 'best practice' and 'best fit' for the universalistic and contingency perspectives, and 'bundling' as the third approach (Richardson and Thompson, 1999). This followed the classification made by Guest (1997) of fit as an ideal set of practices, fit as contingency and fit as bundles.

The best practice model

This model is based on the assumption that there is a set of best HRM practices that are universal in the sense that they are best in any situation, and that adopting them will lead to superior organizational performance.

A number of lists of 'best practices' have been produced, the most quoted being by Pfeffer (1998):

- employment security;
- selective hiring;
- self-managed teams;
- high compensation contingent on performance;
- training to provide a skilled and motivated workforce;
- reduction of status differentials;
- sharing information.

The best fit model

The best fit model is in line with contingency theory. It emphasizes that HR strategies should be congruent with the context and circumstances of the organization. 'Best fit' can be perceived in terms of vertical integration or alignment between the organization's business and HR strategies. There are three models: life cycle, competitive strategy and strategic configuration.

The life cycle model

The life cycle model is based on the theory that the development of a firm takes place in four stages: start-up, growth, maturity and decline. This is in line with product life cycle theory. The basic premise of this model was expressed by Baird and Meshoulam (1988: 117) as follows:

> Human resource management's effectiveness depends on its fit with the organization's stage of development. As the organization grows and develops, human resource management programmes, practices and procedures must change to meet its needs. Consistent with growth and development models it can be suggested that human resource management develops through a series of stages as the organization becomes more complex.

Best fit and competitive strategies

Three strategies aimed at achieving competitive advantage were identified by Porter (1985):

1. *Innovation* – being the unique producer.
2. *Quality* – delivering high-quality goods and services to customers.
3. *Cost leadership* – the planned result of policies aimed at 'managing away' expense.

It was argued by Schuler and Jackson (1987) that to achieve the maximum effect it is necessary to match the role characteristics of people in an organization with the preferred strategy.

Strategic configuration

Another approach to best fit is the proposition that organizations will be more effective if they adopt a policy of strategic configuration (Delery and Doty, 1996). This means matching their strategy to one of the ideal types defined by theories such as those produced by Miles and Snow (1978). They identified the following four types of organizations, classifying the first three types as 'ideal' organizations:

1. *Prospectors*, which operate in an environment characterized by rapid and unpredictable changes. Prospectors have low levels of formalization and specialization and high levels of decentralization. They have relatively few hierarchical levels.
2. *Defenders*, which operate in a more stable and predictable environment than prospectors and engage in more long-term planning. They have more mechanistic or bureaucratic structures than prospectors and obtain coordination through formalization, centralization, specialization and vertical differentiation.
3. *Analysers*, which are a combination of the prospector and defender types. They operate in stable environments, like defenders, and also in markets where new products are constantly required, like prospectors. They are usually not the initiators of change, like prospectors, but they follow the changes more rapidly than defenders.
4. *Reactors*, which are unstable organizations existing in what they believe to be an unpredictable environment. They lack consistent well-articulated strategies and do not undertake long-range planning.

Critical evaluation of the best practice and best fit models

The best practice model

The notion of best practice assumes that there are universally effective HR practices that can readily be transferred. This rubric has been attacked by a number of commentators. Cappelli and Crocker-Hefter (1996: 7) commented that the notion of a single set of best practices has been overstated: 'There are examples in virtually every industry of firms that have very distinctive management practices... Distinctive human resource practices shape the core competencies that determine how firms compete.'

Purcell (1999: 26) noted that 'the search for best practice tends to take on the flavour of a moral crusade'. He has also criticized the best practice or universalist view by pointing out the inconsistency between a belief in best practice and the resource-based view, which focuses on the intangible assets, including HR, that allow the firm to do better than its competitors. He asked how can 'the universalism of best practice be squared with the view that only some resources and routines are important and valuable by being rare and imperfectly imitable?' and stated that: 'The claim that the bundle of best practice HRM is universally applicable leads us into a utopian cul-de-sac' (ibid: 36). Boxall (2007: 5) concluded that he was 'deeply sceptical about claims for universal applicability for particular HRM practices or clusters of practices [but] this does not rule out the search for general principles in the management of work and people'.

However, a knowledge of what is assumed to be best practice can be used to inform decisions on what practices are most likely to fit the needs of the organization, as long as it is understood why a particular practice should be regarded as a best practice and what needs to be done to ensure that it will work in the context of the organization. Becker and Gerhart (1996) argued that the idea of best practice might be more appropriate for identifying the principles underlying the choice of practices, as opposed to the practices themselves.

The best fit model

The best fit model seems to be more realistic than the best practice model. As Dyer and Holder (1988: 31) observed: 'The inescapable conclusion is that what is best depends.' But there are limitations to the concept. Paauwe (2004: 37) emphasized that: 'It is necessary to avoid falling into the trap of "contingent determinism" (ie claiming that the context absolutely determines the strategy). There is, or should be, room for making strategic choices.'

There is a danger of mechanistically matching HR policies and practices with strategy. It is not credible to claim that there are single contextual factors that determine HR strategy, and internal fit cannot therefore be complete. Purcell (1999: 35) pointed out that: 'each firm has to make choices not just on business and operational strategies but on what type of HR system is best for its purposes'. As Boxall (2007: 61) asserted: 'It is clearly impossible to make all HR policies reflective of a chosen competitive or economic mission.' They may have to fit with social legitimacy goals. And Purcell (1999: 37) commented that: 'The search for a contingency or matching model of HRM is also limited by the impossibility of modelling all the contingent variables, the difficulty of showing their interconnection, and the way in which changes in one variable have an impact on others.'

Best fit models tend to be static and don't take account of the processes of change. They neglect the fact that institutional forces shape HRM – it cannot be assumed that employers are free agents able to make independent decisions.

Conclusions

It is often said that best fit is better than best practice but this statement can only be accepted with reservations. As Stavrou *et al* (2010: 952–53) argued:

> There may be merit in both approaches where the debate is between general principles/bundles (training and development, staffing, compensation and benefits, communication and participation, and planning) and the manner in which they are carried out... It seems that the 'best fit' and 'best practice' approaches of the HR-performance relationship are not necessarily mutually exclusive. On the contrary, they may be combined to provide a more holistic picture.

This is particularly the case if the term 'best practice' is replaced by 'good practice', thus avoiding the notion of universality implied by the former term.

For example, the meta-analysis carried out by Schmidt and Hunter (1998) established conclusively that when selecting people, the best levels of predictive validity are achieved by a combination of structured interviews and intelligence tests. But a decision on what sort of structured interview should be adopted and whether or not to use intelligence tests would depend on the situation in which the decision was made.

Bundling

'Bundling' is the development and implementation of several HR practices together so that they are interrelated and therefore complement and reinforce each other. This is the process of horizontal integration, which is also referred to as the use of 'complementarities'. Richardson and Thompson (1999) suggested that a strategy's success turns on combining vertical or external fit and horizontal or internal fit. They concluded that a firm with bundles of associated HR practices should have a higher level of performance, provided it also achieves high levels of fit with its competitive strategy.

Dyer and Reeves (1995: 656–57) noted that: 'The logic in favour of bundling is straightforward... Since employee performance is a function of both ability and motivation, it makes sense to have practices aimed at enhancing both.' Thus there are several ways in which employees can acquire needed skills (such as careful selection and training) and multiple incentives to enhance motivation (different forms of financial and non-financial rewards). Their study of various models listing HR practices that create a link between HRM and business performance found that the activities appearing in most of the models were involvement, careful selection, extensive training and contingent compensation.

The process of bundling HR strategies is an important aspect of the concept of strategic HRM. In a sense, SHRM is holistic: it is concerned with the organization as a total system or entity and addresses what needs to be done across the organization as a whole. It is not interested in isolated programmes and techniques, or in the ad hoc development of HR strategies and practices.

Bundling can take place in a number of ways. Competency frameworks (a set of definitions of the competencies that describe the types of behaviour required for the successful performance of a role) can be devised that have a variety of uses, for example to specify recruitment standards, provide a framework for structured interviews, identify learning and development needs and indicate the standards of behaviour or performance required. Job evaluation can also be used to clarify and define levels in an organization. Grade structures can define career ladders in terms of competency requirements (career family structures) and thus provide the basis for learning and development programmes. Total reward approaches 'bundle' financial and non-financial rewards together. High-performance systems are in effect based on the principle of bundling because they group a number of HR practices together to produce synergy and thus increase their impact.

Critical evaluation of bundling

Bundling sounds like a good idea. The research by MacDuffie (1995) and others has shown that bundling can improve performance. But there are a number of inhibiting factors, namely:

- deciding which bundles are likely to be best – there is no evidence that one bundle is generally better than another;
- actually linking practices together – it is always easier to deal with one practice at a time;
- managing the interdependencies between different parts of a bundle;
- convincing top management and line managers that bundling will benefit the organization and them.

These can be overcome by dedicated HR professionals, but it is hard work. What can be done, with difficulty, is to find ways in which different HR practices can support one another, as in the examples given above.

HR strategies

HR strategies indicate what the organization wants to do about its human resource management policies and practices and how they should be integrated with the business strategy and each other. They set out aspirations that are expressed as intentions, which are then converted into actions. As suggested by Chesters (2011: 32), they should be regarded as a statement of the organization's collective endeavour. They are not just a laundry list of everything that the organization would like to do.

HR strategies were described by Dyer and Reeves (1995: 656) as 'internally consistent bundles of human resource practices'. Richardson and Thompson (1999: 3) observed that:

> A strategy, whether it is an HR strategy or any other kind of management strategy must have two key elements: there must be strategic objectives (ie things the strategy is supposed to achieve), and there must be a plan of action (ie the means by which it is proposed that the objectives will be met).

Purcell (2001: 72) made the point that: 'Strategy in HR, like in other areas, is about continuity and change, about appropriateness in the circumstances, but anticipating when the circumstances change. It is about taking strategic decisions.'

The purpose of HR strategies is to articulate what an organization intends to do about its HRM policies and practices now and in the longer term to ensure that they contribute to the achievement of business objectives. However, it is necessary to bear in mind the dictum of Fombrun *et al* (1984) that business and managers should perform well in the present to succeed in the future.

HR strategies may be defined formally as part of a strategic HRM process that leads to the development of overall or specific strategies for implementation by HR and, vitally, line managers. But an organization that has developed an HR strategy will not be practising SHRM unless that HR strategy has strategic relevance to the organization's success. As Wright and McMahan (1999: 52) indicated, HRM can only be considered to be strategic if 'it enables an organization to achieve its goals'.

Pettigrew and Whipp (1991: 30) emphasized that strategy, 'far from being a straightforward, rational phenomenon, is in fact interpreted by managers according to their own frame of reference, their particular motivations and information'. They were writing about business strategy, but the same applies to HR strategy, which can appear through an emergent, evolutionary and possibly unarticulated process influenced by the business strategy as it develops and changes in the internal and external environment. But there are still strong arguments for a systematic approach to identifying strategic directions that can provide a framework for decision-making and action. The main argument for articulating HR strategies is that unless you know where you are going, you will not know how to get there or when you have arrived.

Because all organizations are different, all HR strategies are different. There is no such thing as a standard strategy. Research into HR strategy conducted by Armstrong and Long (1994) and Armstrong and Baron (2002) revealed many variations. Some strategies are simply very general declarations of intent. Others go into much more detail. The two types of HR strategies are: 1) general strategies such as high-performance working; 2) specific strategies relating to the different aspects of HRM such as learning and development and reward.

General HR strategies

General strategies describe the overall system or bundle of complementary HR practices that the organization proposes to adopt or puts into effect in order to improve organizational performance. The three main approaches are summarized below.

High-performance management

High-performance management aims, through high-performance work systems (bundles of practices that enhance employee performance and facilitate their engagement, motivation and skill enhancement), to make an impact on the performance of the organization in such areas as productivity, quality, levels of customer service, growth and profits. High-performance working practices include rigorous recruitment and selection procedures, extensive and relevant training and management development activities, incentive pay systems and performance management processes.

High-commitment management

One of the defining characteristics of HRM is its emphasis on the importance of enhancing mutual commitment (Walton, 1985). High-commitment management has been described by Wood (1996) as: 'A form of management which is aimed at eliciting a commitment so that behaviour is primarily self-regulated rather than controlled by sanctions and pressures external to the individual, and relations within the organization are based on high levels of trust.'

High-involvement management

As defined by Benson *et al* (2006: 519): 'High-involvement work practices are a specific set of human resource practices that focus on employee decision-making, power, access to information, training and incentives.' Camps and Luna-Arocas (2009: 1057) observed that: 'High-involvement work practices aim to provide employees with the opportunity, skills and motivation to contribute to organizational success in environments demanding greater levels of commitment and involvement.' The term 'high-involvement' was used by Lawler (1986) to describe management systems based on commitment and involvement, as opposed to the old bureaucratic model based on control.

Examples of general HR strategies

- A local authority: as expressed by the chief executive of this borough council, its HR strategy is about 'having a very strong focus on the overall effectiveness of the organization, its direction and how it's performing; there is commitment to, and belief in, and respect for individuals, and I think that these are very important factors.'
- A public utility: 'The only HR strategy you really need is the tangible expression of values and the implementation of values... unless you get the human resource values right you can forget all the rest' (managing director).
- A manufacturing company: 'The HR strategy is to stimulate changes on a broad front aimed ultimately at achieving competitive advantage through the efforts of our people. In an industry of fast followers, those who learn quickest will be the winners' (HR director).
- A retail stores group: 'The biggest challenge will be to maintain [our] competitive advantage and to do that we need to maintain and continue to attract very high calibre people. The key differentiator on anything any company does is fundamentally the people, and I think that people tend to forget that they are the most important asset. Money is easy to get hold of, good people are not. All we do in terms of training and manpower planning is directly linked to business improvement' (managing director).

Specific HR strategies

Specific HR strategies set out what the organization intends to do in areas such as:

- *Human capital management* – obtaining, analysing and reporting on data that informs the direction of value-adding, people management, strategic, investment and operational decisions.
- *Knowledge management* – creating, acquiring, capturing, sharing and using knowledge to enhance learning and performance.
- *Corporate social responsibility* – a commitment to managing the business ethically in order to make a positive impact on society and the environment.
- *Engagement* – the development and implementation of policies designed to increase the level of employees' engagement with their work and the organization.
- *Organization development* – the planning and implementation of programmes designed to enhance the effectiveness with which an organization functions and responds to change.
- *Resourcing* – attracting and retaining high-quality people.
- *Talent management* – how the organization ensures that it has the talented people it needs to achieve success.
- *Learning and development* – providing an environment in which employees are encouraged to learn and develop.
- *Reward* – defining what the organization wants to do in the longer term to develop and implement reward policies, practices and processes that will further the achievement of its business goals and meet the needs of its stakeholders.

- *Employee relations* – defining the intentions of the organization about what needs to be done and what needs to be changed in the ways in which the organization manages its relationships with employees and their trade unions.
- *Employee well-being* – meeting the needs of employees for a healthy, safe and supportive work environment.

The following are some examples of specific HR strategies.

The Children's Society

- Implement the rewards strategy of the society to support the corporate plan and secure the recruitment, retention and motivation of staff to deliver its business objectives.
- Manage the development of the human resources information system to secure productivity improvements in administrative processes.
- Introduce improved performance management processes for managers and staff of the society.
- Implement training and development that supports the business objectives of the society and improves the quality of work with children and young people.

Diageo

There are three broad strands to the *Organization and People Strategy*:

1. *Reward and recognition*: use recognition and reward programmes to stimulate outstanding team and individual performance contributions.
2. *Talent management*: drive the attraction, retention and professional growth of a deep pool of diverse, talented employees.
3. *Organizational effectiveness*: ensure that the business adapts its organization to maximize employee contribution and deliver performance goals.

The strategy provides direction to the company's talent, operational effectiveness and performance and reward agendas. The company's underlying thinking is that the people strategy is not for the human resource function to own but is the responsibility of the whole organization, hence the title 'Organization and People Strategy'.

A government agency

The key components of the HR strategy are:

- Investing in people – improving the level of intellectual capital.
- Performance management – integrating the values contained in the HR strategy into performance management processes and ensuring that reviews concentrate on how well people are performing those values.
- Job design – a key component concerned with how jobs are designed and how they relate to the whole business.
- The reward system – in developing reward strategies, taking into account that this is a very hard-driven business.

A local authority

The focus is on the organization of excellence. The strategy is broken down into eight sections: employee relations, recruitment and retention, training, performance management, pay and benefits, health and safety, absence management and equal opportunities.

Criteria for an effective HR strategy

An effective HR strategy is one that works in the sense that it achieves what it sets out to achieve. Its criteria are that it:

- will satisfy business needs;
- is founded on detailed analysis and study and is evidence-based – it is not just wishful thinking;
- can be turned into actionable programmes that anticipate implementation requirements and problems;

- is coherent and integrated, being composed of components that fit with and support each other;
- takes account of the needs of line managers and employees generally as well as those of the organization and its other stakeholders.

Formulating HR strategy

Research conducted by Wright *et al* (2004) identified two approaches that can be adopted by HR to strategy formulation: 1) the inside-out approach begins with the status quo HR function (in terms of skills, processes, technologies, etc) and then attempts (with varying degrees of success) to identify linkages to the business (usually through focusing on 'people issues'), making minor adjustments to HR activities along the way; 2) the outside-in approach in which the starting point is the business and the customer, competitor and business issues it faces. The HR strategy then derives directly from these challenges to add real value.

Wright *et al* commented that HR strategies are more likely to flow from business strategies dominated by product/market and financial considerations. But there is still room for HR to make an essential contribution at the stage when business strategies are conceived, for example by focusing on resource issues. This contribution may be more significant when strategy formulation is an emergent or evolutionary process – HR strategic issues will then be dealt with as they arise during the course of formulating and implementing the corporate strategy.

Implementing HR strategy

As Gratton (2000: 30) commented: 'There is no great strategy, only great execution.' Strategies cannot be left as generalized aspirations or abstractions. But getting strategies into action is not easy: intent does not always lead to action. Too often, strategists act like Charles Dickens's character Mr Pecksmith, who was compared by Dickens (*Martin Chuzzlewit*, Penguin Classics, 2004: 23) to 'a direction-post which is always telling the way to a place and never goes there.' It is necessary to avoid saying, in effect: 'We need to get from here to there but we don't care how.'

If, in Kanter's (1984) phrase, HR strategies are to be action vehicles, they must be translated into HR policies that provide guidelines on decision-making and HR practices that enable the strategy to work. These can be the basis for implementation programmes with clearly stated objectives and deliverables.

To a large extent, HR strategies are implemented by line managers. As Purcell *et al* (2003: *x*) stressed, it is front-line managers who 'bring policies to life'. They pointed out that:

> Implementing and enacting policies is the task of line managers. It is necessary first to involve line managers in the development of HR strategy – bearing in mind that things done *with* line managers are much more likely to work than things done *to* line managers. Second, ensure that the HR policies they are expected to put into practice are manageable with the resources available. Third, provide managers with the training, supporting processes and on the spot guidance they need.

Key learning points: Strategic HRM

The conceptual basis of strategic HRM

Strategic HRM is the 'interface between HRM and strategic management'. It takes the notion of HRM as a strategic, integrated and coherent approach and develops that in line with the concept of strategic management (Boxall, 1996).

The fundamental characteristics of strategy

- Forward looking.
- The organizational capability of a firm depends on its resource capability.
- Strategic fit – the need when developing HR strategies to achieve congruence between them and the organization's business strategies within the context of its external and internal environment.

How strategy is formulated

An emergent and flexible process of developing a sense of direction, making the best use of resources and ensuring strategic fit.

The aim of SHRM

To generate organizational capability by ensuring that the organization has the skilled, engaged, committed and well-motivated employees it needs to achieve sustained competitive advantage.

Implications of the resource-based view (RBV)

The RBV emphasizes the importance of creating firms that are 'more intelligent and flexible than their competitors' (Boxall, 1996) by hiring and developing more talented staff and by extending the skills base.

Implications of the concept of strategic fit

The concept of strategic fit means developing HR strategies that are integrated with the business strategy and support its achievement (vertical integration or fit), and the use of an integrated approach to the development of HR practices.

Best practice

There is a set of best HRM practices that are universal in the sense that they are best in any situation and adopting them will lead to superior organizational performance. The notion of best practice incorrectly assumes that there are universally effective HR practices that can readily be transferred.

Best fit

HR strategies should be congruent with the context and circumstances of the organization. More realistic than best practice, but there is a danger of mechanistically matching HR policies and practices with strategy.

The significance of bundling

The process of bundling HR strategies is an important aspect of the concept of SHRM, which is concerned with the organization as a total system or entity and addresses what needs to be done across the organization as a whole.

HR strategies

HR strategies set out what the organization intends to do about its HRM policies and practices and how they should be integrated with the business strategy and each other. The two types of HR strategies are: 1) general strategies such as high-performance working; 2) specific strategies relating to the different aspects of HRM such as learning and development and reward.

Questions

1 What is strategic HRM?
2 What is strategic management?
3 What is strategy?
4 What is the resource-based view?
5 What is the meaning and significance of strategic fit?
6 What is the best practice model and to what extent is it valid?
7 What is the best fit model and to what extent is it valid?
8 What is bundling?
9 What are HR strategies?
10 What are the criteria for an effective HR strategy?

References

Abell, D F (1993) *Managing with Dual Strategies: Mastering the present, pre-empting the future*, New York, Free Press

Alvesson, M (2009) Critical perspectives on strategic HRM, in (eds) J Storey, P M Wright and D Ulrich, *The Routledge Companion to Strategic Human Resource Management*, Abingdon, Routledge, pp 52–67

Armstrong, M and Baron, A (2002) *Strategic HRM: The route to improved business performance*, London, CIPD

Armstrong, M and Long, P (1994) *The Reality of Strategic HRM*, London, IPM

Baird, L and Meshoulam, I (1988) Managing two fits of strategic human resource management, *Academy of Management Review*, 13 (1), pp 116–28

Barney, J B (1991) Firm resources and sustained competitive advantage, *Journal of Management Studies*, 17 (1), pp 99–120

Barney, J B (1995) Looking inside for competitive advantage, *Academy of Management Executive*, 9 (4), pp 49–61

Becker, B E and Gerhart, S (1996) The impact of human resource management on organizational performance: progress and prospects, *Academy of Management Journal*, 39 (4), pp 779–801

Benson, G S, Young, S M and Lawler, E E (2006) High involvement work practices and analysts' forecasts of corporate performance, *Human Resource Management*, 45 (4), pp 519–27

Boxall, P F (1996) The strategic HRM debate and the resource-based view of the firm, *Human Resource Management Journal*, 6 (3), pp 59–75

Boxall, P F (2007) The goals of HRM, in (eds) P Boxall, J Purcell and P Wright, *The Oxford Handbook of Human Resource Management*, Oxford, Oxford University Press, pp 48–67

Boxall, P F and Purcell, J (2003) *Strategy and Human Resource Management*, Basingstoke, Palgrave Macmillan

Brewster, C (2004) European perspectives of human resource management, *Human Resource Management Review*, 14 (4), pp 365–82

Camps, J and Luna-Arocas, R (2009) High-involvement work practices and firm performance, *International Journal of Human Resource Management*, 20 (5), pp 1056–77

Cappelli, P and Crocker-Hefter, A (1996) Distinctive human resources are firms' core competencies, *Organizational Dynamics*, Winter, pp 7–22

Chandler, A D (1962) *Strategy and Structure*, Boston, MA, MIT Press

Chesters, J (2011) Creating strategic impact: it's how not what, *People Management*, August, pp 32–35

Delery, J E and Doty, H D (1996) Modes of theorizing in strategic human resource management: tests of universality, contingency and configurational performance predictions, *Academy of Management Journal*, 39 (4), pp 802–35

Dickens, C (1843) *Martin Chuzzlewit*, London, Chapman & Hall (Penguin Classics, 2004)

Digman, L A (1990) *Strategic Management – Concepts, decisions, cases*, Georgetown, Ontario, Irwin

Dyer, L and Holder, G W (1988) Strategic human resource management and planning, in (ed) L Dyer, *Human Resource Management: Evolving roles and responsibilities*, Washington, DC, Bureau of National Affairs

Dyer, L and Reeves, T (1995) Human resource strategies and firm performance: what do we know and where do we need to go?, *The International Journal of Human Resource Management*, 6 (3), pp 656–70

Faulkner, D and Johnson, G (1992) *The Challenge of Strategic Management*, London, Kogan Page
Fombrun, C J, Tichy, N M and Devanna, M A (1984) *Strategic Human Resource Management*, New York, Wiley
Grant, R M (1991) The resource-based theory of competitive advantage: implications for strategy formulation, *California Management Review*, 33 (3), pp 114–35
Gratton, L A (2000) Real step change, *People Management*, 16 March, pp 27–30
Guest, D E (1991) Personnel management: the end of orthodoxy, *British Journal of Industrial Relations*, 29 (2), pp 149–76
Guest, D E (1997) Human resource management and performance; a review of the research agenda, *The International Journal of Human Resource Management*, 8 (3), pp 263–76
Heller, R (1972) *The Naked Manager*, London, Barrie & Jenkins
Hendry, C and Pettigrew, A (1990) Human resource management: an agenda for the 1990s, *International Journal of Human Resource Management*, 1 (1), pp 17–44
Hunt, S (1991) The resource-advantage theory of competition, *Journal of Management Inquiry*, 4 (4), pp 317–22
Johnson, G, Scholes, K and Whittington, R (2005) *Explaining Corporate Strategy*, 7th edn, Harlow, FT Prentice Hall
Kanter, R M (1984) *The Change Masters*, London, Allen & Unwin
Lawler, E E (1986) *High Involvement Management*, San Francisco, CA, Jossey-Bass
Mabey, C, Salaman, G and Storey, J (1998) *Human Resource Management: A strategic introduction*, 2nd edn, Oxford, Blackwell
MacDuffie, J P (1995) Human resource bundles and manufacturing performance, *Industrial Relations Review*, 48 (2), pp 199–221
Miles, R E and Snow, C C (1978) *Organizational Strategy: Structure and process*, New York, McGraw-Hill
Mintzberg, H (1987) Crafting strategy, *Harvard Business Review*, July–August, pp 66–74
Paauwe, J (2004) *HRM and Performance: Achieving long-term viability*, Oxford, Oxford University Press
Penrose, E (1959) *The Theory of the Growth of the Firm*, Oxford, Blackwell
Pettigrew, A and Whipp, R (1991) *Managing Change for Strategic Success*, Oxford, Blackwell
Pfeffer, J (1998) *The Human Equation*, Boston, MA, Harvard Business School Press
Pfeffer, J and Davis-Blake, A (1992) Understanding organizational wage structures: a resource dependence approach, *Academy of Management Journal*, 30, pp 437–55
Porter, M E (1985) *Competitive Advantage: Creating and sustaining superior performance*, New York, The Free Press
Priem, R L and Butler, J E (2001) Is the resource-based theory a useful perspective for strategic management research?, *Academy of Management Review*, 26 (1), pp 22–40
Purcell, J (1999) Best practice or best fit: chimera or cul-de-sac, *Human Resource Management Journal*, 9 (3), pp 26–41
Purcell, J (2001) The meaning of strategy in human resource management, in (ed) J Storey, *Human Resource Management: A critical text*, 2nd edn, London, Thompson Learning, pp 59–77
Purcell, J, Kinnie, K, Hutchinson, R, Rayton, B and Swart, J (2003) *People and Performance: How people management impacts on organizational performance*, London, CIPD
Quinn, J B (1980) *Strategies for Change: Logical incrementalism*, Georgetown, Ontario, Irwin
Richardson, R and Thompson, M (1999) *The Impact of People Management Practices on Business Performance: A literature review*, London, IPD
Schmidt, F L and Hunter, J E (1998) The validity and utility of selection methods in personnel psychology: practical and theoretical implications of 85 years of research findings, *Psychological Bulletin*, 124 (2), pp 262–74
Schuler, R S (1992) Strategic human resource management: linking people with the strategic needs of the business, *Organizational Dynamics*, 21 (1), pp 18–32
Schuler, R S and Jackson, S E (1987) Linking competitive strategies with human resource management practices, *Academy of Management Executive*, 9 (3), pp 207–19
Schuler, R S and Jackson, S E (2007) *Strategic Human Resource Management*, 2nd edn, Oxford, Blackwell
Sparrow, P, Hesketh, A, Hird, M and Cooper, C (2010) Introduction: Performance-led HR, in (eds) P Sparrow, A Hesketh, M Hird and C Cooper, *Leading HR*, Basingstoke, Palgrave Macmillan, pp 1–22
Stavrou, E T, Brewster, C and Charalambousa, C (2010) Human resource management and firm performance in Europe through the lens of business systems: best fit, best practice or both?,

The International Journal of Human Resource Management, 21 (7), pp 933–62
Thompson, A A and Strickland, A J (1996) *Strategic Management, Concepts and Cases*, 9th edn, Chicago, IL, Irwin
Truss, C (1999) Soft and hard models of HRM, in (eds) L Gratton, V H Hailey, P Stiles and C Truss, *Strategic Human Resource Management*, Oxford, Oxford University Press
Tyson, S (1997) Human resource strategy: a process for managing the contribution of HRM to organizational performance, *International Journal of Human Resource Management*, 8 (3), pp 277–90
Ulrich, D (1998) A new mandate for human resources, *Harvard Business Review*, January–February, pp 124–34
Walton, R E (1985) From control to commitment in the workplace, *Harvard Business Review*, March–April, pp 77–84
Wernerfelt, B (1984) A resource-based view of the firm, *Strategic Management Journal*, 5 (2), pp 171–80
Wood, S (1996) High commitment management and organization in the UK, *The International Journal of Human Resource Management*, 7 (1), pp 41–58
Wright, P M and McMahan, G C (1992) Theoretical perspectives for SHRM, *Journal of Management*, 18 (2), pp 295–320
Wright, P M and McMahan, G C (1999) Theoretical perspectives for human resource management, in (eds) R S Schulker and S E Jackson, *Strategic Human Resource Management*, Blackwell, Oxford, pp 49–72
Wright, P M and Snell, S A (1998) Towards a unifying framework for exploring fit and flexibility in strategic human resource management, *Academy of Management Review*, 23 (4), pp 756–72
Wright, P M, Snell, S A and Jacobsen, H H (2004) Current approaches to HR strategies: inside-out versus outside-in, *Human Resource Planning*, 27 (4), pp 36–46

03 Delivering HRM – systems and roles

KEY CONCEPTS AND TERMS

Business partner	Professionalism
Centre of excellence	Shared service centre
HR architecture	Strategic business partner
HR delivery model	The three-legged stool model
HR philosophies, policies, practices	Transactional HR activities
HR system processes and programmes	Transformational HR activities

LEARNING OUTCOMES

On completing this chapter you should be able to define these key concepts. You should also understand:

- The framework for delivering HRM
- What the concept of HR architecture means
- What an HR system looks like
- The HR role of line managers
- The role and organization of the HR function
- The nature of an HR delivery model
- The role of HR professionals

Introduction

The framework for delivering HRM is provided by the HR architecture of an organization, which consists of the HR system, HR practices and the HR delivery model adopted by the HR function. Within that framework the provision of advice and services relating to human resource management is the responsibility of the HR function and the HR professionals who are members of the function. Ultimately, however, the delivery of HRM is up to line managers who put HR policies into practice.

HR techniques such as organization development, selection testing, talent management, performance management and total reward play an important part in the delivery of HRM. But there is the danger that new and seemingly different techniques become 'flavours of the month' only to be quickly forgotten when they fail to deliver. Some time ago McLean (1981: 4) observed that:

> The history of the management of human resources is littered with examples of widely acclaimed techniques enthusiastically introduced by managers who are keen to find solutions to their 'people' problems, only to be discarded and discredited by the same disillusioned and increasingly cynical managers some time later.

Times have not changed. The effective delivery of HRM depends on using techniques which are tried, tested and appropriate, not ones which have been promoted vigorously as 'best practice' without supporting evidence.

HR architecture

HR architecture consists of the HR systems, processes and structure, and employee behaviours. It is a comprehensive representation of all that is involved in HRM, not simply the structure of the HR function. As explained by Becker *et al* (2001: 12): 'We use the term HR architecture to broadly describe the continuum from the HR professionals within the HR function, to the system of HR related policies and practices, through the competencies, motivation and associated behaviours of the firm's employees.'

It was noted by Hird *et al* (2010: 25) that: 'this architecture is seen as a unique combination of the HR function's structure and delivery model, the HR practices and system, and the strategic employee behaviours that these create'.

Purcell (1999: 38) suggested that the focus should be on 'appropriate HR architecture and the processes that contribute to organizational performance'. Becker and Huselid (2006: 899) stated that: 'It is the fit between the HR architecture and the strategic capabilities and business processes that implement strategy that is the basis of HR's contribution to competitive advantage.'

The HR system

The HR system contains the interrelated and jointly supportive HR activities and practices which together enable HRM goals to be achieved. Becker and Huselid (1998: 95) observed that: 'The HRM system is first and foremost a vehicle to implement the firm's strategy.' Later (2006) they argued that it is the HR system that is the key HR asset. Boselie *et al* (2005: 73) pointed out that in its traditional form HRM can be viewed as 'a collection of multiple discrete practices with no explicit or discernible link between them. The more strategically minded system approach views HRM as an integrated and coherent bundle of mutually reinforcing practices.'

As illustrated in Figure 3.1, an HRM system brings together HR philosophies that describe the overarching values and guiding principles adopted in managing people. Taking account of the internal and external environments in which the organization operates, the system incorporates:

- *HR strategies*, which define the direction in which HRM intends to take each of its main areas of activity.
- *HR policies*, which set out what HRM is there to do and provide guidelines defining how specific aspects of HR should be applied and implemented.
- *HR practices*, which consist of the HRM activities involved in managing and developing people and in managing the employment relationship.

FIGURE 3.1 The HRM system

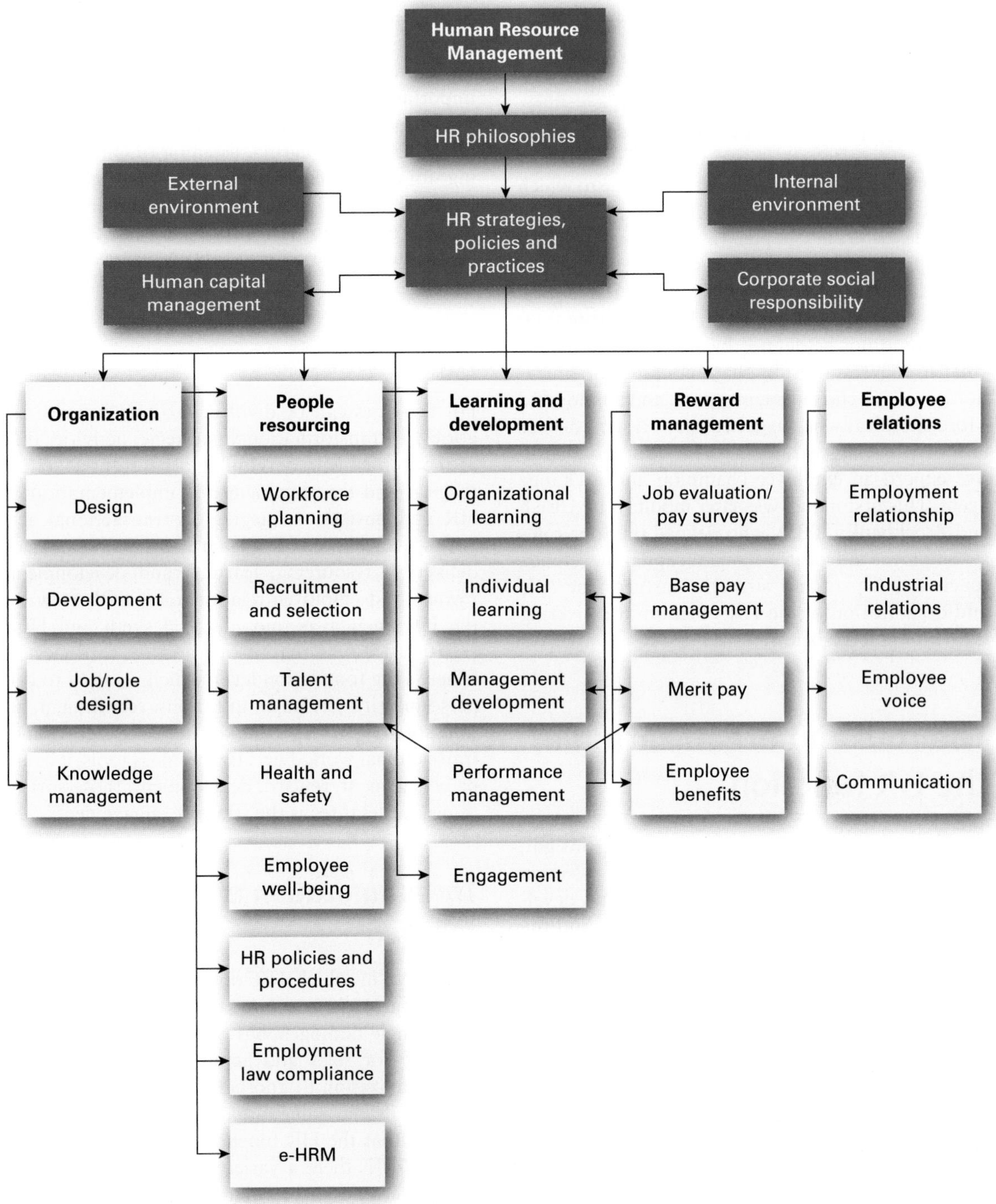

The HR function delivery model

In a sense the HR function is in the delivery business – providing the advice and services that enable organizations and their line managers to get things done through people. The HR delivery model describes how those services are provided. These methods of delivery take place irrespective of the degree to which what is done corresponds with the conceptual HRM model described in Chapter 1.

The most celebrated delivery model was produced by Dave Ulrich. In his influential *Harvard Business Review* article (1998: 124) he wrote that: 'HR should not be defined by what it does but by what it delivers – results that enrich the organization's value to customers, investors, and employees.' More specifically he suggested that HR can deliver in four ways: as a strategic partner, an administrative expert, an employee champion and a change agent. This first model was later modified by Ulrich and Brockbank (2005), who defined the four roles as employee advocate, human capital developer, functional expert and strategic partner. The role and organization of the HR function in delivering HRM is explored below.

The role and organization of the HR function

Members of the HR function provide insight, leadership, advice and services on matters affecting the management, employment, learning and development, reward and well-being of people, and the relationships between management and employees. Importantly, they contribute to the achievement of organizational effectiveness and success (the impact of HRM on performance is considered in Chapter 4).

The basic role of HR is to deliver HRM services. But it does much more than that. It plays a key part in the creation of an environment that enhances engagement by enabling people to make the best use of their capacities, to realize their potential to the benefit of both the organization and themselves, and to achieve satisfaction through their work.

Increasingly, the role of HR is seen to be business-oriented – contributing to the achievement of sustained competitive advantage. Becker and Huselid (1998: 97) argued that HR should be 'a resource that solves real business problems'. But one of the issues explored by Francis and Keegan (2006) through their research is the tendency for a focus on business performance outcomes to obscure the importance of employee well-being in its own right. They quoted the view of Ulrich and Brockbank (2005: 201) that 'caring, listening to, and responding to employees remains a centrepiece of HR work'. The HR function and its members have to be aware of the ethical dimensions of their work (the ethical dimension of HRM is explored in Chapter 8).

HR activities

HR activities can be divided into two broad categories: 1) transformational (strategic) activities that are concerned with developing organizational effectiveness and the alignment and implementation of HR and business strategies; 2) transactional activities, which cover the main areas of HR service delivery – resourcing, learning and development, reward and employee relations. A CEO's view on the HR agenda as quoted by Hesketh and Hird (2010: 105) was that it operates on three levels: 'There's the foundation level, which we used to call personnel, it's just pay and rations, recruitment, all that sort of stuff that makes the world go round, transactional work. Level two to me is tools, it could be engagement, reward, development, those sort of things. Level three is the strategic engagement.'

The organization of the HR function

The ways in which HR operates vary immensely. As Sisson (1990) commented, HR management is not a single homogeneous occupation – it involves a variety of roles and activities that differ from one organization to another and from one level to another in the same organization. Tyson (1987) claimed that the HR function is often 'balkanized' – not only is there a variety of roles and activities but these tend to be relatively self-centred, with little passage between them. Hope-Hailey *et al* (1997: 17) believed that HR could be regarded as a 'chameleon function' in the sense that the diversity of practice established by their research suggests that 'contextual variables dictate different roles for the function and different practices of people management'.

The organization and staffing of the HR function clearly depend on the size of the business, the extent to which operations are decentralized, the type of work carried out, the kind of people employed and the role assigned to the HR function. A survey by Incomes Data Services (IDS, 2010) found that the overall median number of HR staff in the responding organizations was 14: in small and medium-sized companies (with 1–499 staff) the median number was 3.5, and in companies with 500 or more employees it was 20. While, as would be expected, large organizations employed more staff than small and medium-sized enterprises (SMEs), they had on average fewer HR staff per employee. For SMEs the median ratio of employees to HR staff was 62:1; in large employers it was 95:1. The overall ratio was 80:1. The IRS 2012 survey of HR roles and responsibilities found that the median ratio of employees to HR practitioners was 80:1.

A traditional organization might consist of an HR director responsible directly to the chief executive, with functional heads dealing, respectively, with recruitment and employment matters, learning and development, and reward management. Crail (2006: 15) used the responses from 179 organizations to an IRS survey of the HR function to produce a model of an HR department. He suggested that this 'might consist of a team of 12 people serving a workforce of around 1,200. The team would have a director, three managers, one supervisor, three HR officers and four assistants. It would include a number of professionally qualified practitioners, particularly at senior level'. However, there is no such thing as a typical HR function, although the 'three-legged stool' model as described below has attracted a lot of attention.

The three-legged stool model

The notion of delivering HRM through three major areas – centres of expertise, business partners and HR shared service centres – emerged from the HR delivery model produced by Ulrich (1997, 1998), although, as reported by Hird *et al* (2010: 26): 'Ulrich himself has gone on record recently to state that the structures being implemented by HR based on his work are not actually his idea at all but an interpretation of his writing.' They noted that the first reference to the three-legged stool was in an article by Johnson (1999: 44), two years after Ulrich published his delivery model. In this article Johnson quoted David Hilborn, an associate of William Mercer, management consultants, as follows:

> The traditional design [of an HR department] typically includes a vice president of HR, then a manager of compensation and benefits, a manager of HRIS and payroll, a manager of employment and so on. However, the emerging model is more like a three-legged stool. One leg of the stool includes an administrative service centre which processes payroll, benefits and the like and focuses on efficiency in transaction functions. The second leg is a centre of excellence (or expertise) in which managers and specialists work. These employees concentrate on design rather than transactions and will have line managers as their customers. HR business partners make up the third leg. They are generalists who usually report to line managers and indirectly to HR. These employees don't get involved in transactions, but instead act as consultants and planners, linking the business with appropriate HR programmes.

This exposition provided the blueprint for all subsequent versions of the model, which has evolved as follows:

- *Centres of expertise* – these specialize in the provision of high-level advice and services on key HR activities. The CIPD survey on the changing HR function (CIPD, 2007) found that they existed in 28 per cent of respondents' organizations. The most common expertise areas were training and development (79 per cent), recruitment (67 per cent), reward (60 per cent) and employee relations (55 per cent).
- *Strategic business partners* – these work with line managers to help them reach their goals through effective strategy formulation and execution. They are often 'embedded' in business units or departments.
- *HR shared service centres* – these handle all the routine 'transactional' services across the business, which include such activities as recruitment, absence monitoring and advice on dealing with employee issues such as discipline and absenteeism.

Critical evaluation of the three-legged stool model

Although this model has attracted a great deal of attention, the 2007 CIPD survey found that only 18 per cent of respondents had implemented all three 'legs', although 47 per cent had implemented one or two elements, with business partners being the most common (29 per cent).

Moreover, there are difficulties with the notion. Gratton (2003: 18) pointed out that: 'this fragmentation of the HR function is causing all sorts of unintended problems. Senior managers look at the fragments and are not clear how the function as a whole adds value'. And as Reilly (2007) commented, respondents to the CIPD survey mentioned other problems in introducing the new model. These included difficulties in defining roles and accountabilities, especially those of business partners, who risk being 'hung, drawn and quartered by all sides', according to one HR director. At the same time, the segmented nature of the structure gives rise to 'boundary management' difficulties, for example when it comes to separating out transactional tasks from the work of centres of expertise. The model can also hamper communication between those engaged in different HR activities. Other impediments were technological failure, inadequate resources in HR and skills gaps.

Hird *et al* (2010: 31) drew attention to the following issues:

- An 'off the shelf' introduction of a new HR structure without careful thought as to how the model fits the organization's requirements.
- A lack of care in dealing with the boundary issues between elements of the HR structure which can easily be fragmented.
- A lack of attention to the new skill sets needed by business partners to ensure they can play at the strategic level.
- A lack of understanding on the part of managers as to the value of a new HR structure.
- A lack of skill on the part of line managers to make the required shift to greater responsibility for people issues implied by the new model.
- What is referred to as the 'polo' problem: a lack of provision of the execution of HR services as the business partner shifts to strategic work, and the centre of expertise to an advisory role.

However, some benefits were reported by respondents to the CIPD (2007) survey. Centres of expertise provide higher quality advice. Business partners exercise better business focus, line managers are more engaged, and the profile of HR is raised. Also, the introduction of shared services results in improved customer service and allows other parts of HR to spend more time on value-adding activities. It can also cut costs by reducing the number of HR staff required.

Dealing with the issues

The following approach incorporating recommendations by Holley (2009: 8–9) can be used to deal with HR structuring issues:

- ensure that top management are behind the changes;
- involve line managers and the whole of HR in planning and implementation;
- work out exactly who will do what in each area – HR and the line – avoid overlaps and ambiguities, taking particular care in defining the respective responsibilities of business partners and members of shared services centres and centres of expertise;
- ensure that the right balance is achieved between HR strategic (transformational) activities and HR service delivery (transactional) activities;
- ensure that the right people are in the right roles (don't simply switch job titles);
- let everyone know about the changes – why they are taking place, how they will work and any differences in responsibilities;
- define the skills required by both HR staff and line managers and help in their development;
- plan the implementation, phasing it as required to avoid any disruption;
- monitor implementation to ensure that it is going according to plan.

Evaluating the HR function

It is necessary to evaluate the contribution of the HR function to establish how effective it is at both the strategic level and in terms of service delivery and support. The prime criteria for evaluating the work of the function are its ability to operate strategically and its capacity to deliver the levels of services required.

Research conducted by the Institute for Employment Studies (Hirsh, 2008) discovered that the factors that correlated most strongly with line managers' and employees' satisfaction with HR were:

- being well supported in times of change;
- HR giving good advice to employees;
- being well supported when dealing with difficult people or situations;
- HR getting the basics right.

But the results showed that HR could do better in each of these areas. The conclusions reached were that HR must find out what its customers need and what their experiences of HR services are. HR has to be responsive – clear about what it is there for and what services it offers, and easy to contact.

The IRS 2012 survey of HR roles and responsibilities established that the main measures used by respondents to assess HR effectiveness were:

- absence management data – 79 per cent;
- staff turnover data – 75 per cent;
- exit interview feedback – 66 per cent;
- discipline and grievance data – 60 per cent;
- results of employee surveys – 60 per cent;
- anecdotal/informal feedback – 59 per cent;
- number of tribunal cases – 50 per cent;
- benchmarking – 47 per cent;
- spending against budget – 46 per cent;
- time-to-fill vacancies data – 34 per cent;
- cost per hire – 30 per cent.

CASE STUDIES ON THE ORGANIZATION OF THE HR FUNCTION

HR organization at the National Australia Bank Group

HR at the National Australia Bank Group has a number of centres of expertise, business partners, solutions consultants, project managers, a shared services centre, and telephone advisory service for employees (the people advisory helpline).

Centres of expertise

Centres of expertise cover areas such as reward, employment policy, talent management, culture management, diversity and performance. The staff in the centres are specialists in their respective fields, while the other parts of HR can be found in the HR service centre, with the exception of recruitment, which is conducted by line managers.

Business partners

Business partners attend business unit leadership team meetings and set the company's people strategies and deliver the HR requirements emerging from various projects. They tend to work in the areas of talent, performance, leadership, diversity and culture and their job is to facilitate the implementation of corporate people initiatives with the relevant specialist HR partners. Unlike shared services staff, they only get involved in HR's daily operational matters if projects escalate and extra help is required.

Solutions consultants

Solutions consultants deal with operational queries referred to them from the people advisory helpline – mainly issues of case management and other more complex enquiries. They are a key point of contact for people leaders on matters of policy and procedure, although they do participate in some transaction work as well.

Project staff

Project staff work on projects that emerge from strategic discussions.

The HR shared services model at PricewaterhouseCoopers (PwC)

The HR shared services model at PwC consists of transactional and professional areas. Transactional functions include payroll, benefits administration and the joiners/leavers process department. The transactional functions also provide services for their professional counterparts. In contrast, professional areas organized into centres of expertise include functions such as recruitment, learning and development, reward, diversity, and legal and advisory.

The centres of expertise sit within the central human capital services centre but there are definite lines between them. Every centre of expertise is a cost centre, but for the annual budgeting process all are looked at together as part of the HR shared services function.

The result of introducing the centres of expertise has been that specialist knowledge is now organized into discrete units enabling know-how and experience to be more easily shared. The new structure means there is less duplication and the improved efficiencies allow more time to be dedicated to strategic issues. Additionally, a decrease in costs has been achieved via a combination of reductions in headcount, economies of scale and related efficiencies.

Reorganizing HR in the Greater Manchester Fire Service

Following major changes in operations, it was decided by senior management that the role of the fire service's HR function was to provide high-level, strategic advice from advisers who could work closely with them, backed up by specialists. In other words, a business partner model. So the brigade began to recruit business partners – placing a special emphasis on those with expertise in employee relations – and specialists to cover areas such as occupational health, equality and diversity, reward, pensions and recruitment. Finding candidates with sufficient gravitas to act as top-level strategic advisers was difficult. There weren't many true business partners about. A lot of people calling themselves business partners were really HR advisers.

When the team was in place the major developments were:

- to introduce a more transparent promotions process;
- to work on the organizational climate and leadership – a series of away-days for leaders using organizational climate tools such as 360-degree feedback and the Belbin Team Inventory;
- the recruitment process was also modernized by putting together a resourcing team, building a microsite and developing an applicant tracking system;
- to reorganize training;
- a departmental competency framework was put in place to ensure HR staff would be able to move easily within the organization rather than becoming bogged down in specialist areas.

The roles of HR professionals

The roles of HR professionals vary widely according to the extent to which they are generalist (eg HR director, HR manager, HR officer), or specialist (eg head of learning and development, head of talent management, head of reward), the level at which they work (strategic, executive or administrative) the needs of the organization, the view of senior management about their contribution, the context within which they work and their own capabilities. They can act as strategists, business partners, innovators, change agents, internal consultants, facilitators and coaches. Tyson and Fell (1986: 7) believed that they were 'specialists in managing the employment relationship'. The competencies required are demanding. The various roles are described below.

The general role

The CIPD Profession Map (2013: 9) stated that the HR profession is 'an applied business discipline with a people and organization specialism'. Research conducted by the CIPD in 2010 emphasized the need for HR professionals to be 'insight-led'. Sears (2011: 35) reported that the researchers 'found that demonstrating a sense of purpose that spans the whole pyramid demands a wide-awake HR function, with a deep understanding of business, contextual and organizational factors.

HR professionals can play a proactive role, contributing to the formulation of corporate strategy, developing integrated HR strategies and volunteering guidance on matters related to upholding core values and ethical principles. They help to improve organizational capability – the capacity of the organization to perform effectively and thus reach its goals and work with line managers to deliver performance targets. As described later in this chapter, their role in dealing with people issues can be strategic or innovative and they can act as change agents. They can also be regarded as facilitators; in the words of Tyson and Fell (1986: 65): 'Their work allows other managerial work to happen.' But HR professionals are very much concerned with service delivery which, as a basic responsibility of the HR function, is discussed first below.

The service delivery role

The service delivery role of HR professionals operates at a transformational level when HR strategies, programmes and policies are devised and implemented which further the achievement of business goals and help to meet the needs of employees. But for many HR people the emphasis is on transactional activities such as recruitment, training, handling day-to-day employment matters and dealing with employment law matters. The latter is one of the most demanding and time-consuming areas in which they give advice and provide services. A 2002 survey by the CIPD found that two thirds of HR specialists were spending in excess of 20 per cent of their time coping with employment law issues, while a quarter reported that over 40 per cent of their working days were being spent in this way.

For many HR practitioners service delivery is what they do. The importance of this aspect of their work should not be underestimated by focusing too much on strategic or business partner roles. Line managers tend to judge HR professionals on the quality and efficiency of the services they provide, such as recruitment, training and solving people problems, rather than on their strategic capabilities.

The strategic role

HR professionals have a strategic role when they are operating at a transformational (strategic) level as HR directors or heads of the HR function, heads of centres of expertise or key HR functions, and strategic business partners. The strategic HRM skills and knowledge they need to carry out this role are described in Chapter 44. At a transactional level (as an HR officer, adviser or assistant delivering basic HR services such as recruitment or training, or working in an HR shared service centre) their role is not primarily strategic but they can make a contribution to the formulation and implementation of HR strategy.

Strategic level roles

The roles of HR professionals at a strategic level are:

- To formulate and implement, in conjunction with their management colleagues, forward-looking HR strategies that are based on insights into the needs of the organization, aligned to business objectives and integrated with one another. In doing so they adopt an 'outside-in' approach as described by Wright *et al* (2004) in which the starting point is the business, including the customer, competitor and business issues it faces. The HR strategy then derives directly from these challenges in order to create real solutions and add real value.
- To contribute to the development of business strategies. They do this by advising on how the business can achieve its strategic goals by making the best use of its human resources and by demonstrating the particular contribution that can be made by the talented people it employs.
- To work alongside their line management colleagues and provide on an everyday basis continuous support to the implementation of the business or operational strategy of the organization, function or unit.

The strategic contribution of HR advisers or assistants

The role of HR advisers or assistants is primarily that of delivering effective HR services within their function, or as a member of an HR service centre. While they will not be responsible for the formulation of HR strategies they may contribute to them within their own speciality. They will need to understand the business goals of the departments or managers for whom they provide services in order to ensure that these services support the achievement of those goals.

The business partner role

The notion of HR professionals as business partners has seized the imagination of HR people. In essence, the concept is that, as business partners, HR specialists share responsibility with their line management colleagues for the success of the enterprise and get involved with them in implementing business strategy and running the business.

As business partners, HR practitioners work closely with their line management colleagues. They are aware of business strategies and the opportunities and threats facing the organization. They are capable of analysing organizational strengths and weaknesses and diagnosing the issues facing the enterprise and their human resource implications. They understand the business model and know about the critical success factors that will create competitive advantage. They adopt a 'value-added' approach when making a convincing business case for innovations.

The term 'value added' looms large in the concept of the HR business partner. In the language of accounting, where the phrase originated, added value is defined as the value added to the cost of raw materials and bought-out parts by the process of production and distribution. In HR speak, a value-added approach means creating value through HR initiatives that make a significant contribution to organizational success. Strictly speaking, added value is measured by the extent to which the value of that contribution exceeds its cost or generates a return on investment. But the term is often used more generally to signify the business-oriented approach that HR professionals are expected to adopt and how it contributes to the creation of value by the firm. Adding value is about improving performance and results – getting more out of an activity than was put into it.

Critical evaluation of the business partner concept

It can be argued that too much has been made of the business partner model. Perhaps it is preferable to emphasize that the role of HR professionals is to be part of the business rather than merely being partners. There is the danger of overemphasizing the seemingly glamorous role of business or strategic partner at the expense of the service delivery aspect of the HR practitioner's role. Syrett (2006) noted that whatever strategic aspirations senior HR practitioners have, they will amount to nothing if the function they represent cannot deliver the essential transactional services their internal line clients require. As an HR specialist commented to Caldwell (2004): 'My credibility depends on running an extremely efficient and cost-effective administrative machine... If I don't get that right, and consistently, then you can forget about any big ideas.' Another person interviewed during Caldwell's research referred to personnel people as 'reactive pragmatists', a realistic situation in many organizations.

The problem of the overemphasis on the business partner role has been influenced by the erroneous belief that Ulrich was simply focusing on HR executives as business partners. This has had the unfortunate effect of implying that it was their only worthwhile function. But Ulrich cannot be blamed for this. In 1998 he gave equal emphasis to the need for HR people to be administrative experts, employee champions and change agents, and this was confirmed in the revised model (Ulrich and Brockbank, 2005).

Example – business partnering at the Automobile Association (AA)

The key competencies required by the AA for its business partners are concerned with commercial decision-making, commerciality, influencing people and facilitating change. They have to:

- understand the key factors affecting overall costs and profits;
- understand and interpret financial data;
- understand the connectivity between functional areas of the business;
- understand the impact of actions on cash flow and profitability.

The innovation role

A strategic and therefore proactive approach to HRM will mean that HR specialists will need to innovate – to introduce new processes and procedures they believe will increase organizational effectiveness.

The case for innovation should be established by processes of analysis and diagnosis using an evidence-based management approach to identify the business need and the issues to be addressed. 'Benchmarking' can be used to identify 'best practice' in other organizations. But 'best fit' is more important than 'best practice' – in other words, the innovation should meet the particular needs of the business, which are likely to differ from those of other 'best practice' organizations. It has to be demonstrable that the innovation is appropriate, beneficial, practical in the circumstances and can be implemented without too much difficulty in the shape of opposition from those affected by it or the unjustifiable use of resources – financial and the time of those involved.

The danger, according to Marchington (1995), is that HR people may go in for 'impression management' – aiming to make an impact on senior managers and colleagues through publicizing high-profile innovations. HR specialists who try to draw attention to themselves simply by promoting the latest flavour of the month, irrespective of its relevance or practicality, are falling into the trap that Drucker (1955: 243), anticipating Marchington by 40 years, described as follows: 'The constant worry of all personnel administrators is their inability to prove that they are making a contribution to the enterprise. Their preoccupation is with the search for a "gimmick" which will impress their management colleagues.'

As Marchington points out, the risk is that people believe 'all can be improved by a wave of the magic wand and the slaying of a few evil characters along the way'. This facile assumption means that people can too readily devise elegant solutions that do not solve the problem because of the hazards encountered during implementation – for example, the indifference or even open hostility of line managers. These have to be anticipated and catered for.

Guidelines for HR innovations are set out below.

Guidelines for HR innovations

As change agents HR specialists have to be experts in innovation. The following are guidelines on what needs to be done:

- Be clear on what has to be achieved and why.
- Ensure that what you do fits the strategy, culture and circumstances of the organization.
- Don't follow fashion – do your own thing as long as it is relevant and fits the organization's needs.
- Keep it simple – overcomplexity is a common reason for failure.
- Don't rush – it will take longer than you think.
- Don't try to do too much at once – an incremental approach is generally best.
- Assess resource requirements and costs.
- Pay close attention to project planning and management.
- Remember that the success of the innovation rests as much on the effectiveness of the process of implementation (line manager buy-in and skills are crucial) as it does on the quality of the concept, if not more so.
- Focus on change management approaches – communicate, involve and train.

The change agent role

The implementation of strategy means that HR specialists have to act as change agents, facilitating change by providing advice and support on its introduction and management. Caldwell (2001) categorized HR change agents in four dimensions:

1. *Transformational change* – a major change that has a dramatic effect on HR policy and practice across the whole organization.
2. *Incremental change* – gradual adjustments of HR policy and practices which affect single activities or multiple functions.

3. *HR vision* – a set of values and beliefs that affirm the legitimacy of the HR function as a strategic business partner.
4. *HR expertise* – the knowledge and skills that define the unique contribution the HR professional can make to effective people management.

Carrying out the role of the HR professional

How HR professionals carry out these roles depends on the context in which they work (the culture of the organization, the types of activities it carries out and the requirements of senior management), their skills and disposition and, importantly, the values they adopt. They will be affected by ambiguity and questions on the status of the profession and what is involved in being a professional. All this demands competency in a number of areas and requirements to adopt certain behaviours.

The values of HR

The most important aspect of values is the ethical stance HR people take in promoting people management policies and practices that are just, fair and take account of the interests of employees as well as those of the business. The pressure on HR practitioners in the private sector is to promote the interests of the business and thus increase shareholder value. In the public sector, the pressure is to promote the aims of the organization. The problem is that, as observed by Parkes and Davis (2013: 2413): 'HR seems wedded to its allegiance to profitability and distancing itself from any connections with welfare.' They also note that: 'The economic drivers for organizations are important but the danger of relying only on the business-case is that ethics and responsibility become optional.'

Ambiguities in the role of HR practitioners

The activities and roles of HR specialists and the demands made upon them as described above appear to be quite clear cut, but Thurley (1981) pointed out that HR practitioners can be specialists in ambiguity. This continues in the age of Ulrich. As Hope-Hailey *et al* (2005: 51) commented: 'Ulrich highlighted that HR professionals must be both strategic and operational, yet the potential role conflict this could engender was not addressed.' Caldwell (2004: 212) reached the following conclusions on the basis of his research:

> There is the issue of 'powerlessness' or the marginality of HR practitioners in management decision-making processes, especially at a strategic level. The HR function has an inward-looking tendency to identify professional expertise mainly with administrative concerns over who controls HR activities, rather than questions of HR practices or who has responsibility for implementing HR policy.

The difficulties that HR professionals face in dealing with ambiguity was well described by Guest and King (2004: 421):

> Much management activity is typically messy and ambiguous. This appears to apply more strongly to people management than to most other activities. By implication, the challenge lies not in removing or resolving the ambiguities in the role [of HR professionals] but in learning to live with them. To succeed in this requires skills in influencing, negotiating and learning when to compromise. For those with a high tolerance of ambiguity, the role of HR specialist, with its distinctive opportunity to contribute to the management of people in organizations, offers unique challenges; for those only comfortable if they can resolve the ambiguities, the role may become a form of purgatory.

The status of HR

Over the years, the HR profession has suffered from an inferiority complex. This may arise because the role of HR professionals is ill-defined (they are unsure of where they stand), their status is not fully recognized, or top management and line managers have equivocal views about their value to the organization. Tyson and Fell (1986: 68) remarked that 'the ambiguous character of their work contributes to the problems of convincing others of its value'.

Long ago Drucker (1955: 243) observed that: 'The constant worry of all personnel administrators is their inability to prove that they are making a contribution to the organization.' Skinner (1981: 106) in his *Harvard Business Review* article, 'Big hat no cattle', stated that 'the corporate role of personnel has always been problematic'; and Tyson and Fell (1986: 136) argued that: 'Classical personnel management has not been granted a position in decision-making circles because it has frequently not earned one. It has not been concerned with the totality of the organization but often with issues which have not only been parochial but esoteric to boot.'

Watson (1996) referred to the perpetual marginality of the HR function and Caldwell (2004: 212) raised the 'issue of "powerlessness" or the marginality of HR practitioners in management decision-making processes'.

Traditionally, the HR practitioner's reaction to this problem has been, in the words of Drucker (1955: 243) to 'search for a "gimmick" that will impress their management colleagues'. This was later called adopting 'the flavour of the month'. HR professionals have now become more sophisticated. They have enthusiastically supported approaches that appeal to management such as engagement policies and talent management. And in the UK, CIPD spends a lot of time attempting to boost the status of the HR profession by stressing the strategic and business partner role of practitioners.

But research conducted by Guthrie *et al* (2011: 1681) confirmed that: 'HR departments are still often viewed, collectively, as a function that is more bureaucratic than strategic.' They noted previous research, which has shown that 'it is this role – the strategic role – in which line executives believe that HR is particularly deficient' (ibid: 1682). The following perceptive comment was made on this trend by Keegan and Francis (2010: 878):

> Bearing in mind the history of HR practitioners' struggles for acceptance as key organizational players it is hardly surprising that a way of discursively modelling the concept of HR as 'hard' and relating it to others concepts such as 'business driven agendas' and 'strategic management', has become so popular. It offers perhaps a way out of the dualism when they seek to claim a share of strategic decision making while at the same time struggling to attend to the employee centred and administrative aspects of the role.

They also commented that: 'Exhortations for HR practitioners to pursue strategic roles and downplay their historically embedded administrative and employee championing pose a serious threat to the integrity of HR work and claims to professional expertise' (ibid: 894).

What it means to be an HR professional

Professionalism in HR as in other fields can be defined generally as the conduct exhibited by people who are providing advice and services that require expertise and that meet defined or generally accepted standards of behaviour. Work done by a professional is usually distinguished by its reference to a framework of fundamental concepts that reflect the skilful application of specialized education, training and experience. It is accompanied by a sense of responsibility and an acceptance of recognized standards. Even more loosely, people can be described as acting 'professionally' when they do their work well and act responsibly.

Professionalism in HR means working in accordance with a professional ethos. As suggested by Fletcher (2004) this is characterized by:

- the possession of specialized knowledge and skills;
- power and status based on expertise;
- self-discipline and adherence to some aspirational performance standards;
- the opportunity to display high levels of autonomy;
- the ability to apply some independence of judgement;
- operating, and being guided by, a code of ethics.

HR professionals are required to uphold the standards laid down by their professional body, the CIPD, but they must also adhere to their own ethical values. Additionally, they are bound by organizational codes of conduct expressed formally or accepted and understood as core values (the basic values adopted by an organization that set out what is believed to be important about how people and organizations should behave).

HR competencies

The demands made on HR professionals in terms of skills and expected behaviours are considerable although, nowadays, as Keegan and Francis (2010: 884) commented, 'Success in HR roles is measured in terms of developing an effective business rather than people skills.' Brockbank *et al* (1999) conducted research that led to a definition of the key HR competency 'domains' and their components, as set out in Table 3.1.

HR behaviours

The CIPD's HR profession map first issued in June 2009 (CIPD, 2013) listed the following behaviours needed by HR professionals to carry out their activities:

- curious;
- decisive thinker;
- skilled influencer;
- driven to deliver;
- collaborative;
- personally credible;
- courage to challenge;
- role model.

TABLE 3.1 Key HR specialist competency areas (Brockbank *et al*, 1999)

Competency domain	Components
1 Personal credibility	Live the firm's values, maintain relationships founded on trust, act with an 'attitude' (a point of view about how the business can win, backing up opinion with evidence).
2 Ability to manage change	Drive change: ability to diagnose problems, build relationships with clients, articulate a vision, set a leadership agenda, solve problems and implement goals.
3 Ability to manage culture	Act as 'keepers of the culture', identify the culture required to meet the firm's business strategy, frame culture in a way that excites employees, translate desired culture into specific behaviours, encourage executives to behave consistently with the desired culture.
4 Delivery of human resource practices	Expert in the speciality, able to deliver state-of-the-art innovative HR practices in such areas as recruitment, employee development, compensation and communication.
5 Understanding of the business	Strategy, organization, competitors, finance, marketing, sales, operations and IT.

The HR role of line managers

HR can initiate new policies and practices but it is line managers that have the main responsibility for implementing them. In other words, HR proposes but the line disposes. As Guest (1991: 159) observed: 'HRM is too important to be left to personnel managers.'

If line managers are not inclined favourably towards what HR wants them to do they won't do it or, if compelled to, they will be half-hearted about it. On the basis of their research, Guest and King (2004: 421) noted that 'better HR depended not so much on better procedures but better implementation and ownership of implementation by line managers'.

As pointed out by Purcell *et al* (2003), high levels of organizational performance are not achieved simply by having a range of well-conceived HR policies and practices in place. What makes the difference is how these policies and practices are implemented. That is where the role of line managers in people management is crucial: 'managers... play a vital role in making involvement happen, in communicating, in being open to allow employee concerns to be raised and discussed, in allowing people space to influence how they do their job, and in coaching, guiding and recognizing performance and providing help for the future' (ibid: 40). Purcell and his colleagues noted that dealing with people is perhaps the aspect of their work in which line managers can exercise the greatest amount of discretion and they can use that discretion by not putting HR's ideas into practice. As they observed, it is line managers who bring HR policies to life.

A further factor affecting the role of line managers is their ability to do the HR tasks assigned to them. People-centred activities such as defining roles (job design), interviewing, reviewing performance, providing feedback, coaching, and identifying learning and development needs all require special skills. Some managers have them; many don't. Performance management systems and performance-related pay schemes can easily fail because of untrained line managers. The implementation of policies to enhance engagement levels (as described in Chapter 15) depends largely on line managers.

Hutchinson and Purcell (2003) made the following recommendations on how to improve the quality of the contribution line managers make to people management.

Source review

Improving the quality of line managers as people managers – Hutchinson and Purcell (2003)

- Provide them with time to carry out their people management duties, which are often superseded by other management duties.
- Select them carefully with much more attention being paid to the behavioural competencies required.
- Support them with strong organizational values concerning leadership and people management.
- Encourage the development of a good working relationship with their own managers.
- Ensure they receive sufficient skills training to enable them to perform their people management activities such as performance management.

To which can be added that better implementation and better ownership by line managers of HR practices is more likely to be achieved if: 1) the practice demonstrably benefits them; 2) they are involved in the development and, importantly, the testing of the practices; 3) the practice is not too complicated, bureaucratic or time-consuming; 4) their responsibilities are defined and communicated clearly; and 5) they are provided with the guidance, support and training required to implement the practice.

Key learning points: Delivering HRM – systems and roles

HRM delivery

HRM is delivered through the HR architecture of an organization, which includes the HR system, HR practices and the HR delivery model adopted by the HR function.

HR architecture

HR architecture includes the HR systems and processes and employee behaviours as well as the structure of the HR function.

The HR system

The HR system as part of the HR architecture consists of the interrelated and jointly supportive HR activities and practices, which together enable HRM goals to be achieved.

The HR delivery model

The HR delivery model describes how those services are delivered by the HR function. The best known model was produced by Ulrich in 1998; he suggested that HR could be delivered by specialists in four ways: strategic partner, administrative expert, employee champion and change agent.

The 'three-legged stool' model of the HR function

This model identifies three areas of HR activity: centres of expertise, strategic business partners and shared service centres.

Roles of HR professionals

They can act as business partners, strategists, innovators, change agents, internal consultants, facilitators and coaches.

Ambiguities in the role of HR practitioners

The activities and roles of HR specialists and the demands made upon them appear to be quite clear cut but in practice the role can be ambiguous.

Professionalism in HR

Professionalism is defined generally as the conduct exhibited by people who are providing advice and services that require expertise and that meet defined or generally accepted standards of behaviour. HR professionals are required to uphold the standards laid down by their professional body, the CIPD, but they must also adhere to their own ethical values.

The HR role of line managers

Line managers play a crucial role in implementing HR policies but they are not always committed or qualified to do so.

Questions

1 How is HRM delivered?
2 What is HRM architecture?
3 What is an HR system?
4 What are the key HR practices?
5 What is the HR delivery model?
6 What is the 'three-legged stool' model for organizing the HR function?
7 What are the main roles of HR professionals?
8 What are the key HR competency domains or areas identified by Brockbank and his colleagues?
9 What does professionalism in HR involve?
10 What is the HR role of line managers?

References

Becker, B E and Huselid, M A (1998) High performance work systems and firm performance: a synthesis of research and managerial implications, *Research on Personnel and Human Resource Management*, 16, pp 53–101

Becker, B E and Huselid, M A (2006) Strategic human resource management: where do we go from here? *Journal of Management*, 32 (6), pp 898–925

Becker, B E, Huselid, M A and Ulrich, D (2001) *The HR Score Card: Linking people, strategy, and performance*, Boston, MA, Harvard Business School Press

Boselie, P, Dietz, G and Boon, C (2005) Commonalities and contradictions in HRM and performance research, *Human Resource Management Journal*, 15 (3), pp 67–94

Brockbank, W, Ulrich, D and Beatty, D (1999) HR professional development: creating the future creators at the University of Michigan Business School, *Human Resource Management*, 38, Summer, pp 111–17

Caldwell, R (2001) Champions, adapters, consultants and synergists: the new change agents in HRM, *Human Resource Management Journal*, 11 (3), pp 39–52

Caldwell, R (2004) Rhetoric, facts and self-fulfilling prophesies: exploring practitioners' perceptions of progress in implementing HRM, *Industrial Relations Journal*, 35 (3), pp 196–215

Chartered Institute of Personnel and Development (2002) *Employment Law: Survey report*. London, CIPD

Chartered Institute of Personnel and Development (2007) The Changing HR Function, London, CIPD

Chartered Institute of Personnel and Development (2010) CIPD Next Generation, London, CIPD

Chartered Institute of Personnel and Development (2013) HR Profession Map, http://www.cipd.co.uk/hr-profession-map-download.aspx [accessed 25 January 2013]

Crail, M (2006) HR roles and responsibilities 2006: benchmarking the HR function, *IRS Employment Review* 839, 20 January, pp 9–15

Drucker, P (1955) *The Practice of Management*, London, Heinemann

Fletcher, C (2004) *Appraisal and Feedback: Making performance review work*, 3rd edn, London, CIPD

Francis, H and Keegan, A (2006) The changing face of HRM: in search of balance, *Human Resource Management Journal*, 16 (3), pp 231–49

Gratton, L (2003) The Humpty Dumpty effect: a view of a fragmented HR function, *People Management*, 5 January, p 18

Guest, D E (1991) Personnel management: the end of orthodoxy, *British Journal of Industrial Relations*, 29 (2), pp 149–76

Guest, D E and King, Z (2004) Power, innovation and problem-solving: the personnel managers' three steps to heaven?, *Journal of Management Studies*, 41 (3), pp 401–23

Guthrie, J P, Flood, P C, Liu, W, MacCurtain, S and Armstrong, C (2011) Big hat no cattle? The relationship between the use of high performance work systems and managerial perceptions of HR departments, *The International Journal of Human Resource Management*, 22 (8), pp 1672–85

Hesketh, A and Hird, M (2010) Using relationships between leaders to leverage more value from people: building a golden triangle, in (eds) P Sparrow, A Hesketh, M Hird and C Cooper, *Leading HR*, Basingstoke, Palgrave Macmillan, pp 103–21

Hird, M, Sparrow, P and Marsh, C (2010) HR structures: are they working?, in (eds) P Sparrow, A Hesketh, M Hird, and C Cooper, *Leading HR*, Basingstoke, Palgrave Macmillan, pp 23–45

Hirsh, W (2008) What do people want from you?, *People Management*, 18 September, pp 23–6

Holley, N (2009) *HR Models: Lessons from best practice*, Henley, Henley Business School http://www henleyhktest.reading.ac.uk [accessed 26 February 2013]

Hope-Hailey, V, Farndale, E and Truss, C (2005) The HR department's role in organizational performance, *Human Resource Management Journal*, 15 (3), pp 49–66

Hope-Hailey, V, Gratton, L, McGovern, P, Stiles, P and Truss, C (1997) A chameleon function? HRM in the '90s, *Human Resource Management Journal*, 7 (3), pp 5–18

Hoque, K and Noon, M (2001) Counting angels: a comparison of personnel and HR specialists, *Human Resource Management Journal*, 11 (3), pp 5–22

Hutchinson, S and Purcell, J (2003) *Bringing Policies to Life: The vital role of front line managers in people management*, London, CIPD

IDS (2010) HR Function Survey, *HR Study* 928, October, London, IDS

IRS (2012) *HR Roles and Responsibilities* Survey, http://www.xperthr.co.uk/article/106943/hr-role-and-responsibilities-the- 2012-survey [accessed 24 February 2013]

Johnson, C (1999) Changing shapes: trends in human resource reorganizations, *HR Magazine*, 44 (3), pp 40–48

Keegan, A and Francis, H (2010) Practitioner talk: the changing textscape of HRM and emergence of HR business partnership, *The International Journal of Human Resource Management*, 21 (6), pp 873–98

Marchington, M (1995) Fairy tales and magic wands: new employment practices in perspective, *Employee Relations*, Spring, pp 51–66

McLean, A (1981) Organization development: a case of the emperor's new clothes?, *Personnel Review*, 4 (1), pp 3–14

Parkes, C and Davis, A J (2013) Ethics and social responsibility – do HR professionals have 'the courage to challenge' or are they set to be permanent 'bystanders'? *International Journal of Human Resource Management*, 23 (12), pp 2411–34

Purcell, J (1999) Best practice or best fit: chimera or cul-de-sac, *Human Resource Management Journal*, 9 (3), pp 26–41

Purcell, J, Kinnie, K, Hutchinson, R, Rayton, B and Swart, J (2003) *Understanding the People and Performance Link: Unlocking the black box*, London, CIPD

Reilly, P (2007) Facing up to the facts, *People Management*, 20 September, pp 43–45

Sears, L (2011) A new way of seeing: insight-led HR, *People Management*, April, pp 34–37

Sisson, K (1990) Introducing the Human Resource Management Journal, *Human Resource Management Journal*, 1 (1), pp 1–11

Skinner, W (1981) Big hat no cattle: managing human resources, *Harvard Business Review*, September–October, pp 106–14

Storey, J (1992) *Developments in the Management of Human Resources*, Oxford, Blackwell

Syrett, M (2006) *Four Reflections on Developing a Human Capital Measurement Capability: What's the future for human capital?*, London, CIPD

Thurley, K (1981) Personnel management: a case for urgent treatment, *Personnel Management*, August, pp 24–29

Tyson, S (1987) The management of the personnel function, *Journal of Management Studies*, 24 (5), pp 523–32

Tyson, S and Fell, A (1986) *Evaluating the Personnel Function*, London, Hutchinson

Ulrich, D (1997) *Human Resource Champions*, Boston, MA, Harvard Business School Press

Ulrich, D (1998) A new mandate for human resources, *Harvard Business Review*, January–February, pp 124–34

Ulrich, D and Brockbank, W (2005) *The HR Value Proposition*, Cambridge, MA, Harvard Press

Watson, T (1996) *Management, Organisation and Employment Strategy*, London, Routledge

Wright, P M, Snell, S A and Jacobsen, H H (2004) Current approaches to HR strategies: inside-out versus outside-in, *Human Resource Planning*, 27 (4), pp 36–46

04 HRM and performance

KEY CONCEPTS AND TERMS

The black box

Causal ambiguity

High-performance culture

High-performance work system

HR value chain

Performance management

Reversed causality

LEARNING OUTCOMES

On completing this chapter you should be able to define these key concepts. You should also understand:

- What impact HRM can make on performance
- How HRM makes that impact
- The nature of a high-performance culture
- How a high-performance work system functions
- The role of performance management
- How HR can contribute

Introduction

All organizations are under an obligation to their stakeholders to perform well. To do this they depend on the quality, dedication, enthusiasm, expertise and skill of the people working in them at every level. The message of the resource-based view is that HRM delivers added value and helps to achieve sustainable competitive advantage through the strategic development of the organization's rare, hard-to-imitate and hard-to-substitute human resources. As Guest (1997: 269) argued: 'The distinctive feature of HRM is its assumption that improved performance is achieved through the people in the organization.' If, therefore, appropriate HR policies and practices are introduced, it can also be assumed that HRM will impact on firm performance.

The chapter begins with a review of the evidence that HRM makes an impact on performance and of the problems met by researchers in establishing what the link is and how it works. It continues with a description of the concept of a high-performance culture and how it can be achieved through a high-performance work system and performance management.

The impact of HR

Much research has been carried out showing that good HRM practice and firm performance are correlated; notable examples in the UK are Guest *et al* (2000a), Patterson *et al* (1997), Purcell *et al* (2003), Thompson (2002) and West *et al* (2002), summarized in Table 4.1.

How HRM makes an impact

Storey *et al* (2009: 4) observed that: 'The premise is that, in some shape or form, HR policies have an effect on HR practices and these in turn influence staff attitudes and behaviours which will, in turn again, impact on service offerings and customer perceptions of value.' The assumption is that good HRM practices will enhance performance. This is supported by the notion of 'best practice HRM', which as noted in Chapter 2 is illustrated by lists such as Pfeffer's (1998). Bowen and Ostroff (2004) argued that the link between HRM and performance is likely to be greater where what they describe as a 'strong' HR system is in place. Core characteristics of their 'strong' system are high levels of distinctiveness, consistency and consensus. Where these are present there will be an organizational climate that supports HR implementation. But they also made the obvious suggestion that it is not enough to have good practices if they are not properly implemented. As Guest (2011: 6) commented: 'What this does is switch the focus to line management.' Nishii *et al* (2008) argued that it is not just the presence of practices that is important but 'perceptions about the intentions behind the practices'.

An extensive research project conducted by Guest and Conway (2011) led to the finding that consensus on HR effectiveness did not support Bowen and Ostroff's (2004) proposition that a strong HR system would have a significant association with outcomes. Guest and Conway commented that their study revealed very low levels of agreement about HR effectiveness. They concluded that: 'There are three elements in a logical model of HR effectiveness. HR practices must be present, they must be effective and they must be effectively implemented' (ibid: 1700).

Uncertainties about the link between HRM and performance

As noted earlier, much research has demonstrated an association between HRM and performance. But Guest *et al* (2000b) observed that it left uncertainties about cause and effect. Ulrich (1997: 304) pointed out that: 'HR practices seem to matter; logic says it is so; survey findings confirm it. Direct relationships between performance and attention to HR practices are often fuzzy, however, and vary according to the population sampled and the measures used.' Guest (2011: 11) summed up his article on HRM and performance with the comment that: 'After hundreds of research studies we are still in no position to assert with any confidence that good HRM has an impact on organization performance.'

There are two issues that affect the determination of a link between HRM and firm performance: 'causal ambiguity' and 'contingency factors'. These contribute to what is known as the 'black box' phenomenon.

TABLE 4.1 Research on the link between HRM and firm performance

Researcher(s)	Methodology	Outcomes
Patterson *et al* (1997)	The research examined the link between business performance and organization culture and the use of a number of HR practices.	HR practices explained significant variations in profitability and productivity (19% and 18% respectively). Two HR practices were particularly significant: 1) the acquisition and development of employee skills, and 2) job design including flexibility, responsibility and variety.
Guest *et al* (2000a)	An analysis of the 1998 WERS survey, which sampled some 2,000 workplaces and obtained the views of about 28,000 employees.	A strong association exists between HRM and both employee attitudes and workplace performance.
Thompson (2002)	A study of the impact of high-performance work practices such as teamworking, appraisal, job rotation, broad-banded grade structures and sharing of business information in UK aerospace establishments.	The number of HR practices and the proportion of the workforce covered appeared to be the key differentiating factor between more and less successful firms.
West *et al* (2002)	Research conducted in 61 UK hospitals obtaining information on HR strategy, policy and procedures from chief executives and HR directors and mortality rates.	An association between certain HR practices and lower mortality rates was identified. As noted by West: 'If you have HR practices that focus on effort and skill; develop people's skills; encourage cooperation, collaboration, innovation and synergy in teams for most, if not all employees, the whole system functions and performs better.'
Purcell *et al* (2003)	A University of Bath longitudinal study of 12 companies to establish how people management impacts on organizational performance.	The most successful companies had 'the big idea'. They had a clear vision and a set of integrated values. They were concerned with sustaining performance and flexibility. Clear evidence existed between positive attitudes towards HR policies and practices, levels of satisfaction, motivation and commitment, and operational performance. Policy and practice implementation (not the number of HR practices adopted) is the vital ingredient in linking people management to business performance and this is primarily the task of line managers.

TABLE 4.1 Continued

Researcher(s)	Methodology	Outcomes
Birdi *et al* (2008)	A longitudinal research study by the Institute of Work Psychology, University of Sheffield covering 308 companies over 22 years, designed to establish the impact of various HRM and operational practices on company productivity.	It was found that the impact of empowerment (job enrichment) was to produce a gain of nearly 7% of value added per employee, while the gain for extensive training was nearly 6%. But teamwork did not make a significant impact, neither did total quality management or just-in-time.

Causal ambiguity

The term causal ambiguity refers to the numerous, subtle and often hidden interconnections between the factors influencing cause and effect. Boselie *et al* (2005: 75) referred to the causal distance between an HRM input and an output such as financial performance: 'Put simply, so many variables and events, both internal and external, affect organizations that this direct linkage strains credibility.'

A basic reason for ambiguity is multiple causation, which exists when there is more than one possible cause for an effect. HRM may have caused an improvement in performance but there may be many other economic or business factors that did so, and it could be difficult to unravel them. Another factor is the possibility of reversed causality (a situation where A might have caused B but B might well have caused A). As Purcell *et al* (2003: 2) expressed it: 'Although it is nice to believe that more HR practices leads to higher economic return, it is just as possible that it is successful firms that can afford more extensive (and expensive) HRM practices.'

Contingency factors

Causation will additionally be affected by the organization's context, ie the internal and external environmental factors that influence what happens within the organization.

The black box phenomenon

Causal ambiguity also stems from the black box phenomenon, as illustrated in Figure 4.1. This is the situation in which, while it may be possible to observe HRM inputs in the form of HR practices and to measure firm performance outputs, it may be difficult to ascertain, through research, what happened in between – what the HRM outcomes were that converted the input of HR practices into firm performance outputs. Alvesson (2009: 56) suggested that: 'Research does not proceed beyond attempts to find an empirical association between HR practices and organizational performance. The phenomena are in a black box, only input and output are registered and what is happening remains clouded in the dark.'

FIGURE 4.1 The black box phenomenon

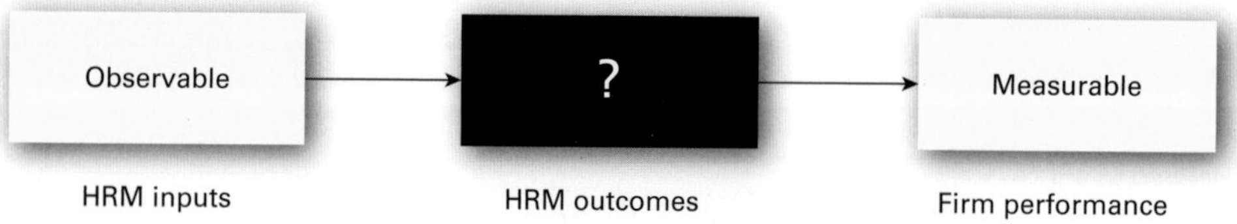

Explanations of how HRM makes an impact

Guest (1997: 268) stated that: 'The assumption is that "appropriate" HRM practices tap the motivation and commitment of employees.' He explained how expectancy theory might help to explain the HR/performance link as follows:

> The expectancy theory of motivation provides one possible basis for developing a more coherent rationale about the link between HRM practices and performance. Although expectancy theory is concerned primarily with motivation, it is also a theory about the link between motivation and performance. Specifically, it proposes that high performance, at the individual level, depends on high motivation plus possession of the necessary skills and abilities and an appropriate role and understanding of that role. It is a short step to specify the HRM practices that encourage high skills and abilities, for example careful selection and high investment in training; high motivation, for example employee involvement and possibly performance-related pay; and an appropriate role structure and role perception, for example job design and extensive communication and feedback.

Following this contribution from Guest, any explanation of the impact of HRM on organizational performance is likely to be based on three propositions: 1) that HR practices can make a direct impact on employee characteristics such as engagement, commitment, motivation and skill; 2) if employees have these characteristics it is probable that organizational performance in terms of productivity, quality and the delivery of high levels of customer service will improve; and 3) if such aspects of organizational performance improve, the financial results achieved by the organization will improve. This can be described as the HR value chain.

The propositions highlight the existence of an intermediate factor between HRM and financial performance. This factor consists of the HRM outcomes in the shape of employee characteristics affected by HR practices. Therefore, HRM does not make a direct impact. A model of the impact of HRM taking into account the considerations of reverse causation and contingency effects mentioned earlier is shown in Figure 4.2.

But high performance is not just about HR practices. The case-based research by Purcell *et al* (2003) showed that the key to activating what they called the 'people-performance' link lies not only in well-crafted 'bundles' of HR practices, but in their conjunction with a powerful and cohering organizational vision (or 'big idea') and corporate leadership, together with front-line leadership's action and use of its discretionary power.

FIGURE 4.2 Impact of HRM on organizational performance (based on Paauwe, 2004)

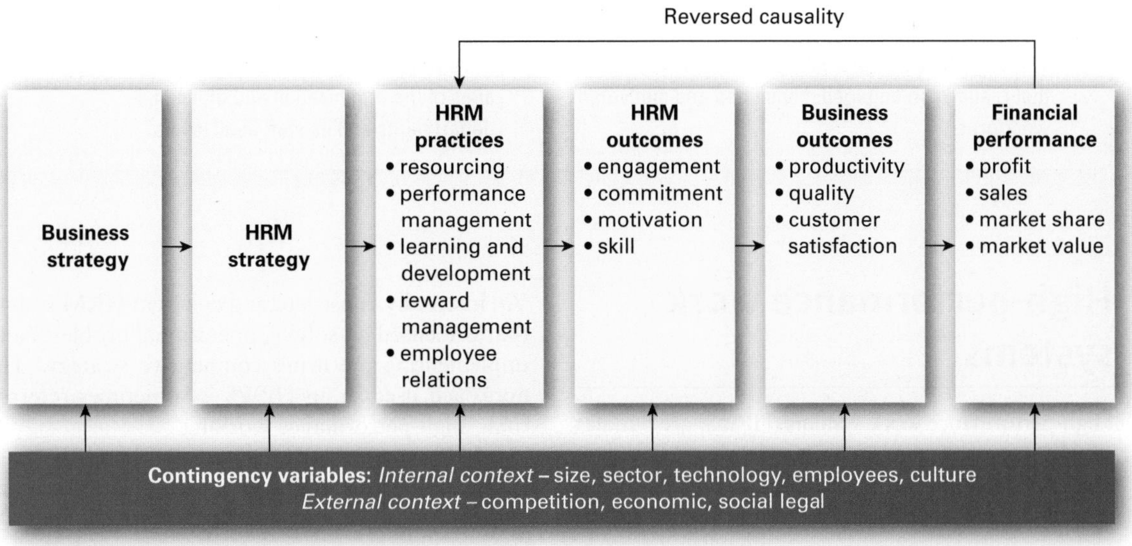

Developing a high-performance culture

Organizations achieve sustained high performance through the systems of work they adopt, but these systems are managed and operated by people. Ultimately, therefore, high-performance working is about improving performance through people. This can be done through the development and implementation of a high-performance culture involving high-performance work systems in which performance management plays an important part.

High-performance cultures are ones in which the achievement of high levels of performance is a way of life. The characteristics of such cultures are set out below.

Characteristics of a high-performance culture

- Management defines what it requires in the shape of performance improvements, sets goals for success and monitors performance to ensure that the goals are achieved.
- Alternative work practices are adopted such as job redesign, autonomous work teams, improvement groups, team briefing and flexible working.
- People know what is expected of them – they understand their goals and accountabilities.
- People feel that their job is worth doing, and there is a strong fit between the job and their capabilities.
- People are empowered to maximize their contribution.
- There is strong leadership from the top that engenders a shared belief in the importance of continuing improvement.
- There is a focus on promoting positive attitudes that result in an engaged, committed and motivated workforce.
- Performance management processes are aligned to business goals to ensure that people are engaged in achieving agreed objectives and standards.
- Capacities of people are developed through learning at all levels to support performance improvement and they are provided with opportunities to make full use of their skills and abilities.
- A pool of talent ensures a continuous supply of high performers in key roles.
- People are valued and rewarded according to their contribution.
- People are involved in developing high-performance practices.
- There is a climate of trust and teamwork, aimed at delivering a distinctive service to the customer.
- A clear line of sight exists between the strategic aims of the organization and those of its departments and its staff at all levels.

High-performance work systems

High-performance work systems (HPWS) are bundles of HR practices that facilitate employee involvement, skill enhancement and motivation. An HPWS was described by Becker and Huselid (1998: 55) as: 'An internally consistent and coherent HRM system that is focused on solving operational problems and implementing the firm's competitive strategy.' The approach used in an HPWS is sometimes referred to as 'high-performance working'.

Performance cultures are created by HPWS that embody ways of thinking about performance in organizations and how it can be improved. They are concerned with developing and implementing bundles of complementary practices that, as an integrated whole, will make a much more powerful impact on performance than if they were dealt with as separate entities. Appelbaum *et al* (2000) stated that HPWS facilitate employee involvement, skill enhancement and motivation.

Features of an HPWS

There is no generally accepted definition of an HPWS and there is no standard list of the features or components of such a system. In spite of this problem of definition, an attempt to describe the basic components of an HPWS was made by Shih *et al* (2005) as follows:

- *Job infrastructure* – workplace arrangements that equip workers with the proper abilities to do their jobs, provide them with the means to do their jobs, and give them the motivation to do their jobs. These practices must be combined to produce their proper effects.
- *Training programmes to enhance employee skills* – investment in increasing employee skills, knowledge and ability.
- *Information sharing and worker involvement mechanisms* – to understand the available alternatives and make correct decisions.
- *Reward and promotion opportunities that provide motivation* – to encourage skilled employees to engage in effective discretionary decision-making in a variety of environmental contingencies.

Many descriptions of high-performance systems include lists of desirable features and therefore embody the notion of 'best practice'. However, Gephart (1995) noted that research has not clearly identified any single set of high-performance practices. Becker *et al* (1997) pointed out that HPWS were highly idiosyncratic and had to fit the organization's individual circumstances. The lists that have been compiled vary considerably, as is shown in the selection set out in Table 4.2.

Examples

The examples in Table 4.3 of firms that adopt high-performance working policies and practices, assembled by Stevens (2005), illustrate the variety and generalized nature of approaches.

Critical evaluation of the high-performance work system approach

Research conducted by Ramsay *et al* (2000) aimed to explore linkages from HPWS practices to employee outcomes, and via these to organizational performance. They referred to the existence of the 'black box', meaning that while the introduction of an HPWS may be associated with improved performance, no researchers have yet established how this happens. They commented that 'the widely held view that positive performance outcomes from HPWS flow via positive employee outcomes has been shown to be highly questionable' (ibid: 521).

Godard (2001) concluded, following his research in Canada, that the actual effects of high-performance work systems can vary considerably and many have a limited lifespan. Following further research, he commented in 2004 that:

> The full adoption of this (high performance) paradigm may not yield outcomes that are appreciably more positive than those yielded by practices that have long been associated with good management, including professional personnel practices (eg job ladders, employment security, grievance systems, formal training, above-market pay), group work organization, information sharing and accommodative union relations policies... There may be positive effects in some workplaces. However, these effects may be inherently more limited than assumed and, in a great many workplaces, may not be sufficient to justify full adoption.

TABLE 4.2 Components of an HPWS

US Department of Labor (1993)	Appelbaum *et al* (2000)	Sung and Ashton (2005)	Thompson and Heron (2005)
• Careful and extensive systems for recruitment, selection and training. • Formal systems for sharing information with employees. • Clear job design. • High-level participation processes. • Monitoring of attitudes. • Performance appraisals. • Properly functioning grievance procedures. • Promotion and compensation schemes that provide for the recognition and reward of high-performing employees.	• Work is organized to permit front-line workers to participate in decisions that alter organizational routines. • Workers require more skills to do their jobs successfully, and many of these skills are firm specific. • Workers experience greater autonomy over their job tasks and methods of work. • Incentive pay motivates workers to extend extra effort on developing skills. • Employment security provides front-line workers with a long-term stake in the company and a reason to invest in its future.	• High-involvement work practices – eg self-directed teams, quality circles and sharing/access to company information. • Human resource practices – eg sophisticated recruitment processes, performance appraisals, work redesign and mentoring. • Reward and commitment practices – eg various financial rewards, family friendly policies, job rotation and flexi-hours.	• Information sharing. • Sophisticated recruitment. • Formal induction programme. • Five or more days of off-the-job training in the last year. • Semi- or totally autonomous work teams; continuous improvement teams; problem-solving groups. • Interpersonal skills development. • Performance feedback. • Involvement – works council, suggestion scheme, opinion survey. • Team-based rewards, employee share ownership scheme, profit-sharing scheme.

But research conducted by Sung and Ashton (2005), Combs *et al* (2006) and Ericksen (2007) indicated that an HPWS can significantly improve performance. Even so, it is still possible to have reservations about causality and there seems to be no agreement on what constitutes an HPWS except for variable lists of 'best practices' – a dubious concept. As Godard (2004) commented, these lists are no more than bundles of long-accepted good personnel practices. Perhaps the virtue of the HPWS model is simply that it makes people think about what can be done to improve performance and how the various approaches can be linked together in a cohesive action programme.

TABLE 4.3 Examples of high-performance working ingredients

Organization	High-performance working ingredients
Halo Foods	A strategy that maintains competitiveness by increasing added value through the efforts and enhanced capability of all staff. The integration of technical advance with people development. Continuing reliance on teamworking and effective leadership, with innovation and self- and team management skills.
Land Registry	Organizational changes to streamline processes, raise skill levels and release talents. Managers who could see that the problems were as much cultural as organizational. Recruitment of people whose attitudes and aptitudes match the needs of high-performance work practices.
Meritor Heavy Vehicle Braking Systems	Skill enhancement, particularly of management and self-management skills using competence frameworks. Teamworking skills and experience used on improvement projects. Linking learning, involvement and performance management.
Orangebox	A strategy that relies on constant reinvention of operational capability. Engagement and development of existing talent and initiative in productivity improvement. Increasing use of cross-departmental projects to tackle wider opportunities.
Perkinelmer	A vision and values worked through by managers and supervisors. Engagement of everyone in the organization and establishment of a continuous improvement culture. Learning as a basis for change.
United Welsh Housing Association	Linking of better employment relations with better performance. Using staff experience to improve customer service. Focusing management development on the cascading of a partnership culture.

Performance management

Performance management can contribute to the development of a high-performance culture in an organization by delivering the message that high performance is important. The management of organizational performance is the continuing responsibility of top management who, with the help and advice of HR, plan, organize, monitor and control activities and provide leadership to achieve strategic objectives and satisfy the needs and requirements of stakeholders. Individual and team performance management systems play an important part, but they function within the context of what is done to manage organizational performance and to develop effective work systems.

The strategic approach adopted by Johnson & Johnson was described by Wortzel-Hoffman and Boltizar (2007) as follows:

> As we embarked on developing an integrated performance and development process into the organization, we knew that driving change and an enhanced process requires a cultural shift within an organization. The best performance management becomes a continuous process and is not a one time event; it takes time and effort and a dedication to developing people. We also knew that from a business standpoint it was critical to build and develop the talent pipeline of the organization to meet the aggressive business goals and dynamically changing marketplace.

Performance management at organizational, team and individual level defines what high performance is and how managers and their teams should achieve it. It explains how performance should be measured and the steps that should be taken to monitor results in comparison with expectations. The means of achieving high performance are provided by defining the performance expectations implicit in the psychological contract, creating high levels of engagement, motivating people and enhancing skills and competencies through feedback, coaching and personal development planning. Performance management systems are described more fully in Chapter 25.

The contribution of HR

HR contributes to enhancing organizational performance by providing insights on the performance issues affecting the organization and its employees. This means identifying the reasons for the issues, exploring their implications for business and people management and conveying these messages to management. The aim is to find new ways of meeting performance challenges.

HR can advise management on the development of a high performance strategy supported by performance and reward initiatives. Additionally, HR can review policies and practices such as those concerned with organizational development, engagement, resourcing, learning and development, and employee relations. Decisions can then be made to enhance existing policies and practices or introduce new ones. Importantly, consideration needs to be given to how integration of these policies and practices can be achieved by linking them together in a 'bundle' so that they are mutually supportive.

HR has then to prepare a business case for any developments or innovations and persuade management to accept it. Line managers and employees should be involved in the development programme and a communications strategy should be created to inform people about what is going on and how it will affect them.

HR will also be involved in producing and project managing an implementation programme. As necessary, learning and development activities and events will be conducted to ensure that line managers and employees have the skills required.

Key learning points: HRM and performance

The impact of HRM

Much research has been carried out showing that good HRM practice and firm performance are correlated; notable examples in the UK are Guest *et al* (2000a), Patterson *et al* (1997), Purcell *et al* (2003), Thompson (2002) and West *et al* (2002).

How HRM makes an impact

Storey *et al* (2009: 4) observed that: 'The premise is that, in some shape or form, HR policies have an effect on HR practices and these in turn influence staff attitudes and behaviours which will, in turn again, impact on service offerings and customer perceptions of value.'

Explanations of how HRM makes an impact

Guest (1997: 268) stated that: 'The assumption is that "appropriate" HRM practices tap the motivation and commitment of employees.'

An explanation of the impact of HRM is based on three propositions: 1) that HR practices can make a direct impact on employee characteristics such as engagement, commitment, motivation and skill; 2) if employees have these characteristics it is probable that organizational performance in terms of productivity, quality and the delivery of high levels of customer service will improve; and 3) if such aspects of organizational performance improve, the financial results achieved by the organization will improve.

Developing a high-performance culture

Organizations achieve sustained high performance through the systems of work they adopt, but these systems are managed and operated by people. Ultimately, high-performance working is about improving performance through people. This can be done through the development and implementation of a high-performance culture involving HPWS in which performance management plays an important part.

High-performance work systems

HPWS are bundles of HR practices that facilitate employee involvement, skill enhancement and motivation. HPWS provide the means for creating a performance culture.

Performance management

Performance management can contribute to the development of a high-performance culture by delivering the message in an organization that high performance is important.

The contribution of HR

HR can contribute to enhancing organizational performance by providing insight on the performance issues affecting the organization and its employees.

Questions

1. How does HRM make an impact on performance?
2. What is a high-performance culture?
3. What is a high-performance work system?
4. What are the typical features of a high-performance work system?
5. How can performance management contribute?

References

Alvesson, M (2009) Critical perspectives on strategic HRM, in (eds) J Storey, P M Wright and D Ulrich, *The Routledge Companion to Strategic Human Resource Management*, Abingdon, Routledge, pp 53–68

Appelbaum, E, Bailey, T, Berg, P and Kalleberg, A L (2000) *Manufacturing Advantage: Why high performance work systems pay off*, Ithaca, NY, ILR Press

Becker, B E and Huselid, M A (1998) High performance work systems and firm performance: a synthesis of research and managerial implications, *Research on Personnel and Human Resource Management*, 16, pp 53–101

Becker, B E, Huselid, M A, Pickus, P S and Spratt, M F (1997) HR as a source of shareholder value: research and recommendations, *Human Resource Management*, Spring, 36 (1), pp 39–47

Birdi, K, Clegg, C, Patterson, M, Robinson, A, Stride, C B, Wall, T D and Wood, S J (2008) The impact of human resource and operational management practices on company productivity: a longitudinal study, *Personnel Psychology*, 61 (3), pp 467–501

Boselie, P, Dietz, G and Boon, C (2005) Commonalities and contradictions in HRM and performance research, *Human Resource Management Journal*, 15 (3), pp 67–94

Bowen, D and Ostroff, C (2004) Understanding HRM – firm performance linkages: the role of the 'strength' of the HRM system, *Academy of Management Review*, 29 (2), pp 203–21

Combs, J, Liu, Y, Hall, A and Ketchen, D (2006) How much do high performance work practices matter? A meta-analysis of their effects on organizational performance, *Personnel Psychology*, 59 (3), pp 501–28

Ericksen, J (2007) High performance work systems: dynamic workforce alignment and firm performance, *Academy of Management Proceedings*, pp 1–6

Gephart, M A (1995) *The road to high performance: steps to create a high performance workplace*, Training and Development, June, p 29

Godard, J (2001) Beyond the high performance paradigm? An analysis of variation in Canadian managerial perceptions of reform programme effectiveness, *British Journal of Industrial Relations*, 39 (1), pp 25–52

Godard, J (2004) A critical assessment of the high performance paradigm, *British Journal of Industrial Relations*, 42 (2), pp 349–78

Guest, D E (1997) Human resource management and performance; a review of the research agenda, *The International Journal of Human Resource Management*, 8 (3), 263–76

Guest, D E (2011) Human resource management and performance: still searching for some answers, *Human Resource Management Journal*, 21 (1), pp 3–13

Guest, D E and Conway, N (2011) The impact of HR practices, HR effectiveness and a 'strong HR system' on organizational outcomes: a stakeholder perspective, *The International Journal of Human Resource Management*, 22 (8), pp 1686–702

Guest, D E, Michie, J, Sheehan, M and Conway, N (2000a) *Employee Relations, HRM and Business Performance: An analysis of the 1998 Workplace Employee Relations Survey*, London, CIPD

Guest, D E, Michie, J, Sheehan, M, Conway, N and Metochi, M (2000b) *Effective People Management: Initial findings of Future of Work survey*, London, CIPD

Nishii, L, Lepak, D and Schneider, B (2008) Employee attributions of the 'why' of HR practices: their affects on employee attitudes and behaviours, and customer satisfaction, *Personnel Psychology*, 61 (3), pp 503–45

Paauwe, J (2004) *HRM and Performance: Achieving long-term viability*, Oxford, Oxford University Press

Patterson, M G, West, M A, Lawthom, R and Nickell, S (1997) *Impact of People Management Practices on Performance*, London, IPD

Pfeffer, J (1998) *The Human Equation*, Boston, MA, Harvard Business School Press

Purcell, J, Kinnie, K, Hutchinson, R, Rayton, B and Swart, J (2003) *Understanding the People and Performance Link: Unlocking the black box*, London, CIPD

Ramsay, H, Scholarios, D and Harley, B (2000) Employees and high performance work systems: testing inside the black box, *British Journal of Industrial Relations*, 38 (4), pp 501–31

Shih, H-A, Chiang, Y-H and Hsu, C-C (2005) Can high performance work systems really lead to better performance?, *Academy of Management Conference Paper*, pp 1–6

Stevens, J (2005) *High Performance Wales: Real experiences, real success*, Cardiff, Wales Management Council

Storey, J, Wright, P M and Ulrich, D (2009) Introduction, in (eds) J Storey, P M Wright and

D Ulrich, *The Routledge Companion to Strategic Human Resource Management*, Abingdon, Routledge, pp 3–13

Sung, J and Ashton, D (2005) *High Performance Work Practices: Linking strategy and skills to performance outcomes*, DTI in association with CIPD, available at http://www.cipd.co.uk/subjects/corpstrtgy/

Thompson, M (2002) *High Performance Work Organization in UK Aerospace*, London, The Society of British Aerospace Companies

Thompson, M and Heron, P (2005) Management capability and high performance work organization, *International Journal of Human Resource Management*, 16 (6), pp 1029–48

Ulrich, D (1997) *Human Resource Champions*, Boston, MA, Harvard Business School Press

US Department of Labor (1993) *High Performance Work Practices and Work Performance*, Washington, DC, US Government Printing Office

West, M A, Borrill, C S, Dawson, C, Scully, J, Carter, M, Anclay, S, Patterson, M and Waring, J (2002) The link between the management of employees and patient mortality in acute hospitals, *International Journal of Human Resource Management*, 13 (8), pp 1299–310

Wortzel-Hoffman, N and Boltizar, S (2007) Performance and development planning: a culture shift perspective, *Organization Development Journal*, 25 (2), pp 195–200

05 Human capital management

KEY CONCEPTS AND TERMS

- Balanced scorecard
- Human capital
- Human capital advantage
- Human capital index – Watson Wyatt
- Human capital management
- Human capital measurement
- Human capital monitor – Andrew Mayo
- Human process advantage
- Intangible resources
- Intellectual capital
- Metrics
- Organizational capital
- Organizational performance model – Mercer HR Consulting
- Social capital

LEARNING OUTCOMES

On completing this chapter you should be able to define these key concepts. You should also understand:

- The nature of human capital management
- The concept of human capital
- Characteristics of human capital
- Constituents of human capital
- Significance of human capital theory
- Importance of human capital measurement
- Reasons for interest in human capital measurement
- Approaches to measurement
- Measurement elements
- Factors affecting choice of measurement
- Criteria for HCM data for managers

Introduction

As defined by Baron and Armstrong (2007: 20), human capital management (HCM) is concerned with obtaining, analysing and reporting on data that inform the direction of value-adding people management, strategic, investment and operational decisions at corporate level and at the level of front-line management. It is, as emphasized by Kearns (2005), ultimately about value.

The nature of human capital management

The Accounting for People Task Force report (2003) stated that HCM involves the systematic analysis, measurement and evaluation of how people policies and practices create value. The report emphasized that HCM should be regarded as an approach to people management that deals with it as a high-level strategic issue rather than a matter to be left to HR. However, Wright and McMahan (2011: 102) warned that human capital should not be treated as a form of capital owned and controlled by the firm: 'To do so would miss the complexity of the construct and continue to ignore the "human" in strategic HRM.'

The defining characteristic of HCM is the use of metrics to guide an approach to managing people that regards them as assets and emphasizes that competitive advantage is achieved by strategic investments in those assets through employee engagement and retention, talent management and learning and development programmes. HCM relates HR strategy to business strategy. The concept of HCM is underpinned by the concept of human capital, as explained below.

The concept of human capital

Adam Smith, cited by Schultz (1981: 140), originated the idea of human capital (like so many other economic concepts) when he wrote that: 'The acquired wealth of nations derives from the acquired abilities of people – their education, experience, skills and health.' Individuals generate, retain and use knowledge and skill (human capital) and create intellectual capital. Their knowledge is enhanced by the interactions between them (social capital) and generates the institutionalized knowledge possessed by an organization (organizational capital). This concept of human capital is explained below.

Human capital defined

Human capital consists of the knowledge, skills and abilities of the people employed in an organization. As Wright and McMahan (2011: 101) explained:

> Each individual in the organization has characteristics that comprise human capital. He/she also engages in the processing of information, interpretation and reaction to that information in making choices about how to feel and behave. The aggregation of human capital, we propose, constitutes the organization or unit's 'human capital'.

Human capital constitutes a key element of the market worth of a company. A research study conducted in 2003 by CFO Research Services estimated that the value of human capital represented over 36 per cent of total revenue in a typical organization.

The significance of the term was emphasized by Schultz (1961), who defined it as follows.

Source review

Human capital defined – Schultz (1961: 1)

Although it is obvious that people acquire useful skills and knowledge, it is not obvious that these skills and knowledge are a form of capital, that this capital is in substantial part a product of deliberate investment, that it has grown in Western countries at a much faster rate than conventional (non-human) capital, and that its growth may well be the most distinctive feature of the economic system.

He also noted that: 'Attributes... which are valuable and can be augmented by appropriate investment will be treated as human capital... Consider all human abilities to be either innate or acquired' (ibid: 21).

A later detailed definition was put forward by Bontis *et al* (1999).

Source review

Human capital defined – Bontis *et al* (1999: 393)

Human capital represents the human factor in the organization; the combined intelligence, skills and expertise that gives the organization its distinctive character. The human elements of the organization are those that are capable of learning, changing, innovating and providing the creative thrust which if properly motivated can ensure the long-term survival of the organization.

Scarborough and Elias (2002: *ix*) commented that: 'The concept of human capital is most usefully viewed as a bridging concept – that is, it defines the link between HR practices and business performance in terms of assets rather than business processes.' They pointed out that human capital is to a large extent 'non-standardized, tacit, dynamic, context dependent and embodied in people'. These characteristics make it difficult to evaluate human capital, bearing in mind that the 'features of human capital that are so crucial to firm performance are the flexibility and creativity of individuals, their ability to develop skills over time and to respond in a motivated way to different contexts' (ibid: *ix*).

It is indeed the knowledge, skills and abilities of individuals that create value, which is why the focus has to be on means of attracting, retaining, developing and maintaining the human capital they represent. Davenport (1999: 7) observed that: 'People possess innate abilities, behaviours and personal time. These elements make up human capital, the currency people bring to invest in their jobs. Workers, not organizations, own this human capital.'

The choices they make include how much discretionary behaviour they are prepared to exercise in carrying out their role (discretionary behaviour refers to the discretion that people at work can exercise about the way they do their jobs and the amount of effort, care, innovation and productive behaviour they display). They can also choose whether or not to remain with the organization.

The constituents of human capital

Human capital consists of intellectual, social and organizational capital.

Intellectual capital

The concept of human capital is associated with the overarching notion of intellectual capital, which is defined as the stocks and flows of knowledge available to an organization. These can be regarded as the intangible resources associated with people, which together with tangible resources (money and physical assets) comprise the market or total value of a business.

Social capital

Social capital is another element of intellectual capital. It consists of the knowledge derived from networks of relationships within and outside the organization. Social capital has been defined by Putnam (1996: 66) as 'the features of social life – networks, norms and trust – that enable participants to act together more effectively to pursue shared objectives'. It is important to take into account social capital considerations, that is, the ways in which knowledge is developed through interaction between people. Bontis *et al* (1999) commented that it is flows as well as stocks that matter. Intellectual capital develops and changes over time and a significant part is played in these processes by people acting together.

Organizational capital

Organizational capital is the institutionalized knowledge possessed by an organization that is stored in databases, manuals, etc (Youndt, 2000). It is often called 'structural capital' (Edvinson and Malone,

1997), but the term 'organizational capital' is preferred by Youndt because, he argues, it conveys more clearly that this is the knowledge that the organization actually owns.

Approaches to people management raised by human capital theory

An approach to people management based on human capital theory involves obtaining answers to these questions:

- What are the key performance drivers that create value?
- What skills do we have?
- What skills do we need now and in the future to meet our strategic aims?
- How are we going to attract, develop and retain these skills?
- How can we develop a culture and environment in which organizational and individual learning takes place that meets both our needs and the needs of our employees?
- How can we provide for both the explicit and tacit knowledge created in our organization to be captured, recorded and used effectively?

Human capital theory helps to determine the impact of people on the business and their contribution to shareholder value. It demonstrates that HR practices produce value for money in terms of, for example, return on investment. It also provides guidance on future HR and business strategies and data that will inform strategies and practices designed to improve the effectiveness of people management in the organization.

Human capital measurement

The role of human capital measurement is to assess the impact of HRM practices and the contribution made by people to organizational performance. Human capital measurement is about finding links, correlations and, ideally, causation, between different sets of (HR) data, using statistical techniques.

The need for human capital measurement

Human capital measurement provides a basis for people management decision-making. It means identifying the people management drivers and modelling the effect of varying them. The recognized importance of achieving human capital advantage has led to an interest in the development of methods of measuring the value and impact of that capital for these reasons:

- People in organizations add value and there is a case for assessing this value to provide a basis for HR planning and for monitoring the effectiveness and impact of HR policies and practices.
- The process of identifying measures and collecting and analysing information relating to them will focus the attention of the organization on what needs to be done to find, keep, develop and make the best use of its human capital.
- Measurements can be used to monitor progress in achieving strategic HR goals and generally to evaluate the effectiveness of HR practices.
- You cannot manage unless you measure.

The need is to develop a framework within which reliable information can be collected and analysed such as added value per employee, productivity, and measures of employee behaviour (attrition and absenteeism rates, the frequency/severity rate of accidents, and cost savings resulting from suggestion schemes).

However, the Institute for Employment Studies (Hartley, 2005) emphasized that reporting on human capital is not simply about measurement. Measures on their own such as those resulting from benchmarking are not enough; they must be clearly linked to business performance. It was established by Scarborough and Elias (2002: *x*), on the basis of their research, that:

> Measures are less important than the activity of measuring – of continuously developing and refining our understanding of the productive role of human capital within particular settings, by embedding such activities in management practices, and linking them to the business strategy of the firm.

Approaches to measurement

Three approaches to measurement are described below.

The human capital index – Watson Wyatt

On the basis of a survey of companies that have linked together HR management practices and market value, Watson Wyatt Worldwide (2002) identified four major categories of HR practice that could be linked to increases in shareholder value creation. These are:

- total rewards and accountability: 16.5 per cent;
- collegial, flexible workforce: 9.0 per cent;
- recruiting and retention excellence: 7.9 per cent;
- communication integrity: 7.1 per cent.

The organizational performance model – Mercer HR Consulting

As described by Nalbantian *et al* (2004) the organizational performance model developed by Mercer HR Consulting is based on the following elements: people, work processes, management structure, information and knowledge, decision-making and rewards, each of which plays out differently within the context of the organization, creating a unique DNA.

The statistical tool 'Internal Labour Market Analysis' used by Mercer draws on the running record of employee and labour market data to analyse the actual experience of employees rather than stated HR programmes and policies. Thus gaps can be identified between what is required in the workforce to support business goals and what is actually being delivered.

The human capital monitor – Andrew Mayo

Andrew Mayo (2001) has developed the 'human capital monitor' to identify the human value of the enterprise or 'human asset worth', which is equal to 'employment cost × individual asset multiplier'. The latter is a weighted average assessment of capability, potential to grow, personal performance (contribution) and alignment to the organization's values set in the context of the workforce environment (ie how leadership, culture, motivation and learning are driving success). The absolute figure is not important. What does matter is that the process of measurement leads you to consider whether human capital is sufficient, increasing, or decreasing, and highlights issues to address. Mayo advises against using too many measures and instead to concentrate on a few organization-wide measures that are critical in creating shareholder value or achieving current and future organizational goals.

He believes that value added per person is a good measure of the effectiveness of human capital, especially for making inter-firm comparisons. But he considers that the most critical indicator for the value of human capital is the level of expertise possessed by an organization. He suggests that this could be analysed under the headings of identified organizational core competencies. The other criteria he mentions are measures of satisfaction derived from employee opinion surveys and levels of attrition and absenteeism.

Measurement data

The main HCM data used for measurement are:

- Basic workforce data – demographic data (numbers by job category, sex, race, age, disability, working arrangements, absence and sickness, turnover and pay).
- People development and performance data – learning and development programmes, performance management/potential assessments, skills and qualifications.
- Perceptual data – attitude/opinion surveys, focus groups, exit interviews.
- Performance data – financial, operational and customer.

A summary of human capital measures and their possible uses is given in Table 5.1.

TABLE 5.1 A summary of human capital measures and their possible uses

Measures	Possible use: analysis leading to action
Workforce composition – gender, race, age, full-time, part-time	Analyse the extent of diversity Assess the implications of a preponderance of employees in different age groups, eg extent of losses through retirement Assess the extent to which the organization is relying on part-time staff
Length of service distribution	Indicate level of success in retaining employees Indicate preponderance of long- or short-serving employees Enable analysis of performance of more experienced employees to be assessed
Skills analysis/assessment – graduates, professionally/technically qualified, skilled workers	Assess skill levels against requirements Indicate where steps have to be taken to deal with shortfalls
Attrition – employee turnover rates for different categories of management and employees	Indicate areas where steps have to be taken to increase retention rates Provide a basis for assessing levels of commitment
Attrition – cost of	Support business case for taking steps to reduce attrition
Absenteeism/sickness rates	Identify problems and need for more effective attendance management policies
Average number of vacancies as a percentage of total workforce	Identify potential shortfall problem areas
Total payroll costs (pay and benefits)	Provide data for productivity analysis
Compa-ratio – actual rates of pay as a percentage of policy rates	Enable control to be exercised over management of pay structure
Percentage of employees in different categories of contingent pay or payment-by-result schemes	Demonstrate the extent to which the organization believes that pay should be related to contribution
Total pay review increases for different categories of employees as a percentage of pay	Compare actual with budgeted payroll increase costs Benchmark pay increases
Average bonuses or contingent pay awards as a % of base pay for different categories of managers and employees	Analyse cost of contingent pay Compare actual and budgeted increases Benchmark increases

TABLE 5.1 Continued

Measures	Possible use: analysis leading to action
Outcome of equal pay reviews	Reveal pay gap between male and female employees
Personal development plans completed as a percentage of employees	Indicate level of learning and development activity
Training hours per employee	Indicate actual amount of training activity (note that this does not reveal the quality of training achieved or its impact)
Percentage of managers taking part in formal management development programmes	Indicate level of learning and development activity
Internal promotion rate (% of promotions filled from within)	Indicate extent to which talent management programmes are successful
Succession planning coverage (% of managerial jobs for which successors have been identified)	Indicate extent to which talent management programmes are successful
Percentage of employees taking part in formal performance reviews	Indicate level of performance management activity
Distribution of performance ratings by category of staff and department	Indicate inconsistencies, questionable distributions and trends in assessments
Accident severity and frequency rates	Assess health and safety programmes
Cost savings/revenue increases resulting from employee suggestion schemes	Measure the value created by employees

Human capital reporting

Internal reporting

Analysing and reporting human capital data to top management and line managers leads to informed decision-making about what needs to be done to improve business results, the ability to recognize problems and take action to deal with them, and the scope to demonstrate the effectiveness of HR solutions and thus support the business case for greater investment in HR practices. Data must be accompanied by analysis and explanation.

External reporting

The EC Accounts Modernization Directive requires companies to prepare a business review. This has to disclose information that is necessary for understanding the development, performance or position of the business of the company, including the analysis of key financial and other performance indicators, and information relating to environmental and employee matters, social and community issues, and any policies of the company in relation to these matters and their effectiveness.

Introducing HCM

As Baron and Armstrong (2007) observed, the development of HCM should be regarded as a journey. It is not an all-or-nothing affair. It does not have to depend on a state-of-the-art HR database or the possession of advanced expertise in statistical analysis. It is not difficult to record and report on basic data and, although analytical ability is necessary, the level required should be possessed by any HR professional.

At the beginning of the journey an organization may do no more than collect basic HR data on, for instance, employee turnover and absence. But anyone who goes a little bit further and analyses that data to draw conclusions on trends and causation – leading to proposals on the action required supported by that analysis – is into HCM. Not in a big way perhaps, but it is a beginning. At the other end of the scale there are the highly sophisticated approaches to HCM operated by such organizations as Nationwide and Standard Chartered Bank.

HCM CASE STUDIES ON APPROACHES TO MEASUREMENT

Nationwide Building Society

Nationwide feeds its human capital information into an intranet-based information system that gives users an assessment of how they are doing against a number of indicators. It uses a dashboard of red, amber and green indicators to give each business unit an idea of how they are faring on a number of key drivers of employee commitment. This is backed up with advice on how improvements might be made.

Standard Chartered Bank

Standard Chartered Bank uses a human capital scorecard to analyse its data. This is produced on a quarterly and annual basis with various cuts of the same data produced for different business segments and countries, in addition to a global report. This comprises a series of slides with commentary to enable managers to understand the data.

The data is also included in twice-yearly board reviews on people strategy and forms part of the annual strategy planning process. The scorecard data is reviewed within each global business by a top team 'People Forum'. At country level, each local chief executive and his or her management committee reviews key trends in order to specify areas they need to focus on.

In addition, the bank uses qualitative analysis to examine trends and this has led it to identify the role of the manager as mediating the relationship between engagement and performance. In turn, this has led to a focus on qualitative research to identify what raises the bank's best managers above the rest. A further example is a qualitative analysis of high performance in selected customer-facing roles to determine the key behaviours that continue to drive customer loyalty.

Key learning points: Human capital management

The concept of human capital

Individuals generate, retain and use knowledge and skill (human capital) and create intellectual capital. Human capital 'defines the link between HR practices and business performance in terms of assets rather than business processes' (Scarborough and Elias, 2002).

Characteristics of human capital

Human capital is non-standardized, tacit, dynamic, context-dependent and embodied in people (Scarborough and Elias, 2002).

Constituents of human capital

Human capital consists of intellectual capital, social capital and organizational capital.

Significance of human capital

Human capital theory regards people as assets and stresses that investment by organizations in people will generate worthwhile returns.

Importance of human capital measurement

Measuring and valuing human capital is an aid to people management decision-making.

Reasons for interest in human capital measurement

- Human capital constitutes a key element of the market worth of a company.
- People in organizations add value.
- Focus attention on what needs to be done to make the best use of its human capital.
- Monitor progress in achieving strategic HR goals and evaluate HR practices.
- You cannot manage unless you measure.

Approaches to measurement

- The human capital index – Watson Wyatt World-wide.
- The organizational performance model – Mercer HR Consulting.
- The human capital monitor – Andrew Mayo.

Measurement elements

Workforce data, people development data, perceptual data and performance data.

Factors affecting choice of measurement

- Type of organization; its business goals and drivers.
- The existing key performance indicators (KPIs).
- Use of balanced scorecard.
- The availability, use and manageability of data.

Criteria for HCM data as a guide to managers

Data will only be useful for managers if:

- it is credible, accurate and trustworthy;
- they understand what it means for them;
- it is accompanied by guidance as to what action can be taken;
- they have the skills and abilities to understand and act upon it.

Questions

1 What is human capital management?
2 What is human capital?
3 What is intellectual capital?
4 What is social capital?
5 What is organizational capital?
6 What is human capital measurement?
7 Why is human capital measurement important?
8 What is the main human capital management data used for measurement?

References

Accounting for People Task Force (2003) *Accounting for People*, London, DTI

Baron, A and Armstrong, M (2007) *Human Capital Management: Achieving added value through people*, London, Kogan Page

Bontis, N, Dragonetti, N C, Jacobsen, K and Roos, G (1999) The knowledge toolbox: a review of the tools available to measure and manage intangible resources, *European Management Journal*, 17 (4), pp 391–402

CFO Research Services (2003) *Human Capital Management: The CFO's perspective*, Boston, MA, CFO Publishing

Davenport, T O (1999) *Human Capital*, San Francisco, CA, Jossey-Bass

Edvinson, L and Malone, M S (1997) *Intellectual Capital: Realizing your company's true value by finding its hidden brainpower*, New York, Harper Business

Hartley, V (2005) *Open for Business: HR and human capital reporting*, Brighton, IES

Kearns, P (2005) *Evaluating the ROI from Learning*, London, CIPD

Mayo, A (2001) *The Human Value of the Enterprise: Valuing people as assets*, London, Nicholas Brealey

Nalbantian, R, Guzzo, R A, Kieffer, D and Doherty, J (2004) *Play to Your Strengths: Managing your internal labour markets for lasting competitive advantage*, New York, McGraw-Hill

Putnam, R D (1996) The strange disappearance of civic America, *The American Prospect*, Winter, pp 34–48

Scarborough, H and Elias, J (2002) *Evaluating Human Capital*, London, CIPD

Schultz, T W (1961) Investment in human capital, *American Economic Review*, 51, March, pp 1–17

Schultz, T W (1981) *Investing in People: The economics of population quality*, Los Angeles, CA, University of California Press

Watson Wyatt Worldwide (2002) *Human Capital Index: Human capital as a lead indicator of shareholder value*, Washington, DC, Watson Wyatt Worldwide

Wright, P M and McMahan, G C (2011) Exploring human capital: putting human back into strategic human resource management, *Human Resource Management Journal*, 21 (2), pp 93–104

Youndt, M A (2000) Human resource considerations and value creation: the mediating role of intellectual capital, *Paper delivered at National Conference of US Academy of Management*, Toronto, August

06 Knowledge management

KEY CONCEPTS AND TERMS

Communities of practice

Data

Explicit knowledge

Information

Knowledge

Knowledge management

Tacit knowledge

LEARNING OUTCOMES

On completing this chapter you should be able to define these key concepts. You should also know about:

- The purpose and significance of knowledge management
- Knowledge management strategies
- Knowledge management systems
- Knowledge management issues
- The contribution HR can make to knowledge management

Introduction

Knowledge management is concerned with storing and sharing the wisdom, understanding and expertise accumulated in an enterprise about its processes, techniques and operations. It treats knowledge as a key resource. It was defined by Tan (2000: 10) as: 'The process of systematically and actively managing and leveraging the stores of knowledge in an organization.' As Ulrich (1998: 126) remarked: 'Knowledge has become a direct competitive advantage for companies selling ideas and relationships.'

There is nothing new about knowledge management. Hansen *et al* (1999: 106) observed that: 'For hundreds of years, owners of family businesses have passed on their commercial wisdom to children, master craftsmen have painstakingly taught their trades to apprentices, and workers have exchanged ideas and know-how on the job.' But they also commented that: 'As the foundation of industrialized economies has shifted from natural resources to intellectual assets, executives have been compelled to examine the knowledge underlying their business and how that knowledge is used' (ibid: 106).

Knowledge management is more concerned with people and how they acquire, exchange and spread knowledge than it is about information technology. That is why it has become an important area for HR practitioners, who are in a strong position to exert influence in this aspect of people management. It is associated with intellectual capital theory (see Chapter 5), in that it refers to the notions of human, social and organizational or structural capital. It is also linked to organizational learning (see Chapter 22).

Knowledge management should be based on an understanding of the concept of knowledge; this is therefore dealt with in the first section of this chapter. In subsequent sections knowledge management is described in more detail, strategies for developing its practice are described and consideration is given to the role of HR.

The concept of knowledge

Knowledge is defined as what people understand about things, concepts, ideas, theories, procedures and practices. It can be described as know-how or, when it is specific, expertise. A distinction was made by Ryle (1949) between 'knowing how' and 'knowing that'. 'Knowing how' is the ability of a person to perform tasks, and 'knowing that' is holding pieces of knowledge in one's mind. According to Blackler (1995: 1023): 'Rather than regarding knowledge as something that people have, it is suggested that knowing is better regarded as something that they do.' He also noted that: 'Knowledge is multifaceted and complex, being both situated and abstract, implicit and explicit, distributed and individual, physical and mental, developing and static, verbal and encoded' (ibid: 1032–33).

Nonaka (1991) suggested that knowledge is held either by individuals or collectively. In Blackler's (1995) terms, embodied or embraced knowledge is individual and embedded, and cultural knowledge is collective. It can be argued (Scarborough and Carter, 2000) that knowledge emerges from the collective experience of work and is shared between members of a particular group or community.

Explicit and tacit knowledge

Nonaka (1991) and Nonaka and Takeuchi (1995) stated that knowledge is either explicit or tacit. Explicit knowledge can be codified – it is recorded and available and is held in databases, in corporate intranets and intellectual property portfolios. Tacit knowledge exists in people's minds. It is difficult to articulate in writing and is acquired through personal experience. As suggested by Hansen *et al* (1999), it includes scientific or technological expertise, operational know-how, insights about an industry and business judgement. The main challenge in knowledge management is how to turn tacit knowledge into explicit knowledge.

Data, information and knowledge

A distinction can be made between data, information and knowledge:

- Data consists of the basic facts – the building blocks – for information and knowledge.
- Information is data that have been processed in a way that is meaningful to individuals; it is available to anyone entitled to gain access to it. As Drucker (1988: 46) put it, 'information is data endowed with meaning and purpose'.

- Knowledge is information used productively; it is personal and often intangible and it can be elusive – the task of tying it down, encoding it and distributing it is tricky.

Knowledge management defined

Knowledge management is about getting knowledge from those who have it to those who need it in order to improve organizational effectiveness. It was defined by Scarborough *et al* (1999: 1) as 'any process or practice of creating, acquiring, capturing, sharing and using knowledge, wherever it resides, to enhance learning and performance in organizations'. They suggested that it focuses on the development of firm-specific knowledge and skills that are the result of organizational learning processes. Knowledge management deals with both stocks and flows of knowledge. Stocks include expertise and encoded knowledge in computer systems. Flows represent the ways in which knowledge is transferred from people to people or from people to a knowledge database.

Knowledge management identifies relevant information and then disseminates it so that learning can take place. It promotes the sharing of knowledge by linking people with people and by linking them to information so that they learn from recorded experiences. As explained by Blake (1988), the purpose of knowledge management is to capture a company's collective expertise and distribute it to wherever it can achieve the biggest payoff. This is in accordance with the resource-based view of the firm, which suggests that the source of competitive advantage lies within the firm (ie in its people and their knowledge), not in how it positions itself in the market. A successful company is a knowledge-creating company.

Knowledge is possessed by organizations and people in organizations. Organizational operational, technical and procedural knowledge can be stored in databanks and found in reports, libraries, policy documents, manuals and presentations. It can also be moved around the organization through information systems and by meetings, workshops, courses, 'master classes', written publications and 'communities of practice', defined by Wenger and Snyder (2000: 139) as 'groups of people informally bound together by shared expertise and a passion for joint enterprise'. The intranet provides an additional and very effective medium.

People possess knowledge that has been acquired through their own experiences at work. But it will not necessarily be shared formally or even informally with their colleagues and crucial knowledge could be lost if it remains locked up in the minds of employees, or taken elsewhere by them if they leave the organization. An important issue in knowledge management is how knowledge can be identified and distributed.

In the information age, knowledge rather than physical assets or financial resources is the key to competitiveness. Knowledge management allows companies to make the best use of their employees' creativity and expertise (Mecklenburg *et al*, 1999). As Boxall and Purcell (2000: 197) noted: 'Managing knowledge inevitably means managing both the company's proprietary technologies and systems (which don't walk out of the door at the end of the day) and the people (who do)'.

Knowledge management strategies

Two approaches to knowledge management strategy have been identified by Hansen *et al* (1999): the codification strategy and the personalization strategy.

The codification strategy

Knowledge is carefully codified and stored in databases where it can be accessed and used easily by anyone in the organization. Knowledge is explicit and is codified using a 'people-to-document' approach. The strategy is therefore document-driven. Knowledge is extracted from the person who developed it, made independent of that person and reused for various purposes. It is stored in an electronic repository for people to use, and allows people to search for and retrieve codified knowledge without having to contact the person who originally developed it. This strategy relies largely on information technology to manage databases and also on the use of the intranet.

The personalization strategy

Knowledge is closely tied to the person who has developed it and is shared mainly through direct person-to-person contacts. This 'person-to-person' approach means providing for tacit knowledge to be passed on. The exchange is achieved by creating networks and encouraging face-to-face communication between people by informal conferences, workshops, communities of practice, brainstorming and one-to-one sessions.

Hansen *et al* (1999) proposed that the choice of strategy should be contingent on the organization: what it does and how it does it. Thus consultancies such as Ernst & Young, using knowledge to deal with recurring problems, may rely on codification so that recorded solutions to similar problems are easily retrievable. Strategy consultancy firms such as McKinsey or Bains, however, rely on a personalization strategy to help them to tackle the high-level strategic problems they are presented with that demand the provision of creative, analytically rigorous advice. They need to channel individual expertise and they find and develop people who are able to use a person-to-person knowledge-sharing approach. Experts can be identified who can be approached by e-mail, telephone or personal contact.

The research conducted by Hansen *et al* (1999) established that companies that use knowledge well adopt either the codification or the personalization strategy predominantly and use the other strategy to support their first choice. They pointed out that those who try to excel at both strategies risk failing at both.

Knowledge management issues

The strategies referred to above do not provide easy answers. The issues that need to be addressed in developing knowledge management practices are discussed below.

The pace of change

One of the main issues in knowledge management is how to keep up with the pace of change and identify what knowledge needs to be captured and shared.

Relating knowledge management strategy to business strategy

As Hansen *et al* (1999) showed, it is not knowledge per se but the way it is applied to strategic objectives that is the critical ingredient in competitiveness. They suggested that 'competitive strategy must drive knowledge management strategy' and that management have to answer the question: 'How does knowledge that resides in the company add value for customers?' (ibid: 114).

Technology and people

Technology may be central to companies adopting a codification strategy, but for those following a personalization strategy IT is best used in a supportive role. Hansen *et al* (1999: 113) commented that:

> In the codification model, managers need to implement a system that is much like a traditional library – it must contain a large cache of documents and include search engines that allow people to find and use the documents they need. In the personalization model, it's more important to have a system that allows people to find other people.

Scarborough *et al* (1999) suggested that technology should be viewed as a means of communication rather than as a means of storing knowledge. Knowledge management is more about people than technology. Research by Davenport (1996) established that managers get two-thirds of their information from face-to-face or telephone conversations.

There is a limit to how much tacit knowledge can be codified. In organizations relying more on tacit than explicit knowledge, a person-to-person approach works best, and IT can only support this process; it cannot replace it.

The significance of process

Blackler (1995) emphasized that a preoccupation with technology may mean that too little attention is paid to the processes (social, technological and organizational) through which knowledge combines and interacts in different ways. The key processes are the interactions between people. This is the social capital of an organization – 'the network of relationships [that] constitute a valuable resource for the conduct of social affairs' (Nahpiet and Ghoshal, 1998: 243). Social networks can be particularly important in ensuring that knowledge is shared. Trust is also required – people are not willing to share knowledge with those they do not trust.

The culture of the company may inhibit knowledge sharing. The norm may be for people to keep knowledge to themselves as much as they can because 'knowledge is power'. An open culture will encourage people to share their ideas and knowledge.

Knowledge workers

Knowledge workers, as defined by Drucker (1993), are individuals who have high levels of education and specialist skills combined with the ability to apply these skills to identify and solve problems. As Argyris (1991: 100) commented, they are: 'The nuts and bolts of management... increasingly consist of guiding and integrating the autonomous but interconnected work of highly skilled people.' Knowledge management is about the management and motivation of knowledge workers who create knowledge and will be the key players in sharing it.

The contribution of HR to knowledge management

HR can make an important contribution to knowledge management simply because knowledge is shared between people; it is not just a matter of capturing explicit knowledge through the use of IT. The role of HR is to see that the organization has the intellectual capital it needs. The resource-based view of the firm emphasizes, in the words of Cappelli and Crocker-Hefter (1996: 7), that 'distinctive human resource practices help to create unique competences that differentiate products and services and, in turn, drive competitiveness'.

HR can contribute by providing advice on culture management, organization design and development, and by establishing learning and communication programmes and systems. There are 10 ways of doing this:

1. Help to develop an open culture in which the values and norms emphasize the importance of sharing knowledge.
2. Promote a climate of commitment and trust.
3. Advise on the design and development of organizations that facilitate knowledge sharing through networks, teamwork and communities of practice.
4. Advise on resourcing policies and provide resourcing services that ensure that valued employees who can contribute to knowledge creation and sharing are attracted and retained.
5. Advise on methods of motivating people to share knowledge and rewarding those who do so.
6. Help in the development of performance management processes that focus on the development and sharing of knowledge.
7. Develop processes of organizational and individual learning that will generate and assist in disseminating knowledge.
8. Set up and organize workshops, conferences, seminars, communities of practice and symposia that enable knowledge to be shared on a person-to-person basis.
9. In conjunction with IT, develop systems for capturing and, as far as possible, codifying explicit and tacit knowledge.
10. Generally, promote the cause of knowledge management with senior managers to encourage them to exert leadership and support knowledge management initiatives.

Key learning points: Knowledge management

The purpose and significance of knowledge management

Knowledge management is about getting knowledge from those who have it to those who need it in order to improve organizational effectiveness.

Knowledge management strategies

The codification strategy – knowledge is carefully codified and stored in databases where it can be accessed and used easily by anyone in the organization. Knowledge is explicit and is codified using a 'people-to-document' approach.

The personalization strategy – knowledge is closely tied to the person who has developed it and is shared mainly through direct person-to-person contacts. This is a 'person-to-person' approach that involves ensuring that tacit knowledge is passed on.

Knowledge management systems

- Creating an intranet.
- Creating 'data warehouses'.
- Using decision support systems.
- Using 'groupware', ie information communication technologies such as e-mail or discussion bases.
- Creating networks or communities of practice or interest of knowledge workers.

Knowledge management issues

- The pace of change.
- Relating knowledge management strategy to business strategy.
- IT is best used in a supportive role.
- Attention must be paid to the processes (social, technological and organizational) through which knowledge combines and interacts in different ways.
- The significance of knowledge workers must be appreciated.

The contribution HR can make to knowledge management

- Help to develop an open culture that emphasizes the importance of sharing knowledge.
- Promote a climate of commitment and trust.
- Advise on the design and development of organizations that facilitate knowledge sharing.
- Ensure that valued employees who can contribute to knowledge creation and sharing are attracted and retained.
- Advise on methods of motivating people to share.
- Help in the development of performance management processes that focus on the development and sharing of knowledge.
- Develop processes of organizational and individual learning that will generate and assist in disseminating knowledge.
- Set up and organize workshops, conferences and communities of practice and symposia that enable knowledge to be shared on a person-to-person basis.
- In conjunction with IT, develop systems for capturing and, as far as possible, codifying explicit and tacit knowledge.
- Generally, promote the cause of knowledge management with senior managers.

Questions

1 What is knowledge management?

2 What is knowledge?

3 What is the difference between explicit and tacit knowledge?

4 What is the distinction between data, information and knowledge?

5 What is the purpose of knowledge management?

6 How can HR help to promote knowledge management?

References

Argyris, C (1991) Teaching smart people how to learn, *Harvard Business Review*, May–June, pp 54–62

Blackler, F (1995) Knowledge, knowledge work and experience, *Organization Studies*, 16 (6), pp 16–36

Blake, P (1988) The knowledge management explosion, *Information Today*, 15 (1), pp 12–13

Boxall, P and Purcell, J (2000) Strategic human resource management: where have we come from and where are we going?, *International Journal of Management Reviews*, 2 (2), pp 183–203

Cappelli, P and Crocker-Hefter, A (1996) Distinctive human resources are firms' core competencies, *Organizational Dynamics*, 24 (3), pp 7–22

Davenport, T H (1996) Why re-engineering failed: the fad that forgot people, *Fast Company*, Premier Issue, pp 70–74

Drucker, P (1988) The coming of the new organization, *Harvard Business Review*, January–February, pp 45–53

Drucker, P (1993) *Post-capitalist Society*, Oxford, Butterworth-Heinemann

Hansen, M T, Nohria, N and Tierney, T (1999) What's your strategy for managing knowledge?, *Harvard Business Review*, March–April, pp 106–16

Mecklenberg, S, Deering, A and Sharp, D (1999) Knowledge management: a secret engine of corporate growth, *Executive Agenda*, 2, pp 5–15

Nahpiet, J and Ghoshal, S (1998) Social capital, intellectual capital and the organizational advantage, *Academy of Management Review*, 23 (2), pp 242–66

Nonaka, I (1991) The knowledge creating company, *Harvard Business Review*, November–December, pp 96–104

Nonaka, I and Takeuchi, H (1995) *The Knowledge Creating Company*, New York, Oxford University Press

Ryle, G (1949) *The Concept of Mind*, Oxford, Oxford University Press

Scarborough, H and Carter, C (2000) *Investigating Knowledge Management*, London, CIPD

Scarborough, H, Swan, J and Preston, J (1999) *Knowledge Management: A literature review*, London, IPD

Tan, J (2000) Knowledge management – just more buzzwords?, *British Journal of Administrative Management*, March–April, pp 10–11

Ulrich, D (1998) A new mandate for human resources, *Harvard Business Review*, January–February, pp 124–34

Wenger, E and Snyder, W M (2000) Communities of practice: the organizational frontier, *Harvard Business Review*, January–February, pp 33–41

07
Competency-based HRM

KEY CONCEPTS AND TERMS

- Behavioural competencies
- Behavioural indicators
- Competency
- Competency-based HRM
- Competency framework
- Criterion referencing
- Emotional intelligence
- Role-specific competencies
- Technical competencies

LEARNING OUTCOMES

On completing this chapter you should be able to define these key concepts. You should also understand:

- The meaning of competency-based HRM
- The different types of competencies
- The contents of competency frameworks
- Reasons for using competencies
- Coverage of competencies
- Applications of competency-based HRM
- How to develop a competency framework
- Keys to success in using competencies
- Competencies and emotional intelligence

Introduction

Competency-based HRM is about using the notion of competency and the results of competency analysis to inform and improve HR processes, especially those concerned with recruitment and selection, learning and development, and performance and reward management. It has an important part to play in a number of HR activities.

Competency defined

The term 'competency' refers to an underlying characteristic of a person that results in effective or superior performance. The leading figure in defining and popularizing the concept of competency was Boyatzis (1982). He conducted research that established that there was no single factor but a range of factors that differentiated successful from less successful performance. These factors included personal qualities, motives, experience and behavioural characteristics. Since his contribution, three types of competencies have been identified: behavioural competencies, technical competencies and NVQs/SNVQs.

Behavioural competencies

Behavioural competencies define behavioural expectations, ie the type of behaviour required to deliver results under such headings as teamworking, communication, leadership and decision-making and are sometimes known as 'soft skills'. Criterion-referencing, ie comparing one measure or situation with a criterion in the form of another measure or outcome, may be used to determine the relationship between them. They can be set out in a 'competency framework', which contains definitions of the behavioural competencies used for all employees in an organization or for particular occupations such as managers. Guidelines on defining behavioural competencies are provided in Chapter 51.

Technical competencies

Technical competencies define what people have to know and be able to do (knowledge and skills) in order to carry out and meet performance expectations and are sometimes known as 'hard skills'. They are related to either generic roles (groups of similar roles), or to individual roles ('role-specific competencies'). They are not usually part of a behavioural-based competency framework, although the two are linked when considering and assessing role demands and requirements.

The terms 'technical competencies' and 'competences' are closely related, although the latter has a particular and more limited meaning when applied to NVQs/SNVQs, as discussed below. Guidelines on defining technical competencies are provided in Chapter 51.

NVQ/SNVQ competences

The concept of competence was conceived in the UK as a fundamental part of the process of developing standards for NVQs/SNVQs. These specify minimum standards for the achievement of set tasks and activities expressed in ways that can be observed and assessed with a view to certification. An element of competence in NVQ language is a description of something that people in a work area should be able to do. They are assessed on being competent or not yet competent. No attempt is made to assess the level of competence.

Competency headings

The most common competencies included in competency in frameworks are people skills, although outcome-based skills, such as focusing on results and solving problems, are also popular. The more common competency headings included in the frameworks of organizations responding to a Competency and Emotional Intelligence survey in 2006/7 are shown in Table 7.1.

The first seven of these were used in over 50 per cent of the respondent organizations. The 49 frameworks included 553 competency headings. No doubt, many of these overlapped. The typical number of competencies was seven, rising to eight where the frameworks applied solely to managers.

TABLE 7.1 Incidence of different competency headings

Competency heading	Summary definition	% used
Team orientation	The ability to work cooperatively and flexibly with other members of the team with a full understanding of the role to be played as a team member.	86
Communication	The ability to communicate clearly and persuasively, orally or in writing.	73
People management	The ability to manage and develop people and gain their trust and cooperation to achieve results.	67
Customer focus	The exercise of unceasing care in looking after the interests of external and internal customers to ensure that their wants, needs and expectations are met or exceeded.	65
Results orientation	The desire to get things done well and the ability to set and meet challenging goals, create own measures of excellence and constantly seek ways of improving performance.	59
Problem solving	The capacity to analyse situations, diagnose problems, identify the key issues, establish and evaluate alternative courses of action and produce a logical, practical and acceptable solution.	57
Planning and organizing	The ability to decide on courses of action, ensuring that the resources required to implement the action will be available and scheduling the programme of work required to achieve a defined end-result.	51
Technical skills	Possession of the knowledge, understanding and expertise required to carry out the work effectively.	49
Leadership	The capacity to inspire individuals to give of their best to achieve a desired result and to maintain effective relationships with individuals and the team as a whole.	43
Business awareness	The capacity continually to identify and explore business opportunities, understand the business needs and priorities of the organization and constantly to seek methods of ensuring that the organization becomes more businesslike.	37

TABLE 7.1 Continued

Competency heading	Summary definition	% used
Decision making	The capacity to make sound and practical decisions that deal effectively with the issues and are based on thorough analysis and diagnosis.	37
Change orientation	The ability to manage and accept change.	33
Developing others	The desire and capacity to foster the development of members of his or her team, providing feedback, support, encouragement and coaching.	33
Influence and persuasion	The ability to convince others to agree on or to take a course of action.	33
Initiative	The capacity to take action independently and to assume responsibility for one's actions.	29
Interpersonal skills	The ability to create and maintain open and constructive relationships with others, to respond helpfully to their requests and to be sensitive to their needs.	29
Strategic orientation	The capacity to take a long-term and visionary view of the direction to be followed in the future.	29
Creativity	The ability to originate new practices, concepts and ideas.	26
Information management	The capacity to originate and use information effectively.	26
Quality focus	The focus on delivering quality and continuous improvement.	24
Self-confidence and assertiveness	Belief in oneself and standing up for one's own rights.	24
Self-development	Managing one's own learning and development.	22
Managing	Managing resources, people, programmes and projects.	20

TABLE 7.2 Example of a basic competency framework

- *Achievement/results orientation.* The desire to get things done well and the ability to set and meet challenging goals, create own measures of excellence and constantly seek ways of improving performance.
- *Business awareness.* The capacity continually to identify and explore business opportunities, understand the business opportunities and priorities of the organization and constantly to seek methods of ensuring that the organization becomes more businesslike.
- *Communication.* The ability to communicate clearly and persuasively, orally or in writing.
- *Customer focus.* The exercise of unceasing care in looking after the interests of external and internal customers to ensure that their wants, needs and expectations are met or exceeded.
- *Developing others.* The desire and capacity to foster the development of members of his or her team, providing feedback, support, encouragement and coaching.
- *Flexibility.* The ability to adapt to and work effectively in different situations and to carry out a variety of tasks.
- *Leadership.* The capacity to inspire individuals to give of their best to achieve a desired result and to maintain effective relationships with individuals and the team as a whole.
- *Planning.* The ability to decide on courses of action, ensuring that the resources required to implement the actions will be available and scheduling the programme of work required to achieve a defined end-result.
- *Problem solving.* The capacity to analyse situations, diagnose problems, identify the key issues, establish and evaluate alternative courses of action and produce a logical, practical and acceptable solution.
- *Teamwork.* The ability to work cooperatively and flexibly with other members of the team with a full understanding of the role to be played as a team member.

Competency frameworks

Competency frameworks provide the basis for the use of competencies in areas such as recruitment and selection, learning and development, and performance management. They may simply contain definitions of each competency heading as in the example given in Table 7.2.

Some frameworks illustrate these definitions with descriptions of acceptable or unacceptable behaviour, which may be expressed as positive or negative indicators as shown in Table 7.3.

Using competencies

A number of approaches to using competencies are adopted, as described below.

The 'menu' approach

A 'menu' approach selects competencies that are relevant to generic or individual roles. Some organizations provide guidelines on the number of competencies to be selected (eg four to eight) and others combine their core framework with a menu so that users are required to select the organization-wide core competencies but can add a number of optional ones.

Role-specific competencies

Role-specific competencies are also used by some organizations for generic or individual roles. These may be incorporated in a role profile in addition to a statement of key result areas. This approach is adopted in performance management processes, in recruitment person specifications and in the preparation of individual learning programmes.

TABLE 7.3 Example of competency framework definition with positive and negative indicators

Competency heading	Manage continuous improvement
Competency definition	Constantly seeking ways of improving the quality of services, the relevance and appeal of those services to the needs of customers and clients, and their effectiveness.
Competency requirement	Set targets for improvement. Develop and implement programmes for managing change. Contribute to the development of quality assurance and control processes and ensure that they are implemented.
Positive indicators	Encourages the development of new ideas and methods especially those concerned with the provision of quality. Conscious of the factors that enable change to take place smoothly. Discusses ideas with colleagues and customers and formulates views on how to improve services and processes.
Negative indicators	Doesn't try anything that hasn't been done before. Complacent, believes that there is no room for improvement. Follows previous practices without considering whether there is any need to change.

Graded competencies

A further, although less common, application of competencies is in graded career or job family structures (career or job families consist of jobs in a function or occupation such as marketing, operations, finance, IT, HR, administration or support services that are related through the activities carried out and the basic knowledge and skills required, but in which the levels of responsibility, knowledge, skill or competence needed differ). In such families, the successive levels in each family are defined in terms of competencies as well as the key activities carried out.

Applications of competency-based HRM

The Competency and Emotional Intelligence 2006/7 survey found that 95 per cent of respondents used behavioural competencies and 66 per cent used technical competencies. It was noted that because the latter deal with specific activities and tasks they inevitably result in different sets of competencies for groups of related roles, functions or activities. The three top areas where competencies were applied are:

- Recruitment and selection: 85 per cent.
- Learning and development: 82 per cent.
- Performance management: 76 per cent.

Only 30 per cent of organizations linked competencies to reward. The ways in which these competencies are used are described below.

Recruitment and selection

Competencies are used in many organizations as a basis for person specifications set out under competency headings developed through role analysis. The competencies defined for a role are used as the framework for recruitment and selection, and competency-based interviews are structured around the competencies listed in the specification.

Learning and development

Role profiles, which are either generic (covering a range of similar jobs) or individual (role-specific), can include statements of the competencies required. These are used to assess the levels of competency achieved by individuals and so identify their learning and development needs. Learning events can be based on competency analysis related to an organization's competency framework.

Competencies are also used in development centres, which help participants build up their understanding of the competencies they require now and in the future so that they can plan their own self-directed learning programmes.

Performance management

Competencies in performance management are used to ensure that performance reviews do not simply focus on outcomes but also consider the behavioural aspects of how the work is carried out that determine those outcomes. Performance reviews conducted on this basis are used to inform personal improvement and development plans and learning programmes.

Reward management

Competency-related pay relates additional awards to assessments of competency but it has never become popular. However, more frequent use is made of contribution-related pay, which provides for people to be rewarded according to both the results they achieve and their level of competence.

Developing a competency framework

A competency framework should be as simple to understand and use as possible. The language should be clear and jargon-free. Without clear language and examples it can be difficult to assess the level of competency achieved. When defining competencies, especially if they are used for performance management or competency-related pay, it is essential to ensure that they can be assessed. They must not be vague or overlap with other competencies and they must specify clearly the sort of behaviour that is expected and the level of technical or functional skills (competencies) required to meet acceptable standards. It is helpful to address the user directly ('you will...') and to give clear and brief examples of how the competency needs to be performed.

Developing a behavioural competency framework that fits the culture and purpose of the organization and provides a sound basis for a number of key HR processes is not to be undertaken lightly. It requires a lot of hard work, much of it concerned with involving staff and communicating with them to achieve understanding and buy-in. The steps required are described below.

Step 1. Programme launch

Decide on the purpose of the framework and the HR processes for which it will be used. Make out a business case for its development, setting out the benefits to the organization in such areas as improved performance, better selection outcomes, more focused performance management, employee development and reward processes. Prepare a project plan that includes an assessment of the resources required and the costs.

Step 2. Involvement and communication

Involve line managers and employees in the design of the framework (Steps 3 and 4) by setting up a task force. Communicate the objectives of the exercise to staff.

Step 3. Framework design – competency list

First, get the task force to draw up a list of the core competencies and values of the business – what it should be good at doing and the values it believes should influence behaviour. This provides a foundation for an analysis of the competencies required by people in the organization. The aim is to identify and define the behaviours that contribute to the achievement of organizational success, and there should be a powerful link between these people competencies and the organization's core competencies (more guidance on defining competencies is provided in Chapter 51).

The list can be drawn up by brainstorming. The list should be compared with examples of other competency frameworks, to avoid replicating other lists. It is essential to produce a competency framework that fits and reflects the organization's own culture, values, core competencies and operations, but referring to other lists will help to clarify the conclusions reached in the initial analysis and serve to check that all relevant areas of competency have been included. When identifying competencies, care must be taken to avoid bias because of sex or race.

Step 4. Framework design – definition of competencies

Care needs to be exercised to ensure that definitions are clear and unambiguous and that they will serve their intended purpose. If, for example, one of the purposes is to provide criteria for conducting performance reviews, then it is necessary to be certain that the way the competency is defined, together with supporting examples, will enable fair assessments to be made. The following four questions have been produced by Mirabile (1998) to test the extent to which a competency is valid and can be used:

1. Can you describe the competency in terms that others understand and agree with?
2. Can you observe it being demonstrated or failing to be demonstrated?
3. Can you measure it?
4. Can you influence it in some way, eg by training, coaching or some other method of development?

It is also important at this stage to ensure that definitions are not biased.

Step 5. Define uses of the competency framework

Define exactly how it is intended that the competency framework should be used, covering such applications as recruitment and selection, learning and development, performance management and reward.

Step 6. Test the framework

Test the framework by gauging the reactions of a balanced selection of line managers and other employees to ensure that they understand it and believe that it is relevant to their roles. Also pilot-test the framework in live situations for each of its proposed applications.

Step 7. Finalize the framework

Amend the framework as necessary following the tests and prepare notes for guidance on how it should be used.

Step 8. Communicate

Let everyone know the outcome of the project – what the framework is, how it will be used and how people will benefit. Group briefings and any other suitable means should be used.

Step 9. Train

Give line managers and HR staff training in how to use the framework.

Step 10. Monitor and evaluate

Monitor and evaluate the use of the framework and amend it as required.

Keys to success in using competencies

- The competencies should reflect the organization's values and its needs, as established by analysis, to determine the behaviours that will lead to high performance.
- Frameworks should not be overcomplex.
- There should not be too many headings in a framework – seven or eight will often suffice.
- The language used should be clear and jargon-free.
- Competencies must be selected and defined in ways that ensure that they can be assessed by managers – the use of 'behavioural indicators' is helpful.
- Frameworks should be regularly updated.

Competencies and emotional intelligence

Emotional intelligence as described fully in Chapter 10 is a combination of skills and abilities such as self-awareness, self-control, empathy and sensitivity to the feelings of others. It covers many of the inter-personal skills included in competency frameworks.

But as Dulewicz and Higgs (1998) pointed out, the concept of emotional intelligence overlaps with that of competency.

Key learning points: Competency-based HRM

Competency-based HRM is about using the notion of competency and the results of competency analysis to inform and improve HR processes, especially those concerned with recruitment and selection, learning and development, and performance and reward management.

Competency defined

The term 'competency' refers to an underlying characteristic of a person that results in effective or superior performance. The different types of competencies are:

1. Behavioural competencies define behavioural expectations, ie the type of behaviour required to deliver results under such headings as teamworking, communication, leadership and decision-making.
2. Technical competencies define what people have to know and be able to do (knowledge and skills) to carry out their roles effectively.
3. NVQ/SNVQ competences specify minimum standards for the achievement of set tasks and activities expressed in ways that can be observed and assessed with a view to certification.

The contents of competency frameworks (the 10 most popular headings)

1. team orientation;
2. communication;
3. people management;
4. customer focus;
5. results orientation;
6. problem solving;
7. planning and organizing;
8. technical skills;
9. leadership;
10. business awareness.

Uses of competencies (2006/7)

- Learning and development: 82 per cent.
- Performance management: 76 per cent.
- Selection: 85 per cent.
- Recruitment: 55 per cent.
- Reward: 30 per cent.

How to develop a competency framework

- Decide on the purpose of the framework and the HR processes for which it will be used.
- Make out a business case for its development, setting out the benefits.
- Prepare a project plan that includes an assessment of the resources required and the costs.
- Involve line managers and employees in the design of the framework.
- Communicate the objectives of the exercise to staff.
- Draw up a list of the core competencies of the business.
- Define the competencies for inclusion in a competency framework.
- Test and finalize and communicate framework.

Keys to success in using competencies

- The competencies should reflect the organization's values and its needs, as established by analysis, to determine the behaviours that will lead to high performance.
- Frameworks should not be overcomplex.
- There should not be too many headings in a framework – seven or eight will often suffice.
- The language used should be clear and jargon-free.
- Competencies must be selected and defined in ways that ensure they can be assessed by managers – the use of 'behavioural indicators' is helpful.
- Frameworks should be regularly updated.

Competencies and emotional intelligence

The emotional intelligence elements of self-awareness, emotional management, empathy, relationships, communication and personal style correspond to competencies such as sensitivity, flexibility, adaptability, resilience, impact, listening, leadership, persuasiveness, motivating others, energy, decisiveness and achievement motivation.

Questions

1 What is competency-based HRM?
2 What is a competency?
3 What are behavioural competencies?
4 What are technical competencies?
5 What is the difference between the concepts of competency and competence?
6 What is a competency framework?
7 What are the main ways in which competencies can be used?

References

Boyatzis, R (1982) *The Competent Manager*, New York, Wiley

Competency and Emotional Intelligence (2006/7) *Raising Performance Through Competencies: The annual benchmarking survey*, London, Competency and Emotional Intelligence

Dulewicz, V and Higgs, M (1999) The seven dimensions of emotional intelligence, *People Management*, 28, October, p 53

Mirabile, R J (1998) Leadership competency development, competitive advantage for the future, *Management Development Forum*, 1 (2), pp 1–15

08
The ethical dimension of HRM

KEY CONCEPTS AND TERMS

- Bounded rationality
- Core values
- Deontological ethics theory
- Discourse
- Distributive justice
- Ethics
- Fair dealing
- Morality
- Natural justice
- Procedural justice
- Social justice
- Stakeholder theory
- Utilitarianism

LEARNING OUTCOMES

On completing this chapter you should be able to define these key concepts. You should also understand:

- The meaning of ethics
- The nature of ethical decisions and judgements
- The ethical concepts of deontology, utilitarianism, stakeholder theory and discourse theory
- The significance of the concepts of equity, justice and fair dealing
- HRM ethical guidelines
- How to resolve ethical dilemmas
- The ethical role of HR

Introduction

The theme of this chapter is the importance of recognizing that there is an ethical dimension to human resource management. As Boxall *et al* (2007: 5) pointed out: 'While HRM does need to support commercial outcomes (often called "the business case"), it also exists to serve organizational needs for social legitimacy.' This means exercising social responsibility, ie being concerned for the interests (well-being) of employees and acting ethically with regard to the needs of people in the organization and the community.

To grasp this ethical dimension it is necessary to understand the nature and principles of ethics, the ethical role of HR and the ethical guidelines they can use. It is also necessary to know about approaches to resolving ethical dilemmas.

The meaning and concerns of ethics

Ethics is defined by the *Compact Oxford Dictionary* as being 'related to morals, treating of moral questions', and ethical is defined as 'relating to morality'. Morality is defined as 'having moral qualities or endowments' and moral is defined as 'of or pertaining to the distinction between right and wrong'. Petrick and Quinn (1997: 42) wrote that ethics 'is the study of individual and collective moral awareness, judgement, character and conduct'. Hamlin *et al* (2001: 98) noted that ethics is concerned with rules or principles that help us to distinguish right and wrong.

Ethics and morality are sometimes treated as being synonymous, although Beauchamp and Bowie (1983: 1–2) suggested that they are different: 'Whereas morality is a social institution with a history and code of learnable rules, ethical theory refers to the philosophical study of the nature of ethical principles, decisions and problems.' Clearly, ethics is concerned with matters of right and wrong and therefore involves moral judgements. Even if ethics and morality are not the same, the two are closely linked. As Clegg *et al* (2007: 111) put it: 'We understand ethics as the social organizing of morality.' Simplistically, ethics could be described as being about behaviour while morality is about beliefs.

Ethics is concerned with making decisions and judgements about what is the right course of action to take. It can be described in terms of a framework that sets out different approaches and can be extended to embrace particular concepts that affect and guide ethical behaviour, namely equity, justice and fair dealing. These approaches and concepts are discussed below.

The nature of ethical decisions and judgements

As defined by Jones (1991: 367), an ethical decision is one that is morally acceptable to the larger community. He also noted that: 'A moral issue is present where a person's actions, when freely performed, may harm or benefit others. In other words, the action or decision must have consequences for others and must involve choice, or volition, on the part of the actor or decision maker' (ibid: 367).

Winstanley and Woodall (2000a: 8–9) observed that:

> Ethics is not about taking statements of morality at face value; it is a critical and challenging tool. There are no universally agreed ethical frameworks... Different situations require ethical insight and flexibility to enable us to encapsulate the grounds upon which competing claims can be made. Decisions are judgements usually involving choices between alternatives, but rarely is the choice between right and wrong... Moral disagreement and judgements are concerned with attitudes and feelings, not facts.

Clegg *et al* (2007: 112) emphasized that: 'Ethical decisions emerge out of dilemmas that cannot be managed in advance through rules.' People have to make choices. Foucault (1997: 284) asked: 'What is ethics, if not the practice of freedom?'

Ethical frameworks

The ethical concepts of deontology, utilitarianism, stakeholder theory and discourse theory, as described below, provide frameworks that can be used to evaluate HRM policies and practices.

Deontological theory

Deontological (from the Greek for 'what is right') theory maintains that some actions are right or wrong irrespective of their consequences. It is associated with Kant's notion of the categorical imperative, which contains two main propositions: a) that one should follow the principle that what is right for one person is right for everyone, and thus you must do to others as you would be done by; and b) in the words of Rawls (1973: 183): 'We must treat persons solely as ends and not in any way as means.'

Utilitarianism

Utilitarianism is the belief that the highest principle of morality is to maximize happiness, the overall balance of pleasure against pain. Actions are justified when they result in the greatest good to the greatest number. As Sandel (2010: 33) explained, utilitarianism says that 'the morality of an action depends solely on the consequences it brings about; the right thing to do will be whatever brings about the best state of affairs.' In other words, actions should be judged in terms of their results. This can be interpreted as supporting the dubious principle that the end justifies the means – torture is all right as long as it prevents terrorism (NB even if this argument were accepted, the effectiveness of torture as a means of preventing terrorism is highly questionable). Utilitarianism has been criticized first because it fails to respect individual rights and second because, as Michael Sandel explained, it implies that all moral judgements can be translated into a single currency of value, but there is no such thing as a 'util'.

Stakeholder theory

In accordance with the ideas of Freeman (1984), stakeholder theory states that the organization should be managed on behalf of its stakeholders: its owners, employees, customers, suppliers and local communities. As Legge (1998: 22) described it, management must act in the interests of the stakeholders as their agent, and also act in the interests of the organization to ensure the survival of the firm, safeguarding the long-term stakes of each group.

Discourse ethics

Foucault (1972) defined discourse as the taken-for-granted ways that people are collectively able to make sense of experience. Discourse ethics, as explained by Winstanley and Woodall (2000a: 14), suggests that 'the role of ethicists is not to provide solutions to ethical problems, but rather to provide a practical process and procedure which is both rational and consensus enhancing, through which issues can be debated and discourse can take place'.

Equity theory

Equity theory, as formulated by Adams (1965), is concerned with the perceptions people have about how they are being treated as compared with others. To be dealt with equitably is to be treated fairly in comparison with another group of people (a reference group) or a relevant other person. Equity involves feelings and perceptions and it is always a comparative process. It is not synonymous with equality, which means treating everyone the same and would be inequitable if they deserve to be treated differently.

Justice

Justice is the process of treating people in a way that is inherently fair, right and proper. The concept of 'justice as fairness' proposed by Rawls (1973: 348) states that 'natural duties and obligations arise only in virtue of ethical principles'. These principles were expressed by Rawls as follows:

> First: every person is to have the equal right to the most extensive basic liberty comparable with a similar liberty for others.
> Second: social and economic inequalities are to be arranged so that they are both (a) reasonably expected to be to everyone's advantage, and (b) attached to positions and offices open to all. (ibid: 60)

There are four types of justice: procedural justice, distributive justice, social justice and natural justice.

Procedural justice

Procedural justice (Adams, 1965; Leventhal, 1980) involves treating people in ways that are fair, consistent, transparent and properly consider their views and needs. In organizations, it is concerned with fair process and the perceptions employees have about the fairness with which company procedures in such areas as performance appraisal, promotion and discipline are being operated. The five factors that affect perceptions of procedural justice, as identified by Tyler and Bies (1990), are:

- Adequate consideration of an employee's viewpoint.
- Suppression of personal bias towards an employee.
- Applying criteria consistently across employees.
- Providing early feedback to employees about the outcome of decisions.
- Providing employees with an adequate explanation of decisions made.

Distributive justice

Distributive justice (Adams, 1965; Leventhal, 1980) means ensuring that people are rewarded equitably in comparison with others in the organization and in accordance with their contribution, and that they receive what was promised to them (management 'delivers the deal').

Social justice

Social justice is based on the concepts of human rights and equality. Rawls (1973: 3–4) rejected the principle of utilitarianism when he asserted that in society: 'Each person possesses an inviolability founded on justice that even the welfare of society as a whole cannot override. For this reason justice denies that the loss of freedom for some is made right by a greater good shared by others.' In organizations, social justice means relating to employees generally in ways that recognize their natural rights to be treated justly, equitably and with respect.

Natural justice

According to the principles of natural justice employees should know the standards they are expected to achieve and the rules to which they are expected to conform. They should be given a clear indication of where they are failing or what rules have been broken and, except in cases of gross misconduct, they should be given a chance to improve before disciplinary action is taken.

HRM ethical guidelines

The guidelines set out below relate to how employees are treated in general and to the major HRM activities of organization development, recruitment and selection, learning and development, performance management, reward management and employee relations. They also relate to employment practices concerning the work environment, employee well-being, equal opportunities, managing diversity, handling disciplinary matters and grievances, job security and redundancy.

General guidelines

- Recognize that the strategic goals of the organization should embrace the rights and needs of employees as well as those of the business.
- Recognize that employees are entitled to be treated as full human beings with personal needs, hopes and anxieties.
- Do not treat employees simply as means to an end or mere factors of production.
- Relate to employees generally in ways that recognize their natural rights to be treated justly, equitably and with respect.

Organization development (OD)

- Agree in advance with clients and individuals the goals, content and risks of an OD programme.

- Make explicit any values or assumptions used in the programme.
- Obtain the maximum involvement of all concerned in the programme so that they understand the processes involved and how they can benefit from them.
- Work with clients to plan and implement change to the benefit of all stakeholders.
- Enable individuals to continue with their development on completing the programme.
- Protect confidentiality.

Recruitment and selection

- Treat candidates with consideration – applications should be acknowledged, candidates should be kept informed without undue delay of decisions made about their application, and they should not be kept waiting for the interview.
- Avoid intrusive or hectoring questioning in interviews.
- Do not put candidates under undue stress in interviews.
- Do not criticize any aspect of the candidate's personality or experience.
- Use relevant selection criteria based on a proper analysis of job requirements.
- Give candidates reasonable opportunity to present their case and to ask questions.
- Avoid jumping to conclusions about candidates on inadequate evidence or as a result of prejudice.
- Give accurate and complete information to candidates about the job, prospects, security and terms and conditions of employment.
- Only use properly validated tests administered by trained testers.
- Do not use discriminating or biased tests.
- Monitor tests for impact and unintended bias.
- Ensure that candidates are not unfairly disadvantaged by testing processes.
- Give candidates feedback on test results unless there are compelling reasons why feedback should not be given.
- Ensure that selection decisions are free of discrimination or bias on the grounds of sex, sexual orientation, race, age or disability.
- Give unsuccessful candidates the reason for the decision if they request it.

Learning and development

- Respect individual rights for dignity, self-esteem, privacy and autonomy.
- Recognize that it is necessary and legitimate to provide individuals with learning opportunities that enable them to gain the knowledge and skills required to perform well in their jobs and develop their potential. But note that individuals should still be allowed autonomy to choose the extent to which they pursue learning and development programmes beyond this basic requirement.
- Accept that while the organization has the right to conduct learning and development activities that enhance performance, individuals also have the right to be provided with opportunities to develop their own knowledge, skills and employability.
- Ensure that people taking part in learning events feel 'psychologically safe' in accordance with the view expressed by Schein (1993: 91) that: 'To make people feel safe in learning, they must have a motive, a sense of direction, and the opportunity to try out new things without the fear of punishment.'
- Avoid manipulating people to accept imposed organizational values.

Performance management

Performance management ethical principles have been defined by Winstanley and Stuart-Smith (1996) as follows:

- *Respect for the individual* – people should be treated as 'ends in themselves' and not merely as 'means to other ends'.
- *Mutual respect* – the parties involved in performance management should respect each other's needs and preoccupations.

- *Procedural fairness* – the procedures incorporated in performance management should be operated fairly in accordance with the principles of procedural justice.
- *Transparency* – people affected by decisions emerging from performance management processes should have the opportunity to scrutinize the basis upon which decisions were made.

Reward management

- Generally apply the principles of procedural and distributive justice.
- Ensure that reward policies and practices are fair, equitable and transparent and that they are applied consistently.
- Reward people according to their contribution.
- Ensure that people know in general the basis upon which rewards are provided and in particular how their own reward package is determined.
- Maintain reasonable and defensible pay differentials.
- Ensure that equal pay is provided for work of equal value.
- Base decisions about performance pay or bonuses on fair and equitable criteria.
- Avoid bonus schemes that encourage undesirable behaviour.
- Do not pay less than the living wage (in the UK in July 2013 it was £7.45 per hour outside London compared with £6.19 for the statutory minimum wage).

Employee relations

- Deliver the deal.
- Be open to employees' input and responsive to justifiable questions and concerns about employment policies and practices.
- Provide genuine opportunities and channels for employees to express their views and influence decisions on matters that affect them.
- Negotiate in good faith.
- Recognize that the interests of management and employees do not necessarily coincide and develop and implement employee relations policies accordingly.

Employment practices

- Create a healthy, safe and fulfilling work environment.
- Promote the well-being of employees by improving the quality of working life provided for them, enhancing work–life balance and developing family-friendly policies.
- Take particular care to minimize the stress to which employees may be subjected.
- Provide equal opportunities for all with regard to recruitment and selection, learning and development, talent management, career progression and promotion.
- Manage diversity by recognizing the differences between people and ensuring that everyone feels valued and that the talents of all employees will be properly utilized.
- Handle disciplinary matters according to the principles of natural justice.
- Recognize that people may have legitimate grievances and respond to them promptly, fully and sympathetically.
- Preserve job security as far as possible and take alternative action to avoid compulsory redundancies.
- If compulsory redundancy is unavoidable, do whatever is possible to alleviate the distress by, for example, helping people to find work.
- Do not allow whistle-blowers who expose wrongdoing to be penalized.

Ethical dilemmas

'Ethics will be enacted in situations of ambiguity where dilemmas and problems will be dealt with without the comfort of consensus or certitude' (Clegg *et al*, 2007: 109). Bauman, quoted in Bauman and Tester (2001: 44), commented that: 'Morality concerns choice first of all – it is the predicament human beings encounter when they must make a selection amongst various possibilities.' And Derrida (1992) observed that ethical responsibility can exceed rational calculation.

Resolving ethical dilemmas

As Adam Smith (1759) wrote in *The Theory of Modern Sentiments* (quoted by Harrison, 2009: 246): 'When ethically perplexed, the question we should always ask is: would a disinterested observer, in full possession of the relevant facts, approve or disapprove of our actions?' This guidance is just as compelling and relevant today.

Woodall and Winstanley (2000: 285) suggested that 'being ethical is not so much about finding one universal principle to govern all action, but more about knowing how to recognize and mediate between often unacknowledged differences of view'. By definition, an ethical dilemma is one that will be difficult to resolve. There may be all sorts of issues surrounding the situation, some of which will be unclear or contentious. The extent to which people react or behave rationally may be limited by their capacity to understand the complexities of the situation they are in and affected by their emotional reactions to it (the concept of bounded rationality). As Harrison (2009: 331) explained:

> Some of the factors that militate against a purely 'rational' approach include confused, excessive, incomplete or unreliable data, incompetent processing or communicating of information, pressures of time, human emotions, and differences in individuals' cognitive processes, mental maps and reasoning capacity.

Faced with factors such as these the process of ethical dilemma resolution can be hard going.

There is no 'one right way' to deal with an ethical issue, but an approach based on systematic questioning, analysis and diagnosis to get at the facts and establish the issues involved is more likely to produce a reasonably satisfactory outcome than one relying purely on 'gut feeling'. The following checklist – used judiciously and selectively according to the circumstances – can provide a basis for such questioning and analysis.

Checklist – dealing with ethical issues

- What are the known facts about the situation and is it possible that there are facts or circumstances that have not come to light, and if so what can be done to uncover them?
- In disciplinary or conduct cases, to what extent does the conduct contravene the organization's code of ethical conduct (if one exists) or any other relevant organizational policy guidelines and rules?
- In disciplinary cases, are there any mitigating circumstances?
- Have different versions or interpretations of the facts and circumstances been offered and, if so, what steps can be taken to obtain the true and full picture?
- Do the facts as established and confirmed justify the proposed action?
- Is the proposed action in line with both the letter and the spirit of the law?
- Is the proposed action and any investigations leading to it consistent with the principles of natural, procedural or distributive justice?
- Will the proposed action benefit the organization and if so how?
- Is there any risk of the proposed action doing harm to the organization's reputation for fair dealing?
- Will the proposed action be harmful to the individual affected or to employees generally in any way and if so how?

The ethical role of HR

Legge (1998: 20–21) commented that: 'In very general terms I would suggest that the experience of HRM is more likely (but not necessarily) to be viewed positively if its underlying principles are ethical.' HR professionals have a special responsibility for guarding and promoting core values in the organization on how people should be managed and treated. They need to take action to achieve fair dealing. This means treating people according to the principles of procedural, distributive, social and natural justice, and seeing that decisions or policies that affect them are transparent in the sense that they are known, understood, clear and applied consistently.

Kochan (2007: 600) suggested that: 'HR derives its social legitimacy from its ability to serve as an effective steward of a social contract in employment relationships capable of balancing and integrating the interests and needs of employers, employees and the society in which these relationships are embedded.' But he also noted that most HR professionals have 'lost any semblance of credibility as stewards of the social contract because most HR professionals have lost their ability to seriously challenge or offer an independent perspective on the policies and practices of the firm' (ibid: 604). And, Parkes and Davis (2013: 2427) pointed out the risk that the HR role can become 'rather passive, favouring communicating standards rather than actively promoting ethical behaviour'.

To overcome this problem and thus fulfil an ethical role Winstanley and Woodall (2000b: 7) remarked that: 'HR professionals have to raise awareness of ethical issues, promote ethical behaviour, disseminate ethical practices widely among line managers, communicate codes of ethical conduct, ensure people learn about what constitutes ethical behaviours, manage compliance and monitor arrangements.'

There are three approaches that HR can adopt. The first is to ensure that HR policies and the actions taken to implement them meet acceptable ethical standards. HR can press for the production of a value statement that sets out how the organization intends to treat its employees. Value statements may be set out under such headings as care and consideration for people, belief that people should be treated justly and equitably and belief that the views of employees about matters that concern them should be listened to.

This requires advocacy skills to persuade management to adopt and act on these policies and the courage and determination to make out the ethical case even when management favours a conflicting business case. But value statements are meaningless until the values are put into practice; the ethical role of HR involves helping to ensure that this takes place.

Second, HR practitioners can act as role models, leading by example and living and breathing good ethical behaviour. As a respondent to the survey conducted by Parkes and Davis (2013: 2426) commented: 'If HR does not act ethically, how can it expect employees to do so?'

The third approach, and the hardest, is to challenge unethical behaviour on the part of management. Such behaviour can take many forms, including management tolerance for exploitation and bullying; the lack of a whistle-blowing policy, which provides routes for reporting malpractice and performance management criteria that emphasize organizational gain over all else. The latter was the case at the Royal Bank of Scotland (RBS) before the financial crisis, where the performance management concentrated on target achievement, ignoring behaviour. The courage to challenge is less likely to be forthcoming in organizations where the culture is one of command and control – and obedience is expected to whatever is dictated by management (features of the pre-crash RBS culture). Power, politics and culture shape norms of behaviour and, as Herb Kelleher (the CEO of Southwest Airlines) put it, culture is 'what people do when no one is looking' (reported by Lee, 1994). One respondent to the Parkes and Davis survey (2013: 2425) commented: 'It can be difficult on a personal level to be speaking out – HR do not have the power'. Another said: 'Speaking out can be career suicide'. It is too easy in these circumstances for HR to be mere bystanders. Neil Roden, former head of HR at RBS, explained HR's position in relation to the financial debacle at the bank as follows: 'I'm not absolving myself totally... (but) I can't see what HR could have done... I wasn't running the bank... the CEO makes the decisions, not me. HR is a support function, no more, no less important than sales or IT.'

An HR director who is a member of an executive board can question decisions from an ethical viewpoint but if the comments are not heeded then the director will either have to accept the decision or resign. It is important to challenge – and the courage to do so is listed by the CIPD as one of the qualities required by an HR professional. But it is difficult and there may be limits to what HR can do. If HR professionals cannot do anything about the way their organization does things they either have to carry on and do whatever they can in other less confrontational ways, or they must leave.

Key learning points: The ethical dimension of HRM

Ethics and morality defined

Ethics is defined by the *Compact Oxford Dictionary* as being 'related to morals, treating of moral questions', and ethical is defined as 'relating to morality'. Morality is defined as 'having moral qualities or endowments' and moral is defined as 'of or pertaining to the distinction between right and wrong'. Simplistically, ethics could be described as being about behaviour while morality is about beliefs.

Ethics is concerned with making ethical decisions and judgements. It can be described in terms of an ethical framework that sets out different approaches and can be extended to embrace particular concepts that affect and guide ethical behaviour, namely equity, justice and fair dealing. An ethical decision is one that is morally acceptable to the larger community.

Ethical concepts

The ethical concepts of deontology, utilitarianism, stakeholder theory and discourse theory provide frameworks that can be used to evaluate HRM policies and practices.

An important role for HR professionals is to do whatever they can to embed the consistent application of ethical values in the organization so that they can become values in use rather than simply professed values in a code of practice or values statement.

Ethical guidelines

Ethical guidelines set out how employees are treated in general, and to the major HRM activities of organization development, recruitment and selection, learning and development, performance management, reward management, employee relations, and employment practices concerning the work environment, employee well-being, equal opportunities, managing diversity, handling disciplinary matters and grievances, job security and redundancy.

Handling ethical dilemmas

There is no 'one right way' to deal with an ethical dilemma but an approach based on systematic questioning, analysis and diagnosis to get at the facts and establish the issues involved is more likely to produce a reasonably satisfactory outcome than one relying purely on 'gut feeling'. An ethical dilemma is one that will be difficult to resolve. There may be all sorts of issues surrounding the situation, some of which will be unclear or contentious.

The role of HR

HR professionals have a special responsibility for guarding and promoting core values in the organization on how people should be managed and treated generally. They are particularly concerned with values relating to just and fair treatment. They can act as role models and challenge unethical practices. But challenging can be difficult.

Questions

1. What are ethics?
2. What is the nature of ethical judgements?
3. What is the deontological theory of ethics?
4. What is the utilitarian theory of ethics?
5. What is stakeholder theory?
6. What is procedural justice?
7. What is distributive justice?
8. What is the ethical dimension of HRM?
9. What are commonly accepted general guidelines on HR ethical behaviour?
10. How should ethical dilemmas be dealt with?

References

Adams, J S (1965) Injustice in social exchange, in (ed) L Berkowitz, *Advances in Experimental Psychology*, New York, Academic Press

Bauman, Z and Tester, K (2001) *Conversations with Zygmunt Bauman*, Cambridge, Polity Press

Beauchamp, T L and Bowie, N E (1983) *Ethical Theory and Business*, 2nd edn, Englewood Cliffs, NJ, Prentice Hall

Boxall, P F, Purcell, J and Wright, P (2007) Human resource management; scope, analysis and significance, in (eds) P Boxall, J Purcell and P Wright, *The Oxford Handbook of Human Resource Management*, Oxford, Oxford University Press, pp 1–18

Clegg, S, Kornberger, M and Rhodes, C (2007) Business ethics as practice, *British Journal of Management*, 18 (2), pp 107–22

Derrida, J (1992) Forces of law: the mystical foundation of authority, in (eds) D Cornell, M Rosenfeld and D G Carlson, *Deconstruction and the Possibility of Justice*, London, Routledge, pp 3–68

Foucault, M (1972) *The Archaeology of Knowledge and the Discourse on Language*, New York, Pantheon Books

Foucault, M (1997) *Ethics, Subjectivity and Truth. Essential Works of Foucault, 1954–1984*, ed P Rabinow, New York, The New Press

Freeman, R E (1984) *Strategic Management: A stakeholder perspective*, Englewood Cliffs, NJ, Prentice Hall

Guest, D E and King, Z (2004) Power, innovation and problem-solving: the personnel managers' three steps to heaven?, *Journal of Management Studies*, 41 (3), pp 401–23

Hamlin, B, Keep, J and Ash, K (2001) *Organizational Change and Development: A reflective guide for managers*, London, FT Pitman

Harrison, R (2009) *Learning and Development*, 5th edn, London, CIPD

HR Magazine (2010) Interview with Neil Roden, former HR Director of RBS, available at http://www.hrmagazine.co.uk/hr/opinion/105196/interview-neil-roden-hr-director-royal-bank-scotland [accessed 6 July 2013]

Jones, T M (1991) Ethical decision making by individuals in organizations: An issue-contingent model, *Academy of Management Review*, 16 (2), pp 366–95

Kochan, T A (2007) Social legitimacy of the HRM profession: a US perspective, in (eds) P Boxall, J Purcell and P Wright, *The Oxford Handbook of Human Resource Management*, Oxford, Oxford University Press, pp 599–619

Lee, W G (1994) A conversation with Herb Kelleher, *Organizational Dynamics*, 23 (2), pp 64–74

Legge, K (1998) The morality of HRM, in (eds) C Mabey, D Skinner and T Clark, *Experiencing Human Resource Management*, London, Sage, pp 14–32

Leventhal, G S (1980) What should be done with equity theory?, in (eds) G K Gergen, M S Greenberg and R H Willis, *Social Exchange: Advances in theory and research*, New York, Plenum

Parkes, C and Davis, A J (2013) Ethics and social responsibility – do HR professionals have 'the courage to challenge' or are they set to be permanent 'bystanders'? *International Journal of Human Resource Management*, 23 (12), pp 2411–34

Petrick, J A and Quinn, J F (1997) *Management Ethics: Integrity at work*, London, Sage

Rawls, J (1973) *A Theory of Justice*, Oxford, Oxford University Press

Sandel, M J (2010) *Justice: What's the right thing to do?* London, Penguin Books

Schein, E (1993) How can organizations learn faster? The challenge of entering the green room, *Sloan Management Review*, 34 (2), pp 85–92

Tyler, T R and Bies, R J (1990) Beyond formal procedures: the interpersonal context of procedural justice, in (ed) J S Carrol, *Applied Social Psychology and Organizational Settings*, Hillsdale, NJ, Lawrence Erlbaum

Winstanley, D and Stuart-Smith, K (1996) Policing performance: the ethics of performance management, *Personnel Review*, 25 (6), pp 66–84

Winstanley, D and Woodall, J (2000a) Introduction, in (eds) D Winstanley and J Woodall, *Ethical Issues in Contemporary Human Resource Management*, Basingstoke, Macmillan, pp 3–22

Winstanley, D and Woodall, J (2000b) The ethical dimension of human resource management, *Human Resource Management Journal*, 10 (2), pp 5–20

Woodall, J and Winstanley, D (2000) Concluding comments: ethical frameworks for action, in (eds) D Winstanley and J Woodall, *Ethical Issues in Contemporary Human Resource Management*, Basingstoke, Macmillan, pp 3–22

09 Corporate social responsibility

KEY CONCEPTS AND TERMS

Corporate social responsibility (CSR)

Stakeholder theory

Strategic CSR

Value statement

LEARNING OUTCOMES

On completing this chapter you should be able to define these key concepts. You should also understand:

- The meaning of corporate social responsibility (CSR)
- CSR activities
- CSR strategy
- Developing a CSR strategy
- The rationale for CSR

Introduction

The notion that businesses should act in a socially responsible way by practising 'corporate social responsibility' (CSR) has been around for some time. J M Keynes wrote in 1923 that: 'The business man is only tolerable so long as his gains can be held to bear some relation to what, roughly and in some sense, his activities have contributed to society.' The aim of this chapter is to explore what CSR means as a concept and a strategy. The rationale for CSR is also considered – the arguments in favour are overwhelming, but reference is made also to powerful opposing views.

HR professionals, because of the ethical dimension of their function (as described in Chapter 8), have an important role to play in furthering CSR. CSR was justified by the CIPD (2009: 1) as a relevant and important HR activity because:

> CSR needs to be embedded in an organization's culture to make a change to actions and attitudes, and the support of the top team is critical to success. HR already works at communicating and implementing ideas, policies, cultural and behavioural change across organizations. Its role in influencing attitudes and links with line managers and the top team means it is ideally placed to do the same with CSR.

HR professionals need to marshal the arguments in favour of CSR, as set out in this chapter, to overcome any overt or covert resistance. They must be able to advise on CSR strategies and how they can be implemented. This is not an easy task and suggestions on the approaches that can be adopted are made in the concluding section of the chapter.

Corporate social responsibility defined

Corporate social responsibility (CSR) is exercised by organizations when they conduct their business in an ethical way, taking account of the social, environmental and economic impact of how they operate, and going beyond compliance. Wood (1991: 695) stated that: 'The basic idea of corporate social responsibility is that business and society are interwoven rather than distinct entities; therefore, society has certain expectations for appropriate business behaviour and outcomes.' As Baron (2001: 11) noted, CSR involves 'providing to others benefits beyond those generated by economic transactions with the firm or required by law'.

McWilliams *et al* (2006: 1) stated that CSR refers to the actions taken by businesses 'that further some social good beyond the interests of the firm and that which is required by law'. CSR has also been described by Husted and Salazar (2006: 76) as being concerned with 'the impact of business behaviour on society' and by Porter and Kramer (2006: 83) as a process of integrating business and society. The latter argued that to advance CSR: 'We must root it in a broad understanding of the interrelationship between a corporation and society while at the same time anchoring it in the strategies and activities of specific companies.'

CSR is concerned generally with how companies function and this includes how they manage their people. The CIPD (2003: 5) emphasized that 'the way a company treats its employees will contribute directly to the picture of a company that is willing to accept its wider responsibilities'.

CSR policy may be expressed in a value statement that sets out the organization's core values under such headings as:

- care and consideration for people;
- competence;
- competitiveness;
- customer service;
- innovation;
- performance;
- quality;
- teamwork.

But espoused values are pointless unless they become values in use and this needs concerted action by management working with employees and supported by HR.

Strategic CSR defined

Strategic CSR is about deciding initially the degree to which the firm should be involved in social issues and then creating a corporate social agenda

– considering what social issues to focus on and to what extent. As Porter and Kramer (2006: 85) observed: 'It is through strategic CSR that the company will make the greatest social impact and reap the greatest business benefits.' They also observed that strategy is always about choice – organizations that 'make the right choices and build focused, proactive and integrated social initiatives in concert with their core strategies will increasingly distance themselves from the pack' (ibid: 91).

CSR strategy needs to be integrated with the business strategy but it is also closely associated with HR strategy. This is because it is concerned with socially responsible behaviour both outside and within the firm – with society generally and with the internal community. In the latter case this means creating a working environment where personal and employment rights are upheld and HR policies and practices provide for the fair and ethical treatment of employees.

CSR activities

CSR activities as listed by McWilliams *et al* (2006) include incorporating social characteristics or features into products and manufacturing processes, adopting progressive HRM practices, achieving higher levels of environmental performance through recycling and pollution abatement, and advancing the goals of community organizations. The information set out below was obtained by Business in the Community research.

Source review

The CSR activities of 120 leading British companies – Business in the Community (2007)

- *Community* – skills and education, employability and social exclusion were frequently identified as key risks and opportunities. Other major activities were support for local community initiatives and being a responsible and safe neighbour.
- *Environment* – most companies reported climate change and resource-use as key issues for their business: 85 per cent of them managed their impacts through an environmental management system.
- *Marketplace* – the issues most frequently mentioned by companies were research and development, procurement and supply chain, responsible selling, responsible marketing and product safety. There was a rising focus on fair treatment of customers, providing appropriate product information and labelling, and on the impacts of products on customer health.
- *Workplace* – this was the strongest management performing area as most companies have established employment management frameworks that can cater for workplace issues as they emerge. Companies recognized the crucial role of employees to achieve responsible business practices. Emphasis was placed on internal communications and training in order to raise awareness and understanding of why CSR is relevant to them and valuable for the business. More attention was paid to health and well-being issues as well as the traditional safety agenda. More work was done on diversity, both to ensure the business attracts a diverse workforce and to communicate the business case for diversity internally.

Business in the Community also reported a growing emphasis on responsible business as a source of competitive advantage as firms move beyond minimizing risk to creating opportunities. A survey conducted by Industrial Relations Services (Egan, 2006) found that:

- most employers believe that employment practices designed to ensure the fair and ethical treatment of staff can boost recruitment and retention;
- relatively few employers are strongly convinced of a positive link to business performance or productivity;
- the issue of ethics in employment is often viewed as part of a broader social responsibility package;
- policies on ethical employment most commonly cover HR practice in the areas of recruitment, diversity, redundancy/dismissal proceedings and employee involvement.

The rationale for CSR

Stakeholder theory, as first propounded by Freeman (1984), suggests that managers must satisfy a variety of constituents (eg workers, customers, suppliers, local community organizations) who can influence firm outcomes. According to this view, it is not sufficient for managers to focus exclusively on the needs of shareholders or the owners of the business. Stakeholder theory implies that it can be beneficial for the firm to engage in certain CSR activities that non-financial stakeholders perceive to be important.

The rationale for CSR, as defined by Hillman and Keim (2001), is based on two propositions. First, there is a moral imperative for businesses to 'do the right thing' without regard to how such decisions affect firm performance (the social issues argument); second, firms can achieve competitive advantage by tying CSR activities to primary stakeholders (the stakeholders argument). Their research in 500 firms implied that investing in stakeholder management may be complementary to shareholder value creation and could indeed provide a basis for competitive advantage as important resources and capabilities are created that differentiate a firm from its competitors. However, participating in social issues beyond the direct stakeholders may adversely affect a firm's ability to create shareholder wealth. Strong arguments for CSR were made by Porter and Kramer (2006).

> **Source review**
>
> ### Arguments supporting CSR – Porter and Kramer (2006)
>
> 1. *The moral appeal* – the argument that companies have a duty to be good citizens. The US business association Business for Social Responsibility (2007) asks its members 'to achieve commercial success in ways that honour ethical values and respect people, communities and the natural environment'.
> 2. *Sustainability* – an emphasis on environmental and community stewardship. This involves meeting the needs of the present without compromising the ability of future generations to meet their own needs.
> 3. *Licence to operate* – every company needs tacit or explicit permission from government, communities and other stakeholders to do business.
> 4. *Reputation* – CSR initiatives can be justified because they improve a company's image, strengthen its brand, enliven morale and even raise the value of its stock.

Moran and Ghoshal (1996: 45) contended that 'what is good for society does not necessarily have to be bad for the firm, and what is good for the firm does not necessarily have to come at a cost to society. Value creation, rather than value appropriation, lies at the heart of effective firm strategies.'

The opposing view

The opposing view is that businesses are there to make a profit, not to exercise social responsibility. The marketing expert Theodore Levitt (1958: 41), in an article in the *Harvard Business Review* on the dangers of social responsibility, posed the questions: 'Are top executives being taken in by pretty words and soft ideas? Are they letting the country in for a nightmare return to feudalism by forgetting that they must be businessmen first, last and almost always?' He did write that CSR can be used as 'a way of maximizing the lifetime of capitalism by taking the wind out of its critics' sails' (ibid: 43). But, writing as an unrestructured capitalist, he suggested that: 'The essence of free enterprise is to go after profit in any way that is consistent with its own survival as an economic system' (ibid: 44).

The Chicago monetarist Milton Friedman (1962: 133–34) questioned the ability of business managers to pursue the social interest. He asked:

> If businessmen do have a social responsibility other than making maximum profits for stockholders, how are they to know what it is? Can self-selected private individuals decide what the social interest is? Can they decide how great a burden they are justified in placing on themselves or their stockholders to serve that social interest?

In 1970 Friedman argued that the social responsibility of business is to maximize profits within the bounds of the law. He maintained that the mere existence of CSR was an agency problem within the firm in that it was a misuse of the resources entrusted to managers by owners, which could be better used on value-added internal projects or returned to the shareholders.

These outspoken views may no longer be supported so openly but they still exist and are still acted on. There is much evidence that CSR is not on the agenda – for example, UK banks that made money by selling worthless investments or insurance policies and then failed to respond adequately to complaints. And, less egregiously, a glance at the 'Your Problems' column in the *Observer* reveals plenty of instances of businesses indulging in antisocial behaviour. It is necessary, therefore, to have a convincing case for the benefits of CSR.

Benefits of CSR

Benefits from CSR listed by the CIPD (2003: 4) include, 'offering distinctive positioning in the market place, protecting reputation, building credibility and trust with customers and employees, redefining corporate purpose or mission and securing the company's licence to operate'.

Much research has been conducted into the relationship between CSR and firm performance. For example, Russo and Fouts (1997) found that there was a positive relationship between environmental performance and financial performance. Hillman and Keim (2001) established that if the socially responsible activity were directly related to primary stakeholders, then investments may benefit not only stakeholders but also result in increased shareholder wealth. However, participation in social issues beyond the direct stakeholders may adversely affect a firm's ability to create such wealth.

The basis for developing a CSR strategy

The basis for developing a CSR strategy is provided by the following competency framework of the CSR Academy (2006), which is made up of six characteristics:

1. *Understanding society* – understanding how business operates in the broader context and knowing the social and environmental impact that the business has on society.
2. *Building capacity* – building the capacity of others to help manage the business effectively. For example, suppliers understand the business's approach to the environment and employees can apply social and environmental concerns in their day-to-day roles.
3. *Questioning business as usual* – individuals continually questioning the business in relation to a more sustainable future and being open to improving the quality of life and the environment.
4. *Stakeholder relations* – understanding who the key stakeholders are and the risks and opportunities they present. Working with them through consultation and taking their views into account.
5. *Strategic view* – ensuring that social and environmental views are included in the business strategy so that they are integral to the way the business operates.
6. *Harnessing diversity* – respecting that people are different, which is reflected in fair and transparent business practices.

Developing and implementing a CSR strategy

To develop and implement a CSR strategy based on these principles it is necessary to:

- understand the business and social environment in which the firm operates;
- understand the business and HR strategies and how the CSR strategy should be aligned to them;
- know who the stakeholders are (including top management) and find out their views on and expectations of CSR;
- produce and deliver persuasive arguments in favour of CSR: if all else fails suggest that there is room for enlightened self-interest that involves doing well by doing good;
- identify the areas in which CSR activities might take place by reference to their relevance in the business context of the organization and an evaluation of their significance to stakeholders;
- prioritize as necessary on the basis of an assessment of the relevance and significance of CSR to the organization and its stakeholders and the practicalities of introducing the activity or practice;
- draw up the strategy and make the business case for it to top management and the stakeholders;
- obtain approval for the CSR strategy from top management and key stakeholders;
- communicate information on the whys and wherefores of the strategy, comprehensively and regularly;
- provide training to employees on the skills they need in implementing the CSR strategy;
- measure and evaluate the effectiveness of CSR.

Key learning points: Corporate social responsibility

The meaning of CSR

CSR activities include incorporating social characteristics or features into products and manufacturing processes, adopting progressive HRM practices, achieving higher levels of environmental performance through recycling and pollution abatement, and advancing the goals of community organizations.

The rationale for CSR

There are two arguments for CSR (Hillman and Keim, 2001): first, there is a moral imperative for businesses to 'do the right thing' without regard to how such decisions affect firm performance (the social issues argument); second, firms can achieve competitive advantage by tying CSR activities to primary stakeholders (the stakeholders argument).

Developing a CSR strategy

- Identify the areas in which CSR activities might take place by reference to their relevance in the business context of the organization and an evaluation of their significance to stakeholders.
- Prioritize as necessary on the basis of an assessment of the relevance and significance of CSR to the organization and its stakeholders and the practicalities of introducing the activity or practice.
- Draw up the strategy and make the case for it to top management and the stakeholders to obtain their approval.
- Communicate information on the strategy, comprehensively and regularly.
- Provide training to employees on the skills they need to use in implementing the CSR strategy.

Questions

1 Is it necessary to have a business case for CSR and, if so, what is it?

2 What is the role of HR in promoting CSR?

3 What sort of approaches to CSR can an organization adopt?

References

Baron, D (2001) Private policies, corporate policies and integrated strategy, *Journal of Economics and Management Strategy*, 10 (1), pp 7–45

Business for Social Responsibility (2007) Annual Report, web@BSR.org [accessed 5 October 2008]

Business in the Community (2007) Benchmarking Responsible Business Practice, bitc.org.uk, accessed 5 October 2008

CIPD (2003) *Corporate Social Responsibility and HR's Role*, London, CIPD

CIPD (2009) *Corporate Social Responsibility*, London, CIPD

CSR Academy (2006) *The CSR Competency Framework*, Norwich, Stationery Office

Egan, J (2006) Doing the decent thing: CSR and ethics in employment, *IRS Employment Review*, 858, 3 November, pp 9–16

Freeman, R E (1984) *Strategic Management: A stakeholder perspective*, Englewood Cliffs, NJ, Prentice Hall

Friedman, M (1962) *Capitalism and Freedom*, Chicago, IL, University of Chicago Press

Friedman, M (1970) The social responsibility of business is to increase its profits, *New York Times Magazine*, September, p 13

Hillman, A and Keim, G (2001) Shareholder value, stakeholder management and social issues: what's the bottom line?, *Strategic Management Journal*, 22 (2), pp 125–39

Husted, B W and Salazar, J (2006) Taking Friedman seriously: maximizing profits and social performance, *Journal of Management Studies*, 43 (1), pp 75–91

Keynes, J M (1923) *A Tract on Monetary Reform*, London, Macmillan

Levitt, T (1958) The dangers of social responsibility, *Harvard Business Review*, September–October, pp 41–50

McWilliams, A, Siegal, D S and Wright, P M (2006) Corporate social responsibility: strategic implications, *Journal of Management Studies*, 43 (1), pp 1–12

Moran, P and Ghoshal, S (1996) Value creation by firms, *Academy of Management Best Paper Proceedings*, pp 41–45

Porter, M E and Kramer, M R (2006) Strategy and society: the link between competitive advantage and corporate social responsibility, *Harvard Business Review*, December, pp 78–92

Russo, M V and Fouts, P A (1997) A resource-based perspective on corporate environmental performance and profitability, *Academy of Management Review*, 40 (3), pp 534–59

Wood, D J (1991) Corporate social performance revisited, *Academy of Management Review*, 16 (4), pp 691–718

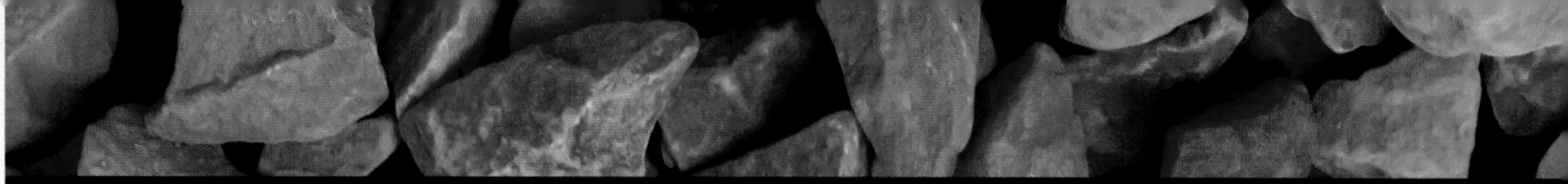

PART II

People and organizations

PART II CONTENTS

Introduction

Human resource management policies and practices need to be based on an understanding of the factors that affect the behaviour of people in organizations. The purpose of this part of the book is to outline a basic set of concepts and to provide analytical tools that will enable HR specialists to diagnose organizational behaviour and to take appropriate actions.

The part starts in Chapter 10 with a general analysis of the concept of organizational behaviour, the term used to describe: 1) how organizations function with regard to their structure, processes and culture; 2) the characteristics of people and how they act in organizations, individually or in groups. Organizational behaviour theory is based on the main behavioural science theories, which have been proved by research. Like all proven theories it provides insights into good practice. Thus it provides guidance on the design of work systems, organizations and jobs, as discussed in Chapter 11, and approaches to organization development (the systematic process of improving organizational capability, which is concerned with process – how things get done) in Chapter 12. It also provides the conceptual framework for approaches to achieving the motivation, commitment and engagement of people, as considered in Part III of this handbook.

10 Organizational behaviour

KEY CONCEPTS AND TERMS

- Behavioural science
- Bounded rationality
- Cognitive dissonance
- Emotional intelligence
- Equity theory
- Expectancy theory
- Extrinsic motivation
- Goal theory
- Intelligence
- Intrinsic motivation
- Lattice organization
- Line and staff organization
- Matrix organization
- Motivation
- Organic organization
- Organization
- Organizational behaviour
- Organizational culture
- Organizational effectiveness
- Organizing
- Personality
- Psychological contract
- Self-efficacy
- Virtual organization

LEARNING OUTCOMES

On completing this chapter you should be able to define these key concepts. You should also know about:

- What is meant by organizational behaviour
- The sources and applications of organizational behaviour theory
- How organizations function
- Organizational culture
- Organizational climate
- Organizational processes
- Characteristics of people
- Implications for HR specialists

Introduction

An understanding of how organizations function and how people behave in them is important to HR professionals, indeed to all managers, as pointed out by Nadler and Tushman (1980).

> **Source review**
>
> **The significance of organizational behaviour theory – Nadler and Tushman (1980: 30)**
>
> Managers perform their jobs within complex social systems called organizations. In many senses, the task of the manager is to influence behaviour in a desired direction, usually towards the accomplishment of a specific task or performance goal. Given this definition of the managerial role, skills in the diagnosis of patterns of organizational behaviour become vital. Specifically, the manager needs to understand the patterns of behaviour that are observed, predict in what direction behaviour will move (particularly in the light of managerial action), and to use this knowledge to control behaviour over the course of time.

Organizational behaviour defined

Organizational behaviour was defined by Huczynski and Buchanan (2007: 843) as the term used to describe 'the study of the structure, functioning, and performance of organizations and the behaviour of groups and individuals within them'. The following are the characteristics of organizational behaviour theory.

> **Source review**
>
> **Characteristics of organizational behaviour – Ivancevich *et al* (2008: 11)**
>
> - It is a way of thinking – about individuals, groups and organizations.
> - It is multidisciplinary – it uses principles, models, theories and methods from other disciplines.
> - There is a distinctly humanistic orientation – people and their attitudes, perceptions, learning capacities, feelings and goals are of major importance.
> - It is performance-oriented – it deals with the factors affecting performance and how it can be improved.
> - The use of scientific method is important in studying variables and relationships.
> - It is applications-oriented in the sense of being concerned with providing useful answers to questions that arise when managing organizations.

The sources and applications of organizational behaviour theory

Organizational behaviour theory is based on the main behavioural science disciplines. These are defined as the fields of enquiry dedicated to the study of human behaviour through sophisticated and rigorous methods. The ways in which they contribute to different aspects of organizational behaviour theory and how they in turn influence HRM practices are summarized in Figure 10.1.

FIGURE 10.1 The sources and applications of organizational behaviour theory

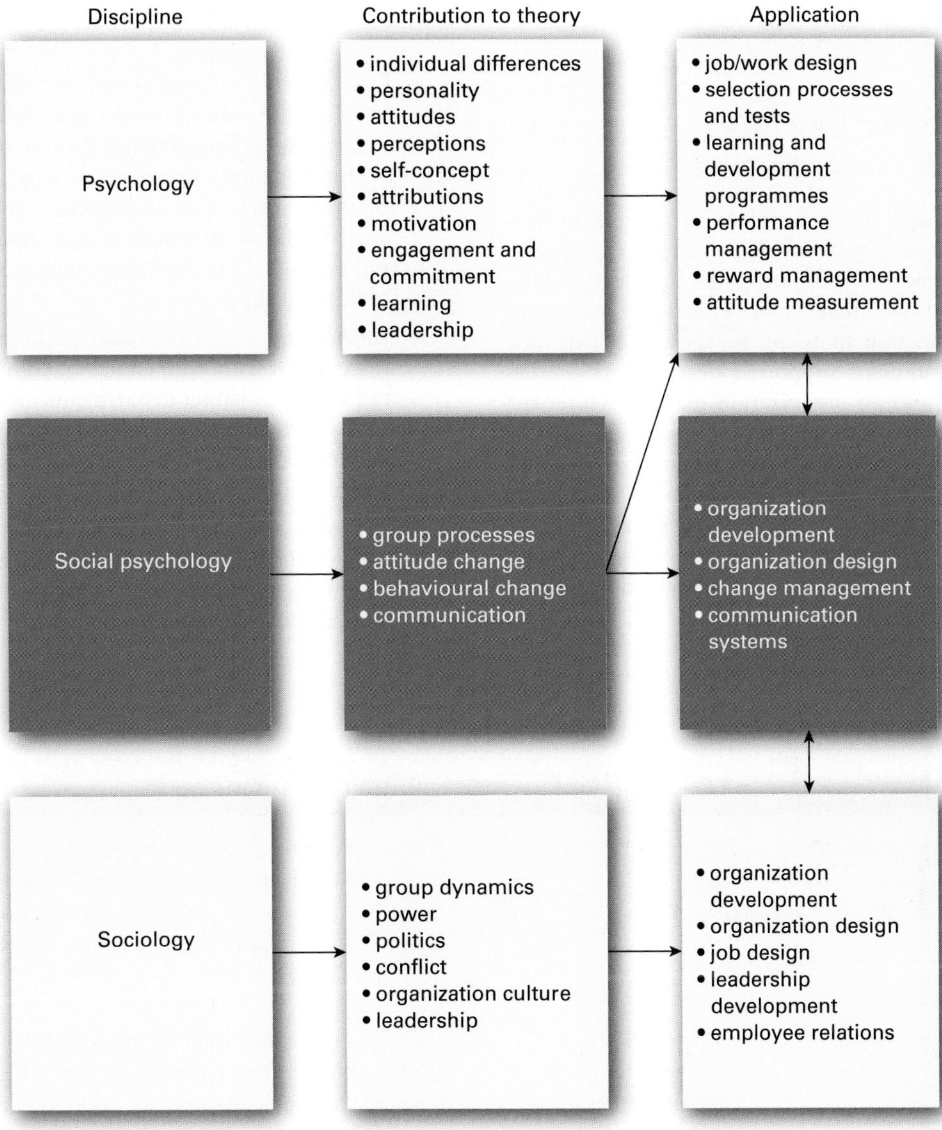

How organizations function

An organization is an entity that exists to achieve a purpose through the collective efforts of the people who work in or for it. Organizing is the process of making arrangements in the form of defined or understood responsibilities and relationships to enable those people to work cooperatively together. Organizations can be described as systems that, as affected by their environment, have a structure that has both formal and informal elements.

Organization structures are frameworks for getting things done. Traditional formal structures were based on laid down hierarchies (lines of command) represented in organization charts, and use was made of closely defined job descriptions. But to varying extents organizations operate informally as well as formally by means of a network of roles and relationships that cut across formal organizational boundaries and lines of command. Organization structures can evolve almost spontaneously as circumstances change and new activities have to be carried out.

Factors affecting how organizations function

The processes that take place in organizations – interaction and networking, leadership, group behaviour, the exercise of power and the use of politics – may well have much more effect on how organizations function than can be shown in a defined organization chart supported by elaborate job descriptions and an organization manual. Moreover, the way in which an organization functions will be largely contingent on its purpose, technology, methods of working and external environment. A number of theories have been developed, summarized in Table 10.1, to explain how organizations function, culminating in the contingency and post-bureaucratic schools that now predominate.

Types of organization

The main types of organization are described briefly below:

- *Line and staff* – a traditional organization based on the military model in which a hierarchy of 'line managers' carry out the fundamental operations such as manufacturing, sales or customer service while the 'staff' functions such as finance and personnel provides them with services, advice and support.
- *Mechanistic* – a formal organization that is hierarchical with rigid chains of command and control, distinct departments and tightly defined and specialized jobs (usually a characteristic of a line and staff organization).
- *Organic* – a relatively informal organization with a non-hierarchical, flat structure where the emphasis is on horizontal processes, the elimination of boundaries between functions,

TABLE 10.1 Schools of organization theory

School	Leading exponents	Summary of theory
The classical school	Taylor (1911), Fayol (1916), Urwick (1947)	Organizations need control, measurement, order and formality to function well. They have to minimize the opportunity for unfortunate and uncontrollable informal relations, leaving room only for the formal ones.
The human relations school	Barnard (1938), Roethlisberger and Dickson (1939)	Barnard emphasized the importance of the informal organization – the network of informal roles and relationships that, for better or worse, strongly influences the way the formal structure operates. In their analysis of the Hawthorne studies Roethlisberger and Dickson stressed the importance of informal groups and decent, humane leadership.
The behavioural science school	Argyris (1957), Herzberg *et al* (1957), McGregor (1960), Likert (1961), Schein (1965)	A humanistic point of view is adopted that is concerned with what people can contribute and how they can best be motivated.

TABLE 10.1 Continued

School	Leading exponents	Summary of theory
The bureaucratic model	Weber (1908) translated in 1947	Max Weber coined the term 'bureaucracy' as a label for a type of formal organization in which impersonality and rationality are developed to the highest degree. Bureaucracy, as he conceived it, was the most efficient form of organization because it was logical and because personalized relationships and non-rational, emotional considerations do not get in its way.
The socio-technical model	Emery (1959), Trist *et al* (1963)	In any system of organization, technical or task aspects are interrelated with the human or social aspects. The emphasis is on interrelationships between, on the one hand, the technical processes of transformation carried out within the organization and, on the other hand, the organization of work groups and the management structures of the enterprise.
The systems school	Miller and Rice (1967)	Organizations should be treated as open systems that are continually dependent upon and influenced by their environments. The basic characteristic of the enterprise as an open system is that it transforms inputs into outputs within its environment.
The contingency school	Burns and Stalker (1961), Woodward (1965), Lawrence and Lorsch (1969)	Members of the contingency school analysed a variety of organizations and concluded that their structures and methods of operation are a function of the circumstances in which they exist. They do not subscribe to the view that there is one best way of designing an organization or that simplistic classifications of organizations as formal or informal, bureaucratic or non-bureaucratic are helpful.
The post-bureaucratic school	Pascale (1990), Ghoshal and Bartlett (1995)	Rather than seeing organizations as a hierarchy of static jobs, members of the post-bureaucratic school think of them as a portfolio of dynamic processes that overlay and often dominate the vertical, authority-based processes of the hierarchical structure. The emphasis is on 'horizontal tasks', collaboration and networking across units rather than on 'vertical tasks' within functional units. Hence the concept of the 'boundaryless organization'.

teamwork and flexible roles (also known as a lattice organization).

- *Matrix organization* – an organization that consists of a functional structure with a number of different disciplines and a project structure consisting of project teams drawn from the disciplines.
- *Network organization* – a collection of interrelated organizations that extends beyond the boundaries of any single organization.
- *Virtual organization* – an organization that mainly uses electronic means for its members to interact with one another thus minimizing face-to-face contacts.

Organizational culture

The culture of an organization has been described by Deal and Kennedy (2000: 4) as 'the way we do things around here'. It is more complex than that, as other definitions given below indicate. But this simplistic definition at least demonstrates that it is an all-pervading notion that affects the way in which people behave and has to be taken into account as a contingency factor in any programme for developing organizations and HR policies and practices. Organizational culture offers a shared system of meanings which is the basis for communications and mutual understanding. If these functions are not fulfilled in a satisfactory way, culture may significantly reduce the effectiveness of an organization. This is why it is important for HR specialists to understand the concept of organizational culture and how it affects organizations.

Organizational culture defined

Organizational or corporate culture is the pattern of values, norms, beliefs, attitudes and assumptions that may not have been articulated but shape the ways in which people in organizations behave and things get done. 'Values' refer to what is believed to be important about how people and organizations behave. 'Norms' are the unwritten rules of behaviour.

This definition emphasizes that organizational culture is concerned with the subjective aspect of what goes on in organizations. It refers to abstractions such as values and norms that pervade the whole or part of a business, which may not be defined, discussed or even noticed. Nevertheless, culture can have a significant influence on people's behaviour. The following are some other definitions of organizational culture:

- A strong culture is a system of informal rules that spells out how people are to behave most of the time. (Deal and Kennedy, 2000: 15)
- The culture of an organization refers to the unique configuration of norms, values, beliefs and ways of behaving that characterize the manner in which groups and individuals combine to get things done. (Eldridge and Crombie, 1974: 89)
- Organizational culture offers a shared system of meanings that is the basis for communications and mutual understanding. (Furnham and Gunter, 1993: 70–71)
- Culture is a pattern of basic assumptions – invented, discovered or developed by a given group as it learns to cope with the problems of external adaptation and internal integration – that has worked well enough to be considered valid and, therefore, to be taught to new members as the correct way to perceive, think and feel in relation to these problems. (Schein, 1990: 110)

How organizational culture develops

The values and norms that are the basis of culture are formed in four ways. First, by the leaders in the organization, especially those who have shaped it in the past. Schein (1990) indicates that people identify with visionary leaders – how they behave and what they expect. They note what such leaders pay attention to and treat them as role models. Second, as Schein also points out, culture is formed around critical incidents – important events from which lessons are learnt about desirable or undesirable behaviour. Third, culture develops from the need to maintain effective working relationships among organization members that establishes values and expectations. Finally, culture is influenced by the organization's environment, which may tend to be dynamic or unchanging.

Culture evolves over time as a result of shared experiences. Schein (1984) suggested that this is a learning process which takes place either through the trauma model, in which members of the organization learn to cope with some threat by the erection of defence mechanisms, or by means of the positive reinforcement model, where things that seem to work become embedded and entrenched. Learning takes place as people adapt to and cope with external pressures, and as they develop successful approaches and mechanisms to handle the internal challenges, processes and technologies in their organization. Where culture has developed over long periods of time and has become firmly embedded it may be difficult to change quickly, if at all, unless a traumatic event occurs.

The diversity of culture

The development process described above may result in a culture that characterizes the whole organization. But there may be different cultures within organizations. For example, the culture of an outward-looking marketing department may be substantially different from that of an internally focused manufacturing function. There may be some common organizational values or norms, but in some respects these will vary between different work environments.

The components of culture

Organizational culture can be described in terms of values, norms, artefacts and management or leadership style.

Values

Values are beliefs in what is best or good for the organization and what should or ought to happen. The 'value set' of an organization may only be recognized at top level, or it may be shared throughout the business, in which case the business could be described as value-driven.

The stronger the values the more they will influence behaviour. This does not depend upon their having been articulated. Implicit values that are deeply embedded in the culture of an organization and are reinforced by the behaviour of management can be influential, while espoused values that are mere rhetoric and are not reflected in managerial behaviour may have little or no effect. When values are acted on they are called 'values in use'. Examples are listed below.

Areas in which values may be expressed – explicitly or implicitly

- Care and consideration for people.
- Competence.
- Competitiveness.
- Customer service.
- Innovation.
- Performance.
- Quality.
- Teamwork.

Values may be expressed through norms and artefacts, as described below. They may also be expressed through the media of language (organizational jargon), rituals, stories and myths.

Norms

Norms are the unwritten rules of behaviour, the 'rules of the game' that provide informal guidelines on how to behave. Norms tell people what they are supposed to be doing, saying, believing, even wearing. They are never expressed in writing – if they were, they would be policies or procedures. They are passed on by word of mouth or behaviour and can be enforced by the reactions of people if they are violated. They can exert very powerful pressure on behaviour because of these reactions – we control others by the way we react to them.

Typical norms

- How managers treat the members of their teams (management style) and how the latter relate to their managers. The prevailing work ethic, eg 'work hard, play hard', 'come in early, stay late', 'if you cannot finish your work during business hours you are obviously inefficient', 'look busy at all times', 'look relaxed at all times'.
- Status – how much importance is attached to it; the existence or lack of obvious status symbols.
- Ambition – naked ambition is expected and approved of, or a more subtle approach is the norm.
- Performance – exacting performance standards are general; the highest praise that can be given in the organization is to be referred to as 'very professional'.
- Power – recognized as a way of life; executed by political means, dependent on expertise and ability rather than position; concentrated at the top; shared at different levels in different parts of the organization.
- Politics – rife throughout the organization and treated as normal behaviour; not accepted as overt behaviour.
- Loyalty – expected, a cradle-to-grave approach to careers; discounted, the emphasis is on results and contribution in the short term.
- Anger – openly expressed; hidden, but expressed through other, possibly political, means.
- Approachability – managers are expected to be approachable and visible; everything happens behind closed doors.
- Formality – a cool, formal approach is the norm; forenames are/are not used at all levels; there are unwritten but clearly understood rules about dress.

Artefacts

Artefacts are the visible and tangible aspects of an organization that people hear, see or feel and which contribute to their understanding of the organization's culture. Artefacts can include such things as the working environment, the tone and language used in e-mails, letters or memoranda, the manner in which people address each other at meetings or over the telephone, the welcome (or lack of welcome) given to visitors and the way in which receptionists deal with outside calls. Artefacts can be very revealing.

Management style

The approach managers use to deal with people – their management or leadership style – is a significant part of the culture of an organization. Management style can be described in terms of the following extremes:

charismatic	↔	non-charismatic
autocratic	↔	democratic
controller	↔	enabler
transactional	↔	transformational

Most managers adopt an approach somewhere between the extremes. Some will vary it according to the situation or their feelings at the time; others will stick to the same style whatever happens. Every manager has his or her own style but this will be influenced by the organizational culture, which may produce a prevailing management style that represents a behavioural norm for managers that is generally expected and adopted.

Classifying organizational culture

There have been many attempts to classify or categorize organizational cultures as a basis for analysis and for taking action to support or change them. Most of these classifications are expressed in four dimensions; three of the best-known ones are summarized below. Note that following the lead of Harrison (1972), there is much common ground between them.

Harrison (1972) – organization ideologies

- *Power-oriented* – competitive, responsive to personality rather than expertise.
- *People-oriented* – consensual, management control rejected.
- *Task-oriented* – focus on competency, dynamic.
- *Role-oriented* – focus on legality, legitimacy and bureaucracy.

Handy (1981) – culture typology

- The *power culture* is one with a central power source that exercises control. There are few rules or procedures and the atmosphere is competitive, power-oriented and political.
- The *role culture* in which work is controlled by procedures and rules and the role, or job description, is more important than the person who fills it. Power is associated with positions not people.
- The *task culture* in which the aim is to bring together the right people and let them get on with it. Influence is based more on expert power than in position or personal power. The culture is adaptable and teamwork is important.
- The *person culture* in which the individual is the central point. The organization exists only to serve and assist the individuals in it.

Schein (1984) – classification of cultures

- *Power culture* in which leadership resides in a few and rests on their ability and tends to be entrepreneurial.
- *Role culture* in which power is balanced between the leader and the bureaucratic structure. The environment is likely to be stable and roles and rules are clearly defined.
- *Achievement culture* in which personal motivation and commitment are stressed and action, excitement and impact are valued.
- *Support culture* in which people contribute out of a sense of commitment and solidarity.

Appropriate cultures

It is not possible to say that one culture is better than another, only that a culture is to a greater or lesser extent appropriate in the sense that it is relevant to the needs and circumstances of the organization and helps rather than hinders its performance. However, embedded cultures can exert considerable influence on organizational behaviour. If there is an appropriate and effective culture it would therefore be desirable to take steps to support or reinforce it. If the culture is inappropriate attempts should be made to determine what needs to be changed and to develop and implement plans for change. A culture will be more effective if it is consistent in its components and shared amongst organizational members, and if it makes the organization unique, thus differentiating it from other organizations.

Organizational climate

As defined by Harrison and Shirom (1999: 263), organizational climate refers to 'members' perceptions of organizational features such as decision-making, leadership and norms about work'. Ivancevich *et al* (2008: 528) described organizational climate as: 'A set of properties of the work environment, perceived directly or indirectly by the employees, that is assumed to be a major force in influencing employee behaviour.'

The term 'organizational climate' is sometimes confused with 'organizational culture' and there has been much debate on what distinguishes them from one another. In Denison's (1996) analysis of this issue, he suggested that 'culture' refers to the deep structure of organizations, which is rooted in the values, beliefs and assumptions held by organizational members. In contrast, 'climate' refers to those aspects of the environment that are consciously perceived by organizational members. Rousseau (1988) stated that climate is a perception and is descriptive. Perceptions are sensations or realizations experienced by an individual. Descriptions are what a person reports of these sensations.

The debate about the meanings of these terms can become academic. It is easiest to regard organizational climate as how people perceive (see and feel about) the culture existing in their organization. French *et al* (1985) distinguish between the actual situation (ie culture) and the perception of it (ie climate).

Organizational processes

A number of social processes take place in organizations that affect how they function. These are: interaction and networking, communication, group behaviour, leadership, power, politics and conflict.

Interaction and networking

Interactions between people criss-cross the organization, creating networks for getting things done and exchanging information that is not catered for in the formal structure. 'Networking' is an increasingly important process in flexible and delayered organizations where more fluid interactions across the structure are required between individuals and teams. Networking means that people canvass opinion and enlist support to promote their projects or ideas. In this way they may get more done than by going through formal channels. People also get things done in organizations by creating alliances – getting agreement on a course of action with other people and joining forces to put the proposed action into effect.

Communications

The communications processes used in organizations have a marked effect on how it functions, especially if they take place through the network, which can then turn into the 'grapevine'. E-mails encourage the instant flow of information (and sometimes produce information overload) but may inhibit face-to-face interactions, which are often the best ways of doing things.

Group behaviour

Organizations consist of groups or teams of people working together. They may be set up formally as part of the structure or they may be informal gatherings. A group can be a permanent or a temporary feature in an organization. Interactions take place within and between groups and the degree to which these processes are formalized varies according to the organizational context.

Formal groups or teams are created by organizations to achieve a defined purpose. People are brought together with the necessary skills to carry out the tasks and a system exists for directing, coordinating and controlling the group's activities. Informal groups are set up by people in organizations who have some affinity for one another. It could be said that formal groups satisfy the needs of the organization while informal groups satisfy the needs of their members.

Groups develop an ideology that affects the attitudes and actions of their members and the degree of satisfaction they feel. If the group ideology is strong and individual members identify closely with the group, it will become increasingly cohesive. Group norms or implicit rules will be evolved that define what is acceptable behaviour and what is not. This is described as a 'reference group', which consists of the group of people with whom an individual identifies. The individual accepts the group's norms and, if in doubt about what to do or say, reference is made to these norms or to other group members before action is taken. Most people in organizations belong to a reference group and this can significantly affect the ways in which they behave.

Four stages of group development were identified by Tuckman (1965):

1. *Forming*, when there is anxiety, dependence on the leader and testing to find out the nature of the situation and the task, and what behaviour is acceptable.
2. *Storming*, where there is conflict, emotional resistance to the demands of the task, resistance to control and even rebellion against the leader.

3 *Norming*, when group cohesion is developed, norms emerge, views are exchanged openly, mutual support and cooperation increase and the group acquires a sense of its identity.
4 *Performing*, when interpersonal problems are resolved, roles are flexible and functional, there are constructive attempts to complete tasks and energy is available for effective work.

Leadership

Organizations largely function by means of managers and supervisors who exercise leadership in order to get their teams into action and ensure that they achieve the results expected of them. Goleman (2000) reported that a study by Hay McBer of 3,871 executives, selected from a database of more than 20,000 executives worldwide, established that leadership had a direct impact on organizational climate, and that climate in turn accounted for nearly one-third of the financial results of organizations. The conclusion from research conducted by Higgs (2006) was that leadership behaviour accounts for almost 50 per cent of the difference between change success and failure. Research by Northouse (2006) into 167 US firms in 13 industries established that over a 20-year period leadership accounted for more variations in performance than any other variable. Leadership skills are described in Chapter 55.

Power

Organizations exist to get things done; in the process of doing this, people or groups exercise power. Directly or indirectly, the use of power in influencing behaviour is a pervading feature of organizations, whether it is exerted by managers, specialists, informal groups or trade union officials. It is a way of achieving results, but it can be misused.

Politics

Political behaviour is an inevitable feature of organizational life. The aim of organizational politicians is to get their own way by influencing people to accept their point of view without going through the usual channels or relying on their authority. Some individuals genuinely believe that the best way to get something done is by using political means, especially when they are frustrated by the normal decision processes. Others unashamedly pursue their own ends. Political behaviour can be harmful when it is underhand and devious, but it can sometimes help to enlist support and overcome obstacles to getting results. All managers need political skills, as described in Chapter 59, but, because of the nature of their role, such skills are particularly important for HR specialists.

Conflict

Conflict is also inevitable in organizations because they function by means of adjustments and compromises among competitive elements in their structure and membership. Conflict also arises when there is change, because it may be seen as a threat to be challenged or resisted, or when there is frustration. Conflict is not always deplorable. It can be a result of progress and change and it can be used constructively.

Characteristics of people

To manage people effectively, it is necessary to take into account the factors that affect how they behave at work. The development of HR processes and the design of organizations are often predicated on the belief that everyone is the same and that they will behave rationally when faced with change or other demands. But the behaviour of people differs because of their characteristics and individual differences and it is not always rational.

The management of people would be much easier if everyone were the same, but they are not. As discussed below, they are, of course, different because of variations in personal characteristics and the influence of their background (the way in which they were brought up). Some people also consider sex, race or disability as factors that affect people's behaviour at work, although holding this view readily leads to discrimination. In addition, there will be differences in ability, intelligence and personality.

Variations in personal characteristics

The headings under which personal characteristics can vary have been classified by Mischel (1968) as follows.

Source review

Variations in personal characteristics – Mischel (1968)

- *Competencies* – abilities and skills.
- *Constructs* – the conceptual frameworks which govern how people perceive their environment.
- *Expectations* – what people have learnt to expect about their own and others' behaviour.
- *Values* – what people believe to be important.
- *Self-regulatory plans* – the goals people set themselves and the plans they make to achieve them.

These characteristics are affected by environmental or situational variables, which include the type of work individuals carry out; the culture, climate and management style in the organization; the social group within which they work; and the 'reference groups' individuals use for comparative purposes (eg comparing conditions of work or pay between one category of employee and another).

The personal characteristics that affect people's behaviour at work, as discussed below, are their ability, intelligence, personality, attitudes, emotions and emotional intelligence.

Ability

Ability is the quality possessed by people that makes an action possible. Abilities have been analysed by Burt (1954) and Vernon (1961). They classified them into two major groups: V:ed – verbal, numerical, memory and reasoning abilities; and K:m – spatial and mechanical abilities, as well as perceptual (memory) and motor skills relating to physical operations such as eye/hand coordination and mental dexterity.

They also suggested that overriding these abilities there is general mental ability (GMA), which accounts for most variations in performance. Following a meta-analysis of 85 years of research findings, Schmidt and Hunter (1998) established that GMA was the most valid predictor of future performance and learning for selecting people without previous experience.

Intelligence

Intelligence has been variously defined as:

- The capacity to solve problems, apply principles, make inferences and perceive relationships. (Argyle, 1989: 53)
- The capacity for abstract thinking and reasoning with a range of different contents and media. (Toplis *et al*, 2004: 20)
- What is measured by intelligence tests. (Wright and Taylor, 1970: 31)

The last, tautological definition is not facetious. As an operational definition, it can be related to the specific aspects of reasoning, inference, cognition (ie knowing, conceiving) and perception (ie understanding, recognition), which intelligence tests attempt to measure.

General intelligence (GI) consists of a number of mental abilities that enable a person to succeed at a wide variety of intellectual tasks that use the faculties of knowing and reasoning. It can be measured by an intelligence test and is sometimes expressed as an intelligence quotient (IQ), which is the ratio of an individual's mental age to the individual's actual age as measured by an intelligence test.

The concept of emotional intelligence (as described later) stresses that emotional maturity – in the sense of the ability to identify, assess and manage the emotions of one's self and others – is also important.

Personality

Personality has been defined by Huczynski and Buchanan (2007: 138) as: 'The psychological qualities that influence an individual's characteristic behaviour patterns in a stable and distinctive manner.' As noted by Ivancevich *et al* (2008), personality appears to be organized into patterns that are, to some degree, observable and measurable and involves both common and unique characteristics – every person is different from every other person in some respects but similar to other people in other respects. Personality is a product of both nature (hereditary) and nurture (the pattern of life experience). Personality can be described in terms of traits or types.

Traits

Traits are predispositions to behave in certain ways in a variety of different situations. The leading model of personality traits is the following 'big five' classification (Costa and McRae, 1992; Digman, 1990):

- *Openness* – inventive/curious or consistent/cautious.
- *Conscientiousness* – efficient/organized or easy-going/careless.
- *Extraversion* – outgoing/energetic or solitary/reserved.
- *Agreeableness* – friendly/compassionate or cold/unkind.
- *Neuroticism* – sensitive/nervous or secure/confident.

The assumption that people are consistent in the ways they express these traits is the basis for making predictions about their future behaviour. We all attribute traits to people in an attempt to understand why they behave in the way they do. But people do not necessarily express the same trait across different situations or even the same trait in the same situation. Different people may exhibit consistency in some traits and exhibit considerable variability in others.

Types

Type theories of personality identify a number of types of personality that can be used to categorize people and may form the basis of a personality test. The types may be linked to descriptions of various traits. One of the most widely used type theories is that of Jung (1923). He identified four major preferences:

- relating to other people – extraversion or introversion;
- gathering information – sensing (dealing with facts that can be objectively verified), or intuitive (generating information through insight);
- using information – thinking (emphasizing logical analysis as the basis for decision-making), or feeling (making decisions based on internal values and beliefs);
- making decisions – perceiving (collecting all the relevant information before making a decision), or judging (resolving the issue without waiting for a large quantity of data).

This is the basis of personality tests such as the Myers-Briggs Types Indicator.

Types should be distinguished from traits. As Huczynski and Buchanan (2007: 142) put it: 'Type approaches fit people into categories possessing common behaviour patterns. A personality trait, on the other hand, is an enduring behaviour that occurs in a variety of settings. While individuals belong to types, traits belong to individuals.'

Attitudes

An attitude can broadly be defined as a settled mode of thinking. Attitudes are evaluative. They are developed through experience but they are less stable than traits and can change as new experiences are gained or influences absorbed. Within organizations they are affected by cultural factors (values and norms); the behaviour of management (management style); policies such as those concerned with pay, recognition, promotion and the quality of working life; and the influence of the 'reference group' (the group with whom people identify). Sometimes there may be a discrepancy between attitudes and behaviour, ie someone may believe in one thing – such as being fair to people – but act differently. This is called 'cognitive dissonance'.

Emotions

Emotions are feelings that arouse people and therefore influence their behaviour such as anger, fear, sadness, joy, anticipation and acceptance. The mildest forms of emotions are called 'moods', which are low intensity, long-lasting emotional states.

Emotional intelligence

The notion of emotional intelligence was first defined by Salovey and Mayer (1990), who proposed that it involves the capacity to perceive emotion, integrate emotion in thought, understand emotion and manage emotions effectively. Goleman (1995) popularized the concept. He defined emotional intelligence as: 'The capacity for recognizing our own feelings and that of others, for motivating ourselves, for managing emotions well in ourselves as well as others.' He suggested that its four components are:

1. *Self-management* – the ability to control or redirect disruptive impulses and moods and regulate own behaviour coupled with a propensity to pursue goals with energy and persistence. The six competencies associated with this component are self-control, trustworthiness and integrity, initiative, adaptability – comfort with ambiguity, openness to change and strong desire to achieve.
2. *Self-awareness* – the ability to recognize and understand your moods, emotions and drives as well as their effect on others. This is linked to three competencies: self-confidence, realistic self-assessment and emotional self-awareness.
3. *Social awareness* – the ability to understand the emotional make-up of other people, and skill in treating people according to their emotional reactions. This is linked to six competencies: empathy, expertise in building and retaining talent, organizational awareness, cross-cultural sensitivity, valuing diversity, and service to clients and customers.
4. *Social skills* – proficiency in managing relationships and building networks to get the desired result from others and reach personal goals, and the ability to find common ground and build rapport. The five competencies associated with this component are: leadership, effectiveness in leading change, conflict management, influence/communication, and expertise in building and leading teams.

According to Goleman, it is not enough to have a high IQ; emotional intelligence is also required. Since Goleman's contribution, three major models of emotional intelligence, as summarized by Clarke (2007), have dominated thinking in this area:

- *Personality models* have become the most popular theory of emotional intelligence following Goleman. Here, emotional intelligence is viewed as comprising a range of emotional dispositions as well as competencies, from individual traits to a number of learnt capabilities. These are all contained within the components of emotional intelligence listed above.
- *Mixed models* comprise aspects of personality as well as abilities to perceive emotional intelligence and manage emotions.
- *The ability model* views emotional intelligence more narrowly as a set of four cognitive abilities that involve the capacity to identify, reason with, and utilize emotions effectively.

As Clarke comments, the first two models have come under criticism in terms of the ambiguity associated with the areas included and the measurement approaches employed. The ability model has received more positive commentary as possessing greater validity.

Critical evaluation of the concept of emotional intelligence

The notion that there is more to being effective as a manager or working with people than having a high IQ is persuasive. What matters is how that intelligence is used, especially when relating to people. The term 'emotional intelligence' has become a convenient and recognizable label for this requirement: someone who is poor at dealing with people is described as lacking in emotional intelligence.

Instruments are available for measuring emotional intelligence such as the Trait Emotional Intelligence Questionnaire (Petrides and Furnham, 2000). On the basis of such questionnaires, learning and development programmes can be created for individuals or groups, which focus on any weaknesses revealed.

But doubts have been expressed about the notion of emotional intelligence. Locke (2005: 426), a well-respected occupational psychologist, made the following observation:

> The concept of emotional intelligence has now become so broad and the components so variegated that no one concept could possibly encompass or integrate all of them, no matter what the concept was called; it is no longer even an intelligible concept. What is the common or integrating element in a concept that includes: introspection about emotions, emotional expression, non-verbal communication with others, empathy, self-regulation, planning, creative thinking and the direction of attention? There is none.

He suggested that emotional intelligence should be renamed as a skill.

Goleman's mixed model of emotional intelligence, although the most popular, has been heavily criticized. Mayer *et al* (2008) described it as mere 'pop psychology'. There is also the question of whether the concept of emotional intelligence adds anything significant to that of behavioural competencies. Dulewicz and Higgs (1999) have produced a detailed analysis of how the emotional intelligence elements of self-awareness, emotional management, empathy, relationships, communication and personal style correspond to competencies such as sensitivity, flexibility, adaptability, resilience, impact, listening, leadership, persuasiveness, motivating others, energy, decisiveness and achievement motivation. They conclude that there are distinct associations between competency modes and elements of emotional intelligence. There is a danger of confusion if emotional intelligence notions and competency frameworks overlap.

Implications for HR specialists

The main implications of organizational behaviour theory for HR specialists are summarized below.

How organizations function

When involved in organization design bear in mind that, while the highly structured classical model with clearly defined roles and lines of control and communication may appear to be the ideal solution, in practice organizations function differently. It is necessary to take into account the post-bureaucratic school and think of the organization as a portfolio of dynamic processes that overlay and often dominate the vertical, authority-based processes of the hierarchical structure. Similarly, organizational development activities should be based on an analysis and understanding of these dynamic processes.

Organizational culture

While it may not be possible to define an ideal culture or to prescribe how it can be developed, it can at least be stated with confidence that embedded cultures exert considerable influence on organizational behaviour and therefore performance. If there is an appropriate and effective culture it is desirable to take steps to support or reinforce it. If the culture is inappropriate, attempts should be made to determine what needs to be changed and to develop and implement plans for change (approaches to culture management are described in Chapter 12). HR innovations need to take account of the culture in which they will operate. They are likely to fail if they are countercultural.

Organizational climate

The perceptions of employees about the organization, which form the organization climate, need to be assessed and understood so that action can be taken to deal with negative factors. Diagnostic tools, as described in Chapter 12, can be used for this purpose.

Organizational processes

The social processes of interaction and networking, communication, group behaviour, leadership, power, politics and conflict need to be understood and considered when considering ways of improving organizational effectiveness (the ability of an organization to achieve its goals by making effective use of the resources available to it). Social and political factors can affect how HR decisions are made and how well they are implemented.

Individual differences

When designing jobs, preparing learning and development programmes, assessing and counselling staff, developing reward systems and dealing with grievances and disciplinary problems, it is necessary to remember that all people are different. What fulfils or motivates one person may not fulfil or motivate another. Abilities, aptitudes and intelligence differ widely and it is necessary to take particular care in fitting the right people in the right jobs and giving them the right training. Personalities, attitudes and emotions also differ. It is important to focus on how to manage diversity. This should take account of individual differences, which will include any issues arising from the employment of women, people from different ethnic groups, those with disabilities and older people. The predictive effectiveness of GMA tests as selection aids should be noted.

Judgements on personality

Personality should not be judged or measured simplistically in terms of stereotyped traits. People are complex and they change, and account has to be taken of this. The problem for HR specialists and managers in general is that, while they have to accept and understand these differences and take full account of them, they have ultimately to proceed on the basis of fitting them to the requirements of the situation, which are essentially what the organization needs to achieve. There is always a limit to the extent to which an organization that relies on collective effort to achieve its goals can adjust itself to the specific needs of individuals. But the organization has to appreciate that the pressures it places on people can result in stress and therefore can become counterproductive.

Key learning points: Organizational behaviour

People perform their roles within complex systems called organizations. The study of organizational behaviour focuses on how this happens.

Organizational behaviour defined

Organizational behaviour was defined by Huczynski and Buchanan (2007) as the term used to describe 'the study of the structure, functioning, and performance of organizations and the behaviour of groups and individuals within them'.

The sources and applications of organizational behaviour theory

Organizational behaviour theory is based on the main behavioural science disciplines. These are defined as the fields of enquiry dedicated to the study of human behaviour through sophisticated and rigorous methods.

How organizations function

- An organization is an entity that exists to achieve a purpose through the collective efforts of the people who work in or for it.
- Organizing is the process of making arrangements in the form of defined or understood responsibilities and relationships to enable those people to work cooperatively together.
- Organizations can be described as systems that, as affected by their environment, have a structure that has both formal and informal elements.
- Organization structures are frameworks for getting things done.
- Traditional formal structures were based on laid-down hierarchies (lines of command) represented in organization charts, and use was made of closely defined job descriptions. But to varying extents organizations operate informally as well as formally by means of a network of roles and relationships that cut across formal organizational boundaries and lines of command.

Organizational culture

The culture of an organization has been described by Deal and Kennedy (2000: 4) as 'the way we do things around here'. Organizational or corporate culture is the pattern of values, norms, beliefs, attitudes and assumptions that may not have been articulated but shape the ways in which people in organizations behave and the ways in which things get done.

How organizational culture develops

The values and norms that are the basis of culture are formed in four ways:

1. By the leaders in the organization, especially those who have shaped it in the past.
2. Around critical incidents – important events from which lessons are learnt about desirable or undesirable behaviour.
3. From the need to maintain effective working relationships among organization members; this establishes values and expectations.
4. Influenced by the organization's environment. The external environment may be relatively dynamic or unchanging.

The components of culture

Organizational culture can be described in terms of values, norms, artefacts and management style.

Classifying organizational culture (Harrison, 1972):

- Power-oriented – competitive, responsive to personality rather than expertise.
- People-oriented – consensual, management control rejected.
- Task-oriented – focus on competency, dynamic.
- Role-oriented – focus on legality, legitimacy and bureaucracy.

Appropriate cultures

It is not possible to say that one culture is better than another, only that a culture is to a greater or lesser extent appropriate in the sense that it is relevant to the needs and circumstances of the organization and helps rather than hinders its performance.

Organizational climate

As defined by Harrison and Shirom (1999), organizational climate refers to 'members' perceptions of organizational features such as decision-making, leadership and norms about work'.

Organizational processes

A number of social processes take place in organizations that affect how they function. These are: interaction and networking, communication, group behaviour, leadership, power, politics and conflict.

Personal characteristics

The personal characteristics that affect people's behaviour at work are their ability, intelligence, personality, attitudes, emotions and emotional intelligence.

Emotional intelligence

Emotional intelligence is a combination of skills and abilities such as self-awareness, self-control, empathy and sensitivity to the feelings of others. Someone with high levels of emotional intelligence should be able to relate to people effectively.

Questions

1 What is organizational behaviour?
2 On what is organizational behaviour theory based?
3 What is an organization?
4 What is organization structure?
5 What is generally agreed to be the most realistic theory of organization?
6 What is organizational culture?
7 How does organizational culture develop?
8 What are the components of culture?
9 How can cultures be classified?
10 What is organizational climate?
11 What are the key organizational processes?
12 What is the 'big five' model?
13 What is emotional intelligence?
14 What are the implications of organization theory for HR specialists?

References

Argyle, M (1989) *The Social Psychology of Work*, Harmondsworth, Penguin

Argyris, C (1957) *Personality and Organization*, New York, Harper & Row

Barnard, C (1938) *The Functions of an Executive*, Boston, MA, Harvard University Press

Burns, T and Stalker, G (1961) *The Management of Innovation*, London, Tavistock

Burt, C (1954) The differentiation of intellectual ability, *British Journal of Educational Psychology*, 24, pp 45–67

Clarke, N (2007) Be selective when choosing emotional intelligence training, *People Management*, 3 May, p 47

Costa, P and McRae, R R (1992) *NEO PI-R: Professional manual*, Odessa, FL, Psychological Assessment Resources

Deal, T and Kennedy, A (2000) *Corporate Cultures*, New York, Perseus Books

Denison, D R (1996) What is the difference between organizational culture and organizational climate? A native's point of view on a decade of paradigm wars, *Academy of Management Review*, 21 (3), pp 619–54

Digman, J M (1990) Personality structure: emergence of the five-factor model, *Annual Review of Psychology*, 41, pp 417–40

Dulewicz, V and Higgs, M (1999) The seven dimensions of emotional intelligence, *People Management*, 28 October, p 53

Eldridge, J and Crombie, A (1974) *The Sociology of Organizations*, London, Allen & Unwin

Emery, F E (1959) *Characteristics of Socio-technical Systems*, London, Tavistock Publications

Fayol, H (1916) *Administration Industrielle et General*, translated by C Storrs (1949) as *General and Industrial Management*, London, Pitman

French, W L, Kast, F E and Rosenzweig, J E (1985) *Understanding Human Behaviour in Organizations*, Harper & Row, New York

Furnham, A and Gunter, B (1993) *Corporate Assessment*, London, Routledge

Ghoshal, S and Bartlett, C A (1995) Changing the role of top management: beyond structure to process, *Harvard Business Review*, January–February, pp 86–96

Goleman, D (1995) *Emotional Intelligence*, New York, Bantam

Goleman, D (2000) Leadership that gets results, *Harvard Business Review*, March–April, pp 78–90

Handy, C (1981) *Understanding Organizations*, Harmondsworth, Penguin Books

Harrison, M and Shirom, A (1999) *Organizational Diagnosis and Assessment*, Thousand Oaks, CA, Sage

Harrison, R (1972) Understanding your organization's character, *Harvard Business Review*, September–October, pp 119–28

Herzberg, F W, Mausner, B and Snyderman, B (1957) *The Motivation to Work*, New York, Wiley

Higgs, M (2006) *Change and its Leadership*, New York, Rowland, Fisher, Lennox Consulting

Huczynski, A A and Buchanan, D A (2007) *Organizational Behaviour*, 6th edn, Harlow, FT Pitman

Ivancevich, J M, Konopaske, R and Matteson, M T (2008) *Organizational Behaviour and Management*, 8th edn, New York, McGraw-Hill/Irwin

Jung, C (1923) *Psychological Types*, London, Routledge Kegan Paul
Lawrence, P R and Lorsch, J W (1969) *Developing Organizations*, Reading, MA, Addison-Wesley
Likert, R (1961) *New Patterns of Management*, New York, Harper & Row
Locke, E A (2005) Why emotional intelligence is an invalid concept, *Journal of Organizational Behavior*, 26 (4), pp 425–31
Mayer, J D, Salovey, P and Caruso, D R (2008) Emotional intelligence: new ability or eclectic traits?, *American Psychologist*, 63 (6), pp 503–17
McGregor, D (1960) *The Human Side of Enterprise*, New York, McGraw-Hill
Miller, E and Rice, A (1967) *Systems of Organization*, London, Tavistock
Mischel, W (1968) *Personality and Assessment*, New York, Wiley
Nadler, D A and Tushman, M L (1980) A congruence model for diagnosing organizational behaviour, in (ed) R H Miles, *Resource Book in Macro-organizational Behaviour*, Santa Monica, CA, Goodyear Publishing, pp 30–49
Northouse, P G (2006) *Leadership: Theory and practice*, 4th edn, Thousand Oaks, CA, Sage
Pascale, R (1990) *Managing on the Edge*, London, Viking
Petrides, K V and Furnham, A (2000) On the dimensional structure of emotional intelligence, *Personality and Individual Differences*, 29, pp 313–20
Roethlisberger, F and Dickson, W (1939) *Management and the Worker*, Cambridge, MA, Harvard University Press
Rousseau, D M (1988) The construction of climate in organizational research, in (eds) L C Cooper and I Robertson, *International Review of Industrial and Organizational Psychology*, Chichester, Wiley
Salovey, P and Mayer, J D (1990) *Emotional Intelligence, Imagination, Cognition and Personality*, 9, pp 185–211
Schein, E H (1965) *Organizational Psychology*, Englewood Cliffs, NJ, Prentice-Hall
Schein, E H (1984) Coming to a new awareness of culture, *Sloan Management Review*, 25 (2), pp 1–15
Schein, E H (1990) Organizational culture, *American Psychologist*, 45, pp 109–19
Schmidt, F L and Hunter, J E (1998) The validity and utility of selection methods in personnel psychology: practical and theoretical implications of 85 years of research findings, *Psychological Bulletin*, 124 (2), pp 262–74
Taylor, F W (1911) *Principles of Scientific Management*, New York, Harper
Toplis, J, Dulewicz, V and Fletcher, C (2004) *Psychological Testing*, Institute of Personnel Management, London
Trist, E L, Higgin, G W, Murray, H and Pollock, A B (1963) *Organizational Choice*, London, Tavistock Publications
Tuckman, B (1965) Development sequences in small groups, *Psychological Bulletin*, 63, pp 123–56
Urwick, L F (1947) *Dynamic Administration*, London, Pitman
Vernon, P E (1961) *The Structure of Human Abilities*, London, Methuen
Weber, M (1908) *The Theory of Social and Economic Organization*, translated by A M Henderson and T Parsons, 1947, Oxford, Oxford University Press
Woodward, J (1965) *Industrial Organization*, Oxford, Oxford University Press
Wright, D S and Taylor, A (1970) *Introducing Psychology*, Harmondsworth, Penguin

11 Work, organization and job design

KEY CONCEPTS AND TERMS

Autonomous working groups
Equifinality
Facility layout
Flexible firm
Fordism
Hot-desking
Intrinsic motivation
Lattice organization
Law of the situation
Line and staff organization
Matrix organization
Mechanistic organization
Minimum critical specification
Multiskilling
Organic organization
Organizational choice
Organizational dilemma
Organization planning
Organizations as systems
Organizing
Self-managed teams
Socio-technical systems theory
Smart working
Strategic choice
System
Taylorism
Work
Work environment
Work system
Work system design

LEARNING OUTCOMES

On completing this chapter you should be able to define these key concepts. You should also understand:

- Work design methodology
- Changes in the nature of work
- Work system design
- Process planning
- Smart working
- Flexible working
- High-performance working
- Lean manufacturing
- Organization design
- Job design

Introduction

Work, organization, and job design are three distinct but closely associated processes that establish what work is done in organizations and how it is done. Work design deals with the ways in which things are done in the work system of a business by teams and individuals. Organization design is concerned with deciding how organizations should be structured. Job design is about establishing what people in individual jobs or roles are there to do. Although these three activities are dealt with separately in this chapter they share one purpose – to ensure that the organization's work systems and structure operate effectively, make the best use of people in their jobs and roles and take account of the needs of people at work.

In theory, to achieve that purpose, work, organization and job design function sequentially. The work system is designed to meet the specific needs of the business and to deliver value to its customers or clients. An organization structure or system (not all organizations are rigidly structured) has to be developed to enable the work system to operate. The structure is made up of jobs or roles (there is a distinction, which will be explained later) that have to be designed in ways that will maximize the extent to which they can be carried out effectively and provide intrinsic motivation, ie motivation from the work itself.

In practice, the processes involved can run concurrently – the work system will involve deciding how the work should be organized, and both the work system and organization design processes will define what sort of jobs or roles are required. At the same time, job design considerations will affect how the work is organized and how the work system functions. This chapter deals with each aspect of design separately, but it should be remembered that the processes interlink and overlap.

Work design

Work design is the creation of systems of work and a working environment that enhance organizational effectiveness and productivity, ensure that the organization becomes 'a great place in which to work' and are conducive to the health, safety and well-being of employees. Work involves the exertion of effort and the application of knowledge and skills to achieve a purpose. Systems of work are the combined processes, methods and techniques used to get work done. The work environment comprises the design of jobs, working conditions and the ways in which people are treated at work by their managers and co-workers as well as the work system. Work design is closely associated with organization and job design in that the latter is conducted within the context of the system of work and the work environment.

To understand the meaning of work design it is necessary first to appreciate what is happening to the world of work and next to review its history.

What is happening to work

The key changes in the contextual and external environment surrounding the world of work have been set out clearly by Parker *et al* (2001). They are:

- a shift away from large-scale industrial production, with a dramatic decline in manufacturing jobs and rise in service work;
- partly as a consequence of this, an increase in customer-facing roles involving some form of emotional behaviour – the requirement for employees to express positive emotions in the way in which they interact with customers;
- significant shifts in the demographics of the workforce in the shape of an increased proportion of women, greater ethnic diversity, more educated employees and an ageing workforce;
- growth in the number of employees engaged in 'knowledge work' – for example, professional services and new product and service development;
- the requirement for a greater variety of products and services and flexibility and agility in responding to customer needs and increased global competition;
- developments in technology affecting the degree to which jobs are involved in IT and become dependent on it;
- shifts from traditional, office or factory-based working to more flexible alternatives, including homeworking;

- a significant increase in the number of employers that an individual employee expects to work for during his or her career.

Work design – a short history

Work design began with the concept of the division of labour originated by Adam Smith (1776). Much later came 'Taylorism', the scientific management movement pioneered by Taylor (1911), which was based on the belief that the most efficient way to do tasks was to remove the responsibility for how to do the work from the individual employee to engineers or managers. The next step was 'Fordism', the moving assembly line introduced by Henry Ford in 1914. Thereafter, the practice of work simplification became embedded in organizations and to a large extent still exists.

The first move away from this situation was provided by the concept of job enrichment popularized by Herzberg (1968: 83), who referred to it as 'vertical job loading'. His definition of the principles and motivators involved is set out in Table 11.1. This was reinforced by job design theory (Hackman and Oldham, 1974).

More recently, the notion of 'smart working' has emerged. Essentially, this means managing the work environment in order to release employees' energy and drive business performance. Smart working, as described in detail later, has been the subject of extensive research conducted by the CIPD (2008).

However, before examining the notion of smart working it is necessary to remember that it takes place within the system of work, and approaches to work system design are therefore examined first.

TABLE 11.1 Vertical job loading (job enrichment) principles and motivators involved

Principles	Motivators involved
Removing some controls while retaining accountability	Responsibility and personal achievement
Increasing the accountability of individuals for own work	Responsibility and personal achievement
Giving a person a complete natural unit of work (module, division, area, and so on)	Responsibility and recognition
Granting additional authority to employees in their activity; job freedom	Responsibility, achievement and recognition
Making periodic reports directly available to the workers themselves rather than to supervisors	Internal recognition
Introducing new and more difficult tasks not previously handled	Growth and learning
Assigning individuals specific or specialized tasks, enabling them to become experts	Responsibility, growth and advancement

SOURCE: Herzberg (1968: 83)

Work system design

A system is a set of practices or activities that fit together and interact to achieve a purpose. Work system design is concerned with how the various processes required to make a product or provide a service should operate. It deals with the set of related activities that combine to give a result that customers want. The structure of the system describes the relations between different operations.

A work system may be centred on activities such as manufacturing, chemical processing, information processing, supply, distribution, transport, the provision of public services or customer service. There is usually a choice between different processes within the work system. As the design of the work system affects costs, quality and productivity it is important to provide the best match between the product or service and the process used to make or deliver it.

Process-centred organizations

Process-centred organizations avoid focusing too closely on the design of a rigid work system but instead concentrate on the stream of products or services required and the processes required to ensure that work flows smoothly to the ultimate satisfaction of the customer or client. They have the following features:

- The focus is on horizontal processes that cut across organizational boundaries.
- The overriding objective will be to maintain a smooth flow of work between functions and to achieve synergy by pooling resources from different functions in task forces or project teams.
- The organization will not be based on the old hierarchical 'command and control' structure, ie one that consists of a functional structure with a number of different disciplines. Instead it will be a 'lattice', or 'matrix' organization (a lattice organization is one with a non-hierarchical, flat structure where the emphasis is on horizontal processes, the elimination of boundaries between functions and teamwork; a matrix organization is one that consists of a functional structure with a number of different disciplines and a project structure consisting of project teams drawn from the disciplines);
- There may still be designated functions for, say, manufacturing, sales and distribution, but the emphasis will be on how these areas work together on multifunctional projects to deal with demands such as product/market development.
- Belief in and reliance on teamwork.
- Expansion of traditional jobs and increased emphasis on flexible roles, with employees making decisions and dealing with all types of customer issues.
- Access to all types of information and knowledge throughout the organization.
- Quality and continuous improvement will be regarded as a common responsibility shared between managers and staff from each function.

Process planning

Work system design covers the planning of processes such as flexible manufacturing systems (computer numerical control machines controlled by a central computer that allows fast and easy changes between products), and supply chain management (the control of products from the original suppliers of materials through to the final customers). It may involve facility layout – the physical arrangement of equipment, offices, rooms, work stations (including 'hot-desks' – individual desks shared between several people) and other resources.

Process planning may determine how manufacturing or the provision of a service should be divided into a series of stages such as machines in a production line, each of which uses resources and adds value.

Requirements to be met in work system design

When designing a work system it is necessary to see that it will:

- fit work requirements for efficiency and flexibility;
- ensure the smooth flow of processes or activities, or of materials from supplier to customer;

- facilitate the effective use of resources and the control of waste;
- as far as possible enable employees to gain fulfilment from their work by providing scope for variety, challenge and autonomy;
- encourage cooperative effort through teamworking;
- provide a good work environment in terms of working conditions;
- take account of the need to provide a healthy and safe system of work ('build safety into the system') bearing in mind the need to minimize stress and pay attention to ergonomic considerations in the design of equipment and work stations to eliminate or at least significantly reduce the risk of such conditions as repetitive strain injury;
- take account of environmental considerations;
- operate generally in accordance with the principles of 'smart working' as described below.

Smart working

As defined by the CIPD (2008: 4), smart working is: 'An approach to organizing work that aims to drive greater efficiency and effectiveness in achieving job outcomes through a combination of flexibility, autonomy and collaboration, in parallel with optimizing tools and working environments for employees.' The characteristics of smart working as established by the CIPD research were:

- self-management – a high degree of autonomy and a philosophy of empowerment;
- the use of virtual teams or work groups;
- focus on outcome-based indicators of performance;
- high-performance working;
- flexibility in work locations and hours;
- use of more advanced communications technology;
- hot-desking and working from home;
- ways of working that are underpinned by or drive high-trust working relationships;
- alignment of smart working with business objectives.

Typical smart working arrangements identified by the CIPD research include flexible working, high-performance working, 'lean' production and designing jobs in which there is a higher degree of freedom to act. The role of each of those arrangements in work design is described below.

Flexible working

Flexible working is a pattern of working practice or working hours that deviates from the standard or normal arrangement. The aim is to provide for greater operational flexibility, improve the use of employees' skills and capacities, increase productivity and reduce employment costs. Flexible working has become increasingly important as a means of enhancing operational effectiveness.

Flexible working means reconsidering traditional employment patterns. This could include operational flexibility, multiskilling, the use of subcontracting and outsourcing, or introducing working arrangements such as flexible hours, job sharing and homeworking.

Forms of operational flexibility

Operational flexibility refers to flexibility in the ways in which work is carried out. The term is sometimes extended to include financial flexibility. The three forms of operational flexibility are:

- *Functional flexibility* so that employees can be redeployed quickly and smoothly between activities and tasks. It may require multiskilling – workers who possess and can apply a number of skills, for example, both mechanical and electrical engineering, or multitasking – workers who carry out a number of different tasks in a work team.
- *Structural flexibility* in a 'flexible firm' where the core of permanent employees is supplemented by a peripheral group of part-time employees, employees on short- or fixed-term contracts or subcontracted workers, as described by Doeringer and Priore (1971) and Atkinson (1984).
- *Numerical flexibility*, which is associated with structural flexibility and means that the

number of employees can be quickly and easily increased or decreased in line with even short-term changes in the level of demand for labour.

Financial flexibility provides for pay levels to reflect the state of supply and demand in the external labour market and also means the use of flexible pay systems that facilitate either functional or numerical flexibility.

Multiskilling

Multiskilling takes place when workers acquire through experience and training a range of different skills they can apply when carrying out different tasks (multitasking). This means that they can be used flexibly, transferring from one task to another as the occasion demands.

A multiskilling strategy will mean providing people with a variety of experience through, for example, moving them between different jobs or tasks (job rotation) and secondments, and by making arrangements for them to acquire new skills through training. It typically includes setting up flexible work teams, the members of which can be deployed on all or many of the team's tasks. A flexible employee resourcing policy can then be established that enables the organization to redeploy people rapidly to meet new demands. This implies abandoning the traditional job description that prescribes the tasks to be carried and replacing it with a role profile, which specifies the range of knowledge and skills that the role holder needs.

Job-sharing

This is an arrangement in which two employees share the work of one full-time position, dividing pay and benefits between them according to the time that each of them works. Job-sharing can mean splitting days or weeks or, less frequently, working alternate weeks. The advantages of job-sharing include reduced employee turnover and absenteeism, because it suits the needs of individuals. Greater continuity results: because if one half of the job-sharing team is ill or leaves, the sharer will continue working for at least half the time. Job-sharing also means that a wider employment pool can be tapped for those who cannot work full-time but want permanent employment. The disadvantages are the administrative costs involved and the risk of responsibility being divided.

Hot-desking

Hot-desking means that individual desks are shared between several people who use them at different times. Those involved do not therefore have a permanent work station. This is convenient for the organization but not everyone likes it.

Homeworking

Home-based employees can carry out such roles as consultants, analysts, designers or programmers, or they can undertake administrative work. The advantages are flexibility to respond rapidly to fluctuations in demand, reduced overheads and lower employment costs if the homeworkers are self-employed (care, however, has to be taken to ensure that they are regarded as self-employed for Income Tax and National Insurance purposes).

Flexible hour arrangements

Flexible hour arrangements can be included in a flexibility plan in one or more of the following ways:

- flexible daily hours – these may follow an agreed pattern day by day according to typical or expected workloads (eg flexitime systems);
- flexible weekly hours – providing for longer weekly hours to be worked at certain peak periods during the year;
- flexible daily and weekly hours – varying daily or weekly hours or a combination of both to match the input of hours to the required output. Such working times, unlike daily or weekly arrangements, may fluctuate between a minimum and a maximum;
- compressed working weeks in which employees work fewer than the five standard days;
- annual hours – scheduling employee hours on the basis of the number of hours to be worked, with provisions for the increase or reduction of hours in any given period, according to the demand for goods or services.

In addition there is the pernicious arrangement of zero-hours contracts in which an employer does not guarantee the employee a fixed number of hours per week. Rather, the employee is expected to be on-call and receive pay only for hours worked. Such contracts are most common in retail, hospitality and restaurants.

High-performance working

High-performance working was defined by Combs *et al* (2006) as the sum of the processes, practices and policies put in place by employers to enable employees to perform to their full potential. They referred to employee participation and flexible working arrangements as examples of such systems that have a direct impact on ways of working and therefore flow through to job design.

Sung and Ashton (2005) defined high-performance work practices as a set or 'bundle' of 35 complementary work practices covering three broad areas:

- High employee involvement work practices – eg self-directed teams, quality circles and sharing/access to company information.
- Human resource practices – eg sophisticated recruitment processes, performance appraisals, mentoring and work redesign.
- Reward and commitment practices – eg various financial rewards, family-friendly policies, job rotation and flexible hours.

Lean manufacturing

Lean manufacturing or lean production, often known simply as 'Lean', is a process improvement methodology developed by Toyota in Japan. Lean focuses on reducing waste and ensuring the flow of production in order to deliver value to customers. It concentrates initially on the design of the process so that waste can be minimized during manufacture. It then examines operations in order to identify opportunities to improve the flow of production, remove wasteful practices and engage in continuous improvement. Various tools are available such as 'FiveS', which is a workplace methodology that uses a list of five words starting with the letter 'S' (sorting, straightening, systematic cleaning, standardizing and sustaining). Reference to these enables a dialogue to take place with employees on how work should be done.

But as noted by the CIPD (2008: 11), the success of Lean depends not so much on the tools but on its approach to work. Lean is implemented by communities of people who carry out and supervise the work and may include stakeholders such as customers. Lean team members are encouraged to think flexibly and be adaptable to change. They have a sense of ownership of what they do and achieve.

CASE STUDIES

Work organization: W L Gore

As described by the CIPD (2008: 25–26), W L Gore, which is best known for its GORE-TEX® fabrics, has a non-hierarchical, flat organization structure (a 'lattice' structure). There are no traditional organization charts, no ranks or job titles and no chains of command nor predetermined channels of communication. What is important when recruiting new people is that they have the right fit with Gore's culture. There are no rigid job specifications. Instead, associates make a commitment to contribute individually and collectively to work areas or projects according to their skills. Individuals are encouraged to take an interest in a wide variety of job areas or projects. Provided the core responsibilities within their role are carried out, associates can then stretch and build on their role to suit their interests, aspirations and the business needs. Gore's 'lattice' structure gives associates the opportunity to use their own judgement, take ownership of work areas and access the resources they need for projects to be successful. Gore's core values and ways of working are built on the principles of 'smart working'. Its unique culture, which fosters creativity, self-motivation, participation and equality, has proved to be a key contributor to associate satisfaction and retention.

Flexible working: B&Q

Flexible working arrangements have been extended at B&Q in association with its diversity strategy. The main components of its flexible working policy are:

- term-time contracts available to parents and grandparents with children/grandchildren up to the age of 16 years (18 if the child is disabled);
- job-share for employees who do not want – or are unable – to work full-time; online job-share register available to help individuals find a job-share partner;
- staggered start/finish times, allowing for personal commitments/interests;
- part-time hours;
- split shifts to fit in with employees' personal commitments;
- dual store contracts, allowing employees to work at more than one location;
- one employee/two roles, allowing employees to develop new and different skills, benefit from multiskilling and work in more than one area of the business;
- home/remote working, allowing employees to work from home or away from their normal workplace on an occasional basis;
- career breaks of 3 to 12 months can be taken for any reason;
- child care vouchers available across the organization;
- maternity, paternity and adoption policies enhanced above the statutory minimum;
- shared maternity/paternity leave; unpaid additional leave can be taken by father/partner where both parents work for B&Q and mother returns to work;
- IVF leave: one week paid time off for IVF treatment;
- paid compassionate or carer's leave: one week off per year.

Organization design

Organization design is the process of deciding how organizations should be structured in terms of the ways in which the responsibility for carrying out the overall task is allocated to individuals and groups of people and how the relationships between them function. The aim is to ensure that people work effectively together to achieve the overall purpose of the organization. The basic question of 'Who does what?' is answered by line managers but HR specialists are also involved in their capacity of helping the business to make the best use of its people. HR professionals can contribute to organization design or redesign activities by using their understanding of the factors affecting organizational behaviour and their knowledge of the business as a whole.

It is generally assumed that organization design is a logical and systematic affair, based on accepted principles and using analytical techniques that produce an inevitable 'best' result. But as explained below there is always organizational choice. There are certain guidelines to which consideration needs to be given, and organization reviews should be based on analysis, as also discussed below. But, ultimately, the ways in which an organization functions and therefore its structure (or sometimes its lack of structure) are contingent on the situation. In accordance with socio-technical theory (see Chapter 10) this consists of the people who work in the organization and the systems and techniques it uses to achieve its purpose.

Organizational choice

There is never one best way of organizing anything. There is always a choice. It is necessary to bear in mind that structural requirements in organizations or organizational units will vary widely according to what they are there to do and the activities they have to carry out. That is why there are no absolute principles such as the traditional precepts of 'unity of command' (one person, one boss) or the need to limit spans of control (the number of functions or people for which a manager is responsible). It all depends. Burns and Stalker (1961) established in their study of electronic companies in Scotland that in stable conditions a highly structured or 'mechanistic' organization will emerge that has specialized functions, clearly defined jobs, strict administrative routines and a hierarchical system of exercising control. However, when the environment is volatile, a rigid system of ranks and routine will inhibit the organization's speed and sensitivity of response. In these circumstances the structure is, or should be, 'organic' in the sense that it is a function of the situation in which the enterprise finds itself rather than conforming to any predetermined and rigid view of how it should operate.

As explained by Cummings and Worley (2005: 516), this means that there are two different types of organization design – mechanistic and organic – the characteristics of which are shown in Table 11.2.

Organization reviews

In exercising organizational choice an organizational review, as described below, will help in the evaluation of the alternatives, but the law of the situation, as described originally by Mary Parker Follett (1924), should prevail. This states that the work that people are required to do depends on the objective requirements of the situation. The final choice will depend upon the context and circumstances of the organization – as Lupton (1975) pointed out, it is important to achieve best fit.

Organizations may evolve organically without any conscious attempt to design them. But if a deliberate design programme is planned this should be based on the evidence that can be produced by a formal organization review conducted in the following stages:

1. *Activity analysis* to establish what work is done and what needs to be done. Two questions need to be answered: 1) are all the activities required properly catered for?; 2) are any unnecessary activities being carried out?
2. *Structural analysis* to determine how activities are grouped together; the number of levels in the hierarchy; the extent to which authority is decentralized to divisions and strategic business units (SBUs); where functions such as finance, HR, IT and research and development are placed in the structure (eg as central functions or integrated into divisions or SBUs); the relationships that exist between different units and functions (with particular attention being given to the way in which they communicate and cooperate with one another). Attention would be paid to such issues as the logic of

TABLE 11.2 Mechanistic and organic design

	Mechanistic design	Organic design
Structure	• Formal • Hierarchical (command and control) • Distinct functional units	• Informal • Flat, lean and flexible-horizontal processes • Lattice structure
Work	• Tightly defined jobs • Minimal scope in jobs for decision-making • Closely controlled work groups	• Flexible roles • Enriched roles with more autonomy • Self-managed teams

the way in which activities are grouped and decentralized; the span of control of managers (the number of separate functions or people they are directly responsible for); any overlap between functions or gaps leading to the neglect of certain activities; the existence of unnecessary departments, units, functions or layers of management; the clarity with which individual responsibilities and accountabilities are defined.

3. *Diagnosis* to identify (on the basis of the activities and structural analyses) the reasons for any structural problems facing the organization or function.
4. The *choice* in the light of the analyses and diagnosis of how the business or part of it should be designed or revised.
5. A *plan* to implement any revisions to the structure, possibly in phases.

Checklists covering the points that should be considered in analysing activities and structures are set out in the organization design toolkit (Chapter 62). When conducting the review the following factors should be taken into account.

Changes in the nature of organizations

As noted by Parker *et al* (2001: 418): 'Organizations... differ from the rather static and inflexible enterprises of earlier times. Greater flexibility is required to enable the rapid delivery of low-cost, high-quality and customized products, and to provide increasingly powerful and demanding customers with seamless service.' They also noted that the use of teamworking and other flexible forms of working continues to grow, distinctions between departments are disappearing as organizations become more integrated, and IT has changed the way in which work is conducted. These considerations may indicate that a traditional hierarchical and rigid structure is inappropriate and a more flexible approach is required.

Minimum critical specification

In accordance with systems theory (see Chapter 10) and the principle of equifinality (the premise that multiple organizational forms are equally effective), Huczynski and Buchanan (2007: 89) suggested that:

'It is not necessary to specify in detail the organization structure and the duties of each member. If an organization can develop its own method of operating and change that as circumstances require, then it will be necessary only to detail the basic and most significant aspects. This approach to organization design is called minimum critical specification.'

Strategic choice

As noted above, there is always choice about what form an organization structure should take. Child (1972) explained that in making such choices the leadership group (the dominant coalition) had to be persuaded to influence the organization structure through an essentially political process. He called this process 'strategic choice'. Choice analysis regards debate and negotiation in the social networks existing in organizations as integral to decision-making on organizational structures.

Successful organization design

Organizations are not static things. Changes are constantly taking place in the business itself, in the environment in which the business operates, and in the people who work in the business. There is no such thing as an 'ideal' organization. The most that can be done is to optimize the processes involved, remembering that whatever structure evolves it will be contingent on the circumstances of the organization. An important point to bear in mind is that organizations consist of people working more or less cooperatively together. Inevitably, and especially at managerial levels, the organization may have to be adjusted to fit the particular strengths and attributes of the people available. The result may not conform to the ideal, but it is more likely to work than a structure that ignores the human element. It is always desirable to have an ideal structure in mind, but it is equally desirable to modify it to meet particular circumstances, as long as there is awareness of any potential problems that may arise. This may seem an obvious point, but it is frequently ignored by management consultants and others who adopt a doctrinaire approach to organization, often with disastrous results.

The worst sin that organization designers can commit is that of imposing their own ideology on the organization. Their job is to be eclectic in their knowledge, sensitive in their analysis of the situation and deliberate in their approach to the evaluation of alternatives.

Research conducted by Whittington and Molloy (2005) indicated that to achieve success in organization design it is necessary to:

- obtain top management support, especially personal commitment and political support;
- avoid piecemeal, uncoordinated change initiatives by making a strategic business case that anticipates implications across the entire organization;
- achieve substantive, rather than tokenistic, employee involvement in the change process, moving beyond communication to active engagement;
- invest in communications with external stakeholders, including customers, suppliers and financial stakeholders;
- involve HR professionals closely, right from the start – involving HR has been proved to positively impact on a range of performance outcomes;
- maintain effective project management disciplines;
- build skilled change management teams – with the right mix of experience and abilities – that can work together.

Job design

Job design specifies the contents of jobs in order to satisfy work requirements and meet the personal needs of the job holder, thus increasing levels of employee engagement. As observed by Wall and Clegg (1998: 265):

> Jobs are created by people for people. Whether deliberately or by default, choices are made about which tasks to group together to form a job, the extent to which job holders should follow prescribed procedures in completing those tasks, how closely the job incumbent will be supervised, and numerous other aspects of the work. Such choices are the essence of job design.

Jobs and roles

A distinction can be made between jobs and roles. A job is an organizational unit consisting of a group of defined tasks or activities to be carried out or duties to be performed. A role is the part played by individuals and the patterns of behaviour expected of them in fulfilling their work requirements. Jobs are about tasks, roles are about people. This distinction means that while jobs may be designed to fit work requirements, roles are developed as people work flexibly, demonstrate that they can do more and take on different responsibilities. Role development (as covered in the next section of this chapter) happens informally, in contrast to the more formal approaches to job design (considered below).

Factors affecting job design

Deciding on the content of a job starts from work requirements because that is why the job exists. When the tasks to be done have been determined it is then necessary to consider how the jobs can be set up to provide the maximum degree of intrinsic motivation for those who have to carry them out with a view to improving performance and productivity. Consideration also has to be given to another important aim of job design: to fulfil the social responsibilities of the organization to the people who work in it by improving the quality of working life, an aim that, as stated in Wilson's (1973) report on this subject, depends upon both efficiency of performance and satisfaction of the worker.

Clearly, the content of a job depends on the work system in which it exists and the organization structure in which it is placed. Job design therefore happens within the context of work and organization design, as described in this chapter, but it is also affected by the following factors:

- the characteristics of jobs;
- the characteristics of task structure;
- the process of intrinsic motivation;
- the job characteristics model;
- the implications of group activities.

The characteristics of jobs

There are three fundamental characteristics shared by all jobs:

1. Job range – the number of operations a job holder performs to complete a task.
2. Job depth – the amount of discretion a job holder has to decide job activities and job outcomes.
3. Job relationships – the interpersonal relationships between job holders and their managers and co-workers.

Task structure

Job design requires the assembly of a number of tasks into a job or a group of jobs. An individual may carry out one main task that consists of a number of interrelated elements or functions. Or task functions may be allocated to a team working closely together in a manufacturing 'cell' or customer service unit, or strung along an assembly line. In more complex jobs, individuals may carry out a variety of connected tasks (multitasking), each with a number of functions, or these tasks may be allocated to a team of workers or be divided between them. In the latter case, the tasks may require a variety of skills that have to be possessed by all members of the team (multiskilling) in order to work flexibly. Complexity in a job may be a reflection of the number and variety of tasks to be carried out, the different skills or competencies to be used, the range and scope of the decisions that have to be made, or the difficulty of predicting the outcome of decisions.

The internal structure of each task consists of three elements: planning (deciding on the course of action, its timing and the resources required), executing (carrying out the plan) and controlling (monitoring performance and progress and taking corrective action when required). A completely integrated job includes all these elements for each of the tasks involved. The worker, or group of workers, having been given objectives in terms of output, quality and cost targets, decides on how the work is to be done, assembles the resources, performs the work, and monitors output, quality and cost standards. Responsibility in a job is measured by the amount of authority that someone has to do all of these things.

The ideal arrangement from the point of view of engagement and motivation is to provide for fully integrated jobs containing all three task elements. In practice, management and team leaders are often entirely responsible for planning and control, leaving the worker responsible for execution. To a degree, this is inevitable, but one of the aims of job design is often to extend the responsibility of workers into the functions of planning and control. This can involve empowerment – giving individuals and teams more responsibility for decision-making and ensuring that they have the training, support and guidance to exercise that responsibility properly.

Intrinsic motivation

The case for using job design techniques is based on the premise that effective performance and genuine satisfaction in work follow mainly from the intrinsic content of the job. This is related to the fundamental concept that people are motivated when they are provided with the means to achieve their goals. Work provides the means to earn money, which as an extrinsic reward satisfies basic needs and is instrumental in providing ways of satisfying higher-level needs. But work also provides intrinsic rewards related to achievement, responsibility and the opportunity to use and develop skills that are more under the control of the worker.

The job characteristics model

The most influential model for job design is the job characteristics model developed by Hackman and Oldham (1974). They identified five core job characteristics:

1. *Skill variety*: the degree to which a job requires an employee to perform activities that challenge his or her skills and abilities.
2. *Task identity*: the degree to which the job requires completion of an identifiable piece of work.
3. *Task significance*: the degree to which the job outcome has a substantial impact on others.
4. *Autonomy*: the degree to which the job gives an employee freedom and discretion in scheduling work and determining how it is performed.
5. *Feedback*: the degree to which an employee gets information about the effectiveness of his or her efforts – with particular emphasis on feedback directly related to the work itself rather than from a third party (for example, a manager).

Hackman and Oldham explained that if the design of a job satisfied the core job characteristics the employee would perceive that the work was worthwhile, would feel responsible for the work and would know if the work had been completed satisfactorily. The outcome of this would be high-quality work performance and high job satisfaction as a result of intrinsic motivation.

The implications of group activities

Jobs should never be considered in isolation. All job holders belong to formal or informal groups and the interrelationships that exist in such groups should be considered when looking at the content of an individual job.

Approaches to job design

Job design starts with an analysis of task requirements, using the job analysis techniques described in Chapter 51. These requirements will be a function of the system of work and the organization structure. As described by Robertson and Smith (1985), the method can be based on the job characteristics model as follows:

- Influence skill variety by providing opportunities for people to do several tasks and by combining tasks.
- Influence task identity by combining tasks to form natural work units.
- Influence task significance by forming natural work units and informing people of the importance of their work.
- Influence autonomy by giving people responsibility for determining their own working systems.
- Influence feedback by establishing good relationships and opening feedback channels.

These methods influence the four approaches to job design described below.

Job rotation

This is the movement of employees from one task to another to reduce monotony by increasing variety.

Job enlargement

This means combining previously fragmented tasks into one job, again to increase the variety and meaning of repetitive work.

Job enrichment

This goes beyond job enlargement to add greater autonomy and responsibility to a job. Job enrichment aims to maximize the interest and challenge of work by providing the employee with a job that has these characteristics:

- it is a complete piece of work in the sense that the worker can identify a series of tasks or activities that end in a recognizable and definable product;
- it affords the employee as much variety, decision-making responsibility and control as possible in carrying out the work;
- it provides direct feedback through the work itself on how well the employee is doing his or her job.

As described by Herzberg (1968), job enrichment is not just increasing the number or variety of tasks, nor is it the provision of opportunities for job rotation. These approaches may relieve boredom, but they do not result in positive increases in motivation.

Self-managing teams (autonomous work groups)

These are self-regulating teams who work largely without direct supervision. The philosophy on which this approach is founded is that of job enrichment but it is also influenced by socio-technical systems theory, which suggests that because the technical aspects of work are interrelated with the social aspects both should be considered when designing jobs.

A self-managing team enlarges individual jobs to include a wider range of operative skills (multi-skilling); decides on methods of work and the planning, scheduling and control of work; distributes tasks itself among its members; and monitors its own performance, taking corrective action when required.

The advocates of self-managing teams or autonomous work groups claim that they represent a more comprehensive view of organizations than the rather simplistic individual motivation theories that underpin job rotation, enlargement and enrichment. Be that as it may, the strength of this system is that in line with socio-technical theory it takes account of the social or group factors and the technology, as well as the individual motivators.

In a study of customer service representatives in a telecommunications company, Batt (1999) found that work organized into self-managed teams led to better service and sales performance (an increase of 9.2 per cent per employee) than traditional work designs, and that the interactive effect of self-managed teams and new technology raised sales by an additional 17.4 per cent.

Choice of approach

Of the four approaches described above, it is generally recognized that, although job rotation and job enlargement have their uses in developing skills and relieving monotony, they do not go to the root of the requirements for intrinsic motivation and for meeting the various motivating characteristics of jobs. These are best satisfied by using, as appropriate, job enrichment, autonomous work groups, or high-performance work design.

High-performance work design

This concentrates on setting up working groups in environments where high levels of performance can be achieved. As described by Buchanan (1987), this requires management to define what it needs in the form of methods of production and the results expected from its introduction. It involves multiskilling – job demarcation lines are eliminated as far as possible and encouragement and training are provided for employees to acquire new skills. Self-managed teams are set up with full responsibility for planning, controlling and monitoring the work.

Role development

Role development is the continuous process through which roles are defined or modified as work proceeds and evolves. Job design as described above takes place when a new job is created or an existing job is changed, often following a reorganization or the introduction of a new work system. But the part that people play in carrying out their roles can evolve over time as people grow into their roles and grow with them, and as incremental changes take place in the scope of the work and the degree to which individuals have freedom to act (their autonomy). Roles will be developed as people develop in them – responding to opportunities and changing demands, acquiring new skills and developing competencies.

Role development takes place in the context of day-to-day work and is therefore a matter between managers and the members of their teams. It means agreeing definitions of accountabilities, objectives and competency requirements as the roles evolve. When these change – as they probably will in all except the most routine jobs – it is desirable to achieve mutual understanding of new expectations.

The process of understanding how roles are developing, and agreeing the implications, can take place through performance management in which the regularly updated performance agreement spells out agreed outcomes (key result areas) and competency requirements. It is necessary to ensure that managers and team leaders define roles within the performance management framework, taking into account the principles of job design set out above.

Key learning points: Work, organization and job design

Work, organization and job design

These are three distinct but closely associated processes that establish what work is done in organizations and how it is done.

Work design

Work design is the creation of systems of work and a working environment that enhance organizational effectiveness and productivity, ensure that the organization becomes 'a great place in which to work' and are conducive to the health, safety and well-being of employees.

Work system design

Work system design is concerned with how the processes required to make a product or provide a service should operate. It deals with the set of related activities that combine to give a result that customers want. The structure of the system describes the relations between different operations.

Smart working

The CIPD (2008: 4) defined smart working as: 'An approach to organizing work that aims to drive greater efficiency and effectiveness in achieving job outcomes through a combination of flexibility, autonomy and collaboration, in parallel with optimizing tools and working environments for employees.'

Flexible working

Flexible working is a pattern of working practice or working hours that deviates from the standard or normal arrangement.

High-performance working

High-performance working was defined by Combs *et al* (2006) as the sum of the processes, practices and policies put in place by employers to enable employees to perform to their full potential.

Lean manufacturing

A process improvement methodology developed by Toyota. 'Lean' focuses on minimizing waste and ensuring the flow of production in order to deliver value to customers.

Aims of organization design

The overall aim of organization design is to optimize the arrangements for conducting the affairs of the business or function and thus achieve the 'best fit' between the structure and what the business or function is there to do.

Organization analysis

The starting point for an organization review is an analysis of the existing circumstances, structure and processes of the organization and an assessment of the strategic issues that might affect it in the future.

Organization diagnosis

The aim of the diagnosis is to establish, on the basis of the analysis, the reasons for any structural problems facing the organization or function.

Organizational choice

There is never one best way of organizing anything. There is always a choice.

Job design

Job design specifies the contents of jobs in order to satisfy work requirements and meet the personal needs of the job holder, thus increasing levels of employee engagement.

Jobs and roles

A job is an organizational unit consisting of a group of defined tasks or activities to be carried out or duties to be performed. A role is the part played by individuals and the patterns of behaviour expected of them in fulfilling their work requirements. Jobs are about tasks, roles are about people.

The job characteristics model

The job characteristics model was developed by Hackman and Oldham (1974). They identified five core job characteristics: skill variety, task identity, task significance, autonomy and feedback.

Approaches to job design

Job design starts with an analysis of task requirements, using job analysis techniques.

Role development

Role development is the continuous process through which roles are defined or modified as work proceeds and evolves.

Questions

1 What is work design?
2 What is work system design?
3 What is smart working?
4 What are the main forms of operational flexibility?
5 What is a flexible firm?
6 What are the overall aims of organization design?
7 What are the stages of an organization review?
8 What is job design?
9 What is the difference between a job and a role?
10 What is the job characteristics model?
11 What is job enrichment?
12 What is role development?

References

Atkinson, J (1984) Manpower strategies for flexible organizations, *Personnel Management*, August, pp 28–31

Batt, R (1999) Work organization, technology and performance in customer service and sales, *Industrial and Labor Relations Review*, 52 (4), pp 539–64

Buchanan, D A (1987) Job enrichment is dead: long live high performance work design!, *Personnel Management*, May, pp 40–43

Burns, T and Stalker, G (1961) *The Management of Innovation*, London, Tavistock

Child, D (1997) Strategic choice in the analysis of action, structure, organizations and environment: retrospective and prospective, *Organizational Studies*, 18 (1), pp 43–76

Child, J (1972) Organizational structure, environment and performance: the role of strategic choice, *Sociology*, 6 (1), pp 1–22

CIPD (2008) *Smart Working: How smart is UK PLC? Findings from organizational practice*, London, CIPD

Combs, J, Liu, Y and Hall, A (2006) How much do high-performance work practices matter? A meta-analysis of their effects on organizational performance, *Personnel Psychology*, 59 (3), pp 501–28

Cummings, T G and Worley, C G (2005) *Organization Development and Change*, Mason, OH, South Western
Doeringer, P and Priore, M (1971) *Internal Labor Markets and Labor Market Analysis*, Lexington, DC, Heath
Emery, E E and Trist, E L (1960) Socio-technical systems, in (eds) C W Churchman and M Verhulst *Management Science, Models and Techniques*, London, Pergamum Press, vol 2, pp 83–97
Emery, F E (1959) *Characteristics of Socio-technical Systems*, London, Tavistock Publications
Follett, M P (1924) *Creative Experience*, New York, Longmans Green
Hackman, J R and Oldham, G R (1974) Motivation through the design of work: test of a theory, *Organizational Behaviour and Human Performance*, 16 (2), pp 250–79
Herzberg, F (1968) One more time: how do you motivate employees? *Harvard Business Review*, January–February, pp 109–20
Huczynski, A A and Buchanan, D A (2007) *Organizational Behaviour*, 6th edn, Harlow, FT Prentice Hall
Lupton, T (1975) Best fit in the design of organizations, *Personnel Review*, 4 (1), pp 15–22
Parker, S K, Wall, T D and Cordery, J L (2001) Future work design research and practice: towards an elaborated model of work design, *Journal of Occupational and Organizational Psychology*, 74 (4), pp 413–40
Robertson, I T and Smith, M (1985) *Motivation and Job Design*, London, IPM
Smith, A (1776) *The Wealth of Nations*, Harmondsworth, Penguin Books, 1986
Sung, J and Ashton, D (2005) *High Performance Work Practices: Linking strategy and skills to performance outcomes*, London, DTI
Taylor, F W (1911) *Principles of Scientific Management*, New York, Harper
Wall, T D and Clegg, C (1998) Job design, in (ed) N Nicholson, *Blackwell's Encyclopaedic Dictionary of Organizational Behaviour*, Oxford, Blackwell, pp 265–68
Whittington, R and Molloy, E (2005) *HR's Role in Organizing: Shaping change*, London, CIPD
Wilson, N A B (1973) *On the Quality of Working Life*, London, HMSO

12 Organization development

KEY CONCEPTS AND TERMS

- Action research
- Behaviour modelling
- Behavioural science
- Business model innovation
- Change management
- Diagnostics
- Forced-field analysis
- Group dynamics
- Humanism
- Integrated strategic change
- Intervention
- Neurolinguistic programming
- Organization capability
- Organization development
- Organizational/corporate culture
- Organizational transformation
- Process
- Process consultation
- Survey feedback
- T-groups
- Transactional analysis

LEARNING OUTCOMES

On completing this chapter you should be able to define these key concepts. You should also understand:

- The meaning of organization development
- The contents of traditional organization development (OD) programmes
- The criticisms made of the original OD concept
- How OD has moved on since it was first introduced
- The nature of organization development today, including the processes of diagnosis and programming

Introduction

Work, organization and job design provide the basic ingredients for operating a business. But it is necessary to see that these processes work well, which is the aim of organization development. In this chapter, organization development is defined and its somewhat chequered history is described, from its origins as 'OD' to the more focused and businesslike approaches adopted today. This leads to a discussion of organization development strategy and an examination of organization development in practice, involving the use of diagnostics as the basis for preparing organization development programmes.

Organization development defined

Organization development is a systematic approach to improving organizational capability, which is concerned with process – how things get done. As expressed by Beer (1980: 10), OD operates as: 'A system wide process of data collection, diagnosis, action planning, intervention and evaluation.'

Organization development in its traditional form as OD was later defined by Rowlandson (1984: 90) as 'an intervention strategy that uses group processes to focus on the whole culture of an organization in order to bring about planned change'. More recently, the CIPD (2010: 1) defined it broadly as a 'planned and systematic approach to enabling sustained organization performance through the involvement of its people'.

The nature of organization development

Organization development in its original version as OD was based on behavioural science concepts, ie the field of enquiry dedicated to the study of human behaviour through sophisticated and rigorous methods. OD was practised through what were called 'interventions'.

However, during the 1980s and 1990s a number of other approaches were introduced. Further changes occurred in the following decade during which a more strategic focus was adopted and more business-focused activities such as smart working and high-performance working came to the fore. It is these changes that led to the broader definition produced by the CIPD.

Organization development used to be the province of specialized consultants who tended to practise it as a mystery, with HR playing a supporting role if it played any role at all. But *HR Magazine* spelt out the close relationship between HR and organization development as follows.

> **Source review**
>
> ### HR and organization development – *HR Magazine* (2007: 1)
>
> To remain competitive in today's global marketplace, organizations must change. One of the most effective tools to promote successful change is organization development (OD). As HR increasingly focuses on building organizational learning, skills and workforce productivity, the effective use of OD to help achieve company business goals and strategies is becoming a broad HR competency as well as a key strategic HR tool. While there are variations regarding the definition of OD, the basic purpose of organization development is to increase an organization's effectiveness through planned interventions related to the organization's processes (often company-wide), resulting in improvements in productivity, return on investment and employee satisfaction.

The CIPD (2010: 3) stated that: 'We place considerable importance on OD, seeing it as one of the ten professional areas within the HR profession map which emphasizes its importance as a HR skill.' The CIPD also commented that:

> OD is not a new discipline and has always had a focus on people but has only relatively recently become considered as a mainstream discipline of

> HR. Supporters of OD argue that its strength is its ability to understand the whole organization and as such it may be inhibiting to root it too firmly in the HR function. However, given the increasing need for the HR profession to act as a business partner, OD and its methods have a part to play in developing HR's strategic role and its involvement in organizational change, organizational culture and employee engagement. (ibid: 3)

The strategic nature of organization development as an integral part of HRM arises because it can play a part in the implementation of business strategy. For example, a strategy for business model innovation (the process followed by an organization to develop a new business model or change an existing one) could result in the need for new organization structures and processes. This would include organization development and change management activities. The aim of this chapter is to explain the purpose of organization development in the light of an analysis of the history of the concept and how it can be applied as part of a strategic HRM approach.

The story of organization development

There are three chapters in the story of organizational development: the original version of the 1960s and 70s, the extensions and modifications to the original approach in the 1980s and 90s, and the new look at organization development of the 2000s.

The first chapter – the original version

Organization development emerged as the 'OD' movement in the 1960s. It was based on the strong humanistic values of its early founders, who wanted to improve the conditions of people's lives in organizations by applying behavioural science knowledge. Its origins can be traced to the writings of behavioural scientists such as Lewin (1947, 1951) on group dynamics (the improvement of group processes through various forms of training, eg team building, interactive skills training, T-groups) and change management. Other behavioural scientists included Maslow (1954) who produced his needs theory of motivation, Herzberg *et al* (1957) who wrote about the motivation to work, and Argyris (1957) who emphasized the need to plan for integration and involvement. McGregor (1960) produced his 'Theory Y', which advocates the recognition of the needs of both the organization and the individual on the basis that, given the chance, people will not only accept but seek responsibility. Likert (1961) added his theory of supportive relationships.

The two founders of the organization development movement were Beckhard (1969) who probably coined the term, and Bennis (1969) who, according to Buchanan and Huczynski (2007: 575), described OD as a 'truth, trust, love and collaboration approach'. Ruona and Gibson (2004: 53) explained that:

> Early OD interventions can be categorized as primarily focusing on individuals and interpersonal relations. OD was established as a social philosophy that emphasized a long-term orientation, the applied behavioural sciences, external and process-oriented consultation, change managed from the top, a strong emphasis on action research and a focus on creating change in collaboration with managers.

The objectives, assumptions and values of the original version of OD

As originally conceived, OD programmes aimed to increase the effectiveness of the various processes that take place in organizations, especially those relating to the ways in which people work together. It was also concerned with improving the quality of people's working lives. The original OD philosophy was that of humanism – the belief that human factors are paramount in the study of organizational behaviour. This had its roots in the conclusions reached from the Hawthorne studies of 1924 to 1932 (Mayo, 1933; Roethlisberger and Dickson, 1939) that the productivity of workers increases when someone they respect takes an interest in them. The focus then turned to the needs of people as individuals and in groups with an emphasis on process – how people worked together and how this could be improved. The assumptions and values of OD were that:

- Most individuals are driven by the need for personal growth and development as long as their environment is both supportive and challenging.

- The work team, especially at the informal level, has great significance for feelings of satisfaction, and the dynamics of such teams have a powerful effect on the behaviour of their members.
- Organizations can be more effective if they learn to diagnose their own strengths and weaknesses.
- Managers often do not know what is wrong and need special help in diagnosing problems, although the outside 'process consultant' ensures that decision-making remains in the hands of the client.

Traditional OD programmes

OD during this time was practised predominantly by external consultants working with senior managers. Personnel specialists were not involved to any great extent. OD programmes consisted then of 'interventions' such as those listed below. In OD jargon an intervention is a planned activity designed to improve organizational effectiveness or manage change. The following are the traditional OD interventions; they still feature in current programmes:

- *Process consultation* – helping clients to generate and analyse information that they can understand and, following a thorough diagnosis, act upon. The information relates to organizational processes such as inter-group relations, interpersonal relations and communications.
- *Change management* – often using the techniques advocated by Lewin (1951), which consisted of processes of managing change by unfreezing, changing and freezing, and force-field analysis (analysing and dealing with the driving forces that affect transition to a future state).
- *Action research* – collecting data from people about process issues and feeding it back in order to identify problems and their likely causes as a basis for an action plan to deal with the problem.
- *Appreciative enquiry* – a methodology that does not focus entirely on finding out what is wrong in order to solve problems. Instead it adopts the more positive approach of identifying 'best practices' – what is working well – and using that information as a basis for planning change. It can be associated with action research.
- *Survey feedback* – a variety of action research in which data is systematically collected about the system through attitude surveys and workshops leading to action plans.
- *Group dynamics* – improving the ways in which people work together by means of programmes that aim to increase the effectiveness of groups through various forms of training, eg team building, interactive skills training and T-groups ('training groups', which aim to increase sensitivity, diagnostic ability and action skills).
- *Personal interventions* – developing interpersonal skills through such processes as transactional analysis (an approach to understanding how people behave and express themselves through transactions with others), behaviour modelling (the use of positive reinforcement and corrective feedback to change behaviour) and neurolinguistic programming or NLP (teaching people to programme their reactions to others and develop unconscious strategies for interacting with them).

The second chapter – criticisms of the original version of OD and new approaches

The OD movement as originally conceived and practised was characterized by what Buchanan and Huczynski (2007: 559) called 'quasi-religious values' with some of the features of a religious movement, which, they claimed, is one reason why it has survived as a concept in spite of the criticisms that began to be levelled at it in the 1980s. Weidner (2004: 39) wrote that: 'OD was something that practitioners felt and lived as much as they *believed*' (original emphasis).

Criticisms of OD

One of the earliest critics was McLean (1981: 4) who noted 'the moral and ethical misgivings concerned with the development of what might be regarded as a sophisticated science of manipulation'. He cited a comment by Strauss (1976) that at times OD is little more than abstract moralization and asserted that:

> It is becoming increasingly apparent that there exists a considerable discrepancy between OD as practised and the prescriptive stances taken by many OD writers... The theory of change and change management which is the foundation of most OD programmes is based on over-simplistic generalizations which offer little specific guidance to practitioners faced with the confusing complexity of a real change situation. (ibid: 13)

Armstrong (1984: 113) commented that: 'Organization development has lost a degree of credibility in recent years because the messianic zeal displayed by some practitioners has been at variance with the circumstances and real needs of the organization.' Burke (1995: 8) stated that 'in the mid-1970s, OD was still associated with T-groups, participative management and consensus, Theory Y, and self-actualization – the soft human, touchy-feely kinds of activities'.

An even more powerful critic was Legge (1995: 212), who observed that the OD rhetoric fitted the era of 'flower power' and that: 'OD was seen, on the one hand as a form of devious manipulation, and on the other as "wishy-washy" and ineffectual.' She noted 'the relative lack of success of OD initiatives in effecting major and lasting cultural change, with the aim of generating commitment to new values in the relatively small number of organizations in which it was tried' (ibid: 213), and produced the following devastating critique.

Source review

A critique of organization development – Legge (1995: 213)

In order to cope with an increasingly complex and changing environment, many of the initiatives were, in retrospect, surprisingly inward looking, involving schemes of management development, work system design, attempts at participation, almost as a good in their own right, without close attention as to how they were to deliver against market-driven organizational success criteria. The long-term nature of OD activities, together with difficulties to clearly establishing to sceptics their contribution to organizational success criteria (and within a UK culture of financial short-termism) rendered the initiatives at best marginal... and at worst to be treated with a cynical contempt.

The main criticisms of OD, as noted by Marsh *et al* (2010: 143), were that it was: 'Oriented to process and tools rather than results... where techniques are considered to be ends in themselves rather than a means to deliver organizational performance.'

New approaches

During the 1980s and 90s an alternative approach emerged, that of culture management, which aimed at achieving cultural change as a means of enhancing organizational capability. Culture change or culture management programmes start with an analysis of the existing culture, which may involve the use of a diagnostic such as the 'Organizational Culture Inventory' devised by Cooke and Lafferty (1989). The desired culture is then defined – one that enables the organization to function effectively and achieve its strategic objectives. As a result, a 'culture gap' is identified, which needs to be filled. This analysis of culture identifies behavioural expectations so that HR processes can be used to develop and reinforce them. This sounds easier than it really is. Culture is a complex and often hard to define notion and it is usually strongly embedded and therefore difficult to change. Anthony (1990: 4) argued that: 'The management of culture... purports to define the meaning of people's lives so that they become concomitant with the organization's view of itself. [It is] the adjustment of human meaning for organizational ends.' He also observed that: 'Published cases do exist of organizations within which major changes in culture have been successfully accomplished and shown to persist but they are rare' (ibid: 5). However, culture management became a process in its own right and OD consultants jumped on the bandwagon.

Culture management involves change management, another important item in the OD toolkit. But as Caldwell (2003: 132) argued: 'It is assumed within most OD models that change can be planned in a "rational" or linear manner, and that the change agent can facilitate this group process, although there is little evidence to support this illusion of "manageability".'

Other movements in this period that could be described as organization development activities but exist as distinct entities included total quality management (TQM) and quality circles. TQM aims to ensure that all activities within an organization happen in the way they have been planned in order to meet the defined needs of customers. Its approach is holistic – quality management is not a separate function to be treated in isolation, but is an integral part of all operations. Quality circles are groups of volunteers engaged in related work who meet regularly to discuss and propose ways of improving working methods under a trained leader.

Another approach more closely related to OD that emerged at this time was organizational transformation. This was defined by Cummins and Worley (2005: 752) as: 'A process of radically altering the organization's strategic direction, including fundamental changes in structures, processes and behaviours.'

Holistic approaches to improving organizational capability emerging in this period, which were not part of what was conventionally known as OD, included high-performance working, high-commitment management, high-involvement management and performance management. The development of these systems in the 2000s led to a radically changed view of what constituted organization development.

The third chapter – changing the focus

The most significant change in the 2000s was the shift to a strategic perspective. As noted by Cummins and Worley (2005: 12): 'Change agents have proposed a variety of large-scale or strategic-change models; each of these models recognizes that strategic change involves multiple layers levels of the organization and a change in its culture, is driven from the top by powerful executives, and has important effects on performance.' They also commented that the practice of organization development therefore went far beyond its humanistic origins. Another development was the emergence of the concept of 'smart working', as described in Chapter 11. This could be described as an OD intervention because it involves taking a fundamental look at methods of improving organizational effectiveness.

There was also more emphasis on associating organization design with organization development. Marsh *et al* (2010) suggested that organization design and organization development need to be merged into one HR capability, with organization design taking precedence. They considered that this should all be brought in-house as a necessary part of the business model innovation process. But as they observed: 'We do not believe that the field of organization development has passed its sell-by date. Far from it. It just needs to be repositioned as an HR capability' (ibid: 143).

However, Weidner (2004: 37) made the following more pessimistic comment about OD: 'Unfortunately, after sixty years – despite the best efforts and intentions of many talented people – OD finds itself increasingly at the margins of business, academe, and practice. The field continues to affirm its values, yet has no identifiable voice.' OD 'interventions' still have a role to play in improving performance but as part of an integrated business and HR strategy planned and implemented by HR in conjunction with senior management, with or without outside help.

The main change that has taken place in the move from traditional OD to organizational development as practised currently is the focus on improving organizational performance and results through organization-wide initiatives. These do encompass the behaviour of people, especially when this relates to their levels of engagement (the degree to which people are committed to their work and the organization and motivated to achieve high levels of performance). But they are also concerned with the organizational processes that affect behaviour and engagement, namely, strategic HRM, work system design, smart working, high-performance working, organization design and job design.

Organization development strategy

Organization development strategy is founded on the aspiration to improve organizational capability, which is broadly the capacity of an organization to function effectively in order to achieve desired results. It has been defined more specifically by Ulrich and Lake (1990: 40) as 'the ability to manage people for competitive advantage'. It is concerned with mapping out intentions on how the work system should be developed in line with the concept of smart working, on how the organization should be structured to meet new demands, on system-wide change in fields such as reward and performance management, on how change should be managed, on what needs to be done to improve organizational processes involving people such as teamwork, communications and participation, and how the organization can acquire, retain, develop and engage the talent it needs. These intentions will be converted into actions on work systems development, structure design, the redesign of jobs and, possibly, OD-type interventions. The latter could take the form of action research, survey feedback and programmes for improving group processes and interpersonal skills, as described earlier in this chapter. The strategy can involve processes of integrated strategic change, as described below, and will be based on organizational diagnosis leading to the design of an organization development programme, as considered in the following sections.

Integrated strategic change

The process of integrated strategic change as conceived by Worley *et al* (1996) can be used to formulate and implement organization development strategies. The steps required are:

- Strategic analysis, a review of the organization's strategic orientation (its strategic intentions within its competitive environment) and a diagnosis of the organization's readiness for change.
- Develop strategic capability – the ability to implement the strategic plan quickly and effectively.
- Integrate individuals and groups throughout the organization into the processes of analysis, planning and implementation to maintain the firm's strategic focus, direct attention and resources to the organization's key competencies, improve coordination and integration within the organization and create higher levels of shared ownership and commitment.
- Create the strategy, gain commitment and support for it and plan its implementation.
- Implement the strategic change plan, drawing on knowledge of motivation, group dynamics and change processes, dealing with issues such as alignment, adaptability, teamwork and organizational and individual learning.
- Allocate resources, provide feedback and solve problems as they arise.

Organizational diagnosis

The practice of organization development is based on an analysis and diagnosis of the circumstances of the organization, the strategic, operational or process issues that are affecting the organization and its ability to perform well. As defined by Manzini (1988: ix): 'An organizational diagnosis is a systematic process of gathering data about a business organization – its problems, challenges, strengths and limitations – and analysing how such factors influence its ability to interact effectively and profitably with its business environment.' This involves the use of the diagnostic cycle with associated analytical and diagnostic tools, which enable those concerned with development to identify areas of concern that can be dealt with in an organization development programme.

The diagnostic cycle

The diagnostic cycle as described by Manzini (1988: 11) consists of:

- data gathering;
- analysis;
- feedback;
- action planning;
- implementation;
- evaluation.

Analytical tools

The two most used analytical tools are SWOT analysis and PESTLE analysis. A SWOT analysis is a 'looking in' and 'looking out' approach that covers the internal organizational factors of strengths and weaknesses and the external factors of opportunities and threats. PESTLE analysis is an environmental scanning tool that covers the following factors: political, economic, social, technological, legal and environmental.

Diagnostics

Diagnostics are tools such as questionnaires or checklists that gather information about a business or on the opinions and attitudes of employees in order to identify issues and problems that can be dealt with in an organization development programme. They enable those concerned with organization development to understand what is happening and why it is happening so that they can do something about it. Diagnostics can be used to assess overall organizational effectiveness in the shape of general strategic, business and operational issues, or they can deal with more specific areas of concern such as a review of the organization's ideology, culture or climate, or a survey of levels of engagement or commitment. Examples of the approach used by various diagnostic instruments are given below.

Organizational ideology questionnaire (Harrison, 1972)

This questionnaire deals with the four orientations defined by Harrison (power, role, task and self). The questionnaire is completed by ranking statements according to views on what is closest to the organization's actual position. The following are examples of statements:

- a good boss is strong, decisive and firm but fair;
- a good subordinate is compliant, hard-working and loyal;
- people who do well in the organization are shrewd and competitive, with a strong need for power;
- the basis of task assignment is the personal needs and judgements of those in authority;
- decisions are made by people with the most knowledge and expertise about the problem.

Organizational culture inventory (Cooke and Lafferty, 1989)

This instrument assesses organizational culture under 12 headings:

1. *Humanistic-helpful* – organizations managed in a participative and person-centred way.
2. *Affiliative* – organizations that place a high priority on constructive relationships.
3. *Approval* – organizations in which conflicts are avoided and interpersonal relationships are pleasant – at least superficially.
4. *Conventional* – conservative, traditional and bureaucratically controlled organizations.
5. *Dependent* – hierarchically controlled and non-participative organizations.
6. *Avoidance* – organizations that fail to reward success but punish mistakes.
7. *Oppositional* – organizations in which confrontation prevails and negativism is rewarded.
8. *Power* – organizations structured on the basis of the authority inherent in members' positions.
9. *Competitive* – a culture in which winning is valued and members are rewarded for out-performing one another.
10. *Competence/perfectionist* – organizations in which perfectionism, persistence and hard work are valued.
11. *Achievement* – organizations that do things well and value members who set and accomplish challenging but realistic goals.
12. *Self-actualization* – organizations that value creativity, quality over quantity, and both task accomplishment and individual growth.

Typical dimensions of organizational climate questionnaires (Koys and De Cotiis, 1991)

- *Autonomy* – the perception of self-determination with respect to work procedures, goals and priorities.
- *Cohesion* – the perception of togetherness or sharing within the organization setting.
- *Trust* – the perception of freedom to communicate openly with members at higher organizational levels about sensitive or personal issues with the expectation that the integrity of such communications will not be violated.
- *Resource* – the perception of time demands with respect to task completion and performance standards.

- *Support* – the perception of the degree to which superiors tolerate members' behaviour, including willingness to let members learn from their mistakes without fear of reprisal.
- *Recognition* – the perception that members' contributions to the organization are acknowledged.
- *Fairness* – the perception that organizational policies are non-arbitrary or capricious.
- *Innovation* – the perception that change and creativity are encouraged, including risk-taking into new areas where the member has little or no prior experience.

Employee attitude or opinion surveys

A number of organizations conduct attitude or opinion surveys on behalf of their clients. Apart from the advantage of being well-tested and professionally administered they also facilitate benchmarking. Surveys provided by such organizations include the CIPD People and Performance employee questionnaire, the IES engagement survey, the Gallup engagement survey and the Saratoga engagement and commitment matrix.

A toolkit for designing and using attitude surveys is provided in Chapter 73 of this handbook. which includes an example of a general attitude survey.

Organization development programmes

The traditional OD programme was behavioural science-based and almost entirely devoted to interpersonal relationships, organizational processes and culture change in the broadest sense. There may still be a need for such interventions today but organization development is a more eclectic affair – anything can be included under the organization development heading as long as it contributes to organizational effectiveness. As explained below there is a choice of activities and some examples are given of approaches to a major organization development initiative, namely culture change.

Organization development activities

The choice is from activities such as those set out in Table 12.1.

These activities can be combined in many ways so that they become mutually supporting. Ones such as culture change and team building can include traditional OD interventions such as action learning, survey feedback and group dynamics. It can be argued that change management is not a separate organization development activity but is a fundamental part of all such activities. Each of those listed above involves change, which has to be managed using the sort of change management skills described in Chapter 54. The following examples of culture change activities drawn from research conducted by the CIPD (2011) illustrate the range of activities covered under the broad heading culture change:

- *Arts Council England Interventions* focused on the organizational structure, embedding the new values and demonstrating leadership commitment for the culture change.
- *Children's Trust Southampton Interventions* focused on the organization's structure, developing values to support the strategy and structure.
- *London Borough of Barnet Interventions* centred on establishing a Lean team to drive the project. Front-line staff were at the heart of the process, which involves them identifying what's wrong with the service and how things could be improved.
- *National Police Improvements Agency* activities include a restructuring of the top management team, a review of existing processes, the involvement of stakeholders and a focus on retaining respect for past ways of working.
- *NP Paribas* focused activities on the organization's structure, processes, values and the importance of leadership.
- *Visa Europe* established a culture change programme that was called 'peak performance'. The process focused on the individual and helping each individual to recognize how their own values and aspirations could be connected with those of the organization in a mutually beneficial way.

TABLE 12.1 Organization development activities

Organization development activity	Brief description	Objective
Business model innovation	The process followed by an organization to develop a new business model or change an existing one.	To obtain insight into the business issues facing the organization, leading to plans for practical interventions that address those issues.
Change management	The process of planning and introducing change systematically, taking into account the likelihood of it being resisted.	To achieve the smooth implementation of change.
Culture change	The process of changing the organization's culture in the shape of its values, norms and beliefs.	To improve organizational effectiveness – the ability of an organization to achieve its goals by making effective use of the resources available to it.
Engagement, enhancement of	The development of improved levels of job and organizational engagement.	To ensure that people are committed to their work and the organization and motivated to achieve high levels of performance.
High-performance working	Developing work system processes, practices and policies to enable employees to perform to their full potential.	To impact on the performance of the organization through its people in such areas as productivity, quality, levels of customer service, growth and profits.
Knowledge management	Storing and sharing the wisdom, understanding and expertise accumulated in an organization about its processes, techniques and operations.	To get knowledge from those who have it to those who need it in order to improve organizational effectiveness.
Lean	A process improvement methodology that focuses on continuous improvement, reducing waste and ensuring the flow of production.	To deliver value to customers.

TABLE 12.1 Continued

Organization development activity	Brief description	Objective
Organizational learning	The acquisition and development of knowledge, understanding, insights, techniques and practices.	To facilitate performance improvement and major changes in strategic direction.
Organization design	The process of deciding how organizations should be structured in terms of the ways in which the responsibility for carrying out the overall task is allocated to individuals and groups of people and how the relationships between them function.	To ensure that people work effectively together to achieve the overall purpose of the organization.
Performance management	A systematic process involving the agreement of performance expectations and the review of how those expectations have been met.	To improve organizational performance by developing the performance of individuals and teams.
Smart working	An approach to organizing work that through a combination of flexibility, autonomy and collaboration, in parallel with optimizing tools and working environments for employees.	To drive greater efficiency and effectiveness in achieving job outcomes.
Team building	Using interactive skills training techniques to improve the ways in which people in teams work together.	To increase group cohesion, mutual support and cooperation.
Total rewards	The combination of financial and non-financial rewards available to employees. It involves integrating the various aspects of reward.	To blend the financial and non-financial elements of reward into a cohesive whole so that together they make a more powerful and longer-lasting impact on job satisfaction and performance.

Conclusions on organization development

Organization development is no longer solely the preserve of external process consultants with behavioural science backgrounds. Instead it is a territory frequently inhabited by business-oriented people based in the organization and acting, in effect, as internal consultants. They include HR specialists who are there not just because they know about HRM but because they are familiar with how businesses operate and where people management fits in.

The organization development processes with which internal specialists and their colleagues are concerned will be determined by the outcome of diagnostic reviews. Because these outcomes will always be different, organizational development programmes will always be different. There is no such thing as a standard 'OD' approach, as was formerly the case. A number of approaches are available, but which to use and how to use is a matter of choice depending on the facts of the situation. This is why the initial analysis and diagnosis is so important. An analytical toolkit for organization development is provided in Chapter 63.

Key learning points: Organization development

Organization development defined

Organization development in its traditional form as 'OD' was defined by Rowlandson (1984: 90) as 'an intervention strategy that uses group processes to focus on the whole culture of an organization in order to bring about planned change'. The CIPD (2010: 1) defined organization development as a 'planned and systematic approach to enabling sustained organization performance through the involvement of its people'.

Strategic nature of organization development

The strategic nature of organization development as an integral part of HRM arises because it can play a significant role in the implementation of business strategy.

Assumptions and values of OD

The assumptions and values of OD as originally conceived were that:

- Most individuals are driven by the need for personal growth and development as long as their environment is both supportive and challenging.
- The work team, especially at the informal level, has great significance for feelings of satisfaction and the dynamics of such teams have a powerful effect on the behaviour of their members.
- OD programmes aim to improve the quality of working life of all members of the organization.
- Organizations can be more effective if they learn to diagnose their own strengths and weaknesses.
- Managers often do not know what is wrong and need special help in diagnosing problems, although the outside 'process consultant' ensures that decision-making remains in the hands of the client.

OD interventions

OD interventions include process consultation, change management, action research, survey feedback, group dynamics and personal interventions.

Criticisms of OD

The main criticisms of OD, as noted by Marsh *et al* (2010: 143), were that it was 'Oriented to process and tools rather than results... where techniques are considered to be ends in themselves rather than a means to deliver organizational performance.'

Organization development strategy

Organization development strategy is based on the aspiration to improve organizational capability, which is broadly the capacity of an organization to function effectively in order to achieve desired results.

The practice of organization development

The practice of organization development is based on an analysis and diagnosis of the circumstances of the organization, the strategic, operational or process issues that are affecting the organization and its ability to perform well. This involves the use of diagnostic tools.

Organization development programmes

The traditional OD programme was behavioural science-based and almost entirely devoted to interpersonal relationships, organizational processes and culture change in the broadest sense. There may still be a need for such interventions today but the emphasis now is on much more focused activities to do with high-performance working, Lean manufacturing, smart working and the enhancement of levels of engagement.

Questions

1. What was the original concept of organization development?
2. What is an OD intervention?
3. What are the most typical types of interventions?
4. What were the main criticisms made of OD in the 1980s and 1990s?
5. How has the approach to OD altered since then?

References

Argyris, C (1957) *Personality and Organization*, New York, Harper & Row

Anthony, P D (1990) The paradox of managing culture or 'he who leads is lost', *Personnel Review*, 19 (4), pp 3–8

Armstrong, M (1984) *A Handbook of Personnel Management Practice*, 2nd edn, London, Kogan Page

Beckhard, R (1969) *Organization Development: Strategy and models*, Reading, MA, Addison-Wesley

Beer, M (1980) *Organization Change and Development: A systems view*, Santa Monica, CA, Goodyear

Bennis, W G (1969) *Organization Development: Its nature, origin and prospects*, Reading, MA, Addison-Wesley

Buchanan, D and Huczynski, A (2007) *Organizational Behaviour*, Harlow, FT Prentice-Hall

Burke, W W (1995) Organization development: then, now and tomorrow, *Organization Development Journal*, 13 (4), pp 7–17

Caldwell, R (2003) Models of change agency: a fourfold classification, *British Journal of Management*, 14 (2), pp 131–42

Chartered Institute of Personnel and Development (2010) *Organization Development*, London, CIPD

Chartered Institute of Personnel and Development (2011) *Developing Organisation Culture: Six case studies*, London, CIPD

Cooke, R and Lafferty, J (1989) *Organizational Culture Inventory*, Plymouth, MI, Human Synergistic

Cummings, T G and Worley, C G (2005) *Organization Development and Change*, Mason, OH, South Western

Harrison, R (1972) Understanding your organization's character, *Harvard Business Review*, 5, pp 119–28

Herzberg, F, Mausner, B and Snyderman, B (1957) *The Motivation to Work*, New York, Wiley

HR Magazine (2007) Organization development: a strategic HR tool, 52 (9), pp 1–10

Koys, D and De Cotiis, T (1991) Inductive measures of organizational climate, *Human Relations*, 44, pp 265–85

Legge, K (1995) *Human Resource Management: Rhetorics and realities*, London, Macmillan

Lewin, K (1947) Frontiers in group dynamics, *Human Relations*, 1 (1), pp 5–42

Lewin, K (1951) *Field Theory in Social Science*, New York, Harper & Row

Likert, R (1961) *New Patterns of Management*, New York, Harper & Row

Manzini, A O (1988) *Organizational Diagnosis*, New York, AMACOM

Marsh, C, Sparrow, P and Hird, M (2010) Improving organization design: The new priority for HR directors, in (eds) P Sparrow, A Hesketh, M Hird and C Cooper, *Leading HR*, Basingstoke, Palgrave Macmillan, pp 136–61

Maslow, A (1954) *Motivation and Personality*, New York, Harper & Row

Mayo, E (1933) *The Human Problems of an Industrial Civilisation*, London, Macmillan

McGregor, D (1960) *The Human Side of Enterprise*, New York, McGraw-Hill

McLean, A (1981) Organization development: a case of the emperor's new clothes?, *Personnel Review*, 4 (1), pp 3–14

Roethlisberger, F and Dickson, W (1939) *Management and the Worker*, Cambridge, MA, Harvard University Press

Rowlandson, P (1984) The oddity of OD, *Management Today*, November, pp 91–93

Ruona, W E A and Gibson, S K (2004) The making of twenty-first century HR: the convergence of HRM, HRD and OD, *Human Resource Management*, 43 (1), pp 49–66

Strauss, G (1976) Organization development, in (ed) R Dubin, Handbook of Work, *Organization and Society*, Chicago, IL, Rand MacNally

Ulrich, D and Lake, D (1990) *Organizational Capability: Competing from the inside out*, New York, Wiley

Weidner, C K (2004) A brand in dire straits: organization development at sixty, *Organization Development Journal*, 22 (2), pp 37–47

Worley, C, Hitchin, D and Ross, W (1996) *Integrated Strategic Change: How organization development builds competitive advantage*, Reading, MA, Addison-Wesley

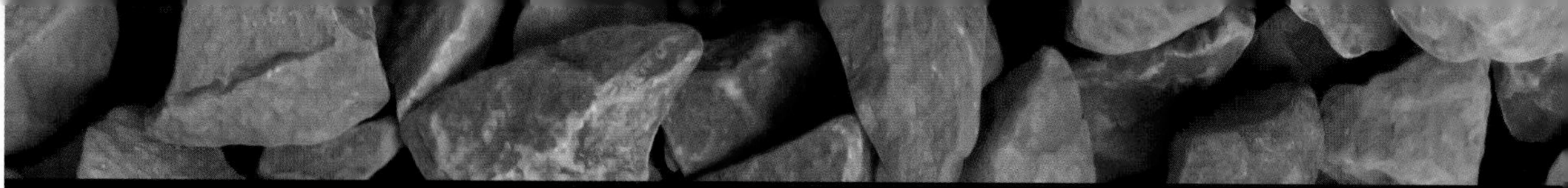

PART III

Factors affecting employee behaviour

PART III CONTENTS

Introduction

A preoccupation shared by all those involved in managing people is how to get the best out of them. 'The best' may be difficult to define. It could be high performance. Or it could be discretionary behaviour (the choice made by people to exercise additional effort, care, innovation and productive behaviour in their jobs). It could be doing more than is contracted for so that the words 'it's not in my job description' or 'this is above my pay grade' are seldom if ever heard. It could be cooperating fully with managers and colleagues or showing loyalty to the organization. It could be any combination of these.

Getting the best out of people is primarily the responsibility of managers and team leaders by exercising effective leadership. But it is also the concern of HR specialists who can help to create a work environment conducive to high performance and can introduce policies and practices that encourage people to do everything expected of them if not more. HR can also provide any advice and help managers to fulfil their people management responsibilities.

To do this, managers and HR specialists need to take into account the general factors that affect how people behave at work, as described in Chapter 10 – namely, ability, intelligence, personality, attitudes, emotions and emotional intelligence. But they should also be aware of the following more specific factors that influence behaviour and therefore performance:

- *Motivation* – the strength and direction of behaviour and the factors that influence people to behave in certain ways.
- *Commitment* – the strength of an individual's identification with, and involvement in, an organization.
- *Engagement* – a situation in which people are committed to their work and the organization and are motivated to achieve high levels of performance.

These are examined in the three chapters of this part.

Of the three constructs (a construct is a conceptual framework that explains how people perceive and react to their environment), motivation is a longstanding one that has been extensively researched and written about since the earlier part of the 20th century. Motivation theory has been used and is still used to inform decisions on how to get more effort and better performance from employees, for example the use of performance-related pay. The importance of the construct of commitment emerged later, notably in the contribution of Richard Walton (1985) whose seminal article in the *Harvard Business Review* advocated the adoption of a commitment strategy rather than one based on control. The most recent construct is that of engagement, which was first presented in a 1990 *Academy of Management Journal* article by William Kahn. He defined engagement as 'the harnessing of organization members' selves to their work roles' (1990: 694).

The construct of engagement contains elements of motivation and commitment, as explained in Chapter 14. It also embraces the notion of organizational citizenship behaviour (OCB), which is positive discretionary behaviour at work that goes beyond role requirements. The relationships between engagement, motivation and OCB are considered in Chapter 15.

However, it is difficult to disentangle the concepts of motivation, commitment and engagement, although an attempt to do so is made in the three chapters of this part. Simplistically, it could be argued that when motivation is extrinsic, ie when things are done to or for people in order to motivate them, such as through pay or recognition, the aim is to make a direct impact on individual performance. In contrast, both commitment and engagement are states of being that can be affected by managerial actions. They are not so direct or immediate as the direct instruments used in the motivation strategies aimed at individuals. Engagement and commitment strategies may be more about taking action that affects employees collectively such as improvements in the work environment.

Three other aspects of the behaviour of people at work are considered in this part. The first of these is job satisfaction, ie the attitudes and feelings that people have about their jobs. This is associated with motivation and engagement but it could be regarded as an outcome of engagement rather than a constituent of it. Whether or not job satisfaction improves performance is considered in Chapters 13 and 15. Second, the relationship between money and motivation is examined in Chapter 13. This is important because it affects policies and practices concerned with the use of pay as an incentive or reward. Third, reference is made in Chapter 15 to the dark side of engagement – burnout – how it happens and what can be done about it.

References

Kahn, W A (1990) Psychological conditions of personal engagement and disengagement at work, *Academy of Management Journal*, 33 (4), pp 692–724

Walton, R E (1985) From control to commitment in the workplace, *Harvard Business Review*, March–April, pp 77–84

13 Motivation

KEY CONCEPTS AND TERMS

Cognitive evaluation
Content (needs) motivation theory
Discretionary behaviour
Discretionary effort
Equity theory
Expectancy theory
Extrinsic motivation
Goal theory
Herzberg's two-factor model of motivation
Intrinsic motivation
Instrumentality
Job characteristics model
Job satisfaction
Law of effect
Line of sight
Management by objectives

LEARNING OUTCOMES

On completing this chapter you should be able to define these key concepts. You should also understand:

- The meaning of motivation
- Types of motivation
- The different motivation theories
- Motivation and job satisfaction
- Approaches to developing a motivation strategy

Introduction

Motivation is the force that energizes, directs and sustains behaviour. High performance is achieved by well-motivated people who are prepared to exercise discretionary effort, ie independently do more than is expected of them. Even in fairly basic roles, Hunter *et al* (1990) found through their research that the difference in value-added discretionary performance between 'superior' and 'standard' performers was 19 per cent. For highly complex jobs it was 48 per cent. The aims of this chapter are to explore the meaning of motivation, define the two main types of motivation – intrinsic and extrinsic, describe and critically evaluate the main theories of motivation, discuss two related aspects of motivation – its relationship to job satisfaction and money, and outline approaches to motivation strategy.

The meaning of motivation

The term 'motivation' derives from the Latin word for movement (*movere*). A motive is a reason for doing something. Motivation is the strength and direction of behaviour and the factors that influence people to behave in certain ways. People are motivated when they expect that a course of action is likely to lead to the attainment of a goal and a valued reward – one that satisfies their needs and wants. The term 'motivation' can refer variously to the goals that individuals have, the ways in which individuals chose their goals and the ways in which others try to change their behaviour. Locke and Latham (2004: 388) observed that: 'The concept of motivation refers to internal factors that impel action and to external factors that can act as inducements to action.'

As described by Arnold *et al* (1991) the three components of motivation are:

1. *Direction* – what a person is trying to do.
2. *Effort* – how hard a person is trying.
3. *Persistence* – how long a person keeps on trying.

Well-motivated people engage in positive discretionary behaviour – they decide to make an effort. Such people may be self-motivated, and as long as this means they are going in the right direction to attain what they are there to achieve, then this is the best form of motivation. But additional motivation provided by the work itself, the quality of leadership, and various forms of recognition and reward, builds on self-motivation and helps people to make the best use of their abilities and to perform well.

There are two types of motivation and a number of theories explaining how it works, as discussed below.

Types of motivation

Intrinsic motivation

Intrinsic motivation takes place when individuals feel that their work is important, interesting and challenging and that it provides them with a reasonable degree of autonomy (freedom to act), opportunities to achieve and advance, and scope to use and develop their skills and abilities. It can be described as motivation by the work itself. It is not created by external incentives. Deci and Ryan (1985) suggested that intrinsic motivation is based on the need to be competent and self-determining (that is, to have a choice). Michael Sandel (2012: 122) remarked that: 'When people are engaged in an activity they consider intrinsically worthwhile, offering money may weaken their motivation by "crowding out" their intrinsic interest or commitment'.

Intrinsic motivation can be enhanced by job design. Katz (1964) suggested that jobs should in themselves provide sufficient variety, complexity, challenge and skill to engage the abilities of the worker. Hackman and Oldham (1974) in their job characteristics model identified the five core characteristics of jobs that result in intrinsic motivation, namely: skill variety, task identity, task significance, autonomy and feedback. Pink (2009) stated that there are three steps that managers can take to improve motivation:

1. *Autonomy* – encourage people to set their own schedule and focus on getting work done not how it is done.
2. *Mastery* – help people to identify the steps they can take to improve and ask them to identify how they will know they are making progress.
3. *Purpose* – when giving instructions explain the *why* as well as the *how*.

Intrinsic motivation is associated with the concept of engagement, as explained in Chapter 15.

Extrinsic motivation

Extrinsic motivation occurs when things are done to or for people in order to motivate them. These include rewards such as incentives, increased pay, praise or promotion; and punishments such as disciplinary action, withholding pay, or criticism.

Extrinsic motivators can have an immediate and powerful effect, but it will not necessarily last long. The intrinsic motivators, which are concerned with the 'quality of working life' (a phrase and movement that emerged from this concept), are likely to have a deeper and longer-term effect because they are inherent in individuals and the work – and are not imposed from outside in such forms as incentive pay.

Motivation theory as described below explains the ways in which intrinsic and extrinsic motivation take place.

Motivation theory

As mentioned by Steers *et al* (2004: 379) the earliest approaches to understanding human motivation date from the time of the Greek philosophers and focus on the concept of hedonism as a principle driving force in behaviour. Individuals were seen as directing their efforts to seeking pleasure and avoiding pain. This principle was later refined and further developed in the works of philosophers such as John Locke and Jeremy Bentham in the 17th and 18th centuries. Motivation theory has moved on from then. It started in the earlier part of the 20th century with the contributions of the exponents of scientific management (instrumentality theory). In the middle years of that century the behavioural scientists entered the field and began to develop the 'content' or 'needs' theory of motivation. The main process theories such as expectancy theory emerged in the in the 1960s and 70s, although the first formulation of the process theory of reinforcement took place in 1911. The three main areas of motivation theory – instrumentality, content and process – are examined below.

Instrumentality theory

Instrumentality theory states in effect that rewards and punishments are the best instruments with which to shape behaviour. It assumes that people will be motivated to work if rewards and penalties are tied directly to their performance; thus the awards are contingent upon effective performance. Instrumentality theory has its roots in the scientific management methods of Taylor (1911: 121) who wrote: 'It is impossible, through any long period of time, to get workmen to work much harder than the average men around them unless they are assured a large and a permanent increase in their pay.'

This theory provides a rationale for financial incentives such as performance-related pay, albeit a dubious one. Motivation using this approach has been and still is widely adopted. It may be successful in some circumstances, eg piece work, but – for reasons explained in Chapter 27 – merit or performance pay is flawed.

Instrumentality theory relies exclusively on a system of external controls and does not recognize a number of other human needs. It also fails to appreciate the fact that the formal control system can be seriously affected by the informal relationship existing between workers.

Content theory

The aim of the content or needs theories produced by Maslow, Alderfer, McClelland, Herzberg, and Deci and Ryan was to identify the factors associated with motivation. The theory focuses on the content of motivation in the shape of needs. Its basis is the belief that an unsatisfied need creates tension and a state of disequilibrium. To restore the balance a goal is identified that will satisfy the need, and a behaviour pathway is selected that will lead to the achievement of the goal and the satisfaction of the need. Behaviour is therefore motivated by unsatisfied needs. A content theory model is shown in Figure 13.1. Content theory, as the term implies, indicates the components of motivation but it does not explain how motivation affects performance – a necessary requirement if the concept is to provide guidance on HR policy and practice. This was the role of expectancy theory, as will be discussed later.

Maslow's hierarchy of needs

The most famous classification of needs is the one formulated by Maslow (1954). He suggested that there are five major need categories that apply to people in general, starting from the fundamental physiological needs and leading through a hierarchy of safety, social and esteem needs to the need for self-fulfilment, the highest need of all. When a lower need is satisfied the next highest becomes dominant and the individual's attention is turned to satisfying this higher need. The need for self-fulfilment, however, can never be satisfied. 'Man is a wanting animal'; only an unsatisfied need can motivate behaviour and the dominant need is the prime motivator of behaviour. Psychological development takes place as people move up the hierarchy of needs, but this is not necessarily a straightforward progression. The lower needs still exist, even if temporarily dormant as motivators, and individuals constantly return to previously satisfied needs.

Maslow's needs hierarchy has an intuitive appeal and has been very popular. But it has not been verified by empirical research such as that conducted by Wahba and Bridwell (1979), and it has been criticized for its apparent rigidity – different people may have different priorities and the underpinning assumption

FIGURE 13.1 The process of motivation according to content theory

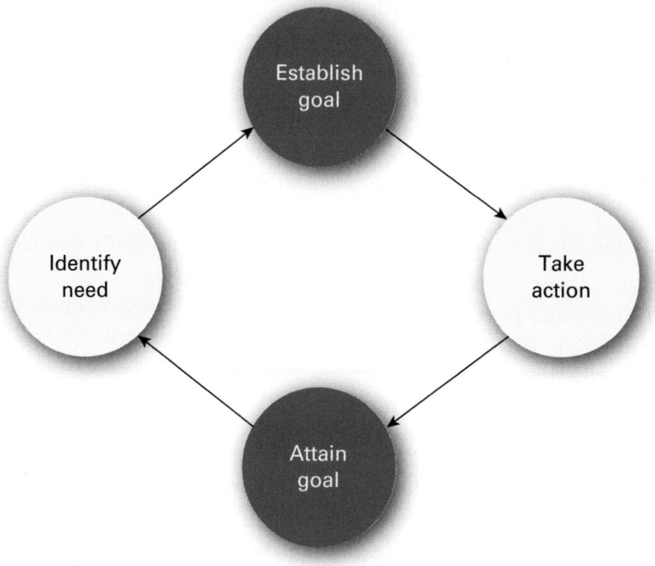

that everyone has the same needs is invalid. It is difficult to accept that needs progress steadily up the hierarchy and Maslow himself expressed doubts about the validity of a strictly ordered hierarchy. But he did emphasize that the higher-order needs are more significant.

ERG theory (Alderfer)

Alderfer (1972) produced a more convincing and simpler theory, which postulated three primary categories of needs:

1. *Existence needs* such as hunger and thirst – pay, fringe benefits and working conditions are other types of existence needs.
2. *Relatedness needs*, which acknowledge that people are not self-contained units but must engage in transactions with their human environment – acceptance, understanding, confirmation and influence are elements of the relatedness process.
3. *Growth needs*, which involve people in finding the opportunities to be what they are most fully and to become what they can. This is the most significant need.

McClelland's achievement motivation

An alternative way of classifying needs was developed by McClelland (1961), who based it mainly on studies of managers. He identified three needs of which the need for achievement was the most important:

1. The need for *achievement*, defined as the need for competitive success measured against a personal standard of excellence.
2. The need for affiliation, defined as the need for warm, friendly, compassionate relationships with others.
3. The need for *power*, defined as the need to control or influence others.

Herzberg's two-factor model

The two-factor model of motivation developed by Herzberg (1957, 1966) was based on an investigation into the sources of job satisfaction and dissatisfaction of accountants and engineers who were asked what made them feel exceptionally good or exceptionally bad about their jobs. According to Herzberg, this research established that there were two factors that affected feelings of satisfaction or dissatisfaction. Motivating factors or 'satisfiers' relate to the job content and consist of the need for achievement, the interest of the work, responsibility and opportunities for advancement. These needs are the intrinsic motivators. He summed this up in the phrase 'motivation by the work itself'.

Hygiene factors relate to the job context, including such things as pay and working conditions. 'Hygiene' is used in the medical use of the term, meaning preventative and environmental. In themselves hygiene factors neither satisfy nor motivate and they serve primarily to prevent job dissatisfaction, while having little effect on positive job attitudes. Pay is not a satisfier but if it is inadequate or inequitable it can cause dissatisfaction. However, its provision does not provide lasting satisfaction.

Herzberg's two-factor theory in effect identifies needs but it has been attacked by, for example, Opsahl and Dunnette (1966). The research method has been criticized because no attempt was made to measure the relationship between satisfaction and performance. It has been claimed that the two-factor nature of the theory is an inevitable result of the questioning method used by the interviewers. It has also been suggested that wide and unwarranted inferences have been drawn from small and specialized samples and that there is no evidence to suggest that the satisfiers do improve productivity. The underpinning assumption that everyone has the same needs is invalid. Denise Rousseau (2006: 263) in her presidential address to the US Academy of Management summed up these views as follows: 'Herzberg's long discredited two-factor theory is typically included in the motivation section of management textbooks, despite the fact that it was discredited as an artefact of method bias over thirty years ago.'

In spite of these objections, the Herzberg two-factor theory continues to thrive; partly because it is easy to understand and seems to be based on real-life rather than academic abstractions, and partly because it convincingly emphasizes the positive value of the intrinsic motivating factors and highlights the need to consider both financial and non-financial factors when developing reward systems. It is also in accord with a fundamental belief in the dignity of labour and the Protestant ethic – that work is good in itself. Herzberg's strength as a proselytizer rather than a researcher meant that he had considerable influence on the job enrichment movement, which sought to design jobs in a way that would maximize the opportunities to obtain intrinsic satisfaction from work and thus improve the quality of working life. Herzberg famously remarked that if you want people to do a good job then give them a good job to do (quoted by Dowling, 1971).

Self-determination theory

As formulated by Deci and Ryan (2000) this theory states that individuals are motivated by the need to achieve three fundamental goals: striving for competence, autonomy and relatedness.

Comment on content theories

Shields (2007: 74) observed that content theories share some common shortcomings. His criticisms were that they incorrectly assume:

- the existence of a universally applicable set of human needs;
- that according to Maslow (1954), needs conform to a simple ordered hierarchy of need importance, when in reality, needs seem to operate in a more flexible, less ordered and predictable way;
- that the link between needs and behaviours is direct and automatic, rather than mediated by human consciousness, values and choice.

In addition, he pointed out that content theories 'underestimate the motivational potency of extrinsic rewards, including financial rewards'.

Process theory

In process theory, the emphasis is on the psychological or mental processes and forces that affect motivation, as well as on basic needs. It is also known as cognitive theory because it refers to people's perceptions of their working environment and the ways in which they interpret and understand it. The main process theories are concerned with reinforcement, expectancy, goals, equity, and cognitive evaluation.

Reinforcement theory

This is the oldest and least complex of the process theories. It is based on 'the law of effect' as formulated by Thorndike (1911), which states that over time people learn about the relationships between their actions and the consequences of them and this understanding guides their future behaviour. In other words, if they believe that something has worked previously then they will do it again. It was later developed by Hull (1943, 1951).

Skinner (1953) and others later built on these principles with the notion of 'operant conditioning', which was influenced by the work of Pavlov and his salivating dogs. As Shields (2007: 76) put it: 'Positive reinforcement of desired behaviour elicits more of the same; punishment of undesired behaviour (negative reinforcement) elicits less of the same.' Reinforcement models continue to thrive today as explanatory vehicles for understanding work motivation and job performance, and as a justification of performance pay.

But reinforcement theory can be criticized for taking an unduly mechanistic view of human nature. It implies that people can be motivated by treating them as machines – by pulling levers. In assuming that the present choices of individuals are based on an understanding of the outcomes of their past choices, reinforcement theory ignores the existing context in which choices are made. In addition, motivational theories based on the principle of reinforcement pay insufficient attention to the influence of expectations – no indication is given of how to distinguish in advance which outcomes would strengthen responses and which would weaken them. Above all, they are limited because they imply, in Allport's (1954) vivid phrase, a hedonism of the past.

Expectancy theory

Expectancy theory states that motivation will be high when people know what they have to do in order to get a reward, expect that they will be able to get the reward and expect that the reward will be worthwhile.

The concept of expectancy was originally contained in the valency-instrumentality-expectancy (VIE) theory that was formulated by Vroom (1964). Valency stands for value; instrumentality is the belief that if we do one thing it will lead to another; and expectancy is the probability that action or effort will lead to an outcome.

The strength of expectations may be based on past experiences (reinforcement), but individuals are frequently presented with new situations – a change in job, payment system, or working conditions imposed by management – where past experience is an inadequate guide to the implications of the change. In these circumstances, motivation may be reduced.

Motivation is only likely when a clearly perceived and usable relationship exists between performance and outcome, and the outcome is seen as a means of satisfying needs. This explains why extrinsic financial motivation – for example, an incentive or bonus scheme – works only if the link (line of sight) between effort and reward is clear and the value of the reward is worth the effort. It also explains why intrinsic motivation arising from the work itself can be more powerful than extrinsic motivation. Intrinsic motivation outcomes are more under the control of individuals, who can place greater reliance on their past experiences to indicate the extent to which positive and advantageous results are likely to be obtained by their behaviour.

This theory was developed by Porter and Lawler (1968) into a model shown in Figure 13.2, which follows Vroom's ideas by suggesting that there are two factors determining the effort that people put into their jobs: first, the value of the rewards to individuals in so far as they satisfy their needs for security, social esteem, autonomy and self-actualization; second, the probability that rewards depend on effort, as perceived by individuals – in other words, their expectations about the relationships between effort and reward. Thus, the greater the value of a set of awards and the higher the probability that receiving each of these rewards depends upon effort, the greater the effort that will be put forth in a given situation.

But, as Porter and Lawler emphasized, mere effort is not enough. It has to be effective effort if it is to produce the desired performance. The two variables additional to effort that affect task achievement are: 1) ability – individual characteristics such as intelligence, knowledge, skills; 2) role perceptions – what the individual wants to do or thinks they are required to do. These are good from the viewpoint of the organization if they correspond with what it thinks the individual ought to be doing. They are poor if the views of the individual and the organization do not coincide.

Alongside goal theory (see below), expectancy theory has become the most influential motivation theory, particularly as it affects performance and

FIGURE 13.2 Motivation model (Porter and Lawler, 1968)

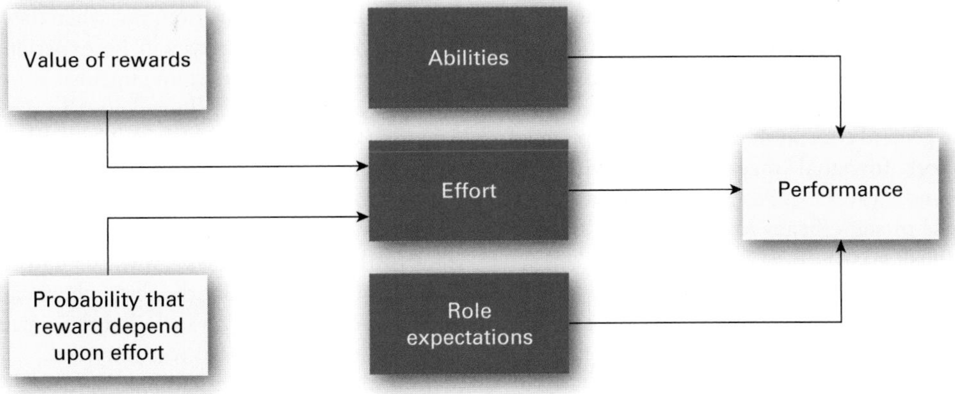

reward management. But reservations have been expressed about it. House *et al* (1974) remarked that: 'Evidence for the validity of the theory is very mixed.' They also established that there were a number of variables affecting expectations that make it difficult to predict how they function. These are:

- Leadership behaviour – the function of the leader in clarifying expectations, guiding, supporting and rewarding subordinates.
- Individual characteristics – the subjects' perception of their ability to perform the required task.
- Nature of the task – whether accomplishing the task provides the necessary reinforcements and rewards.
- The practices of the organization – its reward and control systems and how it functions.

Research conducted by Behling and Starke (1973) established that individuals:

- make crucial personal decisions without clearly understanding the consequences;
- do not in practice consistently evaluate their order of preference for alternative actions;
- have to assign two values when making a decision – its desirability and its achievability – but they tend to be influenced mainly by desirability – they let their tastes influence their beliefs;
- may be able to evaluate the extrinsic rewards they expect but may find it difficult to evaluate the possibility of achieving intrinsic rewards;
- may find it difficult to distinguish the benefits of one possible outcome from another.

They concluded that: 'Expectancy theory can account for some of the variations in work effort but far less than normally attributed to it' (ibid 386).

Shields (2007: 80) commented that a problem with expectancy theory is that it assumes that 'behaviour is rational and premeditated when we know that much workplace behaviour is impulsive and emotional'.

However, in spite of these objections, the simple message of expectancy theory – that people will be motivated if they expect that their behaviour will produce a worthwhile reward – is compelling. And it provides a useful tool to assess the effectiveness of motivating devices such as performance-related pay.

Goal theory

Goal theory as developed by Latham and Locke (1979) following their research states that motivation and performance are higher when individuals are set specific goals, when goals are demanding but accepted, and when there is feedback on performance. Goals must be clearly defined. Participation in goal setting is important as a means of getting agreement to the setting of demanding goals. Feedback is vital in maintaining motivation, particularly towards the achievement of even higher goals.

However, the universality of goal theory has been questioned. For example, Pintrich (2000) noted that people have different goals in different circumstances and that it is hard to justify the assumption that goals are always accessible and conscious. And Harackiewicz *et al* (2002) warned that goals are only effective when they are consistent with and match the general context in which they are pursued. But support for goal theory was provided by Bandura and Cervone (1983) who emphasized the importance of self-efficacy (a belief in one's ability to accomplish goals).

Equity theory

Equity theory, as defined by Adams (1965), is concerned with the perceptions people have about how they are being treated as compared with others. He proposed that employees assess the fairness or otherwise of their rewards (outcomes) in relation to their effort or qualifications (inputs) and that they do this by comparing their own input/output ratio against that of other individuals. If the input/output ratio is perceived to be unfavourable, they will feel that there is reward inequity.

Equity theory explains only one aspect of the processes of motivation and job satisfaction, although it may be significant in terms of morale and, possibly, of performance.

Social learning theory

Social learning theory as developed by Bandura (1977) combines aspects of both reinforcement and expectancy theory. It recognizes the significance of the basic behavioural concept of reinforcement as a determinant of future behaviour but also emphasizes the importance of internal psychological factors, especially expectancies about the value of goals and the individual's ability to reach them. The term 'reciprocal determinism' is used to denote the concept that while the situation will affect individual behaviour individuals will simultaneously influence the situation.

Cognitive evaluation theory

Cognitive evaluation theory contends that the use of extrinsic rewards may destroy the intrinsic motivation that flows from inherent job interest. It was formulated by Deci and Ryan (1985). Referring to their research, they stated that: 'Rewards, like feedback, when used to convey to people a sense of appreciation for work well done, will tend to be experienced informationally and will maintain or enhance intrinsic motivation. But when they are used to motivate people, they will be experienced controllingly and will undermine intrinsic motivation.'

Deci *et al* (1999) followed up this research by carrying out a meta-analysis of 128 experiments on rewards and intrinsic motivation to establish the extent to which intrinsic motivation was undermined by rewards. The results of the study indicated that for high-interest tasks, rewards had significant negative effects on what the researchers called 'free-choice measures', which included the time spent on the task after the reward was removed.

But as noted by Gerhart and Rynes (2003: 52): 'The vast majority of research on this theory has been performed in school rather than work settings, often with elementary school-aged children.' But that did not stop other commentators assuming that the results were equally significant for working adults. It is interesting to note that research in industry conducted by Deci and Ryan (1985), while it found that financial incentives did decrease intrinsic motivation in high-control organizational cultures, also established that in organizations with the opposite high-involvement culture, intrinsic and extrinsic motivation were both increased by monetary incentives. Context is all important. Moreover, a meta-analysis of 145 studies conducted by Cameron *et al* (2001) led to the conclusion that rewards do not inevitably have negative effects on intrinsic motivation.

Purposeful work behaviour

A more recent integrated motivation theory formulated by Barrick and Mount (2013) focused on the impact on motivation of individual factors, such as personality and ability, and situational factors, such as job characteristics. The motivation to engage in purposeful work behaviour depends on both these factors.

Comment on process theories

Process theories are not based on suspect assumptions about the universality of needs, as are content theories. Process theories emphasize the importance of individual decision-making on work behaviour. As pointed out by Shields (2007: 85) They 'acknowledge the importance of social and job context as co-determinants of motivational strength while those other than reinforcement theory also highlight the importance of self-efficacy, task or goal clarity and motivational learning'.

Summary of motivation theories

A summary of motivation theories is set out in Table 13.1.

Conclusions on motivation theory

All the theories referred to above make some contribution to an understanding of the processes that affect motivation. But instrumentality theory provides only a simplistic explanation of how motivation works. Needs and content theories are more sophisticated but have their limitations. As Gerhart and Rynes (2003: 53) commented:

> Although the ideas developed by Maslow, Herzberg and Deci have had considerable appeal to many people, the prevailing view in the academic literature is that the specific predictions of these theories is not supported by empirical evidence. On the other hand it would be a mistake to underestimate the influence that these theories have had on research and practice. Pfeffer, Kohn and others continue to base their argument regarding the ineffectiveness of money as a motivator on such theories.

But, bearing in mind the reservations set out earlier, needs theory still offers an indication of the factors that motivate people and content theory provides useful explanations of how motivation takes place. And while instrumentality and reinforcement theories may be simplistic they still explain some aspects of how rewards affect motivation and performance and they continue to exert influence on the beliefs of some people about the power of incentives to motivate people. Herzberg's research may be flawed but he still contributed to the recognition of the importance of job design.

Motivation theory can explain what makes people tick at work but it is also necessary to consider two other aspects of the impact of motivation – its relationship with job satisfaction and the effect of money on motivation. Strategies for motivation based on the lessons learnt from motivation theory are considered at the end of this chapter.

Motivation and job satisfaction

Job satisfaction can be defined as the attitudes and feelings people have about their work. Positive and favourable attitudes towards the job indicate job satisfaction. Negative and unfavourable attitudes towards the job indicate job dissatisfaction. It can be distinguished from morale, which is a group rather than individual variable, related to the degree to which group members feel attracted to their group and want to remain a member of it.

The factors that affect job satisfaction

Levels of job satisfaction or dissatisfaction are influenced by:

- *The intrinsic motivating factors*. These relate to job content, especially the five dimensions of jobs identified by Hackman and Oldham (1974): skill variety, task identity, task significance, autonomy and feedback (the job characteristics model).
- *The quality of supervision*. The Hawthorne studies (Roethlisberger and Dixon, 1939) resulted in the claim that supervision is the most important determinant of worker attitudes. Elton Mayo (1933) believed that a man's desire to be continuously associated in work with his fellows is a strong, if not the strongest human characteristic.
- *Success or failure*. Success obviously creates satisfaction, especially if it enables individuals to prove to themselves that they are using their abilities to the full. And it is equally obvious that the reverse is true of failure.

Job satisfaction and performance

It is a commonly held and not unreasonable belief that an increase in job satisfaction results in improved performance. The whole human relations movement led by Mayo (1933) and supported by the Roethlisberger and Dixon (1939) research was

TABLE 13.1 Summary of motivation theories

Category	Theory	Summary of theory	Implications
Instrumentality	Taylorism Taylor (1911)	If we do one thing it leads to another. People will be motivated to work if rewards and punishments are directly related to their performance.	Basis of crude attempts to motivate people by incentives. Often used as the implied rationale for performance-related pay although this is seldom an effective motivator.
Content or needs	Hierarchy of needs Maslow (1954)	A hierarchy of needs exists: physiological, safety, social, esteem, self-fulfilment. Needs at a higher level only emerge when a lower need is satisfied.	Focuses attention on the various needs that motivate people and the notion that a satisfied need is no longer a motivator. The concept of a hierarchy has no practical significance.
	ERG Alderfer (1972)	A non-hierarchical theory identifying three basic needs: existence, relatedness and growth.	A simpler and more convincing categorization of needs.
	Achievement motivation McClelland (1961)	Identified three needs for managers: achievement, affiliation and power. Of these, achievement is the most important.	Emphasized the importance to managers of achievement as a motivating factor.
	Two-factor model Herzberg (1957, 1966)	Two groups of factors affect job satisfaction: 1) those intrinsic to the work itself; 2) those extrinsic to the job such as pay and working conditions. The factors that affect positive feelings (the motivating factors) are quite different from those that affect negative feelings (the hygiene factors).	The research methodology has been strongly criticized (it does not support the existence of two factors) and the underpinning assumption that everyone has the same needs is invalid. But it has influenced approaches to job design (job enrichment) and it supports the proposition that reward systems should provide for both financial and non-financial rewards.
	Self-determination Deci and Ryan (2000)	Individuals are motivated to achieve three fundamental goals: striving for competence, autonomy, and relatedness.	Provides an alternative and simpler classification of needs.

TABLE 13.1 Continued

Category	Theory	Summary of theory	Implications
Process	Reinforcement Thorndike (1911) Skinner (1953)	As experience is gained in satisfying needs, people perceive that certain actions help to achieve goals while others are unsuccessful. The successful actions are repeated when a similar need arises.	Provide feedback that positively reinforces effective behaviour.
	Expectancy Vroom (1964) Porter and Lawler (1968)	Effort (motivation) depends on the likelihood that rewards will follow effort and that the reward is worthwhile.	The key theory informing approaches to rewards, ie that they must be a link between effort and reward (line of sight), the reward should be achievable and it should be worthwhile.
	Goal Lathom and Locke (1979)	Motivation will improve if people have demanding but agreed goals and receive feedback	Influences performance management and learning and development practices.
	Equity Adams (1966)	People are better motivated if treated equitably, ie treated fairly in comparison with another group of people (a reference group) or a relevant other person.	Need to have equitable reward and employment practices.
	Social learning Bandura (1977)	Recognizes the significance of reinforcement as a determinant of future behaviour but also emphasizes the importance of expectancies about the value of goals and the individual's ability to reach them.	The emphasis is on expectancies, individual goals and values and the influence of both person and situational factors as well as reinforcement.
	Cognitive evaluation Deci and Ryan (1985)	The use of extrinsic rewards may destroy the intrinsic motivation that flows from inherent job interest.	Emphasizes the importance of non-financial rewards. The conclusions reached from Deci and Ryan's research have been questioned.

based on the belief that productivity could be increased by making workers more satisfied, primarily through pleasant and supportive supervision and by meeting their social needs. But research by Katz *et al* (1950) and Katz *et al* (1951) found that the levels of satisfaction with pay, job status or fellow workers in high productivity units were no different to those in low productivity units.

Meta-analysis by Brayfield and Crocket (1955) of a number of studies concluded that there was little evidence of any simple or appreciable relationship between satisfaction and performance. A later review of research by Vroom (1964) found that the median correlation between job satisfaction and job performance for all these studies was only 0.14, which is not high enough to suggest any marked relationship between them. Spector (1997) came to the same conclusion. Indeed, it can be argued that it is not increases in satisfaction that produce improved performance but improved performance that increases satisfaction. This was confirmed by data on the link between job satisfaction and performance for 177 store managers, analysed by Christen *et al* (2006). It was established that store managers' performance increased their job satisfaction but that job satisfaction had no impact on job performance.

Motivation and money

Money, in the form of pay or some other sort of remuneration, is regarded by many people as the most obvious extrinsic reward. Money seems to provide the carrot that most people want.

Doubts were cast on the effectiveness of money by Herzberg (1968), which although unsupported by his research have some degree of face validity. He claimed that while the lack of money can cause dissatisfaction, its provision does not result in lasting satisfaction. There is something in this, especially for people on fixed salaries or rates of pay who do not benefit directly from an incentive scheme. They may feel good when they get an increase; apart from the extra money, it is a highly tangible form of recognition and an effective means of helping people to feel that they are valued. But this feeling of euphoria can rapidly die away. Other causes of dissatisfaction from Herzberg's list of hygiene factors, such as working conditions or the quality of management, can loom larger in some people's minds when they fail to get the satisfaction they need from the work itself. However, it must be re-emphasized that different people have different needs and wants. Some will be much more motivated by money than others. What cannot be assumed is that money motivates everyone in the same way and to the same extent. Thus it is naive to think that the introduction of a performance-related pay scheme will miraculously transform everyone overnight into well-motivated, high-performing individuals.

Nevertheless, money is a powerful force because it is linked directly or indirectly to the satisfaction of many needs. Money may in itself have no intrinsic meaning, but it acquires significant motivating power because it comes to symbolize so many intangible goals. It acts as a symbol in different ways for different people, and for the same person at different times.

But do financial incentives motivate people? The answer is yes, for those people who are strongly motivated by money and whose expectations are that they will receive a worthwhile financial reward. But less confident employees may not respond to incentives that they do not expect to achieve. It can also be argued that extrinsic rewards may erode intrinsic interest – people who work just for money could find their tasks less pleasurable and may not, therefore, do them so well. What we do know is that a multiplicity of factors is involved in performance improvements and many of those factors are interdependent.

Money can therefore provide positive motivation in the right circumstances not only because people need and want money but also because it serves as a highly tangible means of recognition. But badly designed and managed pay systems can demotivate. Another researcher in this area was Jaques (1961), who emphasized the need for such systems to be perceived as being fair and equitable. In other words, the reward should be clearly related to effort or level of responsibility and people should not receive less money than they deserve compared with their fellow workers. Jaques called this the 'felt-fair' principle.

Motivation strategies

Motivation strategies aim to create a working environment and to develop policies and practices that will provide for higher levels of performance from employees. The factors affecting them and the HR contribution are summarized in Table 13.2.

TABLE 13.2 Factors affecting motivation strategies and the HR contribution

Factors affecting motivation strategies	The HR contribution
The complexity of the process of motivation means that simplistic approaches based on instrumentality or needs theory are unlikely to be successful.	Avoid the trap of developing or supporting strategies that offer prescriptions for motivation based on a simplistic view of the process or fail to recognize individual differences.
People are more likely to be motivated if they work in an environment in which they are valued for what they are and what they do. This means paying attention to the basic need for recognition.	Encourage the development of performance management processes that provide opportunities to agree expectations and to recognize accomplishments.
Extrinsic motivators such as incentive pay can have an immediate and powerful effect, but it will not necessarily last long. The intrinsic motivators, which are concerned with the 'quality of working life' (a phrase and movement that emerged from this concept), are likely to have a deeper and longer-term effect because they are inherent in individuals and the work they do and not imposed from outside in such forms as performance-related pay.	Develop total reward systems that provide opportunities for both financial and non-financial rewards to recognize achievements. Bear in mind, however, that financial rewards systems are not necessarily appropriate and the lessons of expectancy, goal and equity theory need to be taken into account in designing and operating them. Pay particular attention to recognition as a means of motivation. Develop intrinsic motivation by paying attention to job design, ensuring that managers are aware of its importance and their role in designing intrinsically motivating jobs.
Some people will be much more motivated by money than others. It cannot be assumed that money motivates everyone in the same way and to the same extent.	Avoid the introduction of a performance-related pay scheme in the belief that it will miraculously transform everyone overnight into well-motivated, high-performing individuals.
The need for work that provides people with the means to achieve their goals, a reasonable degree of autonomy, and scope for the use of skills and competences.	Advise on processes for the design of jobs that take account of the factors affecting the motivation to work, providing for job enrichment in the shape of variety, decision-making responsibility and as much control as possible in carrying out the work.
The need for the opportunity to grow by developing abilities and careers.	Provide facilities and opportunities for learning through such means as personal development planning processes as well as more formal training. Develop career planning processes.

TABLE 13.2 Continued

Factors affecting motivation strategies	The HR contribution
The cultural environment of the organization in the shape of its values and norms will influence the impact of any attempts to motivate people by direct or indirect means.	Advise on the development of a culture that supports processes of valuing and rewarding employees.
Motivation will be enhanced by leadership, which sets the direction, encourages and stimulates achievement and provides support to employees in their efforts to reach goals and improve their performance generally.	Devise competency frameworks that focus on leadership qualities and the behaviours expected of managers and team leaders. Ensure that leadership potential is identified through performance management and assessment centres. Conduct leadership development programmes.
Achievement motivation is important for managers and those who aspire to greater responsibility.	Pay attention to job design to ensure that people are given the scope to achieve. Develop talent management processes to provide people with opportunities to achieve and performance management processes to provide them with feedback on how well they are achieving and what they must do to achieve more.

Key learning points: Motivation

The process of motivation

Motivation is goal-directed behaviour. People are motivated when they expect that a course of action is likely to lead to the attainment of a goal and a valued reward – one that satisfies their needs and wants.

Types of motivation

The two basic types are intrinsic and extrinsic motivation.

Motivation theories

There are a number of motivation theories that, in the main, are complementary to one another. The most significant theories are those concerned with expectancy, goal setting, equity and cognitive evaluation, which are classified as process or cognitive theories.

Motivation strategies

Motivation strategies aim to create a working environment and to develop policies and practices that will provide for higher levels of performance from employees. They include the design of intrinsically motivating jobs and leadership development programmes and the development of total reward systems and performance management processes.

Questions

1 What is motivation?
2 What is the difference between extrinsic and intrinsic motivation?
3 What is instrumentality?
4 What is reinforcement?
5 What is content or needs theory?
6 How valid is Maslow's concept of the hierarchy of human needs?
7 How valid is Herzberg's two-factor theory of motivation?
8 What is expectancy theory?
9 What is goal theory?
10 What is equity theory?
11 What is cognitive evaluation theory?
12 Which motivation theory provides the best guide on the principles of performance-related pay and why?
13 What message for HR policy is provided by the belief that motivation is a highly complex process?
14 Why is recognition so important as a means of motivation?
15 Why are there limitations in the power of money to motivate?
16 Why is intrinsic motivation through the work itself likely to be more effective in the longer term than extrinsic motivation?

References

Adams, J S (1965) Injustice in social exchange, in (ed) L Berkowitz, *Advances in Experimental Psychology*, New York, Academic Press

Alderfer, C (1972) *Existence, Relatedness and Growth*, New York, The Free Press

Allport, G (1954) The historical background of modern social psychology, in (ed) G Lindzey, *Theoretical Models and Personality*, Cambridge MA, Addison-Wesley

Arnold, J, Robertson, I T and Cooper, C L (1991) *Work Psychology*, London, Pitman

Bandura, A (1977) *Social Learning Theory*, Englewood Cliffs, NJ, Prentice-Hall

Bandura, A and Cervone, D (1983) Self-evaluation and self-efficacy mechanisms governing the motivational effects of goal systems, *Journal of personality and Social Psychology*, 45 (5), pp 1017–28

Barrick, M R and Mount, M K (2013) The theory of purposeful work behavior: the role of personality, higher-order goals, and job characteristics, *Academy of Management Review*, 38, (1), pp 132–53

Behling, O and Starke, F A (1973) The postulates of expectancy theory, *Academy of Management Journal*, 16 (3), pp 375–88

Brayfield, A H and Crockett, W H (1955) Employee attitudes and employee performance, *Psychological Bulletin*, 52, pp 346–424

Cameron, J, Banko, K M and Pierce, W D (2001) Pervasive negative effects of rewards on intrinsic motivation: the myth continues, *The Behavior Analyst*, 24 (1), pp 1–44

Christen, M, Iyler, G and Soberman, D (2006) Job satisfaction, job performance, and effort: a reexamination using agency theory, *Journal of Marketing*, 70, pp 137–50

Connolly, T (1976) Some contested and methodological issues in expectancy models of work performance motivation, *Academy of Management Review*, 1 (4), pp 32–47

Deci, E L and Ryan, R M (1985) *Intrinsic Motivation and Self-determination in Human Behaviour*, New York, Plenum

Deci, E L and Ryan, R M (2000) The "what" and "why" of goal pursuits: human needs and the self-determination of behaviour, *Psychological Inquiry*, 11, pp 227–68

Deci, E L, Koestner, R and Ryan, R M (1999) A meta-analytic review of experiments examining the effects of extrinsic rewards on intrinsic motivation, *Psychological Bulletin*, 25, pp 627–68

Dowling, W E (1971) An interview with Frederick Herzberg, *Management Review*, 60, pp 2–15

Gerhart, B and Rynes, S L (2003) *Compensation: Theory, evidence and strategic implications*, Thousand Oaks CA, Sage

Hackman, J R and Oldham, G R (1974) Motivation through the design of work: test of a theory, *Organizational Behaviour and Human Performance*, 16 (2), pp 250–79

Harackiewicz, J M, Barron, P R, Pintrich, P R, Elliot, A J and Thrash, T M (2002) Revision of goal theory: necessary and illuminating, *Journal of Educational Psychology*, 94 (3), pp 638–45

Herzberg, F (1966) *Work and the Nature of Man*, New York, Staple Press

Herzberg, F (1968) One more time: how do you motivate employees? *Harvard Business Review*, January–February, pp 109–20

Herzberg, F W, Mausner, B and Snyderman, B (1957) *The Motivation to Work*, New York, Wiley

House, R J, Shapiro, H J and Wahba, M A (1974) Expectancy theory as a predictor of work behaviour and attitude: a re-evaluation of empirical evidence, *Decision Sciences*, 5 (3), pp 481–506

Hull, C L (1943) *Principles of Behavior*. New York, Appleton-Century-Crofts

Hull, C (1951) *Essentials of Behaviour*, New Haven CT, Yale University Press

Hunter, J E, Schmidt, F L and Judiesch, M K (1990) Individual differences in output variability as a function of job complexity, *Journal of Applied Psychology*, 75 (1), pp 28–42

Huseman, R C, Hatfield, J D and Milis, E W (1982) A new perception on equity theory: the equity sensitivity constant, *Academy of Management Review*, 12 (2), pp 222–34

Jaques, E (1961) *Equitable Payment*, London, Heinemann

Katz, D (1964) The motivational basis of organizational behaviour, *Behavioural Science*, 9, pp 131–36

Katz, D, Maccoby, N, Gurin, G and Floor, L G (1951) *Productivity, Supervision and Morale in an Office Situation*, Ann Arbor, MI, University of Michigan

Katz, D, Maccoby, N and Morse, N C (1950) *Productivity, Supervision and Morale among Railway Workers*, Ann Arbor, MI, University of Michigan

Latham, G and Locke, E A (1979) Goal setting – a motivational technique that works, *Organizational Dynamics*, Autumn, pp 68–80

Lawler, E E (1988) Pay for performance: making it work, *Personnel*, October, pp 25–29

Locke, E A (1976) The nature and causes of job satisfaction, in (ed) M D Dunnette, *Handbook of Industrial and Organizational Psychology*, Chicago, Rand McNally, pp 1297–349

Locke, E A and Latham, G (2004) What should we do about motivation theory? Six recommendations for the twenty-first century, *Academy of Management Review*, 29 (3), pp 398–403

Maslow, A (1954) *Motivation and Personality*, New York, Harper & Row

Mayo, E (1933) *The Human Problems of an Industrial Civilisation*, London, Macmillan

McClelland, D C (1961) *The Achieving Society*, New York, Van Nostrand

Opsahl, R C and Dunnette, M D (1966) The role of financial compensation in individual motivation, *Psychological Bulletin*, 56, pp 94–118

Pink, D H (2009) *Drive: The surprising truth about workplace motivation*, New York, Riverhead Books

Pintrich, P R (2000) An achievement goal perspective on issues in motivation technology, theory and research, *Contemporary Educational Psychology*, 25, pp 92–104

Porter, L W and Lawler, E E (1968) *Managerial Attitudes and Performance*, Homewood IL, Irwin-Dorsey

Reinharth, L and Wahba, M A (1975) Expectancy theory as a predictor of work motivation, effort expenditure and job performance, *Academy of Management Journal*, 18 (3), pp 520–37

Roethlisberger, F and Dickson, W (1939) *Management and the Worker*, Cambridge, MA, Harvard University Press

Rousseau, D M (2006) Is there such a thing as evidence-based management? *Academy of Management Review*, 31 (2), pp 256–69

Sandel, M (2012) *The Moral Limits of Markets: What money cannot buy*, London, Allen Lane

Shields, J (2007) *Managing Employee Performance and Reward*, Port Melbourne, Cambridge University Press

Skinner, B F (1953) *Science and Human Behavior*, New York, The Free Press

Spector, P E (1997) *Job Satisfaction: Application, assessment, causes and consequences* (Vol 3), London, Sage

Steers, R M, Mowday, R T and Shapiro, D L (2004) Call for papers: the future of work motivation theory, *Academy of Management Review*, 29 (3), pp 379–387

Taylor, F W (1911) *Principles of Scientific Management*, New York, Harper (republished Norton, 1967)

Thorndike, E L (1911) *Animal Intelligence*, New York, Macmillan

Vroom, V (1964) *Work and Motivation*, New York, Wiley

Wahba, M A and Bridwell, L G (1979) Maslow reconsidered: a review of research on the need hierarchy theory, in (eds) R M Sters and L W Porter, *Motivation and Work Behaviour*, New York, McGraw-Hill

14 Commitment

KEY CONCEPTS AND TERMS

- Commitment
- High commitment model
- Mutuality
- Organizational engagement
- Pluralist
- Psychological contract
- Unitarist

LEARNING OUTCOMES

On completing this chapter you should be able to define these key concepts. You should also understand:

- The meaning of organizational commitment
- The importance of commitment
- Commitment and engagement
- Problems with the concept of commitment
- The impact of high commitment
- Factors affecting commitment
- Developing a commitment strategy

Introduction

Commitment represents the strength of an individual's identification with, and involvement in, an organization. It is a concept that has played an important part in HRM philosophy. As Guest (1987: 503) suggested, HRM policies are designed to 'maximize organizational integration, employee commitment, flexibility and quality of work'. Beer *et al* (1984: 20) identified commitment in their concept of HRM as a key dimension because it 'can result not only in more loyalty and better performance for the organization, but also in self-worth, dignity, psychological involvement, and identity for the individual'.

The meaning of organizational commitment

Commitment refers to attachment and loyalty. It is associated with the feelings of individuals about their organization. Mowday (1998) stated that it is characterized by an emotional attachment to one's organization that results from shared values and interests. The three characteristics of commitment identified by Mowday *et al* (1982) are:

1. A strong desire to remain a member of the organization.
2. A strong belief in and acceptance of the values and goals of the organization.
3. A readiness to exert considerable effort on behalf of the organization.

Appelbaum *et al* (2000: 183) rephrased this definition as: 'Organizational commitment is a multidimensional construct that reflects a worker's: identification with the organization (loyalty), attachment to the organization (intention to stay), and willingness to expend effort on the organization's behalf (discretionary effort).' An alternative, although closely related definition of commitment emphasizes the importance of behaviour in creating commitment. Three features of behaviour are important in binding individuals to their acts: the visibility of the acts, the extent to which the outcomes are irrevocable, and the degree to which the person undertakes the action voluntarily. Commitment, according to Salancik (1977) can be increased and harnessed to obtain support for organizational ends and interests through such ploys as participation in decisions about actions.

The importance of commitment

The importance of commitment was highlighted by Walton (1985a). His theme was that improved performance would result if the organization moved away from the traditional control-oriented approach to workforce management, which relies upon establishing order, exercising control and achieving efficiency. He proposed that this approach should be replaced by a commitment strategy that would enable workers 'to respond best – and most creatively – not when they are tightly controlled by management, placed in narrowly defined jobs, and treated like an unwelcome necessity, but, instead, when they are given broader responsibilities, encouraged to contribute and helped to achieve satisfaction in their work' (ibid: 77). He described the commitment-based approach as follows.

Source review

Richard Walton on commitment – Walton (1985a: 79)

Jobs are designed to be broader than before, to combine planning and implementation, and to include efforts to upgrade operations, not just to maintain them. Individual responsibilities are expected to change as conditions change, and teams, not individuals, often are the organizational units accountable for performance. With management hierarchies relatively flat and differences in status minimized, control and lateral coordination depend on shared goals. And expertise rather than formal position determines influence.

Expressed like this, a commitment strategy sounds idealistic ('the American dream' as Guest (1990) put it) but it does not appear to be a crude attempt to manipulate people to accept management's values and goals, as some have suggested. In fact, Walton did not describe it as being instrumental in this manner. His prescription was for a broad HRM approach to the ways in which people are treated, jobs are designed and organizations are managed. He believed that the aim should be to develop 'mutuality', a state that exists when management and employees are interdependent and both benefit from this interdependency. The importance of mutuality and its relationship to commitment was spelt out by Walton (1985b: 64) as follows:

> The new HRM model is composed of policies that promote mutuality – mutual goals, mutual influence, mutual respect, mutual rewards, mutual responsibility. The theory is that policies of mutuality will elicit commitment which in turn will yield both better economic performance and greater human development.

But a review by Guest (1991) of the mainly North American literature, reinforced by the limited UK research available, led him to the conclusion that: 'High organizational commitment is associated with lower labour turnover and absence, but there is no clear link to performance.' Swailes (2002: 164) confirmed that: 'Despite the best efforts of researchers... the evidence for a strong positive link between commitment and performance remains patchy.'

It is probably unwise to expect too much from commitment as a means of making a direct and immediate impact on performance. It is not the same as motivation. It is possible to be dissatisfied with a particular feature of a job while retaining a fairly high level of commitment to the organization as a whole. But it is reasonable to believe that strong commitment to work may result in conscientious and self-directed application to do the job, regular attendance, the need for less supervision and a high level of discretionary effort. Commitment to the organization will certainly be related to the intention to stay there.

Commitment and engagement

The notion of commitment as described above appears to be very similar if not identical to that of organizational engagement that, as defined in Chapter 15, focuses on attachment to, or identification with, the organization as a whole. Are there any differences?

Some commentators have asserted that commitment is a distinct although closely linked entity. As cited by Buchanan (2004: 19), the US Corporate Executive Board divides engagement into two aspects of commitment: 1) rational commitment, which occurs when a job serves employees' financial, developmental or professional self-interest; and 2) emotional commitment, which arises when workers value, enjoy and believe in what they do and has four times the power to affect performance as its more pragmatic counterpart. The Corporate Executive Board (2004: 1) indicated that engagement is 'the extent to which employees commit to someone or something in their organization, how hard they work, and how long they stay as a result of that commitment'. Wellins and Concelman (2005: 1) suggested that 'to be engaged is to be actively committed'. And Macey and Schneider (2008: 8–9) observed that:

> Organizational commitment is an important facet of the state of engagement when it is conceptualized as positive attachment to the larger organizational entity and measured as a willingness to exert energy in support of the organization, to feel pride as an organizational member, and to have personal identification with the organization.

Clearly organizational engagement and commitment are closely associated, and commitment was included by the Institute for Employment Studies in its model (see Chapter 15) as an element of engagement. Appelbaum *et al* (2000: 183) noted that: 'The willingness to exert extra effort is the aspect of organizational commitment that has been shown to be most closely related to an employee's job performance.' Robinson *et al* (2004: 7) suggested that the closest relationship of commitment to engagement was 'affective commitment, ie the satisfaction people get from their jobs and their colleagues and their willingness to go beyond the call of duty for the sake of the organization'. Salanova *et al* (2005) saw commitment as part of engagement but not equivalent to it.

The analysis of the concept of commitment as undertaken in this chapter is based on a considerable body of work exploring its nature and significance, and therefore helps to illuminate the somewhat elusive notion of engagement as discussed in Chapter 15. But there are problems with commitment, as discussed below.

Critical evaluation of the concept of commitment

A number of commentators have raised questions about the concept of commitment. These relate to three main problem areas: 1) the imprecise nature of the term, 2) its unitary frame of reference, and 3) commitment as an inhibitor of flexibility.

The imprecise nature of the term

Guest (1987: 513) raised the question of what commitment really means as follows:

> The case for seeking high commitment among employees seems plausible but the burgeoning research on the topic has identified a number of

problems. One of these concerns the definition of the concept. The first issue is – commitment to what? Most writers are interested in commitment to the organization, but others have examined career commitment and job commitment. Once the general concept of commitment is utilized, then union commitment, workgroup commitment and family commitment should also be considered. The possibility of multiple and perhaps competing commitments creates a more complex set of issues.

Unitary frame of reference

The concept of commitment, especially as put forward by Walton (1985a), can be criticized as being simplistic, even misguided, in adopting a unitary frame of reference that assumes that organizations consist of people with shared interests. It has been suggested by people such as Cyert and March (1963), Mangham (1979) and Mintzberg (1983) that an organization is really a coalition of interest groups where political processes are an inevitable part of everyday life.

Legge (1989: 38) also raised this question in her discussion of strong culture as a key requirement of HRM, which she criticized because it implies 'a shared set of managerially sanctioned values... that assumes an identification of employee and employer interests'. As Coopey and Hartley (1991: 21) put it: 'Commitment is not an all-or-nothing affair (though many managers might like it to be) but a question of multiple or competing commitments for the individual.' A pluralist perspective recognizes the legitimacy of different interests and is more realistic.

It could be argued that values concerned with performance, quality, service, equal opportunity and innovation are not necessarily wrong because they are managerial values. But pursuing a value such as innovation could work against the interests of employees by, for example, resulting in redundancies. And flexibility may sound a good idea but, beyond the rhetoric, as Sisson (1994: 5) observed, the reality may mean that management can do what it wants. It would be quite reasonable for any employee encouraged to behave in accordance with a value supported by management to ask, 'What's in it for me?' It can also be argued that the imposition from above of management's values on employees without their having any part to play in discussing and agreeing them is a form of coercion.

Commitment and flexibility

It was pointed out by Coopey and Hartley (1991: 22) that: 'The problem for a unitarist notion of organizational commitment is that it fosters a conformist approach which not only fails to reflect organizational reality, but can be narrowing and limiting for the organization.' They argued that if employees are expected and encouraged to commit themselves tightly to a single set of values and goals they will not be able to cope with the ambiguities and uncertainties that are endemic in organizational life in times of change. Conformity to 'imposed' values will inhibit creative problem solving, and high commitment to present courses of action will increase both resistance to change and the stress that invariably occurs when change takes place.

If commitment is related to tightly defined plans, this will become a real problem. To avoid it, the emphasis should be on overall strategic directions. These would be communicated to employees with the proviso that changing circumstances will require their amendment. In the meantime, however, everyone can at least be informed in general terms where the organization is heading and, more specifically, the part they are expected to play in helping the organization to get there and, if they can be involved in the decision-making processes on matters that affect them (including management's values for performance, quality and customer service), so much the better.

Values need not necessarily be restrictive. They can be defined in ways that allow for freedom of choice within broad guidelines. In fact, the values themselves can refer to such processes as flexibility, innovation and responsiveness to change. Thus, far from inhibiting creative problem solving, they can encourage it. But they will not do so if they are imposed from above. Employees need to have a say in defining the values they are expected to support.

Factors affecting commitment

Kochan and Dyer (1993) indicated that the factors affecting the level of commitment in what they called 'mutual commitment firms' were as follows:

- *Strategic level*: supportive business strategies, top management value commitment and effective voice for HR in strategy making and governance.
- *Functional (human resource policy) level*: staffing based on employment stabilization, investment in training and development and contingent compensation that reinforces cooperation, participation and contribution.
- *Workplace level*: selection based on high standards, broad task design and teamwork, employee involvement in problem solving and a climate of cooperation and trust.

The research conducted by Purcell *et al* (2003) identified the following key policy and practice factors that influence levels of commitment:

- received training last year;
- satisfied with career opportunities;
- satisfied with the performance appraisal system;
- think managers are good in people management (leadership);
- find their work challenging;
- think their firm helps them achieve a work–life balance;
- satisfied with communication or company performance.

Developing a commitment strategy

A commitment strategy can be based on the high-commitment model incorporating policies and practices in areas of HR such as job design, learning and development, career planning, performance management, reward management, participation, communication and employee well-being. HR should play a major part in developing a high-commitment organization. The 10 steps it can take are:

1. Advise on methods of communicating the values and aims of management and the achievements of the organization so that employees are more likely to identify with the organization as one they are proud to work for.
2. Emphasize to management that commitment is a two-way process; employees cannot be expected to be committed to the organization unless management demonstrates that it is committed to them and recognizes their contribution as stakeholders.
3. Impress on management the need to develop a climate of trust by being honest with people, treating them fairly, justly and consistently, keeping its word, and showing willingness to listen to the comments and suggestions made by employees during processes of consultation and participation.
4. Develop a positive psychological contract (the set of reciprocal but unwritten expectations that exist between individual employees and their employers) by treating people as stakeholders, relying on consensus and cooperation rather than control and coercion, and focusing on the provision of opportunities for learning, development and career progression.
5. Advise on the establishment of partnership agreements with trade unions that emphasize unity of purpose, common approaches to working together and the importance of giving employees a voice in matters that concern them.
6. Recommend and take part in the achievement of single status for all employees (often included in a partnership agreement) so that there is no longer an 'us and them' culture.
7. Encourage management to declare a policy of employment security and ensure that steps are taken to avoid involuntary redundancies.
8. Develop performance management processes that provide for the alignment of organizational and individual objectives.
9. Advise on means of increasing employee identification with the company through rewards related to organizational performance (profit sharing or gainsharing) or employee share ownership schemes.
10. Enhance employee job engagement, ie identification of employees with the job they are doing, through job design processes that aim to create higher levels of job satisfaction (job enrichment).

Key learning points: Commitment

The meaning of commitment

Commitment refers to attachment and loyalty. It is associated with the feelings of individuals about their organization. The three characteristics of commitment identified by Mowday *et al* (1982) are:

1. A strong desire to remain a member of the organization.
2. A strong belief in and acceptance of the values and goals of the organization.
3. A readiness to exert considerable effort on behalf of the organization.

The impact of high commitment

In his seminal *Harvard Business Review* article, Richard Walton (1985a) stated that 'eliciting employee commitment will lead to enhanced performance [and] the evidence shows this belief to be well founded'. The importance of commitment was highlighted by Walton. His theme was that improved performance would result if the organization moved away from the traditional control-oriented approach to workforce management, which relies upon establishing order, exercising control and achieving efficiency. He proposed that this approach should be replaced by a commitment strategy.

Problems with the concept of commitment

There are four main problem areas: 1) the imprecise nature of the term, 2) its unitary frame of reference, 3) commitment as an inhibitor of flexibility, and 4) the extent to which high commitment does in practice result in improved organizational performance.

Engagement and commitment

Organizational engagement and commitment are closely associated. Commitment was included by the IES in its model as an element of engagement. But commitment is a somewhat wider concept in that it is concerned with both job engagement and organizational engagement.

The factors affecting the level of commitment (Kochan and Dyer, 1993)

- *Strategic level*: supportive business strategies, top management value commitment and effective voice for HR in strategy making and governance.
- *Functional (human resource policy) level*: staffing based on employment stabilization, investment in training and development and contingent compensation that reinforces cooperation, participation and contribution.
- *Workplace level*: selection based on high standards, broad task design and teamwork, employee involvement in problem solving and a climate of cooperation and trust.

HR's role in enhancing commitment

HR should play a major part in developing a high-commitment organization. The 10 steps it can take are:

- Advise on methods of communicating the values and aims of management.
- Emphasize to management that commitment is a two-way process.
- Impress on management the need to develop a climate of trust.
- Develop a positive psychological contract.
- Advise on the establishment of partnership agreements with trade unions.
- Recommend and take part in the achievement of single status for all employees.
- Encourage management to declare a policy of employment security.
- Develop performance management processes.
- Advise on means of increasing employee identification with the company.
- Enhance employee job engagement through job design processes.

Questions

1 What is commitment?
2 What is mutuality?
3 What are the three characteristics of commitment?
4 Why is commitment important?
5 What impact can high levels of commitment have on performance?
6 What is the relationship between commitment and engagement?
7 What did the research conducted by Purcell *et al* (2003) tell us about the factors affecting commitment?
8 Is a belief in the virtues of commitment based on an unrealistic unitary view of employment relationships?
9 Do high levels of commitment result in lack of flexibility and, if so, what can be done about it?
10 What are the essential features of a commitment strategy?

References

Appelbaum, E, Bailey, T, Berg, P and Kalleberg, A L (2000) *Manufacturing Advantage: Why high performance work systems pay off*, Ithaca, NY, ILR Press

Beer, M, Spector, B, Lawrence, P, Quinn Mills, D and Walton, R (1984) *Managing Human Assets*, New York, The Free Press

Buchanan, L (2004) The things they do for love, *Harvard Business Review*, December, pp 19–20

Coopey, J and Hartley, J (1991) Reconsidering the case for organizational commitment, *Human Resource Management Journal*, 1 (3), pp 18–31

Corporate Executive Board (2004) *Driving Performance and Retention through Employee Engagement*, www.corporateleadershipcouncil.com/Images/CLC/PDF/CLC12KADBP.pdf [accessed 13 September 2005]

Cyert, R M and March, J G (1963) *A Behavioural Theory of the Firm*, Englewood Cliffs, NJ, Prentice-Hall

Guest, D E (1987) Human resource management and industrial relations, *Journal of Management Studies*, 24 (5), pp 503–21

Guest, D E (1990) HRM and the American dream, *Journal of Management Studies*, 27 (4), pp 377–97

Guest, D E (1991) Personnel management: the end of orthodoxy, *British Journal of Industrial Relations*, 29 (2), pp 149–76

Kochan, T A and Dyer, L (1993) Managing transformational change: the role of human resource professionals, *International Journal of Human Resource Management*, 4 (3), pp 569–90

Legge, K (1989) Human resource management: a critical analysis, in (ed) J Storey, *New Perspectives in Human Resource Management*, London, Routledge, pp 19–40

Macey, W H and Schneider, B (2008) The meaning of employee engagement, *Industrial and Organizational Psychology*, 1, pp 3–30

Mangham, L L (1979) *The Politics of Organizational Change*, London, Associated Business Press

Mintzberg, H (1983) *Power in and around Organizations*, Englewood Cliffs, NJ, Prentice-Hall

Mowday R (1998) Reflections on the study and relevance of organizational commitment. *Human Resource Management Review*, 8, 387–401

Mowday, R, Porter, L and Steers, R (1982) *Employee-organization Linkages: The psychology of commitment, absenteeism and turnover*, London, Academic Press

Purcell, J, Kinnie, K, Hutchinson, R, Rayton, B and Swart, J (2003) *Understanding the People and Performance Link: Unlocking the black box*, London, CIPD

Robinson, D, Perryman, S and Hayday, S (2004) *The Drivers of Employee Engagement*, Brighton, Institute for Employment Studies

Salancik, G R (1977) Commitment and the control of organizational behaviour and belief, in (eds) B M Straw and G R Salancik, *New Directions in Organizational Behaviour*, Chicago, IL, St Clair Press

Salanova, M, Agut, S and Peiro, J M (2005) Linking organizational resources and work engagement to employee performance and customer loyalty: the mediation of service climate, *Journal of Applied Psychology*, 90, pp 1217–27

Sisson, K (1994) Personnel management: paradigms, practice and prospects, in (ed) K Sisson, *Personnel Management*, 2nd edn, Oxford, Blackwell, pp 3–50

Swailes, S (2002) Organizational commitment; a critique of the construct and measures, *International Journal of Management Reviews*, 4 (2), pp 155–78

Walton, R E (1985a) From control to commitment in the workplace, *Harvard Business Review*, March–April, pp 77–84

Walton, R E (1985b) Towards a strategy of eliciting employee commitment based on principles of mutuality, in (eds) R E Walton and P R Lawrence, *HRM Trends and Challenges*, Boston, MA, Harvard Business School Press, pp 35–65

Wellins, R and Concelman, J (2005) *Personal Engagement: Driving growth at the see-level*, www.ddiworld.com/pdf/ddipersonalengagement.ar.pdf [accessed 29 April 2005]

15 Employee engagement

KEY CONCEPTS AND TERMS

Commitment
Discretionary behaviour
Engagement
Extrinsic motivation
Intrinsic motivation
Job engagement
Leader-member exchange
Motivation
Organizational citizenship behaviour
Organizational engagement
Social exchange theory

LEARNING OUTCOMES

On completing this chapter you should be able to define these key concepts. You should also understand:

- The meaning of employee engagement
- Job engagement
- Organizational engagement
- The theory of engagement
- The components of engagement
- The drivers of engagement
- Outcomes of engagement
- Enhancing engagement
- The significance of burnout

Introduction

Engagement takes place when people are committed to their work and the organization and are motivated to achieve high levels of performance. According to the CIPD (2012: 13): 'Engagement has become for practitioners an umbrella concept for capturing the various means by which employers can elicit additional or discretionary effort from employees – a willingness on the part of staff to work beyond contract. It has become a new management mantra.' As David Guest (2013: 231) remarked: 'One of the attractions of engagement is that it is clearly a good thing. Managers are attracted to the concept because they like the idea of having engaged employees and dislike the prospect of having disengaged employees'.

According to Truss *et al* (2013: 1): 'The notion that individuals can be "personally" engaged in their work, investing positive emotional and cognitive energy into their role performance, was first proposed by William Kahn (1990) in his seminal article in the *Academy of Management Journal*'. Schaufeli (2013: 15) commented: 'It is not entirely clear when the term "engagement" was first used in relation to work, but generally the Gallup Organization is credited with coining the term, sometime during the 1990s'.

Reilly and Brown (2008) noted that the terms 'job satisfaction', 'motivation' and 'commitment' are generally being replaced now in business by 'engagement' because it appears to have more descriptive force and face validity. Truss *et al* (2013: 2657) suggested that 'engagement may constitute the mechanism through which HRM practitioners impact individual and organizational performance'.

This chapter starts with an analysis of the meaning of employee engagement and continues with an assessment of the components, drivers and outcomes. This is followed by a discussion of what Macey *et al* describe as burnout, the possibility of which should be taken into account in pursuing the engagement strategies described at the end of the chapter.

The meaning of employee engagement

Kahn (1990: 894) defined employee engagement as 'the harnessing of organization members' selves to their work roles; in engagement, people employ and express themselves physically, cognitively, and emotionally during role performances'. There have been dozens of definitions since the explosion of interest in the concept during the 2000s. Harter *et al* (2002: 269) stated that engagement was 'the individual's involvement and satisfaction with as well as enthusiasm for work. A later definition was produced by Macey *et al* (2009: 7) who defined engagement as 'an individual's purpose and focused energy, evident to others in the display of personal initiative, adaptability, effort and persistence directed towards organizational goals'.

Alfes *et al* (2010: 5) saw engagement as having three core facets:

1 *intellectual engagement* – thinking hard about the job and how to do it better;
2 *affective engagement* – feeling positively about doing a good job;
3 *social engagement* – actively taking opportunities to discuss work-related improvements with others at work.

Job or organizational engagement or both

The term 'engagement' can be used in a specific job-related way to describe what takes place when people are interested in and positive – even excited – about their jobs, exercise discretionary behaviour and are motivated to achieve high levels of performance. It is described as job or work engagement. Truss *et al* (2006: ix) stated that: 'Put simply, engagement means feeling positive about your job.' They went on to explain that: 'The engaged employee is the passionate employee, the employee who is totally immersed in his or her work, energetic, committed and completely dedicated' (ibid: 1).

Organizational engagement focuses on attachment to or identification with the organization as a whole. The Conference Board (2006) defined employee engagement as the heightened connection that employees feel for their organization. Robinson *et al* (2004: 9) emphasized the organizational aspect of engagement when they referred to it as 'a positive attitude held by the employee towards the organization and its values'. This definition of organizational engagement resembles the traditional notion of commitment.

Perhaps the most illuminating and helpful approach to the definition of engagement is to recognize that it involves both job and organizational engagement as suggested by Saks (2006) and Balain and Sparrow (2009).

The theory of engagement

Saks (2006: 603) thought that a strong theoretical rationale for engagement was provided by social exchange theory. As he described it:

> Social exchange theory argues that obligations are generated through a series of interactions between

> parties who are in a state of reciprocal interdependence. A basic tenet of social exchange theory is that relationships evolve over time into trusting, loyal and mutual commitments as long as the parties abide by certain 'rules' of exchange... [These] usually involve reciprocity or repayment rules such that the actions of one party lead to a response or actions by the other party.

He argued that one way for individuals to repay their organization is through their level of engagement. In other words, employees will choose to engage themselves to varying degrees and in response to the resources they receive from their organization. This is consistent with the description of engagement by Robinson *et al* (2004) as a two-way relationship between the employer and the employee. Balain and Sparrow (2009: 16) concluded that:

> To understand what really causes engagement, and what it causes in turn, we need to embed the idea in a well-founded theory. The one that is considered most appropriate is social exchange theory, which sees feelings of loyalty, commitment and discretionary effort as all being forms of social reciprocation by employees to a good employer.

As discussed below, the concept of engagement can be further explored in terms of its make-up (its components), its antecedents (the forces that drive it), and its outcomes.

The components of employee engagement

Engagement can be regarded as having three overlapping components: motivation and commitment as defined in Chapters 13 and 14 and organizational citizenship behaviour (OCB) as defined below. A model of engagement containing these components produced by the Institute for Employment Studies (Armstrong *et al*, 2010) is shown in Figure 15.1. Work or job engagement is also associated with job satisfaction. These components of engagement are considered below.

Engagement and commitment

The concepts of commitment and organizational engagement are closely related, although Robinson *et al* (2004) stated that while engagement contains many of the elements of commitment it is not a perfect match. They suggested that it does not reflect sufficiently two aspects of engagement – its two-way nature, and the extent to which engaged employees are expected to have positive attitudes about their job. However, Storey (2007: 8) referred to the concept of employee engagement as 'a term that broadly equates with the notion of high commitment'.

FIGURE 15.1 IES model of employee engagement

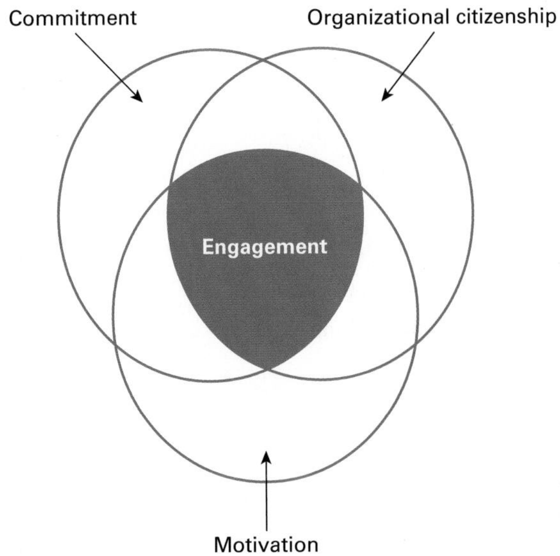

SOURCE: Armstrong *et al* (2000)

Yalabik *et al* (2013: 2803) proposed that 'affective commitment' (ie an emotional attachment to, identification with and involvement with the organization) is an antecedent of work engagement.

Engagement and motivation

The motivation element in engagement is intrinsic. Macey *et al* (2009: 67) commented that: 'When the work itself is meaningful it is also said to have intrinsic motivation. This means that it is not the pay or recognition that yields positive feelings of engagement but the work itself.' They also pointed out that engaged employees 'feel that their jobs are an important part of what they are' (ibid: 127).

Engagement and organizational citizenship behaviour

Organizational citizenship behaviour (OCB), as originally defined by Organ (1988), is employee behaviour that goes above and beyond the call of duty and contributes to organizational effectiveness. It is discretionary and not explicitly recognized by the employing organization's formal reward system.

As Little and Little (2006) observed, OCB is an outcome of the attitudes of job satisfaction and organizational commitment. It is similar to the definitions in the engagement literature of being respectful of and helpful to colleagues and willingness to go the extra mile or work longer hours, try harder, accomplish more and speak positively about the organization. They noted that this desirable behaviour has been shown to be related more to the work situation than to individual dispositions.

Engagement and job satisfaction

Job satisfaction was defined by Locke (1976: 1304) as 'a pleasurable or positive emotional state resulting from the appraisal of one's job and job experiences'. Engaged employees are more likely than not to be satisfied with their jobs.

Job satisfaction, like commitment, is regarded by Yalabik *et al* (2013: 2805) as an antecedent of work engagement. It has been shown to be related to other attitudes and behaviours. Positively, it is related to organizational commitment, job involvement, organizational citizenship behaviours and mental health. Negatively, it is related to turnover and stress.

Drivers of employee engagement

To be able to do anything about engagement it is necessary to understand the factors that affect this – its antecedents and drivers. Crawford *et al* (2013: 59–62) listed the following drivers:

- *Job challenge* – this takes place when the scope of jobs is broad, job responsibility is high and there is a high work load. It enhances engagement because it creates potential for accomplishment and personal growth.
- *Autonomy* – the freedom, independence and discretion allowed to employees in scheduling their work and determining the procedures for carrying it out. It provides a sense of ownership and control over work outcomes.
- *Variety* – jobs which allow individuals to perform many different activities or use many different skills.
- *Feedback* – providing employees with direst and clear information about the effectiveness of their performance.
- *Fit* – the existence of compatibility between an individual and a work environment (eg, job, organization, manager, co-workers) which allows individuals to behave in a manner consistent with how they see or want to see themselves.
- *Opportunities for development* – these make work meaningful because they provide pathways for employee growth and fulfilment.
- *Rewards and recognition* – these represent both direct and indirect returns on the personal investment of one's time in acting out a work role.

In addition, the quality of leadership exercised by line managers is an important driver Hakanen *et al* (2006) established through their research that supervisory support is positively related to employee engagement as is involvement in decision-making and day-to-day control over tasks and schedules. Macey and Schneider (2008) argued that when leaders have clear expectations, are fair, and recognize good performance they will have positive effects on employee engagement by engendering a sense of attachment to the job. Research by MacLeod and Clarke (2009) confirmed that line managers played a key part in promoting engagement by providing clarity of purpose, appreciating employees' effort and contribution, treating their people as individuals and ensuring that work is organized efficiently and effectively so that employees feel they are valued, and equipped and supported to do their job.

Macey *et al* (2009: 11) emphasized the work environment and the jobs people do. They noted that: 'Engagement requires a work environment that does not just demand more but promotes information sharing, provides learning opportunities and fosters a balance in people's lives, thereby creating the bases for sustained energy and personal initiative.'

Outcomes of engagement

Stairs and Galpin (2010) claimed that high levels of engagement have been shown to relate to:

- lower absenteeism and higher employee retention;
- increased employee effort and productivity;
- improved quality and reduced error rates;
- increased sales;
- higher profitability, earnings per share and shareholder returns;
- enhanced customer satisfaction and loyalty;
- faster business growth; and
- higher likelihood of business success.

Alfes *et al* (2010: 2) asserted that engaged employees perform better, are more innovative than others, are more likely to want to stay with their employers, enjoy greater levels of personal well-being and perceive their workload to be more sustainable than others.

However, Sparrow (2013: 102) warned against over-confident claims that high engagement results in high performance. He suggested that it is possible that being in a well-performing unit makes employees engaged, not the other way round a possible. In other words 'reverse causation' (A situation where A might have caused B but it is just as likely that B caused, **A**).

Enhancing employee engagement

Research conducted by Towers Perrin (2003) showed that enhancing engagement is a process that never ends and it rests on the foundation of a meaningful and emotionally enriching work experience. Furthermore, it is not about making people happy, or paying them more money. Important as pay and benefits are in attracting and retaining people, it was found they play a less significant role in engaging people in their work. The elements found to be fundamental for engagement were strong leadership, accountability, autonomy, a sense of control over one's environment and opportunities for development.

Jenkins and Delbridge (2013) proposed that in line with Storey's (1989) contrast between 'hard' and 'soft' HRM it was possible to distinguish between hard and soft management approaches to enhancing engagement. In their case studies of two companies, one adopted a soft approach that centred on work design and promoting positive workplace conditions and relationships between management and employees. Enhanced employee engagement was seen as a positive outcome – productivity was not the primary goal. In the other case, a 'hard' approach concentrated on directly increasing employee effort to improve organizational performance. In the company using a soft approach high levels of engagement were reported, while in the other company high levels of employee disengagement were evident.

To enhance employee engagement employers have to address issues concerning both aspects of engagement – job and organizational engagement. These are interrelated and any actions taken to enhance either aspect will be mutually supporting. However, it is useful to consider what can be done specifically in each area, bearing in mind the particular circumstances and needs of the organization.

Enhancing job engagement

Line managers play a key role in enhancing job engagement with the support of organizational initiatives in the areas of job design, learning programmes, including leadership development for line managers, and performance and reward management systems.

Line managers

According to the Gallup Organization research reported by Coffman and Gonzalez-Molina (2002: 130), to enhance engagement managers should:

- make employees aware of their individual strengths;
- provide continuous feedback on how those strengths are being used;
- 'clear the path' so that employees can do what they do best without unnecessary distractions;
- build trust by showing commitment to the employee's success;
- challenge people within areas of their distinctive strengths;
- focus upon particular skills and knowledge in order to build talent into strength;
- give employees ownership and creation of their outcomes.

Extensive research by Lewis *et al* (2012) for the Chartered Institute of Personnel and Development resulted in the production of the competency framework for employee engagement management set out in Table 15.1.

Job design

Job design is an important factor in enhancing engagement. Macey *et al* (2009: 69) commented that: 'People come to work for pay but get engaged at work because the work they do is meaningful.' Intrinsic motivation and therefore increased engagement can be generated by the work itself if it provides interest and opportunities for achievement and self-fulfilment. Robertson and Smith (1985) suggested that the aim should be to influence: 1) skill variety, 2) task identity, 3) task significance, 4) autonomy, and 5) feedback.

Learning and development programmes

Learning and development programmes can ensure that people have the opportunity and are given the encouragement to learn and grow in their roles. This includes the use of policies that focus on role flexibility – giving people the chance to develop their roles by making better and extended use of their talents. It also means going beyond talent management for the favoured few and developing the abilities of the core people on whom the organization depends.

The strategy should also cover career development opportunities and how individuals can be given the guidance, support and encouragement they need if they are to fulfil their potential and achieve a successful career with the organization in tune with their talents and aspirations. The actions required to provide men and women of promise with a sequence of learning activities and experiences that will equip them for whatever level of responsibility they have the ability to reach should be included in the strategy.

Developing engagement through performance management

Performance management processes as described in Chapter 25 can be used to define individual goals and responsibilities, offer feedback on performance and provide the basis for developing skills and planning career development. Although the organization can create a performance management system, its effectiveness will depend on the interest and competence of line managers.

Developing engagement through reward

Reilly and Brown (2008) asserted that appropriate reward practices and processes, both financial and non-financial and managed in combination (ie a

TABLE 15.1 Employee engagement management competency framework

Competency	Description
Autonomy and empowerment	Trusts and involves employees
Development	Helps to develop employees' careers
Feedback, praise and recognition	Gives positive feedback and praise and rewards good work
Individual interest	Shows concern for employees
Availability	There when needed
Personal manner	Positive approach, leads by example
Ethics	Treats employees fairly
Reviewing and guiding	Helps and advises employees
Clarifying expectations	Sets clear goals and defines what is expected
Managing time and resources	Ensures resources are available to meet workload
Following processes and procedures	Understands and explains processes and procedures

SOURCE: Adapted from Lewis *et al* (2012: 9)

total rewards approach), can help to build and improve employee engagement, and that badly designed or executed rewards can hinder it. Their model, based on research of how reward policies influence performance through engagement, is shown in Figure 15.2.

Enhancing organizational engagement

The approaches that can be used to enhance organizational engagement consist of: 1) high-involvement management; (2) providing more scope for employee voice; (3) developing 'the big idea'; and 4) tackling the work environment.

High-involvement management

Organizational engagement can be developed through high-involvement management – a term first used by Lawler (1986) to describe management systems based on commitment and involvement, as opposed to the old bureaucratic model based on control. The underlying hypothesis is that employees will increase their involvement with the company if they are given the opportunity to manage and understand their work. Lawler claimed that high-involvement practices worked well because they acted as a synergy and had a multiplicative effect.

High-involvement management means treating employees as partners in the enterprise, whose interests are respected. It also means providing employees with a voice, as discussed below.

FIGURE 15.2 How reward policies influence performance through engagement

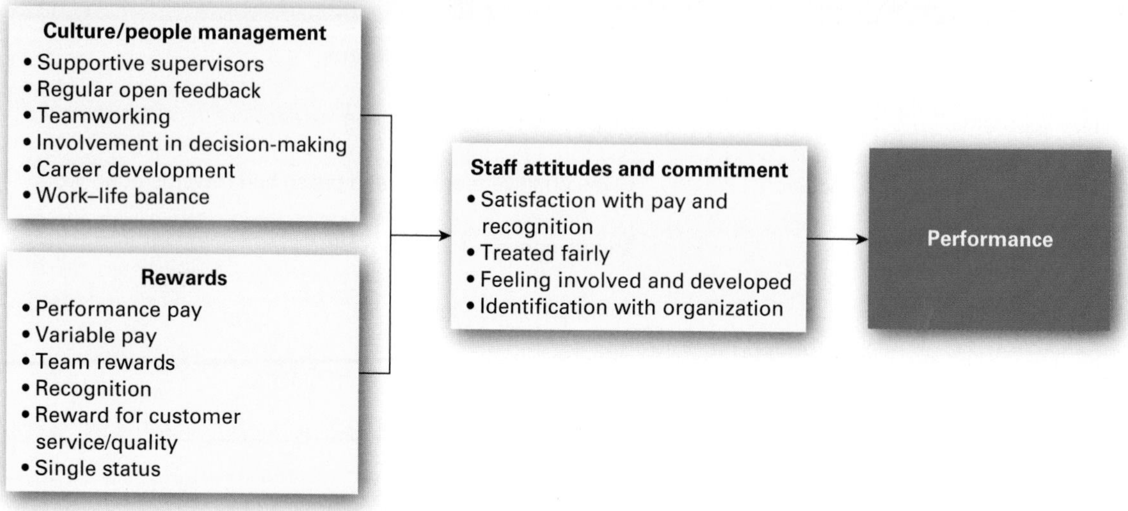

SOURCE: Reilly and Brown (2008)

Employee voice

Employee voice policies enable employees to effectively communicate their concerns to management. Rees *et al* (2013: 2781) suggested that there is a direct relationship between the effectiveness of such policies and levels of employee engagement. They invoked social exchange theory, which states that employees engage in reciprocal relationships that can develop into trusting, loyal and mutual commitments when certain 'rules of exchange' are observed. Employees will demonstrate positive attitudes and behaviours when they perceive that their employer values them and their contribution. They will demonstrate higher levels of performance if the work environment is one in which employees have a voice in the sense that they can share their concerns, opinions and ideas with their employers.

The 'big idea'

A basis for building organizational engagement was established by the longitudinal research in 12 companies conducted by Professor John Purcell and his colleagues (Purcell *et al*, 2003: 13). They found that the most successful companies had 'the big idea'. This was 'a clear sense of mission underpinned by values and a culture expressing what a firm is and its relationship with its customers and employees'.

The work environment

Increasing organizational engagement through the work environment means developing a culture that encourages positive attitudes to work, promoting interest and excitement in the jobs people do, reducing stress and recognizing the importance of social interaction. For example, Lands' End, the clothing company, believes that staff who are enjoying themselves, who are being supported and developed and who feel fulfilled and respected at work, will provide the best service to customers.

It was suggested by Guest (2009) that engagement can be achieved through effective leadership of a strong, positive culture that ensures the enactment of organizational values; through strong management that supports employees' work and well-being; through careful design of systems and jobs to enable employees to contribute through full use of their knowledge and skills; through effective employee voice; and through provision of appropriate resources, tools and information to perform effectively.

Burnout

There is a negative side to engagement – burnout, defined by Maslach and Jackson (1981: 99) as 'a syndrome of emotional exhaustion and cynicism'. Burnout can take place when individuals are placed under too much pressure to perform. It is sometimes called disengagement. Workaholics who put themselves under too much pressure can suffer burnout.

Burnout is a response to high stress caused by excessive job demands, which include attempting to meet challenging, relentless and unreachable standards. It is more likely to happen when workers have no control over their work environment. Burnout can result in failure, absenteeism or leaving the organization.

To avoid the pursuit of engagement resulting in disengagement and burnout, managements need to ensure that employees are not put under too much pressure, are provided with support when required and are recognized for what they can achieve with the resources they have available (including their own skills and ability to exert effort). Alfes *et al* (2010) concluded that a responsible approach to engagement requires a work environment that does not just demand more but fosters a balance in people's lives.

Measuring engagement

Engagement surveys provide the basis for the development and implementation of engagement strategies. A review by Vance (2006) of a number of such surveys identified the following common themes:

- pride in employer;
- satisfaction with employer;
- job satisfaction;
- opportunity to perform well at challenging work;
- recognition and positive feedback for one's contributions;
- personal support from one's supervisor;
- effort above and beyond the minimum;
- understanding the link between one's job and the organization's mission;
- prospects for future growth with one's employer;
- intention to stay with one's employer.

The important thing to do with an engagement survey (an example of which is given in Chapter 64), as with any form of attitude survey, is to ensure that proper use is made of it through the 'triple-A' approach: Analysis, Assessment and Action. It is also important to inform employees of the results of the survey in full and involve them in assessing the results and agreeing actions.

Conclusions

Keenoy (2013: 198) referred to the message delivered by employee engagement prescriptions as 'motherhood and apple pie' and suggested that the term engagement could be replaced by job involvement, empowerment, high performance management or 'any of the other putative solutions' to the problem of getting employees to be more productive. He argued that 'there are powerful generic echoes of McGregor's (1960) Theory Y' – the view that people are creative beings who under proper conditions will not only accept but also seek responsibility.

David Guest (2013: 233) warned that: 'The risk must be that it [employee engagement] will soon join the pantheon of laudable aspirations with which we can all agree, including happiness, quality, growth and sustainability; goals that most of us would like to pursue, concepts that some people think we can measure, but goals that will remain ultimately elusive in many if not most cases'.

However, John Purcell (2013: 247) contended that: 'Employee engagement is worth pursuing, not as an end in itself, but as a means of improving working lives and company performance'. And the CIPD (2012: 1) noted that:

> Engagement is not about driving employees to work harder but about providing the conditions in which they will work more effectively – it is about releasing employees' discretionary behaviour.

CASE STUDY Land Registry – modernizing the public sector

Land Registry is a government executive agency employing 300 people. Engaging and enthusing its staff has been a challenge. The Swansea site was an underperforming office within an otherwise successful organization. Today it is one of the most productive Land Registry offices as a result of a planned high-engagement working change process.

The change process focused on the engagement of individuals at all levels. An internal project board masterminded a series of staff surveys and conferences. Senior management team away-days and line management training and coaching to improve performance management and the development of soft skills were all resourced in-house. Training initially focused on senior management team development, so they could understand and lead the changes, building middle management skills so that they could lead change and create an atmosphere in which employees could have confidence in an open appraisal process, and team building and development. Service to customers was always at the centre of the process. Personal development plans, based on Land Registry's national core competency framework, provided the opportunity to discuss knowledge, skills and 'most importantly' attitudes. The framework bands nine competencies in five main performance areas:

- *Delivering results*: planning and organizing the workload; and dealing effectively with/managing change.
- *Effective teamwork*: contributing to the team's performance; and building and leading a team.
- *Knowledge and experience*: acquiring and applying technical/specialist knowledge.
- *Providing a quality service*: meeting customers' needs; and anticipating problems and achieving solutions.
- *Personal effectiveness*: communicating effectively; and showing initiative and determination.

Each of these competencies can be demonstrated at four levels, from entry to senior management level.

Key learning points: Employee engagement

The meaning of employee engagement

Engagement happens when people are committed to their work and the organization and are motivated to achieve high levels of performance. It has two interrelated aspects: 1) job engagement, which takes place when employees exercise discretionary effort because they find their jobs interesting, challenging and rewarding; and 2) organizational engagement, when they identify with the values and purpose of their organization and believe that it is a great place in which to work and to continue to work.

Components of engagement

The components of engagement are commitment, organizational citizenship behaviour, motivation and job satisfaction.

Theory of engagement

Engagement will have behavioural outcomes leading to what can be described as an 'engaged employee'. A strong theoretical rationale for engagement is provided by social exchange theory.

Drivers of engagement

Macey *et al* (2009) emphasize the importance of the work environment and the jobs people do. Alfes *et al* (2010) established that the main drivers of engagement are meaningful work (the most important), senior management vision and communication, positive perceptions of one's line manager and employee voice – employees having a say in matters that concern them.

Enhancing engagement

Line managers play a key role in enhancing job engagement with the support of organizational initiatives in the areas of job design; learning programmes, including leadership development for line managers; and performance and reward management systems.

The approaches that can be used to enhance organizational engagement include: 1) high-involvement management; (2) developing 'the big idea'; and (3) tackling the work environment.

Burnout

Burnout can take place when individuals are placed under too much pressure to perform. It is sometimes called disengagement.

Measuring engagement

Engagement surveys provide the basis for the development and implementation of engagement strategies.

Questions

1 What is employee engagement?
2 What is job engagement?
3 What is organizational engagement?
4 What are the components of engagement?
5 What is organizational citizenship behaviour?
6 What is the relationship between engagement and commitment?
7 What is the relationship between engagement and motivation?
8 What is the relationship between engagement and organizational citizenship behaviour?
9 What are the main outcomes of engagement (name at least four)?
10 What are the main conclusions about engagement reached by the research conducted by Saks (2006)?
11 What are the main conclusions about engagement reached by the research conducted by Balain and Sparrow (2009)?
12 What are the main conclusions about engagement reached by the research conducted by MacLeod and Clarke (2009)?
13 What are the main conclusions about engagement reached by the research conducted by Alfes *et al* (2010)?
14 What is social exchange theory?
15 What is discretionary behaviour?
16 What are the main drivers of engagement as listed by MacLeod and Clarke (name at least three)?
17 How can job engagement be enhanced?
18 What is the role of job design in job engagement?
19 How can organizational engagement be enhanced?
20 What is high-involvement management?

References

Alfes, K, Truss, C, Soane, E C, Rees, C and Gatenby, M (2010) *Creating an Engaged Workforce*, London, CIPD

Armstrong, M, Brown, D and Reilly, P (2010) *Evidence-based Reward Management*, London, Kogan Page

Balain, S and Sparrow, P (2009) *Engaged to Perform: A new perspective on employee engagement*, Lancaster, Lancaster University Management School

Chartered Institute of Personnel and Development (2012) *Employee Engagement Factsheet*, available at www.cipd.co.uk/hr-resources/factsheets/employee-engagement.aspx [accessed October 2012]

Chartered Institute of Personnel and Development (2012) *Where has all the trust gone?* London, CIPD

Christian, M S, Garza, A S and Slaughter, J E (2011) Work engagement: a quantitative review and test of its relations with task and contextual performance, *Personnel Psychology*, 64 (1), pp 89–136

Coffman, C and Gonzalez-Molina, G (2002) *Follow This Path*, New York, Warner Business Books

Conference Board (2006) *Employee Engagement: A review of current research and its implications*, New York, Conference Board

Crawford, E R, Rich, B L, Buckman, B and Bergeron, J (2013) The antecendents and drivers of employee engagement in (eds) C Truss, R Deldridge, K Afles, A Shantz and E Soane, *Employee Engagement in Theory and Practice*, London, Routledge, pp 57–81

Guest, D (2009) *Review of Employee Engagement: Notes for a discussion* (unpublished), prepared specifically for the MacLeod and Clarke 2009 review of employee engagement.

Guest, D E (2013) Employee engagement: fashionable fad or long-term fixture? in (eds) C Truss, R Deldridge, K Afles, A Shantz and E Soane, *Employee Engagement in Theory and Practice*, London, Routledge, pp 221–235

Hakanen, J J, Bakker, A B and Schaufeli, W B (2006) Burnout and work engagement among teachers, *Journal of School Psychology*, 43, pp 495–513

Harter, J K, Schmidt, F L and Hayes, T L (2002) Business-unit level relationship between employee satisfaction, employee engagement, and business outcomes: a meta-analysis, *Journal of Applied Psychology*, 87, pp 268–79

Jenkins, S and Delbridge, R (2013) Context matters: examining 'soft' and 'hard' approaches to employee engagement in two workplaces, *International Journal of Human Resource Management*, 24 (14), pp 2670–91

Kahn, W A (1990) Psychological conditions of personal engagement and disengagement at work, *Academy of Management Journal*, 33 (4), pp 692–724

Keenoy, T (2013) Engagement: A murmeration of objects? in (eds) C Truss, R Deldridge, K Alfes, A Shantz and E Soane, *Employee Engagement in Theory and Practice*, London, Routledge, pp 198–220

Lawler, E E (1986) *High Involvement Management*, San Francisco, CA, Jossey-Bass

Lewis, R, Donaldson-Feilder, E and Tharani, T (2012) *Management Competencies for Enhancing Employee Engagement*, London, CIPD

Little, B and Little, P (2006) Employee engagement: conceptual issues, *Journal of Organizational Culture, Communications and Conflict*, 10 (1), pp 111–20

Locke, E A (1976) The nature and causes of job satisfaction, in (ed) M D Dunnette, *Handbook of Industrial and Organizational Psychology*, Chicago, Rand McNally, pp 1297–343

Macey, W H and Schneider, B (2008) The meaning of employee engagement, *Industrial and Organizational Psychology: Perspectives on Science and Practice*, 1, pp 3–30

Macey, W H, Schneider, B, Barbera, K M and Young, S A (2009) *Employee Engagement*, Malden, MA, Wiley-Blackwell

MacLeod, D and Clarke, N (2009) *Engaging for Success: Enhancing performance through employee engagement*, London, Department for Business Innovation and Skills

Maslach, C and Jackson, S E (1981) The measurement of experienced burnout, *Journal of Organizational Behaviour*, 2 (2) pp 99–113

McGregor, D (1960) *The Human Side of Enterprise*, New York, McGraw-Hill

Organ, D W (1988) *Organizational Citizenship Behaviour: The good soldier syndrome*, Lexington, MA, Lexington Books

Purcell, J (2013) Employee voice and engagement, in (eds) C Truss, R Deldridge, K Alfes, A Shantz and E Soane, *Employee Engagement in Theory and Practice*, London, Routledge, pp 236–49

Purcell, J, Kinnie, K, Hutchinson, N, Rayton, B and Swart, J (2003) *People and Performance: How people management impacts on organizational performance*, London, CIPD

Rees, C, Alfes, K and Gatenby, M (2013) Employee voice and engagement: connections and consequences, *International Journal of Human Resource Management*, 24 (14), pp 2780–98

Reilly, P and Brown, D (2008) Employee engagement: future focus or fashionable fad for reward management? *WorldatWork Journal*, 17 (4), pp 37–49

Robertson, I T and Smith, M (1985) *Motivation and Job Design*, London, IPM

Robinson, D, Perryman, S and Hayday, S (2004) *The Drivers of Employee Engagement*, Brighton, Institute for Employment Studies

Saks, A M (2006) Antecedents and consequences of employee engagement, *Journal of Managerial Psychology*, 21 (6), pp 600–19

Schaufeli, W B (2013) What is engagement? in (eds) C Truss, R Deldridge, K Alfes, A Shantz and E Soane, *Employee Engagement in Theory and Practice*, London, Routledge, pp 15–35

Sparrow, P (2013) Strategic HRM and employee engagement, in (eds) C Truss, R Deldridge, K Alfes, A Shantz and E Soane, *Employee Engagement in Theory and Practice*, London, Routledge, pp 99–115

Stairs, M and Galpin, M (2010) Positive engagement: from employee engagement to workplace happiness, in (eds) P A Linley, S Harrington and N Garcea, *The Oxford Handbook of Positive Psychology and Work*, New York, Oxford University Press

Storey, J (1989) From personnel management to human resource management, in (ed) J Storey, *New Perspectives on Human Resource Management*, London, Routledge, pp 1–18

Storey, J (2007) What is human resource management?, in (ed) J Storey, *Human Resource Management: A critical text*, London, Thompson Learning, pp 3–19

Towers Perrin (2003) *Working Today: Understanding what drives employee engagement*, New York, Towers Perrin

Truss, C, Deldridge, R, Alfes, K, Shantz, A and Soane, E (2013) Introduction, *Employee Engagement in Theory and Practice*, London, Routledge

Truss, C, Schantz, A, Soane, E, Alfes, K and Delbridge, R, (2013) Employee engagement, organizational performance and individual well-being: exploring the evidence, developing the theory, *International Journal of Human Resource Management*, 24 (14), pp 2657–69

Truss, C, Soane, E, Edwards, C, Wisdom, K, Croll, A and Burnett, J (2006) *Working Life: Employee attitudes and engagement*, London, CIPD

Vance, R J (2006) *Employee Engagement and Commitment: A guide to understanding, measuring and increasing engagement in your organization*, Alexandria, VA, SHRM Foundation

Yalabik, Z Y, Popaitoon, P, Chowne, J A and Rayton, B A (2013) Work engagement as mediator between employee attitudes and outcomes, *International Journal of Human Resource Management*, 24 (14), pp 2799–823

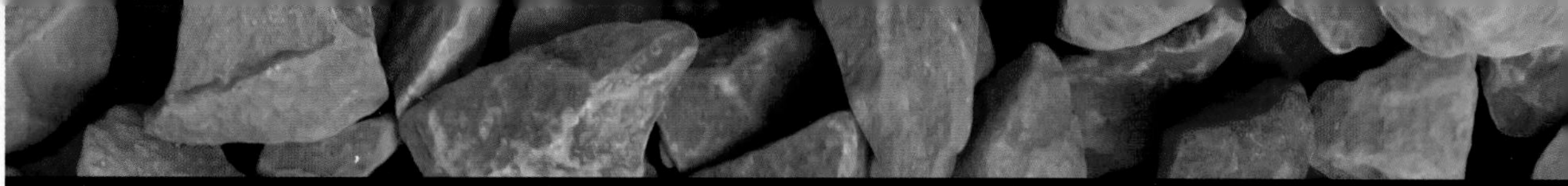

PART IV

People resourcing

PART IV CONTENTS

Introduction

People resourcing, often called 'employee resourcing' or simply 'resourcing', is the term used to cover employment activities that ensure the organization has the people it needs, and deals with employee issues such as turnover and absenteeism issues. The employment activities comprise workforce planning, recruitment and selection, attracting and retaining people, managing employee turnover, absence management and talent management. People resourcing is associated with learning and development programmes that provide for the organization to have the skills and talented people it requires.

Resourcing is a vital organizational activity that recognizes that the strategic capability of a firm depends on its resource capability in the shape of people (the resource-based view). This is the strategic approach to resourcing, as explained in Chapter 16. From this emerges the workforce planning aspect of resourcing covered in Chapter 17, which deals with what sort of workforce the organization requires now and in the future and what steps should be taken to meet those requirements.

The core resourcing activities of recruitment and selection and handling employment issues discussed in the next two chapters are transactional. There are some who are rather dismissive about them, implying that HR is primarily a transformational activity and that recruitment, while necessary, is best left to the sidelined inhabitants of shared service centres so that business partners can get on with what really matters. They could not be more wrong. If HR does not deliver the transactional services expected of it, then no amount of strategizing will save the function from being dismissed as a luxury.

However, talent management as described in Chapter 20 contains both transformational and transactional elements. It recognizes that businesses with the best people win and that the way to transform the organization is to identify and develop those with talent, but it also involves transactional activities such as recruitment and the administration of learning and development events.

16
Strategic resourcing

KEY CONCEPTS AND TERMS

Employee value proposition

Employer brand

Employer of choice

Psychological contract

Talent management

Workforce planning

LEARNING OUTCOMES

On completing this chapter you should be able to define these key concepts. You should also know about:

- The meaning of strategic resourcing
- The objective of strategic resourcing
- The strategic HRM approach to resourcing
- Strategic fit in resourcing
- Integrating business and resourcing strategies
- The components of resourcing strategy

Introduction

Strategic resourcing is a key part of strategic human resource management, ie matching human resources to the strategic and operational requirements of the organization and ensuring the full utilization of those resources. It is concerned not only with obtaining and keeping the number and quality of staff required but also with selecting and promoting people who 'fit' the culture and the strategic requirements of the organization.

The objective of strategic resourcing

Strategic resourcing aims to ensure that the organization has the people it needs to achieve its business goals. Like strategic HRM, strategic resourcing is essentially about the integration of business and employee resourcing strategies so that the latter contribute to the achievement of the former.

The concept that the strategic capability of a firm depends on its resource capability in the shape of people (the resource-based view) provides the rationale for strategic resourcing. The objective is therefore to ensure that a firm achieves competitive advantage by recruiting, retaining and developing more capable people than its rivals. The organization attracts such people by being 'the employer of choice'. It retains them by providing better opportunities, rewards and conditions of employment than others and by developing a positive psychological contract (the set of reciprocal but unwritten expectations that exist between individual employees and their employers), which increases engagement and commitment and creates mutual trust. Furthermore, the organization deploys its people in ways that maximize the added value they supply and develops their talents and skills.

The strategic HRM approach to resourcing

The philosophy behind the strategic approach to resourcing is that it is people who implement the strategic plan. As Quinn Mills (1983) put it, the process is one of 'planning with people in mind'.

The integration of business and resourcing strategies is based on an understanding of the direction in which the organization is going and the determination of:

- the numbers of people required to meet business needs;
- the skills and behaviour required to support the achievement of business strategies;
- the impact of organizational restructuring as a result of rationalization, decentralization, delayering, acquisitions, mergers, product or market development, or the introduction of new technology – for example, cellular manufacturing;
- plans for changing the culture of the organization in such areas as ability to deliver, performance standards, quality, customer service, teamworking and flexibility, which indicate the need for people with different attitudes, beliefs and personal characteristics.

These factors will be strongly influenced by the type of business strategies adopted by the organization and the sort of business it is in. These may be expressed in such terms as Miles and Snow's (1978) typology of defender, prospector and analyser organizations.

Strategic HRM places more emphasis than traditional personnel management on finding people whose attitudes and behaviour are likely to fit what management believes to be appropriate and conducive to success. Townley (1989) commented that organizations are concentrating more on the attitudinal and behavioural characteristics of employees. This tendency has its dangers. Innovative and adaptive organizations need non-conformists, even mavericks, who can 'buck the system'. If managers recruit people 'in their own image' there is the risk of staffing the organization with conformist clones and of perpetuating a dysfunctional culture – one that may have been successful in the past but is no longer appropriate in the face of new challenges.

The resourcing strategies that emerge from the process of strategic resourcing exist to provide the people and skills required to support the business strategy, but they should also contribute to the formulation of that strategy. HR directors have an obligation to point out to their colleagues the human resource opportunities and constraints that will affect the achievement of strategic plans. In mergers or acquisitions, for example, the ability of management within the company to handle the new situation and the quality of management in the new business will be important considerations.

Strategic fit in resourcing

Strategic resourcing places more emphasis than traditional personnel management on finding people whose attitudes and behaviour are likely to fit what management believes to be appropriate and conducive to success. As mentioned above, Townley (1989) felt that organizations are concentrating more on the attitudinal and behavioural characteristics of employees, a tendency that has its dangers.

Bundling resourcing strategies and activities

Employee resourcing is not just about recruitment and selection. It is concerned with any means available to meet the firm's need for certain skills and behaviours. A strategy to ensure the organization has the talented people it needs (a talent management strategy) may start with recruitment and selection but would extend into learning and development to enhance abilities and skills and modify behaviours and succession planning. Performance management processes can be used to identify development needs (skills and behaviours) and motivate people to make the most effective use of their abilities. Competency frameworks and profiles can be prepared to define the skills and behaviours required and can be used in selection, employee development and employee reward processes. The aim should be to develop a reinforcing bundle of strategies along these lines.

The components of strategic employee resourcing

The overarching component of strategic resourcing is the integration of resourcing and business plans. Within this framework strategic resourcing includes specific strategies for:

- *Workforce planning*, alternatively called human resource planning – assessing future business needs and deciding on the numbers and types of people required.
- *Developing the organization's employee value proposition and its employer brand* – the employee value proposition is what an organization offers that prospective or existing employees would value and which would help to persuade them to join or remain with the business; employer brand is the image presented by an organization as a good employer.
- *Resourcing plans* – preparing plans for finding people from within the organization and/or for learning and development programmes to help people learn new skills. If needs cannot be satisfied from within the organization, it involves preparing longer-term plans for ensuring that recruitment and selection processes will satisfy them.
- *Retention plans* – preparing plans for retaining the people the organization needs.
- *Flexibility plans* – planning for increased flexibility in the use of human resources to enable the organization to make the best use of people and adapt swiftly to changing circumstances.
- *Talent management* – ensuring that the organization has the talented people it requires to provide for management succession and meet present and future business needs.

CASE STUDY

Recruitment and retention strategy at Buckingham County Council

Attracting and retaining high-quality staff is considered key to the corporate strategy of Buckingham County Council, which employs around 14,000 people. Resourcing is one of the most important things the council does to improve performance.

Resourcing and people strategy

The resourcing strategy complements and reinforces the people strategy, which has five targets:

1. being the best employer;
2. bringing in additional talent;
3. developing existing talent;
4. championing diversity;
5. transforming the organization.

The people strategy dashboard

A people strategy dashboard has been created to ensure that human resources are managed more effectively. This extends the people strategy targets and is used to monitor progress in achieving them.

Improving recruitment and selection

This involved:

- strengthening the employer brand;
- developing a better recruitment website;
- developing a talent bank to ensure that vacancies were filled quickly;
- streamlining processes to reduce the time to fill vacancies;
- the development of a competency framework used for competency-based selection.

Retaining talent

An holistic approach is adopted to retaining talent. This involves paying attention to every aspect of the employment relationship and setting a best-employer target. A staff survey is used to measure employee engagement.

Total reward strategy

A total reward approach is adopted, including the use of total reward statements.

Talent management

A talent management toolkit is used to identify and develop potential high performers at every level in the organization.

Key learning points: Strategic resourcing

- Employee resourcing, generally known simply as 'resourcing' is the term used to describe activities concerned with the acquisition, retention and development of human resources.
- Strategic resourcing is concerned with ensuring that the organization obtains and retains the people it needs and employs them effectively. It is a key part of the strategic HRM process, which is fundamentally about matching human resources to the strategic and operational needs of the organization and ensuring the full utilization of those resources.
- The aim of strategic resourcing is therefore to ensure that a firm achieves competitive advantage by employing more capable people than its rivals. These people will have a wider and deeper range of skills and will behave in ways that will maximize their contribution.
- Strategic resourcing places more emphasis than traditional personnel management on finding people whose attitudes and behaviour are likely to be congruent with what management believes to be appropriate and conducive to success.
- The philosophy behind the strategic HRM approach to resourcing is that it is people who implement the strategic plan. Resourcing strategies exist to provide the people and skills required to support the business strategy, but they should also contribute to the formulation of that strategy.
- Strategic resourcing is not just about recruitment and selection. It is concerned with any means available to meet the needs of the firm for certain skills and behaviours.
- The overarching component of strategic resourcing is the integration of resourcing and business plans. Within this framework strategic resourcing includes specific strategies for:

  1. workforce planning;
  2. developing the organization's employee value proposition and its employer brand;
  3. resourcing plans;
  4. retention;
  5. flexibility;
  6. talent management.

Questions

1 What is resourcing?
2 What is strategic resourcing?
3 What is the essential nature of strategic resourcing?
4 What is the strategic HRM approach to resourcing?
5 What is meant by integrating business and resourcing strategies?
6 What are the components of resourcing strategy?

References

Miles, R E and Snow, C C (1978) *Organizational Strategy: Structure and process*, New York, McGraw-Hill

Quinn Mills, D (1983) Planning with people in mind, *Harvard Business Review*, November–December, pp 97–105

Townley, B (1989) Selection and appraisal: reconstructing social relations?, in (ed) J Storey, *New Perspectives in Human Resource Management*, London, Routledge

17
Workforce planning

KEY CONCEPTS AND TERMS

Demand forecasting

Hard human resources planning

Human resources planning

PESTLE analysis

Ratio-trend analysis

Scenario planning

Soft human resources planning

Supply forecasting

SWOT analysis

LEARNING OUTCOMES

On completing this chapter you should be able to define these key concepts. You should also understand:

- The nature of workforce planning
- The link between workforce and business planning
- The rationale for workforce planning
- Workforce planning issues
- Approaches to workforce planning

Introduction

Organizations have to know how many people and what sort of people they need to meet present and future business requirements. This is the function of workforce planning. The purpose of this chapter is to describe how workforce planning functions, bearing in mind that it is not as straightforward as it was presented when the notion of 'manpower planning' became popular in the 1960s and 70s. Workforce planning, or human resource planning as it used to be called, may be well established in the HRM vocabulary but it does not seem to be embedded as a key HR activity.

This chapter starts with a definition of workforce planning and continues with a discussion of its aims and the issues involved, including its link with business planning. The final section of the chapter describes the processes used, namely scenario planning, demand and supply forecasting and action planning. A workforce planning toolkit is provided in Chapter 65.

Workforce planning defined

The following definition of workplace planning was produced by the CIPD (2010a: 4): 'Workforce planning is a core process of human resource management that is shaped by the organizational strategy and ensures the right number of people with the right skills, in the right place at the right time to deliver short- and long-term organizational objectives.'

Workforce planning may be conducted as an overall approach to establishing and satisfying people requirements covering all major employee categories and skills. However, it frequently concentrates on key categories of staff, for example, doctors, nurses and other health workers in the National Health Service, skilled operatives in a manufacturing company, sales staff in a retail store or drivers in a transport company.

Rothwell (1995: 194) distinguished between HR planning in the hard sense – 'to serve as an indicator of the likely match or mismatch of the supply and demand for the right number of people with appropriate skills' – and HR planning in the soft sense – 'to alert the organization to the implications of business strategy for people development, culture and attitudes as well as numbers and skills'. The CIPD (2010a: 4) made a similar distinction between 'hard' and 'soft' workforce planning. As the report on their research commented:

> Hard workforce planning is about numbers. In the past this often revolved around using past trends to predict the future, matching supply and demand for labour with the result that plans were often out of date before the ink was dry. Now there is more emphasis on management information that can help understand cause and effect of certain phenomena.

Soft workplace planning focuses on general issues relating to the supply of and demand for people and how they are deployed.

The precursor to workforce planning – manpower planning as conceived in the 1960s – was almost entirely about numbers in the shape of quantitative demand and supply forecasts. It was the failure in many organizations to produce accurate forecasts and therefore prepare meaningful plans that led to its decline if not fall. Workforce planning today covers a wider range of activities such as succession planning, smart working, flexible working and talent planning, and is not such a numbers game.

Incidence of workforce planning

The CIPD Annual Survey of Resourcing and Talent Planning (2010b) found that 61 per cent of organizations conducted workforce planning, although it was most common in the public services sector and in larger organizations: 20 per cent of organizations planned for less than one year, 41 per cent for one to two years and only 2 per cent for more than five years. The CIPD (2010a) research established that the top five planning activities were:

1. succession planning – 62 per cent;
2. flexible working – 53 per cent;
3. demand/supply forecasting – 53 per cent;
4. skills audit/gap analysis – 49 per cent;
5. talent management – 42 per cent.

The link between workforce and business planning

Workforce planning is an integral part of business planning. The strategic planning process defines projected changes in the types of activities carried out by the organization and the scale of those activities. It identifies the core competencies that the organization needs to achieve its goals and therefore its skill and behavioural requirements.

Workforce planning interprets these plans in terms of people requirements. But it may influence the business strategy by drawing attention to the ways in which people could be developed and deployed more effectively to further the achievement of business goals. It will also address issues concerning the supply of suitable people.

Reasons for workforce planning

Research conducted by the Institute for Employment Studies (Reilly, 1999) established that there were three main reasons why organizations engaged in workforce planning:

1. Planning for substantive reasons, that is, to have a practical effect by optimizing the use of resources and/or making them more flexible, acquiring and nurturing skills that take time to develop, identifying potential problems and minimizing the chances of making a bad decision.
2. Planning because of the process benefits, which involves understanding the present in order to confront the future, challenging assumptions and liberating thinking, making explicit decisions that can later be challenged, standing back and providing an overview and ensuring that long-term thinking is not driven out by short-term focus.
3. Planning for organizational reasons, which involves communicating plans so as to obtain support/adherence to them, linking HR plans to business plans so as to influence them, (re)gaining corporate control over operating units and coordinating and integrating organizational decision-making and actions.

Workforce planning issues

The main difficulties faced by those involved in quantitative (hard) workforce planning are the impact of change and trying to predict the future. Many organizations therefore adopt a short-term approach and deal with deficits or surpluses of people as they arise. This problem is compounded by what Rothwell (1995) referred to as the shifting kaleidoscope of policy priorities and strategies within organizations. It sounds like a good idea to adopt an integrated approach to workforce and business planning but it won't work well if business plans are volatile, vague, misleading or non-existent, as they easily can be. Beardwell (2007: 62) commented that HR plans should be treated as 'tentative, flexible, and reviewed and modified on a regular basis'. Cappelli (2009: 10) noted that: 'The competitive environment for businesses is so changeable, and firms adjust their own strategies and practices so frequently that these estimates [of the demand for talent] are rarely accurate and they get much worse the farther out one goes.'

This problem will not be so acute in a stable marketplace, with largely passive (and static) customers, and with scope for long-term forecasting. But these are rare conditions today, even in the public sector where for a long time workplace planning has thrived.

It can be said that workforce planning is more art than science. Perhaps the accuracy of demand and supply forecasts is less important than the overall understanding of what the organization needs in the way of people, which can be generated by a systematic approach to planning.

The systematic approach to workforce planning

A flow chart of the process of workforce planning is shown in Figure 17.1. This identifies the main planning activities described below. Although these are

FIGURE 17.1 Workforce planning flowchart

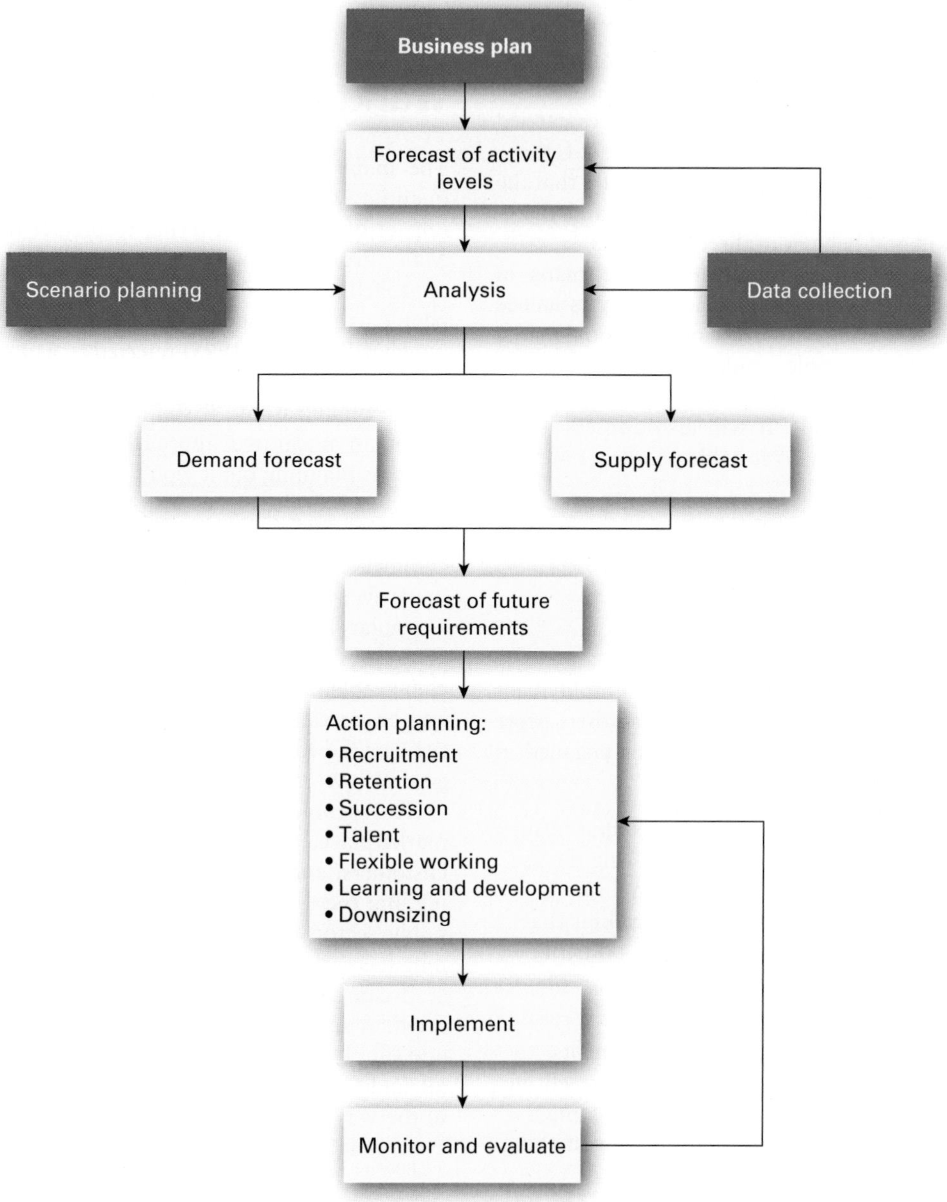

referred to as separate areas, they are interrelated and can overlap. For example, demand forecasts may be prepared on the basis of assumptions about the productivity of employees. But a forecast of the supply of suitable people will also have to consider productivity trends and how they might affect the supply. A more detailed flow chart is given in Chapter 65 (Figure 65.1).

Business planning

The business plan provides the basis for the workforce plan insofar as it sets out what the organization intends to do in terms of activities and the scale of those activities.

Forecast activity levels

Forecasts of future activity levels flow from the business plan, which will have implications for the demand for people. Activity level forecasts will also be affected by external factors, for example demographic and political policy trends, especially in the public sector. Data will need to be collected and analysed for this purpose.

Scenario planning

Scenario planning is an assessment of the environmental changes that are likely to affect the organization so that a prediction can be made of the possible situations that may have to be dealt with in the future. The scenario may list a range of predictions so that different responses can be considered. The scenario is best based on systematic environmental scanning, possibly using the PESTLE approach (an assessment of the political, economic, social, legal, technological and economic factors that might affect the organization). The implications of these factors on the organization's labour markets and what can be done about any human resource issues can then be considered.

Data collection

The information used in workforce planning can be collected under the following headings:

- *Qualitative internal data*: business information on product/market developments, proposed work system and organizational changes; HR information on people (skills, performance, etc).
- *Quantitative internal data*: workforce data on turnover, absence, demographics, skills audits, etc.
- *Qualitative external data*: PESTLE analysis covering the following factors: political, economic, social, technological, legal and environmental.
- *Quantitative external data*: labour market – demographics, skills availability.

Analysis

The analysis stage brings all the information together from the business plan, the activity forecast, scenarios and internal and external data to provide the basis for demand and supply forecasts.

Demand forecasting

Demand forecasting is the process of estimating the future numbers of people required and the likely skills and competences they will need. The basis of the forecast is the annual budget and longer-term business plan, translated into activity levels for each function and department. In a manufacturing company the sales budget would be translated into a manufacturing plan, giving the numbers and types of products to be made in each period. From this information the number of hours to be worked by each skill category to make the quota for each period would be computed.

Details are required of any organizational and work plans that would result in increased or decreased demands for employees. Examples are setting up a new regional organization, creating a new sales department, decentralizing a head office function to the regions, plans for new methods of working, additional outsourcing, increasing productivity and reducing employment costs. The demand forecasting methods for estimating the numbers of people required are described below.

Managerial judgement

The most typical method of forecasting used is managerial judgement. This simply requires managers to sit down, think about their future workloads, and decide how many people they need. It may be quite unscientific and misleading.

Forecasting might be done on a 'bottom-up' basis with line managers submitting proposals for agreement by senior management. Alternatively, a 'top-down' approach can be used, in which company and departmental forecasts are prepared by top management, possibly acting on advice from the personnel departments. These forecasts are reviewed and agreed with departmental managers. A less directive approach is for top management to prepare planning guidelines for departmental managers, setting out the planning assumptions and the targets they should try to meet.

Perhaps the best way of using managerial judgement is to adopt both the 'bottom-up' and 'top-down' approaches. Guidelines for departmental managers should be prepared, indicating broad company assumptions about future activity levels that will affect their departments. Targets are also set where necessary. Armed with these guidelines, departmental managers prepare their forecasts to a laid-down format. They are encouraged to seek help at this stage from the personnel or work study departments. Meanwhile, the HR department, in conjunction as necessary with planning and work study departments, prepares a company forecast. The two sets of forecasts can then be reviewed by a human resource planning committee consisting of functional heads. This committee reconciles with departmental managers any discrepancies between the two forecasts and submits the final amended forecast to top management for approval. This is sometimes called the 'right-angle method'.

Ratio-trend analysis

Ratio-trend analysis is carried out by analysing existing ratios between an activity level and the number of employees working on that activity. The ratio is applied to forecast activity levels to determine an adjusted number of people required. Account can be taken of possible improvements in productivity that would affect the ratio. The analysis may be extended to cover employees connected to but not directly involved in the activity – the indirect workers who provide support to the direct workers responsible for carrying out the activity. The existing ratio of directs to indirects would be applied to the forecast number of directs needed to deal with the new activity levels to forecast the number of indirects needed.

Work study techniques

Work study techniques are used in association with activity level forecasts to calculate how long operations should take and the number of people required. Work study techniques for direct workers can be combined with ratio-trend analysis to calculate the number of indirect workers needed.

Forecasting skill and competency requirements

Forecasting skill and competency requirements is largely a matter of managerial judgement. This judgement should, however, be exercised on the basis of an analysis of the impact of projected product/market developments and the introduction of new technology, either information technology or computerized manufacturing.

Supply forecasting

Supply forecasting measures the number of people likely to be available from within and outside the organization. The internal supply analysis covers the following areas:

- existing number of people employed by occupation, skill and potential;
- potential losses to existing resources through attrition (employee turnover);
- potential changes to existing resources through internal promotions;
- changes to the organization structure, new methods of working (including flexible working) more part-time working and different working hours;
- effect of increases in productivity;
- sources of supply from within the organization – existing employees and the outputs of talent management or training programmes.

The external supply analysis examines the local and national labour markets to assess implications for the availability of future people requirements. It will also take account of environmental changes as revealed by scenario planning.

Forecast of future requirements

To forecast future requirements it is necessary to analyse the demand and supply forecasts to identify any deficits or surpluses. The analysis can be made with the help of spreadsheets. The basic data can be set out as follows:

1	Current number employed	700
2	Annual level of turnover	10 per cent
3	Expected losses during year	70
4	Balance at end year	630
5	Number required at end year	750
6	Number to be obtained	(5 – 4) = 120 during year

The data on the number of employees required may be modified by reference to the impact of any productivity plans, organizational changes, new methods of working or revision of role responsibilities.

Action planning

Action plans are derived from the broad resourcing strategies and the more detailed analysis of demand and supply factors. However, the plans often have to be short term and flexible because of the difficulty of making firm predictions about workforce requirements in times of rapid change. The planning activities start with the identification of internal resources available now or that could be made available through learning and development programmes. They continue with plans for recruitment and retention, succession and talent management, the reduction of employee turnover and absenteeism, flexible working, outsourcing, productivity improvement and the revision of role responsibilities. Learning and development programmes may be prepared to provide for future skill requirements. Regrettably, but sometimes inevitably, plans for downsizing may be necessary, but these can aim to avoid compulsory redundancies by such means as recruitment freezes.

Implementation

The implementation of the action plans will provide a challenge. A flexible approach involving quick responses is needed to cope with unforeseeable changes in people requirements.

Monitoring and evaluation

Because of unpredictable events, the implementation of action plans does not always run smoothly. It is necessary to monitor progress carefully, evaluate the effects and, as required, amend the action plan.

CASE STUDIES

Buckinghamshire County Council

Business need drove the workforce planning project at Buckinghamshire County Council. This recognized that current workforce planning practices would not meet the challenge of the Care Standards Act 2000, or of future service delivery. One of the main issues in working with children and families was recruiting and retaining qualified social workers. There were insufficient numbers of social workers in post. Turnover levels among established and new employees were high.

The council therefore decided to align strategy and workforce planning in social care for children and families. The workforce plan was developed with the input of a team of representatives from social care for children and families. It was recognized that workforce planning was essential to anticipate future areas of skills shortages. This council is now in a position to anticipate skills shortages and has dealt with them innovatively and immediately.

The workforce plan looked at short- and long-term planning. Short-term planning covered immediate action on recruitment and promotion. Long-term planning covered activities that may span the next five years. Workforce planning allowed for an assessment of skills and an exploration of the levels employees need to work at.

Plymouth Primary Care Trust

The trust set up a multidisciplinary team drawn from the workforce planning and development department, finance and public health teams within the organization to introduce workforce planning across the whole organization. The trust's 230 managers and budget holders were then invited to an awareness programme to introduce the Six Steps Workforce Planning Methodology developed by the NHS Workforce Projects Team (2009). The steps are:

1 Define the plan.
2 Map service change.
3 Define the required workforce.
4 Understand workforce availability.
5 Plan to deliver the required workforce.
6 Implement, monitor and refresh.

Managers were informed that, using this framework, they would be required to produce plans over a one-year, two-year and five-year timescale. The guide was applied by asking each manager to define their workforce plan, outline forces for change, assess demand, assess supply, undertake a gap analysis and subsequent action planning and carry out implementation and a review of the plans.

It was found that while some managers were skilled in workforce planning, the majority needed support to link together the financial, workforce and planning elements of the process. The outcomes were:

- trust-wide workforce planning, using electronic staff record and planning tools;
- workforce planning is now part of day-to-day trust business;
- detailed workforce plans across clinical and non-clinical directorates;
- increased awareness of financial position, age profiles, and workforce risk assessment;
- the development of a more efficient workforce by reviewing skill mix and succession planning;
- integration of workforce planning into the corporate management programme.

Reference

Workforce Projects Team (2009) Skills for Health, available at **http://www.healthcareworkforce.nhs.uk/resource/latest_resources/introduction_to_workforce_planning.html** [accessed 29 July 2011]

Siemens (UK)

Workforce planning at Siemens (UK), the engineering and technology services company, (as reported by the CIPD, 2010a), involves obtaining answers to three fundamental questions: What do we have? What do we want? How do we fill the gap?

At the highest level, the corporate people strategy gives the context for workforce planning, the key objective of which is to ensure that Siemens has the right level of capability to execute business strategy. In essence, the process of workforce planning is one in which the business strategy converges with the people strategy.

The workforce planning process starts with a review of the current workforce derived from SAP data [SAP is a business software system] and onto this is overlaid the likely attrition. Future requirements are identified by means of a dialogue between HR business partners and business unit managers. This enables the skills in each job family to be matched to business initiatives and provides the basis for the workforce forecast.

Key learning points: Workforce planning

Workforce planning defined

The following definition of workplace planning was produced by the CIPD (2010a: 4): 'Workforce planning is a core process of human resource management that is shaped by the organizational strategy and ensures the right number of people with the right skills, in the right place at the right time to deliver short- and long-term organizational objectives.'

Incidence of workforce planning

The CIPD (2010a) research revealed that workforce planning in one form or another is taking place in many organizations.

Link to business planning

Workforce planning is an integral part of business planning.

The rationale for workforce planning

Workforce planning provides a basis for a systematic approach to assessing the number and type of people needed and, having taken into account information on the supply of labour and environmental scanning, for the preparation of recruitment, retention, management succession and talent management plans. Workforce planning is important because it encourages employers to develop clear and explicit links between their business and HR plans and to integrate the two more effectively.

Workforce planning issues

The main difficulties faced by those involved in workforce planning are the impact of change and predicting the future.

Approaches to workforce planning

- Business planning.
- Forecast activity levels.
- Scenario planning.
- Data collection.
- Analysis.
- Demand forecasting.
- Supply forecasting.
- Forecast of future requirements.
- Action planning.
- Implementation.
- Monitoring and evaluation.

Questions

1. What is workforce planning?
2. What is the link between business and workforce planning?
3. What is the rationale for workforce planning?
4. What are the main approaches to workforce planning?

References

Beardwell, J (2007) Human resource planning, in (eds) J Beardwell and T Claydon, *Human Resource Management: A contemporary approach*, 5th edn, Essex, Pearson, pp 189–224

Cappelli, P (2009) A supply chain approach to workforce planning, *Organizational Dynamics*, 38 (1), pp 8–15

CIPD (2010a) *Workforce Planning: Right people, right time, right skills*, London, CIPD

CIPD (2010b) *Annual Survey of Resourcing and Talent Planning*, London, CIPD

Reilly, P (1999) *The Human Resource Planning Audit*, Cambridge, Cambridge Strategy Publications

Rothwell, S (1995) Human resource planning, in (ed) J Storey, *Human Resource Management: A critical text*, London, Routledge

18 Recruitment and selection

KEY CONCEPTS AND TERMS

Biodata
Criterion measure
Employer brand
Employer of choice
Intelligence quotient (IQ)
Job board
Knowledge, skills and abilities (KSAs)
Person specification
Predictive ability
Psychological test
Psychometric test
Recruitment
Recruitment process outsourcing (RPO)
Reliability (test)
Role profile
Selection
Validity (test)
Web 2.0

LEARNING OUTCOMES

On completing this chapter you should be able to define these key concepts. You should also understand:

- The recruitment and selection process
- Defining requirements
- Attracting candidates
- Processing applications
- Selection methods – interviewing and tests
- References and offers
- Dealing with recruitment problems

Introduction

Recruitment is the process of finding and engaging the people the organization needs. Selection is that part of the recruitment process concerned with deciding which applicants or candidates should be appointed to jobs. Recruitment can be costly. The 2013 CIPD survey of resourcing and talent planning found that the average recruitment cost of filling a vacancy for a director or senior manager was £8,000 while for other employees it was £3,000.

The recruitment and selection process

The stages of recruitment and selection are:

1. Defining requirements.
2. Attracting candidates.
3. Sifting applications.
4. Interviewing.
5. Testing.
6. Assessing candidates.
7. Obtaining references.
8. Checking applications.
9. Offering employment.
10. Following up.

Defining requirements

The number and categories of people required may be set out in formal workforce plans from which are derived detailed recruitment plans. More typically, requirements are expressed as ad hoc demands for people because of the creation of new posts, expansion into new activities or areas, or the need for a replacement. These short-term demands may put HR under pressure to deliver candidates quickly.

Requirements are set out in the form of role profiles and person specifications. These provide the information required to post vacancies on the company's website or the internet, draft advertisements, brief agencies or recruitment consultants and assess candidates by means of interviews and selection tests.

Role profiles

Role profiles define the overall purpose of the role, its reporting relationships and the key result areas. For recruiting purposes, the profile is extended to include information on terms and conditions (pay, benefits and hours of work); special requirements such as mobility, travelling or unsocial hours; and learning, development and career opportunities. The recruitment role profile provides the basis for a person specification.

Person specification

A person specification, also known as a recruitment or job specification, defines the knowledge, skills and abilities (KSAs) required to carry out the role, the types of behaviour expected from role holders (behavioural competencies) and the education, qualifications, training and experience needed to acquire the necessary KSAs. The specification is set out under the following headings:

- *Knowledge* – what the individual needs to know to carry out the role.
- *Skills and abilities* – what the individual has to be able to do to carry out the role.
- *Behavioural competencies* – the types of behaviour required for successful performance of the role. These should be role-specific, ideally based on an analysis of employees who are carrying out their roles effectively. The behaviours should also be linked to the core values and competency framework of the organization to help in ensuring that candidates will fit and support the organization's culture.
- *Qualifications and training* – the professional, technical or academic qualifications required or the training that the candidate should have undertaken.
- *Experience* – the types of achievements and activities that would be likely to predict success.
- *Specific demands* – anything that the role holder will be expected to achieve in specified areas, eg develop new markets or products; improve sales, productivity or levels of customer service; introduce new systems or processes.

- *Special requirements* – travelling, unsocial hours, mobility, etc.

It is advisable not to overstate the requirements. Perhaps it is natural to go for the best, but setting an unrealistically high level for candidates increases the problems of attracting applicants and results in dissatisfaction among recruits when they find their talents are not being used. Understating requirements can, of course, be equally dangerous, but it happens less frequently.

The KSAs and competencies defined in the role profile form a fundamental feature of the selection process, which becomes more of a person-based than a job-based approach. They are used as the basis for structured interviews and provide guidance on which selection techniques, such as psychological testing or assessment centres, are most likely to be useful.

The following is an example of the key KSA and competencies parts of a person specification for an HR recruitment adviser.

KSA and competency requirements for a recruitment adviser

1 Knowledge of:

- all aspects of recruitment;
- sources of recruits;
- different media for use in recruiting;
- relevant test instruments (OPQ qualified).

2 Skills and abilities in:

- interviewing techniques;
- test administration;
- role analysis.

3 Behavioural competencies:

- able to relate well to others and use interpersonal skills to achieve desired objectives;
- able to influence the behaviour and decisions of people on matters concerning recruitment and other HR or individual issues;
- able to cope with change, to be flexible and to handle uncertainty;
- able to make sense of issues, identify and solve problems and 'think on one's feet';
- focus on achieving results;
- able to maintain appropriately directed energy and stamina, to exercise self-control and to learn new behaviours;
- able to communicate well, orally and on paper.

Attracting candidates

The following steps are required when planning how to attract candidates:

1. Analyse recruitment strengths and weaknesses to develop an employee value proposition and employer brand.
2. Analyse the requirement to establish what sort of person is needed.
3. Identify potential sources of candidates.

Analyse recruitment strengths and weaknesses

Attracting candidates is primarily a matter of identifying, evaluating and using the most appropriate sources of applicants. However, in cases where difficulties in attracting or retaining candidates are being met or anticipated, it may be necessary to carry out a study of the factors that are likely to attract or deter candidates – the strengths and weaknesses of the organization as an employer. The study could make use of an attitude survey to obtain the views of existing employees. The analysis should cover such matters as the national or local reputation of the organization, pay, employee benefits and working conditions, the intrinsic interest of the job, security of employment, opportunities for education and training, career prospects, and the location of the office or plant.

Candidates are, in a sense, selling themselves, but they are also buying what the organization has to offer. If, in the latter sense, the labour market is a buyer's market, then the company selling itself to candidates must study their wants and needs in relation to what it can provide. The study can be used to develop an employee value proposition (what an organization has to offer that prospective or existing employees would value and that would help to persuade them to join the business) and an employee brand (the image presented by an organization as a good employer) incorporating the features set out above. They can contribute to the recruitment material used on corporate websites and in advertisements and brochures to help make the organization 'an employer of choice'.

Analyse the requirement

First it is necessary to establish what jobs have to be filled and by when. Then turn to an existing role profile and person specification or, if not available or out of date, draw up new ones that set out information on responsibilities and competency requirements. This information can be analysed to determine the required education, qualifications and experience.

The next step is to consider where suitable candidates are likely to come from: within the organization, from other organizations or from education establishments, and the parts of the country where they can be found. Next, define the terms and conditions of the job (pay and benefits).

Finally, refer to the analysis of strengths and weaknesses to assess what it is about the job or the organization that is likely to attract good candidates, so that the most can be made of these factors when advertising the vacancy or reaching potential applicants in other ways. Consider also what might put them off, for example the location of the job, so that objections can be anticipated. Analyse previous successes or failures to establish what does or does not work.

Identify sources of candidates

First consideration should be given to internal candidates. In addition, it is always worth trying to persuade former employees to return to the organization or obtain suggestions from existing employees (referrals). Talent banks that record candidate details electronically can be maintained and referred to at this stage.

If these approaches do not work, the sources of candidates are online recruiting, social media, advertising, recruitment agencies, job centres, consultants, recruitment process outsourcing providers and direct approaches to educational establishments. The main sources used by employers, as established by the 2013 CIPD survey, were:

- own corporate website – 62 per cent;
- recruitment agencies – 49 per cent;
- employee referral scheme – 33 per cent;
- professional networking, eg LinkedIn – 32 per cent;
- commercial job boards – 32 per cent;

- local newspaper advertisements – 29 per cent;
- specialist journals – 24 per cent;
- Jobcentre Plus – 19 per cent;
- search consultants – 17 per cent;
- links with educational establishments – 14 per cent;
- national newspaper advertisements – 12 per cent;
- social networking sites – 9 per cent.

Note the predominance of corporate websites and local agencies as sources of candidates. It is also interesting to note that referrals are the third most popular method.

There is usually a choice between different methods or combinations of them. The criteria to use when making the choice are: 1) the likelihood that it will produce good candidates; 2) the speed with which the choice enables recruitment to be completed; and 3) the costs involved, bearing in mind that there may be direct advertising costs or consultants' fees.

Online recruitment

Online or e-recruitment uses the internet to advertise or 'post' vacancies, provides information about jobs and the organization and enables e-mail communications to take place between employers and candidates. The latter can apply for jobs online and can e-mail application forms and CVs to employers or agencies. Tests can be completed online. The main types of online recruitment sites are corporate websites, commercial job boards and agency sites. Social media as described below is also used extensively.

The advantages of online recruiting are that it can reach a wider range of possible applicants. It is quicker and cheaper than traditional methods of advertising, more details of jobs and firms can be supplied on the site, and CVs can be matched and applications can be submitted electronically. More than four-fifths of respondents to the CIPD's 2013 survey reported that it helped them to increase the strength of their employer brand. The disadvantages are that it may produce too many irrelevant or poor applications and it is still not the first choice of many job seekers. Consider using it in conjunction with other recruitment methods to maximize response.

Corporate websites may simply list vacancies and contact details. A more elaborate approach would consist of a dedicated website area that gives details of vacancies, person specifications, benefits and how to apply for jobs, for example by completing online application forms and tests. Such areas may be linked directly to an organization's home page so that general browsers can access them. An intranet link may be available to enable internal staff to access the website. Some organizations are building their own professional communities or talent networks. The management of websites can be outsourced to recruitment consultants or specialized web agencies. The following are guidelines on the use of websites:

- Keep the content of the site up to date.
- Ensure the site is accessible directly or through search engines.
- Provide contact numbers for those with technical problems.
- Take care over the wording of online copy – the criteria for good copy in conventional advertisements apply.

Commercial job boards are operated by specialized firms such as Monster.co.uk and Fish4jobs.com and consist of large databanks of vacancies. Companies pay to have their jobs listed on the sites. Information about vacancies may reproduce an advertisement so that the site is simply an additional form of communication, but some vacancies are only found online. Links may be provided to the organization's website. As recommended by Syedain (2012):

- Go for specialized sites rather than generalist.
- Stick to one or two sites rather than spreading your vacancy everywhere.
- If you are unsure about the best site, Google the job and browse the sites that come up in order to see which is most authoritative.
- Pay to obtain a prominent site.
- Bear in mind that people who look at the site are seeking a job. Job sites are not like print advertisements, which have to attract casual readers.
- Ensure that the information you provide is clear about what you are offering and the achievements, qualifications and experience you are looking for.

Agency sites are run by established recruitment agencies. Candidates register online but may be expected to discuss their details in person before these are forwarded to a prospective employer.

Social media

The use of social media means applying Web 2.0 technologies to search for recruits and find out more about them online on sites such as LinkedIn and Facebook. Potential recruits sometimes provide blogs from existing employees covering their experiences in working for the organization.

The 2013 survey of the Forum for In-House Recruitment Managers (FIRM), whose members tend to be bigger employers, established that 94 per cent used LinkedIn for attracting and recruiting candidates and the remaining 6 per cent intend to do so. LinkedIn recruiter tools enable employers to see how the online population views their employer brand, search the world by sector, job level, specialism and geography and directly approach strangers. Syedain (2013) recommends that to make the most of LinkedIn it is necessary to:

- build and prime a personal network before you recruit;
- set aside time to seek out and engage relevant and promising talent;
- obtain advice or training in how to use LinkedIn as a recruiting tool;
- get buy-in from the top – encourage senior managers to keep their own profiles up to date;
- build the employer brand by encouraging to post information on their status updates that give a sense of the organization;
- talk to managers about who they know or can get introduced to online;
- create an employer page and keep it updated;
- personalize your direct approaches, whether InMails or invitations to connect;
- be selective about the number and type of jobs you publicize – it is easy to overwhelm people's feeds and inboxes.

As reported by Anna Cook (2012), head of CERN's recruitment unit, CERN, the world's largest particle physics laboratory, has successfully made use of social media. All job vacancies are advertised on LinkedIn, Facebook and Twitter. These networks provide much more than simple job boards in that they are used as communication tools to interact with the audience, with candidates and with people who are not necessarily candidates but may know people who may want to apply. Appropriate use is made of each medium. For example, Facebook is used to host a weekly question and answer session between one of CERN's recruiters and anyone who wants to submit a question, whereas the professional network LinkedIn provides a forum for more specialized discussions.

T-Mobile International has created a Facebook site for graduate recruitment. Potential graduate recruits established an individual presence on this invitation-only site. The site was used to provide information on selection procedures and processes, for example criteria and timetables and to allow the potential recruits to communicate with each other. As well as T-Mobile's IT department, an internal 'brand ambassador' was involved in design throughout.

Advertising

Advertising has traditionally been the most obvious method of attracting candidates and it is still fairly important, especially at local level and in specialized journals. However, as the CIPD 2013 survey revealed, many organizations now prefer to use online recruitment, agencies or consultants. A conventional advertisement will have the following aims:

- Generate candidates – attract a sufficient number of good candidates at minimum cost.
- Attract attention – it must compete for the attention of potential candidates against other employees.
- Create and maintain interest – it has to communicate, in an attractive and interesting way, information about the job, the company and the terms and conditions of employment.
- Stimulate action – the message needs to be conveyed in a way that will prompt a sufficient number of replies from candidates with the right qualifications for the job.

To achieve these aims, it is necessary to carry out the actions set out below. A recruitment advertisement should start with a compelling headline and then contain information on the following:

- the organization;
- the job;
- the person required – qualifications, experience, etc;
- the pay and benefits offered;
- the location;
- the action to be taken.

The headline is all important. The simplest and most obvious approach is to set out the job title in bold type. To gain attention, it is advisable to quote the rate of pay and key benefits such as a company car. Applicants are suspicious of clauses such as 'salary will be commensurate with age and experience' or 'salary negotiable'. This often means either that the salary is so low that the company is afraid to reveal it, or that pay policies are so incoherent that the company has no idea what to offer until someone tells them what he or she wants.

The name of the company should be given. Do not use box numbers – if you want to be anonymous, use a consultant. Add any selling points, such as growth or diversification, and any other areas of interest to potential candidates, such as career prospects. The essential features of the job should be conveyed by giving a brief description of what the job holder will do and, as far as space permits, the scope and scale of activities. Create interest in the job but do not oversell it.

The qualifications and experience required should be stated as factually as possible. There is no point in overstating requirements and seldom any point in specifying exactly how much experience is wanted. Be careful about including a string of personal qualities such as drive, determination and initiative. These have no real meaning to candidates. Phrases such as 'proven track record' and 'successful experience' are equally meaningless. No one will admit to not having either of them.

The advertisement should end with information on how the candidate should apply. 'Brief but comprehensive details' is a good phrase. Candidates can be asked to write or e-mail their response, but useful alternatives are to ask them to telephone or to come along for an informal chat at a suitable venue.

Remember the anti-discrimination legislation set out in the Equality Act (2010). This makes it unlawful to discriminate in an advertisement by favouring either sex, the only exceptions being a few jobs that can be done only by one sex. Advertisements must therefore avoid sexist job titles such as 'salesman' or 'stewardess'. They must refer to a neutral title such as 'sales representative', or amplify the description to cover both sexes by stating 'steward or stewardess'. Potential respondents should be referred to only as the 'candidate' or the 'applicant', otherwise you must specify 'man or woman' or 'he or she'. It is accepted, however, that certain job titles are unisex and therefore non-discriminatory, including director, manager, executive and officer.

It is also unlawful to place an advertisement that discriminates against any particular race. As long as race is never mentioned or even implied in an advertisement, you should have no problem in keeping within the law. The Equality Act also makes it unlawful to discriminate against employees on account of their age. Age limits should therefore not be included in advertisements and the wording should not indicate that people below or above a certain age are not wanted.

It is essential to measure the response to advertisements to provide guidance on the relative cost-effectiveness of different media. Cost per reply is the best ratio.

Recruitment agencies

Most recruitment agencies deal with secretarial and office staff who are registered with them. They are usually quick and effective but quite expensive. Agencies can charge a fee for finding someone of 15 per cent or more of the first year's salary. It can be cheaper to advertise or use the internet, especially when the company is in a buyer's market. Shop around to find the agency that suits the organization's needs at a reasonable cost.

Agencies should be briefed carefully on what is wanted. They can produce unsuitable candidates but the risk is reduced if they are clear about the requirements.

Jobcentre Plus

The jobcentres operated by the government are mainly useful for manual and clerical workers and sales or call centre assistants.

Recruitment consultants

Recruitment consultants advertise, interview and produce a shortlist. They provide expertise and reduce workload. The organization can be anonymous if it wishes. Most recruitment consultants charge a fee based on a percentage of the basic salary for the job, usually ranging from 15 to 20 per cent.

When choosing a recruitment consultant check their reputation and expertise, compare fees and meet the person who will work on the assignment to assess his or her quality. To use them effectively:

- Agree terms of reference.
- Brief them on the organization, where the job fits in, why the appointment is to be made, terms and conditions and any special requirements.
- Give them every assistance in defining the job and the person specification – they will do much better if they have comprehensive knowledge of what is required and what type of person is most likely to fit into the organization well.
- Check carefully the proposed programme and the draft text of the advertisement.
- Clarify the arrangements for interviewing and shortlisting.
- Clarify the basis upon which fees and expenses will be charged.
- Ensure that arrangements are made to deal directly with the consultant who will handle the assignment.

Executive search consultants

Use an executive search consultant or 'headhunter' for senior jobs where there is only a limited number of suitable people and a direct lead to them is wanted. Headhunters are not cheap. They charge a fee of 30 to 50 per cent or so of the first year's salary, but they can be quite cost-effective.

Executive search consultants first approach their own contacts in the industry or profession concerned. The good ones have an extensive range of contacts and their own data bank. They will also have researchers who will identify suitable people who may fit the specification or can provide a lead to someone else who may be suitable. The more numerous the contacts, the better the executive search consultant. When a number of potentially suitable and interested people have been assembled, a fairly relaxed and informal meeting takes place and the consultant forwards a shortlist to the client with full reports on candidates.

There are some good and some not so good executive search consultants. Do not use one unless a reliable recommendation is obtained.

Educational and training establishments

Many jobs can, of course, be filled by school leavers. For some organizations the main source of recruits for training schemes will be universities and colleges as well as schools. Graduate recruitment is a major annual exercise for some companies, which go to great efforts to produce glossy brochures, visit campuses on the 'milk run' and use elaborate sifting and selection procedures to vet candidates, including 'biodata' and assessment centres.

Recruitment process outsourcing

Recruitment process outsourcing (RPO) is the term used when an organization commissions a provider to take responsibility for the end-to-end delivery of the recruitment process, covering all vacancies or a selection of them. This involves liaising with hiring managers to define requirements and specifications, deciding on the best ways to attract candidates, processing applications, and setting up and facilitating interviews. Some companies do not hand over all recruitment, using RPO only for high-volume vacancies. They may retain responsibility for senior and specialist jobs.

The advantage of RPO is that it can save time, bring outside expertise to bear on recruitment problems and free up HR for more value-adding activities. The disadvantage is the perception by some HR people and line managers that the provider is too remote to deal with the real issues and that there is a danger of losing control.

Comparison of sources

A summary of sources and an analysis of their advantages and disadvantages is given in Table 18.1.

TABLE 18.1 Summary of sources of candidates

Source	Description	Advantages	Disadvantages
Online recruitment	Company websites, job boards, social media.	Generally, can reach a wider range of possible applicants, and it is quicker and cheaper than traditional methods of advertising. More details of jobs and firms can be supplied on the site and CVs can be matched and applications can be submitted electronically. Websites can use an organization's brand to attract candidates. Job boards are keyword searchable. Job details can be changed and CVs managed electronically. Social media are good for reach – LinkedIn currently has 100 million members worldwide.	Generally, may produce too many irrelevant or poor applications and it is still not the first choice of many job seekers. Websites are expensive and still need other media to drive traffic to the site. Job boards are bad for 'passive seekers'. Social media – employer/recruiter has to manage own profile.
Advertising	Display or classified advertisements in national or local newspapers or journals.	Attract 'passing trade' – people who are not actively looking for a job.	Soon become irrelevant.
Recruitment agencies	Mainly recruit office and sales staff who are registered with them.	Convenient, save time and trouble, draw on an established pool of candidates.	Can produce unsuitable candidates. Pool may be limited.
Jobcentres	Mainly for manual workers and clerical and sales staff.	No cost; usually plenty of choice.	Limited to relatively routine jobs.
Recruitment consultants	Advertise, interview and produce a shortlist.	Provide expertise and reduce workload.	Can be expensive.
Executive search consultants	Conduct searches for senior executives.	Can find top-level people who might not otherwise be interested.	Expensive, limited to top jobs.
Educational establishments	Universities, colleges and schools.	Major source of future talent.	Recruitment campaigns can be costly.
Recruitment process outsourcing	Deliver complete recruiting process.	Save time, bring outside expertise to bear on recruitment problems and free up HR for more value-adding activities.	Feeling that provider is too remote to deal with the real issues and that there is a danger of losing control.

Dealing with applications

If recruitment agencies or consultants are used they will deliver their client a shortlist of candidates for interview. If not, the organization has to sift the applications itself. This means examining the information supplied by applicants, sorting them and drawing up a shortlist of applicants to be interviewed.

Examining information from candidates

Candidates may respond to an online notice or an advertisement with a formal application (by e-mail or letter), usually supported by a CV. Applicants may be asked to provide information about their education, qualifications, training and experience in a standardized format to provide a structured basis for drawing up shortlists, the interview itself and for the subsequent actions in offering an appointment and in setting up records. This ensures that all applicants are considered on the same basis against the person specification.

An application form, as illustrated in Figure 18.1, which sets out the information required, can be completed online (preferable if an online application has been made) or on paper. The following suggestions have been made by Pioro and Baum (2005) on how to use application forms more effectively:

- Decide what the criteria for selection are and how these will be assessed by use of the application form.
- Keep questions clear, relevant and non-discriminatory.
- Ask for only the bare minimum of personal details.
- Widen your pool of applicants by offering different options and guidance for completing and viewing application forms.
- Employers may also refer for further information to social networks or the candidate's own blog.

However, to save time and trouble, recruiters may prefer to make a decision on the details provided in the initial application where it is clear that an applicant meets or does not meet the specification.

Processing applications

When the vacancy or vacancies have been posted or advertised and a fair number of replies received, the initial step is to list the applications on the recruitment database setting out name, date application received and actions taken (reject, hold, interview, shortlist, offer). A standard acknowledgement letter should be sent to each applicant unless an instant decision can be made to interview or reject. The next steps are to sift applications prior to drawing up a shortlist and arranging interviews.

Sorting applications

Applications are sifted by comparing the information available about them with the key criteria in the person specification. The criteria should be analysed with care so that they are fully understood. The criteria can be classified under the following three headings so that they can be applied consistently to guide sifting decisions:

1. *Essential* – applicants will not be considered unless this criterion is satisfied.
2. *Very desirable* – preference will be given to applicants who meet this criterion.
3. *Desirable* – applicants who meet this criterion will be given favourable consideration but it is not an essential requirement. However, if a number of applicants meet the first two criteria, satisfying desirable criteria would be a factor in making a choice.

A highly structured method of sifting applications is provided by the use of biodata. These are items of biographical data that are criterion-based (ie they relate to established criteria in such terms as qualifications and experience that indicate whether individuals are likely to be suitable). These are objectively scored and, by measurements of past achievements, predict future behaviour.

Following the analysis, applicants can be sorted initially into three categories: possible, marginal and unsuitable. The more information made available and the clearer the criteria the easier this process is. When there is a large field of applicants with many 'possibles', sifting may have to be repeated against more stringent criteria until a shortlist for interview is identified.

FIGURE 18.1 Example of application form (compressed)

APPLICATION FORM		
Surname:		***First name:***
Address:		
Tel. (home)	***Tel. (work)***	***e-mail (personal)***
Position applied for:		

Education				
Dates		***Name of secondary school, college or university***	***Main subjects taken***	***Qualifications***
From	***To***			

Specialized training received
Other qualifications and skills (languages, keyboard skills, current driving licence, etc)

Employment history (Give details of all positions held since completing full-time education, start with your present or most recent position and work back)					
Dates		***Name of employer, address and nature of business including any service in the Armed Forces***	***Position and summary of main duties***	***Starting and leaving rate of pay***	***Reasons for leaving or wanting to leave***
From	***To***				

Add any comments you wish to make to support your application
I confirm that the information given on this application form is correct **Signature of applicant**...**Date**......................

Ideally, the numbers on the shortlist should be between four and eight. Fewer than four leaves relatively little choice (although such a limitation may be forced on the recruiter if an insufficient number of good applications have been received). More than eight will mean that too much time is spent on interviewing and there is a danger of diminishing returns.

Draw up an interviewing programme

The time allowed for an interview will vary according to the complexity of the job. For a fairly routine job, 30 minutes or so should suffice. For a more senior job, 60 minutes or more is required. It is best not to schedule too many interviews per day for more senior jobs – interviewers who try to conduct more than five or six exacting interviews will quickly run out of steam and do neither the interviewee nor the organization any justice. It is advisable to leave about 15 minutes between interviews to write up notes and prepare for the next one.

Administering the selection programme

When the interviewing programme has been drawn up shortlisted candidates can be invited for interview, using a standard letter where large numbers are involved. Candidates should be asked to complete an application form if they have not already done so. There is a lot to be said at this stage for sending candidates more details of the organization and the job so that too much time is not spent in going through this information at the interview.

Review the remaining 'possibles' and 'marginals' and decide if any are to be held in reserve. Send reserves a standard 'holding' letter and send the others a standard rejection letter. The latter should thank candidates for the interest shown and inform them briefly, but not too brusquely, that they have not been successful. A typical reject letter might read as follows:

> Since writing to you on... we have given careful consideration to your application for the above position. I regret to inform you, however, that we have decided not to ask you to attend for an interview. We should like to thank you for the interest you have shown.

Selection methods

The aim of selection is to assess the suitability of candidates by predicting the extent to which they will be able to carry out a role successfully. It involves deciding on the degree to which the characteristics of applicants in terms of their KSAs, competencies, experience, qualifications, education and training match the person specification and then using this assessment to make a choice between candidates. The so-called 'classic trio' of selection methods consists of application forms, interviews and references. To these should be added selection tests and assessment centres.

Interviews are normally conducted by means of a face-to-face discussion. But, as established by the CIPD's 2013 survey, a considerable proportion of employers (56 per cent) conduct interviews by telephone. Nearly one-third (30 per cent) use video or Skype interviews, rising to 42 per cent of those who recruit from overseas.

Interviews

The interview is the most familiar method of selection. The aim is to elicit information about candidates that will enable a prediction to be made about how well they will do the job and thus lead to a selection decision.

An interview involves face-to-face discussion. When it is an individual rather than a panel interview, it provides the best opportunity for the establishment of close contact – rapport – between the interviewer and the candidate, thus easing the acquisition of information about the candidate's suitability and how well he or she would fit into the organization. As described below, interviews should be structured (detailed consideration of selection interviewing skills is given in Chapter 50). The advantages and disadvantages of interviews are as follows.

Advantages of interviews

- Provide opportunities for interviewers to ask probing questions about the candidate's experience and to explore the extent to which the candidate's competencies match those specified for the job.

- Enable interviewers to describe the job (a 'realistic job preview') and the organization in more detail, providing some indication of the terms of the psychological contract.
- Provide opportunities for candidates to ask questions about the job and to clarify issues concerning training, career prospects, the organization and terms and conditions of employment.
- Enable a face-to-face encounter to take place so that the interviewer can make an assessment of how the candidate would fit into the organization and what he or she would be like to work with.
- Give the candidate the same opportunity to assess the organization, the interviewer and the job.

Disadvantages of interviews

- Can lack validity as a means of making sound predictions of performance, and lack reliability in the sense of measuring the same things for different candidates.
- Rely on the skill of the interviewer – many people are poor at interviewing, although most think that they are good at it.
- Can lead to biased and subjective judgements by interviewers.

These disadvantages are most common when unstructured interviews are used, but they can be alleviated: first, by using a structured approach as described below; second, by training interviewers. The use of other opinions can also help to reduce bias, especially if the same structured approach is adopted by all the interviewers. Finally, selection tests, especially those measuring intelligence or general ability, can provide valuable information that supplements the interview.

Interview arrangements

Interviews are frequently conducted on a one-to-one basis but there is a case for using a second interviewer in order to avoid a biased or superficial decision. The alternative is a selection board or panel, which is often used in the public sector. This brings together a number of parties interested in the selection decision. But the drawbacks are that questions tend to be unplanned and delivered at random and the candidates are unable to do justice to themselves because they may not be allowed to expand on their responses.

Structured interviews

A structured interview is one based on a defined framework. Within the framework there may be a set of predetermined questions. All candidates are asked the same questions, which will focus on the attributes and behaviours required to succeed in the job. The answers may be scored through a rating system.

The most typical framework is the person specification. Interview questions aim to analyse and build on the information provided by the candidate's CV or application form to establish the extent to which a candidate has the required knowledge, skills and abilities (KSAs). In a competency-based interview the emphasis is on establishing if the candidate has the right level of desirable behavioural competencies. A structured interview may include experience-based questions in which candidates are asked to relate how they handled situations in the past requiring skills and abilities necessary for effective performance in the job for which they are applying. And/or it may include situational questions that provide candidates with hypothetical job-relevant situations and ask how they would deal with them. Research by Pulakos and Schmitt (1995) found that experience-based interviews yielded higher levels of validity than situation-based ones. But as described in Chapter 50, both types of questions may be incorporated in an interview.

Unstructured interviews

Unstructured interviews are essentially a general discussion during which the interviewer asks a few questions that are relevant to what he or she is looking for but without any specific aim in mind other than getting an overall picture of the candidate as an individual. Questions are often random and non-specific. Candidates are judged on the general impression they make and the process is likely to be quite subjective. Research quoted later in this chapter has shown that the predictive validity (the extent to which it predicts performance in a job) of an unstructured interview is fairly low. The preferred method is a structured interview, which when conducted well has a higher level of predictive validity.

Selection testing

Selection tests are used to provide valid and reliable evidence of levels of abilities, intelligence, personality characteristics, aptitudes and attainments. Psychological tests are measuring instruments, which is why they are often referred to as psychometric tests: 'psychometric' means mental measurement. Psychometric tests assess intelligence or personality. They use systematic and standardized procedures to measure differences in individual characteristics, thus enabling selectors to gain a greater understanding of candidates to help in predicting the extent to which they will be successful in a job. The other types of tests described below are ability and aptitude tests.

Intelligence tests

Intelligence tests measure a range of mental abilities that enable a person to succeed at a variety of intellectual tasks using the faculties of abstract thinking and reasoning. They are concerned with general intelligence (termed 'g' by Spearman (1927) one of the pioneers of intelligence testing) and are sometimes called 'general mental ability' (GMA) tests. Intelligence tests measure abilities while cognitive tests measure an individual's learning in a specific subject area. They contain questions, problems and tasks. The meta-analysis conducted by Schmidt and Hunter (1998) showed that intelligence tests had high predictive validity.

The outcome of a test can be expressed as a score that can be compared with the scores of members of the population as a whole, or the population of all or part of the organization using the test (norms). An intelligence test may be recorded as an intelligence quotient (IQ), which is the ratio of an individual's mental age to the individual's actual age as measured by an intelligence test. When the mental and actual age correspond, the IQ is 100. Scores above 100 indicate that the individual's level of average is above the norm for his or her age, and vice versa. It is usual now for IQs to be directly computed as an IQ test score. It is assumed that intelligence is distributed normally throughout the population; that is, the frequency distribution of intelligence corresponds with the normal curve shown in Figure 18.2.

The normal curve is a way of expressing how scores will typically be distributed; for example,

FIGURE 18.2 A normal curve

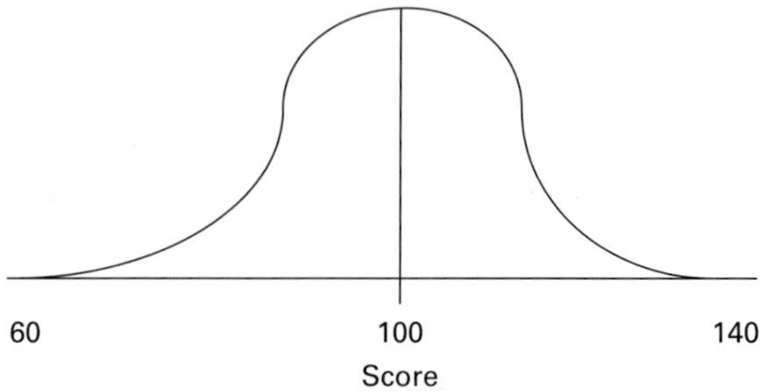

that 60 per cent of the population are likely to get scores between x and y, 20 per cent are likely to get scores below x and 20 per cent are likely to get more than y.

Intelligence tests can be administered to a single individual or to a group. They can also be completed online.

Personality tests

Personality tests attempt to assess the personality of candidates in order to make predictions about their likely behaviour in a role. There are many different theories of personality and, consequently, many different types of personality tests. These include self-report personality questionnaires and other questionnaires that measure interests, values or work behaviour.

Personality tests can provide interesting supplementary information about candidates that is free from the biased reactions that frequently occur in face-to-face interviews, but they have to be used with great care. The tests should have been developed by a reputable psychologist or test agency on the basis of extensive research and field testing, and they must meet the specific needs of the user.

Ability tests

Ability tests establish what people are capable of knowing or doing. They measure the capacity for:

- *verbal reasoning* – the ability to comprehend, interpret and draw conclusions from oral or written language;
- *numerical reasoning* – the ability to comprehend, interpret and draw conclusions from numerical information;

- *spatial reasoning* – the ability to understand and interpret spatial relations between objects;
- *mechanical reasoning* – understanding of everyday physical laws such as force and leverage.

Aptitude tests

Aptitude tests are occupational or job-related tests that assess the extent to which people can do the work. They typically take the form of work sample tests, which replicate an important aspect of the actual work the candidate will have to do, such as using a keyboard or carrying out a skilled task such as repair work. Work sample tests can be used only with applicants who are already familiar with the task through experience or training.

Characteristics of a good test

A good test is one that provides data that enables reliable predictions of behaviour or performance to be made and therefore assists in the process of making objective and reasoned decisions when selecting people for jobs. It will be based on research that has produced standardized criteria derived by using the same measure to test a number of representative people to produce a set of 'norms' for comparison purposes. The test should be capable of being objectively scored by reference to the normal or average performance of the group.

The two key characteristics of a good test are first that it is reliable in the sense that it always measures the same thing: a test aimed at measuring a particular characteristic, such as intelligence, should measure the same characteristic when applied to different people at the same or a different time or to the same person at different times. Second, a test should be valid in the sense that it measures the characteristic that the test is intended to measure. Thus, an intelligence test should measure intelligence (however defined) and not simply verbal facility. A test meant to predict success in a job or in passing examinations should produce reasonably convincing (statistically significant) predictions.

A criterion-related approach is used to assess validity. This means selecting criteria against which the validity of the test can be measured. These criteria must reflect 'true' performance at work as accurately as possible. A single criterion is inadequate: multiple criteria should be used. The extent to which criteria can be contaminated by other factors should also be considered and it should be remembered that criteria are dynamic – they will change over time.

Interpreting test results

Test results can be interpreted by the use of norms or through criterion scores.

Norms

An individual's score in a test is not meaningful on its own. It needs to be compared with the scores achieved by the population on whom the test was standardized – the norm or reference group. A normative score is read from a norms table and might, for example, indicate that someone has performed the test at a level equivalent to the top 30 per cent of the relevant population.

Criterion scores

Norms simply tell us how someone has performed a test relative to other people. A more powerful approach is to use the relationship between test scores and an indication of what the test is designed to measure, such as job success. This is described as a criterion measure.

The use of tests in a selection procedure

Validated intelligence and personality tests will produce useful data, but there is much to be said for combining them in a selection procedure with structured interviews.

Tests are often used as part of a selection procedure for occupations where a large number of recruits are required, and where it is not possible to rely entirely on examination results or information about previous experience as the basis for predicting future performance. In these circumstances it is economical to develop and administer the tests, and a sufficient number of cases can be built up for the essential validation exercise. Tests usually form part of an assessment centre programme. They can be administered online and FIRM's 2013 membership survey showed that they were used for 72 per cent of applications.

Intelligence tests are particularly helpful in situations where intelligence is a key factor and there is no other reliable method of measuring it. Aptitude tests are most useful for jobs where specific and measurable skills are required, such as word-processing and skilled repair work. Personality tests can complement structured interviews and intelligence and aptitude tests. Some organizations use them for jobs such as selling, where they believe that 'personality' is important and where it is not too difficult to obtain quantifiable criteria for validation purposes. They may be used to assess integrity and conscientiousness where these characteristics are deemed to be important.

In some situations a battery of tests may be used, including various types of intelligence, personality and aptitude tests. These may be a standard battery supplied by a test agency, or a custom-built battery may be developed. The biggest pitfall to avoid is adding extra tests just for the sake of it, without ensuring that they make a proper contribution to the success of the predictions for which the battery is being used.

Tests should be administered only by people who have been trained in what the tests are measuring, how they should be used, and how they should be interpreted. Also, it is essential to evaluate all tests by comparing the results at the interview stage with later achievements. To be statistically significant, these evaluations should be carried out over a reasonable period of time and cover as large a number of candidates as possible.

Assessment centres

Assessment centres assemble a group of candidates and use a range of assessment techniques over a concentrated period (one or two days) with the aim of providing a more comprehensive and balanced view of the suitability of individual members of the group. The main features of assessment centres are that:

- exercises are used to capture and simulate the key dimensions of the job;
- these may include one-to-one role-plays and group exercises; it is assumed that performance in these simulations predicts behaviour on the job;
- candidates are interviewed and tested;
- performance is measured in several dimensions in terms of the competencies required to achieve the target level of performance in a particular job or at a particular level in the organization;
- several candidates or participants are assessed together to allow interaction and to make the experience more open and participative;
- several trained assessors or observers are used in order to increase the objectivity of assessments.

The case for assessment centres is that they obtain much more information about candidates than conventional interviews, even when these are supplemented by tests. But research by Schmidt and Hunter (1998) has shown that on their own, the ability of assessment centres to predict how well someone will perform (predictive validity) is lower than that of intelligence tests combined with structured interviews. Assessment centres are expensive and time-consuming and their use tends to be restricted to large organizations for managerial positions or for graduates.

Choice of selection methods

There is a choice between the selection methods. The most important criterion is the ability of a selection method or combination of methods to predict future performance. Predictive ability is expressed as a coefficient – complete validity would be 1.0; no validity would be 0.0.

The meta-analysis on the validity of different selection methods conducted by Schmidt and Hunter (1998: 265), which covered 85 years of research findings, produced the following predictive validity coefficients:

Intelligence tests and structured interviews	.63
Intelligence tests and unstructured interviews	.55
Assessment centres and structured interviews	.53
Intelligence tests only	.51
Structured interviews only	.51
Unstructured interviews only	.38
Assessment centres only	.37
Graphology only	.02

Robertson and Smith (2001) added personality assessments to this list, with a validity coefficient of .37.

Schmidt and Hunter (1998) established that the reason why intelligence (GMA) is such a good predictor of job performance is that more intelligent people acquire job knowledge more rapidly and acquire more of it, and it is this knowledge of how to perform the job that causes their job performance to be higher. Their research clearly indicates that the combination of structured interviews and intelligence tests is the most effective in terms of predictive validity. Graphology is useless.

Provisional offers and obtaining references

After the interviewing and testing procedure has been completed, a provisional decision to make an offer by telephone or in writing can be made. This is normally 'subject to satisfactory references' and the candidate should, of course, be told that these will be taken up. If there is more than one eligible candidate for a job it may be advisable to hold one or two people in reserve. Applicants often withdraw, especially those whose only purpose in applying for the job was to carry out a 'test marketing' operation, or to obtain a lever with which to persuade their present employers to value them more highly.

The main purpose of a reference is to obtain in confidence factual information about a prospective employee. This information is straightforward and essential. It is necessary to confirm the nature of the previous job, the period of time in employment, the reason for leaving (if relevant), the salary or rate of pay and, possibly, the attendance record.

Opinions about character, competence, performance and suitability are unreliable. Referees are reluctant to commit themselves and they are not in any position to assess suitability – only the prospective employer can do that. Personal referees are, of course, entirely useless. All they prove is that the applicant has at least one or two friends.

A written request for a reference could simply ask the previous employer to confirm the candidate's employment record. More precise answers may be obtained if a standard form is provided for the employer to complete. The questions asked on this form should be limited to the following:

- What was the period of employment?
- What was the job title?
- What work was carried out?
- What was the rate of pay or salary?
- How many days' absence were there over the last 12 months?
- Would you re-employ (if not, why not)?

The last question is important, if it is answered honestly.

Telephone references may save time and may be more reliable. They can be used as an alternative or in addition to written references. Ask factual questions only and keep a record of the conversation.

References – legal aspects

The key legal points that should be considered when asking for or giving references are:

- Once the decision has been made to make an offer, the letter should state that 'this is a provisional offer subject to the receipt of satisfactory references'.
- It has been generally held that there is no common law duty on an employer to provide references for a serving or past employee unless there is a term to that effect in the employment contract. But it has been ruled (Spring v. Guardian Assurance 1994) that there might be a moral duty to provide a reference where it is 'natural practice' to require a reference from a previous employer before offering employment, and where the employee could not expect to enter that type of employment without a reference.
- If a reference contains a false or unsubstantiated statement that damages the reputation of the individual, action for damages may result. It is possible to succeed in a claim for damages if it can be shown that the reference provided was negligent because reasonable care had not been taken in preparing it, which includes ensuring that it is factually correct.

Checking applications

It is a sad fact that applicants all too often misinform their prospective employers about their education, qualifications and employment record. This was confirmed by a survey carried out by the CIPD (2008), which found that 25 per cent of employers had to withdraw their offers because applicants had lied or misrepresented their application. It is always advisable to check with universities, professional institutes and previous employers that the facts given by applicants are correct. Other checks can be made such as:

- interview questions about actual (not hypothetical) experiences, with deep probing to ascertain the extent of the individual's personal involvement, decision-making and contribution;
- detailed application forms with open-ended questions about specific learning related to the skills, knowledge and competencies required for the vacancies under consideration;
- identification check;
- electoral register check;
- credit reference agency check (especially appropriate for positions in the financial services sector);
- confirmation of previous employment with HM Revenue and Customs or through the Department of Work and Pensions;
- Criminal Records Bureau check;
- Companies House check (for directors);
- fraud prevention check, including Cifas staff fraud database check (to prevent an employer unwittingly employing people previously dismissed for fraud somewhere else). Cifas is a not-for-profit fraud prevention service.

Offering employment

The final stage in the selection procedure is to confirm the offer of employment after satisfactory references have been obtained, and the applicant has passed the medical examination required for pension and life assurance purposes or because a certain standard of physical fitness is required for the work. The contract of employment should also be prepared at this stage.

Following up

It is essential to follow up newly engaged employees to ensure that they have settled in and to check on how well they are doing. If there are any problems it is much better to identify them at an early stage rather than allowing them to fester.

Following up is also important as a means of checking on the selection procedure. If by any chance a mistake has been made, it is useful to find out how it happened so that the procedure can be improved. Misfits can be attributed to a number of causes; for example: inadequate person specification, poor sourcing of candidates, weak advertising, poor interviewing techniques, inappropriate or invalidated tests, or prejudice on the part of the selector.

Dealing with recruitment problems

Every experienced HR professional who is responsible for recruitment and selection will occasionally come across a vacancy that is particularly difficult to fill. In this situation any compromise that involves appointing someone who does not meet the specification must be avoided. To deal with the problem constructively it is necessary to take the following actions:

- Ensure that all the possible sources of candidates have been used.
- Consider any ways in which the advertisement or website entry could be made more attractive.
- Check that the person specification is realistic – that the requirements have not been overstated.
- Consider whether it might be necessary to improve the package offered to candidates – check market rates to ensure that the level of pay and benefits are competitive.
- In discussion with the line manager, examine the possibility of reshaping the role to increase its attractiveness.
- If the worse comes to the worst, discuss with the manager alternative ways of carrying out the work with existing staff.

CASE STUDIES

Recruitment assessment processes at Embarq

Embarq is the largest independent local telecoms provider in the United States. It suffered catastrophic rates of staff turnover in its call centres; then a new assessment process designed by PreVisor reduced turnover from 33.5 per cent in the first 90 days to 12.5 per cent.

The new process begins with an online screening tool that identifies characteristics and motivations that define long-term success in the roles, such as 'customer focus' and 'persistence'. There follows a behaviour-based structured interview and a sales-based role-play exercise. This exercise takes place over the phone, which tests candidates in the most realistic way possible, and is more convenient and cost-effective.

Sales have since increased by 24 per cent, and customer service has also improved.

Recruitment and retention at Paul UK

Paul UK operates a chain of 22 retail patisserie and bakery shops employing 400 people. Its staff turnover rate of 168 per cent was below the sector's average but still too high. The steps taken to overcome this problem were as follows:

- a robust recruitment process was introduced using branded application forms and centralized recruiting;
- role descriptions and skills specifications were created for posts;
- a competency-based approach to recruitment was introduced – the competencies are closely linked to the company's values and defined the behaviours and attitudes required;
- recruitment literature was professionally designed by an agency;
- an employer brand was built – the promotional leaflet highlights the benefits of working for the company;
- an employee referral scheme was introduced (helped by the employer brand);
- a resource centre for recruitment and training was established;
- a rolling induction training programme was introduced;
- a career progression framework was developed.

The outcome was that within two years staff turnover had dropped by 30 per cent and retention rates had doubled.

Key learning points: Recruitment and selection

Define requirements

Requirements are set out in the form of job descriptions or role profiles and person specifications. These provide the information required to draft advertisements, post vacancies on the internet, brief agencies or recruitment consultants and assess candidates by means of interviews and selection tests.

Analyse recruitment strengths and weaknesses

The analysis should cover such matters as the national or local reputation of the organization, pay, employee benefits and working conditions, the intrinsic interest of the job, security of employment, opportunities for education and training, career prospects, and the location of the office or plant.

Analyse the requirement

- Establish how many jobs have to be filled and by when.
- Set out information on responsibilities and competency requirements.
- Consider where suitable candidates are likely to come from.
- Define the terms and conditions of the job (pay and benefits).
- Consider what is likely to attract good candidates.

Identify sources of candidates

Initially, consideration should be given to internal candidates. An attempt can be made to persuade former employees to return to the organization or obtain suggestions from existing employees (referrals). If these approaches do not work, the main sources of candidates are online recruiting, advertising, agencies and jobcentres, consultants, recruitment process outsourcing providers and direct approaches to educational establishments.

Selection methods

The aim is to assess the suitability of candidates by predicting the extent to which they will be able to carry out a role successfully. It involves deciding on the degree to which the characteristics of applicants match the person specification and using this assessment to make a choice between candidates. The interview is the most familiar method of selection. The aim is to elicit information about candidates that will enable a prediction to be made about how well they will do the job and thus lead to a selection decision.

Structured interviews

A structured interview is one based on a defined framework. Within the framework there may be a set of predetermined questions. All candidates are asked the same questions and the answers may be scored through a rating system.

Competency-based interviews

In its purest form, a competency-based interview is a structured interview that focuses on the required behavioural competencies as set out in the person specification. The questions will be designed to establish the typical behaviour of a candidate in work situations.

Selection tests

Selection tests are used to provide valid and reliable evidence of levels of abilities, intelligence, personality characteristics, aptitudes and attainments.

Choice of selection methods

There is a choice between the selection methods. The most important criterion is the predictive validity of the method or combination of methods. Schmidt and Hunter (1998) found that the best results were obtained by combining intelligence tests with structured interviews.

References and offers

After the interviewing and testing procedure has been completed, a provisional offer by telephone or in writing can be made. This is normally 'subject to satisfactory references'. It is essential to check the information provided by candidates on qualifications and their work experience.

Questions

1 What is the difference between recruitment and selection?
2 What are the main stages of recruitment and selection?
3 What is a person specification?
4 How should recruitment strengths and weaknesses be analysed?
5 What are the main sources of candidates?
6 What is a structured interview?
7 What are the main types of selection tests?
8 What are the main criteria for a good test?
9 How should tests be used in a selection procedure?

References

CIPD (2013) *Survey of Resourcing and Talent Planning*, London, CIPD
Cook, A (2012) Social media can transform the quality of recruitment, *People Management*, October, p 49
Forum for In-House Recruitment Managers – FIRM (2013) *Recruitment Survey*, London, FIRM
Pioro, I and Baum, N (2005) How to design better job application forms, *People Management*, 16 June, pp 42–43
Pulakos, E D and Schmitt, N (1995) Experience-based and situational interviews: studies of validity, *Personnel Psychology*, 48 (2), pp 289–308
Robertson, I T and Smith, M (2001) Personnel selection, *Journal of Occupational and Organizational Psychology*, 74 (4), pp 441–72
Schmidt, F L and Hunter, J E (1998) The validity and utility of selection methods in personnel psychology: practical and theoretical implications of 85 years of research findings, *Psychological Bulletin*, 124 (2), pp 262–74
Spearman, C (1927) *The Abilities of Man*, New York, Macmillan
Syedain, H (2012) *People Management Guide to Recruitment Marketing*, July, p 19
Syedain, H (2013) The new rules of recruitment, *People Management*, July, pp 19–25

19 Resourcing practice

KEY CONCEPTS AND TERMS

- Absence management
- The Bradford factor
- Employee turnover
- Employee turnover index
- Employer of choice
- Half-life index
- Length of service analysis
- Stability index
- Survival rate

LEARNING OUTCOMES

On completing this chapter you should be able to define these key concepts. You should also know about:

- Employee value propositions
- Creating an employer brand
- Measuring employee turnover
- Estimating the cost of employee turnover
- Retention planning
- Risk of leaving analysis
- Absence management
- Flexibility planning

Introduction

This chapter deals with general resourcing practices covering developing an employee value proposition, creating an employer brand, analysing employee turnover, tackling retention problems, managing absence management, introducing people to the organization and releasing them from it.

Employee value proposition

An organization's employee value proposition consists of what it offers to prospective or existing employees that they will value and that will persuade them to join or remain with the business. It will include remuneration – which is important but can be over-emphasized compared with non-financial factors.

The latter may be crucial in attracting and retaining people and include the attractiveness of the organization, the degree to which it acts responsibly, respects diversity and inclusion, work–life balance and opportunities for personal and professional growth. The aim is to become 'an employer of choice', a firm that people want to work for and stay with. The conclusions of Purcell *et al* (2003) on the basis of their research were as follows.

Source review

On being an employer of choice – Purcell *et al* (2003)

What seems to be happening is that successful firms are able to meet people's needs both for a good job and to work 'in a great place'. They create good work and a conducive working environment. In this way they become an 'employer of choice'. People will want to work there because their individual needs are met – for a good job with prospects linked to training, appraisal and working with a good boss who listens and gives some autonomy but helps with coaching and guidance.

To develop an employee value proposition it is necessary first to analyse what the organization has to offer people by reference to:

- its reputation as a business and as an employer;
- its working environment;
- its location;
- the career opportunities available;
- the scope that it provides for learning new skills;
- the terms and conditions of employment it offers.

The next step is to decide how this proposition can be conveyed to potential applicants on the organization's website or by other means.

Employer brand

The employee value proposition can be expressed as an employer brand – the image presented by an organization as a good employer. An employer brand was defined by Walker (2007: 44) as 'a set of attributes and qualities – often intangible – that make an organization distinctive, promise a particular kind of employment experience and appeal to people who will thrive and perform their best in its culture'. Employer branding is the creation of a brand image of the organization for prospective employees.

Creating an employer brand

- Analyse what the best candidates need and want and take this into account in deciding what should be offered and how it should be offered.
- Establish how far the core values of the organization support the creation of an attractive brand and ensure that these are incorporated in the presentation of the brand, as long as they are 'values in use' (lived by members of the organization) rather than simply espoused.
- Define the features of the brand on the basis of an examination and review of each of the areas that affect people's perceptions of the organization as 'a great place to work' – the way people are treated, the provision of a fair deal, opportunities for growth, work–life balance, leadership, the quality of management, involvement with colleagues and how and why the organization is successful.
- Benchmark the approaches of other organizations (the *Sunday Times* list of the 100 best companies to work for is useful) to obtain ideas about what can be done to enhance the brand.
- Be honest and realistic.

CASE STUDY

Developing an employer brand at the Ordnance Survey

The Ordnance Survey was finding it difficult to recruit technological and commercial staff of the right calibre and it was therefore decided to deal with the problem by conducting an employer branding exercise.

Objectives

The objectives of the exercise were to:

- improve external perceptions of Ordnance Survey as an employer;
- get recruitment campaigns 'right first time';
- reduce recruitment costs;
- attract and recruit high-quality people, especially in technology and commercial areas;
- unlock people's potential to deliver great performance;
- match the employee experience to the organization's strong corporate brand.

The research programme

The employee-research company ORC was engaged to conduct internal and external research and consultation. The external research covered four other large employers with which Ordnance Survey compared well. It also included in-depth interviews with recruitment consultants, short-service leavers and those who had been offered a post but not taken it up. Internal research took the form of focus groups, interviews and consultation with recent joiners. The key messages from this external and internal research were fed into the brand development workshop.

The brand development workshop

The workshop consisted of a cross-section of staff who discussed the attributes of Ordnance Survey and the ways in which it presented them. Action groups met to consider particular aspects of the organization and its policies and how the brand could be developed. The focus was on the 'touch points' at which existing and potential employees engaged with the organization. The aim was to create something compelling and achievable with regard to each of these key elements. A leadership development programme was conducted that included looking at the employer brand.

Outcome

The employer brand created by this process was used as a centre point to inform and shape the people strategy and is aligned to the business strategy.

Employee turnover

Employee turnover (sometimes known as 'labour turnover', 'wastage' or 'attrition') is the rate at which people leave an organization. It can be disruptive and costly. The CIPD (2013) survey of resourcing and talent planning found that the average rate of turnover (the number leaving as a percentage of the number employed) in the UK was 11.9 per cent.

It is necessary to measure employee turnover and calculate its costs in order to forecast future losses for planning purposes and to identify the reasons that people leave the organization. Plans can then be made to attack the problems causing unnecessary turnover and to reduce costs. There are a number of different methods of measuring turnover, as outlined below.

Employee turnover index

The employee turnover index as set out below (sometimes referred to as the employee or labour wastage index) is the traditional formula for measuring turnover:

$$\frac{\text{Number of leavers in a specified period (usually 1 year)}}{\text{Average number of employees during the same period}} \times 100$$

This method is in common use because it is easy to calculate and to understand. It is a simple matter to work out that, if last year 30 out of an average force of 150 employees left (20 per cent turnover) and his trend continues, then the company will have to recruit 108 employees during the following year to increase and to hold the workforce at 200 in that year (50 extra employees, plus 40 to replace the 20 per cent wastage of the average 200 employees employed, plus 18 to replace wastage of the 90 recruits).

This formula is simple, but it can be misleading. The problem is that the percentage may be inflated by the high turnover of a relatively small proportion of the workforce, especially in times of heavy recruitment. Thus, a company employing 1,000 people might have had an annual wastage rate of 20 per cent, meaning that 200 jobs had become vacant during the year. But this could have been spread throughout the company, covering all occupations and long- as well as short-service employees. Alternatively, it could have been restricted to a small sector of the workforce – only 20 jobs might have been affected although each of these had to be filled 10 times during the year. These are different situations and unless they are understood inaccurate forecasts would be made of future requirements and inappropriate actions would be taken to deal with the problem. The turnover index is also suspect if the average number of employees upon which the percentage is based is unrepresentative of recent trends because of considerable increases or decreases during the period in the numbers employed.

Stability index

The stability index is considered by many to be an improvement on the turnover index. The formula is:

$$\frac{\text{Number with 1 year's service or more}}{\text{Number employed 1 year ago}} \times 100$$

Survival rate

The survival rate is the proportion of employees who are engaged within a certain period who remain with the organization after so many months or years of service. Thus, an analysis of a cohort of 20 trainees who have completed their training might show that after two years 10 of the original trainees were still with the company, a survival rate of 50 per cent. The distribution of losses for each entry group, or cohort, can be plotted in the form of a survival curve, as shown in Figure 19.1.

FIGURE 19.1 A survival curve

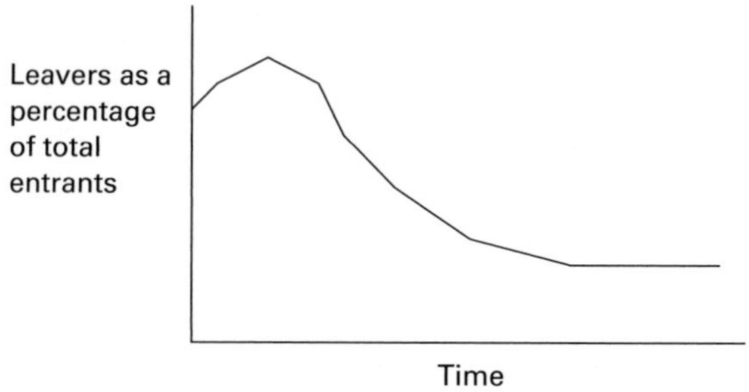

The basic shape of this curve has been found to be similar in many situations, although the peak of the curve may occur further along the time scale and/or may be lower when it relates to more highly skilled or trained entry cohorts. An example of a survival rate analysis is shown in Table 19.1. This indicates that half the number of recruits in any one year may be lost over the next five years, unless something can be done about the factors causing wastage.

The survival rate is useful as a means of tracking a 'cohort' of recruits (eg graduates) to assess the effectiveness of recruitment and retention policies. But it cannot be used as a means of measuring the turnover rates of whole populations in order to allow for future wastage when making supply forecasts.

Half-life index

A simpler concept derived from survival rate analysis is that of the half-life index, which is defined as the time taken for a group or cohort of starters to reduce to half its original size through the wastage process (five years in the above example). Comparisons can then be made for successive entry years or between different groups of employees to show where action may have to be taken to counter undesirable wastage trends.

TABLE 19.1 A survival rate analysis

Entry cohort	Original number	Number surviving to end of year after engagement				
		Year 1	Year 2	Year 3	Year 4	Year 5
A	40	35	28	26	22	20
B	32	25	24	19	18	16
C	48	39	33	30	27	24
D	38	32	27	24	22	19
E	42	36	30	26	23	21
Total	200	167	142	125	112	100
Average survival rate	100%	83%	71%	62%	56%	50%

Leavers' length of service analysis

The information from measures of stability can be enhanced if an analysis is also made of the average length of service of people who leave, as in Figure 19.2. This analysis is still fairly crude, because it deals only with those who leave. A more refined analysis would compare for each designated length of service the numbers leaving with the numbers employed. If, in the example shown, the total number employed with less than three months' service was 80 and the total with more than five years' service was 80, the proportion of leavers in each category would be, respectively, 35 per cent and 14 per cent – more revealing figures.

Choice of measurement

It is difficult to avoid using the conventional employee (labour) turnover index as the easiest and most familiar of all methods of measurement. It provides the simplest basis for assessing future levels of supply by allowing for wastage. But it can usefully be supplemented with some measure of stability (eg survival rate or the length of service of leavers) to identify recruitment or retention problems.

The cost of employee turnover

The cost of employee turnover can be considerable. The CIPD 2008 survey established that the average cost per employee was £5,800, rising to £20,000 for senior managers or directors. Cost estimates are useful as means of backing up a business case for taking action to reduce turnover. The following factors should be considered when calculating costs:

- direct cost of recruiting replacements (advertising, interviewing, testing, etc);
- direct cost of introducing replacements (induction cost);
- direct cost of training replacements in necessary skills;
- leaving costs – payroll and HR administration;
- opportunity cost of time spent by HR and line managers in recruitment, induction and training;
- loss of output from those leaving before they are replaced;
- loss of output because of delays in obtaining replacements;
- loss of output while new starters are on their learning curves acquiring the necessary knowledge and skills.

FIGURE 19.2 Leavers' length of service analysis

Occupation	Leavers by length of service						Total number leaving	Average number employed	Index of employee turnover %
	Less than 3 months	3–6 months	6 months–1 year	1–2 years	3–5 years	5 or more years			
A	5	4	3	3	2	3	20	220	9
B	15	12	10	6	3	4	50	250	20
C	8	6	5	4	3	4	30	100	30
Totals	28	22	18	13	8	11	100	570	18

Research by Phillips (1990) found that the 'visible' (ie direct) costs of recruitment accounted for only 10 to 15 per cent of total costs. By far the highest costs were associated with the inefficiencies arising while the post was vacant (33 per cent) and the inefficiency of new workers (32 per cent). On average, 12.5 months were required for executives to be comfortable in a new position and 13.5 months were required for a new employee to achieve maximum efficiency.

Retention planning

The turnover of key employees can have a disproportionate impact on the business. The people that organizations wish to retain are often the ones most likely to leave. It was claimed by Reed (2001) that every worker is five minutes away from handing in his or her notice, and 150 working hours away from walking out of the door to a better offer. There is no such thing as a job for life and today's workers have few qualms about leaving employers. Action is required to retain talented people, but there are limits to what any organization can do. It is also necessary to encourage higher levels of contribution from existing talent and to value them accordingly.

Factors affecting retention

Retention strategies should be based on an understanding of the factors that affect whether or not employees leave or stay. For early-career employees (30 years old and under) career advancement is significant. For mid-career employees (age 31–50) the ability to manage their careers and satisfaction from their work are important. Late-career employees (aged over 50) will be more interested in security. It is also the case that a younger workforce will change jobs and employers more often than an older workforce, and workforces with a lot of part-timers are less stable than those with predominately full-time staff. The other factors that affect retention are:

- company image;
- the effectiveness of recruitment, selection and deployment (fitting people into jobs that suit them;
- leadership – 'employees join companies and leave managers';

- learning and career opportunities;
- performance recognition and rewards.

A study by Holbeche (1998) of high-flyers found that the factors that aided the retention and motivation of high performers included providing challenge and achievement opportunities (eg assignments), mentors, realistic self-assessment and feedback.

Basis of the retention strategy

A retention strategy takes into account the retention issues the organization is facing and sets out ways in which these issues can be dealt with. This may mean accepting the following argument offered by Cappelli (2000: 104):

> To adopt the new strategy you have to accept the new reality: the market, not your company, will ultimately determine the movement of your employees. Yes, you can make your organization as pleasant and rewarding a place in which to work in as possible – you can fix problems that might push people towards the exits. But you can't counter the pull of the market; you can't shield your people from attractive opportunities and aggressive recruiters. The old goal of HR – to minimize overall employee turnover – needs to be replaced by a new goal: to influence who leaves and when.

The strategy should be based on an analysis of the risks of leaving.

Risk of leaving analysis

As proposed by Bevan *et al* (1997) risk analysis can be used to quantify the seriousness of losing key people or of key posts becoming vacant. Risk analysis can be carried out by initially identifying potential risk areas – the key people who may leave and, for each of them, as individuals or groups, estimate:

- the likelihood of this occurring;
- how serious the effects of a loss would be on the business;
- the ease with which a replacement could be made and the replacement costs.

Each of the estimates could be expressed on a scale, say: very high, high, medium, low, very low. An overview of the ratings under each heading could then indicate where action may need to be taken to retain key people or groups of people.

The analysis should provide information on reasons for leaving, for example:

- more pay;
- better prospects (career move);
- more security;
- more opportunity to develop skills;
- unable to cope with job;
- better working conditions;
- poor relationships with manager/team leader;
- poor relationships with colleagues;
- bullying or harassment;
- personal – pregnancy, illness, moving away from area, etc.

Information on the reasons for leaving, and therefore where action needs to be taken, can be provided by exit interviews, but they are fallible. More reliance can be placed on the results of attitude or opinion surveys to identify areas of dissatisfaction. The retention plan should propose actions that would focus on each of the areas in which there is dissatisfaction or lack of commitment.

Areas for action

Depending on the outcome of the risk and reasons for leaving analyses the possible actions that can be taken are:

- Ensure that selection and promotion procedures match the capacities of individuals to the demands of the work they have to do. Rapid turnover can result simply from poor selection or promotion decisions.
- Reduce the losses of people who cannot adjust to their new job – the 'induction crisis' – by giving them proper training and support when they join the organization.
- Design jobs to maximize skill variety, task significance, autonomy, control over work and feedback, and ensure that they provide opportunities for learning and growth. Some roles can be 'customized' to meet the needs of particular individuals.

- Deal with uncompetitive, inequitable or unfair pay systems. But as Cappelli (2000) pointed out, there is a limit to the extent to which people can be bribed to stay.
- Encourage the development of social ties within the company. In the words of Cappelli (2000: 108), 'loyalty to companies may be disappearing but loyalty to colleagues is not'.
- Take steps to improve work–life balance by developing policies, including flexible working, that recognize the needs of employees outside work.
- Eliminate as far as possible unpleasant working conditions or the imposition of too much stress on employees.
- Select, brief and train managers and team leaders so that they appreciate the positive contribution they can make to improving retention by the ways in which they lead their teams. Bear in mind that people often leave their managers rather than their organization.

Ensure that policies for controlling bullying and harassment are in place and are applied.

Absence management

Absence or attendance management is the development and application of policies and procedures designed to reduce levels of absenteeism. The CIPD (2012) report on absence management revealed that:

- the average length of employee absence was 6.8 days per employee per year;
- larger organizations have higher average levels of absence than smaller organizations;
- on average, two-thirds of working time lost to absence is accounted for by short-term absences of up to seven days; one-fifth is attributed to long-term absences;
- the average cost of absence was £600 per employee per year.

Something needs to be done about it. This means understanding the causes of absence, adopting comprehensive absence management (or, more positively, attendance management) policies, measuring absence and implementing procedures for the management of short- and long-term absence.

Causes of absence

The causes of absence have been analysed by Huczynski and Fitzpatrick (1989) under three headings: job situation factors, personal factors and attendance factors.

Job situation factors

- Job scope – a high degree of task repetitiveness is associated with absenteeism, although job satisfaction itself is a contributory rather than a primary cause of absence.
- Stress – it is estimated that 40 million working days are lost each year in the UK through stress. This can be attributed to work load, poor working conditions, shift work, role ambiguity or conflict, relationships and organizational climate.
- Frequent job transfers increase absenteeism.
- Management style – the quality of management, especially that of immediate supervisors, affects the level of absenteeism.
- Physical working conditions.
- Work group size – the larger the organization the higher the absence rate.

Personal factors

- Employee values – for some workers, doing less work for the same reward improves the deal made with the employer (the effort-reward bargain). The following positive outcomes of absence have been shown by research to be particularly important to employees: break from routine, leisure time, dealing with personal business and a break from co-workers.
- Age – younger employees are more frequently absent than older ones.
- Personality – some people are absence-prone (studies have noted that between 5 and 10 per cent of workers account for about half of the total absence, while a few are never absent at all).

Attendance factors

- Reward systems – as pay increases attendance improves.
- Sick-pay schemes may increase absenteeism.
- Work group norms can exert pressure for or against attendance.

Absence policies

Absence policies should cover:

- methods of measuring absence;
- setting targets for the level of absence;
- deciding on the level of short-term absence that would trigger action, possibly using the Bradford Factor, as explained below;
- the circumstances in which disciplinary action might be taken;
- what employees must do if they are unable to attend work;
- sick-pay arrangements;
- provisions for the reduction and control of absence such as return-to-work interviews;
- other steps that can be taken to reduce absence, such as flexible working patterns.

The skills required to manage absenteeism are examined in Chapter 57.

Recording and measuring absence

As a basis for action, absence levels need to be recorded so that they can be measured and monitored against targets for maintaining absence at a certain level, or reducing absenteeism.

An HR information system (HRIS) can provide the best means of recording absenteeism. If a self-service approach is in place, managers and team leaders have direct access to absence records showing the incidence of absenteeism (number and lengths of absence). This data can be consolidated for use by HR in compiling absence statistics and monitoring against targets. The most common measurement is the percentage of time available that has been lost due to absence.

The Bradford Factor

The Bradford Factor provides a useful measure. This index identifies persistent short-term absence by measuring the number and duration of spells of absence. Its exact origin is a mystery, although IDS (2007) believes that it has some connection with Bradford University's School of Management. It is calculated using the formula S × S × D = Bradford points score, where S is the number of occasions of absence in the last 52 weeks and D is the total number of days' absence in the last 52 weeks. Thus, for employees with a total of 14 days' absence in a 52-week period, the Bradford score can vary enormously depending on the number of occasions involved. For example:

one absence of 14 days is 14 points: 1 × 1 × 14

seven absences of two days each is 686 points: 7 × 7 × 14

14 absences of one day each is 2,744 points: 14 × 14 × 14

The Bradford index can be used as a trigger to initiate action. It is typically set at 250 points so that action would be initiated if, for example, there had been 10 days absence over five spells.

Controlling short-term absence

Short-term absence can be controlled by the following:

- return-to-work interviews conducted by line managers, which can identify problems at an early stage and provide an opportunity for a discussion on ways of reducing absence;
- use of trigger mechanisms such as the Bradford Factor to review attendance;
- invoking disciplinary procedures for unacceptable absence levels;
- training line managers in methods of controlling absence, including return-to-work interviews;
- extending the scope for flexible working.

Managing long-term absence

The best way to manage long-term absence is to keep in contact with employees by letter, telephone or visits to discuss the situation and, where possible, plan the return to work. This plan may include modified working hours or a modified role for a period.

CASE STUDIES

Controlling sickness absence at Wincanton

Distribution company Wincanton had a problem controlling sickness absence because its large workforce is spread over 285 sites. The solution was to outsource absence management to Active Health Partners, which operates a call centre staffed by nurses – employees must report their absences and can receive medical advice. An online absence recording system is also provided, which provides line managers with information on absences and access to absence statistics.

As soon as an employee calls Active Health Partners an e-mail or text is sent to the employee's line manager via an automated system, informing him or her of the absence and the reason for it and giving an approximate return-to-work date. The system also provides various triggers to line managers. For example, once an employee has been away for more than 15 days, the manager receives a message indicating that contact needs to be made. Managers are expected to conduct return-to-work interviews and have more formal discussions when an absence exceeds 15 days. They will explore why there has been this amount of time off, if there is an underlying health issue, if an employee should be referred to Occupational Health and if the disciplinary process should be started.

As a result, Wincanton reduced sickness absence by 10,000 days in six months.

Absence management at Westminster City Council

Monitoring

Sickness absence is recorded by line managers on the intranet system.

Return-to-work interviews

A return-to-work interview is held between the manager and the employee after any length of absence, even one day, although this may only take a couple of minutes. Employees are required to complete a self-certification/return to work form. Employees who have been absent for eight days or more are informed that they will be referred to Occupational Health.

Absence trigger points

An employee who has had more than seven days' sickness absence in any rolling 365-day period is dealt with through the 'enhanced sickness management procedure'. If sickness absence exceeds 20 days, the long-term sickness procedure is applied.

The enhanced sickness management procedure

- Line managers complete a referral form that is forwarded to Occupational Health staff who decide to conduct a face-to-face consultation or make a desktop assessment – and in either case provide any advice necessary to the manager or the individual and send a report to the manager and HR.
- Within 10 days of receiving the report the manager meets the employee to review the sickness record, consider any further explanations for the absence, discuss the report from Occupational Health and agree action to improve attendance and minimize sickness.
- As necessary, especially in cases of disability, Occupational Health will discuss with the manager and the employee any reasonable adaptations to the work environment that may be helpful.

Long-term sickness absence management

- Every four weeks managers review cases of long-term absence with the Occupational Health service and also contact the employee.
- If an employee has been off work the managers and Occupational Health hold a case conference to assess the situation. The employee is required to meet Occupational Health if this is possible.

- The manager makes an assessment following the case conference covering the nature and likely length of the illness, the impact of the absence on the work and how any impact will be managed.
- Following this assessment a face-to-face meeting is held with the employee to ensure that other relevant factors and personal circumstances are taken into account.
- A sickness absence hearing may be called as a result of this meeting and the case conference.

Employee assistance programme

An employee assistance programme (EAP) is available through an external provider. Employees can raise problems with helpline staff, and face-to-face counselling can be made available.

Induction

Induction is the process of receiving and welcoming employees when they first join a company and giving them the basic information they need to settle down quickly and happily and start work. The aims are to:

- smooth the preliminary stages when everything is likely to be strange and unfamiliar to the starter;
- establish quickly a favourable attitude to the organization in the mind of new employees so that they are more likely to stay;
- obtain effective output from the new employee in the shortest possible time;
- reduce the likelihood of the employee leaving quickly.

Introduction to the organization

New starters will be concerned about who they are going to work for (their immediate manager or team leader), who they are going to work with, what work they are going to do on their first day and the geographical layout of their place of work (location of entrances, exits, lavatories, restrooms and the canteen).

Some of this information may be provided by a member of the HR department, or an assistant in the new employee's place of work. But the most important source of information is the immediate manager, supervisor or team leader.

Departmental induction

The departmental induction programme should, wherever possible, start with the departmental manager, not the immediate team leader. The manager may give only a general welcome and a brief description of the work of the department before handing over new employees to their team leaders for the more detailed induction. But it is important for the manager to be involved at this stage so that he or she is not seen as a remote figure by the new employee. At least this means that the starter will not be simply a name or a number to the manager. The detailed induction in the workplace is probably best carried out by the immediate team leader.

Induction to the workplace

The team leader should introduce new starters to their fellow team members. It is best to get one member of the team to act as a guide or 'starter's friend'. There is much to be said for these initial guides being people who have not been long with the organization. As relative newcomers they are likely to remember all the small points that were a source of worry to them when they started work, and so help new employees to settle in quickly.

On-the-job induction training

Most new starters other than those on formal training schemes will learn on-the-job, although this may be supplemented with special off-the-job courses to develop particular skills or knowledge. But on-the-job training can be haphazard, inefficient and wasteful. A planned, systematic approach is desirable. This can incorporate an assessment of what the new starter needs to learn, the use of designated and trained colleagues to act as guides and mentors, and coaching by team leaders or specially appointed and trained departmental trainers.

These on-the-job arrangements can be supplemented by self-managed learning arrangements, offering access to flexible learning packages or providing advice on learning opportunities.

Release from the organization

One of the most demanding areas of human resource management in organizations is that of handling arrangements for releasing people through redundancy, dismissal or retirement.

Redundancy

Redundancy takes place when the organization as a whole is reducing the number of employees (downsizing), when structural changes are being made following mergers and acquisitions, and when individual jobs are no longer needed. If, unfortunately, redundancy has to take place, it is necessary to plan ahead – seeking and implementing methods of avoiding redundancy as far as possible, making arrangements for voluntary redundancy and helping people to find jobs (outplacement). HR usually has the onerous responsibility of handling the redundancy itself.

Planning ahead

Planning ahead means that future reductions in people needs are anticipated and steps are taken to minimize compulsory redundancies. This can be done by freezing recruitment and allowing the normal flow of leavers (natural wastage) to reduce or even eliminate the need for redundancy, calling in outsourced work, reducing or eliminating overtime, reducing the number of part-timers and temporary staff, work-sharing (two people splitting one job between them) or, more reluctantly, reduction in working hours or temporary layoffs.

Voluntary redundancy

Asking for volunteers – with a suitable payoff – is another way of reducing compulsory redundancies. The disadvantage is that the wrong people might go, ie the good workers who find it easy to get other work. It is sometimes useful to offer such people a special loyalty bonus if they stay on.

Outplacement

Outplacement is about helping redundant employees to find other work and to cope with the problems they face. It can take place through specialized outplacement consultants and counselling or by setting up 'job shops'.

Outplacement consultants provide counselling on how people can make the best use of what they can offer to other employers. They can be helped to identify their strengths and achievements, the type of job they are qualified to do and the sort of employer that is most likely to want people with their experience and qualifications. Assistance can be provided in preparing what is sometimes called an 'achievement CV', which spells out what the individual has been successful in and prompts the thought in the employer's mind: 'What the individual has done for them he or she can do for us.'

Counselling involves help and advice in identifying possible moves, preparing CVs and how to make the best impression in interviews. Counselling may be provided by HR staff, but there is much to be said for using specialized outplacement consultants.

Help may be given on an individual basis through counselling or outplacement consultants, but in larger scale redundancies job shops can be set up. The staff of the job shop, who may be from HR or are sometimes members of a specialized outplacement consultancy, scour the travel-to-work area seeking job opportunities, match people to jobs and arrange interviews.

Dismissal

Dismissal takes place when an employer terminates the employment of someone with or without notice. A contract can be terminated as a result of demotion or transfer, as well as dismissal. People can be 'constructively dismissed' if they resign because of their employer's unreasonable behaviour.

Approach to dismissal

Dismissals should be handled in accordance with the following principles of natural justice:

- Individuals should know the standards of performance they are expected to meet and the rules to which they are expected to conform.
- They should be given a clear indication of where they are failing or what rules they have broken.
- Except in cases of gross misconduct, they should be given an opportunity to improve before disciplinary action is taken.

Disciplinary procedure

These principles should form the basis of a disciplinary procedure, which is staged as follows:

1. An informal discussion on the problem.
2. A first written warning.
3. A final written warning.
4. Dismissal or action short of dismissal such as loss of pay or demotion.

Employees should be reminded of their right to be accompanied by a colleague or employee representative in disciplinary hearings. (An example of a full disciplinary procedure incorporating the stages listed above is given in Chapter 41.)

Managers and team leaders should be made aware of the procedure and told what authority they have to take action. It is advisable to have all written warnings and any final action approved by a higher authority. In cases of gross misconduct, managers and team leaders should be given the right to suspend if higher authority is not available, but not to dismiss. The importance of obtaining and recording the facts should be emphasized. Managers should always have a colleague with them when issuing a final warning and should make a note to file of what was said on the spot.

Retirement

Retirement is a major change and should be prepared for. Retirement policies need to specify:

- when people are due to retire;
- the circumstances, if any, in which they can work beyond their normal retirement date;
- the provision of pre-retirement training on such matters as finance, insurance, state pension rights and other benefits, health, working either for money or for a voluntary organization, and sources of advice and help;
- the provision of advice to people about to retire.

Key learning points: Resourcing practice

Employee value proposition

An organization's employee value proposition consists of what it offers to prospective or existing employees that they will value and that will persuade them to join or remain with the business. It can be developed by analysing everything that the organization has to offer potential employees and then conveying that offer to them on the organization's website or by other means.

Employer brand

The employee value proposition can be expressed as an employer brand – the image presented by an organization as a good employer. To create an employer brand:

- analyse what the best candidates need and want;
- establish how far the core values of the organization support the creation of an attractive brand;
- define the features of the brand on the basis of an examination and review of each of the areas that affect the perceptions of people about the organization as 'a great place to work';
- benchmark the approaches of other organizations;
- be honest and realistic.

Measuring employee turnover

It is necessary to measure employee turnover and calculate its costs in order to forecast future losses for planning purposes and to identify the reasons that people leave the organization. Plans can then be made to attack the problems causing unnecessary turnover and to reduce costs. The methods available are: employee turnover index, half-life index, length of service analysis, stability index and survival rate.

Estimating the cost of employee turnover:

- direct cost of recruiting replacements;
- direct cost of introducing replacements;
- direct cost of training replacements;
- leaving costs;
- opportunity cost of time spent by HR and line managers in recruitment, etc;
- loss of output.

Retention planning

Retention strategies should be based on an understanding of the factors that affect whether or not employees leave or stay.

Risk of leaving analysis:

- more pay;
- better prospects (career move);
- more security;
- more opportunity to develop skills;
- unable to cope with job;
- better working conditions;
- poor relationships with manager/team leader;
- poor relationships with colleagues;
- bullying or harassment;
- personal – pregnancy, illness, moving away from area, etc.

Absence policies:

- methods of measuring absence;
- setting targets for the level of absence;
- deciding on the level of short-term absence that would trigger action, possibly using the Bradford Factor;
- the circumstances in which disciplinary action might be taken;
- what employees must do if they are unable to attend work;
- sick-pay arrangements;
- provisions for the reduction and control of absence such as return-to-work interviews;
- other steps that can be taken to reduce absence such as flexible working patterns.

Induction

Induction is the process of receiving and welcoming employees when they first join a company and giving them the basic information they need to settle down quickly and happily and start work.

Release from the organization

One of the most demanding areas of HRM in organizations is in handling arrangements for releasing people through redundancy, dismissal or retirement.

Questions

1 What is an employee value proposition?

2 What is an employer brand?

3 What is the employee turnover index and why can it be misleading?

4 What factors affect employee retention?

5 What should absence policies cover?

6 What are the principles of natural justice?

References

Bevan, S, Barber, I and Robinson, D (1997) *Keeping the Best: A practical guide to retaining key employees*, Brighton, Institute for Employment Studies

Cappelli, P (2000) A market-driven approach to retaining talent, *Harvard Business Review*, January–February, pp 103–11

CIPD (2008) *Survey of Recruitment, Retention and Turnover*, London, CIPD

CIPD (2012) *Survey of Absence Management*, London, CIPD

CIPD (2013) *Survey of Resourcing and Talent Planning*, London, CIPD

Holbeche, L (1998) *Motivating People in Lean Organizations*, Oxford, Butterworth-Heinemann

Huczynski, A and Fitzpatrick, M J (1989) *Managing Employee Absence for a Competitive Edge*, London, Pitman

IDS (2007) Absence Management, *HR Study 810*, London, IDS

Phillips, J D (1990) The price tag of turnover, *Personnel Journal*, December, pp 58–61

Purcell, J, Kinnie, K, Hutchinson, S, Rayton, B and Swart, J (2003) *People and Performance: How people management impacts on organizational performance*, London, CIPD

Reed, A (2001) *Innovation in Human Resource Management*, London, CIPD

Walker, P (2007) Develop an effective employer brand, *People Management*, 18 October, pp 44–45

20 Talent management

KEY CONCEPTS AND TERMS

- Career planning
- Portfolio career
- Protean career
- Succession planning
- Talent
- Talent management
- Talent on demand policies
- Talent pipeline
- Talent planning
- Talent pool
- Talent relationship management
- War for talent

LEARNING OUTCOMES

On completing this chapter you should be able to define these key concepts. You should also know about:

- The meaning of talent management
- The process of talent management
- Developing a talent management strategy
- Management succession planning
- Career management

Introduction

The process of talent management is based on the proposition that 'those with the best people win'. It emerged in the late 1990s when McKinsey and Company coined the phrase 'the war for talent'. It has now been recognized as a major resourcing activity, although its elements are familiar. The fundamental concept of talent management – that it is necessary to engage in talent planning to build a talent pool by means of a talent pipeline – is a key concern of human resource management. Talent management was defined by Tansley and Tietze (2013: 1804) as follows: 'Talent management contains strategies and protocols for the systematic attraction, identification, development, retention and deployment of individuals with high potential who are of particular value to an organization.' However, this definition refers to 'individuals with high potential' and although this may be the usual approach, some people believe that talent management covers everybody – on the grounds that all people have talent and talent management activities should not be restricted to the favoured few.

There are many versions of talent management but in one way or another most incorporate typical HRM activities such as potential assessment, leadership and management development, succession planning and career planning. This chapter covers the meaning of talent management and talent management strategy and the processes involved. Two important aspects of talent management – management succession planning and career management – are dealt with at the end of the chapter.

Talent management defined

Talent management is the process of ensuring that the organization has the talented people it needs to attain its business goals. It involves the strategic management of the flow of talent through an organization by creating and maintaining a talent pipeline. As suggested by Younger *et al* (2007), the approaches required include emphasizing 'growth from within'; regarding talent development as a key element of the business strategy; being clear about the competencies and qualities that matter; maintaining well-defined career paths; taking management development, coaching and mentoring seriously; and demanding high performance.

The term 'talent management' may refer simply to management succession planning and/or management development activities, although this notion does not really add anything to these familiar processes except a new name – admittedly quite an evocative one. It is better to regard talent management as a more comprehensive and integrated bundle of activities, the aim of which is to create a pool of talent in an organization, bearing in mind that talent is a major corporate resource.

According to Lewis and Hackman (2006), talent management is defined in three ways: 1) as a combination of standard human resource management practices such as recruitment, selection and career development; 2) as the creation of a large talent pool, ensuring the quantitative and qualitative flow of employees through the organization (ie akin to succession or human resource planning); (3) as a good based on demographic necessity to manage talent.

Iles *et al* (2010: 127) identified three broad strands of thought about talent management:

1. It is not essentially different from human resource management or human resource development. Both are about getting the right people in the right job at the right time and managing the supply and development of people for the organization.
2. It is simply integrated HRD with a selective focus on a small 'talented' section of the workforce (a 'talent pool').
3. It involves organizationally focused competence development through managing and developing flows of talent through the organization. The focus is on the talent pipeline rather than the talent pool. This strand is closely related to succession and human resource planning.

The extent to which talent management is a new idea or simply a bundle of existing practices has been questioned. Iles and Preece (2010: 244–45) observed that:

> Many current ideas in talent management, now often presented as novel and best practice, such as assessing potential, 360-degree feedback, assessment centres and coaching, come from the 1950s era of large stable bureaucracies and sophisticated succession planning as part of more general 'manpower planning'.

And David Guest, cited by Warren (2006: 29), commented that:

> Organizations espouse a lot of notions about talent management and give it a lot of emphasis, but in practical terms it doesn't have a very different meaning to what most organizations have always done. Talent management is an idea that has been around a long time. It's been relabelled.

But he also noted that the process of bringing together some old ideas gives them a freshness and that it can provide a means of integrating these practices so that a coherent approach is adopted by the use of mutually supportive practices.

Before describing the process of talent management it is necessary to answer three questions:

1. What is talent?
2. What does it mean when reference is made to 'the war for talent'?
3. Who is covered by talent management programmes?

Talent defined

Talent was defined by Michaels *et al* (2001, *xii*) as 'the sum of a person's abilities... his or her intrinsic gifts, skills, knowledge, experience, intelligence, judgement, attitude, character and drive. It also includes his or her ability to learn and grow.'

Talent is what people must have in order to perform well in their roles. They make a difference to organizational performance through their immediate efforts and they have the potential to make an important contribution in the future. Talent management aims to identify, obtain, keep and develop those talented people.

The war for talent

Following the McKinsey lead, the phrase 'the war for talent' has become a familiar metaphor for talent management. Michaels (of McKinsey and Co) *et al* (2001) identified five imperatives that companies need to act on if they are going to win what they called the 'war for managerial talent':

1. Creating a winning employee value proposition that will make your company uniquely attractive to talent.
2. Moving beyond recruiting hype to build a long-term recruiting strategy.
3. Using job experience, coaching and mentoring to cultivate the potential in managers.
4. Strengthening the talent pool by investing in A players, developing B players and acting decisively on C players.
5. Central to this approach is a pervasive mindset – a deep conviction shared by leaders throughout the company that competitive advantage comes from having better talent at all levels.

But Pfeffer (2001: 258) expressed doubts about the war for talent concept, which he believed was the wrong metaphor for organizational success. He argued that:

> Fighting the war for talent can readily create self-fulfilling prophesies that leave a large portion of the workforce demotivated or ready to quit, and produce an arrogant attitude that makes it hard to learn or listen. It can cause the company to focus always on getting better people, mainly from outside, instead of fixing the culture and system of management practices that research has shown are consequential for performance.

He suggested (ibid: 249) that perceiving talent management as a 'war' leads to:

- an invariable emphasis on individual performance thereby damaging team work;
- a tendency to glorify the talents of those outside the company and downplay the skills and abilities of insiders;
- those labelled as less able becoming less able because they are asked to do less and given fewer resources and training;
- a de-emphasis on fixing the systemic, cultural and business issues that are invariably more important for enhancing performance;
- the development of an elitist, arrogant attitude (cf Enron).

The people involved

There are different opinions about who should be involved. On the one hand there is the view that you must pay most attention to the best, while on the other, the view is that everyone has talent and it is not just about the favoured few. Iles and Preece (2010: 248) have identified three main perspectives:

1. Exclusive people – key people with high performance and/or potential irrespective of position.
2. Exclusive position – the right people in the strategically critical jobs.
3. Inclusive people – everyone in the organization is seen as actually or potentially talented, given opportunity and direction.

The first two perspectives, or a combination of the two, are the most common. Many organizations focus on the elite. For example, Microsoft UK is most concerned with its 'A list', the top 10 per cent of performers, regardless of role and level, whilst Six Continents targets executives below board level and high-potential individuals, as the two cadres are likely to provide their leaders of tomorrow. Huselid *et al* (2005) argued that talent management policies should concentrate on 'A positions'. McDonnell and Collings (2011: 58) suggested that talent management is 'primarily concerned with those who add value to the organization... those who possess the potential to have a differential impact on organizational success'. They therefore argued that talent management should focus on these individuals rather than including everyone in the organization.

According to Clarke and Winkler (2006), the inclusive people approach is comparatively rare in practice, although there have been strong advocates of it such as Buckingham and Vosburgh (2001: 18), who wrote that talent is inherent in each person: 'HR's most basic challenge is to help one particular person increase his or her performance; to be successful in the future we must restore our focus on the unique talents of each individual employee, and on the right way to transfer those talents into lasting performance.' If exclusive approaches are adopted there is a danger of talent management being perceived as an elitist process. Creating a talent pool of a limited number of individuals may alienate those who are left out. Thorne and Pellant (2007: 9) argued that: 'No organization should focus all its attention on development of only part of its human capital. What is important, however, is recognizing the needs of different individuals within its community.' The CIPD (2010a: 1) asserted that: 'Talent management and diversity need to be interlinked. Diversity should be threaded through all talent management activities and strategies to ensure that organizations make the best use of the talent and skills of all their employees in ways that are aligned to business objectives.'

The most common view seems to be that the aims of talent management are to obtain, identify and develop people with high potential. But it should not be at the expense of the development needs of people generally. The McKinsey prescription has often been misinterpreted as meaning that talent management is only about obtaining, identifying and nurturing high-flyers, ignoring the point made by Michaels *et al* (2001) that competitive advantage comes from having better talent at all levels.

A case study of a global management consultancy (Tansley and Tietze, 2013) revealed that the consultancy's approach to talent management was both inclusive (everyone is talented) and exclusive (key people were developed in ways different to those adopted for 'everyday talent'. This was expressed by the company's Talent Development Director as follows:

> Talent in the Firm means two things. One I think that everybody is a talented individual. We recruit bright people intellectually. But our business also has the responsibility to help them realize that. So there is a fundamental belief that everyone is talented, and there is a belief that we do need to identify future leaders, who are going to lead key parts or have key roles in the business in the future and these would be quite senior roles. And that identifying talent to these spaces, and helping people to gravitate towards one of these roles, will be the key challenge for us.

These beliefs were put into affect by the firm through a talent progression sequence of four stages:

1. *Rising talent* – highly educated graduate recruits who are given education and training for core technical or professional roles.
2. *Emerging leaders* – who are given training and education for management under the guidance of sponsors or mentors.
3. *Next generation leaders* – who undertake leadership development programmes and may attend a corporate academy.
4. *Corporate next generation leaders* – who are provided with one-to-one development through coaches and mentors and briefed on corporate/governance strategy.

The process of talent management

The process of talent management can be described as a pipeline that, as illustrated in Figure 20.1, operates within the parameters of talent strategy and policy and starts with talent planning, followed by a sequence of resourcing and talent development activities to produce a talent pool.

A more detailed flow chart of the process of talent management is shown in Figure 20.2.

Talent management starts with the business strategy and what it signifies in terms of the future demand for talented people. Ultimately, the aim is to develop and maintain a pool of talented people through the talent pipeline, which consists of the processes of resourcing, career planning and talent

FIGURE 20.1 The talent management pipeline

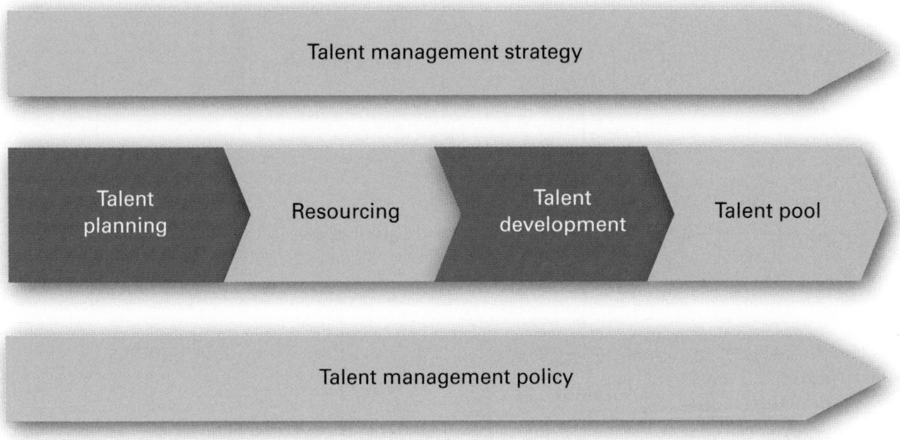

development that maintain the flow of talent needed by the organization. Its elements are:

- *Talent planning* – the process of establishing how many and what sort of talented people are needed now and in the future. It uses the techniques of workforce planning as described in Chapter 17 and leads to the development of policies for attracting and retaining talent and for estimating future requirements as monitored by talent audits.
- *Resourcing* – the outcomes of talent planning are programmes for obtaining people from within and outside the organization (internal and external resourcing). Internally they involve the identification of talent, talent development and career management. Externally they mean the implementation of policies for attracting high-quality people.
- *Talent identification* – the use of talent audits to establish who is eligible to become part of the talent pool and to benefit from learning and development and career management programmes. The information for talent audits can be generated by a performance management system that identifies those with abilities and potential.
- *Talent relationship management* – building effective relationships with people in their roles. It is better to build on an existing relationship rather than try to create a new one when someone leaves. The aims are to recognize the value of individual employees, provide opportunities for growth, treat them fairly and achieve 'talent engagement', ensuring that people are committed to their work and the organization.
- *Talent development* – learning and development policies and programmes are key components of talent management. They aim to ensure that people acquire and enhance the skills and competencies they need. Policies should be formulated by reference to 'employee success profiles', which are described in terms of competencies and define the qualities that need to be developed. Leadership and management development programmes as described in Chapter 24 play an important part.
- *Talent retention* – the implementation of policies designed to ensure that talented people remain as engaged and committed members of the organization (retention planning is covered in Chapter 19).
- *Career management* – as discussed later in this chapter, this is concerned with the provision of opportunities for people to

FIGURE 20.2 The talent management process

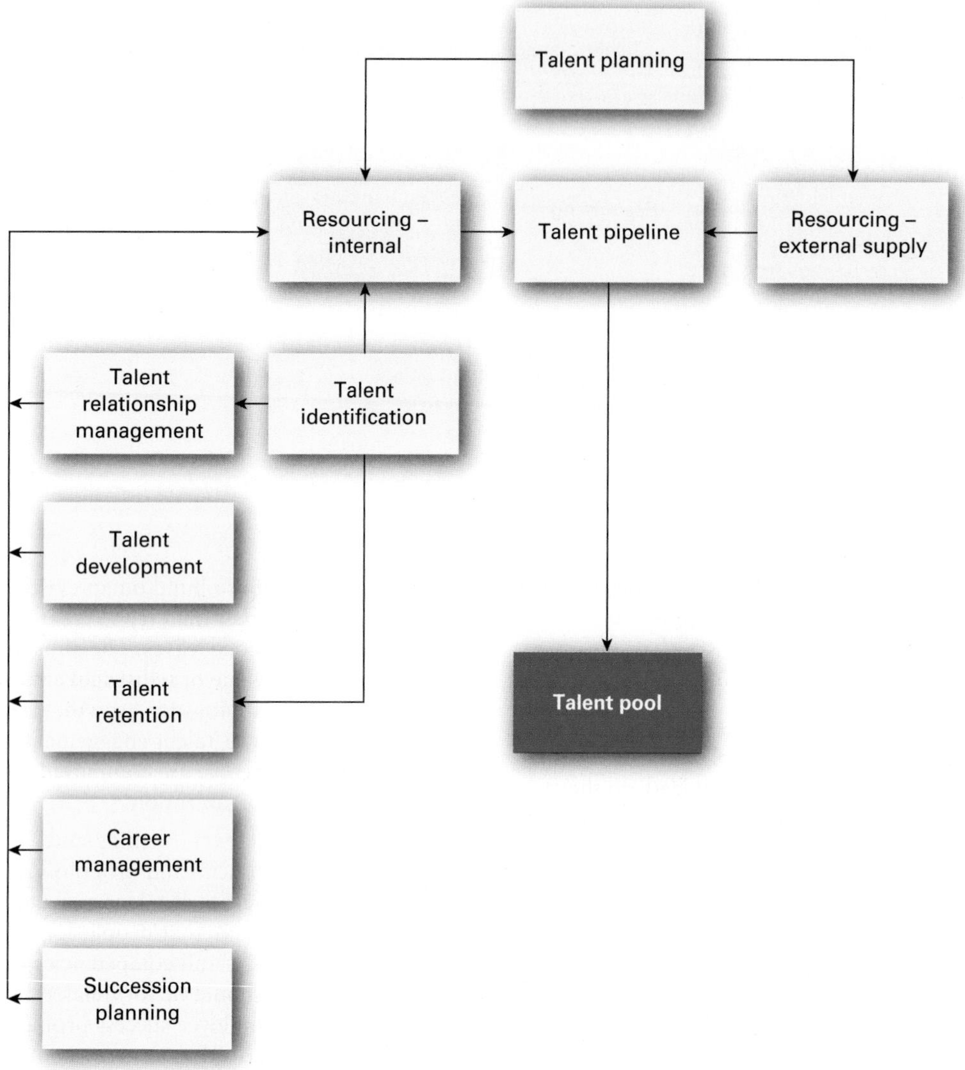

develop their abilities and their careers so that the organization has the flow of talent it needs and they can satisfy their own aspirations.

- *Management succession planning* – as far as possible, the objective is to see that the organization has the managers it requires to meet future business needs. It is considered in detail later in this chapter.
- *The talent pipeline* – the processes of resourcing, talent development and career planning that maintain the flow of talent needed to create the talent pool required by the organization.
- *The talent pool* – the resources of talent available to an organization.

Talent management strategy

Cappelli (2008) suggested that the signs of a successful talent management strategy are that it is inclusive and that it can address and resolve any incongruity between the supply and demand of talent. He stated that too many firms have more employees than they need for available positions, or a talent shortfall, and always at the wrong times. He argued that talent management should not just be about employee development or succession planning, as many of the commonplace definitions suggest, but should focus on helping the firm attain its strategic objectives. His four principles for 'talent on demand' were:

1. Make and buy talent to manage the demand-side risk.
2. Reduce the uncertainty in talent demand.
3. Earn a return on investment in developing employees.
4. Employee interests should be balanced by creating an internal labour market that offers all the advantages of the external labour market to reduce staff turnover and to avoid the associated loss of talent and costs.

A talent management strategy consists of a view on how the processes involved in creating a talent pool should mesh together with an overall objective – to acquire and nurture talent wherever it is and wherever it is needed by using a number of interdependent policies and practices. Talent management is the notion of 'bundling' in action. The strategy should be based on definitions of what is meant by talent in terms of competencies and potential, who the talent management programme should cover, and the future talent requirements of the organization. The aims should be to:

- develop the organization as an 'employer of choice';
- plan and implement recruitment and selection programmes that ensure good-quality people are recruited who are likely to thrive in the organization and stay with it for a reasonable length of time (but not necessarily for life);
- plan and implement talent retention programmes;
- introduce reward policies that help to attract and retain high-quality staff;
- design jobs and develop roles that give people opportunities to apply and grow their skills and provide them with autonomy, interest and challenge;
- implement talent development programmes;
- provide talented staff with opportunities for career development and growth;
- recognize those with talent by rewarding excellence, enterprise and achievement;
- generate and maintain a talent pool so that 'talent on demand' is available to provide for management succession.

It can be difficult to introduce comprehensive talent management processes covering all the activities involved. A phased approach may be best. Resourcing activities take place anyhow, although the advantages of planning them on the basis of assessments of talent requirements are considerable; and it makes sense to devote energies to retaining key staff. But beyond that, the starting point in practice for an extended talent management programme could be a process of identifying people with talent through a performance management system. It would then be possible to concentrate on leadership and management development programmes. Sophisticated approaches to career planning and, possibly, succession planning could be introduced later.

What is happening in talent management

A study by CIPD (2007) of nine UK private and public sector organizations found that:

- What is seen as talent and how it is developed is highly varied.
- There is no one definition of talent management.
- There was little evidence of employers adopting a formal talent management strategy.
- Talent management programmes varied in terms of who they were aimed at and how.
- There were issues relating to the demotivation of individuals not selected for

talent management, especially if this meant that they had fewer resources and opportunities for progression.

- There was often a lack of integration with other HR programmes.

The CIPD 2013 learning and talent development survey revealed that the six most important objectives of respondents' talent management policies were:

1. Growing future senior managers/leaders (62 per cent).
2. Developing high-potential employees (60 per cent).
3. Enabling the achievement of the organization's strategic goals (37 per cent).
4. Retaining key staff (36 per cent).
5. Meeting the future skills requirements of the organization (32 per cent).
6. Attracting and recruiting key staff to the organization (27 per cent).

The most effective approach used by respondents was coaching, followed by development programmes and mentoring.

Career management

Career management is about providing the organization with the flow of talent it needs. But it is also concerned with the provision of opportunities for people to develop their abilities and their careers in order to satisfy their own aspirations. It integrates the needs of the organization with the needs of the individual.

An important part of career management is career planning, which shapes the progression of individuals within an organization in accordance with assessments of organizational needs, defined employee success profiles and the performance, potential and preferences of individual members of the enterprise. Career management also involves career counselling to help people develop their careers to their advantage as well as that of the organization.

Career management has to take account of the fact that many people are not interested in developing their careers in one organization and prefer to look for new experience elsewhere. But as De Vos and Dries (2013: 1828) point out: 'Although careers for life, admittedly, are a reality from a distant past, the organizational career is far from dead.'

Aims

For the organization, the aim of career management is to meet the objectives of its talent management policies, which are to ensure that there is a talent flow that creates and maintains the required talent pool. For employees, the aims of career management policies are: 1) to give them the guidance, support and encouragement they need to fulfil their potential and achieve a successful career with the organization in tune with their talents and ambitions; and 2) to provide those with promise a sequence of experience and learning activities that will equip them for whatever level of responsibility they have the ability to reach.

Career management calls for an approach that explicitly takes into account both organizational needs and employee interests. It calls for creativity in identifying ways to provide development opportunities. Career management policies and practices are best based on an understanding of the stages through which careers progress in organizations.

Career stages

The stages of a career within an organization can be described as a career life cycle. Hall (1984) set this out as follows:

1. Entry to the organization, when the individual can begin the process of self-directed career planning.
2. Progress within particular areas of work, where skills and potential are developed through experience, training, coaching, mentoring and performance management.
3. Mid-career, when some people will still have good career prospects while others may have got as far as they are going to get, or at least feel that they have. It is necessary to ensure that these 'plateaued' people do not lose interest at this stage by taking such steps as providing them with cross-functional moves, job rotation, special assignments, recognition and rewards for effective performance, etc.

4 Later career, when individuals may have settled down at whatever level they have reached but are beginning to be concerned about the future. They need to be treated with respect as people who are still making a contribution and be given opportunities to take on new challenges wherever this is possible. They may also need reassurance about their future with the organization and what is to happen to them when they leave.

5 End of career with the organization – the possibility of phasing disengagement by being given the chance to work part-time for a period before they finally have to go should be considered at this stage.

Career dynamics

Career management should be based on an understanding of career dynamics. This is concerned with how careers progress – the ways in which people move through their careers either upwards when they are promoted, or by enlarging or enriching their roles to take on greater responsibilities or make more use of their skills and abilities. The three stages of career progression – expanding, establishing and maturing – are illustrated in Figure 20.3. This also shows how individuals progress or fail to progress at different rates through these stages.

Career development strategy

A career development strategy might include the following activities:

- a policy of promoting from within wherever possible;
- career routes enabling talented people to move upwards or laterally in the organization as their development and job opportunities take them;
- personal development planning as a major part of the performance management process, to develop each individual's knowledge and skills;
- systems and processes to achieve sharing and development of knowledge (especially tacit) across the firm;
- multidisciplinary project teams, with a shifting membership, to offer developmental opportunities for as wide a range of employees as possible.

FIGURE 20.3 Career progression stages

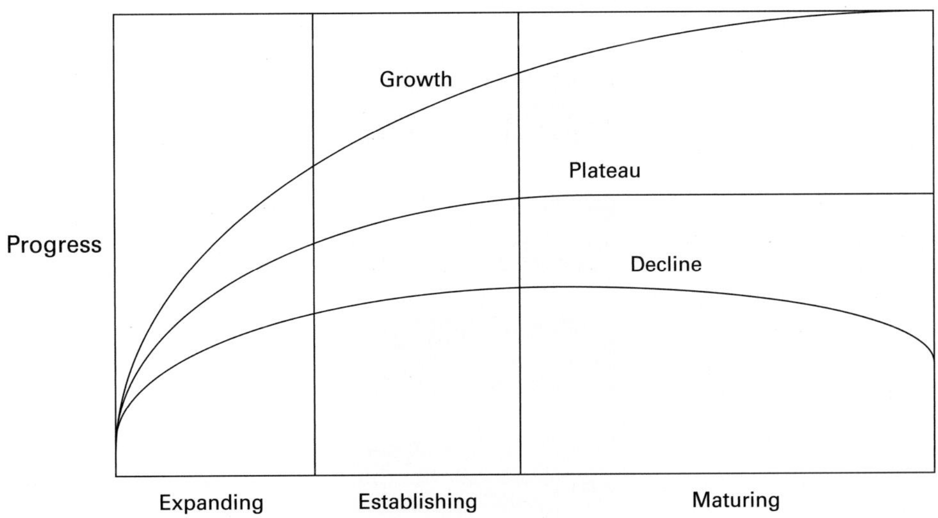

Career management activities

As described by Hirsh and Carter (2002), career management encompasses recruitment, personal development plans, lateral moves, special assignments at home or abroad, development positions, career bridges, lateral moves and support for employees who want to develop.

Baruch and Peiperl (2000) identified 17 career management practices, and their survey of 194 UK companies established a rank order for their use. The practices are listed below in order, from most frequent to least frequent use:

1. Postings regarding internal job openings.
2. Formal education as part of career development.
3. Performance appraisal as a basis for career planning.
4. Career counselling by manager.
5. Lateral moves to create cross-functional experience.
6. Career counselling by HR department.
7. Retirement preparation programmes.
8. Succession planning.
9. Formal mentoring.
10. Common career paths.
11. Dual ladder career paths (parallel hierarchy for professional staff).
12. Books and/or pamphlets on career issues.
13. Written personal career planning (as done by the organization or personally).
14. Assessment centres.
15. Peer appraisal.
16. Career workshops.
17. Upward (subordinate) appraisal.

The process of career management is illustrated in Figure 20.4.

Career management policies

The organization needs to decide on the degree to which it 'makes or buys' talented people, which means answering the questions: to what extent it should grow its own talent (a promotion from within policy); how much it should rely on external recruitment (bringing 'fresh blood' into the organization). The policy may be to recruit potentially high performers who will be good at their present job and are rewarded accordingly. If they are really good, they will be promoted and the enterprise will get what it wants. Deliberately training managers for a future that will never happen is a waste of time.

FIGURE 20.4 The process of career management

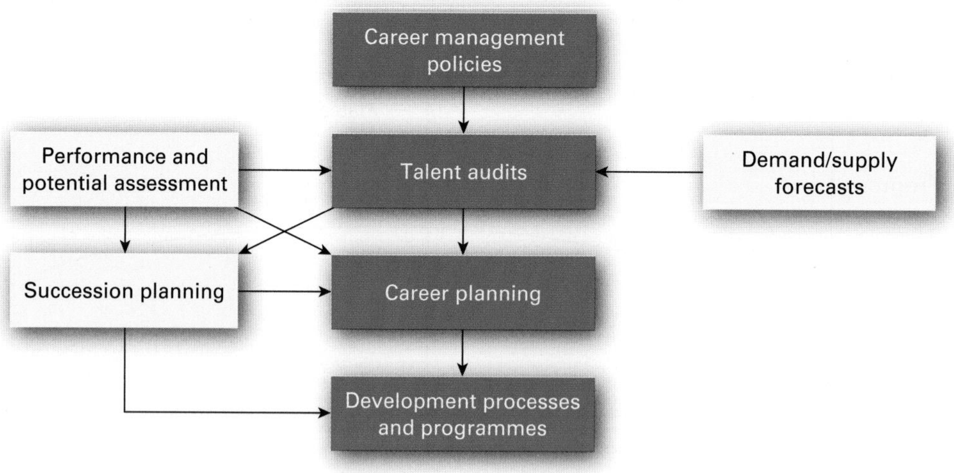

In contrast, and much less frequently, employers who believe in long-term career planning develop structured approaches to career management. These include elaborate reviews of performance and potential, assessment centres to identify talent or confirm that it is there, high-flyer schemes and planned job moves in line with a predetermined programme.

There may also be policies for dealing with the 'plateaued' manager who has got so far but will get no further. Some managers in this position may be reconciled to reaching that level but continue to work effectively. Others will become bored, frustrated and unproductive, especially rising stars who are on the wane. The steps that can be taken to deal with this problem include:

- lateral moves into different functional areas or specialized subsidiaries, to provide new challenges and career breadth;
- temporary assignments and secondments outside the organization;
- appointments as leaders of project teams set up to deal with performance barriers inside the organization such as the slowness of responses to customer complaints.

Career planning

Career planning involves the definition of career paths – the routes people can take to advance their careers within an organization. It uses all the information provided by the organization's assessments of requirements, the assessments of performance and potential and management succession plans, and translates it into the form of individual career development programmes and general arrangements for management development, career counselling and mentoring.

It is possible to define career progression in terms of what people are required to know and be able to do to carry out work to progress up the 'career ladder' (the sequence of jobs at increasing levels of responsibility that constitutes a career). These levels can be described as 'competency bands'. For each band, the competencies needed to achieve a move to that level would be defined in order to produce a career map incorporating 'aiming points' for individuals, as illustrated in Figure 20.5. People would be made aware of the competency levels they must reach to achieve progress in their careers. This would help them to plan their own development, although support and guidance should be provided by their managers, HR specialists and, if they exist, management development advisers or mentors. The provision of additional experience and training could be arranged as appropriate, but it would be important to clarify what individual employees need to do for themselves if they want to progress within the organization. At Procter & Gamble, for example, 'destination jobs' are identified for rising

FIGURE 20.5 Competency band career progression system

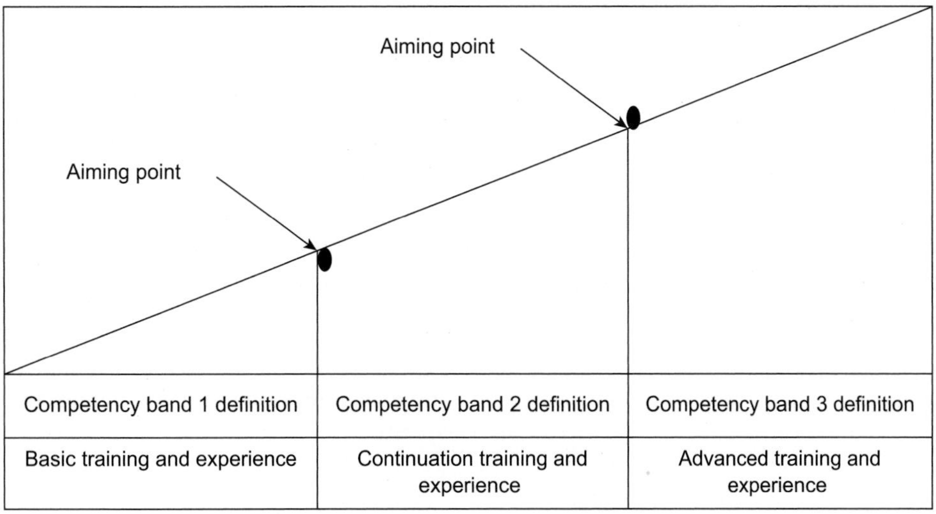

FIGURE 20.6 Career paths in a career family structure

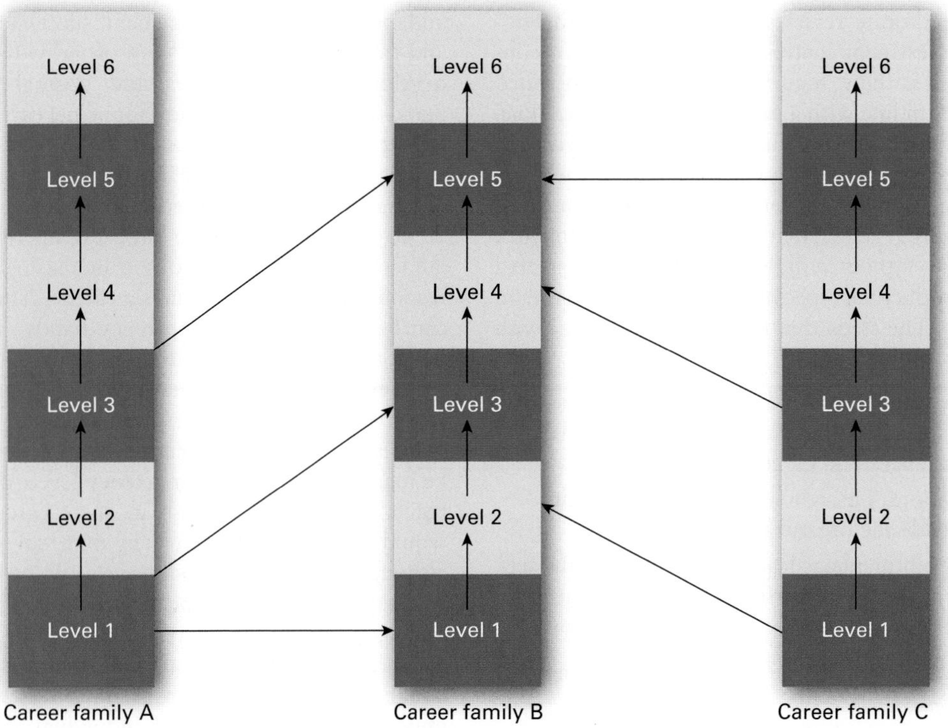

stars, which are attainable only if the employee continues to perform, impress and demonstrate growth potential.

Career family grade structures, as described in Chapter 27, can define levels of competency in each career family and show career paths upwards within families or between families. This is illustrated in Figure 20.6.

Formal career planning may be the ideal but, as noted by Hirsh *et al* (2000), there has been a shift from managed career moves to more open internal job markets. The process of internal job application has become the main way in which employees progress their careers.

Self-managed careers

The organization may need to manage careers as part of its talent management and management succession programmes and can provide support and guidance to people with potential. Ultimately, however, it is up to individuals to manage their own careers within and beyond their present organization. Handy (1984) used the term 'portfolio career' to describe his forecast that people will increasingly change the direction of their careers during the course of their working life. Hall (1996) coined the phrase the 'protean career' in which individuals take responsibility for transforming their career path (the name comes from the Greek god Proteus, who could change his shape at will).

Schein (1978) originated the notion of 'career anchors'. He defined them as the self-concept of people, consisting of self-perceived talents and abilities, basic values and a sense of motives and needs relating to their careers. As people gain work experience, career anchors evolve and function as stabilizing forces, hence the metaphor of 'anchor'.

CASE STUDIES

BT

BT's approach to investing in its talent is primarily focused on responding to individual needs in line with a BT-wide 'Talent Deal'. This is a set of commitments made to individuals in BT's talent pool on the support they can expect in areas such as career planning and movement, opportunities for networking and meeting top executives, and mentoring. It also specifies the commitments expected of BT's talent pool members, such as the contribution they make to supporting the development of other colleagues.

Cargill

The Cargill food business operates a global, corporate-level labour and talent management process. This is structured on the lines of 'food platforms' (collections of around eight business units that operate in the food businesses) and has representatives from Latin America, Europe, Asia, etc, meeting twice per year. They look at the work of the businesses and consider how talent might be managed and succession planned in those businesses. A workable model exists to look at talent management and succession planning at a platform level and at a practical level. Consideration is being given to how to integrate talent management and succession planning on a global basis, and a start has been made on highlighting positive and negative aspects of talent management and succession planning. These will be discussed at corporate level by the board to ensure that Cargill values are embedded in future talent management and succession planning strategy, policies and practices.

GlaxoSmithKline

GlaxoSmithKline is identifying those positions, at both the corporate and business-unit levels, that are critical to the company's success in a rapidly changing competitive environment. As part of that initiative, the company developed a statement of its workforce philosophy and management guidelines. One of these explicitly addresses 'workforce differentiation' and reads, in part: 'It is essential that we have key talent in critical positions and that the careers of these individuals are managed centrally.'

HSBC

As reported by Ready and Conger (2007: 72–73), HSBC has created a system of talent pools that track and manage the careers of employees with high potential. Employees in these pools are selected initially for new assignments within their region or line of business and, over time, are given positions that cross boundaries in order to demonstrate that they have the potential to reach a senior management role. They can then be placed in the group talent pool, which means that they have the potential to reach the senior executive level in three to five years and top management in the longer term. Leaders conduct talent relationship dialogues with members of each pool in order to address their development needs and concerns.

IBM

The overall aim of talent management within IBM is 'to develop the leaders of tomorrow'. Part of what makes it a global company is the importance it places on high-potential people gaining international experience. For employees, being identified as talent therefore drives many opportunities in the company.

Every leader in the company has responsibility for identifying and nurturing talent. The areas for them to look for are aptitude, potential and the ability to grow and develop. The identification of talented individuals is based on their performance against 10 leadership competencies, which are consistent globally. The leadership competencies are used as a development tool for employees at all levels in IBM, not just those already highlighted as having potential.

Readiness for promotion to executive roles is linked to competencies. For example, if an individual needs to get client relationship-building skills, then his or her next job has to include that. Readiness is categorized in terms of 'next job' or 'two jobs away' rather than a number of years.

Standard Chartered Bank

As reported by the CIPD (2010c), Standard Chartered was looking closely at its existing approach to talent management. This has involved:

- re-examining the processes, to ensure that there is greater transparency, education and understanding about the importance of robust talent identification and development;
- embedding talent processes to establish clearer links between our talent processes and other global people processes around performance management and engagement;
- encouraging more experiential-based learning centred more on on-the-job learning and learning from others;
- providing support to help our managers and leaders engage and motivate their teams;
- ensuring that talented staff continue to perform above their peer group, are highly engaged and that they are retained.

Management succession planning

Management succession planning is the process of ensuring that capable managers are available to fill vacant managerial posts. Three questions need to be answered: first, are there enough potential successors available – a supply of people coming through who can take key roles in the longer term? Second, are they good enough? Third, do they have the right skills and competencies for the future? At different stages in their careers, managers may be categorized as being ready to do the next job now, or being ready for a specified higher-grade position in, say, two years' time, or as a high-flyer on the 'A list' who has senior management potential. Such assessments generate development plans such as leadership and development programmes, special assignments and job rotation.

As noted by Iles and Preece (2010: 256), succession planning can be seen in terms of identifying successors for key posts and then planning career moves and/or development activities for these potential successors. They suggested that:

> Processes need to be designed round purpose, population, principles, process and players, with senior management engagement and HR championing. The highest potential employees are thus offered accelerated development and career paths. Of course, the downside is that non-selected employees may feel that they are less valued and have less access to development opportunities.

They also commented that in reality few companies have such programmes and that some are critical of attempts to equate succession planning with talent

FIGURE 20.7 Management succession schedule

MANAGEMENT SUCCESSION SCHEDULE					Department:		Director/manager:	
Existing managers						Potential successors		
Name	Position	Due for replacement	Rating		If promotable, to what position and when?	Names: 1st and 2nd choice	Positions	When
			Performance	Potential				

management, arguing instead for a 'talent on demand' framework, 'based on managing risk (not overestimating the places to be filled) and using talent pools to span functions' (ibid: 256). They reported that some people are more positive about the value of 'leadership pipelines', which enable the organization to:

- focus on development;
- identify critical 'lynchpin' roles;
- create transparent succession management systems;
- regularly measure progress;
- ensure flexibility.

Succession planning is based on the information about managers in supply and demand forecasts, talent audits and performance and potential reviews. In some large organizations where demand and supply forecasts can be made accurately, there are highly formalized succession planning processes based on the sort of management succession schedule illustrated in Figure 20.7.

However, the scope for formal succession planning may be limited in today's more flexible and rapidly changing organizations, where elaborate succession plans could be out of date as soon as they are made. In these circumstances, the most that can be done is to use talent management and management development processes to ensure that there are plenty of talented people around in 'talent pools' to fill vacancies as they arise on the basis of 'talent on demand', bearing in mind that the most talented or ambitious individuals may not want to wait very long.

As McDonnell and Collings (2011: 64) emphasized:

> Succession planning has evolved from the traditional short-term focus on replacing senior managers if they happened to leave without prior warning. There is now a more long-term aim of developing a cadre of key talent who able to take on higher level roles, potentially roles that may not currently exist... The utilization of talent pools consisting of employees with key generic type competencies and skills allows the organization far greater scope when positions become available. Management will be able to select the most suitable candidate from a pool of candidates and train the person into the specific requirements of that particular role.

Key learning points: Talent management

The meaning of talent management

Talented people possess special gifts, abilities and aptitudes that enable them to perform effectively. Talent management is the process of identifying, developing, recruiting, retaining and deploying those talented people.

The process of talent management

Talent management starts with the business strategy and what it signifies in terms of the talented people required by the organization. Ultimately, its aim is to develop and maintain a pool of talented people. Its elements are talent planning, resourcing strategies, retention programmes, talent development, career management and management succession planning.

Developing a talent management strategy

A talent management strategy consists of a view on how the processes should mesh together with an overall objective – to acquire and nurture talent wherever it is and wherever it is needed by using a number of interdependent policies and practices. Talent management is the notion of 'bundling' in action.

Career management

Career management involves the definition of career paths – the routes people can take to advance their careers within an organization. It uses all the information provided by the organization's assessments of requirements, the assessments of performance and potential and management succession plans, and translates it into the form of individual career development programmes and general arrangements for management development, career counselling and mentoring.

Management succession planning

Management succession planning is the process of ensuring that capable managers are available to fill vacant managerial posts. Traditionally it has been regarded as a formal process but it is increasingly that the need is to develop a pool of talented managers so that a 'talent on demand' approach can be adopted.

Questions

1. What is talent management?
2. What is talent?
3. What are the elements of a talent management programme?
4. What is management succession planning?
5. What is career management?

References

Baruch, Y and Peiperl, M (2000) Career management practices: an empirical survey and explanations, *Human Resource Management*, 39 (4), pp 347–66

Buckingham, M and Vosburgh, R (2001) The 21st century human resources function: it's the talent, stupid, *Human Resource Planning*, 24 (4), pp 17–23

Cappelli, P (2008) *Talent on Demand: Managing talent in an uncertain age*, Boston MA, Harvard Business School Press

CIPD (2007) *Talent: Strategy, management, measurement*, London, CIPD

CIPD (2010a) *Opening up Talent for Business Success*, London, CIPD

CIPD (2010b) *War on Talent? Talent management under threat in uncertain times*, Part 1, London, CIPD

CIPD (2010c) *Fighting Back through Talent Innovation: Talent management under threat in uncertain times*, Part 2, London, CIPD

CIPD (2013) *Learning and Talent Development Survey*, London, CIPD

Clarke, R and Winkler, V (2006) *Reflections on Talent Management*, London, CIPD

DeVos, A and Dries, N (2013) Applying a talent management lens to career management: the role of human capital composition and continuity, *International Journal of Human Resource Management*, 24 (9), pp 1816–31

Hall, D T (1984) Human resource development and organizational effectiveness, in (eds) D Fombrun, M A Tichy and M A Devanna, *Strategic Human Resource Management*, New York, Wiley

Hall, D T (1996) *The Career is Dead: Long live the career*, San Francisco, CA, Jossey-Bass

Handy, C (1984) *The Future of Work*, Oxford, Blackwell

Hirsh, W and Carter, A (2002) *New Directions in Management Development*, Paper 387, London, Institute for Employment Studies

Hirsh, W, Pollard, E and Tamkin, P (2000) Management development, *IRS Employee Development Bulletin*, November, pp 8–12

Huselid, M A, Beatty, R W and Becker, B E (2005) A-players or A-positions? The strategic logic of workforce management, *Harvard Business Review*, December, pp 110–17

Iles, P and Preece, D (2010) Talent management and career development, in (eds) J Gold, R Thorpe and A Mumford, *Gower Handbook of Leadership and Management Development*, Farnham, Gower, pp 243–60

Iles, P, Preece, D and Chuai, X (2010) Talent management as a management fashion in HRD: towards a research agenda, *Human Resource Development International*, 13 (2), pp 125–45

Lewis, R E and Hackman, R J (2006) Talent management: a critical review, *Human Resource Management Review*, 16 (2), pp 139–54

McDonnell, A and Collings, D G (2011) Identification and evaluation of talent in MNEs, in H Scullion and D G Collings (eds) *Global Talent Management*, London, Routledge, pp 56–73

Michaels, E G, Handfield-Jones, H and Axelrod, B (2001) *The War for Talent*, Boston, MA, Harvard Business School Press

Pfeffer, J (2001) Fighting the war for talent is hazardous to your organization's health, *Organizational Dynamics*, 29 (4), pp 248–59

Ready, D A and Conger, J A (2007) Make your company a talent factory, *Harvard Business Review*, June, pp 68–77

Schein, E H (1978) *Career Dynamics: Matching individual and organizational needs*, Reading, MA, Addison-Wesley

Tansley, C and Tietze, S (2013) Rites of passage through talent management stages: an identity work perspective, *International Journal of Human Resource Management*, 24 (9), pp 1799–815

Thorne, K and Pellant, A (2007) *The Essential Guide to Managing Talent*, London, Kogan Page

Warren, C (2006) Curtain call, *People Management*, 23 March, pp 24–29

Younger, J, Smallwood, N and Ulrich, D (2007) Developing your organization's brand as a talent developer, *Human Resource Planning*, 30 (2), pp 21–29

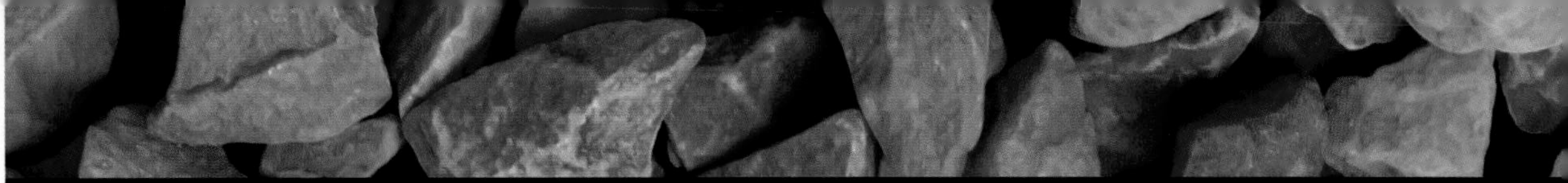

PART V

Learning and development

PART V CONTENTS

Introduction

Learning and development strategies and practices, as described in this part, aim to ensure that people in the organization acquire and develop the knowledge, skills and competencies they need to carry out their work effectively and advance their careers to their own benefit and that of the organization.

The term 'learning and development' (L&D) has largely replaced that of 'human resource development' (HRD), at least for practitioners. Rosemary Harrison (2009: 5) observed that:

> The term human resource development retains its popularity among academics but it has never been attractive to practitioners. They tend to dislike it because they see its reference to people as a 'resource' to be demeaning. Putting people on a par with money, materials and equipment creates the impression of 'development' as an unfeeling, manipulative activity, although the two terms are almost indistinguishable.

The terms are indeed often used interchangeably by commentators and practitioners although the introduction of 'learning' has emphasized the belief that what matters for individuals is that they are given the opportunity to learn, often for themselves, with guidance and support, rather than just being on the receiving end of what the organization provides.

The following definition of strategic HRD, produced by Walton (1999: 82), could serve equally well as a definition of strategic L&D:

> Strategic human resource development involves introducing, eliminating, modifying, directing, and guiding processes in such a way that all individuals and teams are equipped with the skills, knowledge and competences they require to undertake current and future tasks required by the organization.

This part deals with L&D under the following headings:

- strategic learning and development – how L&D is aligned to the business strategy, L&D strategy;
- the process of learning and development – how people and organizations learn, the concept of the learning organization;
- the practice of learning and development – identifying L&D needs, encouraging and supporting workplace learning, planning and implementing learning programmes and events, evaluating L&D;
- leadership and management development – the planning and implementation of processes and programmes for developing leadership qualities and for developing managers generally.

References

Harrison, R (2009) *Learning and Development*, 5th edn, London, CIPD
Walton, J (1999) *Strategic Human Resource Development*, Harlow, FT Prentice Hall

21 Strategic learning and development

KEY CONCEPTS AND TERMS

Development
Individual learning
Learning
Learning culture
Learning and development (L&D)
Organizational learning
Strategic L&D
Training

LEARNING OUTCOMES

On completing this chapter you should be able to define these key concepts. You should also know about:

- The meaning of learning and development (L&D)
- The meaning and aims of strategic L&D
- The basic philosophies that underpin L&D strategy and practice
- How to create a learning culture
- The nature of strategies for promoting individual learning

Introduction

Organizations need people with high and appropriate levels of knowledge, skills and abilities. Steps taken to meet this need are business-led in the sense that they are based on an understanding of the strategic imperatives of the business and support the achievement of its goals. But organizations also need to take account of the personal needs of those they employ for development and growth. This is good in itself but it means that the organization will be a more fulfilling and therefore attractive place in which to work.

This chapter starts with a definition of the process of learning and development and its elements, which leads to a definition of strategic learning and development (L&D) and its aims. Consideration is then given to the philosophy of L&D before examining strategies for creating a learning culture and for promoting organizational and individual learning.

Learning and development defined

Learning and development is defined as the process of ensuring that the organization has the knowledgeable, skilled and engaged workforce it needs. It involves facilitating the acquisition by individuals and teams of knowledge and skills through experience, learning events and programmes provided by the organization, guidance and coaching provided by line managers and others, and self-directed learning activities carried out by individuals. Harrison (2009: 8) defined learning and development more broadly as follows:

> The primary purpose of learning and development as an organizational process is to aid collective progress through the collaborative, expert and ethical stimulation and facilitation of learning and knowledge that support business goals, develop individual potential, and respect and build on diversity.

The components of L&D are:

- *Learning* – the process by which a person acquires and develops knowledge, skills, capabilities, behaviours and attitudes. It involves the modification of behaviour through experience as well as more formal methods of helping people to learn within or outside the workplace.
- *Development* – the growth or realization of a person's ability and potential through the provision of learning and educational experiences.
- *Training* – the systematic application of formal processes to impart knowledge and help people to acquire the skills necessary for them to perform their jobs satisfactorily.
- *Education* – the development of the knowledge, values and understanding required in all aspects of life rather than the knowledge and skills relating to particular areas of activity.

Learning should be distinguished from training. 'Learning is the process by which a person constructs new knowledge, skills and capabilities, whereas training is one of several responses an organization can undertake to promote learning' (Reynolds *et al*, 2002: 9). Learning is what individuals do; training is what organizations do to individuals. The components of learning and development are shown in Figure 21.1.

Strategic L&D defined

Strategic L&D is an approach to helping people to learn and develop that is concerned with how the organization's goals will be achieved through its human resources by means of integrated L&D strategies, policies and practices. Like strategic HRM, it is based on the fundamental proposition that the human resources of an organization play a strategic role in its success. Strategic L&D policies are closely associated with that aspect of strategic HRM concerned with investing in people and developing the organization's human capital.

Aims of strategic L&D

Strategic L&D aims to produce a coherent and comprehensive framework for developing people through the creation of a learning culture and the formulation of organizational and individual learning strategies. It exists to enhance resource capability in accordance with the belief that a firm's human resources are a major source of competitive advantage. It is therefore about developing the intellectual capital required by the organization as well as ensuring that people of the right quality are available to meet present and future needs.

The main thrust of strategic L&D is to provide an environment in which people are encouraged to learn and develop. Although it is business-led, its strategies have to take into account the needs of individual employees. The importance of increasing employability outside as well as within the organization is also a concern.

FIGURE 21.1 Components of learning and development

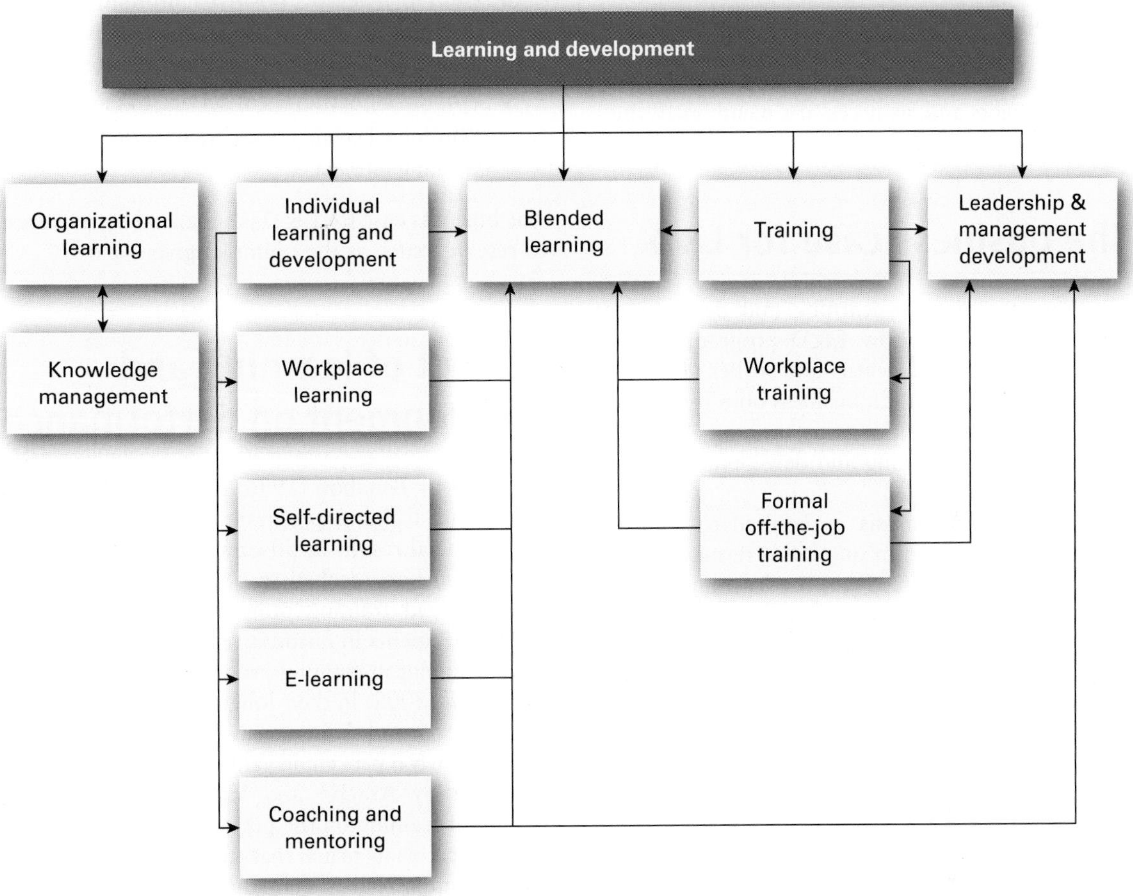

Learning and development philosophy

The philosophy underpinning strategic L&D is as follows:

- Learning and development activities make a major contribution to the successful attainment of the organization's objectives and investment in it benefits all the stakeholders of the organization.
- Learning and development plans and programmes should be integrated with and support the achievement of business and human resource strategies.
- Learning and development should be performance-related – designed to achieve specified improvements in corporate, functional, team and individual performance and make a major contribution to bottom-line results.
- Everyone in the organization should be encouraged and given the opportunity to learn – to develop their skills and knowledge to the maximum of their capacity.
- The framework for individual learning is provided by personal development plans that focus on self-managed learning and are supported by coaching, mentoring and formal training.

- The organization needs to invest in learning and development by providing appropriate learning opportunities and facilities, but the prime responsibility for learning and development rests with individuals, who will be given the guidance and support of their managers and, as necessary, members of the HR department.

The business case for L&D

The business case for learning and development should demonstrate how L&D programmes will meet business needs. Kearns and Miller (1997) go as far as to claim that if a business objective cannot be cited as a basis for designing training and development, then no training and development should be offered.

A cost/benefit analysis is required to compare the benefits expressed in quantified terms as far as possible that will result from the learning activity. The business case has to convince management that there will be an acceptable return on the investment (RoI) in learning and training programmes and events. It can be difficult to produce realistic figures, although the attempt is worth making with the help of finance specialists. The case for investing in L&D can refer to all or any of the following potential benefits:

- Improve individual, team and corporate performance.
- Attract high-quality employees by offering them learning and development opportunities, increasing their levels of competency and enhancing their skills, thus enabling them to obtain more job satisfaction, to gain higher rewards and to progress within the organization.
- Improve operational flexibility by extending the range of skills possessed by employees (multiskilling).
- Increase the commitment of employees by encouraging them to identify with the mission and objectives of the organization.
- Help to manage change by increasing understanding of the reasons for it and providing people with the knowledge and skills they need to adjust to new situations.
- Provide line managers with the skills required to lead, manage and develop their people.
- Help to develop a positive culture in the organization, for example, one that is oriented towards performance improvement.
- Provide higher levels of service to customers.
- Minimize learning costs (reduce the length of learning curves).

The business case for L&D is enhanced by reference to research such as the examples given below.

Impact of learning and development on performance

Research by Benabou (1996) examined the impact of various training programmes on the business and financial results at 50 Canadian organizations. The conclusion reached was that in most cases a well-designed training programme can be linked to improvements in business results and that return on investment in training programmes is very high. Birdi *et al* (2008) in their longitudinal study of 308 companies found that extensive training produced a gain of nearly 6 per cent in value added per employee. Research by Aragon and Valle (2013) into the impact of training on the performance of managers established that firms that train their managers obtain better results than those that do not, and that the intensive training contributes to improved performance.

Learning and development strategies

Learning and development strategies are the active components of an overall approach to strategic L&D. They express the organization's intentions on how L&D activities will take place and provide guidance on how these activities should be planned and implemented. The strategies ensure that an L&D philosophy as set out above is acted upon. They are concerned with developing a learning culture, promoting organizational learning and providing for individual learning.

Strategies for creating a learning culture

A learning culture is one in which learning is recognized by top management, line managers and employees generally as an essential organizational process to which they are committed and in which they engage continuously. The characteristics of a learning culture are self-managed learning not instruction, long-term capacity building not short-term fixes, and empowerment not supervision.

Reynolds (2004: 9) described a learning culture as a 'growth medium', in which 'employees will commit to a range of positive discretionary behaviours, including learning'. He suggested that to create a learning culture it is necessary to develop organizational practices that 'give employees a sense of purpose in the workplace, grant employees opportunities to act upon their commitment, and offer practical support to learning'.

The steps required to create a learning culture as proposed by Reynolds (2004) are:

- Develop and share the vision – belief in a desired and emerging future.
- Empower employees – provide 'supported autonomy'; freedom for employees to manage their work within certain boundaries (policies and expected behaviours) but with support available as required. Adopt a facilitative style of management in which responsibility for decision-making is ceded as far as possible to employees.
- Provide employees with a supportive learning environment where learning capabilities can be discovered and applied, eg peer networks, supportive policies and systems, and protected time for learning.
- Use coaching techniques to draw out the talents of others by encouraging employees to identify options and seek their own solutions to problems.
- Guide employees through their work challenges and provide them with time, resources and, crucially, feedback.
- Recognize the importance of managers acting as role models.
- Encourage networks – communities of practice.
- Align systems to vision – get rid of bureaucratic systems that produce problems rather than facilitate work.

Organizational learning strategies

Organizational learning strategies aim to improve organizational effectiveness through the acquisition and development of knowledge, understanding, insights, techniques and practices. This is in accordance with one of the basic principles of HRM, namely that it is necessary to invest in people in order to develop the human capital required by the organization and to increase its stock of knowledge and skills. As stated by Ehrenberg and Smith (1994: 279–80), human capital theory indicates that: 'The knowledge and skills a worker has – which comes from education and training, including the training that experience brings – generate productive capital.'

Individual learning strategies

Individual learning comprises the processes and programmes used to increase the capabilities of individual employees. Strategies for individual learning are driven by the organization's human resource requirements, which are expressed in terms of the skills and behaviours required to achieve business goals. Strategies should cover:

- how learning needs will be identified;
- the role of self-managed learning;
- the facilitation of workplace learning;
- the support that should be provided for individual learning in the form of guidance, coaching, mentoring, learning resource centres, e-learning and internal or external training programmes and courses.

Key learning points: Strategic learning and development

Learning and development

Learning and development is the process of acquiring and developing knowledge, skills capabilities, behaviours and attitudes through learning or developmental experiences.

Strategic L&D

Strategic L&D is an approach to helping people to learn and develop that is concerned with how the organization's goals will be achieved through its human resources by means of integrated L&D strategies, policies and practices. Strategic L&D aims to produce a coherent and comprehensive framework for developing people through the creation of a learning culture and the formulation of organizational and individual learning strategies.

Learning and development strategies

Learning and development strategies are the active components of an overall approach to strategic L&D. They express the organization's intentions on how L&D activities will take place in the organization and provide guidance on how these activities should be planned and implemented.

Learning culture

A learning culture is one in which learning is recognized by top management, line managers and employees generally as an essential organizational process to which they are committed and in which they engage continuously.

Organizational learning strategies

Organizational learning strategies aim to develop a firm's resource-based capability.

Individual learning strategies

The individual learning strategies of an organization are driven by its human resource requirements, the latter being expressed in terms of the sort of skills and behaviours that will be required to achieve business goals.

Questions

1. What is learning and development (L&D)?
2. What is learning?
3. What is training?
4. What is development?
5. What is education?
6. What is strategic L&D?
7. What are the aims of strategic L&D?
8. What is a learning culture?
9. What is organizational learning strategy?
10. What is individual learning strategy?

References

Aragon, I B and Valle, R S (2013) Does training managers pay off? *The International Journal of Human Resource Management*, 24 (8), pp 1671–84

Benabou, C (1996) Assessing the impact of training programs on the bottom line, *National Productivity Review*, 15 (3), pp 91–99

Birdi, K, Clegg, C, Patterson, M, Robinson, A, Stride, C B, Wall, T D and Wood, S J (2008) The impact of human resource and operational management practices on company productivity: a longitudinal study, *Personnel Psychology*, 61 (3), pp 467–501

Ehrenberg, R G and Smith, R S (1994) *Modern Labor Economics*, New York, Harper Collins

Harrison, R (2009) *Learning and Development*, 5th edn, London, CIPD

Kearns, P and Miller, T (1997) Measuring the impact of training and development on the bottom line, *FT Management Briefings*, London, Pitman

Reynolds, J (2004) *Helping People Learn*, London, CIPD

Reynolds, J, Caley, L and Mason, R (2002) *How Do People Learn?*, London, CIPD

22 The process of learning and development

KEY CONCEPTS AND TERMS

Cognitive learning theory
Discretionary learning
Double-loop learning
Experienced workers standard (EWS)
Experiential learning
Learning organization
Operant conditioning
Organizational learning
Progressive parts method of training
Reinforcement theory
Self-directed (self-managed) learning
Single-loop learning
Social learning theory

LEARNING OUTCOMES

On completing this chapter you should be able to define these key concepts. You should also understand:

- How people learn
- Learning theory
- The motivation to learn
- Learning styles
- Learning to learn
- The learning curve
- The implications of learning theory and concepts
- Operant conditioning
- Organizational learning
- The learning organization
- Self-directed learning

Introduction

The practice of learning and development should be based on an understanding of learning theory and the processes involved in learning and development as described in this chapter. These processes are complex and varied.

How people learn

Individuals learn for themselves but they also learn from other people – their managers and co-workers (social learning). They learn mainly by doing (experiential learning) and to a much lesser extent by instruction. The ways in which individuals learn will differ and what they learn will depend largely on how well they are motivated or self-motivated. Discretionary learning (self-directed or self-managed) takes place when individuals of their own volition actively seek to acquire the knowledge and skills they need to carry out their work effectively. It should be encouraged and supported.

The 70/20/10 model for learning and development is based on research conducted by the Centre for Creative Leadership which was described by Lombardo and Eichinger (1996). The model explains that people's development will be about 70 per cent from work experience, about 20 per cent from social learning (through managers by example and feedback and by fellow workers) and 10 per cent from courses and reading. In other words, by far the majority of learning takes place in the workplace. This should be the guiding principle for learning and development programmes.

Learning theory

The key learning theories are:

- *Reinforcement theory* – based on the work of Skinner (1974) this expresses the belief that changes in behaviour take place as a result of an individual's response to events or stimuli and the ensuing consequences (rewards or punishments). Individuals can be 'conditioned' to repeat the behaviour by positive reinforcement in the form of feedback and knowledge of results. This is known as 'operant conditioning'.
- *Cognitive learning theory* – learning involves gaining knowledge and understanding by absorbing information in the form of principles, concepts and facts and then internalizing it. Learners can be regarded as powerful information-processing machines.
- *Experiential learning theory* – experiential learning takes place when people learn from their experience by absorbing and reflecting on it so that it can be understood and applied. Thus people become active agents of their own learning.
- *Social learning theory* – this states that effective learning requires social interaction. Wenger (1998) suggested that we all participate in 'communities of practice' (groups of people with shared expertise who work together) and that these are our primary sources of learning. Bandura (1977) viewed learning as a series of information-processing steps set in train by social interactions.

The motivation to learn

People will learn more effectively if they are motivated to learn. As Reynolds *et al* (2002: 34) commented: 'The disposition and commitment of the learner – their motivation to learn – is one of the most critical factors affecting training effectiveness. Under the right conditions, a strong disposition to learn, enhanced by solid experience and a positive attitude, can lead to exceptional performance.'

Two motivation theories are particularly relevant to learning. Expectancy theory states that goal-directed behaviour is driven by the expectation of achieving something that the individual regards as desirable. If individuals feel that the outcome of learning is likely to benefit them they will be more inclined to pursue it. When they find that their expectations have been fulfilled, their belief that learning is worthwhile will be reinforced.

Goal theory states that motivation is higher when individuals aim to achieve specific goals, when these goals are accepted and, although difficult, are achievable, and when there is feedback on performance. Learning goals may be set for individuals (but to be effective as motivators they must be agreed) or individuals may set their own goals (self-directed learning).

Learning styles

Learning theories describe in general terms how people learn, but individual learners will have different styles – a preference for a particular approach to learning. The two most familiar classifications of learning styles are those produced by Kolb *et al* (1974) and by Honey and Mumford (1996).

Kolb *et al*'s learning style inventory

Kolb *et al* (1974) identified a learning cycle consisting of four stages, as shown in Figure 22.1. These stages were defined as follows:

1. *Concrete experience* – this can be planned or accidental.
2. *Reflective observation* – this involves actively thinking about the experience and its significance.
3. *Abstract conceptualization (theorizing)* – generalizing from experience to develop various concepts and ideas that can be applied when similar situations are encountered.
4. *Active experimentation* – testing the concepts or ideas in new situations. This gives rise to a new concrete experience and the cycle begins again.

The key to this model is that it is a simple description of how experience is translated into concepts that are then used to guide the choice of new experiences. To learn effectively, individuals must shift from being observers to participants, from direct involvement to a more objective analytical detachment. Every person has his or her own learning style; one of the most important arts that trainers have to develop is to adjust their approaches to the learning styles of trainees. Trainers must acknowledge these learning styles rather than their own preferred approach.

FIGURE 22.1 The Kolb learning cycle

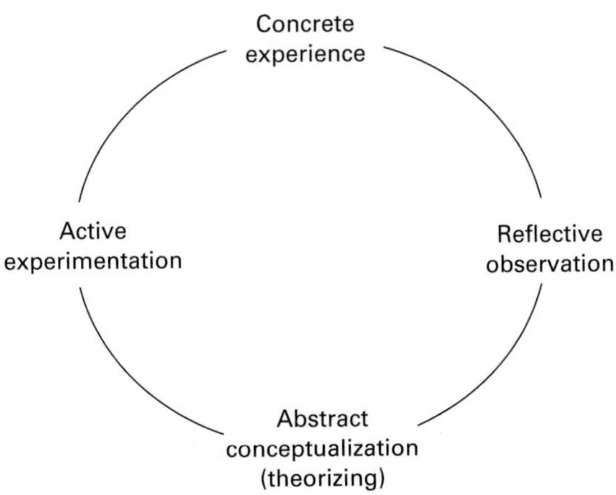

The Honey and Mumford learning styles

Another analysis of learning styles was made by Honey and Mumford (1996). They identified the following four styles:

1. *Activists* – who involve themselves fully without bias in new experiences and revel in new challenges.
2. *Reflectors* – who stand back and observe new experiences from different angles. They collect data, reflect on it and then come to a conclusion.
3. *Theorists* – who adapt and apply their observations in the form of logical theories. They tend to be perfectionists.
4. *Pragmatists* – who are keen to try out new ideas, approaches and concepts to see if they work.

However, none of these four learning styles is exclusive. It is quite possible that one person could be both a reflector and a theorist and someone else could be an activist/pragmatist, a reflector/pragmatist or even a theorist/pragmatist.

Use of learning style theory

Learning style theory can be used in the design and conduct of learning events or personal development programmes. Learning situations can be set up to fit the learning style of participants. The problem is that people do not necessarily have a single learning style and there certainly will be a large range of styles in any learning group. It may therefore be difficult to fit the approach to the style.

Learning to learn

People learn all the time and through doing so acquire knowledge, skills and insight. But they will learn more effectively if they 'learn how to learn'.

As defined by Honey (1998), the process of learning to learn is the acquisition of knowledge, skills and insights about the learning process itself. The aims are to:

- provide a basis for organizing and planning learning;
- pinpoint precisely what has been learnt and what to do better or differently as a consequence;
- share what has been learnt with other people so that they benefit;
- check on the quality of what has been learnt;
- transfer what has been learnt and apply it in different circumstances;
- improve the learning process itself so that *how* people learn, not just *what* people learn, is given constant attention.

The learning curve

The concept of the learning curve refers to the time it takes an inexperienced person to reach the required level of performance in a job or a task, which is sometimes called the experienced worker's standard (EWS). The existence of the learning curve needs to be taken into account when planning and implementing training or instruction programmes. The standard learning curve is illustrated in Figure 22.2.

But rates of learning vary, depending on the effectiveness of the training, the experience and natural aptitude of the learner and the latter's interest in learning. Both the time taken to reach the EWS and the variable speed with which learning takes place at different times affect the shape of the curve, as shown in Figure 22.3.

Learning is often stepped, with one or more plateaus, while further progress is halted. This may be because learners cannot continually increase their skills or speeds of work and need a pause to consolidate what they have already learnt. The existence of steps such as those shown in Figure 22.4 can be used when planning skills training to provide deliberate reinforcement periods when newly acquired skills are practised in order to achieve the expected standards.

When a training module is being prepared that describes what has to be learnt and the training needed to achieve the required levels of skill and speed, it is often desirable to proceed step-by-step, taking one task or part of a task at a time, reinforcing it and then progressively adding other parts, consolidating at each stage. This is called the 'progressive parts method' of training.

FIGURE 22.2 A standard learning curve

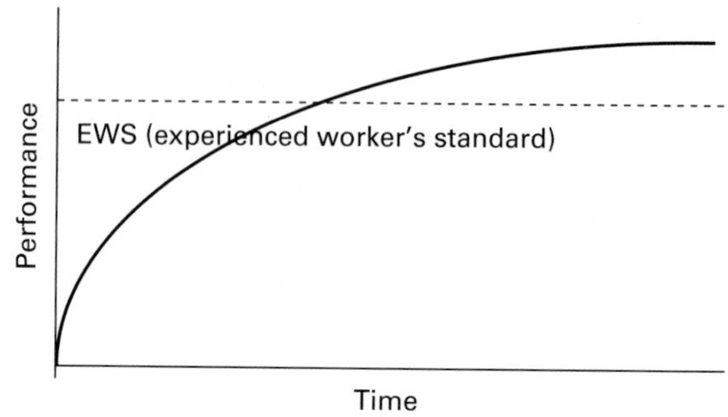

FIGURE 22.3 Different rates of learning

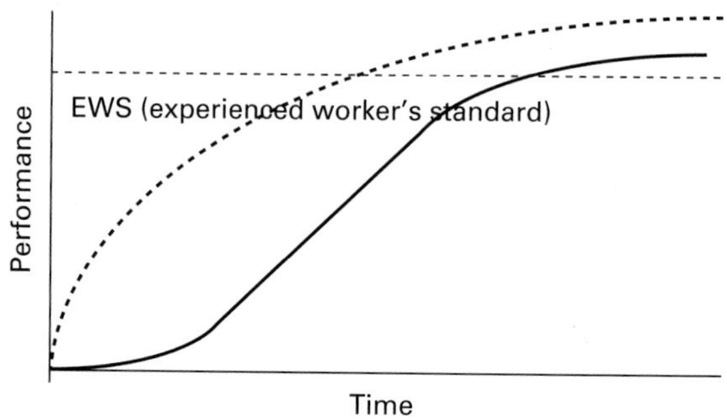

FIGURE 22.4 A stepped learning curve

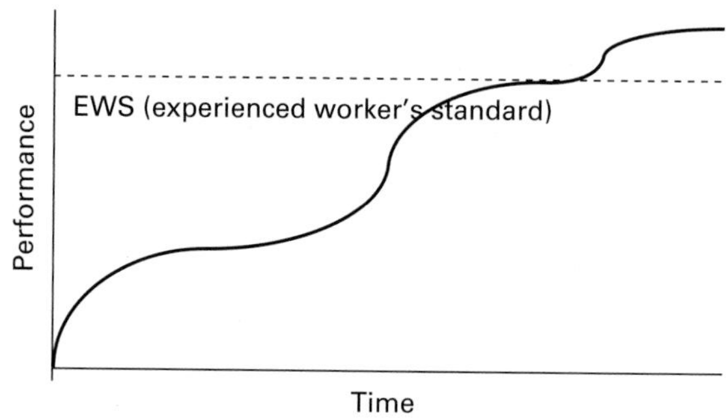

The implications of learning theory and concepts

The practical implications of the learning theories described above are summarized in Table 22.1.

Organizational learning

Organizational learning theory is concerned with how learning takes place in organizations. It focuses on collective learning but takes into account the proposition made by Argyris (1992) that organizations do not perform the actions that produce the learning; it is individual members of the organization who behave in ways that lead to it, although organizations can create conditions that facilitate such learning. The concept of organizational learning recognizes that the way in which this takes place is affected by the context of the organization and its culture.

Organizational learning defined

Organizational learning is concerned with the methods adopted by organizations to promote learning; it is not simply the sum of all the L&D activities that are carried out in an organization.

The process of organizational learning

Organizational learning can be characterized as an intricate three-stage process consisting of knowledge acquisition, dissemination and shared implementation. As such it is closely related to knowledge management. Knowledge may be acquired from direct experience, the experience of others or organizational memory.

Argyris (1992) suggested that organizational learning occurs under two conditions: first, when an organization achieves what is intended and, second, when a mismatch between intentions and outcomes is identified and corrected. He distinguished between single-loop and double-loop learning. These two types of learning have been described as adaptive or generative learning.

Single-loop or *adaptive learning* is incremental learning that does no more than correct deviations from the norm by making small changes and improvements without challenging assumptions, beliefs or decisions. Organizations where single-loop learning is the norm define what Argyris calls the 'governing

TABLE 22.1 The practical implications of learning theory and concepts

Theory/concept	Content	Practical implications
The process of learning	Learning is complex and is achieved in many different ways. The context is important.	Different learning needs require different learning methods, often in combination. Learning effectiveness depends on the extent to which the organization believes in learning and supports it.
Reinforcement theory	Behaviours can be strengthened by reinforcing them with positive feedback (conditioning).	Reinforcement theory underpins training programmes concerned with developing skills through instruction. In these, the learner is conditioned to make a response and receives immediate feedback and progress is made in incremental steps, each directed to a positive outcome.

TABLE 22.1 Continued

Theory/concept	Content	Practical implications
Cognitive learning theory	Learners acquire understanding, which they internalize by being exposed to learning materials and by solving problems.	The knowledge and understanding of learners can be enriched and internalized by presenting them with learning materials (eg e-learning). Case studies, projects and problem-solving activities can also be used for this purpose. Self-directed learning, personal development planning activities and discovery learning processes with help from facilitators, coaches or mentors are underpinned by cognitive learning theory.
Experiential learning theory	People learn by constructing meaning and developing their skills through experience.	Learning through experience in the workplace can be enhanced by encouraging learners to reflect on and make better use of what they learn through their own work and from other people. Self-directed learning and personal development planning activities with help from facilitators, coaches or mentors are also underpinned by experiential learning theory, as is action learning.
Social learning theory	Learning is most effective in a social setting. Individual understanding is shaped by active participation in real situations.	Learning can be encouraged in communities of practice and in project teams and networks.
Learning styles	Every person has their own learning style.	Learning programmes need to be adjusted to cope with different learning styles. Trainers also have to flex their methods. People will learn more effectively if they are helped to 'learn how to learn' by making the best use of their own style but also by experimenting with other styles.
The motivation to learn	People need to be motivated to learn effectively.	Learners should be helped to develop learning goals and to understand the benefits to them of achieving them. Performance management processes leading to personal development plans can provide a means of doing this.
The learning curve	The time required to reach an acceptable standard of skill or competence, which varies between people. Learning may proceed in steps with plateaus rather than being a continuous process.	Recognize that progress may vary and may not be continuous. Enable learners to consolidate their learning and introduce reinforcement periods in training programmes to recognize the existence of learning steps and plateaus.

variables', ie what they expect to achieve in terms of targets and standards and then monitor and review achievements, and take corrective action as necessary, thus completing the loop.

Double-loop or *generative learning* involves challenging assumptions, beliefs, norms and decisions rather than accepting them. On this basis, learning takes place through the examination of the root causes of problems so that a new learning loop is established that goes far deeper than the traditional learning loop provided by single-loop or instrumental learning. It occurs when the monitoring process initiates action to redefine the governing variables to meet the new situation, which may be imposed by the external environment. The organization has learnt something new about what has to be achieved in the light of changed circumstances and can then decide how this should be done. This learning is converted into action. The process is illustrated in Figure 22.5.

As Easterby-Smith and Araujo (1999) commented, single-loop learning could be linked to incremental change. In contrast, double-loop learning is associated with radical change, which may involve a major change in strategic direction. It is generally assumed that double-loop learning is superior, but there are situations when single-loop learning may be more appropriate.

FIGURE 22.5 Single-loop and double-loop learning

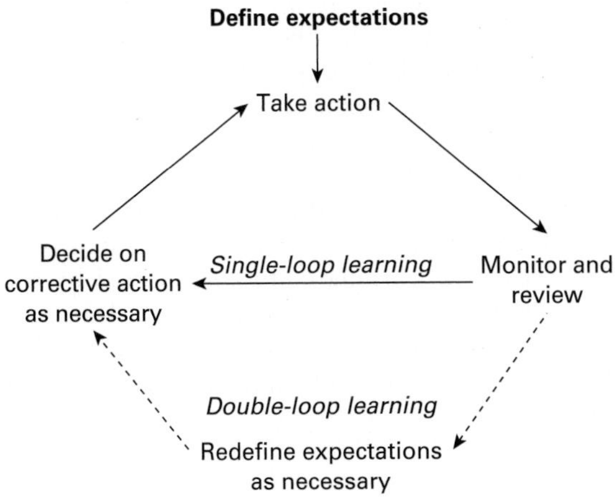

The notion of the learning organization

A learning organization was described by Senge (1990: 3), who originated the idea, as one 'where people continually expand their capacity to create the results they truly desire, where new and expansive patterns of thinking are nurtured, where collective aspiration is set free, and where people are continually learning how to learn together'. Further definitions of a learning organization were provided by Wick and Leon (1995: 299), who stated that it was one that 'continually improves by rapidly creating and refining the capabilities required for future success', and by Pedler *et al* (1997: 3), who referred to it as an organization that 'facilitates the learning of all its members and continually transforms itself'. Garvin (1993) suggested that learning organizations are good at doing five things:

1. Systematic problem solving – which rests heavily on the philosophy and methods of the quality movement. Its underlying ideas include relying on scientific method rather than guesswork for diagnosing problems – what Deming (1986) called the 'plan-do-check-act' cycle and others refer to as 'hypothesis-generating, hypothesis-testing' techniques. Data rather than assumptions are required as the background to decision-making – what quality practitioners call 'fact-based management', and simple statistical tools such as histograms, Pareto charts and cause-and-effect diagrams are used to organize data and draw inferences.
2. Experimentation – this activity involves the systematic search for and testing of new knowledge. Continuous improvement programmes – 'kaizen' – are an important feature in a learning organization.
3. Learning from past experience – learning organizations review their successes and failures, assess them systematically and record the lessons learnt in a way that employees find open and accessible. This process has been called the 'Santayana principle', quoting the philosopher George Santayana who coined the phrase: 'Those who cannot remember the past are condemned to repeat it.'

4 Learning from others – sometimes the most powerful insights come from looking outside one's immediate environment to gain a new perspective. This process has been called SIS, for 'steal ideas shamelessly'. Another more acceptable word for it is 'benchmarking' – a disciplined process of identifying best practice organizations and analysing the extent to which what they are doing can be transferred, with suitable modifications, to one's own environment.
5 Transferring knowledge quickly and efficiently throughout the organization – by seconding people with new expertise, or by education and training programmes, as long as the latter are linked explicitly with implementation.

Critical evaluation of the learning organization notion

The notion of the learning organization is persuasive because it provides a rationale for comprehensive learning and development programmes. However, Scarborough *et al* (1999) argued that the learning organization concept is overconcerned with organization systems and design. Little attention seems to be paid to what individuals want to learn or how they learn. The idea that individuals should be enabled to invest in their own development seems to have escaped learning organization theorists, who are more inclined to focus on the imposition of learning by the organization, rather than creating a climate conducive to learning.

Viewing organizations as learning systems is a limited notion. Argyris and Schon (1996) explained that organizations are products of visions, ideas, norms and beliefs, so that their shape is much more fragile than the organization's material structure. People act as learning agents for the organization in ways that cannot easily be systematized. They are not only individual learners but also have the capacity to learn collaboratively. This is described by organization learning theory and leads to the belief that it is the culture and environment that are important, not the systems approach implied by the concept of the learning organization.

The notion of a learning organization is rather nebulous. It incorporates miscellaneous ideas about human resource development, systematic training, action learning, organizational development and knowledge management, with an infusion of the precepts of total quality management. But they do not add up to a convincing whole. Easterby-Smith (1997) contended that attempts to create a single best-practice framework for understanding the learning organization are fundamentally flawed. There are other problems with the concept: it is idealistic; knowledge management models are beginning to supersede it; few organizations can meet the criteria; and there is little evidence of successful learning organizations.

Burgoyne (1999), one of the earlier exponents of the learning organization, has admitted that there has been some confusion about it and that there have been substantial naiveties in most of the early thinking. He believes that the concept should be integrated with knowledge management initiatives so that different forms of knowledge can be linked, fed by organizational learning and used in adding value.

The learning organization and organizational learning

The notion of the learning organization is often associated with the concept of organizational learning. But they are different. Easterby-Smith and Araujo (1999) explained that the literature on organizational learning focuses on the observation and analysis of the processes of individual and collective learning in organizations, whereas the learning organization literature is concerned with using specific diagnostic and evaluative tools that can help to identify, promote and evaluate the quality of the learning processes inside organizations. In other words, organizational learning is about how people learn in organizations, and the learning organization notion attempts to explain what organizations should do to facilitate the learning of their members.

However, as explained above, learning organization theory provides a dubious base for action. The idea of a learning culture supported by the understanding of how organizations learn, as provided by organizational learning theory and knowledge management initiatives, has more to offer.

Self-directed learning

Self-directed or self-managed learning involves encouraging individuals to take responsibility for their own learning needs, either to improve performance in their present job or to develop their potential and satisfy their career aspirations. It can also be described as 'self-reflective learning' (Mezirow, 1985), which is the kind of learning that involves encouraging individuals to develop new patterns of understanding, thinking and behaving.

Key learning points: The process of learning and development

The processes of L&D

The processes of L&D are complex and varied. They consist of the ways in which individuals and organizations learn as explained by learning theory, the concept of organizational learning, the dubious notion of the learning organization, and the contribution made by individuals to their own learning and development (self-directed or self-managed learning).

How people learn

Individuals learn for themselves and from other people. They learn as members of teams and by interaction with their managers, co-workers and people outside the organization (social learning). People learn by doing and by instruction. The ways in which individuals learn will differ and the extent to which they learn will depend largely on how well they are motivated or self-motivated:

- The key learning theories are reinforcement theory, cognitive learning theory, experiential learning theory and social learning theory.
- People will learn more effectively if they are motivated to learn.
- Learning theories describe in general terms how people learn but individual learners will have different styles – a preference for a particular approach to learning. The two most familiar classifications of learning styles are those produced by Kolb *et al* (1974) and by Honey and Mumford (1996).
- People learn all the time and through doing so acquire knowledge, skills and insight. But they will learn more effectively if they 'learn how to learn'.
- The concept of the learning curve refers to the time it takes an inexperienced person to reach the required level of performance in a job or a task.

Organizational learning

Organizational learning is about the development and acquisition in organizations of knowledge, understanding, insights, techniques and practices in order to improve organizational effectiveness. It is concerned with the processes adopted by organizations in promoting learning; it is not simply the sum of all the learning and development activities that are carried out in an organization.

The learning organization

Defined by Pedler *et al* (1997) as an organization that 'facilitates the learning of all its members and continually transforms itself'. Learning organization theory provides a dubious base for action. The idea of a learning culture, supported by the understanding of how organizations learn, as provided by organizational learning theory and knowledge management initiatives, has more to offer.

Self-directed learning

Self-directed or self-managed learning involves encouraging individuals to take responsibility for their own learning needs, either to improve performance in their present job or to develop their potential and satisfy their career aspirations.

Questions

1 How do people learn?
2 What are the key learning theories?
3 How are people motivated to learn?
4 What is the learning curve and what is its significance?
5 What is organizational learning?
6 What is the notion of a learning organization and how valid is it?
7 Is there any difference between the concepts of organizational learning and the learning organization? If so, what is it?
8 What is self-directed learning?

References

Argyris, C (1992) *On Organizational Learning*, Cambridge, MA, Blackwell

Argyris, C and Schon, D A (1996) *Organizational Learning: A theory of action perspective*, Reading, MA, Addison Wesley

Bandura, A (1977) *Social Learning Theory*, Englewood Cliffs, NJ, Prentice Hall

Burgoyne, J (1999) Design of the times, *People Management*, 3 June, pp 39–44

Deming, W E (1986) *Out of the Crisis*, Cambridge, MA, Massachusetts Institute of Technology Center for Advanced Engineering Studies

Easterby-Smith, M (1997) Disciplines of organizational learning: contributions and critiques, *Human Relations*, 50 (9), pp 1085–113

Easterby-Smith, M and Araujo, J (1999) Organizational learning: current debates and opportunities, in (eds) M Easterby-Smith, J Burgoyne and L Araujo, *Organizational Learning and the Learning Organization*, London, Sage

Garvin, D A (1993) Building a learning organization, *Harvard Business Review*, July–August, pp 78–91

Honey, P (1998) The debate starts here, *People Management*, 1 October, pp 28–29

Honey, P and Mumford, A (1996) *The Manual of Learning Styles*, 3rd edn, Maidenhead, Honey Publications

Kolb, D A, Rubin, I M and McIntyre, J M (1974) *Organizational Psychology: An experimental approach*, Englewood Cliffs, NJ, Prentice Hall

Lombardo, M M and Eichinger, R W (1996) *The Course Architect Development Planner*, Minneapolis, Lominger

Mezirow, J A (1985) A critical theory of self-directed learning, in (ed) S Brookfield, *Self-directed Learning: From theory to practice*, San Francisco, CA, Jossey-Bass

Pedler, M, Burgoyne, J and Boydell, T (1997) *The Learning Company: A strategy for sustainable development*, 2nd edn, Maidenhead, McGraw-Hill

Reynolds, J, Caley, L and Mason, R (2002) *How Do People Learn?*, London, CIPD

Scarborough, H, Swan, J and Preston, J (1999) *Knowledge Management: A literature review*, London, IPM

Senge, P (1990) *The Fifth Discipline: The art and practice of the learning organization*, London, Doubleday

Skinner, B F (1974) *About Behaviourism*, London, Cape

Wenger, E (1998) *Communities of Practice: Learning, meaning and identity*, Cambridge, Cambridge University Press

Wick, C W and Leon, L S (1995) Creating a learning organization: from ideas to action, *Human Resource Management*, 34 (2), pp 299–311

23 The practice of learning and development

KEY CONCEPTS AND TERMS

Action learning
ADDIE model
Bite-sized training
Blended learning
Coaching
Cost/benefit analysis
Criterion behaviour
Development
Discretionary learning
e-learning
Experiential learning
Formal learning
Informal learning
Instruction
Just-in-time training
Learning
Learning and development
Learning contract
Learning culture
Learning evaluation
Learning event
Learning needs analysis
Learning programme
Learning specification
Mentoring
Multitasking
Personal development plan
Planned experience
Return on expectations
Return on investment
Self-directed learning
Systematic training
Terminal behaviour
Training

LEARNING OUTCOMES

On completing this chapter you should be able to define these key concepts. You should also understand:

- The approaches to learning and development
- Workplace learning
- Mentoring
- Planned experience
- Transferring training
- Blended learning
- The role of the L&D function
- Identifying learning needs
- Coaching
- Personal development planning
- Training
- Effective training practices
- Planning and delivering learning events and programmes

Introduction

This chapter deals with the conduct of learning and development (L&D) activities in organizations. It covers how learning needs are identified, the basic approaches of workplace learning and self-directed learning, how workshop learning can be enhanced through activities such as coaching and mentoring, training techniques and programmes, the concept of blended learning, how learning can be evaluated and the responsibility for learning.

Identifying learning needs

All learning activities need to be based on an understanding of what should be done and why it should be done. The purpose of the activities must be defined by identifying and analysing learning needs in the organization and for the groups and individuals within it.

Approaches to learning needs analysis

Learning needs are often established on the basis of general assumptions about what people in particular occupations need to know and be able to do, for example managers need to learn about leadership. This is an easy approach but it can be facile. The assumptions could be so generalized that the resulting learning event will be all things to everybody and nothing for anyone in particular.

So far as possible, evidence should be collected on learning needs through gap analysis and a review of corporate, collective and individual needs. These three areas are interconnected, as shown in Figure 23.1. The analysis of corporate needs will lead to the identification of collective learning needs in different departments, functions or occupations, while these in turn will indicate what individual employees need to learn. The process operates in reverse. As the needs of individual employees are analysed separately, common needs emerge, which can be dealt with on a group basis. The sum of group and individual needs will help to define corporate needs, although there may be some overarching learning requirements that can be related only to the company as a whole to attain its business goals. These areas of analysis are discussed below.

Gap analysis

Learning needs analysis is often described as the process of identifying the learning gap – the gap between what is and what should be, as illustrated in Figure 23.2.

Gap analysis involves identifying the gap between what people know and can do and what they should know and be able to do, so that the learning needed to fill the gap can be specified. Information on the nature of the gap may be obtained by one or more of the methods described below. But this 'deficiency model' of training – only putting things right that have gone wrong – is limited. Learning is much more positive than that. It should be concerned with identifying and satisfying development needs – fitting people to take on extra responsibilities,

FIGURE 23.1 Learning needs analysis – areas and methods

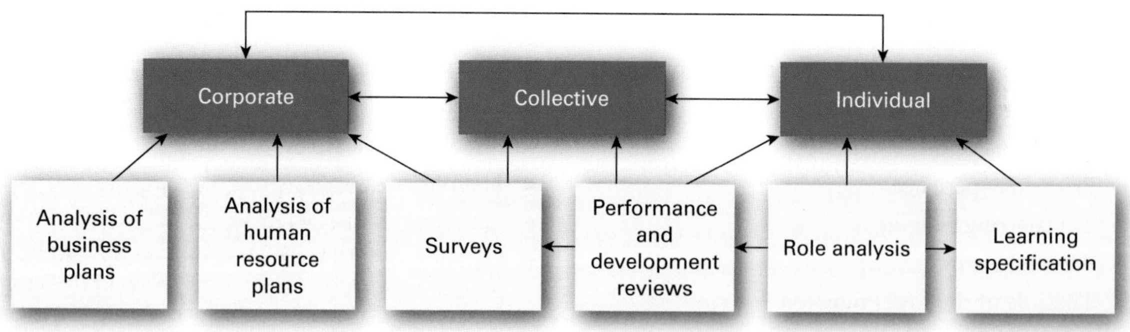

FIGURE 23.2 The learning gap

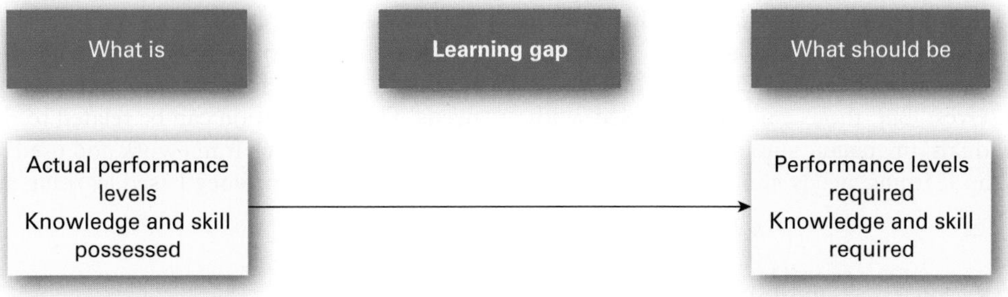

acquire new skills to deal with changing work demands, or develop a range of skills to facilitate multitasking.

Analysis of business and workforce plans

Business and workforce plans should indicate in general terms the types of skills and competencies that may be required in the future and the numbers of people with those skills and competencies who will be needed. An analysis should also be made of any areas where future changes in work processes, methods or job responsibilities are planned and any additional knowledge or skills that may be required. These broad indicators have to be translated into more specific plans that cover, for example, the outputs from training programmes of people with particular skills or a combination of skills (multi-skilling).

Surveys

Special surveys or an interviewing programme can obtain the views of managers and other employees on what they need to learn. However, the material gathered from a survey may be unspecific and, when interviewed, people may find it difficult to articulate what they want. In the latter case it is best to lead with a discussion of the work they do and identify any areas where they believe that their performance and potential could be developed. This could lead to the identification of any additional things they feel they need to know or be able to do. Individual views can be amalgamated to provide a picture of common learning needs.

Performance and development reviews

Performance management processes, as described in Chapter 25, should be a prime source of information about individual learning and development needs. Reviews should include an analysis of role requirements in the shape of knowledge, skills and abilities (KSAs) and the behavioural competencies needed to perform effectively, taking into account any new demands that will be made on the role holder. A joint assessment can then be made of development needs and what sort of development programme is required. The extent to which the individual meets role requirements can be reviewed and agreement reached on what needs to be done to remedy any deficiencies. This can lead to personal development plans and learning contracts, which involve action plans, self-directed learning and an agreement on what support will be provided to the individual by the organization and the manager. An overall analysis of performance and development review reports can reveal any common learning needs that can be satisfied by tailored learning events.

Role analysis

Role analysis is the basis for preparing role profiles that provide a framework for analysing and identifying learning needs. Role profiles set out the key result areas of the role but, importantly, also define the competencies required to perform it. Performance management should ensure that role profiles are updated regularly, and the review can be built on an analysis of the results achieved by reference to the key result areas and agreed objectives.

The competency framework for the role is used to assess the level of competency displayed. An assessment can then be made of any learning required to develop levels of competency. Ideally, this should be a self-assessment by individuals who should be given every encouragement to identify learning needs for themselves. But these can be discussed with the individuals' manager and agreement reached on how the learning needs should be met by the individuals through self-managed learning, and with the help and support of their managers. The output of role analysis could be a learning specification, as illustrated in Figure 23.3.

This method of assessing individual learning needs can generate information on common learning needs. The information can be related to the organization's competency framework and used to inform the design of competency-based learning events.

FIGURE 23.3 A learning specification

LEARNING SPECIFICATION	
Role: Product Manager	**Department:** Marketing
What the role holder must understand	
Learning outcomes	***Learning methods***
• The product market • The product specification • Market research availability • Interpretation of marketing data • Customer service requirements • Techniques of product management	• Coaching: Marketing Manager and Advertising Manager • Coaching: Operations Manager • Coaching: Market Research Manager • Coaching: Market Research Manager • Coaching: Customer Service Manager • Institute of Marketing courses
What the role holder must be able to do	
Learning outcomes	***Learning methods***
• Prepare product budget • Prepare marketing plans • Conduct market reviews • Prepare marketing campaigns • Specify requirements for advertisements and promotional material • Liaise with advertising agents and creative supplier • Analyse results of advertising campaigns • Prepare marketing reports	• Coaching: Budget Accountant • Coaching: Mentor • Coaching: Market Research Department • Read: Product Manager's Manual • Read: Product Manager's Manual • Attachment to agency • Coaching: Mentor, read: analyses • Read: previous reports; observe: marketing review meetings

Skills analysis

Skills analysis, as described in Chapter 51, determines the skills required to achieve an acceptable standard of performance. It is mainly used for technical, craft, manual and office jobs to provide the basis for devising learning and training programmes.

Evaluation

Further information should be obtained from learning evaluations, as described at the end of this chapter.

Approaches to learning and development

Approaches to learning and development are influenced by the learning theory presented in Chapter 22, especially experiential learning theory. This emphasizes that people learn mainly from experience and therefore most learning takes place in the workplace as confirmed by the 70/20/10 model explained on page 292. It also indicates that people learn best when they do it for themselves – self-directed learning. But they need support and help. Experiential and self-directed learning can be enhanced in the workplace by activities such as induction, planned experience, coaching, mentoring and e-learning and planned development. These can be supplemented but not replaced by formal training, which involves the delivery of training events and programmes. The effectiveness of learning is increased by joining up the different methods available (blended learning). The basic approaches of workplace learning and self-directed learning are discussed below. The next section describes ways of enhancing workshop learning and this is followed by descriptions of training and blended learning processes.

Workplace learning

Workplace learning is experiential learning. It is learning by doing and by reflecting on experience so that it can be understood and applied. Workplace learning is largely an informal process, although line managers have an important part to play in facilitating it. It involves self-directed learning and is enhanced by coaching, mentoring, e-learning and more formal planned experience. It can be supplemented by training interventions, but more formal approaches are there simply to extend experiential learning.

A study by Eraut *et al* (1998) established that in organizations adopting a learner-centred perspective, formal education and training provided only a small part of what was learnt at work. Most of the learning described to the researchers was non-formal, neither clearly specified nor planned. It arose naturally from the challenges of work. Effective learning was, however, dependent on the employees' confidence, motivation and capability. Some formal training to develop skills (especially induction training) was usually provided, but learning from experience and other people at work predominated.

Reynolds (2004: 3) observed that:

> The simple act of observing more experienced colleagues can accelerate learning; conversing, swapping stories, cooperating on tasks and offering mutual support deepen and solidify the process... This kind of learning – often very informal in nature – is thought to be vastly more effective in building proficiency than more formalized training methods.

The characteristics of workplace learning were explained by Stern and Sommerlad (1999) as follows:

- *The workplace as a site for learning.* In this case, learning and working are spatially separated with some form of structured learning activity occurring off or near the job. This may be in a 'training island' in the department or on the shop floor where the production process is reproduced for trainees.
- *The workplace as a learning environment.* In this approach, the workplace itself becomes an environment for learning. Various on-the-job activities such as coaching, mentoring, job rotation, job shadowing and cross-functional or cross-site project work can be conducted, which are structured to different degrees. Learning is intentional and planned and the aim is to support, structure and monitor the learning of employees.
- *Learning and working are inextricably mixed.* In this case, learning is informal. It becomes an everyday part of the job and is built into routine tasks. Zuboff (1988) commented that learning was at the heart of productive activity. Workers develop skills,

knowledge and understanding through dealing with the challenges posed by the work. This can be described as continuous learning.

But there are disadvantages. Learning on-the-job was once anathematized as 'sitting by Nellie' (this was when Nellie was a fairly common name), meaning that trainees were left to their own devices to pick up bad habits from their neighbours. It can be argued that formal training has its limits but at least it is planned and systematic. In fact the systematic training movement of the 1960s (discussed later in this chapter) was a reaction against traditional laissez faire approaches.

A further difficulty is that workplace learning depends largely on the willingness and ability of line managers to take responsibility for it. Some will, many won't. This crucial aspect of learning may therefore be neglected unless the HR or L&D function does something about it. And that is not easy, as discussed in the last section of this chapter.

Self-directed learning

Self-directed learning is based on a process of recording achievement and action planning, which means that individuals review what they have learnt, what they have achieved, what their goals are, how they are going to achieve those goals and what new learning they need to acquire. The learning programme can be 'self-paced' in the sense that learners can decide for themselves, up to a point, the rate at which they learn, and are encouraged to measure their own progress and adjust the programme accordingly.

Self-directed learning is based on the principle that people learn and retain more if they find things out for themselves. But they still need to be given guidance on what to look for and help in finding it. Learners have to be encouraged to define, with whatever guidance they need, the knowledge and skills required to do their work. They need to be told where they can get the material or information that will help them to learn and how to make good use of it. This can be done through personal development planning, as described later in this chapter. They also need support from their manager and the organization with the provision of coaching, mentoring and learning facilities, including e-learning.

Enhancing workplace learning

Experiential learning in the workplace is important but it should not be left to chance. It needs to be enhanced by such means as induction learning, planned experience, coaching, mentoring, e-learning and personal development planning, as described below.

Induction

Most new starters other than those on formal training schemes will learn on-the-job, although this may be supplemented with special off-the-job courses to develop particular skills or knowledge. On-the-job training can be haphazard, inefficient and wasteful. A planned, systematic approach is desirable. This can incorporate the definition to new starters of what they are expected to do (their roles), an assessment of what they need to learn (a learning specification), the use of designated and trained colleagues to act as guides and mentors, and coaching by team leaders or specially appointed and trained departmental trainers. A planned experience programme as described below may be desirable. These on-the-job arrangements can be supplemented by self-managed learning arrangements that offer access to e-learning material.

Planned experience

Planned experience is the process of deciding on a sequence of experience that will enable people to obtain the knowledge and skills required in their jobs and prepare them to take on increased responsibilities. This enables experiential learning to take place to meet a learning specification. A programme is drawn up that sets down what people are expected to learn in each department or job in which they are given experience. This should spell out what they are expected to discover for themselves. A suitable person (a mentor) should be available in order to see that people in a development programme are given the right experience and opportunity to learn. Arrangements should be made to check progress. A good way of stimulating people to find out for themselves is to provide them with a list of questions to answer. It is essential, however, to follow up each segment of experience to check what has been learnt and, if necessary, modify the programme.

Coaching

Coaching is a personal (usually one-to-one) approach to helping people develop their skills and knowledge and improve their performance. The need for coaching may arise from formal or informal performance reviews, but opportunities for coaching will emerge during everyday activities. Coaching as part of the normal process of management consists of:

- using whatever situations may arise as opportunities to promote learning;
- controlled delegation – ensuring that individuals not only know what is expected of them but also understand what they need to know and be able to do to complete the task satisfactorily; this gives managers an opportunity to provide guidance at the outset: guidance at a later stage may be seen as interference;
- making people aware of how well they are performing by, for example, asking them questions to establish the extent to which they have thought through what they are doing;
- encouraging people to look at higher-level problems and how they would tackle them.

Coaching has an important role in workplace learning. Executive coaching is used frequently as part of a blended learning approach (ie one that includes a number of complementary learning activities) to leadership and management development. Coaching skills are covered in Chapter 52.

Mentoring

Mentoring is the process of using specially selected and trained individuals to provide guidance, pragmatic advice and continuing support that will help the person or persons allocated to them to learn and develop. Mentors prepare people to perform better in the future and groom them for higher and greater things, ie career advancement. Mentoring can play an important part in a leadership and management development programme.

Mentoring is a method of helping people to learn and develop, as distinct from coaching, which is a relatively directive means of increasing people's competence. Mentoring promotes learning on-the-job, which is always the best way of acquiring the particular skills and knowledge the job holder needs. Mentoring also complements formal training by providing those who benefit from it with individual guidance from experienced managers who are 'wise in the ways of the organization'.

E-learning

E-learning involves the use of computer, networked and web-based technology to provide learning material and guidance to individual employees. It can be delivered through a firm's intranet system.

E-learning enhances learning by extending and supplementing face-to-face learning rather than replacing it. It enables learning to take place when it is most needed (just-in-time as distinct from just-in-case) and when it is most convenient. Learning can be provided in short segments or bites that focus on specific learning objectives. It is 'learner-centric' in that it can be customized to suit an individual's learning needs – learners can choose different learning objects within an overall package. The main drawbacks are the need for learners to be self-motivated, the time and effort required to develop and update e-learning programmes and, sometimes, the availability of computers.

E-learning programmes may cover common business applications and processes, induction programmes and, frequently, IT skills development. They are not so effective for developing soft skills such as team building, communication or presentation that rely on interpersonal contact. But programmes can still cover basic principles that prepare people for practical face-to-face sessions, provide reinforcement through post-event reading, help with self-assessment and lead to chat-room support.

The emphasis is on self-paced learning – learners control the rate at which they learn, although they may be given targets for completion and guidance from tutors on how they should learn. However, the impact of e-learning is strongly influenced by the quality of the support provided to learners. It is the effectiveness of this support rather than the sophistication of the technology that counts.

Performance and development management

Performance and development management processes as described fully in Chapter 26 enable managers and individual members of their teams to work together to identify L&D needs.

Personal development planning

Personal development planning is carried out by individuals with guidance, encouragement and help from their managers, usually on the basis of performance and development reviews. A personal development plan sets out the actions people propose to take to learn and to develop themselves. They take responsibility for formulating and implementing the plan but they receive support from the organization and their managers in doing so. The purpose is to provide what Tamkin *et al* (1995) called a 'self-organized learning framework'.

Stages of personal development planning

- *Analyse current situation and development needs*. This can be done as part of a performance management process.
- *Set goals*. These could include improving performance in the current job, improving or acquiring skills, extending relevant knowledge, developing specified areas of competence, moving across or upwards in the organization, preparing for changes in the current role.
- *Prepare action plan*. The action plan sets out what needs to be done and how it will be done under headings such as outcomes expected (learning objectives), the development activities, the responsibility for development (what individuals are expected to do and the support they will get from their manager, the HR department or other people), and timing. A variety of activities tuned to individual needs should be included in the plan, for example observing what others do, project work, planned use of e-learning programmes and internal learning resource centres, working with a mentor, coaching by the line manager or team leader, experience in new tasks, guided reading, special assignments and action learning. Formal training to develop knowledge and skills may be part of the plan but it is not the most important part.
- *Implement*. Take action as planned.

The plan can be expressed in the form of a learning contract, which is a formal agreement between the manager and the individual on what learning needs to take place, the objectives of such learning and what part the individual, the manager, the L&D function or a mentor will play in ensuring that learning happens. The partners to the contract agree on how the objectives will be achieved and their respective roles. It will spell out learning programmes and indicate what coaching, mentoring and formal training activities should be carried out. It is, in effect, a blueprint for learning.

Training

Training is the use of systematic and planned instruction activities to promote learning. The approach can be summarized in the phrase 'learner-based training'. It is one of several responses an organization can undertake to promote learning.

As Reynolds (2004: 45) pointed out, training has a complementary role to play in accelerating learning: 'It should be reserved for situations that justify a more directed, expert-led approach rather than viewing it as a comprehensive and all-pervasive people development solution.' He also commented that the conventional training model has a tendency to 'emphasize subject-specific knowledge, rather than trying to build core learning abilities'.

The justification for training

Formal training is indeed only one of the ways of ensuring that learning takes place, but it can be justified in the following circumstances:

- The knowledge or skills cannot be acquired satisfactorily in the workplace or by self-directed learning.

- Different skills are required by a number of people, which have to be developed quickly to meet new demands and cannot be gained by relying on experience.
- The tasks to be carried out are so specialized or complex that people are unlikely to master them on their own initiative at a reasonable speed.
- When a learning need common to a number of people has to be met that can readily be dealt with in a training event or programme. For example: induction, essential IT skills, communication skills.

Transferring training

The problem of transferring training was raised by Reynolds (2004: 47) as follows:

> Some types of intervention [can] disrupt self-directed learning by paying insufficient attention to the needs of the learner in the work context. Methods that rely heavily on the transfer of external expertise or content to employees... carry the highest risk in this regard, since their design is often removed from the context in which work is created. As a result it is impossible to meet learning needs adequately.

This is a fundamental problem and applies equally to externally and internally run training courses where what has been taught can be difficult for people to apply in the entirely different circumstances in their workplace. Training can seem to be remote from reality and the skills and knowledge acquired can appear to be irrelevant. Transfer of learning problems often occur after management or supervisory training, but even the manual skills learnt in a training centre can be difficult to transfer.

To tackle this problem it is necessary to make the training as relevant and realistic as possible, anticipating and dealing with any potential transfer difficulties. Individuals are more likely to apply learning when they do not find it too difficult; believe what they learnt is relevant, useful and transferable; are supported by line managers; have job autonomy; believe in themselves; and are committed and engaged. Transfer is also more likely if systematic training and 'just-in-time training' approaches are used, as described below.

Systematic training

Training should be systematic in that it is specifically designed, planned and implemented to meet defined needs. It is provided by people who know how to train and the impact of training is carefully evaluated. The concept was originally developed for the industrial training boards in the 1960s and, as illustrated in Figure 23.4, consists of a simple four-stage model:

1. Identify training needs.
2. Decide what sort of training is required to satisfy these needs.
3. Use experienced and trained trainers to implement training.
4. Follow up and evaluate training to ensure that it is effective.

Just-in-time training

Just-in-time training is training that is closely linked to the pressing and relevant needs of people by its association with immediate or imminent work activities. It is delivered as close as possible to the time when the activity is taking place. The training will be based on an identification of the latest requirements, priorities and plans of the participants, who will be briefed on the live situations in which their learning has to be applied. The training programme will take account of any transfer issues and aim to ensure that what is taught is seen to be applicable in the current work situation.

Bite-sized training

Bite-sized training involves the provision of opportunities to acquire a specific skill or a particular piece of knowledge in a short training session focused on one activity, such as using a particular piece of software, giving feedback, or handling an enquiry about a product or service of the company. It is often carried out through e-learning. It can be a useful means of developing a skill or understanding through a concentrated session or learning activity without diversions, which is readily put to use in the workplace. But it can be weak in expanding individuals' intellectual capacity and holistic (or 'whole view') understanding of the business – essential qualities to enable employees to respond creatively to the challenges of today's knowledge economy.

FIGURE 23.4 Systematic training model

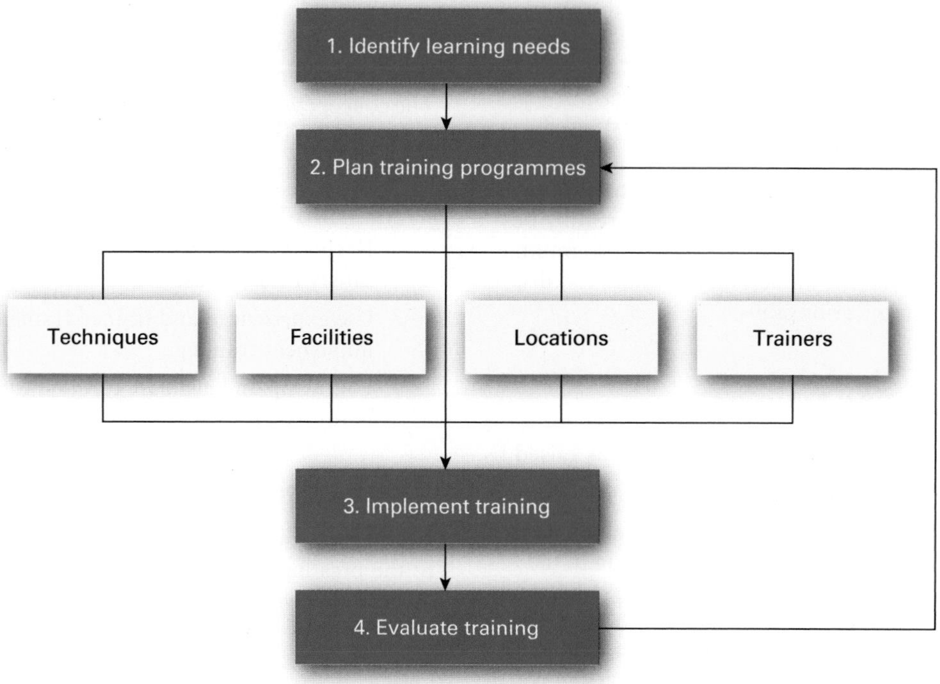

It can also be facile and too restricted and relies on the support of line managers, which is not always forthcoming. It is best for training employees in straightforward techniques that they can use immediately in their work or to complement, not replace, longer courses or developmental processes.

Types of training

Training programmes or events can be concerned with any of the following:

- manual skills, including apprenticeships;
- IT skills;
- team leader or supervisory training;
- management training;
- interpersonal skills, eg leadership, team building, group dynamics, neurolinguistic programming;
- personal skills, eg assertiveness, coaching, communicating, time management;
- training in organizational procedures or practices, eg induction, health and safety, performance management, equal opportunity or managing diversity policy and practice.

Effective training practices

Effective training uses the systematic approach defined above with an emphasis on skills analysis. The purpose of the training should be clearly defined in terms of the behaviour required as a result of training. The focus of the training should be to develop transferable skills. The training should be evaluated on the basis of the extent to which it has achieved its purpose.

Planning and delivering learning events

This process of planning and delivering learning events and programmes is described by the ADDIE model, which has five phases: analysis, design, development, implementation and evaluation.

Analysis phase

In the analysis phase the learning goals and objectives are established and the learning environment and learner's existing knowledge and skills are identified.

Design phase

The design phase deals with subject matter analysis, the programme outline and the use of learning aids and assessment instruments.

Development phase

In the development phase the detailed programme is constructed as conceived in the design phase. This covers the session plan, the outline content and learning outcomes of each session, methods of delivery, preparation of visual aids, handouts, supporting material and exercises, the arrangements for administering the programme (main lecture room, syndicate rooms, projectors, flip charts, etc) and the final printed version of the programme for distribution to nominating managers and, later, to delegates. This will set out the objectives and benefits of the programme and how these will be achieved. The costs of the programme will be calculated to ensure that they are within budget.

Those conducting the programme prepare the detailed contents of their sessions, decide on their method of delivery, rehearse their sessions and work out how the exercises will fit in. The programme director ensures that the efforts of all those involved are coordinated.

Implementation phase

The programme is implemented as planned.

Evaluation phase

Each session is evaluated by the programme director and, at the end, by participants. The impact of the programme on performance is measured and the degree to which it met expectations assessed.

A toolkit for the planning and delivery of learning events is contained in Chapter 67 of this handbook.

Blended learning

Blended learning is the use of a combination of learning methods to increase the overall effectiveness of the learning process by providing for different parts of the learning mix to complement and support one another. A blended learning programme might be planned for an individual using a mix of planned experience, self-directed learning activities defined in a personal development plan, e-learning facilities, group action learning activities, coaching or mentoring, and instruction provided in an in-company or external course.

Generic training for groups of people might include e-learning, planned instruction programmes and selected external courses. Within a training course a complementary mix of different training activities might take place, for example a skills development course for managers or team leaders might include some instruction on basic principles, but much more time would be spent on case studies, simulations, role playing and other exercises.

Evaluation of learning

It is important to evaluate learning to assess its effectiveness in producing the outcomes specified when the activity was planned and to indicate where improvements or changes are required in order to make the training even more effective. As noted by Tamkin *et al* (2002), learning can be modelled as a chain of impact from the planning of learning to meet organizational or individual learning needs to the learning that takes place in a learning event, from learning to changed behaviour, and from changed behaviour to impact on others and the organization as a whole.

Evaluation is an integral feature of learning activities. In essence, it is the comparison of objectives with outcomes to answer the question of how far the event has achieved its purpose. The setting of objectives and the establishment of methods of measuring results are, or should be, an essential part of the planning stage of any L&D programme. Evaluation provides guidance on what needs to be done to ensure that learning activities are effective.

Approach to evaluation

It is at the planning stage that the basis upon which each category of learning event or programme is to be evaluated should be determined. This means defining expectations on the impact that the event will make in terms of criterion behaviour (the performance standards or changes in behaviour on-the-job to be achieved if a learning process is to be regarded as successful) and terminal behaviour (the actual work behaviour of learners when they complete their learning programme). The aim is to establish the extent to which the event has achieved its purpose. At the same time, it is necessary to consider how the information required for evaluation should be obtained and analysed.

The areas that need to be evaluated are:

- *Planning* – the extent to which needs were properly evaluated and objectives set.
- *Conduct* – how well the programme or event was organized and managed, the degree to which the inputs and methods were appropriate and effective, and its cost compared with the budget.
- *Reactions* – what participants felt about the event.
- *Outcomes* – the impact the event made on individual, departmental and organizational performance.

Evaluation can take place at different levels, starting with immediate reactions to the learning event and completed with an assessment of the impact it has had on organizational performance. The best known and most used system of levels was developed by Kirkpatrick (1994).

Levels of evaluation – Kirkpatrick

The four levels of evaluation suggested by Kirkpatrick are as follows.

Level 1: Reaction

At this level, evaluation measures how those who participated in the training have reacted to it. In a sense, it is a measure of immediate customer satisfaction. Kirkpatrick suggested the following guidelines for evaluating reactions:

- determine what you want to find out;
- design a form that will quantify reactions;
- encourage written comments and suggestions;
- get 100 per cent immediate response;
- get honest responses;
- develop acceptable standards;
- measure reactions against standards, and take appropriate action;
- communicate reactions as appropriate.

Research by Warr *et al* (1970) showed that there was relatively little correlation between learner reactions and subsequent measures of changed behaviour. But as Tamkin *et al* (2002) claimed, despite this, organizations are still keen to get reactions to training, and used with caution this can produce useful information on the extent to which learning objectives were perceived to be met and why.

Level 2: Evaluate learning

This level obtains information on the extent to which learning objectives have been attained. It will aim to find how much knowledge was acquired, what skills were developed or improved, and the extent to which attitudes have changed in the desired direction. So far as possible, the evaluation of learning should involve the use of tests before and after the programme – written, oral or performance tests.

Level 3: Evaluate behaviour

This level evaluates the extent to which behaviour has changed as required when people attending the programme have returned to their jobs. The question to be answered is the extent to which knowledge, skills and attitudes have been transferred from the classroom to the workplace. Ideally, the evaluation should take place both before and after the training. Time should be allowed for the change in behaviour to take place. The evaluation needs to assess the extent to which specific learning objectives relating to changes in behaviour and the application of knowledge and skills have been achieved.

Level 4: Evaluate results

This is the ultimate level of evaluation and provides the basis for assessing the benefits of the training against its costs. The objective is to determine the added value of learning and development programmes – how they contribute to raising organizational performance significantly above its previous level. The evaluation has to be based on before-and-after measures and should determine the extent to which the fundamental objectives of the training have been achieved in areas such as increasing sales, raising productivity, reducing accidents or increasing customer satisfaction. Evaluating results is obviously easier when they can be quantified. However, it is not always easy to prove the contribution to improved results made by training as distinct from other factors and, as Kirkpatrick said, that evaluators should be satisfied with evidence, because proof is usually impossible to get. Perhaps the most powerful method of demonstrating that 'learning programmes pay' is to measure the return on investment, as discussed below.

In practice, organizations find it difficult to advance above level 1. That is why there have been moves to use an overall measure such as return on investment or return on expectations.

Return on investment as a method of evaluation

Return on investment (RoI) is advocated by some commentators as a means of assessing the overall impact of training on organizational performance. It is calculated as:

$$\frac{\text{Benefits from training (£)} - \text{costs of training (£)}}{\text{Costs of training (£)}} \times 100$$

Kearns and Miller (1997) believe that only this sort of measure is useful in evaluating the overall impact of training. They argue that particular hard measures should be used to evaluate specific training; for example, if development aims to bring about greater awareness of customers then it should be measured by the eventual effect on customer spend, customer satisfaction and number of customers.

The pressure to produce financial justification for any organizational activity, especially in areas such as learning and development, has increased the interest in RoI. The problem is that while it is easy to record the costs it is much harder to produce convincing financial assessments of the benefits.

Return on expectations

The evaluation of learning has traditionally concentrated on the Kirkpatrick 'levels' approach. But there is a trend to concentrate more on the validation of the total learning process and on the outcomes of learning. This means focusing on return on expectation measures, which assess the extent to which the anticipated benefits of any learning investment have been realized. As described by Anderson (2007: 33): 'This involves focusing on establishing "up front" the anticipated benefits of learning interventions or investments with key stakeholders, and then assessing the extent to which the anticipated benefits have been realized.'

The problem with evaluation

The need for evaluation is generally recognized by L&D specialists and the Kirkpatrick model is well known, but Grove and Ostroff (1990) noted that there were five barriers that appeared to explain why training evaluations were not carried out very effectively in organizations:

1. Senior management often not insisting on or requesting information on the impact of the training that was provided.
2. The lack of expertise among L&D professionals on how to carry out training evaluations.
3. A lack of clear objectives attached to training programmes so that actually knowing what to evaluate against is difficult if not impossible.
4. The limited budgets available to training departments means that resources are devoted to training provision rather than training evaluation.
5. The risks associated with evaluation may be too great, given that the evaluation data might reveal that the training had little impact.

The following comment on the limitations of traditional approaches to evaluation was made by Anderson (2007: 3):

> Traditional approaches to evaluation set out to prove the merit of specific learning interventions and to demonstrate their cost-effective delivery. Such proof, however, while identifying that the trainer has done good work, does not necessarily assess the extent of the training intervention with the organization's strategic priorities... Whereas a traditional approach to evaluation focuses on the reactions and consequences for learners and trainers resulting from discrete and individual

training interventions, a strategic approach requires a focus on the aggregate value contribution made by a more dispersed range of learning processes.

Application of evaluation

The more care that has been taken in the assessment of needs and the more precise the objectives, the greater will be the possibility of effective evaluation. This is the basis for conducting evaluation at various levels.

It could be argued that the only feedback that matters from evaluation is the results in terms of improved unit or organizational performance that learning brings. But if this is hard to measure, a learning event could still be justified in terms of any actual changes in behaviour that the programme was designed to produce. This is based on the assumption that the analysis of learning needs indicated that the behaviour is more than likely to deliver the desired results. Similarly, at the learning level, if a proper analysis of knowledge, skills and attitude requirements and their impact on behaviour has been conducted, it is reasonable to assume that if the knowledge, etc has been acquired, behaviour is likely to change appropriately. Finally, if all else fails, reactions are important in that they provide immediate feedback on the quality of training given (including the performance of the trainer), which can point the way to corrective action.

Responsibility for the implementation of learning

Individuals should be expected to take a considerable degree of responsibility for managing their own learning (self-directed or discretionary learning) but they need the help and support of their line managers and the organization, including the L&D function. Line managers have a key role in planning and facilitating learning by organizing induction training, providing learning opportunities (planned experience), coaching, mentoring, conducting performance and development reviews, agreeing learning contracts and personal development plans with their people, and helping them to implement those plans. But they have to be encouraged to do this. They should understand that the promotion of learning is regarded as an important aspect of their responsibilities and that their performance in carrying it out will be assessed. They also need guidance on how they should carry out their developmental role.

Responsibility for L&D is being increasingly placed on managers and employees rather than on L&D professionals. The latter need to become learning facilitators rather than training providers or instructors. Stewart and Tansley (2002) recommended that training specialists should focus on learning processes rather than the content of training courses. Carter *et al* (2002) argued that changes in training delivery methods are leading to a variety of different role demands. These roles include facilitator and change agent.

What L&D practitioners do

As facilitators, L&D specialists analyse learning needs and make proposals on how these can best be satisfied. They provide facilities such as learning resource centres and e-learning programmes and plan and implement training interventions, often outsourcing training to external providers.

The emphasis in current thinking is on enabling learning rather than just delivering training. The most important activities of L&D specialists are to encourage, guide and help line managers to fulfil their workplace learning responsibilities. But the reality is that many L&D practitioners are still in the training business. As Poell (2005: 85) noted: 'Although it is common nowadays to assert that employees are self-responsible for their own learning and careers, in practice, HRD professionals will spend most of their time coordinating, designing and delivering training to employees.' Sambrook and Stewart (2005: 79), on the basis of their trans-Europe research, concluded that: 'Despite the wishes and, in some cases, the efforts of HRD professionals, learning and development practice still relies to a significant extent on traditional and formalized training interventions.'

It is not difficult to understand why this is happening. The systematic training approach – ie training specifically designed, planned, implemented and evaluated to meet defined needs – is traditionally what professional trainers are expected to do, so they do it. The promotion and facilitation of self-directed and workplace learning are not such recognized requirements and are more difficult, so they don't do it.

CASE STUDIES

Developing a learning strategy for Remploy

Remploy is a government-funded organization that provides employment and development opportunities for disabled people. It operates 83 factories. The company's strategy for learning is explicit and well understood in the organization, and was developed from the bottom-up rather than top-down. Its starting point was recognition that a number of local initiatives in the factories were proving successful and could be developed on a national basis.

The trade unions advocated enhanced opportunities for skill development in basic areas. As a result a national strategy was developed with learning centres as a major element in all 83 sites. Although the use of each learning centre is locally determined, they all have the following in common: a physical location (with at least some PCs); a relationship with a local college whose tutors will visit the site to advise and facilitate; and access to a suite of e-learning programmes, made available from the LearnDirect library (the national e-learning initiative).

Training overhaul for Scottish police

A radical overhaul of training for the Scottish police has created more opportunities for promotion and culminated in a prestigious National Training Award. The improved training scheme uses facilitated learning delivery, where trainees pre-read all information before attending sessions and then discuss issues and learn from each other. Responsibility for learning is now firmly placed on the shoulders of the individual – you have got to want to be a police officer and you have got to want to learn. After 15 weeks of initial training, a two-week 'reconvention' period helps staff with the areas they particularly need to address. This training is tailored to individual requirements: syndicates of recruits with similar needs are put together to receive it. This 'partnership approach' had helped the participants to focus on communication and problem-solving skills. A Certificate of Higher Education in policing, accredited by the University of Stirling, is awarded on completion of the programme. There are also opportunities to take a diploma in management skills.

Integrated e-learning at Cable & Wireless

E-learning at Cable & Wireless is based on the establishment and promotion of a single platform for learning. This has been delivered through an outsourcing arrangement with the e-learning company SkillSoft. The core platform is a learning management system that is available to Cable & Wireless colleagues as a portal labelled 'iLEARN'. All training delivery channels are linked to this portal. The library of generic material consists of some 15,000 items plus about 60 modules commissioned by Cable & Wireless.

In the first year since the e-learning system was launched, three-quarters of the workforce used it and this penetration figure is rising. Some 20,000 e-learning activities were accessed and 15,000 hours of e-learning undertaken in total.

Training and learning at a Customer Support Centre

The Customer Support Centre employs 300 people. Customer service agents work in a group of five, known as a 'pod'. One of the pod members will be a team coach who provides support and advice to his or her agent colleagues.

A working knowledge of each customer support system is essential to do the job and one of the central tasks of the training department is to bring new entrants up to competence as quickly as possible. The following pattern is adopted. New entrants join in cohorts of 8 to 10 and spend their first week in the training room. As the week progresses they spend periods in a pod sitting next to a 'buddy', listening to calls. At the end of that week they are allocated to a pod team and receive close ongoing support from the pod team coach.

Given the emphasis on learning in the workplace, the role of the team coach is critical and there are a number of steps in place to support and enhance their role. A set of skills and needs have been defined and these are delivered to the 30 centre team coaches in 90-minute modules in the training room.

Career coaching at Orange

Within Orange, coaching is used in various ways to support people on-the-job and in leadership and personal development programmes. The career coaching programme uses volunteer line managers who have been trained to provide coaching to staff with whom they have no reporting relationship.

The two objectives for career coaching are: 1) as part of its overall talent management strategy Orange wants to see employees take greater responsibility for their own careers; 2) Orange is in a competitive market as far as skills and resources are concerned and this effort is intended to help with employee retention by engaging employees in conversations about their careers before they look elsewhere. Career coaching is offered to all staff, regardless of grade. The programme consists of three sessions of 90 minutes each, with a line manager coach trained specifically in career coaching.

Employees complete an online application, which must have their line manager's approval, and commit to the time required for the coaching process over an 8–10 week period. Included on this form is the question, 'Why do you want to be coached?' with some examples of the reasons that someone might choose.

The coaching process is tightly structured. The planned outcome is for the employee to develop career goals, which are discussed with the individual's manager at the next performance review. Coaches give employees exercises to work on between the meetings, drawn from a large selection offered by the talent management team.

After the process is completed, individuals are asked to complete an evaluation form describing their experience of the scheme, their coach's style and the outcomes they have achieved.

Coaching at Marks & Spencer

Traditionally M&S trained its customer assistants by taking them off the shop floor for classroom-style training, but the company has introduced a new role, that of coach. When trainees join M&S, their coaches take them through all of the training required for their immediate role, as well as any additional training they may need once qualified. Formal coaching cards are used, which address both service and technical skills and tell the coaches what to assess and what the learning should be. Each trainee is also provided with a booklet summarizing the main learning points.

Implementing a basic skills programme at TNT

TNT UK Ltd has over 9,500 staff working throughout the UK and Ireland. Its core business is express and logistics delivery services both within the UK and internationally.

The basic skills programme was established as a joint initiative between TNT and the Transport and General Workers' Union (T&G). T&G provided the trainers and a contribution from the Union Learning Fund to establish the programme; TNT provided the resources including the office space, computers and refreshments. The role of the T&G's learning representative was crucial in identifying staff with basic skills needs. Individuals were identified and encouraged by the union representative to join the programme. The challenge was to motivate staff to take part in the programme without it being perceived as a stigma. Tactics included selling the benefits of the programme, for example improving communication skills such as reading, rather than focusing on tackling problem areas or deficiencies.

The programme was designed to take place over five days. A continuous course over several days has benefits over a modular approach; for example staff are less likely to lose interest or suffer teasing from colleagues. Areas included reading, writing, numeracy and PC skills. At the end of the programme the participants received certificates from senior managers.

Self-directed learning in Vestas Blades UK Ltd

Vestas Blades UK Ltd is a wind turbine blade research, development and manufacturer based in the Isle of Wight and Southampton. The L&D policy adopted by Vestas was to give ownership of learning to individuals. Learning needed to be continuous, timely and relevant for people whose roles would present new challenges as the business grew. It wanted employees to have a choice about what they learnt, when and how. A menu of training courses not only seemed unattractive but was also seen to have limited effectiveness in terms of the transfer of learning to the workplace. A requirement of any new approach was that it should motivate employees by serving their own individual learning needs while at the same time meeting those of the business.

The self-directed learning programme began by introducing the concept of personal awareness (via the Myers-Briggs Type Indicator) and its relevance to learning. An inquiry tool was developed to help participants identify their own learning needs, known as the Needs Analysis Process (NAP). Individuals decided the learning goals that would have the greatest benefit to them and their part of the business. The NAP focused attention on the impact that the business's strategic and operational objectives had on each participant's current and future level of performance.

Once participants were made aware of the wealth of learning resources available through books or e-learning, they chose the learning group they wanted to join. Each group consisted of four people from across the organization who would meet regularly every six weeks in confidence – serving as a support structure for its members. Such support was critical. The opportunity to talk about how to apply learning in the workplace not only helped group members make sense of the effect that their learning had but also supported fellow learners in the group working on the same or similar topics.

During the first year each group had its own facilitator, drawn primarily from Acuition consultants but also from within the company. The facilitator's role was to accelerate the group's capability to learn.

Measuring the contribution of learning to business performance at Lyreco Ltd (UK)

Lyreco UK is part of a large family-owned office supplies group operating extensively in Europe, Canada and Asia. Metrics are a central part of all management processes at Lyreco and these inform the learning investment and planning processes. In field sales, measures include sales turnover, margin and new business, whilst in customer service the performance and productivity metrics include costs per line, abandoned call rate, average call time, and average wait time. Monthly performance results in all areas are scrutinized to identify areas for attention, and the learning and development team run learning sessions and activities aimed at helping people to improve their performance. When sales margin was identified as an area for attention, over 150 people attended focused workshops and subsequent performance results were tracked to measure improvements. Similarly, warehouse supervisors with the highest staff turnover attended learning programmes and, as a consequence, staff turnover was at its lowest ever levels.

Key learning points: The practice of learning and development

Approach to learning and development

- The starting point for learning and development is the systematic identification of learning needs. This provides the basis for making a choice between the various approaches available and for decisions on the practices that should be adopted for the chosen approach.
- The approaches from which a choice can be made are workplace learning, self-directed learning, e-learning and formal training and development activities involving the delivery of learning events and programmes.
- A blended learning approach should be adopted wherever possible.
- In each case, it is necessary to evaluate the effectiveness of the learning and development process so that improvements can be made if required.

Identifying learning needs

All learning activities need to be based on an understanding of what needs to be done and why. The purpose of the activities must be defined and this is only possible if the learning needs of the organization and the groups and individuals within it have been identified and analysed.

Workplace learning

Workplace learning is experiential learning. It is learning by doing and by reflecting on experience so that it can be understood and applied. Workplace learning is largely an informal process, although line managers have an important part to play in facilitating it.

Self-directed learning

Self-directed or self-managed learning involves encouraging individuals to take responsibility for their own learning needs, either to improve performance in their present job or to develop their potential and satisfy their career aspirations.

Coaching

Coaching is a personal (usually one-to-one) approach to helping people develop their skills and knowledge and improve their performance.

Mentoring

Mentoring is the process of using specially selected and trained individuals to provide guidance, pragmatic advice and continuing support that will help the person or persons allocated to them to learn and develop.

E-learning

E-learning provides for learning via computer, networked and web-based technology. The process comprises defining the system, encouraging access, advising and assisting individual learners and encouraging and facilitating the creation of learning communities.

Personal development planning

Personal development planning is carried out by individuals with guidance, encouragement and help from their managers as required. This should be the outcome of a performance and development review. A personal development plan sets out the actions people propose to take to learn and to develop themselves.

Planned experience

Planned experience is the process of deciding on a sequence of experience that will enable people to obtain the knowledge and skills required in their jobs and prepare them to take on increased responsibilities. This enables experiential learning to take place to meet a learning specification.

Planning and delivering learning programmes and events

The stages are:

- identify learning needs;
- define learning objectives;
- decide on content;
- decide on methods of delivery;
- decide on location, facilities, the budget and who delivers the programme;
- prepare information about the programme or event;
- deliver the programme or event;
- evaluate learning.

Main criteria for effectiveness

- The programme is based on a thorough evaluation of learning needs.
- Clear objectives have been set for the outcomes of the programme.
- Standards are set for the delivery of the programme.
- Success criteria and methods of measuring success have been established.
- A blend of learning and development methods are used – informal and formal – that are appropriate for the established needs of those taking part.
- The outcome of the programme is evaluated.

Blended learning

Blended learning is the use of a combination of learning methods to increase the overall effectiveness of the learning process by providing for different parts of the learning mix to complement and support one another.

Evaluation of learning

Evaluation is an integral feature of learning activities. In essence, it is the comparison of objectives with outcomes to answer the question of how far the event has achieved its purpose. The four levels of evaluation in the Kirkpatrick methodology are: 1) reaction, 2) evaluate learning, 3) evaluate behaviour, 4) evaluate results.

Responsibility for learning

- While individuals should be expected to take a considerable degree of responsibility for managing their own learning, they need the help and support of their line managers and the organization, including the L&D function.
- Line managers have a key role in planning and facilitating learning by conducting performance and development reviews, agreeing learning contracts and personal development plans with their staff, and helping staff to implement those plans through the provision of learning opportunities and coaching.
- Learning and development professionals have to become learning facilitators rather than simply training providers or instructors.

Questions

1. What overall approach should be adopted to learning and development?
2. Why is the identification of learning needs so important?
3. What methods are available for identifying learning needs?
4. What is workplace learning?
5. What is a personal development plan?
6. When is training justified?
7. What constitute effective training practices?
8. How should learning and development events and programmes be planned?
9. What is blended learning?
10. What are the four levels of Kirkpatrick's learning evaluation methodology?

References

Anderson, V (2007) *The Value of Learning: From return on investment to return on expectation*, London, CIPD

Carter, A, Hirsh, W and Aston, J (2002) Resourcing the Training and Development Function, *Report No 390*, Brighton, Institute for Employment Studies

Eraut, M J, Alderton, G, Cole, G and Senker, P (1998) *Development of Knowledge and Skills in Employment*, London, Economic and Social Research Council

Grove, D A and Ostroff, C (1990) Training programme evaluation, in (eds) K N Wexley and J R Hinrichs, *Developing Human Resources*, Washington, DC, Bureau of National Affairs

Kearns, P and Miller, T (1997) Measuring the impact of training and development on the bottom line, *FT Management Briefings*, London, Pitman

Kirkpatrick, D L (1994) *Evaluating Training Programmes*, San Francisco, CA, Berret-Koehler

Poell, R F (2005) HRD beyond what HRD practitioners do, in (eds) C Elliott and S Turnbull, *Critical Thinking in Human Resource Development*, Abingdon, Routledge, pp 85–95

Reynolds, J (2004) *Helping People Learn*, London, CIPD

Sambrook, S and Stewart, J (2005) A critical review of researching human resource development, in (eds) C Elliott and S Turnbull, *Critical Thinking in Human Resource Development*, Abingdon, Routledge, pp 67–84

Stern, E and Sommerlad, E (1999) *Workplace Learning, Culture and Performance*, London, IPD

Stewart, J and Tansley, C (2002) *Training in the Knowledge Economy*, London, CIPD

Tamkin, P, Barber, L and Hirsh, W (1995) *Personal Development Plans: Case studies of practice*, Brighton, Institute for Employment Studies

Tamkin, P, Yarnall, J and Kerrin, M (2002) Kirkpatrick and Beyond: A review of training evaluation, *Report 392*, Brighton, Institute for Employment Studies

Warr, P B, Bird, M W and Rackham, N (1970) *Evaluation of Management Training*, Aldershot, Gower

Zuboff, S (1988) *In the Age of the Smart Machine*, New York, Basic Books

24 Leadership and management development

KEY CONCEPTS AND TERMS

- Action learning
- Development centre
- Leadership
- Leadership and management development
- Leadership development
- Management
- Management development
- Management succession planning
- Outdoor learning

LEARNING OUTCOMES

On completing this chapter you should be able to define these key concepts. You should also understand:

- The nature of leadership and management development
- The nature of leadership and management
- Leadership and management development compared
- Leadership development
- Management development
- Formal approaches to management development
- Informal approaches to management development
- The role of the organization
- The role of the individual
- The role of HR and L&D specialists
- The criteria for leadership and management

Introduction

This chapter is about what organizations can do to develop effective leaders and managers, bearing in mind the point made by Drucker (1955: 158) that: 'The prosperity if not the survival of any business depends on the performance of its managers of tomorrow.'

The chapter starts with a definition of leadership and management development. This leads to a discussion of the nature of leadership and management as a basis for an analysis of what leadership and management development programmes might cover and an examination of the extent, if at all, to which leadership development and management development programmes are different. The conclusion is reached that while they are closely associated, and indeed may be conducted jointly, they are sufficiently different to justify being examined separately, which is undertaken in the next two sections of the chapter.

Leadership and management development defined

Leadership and management development programmes provide for managers to have the leadership and managerial qualities required to achieve success. They form a vital ingredient in talent management, in association with the career planning and career management activities described in Chapter 20. A blended learning approach is used, which combines a number of learning activities such as planned experience, self-directed learning, coaching, mentoring, action learning, outdoor learning and formal education and training in programmes based on an analysis of learning needs.

The nature of leadership and management

There has been much debate on how leadership differs from management. The problem is that leadership involves management and management involves leadership so that it may be difficult to separate the two. There is some consensus on the essential nature of both and the skills involved, as set out below, but there is more disagreement on which is the most important.

Leadership

Leadership means inspiring people to do their best to achieve a desired result. It involves developing and communicating a vision for the future, motivating people and securing their engagement. As defined by Dixon (1994: 214): 'Leadership is no more than exercising such an influence upon others that they tend to act in concert towards achieving a goal which they might not have achieved so readily had they been left to their own devices.' Leadership skills include the ability to:

- inspire others;
- persuade others willingly to behave differently;
- clarify what needs to be done and why;
- communicate a sense of purpose to the team;
- understand, as established by research conducted by Tamkin *et al* (2010), that leaders cannot create performance themselves but are conduits for performance through their influence on others;
- get the team into action so that the task is achieved.

Management

The word 'management' is derived from the Italian verb *maneggiare*, which means 'to handle a horse'. This definition at least states that to manage is to have charge of or responsibility for something, but there is clearly more to it than that. Management has often been defined as 'getting things done through people', thus emphasizing its leadership component. But managers are also responsible for guiding and controlling the business or their part of it by managing their other resources – finance, work systems and technology. Management could therefore be defined as deciding what to do and then getting it done through the effective use of resources.

Research by Tamkin *et al* (2003) established that the abilities managers need are:

- to empower and develop people – understand and practise the process of delivering through the capability of others;

- manage people and performance – managers increasingly need to maintain morale while also maximizing performance;
- work across boundaries, engaging with others, working as a member of a team, thinking differently about problems and their solutions;
- develop relationships and a focus on the customer, building partnerships with both internal and external customers;
- balance technical and generic skills – the technical aspects of management and the management of human relationships.

This list emphasizes the leadership component of management. However, managers are primarily there to get results by ensuring that their function, unit or department operates effectively. They manage people and their other resources, which include time and themselves. They are accountable for attaining goals, having been given authority over those working in their unit or department.

The traditional model of what managers do is that it is a logical and systematic process of planning, organizing, motivating and controlling. But this is misleading. Managers often carry out their work on a day-to-day basis in conditions of variety, turbulence and unpredictability. Managers may have to be specialists in ambiguity, with the ability to cope with conflicting and unclear requirements.

Managers are doers. They deal with events as they occur. But they must also be concerned with where they are going. This requires strategic thinking, especially at higher levels. As strategic thinkers, managers develop a sense of purpose and frameworks for defining intentions and future directions. They are engaged in the process of strategic management.

What are the differences?

Are leadership and management the same or different? Some commentators regard leadership as synonymous with management; others see them as distinct but closely linked and equally necessary activities; others consider management to be a subset of leadership; and yet others praise leadership and demonize management. Bennis (1989) viewed managers as those who promote efficiency, follow the rules and accept the status quo, while leaders focus on challenging the rules and promoting effectiveness. Kotter (1991) saw managers as being the ones who plan, budget, organize and control, while leaders set direction, manage change and motivate people. Hersey and Blanchard (1998) claimed that management merely consists of leadership applied to business situations; or in other words, management forms a subset of the broader process of leadership.

But as Birkinshaw (2010: 23) commented: 'By dichotomizing the work of executives in this way, Kotter, Bennis and others squeezed out the essence of what managers do and basically left them with the boring work that "leaders" don't want.' His view on the leadership-versus-management debate was that: 'Leadership is a process of social influence, concerned with the traits, styles and behaviours of individuals that cause others to follow them. Management is the act of getting people together to accomplish desired goals. To put it simply, we all need to be both leaders and managers' (ibid: 23). Burgoyne (2010: 42) observed that: 'Both [management and leadership] are needed and need to work closely together, often through the same person or team.' Earlier, Mintzberg (2004: 22) summed it all up (as he often did) when he wrote: 'Let's stop the dysfunctional separation of leadership from management. We all know that managers who don't lead are boring, dispiriting. Well, leaders who don't manage are distant, disconnected.'

Leadership and management development compared

In some quarters the term 'leadership development' has replaced 'management development', perhaps because the importance of ensuring that people have leadership qualities has been recognized, while it is believed that they can be safely left to acquire management skills in other ways, eg experience. However, the two are different even though they are closely associated.

A rather simplistic way of differentiating the two is that leadership development tends to be concerned with nurturing the softer skills of leadership through various educational processes, including formal learning events and programmes and coaching. This is illustrated in the three case studies at the end of the next section of this chapter. In contrast, management development relies more on ensuring that managers have the right sequence of experience, which may be supplemented by self-directed learning and courses on management techniques. Further guidance may be provided by coaching and from mentors. But management development programmes traditionally also cover leadership skills.

Leadership development

It is sometimes said that leaders are born not made. This is a rather discouraging statement for those who are not leaders by birthright. It may be true to the extent that some exceptional people seem to be visionaries, have built-in charisma and a natural ability to impose their personality on others. However, even they probably have to develop and hone these qualities when confronted with a situation demanding leadership. Ordinary mortals need not despair: they too can build on their natural capacities and develop their leadership abilities. As Burgoyne (2010: 42) wisely observed: 'The will to lead is largely innate but the ability to do it well is largely learnt.'

As defined by Burgoyne (2010: 43): 'Leadership development in the widest sense involves the acquisition, development and utilization of leadership capability or the potential for it.' Leadership development programmes prepare people for leadership roles and situations beyond their current experience. The essential elements of leadership development, as suggested by Bolden (2010: 129), are reflection, practice, self-awareness, personal support, opportunities to apply learning and relevance to work.

Burgoyne (2010: 44) identified the following leadership development activities:

- job/work placements with leadership capability development as one of the purposes;
- education, training and development of individuals including the 'context sensitive' methods of coaching, mentoring and more formal education, training and development programmes;
- 'soft' organization development processes including culture change, team building and 'hearts and minds' collective mission/ values-creating initiatives.

Yukl (2006) proposed the following conditions for successful leadership development:

- clear learning objectives;
- clear, meaningful content;
- appropriate sequencing of content;
- appropriate mix of training methods;
- opportunity for active practice;
- relevant, timely feedback;
- high trainee confidence;
- appropriate follow-up activities.

But it is not all about subjecting leaders to development programmes. The organization has to play its part in ensuring that leaders are provided with the support and the working conditions they need to carry out their role properly. As Fiedler (1967: 276) emphasized: 'If we wish to increase organizational and group effectiveness we must learn not only to train leaders more effectively but also to build an organizational environment in which the leaders can perform well.'

CASE STUDIES

Cargill

Cargill is an international provider of food, agricultural and risk management products and services. Those in Cargill's different talent pools, such as the 'Next Generation Leaders' and 'Emerging Leaders' undertake both formal and informal development. In Cargill's high-performance Leadership Academy, entrants learn about the fundamentals of leadership and management in the company and work through a number of accelerated leadership modules, gaining the knowledge to enable them to lead Cargill businesses. All of these courses are interspersed with more challenging projects and work assignments. Cargill corporate leaders also take part in the Leadership Academy, where they learn transformational leadership skills and the essentials of coaching and mentoring in formal programmes and informal learning activities, all of which form an important part of their leadership development.

Diageo

At Diageo, the international beverages company, a series of development strategies, particularly for leadership, have been based on Diageo's five values, which were created as the common heartbeat of all the component businesses. The values – 'Be the best', 'Passionate about consumers', 'Proud of what we do', 'Freedom to succeed' and 'Valuing each other' – have become central to Diageo's success, alongside a comprehensive performance management framework. Conversations about performance are now on a 'partnership' basis, where managers, with their employees, are expected to discuss the latter's aspirations and how their growth needs can be satisfied by the business.

The company's first leadership development programme, 1998's 'Building Diageo talent', was designed to help link strategy and organizational performance with individual performance. This had many components, including coaching and benchmarking for leadership development for 4,000 managers. Over the past six years the company's leadership training has evolved to focus more on building 'a core Diageo mindset'. The senior team has prioritized developing a 'total talent strategy' and HR processes have been thoroughly embedded in management thinking worldwide.

HML

As described by Spackman (2010), at HML (a financial services company) the leadership development programme for middle and senior managers consisted of the following elements:

- individual 360-degree feedback;
- orientation event – introduction and contracting;
- action learning sets (sets of six people, three sets in one programme group);
- four modules: profit, client, effectiveness, engagement;
- big event – transformational residential learning;
- self-directed modules;
- individual 360-degree feedback – benchmark scores;
- accreditation and celebration event.

Management development

Management development is concerned with improving the performance of managers in their present roles, preparing them to take on greater responsibilities in the future and also developing their leadership skills. It was defined by Baldwin and Patgett (1994), quoted by Peters (2010: 28), as: 'A complex process by which individuals learn to perform effectively in a management role.' A systematic approach to management development is necessary to meet the needs of organizations for the talented managers they require and because the increasingly onerous demands made on line managers mean that they have to possess a wider range of developed skills than ever before.

The object of management development is to find ways in which the company can produce, mainly from within, a supply of managers better equipped for their jobs at all levels. The principal method of doing this is to ensure that managers gain the right sequence and variety of experience, in good time, that will equip them for whatever level of responsibility they have the ability to reach in the course of their career. This experience can be supplemented – but never replaced – by courses carefully timed and designed to meet particular needs. Management development policies involve the use of both formal and informal approaches.

Formal approaches to management development

Formal approaches to management development consist of processes and events that are planned and provided by the organization. These should be based on the identification of development needs. The methods of defining learning needs described in Chapter 23 can be used to determine collective needs. For individuals, performance management reviews are an important means of producing personal development plans and learning contracts, also described in Chapter 23. This can be done more systematically at development centres. These consist of a concentrated (usually one or two days) programme of exercises, tests and interviews designed to identify managers' development needs and to provide counselling on their careers. Competency frameworks can be used as a means of identifying and expressing development needs and pointing the way to self-managed learning programmes or the provision of learning opportunities by the organization.

The formal approaches that can be used are:

- planned experience – which includes job rotation, job enlargement, taking part in project teams or task groups and secondment outside the organization – this is possibly the most effective approach on the grounds that managers learn to manage mainly by managing;
- coaching – a personal and usually one-to-one approach to helping people develop their skills and levels of competence (coaching skills are dealt with in Chapter 52);
- mentoring – the process of using specially selected and trained individuals (mentors) to provide guidance, pragmatic advice and continuing support that will help the person or persons allocated to them to learn and develop (see also Chapter 52);
- action learning – a method of helping managers develop their talents by exposing them to real problems; they are required to analyse them, formulate recommendations and then take action;
- outdoor learning – getting teams of participants to carry out physical activities so that they can learn about how they act under pressure as team leaders or team members;
- the use of performance management processes to provide feedback and satisfy development needs; these would be competency-based in the sense that they would specify the competencies required and assess the degree to which individuals needed to develop those competencies;
- training by means of internal or external courses;
- structured self-development following a self-directed learning programme set out in a personal development plan and agreed as a learning contract with the manager or a management development adviser.

Informal approaches to management development

Informal approaches to management development make use of the learning experiences managers encounter during the course of their everyday work. Managers are learning every time they are confronted with an unusual problem, an unfamiliar task or a move to a different job. They then have to evolve new ways of dealing with the situation. They will learn if they reflect on what they did, in order to determine how and why it contributed to success or failure. This retrospective or reflective learning will be effective if managers can apply it successfully in the future.

Managers also learn from their managers. This may include how not to do things as well as what to do. Again, they will learn more if they have the capacity to reflect on what they have learnt and apply it to their own circumstances.

Experiential and reflective learning is potentially the most powerful form of learning. It comes naturally to some managers. They seem to absorb, unconsciously and by some process of osmosis, the lessons from their experience, although in fact they have probably developed a capacity for almost instantaneous analysis, which they store in their mental databank to retrieve when necessary.

But many managers either find it difficult to do this sort of analysis or do not recognize the need. This is where informal or at least semi-formal approaches can be used to encourage and help managers to learn more effectively. These comprise:

- emphasizing self-assessment and the identification of development needs by getting managers to assess their own performance against agreed objectives and analyse the factors that contributed to effective or less effective performance – this can be provided through performance management;
- getting managers to produce their own personal development plans – self-directed learning programmes;
- encouraging managers to discuss their problems and opportunities with their manager, colleagues or mentors to establish for themselves what they need to learn or be able to do;
- helping managers to understand their own learning styles so that they can make the best use of their experience and increase the effectiveness of their learning activities (this guidance may have to be provided more formally).

The role of the organization

The traditional view is that the organization need not concern itself with management development. The natural process of selection and the pressure of competition will ensure the survival of the fittest. Managers, in fact, are born not made. Cream rises to the top (but then so does scum). Management development has also been seen as a formal process using management inventories, multicoloured replacement charts, 'Cook's tours' around different departments for newly recruited graduates, detailed job rotation programmes, elaborate points schemes to appraise personal characteristics, and lots of formal courses operating on the 'sheep-dip' principle (ie everyone undergoes them).

The true role of the organization in management development lies somewhere between these two extremes: on the one hand, it is not enough, in conditions of rapid growth (when they exist) and change, to leave everything to chance – to trial and error; on the other hand, elaborate management development programmes cannot successfully be imposed on the organization. A mix of formal and informal methods is required that has to fit the organization's context and specific requirements.

The success of any management development programme depends upon the degree to which there is commitment to it at all levels of management. It is not a separate activity to be handed over to a specialist and forgotten or ignored. The development of subordinates must be recognized as a natural and essential part of any manager's job. But the lead must come from the top.

The role of the individual

As Drucker perceptively wrote many years ago (1955: 162): 'Development is always self-development. Nothing could be more absurd than for the enterprise to assume responsibility for the development of a man. The responsibility rests with the individual, his abilities, his efforts.' But he went on to say:

> Every manager in a business has the opportunity to encourage individual self-development or to stifle it, to direct it or to misdirect it. He should be specifically assigned the responsibility for helping all men working with him to focus, direct and apply their self-development efforts productively. And every company can provide systematic development challenges to its managers.
> (ibid: 163)

The ability to manage is eventually something individuals mainly develop for themselves while carrying out their normal duties. But they will do this much better if they are given encouragement, guidance and opportunities by their organization and their managers. In McGregor's (1960: 192) vivid phrase: managers are grown – they are neither born nor made: 'The individual will grow into what he is capable of becoming, providing we can create the proper conditions for that growth.'

The role of HR and learning and development specialists

However, HR and L&D specialists still have an important role to play. They interpret the needs of the business and advise on how management development as a business-led activity can play its part in meeting these needs. They encourage managers to carry out their developmental activities, providing guidance as required, and they act as coaches or mentors. They also, of course, conduct or manage formal learning events and programmes, but their most important role is to help in developing a climate in which managers can grow.

Criteria for leadership and management development

The effectiveness and value of any approach to management development include the extent to which it:

- links to organizational goals and context – and so has relevance for the organization as well as for individuals;
- builds on and develops the qualities, skills and attitudes of participants;
- is supported by appropriate HR policies to do with recruitment and selection, talent management, succession planning and reward;
- has the full commitment of those responsible for the operation of the process, including line managers;
- is motivating to those encouraged to participate in it.

Key learning points: Leadership and management development

Leadership and management development defined

Leadership and management development programmes ensure that managers have the leadership and managerial qualities required to achieve success.

Leadership

Leadership means inspiring people to do their best to achieve a desired result. It involves developing and communicating a vision for the future, motivating people and securing their engagement.

Management

Defined as deciding what to do and then getting it done through the effective use of resources.

Leadership development compared with management development

Leadership development tends to be concerned with nurturing the softer skills of leadership through various educational processes, including formal learning events and programmes and coaching.

Management development relies more on ensuring that managers have the right sequence of experience, which may be supplemented by self-directed learning and courses on management techniques. Further guidance may be provided by coaching and from mentors. Management development programmes traditionally also cover leadership skills.

Leadership development

Leadership development programmes prepare people for leadership roles and situations beyond their current experience.

Management development

Management development is concerned with improving the performance of managers in their present roles, preparing them to take on greater responsibilities in the future and also developing their leadership skills.

Formal approaches to management development consist of processes and events planned and provided by the organization. They include planned experience, coaching and mentoring, action learning, outdoor learning, performance management, formal training and structured self-development.

Informal approaches to management development make use of the learning experiences that managers encounter during the course of their everyday work.

Responsibility for management development

Individual managers are largely responsible for their own development but need guidance, support and encouragement from their own managers and the HR function.

Questions

1. What is the aim of leadership and management development?
2. What is leadership?
3. What is management?
4. What is the difference between leadership development and management development?
5. What is leadership development?
6. What are the main features of a leadership development programme?
7. What is management development?
8. What formal approaches can be adopted to management development?
9. What is action learning?
10. What informal approaches can be adopted to management development?

References

Baldwin, T T and Patgett, M Y (1994) Management development: a review and a commentary, in (eds) C L Cooper and J T Robertson, *Key Reviews in Management Development*, New York, Wiley

Bennis, W G (1989) *On Becoming a Leader*, New York, Addison Wesley

Birkinshaw, J (2010) An experiment in reinvention, *People Management*, 15 July, pp 22–24

Bolden, R (2010) Leadership, management and organizational development, in (eds) J Gold, R Thorpe and A Mumford, *Gower Handbook of Leadership and Management Development*, Gower, Farnham, pp 118–32

BurgoyneJ (2010) Crafting a leadership and management development strategy, in (eds) J Gold, R Thorpe and A Mumford, *Gower Handbook of Leadership and Management Development*, Farnham, Gower, pp 42–55

Dixon, N F (1994) *On the Psychology of Military Incompetence*, London, Pimlico

Drucker, P (1955) *The Practice of Management*, Oxford, Heinemann

Fiedler, F E (1967) *A Theory of Leadership Effectiveness*, New York, McGraw-Hill

Hersey, P and Blanchard, K H (1998) *Management of Organizational Behaviour*, Englewood Cliffs, NJ, Prentice Hall

Kotter, J P (1991) Power, dependence and effective management, in (ed) J Gabarro, *Managing People and Organizations*, Boston, MA, Harvard Business School Publications

McGregor, D (1960) *The Human Side of Enterprise*, New York, McGraw-Hill

Mintzberg, H (2004) Enough leadership, *Harvard Business Review*, November, p 22

Peters, K (2010) National and international developments in leadership and management development, in (eds) J Gold, R Thorpe and A Mumford, *Gower Handbook of Leadership and Management Development*, Gower, Farnham, pp 23–38

Spackman, T (2010) Crafting a leadership and management development strategy 2, in (eds) J Gold, R Thorpe and A Mumford, *Gower Handbook of Leadership and Management Development*, Gower, Farnham, pp 57–81

Tamkin, P, Hirsh, W and Tyers, C (2003) Chore to champion: the making of better people managers, *Report 389*, Brighton, Institute for Employment Studies

Tamkin, P, Pearson, G, Hirsh, W and Constable, S (2010) *Exceeding Expectation: The principles of outstanding leadership*, London, The Work Foundation

Yukl, G (2006) *Leadership in Organizations*, 6th edn, Upper Saddle River, NJ, Prentice-Hall

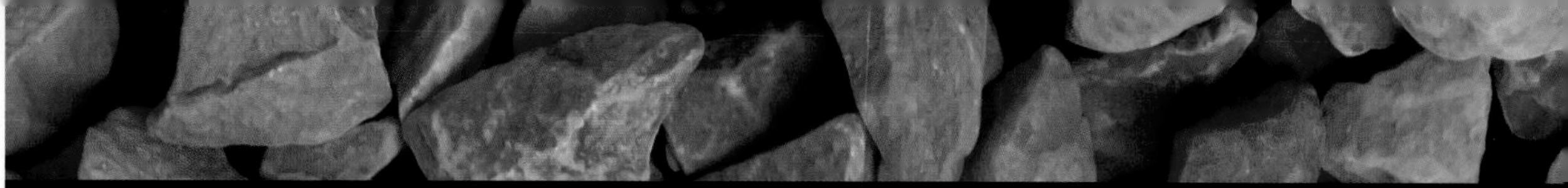

PART VI

Performance and reward

PART VI CONTENTS

Introduction

Performance is concerned with how well something is done and reward is with how people should be recognized for doing it. Performance management and reward management are closely associated topics that play an important part in achieving one of the key goals of HRM – to contribute to the development of a high-performance culture. This is understood by the CIPD, which in its profession map (2013) defines what an HR or reward professional needs to do about performance and reward as follows: 'Builds a high performance culture by delivering programmes that recognize and reward critical skills, capabilities, experience and performance and ensures that reward systems are market-based, equitable and cost-effective.'

The aim of this part is to explore the relationship between performance and reward and how in consort they contribute to the achievement of business goals. It is concerned with: 1) performance management, defined as a systematic process for improving individual, team and organizational performance; 2) reward management, defined as the processes of deciding how people should be rewarded and of ensuring that reward policies and practices are implemented.

Performance is defined as behaviour that accomplishes results. Performance management influences performance by helping people to understand what good performance means and by providing the information needed to improve it. Reward management influences performance by recognizing and rewarding good performance and by providing incentives to improve it.

The part covers: 1) a description of the process of performance management; 2) an analysis of reward management in terms of the basis of reward strategy (strategic reward) and a description of the constituents of a reward system; 3) an examination of the process of reward management, dealing with the main reward activities of job evaluation, market pricing, base pay management, contingent pay, employee benefits; 4) rewarding special groups (executives, knowledge workers, sales and customer service staff and manual workers).

Reference

CIPD (2013) HR Profession Map, http://www.cipd.co.uk/hr-profession-map-download.aspx [accessed 25 January 2013]

25 Performance management

KEY CONCEPTS AND TERMS

Objectives
Performance appraisal
Performance management
Personal development planning
360-degree feedback

LEARNING OUTCOMES

On completing this chapter you should be able to define these key concepts. You should also know about:

- The meaning of performance
- The theories underpinning performance management
- Principles of performance management
- The aims of performance management
- The performance management cycle
- Performance planning
- Managing performance throughout the year
- Reviewing performance
- Assessing performance
- Performance management issues
- The impact of performance management on performance
- Performance management and reward
- 360-degree feedback systems
- Introducing performance management

Introduction

As defined by Aguinis (2005: 2): 'Performance management is a continuous process of identifying, measuring and developing the performance of individuals and teams and aligning performance with the strategic goals of the organization.' Its five elements are agreement, measurement, feedback, positive reinforcement and dialogue.

Cappelli (2008: 196) wrote that: 'When employees fail in their jobs, part of the organization also fails.' Performance management aims to eliminate or at least significantly reduce this possibility. Pulakos (2009: 3) emphasized that: 'Performance management is the key process through which work gets done. It's how organizations communicate expectations and drive behaviour to achieve important goals; it's also about how organizations identify ineffective performers for development programmes or other personnel actions.'

The earliest mention of performance management in the literature was made by Warren (1972). Another early reference to performance management was made by Beer and Ruh (1976). Their thesis was that 'performance is best developed through practical challenges and experiences on the job with guidance and feedback from superiors'. Performance management developed out of merit rating, which originated in the early 20th century and was influenced by the scientific management movement. This was followed by performance appraisal and management by objectives. But it is said that the first known use of merit rating took place during the Wei dynasty (AD 221–265) when the emperor employed an 'imperial rater' whose task it was to evaluate the performance of officials.

Today, the term performance management as an overall description of a process of performance planning and review conducted by managers and individuals has largely replaced the term performance appraisal. The latter has often been relegated to a description of the performance assessment and rating aspect of performance management. Indeed, there are those, including the writers of this handbook, who prefer to avoid the use of the phrase performance appraisal altogether because of its connotations with the worst aspects of traditional merit rating, ie a top-down pronouncement by managers on what they think of their subordinates, which is used as an instrument for command and control. We prefer 'performance review', which signifies that performance management is a joint affair, based on dialogue and agreement.

As considered initially in this chapter, performance management is founded on an understanding of what the word 'performance' means and is underpinned by a number of behavioural theories. It is also based on a number of principles that have emerged from experience in operating it. The chapter continues with a definition of the aims of performance management and an examination of a conceptual model of performance management consisting of the plan-act-monitor-review cycle. The problems of making this concept work are then explored and the chapter ends with analyses of the impact of performance management on performance and reward, a description of a special type of performance management: 360-degree feedback, or multisource assessment, and notes for guidance on introducing performance management.

The basis of performance management

Performance management should be based on an understanding of what the word 'performance' means. Those concerned with introducing and operating performance management should be aware of the underpinning theories and the principles evolved by practitioners from their experience.

The meaning of performance

Performance is defined as behaviour that accomplishes results. As noted by Brumbach (1988: 387):

> Performance means both behaviours and results. Behaviours emanate from the performer and transform performance from abstraction to action. Not just the instruments for results, behaviours are also outcomes in their own right – the product of mental and physical effort applied to tasks – and can be judged apart from results.

Brumbach observed that because of the significance of behaviour there was more to success or failure than whether results were achieved: 'Success is not always positive nor failure always negative' (ibid: 388). This concept of performance leads to the conclusion that when assessing and rewarding the performance of individuals a number of factors have to be considered including both outputs (results) and inputs (behaviour).

Any attempt to manage performance should also bear in mind that it is a complicated notion. Campbell (1990) suggested that performance is the outcome of three determinants:

1. knowledge about facts and things (termed declarative knowledge);
2. knowledge about how things are done and the skills to do them (termed procedural knowledge and skills);
3. motivation to act, to expend effort and to persist (termed motivation).

Underpinning theories

The following three theories underpin performance management.

Goal theory

Goal theory, as developed by Latham and Locke (1979), highlights four mechanisms that connect goals to performance outcomes: 1) they direct attention to priorities; 2) they stimulate effort; 3) they challenge people to bring their knowledge and skills to bear to increase their chances of success; and 4) the more challenging the goal, the more people will draw on their full repertoire of skills. This theory supports the emphasis in performance management on setting and agreeing objectives against which performance can be measured and managed.

Control theory

Control theory focuses attention on feedback as a means of shaping behaviour. As people receive feedback on their behaviour they appreciate the discrepancy between what they are doing and what they are expected to do and take corrective action to overcome the discrepancy. Feedback is recognized as a crucial part of performance management processes.

Social cognitive theory

Social cognitive theory was developed by Bandura (1986). It is based on his central concept of self-efficacy. This suggests that what people believe they can or cannot do powerfully impacts on their performance. Developing and strengthening positive self-belief in employees is therefore an important performance management objective.

Principles of performance management

The research conducted by Armstrong and Baron (1998, 2004) identified the following 10 principles of performance management as stated by practitioners:

1. It's about how we manage people – it's not a system.
2. Performance management is what managers do: a natural process of management.
3. A management tool that helps managers to manage.
4. Driven by corporate purpose and values.
5. To obtain solutions that work.
6. Only interested in things you can do something about and get a visible improvement.
7. Focus on changing behaviour rather than paperwork.
8. Based on accepted principle but operates flexibly.
9. Focus on development not pay.
10. Success depends on what the organization is and needs to be in its performance culture.

Aims of performance management

Performance management is a means of getting better results by providing the means for individuals to perform well within an agreed framework of planned goals, standards and competency requirements. It involves developing a shared understanding about what is to be achieved and how it is to be achieved. The aim is to develop the capacity of people to meet and exceed expectations and to achieve their full potential to the benefit of themselves and the organization. A further aim is to clarify how individuals are expected to contribute to the achievement of organization goals by aligning individual objectives with the strategic objectives of the organization.

Performance management provides the basis for self-development but, importantly, it is also about ensuring that the support and guidance people need to develop and improve are readily available. Performance management can play an important role in rewarding employees by providing them with positive feedback and the recognition of their accomplishments.

Performance management is often seen as primarily a developmental process and may therefore be referred to as 'performance and development management'. It can also be used to generate ratings that inform performance pay decisions.

Shields (2007: 24) explained that a performance management system has a fourfold purpose:

1. Strategic communication – convey to people what doing a good job means and entails.
2. Relationship building – create stronger work relationships by bringing managers and those they manage together regularly to review performance achievements.
3. Employee development – provide performance feedback as a basis for the joint analysis of strengths, weaknesses and areas for improvement and an agreement on a personal development plan and learning contract.
4. Employee evaluation – assess the performance of employees (performance appraisal) as a basis for making decisions on job reassignment, promotion or performance-related reward.

Shields noted that: 'the relationship between the developmental and evaluative purposes is frequently a troubled one and maintaining a harmonious relationship between the two is undoubtedly one of the greatest challenges that awaits the unsuspecting human resource manager' (ibid: 25).

Respondents to an e-reward survey in 2005 identified the following performance management objectives:

- Align individual and organizational objectives – 64 per cent.
- Improve organizational performance – 63 per cent.
- Improve individual performance – 46 per cent.
- Provide the basis for personal development – 37 per cent.
- Develop a performance culture – 32 per cent.
- Inform contribution/performance pay decisions – 21 per cent.

Note the relatively small emphasis on pay.

The following is a statement of objectives from one respondent to the e-reward survey: 'To support culture change by creating a performance culture and reinforcing the values of the organization with an emphasis on the importance of these in getting a balance between "what" is delivered and "how" it is delivered.'

The performance management cycle

Performance management is a natural process of management: it is not an HRM technique or tool. As a natural process of management the performance management cycle, as modelled in Figure 25.1, corresponds with Deming's (1986) plan-do-check-act model.

The processes of performance planning, managing performance, performance reviews, performance assessment recording the agreement and review, and the use of web-enabled technology involved during the cycle are described below.

Performance planning

Performance planning is based on performance agreements. Expectations are defined generally in role profiles that specify key result areas; the knowledge, skills and abilities (KSAs) required and the behavioural competencies needed to perform well. What has to be accomplished in key result areas can be defined in the form of objectives or targets. An important aspect of performance planning is the process of aligning individual goals with the strategic goals of the organization.

The acronym 'SMART' is often used to define a good objective. Traditionally, S stands for specific (sometimes 'stretching'), M for measurable, A for agreed, R for realistic and T for time-related. But as Chamberlin (2011: 26) argued, 'the real aim of setting

FIGURE 25.1 The performance management cycle

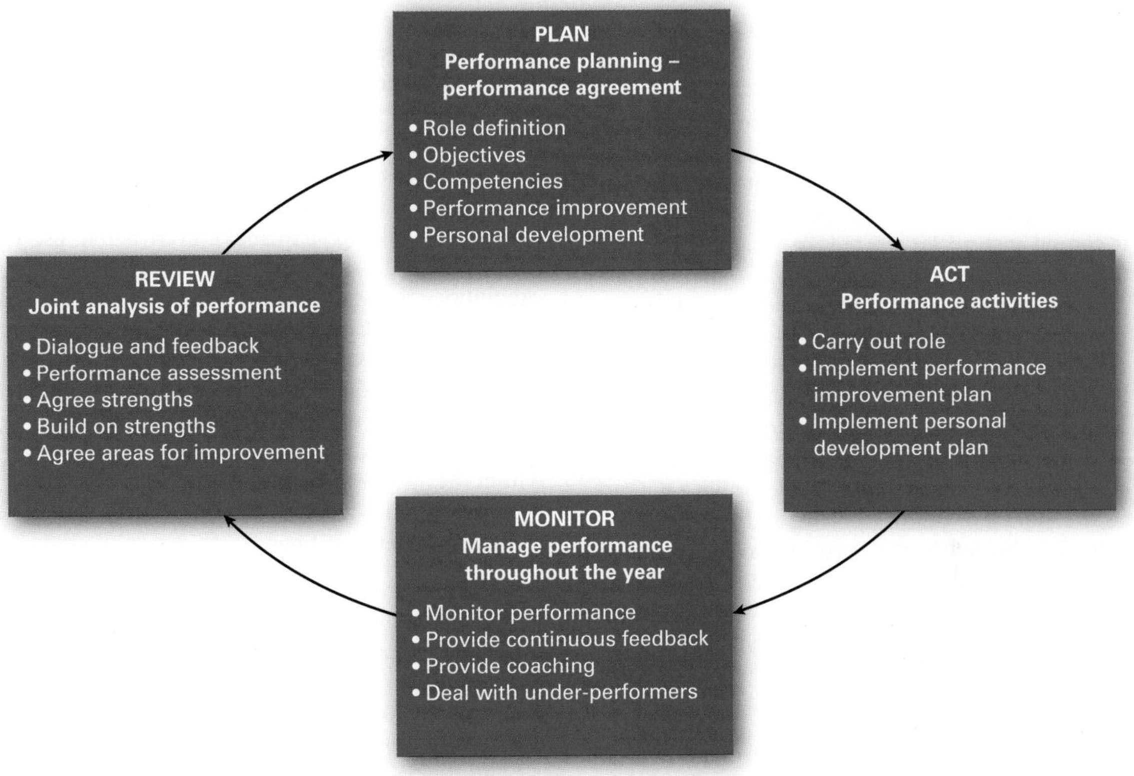

objectives is for people to know exactly what it is they have to do, when they've done it, that they are able to do it, why they have to do it (ie who for) and that it is something they should be doing, and how they are progressing along the way'. Following Blanchard (1989) he suggested that the last three letters of the mnemonic should be amended to read A for attainable, R for relevant and T for trackable. He attached particular importance first to 'relevant', meaning that the objective is to do with the business and its customers. Second, he emphasized 'trackable' because the important thing to do with objectives is to monitor progress over time, ie track it (he rejected 'time-related' because it did not convey this essential feature and was in any case covered already by 'specific').

Performance agreements emerge from the analysis of role requirements and the performance review. An assessment of past performance leads to an analysis of future requirements. The two processes can take place at the same meeting.

Agreement is reached at this stage on how performance will be measured and the evidence that will be used to establish levels of competency. It is important that these measures and evidence requirements should be identified and fully agreed now because they will be used by individuals as well as managers to demonstrate and monitor achievements. The manager and the individual also agree on what the latter needs to do to achieve objectives, raise standards and improve performance.

The agreement may incorporate a personal development plan that provides a learning action programme, which individuals are expected to follow with the support of their managers and the organization. It may include formal training but, more importantly, it will incorporate a wider set of learning and development activities such as self-managed learning, coaching, mentoring, project work and e-learning. If multisource assessment (360-degree feedback) is practised in the organization this will be used to discuss development needs.

Managing performance throughout the year

Perhaps one of the most important features of performance management is that it is a continuous process that reflects normal good management practices of setting direction, monitoring and measuring performance and taking action accordingly. Performance management should not be imposed on managers as something 'special' they have to do. It should instead be treated as a natural function that all good managers carry out.

This approach contrasts with that used in conventional performance appraisal systems, which were usually built around an annual event – the formal review – which tended to dwell on the past. This was carried out at the behest of the personnel department, often perfunctorily, and then forgotten. Managers proceeded to manage without any further reference to the outcome of the review, and the appraisal form was buried in the personnel records system. However, formal reviews that include assessments of performance, as described below, are essential parts of the performance management cycle.

The performance review

A performance review provides a focal point for the consideration of key performance and development issues. The performance review meeting is the means through which the five primary performance management elements of agreement, measurement, feedback, positive reinforcement and dialogue can be put to good use. It leads to the completion of the performance management cycle by informing performance agreements. It involves some form of assessment, as considered in the next section of this chapter.

The review should be rooted in the reality of the individual's performance. It is concrete, not abstract, and it allows managers and individuals to take a positive look together at how performance can become better in the future and how any problems in meeting performance standards and achieving objectives can be resolved. Individuals should be encouraged to assess their own performance and become active agents for change in improving their results. Managers should be encouraged to adopt their proper enabling role: coaching and providing support and guidance.

There should be no surprises in a formal review if performance issues have been dealt with as they should have been – as they arise during the year. Traditional performance appraisals were often no more than an analysis of where those involved are now, and where they have come from. This static and historical approach is not what performance management is about. The true role of performance management is to look forward to what needs to be done by people to achieve the purpose of the job; to meet new challenges; to make even better use of their knowledge, skills and abilities; to develop their capabilities by establishing a self-managed learning agenda; and to reach agreement on any areas where performance needs to be improved and how that improvement should take place. This process also helps managers to improve their ability to lead, guide and develop the individuals and teams for whom they are responsible.

There are 12 golden rules for conducting performance review meetings:

1. *Be prepared.* Managers should prepare by referring to a list of agreed objectives and their notes on performance throughout the year. They should form views about the reasons for success or failure and decide where to give praise, which performance problems should be mentioned and what steps might be undertaken to overcome them. Thought should also be given to any changes that have taken place or are contemplated in the individual's role, and to work and personal objectives for the next period. Individuals should also prepare in order to identify achievements and problems, and to be ready to assess their own performance at the meeting. They should also note any points they wish to raise about their work and prospects.
2. *Work to a clear structure.* The meeting should be planned to cover all the points identified during preparation. Sufficient time should be allowed for a full discussion – hurried meetings will be ineffective. An hour or two is usually necessary to get maximum value from the review.
3. *Create the right atmosphere.* A successful meeting depends on creating an informal environment in which a full, frank but friendly exchange of views can take place. It is best to start with a fairly general discussion before getting into any detail.

4 *Provide good feedback.* Individuals need to know how they are getting on. Feedback should be based on factual evidence. It refers to results, events, critical incidents and significant behaviours that have affected performance in specific ways. The feedback should be presented in a manner that enables individuals to recognize and accept its factual nature – it should be a description of what has happened, not a judgement. Positive feedback should be given on the things that the individual did well in addition to areas for improvement. People are more likely to work at improving their performance and developing their skills if they feel empowered by the process.

5 *Use time productively.* The reviewer should test understanding, obtain information, and seek proposals and support. Time should be allowed for the individual to express his or her views fully and to respond to any comments made by the manager. The meeting should take the form of a dialogue between two interested and involved parties, both of whom are seeking a positive conclusion.

6 *Use praise.* If possible, managers should begin with praise for some specific achievement, but this should be sincere and deserved. Praise helps people to relax – everyone needs encouragement and appreciation.

7 *Let individuals do most of the talking.* This enables them to get things off their chest and helps them to feel that they are getting a fair hearing. Use open-ended questions (ie questions that invite the individual to think about what to reply rather than indicating the expected answer). This is to encourage people to expand.

8 *Invite self-assessment.* This is to see how things look from the individual's point of view and to provide a basis for discussion – many people underestimate themselves.

9 *Discuss performance not personality.* Discussions on performance should be based on factual evidence, not opinion. Always refer to actual events or behaviour and to results compared with agreed performance measures. Individuals should be given plenty of scope to explain why something did or did not happen.

10 *Encourage analysis of performance.* Don't just hand out praise or blame. Analyse jointly and objectively why things went well or badly and what can be done to maintain a high standard or to avoid problems in the future.

11 *Don't deliver unexpected criticisms.* The discussion should only be concerned with events or behaviours that have been noted at the time they took place. Feedback on performance should be immediate; it should not wait until the end of the year. The purpose of the formal review is to reflect briefly on experiences during the review period and, on this basis, to look ahead.

12 *Agree measurable objectives and a plan of action.* The aim should be to end the review meeting on a positive note.

These golden rules may sound straightforward and obvious enough but they will only function properly in a culture that supports this type of approach. This emphasizes the importance of getting and keeping top management support and the need to take special care in developing and introducing the system and in training managers and their staff.

Performance assessment

Most performance management schemes include an assessment, which is usually carried out during or after a performance review meeting. This may be carried out by overall assessment, rating or visual assessment, as described below.

Overall assessment

An overall assessment is based on a general analysis of performance under the headings of the performance agreement. The aim is to reach agreement about future action rather than to produce a summarized and potentially superficial judgement. Managers are expected to reach an understanding with each member of their team as a result of the analysis, which will ensure that the latter will appreciate how well or not so well they are doing. The analysis should also identify the high-flyers and those who are failing to meet acceptable standards. An overall assessment is recorded in a narrative consisting of a written summary of views about the level of performance achieved. This at least ensures that managers have to collect their thoughts together and put them down on paper. But different people will consider different aspects of performance and there will be no consistency in the criteria used for assessment, so it is necessary to have a framework for the analysis. This could be provided on a 'what' and 'how' basis. The 'what' is the achievement of previously agreed objectives related to the headings on a role profile. The 'how' is behaviour in relating to competency framework headings. The results for each 'what' and 'how' heading could be recorded following a joint analysis during a review meeting.

One problem with this form of assessment, indeed any form of assessment, is that we can recognize people at either extreme (top performers and inadequate performers) but cannot accurately distinguish performance differences in the bulk of people lying between those extremes. What managers can do is to tell an individual that he or she has done exceptionally well and that they will therefore be included in the talent management programme, or managers can inform another individual that he or she has not done very well and that they must discuss what needs to be done about it. The others can be told that they are doing a perfectly good job and discussions can take place on how they can build on their strengths or on any learning activity (preferably self-directed) that might help them to do even better. Another problem with overall assessments is that they can be bland, superficial and overgeneralized. This is why many schemes use rating.

Rating

Rating summarizes on a scale the views of the rater on the level of performance achieved. A rating scale is supposed to assist in making judgements and it enables those judgements to be categorized to inform performance- or contribution-pay decisions, or simply to produce an instant summary for the record of how well or not so well someone is doing.

Rating scales can be defined alphabetically (a, b, c, etc), or numerically (1, 2, 3, etc). Initials (ex for excellent, etc) are sometimes used in an attempt to disguise the hierarchical nature of the scale. The alphabetical or numerical points scale may be described adjectivally, for example, a = excellent, b = good, c = satisfactory and d = unsatisfactory. Alternatively, scale levels may be described verbally, as in the following example:

- Exceptional performance: exceeds expectations and consistently makes an outstanding contribution that significantly extends the impact and influence of the role.
- Well-balanced performance: meets objectives and requirements of the role, consistently performs in a thoroughly proficient manner.
- Barely effective performance: does not meet all objectives or role requirements of the role; significant performance improvements are needed.
- Unacceptable performance: fails to meet most objectives or requirements of the role; shows a lack of commitment to performance improvement or a lack of ability, which has been discussed prior to the performance review.

The e-reward 2005 survey of performance management found that overall ratings were used by 70 per cent of respondents. The most popular number of levels was five (43 per cent of respondents). However, some organizations settled for three levels. There is no evidence that any single approach is clearly superior to another, although the greater the number of levels the more is being asked of managers in the shape of discriminatory judgement. It is, however, preferable for level definitions to be positive rather than negative and for them to provide as much guidance as possible on the choice of ratings. It is equally important to ensure that level definitions are compatible with the culture of the organization and that close attention is given to ensuring that managers use them as consistently as possible.

The main problem with ratings is that they are largely subjective and it is difficult to achieve consistency between the ratings given by different managers. Because the notion of 'performance' is often unclear, subjectivity can increase. Even if objectivity is achieved, to sum up the total performance of a person with a single rating is a gross oversimplification of what may be a complex set of factors influencing that performance. To do this after a detailed discussion of strengths and weaknesses suggests that the rating will be a superficial and arbitrary judgement. To label people as 'average' or 'below average', or whatever equivalent terms are used, is both demeaning and demotivating.

The whole performance review session may be dominated by the fact that it will end with a rating, thus severely limiting the forward-looking and developmental focus of the meeting, which is all important. This is particularly the case if the rating governs performance- or contribution-pay increases.

Another problem is that managers may inflate ratings to avoid confrontation with the individuals concerned. Some organizations (8 per cent of the respondents to the performance management survey conducted by Armstrong and Baron (2004)) attempted to counter this by using forced distribution, which requires conforming to a laid down distribution of ratings between different levels, for example: A = 5 per cent, B = 15 per cent, C = 60 per cent, D = 15 per cent and E = 5 per cent. This achieves consistency of a sort but managers and staff rightly resent being forced into this sort of straitjacket.

An alternative to forced distribution is forced ranking. It is most common in the United States where the outcome is sometimes known as a 'vitality curve'. Managers are required to place their staff in order from best to worst. The problem with forced ranking, as with forced distribution, is that the notion of performance may not be defined and is therefore not measurable. In the case of ranking it is therefore unclear what the resulting order of employees truly represents.

Some organizations, mainly in the United States, have gone as far as adopting the practice of annually terminating the employment of 5 to 10 per cent of the consistently lowest performers. This is referred to colloquially as 'rank and hank'. It is claimed that this practice 'raises the bar', ie it is said that it improves the overall level of performance in the business. There is no evidence that this is the case.

Visual assessment

Visual assessment is an alternative to rating. This takes the form of an agreement between the manager and the individual on where the latter should be placed on a matrix or grid, as illustrated in Figure 25.2. The vertical axis of the grid in this example assesses the behavioural style adopted by the individual in carrying out the role, ie inputs. The elements of behaviour to be assessed would be defined in a competency framework and this would be amplified in schedules of what would be regarded as acceptable or unacceptable behaviour for each area of competency. The horizontal axis measures the level of business performance, ie outputs or what the individual delivers. The assessment can place someone anywhere in one of the four quadrants according to behavioural style and delivery. Examples of possible actions are provided. A picture is thus provided of the individual's overall contribution, which is presented visually and as such provides a better basis for analysis and discussion than a mechanistic rating.

Recording the performance agreement and review

The performance agreement and outcomes of a review can be recorded on a performance management form. This should serve as a working document. It should be regularly used by managers and individuals as a reference document on objectives and plans when reviewing progress. It is a means of recording agreements on performance achievements and actions to be taken to improve performance or develop competence and skills. It should be dog-eared from much use – it should not be condemned to moulder away in a file. Examples of forms are given in Figures 25.3a and 25.3b.

Web-enabled performance management

Web-enabled or online performance management makes it easier for managers and employees to record role profiles and performance agreements, monitor progress against the plans, access performance documents, and gather multisource (360-degree appraisal) comments. All this data can be used to assist in performance reviews and record further agreements emerging from the reviews. The aim is to reduce paperwork and simplify the process.

Performance management issues

The many-faceted nature of performance was commented on as follows by Cascio (2010: 334): 'It is an exercise in observation and judgement, it is a feedback process, it is an organizational intervention. It is a measurement process as well as an intensely

FIGURE 25.2 Visual performance assessment matrix

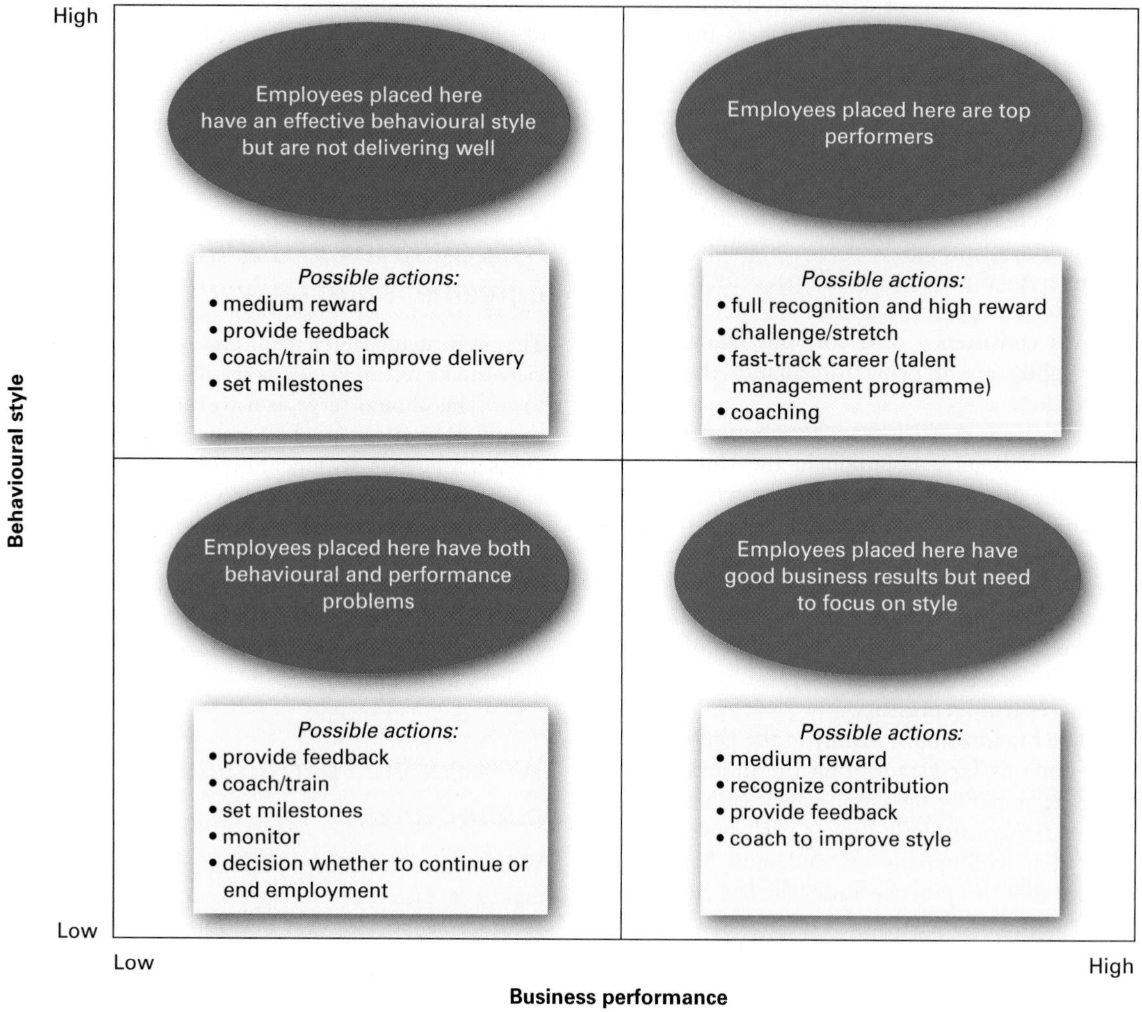

emotional process. Above all, it is an inexact, human process.'

As a human process, performance management can promise more than it achieves. Some years ago Keith Grint (1993: 62), referring to performance appraisal, asserted, famously, that: 'Rarely in the history of business can such a system have promised so much and delivered so little.' More recently, Shields (2007: 6) argued that: 'Ill-chosen, badly designed or poorly implemented performance management schemes can communicate entirely the wrong messages as to what the organization expects from its employees.' Coens and Jenkins (2002: 1) delivered the following judgement:

> Throughout our work lives, most of us have struggled with performance appraisal. No matter how many times we redesign it, retrain the supervisors, or give it a new name, it never comes out right. Again and again, we see supervisors procrastinate or just go through the motions, with little taken to heart. And the supervisors who do take it to heart and give it their best mostly meet disappointment.

Performance management can be modelled convincingly as a system (see above) but the acts or failures to act of fallible human beings prejudice the effectiveness of the system in practice. Duncan Brown (2010) commented that:

FIGURE 25.3a Performance management form (part 1)

PERFORMANCE AGREEMENT AND PERSONAL DEVELOPMENT PLAN	
Name:	Forename(s):
Job title:	Department:
Reviewer's name:	Job title:

PERFORMANCE AGREEMENT	
Objectives	Performance measures
Competencies	Agreed actions

PERSONAL DEVELOPMENT PLAN			
Development need	How it is to be met	Action by whom	Target completion date

FIGURE 25.3b Performance management form (part 2)

PERFORMANCE REVIEW	
Objectives	Achievements
Competencies	Actions taken
Development needs	Actions taken
Comments by reviewer: Signed:	 Date:
Comments by person reviewed: Signed:	 Date:

> The problems [of performance management] are... not of ambition or intent, but rather practice and delivery. Low rates of coverage and even more frequently low quality conversations and non-existent follow-up are commonplace, in the wake of uncommitted directors, incompetent line managers, uncomprehending employees and hectoring HR with their still complex and bureaucratic HR processes.

On the basis of research conducted in 2011 by the Institute for Employment Studies, Brown also observed that: 'The main areas of concern [about performance management] were the skills and attitudes of reviewing managers, the consistency and quality of approach across large organizations, the complexity of the paperwork and the value of outputs... Performance management, it appears, isn't working' (2011: 16).

A survey by WorldatWork and Sibson (2010) established that the top three performance management challenges reported by respondents were: 1) managers lack courage to have difficult performance discussions (63 per cent); 2) performance management is viewed as an 'HR process' instead of as a 'business critical process' (47 per cent); and 3) that they experienced poor goal setting (36 per cent).

However well-designed a performance management system is, its effectiveness mainly depends on the commitment and skills of line managers. Postuma and Campion (2008: 47) remarked that:

> One of the most dreaded tasks managers face is meeting with employees to discuss their job performance. These meetings present a dilemma for managers. On one hand, managers need to give constructive criticism so that employees can improve their performance. On the other hand, managers do not like to give negative feedback because of the bad feelings that often result. It is not surprising, then, that managers avoid giving accurate evaluations, give overly generous evaluations or avoid the process altogether.

They also noted that: 'Too much attention has been placed on the design of a [performance management] system and not enough on how it works when implemented' (ibid: 50).

The e-reward 2005 survey of performance management established that the top four issues concerning respondents about their performance management processes were:

1. Line managers do not have the skills required – 88 per cent.
2. Line managers do not discriminate sufficiently when assessing performance – 84 per cent.
3. Line managers are not committed to performance management – 75 per cent.
4. Line managers are reluctant to conduct performance management reviews – 74 per cent.

When asked how they coped with these problems, respondents to the e-reward survey emphasized the importance of doing the following:

- Involve line managers in the development and introduction of performance management.
- Train and coach line managers – existing managers and, importantly, potential and newly appointed managers.
- Get top management to stress the importance they attach to performance management – by example as well as exhortation.
- Keep it simple – do not impose a bureaucratic system.
- Emphasize whenever possible that performance management is a normal process of management and that one of the criteria for assessing the performance of managers is how well they do it.
- Do whatever can be done to persuade line managers that formal performance reviews need not be stressful occasions if they are conducted properly, but that they can in fact provide 'quality time' for the two parties to engage in a dialogue about performance and development opportunities (eliminating formal ratings helps).

The impact of performance management on performance

Performance management is expected to improve organizational performance generally by creating a performance culture in which the achievement of high performance is a way of life. More specifically, effective performance management ensures that individual goals are aligned with organizational goals, so that key performance indicators for employees are linked to those of the organization, and the contribution people can make to organizational performance is therefore defined.

A description of what performance management should contribute was defined by Jones *et al* (1995) as follows:

- communicate a shared vision throughout the organization to help to establish and support appropriate leadership and management styles;
- define individual requirements and expectation of all employees in terms of the inputs and outputs expected from them thus reducing confusion and ambiguity;
- provide a framework and environment for teams to develop and succeed;
- provide the climate and systems which support reward and communicate how people and the organization can achieve improved performance;
- help people manage ambiguity.

It is assumed that managers and their team members working together on a continuing basis throughout the year to use performance management processes such as goal setting, feedback, performance analysis and coaching will create a situation in which continuous improvement in results will be guaranteed. This could be regarded as an unrealistic aspiration – an optimistic belief – but it is the one that underpins the concept of performance management. The holy grail of performance management is to provide evidence that this belief is justified. But it isn't easy – for the reasons given below.

Establishing the impact

Establishing the impact between human resource management (HRM) practices – including performance management – and firm performance is problematic. This is because causality – determining the link between independent and dependent variables (cause and effect) – is a major issue in research, especially in the HRM field. Correlation does not imply causation. It may be relatively easy to establish correlations in the shape of a demonstration that X is associated with Y; it is much more difficult and sometimes impossible to prove that X causes Y.

Evidence from research

Research projects and other analytical studies that deal with the impact of performance management on overall firm performance, or as aspects of individual performance, are summarized below.

Latham and Locke

As reported by Latham and Locke (1979) field research in a logging company involving 292 supervisors established that those who set specific production goals achieved the highest productivity. A further study of 892 supervisors produced the same result.

Another study in a logging company involved setting a difficult but attainable target for loading trucks. Loggers were told that they would receive no reward for achieving the target but that no one would be criticized for failing to do so. After the third month performance exceeded 90 per cent of the trucks' capacity compared with 58–63 per cent previously. This level has been sustained for the seven years to date.

An analysis of 10 field studies conducted by various researchers for a range of jobs showed that the percentage change in performance after goal setting ranged from 11 per cent to 27 per cent (median 16 per cent).

McDonald and Smith

Research was conducted by McDonald and Smith (1991) covering 437 publicly quoted US companies. The findings were that the 205 respondents with performance management as opposed to the others without had:

- higher profits, better cash flows, stronger stock market performance and higher stock value;
- significant gains over three years in financial performance and productivity;
- higher sales growth per employee;
- lower real growth in number of employees.

The researchers commented that: 'In the successful companies the difference in managing employee performance seems to be that it is regarded as a mainstream business issue, not an isolated "personnel problem".'

This is a classic case of reversed causality. Performance management systems may have generated successful companies but it is just as likely that the successful companies were the ones with the inclination and money to introduce sophisticated practices such as performance management.

Institute of Personnel Management

It was reported by the IPM in 1992 that their extensive research found no evidence that improved performance in the private sector is associated with the pursuit of formal performance management programmes. Poor financial performers were as likely to introduce performance management as good performers. There was no readily available and comparable measures of performance in the public sector to test this link, even through performance management is more likely to be adopted in the public sector.

However, one positive theme that was traced throughout the research was the extent to which performance management raised awareness of the pressures on the organization to perform.

Rodgers and Hunter

A meta-analysis by Rodgers and Hunter (1991) of 70 studies in goal setting, participation in decision-making and objective feedback (as included in typical management-by-objectives programmes) found that 69 of them showed productivity gains and only two showed productivity losses. This led to the conclusion that management by objectives programmes when properly implemented and when supported by top management had an almost universal positive effect on productivity.

Bernadin, Hagan and Kane

Bernardin *et al* (1995) found improvement in subordinate and peer ratings following 360-degree feedback, but no changes in customer ratings or sales volume.

Guest and Conway

An analysis by Guest and Conway (1998) covered the 388 organizations with performance management surveyed by Armstrong and Baron in 1998. The key criteria used for determining the effectiveness of performance management were the achievement of financial targets, development of skills, development of competence, improved customer care and improved quality. Against these criteria, over 90 per cent of respondents rated performance management as being moderately or highly effective. The personnel managers, who in the main responded to the survey, believed that others, and more particularly senior managers, are even more positive in their evaluation. Many also believe that the overall performance of their organization, judged by internal criteria such as quality, productivity and cost, and external criteria such as market share and profitability, are at least as good and are often better than that of their main competitors.

But there were caveats. The analysis indicated that the views of respondents to the survey should all be viewed with extreme caution since they are often based on a very limited form of formal evaluation, or on an absence of any formal evaluation. This raises serious questions about the basis for the generally positive assessment of performance management.

Further, more detailed statistical analysis of the replies to the questionnaire failed to demonstrate consistent evidence of any link between the practice of performance management and outcomes such as the achievement of financial targets, achievement of quality and customer service goals and employee development goals. The conclusion reached was that this survey has produced no convincing evidence that performance management has an impact on overall organizational performance.

Gallup

As reported by Risher (2005) Gallup has analysed its Q 12 survey and found that employers with a formal performance review process have more engaged employees – 33 per cent versus 21 per cent – and fewer disengaged employees – 12 per cent versus 29 per cent.

Sibson and WorldatWork

As reported by Kochanski (2007) a survey by Sibson and WorldatWork found that high performing firms have strong leadership support for performance management. An analysis of total return to shareholders over a three-year period (2003–05) revealed that 64 per cent of the top performing companies had performance management systems that were rated as effective, compared to only 36 per cent of the bottom performing companies. The companies that excelled at performance management: 1) used their systems as the primary way to manage individual performance throughout the company; 2) have strong leadership support; and 3) have more line champions.

Watson Wyatt

As cited by Pulakos *et al* (2008) a recent Watson Wyatt survey found that only 30 per cent of workers felt that their performance management system helped to improve performance. Less than 40 per cent said that the system established clear performance goals or generated honest feedback.

Conclusions

The results of these studies are mixed. But it is still possible to believe in the benefits of performance management to organizations on the assumption that people are more likely to respond positively and are more likely to work to improve their performance and develop their capabilities if they share in the processes of defining expectations and reviewing performance and competency against those expectations, and are involved in creating and implementing plans for developing their skills and competences. If this happens generally (admittedly, often a big if), and if the organization provides the managerial and systems support necessary, than the presumption that this will contribute to overall performance improvement is not unreasonable, even if it cannot be proved.

Performance management as a rewarding process

Performance management, if carried out properly, can reward people by recognition through feedback, the provision of opportunities to achieve, the scope to develop skills, and guidance on career paths. All these are non-financial rewards that can encourage job and organizational engagement and make a longer-lasting and more powerful impact than financial rewards such as performance-related pay.

Performance management is, of course, also associated with pay by generating the information required to decide on pay increases or bonuses related to performance, competency or contribution. In some organizations this is its main purpose, but performance management is, or should be, much more about developing people and rewarding them in the broadest sense.

360-degree feedback

Also known as multisource feedback, 360-degree is assessed and feedback is given by a number of people who may include their manager, subordinates, colleagues and customers. Assessments take the form of ratings against various performance dimensions. The term '360-degree feedback' is sometimes used loosely to describe upward feedback where this is given by subordinates to their managers. This is the most common approach and is more properly described as 180-degree feedback. Feedback may be presented direct to individuals, or to their managers, or both. Expert counselling and coaching for individuals as a result of the feedback may be provided by a member of the HR department or an outside consultant. The 360-degree feedback or a variant of it was used by 30 per cent of the respondents to the 2005 e-reward survey.

Data from questionnaires forms the basis of 360-degree feedback, which measure from different perspectives the behaviours of individuals against a list of competencies. In effect, they ask for an evaluation: 'How well does... do...?' The competency model may be one developed within the organization or the competency headings may be provided by the supplier of a questionnaire. A typical questionnaire may cover aspects of performance such as leadership, teamwork, communication, organizational skills, decisiveness, drive and adaptability. Questionnaires are normally processed with the help of software developed within the organization or, most commonly, provided by external suppliers.

Feedback is presented to individuals, often anonymously but sometimes by their manager. If the purpose of the system is primarily developmental, as is most frequently the case, the action may be left to individuals as part of their personal development plans, but the planning process may be shared between individuals and their managers if they both have access to the information. Even if the data only goes to the individual it can be discussed in a performance review meeting so that joint plans can be made, and there is much to be said for adopting this approach.

The disadvantages can all be minimized if not avoided completely by careful design, communication, training and follow-up. But it is still possible to argue, as did Grint (1995: 68–69), that 360-degree feedback 'merely replaces single-assessor subjectivity with multi-assessor subjectivity'.

Introducing performance management

The programme for introducing performance management should take into account that one of the main reasons why it fails is that either line managers are not interested, or they don't have the skills, or both. It is important to get buy-in from top management so that their leadership can encourage line managers to play their part. Line managers should be involved in planning the scheme and its implementation. They have to be convinced that the time they spend will pay off in terms of improved performance. To encourage buy-in, the process has to be simple (not too much paper). The demanding skills of concluding performance agreements, setting objectives, assessing performance, giving feedback and coaching need to be developed by formal training, supplemented by coaching and the use of mentors.

Excellent practical advice on introducing performance management or making substantial changes to an existing scheme was given by the respondents to the e-Reward 2005 survey. Comments in the form of dos and don'ts are set out in Figure 25.4 in the order of frequency with which they were mentioned.

FIGURE 25.4 Introducing performance management: dos and don'ts

Do	*Don't*
• consult/involve; • provide training; • communicate (process and benefits); • get buy-in from senior management; • align and ensure relevance to organizational/business/stakeholder needs; • keep it simple; • get ownership from line managers; • ensure clear purpose and processes; • monitor and evaluate; • align to culture; • plan and prepare carefully; • align with other HR processes; • run a pilot scheme; • clarify link to reward; • treat as a business process; • be realistic about the scale and pace of change; • define performance expectations.	• just make it a form-filling, paper-intensive exercise; • make it too complicated; • rush in a new system; • underestimate the time it takes to introduce; • keep changing the system; • assume managers have the skills required; • link to pay; • blindly follow others; • neglect communication, consultation and training; • assume that everyone wants it.

Requirements for success

Research by Haines and St-Onge (2012) established that performance management is more likely to be successful when:

- there is more performance management training for managers covering performance coaching and constructive feedback;
- employee recognition is emphasized;
- the corporate culture values engagement;
- performance management is strategically integrated with human resource management and the business plans of the organization;
- human capital is valued;
- there is a positive employee relations climate.

To which could be added two further points. First, the comment made by Lawler and McDermott (2003: 55) that:

> Managers at all levels in a hierarchy can play an important role in the operation of the performance management system. If the performance management system is going to be tied into the business strategy, it is critical that senior management take a role and make the tie between business strategy and the performance management system. The behaviour of management is also an indication of how important the performance management system is and as a result is likely to have a strong influence on how the system is actually executed.

Secondly, performance management systems are more likely to be successful when the culture of the organization is performance-oriented.

CASE STUDIES

Performance management at CEMEX UK

CEMEX UK is a supplier of cement, ready-mixed concrete and aggregates, with 4,000 employees. It is a subsidiary of the Mexican company CEMEX.

Aims

The aims of the Performance and Potential Assessment scheme at CEMEX UK are to:

- promote strategic alignment and respond to business needs;
- facilitate clear communication and understanding of standards;
- ensure objective grading and differentiation of potential levels;
- promote continuous feedback and development;
- reinforce high-performance attitudes.

The annual cycle

Cemex's performance management scheme runs over the calendar year as follows:

1. The company's overall budget is set in January and from this the most senior managers' objectives are established, which are then cascaded down the organization.
2. Around July, there is a mid-year review of initial objectives set and discussions on how the individual is progressing over the first part of the year.
3. Finally, between November and January an ultimate meeting takes place where line managers and individuals meet and staff are rated between one and five by their line managers.

Performance management at DHL

DHL is a global market leader in the international express and logistics industry, with 45,000 staff in Europe.

DHL's annual performance management process begins in August when the bonus framework and core elements of the scheme are designed at the top level. Following this, in mid-November, based on the aims decided upon in August, targets are set for the year by a panel of senior staff. Once devised, these targets are cascaded down the organization into individual personal objectives following discussions between line managers and HR.

The cascading process is designed to ensure that targets are refined and altered to align with each individual's actual job. Further discussions then take place to decide what each target means for employees in practice and their implications for competencies. Around the same time, attainment levels and scoring based on the previous year's performance take place to determine bonus levels and salary rises. Following this, with targets already set, around the middle of January an outline for recording performance targets for personal and financial performance for the coming year is designed, and in mid-February the company's financial results become known. This makes it possible to determine the pot available for bonus payments and salary increases relating to the previous year. Bonuses are paid in either March or April, while salary reviews take place in April.

The initial stage of establishing overall objectives and the target-setting framework sets the tone for the year. From year to year, conditions change, with the priorities of senior management reflecting the current state of affairs. As a result, each year there are a number of overarching themes such as serving customers, for example, or health and safety. These core individual key objectives (IKOs) are strictly adhered to, although local managers can determine themselves how to manage their attainment. In contrast, more flexibility exists for other objectives, with managers at lower levels able to alter them to align with their particular needs. There is further flexibility in the system with regard to its timing.

Performance management tools

To ensure the smooth running of the system, managers and staff alike are provided with a number of tools to help them during the performance management process. These include:

- A performance evaluation template: this template enables the appropriate competency model to be reviewed and evaluated.
- An objective agreement template: this template is located within the performance evaluation template and is used to capture both performance and personal objectives.
- Competency models: available as support tools for personal development planning.
- Technical competencies: these represent a support framework for identifying core technical competencies for key operational roles.
- Development guides: guidelines for use in the support of developing a personal development plan.
- Personal development plan (PDP): a template for assessing an individual against management competencies and developing actions for them to progress their career.
- Career ladder: a guide to support the development of a personal development plan.
- Passport of success: a small booklet retained by the individual (non-management) that identifies completed training.
- Site succession plan: a plan developed utilizing information from the performance review and PDP process.

The annual face-to-face meeting

A key element of the performance management cycle is the face-to-face meeting between line managers and each member of their teams. For operational employees (non-management) the company recommends that, as a minimum, this should be a discussion of around 30 minutes, while for managers a one-hour meeting is suggested. During the meeting, the managers and their direct reports examine performance over the last 12 months with reference to the previous year's objectives. Discussions cover what was achieved, whether support provided was sufficient and, if relevant, what could have been done differently for a more effective result.

Following this they agree performance objectives for the coming year, along with any support in the form of training and development that can be offered. Objectives are documented in a 'target agreement form', information on levels of attainment captured on the 'performance evaluation tool', while training and support needs are recorded in the 'performance development plan'. In addition, as mentioned, further support tools used include competency models, development guides, technical competencies and career ladders.

Unlike performance objectives, development objectives are primarily the individual's responsibility to identify, with support provided by managers via the supply of appropriate resources and by contributing objectivity in discussions on staff potential. In some circumstances, DHL guidance says that it may be appropriate to develop a full performance development action plan, while in others this may not be necessary. In either case, though, the tools mentioned above are available to assist. DHL says it is committed to personal development planning because it supports the growth of individuals across the organization, stating that 'growing its people develops talent to meet the organization's future management and leadership requirements'. Further, it is a 'motivator for the individual and allows development priorities to be clearly identified, creating opportunities to fully achieve their potential'.

Competencies

Closely linked to objectives, competencies play an important part throughout DHL's performance management process. In addition to the management of performance, they are used for recruitment, selection, induction and job sizing and feed into decisions on pay increases. There are different competencies for different roles.

Progress meetings

In addition to the main performance management meetings, managers are advised to arrange progress meetings throughout the year. The number will depend on the individual in question, but the company suggests that there should be at least one every 12 months. In this meeting, discussions cover how attainment against objectives and competencies is progressing, whether training and development support aligns with expectations and whether additional support can be provided. Moreover, in some cases, certain senior employees are consulted on their own aspirations, and questions are asked such as whether they want to move upwards or into a different role, or perhaps to change location.

Performance measurement/scoring

At the end of the year in the subsequent annual meeting the process begins again, while at the same time, ratings for the last 12 months are given based on performance against objectives and the individual's competencies. To aid in the evaluation process, the 'performance evaluation tool' is used, which includes a competency and development needs assessment. Using this, progress against last year's performance evaluation is discussed, particularly drawing on successes during the year. Individual achievement is based on a combination of two ratings. First, there is a measure of achievement against personal objectives – also known as personal targets or individual key objectives (IKOs). This concentrates on what is achieved, as distinct from a second rating that examines *how* things are achieved, drawing on competencies. While there is no particular formula, both ratings are taken into account when making decisions on pay, bonuses and career progression. Under the first measure, target achievement level is linked to IKOs and scores are on a scale of 0 to 133.33 per cent. On-target performance gives a score of 100 per cent. Competency ratings are on a scale of 1 to 5 where 5 is exceptional and 1 unsatisfactory, as follows:

1. *Far exceeds*: consistently demonstrating the competency behaviours effectively, role model.
2. *Exceeds*: demonstrates the competency behaviours beyond what is expected.
3. *Fully meets*: behaviours fully correspond with what is expected in the current role.
4. *Partially meets*: demonstrates minor deficiencies (coachable) in behaviour.
5. *Does not meet*: does not demonstrate behaviours expected in the current role.

When it comes to decisions on salary increases, ratings are moderated by employees' positions in their pay bands, local budget constraints and the market. Ratings are used to determine bonus levels and they also tie in to decisions on promotion and succession planning.

Succession planning

Following the evaluation and rating stage, the line manager's immediate superior reviews the results and, in the light of them, considers, among other things, succession and career planning. By using the overall results, senior managers can determine where there are skills gaps or other deficiencies. In addition, it enables them to take a closer look at individual employees to consider whether they might be more suited to be employed elsewhere in the organization. Similarly, managers can examine strengths and weaknesses, which might flag up a shortage of certain abilities, such as commercial acumen, for example. Such issues can therefore be addressed and recruitment can be directed appropriately. Moreover, it also helps when employees leave the organization, making it simple to determine the corresponding skills and behaviours that go from the organization with that individual. To aid with this task, managers are also able to draw on an additional rating for certain senior staff, termed 'potential for job'. This gauges potential for the future and helps by feeding into future decisions on promotion and succession planning.

Key learning points: Performance management

Performance management defined

Performance management is a systematic process for improving organizational performance by developing the performance of individuals and teams.

The meaning of performance

Performance is defined as behaviour that accomplishes results.

Underpinning theories

- goal theory;
- control theory;
- social cognitive theory.

Aims of performance management

Performance management is a means of getting better results by providing the means for individuals to perform well within an agreed framework of planned goals, standards and competency requirements.

The performance management cycle

The key processes involved during the cycle are concluding performance and development agreements, performance planning, personal development planning, managing performance throughout the year, conducting performance reviews and assessing performance.

Performance management issues

As a human process, performance management can promise more than it achieves. However well designed a performance management system is, its effectiveness mainly depends on the commitment and skills of line managers.

Impact of performance management

Performance management is expected to improve organizational performance, generally by creating a performance culture in which the achievement of high performance is a way of life.

The results of research studies on the impact of performance management are mixed. But it is still possible to believe in the benefits of performance management to organizations on the assumption that people are more likely to respond positively and are more likely to work to improve their performance and develop their capabilities if they share in the processes of defining expectations and reviewing performance and competency against those expectations, and are involved in creating and implementing plans for developing their skills and competences.

Performance management and reward

Performance management, if carried out properly, can reward people by recognition through feedback, the provision of opportunities to achieve, the scope to develop skills, and guidance on career paths.

360-degree feedback

360-degree feedback, also known as multisource feedback, is a process in which someone's performance is assessed and feedback is given by a number of people who may include their manager, subordinates, colleagues and customers.

Introducing performance management

The programme for introducing performance management should take into account that one of the main reasons why it fails is that either line managers are not interested, or they don't have the skills, or both.

The demanding skills of concluding performance agreements, setting objectives, assessing performance, giving feedback and coaching need to be developed by formal training supplemented by coaching and the use of mentors.

Requirements for success

- More performance management training;
- emphasis on employee recognition;
- the corporate culture emphasizes the importance of performance and values engagement;
- performance management is strategically integrated with human resource management and the business plans of the organization;
- a positive employee relations climate.

Questions

1 What are the primary elements of performance management?

2 What are the key processes in the performance management cycle?

3 What are the key issues in performance management?

4 What is 360-degree feedback?

References

Aguinis, H (2005) *Performance Management*, Upper Saddle River NJ, Pearson Education

Armstrong, M and Baron, A (1998) *Performance Management: The new realities*, London, CIPD

Armstrong, M and Baron, A (2004) *Managing Performance: Performance management in action*, London, CIPD

Bandura, A (1977) *Social Learning Theory*, Englewood Cliffs, NJ, Prentice-Hall

Bandura, A (1986) *Social Boundaries of Thought and Action*, Englewood Cliffs, NJ, Prentice-Hall

Beer, M and Ruh, R A (1976) Employee growth through performance management, *Harvard Business Review*, July–August, pp 59–66

Bernadin, H K, Kane, J S, Ross, S, Spina, J D and Johnson, D L (1995) Performance appraisal design, development and implementation, in (eds) G R Ferris, S D Rosen, and D J Barnum, *Handbook of Human Resource Management*, Cambridge, MA Blackwell

Blanchard, K H (1989) *The One Minute Manager – Live!*, London, CareerTrack Publications

Brown, D (2010) Practice what we preach?, posted by Reward Blogger, 6 December, London, CIPD

Brown, D (2011) Performance management – can it ever work?*Manager*, Summer, p 16

Brumbach, G B (1988) Some ideas, issues and predictions about performance management, *Public Personnel Management*, Winter, pp 387–402

Campbell, J P (1990) Modelling the performance prediction problem in industrial and organizational psychology, in (eds) M D Dunnette and L M Hough, *Handbook of Industrial and Organizational Psychology*, Palo Alto CA, Consulting Psychologists Press, pp 687–732

Cappelli, P (2008) *Talent on Demand: Managing talent in an uncertain age*, Boston, MA, Harvard Business School Press

Cascio, W F (2010) *Managing Human Resources: Productivity, quality of work life, profits*, New York, McGraw-Hill Irwin

Chamberlin, J (2011) Who put the 'art' in SMART goals? *Management Services*, Autumn, pp 22–27

Coens, T and Jenkins, M (2002) *Abolishing Performance Appraisals: Why they backfire and what to do instead*, San Francisco, CA, Berrett-Koehler

Deming, W E (1986) *Out of the Crisis*, Cambridge, MA, Massachusetts Institute of Technology Centre for Advanced Engineering Studies

e-reward (2005) *Survey of Performance Management Practice*, Stockport, e-reward

Gheorghe, C and Hack, J (2007) Unified performance management: how one company can tame its many processes, *Business Performance Management*, November, pp 17–19

Grint, K (1993) 'What's wrong with performance appraisal? A critique and a suggestion', *Human Resource Management Journal*, 3 (3) pp 61–77

Grint, K (1995) *Management: A sociological introduction*, Cambridge, Polity Press

Guest, D E and Conway, N (1998) An analysis of the results of the CIPD performance management survey, in M Armstrong and A Baron, *Performance Management: The new realities*, London, CIPD

Haines, V Y and St-Onge, S (2012) Performance management effectiveness: practices or context? *International Journal of Human Resource Management*, 23 (6), pp 1158–75

Institute of Personnel Management (1992) *Performance Management in the UK: An analysis of the issues*, IPM, London

Jones, P, Palmer, J, Whitehead, D and Needham, P (1995) Prisms of performance, *The Ashridge Journal*, April, pp 10–14

Kochanski, J (2007) Sibson reveals secrets of successful performance management, *Employee Benefit News*, September, pp 22–23

Latham, G P and Locke, E A (1979) Goal Setting – a motivational technique that works, *Organizational Dynamics*, Autumn, pp 442–47

Lawler, E E and McDermott, M (2003) Current performance management practices; examining the impacts, *WorldatWork Journal*, 12 (2), pp 49–60

McDonald, D and Smith, A (1991) A proven connection: performance management and business results, *Compensation & Benefits Review*, January–February, pp 59–64

Postuma, R A and Campion, M A (2008) Twenty best practices for just performance reviews, *Compensation & Benefits Review*, January–February, pp 47–55

Pulakos, W D (2009) *Performance Management*, Chichester, Wiley-Blackwell

Pulakos, E D, Mueller-Hanson, R A and O'Leary, R S (2008) Performance management in the US, in (eds) A Varma, P S Budhwar and A DeNisi, *Performance Management Systems: A global perspective*, Routledge, Abingdon

Risher, H (2005) Getting serious about performance management, *Compensation & Benefits Review*, November–December, pp 18–26

Rodgers, R and Hunter, J E (1991) Impact of management by objectives on organizational performance, *Journal of Applied Psychology*, 76 (2), pp 322–36

Shields, J (2007) *Managing Employee Performance and Reward*, Port Melbourne, Cambridge University Press

Warren, M (1972) Performance management: a substitute for supervision, *Management Review*, October, pp 28–42

WorldatWork and Sibson (2010) *The State of Performance Management*, Scottsdale AZ, WorldatWork

26
Reward management – strategy and systems

KEY CONCEPTS AND TERMS

Guiding principles
Reward mix
Reward philosophy
Reward segmentation
Reward strategy
Strategic reward
Total rewards

LEARNING OUTCOMES

On completing this chapter you should be able to define these key concepts. You should also understand:

- The nature of reward strategy
- Reward philosophies
- Formulating and implementing reward strategy
- The nature of a reward system

Introduction

Reward strategy defines what an organization wants to do about reward in the next few years and how it intends to do it. It leads to the development of a reward system that consists of the interrelated processes and practices that combine to ensure that reward management is carried out to the benefit of the organization and the people who work there. This is strategic reward, an approach based on the beliefs that reward and business strategy should be integrated and that it is necessary to be forward looking – to plan ahead and make the plans happen.

Reward strategy should be underpinned by a reward philosophy as described in the first section of this chapter. The chapter continues with a definition of the meaning of reward strategy, a description of its characteristics and how it is designed and implemented. This is followed by a critical evaluation of the concept of reward strategy. The rest of the chapter is devoted to an analysis of the components of a reward system.

Reward philosophy

The reward philosophy of the organization represents its beliefs about how people should be rewarded. Reward philosophies can be expressed as guiding principles that define the approach an organization takes to dealing with reward. They are the basis for reward policies and provide guidelines for the actions contained in the reward strategy. The reward philosophy can be communicated to employees so that they understand the background to the reward policies and practices that affect them.

Guiding principles are often agreed by top management with advice from company reward specialists or external consultants. But they will be more acceptable if members of the organization are involved in their definition. Guiding principles can then be communicated to everyone to increase understanding of what underpins reward policies and practices.

However, employees will suspend their judgement of the principles until they experience how they are applied. What matters to them is not the philosophy itself but the pay practices emanating from it and the messages about the employment 'deal' that they get as a consequence. It is the reality that is important, not the rhetoric.

Reward guiding principles are concerned with matters such as:

- operating the reward system justly, fairly, equitably and transparently in the interests of all stakeholders;
- developing reward policies and practices that support the achievement of business goals;
- rewarding people according to their contribution;
- recognizing the value of everyone who is making an effective contribution, not just the exceptional performers;
- creating an attractive employee value proposition;
- providing rewards that attract and retain people and enlist their engagement;
- helping to develop a high-performance culture;
- maintaining competitive rates of pay;
- maintaining equitable rates of pay;
- allowing a reasonable degree of flexibility in the operation of reward processes and in the choice of benefits by employees;
- devolving more responsibility for reward decisions to line managers.

The following are some examples of reward philosophies and guiding principles.

Examples

The UK Civil Service

1. Meet business need and be affordable:
   - Business, operational and workforce needs are the drivers for a reward strategy.
   - Business cases outline benefits, risks and costs and justify investment.
   - Reward arguments need to be sustainable.
2. Reflect nature of work:
   - Recognize and reflect workforce groups identified by function and skills utilized (eg operational, corporate or policy decisions).
   - Organizations employing similar workforce groups in similar markets are encouraged to consider similar reward arrangements.
3. Recognize performance:
   - Reward reflects the continuing value and the sustained contribution of an employee and their performance in a given position.
   - Value and performance rewarded reflect how jobholders contribute to their organization, impact delivery and meet Professional Government (PSG) requirements.
4. Manage total reward:
   - Reward includes all aspects of the 'employee deal'; tangible and intangible elements of what is offered.
   - Total reward is tailored and promoted to attract, engage and retain the right talent as well as providing personal choice and flexibility.

- Employers/employees need to develop a full understanding and appreciation of the value of the total reward package.

5 Manage all cash:

- Total cash comprises base pay and variable pay.
- Base pay reflects job challenge and individuals' competence in the job.
- Variable pay reflects performance delivered against agreed objectives.

6 Face the market:

- Reward levels, generally and for specific skills, aligned with agreed market positioning to attract, motivate and retain the right talent.
- Reward competitiveness covers each element of total reward (eg base pay, pensions, leave) and the overall deal.

7 Support equal pay:

- Eliminate direct and indirect reward discrimination and reduce any unjustified gender pay gaps.
- Operate reward systems that are perceived by staff to be reasonable and transparent.
- Reward systems and structures evaluated and kept up to date to ensure that they continue to meet the requirements of legislation.

Diageo

1 Performance: rewards are developed that reflect team and individual achievements.

2 Market: rewards reflect the market in which an employee is based, whether that be geographical or functional, and compare favourably with those of competitors.

3 Communication: Diageo aims to explain to 'everyone the components and value of their reward package, the criteria that affect it, and how they can influence it'.

4 Effectiveness: the company seeks 'best practice' and ensures its benefits programmes 'remain effective for the business and our employees'.

Tesco

- We will provide an innovative reward package that is valued by our staff and communicated brilliantly to reinforce the benefits of working for Tesco.
- Reward investment will be linked to company performance so that staff share in the success they create and, by going the extra mile, receive above average reward compared to local competitors.
- All parts of the total reward investment will add value to the business and reinforce our core purpose, goals and values.

Reward strategy

Reward strategy provides the impetus for reward system design and operation in order to achieve three major objectives: performance, competitiveness and fairness. It aims to provide answers to two basic questions: 1) what do we need to do about our reward practices to ensure that they are fit for purpose? and 2) how do we intend to do it? It is a declaration of intent that defines what the organization wants to do in the future to develop and implement reward policies, practices and processes that will further the achievement of its business goals and meet the needs of its stakeholders. The aim is to provide a sense of purpose and direction and a basis for developing reward policies, practices and processes. The strategy is based on an understanding of the needs of the organization and its employees and how they can best be satisfied.

Trevor (2011: 8) observed that strategic reward is:

> ... a means of enhancing company performance and securing competitive advantage, through the alignment of pay strategies, systems, practices and processes to the organizational strategy. As a management tool, pay is no longer purely a cost of hiring necessary labour, but a means of aligning a company's unique and inimitable asset – their employees – to the strategic direction of the organization.

The content of reward strategy

As Armstrong and Murlis (2007: 33) stated: 'Reward strategy will be characterized by diversity and conditioned both by the legacy of the past and the realities of the future.' All reward strategies are different, just as all organizations are different. Of course, similar aspects of reward will be covered in the strategies of different organizations but they will be treated differently in accordance with variations between organizations in their contexts, business strategies and cultures. But the reality of reward strategy is that it is not such a clear-cut process as some believe. It evolves, it changes and it has sometimes to be reactive rather than proactive.

Reward strategy often has to be a balancing act because of potentially conflicting goals. For example, it may be necessary to reconcile the competing claims of being externally competitive and internally equitable – paying a specialist more money to reflect market rate pressures may disrupt internal relativities. Or the belief that a universally applicable reward system is required may conflict with the perceived need to adopt a policy of segmentation (varying the reward package for different jobs, occupations or people to reflect particular knowledge and skills and the types and levels of contribution they make).

Reward strategy may be a broad-brush affair, simply indicating the general direction in which it is thought that reward management should go. Additionally or alternatively, reward strategy may set out a list of specific intentions dealing with particular aspects of reward management, for example:

- the development of a 'total reward' system;
- the introduction of performance pay;
- replacement of an existing contingent pay scheme;
- the introduction of a new grade and pay structure;
- the replacement of a decayed job evaluation scheme;
- the introduction of a formal recognition scheme;
- the development of a flexible benefits system;
- the conduct of equal pay reviews with the objective of ensuring that work of equal value is paid equally.

Examples of key themes in reward strategies

Airbus: Introduce performance pay for all employees; ensure that its rates are competitive with the external market and deal with anomalies caused by previous rigidities, such as grade drift brought about by people having to be promoted to a higher grade to receive additional pay.

AstraZeneca: Promote a culture that values, recognizes and rewards outstanding performance.

Centrica: Establish a link between pay and performance and align pay with the market.

The Children's Society: Develop flexible and fair reward systems that will support our mission and corporate objectives by recognizing contribution, accountability, teamworking and innovation, and are market sensitive but not market led.

Diageo: Release the potential of every employee to deliver Diageo's performance goals.

Kent County Council: Pay people a fair rate for the job and give additional reward for excellent contribution.

National Union of Teachers: Develop a new broad graded pay structure and introduce a new job evaluation scheme as a basis for the structure.

Tesco: Reward staff for their contribution in a way that enables them to benefit directly from the success they help to create.

Formulating reward strategy

The research conducted by Trevor (2011) in seven companies established that in all cases senior management decided on the strategy. They:

- agreed guiding principles;
- provided broad guidelines in the form of expected outcomes;
- reviewed options for action;
- settled the course of action.

This was the basis for the design stage, which was determined largely by benchmarking best practice and internal concerns over relativity, equity (fairness), governance and performance.

A well-designed reward strategy should be based on the answers to the following questions:

- How will it add value?
- How is it going to be put into effect?
- What supporting processes will be needed and can they be made available?
- Who is going to be involved in implementation?
- How are we going to make sure that those involved know what they have to do, know why they are expected to do it, believe that it is worthwhile and have the skills to do it?
- Are people likely to react negatively to the proposed strategy and, if so, how do we deal with their concerns?
- How much time will be needed; how much time have we got?
- Will any additional resources be required and can they be made available?
- Are there any likely implementation problems and how will they be dealt with?

Particular attention should be paid to issues arising from process factors (how the strategy will work) involving people and communicating with them, and the part played by line managers.

Implementing reward strategy

The aim of implementation is to make the reward strategy an operational reality by building the capacity of the organization to put into practice the proposals worked out in the development stage. As Armstrong and Brown (2006: 159) stressed: 'It is always essential to design with implementation in mind.'

But implementation problems can arise for the following reasons:

- *Over-engineering* – reward specialists (both practitioners and consultants) are often tempted to design highly complicated processes that are hard to explain and justify and even harder to operate.
- *Misalignment* – the integration of business and HR strategies is not achieved when formulating the strategy.
- *Precipitant implementation* – new policies and practices are not tested properly to identify potential implementation problems arising from poor design; the absence of adequate supporting processes such as performance management.

There are two ways of dealing with these problems. First, wherever possible, the new or significantly altered reward process should be pilot tested in a division or department or with a selected sample of employees. The second approach, which can be used where there is more than one component of the reward strategy, is to phase the introduction of the different parts. An incremental approach means that people are given the time to absorb and adjust to the new practice, and the resources such as HR support required to deliver the strategy are not overstretched.

Critical evaluation of the concept of reward strategy

The problem with a strategic approach to reward is that it can promise more than it achieves. This contradicts the main message delivered by US writers such as Lawler (1990) in his *Strategic Pay* and Schuster and Zingheim (1992) in their *The New Pay*, which was that it provides a powerful lever for improving business performance. As Thompson (1998: 70) commented:

> The most that companies can hope to do in their approach to reward is to make sure that it does not distort the relationship [between management and employees]. Managing reward is thus a job of damage limitation and perhaps not the 'strategic

> lever for organizational transformation' that appears so seductive in the writing of American commentators.

Trevor (2011) posed the question: to what extent can pay be strategic? He claimed that rationalism is limited and pointed out that pay systems tend to be selected for their legitimacy (best practice as advocated by institutions such as the CIPD and by management consultants) rather than for purely economic reasons. He observed (ibid: 35) that: 'What is desired (approach), and what is intended (design), may not be reflected in what is achieved (operation).' His research into the pay policies and practice of seven large consumer goods companies led to the following conclusions:

> As a result of the gap between intended policy and achieved practice, between the espoused and the realized, pay within a number of the case companies does not fulfil the strategic objectives of motivating managerial, professional and technical employees to work harder. It does not engender commitment or loyalty as outcomes, nor does it equip management with the behavioural 'lever' promised by standard theory. Despite the best efforts of leading companies, and the rhetoric of their espoused pay practice, pay practice is operationally non-strategic. (ibid: 201)

However, it cannot be denied that to have a sense of purpose and direction is a good thing and, with all its limitations, this justifies a strategic approach to reward.

CASE STUDIES: REWARD STRATEGY

Integrated approach to reward at AEGON UK

Like many companies, AEGON UK (a large insurance company) had pay systems and supporting processes such as job evaluation and performance appraisal that used to stand alone, apart from other HR processes. The company adopted a more holistic approach to the development of its new reward system – which it calls the Human Resources Integrated Approach – so that from whatever angle staff now look at the elements of pay management, performance, career development and reward, they are consistent and linked.

The stated objective of this programme is 'to develop a set of HR processes which are integrated with each other and with the business objectives'. In other words, AEGON UK aims to ensure that the processes of recruiting, retaining and motivating people, as well as measuring their performance, are in line with what the business is trying to achieve.

The Human Resources Integrated Approach is underpinned by a competency framework. The established competencies form the basis of the revised HR processes:

- *Recruitment*: competency based with multi-assessment processes as the basic approach.
- *Reward*: market driven with overall performance dictating rate of progress of salaries within broad bands rather than existing grades.
- *Performance management*: not linked to pay, concentrated on personal development, objective setting and competency development.
- *Training and development*: targeted on key competencies and emphasizing self-development.

Reward strategy at BT

Reward strategy at BT (British Telecom) is a fairly broad-brush affair simply indicating the general direction in which it is thought that reward management for the 90,000 staff at BT should go, with an emphasis on adopting a more holistic, total reward approach. It is summarized as follows:

> Use the full range of rewards (salary, bonus, benefits and recognition) to recruit and retain the best people, and to encourage and reward achievement where actions and behaviours are consistent with the BT values.

Guiding principles

BT's reward strategy is underpinned by a set of guiding principles defining the approach that the organization takes to dealing with reward. These guiding principles are the basis for reward policies and provide guidelines for the actions contained in the reward strategy. They express the reward philosophy of the organization – its values and beliefs about how people should be rewarded. The six guiding principles governing the design of the reward system at BT are as follows:

1 business linkage;
2 clarity and transparency;
3 market competitiveness;
4 performance differentiation;
5 choice and flexibility;
6 equal pay.

Broadly speaking, the three principal elements driving individual reward are:

1 The individual's performance and contribution in the role – what does it mean to have high individual performance?
2 The competitiveness of the individual's existing salary, together with the actual (and anticipated) salary movement in relevant local markets – how does salary align to the external market?
3 The company's business results and ability to pay – can the company afford to invest money in terms of additional reward?

Underpinning these pillars are the principles of clarity (a 'focus on roles'), equal pay and choice.

DSG International: aligning reward with the business plan

In a difficult economic environment DSG simplified its complex mix of reward arrangements to establish a close alignment between rewards and the five components of a new business turnaround plan, primarily through the redesign of executive incentive plans. The change was designed to enhance the perception of line-of-sight between individual performance, group performance and reward. It illustrates the vital role of communications to explain the 'why' of reward change, what it means for the business and how each component of reward links to a business plan.

Total reward strategy at GlaxoSmithKline (GSK)

TotalReward, the name by which GSK refers to its approach to reward, consists of three elements:

- total cash (base salary and bonus), plus long-term incentives for managers and executives;
- lifestyle benefits (health care, employee assistance, family support, dental care);
- savings choices (pension plan, ShareSave, ShareReward).

The complete package – the concept of which is based on employees understanding the total value of all the rewards they receive, not just the individual elements – is designed to attract, retain, motivate and develop the best talent. The proposition for employees is that TotalReward gives them the opportunity to share in the company's success, makes it easier to balance home and working life, and helps them to take care of themselves and their families.

The reward system

Strategic reward leads to the design of a reward system. As illustrated in Figure 26.1, this consists of the interrelated processes and practices that combine to ensure that reward management is carried out effectively to the benefit of the organization and the people who work there. The system is driven by the business strategy, which in turn drives the reward strategy. As described below, its major components are financial and non-financial rewards, which are combined to form a total reward system. Performance management plays an important part

FIGURE 26.1 A reward system

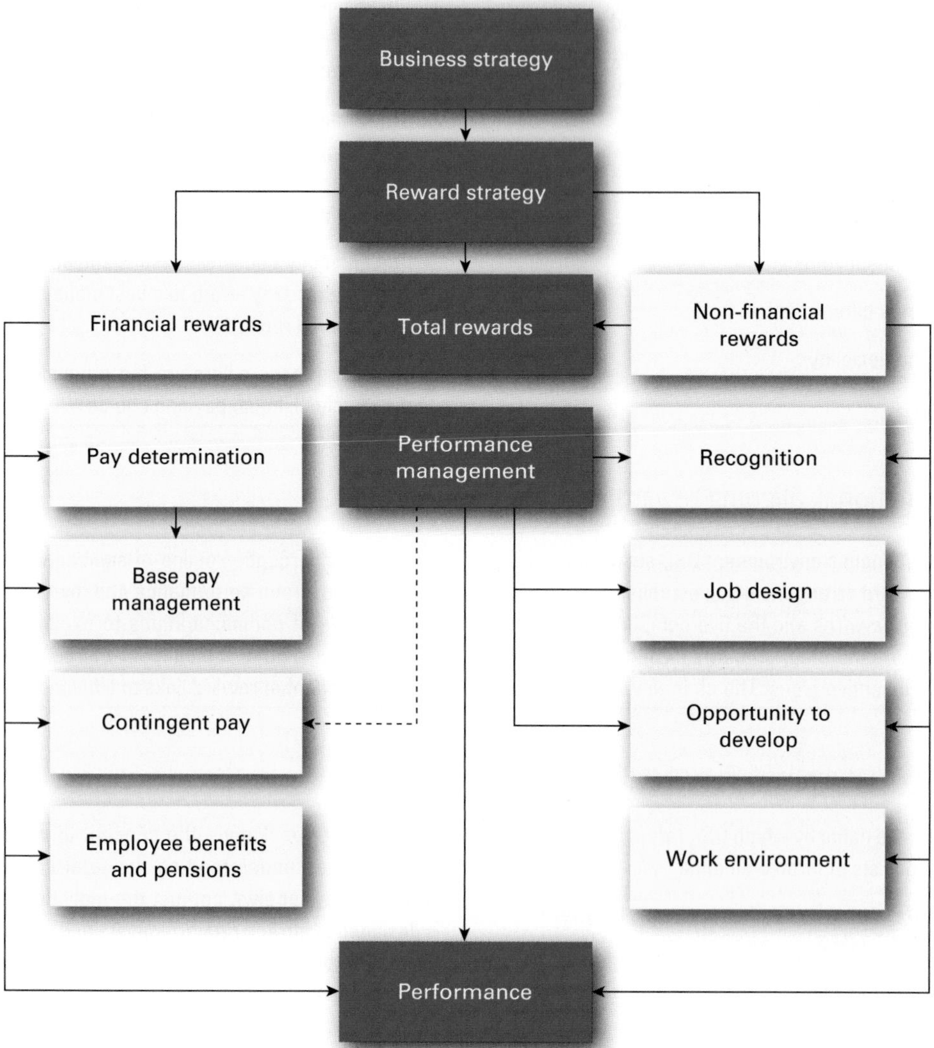

in supporting non-financial rewards and may be used to inform performance or contribution pay decisions. All these components combine to influence levels of performance.

Financial rewards

Financial rewards consist of job-based pay, which provides pay related to the value of the job, and person-based pay, which provides rewards that recognize the individual's contribution. They also include employee benefits and pensions and financial recognition schemes. The management of job and person-based pay involves:

- Pay determination – making decisions on the value of jobs by means of market pricing and job evaluation.
- Base pay management – developing and operating pay structures that group jobs into grades, bands or levels in accordance with

internal and external relativities and usually provide for pay progression.

- Contingent pay – planning and managing schemes that provide for pay progression related to performance, contribution, competence, skill or length of service.

Labour economists distinguish between the incentive effect of financial rewards (generating more engagement and effort) and the sorting effect (attracting better quality employees). The fundamental issue is the extent to which financial rewards provide an incentive effect. The sorting effect is important but creates less controversy, perhaps because it is more difficult to pin down.

The case for and against financial rewards as incentives, and a description of the contingent pay schemes that provide such awards, are set out in the next chapter.

Non-financial rewards

Non-financial rewards focus on the needs people have to varying degrees for recognition, achievement, personal growth and acceptable working conditions. They include the non-financial recognition of achievements, the design of fulfilling jobs, giving people the scope to develop their skills and careers and offering a work environment that provides a high quality of working life and an appropriate relationship between work and private life (work–life balance). Non-financial rewards can be extrinsic, such as praise or recognition, or intrinsic, associated with job challenge and interest and feelings that the work is worthwhile.

Total rewards

Total rewards are the combination of financial and non-financial rewards made available to employees. The various aspects of reward, namely base pay, contingent pay, employee benefits and non-financial rewards, which include intrinsic rewards from the work itself, are linked together and treated as an integrated and coherent whole.

The concept of total rewards describes an approach to reward management that emphasizes the need to consider all aspects of the work experience of value to employees, not just a few such as pay and employee benefits. It aims to blend the financial and non-financial elements of reward into a cohesive whole. A total rewards approach, as shown in Figure 26.2, recognizes that it is necessary to get financial rewards (pay and benefits) right. But it also appreciates the importance of providing people with rewarding experiences that arise from their work environment (the job they do and how they are managed) and the opportunity to develop their skills and careers. It contributes to the production of an employee value proposition that provides a clear, compelling reason why talented people should work for a company.

FIGURE 26.2 The elements of total rewards

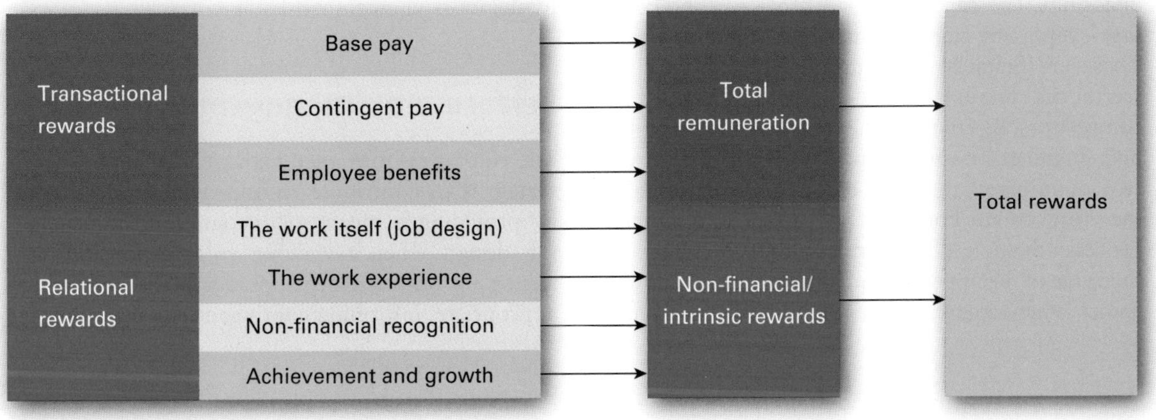

FIGURE 26.3 Model of total rewards: Towers Perrin

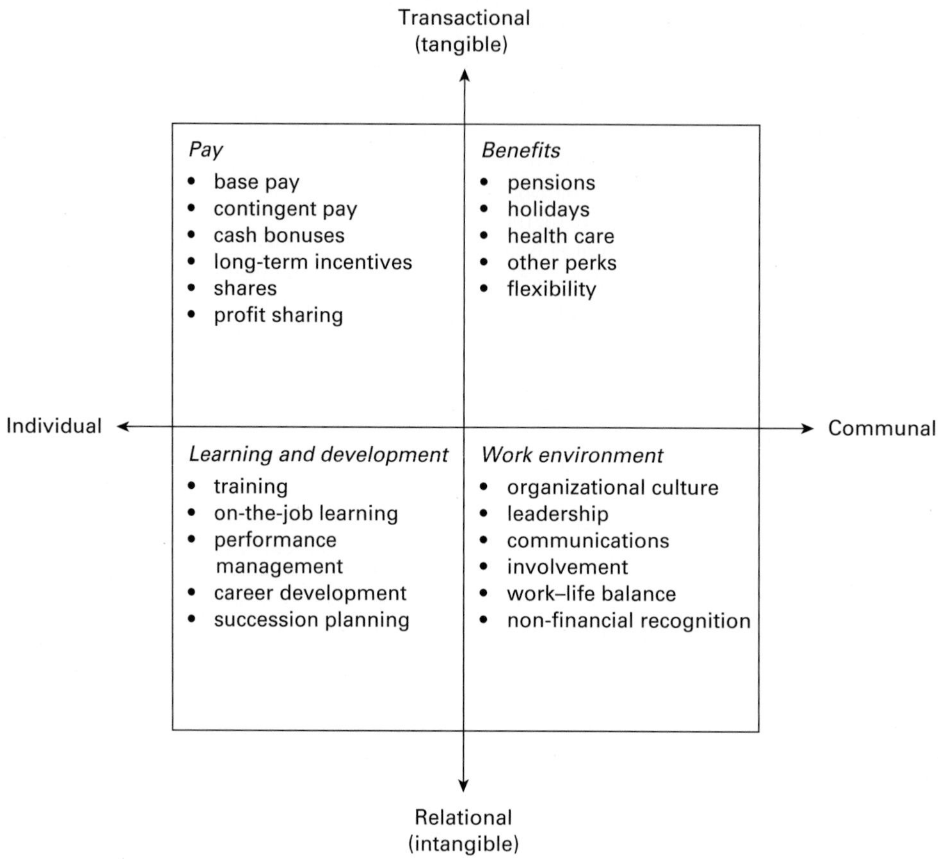

The Towers Perrin model shown in Figure 26.3 is frequently used as the basis for planning a total rewards approach. It consists of a matrix with four quadrants. The upper two quadrants – pay and benefits – represent transactional or tangible rewards. These are financial in nature and are essential to recruit and retain staff but can be easily copied by competitors. By contrast, the relational or intangible non-financial rewards represented in the lower two quadrants cannot be imitated so readily and therefore create both human capital and human process advantage. They are essential to enhancing the value of the upper two quadrants. The real power comes when organizations combine relational and transactional rewards. The model also makes a useful distinction between individual and communal rewards, particularly, in the latter case, those provided by the work environment.

Performance management

The role of performance management in a reward system is to contribute to improving performance by providing a means of recognition, influencing job design when reviewing role responsibilities, setting up personal development plans and, when appropriate, informing contingent pay decisions.

Key learning points: Reward management – strategy and systems

Reward strategy

Reward strategy defines what an organization wants to do about reward in the next few years and how it intends to do it. It may be a broad-brush affair, simply indicating the general direction in which it is thought reward management should go. Additionally or alternatively, reward strategy may set out a list of specific intentions dealing with particular aspects of reward management.

Formulating reward strategy

The thrust of reward strategy is to provide the impetus for reward design and operation in order to achieve three major objectives: performance, competitiveness and fairness.

Implementing reward strategy

The aim of implementation is to make the reward strategy an operating reality by building the capacity of the organization to put into practice the proposals worked out in the development stage.

Reward philosophy

Reward strategy should be underpinned by a reward philosophy that represents the views of the organization on how people should be valued. This can be articulated as a set of principles that guide the development of reward strategy and the design and operation of the reward system.

Reward system

A reward system consists of the interrelated processes and practices of financial and non-financial rewards that combine into a total rewards approach to ensure that reward management is carried out to the benefit of the organization and the people who work there.

Financial rewards consist of job-based pay, which provides pay related to the value of the job, and person-based pay, which provides rewards that recognize the individual's contribution. They also include employee benefits and pensions and financial recognition schemes. Non-financial rewards focus on the needs people have to varying degrees for recognition, achievement, personal growth and acceptable working conditions.

Total rewards are the combination of the financial and non-financial rewards made available to employees.

Questions

1 What is strategic reward?
2 What is the main characteristic of strategic reward?
3 What are the limitations to the concept of strategic reward?
4 What is reward strategy?
5 What are the main objectives of reward strategy?
6 What are the main arguments in favour of having a reward strategy?
7 What are the principal areas covered by a reward strategy?
8 What is reward philosophy?
9 What is the typical approach to formulating reward strategy?
10 What are the main problems organizations meet in implementing reward strategy and how can they be overcome?

References

Armstrong, M and Brown, D (2006) *Strategic Reward: Making it happen*, London, Kogan Page

Armstrong, M and Murlis, H (2007) *Reward Management*, revised 5th edn, London, Kogan Page

Lawler, E E (1990) *Strategic Pay*, San Francisco, CA, Jossey-Bass

Schuster, J R and Zingheim, P K (1992) *The New Pay*, New York, Lexington Books

Thompson, M (1998) Trust and reward, in (eds) S Perkins and St J Sandringham, *Trust, Motivation and Commitment: A reader*, Faringdon, Strategic Remuneration Research Centre

Trevor, J (2011) *Can Pay be Strategic?*, Basingstoke, Palgrave Macmillan

27 The practice of reward management

KEY CONCEPTS AND TERMS

Analytical job matching
Anchor point
Base pay
Base pay management
Broad-banded pay structure
Broad-graded pay structure
Career family pay structure
Compa-ratio
Competency-related pay
Contingent pay
Contribution-related pay
Distributive justice
Evidence-based management
Evidence-based reward management
Extreme market pricing
Factor plan
Financial rewards
Grade
Grade drift
Incentive effect
Job evaluation
Job family pay structure
Job matching
Job size
Job worth
Job-based pay
Line of sight
Lower quartile
Market pricing
Market rate
Median
Merit pay
Mid-point management
Narrow-graded pay structure
Non-financial rewards
Pay progression
Pay range
Pay spine
Pay stance
Payment-by-results
Performance-related pay
Person-based pay
Point-factor job evaluation
Reference point
Remuneration
Reward management
Reward system
Skill-based pay
Sorting effect
Spot rate
Target rate
Time-based pay
Upper quartile

LEARNING OUTCOMES

On completing this chapter you should be able to define these key concepts. You should also understand:

- The meaning and aims of reward management
- Pay determination
- Job evaluation
- Market pricing
- Base pay management
- Contingent pay
- Recognition schemes
- Employee benefits
- The evaluation of reward systems
- The administration of reward

Introduction

The aim of this chapter is to describe how reward management works in practice. It starts with definitions of what reward management is and what it aims to do. The following components of the reward system are then dealt with – pay determination through market pricing and job evaluation, base pay management, contingent pay, recognition, and the provision of employee benefits and pensions. This chapter continues with two sections dealing respectively with the evaluation and management of reward.

Reward management defined

Reward management is concerned with the strategies, policies and practices required to ensure that the value of people and the contribution they make to achieving organizational, departmental and team goals is recognized and rewarded. It is about the design, implementation and maintenance of reward systems that aim to satisfy the needs of both the organization and its stakeholders and to operate fairly, equitably and consistently.

Reward management deals with non-financial rewards such as recognition, learning and development opportunities and increased job responsibility, as well as financial rewards.

Aims of reward management

As Ghoshal and Bartlett (1995) pointed out, reward management is there to add value to people. It is not just about attaching value to them. Its aims are to:

- *Reward people* according to the value they create by providing for them to be recognized and paid in accordance with the degree to which they meet or exceed expectations.
- *Support the achievement of business goals* by helping to ensure that the organization has the talented and engaged people it needs.
- *Promote high performance* by ensuring that the reward system recognizes and encourages it.
- *Support and develop the organization's culture* by linking rewards to behaviour that is in line with core values.
- *Define the right behaviours and outcomes* by defining expectations through performance management and merit pay schemes.

Pay determination

Pay determination is the process of deciding on the level of pay for jobs or people. Its two aims, which often conflict, are: 1) to be externally competitive to attract, engage and retain the people required by the organization; and 2) to be internally equitable in the sense that rates of pay correctly reflect the relativities between jobs. These aims are achieved respectively by market pricing and job evaluation.

Competitive pay

Pay is by no means the only factor that influences people to join or remain with an organization, but it is important. The most significant influence on pay levels is the law of supply and demand. If the demand for labour exceeds supply, pay levels will be higher and vice versa. Organizations pay more to attract and retain high-quality employees in critical positions.

The need to be competitive means that organizations have to take account of market rates when deciding on the level of pay for a job. They bear in mind the saying: 'A job is worth what the market says it's worth.' Consequently, establishing market rates through what is termed 'market pricing', as described in the next section of this chapter, is a vital step in deciding on levels of pay.

Internally equitable pay

Internally equitable pay is fair pay. This means providing equal pay for work of equal value as required by the Equality Act (2010) and supporting case law, and ensuring that the rates of pay for jobs at different levels properly reflect relative values. Internal relativities are established by job evaluation. But there is a tension between external competitiveness and internal equity. Some adopt the slogan, 'the market rules ok' – internal equity considerations are secondary. But if this policy is pursued too vigorously there is a risk of alienating existing employees and contravening the provisions of equal pay legislation. This risk should be assessed.

Market pricing

Market pricing is the process of making decisions on pay structures and individual rates of pay and obtaining information on market rates (market rate analysis). A policy decision is required on the relationship between market rate levels and levels of pay within the organization. This is called the 'pay stance', which may be expressed in such terms as matching median (average) rates or paying upper quartile rates (loosely, within the top 25 per cent).

Use of market pricing

Market pricing informs decisions on base rates of pay, ie, the amount of pay that constitutes the basic rate for the job or the person. The aim is to ensure that the rates are competitive. It helps to develop the pay structure – the pay ranges attached to grades. Information on market rates may lead to the introduction of market supplements for individual jobs or the creation of separate pay structures (market groups) to cater for particular market rate pressures. It is referred to as 'extreme market pricing' when market rates are the sole means of deciding on internal rates of pay and relativities, and conventional job evaluation is not used. An organization that adopts this method is said to be 'market-driven'. Market pricing may be associated with formal job evaluation, which establishes internal relativities and the grade structure.

Acceptability of market pricing

The acceptability of either form of market pricing is dependent on the availability of robust market data and, when looking at external rates, the quality of the job-to-job matching process, ie comparing like with like. It can therefore vary from analysis of data by job titles to detailed matched analysis collected through bespoke surveys focused on real market equivalence. Extreme market pricing can provide guidance on internal relativities. But it can lead to pay discrimination against women, where the market has traditionally been discriminatory, and it does not satisfy UK equal pay legislation.

The concept of a market rate

Market pricing attempts to establish the market rate for jobs, but the notion of a market rate is a more elusive concept than it seems. There is no such thing as a definitive market rate for any job, even when comparing identically sized organizations in the same industry and location. Different market information sources for the same types of jobs produce different results because of variations in the sample, the difficulty of obtaining precise matches between jobs in the organization and jobs elsewhere (job matching), and timing (the dates on which the data is collected may differ).

This means that market rate analysis is most unlikely to produce definite information on the rate for the job. The possibly incomplete data from a number of sources, some more reliable than others, has to be interpreted to indicate what the organization should do about it. This may be expressed as a 'derived market rate', which is a sort of average of a range of pay information – a dubious notion. Data may be available for some jobs but not for others that are unique to the organization.

Market rate analysis

Market rate analysis involves the following steps:

- Identify and define the jobs for which market rate data is required. These are benchmark jobs that are representative of different levels and occupations and can be compared with similar jobs. In conducting the survey the aim will be to 'match' these jobs as closely as possible with jobs elsewhere.
- Identify the sources of information. These can include published surveys conducted by a pay consultancy or research organization, surveys conducted specially by the organization, 'pay clubs' (groups of

employers who exchange pay information) and advertisements. Published surveys are likely to provide the most convenient source of robust information. Special surveys and pay clubs can produce useful data but they are time-consuming. More than one source should be used if possible. Advertisements are useless.

- Collect, analyse and interpret the information. The pay data for jobs may be presented in the form of a range of pay from lowest to highest, the median rate (the midpoint in a distribution of rates of pay) and the upper and lower quartiles (the values which, respectively, are exceeded by a quarter of the values in the distribution or below which a quarter of the values in a distribution occur). Interpreting the data may mean producing a derived market rate from the different sources.
- Apply the information in line with a policy decision on market stance – the pay levels required to be competitive and affordable.

Job evaluation

Job evaluation is a systematic and formal process for defining the relative worth or size of jobs within an organization in order to establish internal relativities. It is carried out through either an analytical or a non-analytical scheme.

Analytical job evaluation schemes

Analytical job evaluation is based on a process of breaking down whole jobs into a number of defined elements or factors and then comparing them factor by factor, either with a graduated scale of points attached to a set of factors, or with grade or role profiles analysed under the same factor headings.

The advantages of an analytical approach are that: first, evaluators have to consider each of the characteristics of the job separately before forming a conclusion about its relative value; second, evaluators are provided with defined yardsticks or guidelines that help to increase the objectivity and consistency of judgements. It can also provide a defence in the UK against an equal pay claim.

A toolkit for designing an analytical job evaluation scheme is provided in Chapter 71. The main analytical schemes, as described below, are point-factor rating and analytical matching.

Point-factor rating

Point-factor schemes are the most common forms of analytical job evaluation. They were used by 70 per cent of the respondents with job evaluation schemes in the e-reward 2003 job evaluation survey.

The basic methodology is to break down jobs into factors. These are the elements in a job such as the level of responsibility, knowledge and skill or decision-making that represent the demands made by the job on job holders. For job evaluation purposes it is assumed that each of the factors will contribute to the value of the job and is an aspect of all the jobs to be evaluated, but to different degrees.

Each factor is divided into a hierarchy of levels, typically five or six. Definitions of these levels are produced to provide guidance on deciding the degree to which the factor applies in the job to be evaluated. A maximum points score is allocated to each factor. The scores available may vary between different factors in accordance with beliefs about their relative significance. This is termed 'explicit weighting'. If the number of levels varies between factors, this means that they are implicitly weighted because the range of scores available will be greater in the factors with more levels.

The total score for a factor is divided between the levels to produce the numerical factor scale. The complete scheme consists of the factor and level definitions and the scoring system (the total score available for each factor and distributed to the factor levels). This comprises the 'factor plan'.

Jobs are 'scored' (ie allocated points) under each factor heading on the basis of the level of the factor in the job. This is done by comparing the features of the job with regard to that factor with the factor level definitions in order to find out which definition provides the best fit. The separate factor scores are then added together to give a total score, which indicates the relative value of each job and can be used to place the jobs in rank order, or allocate them into grades in a graded pay structure that have been defined in terms of job evaluation points.

Analytical job matching

Like point-factor job evaluation, analytical job matching is based on the analysis of a number of defined factors. Profiles of roles to be evaluated that have been analysed and described in terms of job evaluation factors are compared with grade, band or level profiles that have been analysed and described in terms of the same job evaluation factors. The role profiles are then 'matched' with the range of grade or level profiles to establish the best fit and thus grade the job.

Analytical matching can be used to grade jobs or place them in levels following the initial evaluation of a sufficiently large sample of benchmark jobs, ie representative jobs that provide a valid basis for comparisons. This can happen in big organizations when it is believed that it is not necessary to go through the whole process of point-factor evaluation for every job, especially where 'generic' roles are concerned. It takes much less time than using a point-factor scheme and the results can be just as accurate.

Non-analytical job evaluation

Non-analytical job evaluation schemes enable whole jobs to be compared in order to place them in a grade or a rank order – they are not analysed by reference to their elements or factors. They can operate on a job-to-job basis in which a job is compared with another job to decide whether it should be valued more, less, or the same (ranking and 'internal benchmarking' processes). Alternatively, they may function on a job-to-grade basis in which judgements are made by comparing a whole job with a defined hierarchy of job grades (job classification) – this involves matching a job description to a grade description. Non-analytical schemes are simple to introduce and operate but provide no defined standards of judgement. Differences between jobs are not measured and they do not provide a defence in an equal pay case.

Base pay management

Base pay is the amount of pay that constitutes the rate for the job or the person. Base pay management uses the information from market pricing and job evaluation to design and operate grade and pay structures.

Grade and pay structures

Grade and pay structures provide the framework for base pay management as a means of implementing an organization's pay policies. They enable the organization to determine where jobs should be placed in a hierarchy, define pay levels and the scope for pay progression, and provide the basis upon which relativities can be managed, equal pay achieved and the processes of monitoring and controlling the implementation of pay practices can take place. Grade and pay structures also enable organizations to communicate the career and pay opportunities available to employees.

Grade structures

A grade structure consists of a sequence or hierarchy of grades, bands or levels into which groups of jobs that are broadly comparable in size are placed. Narrow-graded structures tend to have 10 or more grades, broad-graded structures have six to eight grades, and broad-banded structures have fewer than six 'bands'. There may be a single structure defined by the number of grades or bands it contains; alternatively the structure may be divided into a number of career or job families, consisting of groups of jobs where the essential nature and purpose of the work are similar but it is carried out at different levels.

Pay structures

A pay structure consists of pay ranges, brackets or scales that are attached to each grade, band or level in a grade structure. Pay structures are defined by the number of grades they contain and, especially in narrow- or broad-graded structures, the span or width of the pay ranges attached to each grade. 'Span' is the scope that the grade provides for pay progression and is usually measured as the difference between the lowest and the highest point in the range as a percentage of the lowest point. Thus a range of £20,000 to £30,000 would have a span of 50 per cent.

Pay can progress within the grades in a narrow- or broad-graded structure on the basis of merit or time served in the grade. Broad-banded structures in theory allow more flexibility, but they often contain pay zones that provide an indication of the extent to which the pay of individuals in a particular role, or cluster of roles, can vary around what is known as an 'anchor point' – the rate for a fully competent person in a role that is aligned to market rates. Another form of pay structure is a pay spine (found mainly in the public and voluntary sectors) consisting of a number of pay points that mark progression on the basis of time served.

Some organizations, especially smaller ones, do not have a formal graded structure and rely entirely on 'spot rates', ie the rates for jobs do not define any scope for the progression of base pay in the form of a pay range or salary bracket, although bonuses may be provided on top of the base rate. A less common method is to have 'individual job grades' which are, in effect, spot rates to which a defined pay range of, say, 20 per cent on either side of the rate has been attached to provide scope for pay progression.

Guiding principles for grade and pay structures

Grade and pay structures should:

- be appropriate to the culture, characteristics and needs of the organization and its employees;
- facilitate the management of relativities and the achievement of equity, fairness, consistency and transparency in managing gradings and pay;
- enable jobs to be graded appropriately and not be subject to grade drift (unjustified upgradings);
- be flexible enough to adapt to pressures arising from market rate changes and skill shortages;
- facilitate operational flexibility and continuous development;
- provide scope as required for pay progression;
- clarify reward, lateral development and career opportunities;
- be constructed logically and clearly so that the basis upon which they operate can readily be communicated to employees;
- enable the organization to exercise control over the implementation of pay policies and budgets.

Types of grade and pay structures

The main types of grade and pay structures and their advantages and disadvantages are summarized in Table 27.1.

Criteria for choice

There is always a choice of structures; the criteria are given in Table 27.2.

Pay progression

Pay progression takes place when base pay advances through pay ranges or brackets in a grade and pay structure, or through promotions or upgradings. The alternative is a spot rate system, which allows for no progression and is entirely job-based. Progression through pay brackets in a person-based approach may be determined formally by means of an individual contingent pay scheme (merit or service-related). Informal progression takes place when there is no contingent pay scheme and increases are not based on a systematic process.

A decision has to be made on whether an individual contingent pay scheme should be used. The alternatives are to use spot rates or some form of bonus scheme based on team or organizational performance (the latter can be offered in addition to individual or team pay).

Contingent pay

Contingent pay provides financial rewards that are related to a factor such as performance or service. It can take the form of consolidated increases to base pay and so provide for pay progression. It can also take the form of cash non-consolidated bonuses. Where consolidated increases for individuals are related to performance, competence, contribution or skill it is known as merit pay. If these are solely related to performance it is known as performance-

TABLE 27.1 Summary description of different grade and pay structures

Type of structure	Features	Advantages	Disadvantages
Narrow-graded	• A sequence of job grades – 10 or more • Narrow pay ranges, eg 20–40% • Progression usually linked to performance	• Clearly indicate pay relativities • Facilitate control • Easy to understand	• Create hierarchical rigidity • Prone to grade drift • Inappropriate in a delayered organization
Broad-graded	• A sequence of between six and nine grades • Fairly broad pay ranges, eg 40–50% • Progression linked to contribution and may be controlled by thresholds or zones	As for narrow-graded structures but in addition: • the broader grades can be defined more clearly • better control can be exercised over grade drift	• Too much scope for pay progression • Control mechanisms can be provided but they can be difficult to manage • May be costly
Broad-banded	• A series of, often, five or six 'broad' bands • Wide pay bands – typically between 50% and 80% • Progression linked to contribution and competence	• More flexible • Reward lateral development and growth in competence • Fit new-style organizations	• Create unrealistic expectations of scope for pay rises • Seem to restrict scope for promotion • Difficult to understand • Equal pay problems
Career family	• Career families identified and defined • Career paths defined for each family in terms of key activities and competence requirements • Same grade and pay structure for each family	• Clarify career paths within and between families • Facilitate the achievement of equity between families and therefore equal pay • Facilitate level definitions	• Could be difficult to manage • May appear to be divisive if 'silos' emerge
Job family	• Separate grade and pay structures for job families containing similar jobs • Progression linked to competence and/or contribution	• Facilitate pay differentiation between market groups • Define career paths against clear criteria	• Can appear to be divisive • May inhibit lateral career development • May be difficult to maintain internal equity between job families unless underpinned by job evaluation
Pay spine	• A series of incremental pay points covering all jobs • Grades may be superimposed • Progression linked to service	• Easy to manage • Pay progression not based on managerial judgement	• No scope for differentiating rewards according to performance • May be costly as staff drift up the spine

TABLE 27.2 Grade and pay structures: criteria for choice

Type of structure	Criteria for choice: the structure may be considered more appropriate when:
Narrow-graded	• the organization is large and bureaucratic with well-defined and extended hierarchies; • pay progression is expected to occur in small but relatively frequent steps; • the culture is one in which much significance is attached to status as indicated by gradings; • when some but not too much scope for pay progression is wanted.
Broad-graded	• it is believed that if there is a relatively limited number of grades it will be possible to define and therefore differentiate them more accurately as an aid to better precision when grading jobs; • an existing narrow-graded structure is the main cause of grade drift; • it is considered that pay progression through grades can be related to contribution and that it is possible to introduce effective control mechanisms.
Broad-banded	• greater flexibility in pay determination and management is required; • it is believed that job evaluation should no longer drive grading decisions; • the focus is on rewarding people for lateral development; • the organization has been delayered.
Career family	• there are distinct families, and different career paths within and between families can be identified and defined; • there is a strong emphasis on career development in the organization; • robust methods of defining competencies exist.
Job family	• there are distinct market groups that need to be rewarded differently; • the range of responsibility and the basis upon which levels exist vary between families; • it is believed that career paths need to be defined in terms of competence requirements.
Pay spine	• this is the traditional approach in public or voluntary sector organizations and it fits the culture; • it is believed to be impossible to measure different levels of contribution fairly and consistently; • ease of administration is an important consideration.

related pay (the most common form). When payments are related to service it is known as service-related pay. Bonuses can be based on individual, team or organizational performance. Wage earners may receive unconsolidated cash payments in addition to their base pay through an incentive scheme. The CIPD 2013 reward survey found that the most common split between total spend on fixed pay and contingent pay were 90 per cent fixed to 10 per cent variable; 71 per cent of the respondents related pay to individual performance.

Merit pay

Decisions on the use of merit or performance-related pay should be based on a critical evaluation of the arguments for and against it and an understanding of the criteria for success.

Arguments for merit pay

The most powerful argument in favour of merit pay is that those who contribute more should be paid more. It can be claimed that it is right and proper to recognize achievement with a financial and therefore tangible reward. This is in accordance with the principle of distributive justice, which while it states that rewards should be provided equitably does not require them to be equal, except when the value of contribution is equal. Financial rewards can also be used to highlight key performance areas, to indicate the behaviours that are valued and generally to emphasize the importance of high performance.

There is plenty of research evidence that financial rewards can improve performance. For example, in the UK this was established by Booth and Frank (1999), Marsden (2004), Prentice *et al* (2007) and Thompson (1998). In the United States, Gupta and Shaw (1998), Jenkins *et al* (1998), Lazear (1999) and Prendergast (1999), amongst others, all found positive relationships between financial incentives and performance.

Arguments against merit pay

A vociferous chorus of disapproval has been heard on the incentive effect of the financial rewards provided by merit pay. One of the best known and most influential voices was that of Alfie Kohn (1993: 62) who stated in the *Harvard Business Review* that: 'Rewards, like punishment, may actually undermine the intrinsic motivation that results in optimal performance. The more a manager stresses what an employee can earn for good work, the less interested that employee will be in the work itself.' His summary was that 'bribes in the workplace simply can't work' (ibid: 63). Jeffrey Pfeffer (1998: 114) concluded in his equally influential *Harvard Business Review* article, 'Six dangerous myths about pay', that: 'Most merit-pay systems share two attributes: they absorb vast amounts of management time and make everybody unhappy.'

There is a strong body of opinion, at least in academic circles, that financial rewards are bad – because they don't work and indeed are harmful, while non-financial rewards are good, at least when they provide intrinsic motivation, ie motivation by the work itself.

The detailed arguments against merit pay are that:

- the extent to which merit pay schemes motivate is questionable – the amounts available for distribution are usually so small that they cannot act as an incentive (the IRS 2012 review of pay trends showed that average merit pay increases were worth only 2.9 per cent);
- the requirements for success are exacting and difficult to achieve;
- money by itself will not result in sustained motivation: intrinsic motivation provided by the work itself goes deeper and lasts longer;
- people react in widely different ways to any form of motivation – it cannot be assumed that money will motivate everyone equally yet that is the premise on which merit pay schemes are based;
- financial rewards may possibly motivate those who receive them but they can demotivate those who don't, and the numbers who are demotivated could be much higher than those who are motivated;
- merit pay schemes can create more dissatisfaction than satisfaction if they are perceived to be unfair, inadequate or badly managed, which can easily be the case;
- employees can be suspicious of schemes because they fear that performance bars will be continuously raised; a scheme may therefore only operate successfully for a limited period;

- schemes depend on the existence of accurate and reliable methods of measuring performance, contribution, competence, or skill, which might not exist;
- individuals are encouraged to emphasize only those aspects of performance that are rewarded;
- merit pay decisions depend on the judgement of managers, which in the absence of reliable criteria can be partial, prejudiced, inconsistent or ill-informed;
- the concept of merit pay is based on the assumption that performance is completely under the control of individuals, when in fact it is affected by the system in which they work;
- merit pay, especially performance-related pay, can militate against quality and teamwork.

These are powerful arguments and further weight to them is supplied by the fact that merit pay schemes are difficult to manage well. Organizations, including the UK Civil Service, rushed into performance-related pay in the 1980s without really understanding how to make it work. Inevitably, problems of implementation arose. Studies such as those conducted by Bowey and Thorpe (1982), Kessler and Purcell (1992), Marsden and Richardson (1994) and Thompson (1992a, 1992b) have all revealed these difficulties. Failures may arise because insufficient attention has been paid to fitting schemes to the context and culture of the organization. But problems are often rooted in implementation and operating difficulties, especially those of inadequate performance management processes, the lack of effective communication and involvement, and line managers who are not capable of or interested in properly carrying out the actions involved. Vicky Wright (1991: 82) remarked that: 'Even the most ardent supporters of performance-related pay recognize that it is difficult to manage well'; Trevor (2011: 201) also questioned the extent to which such systems are manageable.

Critical evaluation of merit pay

The argument that people should be rewarded in accordance with the value of their contribution is a strong one, but it stands alone. The evidence that incentives improve performance is conflicting. In some circumstances, as demonstrated by research projects, it works, but in others it doesn't. Most merit pay schemes are unlikely to provide a direct incentive, simply because they do not match demanding requirements such as line of sight and a worthwhile reward. Their main purpose is to recognize the level of contribution, and even this is questionable because of the difficulty of making fair and consistent assessments of performance as a basis for pay decisions. Such schemes can demotivate more people than they motivate.

But what's the alternative? Should everyone be paid the same rate in a job however well they perform? Or should pay be progressed in line with length of service – paying people for being there? For all its problems, the balance of the argument is in favour of some scheme for relating pay to merit. But the difficulties of doing this should be recognized and every attempt should be made to ensure that pay decisions are fair, consistent and transparent. It is also necessary to consider carefully the exacting criteria for success.

Merit pay – criteria for success

The criteria for effective individual merit pay are:

- Individuals have a clear line of sight between what they do and what they will get for doing it.
- Rewards are worth having.
- Fair and consistent means are available for measuring or assessing performance, competency, contribution or skill.
- People are able to influence their performance by changing their behaviour and developing their competencies and skills.
- The reward follows as closely as possible the accomplishment that generated it.
- The scheme fits the culture of the organization.
- The scheme is manageable and cost-effective.
- The scheme will be supported by well-established methods of measuring performance, competency, contribution or skill.

Choice of merit pay schemes

If a decision is made to go ahead with merit pay, it should be based on an analysis of the features, advantages, disadvantages and appropriateness of the various schemes – shown in Table 27.3 – against the criteria set out above.

Performance-related pay is the most popular scheme. It was used by 84 per cent of the respondents to the e-reward 2009 survey who had merit pay. It was followed by contribution-related pay (57 per cent), competency-related pay (33 per cent) and skill-based pay (21 per cent).

Service-related pay

Pay progression in some organizations, especially in the public and voluntary sectors, can be provided by fixed increments on a pay scale or pay spine related to time in the job (service-related pay). There may sometimes be scope for varying the rate of progress up the scale according to performance. Service-related pay is supported by many public sector unions because they perceive it as being fair – everyone is treated equally. It is felt that linking pay to time in the job rather than performance or competence avoids the partial and ill-informed judgements about people that managers are prone to make. Some people believe that the principle of rewarding people for loyalty through continued service is a good one. Service-related pay is also easy to manage; in fact, it does not need to be managed at all.

The arguments against service-related pay are that:

- it is inequitable in the sense that an equal allocation of pay increases according to service does not recognize the fact that some people will be contributing more than others and should be rewarded accordingly;
- it does not encourage good performance; indeed, it rewards poor performance equally;
- it is based on the assumption that performance improves with experience but this is not automatically the case;
- it can be expensive – everyone may drift to the top of the scale, especially in times of low staff turnover, but the cost of their pay is not justified by the added value they provide.

These arguments have convinced most businesses. However, some are concerned about managing any other kind of formal contingent pay scheme, eg merit pay, and are content to rely on spot rates that they can increase informally at will whenever they think someone is worth more. In the public sector, the UK government in 2013 announced its intention to abolish automatic pay increases. There will be strong resistance from the public sector trade unions to this move.

Team pay

Team pay links payments to members of a formally established team to the performance of that team. The rewards are shared among the members of the team in accordance with a published formula, or on an ad hoc basis in the case of exceptional achievements. Rewards for individuals may also be influenced by assessments of their contribution to team results.

Team pay can enhance cooperative behaviour, encourage flexible working and multiskilling and clarify team goals. It can also persuade less effective performers to improve in order to meet team standards and help to develop self-managed teams. But:

- The effectiveness of team pay depends on the existence of well-defined and mature teams and they may be difficult to identify. Even if they can be, do they need to be motivated by a purely financial reward?
- Team pay may seem unfair to individuals who could feel that their own efforts are unrewarded.
- Pressure to conform, which is accentuated by team pay, could result in the team maintaining its output at lowest common denominator levels – sufficient to gain what is thought collectively to be a reasonable reward but no more.
- It can be difficult to develop performance measures and methods of rating team performance that are seen to be fair – team pay formulae may well be based on arbitrary assumptions about the correct relationship between effort and reward.
- There may be pressure from employees to migrate from poorly performing teams to highly performing teams. If allowed, this

TABLE 27.3 Summary of individual merit pay schemes

Type of scheme	Main features	Advantages	Disadvantages	When most appropriate
Performance-related pay	Increases to basic pay or bonuses are related to assessment of performance	• May motivate (but this is uncertain) • Links rewards to objectives • Meets the need to be rewarded for achievement • Delivers message that good performance is important and will be rewarded	• May *not* motivate • Relies on judgements of performance, which may be subjective • Prejudicial to teamwork • Focuses on outputs, not quality • Relies on good performance management processes • Difficult to manage well	• For people who are likely to be motivated by money • In organizations with a performance-oriented culture • When performance can be measured objectively
Competency-related pay	Pay increases are related to the level of competency	• Focus attention on need to achieve higher levels of competency • Encourages competency development • Can be integrated with other applications of competency-based HR management	• Assessment of competency levels may be difficult • Ignores outputs – danger of paying for competencies that will not be used • Relies on well-trained and committed line managers	• As part of an integrated approach to HRM where competencies are used across a number of activities • Where competency is a key factor where it may be inappropriate or hard to measure outputs • Where well-established competency frameworks exist
Contribution-related pay	Increases in pay or bonuses are related both to inputs (competency) and outputs (performance)	Rewards people not only for what they do but how they do it	As for both PRP and competency-related pay – it may be hard to measure contribution and it is difficult to manage well	When it is believed that a well-rounded approach covering both inputs and outputs is appropriate
Skill-based pay	Increments related to the acquisition of skills	Encourages and rewards the acquisition of skills	Can be expensive when people are paid for skills they don't use	On the shop floor or in retail organizations

could cause disruption and stigmatize the teams from which individuals transfer; if refused it could leave dissatisfied employees in the inadequate teams, making them even worse.

- For many organizations, the disadvantages outweigh the advantages. Perhaps this is why the e-reward 2009 reward survey found that only 11 per cent of respondents had team pay.

Pay for organizational performance

Many organizations believe that their financial reward systems should extend beyond individual merit pay, which does not recognize collective effort, or team pay, which is difficult. They believe that their system should help to enhance engagement and commitment and convince employees that they have a stake in the business as well as providing them with additional pay. The response to this belief is to offer financial rewards that are related to business or organizational performance (sometimes known as 'company-wide' or 'factory-wide' schemes).

The three types of formal business performance schemes are:

- *Profit-sharing* – the payment of sums in cash or shares related to the profits of the business.
- *Share schemes* – employees are given the opportunity to take out share options or participate in a save-as-you-earn scheme of a share incentive plan.
- *Gain-sharing* – the payment of cash sums to employees related to the financial gains made by the company because of its improved performance.

Recognition schemes

Recognition schemes as part of a total reward package enable appreciation to be shown to individuals for their achievements, either informally on a day-to day basis or through formal recognition arrangements. They can take place quietly between managers and their teamworkers or be visible celebrations of success.

A recognition scheme can be formal and organization-wide, providing scope to recognize achievements by gifts or treats or by public applause. Typically, the awards are non-financial but some organizations provide cash awards. Importantly, recognition is also given less formally when managers simply say, 'Well done', 'Thank you', or 'Congratulations' – face-to-face or in a brief note of appreciation.

Employee benefits

Employee benefits consist of arrangements made by employers for their employees that enhance the latter's well-being. They are provided in addition to pay and form important parts of the total reward package. As part of total remuneration, they may be deferred or contingent such as a pension scheme, insurance cover or sick pay, or they may be immediate such as a company car or a loan. Employee benefits also include holidays and leave arrangements, which are not strictly remuneration. Benefits are sometimes referred to dismissively as 'perks' (perquisites) or 'fringe benefits', but when they cater for personal security or personal needs they could hardly be described as 'fringe'. Flexible benefit schemes give employees a choice, within limits, of the type or scale of benefits offered to them by their employers.

Pension provision has undergone considerable change recently. The traditional defined benefit scheme, which provides a pension based on final salary, is disappearing rapidly (too costly) and is being replaced by defined contribution schemes where the retirement pension is whatever annual payment can be purchased with the money accumulated in the fund for a member (cheaper). The 2103 CIPD survey found that the average employer contribution to a defined contribution scheme was 7.9 per cent of salary, while the average employee contribution was 5.0 per cent of salary.

Employee benefits are a costly part of the remuneration package. They can amount to one-third or more of basic pay costs and therefore have to be planned and managed with care.

Evaluating reward

Reward evaluation uses information obtained from reward reviews and reward measurements to assess the level of effectiveness achieved by existing or new reward policies and practices. In essence, it is the comparison of reward outcomes with reward objectives to answer the question of how far the reward system has achieved its purpose. The aims are to:

- find out how well established reward policies and practices are working and identify any problems;
- establish whether reward innovations are functioning as planned and achieving the objectives set for them;
- ensure that value for money is obtained from the different parts of the reward system;
- provide the evidence required to indicate what needs to be done to improve reward effectiveness.

A failure to evaluate pay and reward practices is a critical blind-spot for many of those involved in reward management. This was noted by Pfeffer (1998: 213), who wrote that: 'Little evidence demonstrates the efficacy of rewards, although much evidence indicates that rewards and their design loom large in management attention.' Gerhart and Rynes (2003: 1) commented that:

> Compensation is a complex and often confusing topic. Although compensation costs comprise, on average, 65 per cent to 70 per cent of total costs in the US economy and are likewise substantial elsewhere, most managers are not sure of the likely consequences of spending either more, or less on employees or of paying employees in different ways.

Reward evaluation is a necessary way of improving reward management effectiveness. It is a way of thinking based upon obtaining answers to the following questions posed by Armstrong *et al* (2010: 101):

- What are we trying to do here, what's important to this organization, how do we measure that?
- How are current reward practices helping or hindering what we are trying to do and what evidence do we have of this?
- How might reward changes improve the delivery of the desired outcomes?
- How can we best implement improvements and how can we show ourselves that they are working?

Use of an evidence-based management approach

An evidence-based management approach is required to provide a systematic basis for evaluating reward. As Pfeffer (1998: 196) pointed out: 'Thinking about pay ought to be based on logic and evidence, not on belief or ideology.' Rousseau (2006: 256) explained that: 'Evidence-based management means translating principles based on best evidence into organizational practices.'

Research conducted by Armstrong *et al* (2011) concluded that there are a number of common components to a process of evidence-based reward management, namely: setting strategic objectives, conducting reward reviews of current policies and practices, measuring reward effectiveness, and using the data generated by reviews and measurements to evaluate reward outcomes as a basis for introducing new or improved reward practices. But these are applied in all sorts of ways; sometimes sequentially, sometimes not, depending on the needs of the situation. A model of how the components function in practice is shown in Figure 27.1. It appears to describe a sequential progress in the form of a continuous cycle, from setting objectives and success criteria, through review, measurement, evaluation, and development activities to implementation and further review. This can happen in some circumstances, for example a review by outside consultants. But, as was established from the research case studies of Armstrong *et al*, in practice the components are not necessarily specified or managed in an orderly sequence. They are closely interlinked and they may overlap. Objective setting, review and measurement affect all the other components, as does evaluation. They can take place at any time (or all at once) and they all directly influence the ultimate activities of development and implementation.

Advice on reward evaluation

The following advice on reward evaluation was given by a senior reward practitioner in one of the Armstrong *et al* (2011) case study companies:

1. The best starting point before setting any targets or measuring anything is to decide what the organization wants to achieve.

FIGURE 27.1 A model of the interrelationships between the components of evidence-based reward management

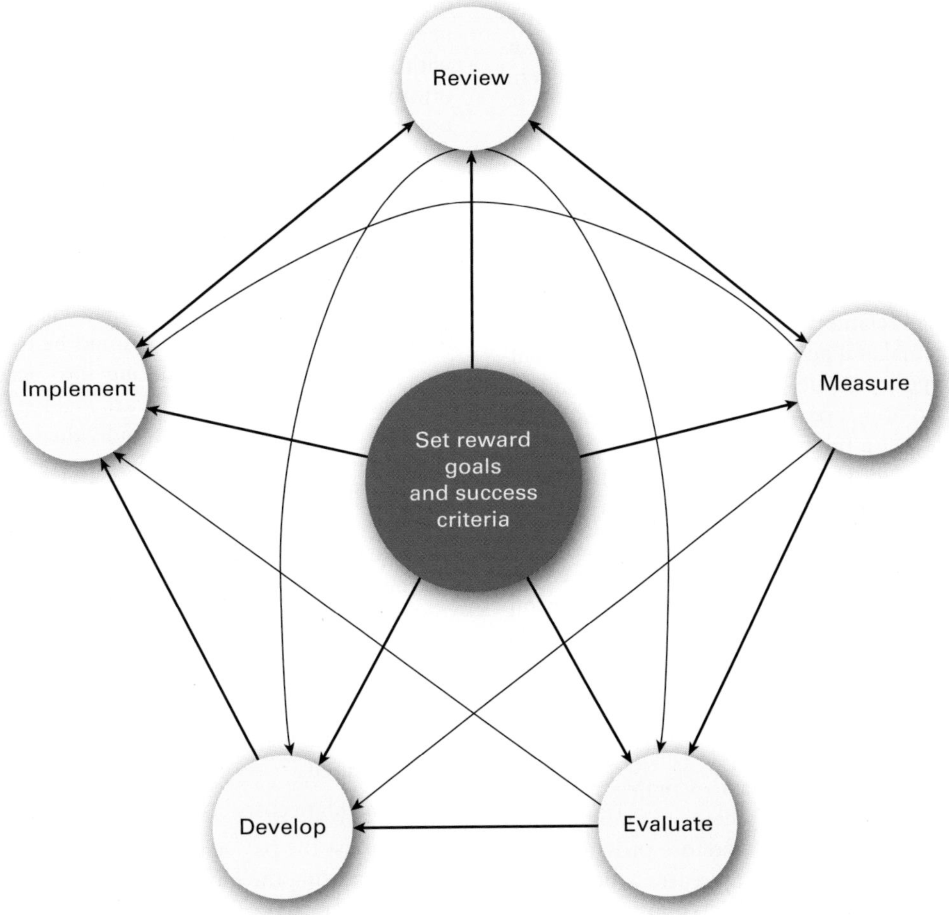

2 Once this has been decided, you should use as much data as you can and benchmark this against the market, before deciding where the company should be positioned.

3 Take care when interpreting data such as high staff satisfaction scores and other perception-related measures – they could simply be reflecting generous, rather than effective, rewards.

4 In some cases evaluation is not necessary – it is plain to see when certain elements of the reward system are working or not.

5 It is your job to place evidence in context and try to interpret what is really happening and why.

Some of the reward evaluation software packages available, although clever, tend only to use quantitative measures, so they don't take account of some of the other factors that might be at work. This is where you come in – to interpret and make sense of the grey as well as black and white areas.

Administering reward management

The administration of reward management is conducted through three main activities: base pay management by means of compa-ratio analysis, general pay reviews and individual pay reviews.

Base pay management through compa-ratio analysis

A compa-ratio (short for 'comparative ratio') measures the relationship in a graded pay structure between actual and policy rates of pay as a percentage. The policy value used is the mid-point or reference point in a pay range, which represents the 'target rate' for a fully competent individual in any job in the grade. This point is aligned with market rates in accordance with the organization's market stance.

Compa-ratios can be used to define the extent to which pay policy is achieved (the relationship between the policy and actual rates of pay). The analysis of compa-ratios indicates what action may have to be taken to slow down or accelerate increases if compa-ratios are too high or too low compared with the policy level. This is sometimes called 'mid-point management'. Compa-ratios can also be used to measure where an individual is placed in a pay range and therefore provide information on the size of pay increases when a pay matrix is used, as described later in this chapter. Compa-ratios are calculated as follows:

$$\frac{\text{actual rate of pay}}{\text{mid or reference point of range}} \times 100$$

A compa-ratio of 100 per cent means that actual pay and policy pay are the same. Compa-ratios higher or lower than 100 per cent mean that, respectively, pay is above or below the policy target rate. For example, if the target (policy) rate in a range were £20,000 and the average pay of all the individuals in the grade were £18,000, the compa-ratio would be 90 per cent. Compa-ratios establish differences between policy and practice. The reasons for such differences need to be established.

General pay reviews

General reviews take place when employees are given an increase in response to general market rate movements, increases in the cost of living, or union negotiations. General reviews are often combined with individual reviews, but employees are usually informed of both the general and individual components of any increase they receive. Alternatively, the general review may be conducted separately to enable better control to be achieved over costs and to focus employees' attention on the performance-related aspect of their remuneration.

Some organizations have completely abandoned the use of across-the-board reviews. They argue that the decision on what people should be paid should be an individual matter, taking into account the personal contribution people are making and their 'market worth' – how they as individuals are valued in the marketplace. This enables the organization to adopt a more flexible approach to allocating pay increases in accordance with the perceived value of individuals to the organization.

The steps required to conduct a general review are:

1. Decide on the budget.
2. Analyse data on pay settlements made by comparable organizations and rates of inflation.
3. Conduct negotiations with trade unions as required.
4. Calculate costs.
5. Adjust the pay structure – by either increasing the pay brackets of each grade by the percentage general increase or by increasing pay reference points by the overall percentage and applying different increases to the upper or lower limits of the bracket, thus altering the shape of the structure.
6. Inform employees.

Individual pay reviews

Individual pay reviews determine contingent pay increases or bonuses. The e-reward 2009 survey of contingent pay found that the average size of the pay awards made by respondents was 3.3 per cent. Individual awards may be based on ratings, an overall assessment that does not depend on ratings, or ranking, as discussed below.

Individual pay reviews based on ratings

Managers propose increases on the basis of their performance management ratings within a given pay review budget and in accordance with pay review guidelines. Of the respondents to the CIPD performance management survey (Armstrong and Baron, 2004) 42 per cent used ratings to inform contingent pay decisions.

There is a choice of methods. The simplest way is to have a direct link between the rating and the pay increase. For example:

Rating	% Increase
A	6
B	4
C	3
D	2
E	0

A more sophisticated approach is to use a pay matrix, as illustrated in Figure 27.2. This indicates the percentage increase payable for different performance ratings according to the position of the individual's pay in the pay range (the individual 'compa-ratio').

Many people argue that linking performance management too explicitly to pay prejudices the essential developmental nature of performance management. However, realistically, it is accepted that decisions on performance-related or contribution-related increases have to be based on some form of assessment. One solution is to 'decouple' performance management and the pay review by holding them several months apart; 45 per cent of the respondents surveyed by Armstrong and Baron (2004) separated performance management reviews from pay reviews (43 per cent of the respondents to the e-reward 2005 survey separated the review). There is still a read-across but it is not so immediate. Some try to do without formulaic approaches (ratings and pay matrices) altogether, although it is impossible to dissociate merit pay completely from some form of assessment.

FIGURE 27.2 A pay matrix

Rating	Percentage pay increase according to performance rating and position in pay range (compa-ratio)			
	Position in pay range			
	80%–90%	91%–100%	101%–110%	111%–120%
Excellent	12%	10%	8%	6%
Very effective	10%	8%	6%	4%
Effective	6%	4%	3%	0
Developing	4%	3%	0	0
Ineligible	0	0	0	0

Guidelines to managers on conducting individual pay reviews

Guidelines have to be issued to managers on how they should conduct reviews. The guidelines will stipulate that they must keep within their budgets and may indicate the maximum and minimum increases that can be awarded, with an indication of how awards could be distributed. For example, in happy days when the budget is 4 per cent overall, it might be suggested that a 3 per cent increase should be given to the majority of staff and the others given higher or lower increases as long as the total percentage increase does not exceed the budget. Managers in some companies are instructed that they must follow a forced pattern of distribution (a forced choice system), but only 8 per cent of the respondents to the CIPD survey (Armstrong and Baron, 2004) used this method.

Steps required

The steps required to conduct an individual pay review are:

- Agree the budget.
- Prepare and issue guidelines on the size, range and distribution of awards and on methods of conducting the review.
- Provide advice and support.
- Review proposals against budget and guidelines and agree modifications to them if necessary.
- Summarize and cost proposals and obtain approval.
- Update the payroll.
- Inform employees.

CASE STUDIES

Kent County Council: successful reward

The council attributes success in its reward policies to a strong and united political direction from the top; a long-term consistency of purpose, but with the appropriate phasing of changes and with adaptation to local circumstances; and a high involvement approach.

McDonald's: demonstrating reward effectiveness

McDonald's is a company with a strong culture of measurement and has built its own people-profit chain methodology to produce impressive evidence that demonstrates how rewards can enhance employee engagement and thereby business performance. The operational and cost focus in the business means that reward arrangements are reviewed regularly and changed if they are not found to be delivering. But the subtler processes of consultation and change management are equally vital in maintaining and strengthening reward effectiveness.

The NSPCC: approaches to achieving reward effectiveness

The experience of the NSPCC was that while measures of organizational and reward effectiveness may differ, the delivery of them is every bit as critical, if not more so, in voluntary organizations. It also shows that limited resources need not be a barrier to assessing and demonstrating effectiveness. Establishing links to the core purpose of the organization was the major driver behind the extensive research undertaken into effectiveness. The culture of the organization and its values were important considerations, as was ensuring that the values of the people in the organization were aligned to them.

Changing the pay structure at Marks & Spencer

Prior to 2005 there were 429 different rates for customer assistants, ranging from £4.94 per hour for new staff, up to £10 per hour for long-serving employees. In May 2005, M&S announced that it would reduce these to four standard rates for customer assistants (with regional variations), which would be tied to specific roles – trainee and qualified, which already existed, and two newly created positions: coach and section coordinator. The move was designed to give staff better career progression opportunities.

Key learning points: The practice of reward management

Reward management defined

Reward management is concerned with the strategies, policies and processes required to ensure that the value of people and the contribution they make to achieving organizational, departmental and team goals is recognized and rewarded.

Pay determination

Pay determination is the process of deciding on the level of pay for jobs or people. The two aims of pay determination, which frequently conflict, are: 1) to be externally competitive in order to attract, engage and retain the people required by the organization; and 2) to be internally equitable in the sense that rates of pay correctly reflect the relativities between jobs.

Market pricing

Market pricing is the process of making decisions on pay structures and individual rates of pay and obtaining information on market rates (market rate analysis). Market rate analysis may be associated with formal job evaluation. The latter establishes internal relativities and the grade structure, and market pricing is used to develop the pay structure – the pay ranges attached to grades. Information on market rates may lead to the introduction of market supplements for individual jobs or the creation of separate pay structures (market groups) to cater for particular market rate pressures.

Job evaluation

Job evaluation is a systematic and formal process for defining the relative worth or size of jobs within an organization in order to establish internal relativities. It is carried out through either an analytical or a non-analytical scheme. Analytical job evaluation is based on a process of breaking down whole jobs into a number of defined elements or factors such as responsibility, decisions and the knowledge and skill required. Non-analytical job evaluation schemes enable whole jobs to be compared in order to place them in a grade or a rank order – they are not analysed by reference to their elements or factors.

Base pay management

The management of base pay uses the information from market pricing and job evaluation to design and operate grade and pay structures that cater for job-based pay and allow scope for pay to progress within the structure through person-based pay.

Grade and pay structures

Grade and pay structures provide a framework within which an organization's pay policies can be implemented. They enable the organization to determine where jobs should be placed in a hierarchy, define pay levels and the scope for pay progression, and provide the basis upon which relativities can be managed, equal pay achieved and the processes of monitoring and controlling the implementation of pay practices can take place.

A grade structure consists of a sequence or hierarchy of grades, bands or levels into which groups of jobs that are broadly comparable in size are placed. A grade structure becomes a pay structure when pay ranges, brackets or scales are attached to each grade, band or level. The main types of grade and pay structures are narrow-graded, broad-graded, broad-banded and pay spines.

Pay progression

Pay progression takes place when base pay advances through pay ranges or brackets in a grade and pay structure, or through promotions or upgradings.

Contingent pay

Contingent pay can be related to individual merit or service or to team or organizational performance or a combination of these.

For salary earners, individual contingent pay can take the form of consolidated increases to base pay that provide for pay progression, or cash bonuses (or both). Wage earners may receive unconsolidated cash payments, in addition to their base pay, through an incentive scheme.

Team pay

Team pay links payments to members of a formally established team to the performance of that team. This is a popular form of reward – the 2009 e-reward reward survey found that 59 per cent of respondents had such schemes.

Pay for organizational performance

The provision of financial rewards that are related to business or organizational performance (sometimes known as 'company-wide' or 'factory-wide' schemes). They include profit-sharing, share schemes and gain-sharing.

Recognition schemes

Recognition schemes as part of a total reward package enable appreciation to be shown to individuals for their achievements, informally on a day-to day basis or through formal recognition arrangements.

Employee benefits

Employee benefits consist of arrangements made by employers for their employees that enhance the latter's well-being. They are provided in addition to pay and form important parts of the total reward package.

Evaluating reward

Reward evaluation uses information obtained from reward reviews and reward measurements to assess the level of effectiveness achieved by existing or new reward policies and practices.

Administering reward management

The administration of reward management is conducted through three main activities: base pay management through compa-ratio analysis, conducting general pay reviews and conducting individual pay reviews.

Questions

1 What is reward management?
2 What are the main aims of reward management?
3 What is a reward system?
4 What is base pay?
5 What is contingent pay?
6 What are financial rewards?
7 What are the main arguments in favour of financial rewards?
8 What are the main arguments against financial rewards?
9 What is a total rewards approach?
10 What is market pricing?
11 What is job evaluation?
12 What are the main types of job evaluation schemes?
13 What is base pay management?
14 What is a grade structure?
15 What is a pay structure?
16 What are the main types of grade and pay structures?
17 What are the guiding principles for grade and pay structures?
18 What is contingent pay?
19 What are the main types of contingent pay?
20 What are the main types of individual contingent pay schemes?
21 What is team pay?
22 What are the main schemes relating rewards to organizational performance?
23 What is evidence-based reward management?
24 What is a compa-ratio and how is it used?
25 What are the steps needed to conduct an individual pay review?

References

Armstrong, M and Baron, A (2004) *Managing Performance: Performance management in action*, London, CIPD

Armstrong, M, Brown, D and O'Reilly, P (2010) *Evidence-based Reward*, London, Kogan Page

Armstrong, M, Brown, D and O'Reilly, P (2011) Increasing the effectiveness of reward: an evidence-based approach, *Employee Relations*, 33 (2), pp 106–20

Booth, A L and Frank, J (1999) Earnings, productivity and performance related pay, *Journal of Labor Economics*, 17 (3), pp 447–63

Bowey, A and Thorpe, R (1982) *The Effects of Incentive Pay Systems*, London, Department of Employment

CIPD (2013) *Reward Management Annual Survey Report*, London, CIPD

e-reward (2003) *Survey of Job Evaluation*, Stockport, e-reward

e-reward (2005) *Survey of Performance Management Practice*, Stockport, e-reward

e-reward (2009) *Survey of Contingent Pay*, Stockport, e-reward

Gerhart, B and Rynes, S L (2003) *Compensation: Theory, evidence and strategic implications*, Thousand Oaks, CA, Sage

Ghoshal, S and Bartlett, C A (1995) Changing the role of top management: beyond structure to process, *Harvard Business Review*, January–February, pp 86–96

Gupta, N and Shaw, J D (1998) Financial incentives, *Compensation & Benefits Review*, March–April, pp 26, 28–32

IRS Employment Review (2012) *Annual Review of Pay Trends*, September, p 1

Jenkins, D G, Mitra, A, Gupta, N and Shaw, J D (1998) Are financial incentives related to performance? A meta-analytic review of empirical research, *Journal of Applied Psychology*, 3, pp 777–87

Kessler, I and Purcell, J (1992) Performance-related pay: objectives and application, *Human Resource Management Journal*, 2 (3), pp 16–33

Kohn, A (1993) Why incentive plans cannot work, *Harvard Business Review*, September–October, pp 54–63

Lazear, E P (1999) Performance pay and productivity, *American Economic Review*, 90, pp 1346–61

Marsden, D (2004) The role of performance-related pay in renegotiating the 'effort bargain': the case of the British public service, *Industrial and Labor Relations Review*, 57 (3), pp 350–70

Marsden, D and Richardson, R (1994) Performing for pay? The effects of 'merit pay' on motivation in a public service, *British Journal of Industrial Relations*, 32 (2), pp 243–61

Pfeffer, J (1998) Six dangerous myths about pay, *Harvard Business Review*, May–June, pp 109–19

Prendergast, C (1999) The provision of financial incentives in firms, *Journal of Economic Literature*, 37, pp 7–63

Prentice, G, Burgess, S and Propper, C (2007) *Performance Pay in the Public Sector: A review of the issues and evidence*, London, Office of Manpower Economics

Rousseau, D M (2006) Is there such a thing as evidence-based management? *Academy of Management Review*, 31 (2), pp 256–69

Thompson, M (1992a) *Pay and Performance: The employer experience*, Brighton, IMS

Thompson, M (1992b) *Pay and Performance: The employee experience*, Brighton, IMS

Thompson, M (1998) HR and the bottom line, *People Management*, 16 April, pp 38–41

Trevor, J (2011) *Can Pay be Strategic?* Basingstoke, Palgrave Macmillan

Wright, V (1991) Performance-related pay, in (ed) E Neale, *The Performance Management Handbook*, London, Institute of Personnel Management

28 Managing reward for special groups

KEY CONCEPTS AND TERMS

Agency theory	Segmentation
Commission	Share option schemes
Deferred bonus schemes	Time rates
Measured day work	Tournament theory
Piece work	Work measurement

LEARNING OUTCOMES

On completing this chapter you should be able to define these key concepts. You should also know about:

- Reward policies and practices for directors and senior executives
- Reward policies and practices for knowledge workers
- Reward policies and practices for sales and customer service staff
- Reward policies and practices for manual workers

Introduction

Many organizations have one reward system applied to all categories of staff below the level of chief executive. However, others find it necessary to cater for the needs of special groups of staff by adopting different reward practices. This is called reward segmentation and, as described in this chapter, frequently applies to the methods used for directors and senior executives, knowledge workers, sales and customer service staff and manual workers.

Rewarding directors and senior executives

Probably no aspect of remuneration has attracted as much attention recently as that of the pay of directors and senior executives, especially since the 2008–09 banking crisis. Searching questions are being asked frequently about the level of remuneration, the basis upon which pay decisions are made, the conditions for earning bonuses, and pension arrangements. A leader in *The Guardian* (2012: 26) commented that: 'Top pay in America and Britain has gone from being a question of how much bosses can earn, to how much some can extract from their companies.'

Executive pay levels

Executive pay is out of control. The High Pay Commission (2011) recorded that in 1999 the average annual pay of chief executives in FTSE 100 companies was £1,234,983 compared with the average annual employee pay of £17,803 – a multiple of 69. Ten years later in 2009 the average pay of chief executives was £3,747,000 compared with the average pay for employees of £25,816 – a multiple of 145. It is even worse in the United States where in 1965 CEOs earned on average about twenty times as much as their typical employee. They now earn about two hundred and seventy times as much (Surowiecki, 2013).

The High Pay Commission found evidence that excessive high pay damages companies, is bad for our economy and has negative impacts on society as a whole. At its worst, excessive high pay bears little relation to company success and is rewarding failure. The commission established that between 1998 and 2009 chief executive remuneration quadrupled while share prices have declined. The remuneration of chief executives of FTSE 100 companies rose by 6.7 per cent per year, while earnings per share fell by 1 per cent per year over the same period.

It has been established by research (Conyon and Leech, 1994; Gomez-Mejia and Balkin, 1992; Gregg *et al* 1993) that there is no evidence that the huge increases in pay have resulted in improved company performance.

Why has executive pay grown so much?

The reasons for the growth in executive rewards as explained by Dymond and Murlis (2009) are:

- Agency theory: shareholders must structure the CEO's pay arrangements to reward behaviours that increase shareholder wealth – this is the most important reason. Agency theory indicates that it is desirable to operate a system of incentives for the agents (directors or managers) of the principles (owners) to motivate and reward acceptable behaviour.
- Tournament theory: the high rewards received by CEOs have little to do with what they deserve. Rather, the main purpose of such rewards is to send signals to senior managers to motivate them to compete for the number one spot. Tournament theory states that the highest prizes (pay) of all are given to the person who wins the tournament by getting the top job.
- The changing nature of companies and the increasing demands made on chief executives.
- Star culture: the creation of the celebrity CEO.
- The talent shortage.
- Pay disclosure in annual reports leading to demands from CEOs to achieve parity.
- Peer group analysis – as Elson and Ferrere (2012: 108) observed: 'Boards typically gravitate in fixing compensation to a set of arbitrary targets – ie, the 50th, 75th, and 90th percentiles of peer group pay. A blind reliance on these pay targets has resulted in a mathematically based upward pay spiral. This dynamic is popularly referred to as the 'Lake Wobegon' effect. [A phrase from the Garrison Keeler book *Lake Wobegon Days* referring to a situation in which all or nearly all of a group claim to be above average].

Corporate governance and executive remuneration

Corporate governance is the internal set of processes and policies that determine the way a corporation is directed and controlled, and serve the needs of shareholders and other stakeholders. It involves the board of a company and includes how members of that board are remunerated. The Combined Code on Corporate Governance produced by the Financial Reporting Council in 2008 laid down general principles of governance and a number of specific principles relating to the remuneration of directors. These are:

- Levels of remuneration should be sufficient to attract, retain and motivate directors of the quality required to run the company successfully, but a company should avoid paying more than is necessary for this purpose. A significant proportion of executive directors' remuneration should be structured so as to link rewards to corporate and individual performance.
- The remuneration committee should judge where to position their company relative to other companies. But they should use such comparisons with caution, in view of the risk of an upward ratchet of remuneration levels with no corresponding improvement in performance. They should also be sensitive to pay and employment conditions elsewhere in the group, especially when determining annual salary increases.
- The performance-related elements of remuneration should form a significant proportion of the total remuneration package of executive directors and should be designed to align their interests with those of shareholders and to give these directors keen incentives to perform at the highest levels.
- The remuneration committee should consider whether the directors should be eligible for annual bonuses. If so, performance conditions should be relevant, stretching and designed to enhance shareholder value. Upper limits should be set and disclosed. There may be a case for part payment in shares to be held for a significant period.
- Payouts or grants under all incentive schemes, including new grants under existing share option schemes, should be subject to challenging performance criteria that reflect the company's objectives. The total rewards potentially available should not be excessive.
- The remuneration committee should consider the pension consequences and associated costs to the company of basic salary increases and any other changes in pensionable remuneration, especially for directors close to retirement.

But it seems that these principles are frequently more honoured in the breach than in the observance.

The elements of executive remuneration

The main elements of executive remuneration are basic pay, short- and long-term bonus or incentive schemes, share option and share ownership schemes, benefits and service contracts. The salary is usually a one-off, negotiated rate and commonly incorporates a golden hello or pay-off deal. It should be set through a remuneration committee that meets good practice guidelines.

Basic pay

Decisions on the base salary of directors and senior executives are usually founded on views about the market worth of the individuals concerned. Remuneration on joining the company is commonly settled by negotiation, often subject to the approval of a remuneration committee. Reviews of base salaries are then undertaken by reference to market movements and success as measured by company performance. Decisions on base salary are important not only in themselves but also because the level may influence decisions on the pay of both senior and middle managers. Bonuses are expressed as a percentage of base salary, share options may be allocated as a declared multiple of basic pay and, commonly, pension will be a generous proportion of final salary.

Bonus schemes

Virtually all major employers in the UK have incentive (bonus) schemes for senior executives. Bonus schemes provide directors and executives with cash sums or shares based on the measures of company and, frequently, individual performance. They are often paid annually but can be deferred for a longer period.

Typically, bonus payments are linked to achievement of profit and/or other financial targets and they are sometimes 'capped'; that is, a restriction is placed on the maximum amount payable. There may also be elements related to achieving specific goals and to individual performance. Bonuses tend to be high – 70 per cent of base salary or more. They are ostensibly intended to motivate directors to achieve performance improvements for the business. A more common although not always disclosed reason for bonuses is to ensure that what is believed to be a competitive remuneration package is available: 'Everyone else is doing it so we must too.'

One of the problems with high bonus expectations is that of the 'moral hazard' involved. For example, directors might be tempted to manipulate reported profits in order to drive up the share price, frequently an important determinant of bonuses. Or they may go for high returns in risky short-term projects, ignoring the possible downside of longer-term losses.

Executives may benefit by receiving bonuses for performance that meets objectives but they do not usually lose pay when their objectives are not achieved. They only gain, they never lose. It can be argued that they should get their base salary for doing their jobs, ie achieving their objectives, and only receive more in the shape of a bonus if they exceed expectations. It could also be argued that if that they fail to meet their objectives they should be penalized by not receiving a portion of their base salary, which would then truly be pay-at-risk. Earn-back pay schemes try to remedy this situation. Such schemes require executives to meet agreed objectives in order to earn back an element of base pay placed at risk. If they do not succeed against the objectives, some or all of the earn-back pay will be lost.

Long-term bonuses

Cash bonus schemes can be extended over periods of more than one year on the grounds that annual bonuses focus too much on short-term results. The most common approach to providing longer-term rewards is through share ownership schemes, as described later.

Deferred bonus schemes

Some companies have adopted deferred bonus schemes under which part of the executive's annual bonus is deferred for, say, two years. The deferred element is converted into shares, each of which is matched with an extra, free share on condition that the executive remains employed by the company at the end of the deferral period. Such a scheme is designed to reward performance and loyalty to the company.

Share option schemes

Many companies have share option schemes that give directors and executives the right to buy a block of shares on some future date at the share price ruling when the option was granted. They are a form of long-term incentive on the assumption that executives will be motivated to perform more effectively if they can anticipate a substantial capital gain when they sell their shares at a price above that prevailing when they took up the option.

Performance share schemes

Some companies have performance share schemes under which executives are provisionally awarded shares. The release of the shares is subject to the company's performance, typically determined on a sliding scale by reference to the company's total shareholder return (a combination of share price growth and dividend yield) ranking against its chosen peer companies over a three-year period. Release is also conditional on the executive remaining employed by the company at the vesting date. Such a scheme rewards loyalty to the company and the value delivered to shareholders in the form of share price performance and dividends but does not link directly to business performance.

Executive restricted share schemes

Under such schemes free shares are provisionally awarded to participants. These shares do not belong to the executive until they are released or vested; hence they are 'restricted'. The number of shares actually released to the executive at the end of a defined period (usually three or, less commonly, five years) will depend on performance over that period against specific targets. Thereafter there may be a further retention period when the shares must be held, although no further performance conditions apply.

Benefits

Employee benefits for executives may amount to over 20 per cent of the total reward package. The most important element is the pension scheme, and directors may be provided with a much higher accrual rate than in a typical final salary scheme. This means that, typically, the maximum two-thirds pension can be achieved after 20 years' service or even less, rather than the 40 years it takes in a typical one-sixtieth scheme. Pensions are easily inflated, as demonstrated in a recent notorious case, by presenting the departing director with a last-minute substantial increase in pensionable salary.

Service contracts

Long-term service contracts for directors – ie more than one year – have been fairly typical, but they are disliked in the City because of the high severance payments to departing chief executives and directors that are made if the contract is two or three years, even when it was suspected or actually the case that they had been voted off the board because of inadequate performance. Rolling contracts for directors are now more likely to be restricted to one year.

Rewarding knowledge workers

Knowledge workers are people whose jobs require expertise. Their work is defined by the knowledge they need to do it. The term therefore embraces such diverse groups as scientists, accountants, HR professionals, IT specialists, lawyers, media workers and researchers. This is an area of reward management where segmentation may be appropriate.

The nature of knowledge work, especially in smaller high-tech organizations such as software houses, means that a more flexible approach to pay is required, which pays close attention to levels of competence and skill. For example, the fluid grading system used in the scientific civil service allows for much more flexibility in rewarding scientists in line with their levels of competence rather than by the levels of responsibility that characterize traditional multigraded structures.

Pay flexibility

The overall approach to rewarding knowledge workers should be flexibility within a framework. This means that a common framework of reward policies exists across the organization but within that framework segmentation can take place. Pay arrangements can then be tailored to suit the needs of particular groups of knowledge and professional workers and the individuals within those groups. Pay flexibility could include market rate supplements to attract and retain specific categories of staff and the use of selected market groups (separate pay structures for certain types of staff).

Pay related to competency

If knowledge workers apply their expertise then it seems reasonable to reward them according to the level of expertise (competency) they possess and apply. There are three ways of doing this: 1) by competency-related pay; 2) through structures in which grades or bands are defined in competency terms; and 3) the incorporation of skills and competencies into job evaluation factor plans.

Job and career families

Job and career-family structures consist of separate families of jobs with similar characteristics. Within each family the successive levels of competency required to carry out typical activities are defined, thus indicating career paths. They are particularly appropriate for knowledge workers because they spell out the career ladders that apply specifically to the different categories employed in an organization.

Reward management for sales and customer service staff

Sales and customer service staff make an immediate impact on business results. This has led to an emphasis on financial incentives, especially for sales representatives and sales staff in retailers, who are often treated quite differently from other employees. The reward system for sales and service staff also has to take account of the fact that they are the people who are in direct contact with customers, and this also applies to people in call centres.

There are no hard-and-fast rules governing how sales representatives or customer service staff should be paid. It depends on the type of company, the products or services it offers its customers and the nature of the sales process – how sales are organized and made.

Rewarding sales representatives

Sales representatives are more likely to be eligible for commission payments or bonuses than other staff, on the grounds that their sales performance will depend on or at least be improved by financial incentives. Many companies believe that the special nature of selling and the type of person they need to attract to their sales force requires some form of additional bonus or commission to be paid. The nature of the work of sales staff means that it is usually easy to specify targets and measure performance against them, and sales incentive schemes are therefore more likely to meet the line of sight requirement (ie that there should be a clear link between effort and performance) than schemes for other staff such as managers and administrators. Sales staff, including those in retail establishments, are often paid spot rates with a commission on sales. See Table 28.1.

TABLE 28.1 Summary of payment and incentive arrangements for sales staff

Method	Features	Advantages	Disadvantages	When appropriate
Salary only	Straight salary, no commission or bonus	Encourage customer service rather than high-pressure selling; deal with the problem of staff who are working in a new or unproductive sales territory; protects income when sales fluctuate for reasons beyond the individual's control	No direct motivation through money; may attract underachieving people who are subsidized by high achievers; increases fixed costs of sales because pay costs are not flexed with sales results	When representing the company is more important than direct selling; staff have little influence on sales volume (they may simply be 'order takers'); customer service is all-important
Salary plus commission	Basic salary plus cash commission calculated as a percentage of sales volume or value	Direct financial motivation is provided, related to what sales staff are there to do, ie generate sales; but they are not entirely dependent on commission – they are cushioned by their base salary	Relating pay to the volume or value of sales is too crude an approach and may result in staff going for volume by concentrating on the easier to sell products not those generating high margins; may encourage high-pressure selling as in some financial services firms in the 1980s and 90s	When it is believed that the way to get more sales is to link extra money to results but a base salary is still needed to attract the many people who want to be assured of a reasonable basic salary that will not fluctuate but who still aspire to increase that salary by their own efforts

TABLE 28.1 Continued

Method	Features	Advantages	Disadvantages	When appropriate
Salary plus bonus	Basic salary plus cash bonus based on achieving and exceeding sales targets or quotas and meeting other selling objectives	Provide financial motivation but targets or objectives can be flexed to ensure that particular sales goals are achieved, eg high margin sales, customer service	Do not have a clear line of sight between effort and reward; may be complex to administer; sales representative may find them hard to understand and resent the use of subjective judgements on performance other than sales	When: flexibility in providing rewards is important; it is felt that sales staff need to be motivated to focus on aspects of their work other than simply maximizing sales volume
Commission only	Only commission based on a percentage of sales volume or value is paid, there is no basic salary	Provide a direct financial incentive; attract high-performing sales staff; ensure that selling costs vary directly with sales; little direct supervision required	Lead to high-pressure selling; may attract the wrong sort of people who are interested only in sales and not customer service; focus attention on high volume rather than profitability	When: sales performance depends mainly on selling ability and can be measured by immediate sales results; staff are not involved in non-selling activities; continuing relationships with customers are relatively unimportant
Additional non-cash rewards	Incentives, prizes, cars, recognition, opportunities to grow	Utilize powerful non-financial motivators	May be difficult to administer; do not provide a direct incentive	When it is believed that other methods of payment need to be enhanced by providing additional motivators

Rewarding customer service staff

Customer service staff work mainly in retail establishments and in call or customer contact centres. Their rewards need to reflect the nature of their duties, ie enhancing levels of customer service as well as selling.

Research conducted by West *et al* (2005) established that most employees in the researched organizations had the opportunity to progress their base pay on the basis of their performance or competence, either through a range or up a pay spine, or between grades/levels of job. Such arrangements have generally supplanted spot rates for service roles in call centres and retail shops. Low base pay/high commission arrangements were rare.

At Boots the chemists, shop staff can progress up through a number of pay points according to their level of performance and skill – from entry level, to experienced, to advanced, to expert/specialist. At B&Q, customer advisers are paid on one of six different spot rates. Pay progression is based on the acquisition – and application on the shop floor – of skills and knowledge. There are four additional spot rates beyond the established rate, designed to reward high performance. Each additional level represents an hourly increase up to a maximum rate. At House of Fraser, employees are allocated to one of four competency bands – training, bronze, silver and gold – with staff assessed for a 'promotion' every six months. At Lands' End, there is a six-grade pay structure for hourly paid staff, with spot rates for starters.

Paying manual workers

The pay of manual workers takes the form of time rates, also known as day rates, day work, flat rates or hourly rates. Incentive payments by means of payment-by-results schemes may be made on top of a base rate.

Time rates

These provide workers with a predetermined rate for the actual hours they work. Time rates on their own are most commonly used when it is thought that it is impossible or undesirable to use a payment-by-results system, for example in maintenance work. From the viewpoint of employees the advantage of time rates is that their earnings are predictable and steady and they do not have to engage in endless arguments with rate fixers and supervisors about piece rate or time allowances. The argument against them is that they do not provide a direct incentive relating the reward to the effort or the results. Two ways of modifying the basic time rate approach are to adopt high day rates, as described below, or measured day work.

Time rates may take the form of what are often called high day rates. These are higher than the minimum time rate and may contain a consolidated bonus rate element. The underlying assumption is that higher base rates will encourage greater effort without the problems created when operating an incentive scheme. High day rates are usually above the local market rates in order to attract and retain workers.

Pay structures

Pay systems for manual workers are seldom graded in the ways described in Chapter 27 unless their conditions have been harmonized. Time rates are usually paid in the form of spot rates: that is, a fixed rate for a job or an individual. However, spot rates may be designated for different levels of skill. A person-based pay system may be adopted with three basic rates of pay attached to people – unskilled, semi-skilled and skilled – above which there might be special rates for highly skilled occupations such as toolmakers. Earnings from payment-by-result schemes were added to these rates. Other arrangements include the use of a more discerning hierarchy of rates linked to skill levels (a type of skills-based pay), a job-based pay system with different rates for different jobs, or individual job grades that are, in effect, spot rates to which there is a defined pay to provide scope for pay progression based on performance.

Payment-by-result schemes

Payment-by–result (PBR) schemes provide incentives to workers by relating their pay or, more usually, part of their pay to the number of items they produce or the time taken to do a certain amount of work. The main types of PBR or incentive schemes for individuals are piece work, work-measured schemes, measured day work and performance-related pay. Team bonus schemes are an alternative to individual PBR, and plant-wide schemes can produce bonuses that are paid instead of individual or team bonuses, or in addition to them. Each of these methods is described in Table 28.2 together with an assessment of their advantages and disadvantages for employers and employees and when they are appropriate.

TABLE 28.2 Comparison of shop floor payment-by-result schemes

Scheme	Main features	For employers		For employees		When appropriate
		Advantages	Disadvantages	Advantages	Disadvantages	
Piece work	Bonus directly related to output.	Direct motivation; simple, easy to operate.	Lose control over output; quality problems.	Predict and control earnings in the short-term; regulate pace of work themselves.	More difficult to predict and control earnings in the longer-term; work may be stressful and produce RSI.	Fairly limited application to work involving unit production controlled by the person, eg agriculture, garment manufacture.
Work-measured schemes	Work measurement used to determine standard output levels over a period or standard times for job/tasks; bonus based by reference to performance ratings compared with actual performance or time saved.	Provides what appears to be a 'scientific' method of relating reward to performance; can produce significant increases in productivity, at least in the short-term.	Schemes are expensive, time-consuming and difficult to run and can too easily degenerate and cause wage drift because of loose rates.	Appear to provide a more objective method of relating pay to performance; employees can be involved in the rating process to ensure fairness.	Ratings are still prone to subjective judgement and earnings can fluctuate because of changes in work requirements outside the control of employees.	For short-cycle repetitive work where changes in the work mix or design changes are infrequent, down time is restricted, and management and supervision are capable of managing and maintaining the scheme.
Measured day work	Pay fixed at a high rate on the understanding that a high level of performance against work-measured standards will be maintained.	Employees are under an obligation to work at the specified level of performance.	Performance targets can become easily attained norms and may be difficult to change.	High predictable earnings are provided.	No opportunities for individuals to be rewarded in line with their own efforts.	Everyone must be totally committed to making it work; high standards of work measurement are essential; good control systems to identify shortfalls on targets.

TABLE 28.2 Continued

Scheme	Main features	For employers		For employees		When appropriate
		Advantages	Disadvantages	Advantages	Disadvantages	
Performance-related pay	Payments on top of base rate are made, related to individual assessments of performance.	Reward individual contribution without resource to work measurement; relevant in high technology manufacturing.	Measuring performance can be difficult; no direct incentive provided.	Opportunity to be rewarded for own efforts without having to submit to a pressured PBR system.	Assessment informing performance pay decisions may be biased, inconsistent or unsupported by evidence.	As part of a reward harmonization (shop floor and staff) programme; as an alternative to work-measured schemes or an enhancement of a high day rate system.
Group or team basis	Groups or teams are paid bonuses on the basis of their performance as indicated by work measurement ratings or the achievement of targets.	Encourage team co-operation and effort; not too individualized.	Direct incentive may be limited; depends on good work measurement or the availability of clear group output or productivity targets.	Bonuses can be related clearly to the joint efforts of the group; fluctuations in earnings minimized.	Depend on effective work measurement, which is not always available; individual effort and contribution not recognized.	When team working is important and team efforts can be accurately measured and assessed; as an alternative to individual PBR if this is not effective.
Factory-wide bonuses	Bonuses related to plant performance – added value or productivity.	Increase commitment by sharing success.	No direct motivation.	Earnings increased without individual pressure.	Bonuses often small and unpredictable.	As an addition to other forms of incentive when increasing commitment is important.

Key learning points: Managing reward for special groups

Segmentation

Many organizations have one reward system applied to all categories of staff below the level of chief executive. However, others find it necessary to cater for the needs of special groups of staff by adopting different reward practices. This is called reward segmentation.

Executive pay levels

Executive pay is out of control. The reasons are:

- Tournament theory: the increasing demands made on chief executives.
- Star culture: the creation of the celebrity CEO.
- The talent shortage.
- Pay disclosure in annual reports lead to demands from CEOs to achieve parity.

Elements of directors' and senior executives' pay

Basic, pay, bonus schemes, share options, executive restricted share schemes.

Rewarding knowledge workers

The nature of knowledge work, especially in smaller high-tech organizations such as software houses, means that a more flexible approach to pay is required that gives close attention to levels of competence and skill.

Payment and incentive schemes for sales staff

Summarized in Table 28.1.

Pay for customer service staff

Customer service staff usually have the opportunity to progress their base pay on the basis of their performance or competence, either through a range or up a pay spine, or between grades/levels of job.

Pay for manual workers

The pay of manual workers takes the form of time rates, also known as day rates, day work, flat rates or hourly rates. Incentive payments by means of payment-by-results scheme, as summarized in Table 28.2, may be made on top of a base rate.

Questions

1 What is the function of a remuneration committee?
2 What is a knowledge worker?
3 How should knowledge workers be rewarded?
4 What are the main methods of rewarding sales staff?
5 What are the advantages and disadvantages for employers and employees of work-measured payment-by-result schemes?

References

Chartered Institute of Personnel and Development (2011) *Annual Reward Survey*, London, CIPD

Chartered Institute of Personnel and Development (2013) *Annual Reward Survey*, London, CIPD

The Combined Code on Corporate Governance (2008) London, The Financial Reporting Council

Conyon, M J and Leech, D (1994) Top pay, company performance and corporate performance, *Oxford Bulletin of Economics and Statistics*, 56 (3), August, pp 229–47

Dymond, J and Murlis, H (2009) Executive rewards: 'don't you just give them loads of money?' in (eds) S Corby, S Palmer and E Lindop, *Rethinking Reward*, Basingstoke, Palgrave Macmillan

Elson, C M and Ferrere, C K (2012) *Executive Superstars, Peer Groups and Over-Compensation–Cause, Effect and Solution*, Available at SSRN 2125979, 2012 – works.bepress.com [accessed 24 October 2013]

The Guardian (2012) *A Culture in Need of Curbing*, 6 February, p 26

Gomez-Mejia, L R and Balkin, D B (1992) *Compensation, Organizational Strategy, and Firm Performance*, Cincinnati OH, South Western

Gregg, P, Machin, S and Szymanski, S (1993) The disappearing relationship between directors' pay and corporate performance, *British Journal of Industrial Relations*, 3 (1), pp 1–9

High Pay Commission (2011) *More for Less: What has happened to pay at the top and does it matter?* London, High Pay Commission

Surowiecki, J (2013) Open season, *The New Yorker*, 21 October, p 31

West, M, Fisher, G, Carter, M, Gould, V and Scully, J (2005) *Rewarding Customer Service? Using reward and recognition to deliver your customer service strategy*, London, CIPD

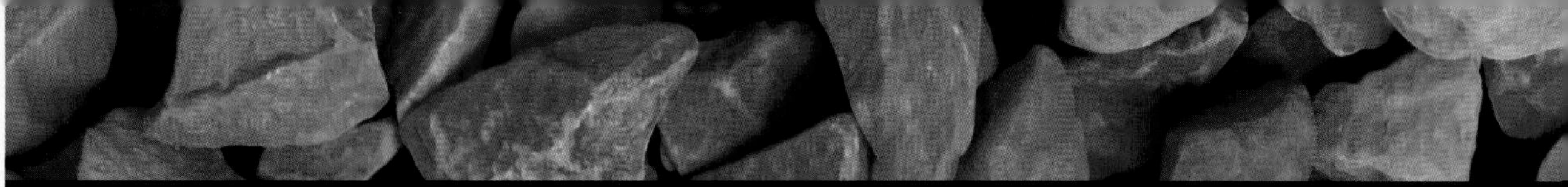

PART VII

Employee relations

PART VII CONTENTS

Introduction

Employee relations are concerned with managing the employment relationship and the psychological contract. They consist of the approaches and methods adopted by employers to deal with employees either collectively through their trade unions or individually. This includes providing employees with a voice and developing communications between them and management.

Employee relations cover a wider spectrum of the employment relationship than industrial relations, which are essentially about what goes on between management and trade union representatives and officials, involving collective agreements, collective bargaining and disputes resolution. This wider definition recognizes the move away from collectivism towards individualism in the ways in which employees relate to their employers.

29 Strategic employee relations

KEY CONCEPTS AND TERMS

- Collectivism
- Derecognition
- Employee relations
- Employee relations climate
- Individualism
- Industrial relations
- Mutuality
- Pay-work bargain
- Pluralist viewpoint
- Single-table bargaining
- Union recognition

LEARNING OUTCOMES

On completing this chapter you should be able to define these key concepts. You should also know about:

- The process of employee relations
- The basis of employee relations
- Employee relations policies
- Employee relations strategies
- The employee relations climate
- Managing with and without unions

Introduction

Strategic employee relations is concerned with the formulation and implementation of plans designed to meet the needs of the business for harmonious and productive relationships and the needs of employees to be treated justly and well. These plans will be based on the organization's policies on how it should relate to employees and their unions.

Against the background of definitions of the process and basis of employee relations, this chapter examines in turn employee relations policies and strategies, the development of a satisfactory employee relations climate and what happens when organizations work with or without unions.

The process of employee relations

Employee relations are concerned with managing and maintaining the employment relationship, taking into account the implications of the notion of the psychological contract (these concepts are discussed in the next two chapters). This means dealing with employees either collectively through their trade unions or individually; handling employment practices, terms and conditions of employment and issues arising from employment; and providing employees with a voice and communicating with employees.

The basis of employee relations

Employee relations are basically about how managements and employees live together and what can be done to make that work. There are two views about the relationship. The unitary viewpoint is the belief that management and employees share the same concerns and it is therefore in both their interests to cooperate. This was expressed by Walton (1985: 64) as the principle of mutuality. A similar belief is expressed in the idea of social partnership, which states that as stakeholders, the parties involved in employee relations should aim to work together to the greater good of all. Partnership agreements, as described in Chapter 32, try to put this idea into practice.

In contrast, the pluralist viewpoint is that the interests of employees will not necessarily coincide with their employers and that the unitary view is naive, unrealistic and against the interests of employees. People of this persuasion don't believe that partnership agreements can work.

The basis of employee relations can be described somewhat simplistically in terms of the pay–work bargain – the agreement made between employers and employees whereby the former undertakes to pay for the work done by the latter. According to this notion, many employers simply want employees who will do what they are told without costing too much. They want engagement and commitment on their own terms. But employees want a 'fair day's pay for a fair day's work' and a say in their terms and conditions of employment and the way in which their work is organized. They want security of employment, good working conditions, a healthy and safe working environment and the scope to raise and resolve grievances. Conflicts of interest can arise between employers and employees on these issues, and where there are unions these conflicts are resolved by the various industrial relations procedures described in Chapter 32. Because of this, employee relations need to be managed by reference to understood and communicated policies and strategies.

Employee relations policies

Employee relations policies express the philosophy of the organization on what sort of relationships are wanted between management and employees and, where necessary, their unions, and how the pay–work bargain should be managed. A social partnership policy will aim to develop and maintain a positive, productive, cooperative and trusting climate of employee relations.

Approaches

There are four approaches to employee relations:

1. Adversarial: the organization decides what it wants to do, and employees are expected to fit in. Employees only exercise power by refusing to cooperate.
2. Traditional: a reasonably good day-to-day working relationship but management proposes and the workforce reacts through its elected representatives, if there are any; if not, employees just accept the situation or walk.
3. Partnership: the organization involves employees in the drawing up and execution of organization policies, but retains the right to manage.
4. Power sharing: employees are involved in both day-to-day and strategic decision-making.

Adversarial approaches are less common now than in the 1960s and 70s. The traditional approach is still the most typical but more interest is being expressed in partnership. Power sharing is rare.

Objectives of employee relations policies

The objectives of employee relations policies may include maintaining good relations with employees and their unions, developing a cooperative and constructive employee relations climate, the effective management of the work process, the control of labour costs, and the development of an engaged and committed workforce. When these policies are articulated, they provide guidelines for taking action on employee relations issues and can help to ensure that these issues are dealt with consistently. They provide the basis for defining management's intentions (its employee relations strategy) on key matters such as union recognition and collective bargaining.

Employee relations policy areas

The areas covered by employee relations policies are:

- *Trade union recognition* – whether trade unions should be recognized or de-recognized, which union or unions the organization would prefer to deal with, and whether or not it is desirable to recognize only one union for collective bargaining and/or employee representational purposes. The policy will have to consider the factors affecting managing with or without unions, as discussed later in this chapter.
- *Collective bargaining* – the extent to which it should be centralized or decentralized and the scope of areas to be covered by collective bargaining.
- *Employee relations procedures* – the nature and scope of procedures for redundancy, grievance handling and discipline.
- *Participation and involvement* – how far the organization is prepared to go in giving employees a voice on matters that concern them.
- *Partnership* – the extent to which a partnership approach is thought to be desirable.
- *The employment relationship* – the extent to which terms and conditions of employment should be governed by collective agreements or based on individual contracts of employment (ie collectivism versus individualism).
- *Harmonization of terms and conditions of employment for staff and manual workers.*
- *Working arrangements* – the degree to which management has the prerogative to determine working arrangements without reference to trade unions or employees (this includes job-based or functional flexibility).

Policy choices

The following policy options for organizations on industrial relations and HRM have been described by Guest (1995):

- *The new realism* – a high emphasis on HRM and industrial relations. The aim is to integrate HRM and industrial relations.
- *Traditional collectivism* – priority to industrial relations without HRM. This involves retaining the traditional industrial relations arrangements within an unchanged industrial relations system. Management may take the view in these circumstances that it is easier to continue to operate with a union, since it provides a useful, well-established channel for communication and for the handling of grievance, discipline and safety issues.
- *Individualized HRM* – high priority to HRM with no industrial relations. According to Guest, this approach is not very common, except in US-owned firms. It is, he believes, essentially piecemeal and opportunistic.
- *The black hole* – no industrial relations. This option is becoming more prevalent in organizations in which HRM is not a policy priority for managements but where they do not see that there is a compelling reason to operate within a traditional industrial relations system. When such organizations

are facing a decision on whether or not to recognize a union, they are increasingly deciding not to do so.

Employee relations strategies

Employee relations strategies set out how employee relations policy aims are to be achieved. The intentions expressed by employee relations strategies may direct the organization towards any of the following:

- Altering the forms of recognition, including single union recognition, or de-recognition.
- Changes in the form and content of procedural agreements.
- New bargaining structures, including decentralization or single-table bargaining (ie bringing all the unions in an organization together as a single bargaining unit).
- The achievement of increased levels of commitment through involvement or participation.
- Deliberately bypassing trade union representatives to communicate directly with employees.
- Increasing the extent to which management controls operations in such areas as flexibility.
- Developing a 'partnership' with trade unions, recognizing that employees are stakeholders and that it is to the advantage of both parties to work together.
- Generally improving the employee relations climate, as discussed below, to produce more harmonious and cooperative relationships.

Employee relations climate

The employee relations climate of an organization refers to the perceptions of management, employees and their representatives about the ways in which employee relations are conducted and how the various parties (managers, employees and trade unions) behave when dealing with one another. An employee relations climate may be created by the management style adopted by management (see below) or by the behaviour of the trade unions or employee representatives (cooperative, hostile, militant, etc) or by the two interacting with one another. It can be good, bad or indifferent according to perceptions about the extent to which:

- management and employees trust one another;
- management treats employees fairly and with consideration;
- management is open about its actions and intentions – employee relations policies and procedures are transparent;
- harmonious relationships are generally maintained on a day-to-day basis that result in willing cooperation rather than grudging submission;
- conflict, when it does arise, is resolved without resort to industrial action and resolution is achieved by integrative processes that result in a 'win-win' solution;
- employees are generally committed to the interests of the organization and, equally, management treat them as stakeholders whose interests should be protected as far as possible.

Management style in employee relations

The term 'management style' refers to the overall approach the management of an organization adopts to the conduct of employee relations. Purcell and Sisson (1983) identified five typical styles:

1. Authoritarian – employee relations are not regarded as important and people issues are not attended to unless something goes wrong.
2. Paternalistic – in some ways this resembles the authoritarian style but a more positive attitude to employees is adopted.
3. Consultative – trade unions are welcomed and employee consultation is a high priority.
4. Constitutional – there is a trade union presence but the management style tends to be adversarial.

5 Opportunistic – management style is determined by local circumstances, which in turn determine whether or not unions are recognized and the extent to which employee involvement is encouraged.

Purcell (1987: 535) defined management style as 'a guiding set of principles which delineate the boundaries and direction of acceptable management action in dealing with employees'. He described two major dimensions: 1) individualism, which refers to the extent to which personnel policies are focused on the rights and capabilities of individual workers; and 2) collectivism, which is concerned with the extent to which management policy is directed towards encouraging the development of collective representation by employees and allowing employees a collective voice in management decision-making. According to Purcell, style is a deliberate choice linked to business policy. Organizations may choose to focus on one or both aspects. Not all firms have a distinctive preferred management style.

Improving the climate

Improvements to the climate can be attained by developing fair employee relations policies and procedures and implementing them consistently. Line managers and team leaders who are largely responsible for the day-to-day conduct of employee relations need to be educated and trained on the approaches they should adopt. Transparency should be achieved by communicating policies to employees, and commitment increased by involvement and participation processes. Problems that need to be resolved can be identified by simply talking to employees, their representatives and their trade union officials. Importantly, as discussed below, the organization can address its obligations to the employees as stakeholders and take steps to build trust.

An ethical approach

Businesses aim to achieve prosperity, growth and survival. Ideally, success should benefit all the stakeholders in the organization – owners, management, employees, customers and suppliers. However, the single-minded pursuit of business objectives can act to the detriment of employees' well-being and security. There may be a tension between accomplishing business purposes and the social and ethical obligations of an organization to its employees. But the chances of attaining a good climate of employee relations are slight if no attempt is made to recognize and act on an organization's obligations to its members.

An ethical approach will be based on high-commitment and high-involvement policies. The commitment will be mutual and the arrangements for involvement will be genuine, ie management will be prepared not only to listen but to act on the views expressed by employees or, at least, if it cannot take action, the reasons will be explained. It will also be transparent and, although the concept of a 'job for life' may no longer be valid in many organizations, an attempt will be made to maintain full employment policies.

Managing with unions

Ideally, managements and trade unions learn to live together, often on a give-and-take basis, the presumption being that neither would benefit from a climate of hostility or by generating constant confrontation. It would be assumed in this ideal situation that mutual advantage would come from acting in accordance with the spirit as well as the letter of agreed joint regulatory procedures. However, both parties would probably adopt a realistic pluralist viewpoint. This means recognizing the inevitability of differences of opinion, even disputes, but believing that with goodwill on both sides they could be settled without resource to industrial action.

Of course, the reality in the 1960s and 70s was often different. In certain businesses, for example in the motor and shipbuilding industries, hostility and confrontation were rife, and newspaper proprietors tended to let their unions hold sway in the interests of peace and profit. Times have changed. Trade union power has diminished in the private sector, if not in the public sector. Managements in the private sector have tended to seize the initiative. They may be content to live with trade unions but they give industrial relations lower priority. They may feel that it is easier to continue to operate with a union because it provides a useful, well-established channel for communication and for the handling of grievance, discipline and safety issues. In the absence of a union, management would need to develop its own alternatives, which would be costly and difficult to operate effectively. The management perspective may be that it is safer to marginalize the unions than formally to derecognize them and risk provoking a confrontation.

The pattern varies considerably but there is general agreement based on studies such as the Workplace Employee Relations Survey (2004) that employers have been able to assert their prerogative – 'management must manage' in the workplace. They seem generally to have regained control over how they organize work, especially with regard to the flexible use of labour and multiskilling. The 'status quo' clause, typical of many agreements in the engineering industry, whereby management could not change working arrangements without union agreement, has virtually disappeared in the private sector.

Four types of industrial relations managements have been identified by Purcell and Sisson (1983):

1. *Traditionalists*, who have unitary beliefs and are anti-union with forceful management.
2. *Sophisticated paternalists*, who are essentially unitary but they do not take it for granted that their employees accept the organization's objectives or automatically legitimize management decision-making. They spend considerable time and resources in ensuring that their employees adopt the right approach.
3. *Sophisticated moderns*, who are either constitutionalists – where the limits of collective bargaining are codified in an agreement but management is free to take decisions on matters that are not the subject of such an agreement; or consulters – they accept collective bargaining but do not want to codify everything in a collective agreement, and instead aim to minimize the amount of joint regulation and emphasize joint consultation with 'problems' having to be solved rather than 'disputes' settled.
4. *Standard moderns*, who are pragmatic or opportunist. Trade unions are recognized, but industrial relations are seen as primarily fire-fighting and are assumed to be non-problematic unless events prove otherwise. This is by far the most typical approach.

On the whole, pluralism prevails and management and unions will inevitably disagree from time to time on employment issues. The aim is to resolve these issues before they become disputes. This means adopting a more positive partnership approach. Where collective agreements are being made, a cooperative or integrative bargaining philosophy can be adopted, based on perceptions about the mutual interdependence of management and employees and the recognition by both parties that this is a means to achieve more for themselves.

Managing without unions

Some firms, especially larger ones, manage without trade unions by adopting a union substitution policy that offers employment policies and pay packages that employees will see as an attractive alternative to trade union membership. They may focus on communications and information sharing but they will basically deal with people individually rather than collectively. Others, especially smaller firms, simply deal with employees individually – sometimes well, sometimes not – and make no attempt to provide substitute arrangements.

Implementing employee relations strategy

The implementation of employee relations strategy needs to take account of the concepts of the employment relationship and the psychological contract, as considered in the next two chapters. The issues involved in implementing strategy in a unionized environment are discussed in Chapter 32, which deals with the practice of industrial relations. Chapters 33 and 34 are concerned with the implementation of employee voice and communications strategy, which are general employee relations matters that affect organizations whether or not they recognize trade unions.

Key learning points: Strategic employee relations

Strategic employee relations

Strategic employee relations is concerned with the policies an organization adopts to managing how it relates to employees and their unions and the strategies it develops to create a situation in which it satisfies the needs of the business for harmonious and productive relationships and the needs of employees to be treated justly and well.

Employee relations

Employee relations are concerned with managing and maintaining the employment relationship, taking into account the implications of the concept of the psychological contract. Employee relations are basically about how managements and employees live together and what can be done to make that work.

Employee relations policies

Employee relations policies express the philosophy of the organization on what sort of relationships between management and employees and their unions is wanted, and how the pay–work bargain should be managed. The areas covered by employee relations policies are trade union recognition, collective bargaining, employee relations procedures, participation and involvement, partnership harmonization and working arrangements.

Employee relations strategies

Employee relations strategies set out how employee relations policy objectives are to be achieved. The intentions expressed by employee relations strategies may direct the organization towards any of the following:

- Altering the forms of recognition, including single union recognition, or derecognition.
- Changes in the form and content of procedural agreements.
- New bargaining structures, including decentralization or single-table bargaining (ie bringing all the unions in an organization together as a single bargaining unit).
- The achievement of increased levels of commitment through involvement or participation.
- Deliberately bypassing trade union representatives to communicate directly with employees.
- Increasing the extent to which management controls operations in such areas as flexibility.
- Developing a 'partnership' with trade unions, recognizing that employees are stakeholders and that it is to the advantage of both parties to work together.
- Generally improving the employee relations climate to produce more harmonious and cooperative relationships.

Employee relations climate

The employee relations climate of an organization refers to the perceptions of management, employees and their representatives about the ways in which employee relations are conducted and how the various parties (managers, employees and trade unions) behave when dealing with one another. An employee relations climate may be created by the management style adopted by management, or by the behaviour of the trade unions or employee representatives (cooperative, hostile, militant, etc), or by the two interacting with one another.

Managing with unions

Ideally, managements and trade unions learn to live together, often on a give-and-take basis, the presumption being that neither would benefit from a climate of hostility or by generating constant confrontation. It would be assumed in this ideal situation that mutual advantage would come from acting in accordance with the spirit as well as the letter of agreed joint regulatory procedures. However, both parties would probably adopt a realistic pluralist viewpoint. This means recognizing the inevitability of differences of opinion, even disputes, but believing that with goodwill on both sides they could be settled without resource to industrial action.

Managing without trade unions

Some firms, especially larger ones, manage without trade unions by adopting a union substitution policy that offers employment policies and pay packages that employees will see as an attractive alternative to trade union membership. They may focus on communications and information sharing but they will basically deal with people individually rather than collectively. Others, especially smaller firms, simply deal with employees individually – sometimes well, sometimes not – and make no attempt to provide substitute arrangements.

Questions

1 What are strategic employee relations?
2 What are employee relations?
3 What are industrial relations?
4 What is the unitary viewpoint?
5 What is the pluralism viewpoint?
6 What are the main areas covered by employee relations policies?
7 What are employee relations strategies?
8 What areas are covered by employee relations strategies?
9 What is an employee relations climate?

References

Guest, D E (1995) Human resource management: trade unions and industrial relations, in (ed) J Storey, *Human Resource Management: A critical text*, London, Routledge

Purcell, J (1987) Mapping management styles in employee relations, *Journal of Management Studies*, 24 (5), pp 78–91

Purcell, J and Sisson, K (1983) Strategies and practice in the management of industrial relations, in (ed) G Bain, *Industrial Relations in Britain*, Oxford, Blackwell

Walton, R E (1985) From control to commitment in the workplace, *Harvard Business Review*, March–April, pp 77–84

Workplace Employee Relations Survey (2004) HMSO, Norwich

30 The employment relationship

KEY CONCEPTS AND TERMS

The employment relationship
High-trust organization
Labour process theory
Mutuality
The pay-work bargain
Psychological contract
Relationship contract
Transactional contract

LEARNING OUTCOMES

On completing this chapter you should be able to define these key concepts. You should also understand:

- The nature of the employment relationship
- Employment relationship contracts
- Managing the employment relationship
- Developing a high-trust organization

Introduction

The employment relationship describes how employers and employees work together. A positive employment relationship is one in which management and employees are interdependent and both benefit from this interdependency, and where there is mutual trust. Such a relationship provides a foundation for employment and employee relations policies. This chapter describes the employment relationship, how it is managed and how a climate of trust can be created.

The nature of the employment relationship

The employment relationship can be expressed formally by what Rubery *et al* (2002) regarded as its cornerstone, namely the contract of employment. The employment relationship can additionally be defined by such means as procedure agreements and work rules.

But the employment relationship is essentially an informal and constant process that happens whenever

FIGURE 30.1 Dimensions of the employment relationship

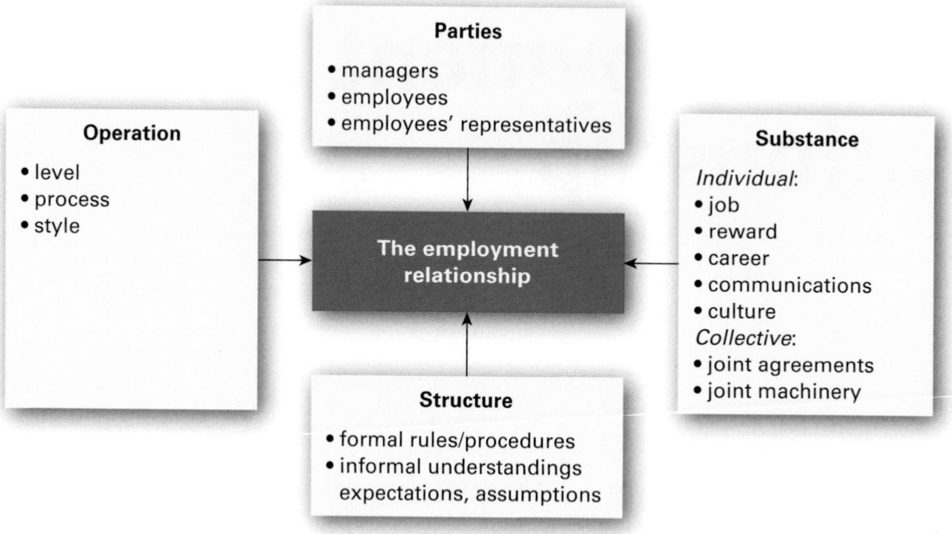

SOURCE: Kessler and Undy (1996)

an employer has dealings with an employee, and vice versa. Underpinning the employment relationship is the psychological contract, which expresses certain assumptions and expectations about what managers and employees have to offer and are willing to deliver. The dimensions of the employment relationship as described by Kessler and Undy (1996) are shown in Figure 30.1.

The basis of the employment relationship

The starting point of the employment relationship is an undertaking by an employee to provide skill and effort to the employer in return for which the employer provides the employee with a salary or a wage (the pay–work bargain). Initially the relationship is founded on a legal contract. This may be a written contract, but the absence of such a contract does not mean that no contractual relationship exists. Employers and employees still have certain implied legal rights and obligations. The employer's obligations include the duty to pay salary or wages, provide a safe workplace, to act in good faith towards the employee and not to act in such a way as to undermine the trust and confidence of the employment relationship. The employee has corresponding obligations, which include obedience, competence, honesty and loyalty. As Marsden (2007: 1263) observed:

> At the heart of the employment relationship lies a 'zone of acceptance' within which employees agree to let management direct their labour. This may relate to the range of tasks that employees are willing to undertake at management's direction, but it may also include the priority to be accorded to different types of work, and the willingness to vary working time according to management's requirements. Depending on how large this zone is, and how its boundaries are drawn, it provides organizations with varying degrees of flexibility to respond to changing production and market requirements.

Marsden and Canibano (2010) referred to this as the 'frontier of control'.

The employment relationship exists at different levels in the organization (management to employees generally, and managers to individual employees and their representatives or groups of people). The operation of the relationship will also be affected by processes such as communications and consultation, and by the management style prevailing throughout the organization or adopted by individual managers.

An important point to remember about the employment relationship is that, generally, it is the employer who has the power to dictate the contractual terms unless they have been fixed by collective bargaining. Individuals, except when they are in demand, have little scope to vary the terms of the contract imposed upon them by employers. Inevitably there are conflicts of interest, between employers who want to control compliant and high-performing employees, and the employees who want to maintain their rights to 'a fair day's pay for a fair day's work'.

Labour process theory and the employment relationship

The employment relationship is sometimes explained by labour process theory. In its original form, as defined by Braverman (1974), this stated that the application of modern management techniques, in combination with mechanization and automation, secures the real subordination of labour, and deskilling of work in the office as well as the shop floor. Thompson and Harley (2007: 149) noted that: 'The notion of the workplace as contested terrain is a central motif of labour process theory.' They pointed out that what is happening is a process of 'capitalizing on humanity' rather than investing in human capital. However, they did comment that: 'In the employment relationship there will always be (actual and potential) conflict, but simultaneously there will be shared interests' (ibid: 156). And they suggested that: 'In an environment where employee skills and commitment are central to organizational success, it is precisely by giving more that organizations will gain more' (ibid: 149).

Employment relationship contracts

Two types of contracts defining the employment relationship have been distinguished by Rousseau and Wade-Benzoni (1994), namely transactional contracts and relational contracts. Transactional contracts are formal contracts that have well-described terms of exchange between employer and employees, often expressed financially. They contain specified performance requirements. Relational contracts are largely informal contracts with more abstract terms and refer to an open-ended membership of the organization. Performance requirements attached to this continuing membership are incomplete or ambiguous. There is also the psychological contract, which is implied rather than stated.

More specifically, the employment relationship is governed by express agreements between employers and employees. These consist of written contracts of employment but they may be conveyed orally at an interview or even set out in an advertisement. In addition, express terms may be included in collective agreements or works rules. The employment relationship is also affected by the terms implied by common law and statutory requirements.

Managing the employment relationship

The dynamic and often nebulous nature of the employment relationship increases the difficulty of managing it. The problem is compounded by the multiplicity of factors that influence the contract – the culture of the organization, the prevailing management style, the values (espoused and practised) of top management, the existence or non-existence of a climate of trust, day-to-day interactions between employees and line managers, and the HR policies and practices of the business.

The latter are particularly important. The nature of the employment relationship is strongly influenced by HR actions. These cover all aspects of HRM. Of particular importance are how people are treated in such areas as recruitment, performance reviews, promotion, career development, reward, involvement and participation, grievance handling, disciplinary procedures and redundancy. The ways in which people are required to carry out their work (including flexibility and multiskilling), how performance expectations are expressed and communicated, how work is organized and how people are managed will also make a significant impact on the employment relationship. HR specialists can contribute to the development of a positive and productive employment relationship in the following ways:

- *during recruitment interviews* – presenting the unfavourable as well as the favourable aspects of a job in a 'realistic job preview';
- *in induction programmes* – communicating to new starters the organization's HR policies and procedures and its core values, indicating to them the standards of performance expected in such areas as quality and customer service, and spelling out requirements for flexibility;
- *by encouraging the maximum amount of contact between managers and team leaders and their team members* – to achieve mutual understanding of expectations and to provide a means of two-way communications;
- *by adopting a general policy of transparency* – ensuring that on all matters affecting them, employees know what is happening, why it is happening and the impact it will make on their employment, development and prospects.

These approaches to managing the employment relationship cover all aspects of people management. It is important to remember, however, that this is a continuous process. The effective management of the relationship means ensuring that values are upheld and that a transparent, consistent and fair approach is adopted in dealing with all aspects of employment. It is also important to remember that perhaps the best way of improving the employment relationship is to develop a climate of trust in the organization.

Developing a climate of trust

Trust, as defined by the *Oxford English Dictionary*, is a firm belief that a person may be relied on. A more complex definition by Rousseau *et al* (1998: 395) indicated that: 'Trust is a psychological state comprising the intention to accept vulnerability based upon positive expectations of the intentions or behaviour of another.'

A climate of trust in the shape of a high-trust organization is an essential ingredient in a positive employment relationship. It has been suggested by Herriot *et al* (1988) that trust should be regarded as social capital – the fund of goodwill in any social group that enables people within it to collaborate with one another. Searle and Skinner (2011) noted that the benefits of increased trust could include:

- improved employee performance;
- higher levels of motivation and positive attitudes (including employees putting more effort into performing and developing their roles);
- reduced cost due to higher productivity, less wastage, lower staff turnover, fewer stoppages, and so on;
- enhanced pro-social behaviour at work, including desirable work-related behaviour and appropriate discretionary behaviour;
- enhanced knowledge-sharing and increased innovation;
- improved cooperative working.

Building trust

As Thompson (1998: 69) noted, trust is an outcome of good management. He also commented that a number of writers have generally concluded that trust is 'not something that can, or should, be directly managed'. He cites Sako (1994) who wrote that: 'Trust is a cultural norm which can rarely be created intentionally because attempts to create trust in a calculative manner would destroy the effective basis of trust.'

In the end, trust is about relationships and mutual support. Trust is created and maintained by managerial behaviour and by the development of better mutual understanding of expectations – employers of employees, and employees of employers. The sort of behaviour that is most likely to engender trust is when management is honest with people, keeps its word (delivers the deal) and practises what it preaches. Organizations that espouse core values ('people are our greatest asset') and then proceed to ignore them will be low-trust organizations. More specifically, trust will be developed if management acts fairly, equitably and consistently; if a policy of transparency is implemented; if intentions and the reasons for proposals or decisions are communicated both to employees generally and to individuals; if there is full involvement in developing reward processes; and if mutual expectations are agreed through performance management. Leaders have a crucial role. As O'Toole and Bennis (2009: 54) pointed out: 'We won't be able to rebuild trust in institutions until leaders learn how to communicate honestly – and create organizations where that's the norm.' The CIPD (2012: 16) suggested that to build trust leaders need to:

- tell the truth;
- be willing to admit mistakes;
- share information openly;
- support transparency;
- seek information from multiple sources and not merely rely on what they are told by their close advisers;
- be candid in their dealings with followers.

Renewing trust

As suggested by Herriot *et al* (1988), if trust is lost, a four-step programme is required to renew it:

1. Admission by top management that it has paid insufficient attention in the past to employees' diverse needs.
2. A limited process of contracting whereby a particular transition to a different way of working for a group of employees is done in a form that takes individual needs into account.
3. Establishing 'knowledge-based' trust, which is based not on a specific transactional deal but on a developing perception of trustworthiness.
4. Achieving trust based on identification in which each party empathizes with each other's needs and therefore takes them on board themselves (although this final state is seldom reached in practice).

Key learning points: The employment relationship

The employment relationship describes how employers and employees work together and relate to one another.

Basis of the employment relationship

The basis of the employment relationship is an undertaking by an employee to provide skill and effort to the employer in return for which the employer provides the employee with a salary or a wage. The employer's obligations also include the duty to provide a safe workplace, to act in good faith towards the employee and not to act in such a way as to undermine the trust and confidence of the employment relationship. The employee has corresponding obligations, which include obedience, competence, honesty and loyalty.

Employment relationship contracts

The three types of employment relationship contracts are transactional, relational and psychological.

Managing the employment relationship

The nature of the employment relationship is strongly influenced by HR actions. These cover all aspects of HRM. Of particular importance are how people are treated in such areas as recruitment, performance reviews, promotion, career development, reward, involvement and participation, grievance handling, disciplinary procedures and redundancy. The ways in which people are required to carry out their work (including flexibility and multiskilling), how performance expectations are expressed and communicated, how work is organized and how people are managed will also make a significant impact on the employment relationship.

Developing a high-trust organization

A high-trust organization exists when management is honest with people, keeps its word (delivers the deal) and practises what it preaches. Trust is created and maintained by managerial behaviour and by the development of better mutual understanding of expectations – employers of employees, and employees of employers.

Questions

1 What is the employment relationship?

2 What is the basis of the employment relationship?

3 How can the employment relationship be managed?

4 How can trust between employers and employees be developed in an organization?

References

Braverman, H (1974) *Labour and Monopoly Capital*, New York, Monthly Review Press

CIPD (2012) *Where has all the trust gone?* London, CIPD

Herriot, P, Hirsh, W and Riley, P (1988) *Trust and Transition: Managing the employment relationship*, Chichester, Wiley

Kessler, S and Undy, R (1996) *The New Employment Relationship: Examining the psychological contract*, London, IPM

Marsden, D (2007) Individual employee voice: renegotiation and performance management in public services, *International Journal of Human Resource Management*, 18 (7), pp 1263–78

Marsden, D and Canibano, A (2010) An economic perspective on employee participation, in (eds) A Wilkinson, P J Gollan, M Marchington and D Lewins, *The Oxford Handbook of Participation in Organizations*, Oxford, Oxford University Press, pp 131–63

O'Toole, J and Bennis, W (2009) What's needed next: a culture of candor, *Harvard Business Review*, June, pp 54–61

Rousseau, D M and Wade-Benzoni, K A (1994) Linking strategy and human resource practices: how employee and customer contracts are created, *Human Resource Management*, 33 (3), pp 463–89

Rousseau, D M, Sitkin, S B, Burt, R S and Camerer, C (1998) Not so different after all: a cross-discipline view of trust, *Academy of Management Review*, 23 (3), pp 393–404

Rubery, J, Earnshaw, J, Marchington, M, Cooke, F L and Vincent, S (2002) Changing organizational forms and the employment relationship, *Journal of Management Studies*, 39 (5), pp 645–72

Sako, M (1994) *The informational requirement of trust in supplier relations: evidence from Japan, the UK and the USA*, unpublished

Searle, R H and Skinner, D (2011) New agendas and perspectives, in (eds) Searle, R H and Skinner, D, *Trust and Human Resource Management*, Cheltenham, Edward Elgar

Thompson, M (1998) Trust and reward, in (eds) S Perkins and St John Sandringham, *Trust, Motivation and Commitment: A reader*, Faringdon, Strategic Remuneration Research Centre, pp 66–71

Thompson, P and Harley, B (2007) HRM and the worker: labour process perspectives, in (eds) P Boxall, J Purcell and P Wright, *Oxford Handbook of Human Resource Management*, Oxford, Oxford University Press, pp 147–65

31 The psychological contract

KEY CONCEPTS AND TERMS

Employability

The psychological contract

Realistic job preview

LEARNING OUTCOMES

On completing this chapter you should be able to define these key concepts. You should also know about:

- The psychological contract defined
- The significance of the psychological contract
- The psychological contract and the employment relationship
- The problem with the psychological contract
- Developing a positive psychological contract

Introduction

The psychological contract underpins the employment relationship. This chapter defines the psychological contract, explains its significance and describes how a positive contract can be developed.

The psychological contract defined

A psychological contract is a set of unwritten expectations that exist between individual employees and their employers. As Guest (2007: 133) explained, it is concerned with: 'The perceptions of both parties to the employment relationship, organization and individual, of the reciprocal promises and obligations implied in that relationship.'

A psychological contract is a system of beliefs that encompasses the actions employees believe are expected of them and what response they expect in return from their employer, and, reciprocally, the actions employers believe are expected of them and what response they expect in return from their employees.

An expanded definition was produced by Rousseau and Wade-Benzoni (1994: 464) as follows:

> Psychological contracts refer to beliefs that individuals hold regarding promises made, accepted and relied upon between themselves and another. (In the case of organizations, these parties include an employee, client, manager, and/or organization as a whole.) Because psychological contracts represent how people interpret promises and commitments, both parties in the same employment relationship (employer and employee) can have different views regarding specific terms.

Within organizations, as Katz and Kahn (1966) pointed out, every role is basically a set of behavioural expectations. These expectations are often implicit – they are not defined in the employment contract. Basic models of motivation such as expectancy theory (Vroom, 1964) maintain that employees behave in ways that they expect will produce positive outcomes. But they do not necessarily know what to expect.

Employees may expect to be treated fairly as human beings, to be provided with work that uses their abilities, to be rewarded equitably in accordance with their contribution, to be able to display competence, to have opportunities for further growth, to know what is required of them and to be given feedback (preferably positive) on how they are doing. Employers may expect employees to do their best on behalf of the organization – 'to put themselves out for the company' – to be fully committed to its values, to be compliant and loyal, and to enhance the image of the organization with its customers and suppliers. Sometimes these assumptions are justified – often they are not. Mutual misunderstandings can cause friction and stress and lead to recriminations and poor performance, or to a termination of the employment relationship. As pointed out by Guest and Conway (1998: *ix*), the psychological contract lacks many of the characteristics of the formal contract: 'It is not generally written down, it is somewhat blurred at the edges, and it cannot be enforced in a court or tribunal.'

The significance of the psychological contract

The concept of the psychological contract highlights the fact that employee/employer expectations take the form of unarticulated assumptions. Disappointments on the part of management as well as employees may therefore be inevitable. These disappointments can, however, be alleviated if managements appreciate that one of their key roles is to manage expectations, which means clarifying what they believe employees should achieve, the competencies they should possess and the values they should uphold. This is a matter not just of articulating and stipulating these requirements but of discussing and agreeing them with individuals and teams.

The psychological contract and the employment relationship

As described by Guest *et al* (1996), the psychological contract may provide some indication of the answers to the two fundamental employment relationship questions that individuals pose: 'what can I reasonably expect from the organization?' and, 'what should I reasonably be expected to contribute in return?' But it is unlikely that the psychological contract, and therefore the employment relationship, will ever be fully understood by either party.

The aspects of the employment relationship covered by the psychological contract will include, from the employees' point of view:

- how they are treated in terms of fairness, equity and consistency;
- security of employment;
- scope to demonstrate competence;

- career expectations and the opportunity to develop skills;
- involvement and influence;
- trust in the management of the organization to keep their promises.

From the employer's point of view, the psychological contract covers such aspects of the employment relationship as competence, effort, compliance, commitment and loyalty. The research conducted by Guest and Conway (2002: 22) led to the conclusion that:

> The management of the psychological contract is a core task of management and acknowledged as such by many senior HR and employment relations managers, and shows that it has a positive association with a range of outcomes within the employment relationship and is a useful way of conceptualizing that relationship.

How psychological contracts develop

Psychological contracts are not developed by means of a single transaction; they evolve over time and can be multifaceted. There are many contract makers who exert influence over the whole duration of an employee's involvement with an organization. Spindler (1994: 326) observed that:

> Every day we create relationships by means other than formal contracts... As individuals form relationships they necessarily bring their accumulated experience and developed personalities with them. In ways unknown to them what they expect from the relationship reflects the sum total of their conscious and unconscious learning to date.

The problem with psychological contracts

The problem with psychological contracts is that employees are often unclear about what they want from the organization or what they can contribute to it. Some employers are equally unclear about what they expect from their employees.

Because of these factors, and because a psychological contract is essentially implicit, it is likely to develop in an unplanned way with unforeseen consequences. Anything that management does or is perceived as doing that affects the interests of employees will modify the psychological contract. Similarly, the actual or perceived behaviour of employees, individually or collectively, will affect an employer's concept of the contract.

Developing and maintaining a positive psychological contract

As Guest *et al* (1996: *v*) explained: 'A positive psychological contract is worth taking seriously because it is strongly linked to higher commitment to the organization, higher employee satisfaction and better employment relations. Again this reinforces the benefits of pursuing a set of progressive HRM practices.' They also emphasized the importance of a high-involvement climate and suggested in particular that HRM practices such as the provision of opportunities for learning, training and development, focus on job security, promotion and careers, minimizing status differentials, fair reward systems and comprehensive communication and involvement processes will all contribute to a positive psychological contract. The steps required to develop such a contract are:

- Define expectations during recruitment and induction programmes.
- Communicate and agree expectations as part of the continuing dialogue implicit in good performance management practices.
- Adopt a policy of transparency on company policies and procedures and on management's proposals and decisions as they affect people.
- Generally treat people as stakeholders, relying on consensus and cooperation rather than control and coercion.

Guest and Conway (2002), on the basis of their research, emphasized the importance of communications in shaping the psychological contract, especially at the recruitment and induction stage when promises and commitments can be made by employers on such matters as interesting work, learning and development opportunities, not making unreasonable demands on employees, feedback on performance, fair treatment, work–life balance, a reasonable degree of security and a safe working environment. At this stage it is advisable to provide what is called a 'realistic job preview', which means communicating to candidates any special demands that will be made on them in the job for which they are applying such as the standards they will be expected to achieve, the working conditions, the hours they may have to work, the travelling they have to do and any requirement for mobility in the UK or abroad.

Guest and Conway concluded that following the recruitment and induction stage, communications are most effective if they are personal and job-related. Top-down communications are less important. They also stressed that a positive psychological contract can only be achieved if management keeps its word – if it does not breach the contract.

Key learning points: The psychological contract

The psychological contract defined

A psychological contract is a set of unwritten expectations that exist between individual employees and their employers. It is a system of beliefs encompassing the actions employees believe are expected of them and the response they expect in return from their employer, and, reciprocally, the actions employers believe are expected of them and the response they expect in return from their employees.

The significance of the psychological contract

The concept of the psychological contract highlights the fact that employee/employer expectations take the form of unarticulated assumptions. Disappointments on the part of management as well as employees may therefore be inevitable.

The psychological contract and the employment relationship

The aspects of the employment relationship covered by the psychological contract will include, from the employees' point of view:

- how they are treated in terms of fairness, equity and consistency;
- security of employment;
- scope to demonstrate competence;
- career expectations and the opportunity to develop skills;
- involvement and influence;
- trust in the management of the organization to keep their promises.

From the employer's point of view, the psychological contract covers such aspects of the employment relationship as competence, effort, compliance, commitment and loyalty.

How psychological contracts develop

Psychological contracts are not developed by means of a single transaction; they evolve over time and can be multifaceted. The steps required to develop a positive psychological contract are:

1. Define expectations during recruitment and induction programmes.
2. Communicate and agree expectations as part of the continuing dialogue implicit in good performance management practices.
3. Adopt a policy of transparency on company policies and procedures and on management's proposals and decisions as they affect people.
4. Generally treat people as stakeholders, relying on consensus and cooperation rather than control and coercion.

Questions

1 What is the psychological contract?

2 What is the significance of the psychological contract?

3 What is the link between the psychological contract and the employment relationship?

4 How do psychological contracts develop?

5 How can a positive psychological contract be developed?

References

Guest, D (2007) HRM and the worker: Towards a new psychological contract, in (eds) P Boxall, J Purcell and P Wright, *Oxford Handbook of Human Resource Management*, Oxford, Oxford University Press, pp 128–46

Guest, D E and Conway, N (1998) *Fairness at Work and the Psychological Contract*, London, IPD

Guest, D E and Conway, N (2002) Communicating the psychological contract: an employee perspective, *Human Resource Management Journal*, 12 (2), pp 22–39

Guest, D E, Conway, N and Briner, T (1996) *The State of the Psychological Contract in Employment*, London, IPD

Katz, D and Kahn, R (1966) *The Social Psychology of Organizations*, New York, John Wiley

Rousseau, D M and Wade-Benzoni, K A (1994) Linking strategy and human resource practices: how employee and customer contracts are created, *Human Resource Management*, 33 (3), pp 463–89

Spindler, G S (1994) Psychological contracts in the workplace: a lawyer's view, *Human Resource Management*, 33 (3), pp 325–33

Vroom, V (1964) *Work and Motivation*, New York, Wiley

32 The practice of industrial relations

KEY CONCEPTS AND TERMS

- Arbitration
- Bargaining power
- Collective agreements
- Collective bargaining
- Conciliation
- Employee relations
- Mediation
- New realism
- New style agreement

LEARNING OUTCOMES

On completing this chapter you should be able to define these key concepts. You should also know about:

- Trade union membership
- Union recognition
- Collective bargaining
- Collective agreements
- Disputes resolution
- Informal industrial relations

Introduction

Industrial relations involve managements and trade unions in concluding collective agreements, collective bargaining, disputes resolution and dealing with issues concerning the employment relationship and the working environment. In this chapter the practice of industrial relations is discussed in terms of the approaches, methods and procedures adopted by employers to deal with employees collectively through their trade unions.

This chapter begins with an analysis of trade union membership and the factors affecting union recognition. It continues with a description of the formal procedures and arrangements that take place when unions are recognized. But industrial relations are also conducted on a daily informal and semi-formal basis, and this is considered in the last section. The employee relations processes of providing employees with a voice and communicating with employees, which can take place in either a unionized or a non-unionized environment, are covered in the next two chapters.

Trade union membership

Trade union membership in the UK in 2011 was 6.4 million. Union density (ie the proportion of those in employment who are union members) was 26.0 per cent of employees – 11.8 per cent in the private sector and 57.1 per cent in the public sector. The overall density in 2011 was down from 32.4 per cent in 1995 (BIS, 2013).

Overall union membership has declined significantly in the UK from its peak of some 12 million in 1979. This has been largely in the private sector for structural reasons – the demise of large manufacturing firms, the rise in the service industries and the growing numbers of part-time workers. Trade unions remain strong in the public sector. The practice of industrial relations still concerns a large proportion of employers; the 2010 Labour Force Survey reported that unions were present in just over 46 per cent of all workplaces.

Union recognition

An employer fully recognizes a union for the purposes of collective bargaining when pay and conditions of employment are jointly agreed between management and trade unions. Partial recognition takes place when employers restrict trade unions to representing their members on issues arising from employment. Full recognition provides unions with negotiating and representational rights; partial recognition only gives unions representational rights. The following discussion of union recognition is only concerned with the much more common practice of full recognition. Unions can be derecognized although, as noted by Blanden *et al* (2006), this is happening less frequently.

Factors influencing recognition or derecognition

Employers in the private sector are in a strong position now to choose whether they recognize a union or not, which union they want to recognize and the terms on which they would grant recognition: for example, a single union and a no-strike agreement.

When setting up on greenfield sites employers may refuse to recognize unions. Alternatively, they can hold 'beauty contests' to select the union they prefer to work with, one that will be prepared to reach an agreement in line with what management wants.

An organization deciding whether or not to recognize a union will take some or all of the following factors into account:

- the perceived value or lack of value of having a process for regulating collective bargaining;
- if there is an existing union, the extent to which management has freedom to manage; for example, to change working arrangements and introduce flexible working or multiskilling;
- the history of relationships with the existing union;
- the proportion of employees who are union members and the degree to which they believe they need the protection that their union provides; a decision on derecognition has to weigh the extent to which its perceived advantages outweigh the disadvantages of upsetting the status quo;
- any preferences as to a particular union, because of its reputation or the extent to which it is believed that a satisfactory relationship can be maintained.

In considering recognition arrangements employers may also consider entering into a 'single union deal', as described later in this chapter.

Collective bargaining

Managing with unions involves collective bargaining – the establishment by negotiation and discussion of agreements on matters of mutual concern to employers and unions covering the employment relationship and terms and conditions of employment.

Collective bargaining is a joint regulating process, dealing with the regulation of management in its relationships with work people as well as the regulation of conditions of employment. It was described by Flanders (1970) as a social process that continually turns disagreements into agreements in an orderly fashion.

Collective bargaining can also be seen as a political relationship in which trade unions, as Chamberlain and Kuhn (1965) noted, share industrial sovereignty or power over those who are governed – the employees. The sovereignty is held jointly by management and union in the collective bargaining process.

Above all, collective bargaining is a power relationship that takes the form of a measure of power-sharing between management and trade unions (although recently the balance of power has shifted markedly in the direction of management in the private sector). Bargaining power is the ability to induce the other side to make a decision or take a course of action that it would otherwise be unwilling to make. Each side is involved in assessing the bargaining preferences and bargaining power of the other side.

Forms of collective bargaining

Walton and McKersie (1965) made the distinction between distributive bargaining, defined as the complex system of activities instrumental to the attainment of one party's goals when they are in basic conflict with those of the other party, and integrative bargaining, defined as the system of activities that are not in fundamental conflict with those of the other party and which therefore can be integrated to some degree.

Another analysis of collective bargaining forms was made by Chamberlain and Kuhn (1965), who distinguished between conjunctive bargaining in which both parties are seeking to reach agreement, and cooperative bargaining, in which it is recognized that each party is dependent on the other and can achieve its objectives more effectively if it wins the support of the other.

Collective agreements

The formal outcomes of collective bargaining are agreements between management and unions dealing with terms and conditions of employment or other aspects of the relationships between the two parties. They consist of substantive agreements, procedural agreements, new style agreements, partnership agreements and employee relations procedures.

Substantive agreements

Substantive agreements set out agreed terms and conditions of employment covering pay, allowances and overtime, working hours, holidays and flexibility arrangements and the achievement of single status or the harmonization of terms and conditions. Single status means that there are no differences in basic conditions of employment. Harmonization is the adoption of a common approach to pay and conditions for all employees, for example, placing all employees in the same grade and pay structure.

Procedural agreements

Procedural agreements set out the methods to be used and the procedures or rules to be followed in the processes of collective bargaining and the settlement of industrial disputes. Their purpose is to regulate the behaviour of the parties to the agreement, but they are not legally enforceable and the degree to which they are followed depends on the goodwill of both parties, or the balance of power between them. Like substantive agreements, procedural agreements are seldom broken and, if so, never lightly – the basic presumption of collective bargaining is that both parties will honour agreements that have been made freely between them.

The scope and content of such agreements can vary widely. Some organizations have limited agreements to the provision of representational rights only, others have taken an entirely different line in concluding single-union deals, which when they first emerged in the 1980s were referred to as the 'new realism'.

Single-union deals

Single-union deals typically agree that there should be a single union representing all employees, flexible working practices, the harmonization of terms and conditions between manual and non-manual employees, the commitment of the organization to involvement and the disclosure of information, the resolution of disputes by such means as arbitration, a commitment to continuity of production, and a 'no-strike' provision.

New style agreements

The so-called 'new style agreements' emerged in the 1990s. These stipulated that negotiating and disputes procedures should be based on the mutually accepted 'rights' of the parties expressed in the recognition agreement. They typically included provision for single-union recognition, single status, labour flexibility, a company council and a no-strike clause to the effect that issues should be resolved without recourse to industrial action.

Partnership agreements

Partnership agreements are based on the concept of social partnership. Both parties (management and the trade union) agree to collaborate to their mutual advantage and to achieve a climate of more cooperative and therefore less adversarial industrial relations. Management may offer job security linked to productivity and the union may agree to more flexible working.

The perceived benefits of partnership agreements are that management and unions will work together in a spirit of cooperation and mutuality. This is clearly preferable to an adversarial relationship. Provision is made for change to be introduced through discussion and agreement rather than by coercion or power.

An analysis by Guest *et al* (2008) of evidence from the 2004 Workplace Employee Relations Survey suggested that partnership practice remains relatively undeveloped and that it is only weakly related to trust between management and employee representatives and to employees' trust in management. Direct forms of participation generally have a more positive association with trust than representative forms.

However, data gathered by Roche (2009) from a large representative sample of employees in Ireland showed that some mutual gains are associated with partnership. Employees gained from enhancement to the intrinsic aspects of their work, eg autonomy, but did not gain security or more pay and did not seem to be more willing to accept change. Employers gained more commitment, an improved climate of employee relations and better supervisor/employee relationships. Unions gained influence and more members.

Dispute resolution

The aim of dispute resolution is to resolve differences between management and a trade union. The aim of collective bargaining is, of course, to reach agreement, preferably to the satisfaction of both parties. Grievance or negotiating procedures provide for various stages of 'failure to agree' and often include a clause providing for some form of dispute resolution in the event of the procedure being exhausted. The types of dispute resolution are conciliation, arbitration and mediation.

Conciliation

Conciliation is the process of reconciling disagreeing parties. It is carried out by a third party, in the UK often an ACAS conciliation officer, who acts in effect as a go-between, attempting to get the employer and trade union representatives to agree on terms. Conciliators can only help the parties to come to an agreement. They do not make recommendations on what that agreement should be: that is the role of an arbitrator or a mediator.

The incentives to seek conciliation are the hope that the conciliator can rebuild bridges and the belief that a determined, if last minute, search for agreement is better than confrontation, even if both parties have to compromise.

Arbitration

Arbitration is the process of settling disputes by getting a third party, the arbitrator, to review and discuss the negotiating stances of the disagreeing parties and make a recommendation on the terms of settlement, which is binding on both parties, who therefore lose control over the settlement of their differences. The arbitrator is impartial and the role is often undertaken in the UK by ACAS officials, although industrial relations academics are sometimes asked to act in this capacity. Arbitration is the means of last resort for reaching a settlement, where disputes cannot be resolved in any other way. Procedure agreements may provide for either side unilaterally to invoke arbitration, in which case the decision of the arbitrator is not binding on both parties. The process of arbitration in its fullest sense, however, only takes place at the request of both parties, who agree in advance to accept the arbitrator's findings. ACAS will not act as an arbitrator unless the consent of both parties is obtained, conciliation is considered, any agreed procedures have been used to the full and a failure to agree has been recorded.

The notion of 'pendulum' or 'final offer' arbitration emerged in the 1980s. It increases the rigidity of the arbitration process by allowing an arbitrator no choice but to recommend either the union's or the employer's final offer – there is no middle ground. The aim is to get the parties to avoid adopting extreme positions. But the evidence from the Workplace Employee Relations Survey (2004) is that the full version of pendulum arbitration as defined here was rare.

Mediation

Mediation takes place when a third party (often ACAS) helps the employer and the union by making recommendations that they are not, however, bound to accept. It is a cheap and informal alternative to an employment tribunal and offers a quick resolution to problems, privacy and confidentiality.

Informal employee relations processes

The formal processes of union recognition, collective bargaining and dispute resolution described in this chapter provide the framework for industrial relations in so far as this is concerned with agreeing terms and conditions of employment and working arrangements, and settling disputes. But within or outside that framework, informal employee relations processes are taking place continuously.

Informal employee relationships happen whenever a line manager or team leader is handling an issue in contact with a union representative, an individual employee or a group of employees. The issue may concern methods of work, allocation of work and overtime, working conditions, health and safety, achieving output and quality targets and standards, discipline, or pay – in the latter case especially if a payment-by-results scheme is in operation, which can generate continuous arguments about times, standards, retimings, payments for waiting time or when carrying out new tasks, and fluctuations or reductions in earnings because of alleged managerial inefficiency.

Line managers and supervisors handle day-to-day grievances arising from any of these issues and are expected to resolve them to the satisfaction of all parties without involving a formal grievance procedure or allowing the issue to become a formal dispute. The thrust for devolving responsibility to line managers for HR matters has increased the onus on them to handle employee relations effectively. A good team leader will establish a working relationship with the union representative of his or her staff that will enable issues arising on the shop floor or with individual employees to be settled amicably before they become a problem.

CASE STUDY

Mediation at the Arts Council of England

When workplace relationships go wrong at the Arts Council of England, staff now turn to TCM, an external provider of mediations services, to manage the conflict and help bring the parties to a workable solution. Mediation will typically be used for a conflict between a line manager and a staff member and, when this happens, a TCM mediator will take over the case until resolution. There is a regular follow-up for a year after that to see how the parties are getting on.

Key learning points: The practice of industrial relations

Union recognition

An employer fully recognizes a union for the purposes of collective bargaining when pay and conditions of employment are jointly agreed between management and trade unions. Partial recognition is when employers restrict trade unions to representing their members on issues arising from employment.

Collective bargaining

Collective bargaining is a joint regulating process, establishing by negotiation and discussion agreements on matters of mutual concern to employers and unions covering the employment relationship and terms and conditions of employment.

Collective agreements

The formal outcomes of collective bargaining are substantive agreements, procedural agreements, new style agreements, partnership agreements and employee relations procedures.

Disputes resolution

The processes of dispute resolution are conciliation, arbitration and mediation.

Informal industrial relations

Informal industrial relations processes take place whenever a line manager or team leader is handling an issue in contact with an individual employee, a group of employees or an employee representative.

Questions

1 What is union recognition?
2 What are the factors affecting union recognition or derecognition?
3 What is collective bargaining?
4 What is a collective agreement?
5 What is a single-union deal?
6 What is a partnership agreement?
7 What are the three methods of disputes resolution?

References

BIS http://data.gov.uk/dataset/trade_union_membership [accessed 28 March 2013]

Blanden, J, Machin, S and Reenen, J V (2006) Have unions turned the corner? New evidence on recent trends in union recognition in UK firms, *British Journal of Industrial Relations*, 44 (2), pp 169–90

Chamberlain, N W and Kuhn, J (1965) *Collective Bargaining*, New York, McGraw-Hill

Flanders, A (1970) *Management and Unions: The theory and reform of industrial relations*, London, Faber and Faber

Guest, D E, Brown, W, Peccei, R and Huxley, K (2008) Does partnership at work increase trust? An analysis based on the 2004 Workplace Employment Relations Survey, *Industrial Relations Journal*, 39 (2), pp 124–52

Labour Force Survey (2010) *London*, BIS

Roche, W K (2009) Who gains from workforce partnership?, *International Journal of Human Resource Management*, 20 (1), pp 1–33

Walton, R E and McKersie, R B (1965) *Behavioural Theory of Labour Negotiations*, New York, McGraw-Hill

Workplace Employee Relations Survey (2004) *London*, DTI

33 Employee voice

KEY CONCEPTS AND TERMS

Employee voice	Joint consultation
Involvement	Participation

LEARNING OUTCOMES

On completing this chapter you should be able to define these key concepts. You should also understand:

- The meaning of employee voice
- The elements of employee voice
- Categorization of employee voice
- Expression of employee voice
- Levels of employee voice
- Stages of employee voice
- Effectiveness of employee voice
- Planning for voice

Introduction

The term 'employee voice' refers to the say that employees have in matters of concern to them in their organization. Participation and involvement are treated as aspects of employee voice in this chapter, although as Wilkinson and Dundon (2010: 168) noted: 'Employee participation, involvement and voice are somewhat elastic terms with considerable width in the range of definitions.'

The meaning of employee voice

As defined by Boxall and Purcell (2003: 162), 'Employee voice is the term increasingly used to cover a whole variety of processes and structures which enable, and sometimes empower employees, directly and indirectly, to contribute to decision-making in the firm.' They declared that employee voice was important because 'it was necessary to recognize a plurality of interests and interest groups which would need to learn to live together and resolve their differences without the use of force' (ibid: 164).

Employee voice describes arrangements for a two-way dialogue to take place that allows employees to influence events at work and includes the processes of involvement, participation, upward problem solving and upward communication. It covers the provision of opportunities for employees to register discontent, express complaints or grievances, and modify the power of management. Direct employee voice takes the form of contacts between management and employees without the involvement of trade unions. Union voice is expressed through representatives and can be power-based. As noted in Chapter 15, providing for employee voice is an important way of enhancing organizational engagement.

The elements of employee voice

The elements of employee voice are participation and involvement. The difference between them was explained by Brewster *et al* (2007: 1248) as follows:

> At the most modest level involvement entails consultation, or soliciting of opinions that may or may not be acted on, rather than bargaining. In contrast, participation accords employees a genuine – clearly demarcated – input into how the firm is governed, even if this input is limited.

As Williams and Adam-Smith (2006) explained, the term 'participation' refers to arrangements that give workers some influence over organizational and workplace decisions, while the term 'involvement' is most usefully applied to management initiatives that are designed to further the flow of communication at work as a means of enhancing the organizational commitment of employees.

Wood (2010: 554) further explained that:

> Participation takes place when employees are accorded some say in the running of the enterprise; in other words, they may make decisions which are likely to be implemented – not merely considered – by management... Employers may seek to involve employees, through regular communication and through soliciting their views on a number of issues, which, however, the employer has no obligation to act on.

Categorization of employee voice

Marchington *et al* (2001) suggested that the elements of employee voice could be categorized as representative participation and upward problem solving.

Representative participation

- *Joint consultation* – a formal mechanism that provides the means for management to consult employee representatives on matters of mutual interest.
- *Collective representation* – the role of trade unions or other forms of staff association in collective bargaining and representing the interests of individual employees and groups of employees. This includes the operation of grievance procedures.
- *Partnership schemes* – these emphasize mutual gains and tackling issues in a spirit of cooperation rather than through traditional, adversarial relationships.
- *European Works Councils* – these may be set up across European sites as required by EC legislation.

Upward problem solving

- *Upward communication* – any means through which employees can make representations to management about their concerns: through their representatives, through established channels (consultative committees, grievance procedures, 'speak-up' programmes, etc) or informally.
- *Attitude surveys* – seeking the opinions of staff through questionnaires.
- *Suggestion schemes* – the encouragement of employees to make suggestions, often accompanied by rewards for accepted ideas.

- *Project teams* – getting groups of employees together with line managers to develop new ideas, processes, services or products or to solve problems (quality circles and improvement groups come into this category, although the former have often failed to survive as a specific method of involvement).

Expression of employee voice

The degree to which employees have a voice will vary considerably. At one end of the scale there will be unilateral management and employees will have no voice at all. At the other end, employees might have complete self-management and control as in a cooperative, although this is very rare. In between, the steps in the degree to which employees have voice, as defined by Boxall and Purcell (2003: 167), are as follows:

- little voice – information provided;
- downward – right to be told;
- some – opportunity to make suggestions;
- two-way – consulted during decision-making;
- two-way plus – consulted at all stages of decision-making and implementation;
- a lot – the right to delay a decision;
- power to affect outcome – the right to veto a decision;
- substantial – equality or co-determination in decision-making.

Levels of employee voice

Participation and involvement take various forms at different levels in an enterprise, as described below:

- *The job level*, at which team leaders and their teams get together to communicate information about work and exchange ideas about how the work should be done. These processes are informal.
- *The management level*, where information can be shared and joint decisions made about working arrangements and conditions. There are limits. Management as a whole, and individual managers, want to retain authority to do what their function requires. Involvement does not imply anarchy, but it does require some degree of willingness on the part of management to share its decision-making powers. At this level, participation and involvement may become more formalized, through consultative committees, briefing groups or other joint bodies involving management and employees or their representatives.
- *The policy-making level*, where the direction in which the business is going is determined and total participation would imply sharing the power to make key decisions. This is seldom practised in the UK, although there may be processes for communicating information on proposed plans (which would almost certainly not reveal proposals for acquisitions or disinvestments, or anything else where commercial security is vital) and discussing the implications of those plans.
- *The ownership level*, where participation implies a share in the equity, which is not meaningful unless the workers have sufficient control through voting rights to determine the composition of the board. This is not a feature of British employee relations.

Stages of employee voice

The stages of employee voice are shown in Figure 33.1. At one end of the scale, management makes decisions unilaterally and exercises its full prerogative; at the other end, decisions are made jointly. Between these extremes there are two intermediate points. The point on this scale at which participation should or can take place at any level in an organization depends on the attitudes, willingness and enthusiasm of both management and employees. Management may be reluctant to give up too much of its authority except under pressure from the unions (which is less likely today), or from European Commission directives on worker consultation.

FIGURE 33.1 Stages of employee voice

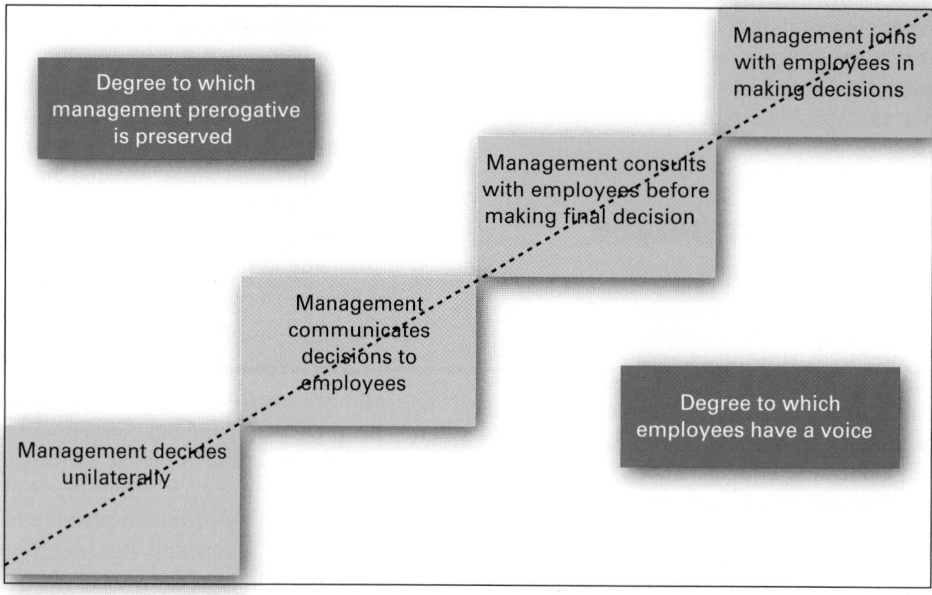

Effectiveness of employee voice

Research by Dundon and Gollan (2007: 9) showed that:

> an integrated approach to employee participation in which such participation is accompanied by related initiatives in employment security, selective employee hiring, variable compensation, extensive training and information sharing with employees is most likely to lead to higher levels of performance.

Later research by Dundon (2009) established that voice could have a positive effect in three ways:

1. valuing employee contributions;
2. improved performance;
3. improved management systems (tapping into employees' ideas).

Research conducted by Cox *et al* (2006) indicated that to be effective, employee involvement and participation mechanisms had to be embedded in the organization – well-established and part of everyday working life. Combinations of involvement and participation practices worked best. The main barriers to effective employee voice appear to be a partial lack of employee enthusiasm, absence of necessary skills to implement and manage employee voice programmes, and issues concerning line managers – such as middle managers acting as blockers through choice or ignorance. Making employee voice effective requires top management support, good leadership skills and finding the right mechanisms for involvement and participation.

Planning for voice

The forms of voice appropriate for an organization depend upon the values and attitudes of management and, if they exist, trade unions, and the current climate of employee relations. Attention has also to be paid to the EC directives on European Works Councils and Information and Consultation of Employees.

Planning should be based on a review of the existing forms of voice, which would include discussions with stakeholders (line managers, employees and trade union representatives) on the effectiveness of existing arrangements and any improvements required. In the light of these discussions, new or revised approaches can be developed, but it is necessary to brief and train those involved on the part that they should play.

CASE STUDIES

Employee involvement at Harrod UK

Harrod UK is a manufacturer of sport equipment. It has adopted the following approach to employee involvement:

- the whole workforce is involved in business planning;
- company-wide meetings are held to plan and review corporate strategy;
- the HR processes of a company training plan and profit-related pay based on the achievement of continuous improvement measures support the consultative culture.

Involving unions in outsourcing decisions at Co-operative Financial Services

When Co-operative Financial Services (CFS) began thinking of outsourcing its life and savings administration business it decided to bring the unions in right at the start of the process. A 'pre-consultation period' enabled Amicus, the National Association of Co-operative Officials and the Transport and General Workers' Union, which between them represent an estimated 70–80 per cent of the CFS workforce, to understand what was being contemplated and to talk to shortlisted outsourcing providers before the company made its final decisions on which ones to choose.

CFS was able to bring one of the outsourcing firms together with its potential new employees to discuss terms and conditions, organizational culture and other issues that mattered to both parties.

Following the success of this process, CFS agreed with the unions a set of principles that would govern any future outsourcing deals between CFS and external partners.

Key learning points: Employee voice

The meaning of employee voice

'Employee voice is the term increasingly used to cover a whole variety of processes and structures which enable, and sometimes empower employees, directly and indirectly, to contribute to decision-making in the firm' (Boxall and Purcell, 2003).

The forms of employee voice

The basic elements of employee voice are participation and involvement. These take the forms of joint consultation, participation, collective representation, upward communication (consultative committees, etc), attitude surveys, suggestion schemes and project teams (quality circles or improvement groups).

Expression of employee voice

The degree to which employees have voice will vary considerably.

Effectiveness of employee involvement and participation

To be effective, employee involvement and participation mechanisms have to be embedded in the organization – well-established and part of everyday working life. According to Cox *et al* (2006), combinations of involvement and participation practices work best.

Planning for voice

Planning should be based on a review of the existing forms of voice, which would include discussions with stakeholders (line managers, employees and trade union representatives) on the effectiveness of existing arrangements and any improvements required. In the light of these discussions, new or revised approaches can be developed, but it is necessary to brief and train those involved on the part they should play.

Questions

1 What is employee voice?
2 What is participation?
3 What is involvement?
4 How can employee voice be categorized?
5 How is employee voice expressed?
6 What are the levels of employee voice?

References

Boxall, P F and Purcell, J (2003) *Strategy and Human Resource Management*, Basingstoke, Palgrave Macmillan

Brewster, C, Croucher, R, Wood, G and Brookes, M (2007) Collective and individual voice: convergence in Europe?, *International Journal of Human Resource Management*, 18 (7), pp 1246–62

Cox, A, Zagelmeyer, S and Marchington, M (2006) Embedding employee involvement and participation at work, *Human Resource Management Journal*, 16 (3), pp 250–67

Dundon, T (2009) Employee participation, in (eds) T Redman and A Wilkinson, *Contemporary Human Resource Management*, London, Pearson

Dundon, T and Gollan, P J (2007) Re-conceptualising voice in the non-union workshop, *International Journal of Human Resource Management*, 18 (7), pp 1182–98

Marchington, M, Wilkinson, A, Ackers, P and Dundon, A (2001) *Management Choice and Employee Voice*, London, CIPD

Wilkinson, A and Dundon, T (2010) Direct employee participation, in (eds) A Wilkinson, P J Gollan, M Marchington and D Lewins, *The Oxford Handbook of Participation in Organizations*, Oxford, Oxford University Press, pp 167–85

Williams, S and Adam-Smith, D (2006) *Contemporary Employment Relations: A critical introduction*, Oxford, Oxford University Press

Wood, G (2010) Participation in developing countries, in (eds) A Wilkinson, P J Gollan, M Marchington and D Lewins, *The Oxford Handbook of Participation in Organizations*, Oxford, Oxford University Press, pp 552–69

34 Employee communications

KEY CONCEPTS AND TERMS

Consultation

Employee communication

Speak-up programme

Team briefing

LEARNING OUTCOMES

On completing this chapter you should be able to define these key concepts. You should also understand:

- The importance of employee communications
- What should be communicated
- The approach to communication
- Communication methods
- Employee communication strategy

Introduction

Employee communication processes and systems provide for 'two-way communication'. In one direction they enable managements to inform employees on matters that concern them. In the other, they provide for upward communication by giving employees a voice, as described in Chapter 33.

Communications should be distinguished from consultation. As the ACAS (2005) guide states, communication is concerned with the exchange of information and ideas within an organization, while consultation goes beyond this and involves managers actively seeking and then taking account of the views of employees before making a decision.

The importance of employee communications

Good communications are important for three reasons:

1. They are a vital part of any change management programme. If any change is proposed – in terms and conditions of employment, HR processes such as merit pay, working methods, technologies, products and services or organization (including mergers and acquisitions) – employees need to know what is proposed and how it will affect them. Resistance to change often arises simply because people do not know what the change is or what it implies for them.
2. Commitment to the organization will be enhanced if employees know what the organization has achieved or is trying to achieve and how this benefits them.
3. Effective communication generates trust as organizations take the trouble to explain what they are doing and why.

It should be emphasized, however, that these three benefits of good communications will only be realized in full if employees are given a voice – the opportunity to comment and respond to the information they obtain from management.

What should be communicated

Managements and individual managers need to communicate to employees about the objectives, strategies, policies and performance of the organization; what they are expected to do; learning and development opportunities; and any proposed changes to conditions of employment, working arrangements and requirements, or the structure, policies and HR practices of the organization. In each case they need to explain why the changes have been made and how they affect employees.

Employees need the opportunity to communicate upwards their comments and reactions to what is proposed will happen or what is actually happening in matters that affect them, for example, pay and other terms of employment, working conditions, work–life balance, equal opportunity, job security, health and safety, and learning and development programmes.

Approach to communication

To be effective, communication needs to be clear, easily understood and concise. Information should be presented systematically on a regular basis and be as relevant, local and timely as possible. Empathy is required by management in the sense of appreciating the concerns of employees and what they want and need to hear. Possible reactions to proposed changes should be assessed and anticipated in the communication. Attitude surveys can be used to find out what information employees want and where they feel there are any gaps that need to be filled.

A variety of communication methods will be needed: via an intranet, spoken and written, direct and indirect. Face-to-face communication to individuals or groups is both direct and swift and it provides an opportunity to gauge the reactions of people who can respond on the spot and ask questions. But it should be supplemented by written material or intranet communications, particularly where the information is important or complex.

Written communication is most effective when the information is important, the topic requires detailed and accurate explanation, the audience is widespread or large, and there is need for a permanent record or a back-up to face-to-face communication. Judicious use should be made of a mix of face-to-face and written communication, using a selection of the methods described below.

Communication methods

Individual face-to-face communication

This is, of course, the most common method of communication but it can be the most problematic. The quality, accuracy and acceptability of the information depend largely on the skill of the managers or team leaders involved and on their commitment to doing it well. Information can be distorted or plain wrong. Briefing notes are helpful but they will not necessarily be used well. Individual communications are inevitable and necessary but should not be relied upon by themselves when the subject matter is important.

Intranet

Organizations are increasingly relying on an internal e-mail system (the intranet) to communicate information, especially in workplaces where all or most of the employees have access to a computer. The advantage of intranet communications is that they can be transmitted swiftly to a wide audience. They can also be used for two-way communications – employees can be invited to respond to questions or surveys.

A communication dashboard can be created for departmental websites, which displays performance metrics in a visual form (as on a car dashboard).

Team briefing

Team briefing (sometimes called cascade briefing) aims to overcome the limited scope for communication through individuals or even joint consultative committees by involving everyone in an organization, level by level, in face-to-face meetings to present, receive and discuss information. It operates as follows:

- *Organization* – covers all levels in the business with the fewest possible steps from top to bottom. There should be between 4 and 18 in each group and the group should be run by its team leader or manager (who must be given training).
- *Subjects* – policies, plans, progress and people.
- *Operation* – work to a brief prepared by the board on key issues. The brief is written up and cascaded down the organization. Briefs are discussed at meetings and comments are fed back to the top to provide for two-way communication.
- *Timing and duration* – meet when there is something to discuss. Meetings last no more than 20–30 minutes.

Team briefing can work well as long as there is enthusiasm for it at the top and this is transmitted throughout the organization. It depends on good briefing, and managers or team leaders who have the necessary communication and interpersonal skills.

Consultative committees

Joint consultation provides a channel for two-way communication. But committees are not always effective. Their discussions can be confined to relatively trivial issues and there is still the problem of disseminating information around the organization – committee members cannot do this on their own. Minutes can be posted on notice boards or through the intranet but may not be read. It is better to highlight key points either on notice boards or through other channels.

Notice boards

Notice boards are the most obvious and familiar means of communication but they can too easily be cluttered up with redundant information. It is necessary to control what goes on to boards and ensure that out-of-date or unauthorized notices are removed.

Speak-up programmes

Speak-up programmes provide unique channels for individual employees to raise points with senior management concerning the organization and its plans and policies. This can be through the intranet.

Magazines

Glossy magazines or house journals are obvious ways to keep employees informed about the activities and achievements of the organization. There is, however, a danger of such magazines being more about public relations than about matters of real interest to employees.

Newsletters and bulletins

Newsletters can appear more frequently than magazines and can angle their contents more to the concerns of employees. They may be distributed in addition to a house magazine, treating the latter mainly as a public relations exercise. Bulletins can be used to give employees immediate information that cannot wait for the next issue of a newsletter.

Employee communication strategy

A strategy for employee communications will deal with what information the organization wants to give to employees and how it wants to provide it. Provision should also be made for upward communications.

Information to be made available

The strategy should be based on an analysis, on a regular basis, of what management wants to say and what employees want to hear. It should also cover provision for upwards communications. The analysis could refer to the areas of interest set out earlier in this chapter.

It may also be necessary to develop a specific communications strategy for any proposed major changes to terms and conditions, working arrangements such as downsizing, or organization structure, including mergers and acquisitions. For example, the introduction of a new pay structure is a major change exercise and will need to be supported by a planned communications strategy.

Providing the information

The strategy should cover the mix of methods that will be used to convey the information – face-to-face (individual or team), notice boards, intranet and magazines, newsletters or bulletins.

Upward communication

The strategy should also provide for upward communication through consultative committees, team briefing, speak-up programmes and the intranet.

Key learning points: Employee communications

The importance of employee communications

Communication is a vital part of a change management programme, in order to increase commitment and generate trust.

What should be communicated

Managements and individual managers need to communicate to employees about terms and conditions of employment; what they are expected to do; learning and development opportunities; the objectives, strategies, policies and performance of the organization; and any proposed changes to conditions of employment, working arrangements and requirements, or the structure and policies of the organization. Employees need the opportunity to communicate upwards their comments and reactions to what is proposed will happen or what is actually happening in matters that affect them.

The approach to communication

Communication needs to be clear, easily understood and concise. Information should be presented systematically on a regular basis and be as relevant, local and timely as possible. More than one medium should be used.

Communication methods

Individual face-to-face communication, intranet, team briefing, consultative committees, notice boards, speak-up programmes, magazines, newsletters and bulletins.

Employee communication strategy

A strategy for employee communications will deal with what information the organization wants to give to employees and how it wants to provide it. Provision should also be made for upward communications.

Questions

1 Why are employee communications important?
2 What should be communicated?
3 What approach to communication should be adopted?
4 What methods of communication are available?

Reference

ACAS (2005) *Guide to Communications*, London, ACAS

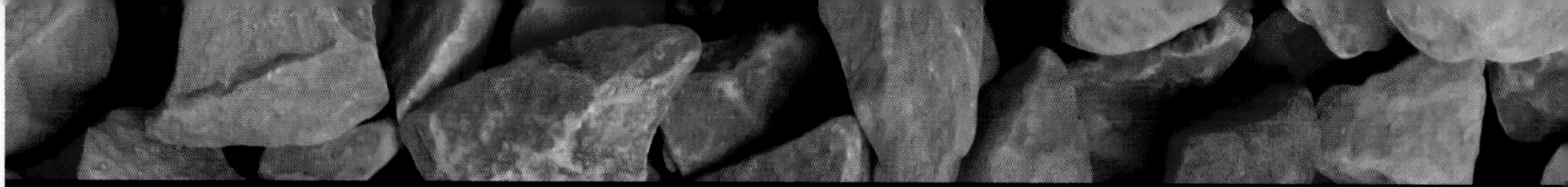

PART VIII

Employee well-being

PART VIII CONTENTS

Introduction

Well-being at work exists when people are happy with their lot – what they do, how they are treated, how they get on with others. The well-being of employees depends on the quality of working life provided by their employers – the feelings of satisfaction and happiness arising from the work itself and the work environment. The concept of the quality of working life emerged in the 1970s (Wilson, 1973) but has been less prominent recently, partly because of the preoccupation with work–life balance. As defined by Taylor (2008), the quality of working life is related to the basic extrinsic job factors of wages, hours and working conditions, and the intrinsic factors of the work itself.

A long time ago, Martin (1967: 21) put up a good case for welfare, as it was then known, as follows: 'People [at work] are entitled to be treated as full human beings with personal needs, hopes and anxieties.' This requirement has not changed since then.

The practice of employee well-being is concerned with creating a satisfactory work environment, dealing with issues affecting people, and providing individual and group services. A key aspect of well-being for employees is their health and safety. Work and job design factors, as covered in Chapter 11, are also important.

References

Martin, A O (1967) *Welfare at Work*, London, Batsford

Taylor, S (2008) *People Resourcing*, London, CIPD

Wilson, N A B (1973) *On the Quality of Working Life*, London, HMSO

35 The practice of employee well-being

KEY CONCEPTS AND TERMS

- Employee assistance programme (EAP)
- Family-friendly policies
- Flexible working
- Flexitime
- Quality of working life
- Work environment
- Work–life balance

LEARNING OUTCOMES

On completing this chapter you should be able to define these key concepts. You should also know about:

- Reasons for concern with employee well-being
- The significance of the work environment
- Managerial behaviour and well-being
- The achievement of work–life balance
- Managing stress
- Sexual harassment
- Bullying
- Services for individuals
- Group employee services

Introduction

The practice of employee well-being as examined in this chapter deals with creating a satisfactory work environment, managing stress, attending to work–life balance issues, dealing with sexual harassment and bullying problems, providing services for individuals including employee assistance programmes, and providing group services such as restaurants and social/sporting facilities. But it is first necessary to consider why organizations should be concerned with employee well-being.

Reasons for concern

The reasons for being concerned about employee well-being are as follows:

- Employers have a duty of care and this means adopting a socially responsible approach to looking after their people.
- It is in the interests of employers to do so because this will increase the likelihood of their employees being committed to the organization and will help to establish it as a 'best place to work'.
- Employers are responsible for creating a good work environment, not only because it is their duty to do so but also as part of the total reward system.

The work environment

The work environment consists of the system of work, the design of jobs, working conditions and the ways in which people are treated at work by their managers and co-workers. When designing the work system – and the jobs in it – well-being is achieved when account is taken of the needs of the people concerned. Working conditions need to meet health and safety requirements. The way people are treated is affected by managerial behaviour, achieving work–life balance and how issues such as stress, harassment and bullying are dealt with.

Managerial behaviour

Lawler (2003) suggests that what managers have to do is 'treat people right'. This means recognizing them as individuals with different needs and wants, rewarding their achievements, helping them to develop and treating them with consideration as human beings.

Work–life balance

Work–life balance is about the achievement by employees of a satisfactory equilibrium between work and non-work activities (eg parental responsibilities and wider caring duties, as well as other activities and interests). Thus employees can reconcile the competing claims of work and home by meeting their own needs as well as those of their employers.

Work–life balance can be enhanced by what are sometimes called 'family-friendly' policies that facilitate flexible working. This covers home-working, part-time working, compressed working weeks, annualized hours, job-sharing, term-time only working and 'flexitime' (an arrangement for providing flexible hours in which employees are contracted to work for a weekly or monthly number of hours; within limits, they may vary their start or finish times as long as they work the hours required during the defined period). It can also involve special leave schemes that provide employees with the freedom to respond to a domestic crisis or to take a career break without jeopardizing their employment status.

Individual requests for a particular working arrangement generally need to be considered on a case-by-case basis, but the culture should not discourage employees from making such requests. In addition to fearing the reaction of line managers, the risk of career-damage is a common reason for poor take-up of work–life balance arrangements. Line management will need to be convinced that work–life balance measures are important and pay off in terms of increased engagement.

Work–life balance policies can lower absence and help to tackle the low morale and high degrees of stress that can lead to retention problems as employees tire of juggling work and life responsibilities. The research conducted by the Institute for Employment Studies (Kodz *et al*, 2002) identified employees who were staying longer with their firms because of access to flexible working arrangements.

Managing stress

There are four main reasons why organizations should be concerned about stress and should do something about it. First, they should act in a socially responsible way to provide a good quality of working life; second, because excessive stress causes illness; third, because it can result in inability to cope with the demands of the job, which of course creates more stress; and fourth, because excessive stress can reduce employee effectiveness and therefore organizational performance. The ways in which stress can be managed by an organization include the following:

- *Job design* – clarifying roles, reducing the danger of role ambiguity and conflict, and giving people more autonomy within a defined structure to manage their responsibilities.
- *Targets and performance standards* – setting reasonable and achievable targets that may stretch people but do not place impossible burdens on them.
- *Job placement* – taking care to place people in jobs that are within their capabilities.
- *Career development* – planning careers and promoting staff in accordance with their capabilities, taking care not to over- or under-promote.
- *Performance management processes* – allowing a dialogue to take place between managers and individuals about the latter's work problems and ambitions.
- *Counselling* – giving individuals the opportunity to talk about their problems with a member of the HR department, or through an employee assistance programme, as described later in this chapter.
- *Anti-bullying campaigns* – bullying at work is a major cause of stress.
- *Management training* – training in what managers can do to alleviate their own stress and reduce it in others.

Sexual harassment

Sadly, sexual harassment has always been a feature of life at work. Perhaps it is not always quite as blatant today as it has been in the past, but it is still there, in more or less subtle forms, and it is just as unpleasant. People who are subject to sexual harassment can take legal action, but it must be the policy of the organization to make it clear that it will not be tolerated and this policy should be backed up by procedures and practices for dealing with harassment.

Problems of dealing with harassment

There are three problems in dealing with harassment. First, it can be difficult to make a clear-cut case. An accusation of harassment can be hard to prove unless there are witnesses, and those who indulge in this practice usually take care to carry it out on a one-to-one basis. In this situation, it may be a case of one person's word against another's. The harasser, usually a man, resorts to two defences: one, that it did not take place ('it was all in her mind'); and two, that if anything did take place it was provoked by the behaviour of the female. When this happens, whoever deals with the case has to exercise judgement and attempt, difficult though it may be, to remove any prejudice in favour of the word of the man, the woman, the boss or the subordinate.

The second problem is that targets of sexual harassment are often unwilling to take action and in practice seldom do so. This is because of the actual or perceived difficulty of proving their case. But they may also feel that they will not get a fair hearing and are worried about the effect that making such accusations will have on how they are treated by their boss or their colleagues in the future, whether or not they have substantiated their accusation.

The third, and perhaps the most deep-rooted and difficult problem is that sexual harassment may be part of the culture of the organization – 'the way we do things around here'; a norm, practised at all levels.

Solutions

There are no easy solutions to these problems. It may be very hard to eradicate sexual harassment completely. But the effort must be made, along the following lines:

- Issue a clear statement by the chief executive that sexual harassment will not be tolerated.
- Back up the statement with a policy directive that spells out in more detail that the organization deplores harassment, why it is not acceptable and what people who believe they are being subjected to harassment can do about it.
- Reinforce the policy statement by behaviour at senior level that demonstrates it is not merely words but that these exhortations have meaning.

- Ensure that the sexual harassment policy is stated clearly in induction courses and is conveyed to everyone. Reinforce this message by regular reminders.
- Make arrangements for employees subjected to sexual harassment to seek advice, support and counselling without any obligation to take a complaint forward. They could talk informally with someone in HR. Alternatively, a counsellor (possibly engaged as part of an employee assistance programme) can usefully offer guidance on harassment problems; assist in resolving them informally by seeking, with the agreement of the complainant, a confidential and voluntary interview with the person complained against to achieve a solution, without recource to a formal disciplinary procedure; assist in submitting a complaint if the employee wishes to raise it formally; and provide counselling to each of the parties on their future conduct.
- Create a special procedure for hearing complaints about sexual harassment. The normal procedure may not be suitable because, for example, the harasser could be the employee's line manager. The procedure should provide for employees to bring their complaint to someone of their own sex, should they so choose.
- Handle complaints about harassment with sensitivity and due respect for the rights of both the complainant and the accused. Ensure that hearings are conducted fairly and that both parties are given an equal opportunity to put their case.
- Where sexual harassment has taken place, crack down on it. It should be stated in the policy that it is regarded as gross industrial misconduct and, if it is proven, makes the individual liable to instant dismissal. Less severe penalties may be reserved for minor cases but there should always be a warning that repetition will result in dismissal.
- Ensure that everyone is aware that the organization does take action, when required, to punish those who indulge in sexual harassment.
- Provide training to line managers and team leaders to ensure that the policy is properly implemented and to make them aware of their direct responsibility to prevent harassment taking place and to take action if it does.

Bullying

Bullying is a form of harassment and can be very unpleasant. It is perhaps one of the most difficult aspects of employee relationships to control. Like sexual harassment, it can be hard to prove that bullying has taken place and employees may be reluctant to complain about a bullying boss, simply because he or she is a bully. But this does not mean that an organization can ignore the problem. A policy should be published stating that bullying is unacceptable behaviour. People who feel that they are being bullied should have the right to discuss the problem with someone in the HR department or a trained counsellor. Bullies should not be punished automatically. They should initially be helped to acknowledge the impact of their behaviours, and to change. Punishment should be reserved for those who persist in spite of this guidance.

Services for individuals

Services may be provided for individuals to help them deal with their problems. This may involve counselling or personal case work where the aim is, as far as possible, to get individuals to help themselves. The areas where counselling and other forms of help may be provided are:

- *Sickness* – the provision of help and advice to employees absent from work for long periods due to illness; this may include sick visits.
- *Bereavement* – advice on how to cope with the death of a partner or close relative.
- *Domestic problems* – normally they should not be the concern of the employer, but if someone is very distressed, help can be offered through a counselling service.

- *Retirement* – advice can be made available to employees who are about to retire in order to prepare them for their new circumstances; continued counselling and visiting services may be provided for retired employees.

Counselling is a skilled business and is best carried out by trained people. This is where employee assistance programmes (EAPs) can be useful. EAP services are provided by external agencies that enable employees to access counselling through a phone service, although face-to-face counselling may also be offered. Employers can refer employees to the service, which is confidential between the agency and the individual.

CASE STUDY

B&Q's employee assistance programme

The aims of the B&Q employee assistance programme are to:

- Support employees of all ages and backgrounds through the full spectrum of life experiences by offering advice, information, practical help and emotional support free of charge and in confidence.
- Support carers of the chronically sick, disabled or elderly by offering advice and information. Locating care options and community resources.
- Save time for working parents by helping them find and arrange good quality, affordable and reliable care arrangements for children of all ages.
- Support parents through a wide range of parenting issues, including understanding and choosing education options, and understanding and monitoring behaviour of children.
- Reduce unplanned absence by encouraging employees with personal, practical, emotional and financial problems to seek early help and advice.
- Offer information and support to managers and HR staff with their personal issues, and issues facing their staff.
- Raise employee morale and commitment by showing the caring face of the employer.
- Improve customer service and productivity by saving employees' time and solving and avoiding work–life conflicts.

Group employee services

Group employee services mainly consist of subsidized restaurants, sports and social clubs, and child care facilities.

Restaurant facilities are desirable in any large establishment where local facilities are limited. Sports or social clubs should not be laid on because they are 'good for morale' – there is no evidence that they are. They may be provided if there is a real need for them arising from a lack of local facilities. In the latter case, the facilities should be shared with the local community. Child care facilities are one of the most popular forms of group services, if they fill a need that cannot be met easily elsewhere.

Key learning points: The practice of employee well-being

Reasons for concern with well-being

Employers have a duty of care and this means adopting a socially responsible approach to looking after their people.

Employers are responsible for creating a good work environment, not only because it is their duty to do so but also as part of the total reward system. It is in the interests of employers to do so because this will increase the likelihood of their employees being committed to the organization and help to establish it as a 'best place to work'.

The significance of the work environment

The work environment consists of the system of work, the design of jobs, working conditions and the ways in which people are treated at work by their managers and co-workers. When designing the work system – and the jobs in it – well-being is achieved when account is taken of the needs of the people concerned. Working conditions need to meet health and safety requirements. The way people are treated is a matter of managerial behaviour, achieving work–life balance and dealing with issues such as stress, harassment and bullying.

The achievement of work–life balance

Flexible working is the most practical solution to establishing an effective work–life balance. This covers flexitime, homeworking, part-time working, compressed working weeks, annualized hours, job-sharing and term-time only working. It also refers to special leave schemes, which provide employees with the freedom to respond to a domestic crisis or to take a career break without jeopardizing their employment status.

Managing stress

Employers have the social responsibility to provide a good quality of working life. Stress can result in inability to cope with the demands of the job, which creates more stress. Excessive stress causes illness and can reduce employee effectiveness and therefore organizational performance.

Sexual harassment

Sexual harassment is difficult to deal with but it is important to make a determined attempt to minimize it through policy statements backed up by special procedures for seeking help and making complaints.

Bullying

A policy should be published stating that bullying is unacceptable behaviour. People who feel that they are being bullied should have the right to discuss the problem with someone in the HR department or a trained counsellor.

Services for individuals

Counselling, possibly through EAP programmes, can be provided for sickness, bereavement, domestic problems and retirement.

Group employee services

These mainly consist of subsidized restaurants, sports and social clubs, and child care facilities.

Questions

1 What does employee well-being mean?
2 What is work–life balance and what can be done about it?
3 How can stress be managed?
4 What are employee assistance programmes (EAPs)?

References

Kodz, J, Harper, H and Dench, S (2002) *Work–life Balance: Beyond the rhetoric*, Report 384, Brighton, Institute for Employment Studies

Lawler, E E (2003) *Treat People Right! How organizations and individuals can propel each other into a virtuous spiral of success*, San Francisco, CA, Jossey-Bass

36
Health and safety

KEY CONCEPTS AND TERMS

Frequency rate	Occupational hygiene
Hazard	Occupational medicine
Health and safety audit	Risk
Health and safety inspection	Risk assessment
Incidence rate	Severity rate
Occupational health programme	Total loss control

LEARNING OUTCOMES

On completing this chapter you should be able to define these key concepts. You should also know about:

- Managing health and safety at work
- Health and safety policies
- Risk assessments
- Health and safety audits
- Health and safety inspections
- Accident prevention
- Occupational health programmes
- Measuring health and safety performance
- Communicating the need for better health and safety practices
- Health and safety training
- Organizing health and safety

Introduction

Health and safety policies and programmes are concerned with protecting employees – and other people affected by what the company produces and does – against the hazards arising from their employment or their links with the company.

Safety programmes deal with the prevention of accidents and with minimizing the resulting loss and damage to people and property. They relate more to systems of work than the working environment, but both health and safety programmes are concerned with protection against hazards, and their aims and methods are clearly interlinked.

Occupational health programmes deal with the prevention of ill-health arising from working conditions. They consist of two elements: 1) occupational medicine, which is a specialized branch of preventive medicine concerned with the identification, diagnosis and prevention of health hazards at work and dealing with any ill-health or stress that has occurred in spite of preventative actions; and 2) occupational hygiene, which is the province of the chemist and the engineer or ergonomist engaged in the measurement and control of environmental hazards.

Managing health and safety at work

The achievement of a healthy and safe place of work and the elimination to the maximum extent possible of hazards to health and safety are the responsibility of everyone employed in an organization, as well as those working there under contract. But the onus is on management to achieve and indeed go beyond the high standard in health and safety matters required by the legislation – the Health and Safety at Work etc Act 1974 and the various regulations and Codes of Practice.

The importance of healthy and safe policies and practices is, sadly, often underestimated by those concerned with managing businesses and by individual managers within those businesses. But the achievement of the highest standards of health and safety in the workplace is important because the elimination, or at least minimization, of health and safety hazards and risks is the moral as well as the legal responsibility of employers – this duty of care is the overriding reason. Close and continuous attention to health and safety is important because ill-health and injuries caused by the system of work or working conditions cause suffering and loss to individuals and their dependents. In addition, accidents and absences through ill-health or injuries result in losses and damage for the organization. This 'business' reason is much less significant than the 'human' reasons, but it is still a consideration, albeit a tangential one.

Health and safety policies

Written health and safety policies are required to demonstrate that top management is concerned about the protection of the organization's employees from hazards at work and to indicate how this protection will be provided. The policies are, therefore: 1) a declaration of intent; 2) a definition of the means by which that intent will be realized; 3) a statement of the guidelines that should be followed by everyone concerned – which means all employees – in implementing the policy.

The policy statement should consist of three parts:

1. The general policy statement.
2. The description of the organization of health and safety.
3. Details of arrangements for implementing the policy.

The general policy statement

The general policy statement should be a declaration of the intention of the employer to safeguard the health and safety of employees. It should emphasize four fundamental points:

1. that the health and safety of employees and the public is of paramount importance;
2. that health and safety takes precedence over expediency;
3. that every effort will be made to involve all managers, team leaders and employees in the development and implementation of health and safety procedures;
4. that health and safety legislation will be complied with in the spirit as well as the letter of the law.

Organization

This section of the policy statement should describe the health and safety organization of the business through which high standards are set and achieved by people at all levels in the organization.

This statement should underline the ultimate responsibility of top management for the health and safety performance of the organization. It should then indicate how key management personnel are held accountable for performance in their areas. The role of safety representatives and safety committees should be defined, and the duties of specialists such as the safety adviser and the medical officer should be summarized.

Implementing health and safety policies

The basis for implementing health and safety policies is provided by three review methods:

- Risk assessments, which identify the existence of hazards.
- Health and safety audits, which provide for a comprehensive review of all aspects of health and safety policies, procedures and practices.
- Health and safety inspections, which locate and define any faults in the system, equipment, plant or machines, or any operational errors that might be a danger to health or the source of accidents.

Conducting risk assessments

Risk assessments are concerned with the identification of hazards and the analysis of the risks attached to them. A hazard is anything that can cause harm (working on roofs, lifting heavy objects, chemicals, electricity, etc). A risk is the chance, large or small, of harm being actually done by the hazard.

The purpose of risk assessments is to initiate preventative action. They enable control measures to be devised on the basis of an understanding of the relative importance of risks. Risk assessments must be recorded if there are five or more employees.

Types of risk assessment

There are two types of risk assessment. The first is quantitative risk assessment, which produces an objective probability estimate based upon risk information that is immediately applicable to the circumstances in which the risk occurs. The second is qualitative risk assessment, which is more subjective and is based on judgement backed by generalized data. Quantitative risk assessment is preferable if the specific data is available. Qualitative risk assessment may be acceptable if there is little or no specific data, as long as it is made systematically on the basis of an analysis of working conditions and hazards and an informed judgement of the likelihood of harm actually being done.

Typical hazards that can be identified by risk assessments include:

- lifting and carrying, eg heavy or unwieldy objects;
- stacking and storage, eg falling materials;
- movement of people and materials, eg falls, collisions;
- processing of raw materials, eg exposure to toxic substances;
- maintenance of buildings, eg roof work, gutter cleaning;
- maintenance of plant and machinery, eg lifting tackle, installation of equipment;
- using electricity, eg using hand tools, extension leads;
- operating machines, eg operating without sufficient clearance or at an unsafe speed; not using safety devices;
- failure to wear protective equipment, eg hats, boots, clothing;
- distribution of products or materials, eg movement of vehicles;
- dealing with emergencies, eg spillages, fires, explosions;
- health hazards arising from the use of equipment or methods of working, eg VDUs, repetitive strain injuries from badly designed work stations or working practices.

Most accidents are caused by a few key activities. Assessors should concentrate initially on those that could cause serious harm. Operations such as roof work, maintenance and transport movement cause far more deaths and injuries each year than many mainstream activities.

When carrying out a risk assessment it is also necessary to consider who might be harmed. This means both employees and visitors (including cleaners and contractors and the public when calling in to buy products or enlist services).

Hazards should be ranked according to their potential. A simple three-point scale can be used such as ‘low’, ‘moderate’ and ‘high’, or ‘negligible’, ‘marginal’ and ‘critical’.

Assessing the risk

When the hazards have been identified it is necessary to assess how high the risks are. This involves answering three questions:

1. What is the worst result?
2. How likely is it to happen?
3. How many people could be hurt if things go wrong?

A probability rating system can be used such as:

- Probable – likely to occur immediately or shortly.
- Reasonably probable – probably will occur in time.
- Remote – may occur in time.
- Extremely remote – unlikely to occur.

Taking action

Risk assessment should lead to action. The type of action can be ranked in order of potential effectiveness in the form of the following safety precedence sequence:

1. *Hazard elimination* – use of alternatives, design improvements, change of process.
2. *Substitution* – for example, replacement of one chemical with another that is less risky.
3. *Use of barriers* – removing the hazard from the worker or removing the worker from the hazard.
4. *Use of procedures* – limitation of exposure, dilution of exposure, safe systems of work (these depend on human response).
5. *Use of warning systems* – signs, instructions, labels (these also depend on human response).
6. *Use of personal protective clothing* – this depends on human response and is used as a side measure only when all other options have been exhausted.

Monitoring and evaluation

Risk assessment is not completed when action has been initiated. It is essential to monitor the hazard and evaluate the effectiveness of the action in eliminating it or at least reducing it to an acceptable level.

Health and safety audits

Risk assessments identify specific hazards and quantify the risks attached to them. Health and safety audits provide for a much more comprehensive review of all aspects of health and safety policies, procedures and practices.

Who carries out a health and safety audit?

Safety audits can be conducted by safety advisers and/or HR specialists, but the more that managers, employees and employee representatives are involved the better. Audits are often carried out under the auspices of a health and safety committee, with its members taking an active part in conducting them. Some organizations also use outside agencies such as the British Safety Institute to conduct independent audits.

Managers can also be held responsible for conducting audits within their departments and, even better, individual members of these departments can be trained to carry out audits in particular areas. The conduct of an audit will be facilitated if checklists are prepared and a simple form used to record results.

What is covered by a health and safety audit?

A health and safety audit should cover policies, procedures and safety practices, as outlined below.

Policies

The following questions should be asked:

- Do health and safety policies meet legal requirements?
- Are senior managers committed to health and safety?
- How committed are other managers, team leaders and supervisors to health and safety?

- Is there a health and safety committee? If not, why not?
- How effective is the committee in getting things done?

Procedures

How effectively do the procedures:

- support the implementation of health and safety policies?
- communicate the need for good health and safety practices?
- provide for systematic risk assessments?
- ensure that accidents are investigated thoroughly?
- record data on health and safety that is used to evaluate performance and initiate action?
- ensure that health and safety considerations are given proper weight when designing systems of work or manufacturing and operational processes (including the design of equipment and work stations, the specification for the product or service, and the use of materials)?
- provide safety training, especially induction training and training when jobs or working methods are changed?

Safety practices

The following questions should be considered:

- To what extent do health and safety practices in all areas of the organization conform to the general requirements of the Health and Safety at Work etc Act and the specific requirements of the various regulations and Codes of Practice?
- What risk assessments have been carried out? What were the findings? What actions were taken?
- What is the health and safety performance of the organization as shown by the performance indicators? Is the trend positive or negative? If the latter, what is being done about it?
- How thoroughly are accidents investigated? What steps have been taken to prevent their recurrence?
- What is the evidence that managers and supervisors are really concerned about health and safety?

What should be done with the audit?

The audit should cover the questions above but its purpose is to generate action. Those conducting the audit will have to assess priorities and costs and draw up action programmes for approval by top management.

Health and safety inspections

Health and safety inspections are designed to examine a specific area of the organization – an operational department or a manufacturing process – to locate and define any faults in the system, equipment, plant or machines, or any operational errors that might be a danger to health or the source of accidents. Health and safety inspections should be carried out on a regular and systematic basis by line managers and supervisors with the advice and help of health and safety specialists. The steps to be taken in carrying out health and safety inspections are as follows:

1. Allocate the responsibility for conducting the inspection.
2. Define the points to be covered in the form of a checklist.
3. Divide the department or plant into areas and list the points to which attention needs to be given in each area.
4. Define the frequency with which inspections should be carried out – daily in critical areas.
5. Use the checklists as the basis for the inspection.
6. Carry out sample or spot checks on a random basis.
7. Carry out special investigations as necessary to deal with special problems, such as operating machinery without guards to increase throughput.

8 Set up a reporting system (a form should be used for recording the results of inspections).
9 Set up a system for monitoring that safety inspections are being conducted properly and on schedule.
10 Ensure that corrective action is taken where necessary.

Accident prevention

The prevention of accidents is achieved by the following actions:

1 Identify the causes of accidents and the conditions under which they are most likely to occur.
2 Take account of safety factors at the design stage – build safety into the system.
3 Design safety equipment and protective devices and provide protective clothing.
4 Carry out regular risk assessments, audits, inspections and checks and take action to eliminate risks.
5 Investigate all accidents resulting in damage or harm in order to establish the cause and to initiate corrective action.
6 Maintain good records and statistics in order to identify problem areas and unsatisfactory trends.
7 Conduct a continuous programme of education and training on safe working habits and methods of avoiding accidents.
8 Encourage approaches to leadership and motivation that do not place excessive demands on people.

Occupational health programmes

Occupational health programmes are designed to minimize the impact of work-related illnesses. The control of occupational health and hygiene problems can be achieved by taking the following actions:

1 Eliminate the hazard at source through design and process engineering.
2 Isolate hazardous processes and substances so that workers do not come into contact with them.
3 Change the processes or substances used in order to promote better protection or eliminate the risk.
4 Provide protective equipment, but only if changes to the design, process or specification cannot completely remove the hazard.
5 Train workers to avoid risk.
6 Maintain plant and equipment to eliminate the possibility of harmful emissions, controlling the use of toxic substances and eliminating radiation hazards.
7 Adopt good housekeeping practices to keep premises and machinery clean and free from toxic substances.
8 Conduct regular inspections to ensure that potential health risks are identified in good time.
9 Carry out pre-employment medical examinations and regular checks on those exposed to risk.
10 Ensure that ergonomic considerations (ie those concerning the design and use of equipment, machines, processes and work stations) are taken into account in design specifications, establishing work routines and training – this is particularly important as a means of minimizing the incidence of repetitive strain injury (RSI).
11 Maintain preventive medicine programmes that develop health standards for each job and involve regular audits of potential health hazards and regular examinations for anyone at risk. Particular attention needs to be exercised in the control of noise, fatigue and stress. The management and control of stress, as considered in Chapter 35, should be a major part of any occupational health programme.

Measuring health and safety performance

It is essential to measure health and safety performance as a means of identifying in good time where actions are necessary. Account should be taken not only of current and recent figures but also trends. The most common measures are:

The frequency rate:

$$\frac{\text{number of injuries}}{\text{number of hours worked}} \times 100{,}000$$

The Incidence rate:

$$\frac{\text{number of injuries}}{\text{average number employed during the period}} \times 1{,}000$$

Some organizations adopt a 'total loss control' approach, which covers the cost of accidents to the business under such headings as 'pay to people off work', 'damage to plant or equipment' and 'loss of production'. A cost severity rate can then be calculated, which is the total cost of accidents per 1,000 hours worked.

Communicating the need for better health and safety practices

It is necessary to deliver the message that health and safety is important; this should supplement rather than replace other initiatives. The following steps can be taken to increase the effectiveness of safety messages:

- *Avoid negatives* – successful safety propaganda should contain positive messages, not warnings of the unpleasant consequences of actions.
- *Expose correctly* – address the message to the right people at the point of danger.
- *Use attention-getting techniques carefully* – lurid images may only be remembered for what they are, not for the message they are trying to convey.
- *Maximize comprehension* – messages should be simple and specific.
- *Messages must be believable* – they should address real issues and be perceived as being delivered by people (ie managers) who believe in what they say and are doing something about it.
- *Messages must point the way to action* – the most effective messages call for positive actions that can be achieved by those who receive them and will offer them a tangible benefit.

Approaches to briefing staff on the importance of health and safety

Advice to a group of staff on the importance of health and safety in the workplace must be based on a thorough understanding of the organization's health and safety policies and procedures and an appreciation of the particular factors affecting the health and safety of the group of people concerned. The latter can be based on information provided by risk assessments, safety audits and accident reports. But the advice must be positive – why health and safety is important and how accidents can be prevented. The advice should not be overweighted by unpleasant warnings. The points to be made include:

- A review of the health and safety policies of the organization with explanations of the reasoning behind them and a positive statement of management's belief that health and safety is a major consideration because: 1) it directly affects the well-being of all concerned; and 2) it can, and does, minimize suffering and loss.
- A review of the procedures used by the organization for the business as a whole, and in the particular area, to assess risks and audit the safety position.
- An explanation of the roles of the members of the group in carrying out their work safely and giving full consideration to the safety of others.

- A reiteration of the statement that one of the core values of the organization is the maintenance of safe systems of work and the promotion of safe working practices.

Health and safety training

Health and safety training is a key part of the preventative programme. It should start as part of the induction course. It should also take place following a transfer to a new job or a change in working methods. Safety training spells out the rules and provides information on potential hazards and how to avoid them. Further refresher training should be provided and special courses laid on to deal with new aspects of health and safety or areas in which safety problems have emerged.

Organizing health and safety

Health and safety concerns everyone in an establishment, although the main responsibility lies with management in general and individual managers in particular. Specific roles should be defined as follows:

- *Management* develops and implements health and safety policies and ensures that procedures for carrying out risk assessments, safety audits and inspections are implemented. Importantly, management has the duty of monitoring and evaluating health and safety performance and taking corrective action as necessary.
- *Managers* can exert a greater influence on health and safety. They are in immediate control and it is up to them to keep a constant watch for unsafe conditions or practices and to take immediate action. They are also directly responsible for ensuring that employees are conscious of health and safety hazards and do not take risks.
- *Employees* should be aware of what constitute safe working practices as they affect them and their fellow workers. While management and managers have the duty to communicate and train, individuals also have the duty to take account of what they have heard and learnt and apply it in the ways that they carry out their work.
- *Health and safety advisers* advise on policies and procedures and on healthy and safe methods of working. They conduct risk assessments, safety audits and investigations into accidents (in conjunction with managers and health and safety representatives), maintain statistics and report on trends and necessary actions.
- *Health and safety representatives* deal with health and safety issues in their areas and are members of health and safety committees.
- *Medical advisers* have two functions: preventative and clinical. The preventative function is most important, especially on occupational health matters. The clinical function is to deal with industrial accidents and diseases and to advise on the steps necessary to recover from injury or illness arising from work. They do not usurp the role of the family doctor in non-work-related illnesses.
- *Safety committees* consisting of health and safety representatives advise on health and safety policies and procedures, help in conducting risk assessments and safety audits, and make suggestions on improving health and safety performance.

Key learning points: Health and safety

Managing health and safety at work

The achievement of a healthy and safe place of work, and the elimination to the maximum extent possible of hazards to health and safety, is the responsibility of everyone employed in an organization, as well as those working there under contract. But the onus is on the management to achieve and indeed go beyond the high standard in health and safety matters required by the legislation – the Health and Safety at Work etc Act 1974 and the various regulations laid down in the Codes of Practice.

Health and safety policies

Written health and safety policies are required to demonstrate that top management is concerned about the protection of the organization's employees from hazards at work and to indicate how this protection will be provided.

Risk assessments

Risk assessments are concerned with the identification of hazards and the analysis of the risks attached to them. The purpose is to initiate preventative action.

Health and safety audits

Health and safety audits provide for a much more comprehensive review of all aspects of health and safety policies, procedures and practices.

Health and safety inspections

Health and safety inspections should be carried out on a regular and systematic basis by line managers and supervisors, with the advice and help of health and safety advisers.

Accident prevention

Checklist:

- Identify the causes of accidents.
- Take account of safety factors at the design stage.
- Design safety equipment and protective devices and provide protective clothing.
- Carry out regular risk assessment audits and inspections and take action to eliminate risks.
- Investigate all accidents.
- Maintain good records and statistics in order to identify problem areas and unsatisfactory trends.
- Conduct a continuous programme of education and training on safe working habits.

Occupational health programmes

Implementing occupational health programmes can:

- Eliminate the hazard at source through design and process engineering.
- Isolate hazardous processes and substances so that workers do not come into contact with them.
- Change the processes or substances used to promote better protection or eliminate the risk.
- Provide protective equipment, but only if changes to the design, process or specification cannot completely remove the hazard.
- Train workers to avoid risk.

Measuring health and safety performance

This is important as a guide to action using the standard measures of frequency, incidence and severity rate.

Communicating the need for better health and safety practices

It is necessary to deliver the message that health and safety is important as long as this supplements rather than replaces other initiatives.

Health and safety training

Health and safety training is a key part of the preventative programme. It should start as part of the induction course. It should also take place following a transfer to a new job or a change in working methods.

Organizing health and safety

Health and safety concerns everyone in an establishment, although the main responsibility lies with management in general and individual managers in particular. The specific roles should be defined for managers and employees, health and safety advisers, medical advisers and the health and safety committee.

Questions

1. What are health and safety and occupational health programmes?
2. What is the purpose of health and safety policies?
3. What is the distinction between risk assessments, health and safety audits and health and safety inspections?
4. What steps need to be taken to prevent accidents?
5. How are occupational health problems controlled?

PART IX

International HRM

PART IX CONTENTS

Introduction

International human resource management (international HRM) is the process of managing people across international boundaries by multinational companies (MNCs). It involves the worldwide management of people, not just the management of expatriates.

It was stated by Brewster *et al* (2005: 949) that: 'A critical challenge for organizations from both the public and private sectors in the 21st century is the need to operate across national boundaries.' As Sparrow *et al* (2011: 50) commented: 'The ultimate aim of multinational companies (MNCs) is to build a core competence of being able to transfer capability across multiple countries, which involves monitoring the implementation of relevant policies and practices, ensuring an adequate corporate culture, establishing the necessary networks, and ensuring all parts of the organization are sensitive to the needs of international staff.'

The fundamental differences between international and domestic HRM are that in an international organization:

- HRM is more complex because it involves operating across national boundaries rather than within only one boundary and therefore takes place in different countries each with its own culture and institutions.
- It is necessary to manage a wider mix of people at headquarters and in foreign subsidiaries that employ local staff (home country nationals) and expatriates from either the parent company (parent company nationals) or other countries (third country nationals).
- Choices have to be made on the extent to which parent company HRM policies and practices should be adopted by subsidiaries – the issue of the degree of convergence required and how it is to be achieved.
- Choices have to be made on the extent to which HR decisions on matters such as appointments, promotions, redeployments and talent management should be centralized or decentralized.
- The management of expatriates involves different approaches to selection, training and career management and special concerns about the adjustment of expatriates to working in foreign countries and to the problems of repatriation.

- HR professionals have to exercise a broader range of expertise covering knowledge about foreign countries, their cultures and their institutions.
- Firms become more involved in the personal lives of their expatriate employees.

In this part, the framework of international HRM is dealt with in Chapter 37, which covers the crucial issue of the degree to which international HRM policies and practices should converge or diverge. Chapter 38 deals with the international HRM practices of workforce planning, resourcing, talent management, reward management and performance management. It also refers to multicultural working and the role of an international HR function. Chapter 39 focuses on expatriates – individuals sent by a parent company on foreign assignments. Although the practices of international HRM as described in Chapter 38 will also apply to expatriates working in foreign subsidiaries, there are a number of special considerations regarding their employment, which are considered in Chapter 39.

References

Brewster, C, Sparrow, P and Harris, H (2005) Towards a new model of globalizing HRM, *The International Journal of Human Resource Management*, 16 (6), pp 949–70

Sparrow, P, Scullion, H and Farndale, E (2011) Global talent management: new roles for the corporate HR function? in H Scullion and D G Collings (eds) *Global Talent Management*, London, Routledge, pp 40–55

37 The international HRM framework

KEY CONCEPTS AND TERMS

- Centralization
- Convergence
- Decentralization
- Divergence
- Ethnocentric orientation
- Geocentric orientation
- Globalization
- Internationalization
- Localization
- MNC or MNE
- Polycentric orientation
- Regiocentric orientation
- Transnational organization

LEARNING OUTCOMES

On completing this chapter you should be able to define these key concepts. You should also understand:

- The international scene
- International strategies
- Contextual factors
- Convergence and divergence

Introduction

International HRM is concerned with human resource management policies and practices in multinational enterprises. Its aim is to ensure that an international organization attracts, deploys, develops and engages the quality of people it requires to achieve its strategic goals. Dr Michael Dickmann of the Cranfield School of Management believes, as reported by Welfare (2006: 8), that the main contrast between national and global HR practice is the need to see the bigger picture: 'The difference is the higher complexity and the need for sensitivity to different cultures and different business environments.' Dickmann stated that understanding the local context is key and that an international HR person needs to be asking questions such as: What is the business environment here? What is the role of the trade unions? What is the local labour law? Are these people different? Are their motivation patterns different?

As discussed in this chapter, international HRM takes place in a framework consisting of the international scene in general, the implications of the different approaches to international strategy and the specific contextual factors associated with differences in culture and institutions.

A key issue in international HRM also considered in this chapter is the extent to which HR policies and practices should converge or diverge. Bartlett and Ghoshal (2002) proposed that strategies in an international context are characterized by conflicting pressures of global standardization (ie internal consistency with the rest of the multinational company (MNC)) and local differentiation (ie external consistency with local environments). Standardization or convergence refers to the degree to which an international parent company's HR policies and practices are adopted by each of its subsidiaries. Localization or divergence refers to the extent to which subsidiaries operate their own HR policies and practices and act and behave as local firms.

The international scene

Internationalization is the process of international economic integration in worldwide markets. Isidor *et al* (2011: 2167) observed that: 'Internationalization offers firms manifold advantages such as realizing economies of scale and scope, learning from international markets, exploiting interrelations between business segments and geographic areas, achieving risk diversification, and cost reduction.'

According to Theodore Levitt (1983), technological, social and economic developments have combined to create a unified world marketplace in which companies must capture global-scale economies to remain competitive. It encompasses globalization – the development of single international markets for goods or services accompanied by an accelerated growth in world trade. Any company that has economic interests or activities extending across a number of international boundaries is a global company.

Globalization raises a number of issues not present when the activities of the firm are confined to one country. As Ulrich (1998: 126) contended, it requires organizations:

> to move people, ideas, products, and information around the world to meet local needs. They must add new and important ingredients to the mix when making strategy: volatile political situations, contentious global trade issues, fluctuating exchange rates, and unfamiliar cultures. They must be more literate in the ways of international customers, commerce, and competition than ever before. In short, globalization requires that organizations increase their ability to learn and collaborate and to manage diversity, complexity, and ambiguity.

Brewster *et al* (2005) identified five distinct, but linked, organizational drivers of this process: efficiency orientation, global service provision, information exchange, core business processes and localization of decision-making. The outcome has been pressure on international businesses to create a federation of global units (in the sense of working together to achieve global strategic goals) rather than national units (in the sense of taking a parochial interest in local concerns and ignoring global requirements). This in turn has increased the move towards standardization (convergence) of HRM policies and procedures and decreased interest in their localization (divergence). Globalization has encouraged the development of international HRM, enhancing the role and authority of international HR functions.

International HRM strategies

International HRM has to function strategically in order to support the achievement of international business strategies.

International HRM strategies will be affected by the different types of business strategies that MNCs can adopt, as identified by Bartlett and Ghoshal (2002: 18–19):

1 Multinational – building strong local presence through sensitivity and responsiveness to local needs.

2 Global – building cost advantages through controlled global-scale operations.
3 International – exploiting parent company knowledge and capabilities through worldwide diffusion and adaptation.
4 Transnational – creating a new organizational model by simultaneously developing global competitiveness, multinational flexibility and worldwide learning capacity.

They suggested that the transnational organization 'is a feasible and necessary response to the changes in the international environment' (ibid: 19) and claimed that adopting the transnational mode allowed companies such as Unilever to deal effectively with these demands. They mentioned that Unilever had developed a strongly held philosophy of management built around independent operating companies whose managers were given maximum responsibility and freedom. The clearly understood role of the Unilever board is to approve plans and budgets, control capital expenditures and appoint and develop executives. At an operating level, local managers have great latitude to develop and implement strategies that reflected the opportunities and constraints of their particular environments. The watchwords that became corporate dogma were 'local initiative and decentralized control'.

In contrast, P&G operations, although regarded by Bartlett and Ghoshal as a transnational organization, were linked back to the parent company in two important respects: not only did foreign subsidiaries depend on the parent for advanced technology and marketing expertise, but they were also structured to operate as replicas of the US company, immersed in the same principles and guided by the same policies.

Contextual factors

All HR activities are affected by the context in which they operate, but the variety of contexts in which international HRM functions are particularly significant. They strongly influence decisions on the dissemination of parent company policies and practices (convergence or divergence) and on the employment of expatriates. As Sparrow *et al* (1994: 269) asserted: 'For global firms to be successful in managing their worldwide work-forces, they need to have an understanding and sensitivity to several local environments. They must utilize local information and adapt it to a broader set of human resource policies that reflect the firm itself.' Cultural differences in local environments are often treated as the most significant factor to be taken into account in managing globally, but differences in local institutions and practices such as collective bargaining can also be important.

Cultural differences

Briscoe *et al* (2012: 114) commented that: 'Many of the most important and difficult challenges to the conduct of international human resource management stem from the differences encountered in various countries' and MNE (Multinational Enterprise)'s cultures.' Variations in national cultures are reflected in people's values, beliefs and behaviour patterns.

Hiltrop (1995) noted the following HRM areas that may be affected by national culture:

- decisions of what makes an effective manager (performance management);
- giving face-to-face feedback;
- readiness to accept international assignments;
- different concepts of social justice;
- pay systems (reward management);
- approaches to organizational structuring.

To which could be added employee relations and communications.

Gerhart and Fang (2005: 974) stated that: 'A misfit between national culture and management practice will reduce effectiveness. For example, using a pay for individual performance plan in a country having a highly collectivist culture will not work well.'

The significance of cultural differences was the influential message delivered by Hofstede (1980) based on his research using worldwide data on IBM employees. He suggested that culture consisted of shared values and involved 'the collective mental programming of people in an environment and broad tendencies to prefer certain states of affairs over others' (ibid: 19). One of the conclusions Hofstede reached was that the cultural values within a nation are substantially more similar than the values of individuals from different nations. This view has been taken up by subsequent commentators such as Adler (2002), who claimed that Hofstede's study explained 50 per cent of the difference between countries in employees' attitudes and behaviours.

But this view has been challenged by Gerhart and Fang (2005). They subjected Hofstede's findings to further analysis and established that at the level of the individual, as distinct from the country, Hofstede's results show that: 'Roughly 2 to 4 per cent of the variance in individual values is explained by national differences. And there is nothing in Hofstede's (1980) study that pertains to individual-level "behaviours". Therefore, Hofstede's work should not be interpreted as showing that national culture explains 50 per cent of behaviours' (ibid: 977). They also established from Hofstede's data that culture varies more between organizations than between countries. In their view, cross-country cultural differences, while real, have been overestimated and may well pale in importance when explaining the effectiveness of HR practices compared with other unique country features such as the character of local institutions. But they accepted that national culture differences can be critical and that insensitivity to national culture differences can and does result in business failure (as well as failure and career consequences for individual expatriate managers).

On the basis of research conducted in 30 multinational companies by the Global HR Research Alliance, Stiles (2007: 37) commented that: 'While national cultural differences were not insignificant, they were less important than we had imagined. Organizational culture actually had more influence on HR practice.' The conclusion from the research was that: 'To think there is one best way to manage human resources is simplistic and wrong, but the variation and contextualization of HR, at least for the companies we studied, owes little to national culture' (ibid: 41).

Institutional differences

Institutional differences include the role of the state and financial sectors, employment law, national systems of education and training, and employment expectations. As described by Gerhart and Fang (2005: 971) other local factors in the environment include 'differences in the centrality of markets, institutions, regulation, collective bargaining and labour-force characteristics'. For example: in Western Europe, collective bargaining coverage is much higher in some countries such as the UK, Germany and Italy than in the United States. Works councils are mandated by law in Western European countries such as Germany, but not in Japan or the United States. In China, Eastern Europe and Mexico, labour costs are lower than in Western Europe, Japan and the United States.

Convergence and divergence

International HRM involves the need to judge the extent to which, on the one hand, an organization should implement similar policies and practices across the world (convergence), or, on the other hand, that it should allow overseas subsidiaries to adopt their own practices or at least modify the policies and practices of the parent company to suit local requirements (divergence). Brewster *et al* (2002) noted that the dilemma facing all multinational corporations is that of achieving a balance between international consistency and local autonomy. As Briscoe *et al* (2012: 48) remarked: 'International HRM strategy has to deal with the issue of whether to standardize HRM policies and practices from headquarters, or to localize them to meet local conditions, or do both (eg combination of core policies established by HQ with localized practices to accommodate local culture and practices).'

Festing and Eidems (2011: 163) reported that: 'In the course of increasing globalization, more and more MNEs are being forced to compete globally and simultaneously adapt their business strategies to changing local demands.' They also suggested that 'firms tend not to standardise a whole HRM system but rather focus on single practices' (ibid: 165).

Convergence and divergence is considered below under the following headings:

- the nature of convergence and divergence;
- factors affecting the degree of convergence or divergence;
- the pressure for convergence;

- advantages and disadvantages of convergence;
- achieving convergence.

The nature of convergence and divergence

There is a natural tendency for managerial traditions in the parent company to shape and standardize the nature of key HR policies and practices throughout an international organization. This can be called a 'one-country' approach. But there are arguments for divergence in the form of allowing subsidiaries to apply their own practices as a means of ensuring that local requirements are sufficiently taken into account (localization). Hence the mantra 'think globally but act nationally'. As Brewster *et al* (2005: 951) pointed out:

> Where global integration and coordination are important, subsidiaries need to be globally integrated with other parts of the organization and/or strategically coordinated by the parent. In contrast, where local responsiveness is important, subsidiaries will have far greater autonomy and there is less need for integration.

But the choice is not between total convergence and total divergence. Frenkel and Peetz (1998: 537) described a globalization-induced trend towards increasing convergence, which finds a counterbalance in national culture, the role of the nation state, and national industrialization strategies. Brewster and Suutari (2005) remarked that strategic alignment (convergence) and localization (divergence) can be regarded as opposite extremes on a continuum. And Brewster *et al* (2005: 952) mentioned that: 'The wider convergence-divergence debate also tends to assume that the HRM system as a whole has to converge or remain divergent, rather than considering whether some parts of the overall HR system might be converging, in some regions or geographies, while other parts might be diverging. Moreover, even within a single HR function there might be convergence at one level but divergence at another'. There is no compulsion to do the same thing everywhere.

Dickmann, as reported by Welfare (2006), instanced organizations such as IBM and Oxfam that operate a model based on universal principles or values across the organization, which are then implemented differently at regional or national level. He suggested that the extent of integration or convergence depends on the business model of the organization: if the company is basically a McDonald's, where there are only limited local variations but the product is essentially the same all over the world, then the approach is likely to be different to a company like Unilever, whose products and processes tend to be much more responsive to the local market (ibid: 9).

Pudelko and Harzing (2007: 536) noted that those who favoured convergence assumed that 'in management, best practices can be defined that are universally valid and applicable, irrespective of national culture or institutional context'. But they also observed that: 'We should not expect every subsidiary to be brought into the best practices scheme in the same way. The subsidiary's strategic role may be of some significance' (ibid: 551).

Brewster *et al* (2005: 953) reported approaches to convergence/divergence in three of their case studies as follows: Shell People Services (web-based provision of international HR services and knowledge transfer across four global businesses through the development of communities of practice); Rolls-Royce PLC (a UK centric company going global and creating a global centre of excellence); Diageo (convergence around core performance capability management, rewards and talent-development processes, and decentralization of international HR through the use of global networks).

The convergence and divergence of HRM policies are associated respectively with centralization and decentralization – but there are differences. As defined by Huczynski and Buchanan (2007: 474), centralization is the concentration of authority and responsibility for decision making in the hands of managers at the top of an organization's hierarchy, and decentralization involves authority and responsibility for decision making being dispersed more widely downwards and given to the operating units, branches and lower-level managers. Centralization and decentralization are mainly concerned with decision making, degrees of autonomy and organizational structures. In contrast, convergence and divergence are primarily about the dissemination or absence of dissemination of specific policies and practices, although they may be linked to processes of centralization or decentralization.

Factors affecting convergence and divergence

The factors affecting convergence and divergence consist of the orientation of international firms as expressed by their attitudes on the role and place of subsidiaries, the drivers of global integration and the institutional and cultural issues influencing the approach to the dissemination of the policies and practices of the parent company.

The orientation of international firms

As described by Perlmutter (1969) there are four types of orientation in international firms:

1. *Ethnocentric orientation* in which fundamental decisions are made at headquarters and foreign subsidiaries possess little autonomy.
2. *Polycentric orientation* in which headquarters considers subsidiaries as independent entities and autonomy is granted to a great extent.
3. *Regiocentric orientation* in which subsidiaries are interconnected and regulated by a regional centre.
4. *Geocentric orientation* in which headquarters and foreign subsidiaries are integrated worldwide and interdependent to a high degree.

More recently, Isidor *et al* (2011: 2171) explained how these orientations developed:

> In the early phase of international firm development, corporations adopt an ethnocentric staffing policy by sending out managers to the host country subsidiaries to transfer parent company culture and to ensure conformity with financial and organizational procedures. After a certain time, they adopt a polycentric staffing policy to management development, promoting, as confidence grows, home country nationals (HCNs) to senior positions in their subsidiaries; yet the polycentric style prevents HCNs from reaching the most senior positions at corporate headquarters. As the company becomes even more international, it adopts a regiocentric and finally a geocentric policy based on developing the best person for the job irrespective of his or her nationality.

Drivers for convergence

Smale (2011) listed three drivers for global integration or convergence:

1. Environmental drivers, which include the removal of trade and investment barriers, the deregulation of markets, the emergence of global customers, the spread of new web-based technologies and the opening up of developing countries such as Brazil, China and India. These drivers force companies to adopt a globally integrated approach to managing the business.
2. Strategic drivers, which capture the business advantages that result from global integration such as global branding, worldwide standardization, the ability to respond quickly to competitive challenges by redeploying resources.
3. Structural drivers, in the form of global structures based on international product divisions that promote integration (while structures based on national units can inhibit it).

Lertxundi and Landeta (2012: 1788) explained that 'organizational practices should be viewed as valuable resources and capacities that it is useful to replicate and exploit throughout the organization'.

Dissemination of HQ policies and practices

Lertxundi and Landeta (2012: 1791) argued that: 'The transferability of best practices is conditional both on cultural/institutional factors as well as organizational ones.' Institutional theory sees the institutions of a country as the determining agents in this dissemination. The cultural approach addresses the issue of dissemination from the point of view of differences in social values and customs. National management methods may be embedded in their institutional and cultural context, which limits the possibility of cross-national learning from so-called best practices.

Choice of convergence

Harris and Brewster (1999) listed the following factors affecting the choice of convergence:

- The extent to which there are well-defined local norms.

- The degree to which an operating unit is embedded in the local environment.
- The strength of the flow of resources – finance, information and people – between the parent and the subsidiary.
- The orientation of the parent to control.
- The nature of the industry – the extent to which it is primarily a domestic industry at local level.
- The specific organizational competencies, including HRM, which are critical for achieving competitive advantage in a global environment.

The pressure for convergence

Brewster (2004) claimed that convergence may be increasing as a result of the power of the markets, the importance of cost, quality and productivity pressures, the emergence of transaction cost economies, the development of like-minded international cadres and benchmarking 'best practice'. Isidor *et al* (2011: 2167) suggested that: 'Internationalization offers firms manifold advantages such as realizing economies of scale and scope, learning from international markets, exploiting interrelations between business segments and geographic areas, achieving risk diversification, and cost reduction.'

Brewster *et al* (2005) thought that it is quite possible for some parts of an HR system to converge while other parts may diverge. Stiles (2007: 41) noted that common practices across borders may be appropriate: 'Organizations seek what works and for HR in multinational companies, the range of options is limited to a few common practices that are believed to secure high performance.' Reilly and Williams (2012: 29) asserted that 'the reasons for commonality are certainly justifiable and organisations may not have any real choice, especially in protecting corporate reputation.'

Advantages and disadvantages of convergence

Convergence can ensure that established good practice in the parent company, which has demonstrably contributed to success, can also contribute to the success of foreign subsidiaries. It can help to ensure that a global mindset exists that enables distinct units to work together to achieve a common purpose, as expressed in the General Motors' mantra – 'One GM one global team'. It can further approaches in each unit that are consistent with the values and beliefs of the parent company. But a misdirected or insensitive policy of convergence can lead to the introduction of inappropriate practices that will fail to operate effectively, alienate local managers and inhibit their willingness and ability to think for themselves.

Research conducted by Reilly and Williams (2012) indicated that the following were the upsides and downsides of what they called a 'one-country' approach by HR, ie convergence:

Upsides:

- promotes common values;
- delivers consistent treatment to staff;
- exports good business practice to all parts of the organization;
- gives greater control over dispersed operations;
- provides cost control.

Downsides:

- harmonization can stifle innovation;
- the centre loses touch with the sharp end of the business;
- ill-conceived policies may be subverted at a local level;
- HR is a focus for frustration as agent of the corporate centre;
- does not easily sit with workforce segmentation.

Perkins and Shortland (2006) noted that strategic choices surrounding employment relationships may be influenced primarily by 'home country' values and practices.

Achieving convergence

If the choice is to adopt convergence to some degree, or in selected areas, it is necessary to remember Tayeb's (2005) proposition that it is generally easier to transfer strategies and policies than practices. Rather than trying to impose central practices, in certain cases it may be preferable simply to set out broad policy guidelines expressing and underpinning the values that the parent company would like to be applied throughout the organization. These could cover, for example, ethical principles on how people should be treated or, more specifically, preferred approaches to the recruitment, selection, induction and reward of employees or to employee participation and communications. It might be necessary to issue guidelines on union recognition and collective bargaining, which recognize that in some countries trade unions will have to be accepted and allowed the rights at least to represent their members and, perhaps, to negotiate on their behalf. It is also necessary to bear in mind that it may not be possible to standardize some aspects of HRM because of local employment law regulations.

Research by Lertxundi and Landeta (2012) found that the practices that reflected the greatest differences between head office and affiliates were those associated with communication and participation. Participation in particular was frequently significantly less in affiliates.

It was established by a Global HR Research Alliance study (Stiles, 2007) that global HR policies and practices were widespread in the areas of maintaining global performance standards, the use of common evaluation processes, common approaches to rewards, the development of senior managers, the application of competency frameworks and the use of common performance management criteria.

Generally, research has indicated that while global HR policies in such areas as talent management, performance management and reward may be developed, communicated and supported by centres of excellence, often through global networking, a fair degree of freedom has frequently been allowed to local management to adopt their own practices in accordance with the local context – as long as in principle these are consistent with global policies.

It was argued by Reilly and Williams (2012: 30) that: 'What HR might need to do is more carefully decide what is common and global, versus what is different and local, against some well thought through criteria. This might mean, for instance, a common HR information system, but local resourcing, or one method of executive reward, yet multiple ways of aligning local pay with the market.' They concluded that: 'It is the essential processes, populations and tools that are the ones to control from the centre, not a crude imposition of one size fits all across the piece' (ibid: 31).

Lertxundi and Landeta (2012) set out two considerations for those making decisions on which HR systems should be exported to their foreign subsidiaries. First, companies with effective HR systems should transfer them to subsidiaries in the same way that they transfer other systems. Second, cultural differences between the parent company's country and the foreign subsidiary should not prevent the export of the general principles of its HR system, although account should be taken of any differences when converting these HR principles into action. HR systems should transfer them to subsidiaries in the same way that they transfer other outstanding systems.

Convergence can be achieved by exercising centralized control; forcing subsidiaries to install the HR policies and practices of the parent company. But managers in subsidiary companies may seek to maintain as much independence as possible and therefore block or at least dilute attempts made by headquarters to enforce its policies. A performance management system complete with standardized forms can readily be installed in foreign companies. But it is easy for local managers to go through the motions and tick the boxes on the forms without conducting performance management properly, in accordance with the precepts of headquarters. Moreover, as reported by Burbach and Royle (2010), when a subsidiary employs a considerable proportion of an MNC's employees it might be able to resist the imposition of an HR system from the centre, simply because the centre could not make it work without the subsidiary's support.

Thus there is a limit to how well compulsion will work. There are other ways of disseminating good practice from headquarters such as information, communication and learning. HR and expatriates can play a major role in these activities. One method of moving practices across boundaries is to establish formal mechanisms to facilitate the transfer of knowledge. For example, Bertelsmann, the German publishing company, has created a number of 'expert committees' for this purpose composed of specialists in such areas as HR, distribution and IT.

Scullion and Starkey (2000: 1074) reported that: 'Our research suggests that MNCs can exert centralized control through the use of expatriates who may be trusted to implement corporate policies and procedures. [This] becomes a de facto centralizing control mechanism. Since network relationships are built and maintained through personal contact, staffing decisions are crucial to the effective management of the linkages that the various subsidiaries have established.' But Edwards *et al* (2011) commented that within a foreign subsidiary of an MNC, home country managers may be able to dilute the influence of expatriates through their greater familiarity with the language and customs of the host country. However, they noted that managers at HQ level also possess sources of power that can be used to overcome resistance at local level and ensure that firms engage in diffusion.

Key learning points: The international HRM framework

International HRM

International HRM is concerned with human resource management policies and practices in multinational enterprises. It has to function strategically in order to support the achievement of international business strategies.

Internationalization and globalization

Internationalization is the process of international economic integration in worldwide markets. Globalization is the development of single international markets for goods or services accompanied by an accelerated growth in world trade. Any company that has economic interests or activities extending across a number of international boundaries is a global company.

Contextual factors affecting international HRM

All HR activities are affected by the context in which they operate, but the variety of contexts in which international HRM functions are particularly significant in the way in which they influence decisions on the dissemination of parent company policies and practices (convergence or divergence) and on the employment of expatriates.

Cultural differences

Briscoe *et al* (2012: 114) commented that: 'Many of the most important and difficult challenges to the conduct of international human resource management stem from the differences encountered in various countries' and MNE's cultures.'

Institutional differences

Institutional differences include the role of the state and financial sectors, employment law, national systems of education and training, and employment expectations.

Convergence and divergence

International HRM involves the need to judge the extent to which, on the one hand, an organization should implement similar policies and practices across the world (convergence) or, on the other, it should allow overseas subsidiaries to adopt their own practices or at least modify the policies and practices of the parent company to suit local requirements (divergence).

Factors affecting convergence and divergence

The factors affecting convergence and divergence consist of the orientation of international firms as expressed by their attitudes on the role and place of subsidiaries, the drivers of global integration and the institutional and cultural issues influencing the approach to the dissemination of the policies and practices of the parent company and to divergence.

Questions

1 What is international human resource management?

2 What are the main issues in international human resource management?

3 What is the significance of cultural differences?

4 What is the significance of institutional differences?

5 What is the significance of the concepts of convergence and divergence?

6 What are the factors that affect the degree of convergence?

References

Adler, N J (2002) *International Dimensions of Organizational Behaviour*, Cincinnati, OH, South-Western

Bartlett, C A and Ghoshal, S (2002) *Managing Across Borders: The transnational solution*, Boston MA, Harvard Business School Press

Brewster, C (2004) European perspectives of human resource management, *Human Resource Management Review*, 14 (4), pp 365–82

Brewster, C, Harris, H and Sparrow, P (2002) *Globalizing HR*, London, CIPD

Brewster, C, Sparrow, P and Harris, H (2005) Towards a new model of globalizing HRM, *The International Journal of Human Resource Management*, 16 (6), pp 949–70

Brewster, C and Suutari, V (2005) Global HRM: Aspects of a research agenda, *Personnel Review*, 34, pp 5–21

Briscoe, D, Schuler, R and Tarique, I (2012) *International Human Resource Management*, 4th edn, New York, Routledge

Burbach, R and Royle, T (2010) Talent on demand? Talent management in the German and Irish subsidiaries of a US multinational corporation, *Personnel Review*, 39 (4), pp 414–31

Edwards, T, Rees, C and Zhang, M (2011) The diffusion of HR practices in MNCs, in (eds) T Edwards and C Rees, *International Human Resource Management*, Harlow, Pearson Education, pp 120–38

Festing, M and Eidems, J (2011) A process perspective on transnational HRM systems – a dynamic capability-based analysis, *Human Resource Management Review*, 21, pp 162–73

Frenkel, S and Peetz, D (1998) Globalization and industrial relations in East Asia: A three-country comparison, *Industrial Relations*, 3, pp 282–310

Gerhart, B and Fang, M (2005) National culture and human resource management: assumptions and evidence, *The International Journal of Human Resource Management*, 16 (6), pp 971–86

Harris, H and Brewster, C (1999) International human resource management: the European contribution, in (eds) C Brewster and H Harris, *International HRM: Contemporary issues in Europe*, London, Routledge

Hiltrop, J M (1995) The changing psychological contract: the human resource challenge of the 1990s, *European Management Journal*, 13 (3), pp 286–94

Hofstede, G (1980) *Cultural Consequences: International differences in work-related values*, Beverley Hills, CA, Sage

Huczynski, A A and Buchanan, D A (2007) *Organizational Behaviour*, 6th edn, Harlow, FT Prentice Hall

Isidor, R, Scwens, C and Kabst, R (2011) Human resource management and early internationalization: is there a leapfrogging in international staffing? *International Journal of Human Resource Management*, 22 (10), pp 2167–84

Lertxundi, A and Landeta, J (2012) The dilemma facing multinational enterprises: transfer or adaptation of their human resource systems, *International Journal of Human Resource Management*, 23 (9), pp 1788–807

Levitt, T (1983) The globalization of markets, *Harvard Business Review*, May–June, pp 92–102

Perkins, S J and Shortland, S M (2006) *Strategic International Human Resource Management*, London, Kogan Page

Perlmutter, H (1969) The torturous evolution of the multinational company, *Columbia Journal of World Business*, Jan–Feb, pp 9–18

Pudelko, M and Harzing, A W K (2007) Country of origin, localization or dominance effect? An empirical investigation of HRM practices in foreign subsidiaries, *Human Resource Management*, 46 (4), pp 535–59

Reilly, P and Williams, T (2012) The challenges of global HR: one way to go? *People Management*, September, pp 28–31

Scullion, H and Starkey, K (2000) In search of the changing role of the corporate human resource function in the international firm, *International Journal of Human Resource Management*, 11 (6), pp 1061–81

Smale, A (2011) Global integration and international RM, in (eds) T Edwards and C Rees, *International Human Resource Management*, Harlow, Pearson Education, pp 98–119

Sparrow, P, Schuler, R S and Jackson, S E (1994) Convergence or divergence: human resource practices and policies for competitive advantage worldwide, *International Journal of Human Resource Management*, 5 (2), pp 267–99

Sparrow, P, Scullion, H and Farndale, E (2011) Global talent management: new roles for the corporate HR function? in (eds) H Scullion and D G Collings, *Global Talent Management*, London, Routledge, pp 40–55

Stiles, P (2007) A world of difference?*People Management*, 15 November, pp 36–41

Tayeb, M H (2005) *International Human Resource Management: A multinational company perspective*, Oxford, Oxford University Press

Ulrich, D (1998) A new mandate for human resources, *Harvard Business Review*, January–February, pp 124–34

Welfare, S (2006) A whole world out there: managing global HR, *IRS Employment Review*, 862, 29 December, pp 8–12

38 The practice of international HRM

KEY CONCEPTS AND TERMS

- Home country nationals (HCNs)
- Parent company nationals (PCNs)
- Talent pipeline
- Talent pool
- Third country nationals (TCNs)

LEARNING OUTCOMES

On completing this chapter you should be able to define these key concepts. You should also understand:

- International workforce planning
- International resourcing
- International talent management
- International reward management
- International performance management
- Multicultural working
- The role of an international HR function

Introduction

The practice of international HRM is concerned with the HR activities conducted by a multinational company (MNC) in managing people throughout the organization. These include headquarters staff, home country nationals (HCNs – employees who are nationals of the country in which the subsidiary is based), third country nationals (TCNs – employees in a subsidiary who are nationals of a country other than the parent company's country), and expatriates (employees assigned to a foreign subsidiary who are nationals of the parent company's country).

The basic HR practices carried out in subsidiaries for their own nationals – recruitment and selection, training, the payment of junior staff and operatives, day-to-day employee relations and HR administration – are similar to those described in earlier chapters of this book. However, they will be affected by local employment legislation, industrial relations practices, customs and cultures and may be influenced by policy guidelines from the centre. These local activities are not covered in this chapter, although one of the roles of an international HR function will be to be aware of local practices and the local contexts that influence them in order to be in a position to provide advice and guidance, especially where they affect the employment of expatriates. HQs will probably not get involved in detailed employee relations but they may issue policy guidelines on union recognition and negotiations and monitor local decisions to ensure that the guidelines are followed, or that there is good reason to ignore them because of local industrial relations practices.

There are, however, a number of HRM areas in which the parent company may play a major part, as discussed in this chapter. Workforce planning for more senior staff may be centralized, as may be resourcing decisions that affect the deployment of parent company or third country nationals. Talent management processes and the remuneration of senior staff and expatriates may also be centralized. While performance management systems will be administered by subsidiaries, the centre may want to ensure that the processes involved conform to what is regarded as best practice within the organization and provide the information required for talent management and staffing decisions. An international HR function may also be concerned with encouraging the actions required to promote multicultural working throughout the organization.

Workforce planning

International resourcing is based on workforce planning processes, which assess how many people are needed throughout the MNC (demand forecasting), set out the sources of people available (supply forecasting) and, in the light of these forecasts, prepare action plans for recruitment, selection or assignment.

Workforce planning may be carried out by the parent company HR function, although it is likely to focus mainly on managers and professional and technical staff throughout the global organization, and is linked to talent planning and talent management. Workforce planning for junior staff and operatives is more likely to be carried out by subsidiaries, although the centre may require information on their plans.

In an international organization, estimates of future people needs can be prepared by each subsidiary for their own workforce planning purposes. The basis of such forecasts is the annual budget and longer-term business plan, translated into activity levels. These are in turn converted to specific requirements expressed in terms of numbers of people in different occupations and levels and with different skills. Assessments can also be made by subsidiaries on how anticipated needs will be met. This may be from inside their organization or in their own labour market (national or international) but it could also include information on how many positions will need to be filled by expatriates from the parent company or from other countries (third country nationals). The role of headquarters may be to review the plans of subsidiaries to make sure that they are realistic and to consolidate information on the requirements for expatriates so as to plan for their availability.

Headquarters may also review the corporate business plan to assess the people implications of any proposals for the expansion of existing businesses and the setting up or acquisition of new businesses. Again, the headquarters HR function has to assess sources of people from within the parent company, or elsewhere, as potential expatriates.

Resourcing

Resourcing in an international organization means making policy decisions on how the staffing requirements of headquarters and the foreign subsidiaries can be met, especially for managers, and professionals and technical staff. For managers, resourcing is conducted by talent management processes. Sparrow *et al* 2011: 42) emphasized that: 'MNC's increasingly demand highly-skilled, highly flexible, mobile employees who can deliver the required results, sometimes in difficult circumstances.'

Paik and Ando (2011: 3006) suggested, on the basis of their research, that: 'To effectively integrate and coordinate activities of foreign affiliates, MNCs need to maintain a higher level of control at headquarters. MNC headquarters want foreign affiliates to act as if they were the headquarters' agents. In this situation, MNCs are inclined to staff foreign affiliates with managers who understand and appreciate headquarters' directives.' However, they also noted that this policy may evolve to rely more on host country staff as headquarters learns how better to integrate activities of foreign affiliates to achieve global efficiency. Cumulatively, headquarters will learn more about managing in the host country and local practices and will build relationships with local suppliers and recruit more local employees.

The four types of orientation in international firms identified by Perlmutter (1969) can result in the following different approaches to the choice of employees:

1. *Ethnocentric orientation.* This means that fundamental decisions are made at headquarters and foreign subsidiaries possess little autonomy. The subsidiaries are likely to be managed by staff from the parent company, ie expatriates. This increases the ability of headquarters to control subsidiary company operations but creates problems in the shape of difficulties in managing expatriates and the frustration of home country nationals.
2. *Polycentric orientation.* Headquarters treats subsidiaries as independent entities with considerable autonomy. The subsidiaries are usually managed by local nationals, which provides for continuity (expatriates come and go) and eliminates the problem of using expatriates, including the likelihood that they are more costly. But, as stressed by Dowling *et al* (2008: 82) this might: 'Isolate the corporate headquarters' staff from the various foreign subsidiaries. The result may be that a multinational firm could become a federation of independent national units with nominal links to corporate headquarters.'
3. *Geocentric orientation.* Headquarters and foreign subsidiaries are integrated worldwide and are highly interdependent. This results in the creation of a worldwide force of international managers who, as 'global managers', can be deployed in any subsidiary. They can help to develop an international global perspective and to ensure that the MNC operates as a global organization. But it may be difficult to build and maintain an international team of managers.
4. *Regiocentric orientation.* Subsidiaries are interconnected and regulated by a regional centre. Staffing policies in regions may resemble those in MNCs with either a polycentric or geocentric orientation.

Whichever orientation exists, an important choice required in staffing subsidiaries in an international firm is between employing parent company or home company nationals or an appropriate combination of the two. Dowling *et al* (2008) listed the advantages and disadvantages of each approach, as shown in Table 38.1.

Additionally, or alternatively, a decision may be made to employ third country nationals (TCNs) in certain posts. TCNs might be easier to obtain than home country nationals and could cost less. But, as pointed out by Dowling *et al* (2008), they might not want to return to their own countries after assignment, the host government may resent the hiring of TCNs, and national animosities (eg India/Pakistan) would have to be considered.

However, there are other ways of meeting staff requirements in foreign subsidiaries. Dowling *et al* (2008) identified the following approaches:

- *Short-term assignments*, which may be for troubleshooting, project management or a stopgap measure until a more permanent arrangement can be made.
- *Extended assignments*, which may last up to one year and involve similar activities as those for short-term assignments.
- *Commuter assignments*, which include special arrangements where the person commutes on a weekly or bi-weekly basis to the place of work in another country.
- *Rotational assignments*, in which employees commute from the home country for a short set period followed by a break in the home country.
- *Virtual assignments*, where the employee does not move to a host location but manages from home some aspect or aspects of the operations in the foreign subsidiary. Use is made of communication technologies such as video conferencing, although the home-based employee may have to visit the host country frequently.

These alternatives are becoming increasingly popular, especially in companies that are finding it difficult to obtain satisfactory expatriates for more conventional assignments. But they can be difficult to manage and stressful for those involved.

TABLE 38.1 Advantages and disadvantages of using PCNs and HCNs

Employment of:	Advantages	Disadvantages
Parent company nationals (PCNs)	• Facilitates control and coordination. • Provides managers with international experience. • Provides people with the best skills for the job. • Promotes the dissemination of the MNC's policies and values.	• Limits the promotional opportunities of HCNs. • Expatriates may find it hard to adapt to the characteristics of the host country's culture and institutions. • Expatriates may impose an inappropriate management style based on that of their parent company. • The remuneration of PCNs and HCNs may differ. • Lack of continuity. • The host country may resent and even limit the deployment of foreigners.
Home country nationals (HCNs)	• Familiar with local culture, institutions and legal requirements. • No language barrier. • Provides continuity. • Morale improved as HCNs see career potential. • Fits local government policy for employing nationals. • Reduces employment costs.	• Unfamiliar with parent company's practices and systems. • Dissemination of HQ practices more difficult. • May not have the immediate skills required. • More difficult to exercise control from the centre.

SOURCE: Adapted from Dowling *et al* (2008: 85)

International talent management

International talent management uses talent management procedures as described in Chapter 20.

Talent management defined

Talent management is the process of ensuring that the organization has the talented people it needs to attain its business goals. It starts with the business strategy and what it signifies in terms of the talented people required by the organization. The aim is to develop and maintain a pool of talented people. This is done through the talent pipeline, which maintains the flow of talent that the organization needs.

International talent management defined

Mellahi and Collings (2010: 143–44) defined international talent management as:

> The systematic identification of key positions which differentially contribute to the organization's sustainable competitive advantage on a global scale, the development of a talent pool of high performing incumbents to fill these roles which reflects the global scope of the multinational enterprise, the development of a differentiated human resource architecture to facilitate filling these positions with the best available incumbent and to ensure their continued commitment to the organization.

The significance of international talent management

Cheese *et al* (2008: 9) argued that: 'talent has become a precious resource fought over by competitors in a global war for talent'. Isidor *et al* (2011: 2168) claimed that: 'The success of global business depends on recruiting the quality of management [required] in the multinational companies.' Mellahi and Collings (2010: 44) suggested that enabling high-performing HCNs to become senior managers improves the performance of an international business by: 1) being better able to respond effectively to the demands of local stakeholders; 2) legitimizing the firm in the host country; 3) providing incentives for retaining and motivating talents.

But a study of 40 global organizations by Ready and Conger (2007) found that virtually all the surveyed companies identified a lack of a sufficient talent pipeline to fill strategic positions within the organization. This severely constrained their ability to grow their business.

The process of international talent management

The conduct of international talent management involves basically the same methods as those used in a domestic setting, namely, a pipeline consisting of processes for:

1. *Talent planning* – defining what is meant by talent and establishing how many and what sort of talented people are needed now and in the future.
2. *Talent pool definition* – on the basis of talent planning data deciding what sort of talent pool is required. This would consist of the resources of talent available to an organization in terms of numbers, competencies and skills. As noted by Karaevli and Hall (2003) there is a move towards identifying pools of talent that possess the potential to move into a number of roles. This replaces the traditional objective of succession planning, with its short-term focus on finding replacements for managers who leave. The talent pool is filled mainly from within the organization with additions from outside as required. The pool is not managed rigidly. It can be expanded or contracted as demands for talent change; new members can be included and existing members removed if they are no longer eligible.
3. *Identifying talent internally* – by reference to the definitions of talent pool, using assessments of existing staff to decide who is qualified to be included in the talent pool.
4. *Recruiting talent* – bringing in talented people from outside the company to supplement internal talent and become additional members of the talent pool.
5. *Performance management* – talent is not fixed and therefore needs to be reviewed regularly; performance management also provides information on learning and development needs.
6. *Management development and career planning* – a continuous programme of developing the abilities of members of the talent pool and, so far as this is possible, planning their careers.
7. *Assignment or promotion* – talent pool members are assigned to positions in headquarters or, as expatriates, in foreign subsidiaries. Alternatively, they may be promoted within headquarters or a subsidiary. Although in a fully formed talent management system the talent pool is considered to be the major source for senior assignments or for promotions, people not actually in the pool may still be eligible. If no one suitable is available in the pool it may be necessary to recruit externally. Those assigned or promoted will still be included in the talent pool.

Computerized talent management systems can be used to take stock of organizational talent, although they cannot show firms how to manage talent. As McDonnell and Collings (2011: 68) pointed out: 'The global nature of MNCs makes talent management a particularly complex issue.' Mellahi and Collings (2010) identified three reasons why global talent management often fails:

1. Subsidiary managers may believe that it is in their interests to keep their own best talent rather than bring them to the attention of headquarters or other subsidiaries.
2. Decision makers at the centre do not always have access to accurate information about the availability of talent elsewhere in the organization.
3. Even when information is available, the sheer volume, diversity and, possibly, unreliability of the data hinders the centre's ability effectively to manage talent in subsidiaries.

And Sparrow *et al* (2011: 48) commented that: 'The coordination of international talent management strategies in highly decentralized MNCs is more problematic due to greater tensions between the short-term needs of the operating companies and the long-term strategic needs of the business.'

International talent management in action

As reported by Ready and Conger (2007: 71) HSBC has created a system of talent pools that track and manage the careers of high potentials within the company. After those employees have been identified, they are assigned to regional or business unit talent pools, which are managed by local human resources and business unit leaders. They are then selected initially for new assignments within their region or business and may later be given positions that cross boundaries. Managers of the pools single out people to recommend for the group talent pool, which represents the most senior cadre of general managers and is administered centrally.

Ready and Conger (ibid: 73) reported that at Procter & Gamble hiring and promotions are the responsibility of local managers, but high-potential prospects are identified globally. People and positions are tracked in a technology-based talent management system that can accommodate all the company's 135,000 employees but is primarily used to track 13,000 middle- and upper-management employees. Procter & Gamble also conducts a global talent review – a process by which every country, function and business is assessed for its capacity to find, develop, deploy, engage and retain skilled people.

But a case study by Burbach and Royle (2010) revealed that international talent management systems do not always work as well as their sponsors hope. Some employees were unwilling to complete their 'talent profiles' – an essential part of the talent management system used by the company, which were in effect online CVs that every employee was supposed to fill in. The result was that the firm had to force compliance by stipulating that no employees would be promoted unless they completed their profile.

International performance management

Performance management systems in subsidiaries covering home and third country nationals are the area of HRM, where there is likely to be the most convergence. This means that a system based on the one used in the parent company is applied completely or partly worldwide. As Briscoe *et al* (2012: 347) observed: 'There are some valid reasons which suggest that... a standardized approach may be warranted for the sake of global integration, culture cohesiveness, fairness, mobility of global employees, and as a control mechanism.'

Approaches to international performance management

While the arguments in favour of standardization are powerful, and a convergent approach is often adopted, the degree of convergence or divergence in international performance management systems can vary in a number of ways:

1. *Total convergence (standardization)* – using the parent company's scheme throughout the international organization.

2 *Total divergence (localization)* – foreign subsidiaries use their own systems.
3 *Partial convergence* – foreign subsidiaries use a version of the parent company's system, modified to take account of local factors such as culture and work systems. Alternatively, they ensure that their own systems conform to policy guidelines issued by headquarters, possibly including certain requirements such as the design of the forms or methods of rating.
4 *Dual system* – using the headquarters scheme for expatriates (parent company nationals), and local, possibly partly converged schemes, for home country and third country nationals (the special considerations affecting performance management for expatriates are dealt with in Chapter 39).

The trend towards convergence was confirmed by the Global HR Research Alliance research, as reported by Stiles (2007: 39), which concluded that: 'In performance management we found little or no difference across the world. We witnessed a concerted effort on the part of group HR departments to maintain global standards supported by global competencies (at foundation, managerial, technical and leadership level), common evaluation processes and common approaches to rewards. It was difficult, therefore, to find many distinctive local practices.'

International performance management systems

International performance management systems basically contain the following elements that correspond to those found in domestic systems, as described in Chapter 25:

- *Performance agreement* – the manager and the individual jointly decide on the goals that the latter is expected to achieve. These may be hard goals that define the results expected, as far as possible expressed in quantitative terms, or soft goals that are qualitative and refer to behaviours or traits such as upholding corporate values, leadership, interpersonal relationships and customer relations. The agreement may also clarify the level of competency required by the individual by reference to a competency framework.
- *Performance management throughout the year* – this involves regular dialogues between the manager and the individual about the latter's performance, coaching, and taking action to improve performance.
- *Performance review* – a formal review of performance in achieving agreed goals and in meeting competency requirements. The review may incorporate ratings of performance and potential and will be summarized on a performance review form. The review provides the basis for a new performance agreement and for a programme of development to enhance abilities and skills. It may also inform performance-related pay decisions.

International performance management issues

The effectiveness of international performance management is affected overall by the sheer complexity of international business and the distance separating headquarters and subsidiaries. Briscoe and Claus (2008) noted that a challenge is provided by 'the major differences that arise between host national perceptions and those of the home office regarding what was being accomplished and the circumstances under which it was being achieved'. Briscoe and Schuler (2004: 354) mentioned the following difficulties:

- problems with the choice of evaluator (eg in the local or parent company) and that person's amount of contact with the rate;
- the host country's perceptions of performance, which may differ from those in the parent company;
- problems with long-distance communication;
- inadequate contact between parent company rater and subsidiary company rater;
- unclear or contradictory performance objectives for foreign operations;
- lack of understanding by the parent company of the foreign environment and culture;
- indifference to the foreign experience of the expatriate.

The particular issues affecting international performance management are the increased difficulty in influencing and controlling line managers; cultural differences; the problem of achieving consistent rating results; and variable levels of maturity among subsidiaries, which affect relative performance. These issues, as discussed below, need to be taken into account when deciding on the extent to which standardized performance management systems are desirable and, in so far as they are standardized, how they should be managed. There are no easy solutions. Each case has to be decided in accordance with individual circumstances. But it is helpful to be aware of the potential pitfalls so that action can be taken in advance to avoid them, as far as possible.

Line managers

Even in a one-country domestic setting, performance management can easily fail because the line managers on whom the system depends lack the skill or the inclination to do it properly. In an international organization control over the how line managers implement performance management will be even more difficult owing to the diversity of operations, the geographical separation between headquarters and foreign subsidiaries and, possibly, the unwillingness of local managers to take much notice of commands from a remote centre.

Cultural differences

Cultural differences may also affect the ability of an MNC to implement a standardized international system. Shen (2005: 72) noted that: 'For example, in some Asian countries such as China and Japan, feedback is not normally given in order to "save face" and group meetings are often held in performance management processes to achieve group harmony. This aspect of Asian culture is very different from Western culture where individualism is emphasized.'

Rating problems

The achievement of reliable and consistent appraisal ratings in a domestic setting is difficult; in an international operation it is virtually impossible. Care should therefore be taken in designing and interpreting rating systems. It may be best to leave them to the local subsidiary and not try to introduce a suspect universal system.

Variable levels of maturity

The maturity of subsidiaries in terms of their productivity, ability to penetrate markets, availability of skilled employees and work practices will vary and it may be more difficult for some subsidiaries to meet the standards of performance expected by the parent company. Environmental differences such as levels of political stability and standards of living will also affect the results achieved by subsidiaries. Account should be taken of these differences but it is too easy for a remote headquarters to be unaware of how local factors affect performance levels.

International performance management in action

Chartered Standard Bank

The international performance management process used by Chartered Standard Bank is illustrated in Figure 38.1.

Serono SA

As reported by Coleman and Chambers (2005), Serono SA, the Swiss biotechnology company with offices around the world, needed a performance management, pay-for-performance and compensation system that was not only consistent but was also flexible enough to adjust to the laws governing employment in each of its far-flung operations.

Each Serono operating unit has its own objectives, which are aligned to overarching corporate goals. Units in each country tailor their performance management and reward systems for compliance with local laws, customs and budgets. An information technology system was developed to automate performance management and compensation for Serono's global operations. The analytical tools built into this system enable HR at the centre to gain an overview of how the organization as a whole is evaluating its employees. For example, data on assessments presented as bell curves (graphs showing distributions in the form of a curve shaped like a bell), reveal the extent to which appraisal scores are out of line with what is regarded as a normal distribution.

FIGURE 38.1 International performance management system – Standard Chartered Bank

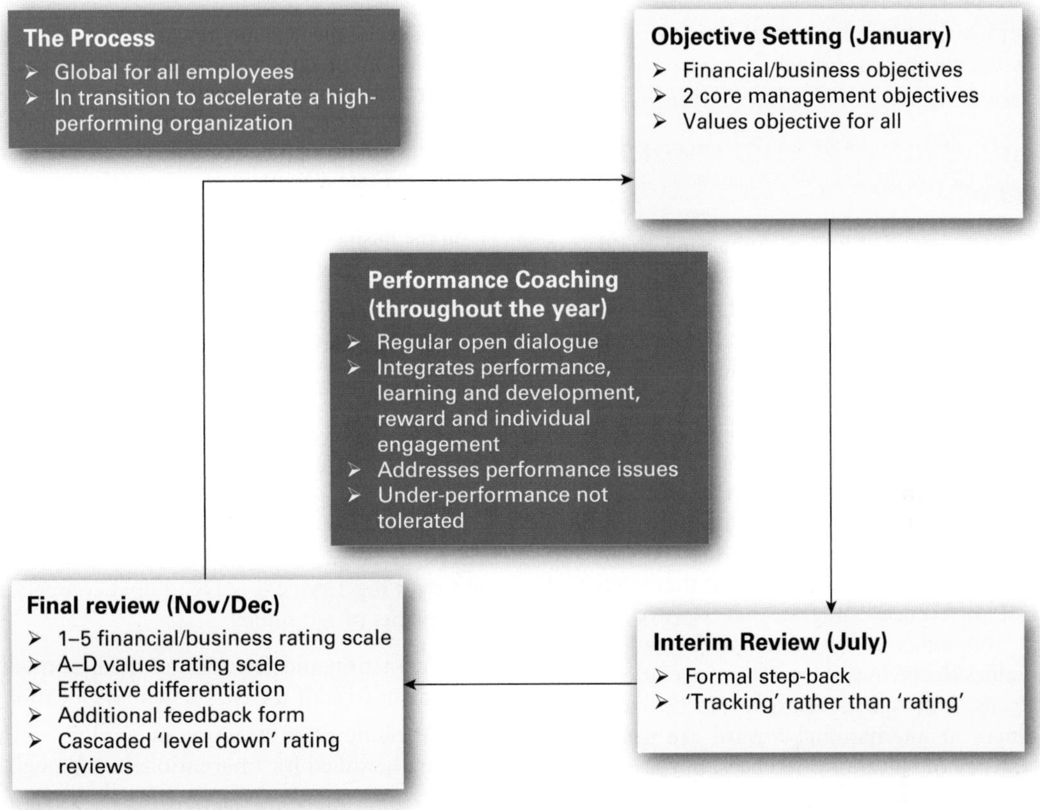

SOURCE: Armstrong and Baron (2005)

Reward management

International reward management involves the management of all aspects of rewards in organizations operating worldwide or a least in a number of countries. It is not just the management of expatriate remuneration.

Traditionally, discussions of international reward strategies and practices have tended to focus on an elite of expatriate workers, sourced from headquarter locations and rewarded in isolation from local country staff. Today, a diverse and complex pattern is emerging, requiring a more strategic approach than simply copying the practices of other multinationals.

Stephen Perkins (2006) explained that achieving an appropriate global/local balance between global and local requirements in international staffing and rewards has therefore become a much more strategic and challenging issue for HR and reward managers. Major organizations such as BP and the World Bank have overhauled their policies in recent years to achieve their key strategic reward goals of mobility and affordability in this more demanding global context.

Baeten and Leuven (2010) listed the following main concerns in global compensation:

- the extent of centralization or decentralization of compensation policies and practices;
- balancing corporate and national cultures;
- the sustainability and span of global compensation policies;

- the choice of compensation instruments to be included in global compensation policies;
- global benchmarking;
- measuring the efficiency of a global compensation approach.

Design of international reward systems

The factors that are likely to impact on the design of reward systems, as suggested by Bradley *et al* (1999), are the corporate culture of the multinational enterprise, expatriate and local labour markets, local cultural sensitivities, and legal and institutional factors. They refer to the choice that has to be made between, on the one hand seeking internal consistency by developing common reward policies in order to facilitate the movement of employees across borders and preserve internal equity, and on the other hand, responding to pressures to conform to local practices. But they point out that studies of cultural differences suggest that reward system design and management needs to be tailored to local values to enhance the performance of overseas operations. Although, as Sparrow (1999) indicated, differences in international reward are not just a consequence of cultural differences, but also of differences in international influences, national business systems and the role and competence of managers in the sphere of HRM.

International reward strategy

International reward strategy is concerned with the development of an integrated approach to building reward policies and practices across international boundaries. It should be integrated, in the sense that it takes into account the business goals and drivers of the parent company while at the same time fitting the strategy to the different contexts and cultures across the globe. The issue of the extent to which the reward strategy should be centralized or decentralized (convergence or divergence) needs to be addressed.

As White (2005: 25) stated: 'Best practice tells us that global rewards must not be considered piecemeal'. He explained that:

> The development of any reward programme calls for an integrated approach whereby each individual element of reward supports the others to reinforce organizational objectives. A global rewards philosophy and total rewards approach can facilitate alignment of an organization's rewards with business strategy, focus employees on the business goals, and reinforce consistent pay practices.

But he also commented that 'different local market practices, regulations and culture are indicators that a one size fits all system will not be truly effective'.

International reward management objectives

Briscoe *et al* (2012: 291–92) gave the following objectives for a typical MNC global compensation and benefits programme:

- Attraction and retention of the best-qualified talent to staff the MNC in all its locations.
- Attraction and retention of employees who are qualified for international assignments.
- Facilitation of transfers between different locations within the MNC.
- Establishment and maintenance of consistent and reasonable relationships between the compensation of employees at home and abroad.
- Maintenance of compensation which is reasonable in relation to the practices of competitors yet minimizes costs to the extent possible.

They noted that national and organizational cultures influence how people perceive the value of the various reward available and commented that: 'The culture may be performance-driven (and pay-for performance is an established norm) or it may be entitlement-oriented (with longevity of service rewarded. In some cultures people are more willing to accept risk in their compensation while in others people are quite risk-averse)' (ibid: 293).

The convergence or divergence of international reward management policy and practice

White (2005: 23) argued that: 'Global consistency in management's messages to employees, as well as in the reward programs that reinforce these messages is critical in building a cohesive entity that will create shareholder value.'

A consistent approach to international reward management will be developed if a global business strategy exists that encourages similarities in reward management policies and practices amongst MNC subsidiaries. But this might violate local cultural norms or business conditions. International reward management practices are affected by differences in three areas: 1) the labour market where in each country there will be unique labour demand and supply pattern; 2) institutions such as government regulations, tax systems and trade unions; 3) national cultures where, for example, there may be difference in the extent to which financial incentives will affect motivation.

As Yanadori (2011: 3867) stated:

> Managing employee compensation in multinational corporations (MNCs) involves carefully balancing two pressures: localization and strategic alignment. On the one hand, the compensation systems in foreign subsidiaries need to be customized to address unique local contexts... On the other hand, MNCs are increasingly interested in establishing, across different subsidiaries, consistent compensation systems that are aligned with their global business strategies.

His research in a multinational finance firm established that different pay rates were adopted to reflect differences in the local labour market.

Research by Baeten and Leuven (2010) in 31 international companies aimed at providing answers to the issue of centralization versus decentralization of compensation policies and systems. It was established that the degree of centralization was very high for senior management (94 per cent), moderate for middle management (54 per cent) and low for operational employees (12 per cent). Decision-making on base pay and incentives was centralized for senior managers. In the case of middle managers, it was centralized for some issues such as grading and criteria for pay reviews, but decentralized for others such as pay ranges and actual base pay increases. It was mainly decentralized for operational employees.

There are four levels of convergence, as set out in Table 38.2.

Briscoe *et al* (2012: 297) listed the following options for establishing a worldwide compensation system:

- Create worldwide salary levels at HQ with differentials for each subsidiary according to their differing costs of living.
- Base pay on local levels (usually excluding executives and globally mobile employees).
- Establish a global base per position where there is a global market for particular occupations or for senior managers and global employees.
- Set up two classifications – local and national for pay. All local nationals above a certain level are placed on the headquarters scale. The others are paid on a local scale.

TABLE 38.2 Levels of convergence in reward management policy and practice

Level 1: Total convergence	Central reward policies and practices have to be followed by each operating unit in accordance with a set of guiding principles. These may include a standard job evaluation scheme, uniform grade and pay structure (with scope for local market differentiation), a common approach to incentives and a common set of benefits.
Level 2: Partial convergence	Central reward policies are applied in some but not all aspects of reward management. Centralization may be limited to senior management or international staff (expatriates or nationals from countries other than the parent company working in the local country – third country nationals). Reward policies and practices for local nationals are decentralized.
Level 3: Partial divergence	Corporate job evaluation schemes and grade structures are recommended but modification is permitted to fit local conditions. However, all locations are expected to comply with the international guiding principles for reward. There may still be centralized policies for senior managers, expatriates, and third country nationals, and some benefits may be standardized. But pay levels and pay progression and incentive arrangements are determined locally.
Level 4: Total divergence	Local companies have complete freedom to develop and apply their own reward policies and practices, although they may be made aware of the international guiding principles.

International reward management in action

CASE STUDIES

US-owned MNC

A case study by Almond *et al* (2005) of the pay policies of a large US-owned MNC operating in Europe found that over the years the degree of centralization or decentralization changed frequently. Until the 1980s, corporate HQ issued a number of global policies that national managers were expected to implement. Some room was given for the policies to be adapted to fit local circumstances but management in subsidiaries had to justify these changes to headquarters.

During the late 1980s, the firm moved away from this highly centralized approach, allowing more scope for subsidiaries to develop policies that suited their own situation. For example, job evaluation systems could be developed independently of the US system. The decentralizing tendency was reversed in the early 1990s, and there has followed a period during which strong coordination of HR policies between countries and central control has been re-established.

General Motors (GM)

As reported by Mercer Human Resource Consulting (2009) GM moves people around the globe frequently because its products are designed and built on global platforms. The international philosophy of GM is expressed in the mantras 'One GM one global team' and 'Global perspective: local engagement'.

But different locations were using different level pay structures and job evaluation schemes. A 'leading change' programme involved compensation chiefs around the world. Under the banner of the phrase 'Global compensation takes the approach that what can be should be' the global team:

- analysed the various strategies, structures and practices in place around the world;
- used corporate governance to decide what needed to be global, regional or local;
- identified 'best practices' in compensation to establish a common philosophy, tools and structure for the salaried workforce;
- engaged key stakeholders in the process;
- provided tools, support and education;
- created with the help of Mercer Consultants more than 200 benchmarks in 30 job functions and then slotted them into global salary grades.

Source review

Research by Scullion and Starkey (2000: 1068)

This research established that in the global companies they analysed, centralized control was reinforced through corporate HR control over the design and management of the rewards system for the top 250 to 400 managers worldwide. Reflecting the more general trend to align HRM with the strategic goals of the organization, senior managerial rewards were aligned not only with short-term divisional or business unit objectives but increasingly with longer-term corporate objectives. A major advantage of a global reward system for top executives over a multifocal strategy, which reflected a significant reform to international rewards for many organizations, was the aligning of reward strategy with global business strategy.

Multicultural working

A fundamental feature of international operations is that multinational and therefore multicultural teams have to work together in foreign subsidiaries. Haas and Nüesch (2012) conducted research which showed that on the one hand multinational teams may have access to a greater variety of task-relevant experience. On the other hand, national diversity may complicate team collaboration and increase team conflict. Evidence was found that multinational teams perform worse than teams with less national diversity. It is therefore necessary for international organizations to develop ways of improving multi-cultural working.

The following 10 tips for managing a multicultural team were devised by Sharon Varney of the Roffey Park Institute (quoted by Craig, 2008):

1. Adopt a 'cultural lens'. Be prepared to set aside tried-and-tested management techniques that may have served you well in the past.
2. Invest in managing new starters' expectations. Allow more time for team formation, induction and establishing goals.
3. Build relationships across cultures. Find time for face-to-face meetings and social activities. However intermittent, time together is of great value.
4. Communicate across cultures. Keep in contact and always check that communications are understood in the way that was intended.
5. Encourage participation in cross-cultural teams. Vary communication styles and methods. Using visuals can help overcome language barriers.

6 Motivate cross-cultural teams. Focus both on team and individual goals. Remember that rewards and incentives can be seen very differently.

7 Manage performance across cultures. Take extra care introducing performance management systems, as one size does not fit all.

8 Raise cultural awareness and understanding. Bring people from different cultures together for specific projects and assignments to promote greater understanding.

9 Manage cross-cultural conflict. Help people clarify their assumptions. Even understanding what the issue is can be difficult.

10 Encourage ethical standards in cross-cultural teams. Ways of conducting business can vary across geographies, so provide clear company guidelines and be ready to deal with any ethical issues in a timely manner.

Role of the international HR function

An international HR function is responsible for developing and operating a transnational HR system, which was defined by Festing and Eidems (2011: 162) as 'the sum of HRM policies and practices that a multinational enterprise uses to attract, develop and maintain its human resources including globally standardized and locally adapted structures and processes'. Briscoe *et al* (2012: 413) indicated that the role of an international HR department should be to:

- contribute as an integral partner in formulating the global strategy for the firm;
- develop processes and concepts for top management as they develop the global strategy;
- help top management to understand the people implications of globalization;
- identify the key skills required in the global organization – both line and HR management;
- share the responsibility for HRM with line managers.

To carry out this role the HR function has to operate strategically and focus on providing advice and support to line executives.

Research by Scullion and Starkey (2000) highlighted a considerable variation in the roles of the HR function in different types of international firms. In centralized global firms the function undertook a wide range of activities and the key roles were management development, succession planning, career planning, strategic staffing, top management rewards and managing the mobility of international managers. In highly decentralized firms a lower degree of coordination and integration existed and HR executives were more limited in the scope of their roles, focusing on management development and succession planning for senior executives.

On the basis of a survey of 64 companies, Brewster *et al* (2005) observed that global HR professionals are acting as the guardians of culture, operating global values and systems. They referred to the 'greater complexity and strategic importance of the [HR function] international role' (ibid: 951) and commented as follows on the role of a central HR philosophy:

> Also helping the HR function deliver against the organizational strategy was what we have termed a central HR philosophy. This consisted of two elements: centralization of HR decision-making and industry-wide convergence of HR practice... The transfer and mutual learning from varied global practice is critically important. However, there was also a drive within organizations to develop some central command and co-ordination over this knowledge. In 21 per cent of firms the HR enabling recipe involved a centralized HR philosophy. These elements involve a degree of convergence and assumptions of best practice. (ibid: 964)

In decentralized firms Sparrow *et al* (2011: 48) noted that 'attempts are made to maintain control over the mobility and careers of international managers, however, this is more fragmented and less systematic than in the globally integrated companies... Corporate HR often has less influence on the operating companies and is frequently not responsible for finding re-entry positions for expatriates; and there are less well-developed career and succession planning systems.'

Key learning points: The practice of international HRM

The practice of international HRM

The practice of international HRM is concerned with the HR activities conducted by a multinational company (MNC) in managing people throughout the organization. These include headquarters staff, home country nationals (HCNs – employees who are nationals of the country in which the subsidiary is based), third country nationals (TCNs – employees in a subsidiary who are nationals of a country other than the parent company's country), and expatriates (employees assigned to a foreign subsidiary who are nationals of the parent company's country.

Workforce planning

International resourcing is based on workforce planning processes, which assess how many people are needed throughout the MNC (demand forecasting), set out the sources of people available (supply forecasting) and, in the light of these forecasts, prepare action plans for recruitment, selection or assignment.

Resourcing

Resourcing in an international organization means making policy decisions on how the staffing requirements of headquarters and the foreign subsidiaries can be met, especially for managers, professionals and technical staff.

An important choice required in staffing subsidiaries in an international firm is between employing parent company or home company nationals or an appropriate combination of the two.

Talent management

Talent management is the process of ensuring that the organization has the talented people it needs to attain its business goals.

The conduct of international talent management involves basically the same methods as those used in a domestic setting, namely, a pipeline consisting of processes for talent planning, talent pool definition, identifying talent internally, recruiting talent, performance management, management development and career planning, assignment or promotion.

International performance management systems

International performance management systems basically contain the following elements, which correspond to those found in domestic systems: performance agreement, performance management throughout the year, performance review.

The effectiveness of international performance management is affected overall by the sheer complexity of international business and the distance separating headquarters and subsidiaries.

The particular issues affecting international performance management are the increased difficulty in influencing and controlling line managers, cultural differences, the problem of achieving consistent rating results, and variable levels of maturity among subsidiaries, which affect relative performance.

Reward management

International reward management involves the management of all aspects of rewards in organizations operating worldwide, or a least in a number of countries.

The factors that are likely to impact on the design of reward systems, as suggested by Bradley *et al* (1999), are the corporate culture of the multinational enterprise, expatriate and local labour markets, local cultural sensitivities and legal and institutional factors.

International reward strategy is concerned with the development of an integrated approach to building reward policies and practices across international boundaries.

Multicultural working

A fundamental feature of international operations is that multinational and therefore multicultural teams have to work together in foreign subsidiaries.

Role of the international HR function

An international HR function is responsible for developing and operating a transnational HR system, which was defined by Festing and Eidems (2011: 162) as 'the sum of HRM policies and practices that a multinational enterprise uses to attract, develop and maintain its human resources including globally standardized and locally adapted structures and processes.'

Questions

1. What are the key areas in which international HRM is practised?
2. How can workforce planning be carried out in an international organization?
3. What are the advantages and disadvantages of employing parent company nationals in a foreign subsidiary?
4. What are the advantages and disadvantages of employing home country nationals in a foreign subsidiary?
5. Why can talent management fail in an international organization?
6. What are the main issues affecting performance management in an international organization?
7. What are the factors that affect the design of reward systems in an international organization?
8. How can multicultural working be encouraged?
9. What is the role of an HR department in an international organization?

References

Almond, P, Edwards, T, Colling, T, Ferner, A, Gunnigle, P, Müller-Camen, M, Quintanilla, J and Wächter, H (2005) Unravelling home and host country effects: an investigation of the HR policies of an American multinational in four European countries, *Industrial Relations*, 44 (2), pp 276–306

Armstrong, M and Baron, A (2005) *Managing Performance: Performance Management in Action*, London, CIPD

Baeten, X and Leuven, V (2010) Global compensation and benefits management: the need for communication and coordination, *Compensation & Benefits Review*, 42 (3), pp 392–402

Bradley, P, Hendry, C and Perkins, P (1999) Global or multi-local? The significance of international values in reward strategy, in (eds) C Brewster and H Harris, *International HRM: Contemporary issues in Europe*, London, Routledge

Brewster, C, Sparrow, P and Harris, H (2005) Towards a new model of globalizing HRM, *International Journal of Human Resource Management*, 16 (6), pp 949–70

Briscoe, D R and Claus, L M (2008) Employee performance management, in (eds) A Varma, P S Budhwar and A DeNisi, *Performance Management Systems: A global perspective*, Abingdon, Routledge, pp 15–39

Briscoe, D R and Schuler, R S (2004) *International Human Resource Management*, 2nd edn, New York, Routledge

Briscoe, D, Schuler, R and Tarique (2012) *International Human Resource Management*, 4th edn, New York, Routledge

Burbach, R and Royle, T (2010) Talent on demand? Talent management in the German and Irish subsidiaries of a US multinational corporation, *Personnel Review*, 39 (4), pp 414–31

Cheese, P, Thomas, K J and Craig, E (2008) *The Talent Powered Organization*, London, Kogan Page

Coleman, T and Chambers, T (2005) Serono case study: global performance, evaluations and compensation, *Compensation & Benefits Review*, July–August, pp 61–65

Craig, T (2008) Different strokes, *Personnel Today*, 25 November, pp 25–29

Dowling, P J, Festing, M and Engle, A D (2008) *International Human Resource Management*, 5th edn, Andover, Cengage Learning EMEA

Festing, M and Eidems, J (2011) A process perspective on transnational HRM systems – a dynamic capability-based analysis, *Human Resource Management Review*, 21, pp 162–73

Haas, H and Nüesch, S (2012) Are multinational teams more successful? *International Journal of Human Resource Management*, 23 (15), pp 3105–13

Isidor, R, Scwens, C and Kabst, R (2011) Human resource management and early internationalization: is there a leapfrogging in international staffing? *International Journal of Human Resource Management*, 22 (10), pp 2167–84

Karaevli, A and Hall, D T (2003) Growing leaders for turbulent times: Is succession planning up to the challenge? *Organizational Dynamics*, 32 (1), 2003, pp 62–79

McDonnell, A and Collings, D G (2011) Identification and evaluation of talent in MNEs, in (eds) H Scullion and D G Collings, *Global Talent Management*, London, Routledge, pp 56–73

Mellahi, K and Collings, D G (2010) The barriers to effective global talent management: the example of corporate elites in MNEs, *Journal of World Business*, 45, pp 143–44

Mercer Human Resource Consulting (2009) *A Whole New World*, New York, Mercer

Paik, Y and Ando, N (2011) MNC's competitive strategies, experiences, and staffing policies for foreign affiliates, *International Journal of Human Resource Management*, 22 (15), pp 3003–19

Perkins, S (2006) *Guide to International Reward and Recognition*, London, CIPD

Perlmutter, H (1969) The torturous evolution of the multinational company, *Columbia Journal of World Business*, Jan–Feb, pp 9–18

Ready, D A and Conger, J A (2007) Make your company a talent factory, *Harvard Business Review*, June, pp 69–77

Scullion, H and Starkey, K (2000) In search of the changing role of the corporate human resource function in the international firm, *The International Journal of Human Resource Management*, 11 (6), pp 1061–81

Shen, J (2005) Effective international performance appraisals: easily said, hard to do, *Compensation and Benefits Review*, July–August, pp 70–79

Sparrow, P R (1999) *The IPD Guide on International Recruitment, Selection and Assessment*, London, IPD

Sparrow, P, Scullion, H and Farndale, E (2011) Global talent management: new roles for the corporate HR function? in (eds) H Scullion and D G Collings, *Global Talent Management*, London, Routledge, pp 40–55

Stiles, P (2007) A world of difference? *People Management*, 15 November, pp 36–41

Varma, A, Budhwar, P S and DeNisi, A (2008) *Performance Management Systems: A global perspective*, Abingdon, Routledge

Welfare, S (2006) A whole world out there: managing global HR, *IRS Employment Review*, 862, 29 December, pp 8–12

White, R (2005) A strategic approach to building a consistent global rewards program, *Compensation & Benefits Review*, July–August, pp 23–40

Yanadori, Y (2011) Paying both globally and locally: an examination of the compensation management of a US multinational finance firm in the Asia pacific region, *The International Journal of Human Resource Management*, 22 (18), pp 3867–87

39 Managing expatriates

KEY CONCEPTS AND TERMS

Acculturization

Cross-cultural awareness

Expatriate

Home-based pay

Host-based pay

LEARNING OUTCOMES

On completing this chapter you should be able to define these key concepts. You should also understand:

- Why use expatriates?
- RoI on international assignments
- The process of managing expatriates
- Resourcing policies
- Recruitment and selection policies
- Preparation policy
- Assimilation and support
- Career management
- Expatriate performance
- Re-entry policies
- Pay and allowances policies
- Case studies

Introduction

An expatriate was defined by Lee and Donohue (2012: 1198) as 'any individual who relocates from his/her home base to an international location for business or work purposes and sets up temporary residence in the host country'.

The management of expatriates on international assignments is a major factor determining success or failure in a global business. Expatriates are expensive. They can be difficult to manage because of the problems associated with adapting to and working in unfamiliar environments and cultures, concerns about their development and careers, difficulties encountered when they re-enter their parent company after a foreign assignment, and questions about how they should be remunerated. It is therefore necessary to consider why expatriates should be employed and how the costs and benefits of using them can be evaluated. In this chapter these issues are dealt with first. The rest of the chapter is devoted to an examination of the various policies and practices required to manage expatriates.

Why use expatriates?

Altman and Baruch (2012) defined the strategic value of international assignments as being:

- to transfer business and technological know-how;
- to develop personnel;
- to facilitate and improve communications between subsidiaries and headquarters;
- to further a unified organizational policy.

They noted that international assignments, from the point of view of individual expatriates, could widen their career perspectives and choice through exposure to work in a foreign environment and enable them to gain a deeper understanding of how an international organization functions.

Pinto *et al* (2012: 2295–96) observed that:

> In the age of globalization, the management of an international workforce is increasingly central to both the competitive advantage of the organization and the mission of international human resource management (IHRM) departments... Organizations use international assignments mainly for: (1) subsidiary control and coordination; (2) skills and knowledge transfer; and (3) managers' development.

RoI on international assignments

International assignments are investments in the use of human capital, which involve costs as well as benefits. It is therefore advisable to calculate the return on investment (RoI) that they generate. Doherty and Dickmann (2012: 3435) defined RoI as 'the comparison of the financial and non-financial costs and benefits relative to the assignment purpose'. They noted that it is important to evaluate the benefits of international mobility to careers, to expatriate retention and to performance over time. They observed that: 'It is possible for corporate executives to construct an evidence-based business case for expatriation by attributing a value to performance improvement, higher retention of staff and promotions, and contrasting these with investment data' (ibid: 3448).

The need for this is driven by the costs of employing expatriates. The Doherty and Dickmann research established that in the nine organizations they studied, employing 3,450 expatriates, the average expatriate investment (pay, benefits and allowances) was £171,022 and the total average cost per expatriate was £462, 212. The average expatriate covered by the survey cost the organization 68 per cent more than managers working domestically.

The key cost metrics identified by Doherty and Dickmann were overall remuneration (pay, benefits and allowances), the management of the international assignment programme including learning and development costs, and outsourcing expenditure (fees paid to external parties, eg relocation services, house search and cultural training). The key benefit metrics were performance, career progression and retention. Collings and Scullion (2006) suggested that expatriation outcomes can be measured on four criteria: 1) assignment costs; 2) earlier termination; 3) expatriate performance; and 4) repatriate turnover.

The calculation of RoI on the employment of expatriates should be seen as an essential part of the process of managing them, as described below.

The process of managing expatriates

The process of managing expatriates has been summarized by Sparrow *et al* (2004: 145) as a global assignment cycle, the three phases of which are:

1. *Pre-departure* – planning the assignment, selecting the individual, administering the relocation programme and conducting preparatory training and development.
2. *Assignment* – performance management, pay and benefits, family support and preparation for repatriation or reassignment.

3 *Post-assignment* – retention by reintegrating returning international assignees into organizational career systems.

Doherty and Dickmann (2012: 3438) explained that: 'The task for HR practitioners is the development and use of congruent HR policies which will activate the successful completion of an assignment and repatriation into the home organization to engender a willingness among employees to go on assignment.'

However, carrying out this task is not easy. The following questions need to be answered:

- How do we decide on our expatriate resourcing policy – the extent to which we need to assign parent company nationals to positions in foreign subsidiaries as expatriates?
- How do we select expatriates who are willing and able to undertake assignments in foreign subsidiaries?
- How do we prepare people for their assignments?
- How do we provide the support that expatriates need when on assignment?
- How do we manage the careers of expatriates?
- How do we manage and measure the performance of expatriates?
- How do we assimilate expatriates in the parent company when they complete their assignment?
- How do we remunerate expatriates?

There are no easy answers to these questions and every international organization will have to develop its own approach. But in doing so there are certain considerations that can be taken into account, as described in the remaining sections of this chapter.

Resourcing policies

Policies are required on the employment of local nationals and the use of expatriates for long periods or shorter assignments. The advantages of employing local nationals are that they:

- are familiar with local markets, the local communities, the cultural setting and the local economy;
- speak the local language and are culturally assimilated;
- can take a long-term view and contribute for a long period (as distinct from expatriates who are more likely to adopt a short-term perspective);
- do not take the patronizing (neocolonial) attitude that expatriates sometimes adopt.

Expatriates may be required to provide the experience and expertise that local nationals lack, at least for the time being. But there is much to be said for a long-term resourcing policy which states that the aim is to fill all or the great majority of posts with local people. Parent companies who staff their overseas subsidiaries with local nationals always have the scope to 'parachute in' specialist staff to deal with particular issues such as the start-up of a new product or service.

Talent management programmes, as described in Chapter 20, can create a talent pool from which people could be selected for foreign assignments. If a talent pool does not exist it will be necessary to identify people who are potential assignees and, in effect, create a special pool for them.

Qualities and behaviours

The qualities and behaviours required for those who might work internationally need to be specified. Leblanc (2001) suggested that they should be able to:

- Recognize the diversity of overseas countries.
- Accept differences between countries as a fact and adjust to these differences effectively.
- Tolerate and adjust to local conditions.
- Cope in the long term with a large variety of foreign contexts.
- Manage local operations and personnel abroad effectively.
- Gain acceptance as a representative of their company abroad.
- Obtain and interpret information about foreign national contexts (institutions, legislations, practices, market specifics etc).

- Inform and communicate effectively with a foreign environment about the home company's policies.
- Take into account the foreign environment when negotiating contracts and partnerships.
- Identify and accept adjustments to basic product specifications in order to meet the needs of the foreign market.
- Develop elements of a common framework for company strategies, policies and operations.
- Accept that the practices that will operate best in an overseas environment will not necessarily be the same as the company's 'home' practices.

Of these qualities the first four refer to the critical requirement of cross-cultural awareness, ie the ability to understand and work within different national cultures.

Alternative approaches to resourcing

The problems involved in the management of expatriates indicate, as suggested by Pinto *et al* (2012: 2312) that 'organizations should re-evaluate their global staffing options and consider other forms of talent (locals and self-assigned individuals) and alternative forms of mobility (eg business travel, virtual teams, short-term assignments and commuting), often equally effective and more compatible with individuals' interests'.

Recruitment and selection policies

People for international assignments can be recruited from a defined pool within the company by identifying individuals with the required qualifications, or by internal advertisements. It may be necessary to seek recruits outside the firm. It is important to be clear about what sort of people are required, by reference to role specifications that spell out the special qualities required for working abroad. It is also advisable to select people who believe that an overseas assignment will be beneficial to them, and who will be capable of working in a different culture. To reduce the assimilation problems that can be faced by an expatriate when working in a foreign location, realistic previews of the conditions they will meet are necessary.

Use of role specifications

Selection should be based on role specifications, which might contain some or all of the points included in the list of qualities and behaviours set out above, modified to take account of any special conditions attached to a particular assignment.

It is useful to build a competency framework as a basis for recruitment and, later, for management development. The following list of the competencies required by global executives was produced by Briscoe and Schuler (2004: 277):

- open-minded and flexible in thought and tactics;
- cultural interest and sensitivity;
- able to deal with complexity;
- resilient, resourceful, optimistic and energetic;
- honesty and integrity;
- stable personal life;
- value-added technical or business skills.

Desire to work abroad

An important recruitment issue is whether or not people want to work abroad. Research by Mol *et al* (2009) revealed that employees are often unwilling to accept an assignment entailing international mobility. As Kim and Froese (2012: 3415) explained:

> An employee's decision whether to accept an expatriate assignment can be a dilemma as the employee must consider both work and family issues. On the one hand, an expatriate assignment might be an important career step. On the other hand, family reasons such as marriage are often cited as a major reason for not accepting international assignments... Other critical factors related to work-family issues in international assignments are host-country attributes; these attributes include

the level of economic development and the country's language – employees who value their occupational role have a strong preference for advanced countries.

Doherty and Dickmann (2012: 3448) commented that: 'The attractiveness of career and development prospects is highly pertinent to an individual's decisions to go abroad.' And research by Pinto *et al* (2012: 2300) confirmed that the challenges, (both personal and professional) and career prospects were the two main motives for accepting an international assignment.

Realistic previews

At interviews for candidates from outside the organization, and when talking to internal staff about the possibility of an overseas assignment, it is advisable to have a policy of providing a realistic preview of the job. The preview should provide information on the overseas operation, any special features of the work, what will need to be done to adjust to local conditions, career progression overseas, re-entry policy on completion of the assignment, pay, and special benefits such as home leave and children's education.

Preparation policy

The preparation policy for overseas assignments should include the provision of cultural familiarization for the country in which the expatriate will work (sometimes called 'acculturization'), information on how to work in multicultural teams, and the business and HR policies that will apply. A pre-assignment training programme should be provided that, as proposed by Tarique and Caligiri (1995), could be designed by taking the following steps:

1. Identify the type of global assignment, eg technical, functional, tactical, developmental or strategic/executive.
2. Conduct a cross-cultural training needs analysis covering organizational analysis and requirements, assignment analysis of key tasks and individual analysis of skills.
3. Establish training goals and measures – cognitive (eg understanding the role of cultural values and norms) and affective (modifying perception about culture and increasing confidence in dealing with individual behaviours to form adaptive behaviours such as interpersonal skills).
4. Develop and deliver the programme – the content should cover both general and specific cultural orientation; a variety of methods should be used.
5. Evaluate training given.

Assimilation and support

Farh *et al* (2010: 439) observed that: 'Expatriates experience high levels of uncertainty in the host country, not only because the problems they encounter in the host country are qualitatively different from those they encountered back home but also because the informational and emotional resources they relied on in the home country are no longer as present or relevant.'

Studies such as those by Stroh *et al* (2005) have shown that even when employees accept an international assignment, they often return early for reasons such as difficulties in adapting to their host countries. Many of those who return early tend to do so after a few months, thus incurring great costs for their firms. As Wu and Ang (2011: 2689) pointed out following their research: 'The ability of expatriates to adjust to their new work environment greatly affects their success in that particular assignment.' They also emphasized that: 'A systems approach to expatriate supporting practices is essential for expatriate adjustments and outcomes' (ibid: 2696).

Assimilation and support policies provide for the adaptation of expatriates to overseas posts and for their progress in them to be monitored and reviewed. Progress may be monitored by conventional performance management processes, but additional information may be provided on potential and the ability of individuals to cope with overseas conditions.

When a number of expatriates are employed it is customary for people to be appointed at headquarters to provide support. Briscoe *et al* (2012) reported that some firms appoint sponsors who look after the interests and prospects of expatriates while they are on assignment, but who also provide an avenue for keeping them informed about what is going on back home.

It may be up to expatriates to seek any support they need from headquarters or elsewhere by direct approaches and networking. But some expatriates are better at this than others. As Farh *et al* (2010: 450) recommended: 'To ensure that expatriates will actually seek support, organizations should reduce the perceived risk associated with support seeking by creating a psychologically safe culture, since asking for help can sometimes be interpreted as a sign of weakness.'

Career experiences and expectations are also important. According to Haslberger and Brewster (2009), when expatriates are clear about the career benefits generated from international careers, they are more likely to adjust to their job and the host culture, and will eventually decide to stay on in the assignment.

As suggested by Briscoe *et al* (2012: 249), support should be based on 'clear, consistent and regular communication between the home office and the expatriates'. The expatriates should be provided with opportunities to travel back to their home country to share experience and knowledge with other members of the organization.

The specific support areas proposed by Wu and Ang (2011) were:

1. Pre-departure preparation should cover cross-cultural training, adequate preparation time and orientation visits to ease the transition process.
2. Companies need to provide appropriate financial assistance to compensate for any hardship involved in expatriation.
3. Companies need to reassure expatriates that a posting will help their career prospects. Farh *et al* (2010: 450) advised that 'organizations may want to employ formal mentoring programs and ensure that the fit between the characteristics of the mentor and mentee is most conducive to the exchange of high-quality support'.

Career management

Special attention has to be paid to managing the careers of expatriates either as part of their experience overseas or when they return permanently or for a period to their home country. As proposed by Briscoe *et al* (2012: 248) career management processes need to begin prior to an international assignment and be updated regularly. The assignment should be part of a larger plan for the firm so that repatriates return to positions that use their international learning and experience.

Career management practices in international organizations may be based on the methods described in Chapter 20. These include the definition of common career paths, career counselling and individual career plans based on the outcome of performance management reviews. The responsibility for ensuring that these activities take place systematically for expatriates can be given to whoever is in charge of talent management or management development at headquarters. Mentors based at head office can be involved by keeping in touch with expatriates before they return to the parent company.

Performance management

Standard performance management systems such as those described in Chapter 25 can be used for assessing expatriate performance. But there are unique circumstances surrounding the work of expatriates, including the need for cross-cultural competence, problems of adjustment, and distance from headquarters and the support it can provide. These combine to suggest that special arrangements should be made for assessing expatriate performance and particular care should be taken to allow for the factors that affect performance.

Assessing performance

Performance management processes for expatriates need to take account of the challenges they face. These are of a different order to those staying at home. Expatriate performance has been broken down into four dimensions by Caligiuri (1997):

technical performance, contextual/pro-social performance, contextual/managerial performance and expatriate specific dimensions.

Kramer and Wayne (2004) produced the following list of expatriate success constructs:

- performing well on the job;
- remaining in the assignment until the end of term;
- adjusting to living conditions.

Lee and Donohue (2012) developed and tested an expatriate performance scale consisting of six factors:

- task performance;
- management and administration;
- teamwork and leadership;
- demonstrating effort;
- communication performance;
- maintaining self-discipline.

Factors affecting expatriate performance

Issues such as culture shock and cross-cultural adjustment may adversely impact on the performance of expatriates. Pinto *et al* (2012: 2297) commented that: 'Socio-cultural adjustment and psychological well-being of expatriates and their families are preconditions for their success.' Evidence collected by Solomon (1995) indicated that expatriate failure is largely due to firms' overemphasis on selection based on technical expertise rather than cross-cultural competence. And Dickmann *et al* (2008) provided evidence that organizations seem to overestimate financial and family motives and undervalue career and work–life balance considerations favoured by expatriates.

Kim and Froese (2012: 3415) explained that: 'The individuals' reluctance to accept an assignment might have influenced their efforts to adjust, their satisfaction with the assignment and ultimately their withdrawal intention. In contrast, individuals seeking or willing to accept an assignment are perhaps more likely to overcome adjustment difficulties, feel more satisfied with the assignment and show intentions to remain until the end of the assignment.'

Re-entry policies

Re-entry policies should be designed to minimize the problems that can arise when expatriates return to their parent company after a foreign posting. They want to be assured that they will be given positions appropriate to their qualifications, and they will be concerned about their careers, suspecting that their overseas experience will not be taken into account. Policies should allow time for expatriates to adjust. The provision of mentors or counsellors is desirable.

Doherty and Dickmann (2012: 3447) found through their research that turnover rates in the first period after expatriates return to their parent company averaged 15 per cent compared with the normal rate of 7 per cent for employees permanently working at headquarters. Turnover risks were due to repatriates having more marketable skills, lack of recognition by the employer of the skills acquired on assignment, or reduced responsibility or status on return. The firm with the highest repatriation turnover rate in the sample (40 per cent) responded by introducing a longer-term career planning process.

Sparrow *et al* (2011: 48) emphasized that the problems of managing repatriations are more complex in highly decentralized MNCs than in the more centralized global companies.

Pay and allowances policies

The policy of most organizations is to ensure that expatriates are no worse off because they have been posted abroad. In practice, various additional allowances or payments, such as hardship allowances, mean that they are usually better off financially than if they had stayed at home. The basic choice is whether to adopt a home-based or host-based policy.

Home-based pay

The home-based pay approach aims to ensure that the value of the remuneration (pay, benefits and allowances) of expatriates is the same as in their home country. The home-base salary may be a *notional* one for long-term assignments (ie the salary that it is assumed would be paid to expatriates were they employed in a job of equivalent level at the parent company). For shorter-term assignments it may be the *actual* salary of the individual. The notional or actual home-base salary is used as the foundation upon which the total remuneration package is built. This is sometimes called the 'build-up' or 'balance sheet' approach.

The salary 'build-up' starts with the actual or notional home-base salary. To this is added a cost-of-living adjustment that is applied to 'spendable income' – the portion of salary that would be used at home for everyday living. It usually excludes income tax, social security, pensions and insurance and can exclude discretionary expenditure on major purchases or holidays on the grounds that these do not constitute day-to-day living expenses.

The expatriate's salary would then consist of the actual or notional home-base salary plus the cost-of-living adjustment. In addition, it may be necessary to adjust salaries to take account of the host country's tax regime in order to achieve tax equalization. Moves of less than one year, which might give rise to double taxation, require particular attention. Some or all of the following allowances may be added to this salary:

- 'incentive to work abroad' premium;
- hardship and location;
- housing and utilities;
- school fees;
- 'rest and recuperation' leave.

Host-based pay

The host-based pay approach provides expatriates with salaries and benefits such as company cars and holidays that are in line with those given to nationals of the host country in similar jobs. This method ensures equity between expatriates and host country nationals. It is adopted by companies using the so-called market rate system, which ensures that the salaries of expatriates match the market levels of pay in the host country.

Companies using the host-based approach commonly pay additional allowances such as school fees, accommodation and medical insurance. They may also fund long-term benefits such as social security, life assurance and pensions from home.

The host-based method is certainly equitable from the viewpoint of local nationals, and it can be less expensive than home-based pay. But it may be much less attractive as an inducement for employees to work abroad, especially in unpleasant locations, and it can be difficult to collect market rate data locally to provide a basis for setting pay levels.

CASE STUDIES

Oxfam

Oxfam is a highly devolved international organization with a strategy of building up local management. Reporting lines for HR staff reflect this devolved approach. Country-based HR staff report to regional HR managers The latter report direct to their regional director but have a 'dotted line' (functional) relationship with Oxfam's head of international HR. This means that they must take account of the principles of Oxfam's international people strategy and its associated policies covering pay, benefits, performance management and other practices that apply to every region.

Thus regions will follow Oxfam's international people strategy, pay and benefits framework and other HR procedures; unless local legislation has to take precedent, they ultimately decide how to implement policies and pay staff within regional budgets. Oxfam recruits locally when it can but it may be necessary to look elsewhere for people with some specialist skills, although this labour pool is from a global labour market rather than a Western one.

IBM

IBM has over 300,000 employees in more than 160 countries. It has evolved in recent years from a predominately IT manufacturing and sales company to become a business services company.

The company is structured into three regions and describes itself as a globally integrated company. Strategy is global but the human front-end of HR is local, staffed with local nationals. A generally integrated approach to HR is adopted, although the extent to which HR policies are tailored to local circumstances varies. This is affected by the need to conform to different legal requirements in each company, which particularly affects employee relations policies. However, total reward and performance management policies and practices are common across the world. The company claims that it acts on its values, for example equal opportunities, even when they may prove controversial locally. Levels of international mobility are high, especially staff working in HR, finance and IT.

Key learning points: Managing expatriates

Expatriates

An expatriate was defined by Lee and Donohue (2012: 1198) as 'any individual who relocates from his/her home base to an international location for business or work purposes and sets up temporary residence in the host country'.

Managing expatriates

The management of expatriates on international assignments is a major factor determining success or failure in a global business. Expatriates are expensive. They can be difficult to manage because of the problems associated with adapting to and working in unfamiliar environments and cultures, concerns about their development and careers, difficulties encountered when they re-enter their parent company after a foreign assignment, and questions about how they should be remunerated.

Use of expatriates

Organizations use international assignments mainly for: 1) subsidiary control and coordination; 2) skills and knowledge transfer; 3) managers' development.

RoI on international assignments

International assignments are investments in the use of human capital, which involve costs as well as benefits. It is therefore advisable to calculate the return on investment (RoI) that they generate.

The process of managing expatriates

The process of managing expatriates has been summarized by Sparrow *et al* (2004: 145) as a global assignment cycle, the three phases of which are: pre-departure, assignment and post-assignment.

Resourcing

Policies are required on the employment of local nationals and the use of expatriates for long periods or shorter assignments.

Expatriates may be required to provide the experience and expertise that local nationals lack, at least for the time being. But there is much to be said for a long-term resourcing policy which states that the aim is to fill all or the great majority of posts with local people.

Recruitment and selection policies

- People for international assignments can be recruited from within the company from a defined pool, by identifying individuals with the required qualifications, or internal advertisements. It may be necessary to seek recruits outside the firm.

- Other sources of people (locals and self-assigned individuals) and alternative forms of mobility (eg business travel, virtual teams, short-term assignments and commuting) should be considered.
- The critical requirement that expatriates should meet is cross-cultural awareness, ie the ability to understand and work within different national cultures.

Preparation policy

The preparation policy for overseas assignments should include the provision of cultural familiarization for the country in which the expatriate will work, information on how to work in multicultural teams, and the business and HR policies that will apply. A pre-assignment training programme should be provided.

Assimilation and support policies

- Assimilation and support policies provide for the adaptation of expatriates to overseas posts and their progress in them to be monitored and reviewed.
- Progress may be monitored by conventional performance management processes, but additional information may be provided on potential and the ability of individuals to cope with overseas conditions.
- Mentors may be appointed to look after the interests of expatriates.

Career management

Special attention has to be paid to managing the careers of expatriates, either as part of their experience overseas or when they return permanently or for a period to their home country.

Expatriate performance

Standard performance management systems can be used for assessing expatriate performance. But there are unique circumstances surrounding the work of expatriates, including the need for cross-cultural competence, problems of adjustment, and distance from headquarters and the support it can provide. These combine to suggest that special arrangements should be made for assessing their performance and particular care should be taken to allow for the factors that affect performance.

Pay and allowances policies

The policy of most organizations is to ensure that expatriates are no worse off because they have been posted abroad. In practice, various additional allowances or payments, such as hardship allowances, mean that they are usually better off financially than if they had stayed at home. The basic choice for expatriate pay is whether to adopt a home-based or host-based policy.

Questions

1. Why should expatriates be used?
2. How can the return on investment for expatriates be calculated?
3. What are the main phases of the employment of expatriates?
4. What qualities should expatriates possess?
5. What factors influence an individual's decision to accept an international assignment?
6. How can support be provided for expatriates?
7. How can the performance of expatriates be assessed?
8. What should re-entry policies for expatriates aim to achieve?
9. What policies can international organizations adopt for the pay of expatriates?
10. What are host-based and home-based pay policies?

References

Altman, Y and Baruch, Y (2012) Global self-initiated corporate expatriate careers: a new era in international assignments, *Personnel Review*, 41 (2) pp 233–55

Briscoe, D and Schuler, R (2004) *International Human Resource Management*, London, Routledge

Briscoe, D, Schuler, R and Tarique, I (2012) *International Human Resource Management*, 4th edn, New York, Routledge

Caligiuri, P (1997) Assessing expatriate success: Beyond just being there, in (ed) Z Aycan, *New Approaches to Employee Management – Theory and Research*, Greenwich, JAI Press, pp 117–40

Collings, D and Scullion, H (2006) Global staffing, in G K Stahl and I Björkman (eds) *Handbook of Research in International Human Resource Management*, Cheltenham, Edward Elgar pp 141–57

Dickmann, M, Doherty, N, Mills, T and Brewster, C (2008) Why do they go? Individual and corporate perspectives on the factors influencing the decision to accept an international assignment, *International Journal of Human Resource Management*, 39 (1), pp 116–34

Doherty, N T and Dickmann, M (2012) Measuring the return on investment in international assignments: an action research approach, *International Journal of Human Resource Management*, 23 (16), pp 3434–54

Farh, C I, Bartol, K M, Shapiro, D L and Shin, J (2010) Networking abroad: a process model of how expatriates form support ties to facilitate adjustment, *Academy of Management Review*, 35 (3), pp 434–54.

Haslberger, A and Brewster, C (2009) Capital gains: expatriate adjustment and the psychological contract in international careers, *Human Resource Management*, 48 (3), pp 379–97

Kim, J and Froese, J (2012) Expatriate willingness in Asia: the importance of host-country characteristics and employees' role commitments, *International Journal of Human Resource Management*, 23 (16), pp 3414–33

Kramer, M L and Wayne, S J (2004) An examination of perceived organizational support as a multidimensional construct in the context of an expatriate assignment, *Journal of Management*, 30, pp 209–37

Leblanc, B (2001) European competitiveness – some guidelines for companies, in (ed) M H Albrecht, *International HRM*, Oxford, Blackwell

Lee, L and Donohue, R (2012) The construction and validation of a measure of expatriate job performance, *International Journal of Human Resource Management*, 23 (6), pp 1197–215

Mol, S T, Born, M P, Willemsen, M E, Henk, T V and Derous, E (2009) When selection ratios are high: Predicting the expatriation willingness of prospective entry-level job applicants, *Human Performance*, 22, pp 111–29

Pinto, L H, Cabral-Cardoso, C and Werther, W B (2012) Compelled to go abroad: Motives and outcomes of international assignments, *International Journal of Human Resource Management*, 23 (11), pp 2295–314

Solomon, C M (1995) Success abroad depends on more than just job skills, *Personnel Journal*, 73 (4), pp 51–54

Sparrow, P, Brewster, C and Harris, H (2004) *Globalizing Human Resource Management*, London, Routledge

Sparrow, P, Scullion, H and Farndale, E (2011) Global talent management: new roles for the corporate HR function? in (eds) H Scullion and D G Collings, *Global Talent Management*, London, Routledge, pp 40–55

Stroh, L K, Black, J S, Mendenhall, M E and Gregersob, H B (2005), *International Assignments: An integration of strategy, research and* practice, Mahwah NJ, Lawrence Erlbaum Associates

Tarique, I and Caligiri, P (1995) Training and development of international staff, in (eds) A W Herzorg and J V Ruyssevelde, *International Human Resource Management*, London, Sage Publications

Wu, P D and Ang, S H (2011) The impact of expatriate supporting practices and cultural intelligence on cross-cultural adjustment and performance of expatriates in Singapore, *International Journal of Human Resource Management*, 22 (13), pp 2683–702

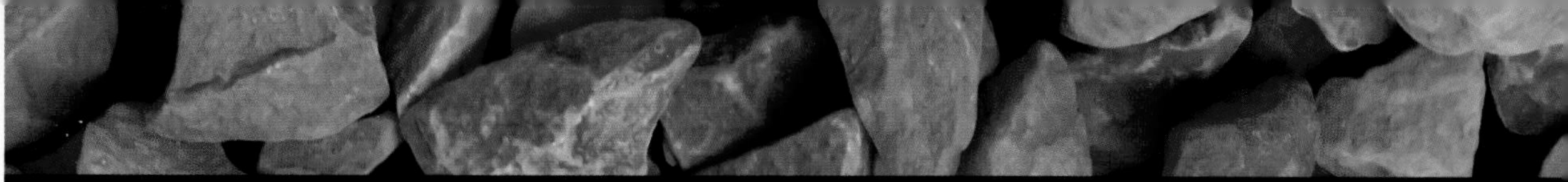

PART X

HRM policy and practice

PART X CONTENTS

Introduction

The HR function is responsible for managing practices that ensure that a consistent, fair and thorough approach is adopted to dealing with HRM issues, that systems are in place that provide for the efficient administration of HR matters, that information is available that guides HRM decisions, and that the spirit as well as the letter of employment law is put into practice. As described in this part, these responsibilities are fulfilled by the development and administration of:

- HR policies that set out the approaches used by the organization to deal with key aspects of HRM and provide guidelines to ensure the consistent application of these approaches;
- HR procedures that are formalized ways of dealing with specific employment matters such as discipline, redundancy and grievance handling;
- HR systems that are computer-based processes for managing the HRM and providing HR information, also known as e-HRM;
- HR practices that meet employment law requirements.

40 HR policies

KEY CONCEPTS AND TERMS

Diversity

Equal opportunities

LEARNING OUTCOMES

On completing this chapter you should be able to define these key concepts. You should also know about:

- The reasons for having HR policies
- Overall HR policy
- Specific HR policies
- Formulating HR policies
- Implementing HR policies

Introduction

HR policies set out the approaches that the organization adopts to dealing with key aspects of HRM and provide continuing guidelines on how these approaches should be applied. They define the philosophies and values of the organization on how people should be treated, and from these are derived the principles upon which managers are expected to act when dealing with HR matters.

HR policies should be distinguished from HR procedures. A policy provides generalized guidance on how HR issues should be dealt with. A procedure spells out precisely what steps should be taken to deal with major employment issues such as grievances, discipline, capability and redundancy.

Why have HR policies?

HR policies define how the organization wants to handle key aspects of people management. As guidelines the aim is to ensure that any HR issues are dealt with consistently in accordance with the values of the organization and in line with certain defined principles. All organizations have HR policies. Some, however, exist implicitly as a philosophy of management and an attitude to employees that is expressed in the way in which HR issues are handled; for example, the introduction of a new grade and pay structure. The advantage of explicit policies in terms of consistency and understanding may appear to be obvious, but there are disadvantages: written policies can be inflexible, constrictive, platitudinous, or all three. To a degree, policies have often to be expressed in abstract terms and managers do not generally care for abstractions. But they do want to know where they stand – people like structure – and formalized HR policies can provide the guidelines they need.

Formalized HR policies can be used in induction, team leader and management training to help participants understand the philosophies and values of the organization and how they are expected to behave within that context. They are a means for defining the employment relationship and the psychological contract. HR policies can be expressed formally as overall statements of the values of the organization or in relation to specific areas, as discussed in this chapter.

Overall HR policy

The overall HR policy defines how the organization fulfils its social responsibilities for its employees and sets out its attitudes towards them. It is an expression of its values or beliefs about how people should be treated. The values expressed in an overall statement of HR policies may explicitly or implicitly refer to the following concepts:

- *Equity* – treating employees fairly and justly by adopting an 'even-handed' approach. This includes protecting individuals from any unfair decisions made by their managers, providing equal opportunities for employment and promotion, and operating an equitable payment system.
- *Consideration* – taking account of individual circumstances when making decisions that affect the prospects, security or self-respect of employees.
- *Organizational learning* – a belief in the need to promote the learning and development of all the members of the organization by providing the processes and support required.
- *Performance through people* – the importance attached to developing a performance culture and to continuous improvement; the significance of performance management as a means of defining and agreeing mutual expectations; the provision of fair feedback to people on how well they are performing.
- *Quality of working life* – consciously and continually aiming to improve the quality of working life. This involves increasing the sense of satisfaction that people obtain from their work by – so far as possible – reducing monotony; increasing variety, autonomy and responsibility; avoiding placing people under too much stress; providing for an acceptable balance between work and life outside work.
- *Working conditions* – providing healthy, safe and – so far as practicable – pleasant working conditions.

These values are espoused by many organizations in one form or another. But to what extent are they practised when making 'business-led' decisions (which can, of course, be highly detrimental to employees if, for example, they lead to redundancy)? One of the dilemmas facing all those who formulate HR policies is: how can we pursue policies focusing on business success and at the same time fulfil our obligations to employees in such terms as equity, consideration, quality of working life, security and working conditions? To argue, as some do, that HR policies should be entirely business-led implies that human considerations are unimportant. Yet organizations have obligations to all their stakeholders, not just their owners.

It may be difficult to express these overall policies in anything but generalized terms, but employers increasingly have to recognize that they are subject to external as well as internal pressures and moral imperatives, which act as constraints on the extent to which they can disregard the higher standards of behaviour towards their employees that are expected of them. What needs to be done to avoid accusations that general HR policy statements are mere rhetoric is to convert them into reality through specific HR policies and enforce their application.

Specific HR policies

The most common areas in which specific HR policies exist are age and employment, AIDS, bullying, discipline, diversity management, e-mails and the internet, employee development, employee relations, employee voice, the employment relationship, equal opportunity, grievances, health and safety, new technology, promotion, redundancy, reward, sexual harassment, substance abuse, whistleblowing and work–life balance.

Age and employment

The policy on age and employment should take into account the UK legislation on age discrimination and the following facts:

- Age is a poor predictor of job performance.
- It is misleading to equate physical and mental ability with age.
- More of the population are living active, healthy lives as they get older.

AIDS

An AIDS policy could include the following points:

- The risk through infection in the workplace is negligible.
- Where the occupation does involve blood contact – as in hospitals, doctors' surgeries and laboratories – the special precautions advised by the Health and Safety Commission will be implemented.
- Employees who know that they are infected with AIDS will not be obliged to disclose the fact to the company, but if they do it will remain completely confidential.
- There will be no discrimination against anyone with or at risk of acquiring AIDS.
- Employees infected by HIV or suffering from AIDS will be treated no differently from anyone else suffering a severe illness.

Bullying

An anti-bullying policy will state that bullying will not be tolerated by the organization and that those who persist in bullying staff will be subject to disciplinary action, which could be severe in particularly bad cases. The policy will make it clear that individuals who are being bullied should have the right to discuss the problem with another person, a representative or a member of the HR function, and to make a complaint. The policy should emphasize that if a complaint is received it will be thoroughly investigated.

Discipline

The disciplinary policy should state that employees have the right to know what is expected of them and what could happen if they infringe the organization's rules. It should also make the point that, in handling disciplinary cases, the organization will treat employees in accordance with the principles of natural justice. It should be supported by a disciplinary procedure (see Chapter 41).

Diversity management

A policy on managing diversity recognizes that there are differences among employees and that these differences, if properly managed, will enable work to be done more efficiently and effectively. It does not focus exclusively on issues of discrimination but instead concentrates on recognizing the differences between people.

Managing diversity is a concept that recognizes the benefits to be gained from differences. It is not the same as equal opportunity, which aims to legislate against discrimination, assumes that people should be assimilated into the organization and, often, relies on affirmative action. A management of diversity policy could:

- acknowledge cultural and individual differences in the workplace;
- state that the organization values the different qualities that people bring to their jobs;
- emphasize the need to eliminate bias in such areas as selection, promotion, performance assessment, pay and learning opportunities;
- focus attention on individual differences rather than group differences.

The policy can be strengthened by the development of diversity networks. These act as support groups for minority staff to share problems and swap tips. But they can additionally help organizations to understand the people who work for them and help the business to perform better:

- At Cisco, the women's network helps business development by hosting events for prospective and existing customers.

- At PwC there are four main networks: for women, ethnic minorities, disabled people and GLEE (an inclusive business network for gays, lesbians and everyone else).
- At BT a disability network focuses on awareness raising about different disabilities to help managers understand them and get the best from people living with a disability. 'Knowledge calls' are provided, which consist of presentations done via conference calls and desktop technology with expert speakers on particular subjects such as Parkinson's and migraines. They typically include someone who has experienced the condition, a Q&A session and inputs from HR relating to the condition or disability. There are online forums and subgroups offering support.

E-mails and use of the internet

The policy on e-mails could state that the sending or downloading of offensive e-mails is prohibited and that the senders or downloaders of such messages are subject to normal disciplinary procedures. The policy may also prohibit internet browsing, for example of social networks, or downloading material not related to the business, although this can be difficult to enforce. Some companies have always believed that reasonable use of the telephone is acceptable and that policy may be extended to the internet.

If it is decided that employees' e-mails should be monitored to check on excessive or unacceptable use, this should be included in an e-mail policy, which would therefore be part of the contractual arrangements. A policy statement could be included to the effect that: 'The company reserves the right to access and monitor all e-mail messages created, sent, received or stored on the company's system.'

Employee development

The employee development policy could express the organization's commitment to the continuous development of the skills and abilities of employees in order to maximize their contribution and to give them the opportunity to enhance their skills, realize their potential, advance their careers and increase their employability, both within and outside the organization. The policy could also express the belief that age should not be a barrier to learning opportunities from which everyone can benefit, irrespective of how old they are.

Employee relations

The employee relations policy will set out the organization's approach to the rights of employees to have their interests represented to management through trade unions, staff associations or some other form of representative system. It will also cover the basis upon which the organization works with trade unions, eg emphasizing that this should be regarded as a partnership.

Employee voice

The employee voice policy should spell out the organization's belief in giving employees an opportunity to have a say in matters that affect them. It should define the mechanisms for employee voice such as joint consultation and suggestion schemes.

The employment relationship

Employment policies should be concerned with fundamental aspects of the employment relationship. They should take account of the requirements of relevant UK and European legislation and case law, as covered in Chapter 43.

Equal opportunity

The equal opportunity policy should spell out the organization's determination to give equal opportunities to all, irrespective of sex, sexual orientation, race, creed, disability, age or marital status. The policy should also deal with the extent to which the organization wants to take 'affirmative action' to redress imbalances between the numbers employed according to sex or race or to differences in the levels of qualifications and skills they have achieved. The policy could be set out as follows:

1. We are an equal opportunity employer. This means that we do not permit direct or

indirect discrimination against any employee on the grounds of race, nationality, sex, sexual orientation, disability, religion, marital status or age.

2 Direct discrimination takes place when a person is treated less favourably than others are or would be treated in similar circumstances.

3 Indirect discrimination takes place when, whether intentional or not, a condition is applied that adversely affects a considerable proportion of people of one race, nationality, sex, sexual orientation, religion or marital status, or those with disabilities or older employees.

4 The firm will ensure that equal opportunity principles are applied in all its HR policies and in particular to the procedures relating to the recruitment, training, development and promotion of its employees.

5 Where appropriate and where permissible under the relevant legislation and codes of practice, employees of under-represented groups will be given positive training and encouragement to achieve equal opportunity.

Grievances

The policy on grievances could state that employees have the right to raise their grievances with their manager, to be accompanied by a representative if they so wish, and to appeal to a higher level if they feel that their grievance has not been resolved satisfactorily. The policy should be supported by a grievance procedure (see Chapter 41).

Health and safety

Health and safety policies cover how the organization intends to provide healthy and safe places and systems of work (see Chapter 36).

New technology

A new technology policy statement could state that there will be consultation about the introduction of new technology and the steps that would be taken by the organization to minimize the risk of compulsory redundancy or adverse effects on other terms and conditions or working arrangements.

Promotion

A promotion policy could state the organization's intention to promote from within wherever this is appropriate as a means of satisfying its requirements for high-quality staff. The policy could, however, recognize that there will be occasions when the organization's present and future needs can only be met by recruitment from outside. The point could be made that a vigorous organization needs infusions of fresh blood from time to time if it is not to stagnate. In addition, the policy might state that employees will be encouraged to apply for internally advertised jobs and will not be held back from promotion by their managers, however reluctant the latter may be to lose them. The policy should define the approach that the organization adopts to engaging, promoting and training older employees. It should emphasize that the only criterion for selection or promotion should be ability to do the job.

Redundancy

The redundancy policy should state that the aim of the organization is to provide for employment security. It is the organization's intention to use its best endeavours to avoid involuntary redundancy through its redeployment and retraining programmes. However, if redundancy is unavoidable, those affected will be given fair and equitable treatment, the maximum amount of warning and every help that can be provided to obtain suitable alternative employment. The policy should be supported by a redundancy procedure (see Chapter 39).

Reward

The reward policy could cover such matters as:

- providing an equitable pay system;
- equal pay for work of equal value;
- paying for performance, competence, skill or contribution;
- sharing in the success of the organization (gain sharing or profit sharing);

- the relationship between levels of pay in the organization and market rates;
- the provision of employee benefits, including flexible benefits, if appropriate;
- the importance attached to the non-financial rewards resulting from recognition, accomplishment, autonomy and the opportunity to develop.

Sexual harassment

The sexual harassment policy should state that:

- Sexual harassment will not be tolerated.
- Employees subjected to sexual harassment will be given advice, support and counselling as required.
- Every attempt will be made to resolve the problem informally with the person complained against.
- Assistance will be given to the employee to complain formally if informal discussions fail.
- A special process will be available for hearing complaints about sexual harassment. This will provide for employees to bring their complaint to someone of their own sex if they so wish.
- Complaints will be handled sensitively and with due respect for the rights of both the complainant and the accused.
- Sexual harassment is regarded as gross misconduct and, if proved, makes the individual liable for instant dismissal. Less severe penalties may be reserved for minor cases, but there will always be a warning that repetition will result in dismissal.

Substance abuse

A substance abuse policy could include assurances that:

- employees identified as having substance abuse problems will be offered advice and help;
- any reasonable absence from work necessary to receive treatment will be granted under the organization's sickness scheme, provided there is full cooperation from the employee;
- an opportunity will be given to discuss the matter once it has become evident or suspected that work performance is being affected by substance-related problems;
- the right to be accompanied by a friend or employee representative in any such discussion;
- agencies will be recommended to which the employee can go for help if necessary;
- employment rights will be safeguarded during any reasonable period of treatment.

Whistle-blowing

Whistle-blowing takes place when someone reports a suspected wrongdoing at work. Dismissal of an employee for whistle-blowing is deemed in law as automatic unfair dismissal if a 'protected disclosure', for example referring to a criminal offence by the employer, is made and the employee 'reasonably believes' that the disclosure is in the 'public interest'. Obviously employers want to avoid that situation and employees need guidance on what they can and can't do and how they should act. Hence the need for a whistle-blowing policy that will:

1. Explain that the organization believes that it is important to deal with any wrongdoing, especially those malpractices specifically referred to in the Public Interest Disclosure Act 1998, including criminal offences, risks to health and safety, failure to comply with a legal obligation, a miscarriage of justice and environmental damage. Specific examples of unacceptable behaviour could be given.
2. Indicate that if anyone becomes aware of an issue that needs to be dealt with they should raise the matter inside the organization, either with their line manager or, if the allegation is about their line manager, to a more senior manager.
3. State that employees will not be penalized for informing management about a malpractice.

Work–life balance

Work–life balance policies define how the organization intends to allow employees greater flexibility in their working patterns so that they can balance what they do at work with the responsibilities and interests they have outside work. The policy will indicate how flexible work practices can be developed and implemented. It will emphasize that the numbers of hours worked must not be treated as a criterion for assessing performance. It will set out guidelines on the specific arrangements that can be made, such as flexible hours, compressed working week, term-time working contracts, working at home, special leave for parents and carers, career breaks and various kinds of child care.

A flexibility policy will need to take account of the Work and Families Act 2006, as described in Chapter 43.

Formulating HR policies

HR policies need to address the key HR issues that have been identified in the organization. They must also take account of external factors such as legislation. The maximum amount of consultation should take place with managers, employees and their representatives and the policies should be communicated widely with guidelines on their application. The following steps should be taken when formulating HR policies:

1. Gain understanding of the corporate culture and its shared values.
2. Analyse existing policies – written and unwritten. HR policies will exist in any organization, even if they are implicit rather than expressed formally.
3. Analyse external factors. HR policies are subject to the requirements of UK employment legislation, European Commission employment regulations, and the official Codes of Practice issued by bodies in the UK, such as ACAS (the Advisory, Conciliation and Arbitration Service), the Commission for Equality and Human Rights and the Health and Safety Executive. The Codes of Practice issued by relevant professional institutions, such as the CIPD, should also be consulted.
4. Assess any areas where new policies are needed or existing policies are inadequate.
5. Check with managers, preferably starting at the top, on their views about HR policies and where they think they could be improved.
6. Seek the views of employees about the HR policies, especially the extent to which they are inherently fair and equitable and are implemented fairly and consistently. Consider doing this through an attitude survey.
7. Seek the views of union representatives.
8. Analyse the information obtained in the first seven steps and prepare draft policies.
9. Consult, discuss and agree policies with management and union representatives.
10. Communicate the policies with guidance notes on their implementation as required (although they should be as self-explanatory as possible). Supplement this communication with training.

Implementing HR policies

The aim will be to implement policies fairly and consistently. Line managers have an important role in doing this. It is they who will be largely responsible for policy implementation. Members of the HR function can give guidance, but it is line managers who are on the spot and have to make decisions about people. The role of HR is to communicate and interpret the policies, convince line managers that they are necessary, and provide training and support that will equip managers to implement them. As Purcell *et al* (2003) emphasized, it is line managers who bring HR policies to life.

Key learning points: HR policies

The reasons for having HR policies

HR policies provide guidelines on how key aspects of people management should be handled. The aim is to ensure that any HR issues are dealt with consistently in accordance with the values of the organization and in line with certain defined principles.

Overall HR policy

The overall HR policy defines how the organization fulfils its social responsibilities for its employees and sets out its attitudes towards them. It is an expression of its values or beliefs about how people should be treated.

Specific HR policies

Specific HR policies cover age and employment, AIDS, bullying, discipline, e-mails and the internet, employee development, diversity management, employee relations, employee voice, the employment relationship, equal opportunity, grievances, health and safety, new technology, promotion, redundancy, reward, sexual harassment, substance abuse and work–life balance.

Formulating HR policies

HR policies need to address the key HR issues that have been identified in the organization. They must also take account of external factors such as legislation. The maximum amount of consultation should take place with managers, employees and their representatives, and the policies should be communicated widely with guidelines on their application.

Implementing HR policies

The aim will be to implement policies fairly and consistently. Line managers have a key role in doing this.

Questions

1. What are HR policies?
2. Why have HR policies?
3. What values may be expressed in overall HR policy?
4. What are the areas in which specific HR policies may be required?
5. How should HR policies be formulated?

Reference

Purcell, J, Kinnie, K, Hutchinson, S, Rayton, B and Swart, J (2003) *Understanding the People and Performance Link: Unlocking the black box*, London, CIPD

41
HR procedures

KEY CONCEPTS AND TERMS

Capability
Discipline
Grievance
HR procedure
Redundancy

LEARNING OUTCOMES

On completing this chapter you should be able to define these key concepts. You should also:

- Be able to define what HR procedures are
- Know about the main HR procedures

What are HR procedures?

HR procedures set out the ways in which certain actions concerning people should be carried out by the management or individual managers. In effect, they constitute a formalized approach to dealing with specific matters of policy and practice.

They should be distinguished from HR policies, as described in Chapter 40, which serve as guidelines on people management practices but do not necessarily lay down precisely the steps that should be taken in particular situations. Procedures are more exacting. They state what must be done as well as spelling out how to do it.

It is desirable to have the key HR procedures written down in order to ensure that HR policies are applied consistently and in accordance with both legal requirements and ethical considerations. The existence of a written and well-publicized procedure ensures that everyone knows precisely what steps need to be taken when dealing with certain significant and possibly recurring employment issues.

The introduction or development of HR procedures should be carried out in consultation with employees and, where appropriate, their representatives. It is essential to brief everyone on how the procedures operate and they should be published either in an employee handbook or as a separate document. Line managers may need special training on how they should apply the procedures, and the HR department should provide guidance wherever necessary. HR will normally have the responsibility of ensuring that procedures are followed consistently.

Procedures are required to deal with capability and disciplinary issues, grievances and redundancy, as discussed below.

Capability procedure

Some organizations deal with matters of capability under a disciplinary procedure, but there is much to be said for dealing with poor performance issues separately, leaving the disciplinary procedure to be invoked for misconduct cases. An example of a capability procedure is given below.

Example: Capability procedure

Policy

The company aims are to ensure that performance expectations and standards are defined, performance is monitored and employees are given appropriate feedback, training and support to meet these standards.

Procedure

1 If a manager/team leader believes that an employee's performance is not up to standard, an informal discussion will be held with the employee to try to establish the reason and to agree the actions required to improve performance by the employee and/or the manager/team leader. If, however:
   - it is agreed that the established standards are not reasonably attainable, they will be reviewed;
   - it is established that the performance problems are related to the employee's personal life, the necessary counselling/support will be provided;
   - it is decided that the poor performance emanates from a change in the organization's standards, those standards will be explained to the employee and help will be offered to obtain conformity with the standards;
   - it is apparent that the poor performance constitutes misconduct, the disciplinary procedure will be invoked.

2 Should the employee show no (or insufficient) improvement over a defined period (weeks/months), a formal interview will be arranged with the employee (together with a representative if so desired). The aims of this interview will be to:
   - explain clearly the shortfall between the employee's performance and the required standard;
   - identify the cause(s) of the unsatisfactory performance and to determine what – if any – remedial treatment (training, retraining, support, etc) can be given;
   - obtain the employee's commitment to reaching that standard;
   - set a reasonable period for the employee to reach the standard and agree on a monitoring system during that period;
   - tell the employee what will happen if that standard is not met.

3 The outcome of this interview will be recorded in writing and a copy will be given to the employee.

4 At the end of the review period a further formal interview will be held, at which time:
   - if the required improvement has been made, the employee will be told of this and encouraged to maintain the improvement;
   - if some improvement has been made but the standard has not yet been met, the review period will be extended;
   - if there has been no discernible improvement and performance is still well below an acceptable standard this will be indicated to the employee and consideration will be given to whether there are alternative vacancies that the employee would be competent to fill; if there are, the employee will be given the option of accepting such a vacancy or being considered for dismissal;
   - if such vacancies are available, the employee will be given full details of them in writing before being required to make a decision;
   - in the absence of suitable alternative work, the employee will be informed and invited to give his or her views on this before the final decision is taken.

5 Employees may appeal against their dismissal. The appeal must be made within three working days.

Disciplinary procedure

A disciplinary procedure sets out the stages through which any disciplinary action should proceed. An example is given below.

Example: Disciplinary procedure (part 1)

Policy

It is the policy of the company that if disciplinary action has to be taken against employees it should:

- be undertaken only in cases where good reason and clear evidence exists;
- be appropriate to the nature of the offence that has been committed;
- be demonstrably fair and consistent with previous action in similar circumstances;
- take place only when employees are aware of the standards that are expected of them or the rules with which they are required to conform;
- allow employees the right to be represented by a representative or colleague during any formal proceedings;
- allow employees the right to know exactly what charges are being made against them and to respond to those charges;
- allow employees the right of appeal against any disciplinary action.

Disciplinary rules

The company is responsible for ensuring that up-to-date disciplinary rules are published and available to all employees. These will set out the circumstances in which an employee could be dismissed for gross misconduct.

Procedure

The procedure is carried out in the following stages:

1. *Informal warning.* A verbal or informal warning is given to the employee in the first instance or instances of minor offences. The warning is administered by the employee's immediate manager or team leader.
2. *Formal warning.* A written formal warning is given to the employee in the first instance of more serious offences or after repeated instances of minor offences. The warning is administered by the employee's immediate manager or team leader. It states the exact nature of the offence and indicates any future disciplinary action that will be taken against the employee if the offence is repeated within a specified time limit. A copy of the written warning is placed in the employee's personal record file but is destroyed 12 months after the date on which it was given, if the intervening service has been satisfactory. The employee is required to read and sign the formal warning and has the right to appeal to higher management if he or she thinks the warning is unjustified. The HR manager should be asked to advise on the text of the written warning.
3. *Further disciplinary action.* If, despite previous warnings, an employee still fails to reach the required standards in a reasonable period of time, it may become necessary to consider further disciplinary action. The action taken may be up to three days' suspension without pay, or dismissal. In either case the departmental manager should discuss the matter with the HR manager before taking action. Staff below the rank of departmental manager may only recommend disciplinary action to higher management, except when their manager is not present (for example, on night-shift), when they may suspend the employee for up to one day pending an inquiry on the following day. Disciplinary action should not be confirmed until the appeal procedure has been carried out.

Example: Disciplinary procedure (part 2)

Summary dismissal

An employee may be summarily dismissed (ie given instant dismissal without notice) only in the event of gross misconduct, as defined in company rules. Only departmental managers and above can recommend summary dismissal, and the action should not be finalized until the case has been discussed with the HR manager and the appeal procedure has been carried out. To enable this review to take place, employees should be suspended pending further investigation, which must take place within 24 hours.

Appeals

In all circumstances, an employee may appeal against suspension, dismissal with notice, or summary dismissal. The appeal is conducted by a member of management who is more senior than the manager who initially administered the disciplinary action. The HR manager should also be present at the hearing. If he or she wishes, the employee may be represented at the appeal by a fellow employee of his or her own choice. Appeal against summary dismissal or suspension should be heard immediately. Appeals against dismissal with notice should be held within two days. No disciplinary action that is subject to appeal is confirmed until the outcome of the appeal.

If an appeal against dismissal (but not suspension) is rejected at this level, the employee has the right to appeal to the chief executive. The head of HR and, if required, the employee's representative should be present at this appeal.

Grievance procedure

A grievance procedure spells out the policy on handling grievances and the approach to dealing with them. An example of a grievance procedure is given below.

Example: Grievance procedure

Policy

It is the policy of the company that employees should:

- be given a fair hearing by their immediate supervisor or manager concerning any grievances they may wish to raise;
- have the right to appeal to a more senior manager against a decision made by their immediate supervisor or manager;
- have the right to be accompanied by a fellow employee of their own choice when raising a grievance or appealing against a decision.

The aim of the procedure is to settle the grievance as nearly as possible to its point of origin.

Procedure

The main stages through which a grievance may be raised are as follows:

1. The employee raises the matter with his or her immediate manager or team leader and may be accompanied by a fellow employee of his or her own choice.
2. If the employee is not satisfied with the decision, the employee requests a meeting with a member of management who is more senior than the manager or team leader who initially heard the grievance. This meeting takes place within five working days of the request and is attended by the manager, a HR manager or business partner, the employee appealing against the decision, and, if desired, his or her representative. The HR manager records the results of the meeting in writing and issues copies to all concerned.
3. If the employee is still not satisfied with the decision, he or she may appeal to the appropriate director. The meeting to hear this appeal is held within five working days of the request and is attended by the director, the head of HR, the employee making the appeal and, if desired, his or her representative. The manager responsible for HR records the result of this meeting in writing and issues copies to all concerned. No further appeal can be made beyond this stage.

Redundancy procedure

A redundancy procedure aims to meet statutory, ethical and practical considerations when dealing with this painful process. An example of a procedure is given below.

Example: Redundancy procedure (part 1)

Definition

Redundancy is defined as the situation in which management decides that an employee or employees are surplus to requirements in a particular occupation and cannot be offered suitable alternative work.

Employees may be surplus to requirements because changes in the economic circumstances of the company mean that fewer employees are required, or because changes in methods of working mean that a job no longer exists in its previous form. An employee who is given notice because he or she is unsuitable or inefficient is not regarded as redundant and would be dealt with in accordance with the usual disciplinary or capability procedure.

Objectives

The objectives of the procedure are to ensure that:

- employees who may be affected by the discontinuance of their work are given fair and equitable treatment;
- the minimum disruption is caused to employees and the company;
- as far as possible, changes are effected with the understanding and agreement of the unions and employees concerned.

Principles

The principles governing the procedure are as follows:

- The trade unions concerned will be informed as soon as the possibility of redundancy is foreseen.
- Every attempt will be made to:
  - absorb redundancy by the natural wastage of employees;
  - find suitable alternative employment within the company for employees who might be affected, and provide training if this is necessary;
  - give individuals reasonable warning of pending redundancy in addition to the statutory period of notice.
- If alternative employment in the company is not available and more than one individual is affected, the factors to be taken into consideration in deciding who should be made redundant will be:
  - length of service with the company;
  - value to the company;
  - other things being equal, length of service should be the determining factor.
- The company will make every endeavour to help employees find alternative work if that is necessary.

Example: Redundancy procedure (part 2)

The procedure for dealing with employees who are surplus to requirements is set out below.

Review of employee requirements

Management will continuously keep under review possible future developments that might affect the number of employees required, and will prepare overall plans for dealing with possible redundancies.

Measures to avoid redundancies

If the likelihood of redundancy is foreseen, the company will inform the union(s), explaining the reasons, and in consultation with the union(s) will give consideration to taking appropriate measures to prevent redundancy.

Departmental managers will be warned by the management of future developments that might affect them so that detailed plans can be made for running down the numbers of employees by allowing natural wastage to take place without replacements, retraining, or transfers.

Departmental managers will be expected to keep under review the work situation in their departments so that contingency plans can be prepared and the HR manager is informed of any likely surpluses.

Consultation on redundancies

If all measures to avoid redundancy fail, the company will consult the union(s) at the earliest opportunity in order to reach agreement.

Selection of redundant employees

In the event of impending redundancy, the individuals who might be surplus to requirements should be selected by the departmental manager with the advice of the HR manager on the principles that should be adopted.

The HR manager should explore the possibilities of transferring affected employees to alternative work. The HR manager should inform management of proposed action (either redundancy or transfer) to obtain approval.

The union(s) will be informed of the numbers affected, but not of individual names.

The departmental manager and the HR manager will jointly interview the employees affected either to offer a transfer or, if a suitable alternative is not available, to inform them that they will be redundant. At this interview, full information should be available to give to the employee on the following, as appropriate:

- the reasons for being surplus;
- the alternative jobs that are available;
- the date when the employee will become surplus (that is, the period of notice);
- the entitlement to redundancy pay;
- the employee's right to appeal to an appropriate director;
- the help the company will provide.

Example: Redundancy procedure (part 3)

An appropriate director will hear any appeals with the HR manager.

The HR manager will ensure that all the required administrative arrangements are made.

If the union(s) have any points to raise about the selection of employees or the actions taken by the company, these should be discussed in the first place with the HR manager. If the results of these discussions are unsatisfactory, a meeting will be arranged with an appropriate director.

Alternative work within the company

If an employee is offered and accepts suitable alternative work within the company, it will take effect without a break from the previous employment and will be confirmed in writing. Employees will receive appropriate training and will be entitled to a four-week trial period to see if the work is suitable. This trial period may be extended by mutual agreement to provide additional training. During this period, employees are free to terminate their employment and, if they do, would be treated as if they had been made redundant on the day their old job ended. They would then receive any redundancy pay to which they are entitled.

Alternative employment

Employees for whom no suitable work is available in the company will be given reasonable opportunities to look for alternative employment.

Key learning points: HR procedures

- HR procedures set out the ways in which certain actions concerning people should be carried out by the management or individual managers. In effect, they constitute a formalized approach to dealing with specific matters of policy and practice.
- They should be distinguished from HR policies, which serve as guidelines on people management practices but do not necessarily lay down precisely the steps that should be taken in particular situations. Procedures are more exacting: they state what must be done as well as spelling out how to do it.
- It is desirable to have the key HR procedures written down to ensure that HR policies are applied consistently and in accordance with both legal requirements and ethical considerations.
- The existence of a written and well-publicized procedure ensures that everyone knows precisely what steps need to be taken when dealing with certain significant and possibly recurring employment issues.
- The introduction or development of HR procedures should be carried out in consultation with employees and, where appropriate, their representatives.
- It is essential to brief everyone on how the procedures operate, and they should be published either in an employee handbook or as a separate document.
- Line managers may need special training on how they should apply the procedures and the HR department should provide guidance wherever necessary. HR will normally have the responsibility of ensuring that procedures are followed consistently.
- Procedures are required to deal with capability and disciplinary issues, grievances and redundancy.

Questions

1 What are HR procedures?

2 What are the characteristics of a good procedure?

3 What would you expect a capability procedure to cover?

4 What would you expect a disciplinary procedure to cover?

5 What would you expect a grievance procedure to cover?

6 What would you expect a redundancy procedure to cover?

42 HR information systems

KEY CONCEPTS AND TERMS

Cloud computing
e-HR
Enterprise resource planning (ERP) system
Functionality
HR information system (HRIS)
Intranet
Self-service
Software as a service (SaaS)
Vanilla system

LEARNING OUTCOMES

On completing this chapter you should be able to define these key concepts. You should also know about:

- Reasons for using an HRIS
- Functions of an HRIS
- Features of an HRIS
- Introducing an HRIS

Introduction

An HR information system (HRIS) is a computer-based information system for managing the administration of HR processes and procedures. 'e-HRM' is an alternative term for the use of computer technology within the HR function. Parry and Tyson (2011: 335) defined an HRIS as: 'A way of implementing HR strategies, policies and practices in organizations through a conscious and directed support of and/or with the full use of web technology-based channels.' They listed five goals for e-HRM: efficiency, service delivery, strategic orientation, manager empowerment and standardization (ibid: 335).

Reasons for introducing an HRIS

The CIPD (2007) survey established that the top 10 reasons for introducing an HRIS were:

1. To improve quality of information available.
2. To reduce administrative burden on the HR department.
3. To improve speed at which information is available.
4. To improve flexibility of information to support business planning.

5 To improve services to employees.
6 To produce HR metrics.
7 To aid human capital reporting.
8 To improve productivity.
9 To reduce operational costs.
10 To manage people's working time more effectively.

The functions of an HRIS

The functions that an HRIS can perform (its 'functionality') are set out below. They cover almost every aspect of HRM.

The functions that an HRIS can perform

- absence recording and management;
- employee records;
- employee surveys;
- employee turnover analysis;
- e-learning;
- equal opportunity modelling;
- expenses;
- HR planning and forecasting;
- job evaluation;
- knowledge management;
- intranet;
- manage diversity;
- manager and employee self-service;
- metrics and human capital reporting;
- online recruitment;
- online performance management systems and 360-degree feedback;
- payroll administration;
- pay reviews;
- pensions and benefits administration.

The 2007 CIPD survey found that the 10 most popular uses to which respondents put their HRIS were:

1 Absence management.
2 Training and development.
3 Rewards.
4 Managing diversity.
5 Recruitment and selection.
6 Other (usually payroll).
7 Appraisal/performance management.
8 HR planning.
9 Knowledge management.
10 Expenses.

Features of an HRIS

The features of particular interest in an HRIS system are the use of software, integration with other IT systems in the organization, use of the intranet, and provisions for self-service.

Use of software

It is customary to buy software from an external supplier. There is a choice between buying a 'vanilla system' (ie an 'off-the-shelf' system without any upgrades) or customizing the supplier's system to meet specified business requirements. Extensive customization can make future upgrades problematic and expensive, so it is important to limit it to what is absolutely necessary.

If an external supplier is used the choice should be made as follows:

- research HR software market through trade exhibitions and publications;
- review HR processes and existing systems;
- produce a specification of system requirements;
- send an invitation to tender to several suppliers;
- invite suppliers to demonstrate their products;
- obtain references from existing customers, including site visits;
- analyse and score the product against the specification.

Alternative approaches

There are ways of providing IT services other than doing it yourself. It is possible to choose 'cloud computing' (the provision of services via an external network or across the internet). 'Software as a service' (SaaS) is an on-demand software delivery model in which users are charged for accessing and managing HR IT provision via a network.

Integration

Enterprise resource planning (ERP) systems integrate all data and processes of an organization into a unified system with the same database. HR systems are not frequently integrated to this extent although they often link payroll administration with other HR functions. Integration of the HR system with IT systems in the wider organization so that they can 'talk to one another' will enable the more effective management of HR data. However, many HR functions retain stand-alone systems, because they believe integration would compromise their own system, potential lack of confidentiality, and the cost and perceived risks involved.

Intranet

An intranet system is one where computer terminals are linked so that they can share information within an organization or within part of an organization. The scope of the information that can be shared across terminals can be limited to preserve confidentiality and this security can be enhanced by using passwords. HR intranet systems can be used for purposes such as updating personal details, applications for internal jobs online, requests for training, access to e-learning, administration of queries and communications.

Self-service

A human resource self-service system (HRSS) allows managers and employees access to information and the facility to interact with the system to input information or make choices of their own. This can operate through an HR portal (a site that functions as a point of access to information on the intranet), which may be specially designed to produce a brand image of the HR function. This is sometimes referred to as a 'business-to-employees' (B2E) portal.

For managers, self-service means that they can access information immediately. This might be HR metrics (human capital reporting measures) in such areas as absenteeism, personal details, performance management data, learning and development progress, and pay (as a basis for pay reviews). They can also input data on their staff. This facilitates the devolution of responsibility to line managers and reduces the administrative burden on HR.

Employees can also access information, input data about themselves, request training and apply for jobs online.

Introducing an HRIS

The steps required are illustrated in Figure 42.1.

The points to consider when introducing an HRIS are:

1. Make sure you really know what you need now and what you are likely to need in the near future so that you can give clear guidelines to the software provider.
2. Involve end-users and other stakeholders in the decision-making process.
3. It is useful to include a member of staff with IT expertise on the decision-making team, even if they're not HR professionals.
4. Go for something clear and straightforward that adds value. Don't go for all the 'bells and whistles': they may cost more, take more time to administer and you will probably end up not using them anyway.
5. Evaluate the range of systems on offer in terms of how they report, and how easy and quick it is to produce the types of report you need on a regular basis. Look at how reports are presented: can you download them into an Excel spreadsheet or into Access so that you can manipulate the data yourself? How easy is it to do mail merge with the information reported?
6. When buying an off-the-shelf system, don't customize it unless it's critical. Each time the system is upgraded, it's these modifications that may cause you difficulties. If you do have modifications, budget for these to be managed on an ongoing basis.

FIGURE 42.1 Introducing an HRIS

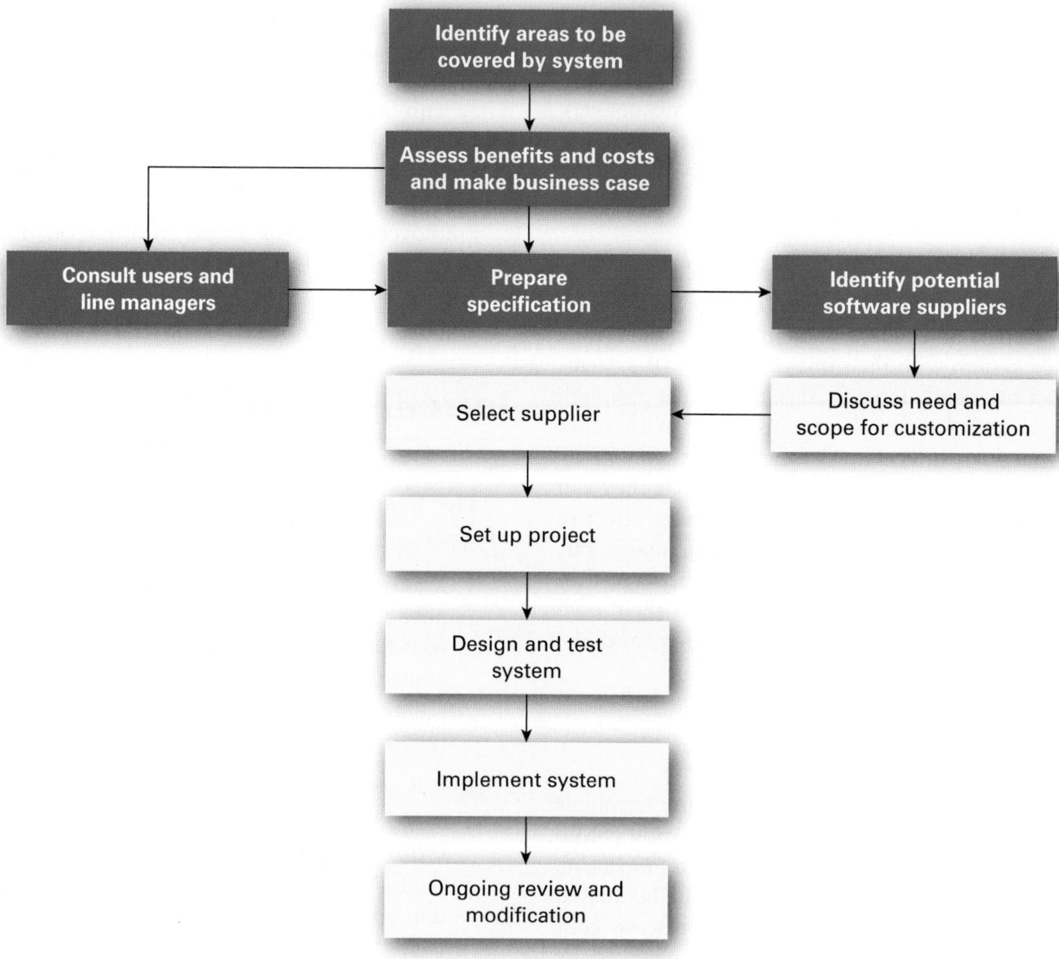

E-HRM achievements

Research conducted by Parry and Tyson (2011) in 10 case study organizations established that efficiency goals were achieved by most of the organizations. Service delivery improvements were generally achieved, supporting improved effectiveness of the HR function. The findings showed that a potential goal for e-HRM is to standardize operational procedures across an organization, but they noted that: 'The realization of improved efficiency and effectiveness is dependent on the design and implementation of the system, and increased effectiveness and involvement in delivering the business strategy may depend on appropriate redeployment and up-skilling of HR staff' (ibid: 352).

Below are some case studies, as reported by Parry and Tyson (2011: 341).

CASE STUDIES

AVISA

An Oracle HR system is used with extensive management self-service for performing salary changes, cost centre and allowance changes, processing leavers, updating and reporting absence, processing overtime payments and comparing performance ratings. Employee self-service is available to maintain personal details, look at payslips, request holidays and record absence. In addition, an Ask-Jeeves system to answer generic HR queries has been introduced.

BOC

BOC has used a SAP HR system since 1999 to hold HR data and allow managers to access this data via their desktop to record absence and enter bonus ratings salary review details. The system drove the payroll process. An e-recruitment system was introduced in 2003 with a recruitment database that sat centrally and was connected to a number of different career centres. The HR intranet has also recently been relaunched.

Marks & Spencer

The range of technological HRM tools include main HRIS plus payroll and personnel data, pensions and absence management systems and an HR portal for information on policies and practices.

Key learning points: HR information systems

Reasons for using an HRIS

The top five reasons are (CIPD, 2007):

- to improve quality of information available;
- to reduce administrative burden on the HR department;
- to improve speed at which information is available;
- to improve flexibility of information to support business planning;
- to improve services to employees.

Functions of an HRIS

Top five uses of an HRIS (CIPD, 2007):

- absence management;
- training and development;
- rewards;
- managing diversity;
- recruitment and selection.

Features of an HRIS

The features of particular interest in an HRIS system are:

- the use of software;
- integration with other IT systems in the organization;
- use of the intranet;
- provisions for self-service.

Introducing an HRIS

See Figure 42.1.

Questions

1 What are the main reasons for having a comprehensive human resource information system?

2 What are the five most popular applications of an HRIS?

3 What is self-service and why is it important?

References

CIPD (2007) *HR and Technology: Impact and advantages*, London, CIPD

Parry, E and Tyson, S (2011) Desired goals and actual outcomes of e-HRM, *Human Resource Management Journal*, 21 (3), pp 335–54

43 Employment law

KEY CONCEPTS AND TERMS

Advisory, Conciliation and Arbitration Service (ACAS)
Constructive dismissal
Discrimination law
Employment regulation
Employment tribunal
Health and safety executive
Maternity pay and leave
Paternity pay and leave
Personal injury claim
National Minimum Wage
Working Time Regulations
Wrongful dismissal
Unfair dismissal

LEARNING OUTCOMES

On completing this chapter you should be able to define these key concepts. You should also know about:

- The objectives of employment law
- The major ways in which the law protects workers
- The ways that employment law is enforced
- The impact of employment law on HRM practice

Introduction

The employment relationship is subject to a great deal of regulation in all industrialized counties and is increasingly a feature of HRM practice in developing economies too. While the details and extent of regulatory protection, as well as the enforcement mechanisms vary from country to country, the aims of employment legislation are remarkably similar (Ashiagbor 2005; Slattery and Broadbent 2013). It is also the case that in all countries the trend in recent years has been towards greater levels of employment regulation, not least due to the actions of supranational bodies such as the International Labour Organization (ILO) and the European Union (EU), which have persistently promoted higher standards of employment practice underpinned by law.

For employers in the UK the adjustment required by the introduction of extensive employment law has often been problematic as the UK's labour market was historically one of the least regulated in the world. There thus remains a strong tendency for employers and their representatives to resist the introduction of new regulation and to campaign for a reduction in the existing 'regulatory burden' on the grounds that it both deters organizations from taking on new staff, while also making the UK economy as a whole less globally competitive than it would otherwise be. Despite these misgivings, it is clear that employment law is here to stay and that it makes good business sense to comply with its requirements. Most employers have to face employment tribunal claims from time to time and most HR professionals have to deal with their consequences on a fairly regular basis.

The purpose of employment law

There has never been any grand strategy behind the construction of modern employment law. Instead it has been built up steadily over 40 years, step by step, new laws being introduced in response to political pressure of one kind or another, and only rarely being repealed. Sometimes the impetus for new regulation has come from European institutions, such as the transfer of undertakings regulations that protect employees' terms and conditions when their organizations are acquired by others, outsourced or merged. On other occasions governments have used employment law to increase their popularity and try to ensure re-election. A good example is the plan by the UK's current coalition government to introduce substantially improved maternity and paternity rights in April 2015 just ahead of a planned general election. New employment law can be introduced in response to events (eg stricter laws on industrial action in the 1980s following major strikes) or campaigns by trade unions and other groups (eg the National Minimum Wage and disability discrimination laws).

Despite this apparent lack of coherence in the development of employment law, it is nonetheless possible to identify a number of key aims that governments hope to achieve by regulating the labour market. In 2013 the UK government issued a progress report on its programme of employment regulation in which three distinct objectives were set out (DBIS 2013a). Here, ministers stated that they sought to create a labour market that was:

- flexible – encouraging job creation and making it easy for people to stay in work and find work;
- effective – enabling employers to manage staff productivity;
- fair – employers competing on a level playing field and workers benefiting from core employment protections.

The idea of a level playing field is particularly important in the context of European Union employment regulation. The aim here is to help ensure that defined minimum standards are observed across all member states so that no one country is able to undercut its labour costs in order to steal an unfair competitive march on the others.

In practice most employment law exists to protect employees from unjust exploitation or unfair treatment by their employers. It is necessary because, for the vast majority of workers, the employment relationship is very unequal in terms of the power that each side is able to exercise over the other. Employers are vastly more powerful, making it relatively easy for them to abuse that power by treating their employees poorly, by dismissing them or discriminating against them for no good reason, underpaying and overworking them, or causing them to risk their heath, safety and welfare while at work. In the early and middle years of the 20th century, trade unions tended to offer employees a much greater level of protection than they are now able to, and so to a considerable extent the state has had to step in to provide protection of the kind that strong unions with high levels of membership once were able to provide.

There are, however, two major further reasons behind employment regulation in today's economic context. First, governments have sought to use employment law to promote good practice in the employment relationship. Ministers are always mindful of the presence of skill shortages and of the presence in our labour market of large numbers of people (typically 20 per cent) who are economically inactive despite being of working age. One aim is to encourage people off welfare and into work, another is to encourage people who could work but who choose not to (eg early retirees) to put their skills at the disposal of the economy. Governments have also wanted to make their countries an attractive destination to highly skilled migrants from overseas who might otherwise choose to settle elsewhere. Ensuring that employers operate fairly and promoting partnership approaches both serve to help meet these objectives. Second, governments are keen to promote flexibility and competition in the labour market. They want to ensure that employees are free to leave their employment and join another organization easily and that they are not prevented from working because of domestic commitments. They also want to ensure that when people persistently perform their jobs poorly, or when their jobs are genuinely redundant, employers are able to terminate their contracts swiftly and cheaply. Above all, ministers want to avoid a situation in which employers are deterred from creating new jobs due to fear of employment legislation. There is thus always a need to balance legitimate protection of employees' rights with the need of employers to hire and fire with relative ease.

Employment law also incorporates the regulation of trade unions. And here too the aim is to achieve a balance between the need to protect the right of all workers to form and join trade unions and the need to ensure that trade unions do not become so powerful as to threaten the economic interests of the majority of people. Finding this balance has always been difficult and controversial, and the position varies considerably from country to country. In the UK, for example, the law makes it very difficult indeed for an employer to dismiss someone for a trade union reason or to prevent a union from organizing a strike that its members have voted for. On the other hand, the way that unions are governed and the extent to which they can gain power over an employer are limited very effectively by the law.

How are these objectives achieved?

Over many decades, but particularly in more recent years, a large body of employment regulation has been built up in order to achieve the purposes set out above. The precise mechanisms vary a great deal internationally, but there is now considerable convergence across Europe, and we are increasingly seeing examples of similar types of regulation being established in newly industrialized countries. China, for example, introduced three major pieces of new employment regulation in 2008, which aim both to promote employment and protect the rights of employees (Lee Cooke 2012: 156–79). Employment law in the UK is in many respects typical in terms of its scope and impact. From an employer perspective our regulation is rather less restrictive than that of some jurisdictions (eg France and the Netherlands), but more restrictive than that of others (eg the United States and Australia). In the UK the objectives of employment regulation are largely met through several distinct bodies of well-established legislation, a number of which have a European origin. The most significant are discrimination law, dismissal law, health and safety law, hours and wages regulations, family-friendly employment law and whistle-blowing law. These are outlined below.

Discrimination law

The underpinning principle here is that it is unlawful to cause a detriment to a worker, a job applicant or someone an organization has employed in the past. The term 'detriment' is widely defined to include financial loss, loss of opportunity or any significant injury to someone's dignity or feelings. Much of the relevant law has now been consolidated and, to an extent, harmonized in the Equality Act 2010, which extends discrimination rights to people who have certain 'protected characteristics'. These include, sex, sexual orientation, race, disability, religion or belief, pregnancy, marital status and age. There are four headings under which an employer's actions can be challenged in court:

- direct discrimination (eg failing to promote a woman because she is a woman);
- indirect discrimination (eg requiring a devout employee to work on a holy day);
- victimization (eg refusing to give a reference to a former employee who brought a race discrimination claim against the organization);
- harassment (eg teasing someone about their sexual orientation).

The defences available to employers are limited. Direct discrimination and victimization on most grounds are almost always unlawful, although in the cases of discrimination on grounds of disability and age the former can be defended where there is a good, genuine business reason. Direct discrimination is also lawful when the nature of a job requires that it is reserved for members of one sex (eg acting and modelling jobs) or a particular race (eg waiters in ethnic restaurants) or religion (eg clerical roles). Indirect discrimination occurs when an organization has a rule or policy in place that has the effect of causing a disadvantage to one group or another, even though this may be entirely unintentional. This can be defended when the rule can be shown to be 'a proportionate means of achieving a legitimate aim', in other words, an objective business need. Harassment can be defended when an incident occurs outside work or when an employer can show that it: 1) acted swiftly and appropriately when it received a complaint; 2) had taken all reasonable steps to prevent such an incident from occurring.

Other statutes give a measure of protection from discrimination to ex-offenders, whistle-blowers, fixed-term employees, part-time workers, agency workers, trade union members and people who do not wish to join a trade union. But in each case the law operates rather differently than is the case for the protected characteristics covered by the Equality Act.

A further significant part of the Equality Act requires that men and women working for the same employer (or associated employers) are paid equally for doing the same job, jobs that have been graded at the same level following a job evaluation exercise and jobs that are dissimilar but nonetheless of equal value to the employer.

In the UK there are only very limited numbers of situations in which positive discrimination or affirmative action is permitted. In this respect our law varies from that of many jurisdictions in which employers are obliged to take positive steps to improve the position of disadvantaged groups. It is common in many EU countries, for example, for companies to be required to appoint a minimum number of women to senior board positions. Elsewhere in the world quota systems apply for the employment of different racial or ethnic groups in order to assure fairness, particularly in the public sector. In practice, this means that some jobs are reserved for members of a particular racial origin or caste (Klarsfeld *et al* 2012).

Dismissal law

Former employees who have completed more than two years' service (one year if employed prior to April 2012) are entitled to seek compensation or reinstatement when they have been unfairly dismissed. This means that they have either been sacked for an unfair reason (eg pregnancy, refusal to work in unsafe conditions) or for a lawful reason (eg misconduct, incapability, redundancy) but in an unreasonable manner. In practice, the large majority of cases concern the manner in which someone has been dismissed, and here the law is very helpful from an employer's point of view. The test that is used to judge 'reasonableness' is known as 'the band of reasonable responses test'. When applying this, a tribunal is required to refrain from judging the matter with reference to what the judge would have done in similar circumstances, or even from making a general judgement as to what most people would consider 'reasonable'. Instead the requirement is to ask the question: could the employer's actions in dismissing the employee be said to have been reasonable?

This means that dismissals that 90 per cent of people would consider to have been unreasonable can nonetheless be found to have been reasonable in law, simply because a case for their reasonableness can be put. In practice, this means that many dismissals fall into the 'harsh but fair' category.

That said, in order to be lawful it is essential that any dismissal is managed in accordance with a fair procedure. In a case of poor work performance this means that an employee must be invited to a formal meeting, given a formal warning in writing, allowed an opportunity to appeal, given a reasonable opportunity to improve and, only then, dismissed following a further formal meeting with a right to appeal. Formal warnings are also required in cases of long-term ill-health (where disability discrimination law can also be highly relevant) and relatively minor acts of misconduct. Only when an employee is guilty of gross misconduct such as stealing, fighting or serious insubordination, is an employer entitled to dismiss summarily without notice. Here too, though, a fair procedure must always be followed, the employee being given every opportunity to defend themselves and to appeal the dismissal. A further requirement is that employees facing hearings at which they may be dismissed must always be allowed to be accompanied by a work colleague and represented by a trade union official.

Aside from unfair dismissal, UK law provides that employees can be wrongfully dismissed or constructively dismissed. Wrongful dismissals occur when the manner of a dismissal breaches the contract of employment. It occurs most commonly when an employee's contract stipulates a notice period that is not then observed when notice is given. So if someone with the right to eight weeks' notice is dismissed with one week's notice, they would be able to bring a claim for compensation.

Constructive dismissals are actually resignations. The law in this area was introduced alongside unfair dismissal law in 1971 in order to prevent employers from circumventing the new rights by treating their employees so badly that they resigned without needing to be dismissed. The test that is now used is contractual. This means that an employee resigns in response to (and soon after) their employer has breached their contract. In such circumstances the tribunals treat the incident as if it were a dismissal and order that appropriate compensation is paid. Importantly, relevant breaches of contract can involve either express or implied terms. Express terms are those that the parties agree at the time they first form their relationship. So, for example, if an employer was to cut someone's contractual pay and the employee was to resign in protest, that would generally constitute a constructive dismissal. Implied terms are many and varied, but are deemed to be present in every contract. The most significant is the 'duty to maintain a relationship of mutual trust and confidence'. If that is broken by an employer, as happens for example in cases of serious bullying at work, the employee is entitled to resign and claim constructive dismissal.

Health and safety law

UK health and safety law can be divided into two very distinct parts. On the one hand, we have the *criminal law* that is enforced by health and safety inspectors employed by local authorities and, at national level, by the Health and Safety Executive (HSE). On the other hand, we have *personal injury law* under which a worker who suffers an injury at work or falls ill as a result of their work can sue their employer for damages.

Health and safety inspectors carry out routine inspections of employers' premises without warning, following which they can issue improvement notices requiring that changes are made to operations, or prohibition notices that prevent the employer from using a piece of equipment or operating a system until recommended changes have been made. In either case, a failure to make the required changes can result in a criminal prosecution. Such prosecutions are also brought when an employer's negligence or recklessness leads either to a death or a serious injury. In the most serious cases, charges of corporate manslaughter can be brought against an organization.

Most personal injury claims also involve demonstrating that an employer or a fellow employee has acted negligently. Importantly, the doctrine of vicarious liability applies here, meaning that employers are deemed to be legally responsible for the actions of their employees while at work. So if an accident is caused as result of a fellow employee's negligence, the injured person brings the case against the employer rather than the colleague whose fault the accident was. There are a number of defences that employers can deploy when faced with personal injury claims. The most common involves satisfying the court that the accident 'was not reasonably foreseeable'. In practice, this requires an employer to have carried out formal risk assessments and to have recorded these. Managers then need to show that the injury was sustained in spite of the fact that the risks were low, that full training had been provided and that safe systems of work were always observed.

In recent years many claims of this kind have related to mental breakdowns brought about through stressful work situations. These are not at all easy for workers to win, because unless they have suffered two breakdowns, the second after returning to work, it is difficult to show that an excessive workload was the main trigger for the illness.

Hours and wages

A variety of laws regulate working time and the amount of money that workers should be paid. The most important statute covering hours of work is the Working Time Regulations 1998. This is European law, which has always been controversial in the UK where we have a tradition of working long hours and claiming overtime payments in return. The key right here is not to be required to work in excess of 48 hours per week. However, in practice, many employees continue to do so. This is partly because actually the law only limits working time to 48 hours averaged over 17 weeks. So employers can lawfully require their staff to work many more hours in particularly busy weeks, provided that on average over any 17-week period the 48-hour rule is observed. In the UK there is also an opt-out system in place, under which employees can remove themselves from the right not to work more than 48 hours per week. This is common because employers can lawfully require new starters to sign opt-out agreements as a condition of being offered a job. There is also a right to opt back in to the regulations without suffering any detriment, but this is not widely known. The Working Time Regulations also provide that minimum rest breaks are provided during a day's work and between shifts. Moreover, they give all workers the right to take 28 days paid holiday per year (pro rata for part-timers), comprising eight bank holidays and 20 further days statutory annual leave.

The National Minimum Wage (NMW) regulations also date from 1998. These require that all workers are paid a minimum amount for every hour that they work, rates being set by the government each year after consulting with the Low Pay Commission. From October 2013 the full adult rate that applies to the vast majority of people is £6.31 per hour. This will apply until October 2014 when the rate will rise again. In addition there is a lower rate for younger workers and workers in training (£5.03 in 2013–14), a youth rate for 16- and 17-year-olds (£3.72) and an apprentice rate (£2.68). Failure to pay the NMW is not only a civil offence, which can result in any back pay that is owed being paid to a claimant, but also a criminal offence that can result in large fines being paid as well.

Another significant area of employment law concerns the situations in which an employer can and cannot make deductions from a worker's pay packet. These are fairly limited, in most cases requiring prior consent on the part of an employee (eg trade union dues), authorization via statute (eg tax) or a court order (eg in order to pay a fine). Importantly, this means that as a rule employers cannot deduct wages as part of a disciplinary process. If suspended from work for any reason an employee must continue to be paid while a matter is investigated. Moreover, if found to have committed an act of misconduct, the employer cannot lawfully fine a worker by way of a punishment.

Family-friendly employment law

In recent years the biggest changes in regulations have been made in the area of family-friendly employment rights. Every two or three years since the mid-1990s new rights have been introduced, while existing rights have been extended. This step-by-step approach has disguised the radical improvement in employment rights that has occurred over time. Moreover, further major extensions of rights are planned for April 2014 and April 2015. The major family-friendly rights that applied in 2013 for most employees were as follows:

- up to one year of maternity or adoptive leave;
- nine months of maternity or adoptive pay;
- the right to paid time off to attend ante-natal appointments;
- two weeks' statutory paternity leave;
- additional paternity leave of up to 32 weeks once a new mother has returned to work;
- the right to time off to deal with family emergencies;
- 18 weeks' unpaid parental leave during the first five years of a child's life;
- the right to request a change of contract in order to work more flexibly.

Until April 2014 this last right only applies to employees with children. After April 2014 all employees with six months' service can request flexible working. Employers can only lawfully turn down a request when one of eight straightforward business reasons apply, and must in any event handle requests reasonably.

After April 2015 it is planned that the whole existing maternity/paternity leave regime will be reformed so as to make it far more flexible. Both parents will be able to take long periods of paid leave and will be able to do so concurrently in the months immediately following the birth or adoption of a child.

Whistle-blowing law

The Public Interest Disclosure Act 1998 protects employees who make a 'protected disclosure' from being treated badly or being dismissed. The situations covered include criminal offences, risks to health and safety, failure to comply with a legal obligation, a miscarriage of justice and environmental damage.

The Enterprise and Regulatory Reform Act 2013 introduced a public interest test. Employees will have legal protection only if they can show that they 'reasonably believe' that the disclosure they have made is in 'the public interest'. Disclosures made before the date when this provision comes into force (25 June 2013) need only to have been made 'in good faith'.

A disclosure outside the organization must usually be made to an appropriate body. For example, disclosing a health and safety issue to the Health and Safety Executive is likely to be protected, but justified disclosures to the media may be protected in certain cases. The employment tribunal claim form asks employees if they agree for the matters raised in their claim to be referred to the appropriate regulatory body.

Dismissing employees for whistle-blowing who can show that they have acted in the public interest is deemed to be automatic unfair dismissal. There is no qualified period of service required and no cap on compensation.

How is employment law enforced?

It is in the area of enforcement and remedies that employment law varies most from country to country (Slattery and Broadbent 2013). In many countries, including Australia, Germany, India and Japan, specialized employment tribunals are charged with deciding cases that are brought by aggrieved employees or ex-employees who believe that an employer has treated them in an unlawful manner. Sometimes these institutions take an arbitration approach, seeking to promote a settlement to the dispute between the parties. In other jurisdictions tribunals are more clearly part of a court system, simply deciding cases in favour of one party or the other after hearing evidence. Elsewhere, notably in the United States, cases are heard by standard civil courts with no specialist brief in the field of employment. A rather different type of system operates in countries where the criminal law plays a much greater role in employment matters. Here local labour officials or inspectors have a central place in the administration of the law. In some jurisdictions, such as the Netherlands, employers are obliged to seek their approval before dismissing staff. Elsewhere, officials bring criminal prosecutions when they have evidence that an employer has acted unlawfully. In France, for example, even when an employer settles a discrimination claim with an employee, it can still find itself having to defend its actions in the criminal courts.

In the UK the inspectorate model is used in the enforcement of health and safety law, in matters concerning the illegal employment of overseas migrants and, to an extent, in the enforcement of the National Minimum Wage. But, in most areas of employment law, criminal sanctions play no role. The onus is overwhelmingly on aggrieved employees and, more commonly, former employees to bring their cases before the civil courts. When a complaint relates to the alleged breach of an employment statute such as unfair dismissal or unlawful discrimination, claimants bring their cases before their local Employment Tribunal. Here the case will either be heard by an Employment Judge sitting alone, or sometimes by a panel of three in which the judge is assisted by two lay members who have industrial experience. In most cases the burden of proof lies with the claimant (ie the person bringing the case), but on some questions of law it can reverse so that the respondent (ie the employer) must satisfy the tribunal that it did not act unlawfully as is alleged. Employment tribunals then decide cases 'on the balance of probabilities', having weighed the evidence that is presented to them by each party or its representatives.

Employment tribunals operate in a relatively informal way. Anyone can carry out the duty of representing a party, the role being in no way restricted to professional lawyers. Sometimes claimants represent themselves or are represented by a family member or a friend. Trade union officials increasingly carry out this kind of work too. Respondents are more likely to employ lawyers to represent them, but sometimes represent themselves too. As a result, the Employment Tribunal provides a relatively swift and low-cost forum in which a case can be decided. Appeals on questions of law can be taken to the Employment Appeals Tribunal and, subsequently, on to the Court of Appeal, Supreme Court and, if appropriate, the European Court of Justice. But appealing a case is usually more costly.

Employment tribunals do not hear cases that relate to breaches of contract or alleged committing of torts such as negligence. So people wanting to pursue wrongful dismissal cases or personal injury claims must instead take their case to the County Court or High Court. In practice this requires them to hire lawyers and to be represented by a barrister. Costs are awarded against losing parties too, making this a riskier and potentially expensive route to take.

In practice, awards against losing respondents are rarely very high. Ahead of a case, solicitors representing claimants often set out a schedule of losses, which is a good deal inflated and does not realistically represent the actual sum that would be won following a successful hearing in court. This is done in a bid to frighten unwary employers into settling the case for a higher sum than they need to in order to avoid the hassle of defending the case in court. The truth, according to the annual statistics published by the Employment Tribunal Service is that the sums awarded are typically much lower than claimants might in theory hope to gain (see Table 43.1).

TABLE 43.1 Median awards made in different types of employment tribunal case 2011–12

Unfair dismissal	£4,560
Race discrimination	£5,256
Sex discrimination	£6,746
Disability discrimination	£8,928
Religious discrimination	£4,267
Sexual orientation discrimination	£13,505
Age discrimination	£6,065

SOURCE: ETS Annual Report 2012

HRM and employment law

The extent to which employment law influences the way that people are managed in organizations varies considerably. Larger corporations with high-profile reputations to defend have a tendency to settle claims ahead of any tribunal hearing in order to avoid negative publicity in the media. The estimated costs associated with defending a claim also typically dwarf the size of the award that the claimant can hope to win. So rather than tie up days of management time defending a case, claimants are simply paid off on condition that they sign a settlement agreement that precludes them from publicizing the case (CBI 2012: 29). The advantage of such a policy is that it effectively enables managers to run their organizations without taking too much notice of the expectations of employment law. The disadvantage, of course, is that it encourages people whose claims are not strong in law to bring cases in any event, in the hope of securing a payout.

A very different approach is typically taken in the public and third sectors where considerable efforts are made to comply with employment legislation. Here, HR departments often gain a reputation for being overcautious in the way that they handle employee grievances, so great is their wish to avoid having to defend a case in the Employment Tribunal. This means that, in practice, the vast majority of tribunal hearings involve smaller private sector enterprises that neither have the resources available to pay people off as a matter of routine, nor to ensure that they are complying with the requirements of the law. Managers in smaller enterprises also tend to prefer an informal management style, which can make legal challenges more likely (DBIS 2013b).

Published evidence suggests that, in practice, employment law has a major impact on the way that HR managers approach their work. As long ago as 2002, when the volume of employment legislation was a good deal less than it is now, the Chartered Institute of Personnel and Development established that two-thirds of HR specialists were spending in excess of 20 per cent of their time 'dealing with employment law issues', while one-quarter reported that over 40 per cent of their working days were being spent in this way (CIPD 2002). A further CIPD survey of HR professionals, carried out five years later, reported that 40 per cent of respondents rated 'securing compliance with employment regulations' as one of their top five objectives, while 90 per cent saw employment regulation as likely to become more important for their organizations in the future (CIPD 2007). These findings are unsurprising when it is considered that around half a million people are dismissed for one reason or another in the UK each year (DBIS 2013b: 23) and that at least one in seven of those who are entitled to do so subsequently challenge their dismissals in the tribunal (Knight and Latreille, 2000). All in all, between 150,000 and 240,000 people lodge employment tribunal claims each year (ETS 2012), meaning that around half of all larger employers face the prospect of having to defend at least one claim every year (CBI 2012: 28).

Surveys of employer opinion regularly report that managers find the volume of employment regulation that they have to comply with to be burdensome, but it is not generally the principles that causes them to complain. The aims of the law are generally supported by employers. What they dislike is its complexity and the time that they are obliged to devote to keeping up with changes (CIPD 2005). As a result, particularly in the case of smaller firms, managers have a strong tendency to worry that they may be found not to be complying with all the expectations of the law. It is fear of the tribunal, as much as their personal experience, that causes them to consider employment law to be a burden (DBIS 2013b).

In fact, the chances are slim that any job applicant, employee or former employee will win a claim against an employer. Employers end up winning four out of five of the claims that are heard in the UK employment tribunals, while over 30 per cent of those that are lodged are withdrawn without a settlement before the case ever comes to court. Avoiding tribunal claims that have any serious prospect of winning is thus not at all difficult. It is really just a question of adhering to the major principles of the law, such as paying staff the National Minimum Wage and avoiding unlawful discrimination, while also taking care to handle dismissals in a procedurally fair manner. Moreover, in 90 per cent of situations that arise in the workplace, there is no need for managers to pay for legal advice. Free guidance is available on numerous websites, including the government's own employment webpages (**www.gov.uk/browse/employing-people**) and those provided by the Advisory, Conciliation and Arbitration Service (ACAS) (**www.acas.org.uk/index.aspx?articleid=1339**). ACAS also provide a free, confidential telephone helpline staffed by advisors who give excellent advice about all employment law issues.

CASE STUDIES

Jenkins v Legoland Windsor Park Ltd (2003)

Mr Jenkins was employed at the Legoland theme park in Windsor Great Park as an 'attractions team leader'. Due to a motorbike accident he had suffered at the age of 16, Mr Jenkins' left arm was very seriously injured. This required him to use a sling at all times. In March 2001 the company held a ceremony at which long service awards were given to all employees who had completed over three years' service. Mr Jenkins was one of the 58 employees who received awards at this ceremony. Each award took the form of a human model made out of Lego. Most of the employees received models that related directly in some way to their work. Cafe staff, for example, were given models of people eating pizzas or drinking coffee, parking attendants got models of people holding traffic cones, and managers got models holding clipboards. Mr Jenkins, however, was presented with a model of a man with his right arm in a sling. The day after the ceremony Mr Jenkins was absent and never returned to work. He was diagnosed by a consultant psychologist as 'suffering from a depressive episode triggered by an insensitive experience at his place of work'. He then brought a disability discrimination claim to the employment tribunal. He argued that he had suffered a detriment as he had been singled out at a presentation ceremony and identified by a wrongly characterized disability. Mr Jenkins won his case at the Employment Appeals Tribunal (EAT) after having lost at the tribunal. It was found that he had been subjected to a detriment for a reason related to his disability. The employer had not been unable to objectively justify its actions. Mr Jenkins won damages of over £30,000 to compensate him for financial losses and injury to feelings.

West Bromwich Building Society Ltd v Townsend (1983)

A building society branch in Wolverhampton was subjected to a routine health and safety inspection by a local authority environmental health officer called Mr Townsend. Following his inspection, Mr Townsend took the decision to use the branch as a test case and to issue an improvement notice requiring the building society to install 'anti-bandit screens' to protect staff from the possibility of a violent robbery. The notice stated that it was Mr Townsend's opinion that the employer was contravening the Health and Safety at Work Act (HSWA) 1974 by not providing such screens:

> The reasons for my said opinion are that staff engaged in the handling of money and in general office duties in the premises are not protected as far as is reasonably practicable from the risk of attack or personal injury from persons frequenting the area of the premises normally open to the general public and I hereby require you to remedy the said contraventions or, as the case may be, the matter occasioning them by September 22nd 1982, in the manner stated in the schedule which forms part of this notice.

The employer appealed against the improvement notice in the employment tribunal. In doing so it made the following points:

1 The building society had considered how it could best protect its employees and included such considerations in risk assessments that were regularly kept under review.

2 The cost of installing protective screens in all its 86 branches would be over £500,000, yet the amount of cash kept on any one of its premises at any one time was only £3,500 maximum.

3 The improvement notice merely stated that it was Mr Townsend's opinion that the building society was in contravention of the HSWA 1974. No particulars were given about which clause in the Act was being contravened and no justification given to back up the general opinion.

4 The improvement notice was not really concerned with bringing about necessary improvements in health and safety at the particular branch concerned. Its real aim was to create a precedent that would apply to all building society branches across the whole country.

The appeal was successful. The tribunal considered that the costs associated with complying with the order would be disproportionate given the level of risk from a health and safety point of view.

Proctor v British Gypsum Ltd (1992)

Mr Proctor was employed as a foreman by the British Gypsum company. He was summarily dismissed from this job after one of his subordinates claimed to have been assaulted by him. In his defence, Mr Proctor presented evidence to show: 1) that he had been provoked; 2) that in the past, employees had not been dismissed for rather more serious incidents of fighting and assault. He therefore claimed that the employer had acted unreasonably in summarily dismissing him – on grounds of inconsistency. Moreover, his previous record of conduct had been impeccable. The employer claimed that the other incidents had occurred some time previously and that their policy on such matters had toughened in the years since. They also claimed that Mr Proctor's position as a foreman made his case materially different. Mr Proctor lost his case. The EAT took the opportunity to set out the circumstances in which consistency/inconsistency is significant. They said that time was significant as no employer could be expected to act consistently with cases that were some years old – management had the right to tighten up in the way that British Gypsum had. The main purpose of the inconsistency rule was to stop victimization – employees who were being picked on and, really, dismissed for other reasons (eg not getting on with their boss).

Each case had to be looked at on its merits: the employers had acted reasonably in expecting higher standards from this man, given his position.

Key learning points: Employment law

The purpose of employment law

The major purpose of employment law is to deter employers from treating their employees unfairly or from exploiting them unjustly. However, governments also use employment regulation to help make work more attractive to people and to promote flexibility in the labour market.

How are these objectives achieved?

In most jurisdictions employment laws give employees a strong measure of protection from unfair discrimination and unfair dismissal. Regulation also helps to ensure that high levels of health and safety practice are observed and that workers are paid reasonably and are not overworked. Family-friendly employment law helps people to achieve an effective work–life balance.

Enforcing employment law

Enforcement is mainly something employees do for themselves by bringing claims to the Employment Tribunal. However, in the field of health and safety, the government employs inspectors to carry out the main enforcement duties.

Employment law and HRM

Published evidence demonstrates that employment law can have a major impact on the way that employers carry out HRM activities. It consumes a great deal of HR professionals' time and is high on their agendas. A variety of good sources of free advice about the expectations of employment law are available to managers.

Questions

1. Why has the volume of employment law grown so much recently?
2. Why does the European Union introduce employment regulation?
3. How does employment law promote flexibility?
4. What are protected characteristics?
5. What is the difference between direct discrimination and indirect discrimination?
6. When is a dismissal unfair in law?
7. What is wrongful dismissal?
8. What is constructive dismissal?
9. What is a personal injury claim?
10. How much is the National Minimum Wage?
11. How much paid holiday are full time workers entitled to?
12. How much paid maternity leave can a mother take from her job?
13. What is an Employment Tribunal?
14. Why do employers settle tribunal claims before a hearing?
15. Where can employers source free advice on employment law issues?

References

Ashiagbor, D (2005) *The European Employment Strategy: Labour market regulation and new governance*, Oxford, Oxford University Press

CBI (2012) *Facing the Future*, Confederation of British Industry

CIPD (2002) *Employment Law: Survey report*, London, Chartered Institute of Personnel and Development

CIPD (2005) *Employment and the Law: Burden or benefit?*, London, Chartered Institute of Personnel and Development

CIPD (2007) *The Changing HR Function: A survey report*, London, Chartered Institute of Personnel and Development

DBIS (2013a) *Employment Law 2013: Progress on reform*, London, Department for Business, Innovation and Skills

DBIS (2013b) *Employment Regulation: Employer perceptions and the impact of employment regulation*, London, Department for Business, Innovation and Skills

ETS (2012) *Annual Report and Statistics*, London, Employment Tribunals Service

Klarsfeld, A, Combs, G M, Susaeta, L and Belizon, M (2012) International perspectives on diversity and equal treatment policies and practices, in (eds) C Brewster and W Mayrhofer, *Handbook of Research on Comparative Human Resource Management*, Cheltenham, Edward Elgar

Knight, K G and Latreille, P L (2000) Discipline, dismissals and complaints to employment tribunals, *British Journal of Industrial Relations*, 38 (4), p 533

Lee Cooke, F (2012) *Human Resource Management in China: New trends and practices*, London, Routledge

Slattery, E and Broadbent, J (2013) *The International Comparative Legal Guide to Employment and Labour Law*, 3rd edn, London, Global Legal Group

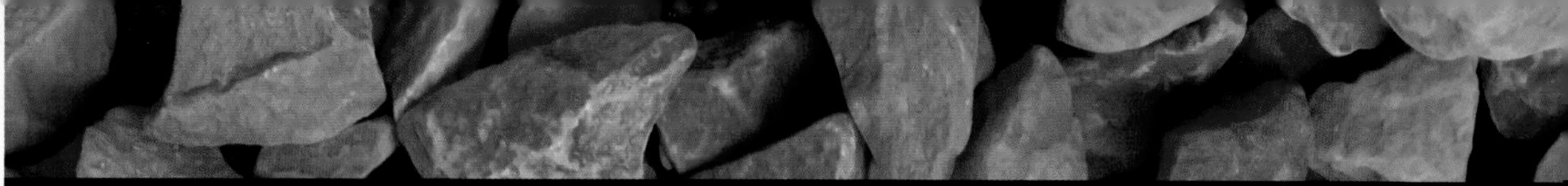

PART XI

HR skills

PART XI CONTENTS

Introduction

It can be argued that fully fledged HR professionals have to be able to deploy a range of skills supported by knowledge that is wider than that required by any other professional working in organizations. Even if this claim cannot be substantiated, it is incontrovertible that a very wide variety of skills have to be used by HR specialists on a day-to-day basis.

As business partners they need strategic and business skills. As professionals constantly faced with the need to gain insight into the organizational and business issues they have to address, they need problem-solving, analytical and critical skills. HR professionals need to know about research methodology to understand the contribution of HR research and, increasingly, to take part in research projects. They must be able to analyse and present information on what is happening in their organizations by using statistical skills.

Another major group of skills that HR professionals need to have are those concerned with HRM practices, especially selection interviewing, job and competency analysis, learning and development techniques and negotiating. Then there are the skills they need because they have a complex role to play within their organizations. They are involved in leading change and exercising leadership in their own functions and, indirectly, in their dealings with line managers – providing guidance and advice. They have to exert influence, not just by using the authority of their position but by the effective exercise of skills in persuading managers to agree to innovations or adopt different courses of action in people management. They will be constantly involved in handling people problems and, from time to time, in managing conflict. Politics is a feature of life in organizations and HR people must know how to cope with political situations.

The purpose of this part is to provide guidance on the application of all the skills mentioned together with any supporting knowledge required.

44 Strategic HRM skills

KEY CONCEPTS AND TERMS

Business model

Business partner

Competitive advantage

Strategic business partner

LEARNING OUTCOMES

On completing this chapter you should be able to define these key concepts. You should also know about:

- The strategic role of the HR professional
- The strategic business partner model
- The strategic role of HR directors
- The strategic role of heads of HR functions
- The strategic role of HR business partners
- The strategic contribution of HR advisers or assistants
- The strategic skills required
- HR strategic skills as defined by the CIPD

Introduction

HR professionals are constantly being urged to be strategic. This chapter examines what this means and describes the knowledge and skills required.

The strategic role of the HR professional

HR strategic activities support the achievement of the organization's goals and values by aligning HR strategies with business strategies. HR professionals are involved in the development and implementation of forward-looking HR strategies that are integrated with one another. Importantly, they work with their line management colleagues in the continuous formulation and execution of the business strategy.

HR professionals, especially at the highest level, make a strategic contribution that ensures that the organization has the quality of skilled and engaged people it needs. Sparrow *et al* (2010: 88) observed that: 'HR must be fully responsive to the strategy and business model of the business. HR is not a rule to itself. It is not "HR for HR", but HR (as broadly defined across the competing stakeholders whom HR has to satisfy) for the business.' The strategic nature of HR has been expressed in the strategic business partner model, as described below.

The strategic business partner model

HR professionals as strategic business partners work closely with management, influencing the business strategy and contributing to its implementation. They share responsibility with their line management colleagues for the success of the enterprise. Ulrich (1998: 127) remarked that: 'To be full-fledged strategic partners with senior management HR executives should impel and guide serious discussion of how the company should be organized to carry out its strategy.'

In 1985, Tyson, anticipating Ulrich, described HR professionals as business managers who have the capacity to identify business opportunities, to see the broad picture, and to understand how their role can help to achieve the company's business objectives. They integrate their activities closely with top management and ensure that they serve a long-term strategic purpose. They anticipate needs, act flexibly and are proactive.

The notion of strategic partner was introduced by Dyer and Holder (1988), not Ulrich, as is generally assumed. Their description of the role is set out in the source review below.

Ulrich and Lake (1990) popularized the idea. They argued that:

> To ensure that management practices become a means for gaining a sustained competitive advantage, human resource professionals need to become strategic business partners and gear their activities to improving business performance. To do this they require a good working knowledge of the organization and its strategies. In assessing the role of human resources in an organization, management needs to determine the extent to which these professionals meet the following criteria:
>
> 1 Spend time with customers and clients – diagnosing, discussing and responding to needs.
>
> 2 Actively participate in business planning meetings and offer informed insights on strategic, technological and financial capabilities.
>
> 3 Understand business conditions.
>
> 4 Demonstrate competence in business knowledge, particularly customer relations, delivery of world-class management practices and management of change.

Source review

The strategic partner role for HR – Dyer and Holder (1988: 31–32)

The recommended role for the HR function is that of 'strategic partner'. This role typically has four aspects: (1) top HR executives cooperate with their line counterparts in formulating HR strategies, (2) top HR executives fully participate in all business strategy sessions as equals to CFOs and other top executives thus permitting early evaluation of proposals from an HR perspective, (3) HR executives work closely with line managers on an ongoing basis to ensure that all components of the business strategies are adequately implemented, and (4) the HR function itself is managed strategically.

Schuler and Jackson (2007: *xiv*) made a similar point when they wrote: 'Today, human resource professionals are being challenged to learn more about the business, its strategy, its environment, its customers, and its competitors.'

Note that none of these comments indicated that HR should be aware of ethical as well as business considerations and act accordingly. However, to do Ulrich justice, he did write later that HR professionals should 'represent both employee needs and implement management agendas' (Ulrich, 1997: 5).

The term 'strategic business partner' has been shortened in common parlance to 'business partner', a term that has been taken up enthusiastically within the HR profession and its professional body in the UK – the CIPD. HR business partners work closely with line managers and enable them to achieve their objectives through their people.

The strategic role of HR professionals varies in accordance with their level or function as HR directors, heads of HR functions, business partners, or HR advisers and assistants.

The strategic role of HR directors

The strategic role of HR directors is to promote the achievement of the organization's goals and values by: 1) developing and implementing HR strategies that are integrated with the business strategy and are coherent and mutually supportive; 2) ensuring that a strategic approach is adopted that provides that HR activities support the business and add value; and 3) taking into account the ethical dimension of HRM. To carry out this role HR directors need to:

- understand the strategic goals of the organization;
- appreciate the business imperatives and performance drivers relative to these goals;
- understand the business model of the organization (how it makes money) and play a part in business model innovation;
- comprehend how sustainable competitive advantage can be obtained through the human capital of the organization and know how HR practices can contribute to the achievement of strategic goals;
- contribute to the development of the business strategy on an 'outside-in' basis (Wright *et al*, 2004), starting from an analysis of the customer, competitor and business issues that the organization faces – the HR strategy then derives directly from these challenges to create solutions, add value and ensure that the organization has the distinctive human capital required to make an impact;
- contribute to the development for the business of a clear vision and a set of integrated values;
- ensure that senior management understands the HR implications of its business strategy;
- see the big picture, including the broader context (the competitive environment and the business, economic, social, legal factors that affect it) in which the organization operates;
- think in the long term of where HR should go and how to get there;
- understand the kinds of employee behaviour required to execute the business strategy successfully;
- believe in and practise evidence-based management;
- be capable of making a powerful business case for any proposals on the development of HR strategies;
- fully embrace ethical considerations when developing and implementing HR strategy.

The strategic role of heads of HR functions

The strategic role of heads of HR functions is fundamentally the same for their function as that of HR directors for the whole organization. They promote the achievement of the organization's business goals by developing and implementing functional strategies that are aligned with the business strategy and integrated with the strategies for other HR functions, and adopt a strategic approach in the sense of ensuring that HR activities support the business, add value and are ethical. To carry out this role, heads of HR functions should:

- understand the strategic goals of the organization as they affect their function;
- appreciate the business imperatives and performance drivers relative to these goals;
- help senior management to understand the implications of its strategy for the HR function;
- know how HR practices in the function can contribute to the achievement of the strategic goals;
- ensure that their activities provide added value for the organization;
- be aware of the broader context (the competitive environment and the business,

economic, social and legal factors that affect it) in which the function operates;

- think in terms of the bigger and longer-term picture of where HR strategies for the function should go and how to get there;
- believe in and practise evidence-based management;
- be capable of making a powerful business case for any proposals on the development of HR strategies for the function;
- fully embrace ethical considerations when developing and implementing HR strategy for the function.

The strategic role of HR business partners

The strategic role of HR business partners is to promote the achievement of the business goals of the organizational unit or function in which they operate. To carry out this role they should:

- understand the business and its competitive environment;
- understand the goals of their part of the business and its plans to attain them;
- ensure that their activities provide added value for the unit or function;
- build relationships founded on trust with their line management clients;
- provide support to the strategic activities of their colleagues;
- align their activities with business requirements;
- believe in and practise evidence-based management;
- be proactive, anticipating requirements, identifying problems and producing innovative and evidence-based solutions to them;
- see the broad picture and rise above the day-to-day detail;
- fully take into account ethical considerations when performing their business partner role.

The strategic contribution of HR advisers or assistants

The role of HR advisers or assistants is primarily that of delivering effective HR services within their function or as a member of an HR service centre. While they are unlikely to be responsible for the formulation of HR strategies they may contribute to them within their own speciality. They will need to understand the business goals of the departments or managers for whom they provide services in order to ensure that these services support the achievement of those goals. They should also fully take into account ethical considerations when performing their role.

The strategic skills required

HR professionals who act strategically will think about what the organization wants to be and become and what they can do to ensure this happens. They will have insight into the real needs of the business and its people and will take a broad view of where the business is going. They will be capable of seeing 'the big picture', looking beyond the confines of the immediate problems they and the business face to what lies ahead, how these problems can be solved and what they can do to support the efforts of other people. This means that they need business, problem-solving and analytical skills, as described in the next three chapters of this book.

The HR Profession Map as issued by the CIPD in 2013 sets out what HR professionals do and need to know in the area of 'strategy, insights and solutions'.

HR strategic activities and skills as defined by the CIPD

In general, according to the CIPD (2013: 9), the strategic role of an HR professional involves the development of 'actionable insights and solutions, prioritised and tailored around a deep understanding of business, contextual and organisational understanding'. In particular, the CIPD (ibid: 10) states that the strategic activities of an HR professional include:

- using a range of analytical tools, personal experience and management information to develop an understanding of what's happening in the organization and externally;
- considering the bigger picture at all times, observing connections, and drawing conclusions about the impact of events and activities on each other;
- developing insights about potential opportunities or risks for the organization from experience;
- using insights to identify opportunities, priorities and potential risks;
- developing and implementing HR solutions that address actions emanating from insights, either to mitigate critical risk or capitalize on opportunity.

The CIPD (ibid: 12–13) also states that to carry out these strategic activities the knowledge required by HR professionals should include the following:

- The vision and purpose of the organization and how to build functional alignment (organization design, strategy and plans) to this vision and purpose. Deep understanding of how things really work in the organization and the barriers to change.
- The rationale for current organization structures and espoused values and behaviour frameworks.
- The differentiating capabilities and skills that drive competitive advantage for the organization – how these can be built, bought or developed.
- What the key organization, commercial and value drivers are and how they impact on HR solutions for the business.

HR as an insight-driven discipline

The CIPD (2010: 4) expanded on what it meant by the use of 'insight' as follows:

> The best HR functions understand exactly how their organization in their market facing their specific challenges can respond in a way unique to it. Indeed in the same way as marketing has become a consumer insight-driven function, so some HR functions are delivering unique organization insight, helping organizations to find new ways of meeting current and future challenges. In these functions, there is a new relationship to data-gathering and analysis – generating true insight.

10 things to do if you want to be strategic

1. Exercise insight – understand the business and its competitive environment, what makes it successful and the external and internal political, social, competitive and economic factors that affect its performance.
2. Be aware of the goals of the business and its plans to attain them and understand the business model – 'how it makes money'.
3. Align what you are doing with the organization's business strategy.
4. Know where you are going and how you are going to get there.
5. Remember that formal strategic plans do not guarantee success; it is the implementation of the plans that delivers results.
6. Know how to plan the use of resources to make the best use of business opportunities.
7. Understand how you can contribute to the achievement of the objectives of the key functions in the business and support the strategic activities of your colleagues.
8. Be able to foresee longer-term developments, envisage options and their probable consequences, and select sound courses of action.
9. Rise above the day-to-day detail and see the broad picture.
10. Challenge the status quo.

Key learning points: Strategic HRM skills

The strategic role of the HR professional

HR strategic activities support the achievement of the organization's goals and values by aligning HR strategies to business strategies. HR professionals are involved in the development and implementation of forward-looking HR strategies that are integrated with one another. Importantly, they work with their line management colleagues in the continuous formulation and execution of the business strategy.

The strategic business partner model

HR practitioners share responsibility with their line management colleagues for the success of the enterprise. In 1985, Tyson described HR practitioners as business managers who have the capacity to identify business opportunities, to see the broad picture and to understand how their role can help to achieve the company's business objectives. They integrate their activities closely with top management and ensure that they serve a long-term strategic purpose. They anticipate needs, act flexibly and are proactive.

The strategic role of HR directors

The strategic role of HR directors is to promote the achievement of the organization's goals and values by: 1) developing and implementing HR strategies that are integrated with the business strategy and are coherent and mutually supportive; 2) ensuring that a strategic approach is adopted that provides that HR activities support the business and add value; and 3) taking into account the ethical dimension of HRM.

The strategic role of heads of HR functions

The strategic role of heads of HR functions is fundamentally the same for their function as that of HR directors for the whole organization. They promote the achievement of the organization's business goals by developing and implementing functional strategies that are aligned with the business strategy and integrated with the strategies for other HR functions, and adopt a strategic approach in the sense of ensuring that HR activities support the business, add value and are ethical.

The strategic role of HR business partners

The strategic role of HR business partners is to promote the achievement of the business goals of the organizational unit or function in which they operate.

The strategic contribution of HR advisers or assistants

The role of HR advisers or assistants is primarily that of delivering effective HR services within their function or as a member of an HR service centre. While they will not be responsible for formulating HR strategies, they may contribute to them within their own specialty.

The strategic skills required

HR professionals who act strategically will think about what the organization wants to be and become and what they can do to ensure this happens. They will have insight into the real needs of the business and its people and will take a broad view of where the business is going. They will be capable of seeing 'the big picture', looking beyond the confines of the immediate problems they and the business face to what lies ahead, how these problems can be solved and what they can do to support the efforts of other people.

Questions

1 What is the strategic role of HR professionals?
2 What is the strategic business partner model?
3 What is the strategic role of HR directors?
4 What are the main strategic skills required?

References

CIPD (2013) *HR Profession Map*, http://www.cipd.co.uk/hr-profession-map-download.aspx [accessed 1 April 2013]

CIPD (2010) *CIPD Next Generation*, London, CIPD

Dyer, L and Holder, G W (1988) Strategic human resource management and planning, in (ed) L Dyer, *Human Resource Management: Evolving roles and responsibilities*, Washington, DC, Bureau of National Affairs, pp 1–46

Schuler, R S and Jackson, S E (2007) *Strategic Human Resource Management*, 2nd edn, Oxford, Blackwell

Sparrow, P, Hesketh, A, Hird, M, Marsh, C and Balain, S (2010) Using business model change to tie HR into strategy: reversing the arrow, in (eds) P Sparrow, A Hesketh, M Hird and C Cooper, *Leading HR*, Basingstoke, Palgrave Macmillan, pp 68–89

Tyson, S (1985) Is this the very model of a modern personnel manager?, *Personnel Management*, May, pp 22–25

Ulrich, D (1997) *Human Resource Champions*, Boston, MA, Harvard Business School Press

Ulrich, D (1998) A new mandate for human resources, *Harvard Business Review*, January–February, pp 124–34

Ulrich, D and Lake, D (1990) *Organizational Capability: Competing from the inside out*, New York, Wiley

Wright, P M, Snell, S A and Jacobsen, H H (2004) Current approaches to HR strategies: inside-out versus outside-in, *Human Resource Planning*, 27 (4), pp 36–46

45
Business skills

KEY CONCEPTS AND TERMS

Absorption costing
The acid test
Activity-based costing
Assets
Balance sheet
Budgetary control
Budgets
Business model
Business model innovation
Cash flow
Cash flow statement
Core competency
Costing
Current liabilities
Direct costs
Earnings per share
Economic value added (EVA)
Gearing
Gross margin
Gross profit
Indirect costs
Key performance indicator (KPI)
Liquidity analysis
Marginal costing
Net profit
Operating or trading profit
Overheads
Overtrading
Price/earnings (P/E) ratio
Profit
Profit and loss account
Profit before taxation
Profitability
The resource-based view
Return on capital employed
Return on equity
Shareholder value
Standard costing
Trading statement or account
Working capital
The working capital ratio

LEARNING OUTCOMES

On completing this chapter you should be able to define these key concepts. You should also understand:

- What it means to be businesslike
- How profits are classified
- The meaning of profitability and the key profitability ratios
- The purpose of cash management
- Business models
- How to interpret a balance sheet
- The purpose of trading and profit and loss statements
- How budgeting and budgetary control work
- Methods of costing
- Business model innovation

Introduction

HR professionals can be regarded as business people with particular expertise in people, rather than as HR people who happen to work for a business. To make an effective contribution, they must possess business and financial skills. They need to understand, as well as skills in dealing with people how their organization delivers value to its customers and how the business achieves competitive advantage and makes money. They need to understand and be able to use the language of the business and, because this will generally be expressed in monetary terms, they need to appreciate how the financial systems of the business work. They also need to know about the concepts of the business model and business model innovation in order to understand how the business makes money now and intends to do so in the future so that they can do something about it.

Equipped with this knowledge, HR professionals can develop the skills needed to interpret the organization's business or corporate strategies, to contribute to the formulation of those strategies and to develop integrated HR strategies. This requirement was spelt out by Ulrich (1997: 7) when he wrote that: 'HR professionals must know the business which includes a mastery of finance, strategy, marketing, and operations.' Research by the CIPD (2010: 5) led to the following conclusion:

> It is also evident that for some HR functions, they see HR as an applied business discipline first and a people discipline second. The ability to understand the business agenda in a deep way means that they are then able to help the business see how critical objectives can only truly be delivered if the people and cultural issues are fully factored in – insight into what it would take to truly deliver. In these places HR has a real share of voice and credibility... Where HR is grounded in the business and delivering the fundamentals well, then it is able to engage in higher value-adding 'OD' and talent-related activities that speak to the critical challenges faced in that organization.

Business skills

Business skills are required to adopt a businesslike approach to management – one that focuses on allocating resources to business opportunities and making the best use of them to achieve the required results. Managers who are businesslike understand and act upon:

- the business imperatives of the organization – its mission and its strategic goals;
- the organization's business model – the basis upon which its business is done (how its mission and strategic goals will be achieved);
- the organization's business drivers – the characteristics of the business that move it forward;
- the organization's core competencies – what the business is good at doing;
- the factors that will ensure the effectiveness of its activities, including specific issues concerning profitability, productivity, financial budgeting and control, costs and benefits, customer service and operational performance;
- the key performance indicators (KPIs) of the business (the results or outcomes identified as being crucial to the achievement of high performance) that can be used to measure progress towards attaining goals;
- the factors that will ensure that the firm's resources, especially its human resources, create sustained competitive advantage because they are valuable, imperfectly imitable and non-substitutable (the resource-based view).

Financial skills

A businesslike approach means using financial skills to know how to analyse and interpret balance sheets, cash flow and trading statements, and profit and loss accounts, and to understand and make use of the financial techniques of budgeting and budgetary control, cash budgeting and costing.

Interpreting balance sheets

A balance sheet is a statement on the last day of the accounting period of the company's assets and liabilities and the share capital or the shareholders' investment in the company. Balance sheet analysis assesses the financial strengths and weaknesses of the company, primarily from the point of view of the shareholders and potential investors, but also as part of management's task to exercise proper stewardship over the funds invested in the company and the assets in its care. With the help of balance sheet ratios, the analysis focuses on the balance sheet equation, considers the make-up of the balance sheet in terms of assets and liabilities, and examines the liquidity position (how much cash or easily realizable assets are available) and capital structure.

The balance sheet equation

The balance sheet equation is: Capital + Liabilities = Assets. Capital plus liabilities shows where the money comes from, and assets indicate where the money is now.

Make-up of the balance sheet

The balance sheet contains four major sections:

1. *Assets or capital in use*, which is divided into long-term or fixed assets (eg land, buildings and plant) and current or short-term assets, which include bank balances and cash, debtors, stocks of goods and materials and work-in-progress.
2. *Current liabilities*, which are the amounts that will have to be paid within 12 months of the balance sheet date.
3. *Net current assets or working capital*, which are current assets less current liabilities. Careful control of working capital lies at the heart of efficient business performance.
4. *Sources of capital*, which comprise share capital, reserves including retained profits, and long-term loans.

Liquidity analysis

Liquidity analysis is concerned with the extent to which the organization has an acceptable quantity of cash and easily realizable assets to meet its needs. The analysis may be based on the ratio of current assets (cash, working capital, etc) to current liabilities (the working capital ratio). Too low a ratio may mean that the liquid resources are insufficient to cover short-term payments. Too high a ratio might indicate that there is too much cash or working capital and that they are therefore being badly managed. The working capital ratio is susceptible to 'window dressing', which is the manipulation of the working capital position by accelerating or delaying transactions near the year end.

Liquidity analysis also uses the 'quick ratio' of current assets minus stocks to current liabilities. This concentrates on the more realizable of the current assets and therefore provides a stricter test of liquidity than the working capital ratio. It is therefore called 'the acid test'.

Capital structure analysis

Capital structure analysis examines the overall means by which a company finances its operations, which is partly by the funds of their ordinary shareholders (equity) and partly by loans from banks and other lenders (debt). The ratio of long-term debt to ordinary shareholder's funds indicates 'gearing'. A company is said to be highly geared when it has a high level of loan capital as distinct from equity capital.

Classification of profits

Profit is basically the amount by which revenues exceed costs. It is classified in trading statements and profit and loss accounts in the following four ways:

1. *Gross profit* – the difference between sales revenue and the cost of goods sold. This is also referred to as gross margin, especially in the retail industry.
2. *Operating or trading profit* – the gross profit less sales, marketing and distribution costs, administrative costs and research and development expenditure.
3. *Profit before taxation* – operating profit plus invested income minus interest payable.
4. *Net profit* – profit minus taxation.

Trading statements

Trading statements or accounts show the cost of goods manufactured, the cost of sales, sales revenue and the gross profit, which is transferred to the profit and loss account.

Profit and loss accounts

Profit and loss accounts provide the information required to assess a company's profitability – the return in the shape of profits that shareholders obtain for their investment in the company. This is the primary aim and best measure of efficiency in competitive business. Profit and loss accounts show:

1 the gross profit from the trading account;
2 selling and administration expenses;
3 the operating profit (1 minus 2);
4 investment income;
5 profit before interest and taxation (3 plus 4);
6 profit before taxation (5 minus loan interest);
7 taxation;
8 net profit (6 minus 7).

Profitability analysis ratios

Profitability is expressed by the following ratios:

- *Return on equity* – profit after interest and preference dividends before tax in relation to ordinary share capital, reserves and retained profit. This focuses attention on the efficiency of the company in earning profits on behalf of its shareholders; some analysts regard it as the best profitability ratio.
- *Return on capital employed* – trading or operating profit to capital employed. This measures the efficiency with which capital is employed.
- *Earnings per share* – profit after interest, taxation and preference dividends in relation to the number of issued ordinary shares. This is an alternative to return on equity as a measure of the generation of 'shareholder value' (the value of the investment made by shareholders in the company in terms of the return they get on that investment). Its drawback is that it depends on the number of shares issued, although it is often referred to within companies as the means by which their obligations to shareholders should be assessed.
- *Price-earnings (P/E) ratio* – market price of ordinary shares in relation to earnings per share. This ratio is often used by investment analysts.
- *Economic value added (EVA)* – post-tax operating profit minus the cost of capital invested in the business. This measures how effectively the company uses its funds.

Financial budgeting

Budgets translate policy into financial terms. They are statements of the planned allocation and use of the company's resources. They are needed to: 1) show the financial implications of plans; 2) define the resources required to achieve the plans; and 3) provide the means of measuring, monitoring and controlling results against the plans.

The procedure for preparing financial budgets consists of the following steps:

1 Budget guidelines are prepared that have been derived from the corporate plan and forecasts. They will include the activity levels for which budgets have to be created and the ratios to be achieved. The assumptions to be used in budgeting are also given. These could include rates of inflation and increases in costs and prices.
2 Initial budgets for a budget or cost centre are prepared by departmental managers with the help of budget accountants.
3 Departmental budgets are collated and analysed to produce the master budget, which is reviewed by top management, who may require changes at departmental level to bring it into line with corporate financial objectives and plans.
4 The master budget is finally approved by top management and issued to each departmental (budget centre) manager for planning and control purposes.

Budgetary control

Budgetary control ensures that financial budgets are met and that any variances are identified and dealt with. Control starts with the budget for the cost centre, which sets out the budgeted expenditure under cost headings against activity levels. A system of measurement or recording is used to allocate expenditures to cost headings and record activity levels achieved. The actual expenditures and activity levels are compared and positive and negative variances noted. Cost centre managers then act to deal with the variances and report their results to higher management.

Cash management

Cash management involves forecasting and controlling cash flows (inflows or outflows of cash to or from the company). It is an important and systematic process of ensuring that problems of liquidity are minimized and that funds are managed effectively. The aim is to ensure that the company is not overtrading, ie that the cost of its operations does not significantly exceed the amount of cash available to finance them. The old adage is that whatever else is done, ensure that 'cash in exceeds cash out'.

Cash flow statements report the amounts of cash generated and cash used for a period. They are used to provide information on liquidity (the availability of cash), solvency and financial adaptability.

Cash budgeting

An operating cash budget deals with budgeted receipts (forecast cash inflows) and budgeted payments (forecast cash outflows). It includes all the revenue expenditure incurred in financing current operations, ie the costs of running the business in order to generate sales.

Costing

Costing techniques provide information for decision-making and control. They are used to establish the total cost of a product for stock valuation, pricing and estimating purposes and to enable the company to establish that the proposed selling price will enable a profit to be made.

Costing involves measuring the direct costs of material and labour plus the indirect costs (overheads) originating in the factory (factory overheads) and elsewhere in the company (sales, distribution, marketing, research and development and administration). Overheads are charged to cost units – this process is called 'overhead recovery'. It provides information on total costs. There are four main methods of doing this:

- *Absorption costing* – this involves allocating all fixed and variable costs to cost units and is the most widely used method, although it can be arbitrary.
- *Activity-based costing* – costs are assigned to activities on the basis of an individual product's demand for each activity.
- *Marginal costing* – this segregates fixed costs and apportions the variable or marginal costs to products.
- *Standard costing* – is the preparation of predetermined or standard costs, which are compared with actual costs to identify variances. It is used to measure performance.

Business models

HR professionals also need to know about the concept of business models and how this influences their activities. A business model provides a picture of an organization, explaining how it achieves competitive advantage and makes money. As defined by Magretta (2002: 87), business models 'are at heart stories – stories that explain how enterprises work... They answer the fundamental questions every manager needs to ask: How do we make money in this business? What is the underlying economic logic that explains how we can deliver value to customers at an appropriate cost?' She explained that a business model 'focuses attention on how all the elements in a system fit into a working whole' (ibid: 90).

Elements of a business model

Johnson *et al* (2008: 52) stated that: 'A business model, from our point of view, consists of four interlocking elements that, taken together, create and deliver value.' These are:

- *The customer value proposition*: how the business will create value for its customers; this is the most important element.
- *The profit formula*: the blueprint that defines how the company creates value for itself while providing value to the customer. It consists of the revenue model, cost structure, margin model (the contribution needed from each transaction to achieve desired profits) and resource velocity (how fast the business needs to turn over inventory and assets and how well resources should be utilized).
- *Key resources:* the assets such as people, technology, products, facilities, equipment, channels and brand required to deliver the value proposition to the targeted customer.

- *Key processes:* recurrent tasks such as training, development, manufacturing, budgeting, planning and sales that allow firms to deliver value in a way they can successfully repeat and increase in scale. Key processes also include a company's rules, metrics and norms.

Business model innovation

Business model innovation is the process of developing new business models or changing existing ones in order to deliver better value to customers, achieve competitive advantage and increase profitability. Johnson (2010: 20) defined the concept in more detail as follows:

> Business model innovation (BMI) refers to the creation or reinvention of a business. Though innovation is more often seen in the form of a new product or service offering, a business model innovation results in an entirely different type of company that competes not only on the value proposition of its offerings, but aligns its profit formula, resources, and processes to enhance that value proposition, capture new market segments, and alienate competitors.

He also observed that: 'Business model innovation thrives in cultures of inquiry, environments in which new value propositions and ideas for new business models are met with interest and encouragement' (ibid: 177).

Business model analysis and design

Business model analysis is a necessary part of business model innovation. It is concerned with two key issues: 1) how the organization creates value; and 2) how the organization establishes unique resources, assets or positions that will achieve competitive advantage. It may involve an analysis of how value is generated at each stage of the value chain (a value chain identifies the sequence of activities in a firm that are strategically relevant and underlie its key capabilities).

The role of HR in business model innovation

On the basis of extensive research into how HR departments dealt with business model innovation, their role was spelt out by Sparrow *et al* (2010: 14–15) as follows:

> A central task for HR directors is to identify how they as leaders, and how their function's own delivery model, structure, and the people processes it manages, add value during periods of business model change. In order for organizations to make their models work, they have to understand the potentially deep implications they have for people management. People management experts have to make sure that those engineering the new business models are working on assumptions that can reasonably be executed.

To play their part in business model innovation, heads of HR need to:

- understand the implications of the existing and potential business model in terms of the organization structure and the new or enhanced capabilities that the people involved will require;
- contribute to the redesign of the organization to meet the requirements of the business model change programme;
- plan organization development activities that systematically improve organizational capability in terms of process – how things get done;
- mastermind change management programmes that provide for the acceptance and smooth implementation of change;
- conduct workforce planning exercises that identify more specifically the numbers of people required with specified skills and knowledge;
- formulate and implement talent management strategies that provide for the development, deployment, recruitment and retention of talented people – those individuals who can make a difference to organizational performance through their immediate contribution and in the longer term;

- develop performance management and contingent reward systems – what Sparrow *et al* (2010: 16) call 'performance-driven processes';
- plan and manage learning programmes to ensure that people have the skills required to implement the new or changed business model;
- establish knowledge management procedures for storing and sharing the wisdom, understanding and expertise accumulated in the organization about its processes, techniques and operations.

In addition, as Schuler and Jackson (2007: 31) pointed out, 'because an innovation strategy requires risk taking and tolerance of inevitable failures, HRM in firms pursuing this strategy should be used to give employees a sense of security and encourage a long-term commitment'.

Key learning points: Business skills

The need for business and financial skills

To make an effective contribution, HR professionals must have business and financial skills. They need to understand what the business model is – how the organization delivers value to its customers and, in commercial organizations, how the business achieves competitive advantage and makes money.

Business skills

Business skills are required to adopt a businesslike approach to management – one that focuses on allocating resources to business opportunities and making the best use of them to achieve the required results.

Financial skills

A businesslike approach means using financial skills to analyse and interpret balance sheets, cash flow and trading statements, and profit and loss accounts, and to understand and make use of the financial techniques of budgeting and budgetary control, cash budgeting and costing.

Interpreting balance sheets

A balance sheet is a statement on the last day of the accounting period of the company's assets and liabilities and the share capital or reserves or shareholders' investment in the company. Balance sheet analysis assesses the financial strengths and weaknesses of the company primarily from the point of view of the shareholders and potential investors, but also as part of management's task to exercise proper stewardship over the funds invested in the company and the assets in its care.

Classification of profits

It is necessary to understand the different ways in which profits can be classified as recorded in trading statements and profit and loss accounts. There are four headings: gross profit, operating or trading profit, profit before tax and net profit.

Trading statements

Trading statements or accounts show the cost of goods manufactured, the cost of sales, sales revenue and the gross profit, which is transferred to the profit and loss account.

Profit and loss accounts

Profit and loss accounts provide the information required to assess a company's profitability – the primary aim and best measure of efficiency in competitive business. Profitability is a measure of the return in the shape of profits that shareholders obtain for their investment in the company. It is expressed in the following ratios: return on equity, return on capital employed, earnings per share, price-earnings (P/E) ratio and economic value added (EVA).

Financial budgeting

Budgets translate policy into financial terms. They are statements of the planned allocation and use of the company's resources.

Budgetary control

Budgetary control ensures that financial budgets are met and that any variances are identified and dealt with.

Cash management

Cash management involves forecasting and controlling cash flows (inflows or outflows of cash). An operating cash budget deals with budgeted receipts (forecast cash inflows) and budgeted payment (forecast cash outflows).

Costing

Costing techniques provide information for decision-making and control. They are used to establish the total cost of a product for stock valuation, pricing and estimating purposes, and to enable the company to establish that the proposed selling price will enable a profit to be made.

Overheads are charged to cost units to provide information on total costs – this is called 'overhead recovery'. There are four methods of doing this: absorption costing, activity-based costing, marginal costing and standard costing.

Business model

A business model provides a picture of an organization that explains how it achieves competitive advantage and makes money. Business model innovation is the process of developing new business models or changing existing ones to deliver better value to customers, achieve competitive advantage and increase profitability.

Questions

1 What is involved in being 'businesslike'?
2 What are the essential financial skills that HR professionals need?
3 What is a balance sheet?
4 What is involved in balance sheet analysis?
5 What is liquidity analysis?
6 What is capital structure analysis?
7 What are the different ways of classifying profits?
8 What is a trading statement?
9 What is a profit and loss account?
10 What are the main components of a profit and loss account?
11 What is profitability?
12 What is return on equity?
13 What is return on capital employed?
14 What are earnings per share?
15 What is the price/earnings ratio?
16 What is financial budgeting?
17 What is budgetary control?
18 What does cash management involve?
19 What is an operating cash budget?
20 What does costing involve?
21 What is a business model?
22 What is business model innovation?

References

CIPD (2010) *Next Generation*, London, CIPD

Johnson, M (2010) *Seizing the White Space*, Boston, MA, Harvard Business Press

Johnson, M, Christensen, C and Kagermann, H (2008) Reinventing your business model, *Harvard Business Review*, December, pp 52–59

Magretta, J (2002) Why business models matter, *Harvard Business Review*, May, pp 86–93

Schuler, R S and Jackson, S E (2007) Understanding human resource management in the context of organizations and their environments, in (eds) R S Schuler and S E Jackson, *Strategic Human Resource Management*, Oxford, Blackwell, pp 23–48

Sparrow, P, Hesketh, A, Hird, M and Cooper, C (2010) Introduction: Performance-led HR, in (eds) P Sparrow, A Hesketh, M Hird, and C Cooper, *Leading HR*, Basingstoke, Palgrave Macmillan

Ulrich, D (1997) Judge me by my future not my past, *Human Resource Management*, 36 (1), pp 5–8

46 Problem-solving skills

KEY CONCEPTS AND TERMS

Occam's razor

Problem solving

LEARNING OUTCOMES

On completing this chapter you should be able to define these key concepts. You should also understand:

- How to improve problem-solving skills
- How to solve a problem

Introduction

Problem solving is a constant feature of life in organizations and elsewhere. It is something that HR professionals do all the time. A logical approach is desirable but this is not easy – the situations where problems have to be solved are often messy, with conflicting evidence, lack of data, and political and emotional issues affecting those involved. But the principles – of getting and analysing what information is available, considering alternatives and making the best choice based on the evidence, an analysis of the context and an assessment of the possible consequences – remain the same, even if it is not possible to apply neat, logical and sequential methods.

Problem solving

Problem solving is the process of analysing and understanding a problem, diagnosing its cause and deciding on a solution that solves the problem and prevents it being repeated. You will often have to react to problems as they arise, but as far as possible a proactive approach is desirable, involving being able to anticipate potential problems and dealing with them in advance by taking preventative action using the normal approaches to problem solving set out below. Proactive problem solving may require creative thinking.

Problems and opportunities

It is often said that 'there are no problems, only opportunities'. This is not universally true, of course, but it does emphasize the point that a problem should lead to positive thinking about what is to be done now, rather than to recriminations. If a mistake has been made, the reasons for it should be analysed to ensure that it does not happen again.

Improving your skills

How can you improve your ability to solve problems? There are a few basic approaches you should use, as discussed below.

Improve your analytical ability

A complicated situation can often be resolved by separating the whole into its component parts. Such an analysis should relate to facts, although, as Drucker (1955) points out, when trying to understand the root causes of a problem you may have to start with an opinion. Even if you ask people to search for the facts first, they will probably look for those facts that fit the conclusion they have already reached.

Opinions are a perfectly good starting point as long as they are brought out into the open at once and then tested against reality. Analyse each hypothesis and pick out the parts that need to be studied and tested (analytical skills are covered in Chapter 47). Follett's (1924) 'law of the situation' – the logic of facts and events – should rule in the end.

Be creative

A strictly logical answer to the problem may not be the best one. Creative thinking is often necessary to develop an entirely new approach.

Keep it simple

One of the basic principles of problem solving is known as Occam's razor. It states that: 'entities are not to be multiplied without necessity'. That is, always believe the simplest of several explanations.

Focus on implementation

A problem has not been solved until the decision has been implemented. Think carefully not only about how a thing is to be done (by whom, with what resources and by when) but also about what will happen when it is put into effect – its impact on the organization and the people concerned and the extent to which they will cooperate. Unforeseen consequences can upset the most carefully prepared plans.

Involve people

You will get less cooperation if you impose a solution. The best method is to arrange things so that everyone arrives jointly at a solution, freely agreed to be the one best suited to the situation (the law of the situation again).

Further consideration of the processes of evaluating evidence and options and to the consulting skills used in problem solving is given in the next chapter.

12 problem-solving steps

The 12 steps of problem solving are:

1 *Define the situation* – establish what has gone wrong or is about to go wrong.

2 *Specify objectives* – define what is to be achieved now or in the future to deal with an actual or potential problem or a change in circumstances.

3 *Develop hypotheses* – develop hypotheses about what has caused the problem.

4 *Get the facts* – find out what has actually happened and contrast this with an assessment of what ought to have happened. This is easier said than done. Insidious political factors may have contributed to the problem and could be difficult to identify and deal with. The facts may not be clear cut. They could be obscured by a mass of conflicting material. There may be lots of opinions but few verifiable facts. Remember that people will see what has happened in terms of their own position and feelings (their framework of reference). Try to understand the political climate and the attitudes and motivation of those concerned. Bear in mind that, as Pfeffer (1996: 36) commented, 'smart organizations

occasionally do dumb things'. Obtain information about internal or external constraints that affect the situation.

5 *Analyse the facts* – determine what is relevant and what is irrelevant. Diagnose the likely cause or causes of the problem. Do not be tempted to focus on symptoms rather than root causes. Test any assumptions. Distinguish between opinions and facts. Dig into what lies behind the problem.

6 *Identify possible courses of action* – spell out what each involves.

7 *Evaluate alternative courses of action* – assess the extent to which they are likely to achieve the objectives, the cost of implementation, any practical difficulties that might emerge and the possible reactions of stakeholders. Consider possible consequences. Critical evaluation techniques, as described in Chapter 47, can be used for this purpose.

8 *Weigh and decide* – determine which alternative is likely to result in the most practical and acceptable solution to the problem. This is often a balanced judgement.

9 *Decide on the objective* – set out goals for implementation of the decision.

10 *Adopt a 'means-end' approach where appropriate* – in complicated situations with long-term implications it may be useful to identify the steps required and select an action at each step that will move the process closer to the goal.

11 *Plan implementation* – prepare a timetable and identify and assemble the resources required.

12 *Implement* – monitor progress and evaluate success. Remember that a problem has not been solved until the decision has been implemented. Always work out the solution to a problem with implementation in mind.

Key learning points: Problem-solving skills

Problem solving is a constant feature of life in organizations and elsewhere. It is the process of analysing and understanding a problem, diagnosing its cause and deciding on a solution that solves the problem and prevents it being repeated.

To improve problem-solving skills it is necessary to: improve your analytical ability, be creative, keep it simple and focus on implementation.

The 12 steps of problem solving are:

1 define the situation;
2 specify objectives;
3 develop hypotheses;
4 get the facts;
5 analyse the facts;
6 identify possible courses of action;
7 evaluate alternative courses of action;
8 weigh and decide;
9 decide on the objective;
10 adopt a 'means-end' approach where appropriate;
11 plan implementation;
12 implement.

Questions

1 What is the nature of problem solving?
2 What is the purpose of analysis in problem solving?
3 What are the key steps that should be taken in problem solving?

References

Drucker, P (1955) *The Practice of Management*, London, Heinemann
Follett, M P (1924) *Creative Experience*, New York, Longmans Green
Pfeffer, J (1996) When it comes to 'best practices', why do smart organizations occasionally do dumb things?, *Organizational Dynamics*, Summer, pp 33–44

47

Analytical and critical skills

KEY CONCEPTS AND TERMS

Analysis

Critical evaluation

Critical thinking

Evidence-based management

Fallacy

LEARNING OUTCOMES

On completing this chapter you should be able to define these key concepts. You should also understand:

- The meaning of evidence-based management
- The nature of critical evaluation
- The nature of critical thinking
- The nature of logical reasoning
- The use of analytical skills

Introduction

Rousseau and Barends (2011: 221) remarked that: 'Blind faith has no place in professional practice.' The effectiveness of HR initiatives and the processes of problem solving and decision-making in which HR practitioners are constantly involved depend largely on thorough analysis and critical thinking, as covered in this chapter. The basis of all these is provided by evidence-based management, as discussed below.

Evidence-based management

Evidence-based management is a method of informing decision-making by making use of appropriate information derived from the analysis of policy and practices and surveys of employee opinion within the organization, systematic benchmarking, and the messages delivered by relevant research. It was defined by Rousseau and Barends (2011: 221) as:

'A decision-making process combining critical thinking with the use of the best available scientific evidence and business information.'

The following comments on evidence-based management were made by Pfeffer and Sutton (2006: 70):

> Nurture an evidence-based approach immediately by doing a few simple things that reflect the proper mindset. If you ask for evidence of efficacy every time a change is proposed, people will sit up and take notice. If you take the time to pursue the logic behind that evidence, people will become more disciplined in their own thinking. If you treat the organization like an unfinished prototype and encourage trial programs, pilot studies, and experimentation – and reward learning from these activities, even when something new fails – your organization will begin to develop its own evidence base.

The need for evidence-based management

Rousseau and Barends (2011: 221) observed that:

> Evidence-based HR is motivated by a basic fact: faulty practices and decision-making abound in HR. Companies persist in using unstructured interviews to assess a job candidate's fit even though there is little evidence to support that. HR departments often pursue one-size-fits-all standardization in their policies, despite considerable evidence that programmes promoting flexibility benefit. In all honesty, can you answer 'yes' to the question, 'Do you know the scientific evidence for ANY of the HR practices your company uses?' Recent surveys of HR practitioners lead us to suspect that the frank response from many readers is 'no'.

The approach to evidence-based management

Rousseau (2006: 2012) suggested that at its core, evidence-based management combines four fundamental features in everyday management practice and decision-making:

- use of the best-available evidence from peer-reviewed sources;
- systematic gathering of organizational facts, indicators and metrics to better act on the evidence;
- practitioner judgement assisted by procedures, practices and framework that reduce bias, improve decision quality and create more vivid learning over time;
- ethical considerations weighing the short- and long-term impacts of decisions on stakeholders and society.

A five-step approach was recommended by Briner *et al* (2009: 23):

1. Practitioners or managers gain understanding of the problem or issue.
2. Internal evidence is gathered about the issue or problem leading, possibly, to a reformulation of the problem to make it more specific.
3. External evidence is gathered from published research.
4. The views of stakeholders are obtained.
5. All the sources of information are examined and critically appraised.

What is done in organizations with the evidence depends largely on the context in which it is done. Cultural, social and political factors influence perceptions and judgements, and the extent to which people behave rationally is limited by their capacity to understand the complexities of the situation they are in and by their emotional reactions to it – the concept of bounded rationality, as expressed by Simon (1957).

We need to understand the context – its impact on what is happening and how things are done. We need then to understand what actions can be taken to deal with the issues emerging from the situation. We need evidence that tells us what is going on within the organization, what has worked well elsewhere that might fit our requirements, and what research has revealed about policies and practices that will guide us in making our decisions. And we need to use that evidence as the basis for our choice of the actions we intend to take. In other words, we need to practice evidence-based management using the analytical, logical reasoning and critical thinking skills described in the rest of this chapter.

Analytical skills

Analysis is the process of breaking down a condition or state of affairs into its constituent parts and establishing the relationships between them. It involves discerning the particular features of a situation.

Analytical skills are used to gain a better understanding of a complex situation or problem. They involve the ability to visualize, articulate and solve complex problems and concepts and make decisions based on available information. Analytical skills include the capacity to evaluate that information to assess its significance, and the ability to apply logical and critical thinking to the situation. They provide the basis for a diagnosis of the cause or causes of a problem and, therefore, for its solution. Importantly, they are a means of gaining insight into issues that affect the success of the business and that influence business and HR strategy.

Logical reasoning

If you say that people are logical, you mean that they draw reasonable inferences – their conclusions can be proved by reference to the facts used to support them – and they avoid ill-founded and tendentious arguments, generalizations and irrelevancies. Logical reasoning is the basis of critical thinking and evaluation. It takes place when there is a clear relationship (a line of reasoning) between the premise (the original proposition) and the conclusion, which is supported by valid and reliable evidence and does not rely on fallacious or misleading argument. Logical reasoning is what Stebbing (1959) called 'thinking to some purpose'. Clear thinking is required to establish the validity of a proposition, concept or idea.

It is necessary to question assumptions, especially when a belief is expressed as a fact. You need to ask yourself – and others – 'what's the evidence for that?' You have to spot fallacious and misleading arguments. A fallacy is an unsound form of argument leading to an error in reasoning or a misleading impression. The most common form of fallacies that need to be discerned in other people's arguments, or avoided in one's own, are summarized below:

- *Affirming the consequent* – leaping to the conclusion that a hypothesis is true because a single cause of the consequence has been observed.
- *Begging the question* – taking for granted what has yet to be proved.
- *Chop logic* – 'Contrarywise', said Tweedledee, 'if it was so, it might be, and if it were so, it would be; but as it isn't it ain't. That's logic'. Chop logic may not always be as bad as that, but it is about drawing false conclusions and using dubious methods of argument. For example: selecting instances favourable to a contention while ignoring those that are counter to it, twisting an argument used by an opponent to mean something quite different from what was intended, diverting opponents by throwing on them the burden of proof for something they have not maintained, ignoring the point in dispute, changing the question to one that is less awkward to answer, and reiterating what has been denied and ignoring what has been asserted. Politicians know all about chop logic.
- *Confusing correlation with causation* – assuming that because A is associated with B it has caused B. It may or may not.
- *False choice* – a situation in which only two alternatives are considered, when in fact there are additional options.
- *Potted thinking* – using slogans and catchphrases to extend an assertion in an unwarrantable fashion.
- *Reaching false conclusions* – forming the view that because some are, then all are. An assertion about several cases is twisted into an assertion about all cases. The conclusion does not follow the premise. This is what logicians call the 'undistributed middle'.
- *Selective reasoning* – selecting instances favourable to a contention while ignoring those that conflict with it.
- *Sweeping statements* – oversimplifying the facts.
- *Special pleading* – focusing too much on one's own case and failing to see that there may be other points of view.

Critical thinking

Critical thinking is the process of analysing and evaluating the quality of ideas, theories and concepts to establish the degree to which they are valid and supported by the evidence, and the extent to which they are biased. It involves reflecting on and interpreting data, drawing warranted conclusions and recognizing ill-defined assumptions.

'Critical' in this context does not mean disapproval or being negative. There are many positive uses of critical thinking, for example testing a hypothesis, proving a proposition or evaluating a concept, theory or argument. Critical thinking can occur whenever people weigh up evidence and make a judgement, solve a problem or reach a decision. The aim is to come to well-reasoned conclusions and solutions and to test them against relevant criteria and standards. Critical thinking calls for the ability to:

- recognize problems and establish ways of dealing with them;
- gather and marshal pertinent (relevant) information;
- identify unstated assumptions and values;
- interpret data, to appraise evidence and to evaluate arguments;
- recognize the existence (or non-existence) of logical relationships between propositions;
- draw warranted conclusions and make valid generalizations;
- test assertions, conclusions and generalizations;
- reconstruct ideas or beliefs by examining and analysing relevant evidence.

Critical evaluation

Critical evaluation is the process of making informed judgements about the validity, relevance and usefulness of ideas and arguments. Critical evaluation means not taking anything for granted and, where necessary, challenging propositions. It involves making informed judgements about the value of ideas and arguments. It uses critical thinking by analysing and evaluating the quality of theories and concepts to establish the degree to which they are valid and supported by the evidence (evidence-based) and the extent to which they are biased. The arguments for and against are weighed and the strength of the evidence on both sides is assessed. On the basis of this assessment, a conclusion is reached on which proposition or argument is to be preferred. Critical evaluation is required when testing propositions and evaluating the outcomes of research.

Testing propositions

Propositions based on research investigations and evidence can be tested by using the following checklist.

Checklist

- Was the scope of the investigation sufficiently comprehensive?
- Are the instances representative or are they selected simply to support a point of view?
- Are there contradictory instances that have not been looked for?
- Does the proposition conflict with other propositions for which there are equally good grounds?
- If there are any conflicting beliefs or contradictory items of evidence, have they been put to the test against the original proposition?
- Could the evidence lead to other equally valid conclusions?
- Are there any other factors that have not been taken into account that may have influenced the evidence and, therefore, the conclusion?

Critically evaluating research

Putting the outcomes of research, for example material published in academic journals, to the test requires critical evaluation and the following checklist can be used.

Checklist

- Is the research methodology sufficiently rigorous and appropriate?
- Are the results and conclusions consistent with the methodology used and its outcomes?
- Is the perspective adopted by the researchers stated clearly?
- Have hypotheses been stated clearly and tested thoroughly?
- Do there appear to be any misleading errors of omission or bias?
- Are any of the arguments tendentious?
- Are inferences, findings and conclusions derived from reliable and convincing evidence?
- Has a balanced approach been adopted?
- Have any underlying assumptions been identified and justified?
- Have the component parts been covered in terms of their interrelationships and their relationship with the whole?
- Have these component parts been disaggregated for close examination?
- Have they been reconstructed into a coherent whole based on underlying principles?

It is worth repeating that critical evaluation does not necessarily mean negative criticism; it means reaching a judgement based on analysis and evidence, and the judgement can be positive as well as negative.

Developing and justifying original arguments

An argument as an aspect of critical thinking consists of a presentation of reasons that support a contention. It consists of:

- a proposition or statement that expresses a point of view or belief;
- the reasoning that makes a case for the proposition or point of view;
- a discussion, the aim of which is to get the reader or listener to agree with the case that has been made;
- a conclusion that sums up the argument and its significance.

Developing an argument

An argument is based (predicated) on a premise (the proposition) that sets out the underpinning assumption. There may be more than one proposition or assumption. It could be phrased something like this: 'The argument is that A is the case. It is predicated on the assumption that B and C apply.' In a sense, this suggests what conclusion the argument is intended to reach but it also indicates that this conclusion depends on the validity of the assumptions, which will have to be proved (there are such things as false premises).

Justifying an argument

The argument continues by supplying reasons to accept the proposition or point of view. These reasons have to be supported by evidence, which should be based on valid research, rigorous observation, or relevant and verifiable experience, not on hearsay. It involves logical reasoning, which avoids the fallacies referred to earlier and requires critical thinking, which means coming to well-reasoned conclusions and solutions and testing them against relevant criteria and standards. It also demands critical evaluation, which means reflecting on and interpreting data, drawing warranted conclusions and identifying faulty reasoning, assumptions and biases. Assumptions have to be tested rigorously and research evidence has to be evaluated. The checklists set out above can be used for this purpose.

Key learning points: Analytical and critical skills

Basis of the processes of problem-solving and decision-making

The processes of problem-solving and decision-making depend largely on effective analysis, critical thinking and evaluation.

Evidence-based management

Evidence-based management is a method of informing decision-making by making use of appropriate information derived from the analysis of HR policy and practices and surveys of employee opinion within the organization, systematic benchmarking, and the messages delivered by relevant research.

Analytical skills

Analysis is the process of gaining a better understanding of a complex situation or problem by breaking it down into its constituent parts and establishing the relationships between them.

Logical reasoning

Logical reasoning involves clear thinking to establish the validity of a proposition, concept or idea.

Critical thinking

Critical thinking clarifies goals, examines assumptions, discerns hidden values, evaluates evidence, accomplishes actions and assesses conclusions.

Critical evaluation

Critical evaluation involves making informed judgements about the value of ideas and arguments.

Developing and justifying original arguments

An argument as an aspect of critical thinking consists of a presentation of reasons that support a contention.

Questions

1 What is evidence-based management?
2 What does analysis involve?
3 What is logical reasoning?
4 What is a fallacy? (give examples of three typical fallacies)
5 What does critical thinking involve?
6 What is critical evaluation?
7 What approaches can be used to test propositions?
8 How do you critically evaluate research?
9 What does an argument consist of?
10 How do you develop an argument?
11 How do you justify an argument?

References

Briner, R B, Denyer, D and Rousseau, D M (2009) Evidence-based management: concept clean-up time? *Academy of Management Perspectives*, September, pp 19–32

Pfeffer, J and Sutton, R I (2006) Evidence-based management, *Harvard Business Review*, January, pp 62–74

Rousseau, D M (2006) Is there such a thing as evidence-based management? *Academy of Management Review*, 31 (2), pp 256–69

Rousseau, D M and Barends, E G (2011) Becoming an evidence-based HR practitioner, *Human Resource Management Journal*, 21 (3), pp 221–35

Simon, H (1957) *Administrative Behaviour*, New York, Macmillan

Stebbing, S (1959) *Thinking to Some Purpose*, Harmondsworth, Penguin Books

48
Research skills

KEY CONCEPTS AND TERMS

- Critical evaluation
- Cross-lagged model
- Deduction
- Evidence-based
- Experimental design
- Falsification
- Grounded theory
- Hypothesis
- Induction
- Likert scale
- Multivariate analysis
- Paradigm
- Phenomenology
- Positivism
- Proposition
- Qualitative research
- Quantitative research
- Reductionism
- The research question
- Theory
- Triangulation

LEARNING OUTCOMES

On completing this chapter you should be able to define these key concepts. You should also understand:

- The nature of research
- Planning and conducting research programmes
- Research methodology
- Methods of collecting data
- Processes involved in research

Introduction

HRM specialists and those studying for HR professional qualifications may be involved in conducting or taking part in research projects. Qualified HR specialists should keep up to date as part of their continuous professional development by studying publications that present research findings, such as those produced by the CIPD, or by reading articles in academic journals. Students must extend their understanding of HRM through reading about research findings.

The purpose of this chapter is to describe the skills and techniques used in research and explain what is involved in planning and conducting research projects. This will be done against the background of a brief review of the nature and philosophy of research.

The nature of research

Research is concerned with establishing what *is* – and from this predicting what will be. It does not decide what ought to be; that is for people interpreting the lessons from research in their own context. Research is about the conception and testing of ideas and hypotheses. This is a creative and imaginative process, although new information is normally obtained within the framework of existing theory and knowledge. Logic and rational argument are methods of testing ideas after they have been created.

What emerges from research is a theory – a well-established explanatory principle that has been tested and can be used to make predictions of future developments. Kurt Lewin (1945: 129) wrote that 'Nothing is as practical as a good theory'. A 'good' theory is produced by clear, logical and linear development of an argument with a close relationship between information, hypothesis and conclusion. Quality of information is a criterion for good research, as is the use of critical evaluation techniques.

The production of narratives that depict events (case studies) or the collection of data through surveys are elements in research programmes, but they can stand alone as useful pieces of information that illustrate practice. Research can be based on a philosophy of positivism or phenomenology.

Positivism

Positivism is the belief that researchers should focus on facts (observable reality), look for causality and fundamental laws, reduce phenomena to their simplest elements (reductionism), formulate hypotheses and then test them. Researchers are objective analysts. The emphasis in positivism is on quantifiable observations that lend themselves to statistical analysis. It tends to be deductive.

Phenomenology

Phenomenology focuses more on the meaning of phenomena than on the facts associated with them. Researchers adopting this philosophy try to understand what is happening. Their approach is holistic, covering the complete picture, rather than reductionist. Researchers collect and analyse evidence, but their purpose is to use this data to develop ideas that explain the meaning of things. They believe that reality is socially constructed rather than objectively determined. Using a phenomenological approach means that the research unfolds as it proceeds – early evidence is used to indicate how to move on to the next stage of evidence collection and analysis, and so on. It tends to be inductive.

Planning and conducting research programmes

Against this background, the steps required to plan and conduct a research programme are:

1. *Define research area.* This should be one that interests the researcher and has a clear link to an accepted theory or an important issue worth exploring. The research should generate fresh insights into the topic. It is necessary to undertake background reading at this stage by means of a preliminary review of the literature (particularly academic journals but also books, especially those based on research) to identify what has already been achieved in this area and any gaps (academic articles often include

proposals on further research). The context within which the research is to be carried out needs to be explained and justified.

2 *Formulate initial research question.* This provides a rationale for the research. It is in effect a statement that answers the questions: what is this research project intended to address and what is its potential contribution to increasing knowledge? At this stage it is based on the outcome of the initial work carried out in step 1, but it will be refined and reformulated at a later stage when more information about the research has been made available.

3 *Review literature.* A literature review will focus mainly on academic journals. The aim is to establish what is already known about the topic, identify existing theoretical frameworks and find out what other relevant research has been carried out.

4 *Develop theoretical framework.* It is necessary to conduct the research within a clear theoretical framework. This will set out the models, concepts and theories that can be drawn on and developed to provide an answer to the research question. If an appropriate framework does not exist, a grounded theory approach may be required in which the researcher uses empirical evidence directly to establish the concepts and relationships that will be contained in the theory adopted as the research framework. It is important to be clear about the assumptions, conditions and limitations that impinge on the investigation.

5 *Finalize the research question.* The initial research question needs to be finalized in the light of the outcome of the earlier steps. The final research question will identify the issues to be explored and the problems to be investigated. It will include a statement of intent, which will set out what the research is to achieve. This statement leads to the formulation of the hypotheses or propositions that will be tested by survey or experiment during the research programme.

6 *Formulate hypotheses or propositions.* A hypothesis provisionally states a relationship between two concepts in such a way that the consequences of the statement being true can be tested. Hypotheses (there may be more than one) indicate the form that the research project will take in the shape of obtaining and analysing the evidence required to test them. Hypotheses may be attached to the statement of the research question. A proposition is a proposal put forward as an explanation of an event, a possible situation or a form of behaviour that will be tested by the research.

7 *Design the research.* This means considering initially what research philosophy will be adopted. Is it to be positivist, phenomenological, or both? It is then necessary to establish the methodology. A decision will need to be made as to the extent to which the research will be quantitative, qualitative or, again, a combination of the two. A decision will also need to be made on the methods to be used, as described below. The research programme then needs to be drawn up. This will cover how the research will be conducted, the timetable and the required resources (funding, people, software, etc). Careful project planning is essential.

8 *Prepare and submit proposal.* This will justify the research by setting out the research question, the proposed methodology, and how the research is intended to increase knowledge and understanding. It will also describe the programme and the resources required.

9 *Conduct the research project.* This includes obtaining and analysing the evidence from the various sources needed to answer the research question and prove or disprove hypotheses. The significance of the findings in relation to the research question and the hypotheses will be discussed and reference will be made to relevant information provided in the literature. This involves an extended literary review; data collection; the use of logical, analytical and critical thinking processes; and the use of statistical analysis where relevant.

10 *Develop conclusions.* These draw together all the evidence. They provide the answer to

the research question and explain why hypotheses have been accepted or rejected. The significance of the findings will also be assessed in terms of how they contribute to the development of existing knowledge and understanding. Any limitations to the study should also be mentioned.

11 *Make recommendations*. These set out any guidelines emerging from the research. They may also indicate any follow-up actions required if the research has been conducted within an organization.

Research methodology

Research methodology involves the collection and analysis of evidence and testing hypotheses or propositions. The sources of evidence and how they will be accessed will be identified. This will include the analysis of primary and secondary source documents, further literature reviews, interviews, surveys and field work. The methodology can include as appropriate the use of triangulation, cross-lagged models and quantitative or qualitative research.

Triangulation

Triangulation takes place when information is obtained from more than two sources, for example, surveys, case studies and literature reviews. Greater confidence can be attached to a result if different methods lead to the same answer. If a researcher uses only one source this may be misleading or random. If two sources are used the results may clash. If three sources are used, the hope is that two of the three will produce similar answers, or if three clashing answers are produced, the researcher knows that the question needs to be reframed, methods reconsidered, or both.

Cross-lagged models

Cross-lagged models are longitudinal statistical panel studies in which two or more variables are measured for a large number of subjects at each of several waves or points in time. The variables divide naturally into two sets and the primary purpose of the analysis is to estimate and test the cross-effects between these two sets.

Quantitative research

Quantitative research is empirical – based on the collection of factual data, which is measured and quantified. It answers research questions from the viewpoint of the researcher. It may involve a considerable amount of statistical analysis, using methods for collecting the data through questionnaires, surveys, observation and experiment. The collection of data is distinct from its analysis.

Qualitative research

Qualitative research aims to generate insights into situations and behaviour so that the meaning of what is happening can be understood. It emphasizes the interpretation of behaviour from the viewpoint of the participants. It is based on evidence that may not be easily reduced to numbers. It makes use of interviews, case studies and observation but it may also draw on the information obtained from surveys. It may produce narratives or 'stories' describing situations, events or processes.

Methods of collecting data

The main methods of collecting data are interviews, questionnaires, surveys, case studies, observation, diaries and experimental designs.

Interviews

Interviews are an important research method. They obtain factual data and insights into attitudes and feelings and can take three forms:

1 *Structured*, which means that they obtain answers to a pre-prepared set of questions. This ensures that every topic is covered and minimizes variations between respondents. But they may be too rigid and inhibit spontaneous and revealing reactions.

2 *Unstructured*, which means that no questions have been prepared in advance and the person being interviewed is left free to talk about the subject without interruption or intervention. Such 'non-directive' interviews are intended to provide greater insight into the interviewee's perspective, avoid fitting

respondents into predetermined categories and enable interviewers to explore issues as they arise. But they can be inconsequential and lead to poor data that is difficult to analyse.

3 *Semi-structured*, which means that the areas of interest have been predetermined and the key questions to be asked or information to be obtained have been identified. The interviewer may have a checklist but does not follow this rigidly. This approach enables the interviewer to phrase questions and vary their order to suit the special characteristics of each interviewee. It may avoid the problems of the completely structured or unstructured interview but it does require a considerable degree of skill on the part of the interviewer.

Interviews are basically qualitative but they can become more quantitative by the use of content analysis. This records the number of times references are made in an interview to the key issues or areas of interest it was intended to cover.

The advantages of interviews are that they obtain information directly from people involved in the area being researched and can provide insights into attitudes and perspectives that questionnaires and surveys will not reveal, thus promoting in-depth understanding. They enable the interviewer to probe answers and check that questions had been understood. But the disadvantages are that:

- the construction of the interview questions may result in leading questions or bland answers;
- interviewers may influence the interviewees' reactions by imposing their own reference frame;
- respondents may tell interviewers what they want to hear;
- they are time-consuming – to set up, to conduct and to analyse;
- they require considerable interviewing skills, including the abilities to recognize what is important and relevant, to probe when necessary, to listen and to control the interview so that it covers the ground it was intended to cover.

Questionnaires

Questionnaires collect data systematically by obtaining answers on the key issues and opinions that need to be explored in a research project. They are frequently used as a means of gathering information on matters of fact or opinion. They use a variety of methods, namely: closed questions that require a yes or no answer, ranking in order of importance or value, or Likert scales. The latter, named after Rensis Likert, the American sociologist who invented them, ask respondents to indicate the extent to which they agree or disagree with a statement. For example, in response to a statement such as 'I like my job' the choice may be: 1 – strongly agree, 2 – agree, 3 – disagree, 4 – strongly disagree. Alternatively, an extended scale may be used and respondents asked to ring round the number that reflects their view about the statement (the higher the number the greater the agreement), for example: My contribution is fully recognized – 1 2 3 4 5 6 7. Extended scales facilitate the quantitative analysis of responses to questionnaires.

To construct and use a questionnaire effectively it is necessary to:

1 Identify the key issues and potential questions.
2 Ensure questions are clear.
3 Avoid asking two questions in one item.
4 Avoid leading questions that supply their own answers.
5 Decide on the structure of the questionnaire including its length (not too many items) and the type of scale to be used.
6 Code questions for ease of analysis.
7 Start with simple factual questions, moving on later to items of opinion or values.
8 Add variety and the opportunity to check consistency by interspersing positive statements such as 'I like working for my boss' with occasional associated negative ones such as 'I do not get adequate support from my boss'.
9 Pilot test the questionnaire.
10 Code results and analyse. Where rating scales have been used, the analysis can be quantified for comparison purposes. Content analysis can be used to analyse narrative answers to open-ended questions.

Questionnaires can effectively gather factual evidence but are not so useful for researchers who are investigating how or why things are happening. It is also impossible to assess the degree of subjectivity that has crept in when expressing opinions. For example, HR managers may give an opinion of the extent to which a performance-related pay scheme has in fact improved performance but the evidence to support that opinion will be lacking. This is where interviews can be more informative.

Surveys

Surveys obtain information from a defined population of people. Typically, they are based on questionnaires but they can provide more powerful data than other methods by using a combination of questionnaires and interviews and, possibly, focus groups (groups of people gathered together to answer and discuss specific questions). When developing and administering surveys the issues are:

1. The definition of the purpose of the survey and the outcomes hoped for – these must be as precise as possible.
2. The population to be covered – this may involve a census of the whole population. Alternatively, if the population is large, sampling will be necessary (see below).
3. The choice of methods – relying entirely on questionnaires may limit the validity of the findings. It is better, if time and the availability of finance permit, to complement them with interviews and, possibly, focus groups. Consideration has to be give to the extent to which triangulation (comparing the information obtained from more than two sources) is appropriate.
4. The questions to which answers are required, whichever method is used.
5. The design of questionnaires and the ways in which interview or focus groups, if used, should be structured.
6. How the outcome of the survey will be analysed and presented, including the use of case studies.

Sampling

In using surveys, and possibly other methods, it may not be feasible to cover the whole population (the sampling frame) and sampling will therefore be necessary. Sampling means that a proportion of the total population is selected for study and the aim is to see that this proportion represents the characteristics of the whole population. The sample must not be biased and that is why, in large-scale surveys, use is made of random sampling, ie the individuals covered by a survey are not selected in accordance with any criteria except that they exist in the population and can be reached by the survey. It is the equivalent of drawing numbers out of a hat. However, if the sample frame is considered to be already arranged randomly, as in the electoral roll, then structured sampling – that is, sampling at regular intervals – can be employed.

Sampling can produce varying degrees of error depending on the size of the sample. Statistical techniques can be used to establish sample errors and confidence limits. For example, they might establish that a sampling error is 3 per cent and the confidence limit is 95 per cent. This could be reasonably satisfactory, depending on the nature of the research (medical research aims to achieve 100 per cent confidence).

Case studies

A research case study is a description of a situation or a history of an event or sequence of events in a real-life setting that illustrates a particular area of interest, for example, how a performance management system has been developed and works. In learning and development, case studies are analysed by those involved to learn something by diagnosing the causes of a problem and working out how to solve it.

Case studies are used extensively in HRM research as a means of collecting empirical evidence in a real-life context. Information is obtained about a situation, an event or a set of events that establishes what has happened, how it happened and why. Case studies provide information that contributes to the creation of a theory as part of a grounded theory approach, or the validation of an established theory. In addition, they can take the form of stories or narratives that illuminate a decision or a set of decisions, why they were taken, how they were implemented and with what result. They can illustrate a total situation and describe the processes involved and how individuals and groups behave in a social setting.

Case study protocol sets out the objectives of the research; how the case study will support the achievement of those objectives, including the evidence required; and how the work of producing the case study will be conducted. The methodology covers:

- sources of evidence – interviews, observation, documents and records;
- the need to use multiple sources of evidence (triangulation) as far as possible;
- the questions to which answers need to be obtained;
- how the case study should be set up, including informing those involved of what is taking place and enlisting their support;
- the schedule of interviews and other evidence-collection activities;
- how the case study database recording the evidence will be set up and maintained;
- how the case study will be presented – including the chain of evidence so that the reader can follow the argument and trace the development of events, the headings and report guidelines (these may be finalized during the course of the exercise) and whether or not the name of the organization will be revealed on publication (named cases studies are more convincing than anonymous ones);
- how approval will be sought for the publication of the case study, especially if it reveals the name of the organization.

Case studies are useful ways of collecting information on the reality of organizational life and processes. But there is a danger of case studies being no more than a story or an anecdote that does not contribute to greater knowledge or understanding. Much skill and persistence are required from the researcher in gaining support, ensuring that relevant and revealing information is obtained, and presenting the case study as a convincing narrative from which valid and interesting conclusions can be derived. All this must be done without taking a biased view, which can be difficult.

Observation

Observation of individuals or groups at work is a method of getting a direct and realistic impression of what is happening. It can be done by a detached or an involved observer, or by participant observation.

Detached observers who simply study what is going on without getting involved with the people concerned may only get a superficial impression of what is happening and may be resented by the people under observation as 'eavesdropping'. In an HR context, involved observers work closely with employees and can move around, observe and participate as appropriate. This means that they can get closer to events and are more likely to be accepted, especially if the objectives and methods have been agreed in advance. Participant observation in the fullest sense means that the researcher becomes an employee and experiences the work and the social processes that take place at first hand. This can provide powerful insights but is time-consuming and requires considerable skill and persistence.

The issues with any form of observation are in getting close enough to events to understand their significance and then analysing the mass of information that might be produced in order to come up with findings that contribute to answering the research question.

Diaries

Getting people to complete diaries of what they do is a method of building a realistic picture of how people, especially managers, spend their time.

Experimental designs

Experimental designs involve setting up an experimental group and a control group and then placing subjects at random in one or other group. The conditions under which the experimental group functions are then manipulated and the outcomes compared with the control group, whose conditions remain unchanged. The classic case of an experimental design was the Hawthorne study, the results of which had a major impact on thinking about how groups function and on the human relations movement. But this was exceptional. It is much easier to use experiments in a laboratory setting, which has been done many times with students. But there is always the feeling that such experiments do not reflect real-life conditions.

Processes involved in research

This section describes the logical, analytical and critical thinking processes that are used in research: deduction, induction, hypothesis testing, grounded theory, paradigms and critical evaluation.

Deduction

Research involves deduction, which is the process of using logical reasoning to reach a conclusion that necessarily follows from general or universal premises. If the premises are correct, so is the deduction. The conclusion is therefore contained within the evidence. It is not a creative or imaginative argument that produces new ideas.

Induction

Research can also be based on induction, which is the process of reaching generalized conclusions from the observation of particular instances. In contrast to deduction, inductive conclusions may be tentative but they contain new ideas. In research, both deductive and inductive reasoning can be used in hypothesis testing.

Hypothesis testing

Formulating a hypothesis is an important element in a research project in that it provides a basis for the development of theory and the collection and analysis of data. A hypothesis is a supposition – a tentative explanation of something. It is a provisional statement that is taken to be true for the purpose of argument or a study and usually relates to an existing wider body of knowledge or theory. A hypothesis has to be tested and should be distinguished from a theory, which, by definition, has been tested. A good hypothesis contains two concepts and proposes a relationship between the two. A working hypothesis is a general hypothesis that has been operationalized so that it can be tested.

Hypothesis formulation and testing uses the strengths of both deductive and inductive processes; the former entirely conclusive but unimaginative, the latter tentative but creative. Induction produces ideas and deduction tests them.

To test a hypothesis, data has to be obtained that will demonstrate that its predicted consequences are true or false. Simply leaping to the conclusion that a hypothesis is true, because a single cause of the consequence has been observed, falls into the trap of what logicians call the 'fallacy of affirming the consequent'. There may be alternative and more valid causes. The preferred method of testing is that of denying the consequent. This is 'falsification', as advocated by Popper (1959). His view was that however much data may be assembled to support a hypothesis, it is not possible to reach a conclusive proof of the truth of that hypothesis. Popper therefore proposed that it was insufficient simply to assemble confirmatory evidence: what must also be obtained is evidence that refutes the hypothesis. Only one instance of refutation is needed to falsify a theory, whereas however many confirmations of the theory exist it will still not be proved conclusively.

Grounded theory

Grounded theory is an inductive method of developing the general features of a theory by grounding the account in empirical observations or evidence. The researcher uses empirical evidence directly to establish the concepts and relationships that will be contained in the theory. Evidence is collected from both primary sources (ie obtained directly by the researcher from the originator of the evidence) and secondary sources (ie information that is already available in the literature or on the internet). Use is made of triangulation.

Paradigm

The term 'paradigm' has become popularized as meaning a way of looking at things. It is often used loosely, but properly it means the philosophical and theoretical framework of a scientific school or discipline within which theories, laws and generalizations – and the experiments performed in support of them – are formulated. In other words, it is a common perspective that underpins the work of theorists so that they use the same approach to conducting research.

Critical evaluation

Critical evaluation involves making informed judgements about the value of ideas and arguments. It uses critical thinking, which is the process of analysing and evaluating the quality of ideas, theories and concepts to establish the degree to which they are valid and supported by the evidence (evidence-based) and the extent to which they are biased. It means reflecting on and interpreting data, drawing warranted conclusions and identifying faulty reasoning, assumptions and biases. A creative leap may be required to reach a judgement; it was described fully in Chapter 47.

Key learning points: Research skills

The nature of research

Research is concerned with establishing what *is* – and from this predicting what will be. It is about the conception and testing of ideas.

Research philosophy

Research design can be based on a philosophy of positivism or phenomenology. Positivism is the belief that researchers should focus on facts (observable reality), look for causality and fundamental laws. Phenomenology is concerned more with the meaning of phenomena than the facts associated with them.

Planning and conducting research programmes

1. Define research area.
2. Formulate initial research question.
3. Review literature.
4. Assess existing theoretical frameworks.
5. Formalize the research question.
6. Formulate hypotheses.
7. Establish the methodology.
8. Draw up research programme.
9. Prepare and submit proposal.
10. Collect and analyse evidence.
11. Develop conclusions.

Approaches to research

- Research can be quantitative or qualitative.
- It can use inductive or deductive methods.
- It involves the testing of hypotheses and may adopt a grounded theory approach, ie an inductive method of developing the general features of a theory by grounding the account in empirical observations or evidence.
- Use may be made of paradigms – common perspectives that underpin the work of theorists so that they use the same approach to conducting research.
- Informed judgements about the value of ideas and arguments are made through critical evaluation.
- It makes use of critical thinking, which is the process of analysing and evaluating the quality of ideas, theories and concepts to establish the degree to which they are valid and supported by the evidence.

Methods of collecting data

- Interviews obtain factual data and insights into attitudes and feelings and can be structured, unstructured or semi-structured.
- Questionnaires collect data systematically by obtaining answers on the key issues and opinions that need to be explored in a research project.
- Surveys obtain information from a defined population of people.
- Case studies collect empirical evidence in a real-life context.

Questions

1 What is the nature of research?
2 What are the steps required to conduct a research project?
3 What are the advantages and disadvantages of interviews as a research technique?
4 What are the advantages and disadvantages of case studies as a research technique?
5 What is induction?
6 What is deduction?
7 What is grounded theory?
8 What is triangulation?
9 What is the difference between a hypothesis and a theory?
10 What is a paradigm?

References

Popper, K (1959) *The Logic of Scientific Discovery*, London, Hutchinson

Lewin, K (1945) The research centre for group dynamics at Massachusetts Institute of Technology, Scrometry, 8, pp 126–36

49
Statistical skills

KEY CONCEPTS AND TERMS

- Average
- Causality
- Chi-squared test
- Correlation
- Dispersion
- Frequency
- Frequency distribution
- Line of best fit
- Lower quartile
- Mean
- Median
- Mode
- Multi-regression analysis
- Multi-variant analysis
- Regression
- Reverse causation
- Scattergram
- Significance
- Standard deviation
- Trend line
- Upper quartile
- Variance

LEARNING OUTCOMES

On completing this chapter you should be able to define these key concepts. You should also understand:

- The use of statistics
- Frequency analysis
- Measures of central tendency
- Measures of dispersion
- Correlation
- Regression
- Tests of significance
- Tests of hypotheses

Introduction

HR professionals need skills in using statistics in order to analyse and present quantitative information that can be used to guide decisions and monitor outcomes. Statistical skills are an essential element in human capital management and are also important in such fields as performance management (the analysis of appraisal results and levels of performance) and reward management (the analysis of market rates, pay reviews, the distribution of pay, and equal pay). Statistics play a major part in the analysis of surveys and research evidence.

HR professionals do not need advanced statistical skills unless they are conducting or taking part in detailed research projects. The main statistics they will use regularly, as described in this chapter, are concerned with the analysis of the incidence of events or activities (frequencies), the use of averages (measures of central tendency), how items in a population are distributed (dispersion) and the relationship between two variables (regression). But they should also be familiar with the concepts of correlation and causation, and at least understand the meaning of more advanced statistical techniques used by researchers such as tests of significance, the chi-squared test and null-hypothesis testing.

Using statistics

Statistics describe and summarize data relating to a 'population', ie a homogeneous set of items with variable individual values. This involves measuring frequencies, central tendencies and dispersion. Statistics can also measure the relationships between variables (correlation and regression), establish the relation between cause and effect (causality), assess the degree of confidence that can be attached to conclusions (tests of significance) and test hypotheses (the chi-squared test and null-hypothesis testing). A wide variety of software is available to conduct the more sophisticated analyses.

Frequency

Frequency is the number of times that individual items in a population or set occur. It is represented in frequency distributions expressed in tabular form or graphically. Commonly used graphs are illustrated in Figure 49.1.

Measures of central tendency

Measures of central tendency identify the middle or centre of a set of data. There are three types:

- Arithmetic average or mean – the total of items or scores in a set divided by the number of individual items in the set. It may give a distorted picture because of large items at either end of the scale.
- Median – the middle item in a range of items (often used in pay surveys when the arithmetic mean is likely to be distorted).
- Mode – the most commonly occurring item in a set of data.

FIGURE 49.1 Examples of charts

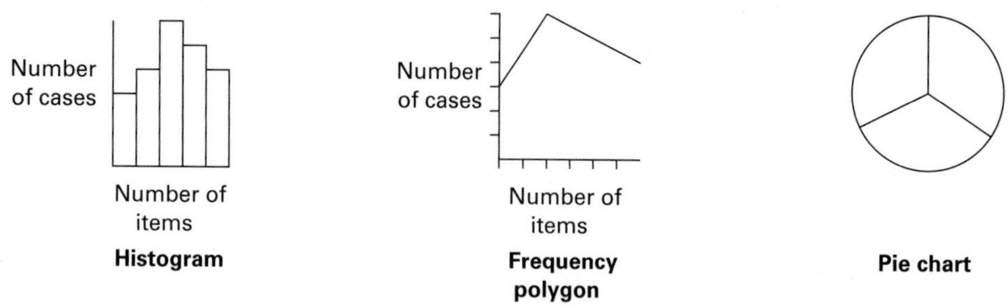

Measures of dispersion

It is often useful to measure the extent to which the items in a set are dispersed or spread over a range of data. This can be done in five ways:

1. By identifying the upper quartile or lower quartile of a range of data. The strict definition of an upper quartile is that it is the value that 25 per cent of the values in the distribution exceed, and the lower quartile is the value below which 25 per cent of the values in a distribution occur. More loosely, especially when looking at pay distributions, the upper and lower quartiles are treated as ranges rather than points in a scale and represent the top and the bottom 25 per cent of the distribution respectively.
2. By presenting the total range of values from top to bottom; this may be misleading if there are exceptional items at either end.
3. By calculating the interquartile range, which is the range between the value of the upper quartile and that of the lower quartile. This can present more revealing information of the distribution than the total range.
4. By calculating the standard deviation, which is used to indicate the extent to which the items or values in a distribution are grouped together or dispersed in a normal distribution, ie one that is reasonably symmetrical around its average. As a rule of thumb, two-thirds of the distribution will be less than one standard deviation from the mean, 95 per cent of the distribution will be less than two standard deviations from the mean, and less than 1 per cent of the distribution will be more than three standard deviations from the mean.
5. By calculating variance, which is the square of a standard deviation.

Correlation

Correlation represents the relationship between two variables. If they are highly correlated they are strongly connected to one another, and vice versa. In statistics, correlation is measured by the coefficient of correlation, which varies between –1 and +1 to indicate totally negative and totally positive correlations respectively. A correlation of zero means that there is no relationship between the variables. Establishing the extent to which variables are correlated is an important feature of HRM research in assessing, for example, the degree to which a performance management system improves organizational performance. But correlations do not indicate causal relationships. Multiple correlation looks at the relationship between more than two variables.

Regression

Regression is another way of looking at the relationship between variables. It expresses how changes in levels of one item relate to changes in levels of another. A regression line (a trend line, or line of best fit) can be traced on a scattergram expressing values of one variable on one axis and values of the other variable on another axis, as shown in Figure 49.2.

FIGURE 49.2 A scattergram with regression (trend) line

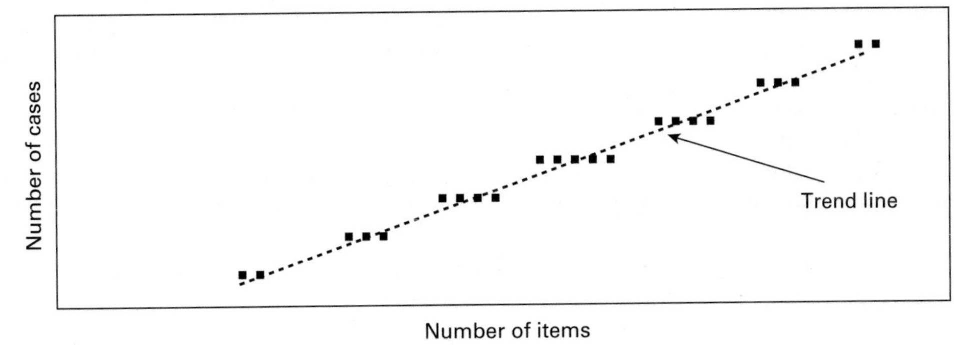

A trend line can be drawn by hand as a line of best fit, but it can be calculated mathematically with greater accuracy. The distances of points from the trend line (the residuals) can be calculated as a check on the reliability of the line.

Multiple regression analysis can be conducted with the aid of a computer in order to express how changes in the levels of a number of items relate to changes in levels of other items.

Causality

Causality is the representation of cause and effect, ie the link between independent and dependent variables. To establish causality is to explain how one thing leads to another. Causality is a major issue in research, including in the HRM field. It may be relatively easy to establish correlations in the shape of a demonstration that X is associated with Y; it is much more difficult and sometimes impossible to prove that X causes Y. There are a number of reasons for this, of which the two set out below are the most important.

First, complications arise because of the phenomenon of multiple causation. There may be a number of factors contributing to a result. In HRM, researchers pursuing the holy grail of trying to establish what HRM contributes to an organization's performance are usually confronted with a number of reasons why an organization has done well in addition to adopting 'best practice' HRM, whatever that is. Statistical techniques can be used to 'control' some variables, ie eliminate them from the analysis, but it is difficult if not impossible to ensure that HRM practices have been completely isolated and that their direct impact on the organization's performance has been measured. Multivariate analysis is used where there is more than one dependent variable and where the dependent variables cannot be combined.

Second, there is the phenomenon of reverse causation, when a cause may be pre-dated by an effect – A might have caused B but, alternatively, B might have come first and be responsible for A. For example, it is possible to demonstrate that organizations with effective performance management schemes do better than those without. But it might equally be the case that it is high-performing organizations that introduce effective performance management. It can be hard to be certain. A good example of reversed causation was provided by Reinhart and Rogoff (2009) whose seminal paper argued that growth rates fell sharply when a nation's debt as a proportion of its annual output reached 90 per cent. This paper provided a justification for the austerity programmes in the UK and Europe in 2011 and later. However, as pointed out by Larry Elliott (2013), Reinhart and Rogoff confused cause and effect; countries might well have high debt levels because they have slow growth, rather than having slow growth because they are heavily indebted. This was apart from the fact noted by Elliott that Reinhart and Rogoff's paper contained basic spreadsheet errors in its original calculations, which meant that the 90 per cent cliff does not exist.

Tests of significance

Significance as a statistical concept refers to the degree to which an event could have occurred by chance. At the heart of statistical science lies a simple idea, which is that the chance or probability of various patterns of events can be predicted. When a particular pattern is observed it is possible to work out what the chances of its occurrence may be, given our existing state of knowledge or by making certain assumptions. If something has been observed that is unlikely to have occurred by chance, this occurrence can be accepted as significant. The problem is that any attempt to reach general conclusions may have to rely on fragmentary data. It is usually necessary to rely on samples of the population being studied, and all sampling is subject to experimental error – the result can only be expressed in terms of probability, and confidence limits will have to be placed on it. These can be calculated in terms of the standard error that might be expected from a sample. A standard error is the estimated standard deviation of a sample mean from a true mean. This implies that on approximately 95 per cent of occasions the estimate of the mean provided by the sample will be within two standard errors of the true mean.

Testing hypotheses

The chi-squared test uses a statistical formula to assess the degree of agreement between the data actually obtained and that expected under a particular hypothesis.

A *null hypothesis* is a method of testing a hypothesis that is frequently used by researchers in which it is assumed that there is no relationship between two or more variables. It asks the question: could the hypothetical relationship have been caused by chance? If the answer is 'no', then the hypothesis is worth pursuing. However, it does not prove that the hypothesis is correct; it only indicates that something is worth pursuing. It can be associated with the chi-squared test.

Key learning points: Statistical skills

Use of statistics

Statistics are used to describe and summarize data relating to a 'population', ie a homogeneous set of items with variable individual values. This involves measuring frequencies, central tendencies and dispersion.

Statistics are also used to measure the relationships between variables (correlation and regression), to establish the relation between cause and effect (causality), to assess the degree of confidence that can be attached to conclusions (tests of significance) and to test hypotheses (the chi-squared test and null-hypothesis testing).

Statistics are used extensively in HRM to analyse and present quantitative information that can be used to guide decisions and monitor outcomes.

Measures of central tendency

Measures of central tendency identify the middle or centre of a set of data. There are three types: arithmetic average (or mean), median and mode.

Measures of dispersion

It is useful to measure the extent to which the items in a set are dispersed or spread over a range of data.

Correlation

Correlation represents the relationship between two variables. If they are highly correlated they are strongly connected to one another, and vice versa.

Regression

Regression is another way of looking at the relationship between variables. It expresses how changes in levels of one item relate to changes in levels of another.

Causality

Determining the link between independent and dependent variables (cause and effect) – is a major issue in research, especially in the HRM field. It may be relatively easy to establish correlations in the shape of a demonstration that X is associated with Y; it is much more difficult and sometimes impossible to prove that X causes Y.

Tests of significance

Significance as a statistical concept refers to the degree to which an event could have occurred by chance.

Questions

1 How are statistics used?
2 What use is made by HR specialists of statistics?
3 What is frequency in statistics?
4 What are the three measures of central tendency?
5 What is dispersion and how is it measured?
6 What is correlation?
7 What is regression?
8 What is causality?
9 What are the problems of establishing causation?
10 What is a test of significance?
11 How can hypotheses be tested?

References

Elliott, L (2013) 'Stonewall' Osborne falls victim to friendly fire, *The Guardian*, 22 April, p 22

Reinhart, C M and Rogoff, K S (2009) *The Aftermath of Financial Crisis*, NBER Woking Paper No 14656, January

50 Selection interviewing skills

KEY CONCEPTS AND TERMS

Behavioural-based interview
Closed question
Competency-based interview
Halo effect
Horns effect
Interview
Open question
Situational-based interview
Structured interview

LEARNING OUTCOMES

On completing this chapter you should be able to define these key concepts. You should also understand:

- Selection interviewing skills
- Preparing for the interview
- Planning the interview
- Questioning techniques
- Coming to a conclusion
- Dos and don'ts of selection interviewing

Introduction

The purpose of a selection interview is to establish the extent to which a candidate will be able to do the job. This means finding out how well a candidate's levels of skill, knowledge, abilities and competency fit a person specification for the job that sets out these requirements. Selection interviewing is a skilled process, and this chapter starts with a description of the basic skills required. It then deals with the three areas in which these skills are applied: preparing for the interview, conducting the interview and reaching a conclusion.

Selection interviewing skills

An interview is a conversation with a purpose. It is a conversation because candidates should be given the opportunity to talk freely about themselves and their careers. But the conversation has to be planned, directed and controlled in order to achieve your aims in the time available. Overall, an effective approach to interviewing can be summed up as the three Cs:

- *Content* – the information you want and the questions you ask to get it.
- *Contact* – your ability to make and maintain good contact with candidates; to establish the sort of rapport that will encourage them to talk freely, thus revealing their strengths and their weaknesses.
- *Control* – your ability to control the interview so that you get the information you want.

This involves using the following interviewing skills: establishing rapport, questioning, listening, maintaining continuity, keeping control and note taking.

Establishing rapport

Establishing rapport means establishing a good relationship with candidates – getting on their wavelength, putting them at ease, encouraging them to respond and generally being friendly. This is not just a question of being 'nice' to them. If you achieve rapport you are more likely to get them to talk freely about both their strengths and weaknesses.

Good rapport is created by the way in which you greet candidates, how you start the interview and how you put your questions and respond to replies. Questions should not be posed aggressively or imply that you are criticizing some aspect of the candidate's career. Some people like the idea of 'stress' interviews, but they are counterproductive. Candidates clam up and gain a negative impression of you and the organization.

When responding to answers you should be appreciative, not critical: 'Thank you, that was very helpful; now can we go on to...?' not, 'Well, it seems to me that things did not go according to plan.'

Body language can also be important. If you maintain natural eye contact, avoid slumping in your seat, nod and make encouraging comments when appropriate, you will establish better rapport and get more out of the interview.

Questioning

Questioning is the key skill that interviewers need to possess. Their purpose is to draw candidates out and elicit the information the interviewer has decided must be obtained to reach a conclusion. Questioning is a fundamental part of a structured interview. There are a number of different types of questions, described later in the section on questioning techniques.

Listening

If an interview is a conversation with a purpose, listening skills are important. You need not only to hear but also to understand what candidates are saying. When interviewing you must concentrate on what candidates are telling you. Summarizing at regular intervals forces you to listen: if you play back to candidates your understanding of what they have told you, for them to confirm or amend, it will ensure that you have fully comprehended the messages they are delivering.

Maintaining continuity

So far as possible link your questions to a candidate's last reply so that the interview progresses logically and a cumulative set of data is built up. You can put bridging questions to candidates such as: 'Thank you, that was an interesting summary of what you have been doing in this aspect of your work. Now, could you tell me something about your other key responsibilities?'

Keeping control

You want candidates to talk, but not too much. When preparing for the interview you should have drawn up an agenda and you must try to stick to it. Don't cut candidates short too brutally but say something like: 'Thank you, I've got a good picture of that, now what about...?'

Focus on specifics as much as you can. If candidates ramble on a bit, ask a pointed question (a 'probe' question) that asks for an example illustrating the particular aspect of their work that you are considering.

Note taking

You won't remember everything that candidates tell you. It is useful to take notes of the key points they make, discreetly, but not surreptitiously. However, don't put candidates off by frowning or tut-tutting when you are making a negative note. It may be helpful to ask candidates if they would mind if you take notes. They can't really object, but will appreciate the fact that they have been asked.

Preparing for the interview

Your first step in preparing for an interview is to familiarize or refamiliarize yourself with the person specification, which (as mentioned in Chapter 18) should be set out under the following headings:

- *Knowledge* – what the individual needs to know to carry out the role.
- *Skills and abilities* – what the individual has to be able to do to carry out the role.
- *Behavioural competencies* – the types of behaviour required for successful performance of the role. These should be role-specific, ideally based on an analysis of employees who are carrying out their roles effectively. The behaviours should also be linked to the core values and competency framework of the organization to help in ensuring that candidates will fit and support the organization's culture.
- *Qualifications and training* – the professional, technical or academic qualifications required or the training that the candidate should have undertaken.
- *Experience* – the types of achievements and activities likely to predict success.
- *Specific demands* – anything that the role holder will be expected to achieve in specified areas, eg develop new markets or products; improve sales, productivity or levels of customer service; introduce new systems or processes.
- *Special requirements* – travelling, unsocial hours, mobility, etc.

You should then read the candidates' CVs and, if available, their application forms or letters and refer to any other information about them obtained from the internet. This will identify any special questions you should ask about their career. For example, it may be necessary to fill in any gaps: 'What does this gap between jobs C and D signify?' (although you would not put the question as baldly as that – it would be better to say something like: 'I see there was a gap of six months between when you left your job in C and started in D. Would you mind telling me what you were doing during this time?')

Finally, you should consider how you will structure and plan the interview.

Structuring the interview

A structured interview is one that is based on a defined framework within which there is a set of predetermined questions. All candidates are asked the same questions and the answers may be scored through a rating system. Questions will focus on the attributes and behaviours required to succeed in the job.

The most typical framework is the person specification. Interview questions aim to analyse and build on the information provided by the candidate's CV or application form to establish the extent to which a candidate has the required knowledge, skills and abilities (KSAs). In a so-called competency-based interview the emphasis is on establishing if the candidate has the right level of desirable behavioural competencies. The interview may include experience-based questions in which candidates are asked to relate how they handled situations in the past requiring skills and abilities necessary for effective performance in the job for which they are applying. And/or it may include situational questions, which provide candidates with hypothetical job-relevant situations and ask how they would deal with them.

Planning the interview

Structured interviews need to be planned in terms of their three main parts (beginning, middle and end), the questions to be put to candidates and how the questions will be sequenced.

The parts of an interview

The content of an interview can be analysed into three parts: its beginning, middle and end.

Beginning

At the start of the interview you should put candidates at their ease. You want them to talk freely in response to your questions. They won't do this if you plunge in too abruptly. Welcome them and thank them for coming to the interview, expressing genuine pleasure about the meeting. But don't waste too much time talking about their journey or the weather.

Some interviewers start by describing the company and the job. Wherever possible it is best to eliminate this part of the interview by sending candidates a brief job description and something about the organization.

If you are not careful you will spend too much time at this stage, especially if the candidate later turns out to be unsuitable. A brief reference to the job should suffice, and this can be extended at the end of the interview.

Middle

This is when you ask questions designed to provide information on; 1) the extent to which the knowledge, skills, capabilities and personal qualities of candidates meet the person specification; 2) the career history and ambitions of candidates; and (sometimes) 3) on certain aspects of their behaviour at work such as sickness and absenteeism.

This part should take at least 80 per cent of the time, leaving, say, 5 per cent at the beginning and 15 per cent at the end.

End

At the end of the interview you should give candidates the opportunity to ask about the job and the company. How they do this can often give you clues as to the degree to which applicants are interested and their ability to ask pertinent questions.

You may want to expand a little on the job. If candidates are promising, some interviewers at this stage extol the attractive features of the job. This is fine as long as these are not exaggerated. To give a 'realistic preview', the possible downsides should be mentioned, for example the need to travel or unsocial working hours. If candidates are clearly unsuitable you can tactfully help them to deselect themselves by referring to aspects of the work that may not appeal to them, or for which they are not really qualified. It is best not to spell out these points too strongly. It is often sufficient simply to put the question: 'This is a key requirement of the job, how do you feel about it?' You can follow up this general question by more specific questions: 'Do you feel you have the right sort of experience?', 'Are you happy about (this aspect of the job)?'

At this stage you should ask final questions about the availability of candidates, as long as they are promising. You can ask when they would be able to start and about any holiday arrangements to which they are committed.

You should also ask their permission to obtain references from their present and previous employers. They might not want you to approach their present employer. But you should tell them that if they are made an offer of employment it would be conditional on a satisfactory reference from that employer. It is useful to ensure that you have the names of people you can approach.

Finally, inform candidates of what happens next. If it might be some time before they hear from you, they should be told that you will be writing as soon as possible but that there will be some delay (don't make a promise you can't keep).

It is not normally good practice to inform candidates of your decision at the end of the interview. You should take time to reflect on their suitability and you don't want to give them the impression that you are making a snap judgement.

Deciding on the questions

The key questions in structured interviews should be planned in advance. This particularly applies to situational questions, which are designed to reveal how a candidate would behave in a typical situation and therefore provide information about levels of behavioural competency. Such questions are linked to the behavioural competencies required in the role.

Capability questions can be planned to establish what candidates know, the skills they possess and what they are capable of doing. An appropriate mix of situational, experience-based and capability questions may be used.

Sequencing the questions

When planning interviews you should give some thought to how you are going to sequence your questions, especially in the middle part. There are two basic approaches, as described below.

Biographical approach

The biographical approach is probably the most popular because it is simple to use and appears to be logical. The interview can be sequenced chronologically, starting with the first job or even before that at school and, if appropriate, college or university. The succeeding jobs, if any, are then dealt with in turn, ending with the present job – to which most attention is given if the candidate has been in it for some time.

However, if you are not careful, using the chronological method for someone who has had a number of jobs can mean spending too much time on the earlier jobs, leaving insufficient time for the most important recent experience. To overcome this problem, an alternative biographical approach is to start with the present job, which is discussed in some depth. The interviewer then works backwards, job by job, but only concentrating on particularly interesting or relevant experience in earlier jobs.

The problem with the biographical approach is that it is predictable. Experienced candidates are familiar with it and have their story ready, glossing over any weak points. It can also be unreliable. You can easily miss an important piece of information by concentrating on a succession of jobs rather than focusing on key aspects of the candidates' experience that illustrate their capabilities. This is why the alternative targeted approach may be preferred.

Targeted or criteria-based approach

A target-based interview is a form of structured interview. It is based on an analysis of the person specification from which criteria are identified for judging the suitability of the candidate. Interview questions can then 'target' these criteria by asking for specific information on what candidates know, what they can do and how they would typically behave in certain situations. They would be asked to support their answers with evidence from their practical experience and their education or training. Responses can be compared with the criteria to assess the extent to which candidates meet the specification. This is probably the best way of focusing your interview to ensure that you get all the information you require about candidates for comparison with the person specification.

Questioning techniques

As mentioned earlier, an interview is a conversation with a purpose. The interviewer's job is to draw the candidate out, at the same time ensuring that the information required is obtained. To this end it is desirable to ask a number of open-ended questions – questions that cannot be answered by 'yes' or 'no' and which promote a full response. But a good interviewer will have an armoury of other types of questions to be asked when appropriate, as described below.

When questioning it is important for interviewers to remember that there will be a natural tendency for candidates to try and provide them with the answers that the interviewer seems to want to hear. It is therefore necessary to phrase questions in ways that do not give away the preferred answer. Open-ended questions may reduce this problem, as do closed questions that focus on factual information.

Open-ended questions

Open-ended questions are phrased generally, give no indication of the expected reply and cannot be answered by 'yes' or 'no'. They encourage candidates to talk – drawing them out and obtaining a full response. Single-word answers are seldom illuminating. It is a good idea to begin the interview with some open questions in order to obtain a general picture of candidates, thus helping them to settle in. Open questions or phrases inviting a response can be phrased as follows:

- I'd like you to tell me about the sort of work you are doing in your present job.
- What do you know about...?
- Could you give me some examples of...?
- In what ways do you think your experience fits you to do the job for which you have applied?
- How have you tackled...?
- What have been the most challenging aspects of your job?
- Please tell me about some of the interesting things you have been doing at work recently.

Open questions can provide a lot of useful information, but you may not get exactly what you want and answers can go into too much detail. For example, the question: 'What has been the main feature of your work in recent months?' may result in a one-word reply – 'marketing'. Or it may produce a lengthy explanation that takes up too much time. Replies to open questions can get bogged down in too much detail, or miss out some key points. They can come to a sudden halt or lose their way. You need to ensure that you get all the facts, keep the flow going and maintain control. Remember that you are in charge. Hence the value of probing, closed and the other types of questions. And candidates faced with open-ended questions can still attempt to provide what they believe the interviewer wants to hear.

Closed questions

Closed questions aim to clarify a point of fact. The expected reply will be an explicit single word or brief sentence. A closed question aims to produce a succinct factual statement without going into detail. When you ask a closed question you intend to find out the following:

- What the candidate has or has not done – 'What did you do then?'
- Why something took place – 'Why did that happen?'
- When something took place – 'When did that happen?'
- How something happened – 'How did that situation arise?'
- Where something happened – 'Where were you at the time?'
- Who took part – 'Who else was involved?'

Probing questions

Probing questions ask for further details and explanations to ensure that you are getting all the facts. You ask probing questions when answers have been too generalized or when you suspect that there may be some more relevant information that candidates have not disclosed. A candidate may claim to have done something and it may be useful to find out more about exactly what contribution was made. Poor interviewers tend to let general and uninformative answers pass by without probing for further details, simply because they are sticking rigidly to a predetermined list of open questions. Skilled interviewers are able to flex their approach to ensure they get the facts while still keeping control to ensure that the interview is completed on time.

A candidate could say to you something like: 'I was involved in a major exercise that produced significant improvements in the flow of work through the factory.' This statement conveys nothing about what the candidate actually did. You have to ask probing questions, such as the examples below:

- You've informed me that you have had experience in... Could you tell me more about what you did?
- What sort of targets or standards have you been expected to achieve?
- How successful have you been in achieving those targets or standards? Please give examples.
- Could you give an example of any project you have undertaken?
- What was your precise role in this project?
- What exactly was the contribution you made to its success?
- What knowledge and skills were you able to apply to the project?
- Were you responsible for monitoring progress?

- Did you prepare the final recommendations in full or in part? If in part, which part?
- Could you describe in more detail the equipment you used?

Behavioural event/situation-based questions

Behavioural event or situation-based questions are hypothetical questions used in structured interviews. They describe a situation to candidates who are asked how they would deal with it. Questions can be prepared in advance to test how candidates would approach a typical problem or issue they might meet in the job for which they are being considered and that is critical to successful job performance. The assumption upon which such questions are based is that the ways in which people describe how they would behave in dealing with or reacting to events is a good predictor of future behaviour. In general, a situational question may take the form: 'What would you do if...?' Other examples of behavioural event or situational questions are:

- Could you give an instance of when you persuaded others to take an unusual course of action?
- Could you describe an occasion when you completed a project or task in the face of great difficulties?
- Could you describe any contribution you have made as a member of a team in achieving an unusually successful result?
- Could you give an instance of when you took the lead in a difficult situation in getting something worthwhile done?
- Could you tell me about a recent achievement of which you are particularly proud?
- Could you give an example of when you successfully introduced an innovation at work?
- Could you describe a situation in which you had to convince others to do something they weren't particularly keen on?
- Could you tell me about a difficult situation with a member of your staff that you have handled particularly well?
- What would you do if someone rudely disagreed with you during a meeting?
- What would you do if you were ordered by your boss to do something that you knew was unethical?
- What would you do if a member of your team refused to carry out what you considered to be a reasonable request?
- How would you deal with a subordinate whose performance is good but who is persistently late coming to work?
- How would you improve the quality of team work in a group?
- What do you think is the best way to motivate people?

When behavioural or situation-based questions lie well within the candidate's expertise and experience the answers can be illuminating. But it could be unfair to ask candidates to say how they would deal with a problem without knowing more about the context in which the problem arose. It can also be argued that what candidates say they would do and what they actually do could be quite different. Hypothetical questions can produce hypothetical answers. The best data upon which judgements about candidates can be made are what they have actually done or achieved. You need to find out if they have successfully dealt with the sort of issues and problems they may be faced with if they join your organization.

Capability questions

Capability questions aim to establish what candidates know, the skills they possess and what they are capable of doing. They can be open, probing or closed, but they will always be focused as precisely as possible on the contents of the person specification, referring to knowledge, skills and competences.

Capability questions should therefore be explicit – focused on what candidates must know and be able to do. Their purpose is to obtain evidence from candidates that shows the extent to which they meet the specification in each of its key areas. Because time is always limited it is best to concentrate on the most important aspects of the work, and it is always best to prepare the questions in advance. The sort of capability questions you can ask are set out below:

- What do you know about...?
- How did you gain this knowledge?
- What are the key skills you are expected to use in your work?
- How would your present employer rate the level of skill you have reached in...?
- Could you please tell me exactly what sort and how much experience you have had in...?
- Could you tell me more about what you have actually been doing in this aspect of your work?
- Can you give me any examples of the sort of work you have done that would qualify you to do this job?
- What are the most typical problems you have to deal with?
- Would you tell me about any instances when you have had to deal with an unexpected problem or a crisis?

Motivation questions

The degree to which candidates are motivated is a personal quality to which it is necessary to give special attention if it is to be properly assessed. This is usually achieved by inference rather than direct questions. 'How well are you motivated?' is a leading question that will usually produce the response: 'Highly'. You can make inferences about the level of motivation of candidates by asking questions on the following subjects:

- *Their career* – replies to such questions as: 'Why did you decide to move on from there?' can give an indication of the extent to which they have been well-motivated in progressing their career.
- *Achievements* – not just, 'What did you achieve?' but, 'How did you achieve it?' and, 'What difficulties did you overcome?'
- *Triumphing over disadvantages* – candidates who have done well in spite of an unpromising upbringing and relatively poor education may be more highly motivated than those with all the advantages that upbringing and education can bestow, but who have not made good use of these advantages.
- *Spare time interests* – don't accept at its face value a reply to a question about spare time interests that, for example, reveals that a candidate collects stamps. Find out if the candidate is well-motivated enough to pursue the interest with determination and to achieve something in the process.

Continuity questions

Continuity questions aim to keep the flow going in an interview and encourage candidates to enlarge on what they have told you, within limits. Here are some examples:

- What happened next?
- What did you do then?
- Can we talk about your next job?
- Can we move on now to...?
- Could you tell me more about...?

It has been said that to keep the conversation going during an interview the best thing an interviewer can do is to make encouraging grunts at appropriate moments. There is more to interviewing than that, but single words or phrases like 'good', 'fine', 'that's interesting', 'carry on' can help things along.

Play-back questions

Play-back questions test your understanding of what candidates have said by putting to them a statement of what it appears they have told you, and asking them if they agree or disagree with your version. For example, you could say: 'As I understand it, you resigned from your last position because you disagreed with your boss on a number of fundamental issues – have I got that right?' The answer might simply be 'yes' to this closed question, in which case you might probe to find out more about what happened. Or the candidate may reply 'Not exactly', in which case you ask for the full story.

Career questions

As mentioned earlier, questions about the career history of candidates can provide some insight into motivation as well as establishing how they have progressed in acquiring useful and relevant knowledge, skills and experience. You can ask questions such as those given below:

- What did you learn from that new job?
- What different skills did you have to use when you were promoted?
- Why did you leave that job?
- What happened after you left that job?
- In what ways do you think this job will advance your career?

Focused work questions

These are questions designed to tell you more about particular aspects of the candidate's work history, such as those shown below:

- How many days absence from work did you have last year?
- How many times were you late last year?
- Have you been absent from work for any medical reason not shown on your application form?
- Do you have a clean driving licence (for those whose work will involve driving)?

Unhelpful questions

- *Multiple questions* such as: 'What skills do you use most frequently in your job? Are they technical skills, leadership skills, teamworking skills or communicating skills?' will only confuse candidates. You will probably get a partial or misleading reply. Ask only one question at a time.
- *Leading questions* that indicate the reply you expect are also unhelpful. If you ask a question such as: 'That's what you think, isn't it?' you will get the reply: 'Yes, I do.' If you ask a question such as: 'I take it that you don't really believe that...?' you will get the reply: 'No, I don't.' Neither of these replies will get you anywhere.

Questions to be avoided

Avoid any questions such as those given below that could be construed as being biased on the grounds of sex, race, disability or age:

- Who is going to look after the children?
- Are you planning to have any more children?
- Are you concerned at all about racial prejudice?
- Would it worry you being the only immigrant around here?
- With your disability, do you think you can cope with the job?
- Do you think that at your time of life you will be able to learn the new skills associated with this job?

Ten useful questions

- What are the most important aspects of your present job?
- What do you think have been your most notable achievements in your career to date?
- What sort of problems have you successfully solved recently in your job?
- What have you learnt from your present job?
- What has been your experience in...?
- What do you know about...?
- What particularly interests you in this job and why?
- Now you have heard more about the job, would you please tell me which aspects of your experience are most relevant?
- What do you think you can bring to this job?
- Is there anything else about your career that hasn't come out yet in this interview but you think I ought to hear?

Coming to a conclusion

It is essential not to be beguiled by a pleasant, articulate and confident interviewee who is all surface and no substance. Beware of the 'halo' effect, which occurs when one or two good points are seized upon, leading to the neglect of negative indicators. The opposite 'horns' effect of focusing on the negatives should also be avoided.

Individual candidates should be assessed against the criteria. These could be set out under the headings of knowledge and skills, competencies, education, qualifications, training, experience and overall suitability. Ratings can be given against each heading, for example: very acceptable, acceptable, marginally acceptable, unacceptable. If you have used situational or behaviourally based questions you can indicate against each question whether the reply was good, just acceptable or poor. These assessments can inform your overall assessment of knowledge, skills and competencies.

Next, compare your assessment of each of the candidates against one another. You can then make a conclusion on those preferred by reference to their assessments under each heading.

In the end, your decision between qualified candidates could well be judgemental. There may be one suitable candidate but there could be two or three (although sometimes there may be none at all). Where there is a choice you have to come to a balanced view by reference to your notes and ratings on which particular candidate is more likely to fit the job and the organization and have potential for a long-term career, if this is possible. Don't, however, settle for second best in desperation. It is better to try again.

Remember to make and keep notes of the reasons for your choice and why candidates have been rejected. These, together with the applications, should be kept for at least six months just in case your decision is challenged as being discriminatory. An example of an interview rating form is given in Figure 50.1.

FIGURE 50.1 Example of an interview rating form

Area	Assessment				Comments
	Very acceptable	Acceptable	Marginally acceptable	Unacceptable	
Experience					
Knowledge and skills					
Competencies					
Education and qualifications					
Training					
Overall suitability					

Dos and don'ts of selection interviewing

Do

- Plan the interview.
- Give yourself sufficient time.
- Use a structured interview approach wherever possible.
- Create the right atmosphere.
- Establish an easy and informal relationship – start with open questions.
- Encourage the candidate to talk.
- Cover the ground as planned, ensuring that you complete a prepared agenda and maintain continuity.
- Analyse the candidate's career to reveal strengths, weaknesses and patterns of interest.
- Make use of open questions that invite people to talk.
- Ensure that questions are clear and unambiguous.
- Get examples and instances of the successful application of knowledge, skills and the effective use of capabilities.
- Make judgements on the basis of the factual information you have obtained about candidates' experience and attributes in relation to the person specification.
- Keep control over the content and timing of the interview.

Don't

- Start the interview unprepared.
- Plunge too quickly into demanding (probing) questions.
- Ask multiple or leading questions.
- Pay too much attention to isolated strengths or weaknesses.
- Allow candidates to gloss over important facts.
- Talk too much or allow candidates to ramble on.
- Allow your prejudices to get the better of your capacity to make objective judgements.
- Fall into the halo effect trap, ie drawing conclusions about a person on the basis of one or two good points, leading to the neglect of negative indicators. Or into the horns trap – focusing too much on one or two weak points.
- Ask questions or make remarks that could be construed as in any way discriminatory.
- Attempt too many interviews in a row.

Key learning points: Selection interviewing skills

Purpose of an interview

The purpose of a selection interview is to establish the extent to which a candidate will be able to do the job. This means finding out how well a candidate's levels of skill, knowledge, abilities and competency fit a person specification for the job that sets out these requirements.

Nature of an interview

An interview is a conversation with a purpose. It is a conversation in that candidates should be given the opportunity to talk freely about themselves and their careers. But the conversation has to be planned, directed and controlled in order to achieve your aims in the time available.

Interviewing skills

- Establishing rapport – creating a good relationship with candidates, getting on their wavelength, putting them at ease, encouraging them to respond and generally being friendly.
- Questioning is the key skill that interviewers need to possess. Their purpose is to draw candidates out and elicit the information the interviewer has decided must be obtained to reach a conclusion.
- If an interview is a conversation with a purpose, listening skills are important. You need not only to hear but also to understand what candidates are saying. When interviewing you must concentrate on what candidates are telling you.
- So far as possible link your questions to a candidate's last reply so that the interview progresses logically and a cumulative set of data is built up.
- You want candidates to talk, but not too much.
- It is useful to take notes of the key points they make, discreetly, but not surreptitiously.

Preparing for the interview

Your first step in preparing for an interview is to familiarize or refamiliarize yourself with the person specification.

Planning the interview

Interviews need to be planned in terms of their three main parts (beginning, middle and end), the structure of questions and how the questions will be sequenced.

The parts of an interview

The content of an interview is in three parts: its beginning, middle and end.

Structuring the interview

A structured interview is one based on a defined framework within which there is a set of predetermined questions. All candidates are asked the same questions and the answers may be scored through a rating system. The most typical framework is the person specification.

Sequencing the interview

When planning interviews you should give some thought to how you are going to sequence your questions, especially in the middle part. There are two basic approaches. The biographical approach is probably the most popular because it is simple to use and appears to be logical. This approach is often referred to as a 'structured interview'. The targeted approach is based on an analysis of the person specification from which criteria are identified for judging the suitability of the candidate. Interview questions can then 'target' these criteria by asking for specific information on what candidates know, what they can do and how they would typically behave in certain situations.

Questioning techniques

- The interviewer's job is to draw the candidate out, at the same time ensuring that the information required is obtained.
- To this end it is desirable to ask a number of open-ended questions – questions that cannot be answered by 'yes' or 'no' and that promote a full response – but a good interviewer will have an armoury of other types of questions to be asked when appropriate.
- Individual candidates should be assessed against the criteria. These could be set out under the headings of knowledge and skills, competencies, education, qualifications, training, experience and overall suitability.
- Ratings can be given against each heading, for example: very acceptable, acceptable, marginally acceptable, unacceptable. If you have used situational or behaviourally based questions you can indicate against each question whether the reply was good, just acceptable or poor. These assessments can inform your overall assessment of knowledge, skills and competencies.

Questions

1. What is the purpose of a selection interview?
2. Why is an interview described as 'a conversation with a purpose'?
3. What are the main interviewing skills?
4. How should interviews be planned?
5. What is a structured interview?
6. What is a biographical interview?
7. What is a targeted interview?
8. What is an open question?
9. What is a closed question?
10. What questions should be avoided?

51 Job, role and skills analysis and competency modelling

KEY CONCEPTS AND TERMS

Accountability profile
Competence
Competency
Competency analysis
Competency modelling
Critical-incident technique
Descriptor
Faults analysis
Functional analysis
Generic role
Job
Job analysis
Job breakdown
Job description
Job learning analysis
KSA (knowledge, skills and abilities statement)
Learning specification
Manual skills analysis
Outcome
Output
Person specification
Personal construct
Repertory grid analysis
Role
Role analysis
Role profile
Skills analysis
Task analysis

LEARNING OUTCOMES

On completing this chapter you should be able to define these key concepts. You should also understand:

- Job analysis methodology and techniques
- Job descriptions
- Role analysis methodology
- Competency modelling

Introduction

The analysis of jobs, roles, and skills and competency modelling are some of the key techniques in human resource management. They provide the information required to produce job descriptions, role profiles, and person and learning specifications. They are of fundamental importance in organization and job design, recruitment and selection, performance management, learning and development, management development, career management, job evaluation and the design of grade and pay structures. These constitute most of the key HRM activities.

This chapter starts with definitions of the terms used in job and role analysis and then deals with the skills required to analyse jobs, roles and skills in order to produce job descriptions and role profiles, and to model competencies to produce competency frameworks.

Definitions

Jobs and roles

The terms 'job' and 'role' are often used interchangeably, but they are different. A job is an organizational unit consisting of a group of defined tasks or activities to be carried out or duties to be performed. A role is the part people play in their work – the emphasis is on the expected patterns of behaviour to achieve agreed outcomes. Roles are about people. Jobs are about tasks and duties.

Job description

A job description defines what job holders are required to do in terms of activities, duties or tasks. It is prescriptive and inflexible, giving people the opportunity to say: 'It's not in my job description', meaning that they only need to do the tasks listed there. A job description is more concerned with tasks than outcomes, and with the duties to be performed than the competencies required to perform them (technical competencies covering knowledge and skills, and behavioural competencies).

Job analysis

Job analysis is the process of collecting, analysing and setting out information about jobs in order to provide the basis for a job description and data for recruitment, training, job evaluation and performance management. Job analysis concentrates on what job holders do and achieve. It identifies the tasks that job holders undertake and the outcomes and outputs they are expected to produce. Outcomes are the results of performance expressed as something that has been attained, such as a task or a project. Outputs are the results of performance expressed in quantified terms such as sales volume, income generated or units of production.

Role profile

A role profile defines key result areas, accountabilities and competencies for an individual role. It concentrates on outcomes rather than duties and therefore provides better guidance on expectations than a job description. It does not constrain people by prescribing their tasks. Outcomes may be expressed as 'key result areas' – elements of the role for which clear outputs and standards can be defined, each of which makes a significant contribution to achieving its overall purpose. Alternatively, they may be termed 'accountabilities' – areas of the role for which role holders are responsible in the form of being held to account for what they do and what they achieve.

A role profile does not prescribe in detail what has to be done to achieve the required outcomes. It therefore allows for greater flexibility than a job description and is more easily updated to reflect changing demands.

Role profiles are person-oriented. A role can be described in behavioural terms – given certain expectations, this is how the person needs to behave to meet them. Because it identifies knowledge, skill and competency requirements it also provides a better basis for recruitment and selection, performance management, and learning and development purposes.

Accountability profile

An accountability profile is a type of role profile that focuses on what role holders will be held to account for in terms of what they do and what they achieve. It may be set out as a list of main accountabilities.

Generic role

A generic role is a role in which essentially similar activities are carried out by a number of people, for example a team leader or a call centre agent. In effect, it covers an occupation rather than a single role. It is described in a generic role profile.

Learning specification

A learning specification defines the knowledge and skills needed to achieve an acceptable level of performance. It is used as the basis for devising learning and development programmes. Learning specifications may be drawn up on the basis of competency and skills analysis.

Person specification

A person specification, also known as a job or role specification, defines the knowledge, skills and abilities (KSAs) required to carry out a role and the education, training, qualifications and experience needed to acquire the necessary KSAs. It may also refer specifically to the competencies required for effective job performance.

Role analysis

Role analysis finds out what people are expected to achieve when carrying out their work and the competencies and skills required to meet those expectations. Role analysis uses similar techniques to job analysis, although the objective of the analysis will be different.

Skills analysis

Skills analysis determines the skills required to achieve an acceptable level of performance.

Competency modelling

Competency modelling is concerned with behavioural analysis to establish the behavioural dimensions that affect job performance, and functional analysis to determine technical or work-based competencies. Behavioural or personal competencies are the personal characteristics of individuals that they bring to their work roles. Technical or work-based competencies refer to expectations of workplace performance and the standards and outputs that people carrying out specified roles are expected to attain. They are also described as competences.

Job analysis

Job analysis produces the following information about a job:

- *Overall purpose* – why the job exists and, in essence, what the job holder is expected to contribute.
- *Organization* – to whom the job holder reports and who reports to the job holder.
- *Content* – the nature and scope of the job in terms of the tasks and operations to be performed and the duties to be carried out.

If the outcome of the job analysis is to be used for job evaluation purposes, the job will also be analysed in terms of the factors or criteria used in the job evaluation scheme.

Job analysis methodology

The essence of job analysis is the application of systematic methods to the collection of information about job content. It is essentially about data collection and the basic steps are:

1. Obtain documents such as existing organization, procedure or training manuals that give information about the job.
2. Obtain from managers fundamental information concerning the job.
3. Obtain from job holders similar information about their jobs.

There are a number of job analysis techniques used for data collection, as described below.

Interviews

The full flavour of a job is best obtained by interviewing job holders and checking findings with their managers or team leaders. The aim of the interview should be to obtain the relevant facts about the job, namely the job title, organizational details (reporting relationships as described in an organization chart) and a list of the tasks or duties performed by the job holder. The interview should also establish outcomes and outputs.

For recruitment, training or job evaluation purposes these basic details can be supplemented by questions designed to elicit from the job holders more information about the level of their responsibilities and the demands made upon them by the job. These can cover the amount of supervision received, the degree of discretion allowed in making decisions, the typical problems to be solved, the amount of guidance available when solving the problems, the relative difficulty of the tasks to be performed and the qualifications and skills required to carry out the work. The following are the steps required to conduct a job analysis interview:

1 Work to a logical sequence of questions that help interviewees to order their thoughts about the job.
2 Probe as necessary to establish what people really do in terms of outputs and outcomes – answers to questions are often vague and information may be given by means of untypical instances.
3 Ensure that job holders are not allowed to get away with vague or inflated descriptions of their work – if, for example, the interview is part of a job evaluation exercise, they would not be human if they did not present the job in the best possible light.
4 Sort out the wheat from the chaff; answers to questions may produce a lot of irrelevant data that must be sifted before preparing the job description.
5 Obtain a clear statement from job holders about their authority to make decisions and the amount of guidance they receive from their manager or team leader. This is not easy: if asked what decisions they are authorized to make, most people look blank because they think about their job in terms of duties and tasks rather than abstract decisions.
6 Avoid asking leading questions that make the expected answer obvious.
7 Allow the job holder ample opportunity to talk by creating an atmosphere of trust.

It is helpful to use a checklist when conducting the interview. Elaborate checklists are not necessary – they only confuse people. The basic questions to be answered are as follows:

1 What is the title of your job?
2 To whom are you responsible?
3 Who is responsible to you? (An organization chart is helpful.)
4 What is the main purpose of your job in overall terms, ie what are you expected to do?
5 What are the key activities you have to carry out in your role? (Try to group them under no more than 10 headings.)
6 What are the results you are expected to achieve in each of those key activities?
7 What are you expected to know to be able to carry out your job?
8 What skills should you have to carry out your job?

The answers to these questions may need to be sorted out – they can often result in a mass of jumbled information that has to be analysed so that the various activities can be distinguished and refined to seven or eight key areas.

The advantages of the interviewing method are that it is flexible, can provide in-depth information and is easy to organize and prepare. It is therefore the most common approach. But interviewing can be time-consuming, which is why in large job analysis exercises, questionnaires may be used to provide advance information about the job. This speeds up the interviewing process or even replaces the interview altogether, although this means that much of the 'flavour' of the job – ie what it is really like – may be lost.

Questionnaires

Questionnaires about their roles can be completed by role holders and approved by the role holder's manager or team leader. They are helpful when a large number of roles have to be covered. They can also save interviewing time by recording purely factual information and by enabling the analyst to structure questions in advance to cover areas that need to be explored in greater depth. The simpler the questionnaire the better: it need only cover the eight questions listed above.

The advantage of questionnaires is that they can produce information quickly and cheaply for a large number of jobs. But a substantial sample is needed and the construction of a questionnaire is a skilled job, which should only be carried out on the basis of some preliminary fieldwork. It is highly advisable to pilot-test questionnaires before launching into a full-scale exercise. The accuracy of the results also depends on the willingness and ability of job holders to complete questionnaires. Many people find it difficult to express themselves in writing about their work.

Observation

Observation means studying role holders at work, noting what they do, how they do it, and how much time it takes. This method is most appropriate for routine administrative or manual roles but it is seldom used because of the time it takes.

Job descriptions

Job descriptions should be based on the job analysis and should be as brief and factual as possible. The headings under which the job description should be written, and notes for guidance on completing each section, are set out below.

Job title

The existing or proposed job title should indicate as clearly as possible the function in which the job is carried out and the level of the job within that function. The use of terms such as 'manager', 'assistant manager' or 'senior' to describe job levels should be reasonably consistent between functions with regard to grading of the jobs.

Reporting to

The job title of the manager or team leader to whom the job holder is directly responsible should be given under this heading. No attempt should be made to indicate here any functional relationships the job holder might have to other people.

Reporting to job holder

The job titles of all the posts directly reporting to the job holder should be given under this heading. Again, no attempt should be made here to indicate any functional relationships that might exist between the job holder and other employees.

Overall purpose

This section should describe as concisely as possible the overall purpose of the job. The aim should be to convey in one sentence a broad picture of the job that will clearly distinguish it from other jobs and establish the role of job holders and the contribution they should make towards achieving the objectives of the company and their own function or unit. No attempt should be made to describe the activities carried out under this heading, but the overall summary should lead naturally to the analysis of activities in the next section. When preparing the job description, it is often best to defer writing down the definition of overall responsibilities until the activities have been analysed and described.

Main activities, tasks or duties

The following method of describing activities, tasks or duties should be adopted:

1. Group the various activities identified by the job analysis together so that no more than seven or eight areas remain. If the number is extended much beyond that, the job description will become overcomplex and it will be difficult to be specific about tasks or duties.
2. Define each activity in one sentence, starting with a verb in the active voice, to provide a positive indication of what has to be done and eliminate unnecessary wording. Examples are: plan, prepare, produce, implement, process, provide, schedule, complete, dispatch, maintain, liaises with, and collaborates with.
3. Describe what is done as succinctly as possible, for example: test new systems, post

cash to the nominal and sales ledgers, dispatch packed output to the warehouse, schedule production, ensure that management accounts are produced, prepare marketing plans.

4 State briefly the purpose of the activity in terms of outcomes, outputs or standards to be achieved. For example: test new systems to ensure they meet agreed systems specifications; post cash to the nominal and sales ledgers in order to provide up-to-date and accurate financial information; dispatch to the warehouse planned output so that all items are removed by carriers on the same day they are packed; schedule production to meet laid-down output and delivery targets; ensure that management accounts are produced that provide the required level of information to management and individual managers on financial performance against budget and on any variances; prepare marketing plans that support the achievement of the marketing strategies of the enterprise, are realistic, and provide clear guidance on the actions to be taken by the development, production, marketing and sales departments; plan and implement sales campaigns to meet sales targets.

An example of a job description is given in Figure 51.1.

Role analysis and role profiles

Role analysis uses the same techniques as job analysis but the focus is on identifying inputs – KSAs (knowledge, skill and abilities), competency requirements and required outcomes (key result areas or accountabilities) rather than simply listing the tasks to be carried out. A role profile is initially set out under the same headings as a job description, ie role title, responsible to, responsible to role holder, and the purpose of the role, but it then focuses on the following aspects of the role: key result areas; knowledge, skills and abilities required; behavioural competencies.

FIGURE 51.1 Example of job description

Job title:	HR adviser; recruitment
Reports to:	HR Service Centre Manager
Reports to job holder:	none
Overall purpose:	To provide recruitment services to line managers for jobs below management level

Main activities:

1 Respond promptly to requests from line managers to assist in recruiting staff.

2 Produce person specifications that clearly indicate requirements for recruitment purposes.

3 Agree on the use of sources of applicants such as web-based recruitment, agencies or media advertisements that will generate high-calibre candidates at a reasonable cost.

4 Brief and liaise with agencies and/or draft advertisements for jobs for approval by line managers and place advertisements or information on vacancies using the media and/or the internet.

5 Process replies and draw up shortlists that enable a choice to be made between well-qualified candidates.

6 Conduct preliminary interviews independently or conduct shortlist interviews with line managers that identify candidates who meet the specification.

7 Agree offer terms with line manager, take up references and confirm the offer.

8 Review and evaluate sources of candidates and analyse recruitment costs.

Key result areas

A key result area is an element of a role for which clear outputs and outcomes can be defined, each of which makes a significant contribution to achieving the overall purpose of the role. It may be described as an 'accountability' – an aspect of the role for which the role holder is responsible (held to account for).

The number of key result areas is unlikely to be more than seven or eight, certainly not more than 10. The basic structure of a key result area definition should resemble that of a job description task definition, ie it should be expressed in one sentence starting with an active verb. However, the content of the definition should focus more on the specific purpose of the activity in terms of outputs or standards to be achieved rather than on describing in detail the duties involved.

Knowledge, skills and abilities required

Knowledge, skills and abilities should be expressed in terms of 'need to know' – the required knowledge of techniques, processes, procedures, systems and the business generally (its products or services and its competitors and customers), and 'need to be able to do' – the skills required in each area of activity. These are the technical competencies required by the job.

Behavioural competencies

Behavioural competencies describe how the role holder is expected to behave when carrying out the role. They may be linked to the organization's competency framework and cover such areas as teamworking, communication, people management and development, and customer relations. An example of a role profile is given in Figure 51.2.

Generic role profiles

Generic role profiles cover occupations rather than individual roles. They tend to be more generalized and may be somewhat simpler than individual role profiles, for example by restricting the profile to lists of key result areas and competency dimensions. An example of a generic role profile is given in Figure 51.3.

Skills analysis

Skills analysis determines the skills required to achieve an acceptable standard of performance. It is mainly used for technical, craft, manual and office jobs to provide the basis for devising learning and training programmes. Skills analysis starts from a broad job analysis but goes into details of not only what job holders have to do but also the particular abilities and skills they need to do it. Skills analysis techniques are described below.

Job breakdown

The job breakdown technique analyses a job into separate operations, processes or tasks that can be used as the elements of an instruction sequence. A job breakdown analysis is recorded in a standard format of three columns:

1. *The stage column* – in which the different steps in the job are described – most semi-skilled jobs can easily be broken down into their constituent parts.
2. *The instruction column* – in which a note is made against each step of how the task should be done. This, in effect, describes what has to be learnt by the trainee.
3. *The key points column* – in which any special points such as quality standards or safety instructions are noted against each step so that they can be emphasized to a trainee learning the job.

Manual skills analysis

Manual skills analysis is a technique developed from work study. It isolates for instructional purposes the skills and knowledge employed by experienced workers in performing tasks that require manual dexterity. It is used to analyse short-cycle, repetitive operations such as assembly tasks and other similar factory work.

FIGURE 51.2 Example of a role profile

Role title:	Database administrator
Department:	Information systems
Purpose of role:	Responsible for the development and support of databases and their underlying environment

Key result areas

- Identify database requirements for all projects that require data management in order to meet the needs of internal customers.
- Develop project plans collaboratively with colleagues to deliver against their database needs.
- Support underlying database infrastructure.
- Liaise with system and software providers to obtain product information and support.
- Manage project resources (people and equipment) within predefined budget and criteria, as agreed with line manager and originating department.
- Allocate work to and supervise contractors on a day-to-day basis.
- Ensure security of the underlying database infrastructure through adherence to established protocols and to develop additional security protocols where needed.

Need to know

- Oracle database administration.
- Operation of Designer 2000 and oracle forms SQL/PLSQL, Unix administration, shell programming.

Able to

- Analyse and choose between options where the solution is not always obvious.
- Develop project plans and organize own workload on a timescale of 1–2 months.
- Adapt to rapidly changing needs and priorities without losing sight of overall plans and priorities.
- Interpret budgets in order to manage resources effectively within them.
- Negotiate with suppliers.
- Keep abreast of technical developments and trends, bring these into day-to-day work when feasible and build them into new project developments.

Behavioural competencies

- Aim to get things done well and set and meet challenging goals, create own measures of excellence and constantly seek ways of improving performance.
- Analyse information from a range of sources and develop effective solutions/recommendations.
- Communicate clearly and persuasively, orally or in writing, dealing with technical issues in a non-technical manner.
- Work participatively on projects with technical and non-technical colleagues.
- Develop positive relationships with colleagues as the supplier of an internal service.

FIGURE 51.3 Example of a generic role profile

Generic role title: Team leader

Overall purpose of role: To lead teams in order to attain team goals and further the achievement of the organization's objectives.

Key result areas

1. Agree targets and standards with team members that support the attainment of the organization's objectives.
2. Plan with team members work schedules and resource requirements that will ensure that team targets will be reached, indeed exceeded.
3. Agree performance measures and quality assurance processes with team members that will clarify output and quality expectations.
4. Agree with team members the allocation of tasks, rotating responsibilities as appropriate to achieve flexibility and the best use of the skills and capabilities of team members.
5. Coordinate the work of the team to ensure that team goals are achieved.
6. Ensure that the team members collectively monitor the team's performance in terms of achieving output, speed of response and quality targets and standards, and agree with team members any corrective action required to ensure that team goals are achieved.
7. Conduct team reviews of performance to agree areas for improvement and actions required.

Competencies

- Build effective team relationships, ensuring that team members are committed to the common purpose.
- Encourage self-direction amongst team members but provide guidance and clear direction as required.
- Share information with team members.
- Trust team members to get on with things – not continually checking.
- Treat team members fairly and consistently.
- Support and guide team members to make the best use of their capabilities.
- Encourage self-development by example.
- Actively offer constructive feedback to team members and positively seek and be open to constructive feedback from them.
- Contribute to the development of team members, encouraging the acquisition of additional skills and providing opportunities for them to be used effectively.

The hand, finger and other body movements of experienced operatives are observed and recorded in detail as they carry out their work. The analysis concentrates on the tricky parts of the job, which while presenting no difficulty to the experienced operative have to be analysed in depth before they can be taught to trainees. Not only are the hand movements recorded, but particulars are also noted of the cues (visual and other senses) that the operative absorbs when performing the tasks. Explanatory comments are added when necessary.

Task analysis

Task analysis is a systematic analysis of the behaviour required to carry out a task with a view to identifying areas of difficulty and the appropriate training techniques and learning aids necessary for successful instruction. It can be used for all types of jobs but is specifically relevant to administrative tasks.

The analytical approach used in task analysis is similar to those adopted in the job breakdown and manual skills analysis techniques. The results of the analysis are usually recorded in a standard format of four columns, as follows:

1. *Task* – a brief description of each element.
2. *Level of importance* – the relative significance of each task to the successful performance of the role.
3. *Degree of difficulty* – the level of skill or knowledge required to perform each task.
4. *Training method* – the instructional techniques, practice and experience required.

Faults analysis

Faults analysis is the process of analysing the typical faults that occur when performing a task, especially the more costly faults. It is carried out when the incidence of faults is high. A study is made of the job and, by questioning workers and team leaders, the most commonly occurring faults are identified. A faults specification is then produced, which provides trainees with information on what faults can occur, how they can be recognized, what causes them, what effect they have, who is responsible for them, what action the trainees should take when a particular fault occurs, and how a fault can be prevented from recurring.

Job learning analysis

Job learning analysis, as described by Pearn and Kandola (1993), concentrates on the inputs and process rather than the content of the job. It analyses nine learning skills that contribute to satisfactory performance. A learning skill is one used to increase other skills or knowledge and represents broad categories of job behaviour that need to be learnt. The learning skills are the following:

- physical skills requiring practice and repetition to get right;
- complex procedures or sequences of activity that are memorized or followed with the aid of written material such as manuals;
- non-verbal information such as sight, sound, smell, taste and touch – used to check, assess or discriminate, and which usually takes practice to get right;
- memorizing facts or information;
- ordering, prioritizing and planning, which refer to the degree to which a role holder has any responsibility for, and flexibility in, determining the way a particular activity is performed;
- looking ahead and anticipating;
- diagnosing, analysing and problem solving, with or without help;
- interpreting or using written manuals and other sources of information such as diagrams or charts;
- adapting to new ideas and systems.

In conducting a job learning analysis interview, the interviewer obtains information on the main aims and principal activities of the job and then, using question cards for each of the nine learning skills, analyses each activity in more depth, recording responses and obtaining as many examples as possible under each heading.

Competency modelling

As defined by Shippmann *et al* (2000: 727):

> Competency modelling approaches typically provide descriptions of the individual-level competencies that are core, or common, for an occupational group, entire level of jobs (eg, executive, management, supervisory, hourly), or for the organization as a whole. The focus is on broad applicability and leveraging what is in common or universal. Even when the modelling effort targets a narrowly defined job group (eg, sales managers), the resulting descriptions are typically at a fairly high level and general in nature.

Competency modelling is the basis for defining behavioural and technical competencies (see Chapter 7).

Behavioural competency modelling

Behavioural competency modelling is the method used to identify, analyse and describe behavioural competencies. These define the behaviours that organizations expect their employees to practise in their work in order to reach an acceptable level of performance. They have an important part to play in providing information that contributes to a number of HRM activities, for example, recruitment, learning and development, and performance management. Examples of competencies and competency frameworks were given in Chapter 7, and suggestions were made about how a competency framework should be constructed. Table 51.1 shows guidance on the criteria for a fully rigorous competency definition, as produced by Shippmann *et al* (2000). These are exacting criteria. The emphasis is on the systematic collection and analysis of data. There are five approaches to behavioural competency analysis: in ascending order of complexity these are:

1 expert opinion;
2 structured interview;
3 workshops;
4 critical-incident technique;
5 repertory grid analysis.

Expert opinion

The basic, crudest and least satisfactory method is for an 'expert' member of the HR department, possibly in discussion with other 'experts' from the same department, to draw up a list from their own understanding of 'what counts', coupled with an analysis of other published lists. This is unsatisfactory because the likelihood of the competencies being appropriate, realistic and measurable in the absence of detailed analysis is fairly remote. The list tends to be bland and, because line managers and job holders have not been involved, unacceptable.

Structured interview

This method begins with a list of competencies drawn up by 'experts' and proceeds by subjecting a number of role holders to a structured interview. The interviewer starts by identifying the key result areas of the role and goes on to analyse the behavioural characteristics that distinguish performers at different levels of competence. The basic question is: What are the positive or negative indicators of behaviour conducive or non-conducive to achieving high levels of performance? These may be analysed under headings such as those set out below:

- Personal drive (achievement motivation).
- Impact on results.
- Analytical power.
- Strategic thinking.
- Creative thinking (ability to innovate).
- Decisiveness.
- Commercial judgement.
- Team management and leadership.
- Interpersonal relationships.
- Ability to communicate.
- Ability to adapt and cope with change and pressure.
- Ability to plan and control projects.

One of the problems with this approach is that it relies too much on the ability of the expert to draw out information from interviewees. It is also undesirable to use a deductive approach that pre-empts the analysis with a prepared list of competency headings. It is better to do this by means of an inductive approach, which starts from specific types of behaviour and then groups them under competency headings. This can be done in a workshop by analysing positive and negative indicators to gain an understanding of the competence dimensions of an occupation or job, as described below.

Workshops

Workshops bring together a group of people who have 'expert' knowledge or experience of the role – managers and role holders as appropriate – with a facilitator, usually but not necessarily a member of the HR department or an outside consultant.

The members of the workshop begin by getting agreement to the overall purpose of the role and its key result areas. They then develop examples of effective and less effective behaviour for each area, which are recorded on flip charts. For example, one of the key result areas for a divisional HR director might be workforce planning, defined as: 'Prepares forecasts of human resource requirements and plans for the acquisition, retention and effective utilization of employees, which ensure that the company's needs for people are met.'

TABLE 51.1 Criteria for a fully rigorous competency definition

Variable	Conditions required to meet high rigorous criteria
Method of investigation	A logically selected mix of multiple methods are used to obtain information, eg interviews, focus groups, questionnaires.
Type of descriptor content collected	Variable combinations of multiple types of information are collected, eg work activities, KSAs (knowledge, skills and abilities statements) and performance standards.
Procedures for developing descriptors	Information collected from content experts using a structured protocol and a representative sample.
Detail of descriptor content	Use of a number of labels representing discrete categories of content which operationally define each category and leave no room for misinterpretation.
Link to business goals and strategies	Steps taken to ensure that results are aligned with the broader goals and longer-term strategies of the organization.
Content review	Formal review takes place to ensure that: • item level descriptions are clear; • content categories do not overlap, content categories are internally consistent; • items represent measurable content appropriate for the intended application.
Ranking descriptor content	The set of descriptors are prioritized and ranked.
Assessment of reliability	Content category labels are matched with item-level descriptors and rated according to their relative importance for successful job performance.
Item retention criteria	Multiple, clear, logical criteria are consistently applied to items to determine whether content is retained or deleted.
Documentation	Clear definitions are made of the procedures to be employed in applying the competency framework.

SOURCE: Shippman *et al* (2000)

The positive indicators for this competency area could include:

- seeks involvement in business strategy formulation;
- contributes to business planning by taking a strategic view of longer-term human resource issues that are likely to affect business strategy;
- networks with senior management colleagues to understand and respond to the human resource planning issues they raise;
- suggests practical ways to improve the use of human resources, for example, the introduction of annual hours.

Negative indicators could include:

- takes a narrow view of HR planning – does not seem to be interested in or understand the wider business context;
- lacks the determination to overcome problems and deliver forecasts;
- fails to anticipate skills shortages; for example, unable to meet the multiskilling requirements implicit in the new computer-integrated manufacturing system;
- does not seem to talk the same language as line management colleagues – fails to understand their requirements;
- slow in responding to requests for help.

When the positive and negative indicators have been agreed, the next step is to distil the competency dimensions that can be inferred from the lists. In this example they could be:

- strategic capability;
- business understanding;
- achievement motivation;
- interpersonal skills;
- communication skills;
- consultancy skills.

These dimensions might also be reflected in the analysis of other areas of competency so that, progressively, a picture of the competencies is built up, which is linked to actual behaviour in the workplace.

The facilitator's job is to prompt, help the group to analyse its findings and assist generally in the production of a set of competence dimensions that can be illustrated by behaviour-based examples. The facilitator may have some ideas about the sort of headings that may emerge from this process but should not try to influence the group to come to a conclusion that it has not worked out for itself, albeit with some assistance from the facilitator.

Workshops can use the critical-incident or repertory grid techniques, as described below.

Critical-incident technique

The critical-incident technique is a means of eliciting data about effective or less effective behaviour related to examples of actual events – critical incidents. The technique is used with groups of job holders and/or their managers or other 'experts' (sometimes, less effectively, with individuals) as follows:

1. Explain what the technique is and what it is used for, ie 'to assess what constitutes good or poor performance by analysing events that have been observed to have a noticeably successful or unsuccessful outcome, thus providing more factual and "real" information than by simply listing tasks and guessing performance requirements'.
2. Agree and list the key results in the role to be analysed. To save time, the analyst can establish these prior to the meeting but it is necessary to ensure that they are agreed provisionally by the group, which can be told that the list may well be amended in the light of the forthcoming analysis.
3. Take each area of the role in turn and ask the group for examples of critical incidents. If, for instance, one of the job responsibilities is dealing with customers, the following request could be made: 'I want you to tell me about a particular occasion at work which involved you – or that you observed – in dealing with a customer. Think about what the circumstances were, eg who took part, what the customer asked for, what you or the other member of the staff did and what the outcome was.'
4. Collect information about the critical incident under the following headings:
   - what the circumstances were;
   - what the individual did;
   - the outcome of what the individual did.

5 Record this information on a flip chart.

6 Continue this process for each key result area.

7 Refer to the flip chart and analyse each incident by obtaining ratings of the recorded behaviour on a scale such as 1 for least effective to 5 for most effective.

8 Discuss these ratings to get initial definitions of effective and ineffective performance for each of the key result areas.

9 Refine these definitions as necessary after the meeting – it can be difficult to get a group to produce finished definitions.

10 Produce the final analysis, which can list the competencies required and include performance indicators or standards of performance for each key result area.

This is a thorough, indeed exhaustive approach, but it is time-consuming and requires skill to manage.

Repertory grid

Like the critical-incident technique, the repertory grid can be used to identify the dimensions that distinguish good from poor standards of performance. The technique is based on Kelly's (1955) personal construct theory. Personal constructs are the ways in which we view the world. They are personal because they are highly individual and they influence the way we behave or view other people's behaviour. The aspects of the role to which these 'constructs' or judgements apply are called 'elements'.

To elicit judgements, a group of people are asked to concentrate on certain elements, which are the tasks carried out by role holders, and to develop constructs about these elements. This enables them to define the qualities that indicate the essential requirements for successful performance.

The procedure followed by the analyst is known as the 'triadic method of elicitation' (a sort of three-card trick) and involves the following steps:

1 Identify the tasks or elements of the role to be subjected to repertory grid analysis. This is done by one of the other forms of job analysis, eg interviewing.

2 List the tasks on cards.

3 Draw three cards at random from the pack and ask the members of the group to nominate which of these tasks is the odd one out from the point of view of the qualities and characteristics needed to perform it.

4 Probe to obtain more specific definitions of these qualities or characteristics in the form of expected behaviour. If, for example, a characteristic has been described as the 'ability to plan and organize', ask questions such as: 'What sort of behaviour or actions indicate that someone is planning effectively?' or, 'How can we tell if someone is not organizing his or her work particularly well?'

5 Draw three more cards from the pack and repeat steps 3 and 4.

6 Repeat this process until all the cards have been analysed and there are no more constructs to be identified.

7 List the constructs and ask the group members to rate each task on every quality, using a six- or seven-point scale.

8 Collect and analyse the scores to assess their relative importance.

Like the critical-incident technique, repertory grid analysis helps people to articulate their views by reference to specific examples. An additional advantage is that the repertory grid makes it easier for them to identify the behavioural characteristics or competencies required in a job by limiting the area of comparison through the triadic technique. Although a full statistical analysis of the outcome of a repertory grid exercise is helpful, the most important results that can be obtained are the descriptions of what constitute good or poor performance in each element of the job.

Like the critical-incident technique, the repertory grid requires a skilled analyst who can probe and draw out the descriptions of job characteristics. It is quite detailed and time-consuming, but even if the full process is not followed much of the methodology is of use in a less elaborate approach to competency modelling.

Choice of approach

Workshops are probably the best approach. They get people involved and do not rely on 'expert' opinion. Critical-incident or repertory grid techniques are more sophisticated and can be associated with workshops but they are time-consuming and considerable expertise is required to run them.

Technical competency modelling

Technical competencies or competences can be modelled through the process of functional analysis, which is used to produce definitions of the competences contained in NVQ (National Vocational Qualification) frameworks. Functional analysis focuses on the outcomes of work performance. Note that the analysis is not simply concerned with outputs in the form of quantifiable results but deals with the broader results that have to be achieved by role holders. An outcome could be a satisfied customer, a more highly motivated subordinate or a better-functioning team.

Functional analysis deals with processes such as developing staff, providing feedback and monitoring performance as well as tasks. It starts with an analysis of the roles fulfilled by an individual in order to arrive at a description of the separate components or 'units' of performance that make up that role. The resulting units consist of performance criteria, described in terms of outcomes, and a description of the knowledge and skill requirements that underpin successful performance. The techniques used in functional analysis are similar to those used in job analysis, described earlier in this chapter.

Key learning points: Job, role and skills analysis and competency modelling

Job analysis methodology and techniques

The essence of job analysis is the application of systematic methods to the collection of information about job content. It is essentially about data collection and the basic steps are:

- obtain documents such as existing organization, procedure or training manuals that give information about the job;
- obtain from managers fundamental information concerning the job;
- obtain from job holders similar information about their jobs.

Job descriptions

Job descriptions should be based on the job analysis and should be as brief and factual as possible. The headings should be: job title, reporting to, reporting to job holder, main purpose of job, main activities, tasks or duties.

Role analysis methodology

Role analysis uses the same techniques as job analysis but the focus is on identifying inputs (knowledge, skill and competency requirements) and required outcomes (key result areas) rather than simply listing the tasks to be carried out.

Behavioural competency modelling

Behavioural competency modelling is used for identifying, analysing and describing behavioural competencies that define the behaviours that organizations expect their staff to practise in their work in order to reach an acceptable level of performance. The emphasis is on the systematic collection and analysis of data. There are five approaches to behavioural competency analysis. In ascending order of complexity these are: expert opinion, structured interview, workshops, critical-incident technique, and repertory grid analysis.

Analysing technical competencies

Functional analysis starts with an analysis of the roles fulfilled by an individual in order to arrive at a description of the separate components or 'units' of performance that make up that role. The resulting units consist of performance criteria, described in terms of outcomes, and a description of the knowledge and skill requirements that underpin successful performance.

Skills analysis

Skills analysis determines the skills required to achieve an acceptable standard of performance. It is mainly used for technical, craft, manual and office jobs to provide the basis for devising learning and training programmes. Skills analysis starts from a broad job analysis but goes into details of what job holders have to do and the particular abilities and skills they need to do it. Skills analysis techniques include job breakdown, manual skills analysis, faults analysis and job learning analysis.

Questions

1 What is the difference between a job and a role?
2 What is a job description?
3 What is a role profile?
4 What is a generic role profile?
5 How should a job analysis interview be conducted?
6 What are the advantages and disadvantages of questionnaires as a method of analysing jobs?

References

Kelly, G (1955) *The Psychology of Personal Constructs*, New York, Norton

Pearn, K and Kandola, R (1993) *Job Analysis: A manager's guide*, London, IPM

Shippmann, J S, Ash, R A and Battista, M (2000) The practice of competency modelling, *Personnel Psychology*, 53 (3), pp 703–40

52 Learning and development skills

KEY CONCEPTS AND TERMS

Coaching

Job instruction

Mentoring

LEARNING OUTCOMES

On completing this chapter you should be able to define these key concepts. You should also know about coaching, mentoring and job instruction skills.

Introduction

HR professionals need skills in coaching and mentoring in order to fulfil their important responsibilities for enhancing the knowledge and skills of employees and for providing guidance to line managers on conducting their learning and development activities.

Coaching

Coaching is a personal (usually one-to-one) approach that enables people to develop their skills and knowledge and improve their performance. As Whitmore (2002: 8) suggested: 'Coaching is unlocking a person's potential to maximize their own performance. It is helping them to learn rather than teaching them.' Clutterbuck (2004: 23) noted that: 'Coaching is primarily focused on performance within the current job and emphasizes the development of skills.'

Coaching is often provided by specialists from inside or outside the organization who concentrate on specific areas of skills or behaviour, for example leadership. But it is also something that HR professionals have to be prepared to do as part of their normal learning and development duties, and this means deploying the skills described below.

The approach to coaching

To succeed in coaching you need to understand that your role is to help people to learn and ensure that they are motivated to learn. They should be aware of the advantages to them as well as the organization of developing their present level of knowledge or skill or modifying their behaviour. Individuals should be given guidance on what they should be learning and feedback on how they are doing and, because learning is an active not a passive process, they should be actively involved with their coach.

Coaching is sometimes informal but it has to be planned. It is not simply checking from time to time on what people are doing and then advising them on how to do it better. Nor is it occasionally telling people where they have gone wrong and throwing in a lecture for good measure. As far as possible, coaching should take place within the framework of a general plan of the areas and direction in which individuals will benefit from further development. Coaching plans should be incorporated into the personal development plans set out in a performance agreement.

Coaching should provide motivation, structure and effective feedback. As a coach, you should believe that people can succeed and that they can contribute to their own success.

Coaching styles

Clutterbuck and Megginson (2005: 52) identified four coaching styles:

1. *Assessor* – this is akin to instruction and involves telling people the way to do something.
2. *Demonstrator* – this is less directive than the assessor style. It involves showing learners how to do something and then getting them to do it with guidance and comments from the coach as required.
3. *Tutor* – this involves encouraging learners to find out how to do things for themselves. It is still relatively directive as it is the coach who suggests what learners should look for.
4. *Stimulator* – this helps learners to teach themselves by guiding their thinking through the use of insight-provoking questions.

Criteria for effectiveness

The following criteria for evaluating the performance of a coach were listed by Gray (2010: 379):

- establishes rapport;
- creates trust and respect;
- demonstrates effective communication skills;
- promotes self-awareness and self-knowledge;
- uses active listening and questioning techniques;
- assists goal development and setting;
- motivates;
- encourages alternative perspectives;
- assists in making sense of a situation;
- identifies significant patterns of thinking and behaving;
- provides an appropriate mix of challenge and support;
- facilitates depth of understanding;
- shows compassion;
- acts ethically;
- inspires curiosity;
- acts as a role model;
- values diversity and difference;
- promotes action and reflection.

Mentoring

Mentors offer guidance, pragmatic advice and continuing support to help those allocated to them to learn and develop. It is a method of helping people to learn, as distinct from coaching, which can be a relatively directive means of increasing people's competence. Mentors may be line managers. They are often appointed and trained by learning and development (L&D) specialists who therefore need to be aware of the skills required. L&D professionals may act as mentors themselves, although experienced managers are best if they have the skills and enthusiasm required.

Mentors provide people with:

- advice in drawing up self-development programmes or learning contracts;
- general help with learning programmes;
- guidance on how to acquire the necessary knowledge and skills to do a new job;
- advice on dealing with any administrative, technical or people problems that individuals meet, especially in the early stages of their careers;

- information on 'the way things are done around here' – the corporate culture in terms of expected behaviour;
- coaching in specific skills;
- help in tackling projects – not by doing it for them but by pointing them in the right direction, helping people to help themselves;
- a parental figure with whom individuals can discuss their aspirations and concerns and who will lend a sympathetic ear to their problems.

Mentors need to adopt a non-directive but supportive approach to helping the person or persons they are dealing with.

Job instruction

When people learn specific tasks, especially those involving basic administrative or manual skills, the learning will be more effective if job instruction techniques are used. HR professionals may possibly be involved in providing direct instruction, but their most typical role is that of promoting effective instruction techniques for use by line managers and others involved in workplace learning or running formal training programmes. They should therefore be aware of the sequence of instruction – preparation, presentation, demonstration, follow up – as described below.

Preparation

Preparation for each instruction period means that the trainer must have a plan for presenting the subject matter and using appropriate teaching methods, visual aids and demonstration aids. It also means preparing trainees for the instruction that is to follow. They should want to learn. They must perceive that the learning will be relevant and useful to them personally. They should be encouraged to take pride in their job and to appreciate the satisfaction that comes from skilled performance.

Presentation

Presentation should consist of a combination of telling and showing – explanation and demonstration. Explanation should be as simple and direct as possible: the trainer explains briefly the ground to be covered and what to look for. He or she makes the maximum use of charts, diagrams and other visual aids. The aim should be to teach first things first and then proceed from the known to the unknown, the simple to the complex, the concrete to the abstract, the general to the particular, the observation to reasoning, and the whole to the parts and back to the whole again.

Demonstration

Demonstration is an essential stage in instruction, especially when the skill to be learnt is mainly a 'doing' skill. Demonstration can take place in three stages:

1. The complete operation is shown at normal speed to show the trainee how the task should be carried out eventually.
2. The operation is demonstrated slowly and in correct sequence, element by element, to indicate clearly what is done and the order in which each task is carried out.
3. The operation is demonstrated again slowly, at least two or three times, to stress the how, when and why of successive movements.

The learner then practises by imitating the instructor and constantly repeating the operation under guidance. The aim is to reach the target level of performance for each element of the total task, but the instructor must constantly strive to develop co-ordinated and integrated performance – that is, the smooth combination of the separate elements of the task into a whole job pattern.

Follow up

Follow up continues during the training period for all the time required by the learner to reach a level of performance equal to that of the normal experienced worker in terms of quality, speed and attention to safety. During the follow-up stage, the learner will continue to need help with particularly difficult tasks or to overcome temporary setbacks that result in a deterioration of performance. The instructor may have to repeat the presentation, and supervise practice more closely until the trainee regains confidence or masters the task.

Key learning points: Learning and development skills

The requirement

HR professionals need skills in coaching and mentoring in order to fulfil their important responsibilities for enhancing the knowledge and skills of employees and for providing guidance to line managers on conducting their learning and development activities.

Coaching

Coaching is a personal (usually one-to-one) approach that enables people to develop their skills and knowledge and improve their performance.

The approach to coaching

- To succeed in coaching you need to understand that your role is to help people to learn and to see that they are motivated to learn.
- Coaching is sometimes informal but it has to be planned. It is not simply checking from time to time on what people are doing and then advising them on how to do it better, or occasionally telling people where they have gone wrong and throwing in a lecture.
- Coaching should provide motivation, structure and effective feedback. As a coach, you should believe that people can succeed and that they can contribute to their own success.

Mentoring

Mentors offer guidance, pragmatic advice and continuing support to help those allocated to them to learn and develop. It is a method of helping people to learn, as distinct from coaching, which can be a relatively directive means of increasing people's competence. Mentors provide people with:

- advice in drawing up self-development programmes or learning contracts;
- general help with learning programmes;
- guidance on how to acquire the necessary knowledge and skills to do a new job;
- advice on dealing with any administrative, technical or people problems that individuals meet, especially in the early stages of their careers;
- information on 'the way things are done around here' – the corporate culture in terms of expected behaviour;
- coaching in specific skills;
- help in tackling projects – not by doing it for them but by pointing them in the right direction, helping people to help themselves;
- a parental figure with whom individuals can discuss their aspirations and concerns and who will lend a sympathetic ear to their problems.

Job instruction

When people learn specific tasks, especially those involving basic administrative or manual skills, the learning will be more effective if job instruction techniques are used. The sequence of instruction is:

1. Preparation for each instruction period means that the trainer must have a plan for presenting the subject matter and using appropriate teaching methods, visual aids and demonstration aids. It also means preparing trainees for the instruction that is to follow.
2. Presentation should consist of a combination of telling and showing – explanation and demonstration. Demonstration is an essential stage in instruction, especially when the skill to be learnt is mainly a 'doing' skill.
3. Follow up continues during the training period for all the time required by the learner to reach a level of performance equal to that of the normal experienced worker in terms of quality, speed and attention to safety.

Questions

1 What is coaching?
2 What approach should be adopted to coaching?
3 What is mentoring?
4 What do mentors do?
5 What is the job instruction sequence?

References

Clutterbuck, D (2004) *Everyone Needs a Mentor: Fostering talent in your organization*, 4th edn, London, CIPD

Clutterbuck, D and Megginson, D (2005) *Making Coaching Work: Creating a coaching culture*, London, CIPD

Gray, D A (2010) Building quality into executive coaching, in (eds) J Gold, R Thorpe and A Mumford, *Gower Handbook of Leadership and Management Development*, Farnham, Gower, pp 367–85

Whitmore, J (2002) *Coaching for Performance*, 3rd edn, London, Nicholas Brealey

53 Negotiating skills

KEY CONCEPTS AND TERMS

Aspiration grid

Bargaining

Corridor negotiations

Negotiating

Zero-sum game

LEARNING OUTCOMES

On completing this chapter you should be able to define these key concepts. You should also understand:

- The process of negotiation
- The stages of a negotiation
- Negotiating and bargaining skills

Introduction

HR practitioners who are involved in industrial relations may conduct or take part in negotiations with trade union representatives or officials. Negotiating is a process that requires considerable skill.

Negotiation involves bargaining, which is reaching the most advantageous position in discussion with another party through a process of offer and counter-offer. It is a process in which two parties – management and the trade union – get together with the aim of getting the best deal possible for their business or their members.

Negotiations involve a conflict of interest. In pay negotiations unions want the highest settlement they can get; management wants the lowest. In negotiations about other terms and conditions, unions will want the best result for their members while management will want to avoid agreeing to anything other than what they think is reasonable from their viewpoint. It can be a zero-sum game – what one side gains the other loses. No one likes to lose, so there is scope for conflict, which has to be managed if an amicable agreement is to be achieved. And negotiators do, or should, try to end up on friendly terms, whatever differences of opinion have occurred on the way. After all, they may well meet again.

TABLE 53.1 Commercial and industrial relations negotiations compared

Industrial relations negotiations	Commercial negotiations
• Assume an ongoing relationship – negotiators cannot walk away.	• Negotiators can walk away.
• The agreement is not legally binding.	• The contract is legally binding.
• Conducted on a face-to-face basis.	• May be conducted at a distance.
• Carried out by representatives responsible to constituents.	• Carried out directly with the parties being responsible to a line manager.
• Make frequent use of adjournments.	• Usually conducted on a continuing basis.
• May be conducted in an atmosphere of distrust, even hostility.	• Usually conducted on a 'willing buyer/willing seller' basis.

The process of negotiation

Negotiating takes place when two parties meet to reach an agreement concerning a proposition, such as a pay claim, which one party has put to the other. Negotiation can be convergent when both parties are equally keen to reach a win-win agreement (in commercial terms, a willing buyer/willing seller arrangement). It can be divergent when one or both of the parties aim to win as much as they can from the other while giving away as little as possible. Negotiations in an industrial relations setting differ from commercial negotiations in the respects shown in Table 53.1.

In negotiations on pay or other terms and conditions of service, management represents the employer's interests and employee representatives represent the interests of employees. Both sides are of equal status. Negotiations take place in an atmosphere of uncertainty. Neither side knows how strong the other side's bargaining position is or what it really wants and will be prepared to accept.

Stages of negotiation

Negotiations are conducted in four stages: initial steps, opening, bargaining and closing.

Initial steps

In a pay negotiation, unions making the claim will define for themselves three things: a) the target they would like to achieve, b) the minimum they will accept, and c) the opening claim they believe will be most likely to achieve the target. Employers define three related things: 1) the target settlement they would like to achieve, 2) the maximum they would be prepared to concede, and 3) the opening offer that will provide them with sufficient room to manoeuvre in reaching their target. The difference between a union's claim and an employer's offer is the negotiating range. If the maximum the employer will offer exceeds the minimum the union will accept the difference will be the settlement range, in which case a settlement will be easily reached. If, however, the maximum the employer will offer is less than the minimum the union will accept, negotiations will be more difficult and a settlement will only be reached if the expectations of either side are adjusted during the bargaining stage. The extent to which this will happen depends on the relative power of the two parties. The strength of the arguments put forward by either party will also be a factor, but the major consideration is usually power.

Preparation for negotiation by either party involves:

- deciding on the strategy and tactics to be used;

- listing the arguments to be used in supporting their case;
- listing the arguments or counter-arguments that the other party is likely to use;
- obtaining supporting data;
- selecting the negotiating team, briefing them on the strategy and tactics and rehearsing them in their roles.

Opening

Tactics in the opening phase of a negotiation are as follows:

- open realistically and move moderately;
- challenge the other side's position as it stands; do not destroy their ability to move;
- observe behaviour, ask questions and listen attentively in order to assess the other side's strengths and weaknesses, their tactics and the extent to which they may be bluffing;
- make no concessions at this stage;
- be non-committal about proposals and explanations – do not talk too much.

Bargaining

After the opening moves, the main bargaining phase takes place in which the gap is narrowed between the initial positions. The attempt is made to persuade each other that their case is strong enough to force the other side to close at a less advantageous point than they had planned. Bargaining is often as much about concealing as revealing – keeping arguments in reserve to deploy when they will make the greatest impact.

The following tactics are used:

- Always make conditional proposals: 'If you will do this, then I will consider doing that' – the words to remember are: 'if... then...'
- Never make one-sided concessions: always trade off against a concession from the other party: 'If I concede x, then I expect you to concede y'.
- Negotiate on the whole package: negotiations should not allow the other side to pick off item by item (salami negotiation).
- Keep the issues open to extract the maximum benefit from potential trade-offs.

There are certain bargaining conventions that experienced negotiators follow, because they appreciate that by so doing they create the atmosphere of trust and understanding that is essential to the sort of stable bargaining relationship that benefits both sides. Some of the more generally accepted conventions are as follows:

- Whatever happens during the bargaining, both parties are hoping to reach a settlement.
- Negotiators should show that they respect the views of the other side and take them seriously even if they disagree with them.
- While it is preferable to conduct negotiations in a civilized and friendly manner, attacks, hard words, threats and controlled losses of temper may be used by negotiators to underline determination to get their way and to shake their opponent's confidence and self-possession. But these should be treated by both sides as legitimate tactics and should not be allowed to shake the basic belief in each other's integrity or desire to settle without taking drastic action.
- Off-the-record discussions ('corridor negotiations') can be mutually beneficial as a means of probing attitudes and intentions and smoothing the way to a settlement, but they should not be referred to specifically in formal bargaining sessions unless both sides agree in advance.
- Each side should be prepared to move from its original position.
- It is normal, although not inevitable, for the negotiation to proceed by alternate offers and counter-offers from each side, leading steadily towards a settlement.
- Third parties should not be brought in until both sides agree that no further progress can be made without them.
- Concessions, once made, cannot be withdrawn.
- If negotiators want to avoid committing themselves to 'a final offer', with the risk of devaluing the term if they are forced to make concessions, they should state as positively as they can that this is as far as they can go. But

bargaining conventions allow further moves from this position on a quid pro quo basis.

- Firm offers must not be withdrawn.
- The final agreement should mean exactly what it says. There should be no trickery and the agreed terms should be implemented without amendment.
- So far as possible the final settlement should be framed and communicated in such a way as to reduce the extent to which the other party loses face or credibility.

When bargaining, the parties have to identify the basis for a possible agreement; that is, the common ground. One way of doing this is to use the aspiration grid technique. The grid sets out the parameters for the anticipated outcome of the negotiations. It shows the expected issues that one of the parties is prepared to trade, as well as the anticipated attitude to the bargaining agenda of the other party. The grid also gives the parameters within which the forthcoming bargaining sessions might be expected to develop. It helps to identify the information required from the other party and the information required to be conveyed by one party to the other party. If the receipt of this information shows expectations as to the behaviour of the other party to be wrong, then the aspiration grid has to be reassessed and modified.

Closing

There are various closing techniques:

- Make a concession from the package, preferably in a minor way, which is traded off against an agreement to settle. The concession can be offered more positively than in the bargaining stage: 'If you will agree to settle at x then I will concede y.'
- Do a deal, split the difference or bring in something new, such as extending the settlement timescale, agreeing to back-payments, phasing increases, or making a joint declaration of intent to do something in the future.
- Summarize what has happened so far, emphasize the concessions that have been made and the extent of movement from the original position, and indicate that the limit has been reached.
- Apply pressure through a threat of the dire consequences that will follow if a 'final' claim is not agreed or a 'final offer' is not accepted.

Employers should not make a final offer unless they mean it. If it is not really their final offer and the union calls their bluff, they may have to make further concessions and their credibility will be undermined. Each party will attempt to force the other side into revealing the extent to which they have reached their final position. But negotiators should not allow themselves to be pressurized. They have to use their judgement on when to say 'this is as far as we can go'. That judgement will be based on their understanding that the stage when a settlement is possible has been reached.

Negotiating and bargaining skills

The skills required to be effective in negotiations and bargaining are:

- *Analytical ability* – the capacity to assess the factors that affect the negotiating stance and tactics of both parties.
- *Empathy* – the ability to put oneself in the other party's shoes.
- *Interactive skills* – the ability to relate well with other people.
- *Communicating skills* – the ability to convey information and arguments clearly, positively and logically.
- *Keeping cards close to the chest* – not giving away what you really want or are prepared to concede until you are ready to do so (in the marketplace it is always easier for sellers to drive a hard bargain with buyers who have revealed somehow that they covet the article).
- *Flexible realism* – the capacity to make realistic moves during the bargaining process in order to reduce the claim or increase the offer, which will demonstrate that the bargainer is seeking a reasonable settlement and is prepared to respond appropriately to movements from the other side.

Key learning points: Negotiation skills

The process of negotiation

Negotiation is the process of coming to terms and, in so doing, getting the best deal possible. Negotiation involves bargaining, which is reaching the most advantageous position in discussion with another party through a process of offer and counter-offer.

Negotiating takes place when two parties meet to reach an agreement on a proposition, such as a pay claim, which one party has put to the other. Negotiation can be convergent when both parties are equally keen to reach a win-win agreement (in commercial terms, a willing buyer/willing seller arrangement). It can be divergent when one or both of the parties aim to win as much as they can from the other while giving away as little as possible.

Stages of negotiation

Negotiations are conducted in four stages: initial steps, opening, bargaining and closing.

Negotiating and bargaining skills

- Analytical ability – the capacity to assess the factors that affect the negotiating stance and tactics of both parties.
- Empathy – the ability to put oneself in the other party's shoes.
- Interactive skills – the ability to relate well with other people.
- Communicating skills – the ability to convey information and arguments clearly, positively and logically.
- Keeping cards close to the chest – not giving away what you really want or are prepared to concede until you are ready to do so.
- Flexible realism – the capacity to make realistic moves during the bargaining process in order to reduce the claim or increase the offer, which will demonstrate that the bargainer is seeking a reasonable settlement and is prepared to respond appropriately to movements from the other side.

Questions

1 What is the process of negotiation?
2 What are the main stages of a negotiation?
3 What are the required negotiating and bargaining skills?

54 Leading and facilitating change

KEY CONCEPTS AND TERMS

Change agent	Field force analysis
Change management	Organizational capability
Culture change	Organizational effectiveness

LEARNING OUTCOMES

On completing this chapter you should be able to define these key concepts. You should also understand:

- The role of HR in leading change
- The change process
- Change models
- Reasons for resistance to change
- Overcoming resistance to change
- Implementing change

Introduction

Leading and facilitating change is about initiating and achieving the smooth implementation of new developments and initiatives by planning and introducing them systematically, allowing for the possibility of their being resisted or, at least, misunderstood. Kotter (1996) emphasized the importance of leading change rather than simply managing it.

The role of HR in leading and facilitating change

Leading and facilitating change is probably the most demanding of all HR roles. If HR is concerned – as it should be – in playing a major part in the achievement of continuous improvement and in the HR processes that support that improvement, then it will need to be involved in facilitating change. Caldwell (2001) stated that the change agent roles that can be carried out by HR professionals are those of change champions, change adapters, change consultants and change synergists.

Leading change

Leading change involves initiating and managing culture change (the process of changing the organization's culture in the shape of its values, norms and beliefs) and the introduction of new structures, systems, working practices and people management processes. The aim is to increase organizational capability (the potential ability of the organization to perform well) and organizational effectiveness (how well the organization actually performs).

Ulrich (1997: 7) observed that HR professionals should be 'as explicit about culture change as they are today about the requirements for a successful training program or hiring strategy'. He later emphasized that: 'HR should become an agent of continuous transformation, shaping processes and a culture that together improve an organization's capacity for change' (1998: 125).

Change leadership means:

- identifying where change is required;
- specifying what changes should take place;
- assessing the benefits of the change and what it will cost;
- establishing the consequences of the change;
- assessing any problems that the change may create, eg resistance to the change, and any risks involved;
- persuading management and anyone else affected by the change that it is necessary, spelling out the benefits and indicating what will be done to deal with potential problems;
- planning how the change should be implemented, including nominating and briefing change agents (people responsible for achieving change), minimizing potential resistance through communication and involvement, and managing risks;
- facilitating the introduction and management of the change;
- ensuring that the change is embedded successfully – 'holding the gains'.

Facilitating change

Facilitating change is about making it happen. As Hamlin and Davies (2001: 13) observed, one of the major challenges facing HR 'is how to help people through the transitions of change, and how to survive in working conditions that are in a constant state of flux'. Brown and Eisenhardt (1997: 21) noted that managers who were successful in the art of continuous change: 'carefully managed the transition between the past and the future. Much like the pit stop in a car race or the baton pass in track, this transition appeared critical.'

The role of HR in facilitating change was described by Vere and Butler (2007: 34) as follows:

- The issue needs to be on the strategic business agenda and managers must see how action will improve business results: that is, there needs to be a sound business case for the initiative. HR managers need to be able to demonstrate the return on the planned investment.
- The change needs to have the active backing of those at the top of the organization, so it is for the HR director to gain the commitment of the top team and engage them in a practical way in taking the work forward.
- HR needs to engage managers in the design of change from the outset (or, if this is a business-driven change, HR needs to be involved at the outset).
- The programme needs to be framed in the language of the business in order to have real meaning and achieve 'buy in' for all parties; if there is too much HR jargon, this will be a turn-off.
- Project and people management skills are crucial to ensure the programme is well planned and resourced and that risks are assessed and managed.
- As in all change programmes, the importance of communication is paramount – to explain, engage and commit people to the programme.
- In this respect the crucial role that HR can play is to ensure that employees are fully engaged in the design and implementation of the change.
- HR needs to draw on others' experience and learning.

To do all this, Ulrich (1997: 8) pointed out that: 'HR professionals need a model of change and the ability to apply the model to a specific situation.' The models described later in this chapter need to be understood and applied as appropriate. The other qualities required are insight – to understand the need for change; courage – to pursue change; and determination – to achieve change.

Leading and facilitating change is hard work. As Alfes *et al* (2010: 111) observed on the basis of their research: 'The role [of HR] is generally constrained and reactive.' They also noted that: 'HR professionals may find their roles circumscribed by expectations of their role, the nature of the change process, capability and capacity' (ibid: 125).

Ulrich (1997) emphasized that one of the key roles of HR professionals is to act as change agents, but it is a difficult role to play. Perhaps, as Thornhill *et al* (2000) noted, the main contribution HR can make is to generate and support change where a core feature is the development and alignment of HRM practices such as culture management, performance management, learning and development, reward management and employee relations.

To lead change it is necessary to understand how the process works. It is important to bear in mind that while those leading change need to be constant about ends, they have to be flexible about means. This requires them to come to an understanding of the various models of change that have been developed and of the factors that create resistance to change and how to minimize such resistance. In the light of an understanding of these models, and the phenomenon of resistance to change, they will be better equipped to make use of the guidelines for change set out at the end of this chapter.

The change process

Conceptually, the change process starts with an awareness of the need for change. An analysis of the situation and the factors that have created it leads to a diagnosis of their distinctive characteristics and an indication of the direction in which action needs to be taken. Possible courses of action can next be identified and evaluated and a choice made of the preferred action.

It is then necessary to decide how to get from here to there. Managing change during this transition state is a critical phase in the change process. It is here that the problems of introducing change emerge and have to be managed. These problems can include resistance to change, instability, high levels of stress, misdirected energy, conflict, and loss of momentum. Hence the need to do everything possible to anticipate reactions and likely impediments to the introduction of change.

The final stage, in which the new structure, system or process is installed, can also be demanding, indeed painful. As described by Pettigrew and Whipp (1991: 27), the implementation of change is an 'iterative, cumulative and reformulation-in-use process'.

The next issue is how to 'hold the gains', ie how to ensure that the change is embedded and maintained. This means continuously monitoring the effects and impact of the change and taking corrective action where necessary to ensure that it continues to work well. The change process has been described in the various change models set out below.

Change models

Change models explain the mechanisms for change and the factors that affect its success. The best known change models are those developed by Lewin (1951) and Beckhard (1969), but other important contributions to an understanding of the mechanisms for change have been made by Thurley (1979) and Beer *et al* (1990).

Lewin

The basic mechanisms for managing change as set out by Lewin (1951) are:

- *Unfreezing* – altering the present stable equilibrium that supports existing behaviours and attitudes. This process must take account of the inherent threats that change presents to people and the need to motivate those affected in order to attain the natural state of equilibrium by accepting change.
- *Changing* – developing new responses based on new information.
- *Refreezing* – stabilizing, supporting and reinforcing the new changed conditions.

Lewin also suggested the following methodology for analysing change, which he called 'field force analysis':

- Analyse the restraining or driving forces that will affect the transition to the future state – these restraining forces will include the reactions of those who see change as unnecessary or as constituting a threat.
- Assess which of the driving or restraining forces are critical.
- Take steps both to increase the critical driving forces and to decrease the critical restraining forces.

Beckhard

Beckhard (1969) proposed that a change programme should incorporate the following processes:

- Set goals and define the future state or organizational conditions desired after the change.
- Diagnose the present condition in relation to these goals.
- Define the transition state activities and commitments required to meet the future state.
- Develop strategies and action plans for managing this transition in the light of an analysis of the factors likely to affect the introduction of change.

Thurley

Thurley (1979) described the following five approaches to managing change:

- *Directive* – the imposition of change in crisis situations or when other methods have failed. This is done by the exercise of managerial power without consultation.
- *Bargained* – this approach recognizes that power is shared between the employer and the employed and change requires negotiation, compromise and agreement before being implemented.
- *'Hearts and minds'* – an all-embracing thrust to change the attitudes, values and beliefs of the whole workforce. This 'normative' approach (ie one that starts from a definition of what management thinks is right or 'normal') seeks 'commitment' and 'shared vision' but does not necessarily include involvement or participation.
- *Analytical* – a theoretical approach to the change process using models of change such as those described above. It proceeds sequentially from the analysis and diagnosis of the situation, through the setting of objectives, the design of the change process, the evaluation of the results and, finally, the determination of the objectives for the next stage in the change process. This is the rational and logical approach much favoured by consultants – external and internal. But change seldom proceeds as smoothly as this model would suggest. Emotions, power politics and external pressures mean that the rational approach, although it might be the right way to start, is difficult to sustain.
- *Action-based* – this recognizes that the way managers behave in practice bears little resemblance to the analytical, theoretical model. The distinction between managerial thought and managerial action blurs in practice to the point of invisibility. What managers *think* is what they do. Real life therefore often results in a 'ready, aim, fire' approach to change management. This typical approach to change starts with a broad belief that some sort of problem exists, although it may not be well defined. The identification of possible solutions, often on a trial and error basis, leads to a clarification of the nature of the problem and a shared understanding of a possible optimal solution, or at least a framework within which solutions can be discovered.

Beer, Eisenstat and Spector

Beer *et al* (1990) suggested in a seminal *Harvard Business Review* article, 'Why change programs don't produce change', that most such programmes are guided by a theory of change that is fundamentally flawed. This theory states that changes in attitudes lead to changes in behaviour: 'According to this model, change is like a conversion experience. Once people get religion, changes in their behaviour will surely follow' (ibid: 159). They thought that this theory gets the change process backwards and made the following comment on it:

> In fact, individual behaviour is powerfully shaped by the organizational roles people play. The most effective way to change behaviour, therefore, is to put people into a new organizational context, which imposes new roles, responsibilities and relationships on them. This creates a situation that in a sense 'forces' new attitudes and behaviour on people. (ibid: 159)

They prescribe six steps to effective change that concentrate on what they call 'task alignment' – reorganizing employees' roles, responsibilities and relationships in order to solve specific business problems in small units where goals and tasks can be clearly defined. The aim of following the overlapping steps is to build a self-reinforcing cycle of commitment, coordination and competence:

1. Mobilize commitment to change through the joint analysis of problems.
2. Develop a shared vision of how to organize and manage to achieve goals such as competitiveness.
3. Foster consensus for the new vision, competence to enact it, and cohesion to move it along.
4. Spread revitalization to all departments without pushing it from the top – don't force the issue: let each department find its own way to the new organization.
5. Institutionalize revitalization through formal policies, systems and structures.
6. Monitor and adjust strategies in response to problems in the revitalization process.

Resistance to change

People resist change because it is seen as a threat to familiar patterns of behaviour as well as to status and financial rewards. Woodward (1968: 80) made this point clearly:

> When we talk about resistance to change we tend to imply that management is always rational in changing its direction, and that employees are stupid, emotional or irrational in not responding in the way they should. But if an individual is going to be worse off, explicitly or implicitly, when the proposed changes have been made, any resistance is entirely rational in terms of his own best interest. The interests of the organization and the individual do not always coincide.

Hamlin and Davies (2001: 58) commented that: 'Any change creates stress and anxiety; this is because as human beings we deal individually with uncertainty in different ways.' However, some people will welcome change as an opportunity. These people need to be identified and, where feasible, they can help in the introduction of change as change agents.

Reasons for resisting change

Specifically, the reasons for resisting change are:

- *The shock of the new* – people are suspicious of anything they perceive will upset their established routines, methods of working or conditions of employment. They do not want to lose the security of what is familiar to them. They may not believe, sometimes with good reason, statements by management that the change is for their benefit as well as that of the organization. They may feel that management has ulterior motives and, sometimes, the louder the protestations of management, the less they will be believed.
- *Economic fears* – loss of money, threats to job security.
- *Inconvenience* – the change will make life more difficult.
- *Uncertainty* – change can be worrying because of uncertainty about its likely impact.
- *Symbolic fears* – a small change that may affect some treasured symbol, such as a separate office or a reserved parking space, may symbolize big ones, especially when employees are uncertain about how extensive the programme of change will be.
- *Threat to interpersonal relationships* – anything that disrupts the customary social relationships and standards of the group will be resisted.

- *Threat to status or skill* – the change is perceived as reducing the status of individuals or as deskilling them.
- *Competence fears* – concern about the ability to cope with new demands or to acquire new skills.

Overcoming resistance to change

Resistance to change can be difficult to overcome, even when the change is not detrimental to those concerned. But the attempt must be made. The starting point is an analysis of the potential impact of change by considering how it will affect people in their jobs. The reasons for resisting change, set out above, can be used as a checklist to establish where there might be problems, with groups or with individuals.

The analysis should indicate what aspects of the proposed change may be supported generally or by specified individuals and which aspects may be resisted. So far as possible, the potentially hostile or negative reactions of people and the reasons for them should be identified. It is necessary to try and understand the likely feelings and fears of those affected so that worries can be relieved and, as far as possible, ambiguities can be resolved. In making this analysis, the individual introducing the change – the change agent – should recognize that new ideas are likely to be suspect and should make ample provision for the discussion of reactions to proposals in order to ensure complete understanding of them.

Involvement in the change process gives people the chance to raise and resolve their concerns and make suggestions about the form of the change and how it should be introduced. The aim is to get 'ownership' – a feeling amongst people that the change is something that they are happy to live with because they have been involved in its planning and introduction – it has become their change.

A communication strategy to explain the proposed change should be prepared and implemented so that unnecessary fears are allayed. All the available channels should be used, but face-to-face communications direct from managers to individuals or through a team briefing system are best.

Implementing change

The problems of implementing strategic change were summed up by Lawler and Mohrman (2003: 24) as follows:

> Most strategies, like most mergers, fail not because of poor thinking, but because of poor implementation. Implementation failures usually involve the failure to acknowledge and build the needed skills and organizational capabilities, to gain support of the workforce, and to support the organizational changes and learning required to behave in new ways. In short, execution failures are often the result of poor human capital management. This opens the door for HR to add important value if it can deliver change strategies, plans and thinking that aid in the development and execution of business strategy.

Implementing change can indeed be difficult. Research by Carnall (1991) in 93 organizations identified the following explanations for failures to implement change effectively:

- implementation took more time than originally allowed;
- major problems that had not been identified beforehand emerged during implementation;
- coordination of implementation activities was not effective enough;
- competing activities and other crises distracted management from implementing the change decision;
- the capabilities of the employees involved were not sufficient;
- training and instruction to lower level employees was inadequate;
- uncontrollable factors in the external environment had an adverse effect on implementation.

The following suggestions on how to minimize such problems were put forward by Nadler and Tushman (1980):

- *Motivate* in order to achieve changes in behaviour by individuals.

- *Manage the transition* by making organizational arrangements designed to ensure that control is maintained during and after the transition and by developing and communicating a clear image of the future.
- *Shape the political dynamics of change* so that power centres develop that support the change rather than block it.
- *Build in stability of structures and processes* to serve as anchors for people to hold on to – organizations and individuals can only stand so much uncertainty and turbulence, hence the emphasis by Quinn (1980) on the need for an incremental approach.

As reported by Surowiecki (2013: 44), Professor Michael Roberto of Bryant University suggested that: 'Anytime you're trying to change the ways you do things, small wins are important. Small wins help you build support both internally and externally, and they make it easier for people to buy in.'

The role of change agents

The change process will take place more smoothly with the help of credible internal or external change agents – people who help to manage change by providing advice and support on its introduction and management. A change agent was defined by Caldwell (2003: 139–40) as 'an internal or external individual or team responsible for initiating, sponsoring, managing and implementing a specific change initiative or complete change programme'. As described by Balugon and Hope-Hailey (2004), the role of the change agent is to lead change. Alfes *et al* (2010) noted that change agents establish what is required, involve people in planning and managing change, advise on how change should be implemented and communicate to people the implications of change.

Keep (2001: 89) listed the following change agent competencies:

- Project management – planning and resource allocation.
- Contracting with clients – defining the task, establishing relationships.
- Team building – defining roles, maintaining good working relationships.
- Analysis and diagnosis – data collection, problem solving, systems thinking.
- Data utilization – qualitative or quantitative data, paper-based review, survey techniques.
- Interpersonal skills – dealing with people, leadership.
- Communication skills – speaking, written presentations/reports, listening.
- Political awareness – sensitivity, influencing.
- Intervention implementation – participation, involvement.
- Monitoring and evaluation – criteria setting and reviewing, measuring effectiveness.
- Technical skills – financial interpretation, psychometrics.
- Process skills – facilitation.
- Insight – reflection, awareness of key issues, critical thinking, intuition.

It is often assumed that only people from outside the organization can take on the change agent role because they are independent and do not 'carry any baggage'. They can be useful, but people from within the firm who are respected and credible can do the job well. This is often the role of HR specialists, but the use of line managers adds extra value.

Guidelines for change management

- The achievement of sustainable change requires strong commitment and visionary leadership from the top.
- Understanding is necessary of the culture of the organization and the levers for change that are most likely to be effective in that culture.
- Those concerned with managing change at all levels should have the temperament and leadership skills appropriate to the circumstances of the organization and its change strategies.
- Change is more likely to be successful if there is a 'burning platform' to justify it, ie a powerful and convincing reason for change.
- It is important to build a working environment that is conducive to change. Learning and development programmes can help to do this.
- It is easier to change behaviour by changing processes, structure and systems than to change attitudes or the organizational culture.
- People support what they help to create. Commitment to change is improved if those affected by change are allowed to participate as fully as possible in planning and implementing it. The aim should be to get them to 'own' the change as something they want and will be glad to live with.
- The reward system should encourage innovation and recognize success in achieving change.
- Change will always involve failure as well as success. The failures must be expected and learnt from.
- Hard evidence and data on the need for change are the most powerful tools for its achievement, but establishing the need for change is easier than deciding how to satisfy it.
- There are always people in organizations who can act as champions of change. They will welcome the challenges and opportunities that change can provide. They are the ones to be chosen as change agents.
- Resistance to change is inevitable if the individuals concerned feel that they are going to be worse off – implicitly or explicitly. The inept management of change will produce that reaction.
- In an age of global competition, technological innovation, turbulence, discontinuity, even chaos, change is inevitable and necessary. The organization must do all it can to explain why change is essential and how it will affect everyone. Moreover, every effort must be made to protect the interests of those affected by change.

Key learning points: Leading and facilitating change

The role of HR in leading and facilitating change

Leading and facilitating change are two of the key roles of HR professionals. In practice, they are probably the most demanding of all HR roles.

Leading change

Leading change involves initiating and managing culture change (the process of changing the organization's culture in the shape of its values, norms and beliefs) and the introduction of new structures, systems, working practices and people management processes.

Facilitating change

Change management is largely about facilitation.

The change process

The change process starts with an awareness of the need for change. An analysis of this situation and the factors that have created it leads to a diagnosis of their distinctive characteristics and an indication of the direction in which action needs to be taken. Possible courses of action can then be identified and evaluated and a choice made of the preferred action.

Change models

The main change models are those produced by Lewin, Beckhard, Thurley and Beer *et al.*

Reasons for resistance to change

The shock of the new, economic fears, inconvenience, uncertainty, symbolic fears, threat to interpersonal relationships, threat to status or skills, competence fears.

Overcoming resistance to change

- Analyse the potential impact of change by considering how it will affect people in their jobs.
- Identify the potentially hostile or negative reactions of people.
- Make ample provision for the discussion of reactions to proposals in order to ensure complete understanding of them.
- Get 'ownership' – a feeling amongst people that the change is something they are happy to live with because they have been involved in its planning and introduction.
- Prepare and implement a communication strategy to explain the proposed change.

Implementing change

Implementation failures usually involve the failure to: acknowledge and build the needed skills and organizational capabilities, to gain support of the workforce, and to support the organizational changes and learning required to behave in new ways.

Questions

1 What is the role of HR in leading and facilitating change?
2 What does leading change involve?
3 What does facilitating change involve?
4 What is the change process?
5 What are the main problems in implementing change?
6 What is Lewin's change model?
7 What is field force analysis?
8 Why do people resist change?
9 How can resistance to change be overcome?
10 What is the role of a change agent?
11 What are the key guidelines for change management?

References

Alfes, K, Truss, C and Gill, J (2010) The HR manager as change agent: evidence from the public sector, *Journal of Change Management*, 10 (1), pp 109–27

Balugon, J and Hope-Hailey, V (2004) *Exploring Strategic Change*, 2nd edn, London, Prentice Hall

Beckhard, R (1969) *Organization Development: Strategy and models*, Reading, MA, Addison-Wesley

Beer, M, Eisenstat, R and Spector, B (1990) Why change programs don't produce change, *Harvard Business Review*, November–December, pp 158–66

Brown, S L and Eisenhardt, K M (1997) The art of continuous change: linking complexity theory and time-paced evolution in relentlessly shifting organizations, *Administrative Science Quarterly*, 42 (1), pp 1–24

Caldwell, R (2001) Champions, adapters, consultants and synergists: the new change agents, *Human Resource Management Journal*, 11 (3), pp 39–52

Caldwell, R (2003) Models of change agency: a fourfold classification, *British Journal of Management*, 14 (2), pp 131–42

Carnall, C (1991) *Managing Change*, London, Routledge

Hamlin, B and Davies, G (2001) Managers, trainers and developers as change agents, in (eds) B Hamlin, J Keep and K Ash, *Organizational Change and Development: A reflective guide for managers, trainers and developers*, Harlow, Pearson Education, pp 39–60

Keep, J (2001) The change practitioner: perspectives on role, effectiveness, dilemmas and challenges, in (eds) B Hamlin, J Keep and K Ash, *Organizational Change and Development: A reflective guide for managers, trainers and developers*, Harlow, Pearson Education, pp 13–38

Kotter, J J (1996) *Leading Change*, Boston, MA, Harvard University Press

Lawler, E E and Mohrman, S A (2003) HR as a strategic partner: What does it take to make it happen?, *Human Resource Planning*, 26 (3), pp 15–29

Lewin, K (1951) *Field Theory in Social Science*, New York, Harper & Row

Nadler, D A and Tushman, M L (1980) A congruence model for diagnosing organizational behaviour, in (ed) R H Miles, *Resource Book in Macro-organizational Behaviour*, Santa Monica, CA, Goodyear Publishing

Pettigrew, A and Whipp, R (1991) *Managing Change for Competitive Success*, Oxford, Blackwell

Quinn, J B (1980) Managing strategic change, *Sloane Management Review*, 11 (4/5), pp 3–30

Surowiecki, J (2013) The turnaround trap, *The New Yorker*, 25 March, p 44

Thornhill, A, Lewis, P, Saunders, M and Millmore, M (2000) *Managing Change: A human resource strategy approach*, Harlow, FT Prentice Hall

Thurley, K (1979) *Supervision: A Reappraisal*, London, Heinemann

Ulrich, D (1997) *Human Resource Champions*, Boston, MA, Harvard Business School Press

Ulrich, D (1998) A new mandate for human resources, *Harvard Business Review*, January–February, pp 124–34

Vere, D and Butler, L (2007) *Fit for Business: Transforming HR in the public service*, London, CIPD

Woodward, J (1968) Resistance to change, *Management International Review*, 8, pp 78–93

55 Leadership skills

KEY CONCEPTS AND TERMS

Authentic leaders
Charismatic leaders
Contingent leadership
Distributed leadership
Emotional intelligence
Leadership
Leadership development
Situational leadership
Trait
Transactional leaders
Transformational leaders
Visionary leaders

LEARNING OUTCOMES

On completing this chapter you should be able to define these key concepts. You should also know about:

- The meaning of leadership
- What leaders do
- The qualities of a good leader
- What makes an effective leader
- The main leadership theories
- The main leadership styles
- The process of leadership development

Introduction

HR professionals need to know about leadership for four reasons: 1) they have to exercise leadership in persuading others to do things; 2) they are, or should be, concerned with the development of leaders in the organization; 3) at a senior level they have to lead their own function; and 4) they are involved in leading change. The purpose of this chapter is to meet this need by analysing the process of leadership and the skills involved.

The meaning of leadership

To lead people is to inspire, influence and guide. Leadership can be described as the ability to persuade others willingly to behave differently. It is the process of getting people to do their best to achieve a desired result. It involves developing and communicating a vision for the future, motivating people and securing their engagement. As Stogdill (1950: 3) explained, leadership is an 'influencing process aimed at goal achievement'.

Leadership theories

Leadership is a complicated notion and a number of theories have been produced to explain it. These theories, as summarized below, have developed over the years and explore a number of different facets of leadership and leadership behaviour. In many ways they complement one another and together they help to gain a comprehensive understanding of what the process of leadership is about.

Trait theory, which explains leadership by reference to the qualities that leaders have, is the basic and to many people the most familiar theory. But it has its limitations, and pragmatic research was carried out to identify what types of behaviour characterized leadership rather than focusing on the personalities of leaders. The key leadership behaviour studies conducted by the Universities of Michigan and Ohio State led to the identification of two dimensions of leadership behaviour, respectively: employee as distinct from job-centred behaviour, and the processes of consideration and initiating structure.

The next step in the development of leadership theory was the recognition by researchers that what leaders did and how they did it was dependent or contingent on the situation they were in (Fiedler, 1967). Different traits became important; different behaviours or styles of leadership had to be used to achieve effectiveness in different situations. These studies resulted in the theories of contingent and situational leadership.

Next, traits theory was in effect revived by Goleman (2001) in the notion of emotional intelligence as a necessary attribute of leaders. Most recently Ulrich put his oar in alongside his colleague Smallwood (2007) with the notion of the leadership brand as a comprehensive approach to leadership by organizations.

The problem with leadership theories

Despite all of the research and theorizing, the concept of leadership is still problematic. As Meindl *et al* (1985: 78) commented: 'It has become apparent that, after years of trying, we have been unable to generate an understanding of leadership that is both intellectually compelling and emotionally satisfying. The concept of leadership remains elusive and enigmatic.'

These problems may arise because leadership, as a notion, is difficult to pin down. There are many different types of situations in which leaders operate, many different types of leaders and many different leadership styles. Producing one theory that covers all these variables is difficult if not impossible. All that can be done is to draw on the various theories that exist in order to explain different facets of leadership without necessarily relying on any one of them for a comprehensive explanation of what is involved.

Perhaps leadership is best defined by considering what leaders do and how they do it (the different styles they adopt), examining what sort of leaders carry out these activities and practise these styles, and looking at any empirical evidence available on what makes them good leaders. These are all covered in the next four sections of this chapter.

What leaders do

The most convincing analysis of what leaders do was produced by Adair (1973). He explained that the three essential roles of leaders are to:

1. *Define the task* – they make it quite clear what the group is expected to do.
2. *Achieve the task* – that is why the group exists. Leaders ensure that the group's purpose is fulfilled. If it is not, the result is frustration, disharmony, criticism and, eventually perhaps, disintegration of the group.
3. *Maintain effective relationships* – between themselves and the members of the group, and between the people within the group. These relationships are effective if they contribute to achieving the task. They can be divided into those concerned with the team and its morale and sense of common purpose, and those concerned with individuals and how they are motivated.

Adair suggested that demands on leaders are best expressed as three areas of need that they must satisfy. These are: 1) task needs – to get the job done; 2) individual needs – to harmonize the needs

FIGURE 55.1 John Adair's model of leadership

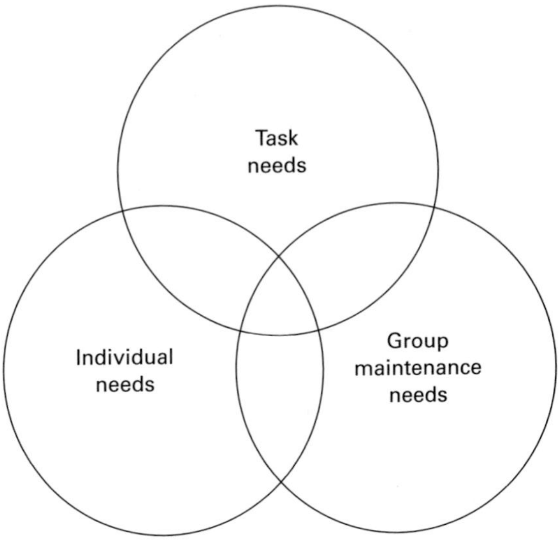

of the individual with the needs of the task and the group; and 3) group maintenance needs – to build and maintain team spirit. As can be seen in Figure 55.1, he modelled these demands as three interlocking circles.

This model indicates that the task, individual and group needs are interdependent. Satisfying task needs will also satisfy group and individual needs. Task needs, however, cannot be met unless attention is paid to individual and group needs, and looking after individual needs will also contribute to satisfying group needs, and vice versa. There is a risk of becoming so task-oriented that leaders ignore individual and group or team needs. It is just as dangerous to be too people-oriented, focusing on meeting individual or group needs at the expense of the task. The best leaders are those who keep these three needs satisfied and in balance, according to the demands of the situation.

Leadership styles

Leadership style is the approach that managers use in exercising leadership when they are relating to their team members. It is sometimes called 'management style'. There are many styles of leadership and no one style is necessarily better than the other in any situation. To greater or lesser degrees, leaders can be autocratic or democratic, controlling or enabling, task-oriented or people-centred. The Hay/McBer research reported by Goleman (2000) identified the following six styles and indicated when they might be used:

1. *Coercive* – demands compliance (use in a crisis or with problem people).
2. *Authoritative* – mobilizes people (use when new vision and direction is needed).
3. *Affiliative* – creates harmony (use to heal wounds and to motivate people under stress).
4. *Democratic* – forges consensus (use to build agreement and get contributions).
5. *Pacesetting* – sets high standards (use to get fast results from a motivated team).
6. *Coaching* – develops people (to improve performance and develop strengths).

In line with contingency and situational theories it should not be assumed that any one style is right in any circumstances. There is no such thing as an ideal leadership style. It all depends. The factors affecting the degree to which a style is appropriate will be the type of organization, the nature of the task, the characteristics of the individuals in the leader's team (the followers) and of the group as a whole and, importantly, the personality of the leader.

Effective leaders are capable of flexing their style to meet the demands of the situation. Normally, democratic leaders may have to shift into more of a directive mode when faced with a crisis, but they make clear what they are doing and why. Poor leaders change their style arbitrarily so that their team members are confused and do not know what to expect next.

Good leaders may also flex their style when dealing with individual team members according to their characteristics. Some people need more positive directions than others. Others respond best if they are involved in decision-making with their boss. But there is a limit to the degree of flexibility that should be used. It is unwise to differentiate too much between the ways in which individuals are treated, or to be inconsistent in one's approach.

Types of leaders

To understand the process of leadership (and, incidentally, provide a basis for leadership development programmes) it is useful not only to analyse the styles that leaders can adopt but also to classify the different types of leaders that apply those styles. As described below, leaders can be charismatic, visionary, transformational, transactional or 'authentic'. However, typical leaders may exhibit any or even all of these characteristics, either consistently or in response to the situation in which they find themselves.

Leadership may be exercised by a few selected authoritative individuals and many studies focus on top managers as 'charismatic' or 'visionary' leaders. But it may and indeed should take the form of distributed leadership, which is spread through the organization amongst people working together by processes of influence and interdependencies. As Huczynski and Buchanan (2007: 720) commented: 'leadership is a widely distributed phenomenon. Leadership functions are best carried out by those who have the interest, knowledge, skills and motivation to perform them effectively.' The possibility that people who become managers may not have these qualities to a desirable extent creates a need for systematic leadership development programmes.

Charismatic leaders

Charismatic leaders rely on their personality, their inspirational qualities and their 'aura' to get people to follow them. Burns (1978), who coined the term, suggested that charismatic leaders were set apart from ordinary people and were treated as being endowed with exceptional powers or qualities that inspire followers.

Conger and Kanungo (1998) described charismatic leadership as a process of formulating an inspiring vision of the future and then demonstrating the importance of the articulated vision. This may involve unconventional behaviour that conveys important goals that are part of the vision and demonstrates means to achieve these goals. Charismatic leaders also take risks and motivate followers by setting a personal example. In this sense, charismatic leaders operate as visionary and transformational leaders, as described below.

But Carey (1992: 232) warned that: 'when the gifts of charisma, inspiration, consideration and intellectual strength are abused for the self-interest of the leader, the effect on followers ceases to be liberating and moral and becomes instead oppressive and ideological'. And Bennis (2010: 4) commented that: 'the ability to inspire trust, not charisma, is what enables leaders to recruit others to a cause'.

Visionary leaders

Visionary leaders are inspired by a clear vision of an exciting future and inspire their followers by successfully conveying that vision to them. Bennis and Nanus (1985: 89) defined a vision as 'a target that beckons'. Their notion of visionary leadership was explained as follows:

> To choose a direction, a leader must first have developed a mental image of a possible and desirable future state of the organization. This image, which we call a vision, may be as vague as a dream or as precise as a goal or mission statement. The critical point is that a vision articulates a view of a realistic, credible and attractive future for the organization, a condition that is different in some important ways from one that now exists. (ibid: 89)

Kouzes and Posner (2003: 112) claimed that: 'One of the most important practices of leadership is giving life and work a sense of meaning and purpose by offering an exciting vision.'

Transformational leaders

Transformational leaders are able, by their force of personality, to make significant changes in the behaviour of their followers in order to achieve the leader's vision or goals. As described by Burns (1978), what he called 'transforming leadership' involves motivating people to strive for higher goals. He believed that good leadership implies a moral responsibility to respond to the values and needs of people in a way that is conducive to the highest form of human relations. As he put it: 'The ultimate test of moral leadership is its capacity to transcend the claims of the multiplicity of everyday needs, wants and expectations' (ibid: 46).

Another researcher, Bass (1985), extended the work of Burns by explaining the psychological mechanisms that underlie transforming leadership. He pointed out that the extent to which leaders are transformational is measured by their influence on their followers in terms of the degree to which they feel trust, admiration, loyalty and respect for the leader and are willing to work harder than originally expected. According to Bass, this occurs because the leader transforms and motivates through an inspiring mission and vision and gives them an identity. Tichy and Devanna (1986) concluded that the transformational leader has three main roles: recognizing the need for revitalization, creating a new vision and institutionalizing change.

Yukl (1999) advised that transformational leaders should:

- develop a challenging and attractive vision together with employees;
- tie the vision to a strategy for its achievement;
- develop the vision, specify and translate it to actions;
- express confidence, decisiveness and optimism about the vision and its implementation;
- realize the vision through small planned steps and small successes on the path to its full implementation.

Transactional leaders

Transactional leaders trade money, jobs and security for compliance. As Burns (1978: 19) noted: 'Such leadership occurs when a person takes the initiative in making contact with others for the purpose of an exchange of valued things.' Tavanti (2008: 169) stated that: 'Transactional leaders exhibit specific leadership skills usually associated with the ability to obtain results, to control through structures and processes, to solve problems, to plan and organize, and work within the structures and boundaries of the organization.' Put like this, a transactional leader conforms to the stereotype of the manager rather than the leader. Bass (1985) argued that leaders can display both transformational and transactional characteristics. Tavanti (2008) also observed that transactional leadership behaviour is used to one degree or another by most leaders, but that: 'Particular instances of transactional leadership are motivated simply by people's wants and preferences. This form of leadership uncritically responds to our preferences, that is, even when they are grounded in base motivations or an undeveloped moral sense' (ibid: 171).

Authentic leaders

The concept of the authentic leader was originally defined by George (2003: 12) as follows:

> Authentic leaders genuinely desire to serve others through their leadership. They are more interested in empowering the people they lead to make a difference than they are in power, money or prestige for themselves. They lead with purpose, meaning and values. They build enduring relationships with them. Others follow them because they know where they stand. They are consistent and self-disciplined.

Authenticity was described by Harter (2002: 382) as 'owning one's personal experiences, be they thoughts, emotions, needs, preferences, or beliefs, processes captured by the injunction to know oneself and behaving in accordance with the true self'. Authentic leadership is based on a positive moral perspective characterized by high ethical standards that guide decision-making and behaviour (May *et al*, 2003). As Avolio *et al* (2004) explained, authentic leaders act in accordance with deep personal values and convictions to build credibility and win the respect and trust of followers. By encouraging diverse viewpoints and building networks of collaborative relationships with followers, they lead in a manner that followers perceive and describe as *authentic*.

George *et al* (2007: 129) set out the basis of authentic leadership as follows:

> We all have the capacity to inspire and empower others. But we must first be willing to devote ourselves to our personal growth and development as leaders... No one can be authentic by trying to imitate someone else. You can learn from others' experiences, but there is no way you can be successful when you are trying to be like them. People trust you when you are genuine and authentic, not a replica of someone else.

Authentic leadership is, in essence, ethical leadership. Walumbwa *et al* (2008) claimed that it can lead to enhanced trust, job satisfaction and performance.

The reality of leadership

The reality of leadership is that many first-line managers and team leaders are appointed or promoted to their posts with some idea, possibly, of what their managerial or supervisory duties are, but with no appreciation of the leadership skills they need. They see their role as being to tell people what to do and then see that they do it. They may tend to adopt a transactional approach, focusing on getting the job done and neglecting everything else. They may not be charismatic, visionary or transformational leaders because, even if they have the latent qualities required, their situation does not seem to require or encourage any of these approaches.

However, the better ones will rely on their know-how (authority goes to the person who knows), their quiet confidence and their cool, analytical approach to dealing with problems. Any newly appointed leader or individual who is progressing to a higher level of leadership will benefit from a leadership development programme (see Chapter 24), which will help them to understand and apply the skills they need.

The qualities of a good leader

As mentioned earlier, the trait theory of leadership has its limitations but there is still some value in studying the qualities required by good leaders. It is generally accepted that one of the key skills a leader or manager needs is an ability to analyse and read situations and to establish order and clarity in situations of ambiguity. Gold *et al* (2010: 6) stated that: 'Leadership demands a sense of purpose, and an ability to influence others, interpret situations, negotiate and express their views, often in the face of opposition.'

Research conducted by the Work Foundation (Tamkin *et al*, 2010), involving 260 in-depth interviews conducted with 77 business leaders from six high-profile organizations, found that outstanding leaders:

- viewed things as a whole rather than compartmentalizing them;
- connect the parts through a guiding sense of purpose;
- are highly motivated to achieve excellence and are focused on organizational outcomes, vision and purpose;
- understand they cannot create performance themselves but are conduits for performance through their influence on others;
- watch themselves carefully and act consistently to achieve excellence through their interactions and their embodiment of the leadership role.

Effective leadership

Effective leaders are confident and know where they want to go and what they want to do. They have the ability to take charge, convey their vision to their team, get their team members into action and ensure that they achieve their agreed goals. They are trustworthy, good at influencing people and earn the respect of their team. They are aware of their own strengths and weaknesses and are skilled at understanding what will motivate their team members. They appreciate the advantages of consulting and involving people in decision-making. They can switch flexibly from one leadership style to another to meet the demands of different situations and people. They have to answer the following questions about the individuals in the group and the team.

Individuals in the group

- What are their strengths and weaknesses?
- What are their needs, attitudes, perspectives and preferences?
- What are likely to be the best ways of motivating them?
- What tasks are they best at doing?
- Is there scope to increase flexibility by developing new skills?
- How well do they perform in achieving targets and performance standards?
- To what extent can they manage their own performance and development?
- Are there any areas where there is a need to develop skill or competence?

- How can I provide them with the sort of support and guidance that will improve their performance?
- What can be done to improve the performance of any individuals in the group by coaching or mentoring?

The team

- How well is the team organized?
- Is the team clear about what is expected of it?
- Do the members of the team work well together?
- If there is any conflict between team members, how can I resolve it?
- How can the commitment and motivation of the team be achieved?
- Are team members flexible – capable of carrying out different tasks?
- To what extent can the team manage its own performance?
- Is there scope to empower the team so that it can take on greater responsibility for setting standards, monitoring performance and taking corrective action?
- Can the team be encouraged to work together to produce ideas for improving performance?
- What is the team good and not so good at doing?
- What can I do to improve the performance of the team through coaching and mentoring?

Key learning points: Leadership skills

Leadership defined

Leadership is the process of influencing the behaviour of others to achieve results.

Leadership theories

The main leadership theories are trait theory, leadership behaviour theory, contingent and situational theories, emotional intelligence theory and the leadership brand.

What leaders do

Adair (1973) explained that the three essential roles of leaders are to define the task, achieve the task, and maintain effective relationships. Leaders have to satisfy interdependent task, individual and group needs.

Types of leaders

Leaders can be charismatic, visionary, transformational, transactional or 'authentic'.

The qualities of a good leader

Leaders need the ability to analyse and read situations and to establish order and clarity in situations of ambiguity. Leadership demands a sense of purpose and an ability to influence others, interpret situations, negotiate and express their views, often in the face of opposition (Gold *et al*, 2010: 6).

The reality of leadership is that many first-line managers and supervisors are appointed or promoted to their posts with some idea, possibly, of what their managerial or supervisory duties are, but with no appreciation of the leadership skills they need to get the results they want with the help of their team.

Leadership development

Leadership development programmes prepare people for leadership roles and situations beyond their current experience. 'Leadership development in the widest sense involves the acquisition, development and utilization of leadership capability or the potential for it' Burgoyne (2010: 43).

Questions

1 What is leadership?
2 What is the trait theory of leadership?
3 What are the two dimensions of leadership behaviour?
4 What is the contingent theory of leadership?
5 What is a transactional leader?
6 What is a transformational leader?
7 What is a charismatic leader?
8 What is an authentic leader?
9 What do leaders do – their essential roles?
10 What are the three needs that leaders must satisfy, as defined by Adair?
11 What are the main types of leadership styles?
12 What are the leadership styles identified by Hay/McBer?
13 What choice of style do leaders have?
14 What qualities do good leaders have?

References

Adair, J (1973) *The Action-centred Leader*, London, McGraw-Hill
Avolio, B J, Gardner, W L, Walumbwa, F O, Luthans, F and May, D R (2004) Unlocking the mask: a look at the process by which authentic leaders impact follower attitudes and behaviours, *Leadership Quarterly*, 15, pp 801–23
Bass, B M (1985) *Leadership and Performance*, New York, Free Press
Bennis, W (2010) We need leaders, *Leadership Excellence*, 27 (12), p 4
Bennis, W and Nanus, B (1985) *Leadership: The strategies for taking charge*, New York, Harper & Row
Burgoyne, J (2010) Crafting a leadership and management development strategy, in (eds) J Gold, R Thorpe and A Mumford, *Gower Handbook of Leadership and Management Development*, Farnham, Gower, pp 42–55
Burns, J M (1978) *Leadership*, New York, Harper & Row
Carey, M R (1992) Transformational leadership and the fundamental option for self-transcendence, *Leadership Quarterly*, 3, pp 217–36
Conger, J A and Kanungo, R N (1998) *Charismatic Leadership in Organizations*, Thousand Oaks, CA, Sage
Fiedler, F E (1967) *A Theory of Leadership Effectiveness*, New York, McGraw-Hill
George, B (2003) *Authentic Leadership*, San Francisco, CA, Jossey-Bass
George, B, Sims, P, McLean, A N and Mayer, D (2007) Discovering your authentic leadership, *Harvard Business Review*, February, pp 129–38
Gold, J, Thorpe, R and Mumford, A (2010) *Gower Handbook of Leadership and Management Development*, Farnham, Gower
Goleman, D (2000) Leadership that gets results, *Harvard Business Review*, March–April, pp 78–90
Goleman, D (2001) *What Makes a Leader*, Boston, MA, Harvard Business School Press
Harter, S (2002) Authenticity, in (eds) C R Snyder and S J Lopez, *Handbook of Positive Psychology*, Oxford, Oxford University Press, pp 382–94
Huczynski, A A and Buchanan, D A (2007) *Organizational Behaviour*, 6th edn, Harlow, FT Prentice Hall
Kouzes, J and Posner, B (2003) *The Leadership Challenge*, San Francisco, CA, Jossey-Bass
May, D R, Chan, A, Hodges, T and Avolio, B J (2003) Developing the moral component of authentic leadership, *Organizational Dynamics*, 32 (3), pp 247–60
Meindl, J R, Ehrlich, S B and Dukerich, J M (1985) The romance of leadership, *Administrative Science Quarterly*, 30 (1), pp 78–102
Stogdill, R M (1950) Leaders, membership and organization, *Psychological Bulletin*, 25, pp 1–14

Tamkin, P, Pearson, G, Hirsh, W and Constable, S (2010) *Exceeding Expectation: The principles of outstanding leadership*, London, The Work Foundation

Tavanti, M (2008) Transactional leadership, in (eds) A Marturano and J Gosling, *Leadership: The key concepts*, London, Routledge, pp 166–70

Tichy, N M and Devanna, M A (1986) *The Transformational Leader*, New York, Wiley

Ulrich, D and Smallwood, N (2007) *Leadership Brand: Developing customer-focused leaders to drive performance and build lasting value*, Boston, MA, Harvard Business School Press

Walumbwa, F O, Avolio, B J, Gardner, W L, Wernsing, T S and Peterson, S J (2008) Authentic leadership: development and validation of a theory-based measure, *Journal of Management*, 34 (1), pp 89–126

Yukl, G (1999) An evaluation of conceptual weaknesses in transformational and charismatic leadership theories, *Leadership Quarterly*, 10, pp 285–305

56 Influencing skills

KEY CONCEPTS AND TERMS

Added value

Business case

Culture change

Facilitating

Return on investment (RoI)

LEARNING OUTCOMES

On completing this chapter you should be able to define these key concepts. You should also understand:

- How to persuade
- How to present a case
- How to make a business case
- Facilitating meetings
- Coordinating discussion

Introduction

HR professionals are in the business of influencing people. They have to persuade senior management, line managers and employees generally to accept their advice or proposals. Influencing involves case presentation and submitting business cases. HR professionals can often be concerned with more subtle forms of influencing people by acting as facilitators and leading discussions.

Persuading people

HR specialists spend a lot of time persuading other people to accept their ideas and suggestions. Persuasion is akin to selling. You may feel that good ideas should sell themselves, but life is not like that. People resist change and anything new is usually treated with suspicion. Here are 10 rules for effective persuasion:

1 *Define your objective and get the facts.* If you are persuading someone to agree to a proposal, first decide what you want to achieve and why. Assemble all the facts that you need to support your case. Eliminate emotional arguments so that you and others can judge the proposition on the facts alone.

2 *Define the problem.* If there is a problem to resolve and you are trying to persuade someone to accept your views on what should be done about it, first decide whether the problem is a misunderstanding (a failure to understand each other accurately) or a true disagreement (a failure to agree even when both parties understand one another). It is not necessarily possible to resolve a true disagreement by understanding each other better. People generally believe that an argument is a battle to understand who is correct. More often, it is a battle to decide who is more stubborn.

3 *Find out what the other party wants.* The key to all persuasion is to see your proposition from the other person's point of view. Find out how they look at things. Establish what they need and want.

4 *Accentuate the benefits.* Present your case in a way that highlights the benefits to the other party or at least reduces any objections or fears.

5 *Predict the other person's response.* Everything we say should be focused on that likely response. Anticipate objections by asking yourself how the other party might react negatively to your proposition and thinking up ways of responding to them.

6 *Create the other person's next move.* It is not a question of deciding what we want to do but what we want the other person to do.

7 *Convince people by reference to their own perceptions.* People decide on what to do on the basis of their own perceptions, not yours.

8 *Prepare a simple and attractive proposition.* Make it as straightforward as possible. Present the case 'sunny side up', emphasizing its benefits. Break the problem into manageable pieces and deal with them one step at a time.

9 *Make the other person a party to your ideas.* Get them to contribute. Find some common ground so that you can start with agreement. Don't try to defeat them in an argument – you will only antagonize them.

10 *Clinch and take action.* Choose the right moment to clinch the proposal – don't prolong the discussion and risk losing it. But follow up promptly.

Case presentation

Persuasion frequently means making a case for what you think should be done. You have to convince people to believe in your views and accept your recommendations. To do this, you must have a clear idea of what you want, and you have to show that you believe in it yourself. Above all, the effectiveness of your presentation will depend upon the care with which you have prepared it.

Thorough preparation is vital. You must think through not only what should be done and why, but also how people will react. Only then can you decide how to make your case: stressing the benefits without underestimating the costs, and anticipating objections. The four steps you should take are:

1 Show that your proposal is based on a thorough analysis of the facts and that the alternatives were properly evaluated before the conclusion was reached. If you have made assumptions, you must demonstrate that these are reasonable on the basis of relevant experience and justifiable projections, which allow for the unexpected. Bear in mind that a proposal is only as strong as its weakest assumption.

2 Spell out the benefits – to the company and/or the individuals to whom the case is being made. Wherever possible, express benefits in financial terms. Abstract benefits, such as customer satisfaction or workers' morale, are difficult to sell. But don't produce 'funny numbers' – financial justification that will not stand up to examination.

3 Reveal costs. Don't try to disguise them in any way. And be realistic. Your proposition will be destroyed if anyone can show that you have underestimated the costs.

4 Remember, senior management decision makers want to know in precise terms what they will get for their money. Most are likely to be cautious, being unwilling and often unable to take much risk. For this reason, it can be difficult to make a case for experiments or pilot schemes unless the decision maker can see what the benefits and the ultimate bill will be.

Making a business case

You may be asked specifically to produce a business case. This will set out the reasons why a proposed course of action will benefit the business, how it will provide that benefit and how much it will cost. A business case is a particular form of persuasion and all the points made above apply to its preparation and presentation. But there are some special features about business cases, as described below.

A business case is typically made either in added-value terms (ie the income generated by the proposal will significantly exceed the cost of implementing it), or on the basis of the return on investment (RoI) (ie the cost of the investment, say in training, is justified by the financial returns in such areas as increased productivity). Clearly, a business case is more convincing when it is accompanied by realistic projections of added value or return on investment. When people make out a case for capital expenditure they analyse the cash flows associated with the investment and calculate the benefits – in financial terms as far as possible – that are likely to arise from them. The objective is to demonstrate that in return for paying out a given amount of cash today, a larger amount will be received over a period of time.

It can be more difficult to make out a business case for an HRM innovation in financial terms. The costs can and should be calculated but the benefits may have to be expressed in qualitative terms. A business case will be enhanced if:

- Data is available on the impact that the proposal is likely to make on key areas of the organization's operations, eg customer service levels, quality, shareholder value, productivity, income generation, innovation, skills development, talent management.
- It can be shown that the proposal will increase the competitive edge of the business, for example enlarging the skill base or multiskilling to ensure that it can achieve competitive advantage through innovation and/or reducing time-to-market.
- There is proof that the innovation has already worked well within the organization (perhaps as a pilot scheme) or represents 'good practice' that is likely to be transferable to the organization.
- It can be implemented without too much trouble, for example not taking up a lot of managers' time, or not meeting with strong opposition from line managers, employees or trade unions (it is as well to check the likely reaction before launching a proposal).
- It will add to the reputation of the company by showing that it is a 'world class' organization, ie what it does is as good as, if not better than, the world leaders in the sector in which the business operates (a promise that publicity will be achieved through articles in professional journals, press releases and conference presentations will help).
- It will enhance the 'employer brand' of the company by making it a 'best place to work'.
- The proposal is brief, to the point and well argued – it should take no more than five minutes to present orally and should be summarized in writing on the proverbial one side of one sheet of paper (supplementary details can be included in appendices).

Making the business case is obviously easier where management is preconditioned to agree to the proposition. For example, it is not hard to convince top managers that performance-related pay is a good thing – they may well be receiving bonus payments themselves and believe, rightly or wrongly, that because it motivates them it will motivate everyone else. Talent management is another process where top management needs little persuasion that things need to be done to enhance and preserve the talent flow, although they will have to be convinced that, in practice, innovations will achieve that aim.

Performance management may be slightly more difficult because it is hard to demonstrate that it can produce measurable improvements in performance, but senior managers are predisposed towards an approach that at least promises to improve the level of performance.

The toughest area for justification in added-value terms can be expenditure on learning and development (L&D) programmes. This is where an RoI approach is desirable. The business case for learning and development should demonstrate how learning, training and development programmes will meet business needs. The following points could be made to support an L&D initiative:

- Improve individual, team and corporate performance in terms of output, quality, speed and overall productivity.
- Attract high-quality employees by offering them learning and development opportunities, increasing their levels of competence and enhancing their skills, thus enabling them to obtain more job satisfaction, to gain higher rewards and to progress within the organization.
- Provide additional non-financial rewards (growth and career opportunities) as part of a total reward policy in order to enhance engagement.
- Improve operational flexibility by extending the range of skills possessed by employees (multiskilling).
- Increase the commitment of employees by encouraging them to identify with the mission and objectives of the organization.
- Help to manage change by increasing understanding of the reasons for change and providing people with the knowledge and skills they need to adjust to new situations.
- Provide line managers with the skills required to manage and develop their people.
- Help to develop a positive culture in the organization, for example, one that is oriented towards performance improvement.
- Provide higher levels of service to customers.
- Minimize learning costs (reduce the length of learning curves).

Facilitating

Facilitating in this context is the process of helping a group reach conclusions in the shape of ideas and solutions. Facilitators do not exist to 'chair' the meeting in the sense of controlling the discussion and pressurizing the group to agree to a course of action. The group is there to make up its own mind and the facilitator helps it to do so. The facilitator is exerting influence, but indirectly.

Help in reaching conclusions is provided by asking questions that encourage the group members to think for themselves. These can be challenging and probing questions but the facilitator does not provide the answers – that is the role of the group. Neither do facilitators allow their own opinions to intrude – they are there to help the group marshal its opinions, not to enforce their own ideas. However, by using questioning techniques carefully, facilitators can ensure that the group thoroughly discusses and analyses the issues and reaches conclusions by consensus rather than allowing anyone to dominate the process.

Facilitators ensure that everyone has their say and that they are listened to. They step in quickly to defuse unproductive arguments. They see that the group defines and understands its objectives and any methodology they might use. They summarize from time to time the progress made in achieving the objectives, without bringing their own views to bear. Facilitators are there to ensure that the group makes progress and does not get stuck in fruitless or disruptive arguments. They encourage the group rather than drive it forward.

The aim of the facilitator is to guide the group's thinking. He or she may, therefore, be more concerned with shaping attitudes than convincing people about what to do or imparting new knowledge. The facilitator has unobtrusively to stimulate people to talk, guide the discussion along predetermined lines (there must be a plan and an ultimate objective), and provide interim summaries and a final summary.

Coordinating discussions

Coordinating discussions is a matter of getting active participation and then ensuring that the discussion informs people of the issues related to the subject and leads to a conclusion that satisfies the participants. HR practitioners lead discussions when they are taking part in L&D activities. Importantly, discussion is also a means of persuading people to do or accept something by getting them to participate in analysing the issues and reaching a joint and acceptable conclusion.

The following techniques can be used to get active participation and to coordinate the process:

- Ask for contributions by direct questions.
- Use open-ended questions that will stimulate thought.
- Check understanding; make sure that everyone is following the argument.
- Encourage participation by providing support rather than criticism.
- Prevent domination by individual members of the group by bringing in other people and asking cross-reference questions.
- Avoid dominating the group yourself. The leader's job is to guide the discussion, maintain control and summarize from time to time. If necessary, 'reflect' opinions expressed by individuals back to the group to make sure they find the answer for themselves. The leader is there to help the group reach a conclusion, not to do it for them.
- Maintain control – ensure that the discussion is progressing along the right lines towards a firm conclusion.

Key learning points: Influencing skills

Influencing people

HR professionals are often involved in influencing other's thinking and decision-making. They must know about persuading people and case presentation.

Persuading people

HR specialists spend a lot of time persuading other people to accept their ideas and suggestions. Persuasion is akin to selling. You may feel that good ideas should sell themselves, but life is not like that. People resist change and anything new is usually treated with suspicion.

Case presentation

Persuasion frequently means making a case for what you think should be done. You have to convince people to believe in your views and accept your recommendations. To do this, you must have a clear idea of what you want, and you have to show that you believe in it yourself.

Making a business case

A business case sets out the reasons why a proposed course of action will benefit the business, how it will provide that benefit and how much it will cost.

Facilitating

Facilitating is the process of helping a group reach conclusions in the shape of ideas and solutions.

Coordinating discussions

Coordinating discussions is a matter of getting active participation and then ensuring that the discussion informs people of the issues related to the subject and leads to a conclusion that satisfies the participants.

Questions

1. What are the most important rules for effective persuasion?
2. What are the key steps required for effective case presentation?
3. How should a business case be made?
4. What is facilitating?
5. How should facilitation be carried out?
6. How should discussions be conducted?

57 Handling people problems

KEY CONCEPTS AND TERMS

Capability procedure	Improvement period
Disciplinary procedure	Return to work interview

LEARNING OUTCOMES

On completing this chapter you should be able to define these key concepts. You should also understand:

- Disciplinary issues
- Absenteeism
- Poor timekeeping
- Negative behaviour
- Underperformance

Introduction

An important part of the transactional role of HR professionals is handling people problems directly or by providing advice and guidance to line managers. Problem-solving skills, described in Chapter 46, are required but it is also necessary to advise overall on how to handle disciplinary problems and how to deal with absenteeism, poor timekeeping, negative behaviour and underperformance.

Disciplinary issues

Employees can be dismissed because they are not capable of doing the work, or for misconduct. It is normal to go through a formal disciplinary procedure containing staged warnings, but instant dismissal can be justified for gross misconduct (eg serious theft), which should be defined in the company's disciplinary procedure or employee handbook. Anyone who has completed more than two years' service (one year if employed prior to April 2012) can claim unfair dismissal if their employer cannot show that one of these reasons applied, if the dismissal was not reasonable in the circumstances, if a constructive dismissal has taken place, or if there has been a breach of a customary or agreed redundancy procedure and there are no valid reasons for departing from that procedure.

Even if the employer can show to an employment tribunal that there was good reason to dismiss the employee, the tribunal will still have to decide whether or not the employer acted in a reasonable way at the time of dismissal. The principles defining 'reasonable' behaviour are in line with the principles of natural justice and are as follows:

- the employee should be informed of the nature of the complaint;
- the employee should be given the chance to explain;
- the employee should be given the opportunity to improve, except in cases of particularly gross incapability or misconduct;
- the employee should be warned of the consequences in the shape of dismissal if specified improvements do not take place;
- the employer's decision to dismiss should be based on sufficient evidence;
- the employer should take any mitigating circumstances into account;
- dismissal should only take place if the offence or misbehaviour deserves it rather than some lesser penalty.

The organization should have a statutory disciplinary procedure (see Chapter 41). Managers need to know what that procedure is and the part they are expected to play in implementing it. Whether or not there is a formal procedure, if it is believed that disciplinary action is necessary the following steps should be taken by the manager, as guided by HR, in planning and conducting a disciplinary interview.

Planning and conducting a disciplinary meeting

1. Get all the facts in advance, including statements from the people involved.
2. Invite the employee to the meeting in writing, explaining why it is being held and that he or she has the right to have someone present at the meeting on his or her behalf.
3. Ensure that the employee has reasonable notice (ideally at least two days).
4. Plan how to conduct the meeting.
5. Line up another member of management to attend the meeting to take notes (they can be important if there is an appeal), generally provide support and witness the proceedings.
6. Start the interview by stating the complaint to the employee and referring to the evidence.
7. Give the employee plenty of time to respond and state his or her case.
8. Take a break as required to consider the points raised and to relieve any pressure in the meeting.
9. Consider what action is appropriate, if any. Actions should be staged, starting with a recorded warning followed, if the problem continues, by a first written warning, then a final written warning and lastly, if the earlier stages have been exhausted, disciplinary action, which would be dismissal in serious cases.
10. Deliver the decision, explaining why it has been taken and confirm it in writing. If possible, meet when everything is quiet, preferably on a Friday.

If all the stages in the disciplinary procedure have been completed and the employee has to be dismissed, or where immediate dismissal can be justified on the grounds of gross misconduct, a manager may have to carry out the unpleasant duty of dismissing the employee. This should be guided by HR and it is advisable that an HR specialist is involved in the dismissal meeting. This is best conducted as follows:

- Keep the meeting formal and organized.
- Write down what is going to be said in advance, giving the reason and getting your facts, dates and figures right.
- Be polite but firm – read out what has been written down and make it clear that it is not open for discussion.
- Ensure that the employee clears his or her desk and has no opportunity to take away confidential material or use his or her computer.
- See the employee off the premises – some companies use security guards as escorts; this might be rather heavy-handed, although it could be useful to have someone on call in case of difficulties.

Absenteeism

A frequent people problem that managers and HR professionals have to face is absenteeism. It may be necessary to deal with recurrent short-term (one or two days) absence or longer-term sickness absence.

Recurrent short-term absence

Dealing with people who are repeatedly absent for short periods can be difficult. This is because it may be hard to determine when occasional absence becomes a problem or whether it is justifiable, perhaps on medical grounds.

So what can be done about it? Many organizations provide guidelines to managers on the 'trigger points' for action (the amount of absence that needs to be investigated), perhaps based on analyses of the incidence of short-term absence and the level at which it is regarded as acceptable (there may be software to generate analyses and data that can be made available direct to managers through a self-service system). If guidelines do not exist, HR specialists should be available to provide advice.

It is necessary to decide when something needs to be done and then what to do about it. A day off every other month may not be too serious, although if it happens regularly on a Monday or a Friday you may feel like having a word with the individual, not as a warning but just to let him or her know that you are aware of what is going on. There may, of course, be a medical or other acceptable explanation. Return-to-work interviews can provide valuable information and an opportunity to discuss any problems. The individual is seen and given the chance to explain the absence.

In persistent cases of absenteeism an absence review meeting can be held. Although this would be more comprehensive than a return-to-work interview it should not at this stage be presented as part of a disciplinary process. The meeting should be positive and constructive. If absence results from a health problem it can be established what is being done about it, and if necessary suggest that his or her doctor should be consulted. Or absences may be caused by problems facing a parent or a carer. In such cases it is right to be sympathetic but it would be reasonable to discuss with the individual what steps can be taken to reduce the problem or whether flexible working could be arranged. The aim is to get the employee to discuss as openly as possible any factors affecting his or her attendance and to agree any constructive steps.

If after holding an attendance review meeting – and, it is to be hoped, agreeing the steps necessary to reduce absenteeism – short-term absence persists without a satisfactory explanation, then another meeting can be held that emphasizes the employee's responsibility for attending work. Depending on the circumstances (each case should be dealt with on its merits), at this meeting it can be indicated that absence levels should improve over a defined timescale (an improvement period). If this does not happen, the individual can expect more formal disciplinary action.

Dealing with long-term absence

Dealing with long-term absence can also be difficult. The aim should be to facilitate the employee's return to work at the earliest reasonable point while recognizing that in extreme cases the person may not be able to come back. In that case he or she can fairly be dismissed for lack of capability as long as:

- the employee has been consulted at all stages;
- contact has been maintained with the employee – this is something you can usefully do as long as you do not appear to be pressing him or her to return to work before he or she is ready;
- appropriate medical advice has been sought from the employee's own doctor, but the employee's consent is needed and employees have the right to see the report – it may be desirable to obtain a second opinion;
- all reasonable options for alternative employment have been reviewed as well any other means of facilitating a return to work.

The decision to dismiss should only be taken if these conditions are satisfied. It is a tricky one and it may be advisable to seek advice from an employment law expert.

Handling poor timekeeping

A poor timekeeping record may initially be dealt with by an informal warning. But if in spite of the warning lateness persists it may be necessary to invoke the disciplinary procedure. This would go through the successive stages of a recorded oral warning, a written warning and a final written warning, which would indicate that timekeeping must improve by a certain date (the improvement period) otherwise disciplinary action will take place. If the final warning does not work, such action would be taken; in serious cases this would mean dismissal.

Note that this raises the difficult question of time limits, which may be given when a final warning is given. If timekeeping does improve by that date, and the slate is wiped clean, it might be assumed that the disciplinary procedure starts again from scratch if timekeeping deteriorates again. But it is in the nature of things that some people cannot sustain efforts to get to work on time for long, and deterioration often occurs. In these circumstances, is it necessary to keep on going through the warning cycles time after time? The answer ought to be no, and the best approach seems to be to avoid stating a finite end date to a final warning period that implies a 'wipe the slate clean' approach. Instead, the warning should simply say that timekeeping performance will be reviewed on a stated date. If it has not improved, disciplinary action can be taken. If it has, no action will be taken, but the employee is warned that further deterioration will make him or her liable to disciplinary action, which may well speed up the normal procedure, perhaps by only using the final warning stage and by reducing the elapsed time between the warning and the review date. There will come a time, if poor timekeeping persists, when you can say 'enough is enough' and initiate disciplinary action.

Handling negative behaviour

Negative behaviour may take the form of lack of interest in the work, unwillingness to cooperate with team leaders or other members of the team, making unjustified complaints about the work or working conditions, grumbling at being asked to carry out a perfectly reasonable task, objecting strongly to being asked to do something extra (or even refusing to do it) – 'It's not in my job description', or, in extreme cases, insolence. People exhibiting negative behaviour may be quietly resentful rather than openly disruptive. They mutter away in the background at meetings and lack enthusiasm.

Managers have to tolerate a certain amount of negative behaviour as long as the individual works reasonably well and does not upset other team members. They have simply to say to themselves, 'It takes all sorts...' and put up with it, although they might calmly say during a review meeting, 'You're doing a good job but...'. If, however, they take this line they have to be specific. They must cite actual instances. It is no good making generalized accusations that will either be openly refuted or internalized by the receiver, making him or her even more resentful.

If the negative behaviour means that the individual's contribution is not acceptable and is disruptive, action has to be taken. Negative people are usually angry about something; their negative behaviour is an easy way of expressing their anger. To deal with the problem it is necessary to find out what has made them angry.

Causes of negative behaviour

There are many possible causes of negative behaviour, which could include one or more of the following:

- a real or imagined slight from their manager or a colleague;
- a feeling of being put upon;
- a belief that the contribution they make is neither appreciated nor rewarded properly in terms of pay or promotion;
- resentment at what was perceived to be unfair criticism;
- anger directed at the company or their manager because what was considered to be a reasonable request (such as for leave or a transfer) was turned down, or because of an unfair accusation.

Dealing with the problem

It is because there can be such a variety of real or imagined causes of negative behaviour that dealing with it becomes one of the most difficult tasks that line managers and HR people have to undertake. If the action taken is crude or insensitive, the negative behaviour will only be intensified. This might mean having to invoke the disciplinary procedure, which should be a last resort.

In one sense, it is easier to deal with an actual example of negative behaviour. This can be handled on the spot. If the problem is one of general attitude rather than specific actions it is more difficult to cope with. Hard evidence may not be available. When individuals are accused of being, for example, generally unenthusiastic or uncooperative, they can simply go into denial and accuse you of being prejudiced. Their negative behaviour may be reinforced.

It is best to deal with this sort of problem informally, either when it arises or at any point during the year when it is felt that something has to be done about it. An annual formal performance review or appraisal meeting is not the right time, especially if it produces ratings that are linked to a pay increase. Raising the issue then will only put individuals on the defensive and a productive discussion will be impossible.

The discussion may be informal but it should have three clear objectives:

1. To review the situation with individuals, the aim being if possible to get them to recognize for themselves that they are behaving negatively. If this cannot be achieved, then the objective is to bring to the attention of individuals your belief that their behaviour is unacceptable in certain ways.
2. To establish the reasons for the individuals' negative behaviour so far as this is feasible.
3. To agree any actions that individuals could take to behave more positively, or what you or the organization could do to remove the causes of the behaviour.

Discussing the problem

The starting point should be general questions about how individuals feel about their work. Do they have any problems in carrying it out? Are they happy with the support they get from you or their colleagues? Are they satisfied that they are pulling their weight to the best of their ability?

This generalized start provides the basis for the next two stages – identifying causes and any remedies. It is best if individuals are encouraged to decide for themselves that there is a problem, but in many cases, if not the majority, this is unlikely to happen. Individuals may not recognize that they are behaving negatively or will not be prepared to admit it.

It is then necessary to discuss the problem. They should be given time to say their piece. The response should spell out how justifiable grievances will be dealt with or why no action is necessary. In the latter case, an explanation should be given as to why the individual's behaviour gives the impression of being negative. This should be specific, bringing up actual instances. For example, a discussion could be based on the following questions: 'Do you recall yesterday's team meeting?', 'How did you think it went?', 'How helpful do you think you were in dealing with the problem?', 'Do you remember saying...?', 'How helpful do you think that remark was?', 'Would it surprise you to learn that I felt you had not been particularly helpful in the following ways...?'

Of course, even if this careful approach is adopted, individuals may still refuse to admit that there is anything wrong with their behaviour. If this impasse is reached, then there is no alternative but to spell out where it is believed they have gone wrong. But this should be done in a positive way:

'Then I think that it is only fair for me to point out to you that your contribution (to the meeting) would have been more helpful if you had...'.

Establishing causes

If the negative behaviour is because of a real or imagined grievance about what the manager, colleagues or the organization have done, then the individual has to be persuaded to spell this out as precisely as possible. At this point, the job of the manager or HR practitioner is to listen, not to judge. People can be just as angry about imaginary slights as they can about real slights. You have to find out how they perceive the problem before you can deal with it.

It may emerge during the discussion that the problem has nothing to do with the manager or the company. It may be family troubles or worries about health or finance. If this is the case, a sympathetic approach is appropriate, which may involve suggesting remedies in the form of counselling or practical advice from within or outside the organization. If the perceived problem is the manager, colleagues or the organization, try to get chapter and verse on what it is so that remedial action can be taken.

Taking remedial action

If the problem rests with the individual, the objective is, of course, to get them to recognize for themselves that corrective action is necessary and what they need to do about it – with help as necessary. In some situations you might suggest counselling, or a source of advice might be recommended. But care needs to be taken: there should be no implication made to the individual that there is something wrong with them. It is best to go no further than suggesting that individuals may find counselling helpful – they don't need it but they could benefit from it. Managers or HR specialists should not offer counselling themselves. This is better done by professional counsellors.

If there is anything specific that the parties involved in the situation can do, then the line to take is that the problem can be tackled together: 'This is what I will do', 'This is what the company will do', 'What do you think you should do?' If there is no response to the last question, this is the point where it is needed to spell out the necessary action. This should be as specific as possible and expressed as suggestions, not commands. A joint problem-solving approach is always best.

10 approaches to handling negative behaviour

1. Define the type of negative behaviour that is being exhibited. Make notes of examples.
2. Discuss the behaviour with the individual as soon as possible, aiming to get agreement about what it is and the impact it makes.
3. If agreement is not obtained, give actual examples of behaviour and explain why you believe them to be negative.
4. Discuss and, so far as possible, agree reasons for the negative behaviour, including those attributed to the individual, yourself and the organization.
5. Discuss and agree possible remedies – actions on the part of the individual, yourself or the organization.
6. Monitor the actions taken and the results obtained.
7. If improvement is not achieved and the negative behaviour is significantly affecting the performance of the individual and the team, then invoke the disciplinary procedure.
8. Start with a verbal warning, indicating the ways in which behaviour must improve and give a time scale and offers of further support and help as required.
9. If there is no improvement, issue a formal warning, setting out as specifically as possible what must be achieved over a defined period of time, indicating the disciplinary action that could be taken.
10. If the negative behaviour persists and continues seriously to affect performance, take the disciplinary action.

Dealing with underperformance

Poor performance can be the fault of the individual but it could also arise because of poor leadership or problems in the system of work. In the case of an individual, the reason may be that he or she:

- could not do it – ability;
- did not know how to do it – skill;
- would not do it – attitude;
- did not fully understand what was expected of him or her.

Inadequate leadership from managers can be the cause of poor performance from individuals. It is the manager's responsibility to specify the results expected and the levels of skill and competence required. As likely as not, when people do not understand what they have to do it is their manager who is to blame.

Performance can also be affected by the system of work. If this is badly planned and organized, or does not function well, individuals cannot be blamed for the poor performance that results. This is the fault of management and they must put it right.

If inadequate individual performance cannot be attributed to poor leadership or the system of work, there are seven steps that can be taken to deal with it:

1. Identify the areas of underperformance – be specific.
2. Establish the causes of poor performance.
3. Agree on the action required.
4. Ensure that the necessary support (coaching, training, extra resources etc) is provided to ensure that the action is successful.
5. Monitor progress and provide feedback.
6. Provide additional guidance as required.
7. As a last resort, invoke the capability or disciplinary procedure (see Chapter 41), starting with an informal warning.

Key learning points: Handling people problems

The HR role in handling people problems

An important part of the transactional role of HR professionals is handling people problems by providing advice and guidance to line managers or directly.

Disciplinary issues

Employees can be dismissed because they are not capable of doing the work or for misconduct. It is normal to go through a formal disciplinary procedure containing staged warnings, but instant dismissal can be justified for gross misconduct (eg serious theft), which should be defined in the company's disciplinary procedure or employee handbook.

The organization should have a statutory disciplinary procedure. Managers need to know what that procedure is and the part they are expected to play in implementing it.

Absenteeism

A frequent people problem that managers and HR professionals have to face is that of dealing with absenteeism. It may be necessary to deal with recurrent short-term (one or two days) absence or longer-term sickness absence.

Many organizations provide guidelines to managers on the 'trigger points' for action (the amount of absence that needs to be investigated), perhaps based on analyses of the incidence of short-term absence and the level at which it is regarded as acceptable. If guidelines do not exist, HR specialists should be available to provide advice.

Handling poor timekeeping

Faced with persistent lateness and when informal warnings to the individual concerned seem to have little effect, it may be necessary to invoke the disciplinary procedure. If timekeeping does not improve this could go through the successive stages of a recorded oral warning, a written warning and a final written warning. If the final warning does not work, disciplinary action would have to be taken; in serious cases this would mean dismissal.

Handling negative behaviour

Negative behaviour may take the form of lack of interest in the work, unwillingness to cooperate with team leaders or other members of the team, making unjustified complaints about the work or working conditions, grumbling at being asked to carry out a perfectly reasonable task, objecting strongly to being asked to do something extra (or even refusing to do it), or, in extreme cases, insolence.

It is because there can be such a variety of real or imagined causes of negative behaviour that dealing with it becomes one of the most difficult tasks that line managers and HR people have to undertake. If the action taken is crude or insensitive the negative behaviour will only be intensified. This might mean having to invoke the disciplinary procedure, which should be a last resort.

In one sense, it is easier to deal with an actual example of negative behaviour. This can be handled on the spot. If the problem is one of general attitude rather than specific actions it is more difficult to cope with. It is best to deal with this sort of problem informally, either when it arises or at any point during the year when it is felt that something has to be done about it.

Dealing with underperformance

Poor performance can be the fault of the individual, but it could arise because of poor leadership or problems in the system of work. To deal with it:

1. Identify the areas of underperformance – be specific.
2. Establish the causes of poor performance.
3. Agree on the action required.
4. Ensure that the necessary support (coaching, training, extra resources, etc) is provided to ensure that the action is successful.
5. Monitor progress and provide feedback.
6. Provide additional guidance as required.
7. As a last resort, invoke the capability or disciplinary procedure (see Chapter 41), starting with an informal warning.

Questions

1. What are the principles of natural justice?
2. How should a disciplinary meeting be conducted?
3. How should short-term absence be dealt with?
4. How should long-term absence be dealt with?
5. How should poor timekeeping be dealt with?
6. How should negative behaviour be handled?
7. How should underperformance be dealt with?

58 Managing conflict

KEY CONCEPTS AND TERMS

Conflict resolution

Constructive confrontation

Creative conflict

LEARNING OUTCOMES

On completing this chapter you should be able to define these key concepts. You should also know about:

- Handling inter-group conflict
- Handling interpersonal conflict
- Handling conflict between team members

Introduction

Conflict is inevitable in organizations because they function by means of adjustments and compromises among competitive elements in their structure and membership. Conflict also arises when there is change, because it may be seen as a threat to be challenged or resisted, or when there is frustration – this may produce an aggressive reaction: fight rather than flight.

Conflict is not to be deplored. It results from progress and change and it can and should be used constructively. Bland agreement on everything would be unnatural and enervating. There should be clashes of ideas about tasks and projects, and disagreements should not be suppressed. They should come out into the open because that is the only way to ensure that the issues are explored and conflicts are resolved.

There is such a thing as creative conflict – new or modified ideas, insights, approaches and solutions can be generated by a joint re-examination of different points of view, as long as this is based on an objective and rational exchange of information and opinions. But conflict becomes counterproductive when it is based on personality clashes, or when it is treated as an unseemly mess to be hurriedly cleared away, rather than as a problem to be worked through. Conflict resolution deals with ways of settling differences between groups, individuals and team members.

Handling inter-group conflict

There are three principal ways of resolving inter-group conflict: peaceful coexistence, compromise and problem solving.

Peaceful coexistence

The aim here is to smooth out differences and emphasize the common ground. People are encouraged to learn to live together; there is a good deal of information, contact and exchange of views; and individuals move freely between groups (for example, between headquarters and the field, or between sales and marketing).

This is a pleasant ideal, but it may not be practicable in many situations. There is much evidence that conflict is not necessarily resolved by bringing people together. Improved communications and techniques such as briefing groups may appear to be good ideas but are useless if management has nothing to say that people want to hear. There is also the danger that the real issues, submerged for the moment in an atmosphere of superficial bonhomie, will surface again later.

Compromise

The issue is resolved by negotiation or bargaining and neither party wins or loses. This concept of splitting the difference is essentially pessimistic. The hallmark of this approach is that there is no 'right' or 'best' answer. Agreements only accommodate differences. Real issues are not likely to be solved.

Problem solving

An attempt is made to find a genuine solution to the problem rather than just accommodating different points of view. This is where the apparent paradox of 'creative conflict' comes in. Conflict situations can be used to advantage to create better solutions.

If solutions are to be developed by problem solving, they have to be generated by those who share the responsibility for seeing that the solutions work. The sequence of actions is: first, those concerned work to define the problem and agree on the objectives to be attained in reaching a solution; second, the group develops alternative solutions and debates their merits; and third, agreement is reached on the preferred course of action and how it should be implemented.

Handling interpersonal conflict

Handling conflict between individuals can be even more difficult than resolving conflicts between groups. Whether the conflict is openly hostile or subtly covert, strong personal feelings may be involved. However, interpersonal conflict, like inter-group conflict, is an organizational reality that is not necessarily good or bad. It can be destructive, but it can also play a productive role. The approaches to dealing with it are withdrawal, smoothing over differences, reaching a compromise, counselling and constructive confrontation.

Withdrawal

The reaction to interpersonal conflict may be the withdrawal of either party, leaving the other one to hold the field. This is the classic 'win-lose' situation. The problem has been resolved by force, but this may not be the best solution if it represents one person's point of view that has ignored counter-arguments and has, in fact, steamrollered over them. The winner may be triumphant but the loser will be aggrieved and either demotivated or resolved to fight again another day. There will have been a lull in the conflict, but not an end to it.

Smoothing over differences

Another approach is to smooth over differences and pretend that the conflict does not exist, although no attempt has been made to tackle the root causes. Again, this is an unsatisfactory solution. The issue is likely to re-emerge and the battle will recommence.

Reaching a compromise

Yet another approach is bargaining to reach a compromise. This means that both sides are prepared to lose as well as win some points and the aim is to reach a solution acceptable to both sides. Bargaining, however, involves all sorts of tactical and often counterproductive games, and the parties are often more anxious to seek acceptable compromises than to achieve sound solutions.

Counselling

Personal counselling is an approach that does not address the conflict itself but focuses on how the two people are reacting. It gives people a chance to release pent-up tensions and may encourage them to think about new ways of resolving the conflict. But it does not address the essential nature of the conflict, which is the relationship between two people. That is why constructive confrontation offers the best hope of a long-term solution.

Constructive confrontation

Constructive confrontation is a method of bringing the individuals in conflict together with a third party whose function is to help build an exploratory and cooperative climate. Constructive confrontation aims to get the contending parties to understand and explore the other's perceptions and feelings. It is a process of developing mutual understanding to produce a win-win situation. The issues will be confronted but on the basis of a joint analysis, with the help of the third party, of facts relating to the situation and the actual behaviour of those involved. Feelings will be expressed but they will be analysed by reference to specific events and behaviours rather than inferences or speculations about motives. Third parties have a key role in this process, and it is not an easy one. They have to get agreement to the ground rules for discussions aimed at bringing out the facts and minimizing hostile behaviour. They must monitor the ways in which negative feelings are expressed and encourage the parties to produce new definitions of the problem and its cause or causes and new motives to reach a common solution. Third parties must avoid the temptation to support or appear to support either of those in contention. They should adopt a counselling approach, as follows:

- listen actively;
- observe as well as listen;
- help people to understand and define the problem by asking pertinent, open-ended questions;
- recognize feelings and allow them to be expressed;
- help people to define problems for themselves;
- encourage people to explore alternative solutions;
- get people to develop their own implementation plans but provide advice and help if asked.

To conclude, conflict, as has been said, is in itself not to be deplored: it is an inevitable concomitant of progress and change. What is regrettable is the failure to use conflict constructively. Effective problem solving and constructive confrontation both resolve conflicts and open up channels of discussion and cooperative action.

Many years ago, one of the pioneering and most influential writers on management, Follett (1924), wrote something on managing conflict that is as valid today as it was then. She said that differences can be made to contribute to the common cause if they are resolved by integration rather than domination or compromise.

Resolving conflict between team members

To resolve conflict between team members the following actions can be taken:

1. Obtain an overview of the situation from your own observations.
2. Find out who is involved.
3. Talk to each of the parties to the conflict to obtain their side of the story.
4. Talk to other members of the group to get their views, being careful to be dispassionate and strictly neutral.
5. Evaluate what you hear from both parties and other people against your knowledge of what has been happening, any history of conflict and the dispositions and previous behaviour of the people involved.

6 Reach preliminary conclusions on the facts, the reasons for the dispute and the extent to which either of the parties or both of them are to blame (but keep these to yourself at this stage).

7 Bring the parties together to discuss the situation. The initial aim of this meeting would be to bring the problem out into the open, get the facts and defuse any emotions that may prejudice a solution to the problem. Both parties should be allowed to have their say but, as the facilitator of this meeting, you should do your best to ensure that they stick to the facts and explain their point of view dispassionately. You should not even remotely give the impression that you are taking sides.

8 Try to defuse the situation so that a solution can be reached that on the whole will be acceptable to all concerned. Ideally, this should be an integrated solution reached by agreement on the basis of collaboration along the lines of: 'Let's get together to find the best solution on the basis of the facts.' It may be necessary to reach a compromise or accommodation – something that everyone can live with.

9 Only if all else fails, or the parties are so recalcitrant in holding an untenable position that no integrated, compromise or accommodating solution can be reached, should you resort to direct action – instructing one or both of the parties to bury their differences and get on with their work. If worse comes to the worst this may involve disciplinary action, beginning with a formal warning.

Key learning points: Managing conflict

The manifestation of conflict

Conflict is inevitable in organizations because they function by means of adjustments and compromises among competitive elements in their structure and membership. Conflict also arises when there is change, because it may be seen as a threat to be challenged or resisted, or when there is frustration – this may produce an aggressive reaction: fight rather than flight.

Handling inter-group conflict

There are three principal ways of resolving inter-group conflict: peaceful coexistence, compromise and problem solving.

Handling interpersonal conflict

The approaches to dealing with interpersonal conflict are withdrawal, smoothing over differences, reaching a compromise, counselling and constructive confrontation.

Resolving conflict between team members

- Obtain an overview of the situation.
- Find out who is involved.
- Talk to each of the parties to the conflict to obtain their side of the story.
- Talk to other members of the group.
- Evaluate what you hear.
- Reach preliminary conclusions on the facts and the reasons for the dispute.
- Bring the parties together to discuss the situation.
- Only resort to direct action if all else fails.

Questions

1. What are the three main ways of handling inter-group conflict?
2. What approaches can be used to deal with interpersonal conflict?
3. How should counselling be handled when dealing with interpersonal conflict?
4. How can conflict between team members be resolved?

Reference

Follett, M P (1924) *Creative Experience*, New York, Longmans Green

59
Political skills

KEY CONCEPTS AND TERMS

Dominant coalition

Networking

Politics

LEARNING OUTCOMES

On completing this chapter you should be able to define these key concepts. You should also understand:

- Typical political approaches
- Using political means to get things done
- Political sensitivity
- Dangers of politics
- Dealing with organizational politics

Introduction

To be politic, according to the *Oxford English Dictionary*, you can be sagacious, prudent, judicious, expedient, scheming or crafty. So political behaviour in an organization could be desirable or undesirable.

Organizations consist of individuals who, while they are ostensibly there to achieve a common purpose, will, at the same time, be driven by their own needs to achieve their own goals. Effective management is the process of harmonizing individual endeavour and ambition to the common good. Some individuals will genuinely believe that using political means to achieve their aims will benefit the organization as well as themselves. Others will rationalize this belief. Yet others will unashamedly pursue their own ends. They may use all their powers of persuasion to legitimize these ends to their colleagues, but self-interest remains the primary drive. These are the corporate politicians that the *Oxford English Dictionary* describes as 'shrewd schemers, crafty plotters or intriguers'. Politicians within organizations can be like this. They manoeuvre behind people's backs, blocking proposals they do not like. They advance their own reputation and career at the expense of other people's. They can be envious and jealous and act accordingly. They are bad news.

But it can also be argued that a political approach to management is inevitable and even desirable in any organization where the clarity of goals is not absolute, where the decision-making process is not clear-cut and where the authority to make decisions is not evenly or appropriately distributed. And there can be few organizations where one or more of these conditions do not apply.

It was suggested by Kakabadse (1983) that politics in an organization is a process of influencing individuals and groups of people to your point of view, where you cannot rely on authority. In this sense, a political approach can be legitimate as long as the ends are justifiable from the viewpoint of the organization. Whether or not that is the case, political skills and political sensitivity, as described in this chapter, are required to thrive and sometimes even survive in organizations. This applies particularly to HR specialists who may lack the power-base that others possess and may feel they have to pursue the achievement of their ends and exert influence through political as well as more open means. But it is also essential for them to gain insight into the political situation in their organization in order to understand what is happening, why it is happening and what they need to do about it.

Typical political approaches

Kakabadse (1983) identified seven approaches that organizational politicians adopt, some of which are more legitimate than others:

1. *Identify the stakeholders*, those who have commitment to act in a particular way.
2. *Keep the stakeholders comfortable*, concentrating on behaviour, values, attitudes, fears and drives that the individuals will accept, tolerate and manage (comfort zones).
3. *Fit the image* – work on the comfort zones and align their image to that of the people with power.
4. *Use the network* – identify the interest groups and people of influence.
5. *Enter the network* – identify the gatekeepers, adhere to the norms.
6. *Make deals* – agree to support other people where this is of mutual benefit.
7. *Withhold and withdraw* – withhold information as appropriate and withdraw judiciously when the going gets rough.

Using political means to get things done

People acting politically get things done by lobbying decision-makers and doing deals. This may not always be desirable, but it does happen, and some people rationalize it on the basis that the end justifies the means (always a dubious stance). Other ploys include withholding information, which is not legitimate but people do indulge in it – which recognizes the fact that knowledge is power. Organizational politicians can go behind people's backs, hatch up plots in dark corners, 'sew things up' before meetings (lobbying) and exert undue influence on weaker brethren. You may not deign to practise these political black arts but it is useful to be aware of the possibility that others will – so that you are prepared for that eventuality.

The reality of politics in organizational life means that HR specialists who are proposing new initiatives to managers need to identify the key decision makers before coming to a final conclusion and launching a fully fledged proposal at a committee or in a memorandum. It makes good sense to test opinion and find out how other people may react, especially when it is possible that there will be some opposition or indifference. This testing process enables the anticipation of counter-arguments and the modification of proposals, either to meet legitimate objections or, when there is no alternative, to accommodate other people's requirements.

Political sensitivity

Organizational politicians exert hidden influence to get their way, and 'politicking' in some form takes place in most organizations. A degree of political sensitivity is desirable – knowing what is going on so that influence can be exerted properly. This means that it is necessary to:

- know 'how things are done around here';
- know how key decisions are made and who makes them;
- understand the factors that are likely to affect decisions;
- know where the power base is in the organization (sometimes called the 'dominant coalition') – who makes the running, who are the people who count when decisions are taken;
- be aware of what is going on behind the scenes;
- know who is a rising star and whose reputation is fading;
- identify any 'hidden agendas' – try to understand what people are really getting at beneath the surface by getting answers to the question: 'Where are they coming from?';
- find out what other people are thinking and seeking;
- network – identify the interest groups and keep in contact with them.

Dangers of politics

Much of this behaviour is legitimate, but there are dangers. Politicking can be carried out to excess, and it can then seriously harm the effectiveness of an organization. The signs of excessive indulgence in political behaviour include:

- backbiting;
- buck-passing;
- secret meetings and hidden decisions;
- feuds between people and departments;
- e-mail or paper wars between armed camps – arguing by e-mail or memoranda rather than meeting people face-to-face is a sign of distrust;
- a multiplicity of snide comments and criticisms;
- excessive and counterproductive lobbying;
- the formation of cabals – cliques that spend their time intriguing.

Dealing with organizational politics

One way to deal with this sort of behaviour is to find out who is going in for it and openly confront them with the damage they are doing. They will, of course, deny that they are behaving politically (they wouldn't be politicians if they didn't), but the fact that they have been identified might lead them to modify their approach. It could, of course, only serve to drive them further underground, in which case their behaviour would have to be observed even more closely and action taken to restrain it.

A more positive approach to keeping politics operating at an acceptable level is for the organization to manage its operations as transparently as possible. The aim should be to ensure that issues are debated fully, that differences of opinion are dealt with frankly and that disagreements are depersonalized, so far as this is possible. Political processes can then be seen as a way of helping to maintain the momentum of the organization as a complex decision-making and problem-solving entity. HR professionals, in their organization development role, can exert influence in achieving these aims.

Key learning points: Political skills

Organizational politics

Politics in an organization is a process of influencing individuals and groups of people to your point of view, where you cannot rely on authority (Kakabadse, 1983). In this sense, a political approach can be legitimate as long as the ends are justifiable from the viewpoint of the organization.

Approaches adopted by organizational politicians are:

1. Identify the stakeholders.
2. Keep the stakeholders comfortable, concentrating on their comfort zones.
3. Work on the comfort zones and align their image to that of the people with power.

4 Use the network – identify the interest groups and people of influence.

5 Enter the network – identify the gatekeepers, adhere to the norms.

6 Make deals – agree to support other people where this is of mutual benefit.

7 Withhold information as appropriate and withdraw judiciously when the going gets rough.

Using political means to get things done

People acting politically get things done by lobbying decision makers and doing deals. Other ploys include withholding information, which is not legitimate, in recognition of the fact that knowledge is power. Organizational politicians can go behind people's backs, hatch up plots in dark corners, 'sew things up' before meetings and exert undue influence on weaker brethren.

Political sensitivity

To be politically sensitive it is necessary to:

- know 'how things are done around here';
- know how key decisions are made and who makes them;
- understand the factors that are likely to affect decisions;
- know where the power base is in the organization;
- be aware of what is going on behind the scenes;
- know who is a rising star and whose reputation is fading;
- identify any 'hidden agendas' – try to understand what people are really getting at beneath the surface;
- find out what other people are thinking and seeking;
- network – identify the interest groups and keep in contact with them.

Dealing with organizational politicians

To keep politics operating at an acceptable level the organization should manage its operations as transparently as possible. The aim should be to ensure that issues are debated fully, that differences of opinion are dealt with frankly and that disagreements are depersonalized.

Questions

1 What are organizational politics?
2 What are typical political approaches?
3 How can political sensitivity be achieved?
4 How should organizational politics be dealt with?

Reference

Kakabadse, A (1983) *The Politics of Management*, Aldershot, Gower

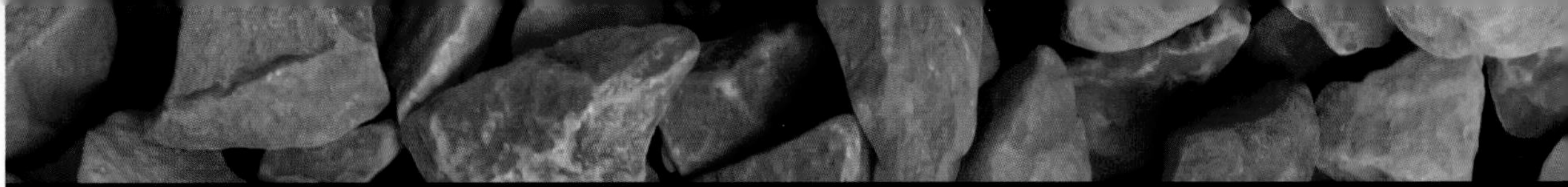

PART XII

HRM toolkits

PART XII CONTENTS

Introduction

The purpose of the HRM toolkits in this part is to provide practical guidance on the steps required to develop and implement HRM innovations and to manage key HR practices. The toolkits consist of questionnaires and checklists that can be used to conduct surveys, to analyse HR practices and the context in which they take place, to assist in the diagnosis of problems and issues, and to plan development and implementation programmes.

The toolkits set out a step-by-step process of analysis and diagnosis. Questionnaires and checklists are provided to elicit views, summarize arrangements and issues, and provide a framework for decision-making. However, the processes are in practice not always as sequential as the layouts of the toolkits suggest. The toolkits should not, indeed cannot, be used rigidly. It is often necessary to use them in accordance with the circumstances.

It is helpful in the first place to read through the whole toolkit to understand its structure and gain familiarity with the instruments it contains. How it is used can then be planned in accordance with the requirements presented by the situation facing the organization. Account needs to be taken of the priorities imposed by internal and external pressures. A speedy solution may be required to a pressing problem and this will mean selecting the relevant parts of the toolkits and focusing on these. Only a limited number of the instruments may therefore be used.

The toolkits have been designed to provide a range of instruments from which a selection can be made. These instruments contain statements or questions that are likely to be generally relevant, but these are only intended to provide guidelines and can be amended to suit the requirements of the situation. Thus questions could be added or deleted, or the instrument could be shortened to ease administration.

Used on this selective basis, the toolkits can provide the basis for programme planning, whether it is a survey, a risk assessment exercise, a fundamental strategic review, a study of particular aspects of human resource management or the evaluation of HR effectiveness. Instruments from within the toolkits can be selected for use in surveys and in involvement activities. They can elicit the information upon which communication plans can be based.

60 Strategic HRM toolkit

Purpose of the toolkit

Strategic HRM is concerned with how the organization's goals will be achieved through its human resources by means of integrated HR strategies, policies and practices. It involves a systematic analysis of the business context and needs, and the effectiveness of existing HRM policies and practices in operating within the context and satisfying the needs. The purpose of this toolkit is to describe the methods of analysis that can be used within a strategic HRM framework.

The strategic HRM framework

Strategic HRM involves a sequence of activities as set out in Figure 60.1.

Analyse:
• what's happening?
• what's good and not so good about it?
• what are the issues?
• what are the problems?
• what's the business need?
Diagnose:
• why do these issues exist?
• what are the causes of the problems?
• what factors are influencing the situation (competition, environmental, political, etc)?
Conclusions and recommendations:
• what are our conclusions from the analysis/diagnosis?
• what alternative strategies are available?
• which alternative is recommended and why?
Action planning:
• what actions do we need to take to implement the proposals?
• what problems may we meet and how will we overcome them?
• who takes the action and when?
Resource planning:
• what resources will we need (money, people, time)?
• how will we obtain these resources?
• how do we convince management that these resources are required?
Benefits:
• what are the benefits to the organization of implementing these proposals?
• how do they benefit individual employees?
• how do they satisfy business needs?

FIGURE 60.1
The sequence of strategic HRM

Strategic HRM activities

The strategic HRM activities conducted within this framework as set out in the rest of the toolkit are to:

- analyse the internal environment (Exhibit 60.1);
- analyse the external environment (Exhibit 60.2);
- analyse the HR implications of business strategy and business drivers (Exhibit 60.3);
- conduct a human resource management attitude survey (Exhibit 60.4);
- analyse the effectiveness of existing HR strategies (Exhibit 60.5);
- conduct a strategic HRM gap analysis (Exhibit 60.6);
- develop a diagnostic framework (Exhibit 60.7).

EXHIBIT 60.1 Analysis of internal environment

Question	Response	Implications for HR strategy
What are the key objectives of our business strategy?		
What are the main drivers of success in our business?		
What are the core values of the organization?		
What evidence is there that these values are used in the everyday life of the organization?		
What are the implications of the type of business we are in on our reward strategy?		
To what extent do we manage centrally or devolve responsibility?		
What is it like to work for this organization?		
What characteristics do we look for in our people?		
What do the people we want, want?		
What is our employee value proposition and does it help to attract and retain high-quality people?		
What do we do to ensure the engagement of our people, and is it enough?		

EXHIBIT 60.2 Analysis of external environment

External factor	Impact on HR policy and practice
Competitive pressures	
Business/economic downturn	
Globalization	
Employment and demographic trends	
Legislation/regulations	
Availability of key skills	
Market rates of pay and trends	

EXHIBIT 60.3 HR implications of business strategy and business drivers

	Content	Possible HR supporting activities	To what extent do we have the effective HR activities required?			What should we do about it?
			Wholly	Partly	Not at all	
Business strategy	• Growth – revenue/profit • Maximize shareholder value • Growth through acquisitions/ mergers • Product development • Market development • Cost leadership	• Workforce planning				
		• Talent management				
		• Skills development				
		• Targeted recruitment				
		• Retention policies				
		• Leadership development				
Business drivers	• Innovation • Maximize added value • Productivity • Customer service • Quality • Satisfy stakeholders – investors, shareholders, employees, elected representatives	• Total reward management				
		• Performance management				
		• High performance working				
		• Enhance engagement				

EXHIBIT 60.4 Human resource management attitude survey

Please state the extent to which you agree or disagree with the following statements about human resource management in this organization by placing a circle around the number which most closely matches your opinion.

		Strongly agree	Agree	Disagree	Strongly disagree
1.	I think this organization is a great place in which to work.	1	2	3	4
2.	I am happy about the values of this organization and the ways in which it conducts its business.	1	2	3	4
3.	I get plenty of opportunities to learn in this job.	1	2	3	4
4.	I get good advice on how I can develop my career.	1	2	3	4
5.	I am given plenty of opportunities to achieve in my job.	1	2	3	4
6.	I get ample opportunity to use my skills in my job.	1	2	3	4
7.	I have been properly trained to do my job.	1	2	3	4
8.	My contribution is adequately rewarded.	1	2	3	4
9.	My performance is recognized properly.	1	2	3	4
10.	The performance pay scheme encourages better performance.	1	2	3	4
11.	I understand how the job evaluation scheme works.	1	2	3	4
12.	Pay increases are handled fairly.	1	2	3	4
13.	I get good feedback on my performance throughout the year.	1	2	3	4
14.	I am kept well informed about changes that affect me in the organization.	1	2	3	4
15.	I feel that management is prepared to listen to employees.	1	2	3	4
16.	The organization treats me fairly.	1	2	3	4
17.	The organization makes every effort to achieve job security.	1	2	3	4
18.	The organization makes every effort to ensure the well-being of its employees.	1	2	3	4
19.	The organization is committed to ensuring the health and safety of its employees.	1	2	3	4
20.	The working conditions in my department encourage good work.	1	2	3	4

EXHIBIT 60.5 Analysis of the effectiveness of existing HR strategies

	Wholly	Partly	Not at all	If partly or not at all, what needs to be done about it?
To what extent does the HR strategy support the achievement of business goals?				
To what extent does the HR strategy promote the well-being of all employees?				
To what extent are the HR strategies in different areas integrated with one another?				
To what extent does HR strategy enable the organization to recruit and retain the skilled people it needs?				
To what extent does HR strategy enable the organization to develop the talented people it needs?				
To what extent does HR strategy ensure that people are rewarded according to their contribution?				
To what extent does HR strategy contribute to the creation of a positive employee relations climate?				

EXHIBIT 60.6 Strategic HRM gap analysis

	1 2 3 4 5 6	
Effective high performance work system in place		No systematic attempt is made to encourage high performance
Integrated talent management programmes are operating effectively		Talent management, if it happens at all, is haphazard or ineffective
Sophisticated techniques are used to recruit employees		A traditional approach is adopted to recruitment
Focus on using blended learning and development processes		Reliance on the delivery of traditional training courses
A total reward approach is used successfully		Reward programmes limited to financial incentives
Employees given a voice on all matters that concern them		Only lip service is paid to employee participation and involvement
Employee well-being given the close attention of management		Little or no concern by management for employee well-being

Mark on the scale X for current, 0 for desired – eg:

High-quality HR practices	O ← X	Poor-quality HR practices

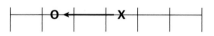

EXHIBIT 60.7 Diagnostic framework

Issues identified by analysis in Exhibits 60.3 to 60.6	Reasons for issues	Action proposed to deal with issues

61 Human capital management toolkit

Purpose of the toolkit

The purpose of this toolkit is to provide guidance on introducing and operating human capital management processes within an organization. It is designed to help you answer the following questions:

- What is a human capital management (HCM) approach?
- Do we need to adopt one?
- If so, how do we do it?
- How do we introduce HCM?

The human capital management approach

An HCM approach starts with an appreciation of the meaning and importance of human capital. It is based on the belief that the process of measuring key aspects of the ways in which human capital is developed and managed, and of assessing the impact it makes on organizational performance, ie human capital management, will guide managements on what needs to be done to obtain added value from people and improve business results.

The process of human capital management

The process of human capital management is illustrated in Figure 61.1.

Reasons for adopting an HCM approach

To assist in deciding whether or not human capital management is for you – and, if it is, why – complete Exhibit 61.1.

Adopting a human capital management approach

If a good case has been established, three questions need to be answered in considering how an HCM approach should be adopted:

1. What use are we going to make of HCM? (See Exhibit 61.2.)
2. How do we make the case to management? (See Exhibit 61.3.)
3. What are the considerations when introducing HCM? (See Exhibit 61.4.)

FIGURE 61.1 The process of human capital management

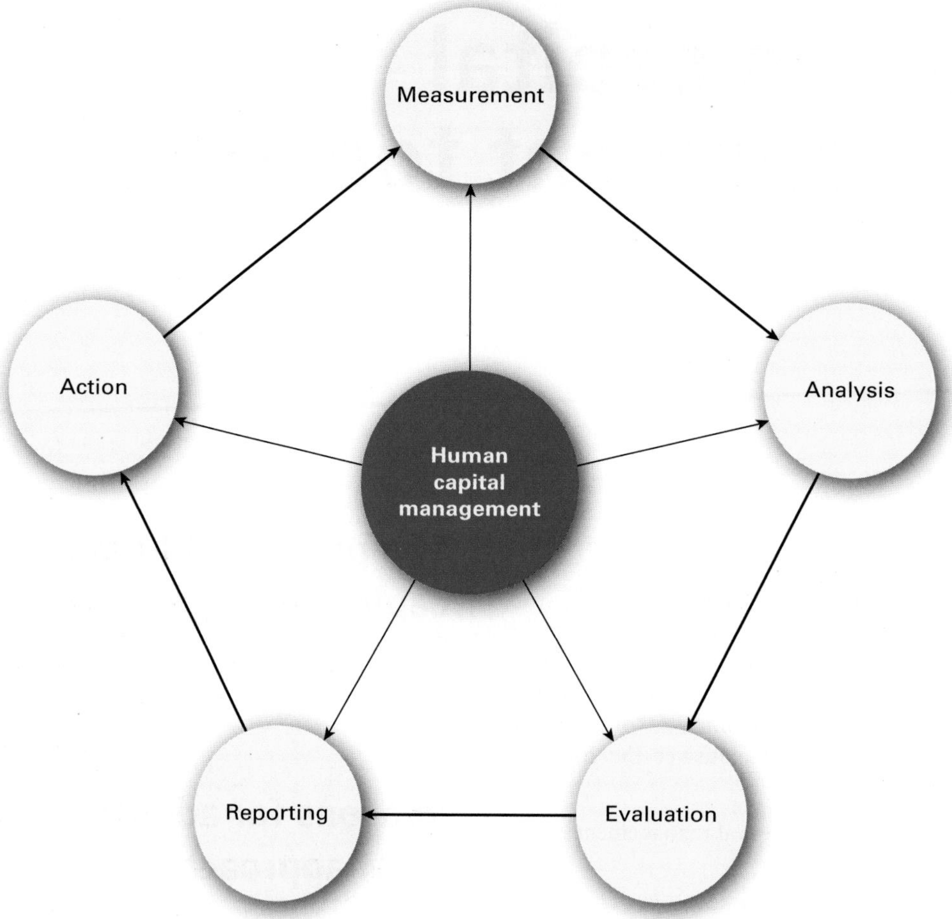

EXHIBIT 61.1 The case for human capital management

Statement on human capital management (HCM)	Indicate the extent to which you agree or disagree with the statement			
	Fully agree	Partially agree	Partially disagree	Wholly disagree
1. I like the idea of HCM but believe that the effort required to introduce it would not be worthwhile.				
2. I am satisfied that we have all the data required to measure the effectiveness and impact of HR policies and that we use it productively.				
3. I am convinced that we do not need to do anything more with our data than we already do.				
4. Top management would appreciate more information on the effectiveness and impact on the business of HR policies and practices.				
5. Line managers would benefit from having more information on how effective they are as people managers.				
6. HCM would provide me with invaluable data to support any business case I would want to make for an HR initiative.				
7. HCM is essential as a guide to the development of HR and business strategy.				
8. HCM would provide invaluable information to me and my colleagues on the effectiveness of the HR function.				
9. HCM is essential as a means of generating meaningful information on human capital issues for the Operating and Financial Report (OFR).				
10. I or my colleagues have all the skills required to develop HCM.				

EXHIBIT 61.2 What use are we going to make of HCM?

What are the possible uses of HCM?	Which of these uses are we going to adopt and why?	What is the preferred timescale for introducing this aspect of HCM?	If applicable, why don't we want to adopt this use?
• Identify need for remedial action • Take immediate or longer-term action: – attraction and retention policies – absence management policies – human resource plans – employee relations policies – other HR policies • Report to line managers on their performance as people managers			
• Monitor performance of HR • Identify areas for improvement • Report to HR staff on their performance			
• Identify and take action on general employee issues concerning commitment, engagement, motivation and morale • Identify and take action on specific employee issues • Report to line managers on performance • Provide guide to longer-term HR strategies			
• Report on performance to management • Identify areas for remedial action • Guide to business and HR strategy			
• Produce eternal reports (business review)			
• Identify impact of HR policies and practices on business performance • Guide the development of business and HR strategy • Support business cases for HR initiatives			

EXHIBIT 61.3 Making the business case for HCM

General arguments in favour of HCM	Degree of relevance to the organization (high, moderate, low)	Specific benefits to the organization
Develop an understanding of what translates human capital into business value as a basis for developing realistic HR and business strategies.		
Establish a clear line of sight between HR interventions and business success (Kearns, 2005).		
Demonstrate that HR practices produce value for money in terms, for example, of return on investment.		
Provide data for internal reports that identify areas for improvement in HR practice.		
Provide data for internal reports that indicate levels of people performance in the organization and identify areas for improvement.		
Provide data for internal reports on the effectiveness of line managers as people managers.		
Provide data for internal reports on the effectiveness of the HR function and identify areas for improvement.		
Provide information on the value of the organization's human capital.		
Provide data for external reports (eg the OFR) that demonstrate that the organization is implementing innovative and productive policies to enhance the value obtained from its human capital.		

EXHIBIT 61.4 Considerations when introducing HCM

What points do we need to cover?	How are we going to deal with them?
How do we make the business case for HCM to management?	
How do we brief line managers and employees generally on the purpose and use of HCM and how it affects them?	
How do we train line managers on the use they can make for HCM?	
How do we stage the introduction of HCM?	
What data do we need?	
How do we collect the data?	
How do we ensure that HR has the HCM skills it needs?	
What internal reports should we produce?	
What information are we going to provide for external reports?	
How are we going to use HCM data as a basis for developing HR strategy?	
How will HCM influence business strategy?	

Introducing HCM

A programme for introducing human capital management is illustrated in Figure 61.2.

FIGURE 61.2 Programme for introducing human capital management

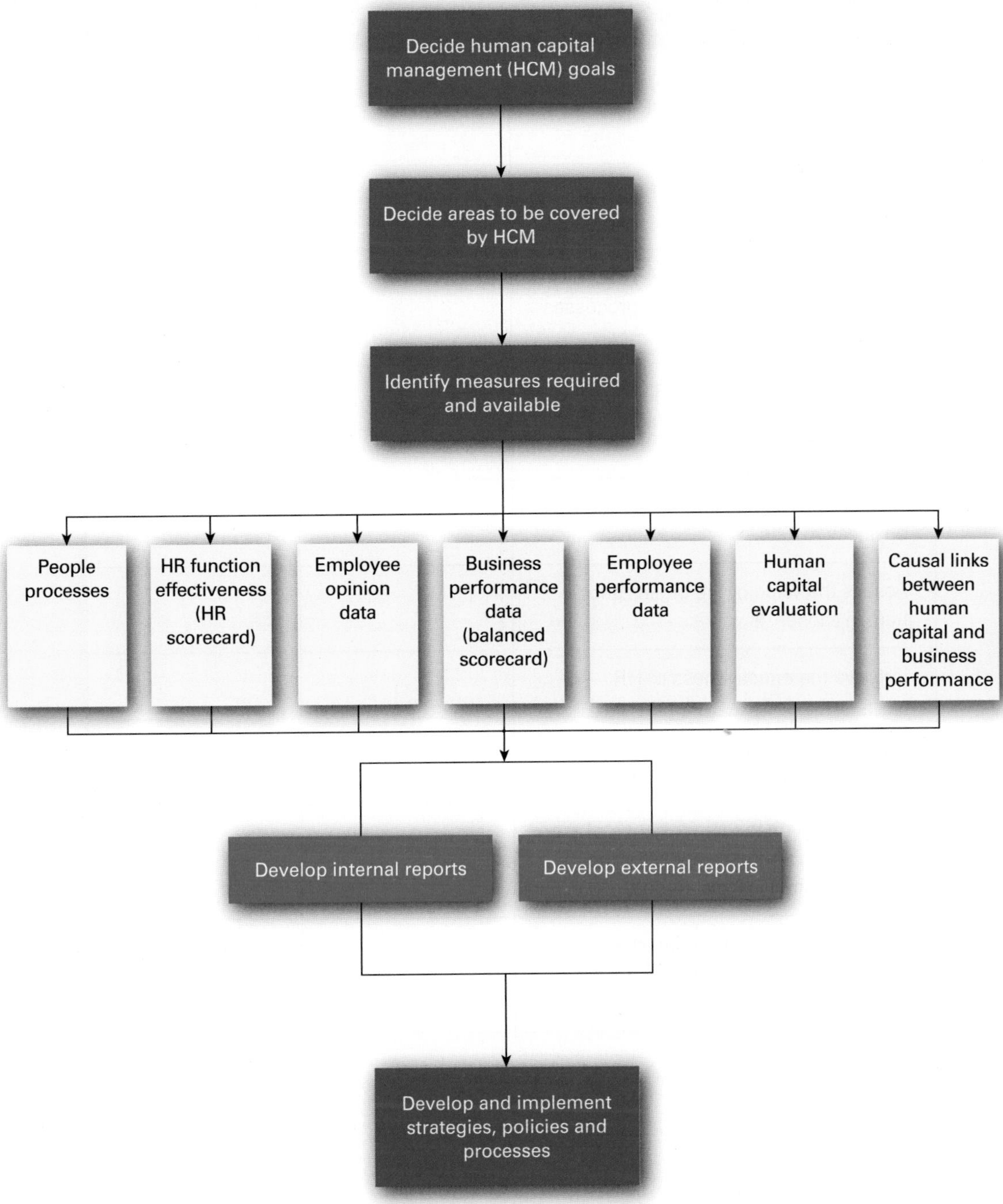

Decide HCM goals

It is necessary to be clear about HCM goals and the questionnaire in Exhibit 61.5 can be used for this purpose. This questionnaire could usefully be completed jointly by HR and senior and line management.

EXHIBIT 61.5 HCM goals

Goal	Importance*	Effectiveness*
Obtain, analyse and report on data that inform the direction of HR strategies and processes		
Inform the development of business strategy		
Use measurements to prove that superior HRM strategies and processes deliver superior results		
Reinforce the belief that HRM strategies and processes create value through people		
Determine the impact of people on business results		
Assess the value of the organization's human capital		
Improve the effectiveness of HR		
Improve the effectiveness of line managers as people managers		
Provide data on the performance of the organization's human capital for the Operating and Financial Report		
Demonstrate that HR processes provide value for money in terms of return on capital employed		

* Scale: 10 = high, 0 = low

Decide areas to be covered by HCM

Use the questionnaire in Exhibit 61.6 to decide on the priority to be given to developing different aspects of HCM.

EXHIBIT 61.6 HCM priorities

HCM area	Priority*	Introduce by:
Make better use of existing people process data		
Develop improved people process data		
Obtain and use better quantitative data on the performance of HR		
Develop HR score card		
Obtain and use data on the people management performance of line managers		
Develop balanced score card		
Conduct employee opinion surveys		
Calculate return on investment in training		
Calculate impact of HR policies and practices on business performance		
Estimate value of human capital		

* Scale: 10 = highest priority; 0 = no priority

Analysis of measures requirements

It is necessary at this stage to analyse the requirements for measures or metrics. Use the questionnaire in Exhibit 61.7 for this purpose.

EXHIBIT 61.7 Analysis of measures requirements – people data and processes

Measures	Possible use – analysis leading to action	Required √	Available now √	To be made available √
Workforce composition – gender, race, age, full-time, part-time	• Analyse the extent of diversity • Assess the implications of a preponderance of employees in different age groups, eg extent of losses through retirement • Assess the extent to which the organization is relying on part-time staff			
Length of service distribution	• Indicate level of success in retaining employees • Indicate preponderance of long or short-serving employees • Enable analyses of performance of more experienced employees to be assessed			
Skills analysis/assessment – graduates, professionally/ technically qualified, skilled workers	• Assess skill levels against requirements • Indicate where steps have to be taken to deal with shortfalls			
Attrition – employee turnover rates for different categories of management and employees	• Indicate areas where steps have to be taken to increase retention rates • Provide a basis for assessing levels of commitment			
Attrition – cost of	• Support business case for taking steps to reduce attrition			
Absenteeism/sickness rates	• Identify problems and need for more effective attendance management policies			

EXHIBIT 61.7 Continued

Measures	Possible use – analysis leading to action	Required √	Available now √	To be made available √
Average number of vacancies as a percentage of total workforce	• Identify potential shortfall problem areas			
Total payroll costs (pay and benefits)	• Provide data for productivity analysis			
Compa-ratio – actual rates of pay as a percentage of policy rates	• Enable control to be exercised over management of pay structure			
Percentage of employees in different categories of contingent pay or payment-by-result schemes	• Demonstrate the extent to which the organization believes that pay should be related to contribution			
Total pay review increases for different categories of employees as a percentage of pay	• Compare actual with budgeted payroll increase costs • Benchmark pay increases			
Average bonuses or contingent pay awards as % of base pay for different categories of managers and employees	• Analyse cost of contingent pay • Compare actual and budgeted increases • Benchmark increases			
Outcome of equal pay reviews	• Reveal pay gap between male and female employees			
Personal development plans completed as a percentage of employees	• Indicate level of learning and development activity			
Training hours per employee	• Indicate actual amount of training activity (note that this does not reveal the quality of training achieved or its impact)			
Percentage of managers taking part in formal management development programmes	• Indicate level of learning and development activity			

EXHIBIT 61.7 Continued

Measures	Possible use – analysis leading to action	Required √	Available now √	To be made available √
Internal promotion rate (% of promotions filled from within)	• Indicate extent to which talent management programmes are successful			
Succession planning coverage (% of managerial jobs for which successors have been identified)	• Indicate extent to which talent management programmes are successful			
Percentage of employees taking part in formal performance reviews	• Indicate level of performance management activity			
Distribution of performance ratings by category of staff and department	• Indicate inconsistencies, questionable distributions and trends in assessments			
Accident severity and frequency rates	• Assess health and safety programmes			
Cost savings/revenue increases resulting from employee suggestion schemes	• Measure the value created by employees			

Reference

Kearns, P (2005) *Evaluating the ROI from Learning*, London, CIPD

62
Organization design toolkit

Purpose of the toolkit

This toolkit provides a set of analytical and diagnostic organization design tools for use in a design and organization development programme, as set out in Figure 62.1.

FIGURE 62.1 Organization design programme

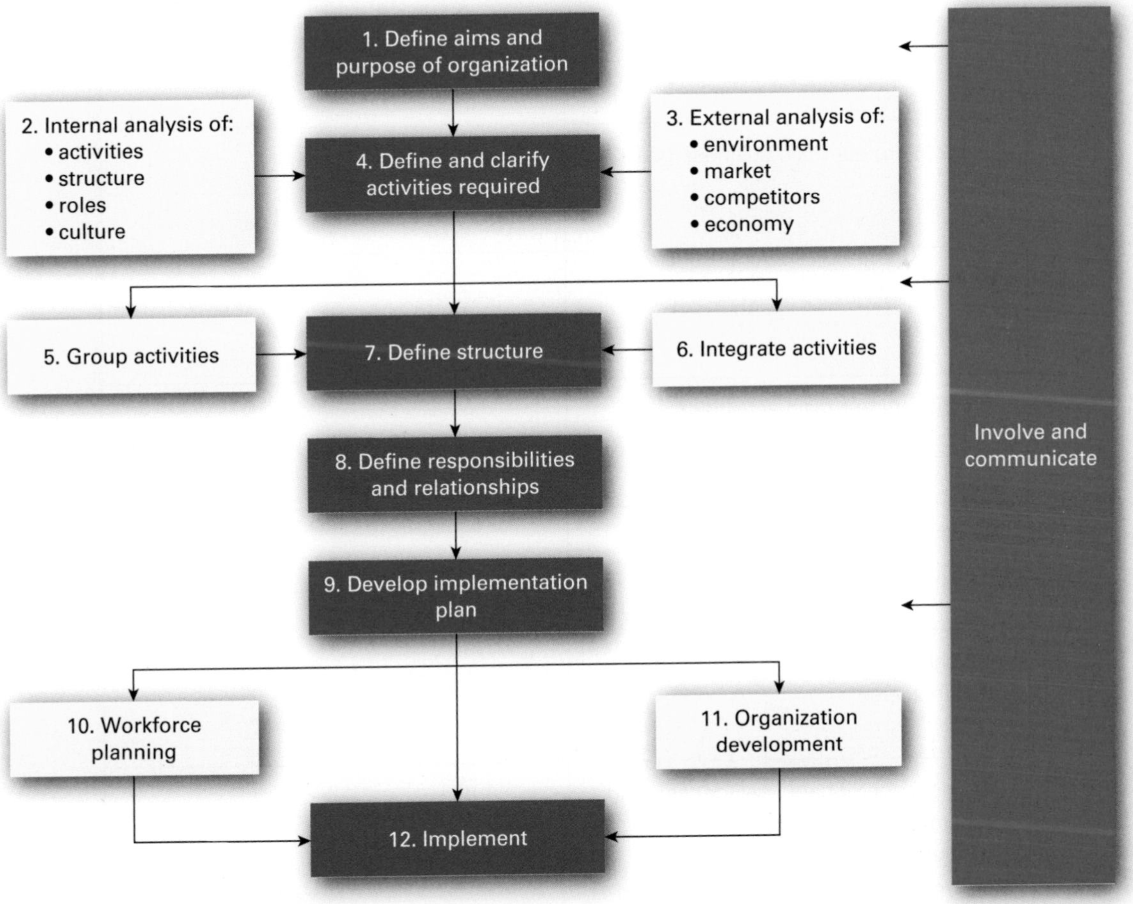

Analysis of aims and purpose of the organization

Use Exhibit 62.1 to analyse the aims and purpose of the organization.

EXHIBIT 62.1 Analysis of overall aims and purpose

Question	Answer
1. What business are we in?	
2. What is our business model?	
3. How do we make money?	
4. What is our mission?	
5. What are our main business goals?	
6. What are our core values?	
7. What are our main activities?	
8. Who are our customers/clients?	
9. Who are our other main stakeholders?	
10. How appropriate, well-defined and understood are our mission and business goals?	

Activities and structure analysis

Use Exhibit 62.2 to analyse activities and structure.

EXHIBIT 62.2 Activities and structure analysis

	Question	Answer
Activities	Are all the activities required to achieve objectives properly catered for?	
	Are any unnecessary activities being carried out?	
	Is there any unnecessary duplication of activities?	
Structure	On what basis are activities grouped together – by product, by function or process, by region or area, by customer or client or by a combination of any of these?	
	Is the basis upon which activities are grouped appropriate in relation to the markets and customers of the organization and its technology, environment and geographical coverage?	
	If grouping is on a product, customer or regional basis, has this resulted in too much duplication of activities, unnecessary numbers of staff or duplication of group or central service functions?	
	If grouping is on a functional or process basis has this resulted in too much task specialization, insufficient identification with the end product and the consultant, or managers not having adequate responsibility for the range of resources they need?	
	Does the basis upon which activities are grouped create boundary difficulties between them?	
	Is the organization a process-based one, in the sense defined by Ghoshal and Bartlett (1995)? Managers are beginning to deal with their organizations in different ways. Rather than seeing them as a hierarchy of static roles, they think of them as a portfolio of dynamic processes. They see core organizational processes that overlay and often dominate the vertical, authority-based processes of the hierarchical structure. Or should it be?	
	Is the flow of work across organizational boundaries smooth and uninterrupted?	
	Is there sufficient degree of flexibility in grouping activities and defining group boundaries to facilitate rapid adjustments to changing requirements?	
	Is there any scope for grouping activities more closely together or removing boundaries between them to facilitate integration and smooth, economical work flows?	
	Does the nature of the work indicate that a looser form of boundaryless organization or a matrix organization would be more appropriate?	
	Should the emphasis be more on creating a climate in which networking can take place and hierarchical decision-making becomes less important?	
	Are there too many levels in the organization and, if so, what is the scope for reducing them?	
	Are there any cases of a 'one-over-one' situation in which managers have an assistant manager between them and the next level, thus creating confusion and duplication?	
	Have any managers more people reporting to them than they can conveniently and effectively control?	
	Does the structure inhibit in any way clear and rapid communications on matters affecting the business and how it is managed?	

Role analysis

Use Exhibit 62.3 to conduct role analysis.

EXHIBIT 62.3 Role analysis

Question	Answer
Are any role holders unclear about what they are expected to do?	
Are any role holders unclear about who they report to for what?	
Are any role holders unclear about their reporting relationship to their line manager and to any other person with whom they have a functional relationship?	
Are any role holders expected to do too much or too little?	
Are any role holders carrying out a range of miscellaneous tasks that do not seem to be logically grouped together?	
Do any role holders lack the authority, resources or information that would enable them to carry out their job effectively?	
Are there any role holders who are clearly unable to carry out their work properly?	
Is there a sufficient degree of flexibility in the ways in which roles are defined to enable role holders to adjust readily to new or changed demands?	
To what extent are roles designed to provide an appropriate degree of challenge, responsibility, autonomy and scope for growth?	
Are managers aware of the principles of job design and do they take them into account in designing jobs in their departments?	
Are there any cases where roles have been inappropriately structured around the capacities or personalities of role holders?	

Reference

Ghoshal, S and Bartlett, C A (1995) Changing the role of top management: beyond structure to process, *Harvard Business Review*, January–February, pp 86–96

63 Organization development toolkit

Purpose of the toolkit

The purpose of this toolkit is to provide the basis for organizational development programmes through a number of diagnostics and checklists covering major aspects of organizational culture and behaviour.

The toolkit contains the following exhibits:

- Exhibit 63.1 Organizational effectiveness – diagnostic checklist
- Exhibit 63.2 Culture analysis
- Exhibit 63.3 Values analysis
- Exhibit 63.4 Norms analysis
- Exhibit 63.5 Artefacts analysis
- Exhibit 63.6 Management style analysis
- Exhibit 63.7 Teamwork analysis
- Exhibit 63.8 Organizational development action plan
- Exhibit 63.9 Choice of organization development activities

EXHIBIT 63.1 Organizational effectiveness – diagnostic checklist

Question	Response
How well is the business performing in terms of financial results, growth, innovation, productivity, reputation (views of stakeholders), operational efficiency, social and environmental responsibility?	
Is the organization delivering quality and value to its clients and customers?	
Is there a clear and relevant business strategy that is acted upon effectively?	
Is the business model (the picture of an organization that explains how it achieves competitive advantage and makes money) appropriate, realistic and understood by all concerned?	
Is there a need and scope for business model innovation (developing a new business model or changing the existing one)?	

EXHIBIT 63.1 Continued

Question	Response
Is there a well-defined and understood set of core values expressed in a values statement, including an ethical approach to business, which are 'values in use' rather than mere rhetoric?	
Are the work systems operating effectively?	
Has a 'smart working' approach been put into operation that incorporates high-performance working and flexibility?	
Is the organization's structure appropriate and working well?	
Is there any evidence of an over-hierarchical approach to management?	
How well do teams work well together?	
Has the organization got the resources required (including people) and are they being managed and used effectively?	

EXHIBIT 63.2 Culture analysis

Types of culture (Handy, 1981)	To what extent does the culture of the organization correspond to any of these types?
The power culture is one with a central power source that exercises control. There are few rules or procedures and the atmosphere is competitive, power-oriented and political.	
The role culture in which work is controlled by procedures and rules and the role, or job description, is more important than the person who fills it. Power is associated with positions not people.	
The task culture in which the aim is to bring together the right people and let them get on with it. Influence is based more on expert power than in position or personal power. The culture is adaptable and teamwork is important.	
The person culture in which the individual is the central point. The organization exists only to serve and assist the individuals in it.	

EXHIBIT 63.3 Values analysis

Question	Answer
Is it possible to say that the organization has a set of core values? If so:	
What are they? eg: • Care and consideration for people • Competence • Competitiveness • Customer service • Innovation • Performance • Quality • Teamwork	
Have they been articulated?	
Have employees been involved in describing them?	
To what extent are they 'values in use' rather than just 'espoused values'?	
Have any efforts been made by the organization to operationalize the values?	
Does anything more need to be done to operationalize the values?	

EXHIBIT 63.4 Norms analysis

Possible norms	To what extent do they apply?
How managers treat the members of their teams (management style) and how the latter relate to their managers.	
The prevailing work ethic, eg 'work hard, play hard', 'come in early, stay late', 'if you cannot finish your work during business hours you are obviously inefficient', 'look busy at all times', 'look relaxed at all times'.	
Status – how much importance is attached to it; the existence or lack of obvious status symbols.	
Ambition – naked ambition is expected and approved of, or a more subtle approach is the norm.	
Performance – exacting performance standards are general; the highest praise that can be given in the organization is to be referred to as very professional.	
Power – recognized as a way of life; executed by political means, dependent on expertise and ability rather than position; concentrated at the top; shared at different levels in different parts of the organization.	
Politics – rife throughout the organization and treated as normal behaviour; not accepted as overt behaviour.	
Loyalty – expected, a cradle-to-grave approach to careers; discounted, the emphasis is on results and contribution in the short term.	
Anger – openly expressed; hidden, but expressed through other, possibly political, means.	
Approachability – managers are expected to be approachable and visible; everything happens behind closed doors.	
Formality – a cool, formal approach is the norm; the atmosphere is relaxed and highly informal.	

EXHIBIT 63.5 Artefacts analysis

Examples of artefacts	How are they evidenced?
The working environment	
The tone and language used in e-mails, letters or memoranda	
The manner in which people address each other at meetings, in e-mails or over the telephone	
The welcome (or lack of welcome) given to visitors	
The way in which receptionists deal with outside calls	

EXHIBIT 63.6 Management style analysis

Indicate the prevailing management style in each of the listed categories on a scale of 1 to 10

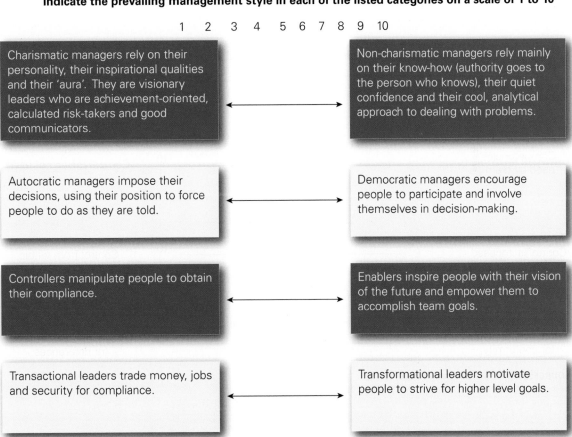

	1 2 3 4 5 6 7 8 9 10	
Charismatic managers rely on their personality, their inspirational qualities and their 'aura'. They are visionary leaders who are achievement-oriented, calculated risk-takers and good communicators.	←→	Non-charismatic managers rely mainly on their know-how (authority goes to the person who knows), their quiet confidence and their cool, analytical approach to dealing with problems.
Autocratic managers impose their decisions, using their position to force people to do as they are told.	←→	Democratic managers encourage people to participate and involve themselves in decision-making.
Controllers manipulate people to obtain their compliance.	←→	Enablers inspire people with their vision of the future and empower them to accomplish team goals.
Transactional leaders trade money, jobs and security for compliance.	←→	Transformational leaders motivate people to strive for higher level goals.

EXHIBIT 63.7 Teamwork analysis

		Scale		
		Degree of mutual trust		
High suspicion	1	________________	10	High trust
		Communications		
Guarded, cautious	1	________________	10	Open, authentic
		Degree of mutual support		
Everyone for themselves	1	________________	10	Genuine concern for each other
		Team objectives		
Not understood	1	________________	10	Clearly understood
		Handling conflict within team		
Through denial, avoidance	1	________________	10	Acceptance and 'working through' conflicts
		Use of member resources		
Competencies used by team	1	________________	10	Competencies not used
		Control methods		
Control is imposed	1	________________	10	Control from within
		Organizational environment		
Restrictive, pressure for conformity	1	________________	10	Free, supportive, respect for differences

SOURCE: adapted from Douglas McGregor (1960)

EXHIBIT 63.8 Organizational development action plan

Area of analysis	Implications for organizational development
Culture analysis	
Values analysis	
Norms analysis	
Artefacts analysis	
Management style analysis	
Teamwork analysis	

EXHIBIT 63.9 Choice of organization development activities

Organization development activity	Brief description	Indicate choice of programme, the reason for the choice and its objective
Business model innovation	The process followed by an organization to develop a new business model or change an existing one.	
Change management	The process of planning and introducing change systematically, taking into account the likelihood of it being resisted.	
Culture change	The process of changing the organization's culture in the shape of its values, norms and beliefs.	
Engagement, enhancement of	The development of improved levels of job and organizational engagement.	
High-performance working	Developing work system processes, practices and policies to enable employees to perform to their full potential.	

EXHIBIT 63.9 Continued

Organization development activity	Brief description	Indicate choice of programme, the reason for the choice and its objective
Knowledge management	Storing and sharing the wisdom, understanding and expertise accumulated in an organization about its processes, techniques and operations.	
Lean	A process improvement methodology that focuses on continuous improvement, reducing waste and ensuring the flow of production.	
Organizational learning	The acquisition and development of knowledge, understanding, insights, techniques and practices.	
Organization design	The process of deciding how organizations should be structured in terms of the ways in which the responsibility for carrying out the overall task is allocated to individuals and groups of people and how the relationships between them function.	
Smart working	An approach to organizing work through a combination of flexibility, autonomy and collaboration, in parallel with optimizing tools and working environments for employees.	
Team building	Using interactive skills training techniques to improve the ways in which people in teams work together.	
Total rewards	The combination of financial and non-financial rewards available to employees. It involves integrating the various aspects of reward.	

References

Handy, C (1981) *Understanding Organizations*, 3rd edn, Harmondsworth, Penguin Books

McGregor, D (1960) *The Human Side of Enterprise*, New York, McGraw-Hill

64 Employee engagement toolkit

Purpose of the toolkit

A high level of employee engagement is the Holy Grail sought by management everywhere. But they are not always clear about what engagement is, what drives engagement and what to do about it. The aim of this toolkit is to clarify these points as a basis for action.

The toolkit contains the questionnaires, checklists and examples of surveys that define the journey required to enhance engagement, as illustrated in Figure 64.1 and Figure 64.2.

FIGURE 64.1 The engagement journey

FIGURE 64.2 Definitions of engagement

Definition	Source
Engaged employees perform better, are more innovative than others, are more likely to want to stay with their employees, enjoy greater levels of personal well-being and perceive their workload to be more sustainable than others.	Alfes *et al* (2010)
Employee engagement is the heightened connection that employees feel for their organization.	The Conference Board (2006)
Engaged employees: work with passion and feel profound connection to their organization. They drive innovation and move the organization forward.	Gallup (quoted by Balain and Sparrow, 2009)
Engagement is an individual's purpose and focused energy, evident to others in the display of personal initiative, adaptability, effort and persistence directed towards organizational goals. Engaged employees feel that their jobs are an important part of who they are.	Macey *et al* (2009)
Employee engagement is a workplace approach designed to ensure that employees are committed to their organization's goals and values, motivated to contribute to organizational success, and are able at the same time to enhance their own sense of well-being.	MacLeod and Clarke (2009)
Engagement is a positive, fulfilling, work-related state of mind that is characterized by vigour, dedication and absorption.	Maslach *et al* (2001)
Engaged performance is a result that is achieved by stimulating employees' enthusiasm for their work and directing it towards organizational success. This result can only be achieved when employers offer an implied contract to their employees that elicits specific positive behaviours aligned with the organization's goals.	Murlis and Watson (2001)
An engaged employee is someone who believes in, and identifies with, the organization.	Robinson *et al* (2004)
The extent to which employees put discretionary effort into their work, beyond the minimum to get the job done, in the form of extra time, brainpower or energy.	Towers Perrin (2007)
Engagement means feeling positive about your job. The engaged employee is the passionate employee, the employee who is totally immersed in his or her work, energetic, committed and completely dedicated.	Truss *et al* (2006)

Drivers of engagement

It is necessary to determine what drives engagement in your organization as a basis for deciding how to measure it and what to do about it. Exhibit 64.1 sets out a list of possible drivers from which to choose.

EXHIBIT 64.1 Drivers of employee engagement

Driver	How relevant is this driver in your organization?		
	Highly	Fairly	Not very
Managers who show that they appreciate the efforts and contribution of people, treat them as individuals and ensure that work is organized so that employees feel they are valued, and are equipped and supported to do their job.			
An organization that lives its values and demonstrates its concern for the well-being and health and safety of employees.			
A work environment that promotes information sharing, provides learning opportunities and fosters a balance in people's lives.			
Meaningful work that uses and develops skills and provides employees with a reasonable degree of autonomy.			
Employees who feel that they are able to voice their ideas and are listened to.			

Measuring engagement

Levels of engagement can be measured by an engagement survey as illustrated in Exhibit 64.2.

EXHIBIT 64.2 Engagement survey

ENGAGEMENT SURVEY

Please place a tick in the box that most closely fits your opinion

Opinion	Strongly agree	Inclined to agree	Neither agree nor disagree	Inclined to disagree	Strongly disagree
1. I am very satisfied with the work I do					
2. My job is interesting					
3. I know exactly what I am expected to do					
4. I am prepared to put myself out to do my work					
5. My job is not very challenging					
6. I am given plenty of freedom to decide how to do my work					
7. I get plenty of opportunities to learn in this job					
8. The facilities/equipment/tools provided are excellent					
9. I do not get adequate support from my boss					
10. I like working for my boss					
11. My contribution is fully recognized					
12. The experience I am getting now will be a great help in advancing my future career					
13. I find it difficult to keep up with the demands of my job					
14. I have no problems in achieving a balance between my work and my private life					
15. I get on well with my work colleagues					
16. I think this organization is a great place in which to work					
17. I believe I have a good future in this organization					
18. I intend to go on working for this organization					
19. I am not happy about the values of this organization – the ways in which it conducts its business					
20. The products/services provided by this organization are excellent					

Engagement gap analysis

An engagement gap analysis compares the current and desired HRM practices for enhancing engagement using the framework set out in Exhibit 64.3. Comparing the largest gaps with the current situation helps to indicate the priority issues to be addressed. It can be used in workshops and focus groups as a means of obtaining the views of line managers and employees on where things need to be done.

EXHIBIT 64.3 Engagement gap analysis

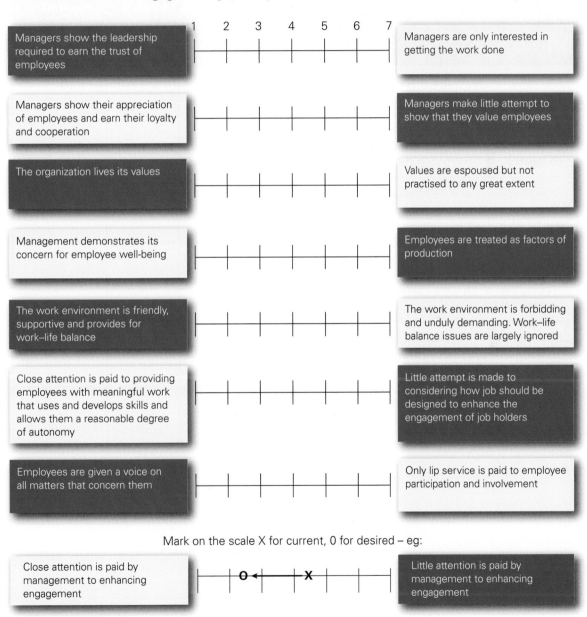

	1	2	3	4	5	6	7	
Managers show the leadership required to earn the trust of employees								Managers are only interested in getting the work done
Managers show their appreciation of employees and earn their loyalty and cooperation								Managers make little attempt to show that they value employees
The organization lives its values								Values are espoused but not practised to any great extent
Management demonstrates its concern for employee well-being								Employees are treated as factors of production
The work environment is friendly, supportive and provides for work–life balance								The work environment is forbidding and unduly demanding. Work–life balance issues are largely ignored
Close attention is paid to providing employees with meaningful work that uses and develops skills and allows them a reasonable degree of autonomy								Little attempt is made to considering how job should be designed to enhance the engagement of job holders
Employees are given a voice on all matters that concern them								Only lip service is paid to employee participation and involvement

Mark on the scale X for current, 0 for desired – eg:

	1	2	3	4	5	6	7	
Close attention is paid by management to enhancing engagement		O ←		X				Little attention is paid by management to enhancing engagement

Diagnosis

A diagnostic framework making use of data on the drivers of engagement, engagement surveys and a gap analysis is shown in Exhibit 64.4.

EXHIBIT 64.4 Engagement diagnostic framework

Engagement driver	Level of concern arising from analysis (Exhibits 64.1 to 64.3)			Any action required
	High concern	Some concern	No concern	
Managers who show that they appreciate the efforts and contribution of people, treat them as individuals and ensure that work is organized so that employees feel they are valued, and are equipped and supported to do their job.				
An organization that lives its values and demonstrates its concern for the well-being and health and safety of employees.				
A work environment that promotes information sharing, provides learning opportunities and fosters a balance in people's lives.				
Meaningful work that uses and develops skills and provides employees with a reasonable degree of autonomy.				
Employees who feel that they are able to voice their ideas and are listened to.				

References

Alfes, K, Truss, C, Soane, E C, Rees, C and Gatenby, M (2010) *Creating an Engaged Workforce*, London, CIPD

Balain, S and Sparrow, P (2009) *Engaged to Perform: A new perspective on employee engagement*, Lancaster, Lancaster University Management School

Conference Board (2006) *Employee Engagement: A review of current research and its implications*, New York, Conference Board

Macey, W H, Schneider, B, Barbera, K M and Young, S A (2009) *Employee Engagement*, Malden, MA, Wiley-Blackwell

MacLeod, D and Clarke, N (2009) *Engaging for Success: Enhancing performance through employee engagement*, London, Department for Business Innovation and Skills

Maslach, C, Schaufeli, W B and Leiter, M P (2001) Job burnout, *Annual Review of Psychology*, 52, pp 397–422

Murlis, H and Watson, S (2001) Creating employee engagement – transforming the employment deal, *Benefits and Compensation International*, 30 (8), pp 6–17

Robinson, D, Perryman, S and Hayday, S (2004) *The Drivers of Employee Engagement*, Brighton, Institute for Employment Studies

Towers Perrin (2007) *Global Workforce Study*, at http://www.towersperrin.com [accessed 1 August 2011]

Truss, C, Soane, E, Edwards, C, Wisdom, K, Croll, A and Burnett, J (2006) *Working Life: Employee attitudes and engagement*, London, CIPD

65 Workforce planning toolkit

Purpose of the toolkit

The purpose of the toolkit is to provide a guide to workforce planning, defined as a process in which an organization attempts to estimate the demand for employees and evaluate the size, nature and sources of supply that will be required to meet the demand. Workforce planning often focuses on key categories of staff, for example doctors, nurses and radiographers in the National Health Service, or skilled operatives in a manufacturing company. A workforce planning flowchart is shown in Figure 65.1.

FIGURE 65.1 Workforce planning flow chart

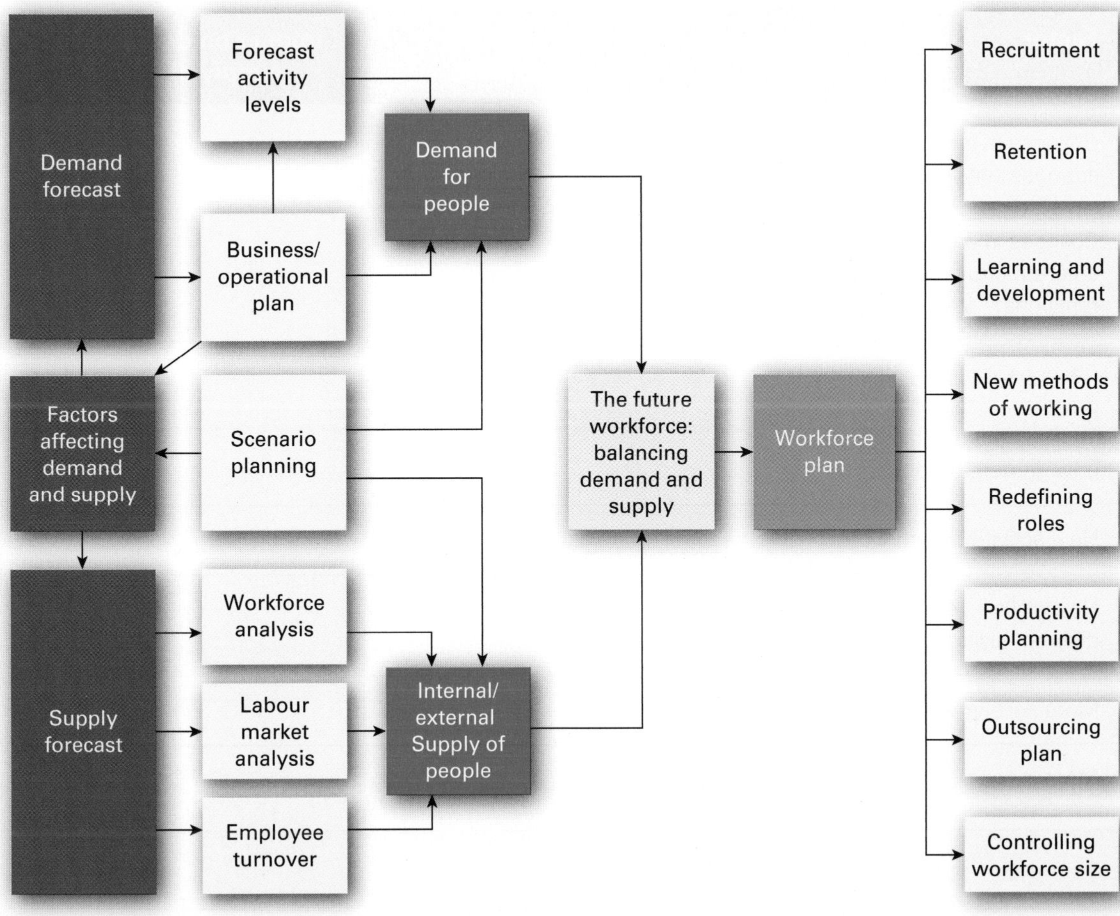

The following tools are provided:

- Exhibit 65.1 Internal factors affecting demand and supply of people
- Exhibit 65.2 Scenario planning
- Exhibit 65.3 Forecasting activity levels
- Exhibit 65.4 Workforce implications of the business plan
- Exhibit 65.5 Demand forecasting methods
- Exhibit 65.6 Demand forecast schedule
- Exhibit 65.7 Workforce analysis
- Exhibit 65.8 Measuring employee turnover
- Exhibit 65.9 Forecasting the supply of people
- Exhibit 65.10 Balancing demand and supply
- Exhibit 65.11 Action planning

Factors affecting demand and supply

The starting point of the workforce planning process is an analysis of the factors affecting the demand and supply of people. Exhibit 65.1 shows the internal factors that need to be considered by reference to business and organizational plans. The external factors are identified by means of scenario planning (Exhibit 65.2).

EXHIBIT 65.1 Internal factors affecting demand and supply of people

Factor	Occurrence in organization	Impact on demand and supply of people
Changes in working arrangements – hours, flexibility		
Changes in organization – different structures, new functions		
Changes in roles – new jobs, greater role flexibility, amalgamation of existing roles, enlargement of roles		
New activities or services		
New skills – demand for new or different skills		
More part-time working		
More outsourcing of work		

EXHIBIT 65.2 Scenario planning

Factors	Assessment of developments that are likely to affect the organization	Workforce plan implications
Political		
Economic		
Social		
Technological		
Legal		
Environmental		

Scenario planning

Scenario planning assesses the environmental changes that are likely to affect the organization so that the implications of these changes on the organization's labour markets and the supply of people can be taken into account in the workforce plan. The PESTLE scanning approach, as shown in Exhibit 65.2, can be used.

Forecasting activity levels

The raw data for preparing demand forecasts is provided by forecast activity levels. Obviously, the activities will vary according to the type of business or organization. The following are examples of different types of activities for which forecasts could be made:

- call outs;
- claims dealt with;
- customers/clients/patients;
- deliveries;
- dispatches;
- enquiries dealt with;
- examinations/inspections made;
- orders processed;
- policies underwritten;
- routes/journeys undertaken;
- telephone calls received/made;
- tests conducted;
- transactions;
- units manufactured or processed;
- volume of items/material manufactured or processed.

An analysis should be made of the current level of activity. The number of people involved and the ratio of people to activity levels are included to provide data for demand forecasts (see Exhibit 65.3).

EXHIBIT 65.3 Forecasting activity levels

Activity	Applicable role(s)	Current level of activity	Current number in role(s)	Ratio: roles to activity*	Forecast level of activity on:		
					Date:	Date:	Date:

* For use in ratio-trend analysis (see Exhibit 65.5)

EXHIBIT 65.4 Workforce implications of the business plan

Question	Answer
What are the key features of the business/operational plan?	
What are the implications of the business/operational plan for the need for new or different skills?	
What are the implications of the business/operational plan for the numbers of different categories of people required?	

Workforce implications of business plan

Business or operational plans indicate projected levels of activity, which feed into the activity level forecast and through that to the demand forecast. They also provide information on the likely demands for new or different skills to meet plans for business model innovation or the introduction of new technology. A checklist is set out in Exhibit 65.4.

Demand forecast methods

Demand forecasts are based on data relating to forecast activity levels and the implications of business and operational plans, together with information from scenario planning. There are three basic forecasting methods, as set out in Exhibit 65.5. Of these, managerial judgement is the most typical, followed by ratio trend analysis.

EXHIBIT 65.5 Demand forecasting methods

Method	Description	Advantages	Disadvantages
Managerial judgement	Managers think about their future workloads and other factors affecting the demand and estimate how many people they need on the basis of judgement and experience. Potential changes in productivity can be factored in.	Simple and quick and makes use of the experience of line managers. An assessment, albeit a qualitative one, can be made of the impact of other factors affecting demand as set out in Exhibit 65.1.	Highly judgemental – the forecasts can be generalized and misleading and may not provide an accurate basis for recruitment planning.
Ratio-trend analysis	Existing ratios between an activity level and the number of employees working on that activity are analysed. The ratio is applied to forecast activity levels to determine an adjusted number of people required. The analysis may be extended to cover employees connected to but not directly involved in the activity, for example indirect workers who support direct workers. The existing ratio of directs to indirects would be applied to the forecast number of directs needed to deal with the new activity levels to determine the number of directs. Potential changes in productivity can be factored in.	Based on factual data about ratios, which can then be linked to quantified estimates of future activity levels. At least gives the appearance of being reasonably scientific.	Relies on forecasts of activity levels that could be little more than inspired guess work. The existing ratios may be related to poor levels of productivity, which the forecast would perpetuate unless real efforts were made to factor in specific productivity improvement plans. Ignores other factors affecting demand because account is only taken of activity levels.
Work study	Work study techniques are used in association with activity level forecasts to calculate how long operations should take and the number of people required.	In the right circumstances, this can produce accurate forecasts.	Limited to situations (eg manufacturing) when work study techniques can be applied.
Choice	Managerial judgement is the easiest although limited option. At least some attempt can be made to allow for the less quantifiable factors that will affect demand. Ratio-trend analysis provides quantified information that could be combined with more qualitative managerial judgements covering the other factors.		

EXHIBIT 65.6 Demand forecast schedule

Occupation	Present number	Forecast numbers required on:			Basis for forecast
		Date:	Date:	Date:	

Demand forecast schedule

A demand forecast schedule, as shown in Exhibit 65.6, shows the forecast number of people requirements for specified occupations based on one of the forecasting methods listed in Exhibit 65.5. An explanation should be made of the basis for the forecast, covering the ratios if ratio-trend analysis is used and the other factors taken into account.

Workforce analysis

Workforce analysis is the first step in assessing the supply of people. It sets out the numbers available in each major occupational group, as in the examples illustrated in Exhibit 65.7.

Employee turnover

The number of existing people as determined by workforce analysis will be eroded by employee turnover (labour attrition or wastage). It is therefore necessary to decide how to measure turnover and then collect and analyse the data before adjusting forecast supply exhibits to take account of wastage. Different methods of measuring wastage are itemized in Exhibit 65.8.

EXHIBIT 65.7 Workforce analysis

Occupational group	Number
Senior managers	
Middle managers	
Junior managers	
Supervisors/team leaders	
Senior professional staff	
Professional staff	
Senior technical staff	
Technical staff	
Senior sales and service staff	
Sales and service staff	
Senior administrative staff	
Administrative staff	
Skilled operatives	
Semi-skilled operatives	
Unskilled operatives	
Senior support and service staff	
Support and service staff	
Drivers	
Others	

EXHIBIT 65.8 Measuring employee turnover

Type of measure	Description	Advantages	Disadvantages
Employee turnover index	$\frac{\text{Number of leavers in a specified period (usually 1 year)}}{\text{Average number of employees during the same period}} \times 100$	Easily understood and applied – most commonly used index.	The percentage may be inflated by the high turnover of a relatively small proportion of the workforce, especially in times of heavy recruitment.
Stability index	$\frac{\text{Number with 1 year's service or more}}{\text{Number employed 1 year ago}} \times 100$	Provides an indication of the tendency for longer-service employees to remain with the company, and therefore shows the degree to which there is continuity of employment.	The index will not reveal the different situations that exist in an organization with a high proportion of long-serving employees in comparison with one where the majority of employees are short service.
Survival rate	The proportion of employees who are engaged within a certain period who remain with the organization after so many months or years of service.	Useful as a means of tracking a cohort of recruits, eg graduates, to assess the effectiveness of recruitment and retention policies.	Cannot be used as a means of measuring the turnover rates of whole populations in order to allow for future wastage as a basis for supply forecasts.
Half-life index	The time taken for a group or cohort of starters to reduce to half its original size through the wastage process.	A simpler form of survival rate. Comparisons can then be made for successive entry years or between different groups of employees to show where action may have to be taken to counter undesirable wastage trends.	As for survival rate.
Leavers' length of service analysis	An analysis is made of the average length of service of leavers. A more refined analysis compares, for designated length of service categories, the numbers leaving with the numbers employed.	An alternative survival rate measure that can be used to assess the effectiveness of recruitment and retention policies.	As for survival rate.

EXHIBIT 65.9 Forecasting the supply of people

Occupation	Present number available	Forecast numbers available on:			Basis for forecast
		Date:	Date:	Date:	

Forecasting internal supply of people

Internal supply forecasting measures the number of people likely to be available from within the organization, having allowed for the output of training programmes, internal movements and promotions, and the impact of employee turnover and changes in hours and other conditions of work. It involves taking the existing numbers in major employment categories (if this is a comprehensive plan), or in the specific categories to be covered by the plan, and adjusting the numbers to take account of losses through employee turnover. Because turnover rates may vary according to the type of occupation, ideally figures for different types would be available. This initial analysis may need to be adjusted to take into account other factors affecting the supply, as listed in Exhibit 65.1. The basis upon which this is done should be explained. A supply forecast schedule is shown in Exhibit 65.9.

Balancing demand and supply

Balancing demand and supply involves taking the demand and supply forecasts and identifying the gaps in the form of deficits or surpluses. This provides the basis for preparing a workforce plan to deal with gaps. A schedule for recording the balance and indicating in headline form the proposed planning actions is shown in Exhibit 65.10.

Action planning

Possible planning actions are defined in Exhibit 65.11 but would, of course, need to be expanded in more detail in the full plan with explanations of the actions required, timescale, responsibilities for the action and the costs and benefits of the proposed action.

EXHIBIT 65.10 Balancing demand and supply

Occupation	Forecast for (date):			Forecast for (date):			Forecast for (date):			Proposed action heading(s)*
	Demand	Supply	Deficit (–) or surplus (+)	Demand	Supply	Deficit (–) or surplus (+)	Demand	Supply	Deficit (–) or surplus (+)	

* Headings:
- Recruitment/procurement plan
- Retention plan
- Learning and development plan
- New methods of working
- Redefining roles
- Productivity plan
- Controlling workforce size

EXHIBIT 65.11 Action planning

Action plan headline	Summary of possible actions
Recruitment/ procurement plan	• Numbers and types of people needed to make up any deficits and when needed. • Likely sources of external recruits. • Proposals for attracting good candidates. • Proposals for dealing with any recruitment problems. • The recruitment programme. • Other sources of people from training programmes or by retraining/reallocation. • Develop talent management programmes.
Retention plan	• Analysis of the factors affecting retention. • Plans for overcoming weaknesses in policies and practices leading to wastage.
Learning and development plan	• New skills required and how they will be developed. • Number of trainees/apprentices required and proposals for recruiting and training them. • Number of existing staff who need training or retraining and the programmes required. • New courses to be developed or changes to be made to existing ones.
New methods of working	• Increase operational flexibility by introducing flexible patterns of work. • Provide more scope for flexible hours. • Review traditional employment patterns. • More outsourcing. • More subcontracting. • Use more temporary and part-time staff and job sharing.
Redefining roles	• Enhance role flexibility. • Encourage multitasking and multiskilling.
Productivity plan	• Improve or streamline methods, procedures and systems. • Deploy more technology, including computers. • Reduce duplication and waste. • Enhance engagement.
Controlling workforce size	If a reduction in numbers is unavoidable (ie if methods mentioned above are insufficient) consider the following options (in order of preference): • Freeze recruitment. • Reduce working hours. • Encourage voluntary redundancy. • As a last resort, use compulsory redundancy.

66 Talent management toolkit

Purpose of the toolkit

Talent management is the process of ensuring that the organization has the talented people it needs to attain its business goals. It involves the management of the flow of talent through an organization by creating and maintaining a talent pipeline, as shown in Chapter 20 (Figure 20.1).

Talent management strategy

A talent management strategy consists of a declaration of intent on how the talent management process of planning, auditing, resourcing, succession planning and development should mesh together to achieve an overall objective – to acquire and nurture talent wherever it is and wherever it is needed by using a number of interdependent policies and practices. The rating framework shown in Exhibit 66.1 can be used to obtain overall views and generate discussion on the strategy.

Talent management policy

Talent management policy can be reviewed by answering the questions set out in Exhibit 66.2.

Talent planning

Talent planning is the process of establishing how many and what sort of talented people are needed now and in the future. The questions set out in Exhibit 66.3 deal with what should be covered.

EXHIBIT 66.1 Rating framework for talent management strategy goals

Objectives	Importance*	Effectiveness*
Reinforce the achievement of organizational goals.		
Identify talented people through performance management and potential assessment processes.		
Recruit and retain talented people.		
Ensure that the talent required is available within the organization.		
Provide for management succession.		
Design jobs and develop roles that give people opportunities to apply and grow their skills and provide them with autonomy, interest and challenge.		
Guide career management.		
Provide talented staff with opportunities for career development and growth.		
Develop leadership and management skills through systematic leadership and management development programmes.		
Recognize those with talent by rewarding excellence, enterprise and achievement.		
Communicate talent management policies to employees.		
Manage programmes effectively.		
Involve experienced line managers in talent management activities.		

* Scale: 10 = high; 1 = low

EXHIBIT 66.2 Talent management policy checklist

Policy question	Answer
What do we mean by talent in this organization?	
What do we mean by talent management in this organization?	
Who should be included in a talent management programme?	
Who should be responsible for talent management?	
To what extent is the policy to make or buy, ie develop internally or recruit from outside?	

EXHIBIT 66.3 Talent planning checklist

Question	Answer
How is talent classified in the organization?	
How many people have we now in each talent category?	
How many people in each category will we need:	In one year's time?
	In two years' time?
	In three years' time?
	In five years' time?
What problems could we have in obtaining the talent required?	
How should we deal with these problems?	

Talent audit

A talent audit identifies those with talent and potential, often through performance management. It provides the basis for career planning and development – ensuring that talented people have the sequence of experience supplemented by coaching and learning programmes that will equip them to carry out more demanding roles in the future. A talent audit checklist is set out in Exhibit 66.4.

EXHIBIT 66.4 Talent audit checklist

Question	Answer
Does a system for assessing talent and potential exist?	
To what extent is the system used properly by line managers?	
How are talented people classified by the system?	
How many people have been assessed in each category?	
Is the number in the higher categories adequate?	
What needs to be done about any problems raised in the answers to the above questions?	

Resourcing talent

Resourcing policies and programmes ensure that the organization gets and keeps the talent it needs. Attraction policies influence programmes for external resourcing. Retention policies are designed to ensure that people continue as engaged and committed members of the organization. Line managers can be asked to carry out separate 'risk analyses' for any key staff in order to assess the likelihood of their leaving, so that steps can be taken to encourage them to stay. The outcome of these policies is a talent flow, which creates and maintains the talent pool. An analysis of the effectiveness of resourcing practices can be made by using the checklist in Exhibit 66.5.

EXHIBIT 66.5 Analysis of effectiveness of resourcing practices

Resourcing aims	Extent to which achieved			Actions required
	Fully	Partly	Not at all	
Identify the talents/skills required.				
Plan and implement recruitment activities and programmes that deliver the talented people required in accordance with make-or-buy policy.				
Develop talented people within the organization in accordance with make-or-buy policy.				
Formulate a retention strategy designed to minimize the loss of talented people.				
Conduct risk analyses of the likelihood of talented people leaving.				
Take action to retain talented people, especially those who are at risk.				
Ensure that the talent pool available is sufficient to satisfy management succession needs.				

Talent development

Learning and development policies and programmes are essential components in the process of talent management – ensuring that people acquire and enhance the skills and competencies they need. Policies should be formulated by reference to 'employee success profiles', which are described in terms of competencies and define the qualities that need to be developed. Employee success profiles can be incorporated in role profiles. A talent development checklist is provided in Exhibit 66.6.

Overall analysis

An overall analysis can be carried out using the questionnaire in Exhibit 66.7 to assess how effectively talent management is being carried out.

EXHIBIT 66.6 Talent development checklist

Question	Answer	Action required
Are there well-established leadership and management development programmes?		
Has the effectiveness of any programmes been evaluated and, if so, what was the result?		
Do development programmes include executive coaching or mentoring? If so, how effective are they?		
Do career planning/management procedures exist that provide to those with promise a sequence of experience and learning activities that will equip them for whatever level of responsibility they have the ability to reach?		
Are those with potential given the opportunity to broaden their experience and develop their skills through lateral moves (job rotation) or special assignments?		

EXHIBIT 66.7 Overall analysis and assessment of talent management practice

	What should be happening	What is happening	What needs to be done?
1.	The strategic management of the flow of talent through an organization is achieved by creating and maintaining a talent pipeline.		
2.	The organization is clear on what is meant by talent in its environment and who the talented people are who will be covered by talent management policies.		
3.	Talent management starts with the business strategy and what it signifies in terms of the talented people required by the organization.		
4.	A well-defined talent pipeline exists, consisting of the processes of resourcing, retention planning, career planning and learning and development (especially leadership and management development) that maintain the flow of talent needed by the organization.		
5.	Talent planning processes are in place that lead to the development of policies for attracting and retaining talent and the determination of future requirements as monitored by talent audits. They also influence the development of the roles that talented people carry out.		
6.	A talent audit process successfully identifies those with potential and provides the basis for career planning and development.		
7.	Talent relationship management activities build effective relationships with people in their roles. They recognize the value of individual employees, provide opportunities for growth, treat them fairly and achieve 'talent engagement', ensuring that people are committed to their work and the organization.		
8.	Performance management processes, including 360-degree feedback, provide a means of building relationships with people, identifying talent and potential, planning learning and development activities and making the most of the talent possessed by the organization.		
9.	'Employee success profiles' are prepared that set out the competencies and qualities required to be classified as having high potential.		
10.	Talented people are provided with the sequence of experience supplemented by coaching, mentoring and learning programmes that will equip them to carry out more demanding roles in the future.		

67 Planning and delivering learning events toolkit

Purpose of the toolkit

Learning events or formal training courses need to be planned and delivered with care. The purpose of this toolkit is to provide a basis for putting the sequence of activities into effect.

Planning learning events

The sequence of activities required is:

1. Establish learning needs.
2. Define objectives.
3. Decide on content and delivery.
4. Decide on arrangements.
5. Distribute information on the event.
6. Deliver the learning.
7. Evaluate.

Establish learning needs

Learning events should be planned to meet well-established and clearly defined learning needs. There are a number of ways of doing this, as listed in Exhibit 67.1, together with an assessment of their advantages and disadvantages. In practice, the methods may be used in combination to provide an overall picture.

Define objectives

It is essential to be clear about what the programme or event is required to achieve – its learning objectives and outcomes. These are defined to satisfy established learning needs and to provide the basis for planning content and evaluating results.

Objectives can be defined as criterion behaviour (the performance standards or changes in behaviour on-the-job to be achieved if a learning process is to be regarded as successful) and terminal behaviour (what actually happened following the learning event). Any gap between criterion and terminal behaviour will indicate deficiencies in the programme. A behavioural objective could be set out as follows.

> At the end of the programme managers will be able to take greater responsibility for the development of their staff. Indicative activities will include:
>
> - the conduct of satisfactory performance and development reviews;
> - the agreement of personal development plans;
> - enabling team members to carry out self-directed learning activities;
> - the ability to use coaching skills to improve performance.

EXHIBIT 67.1 Establishing learning needs

Method	Description	Advantages	Disadvantages
Assumption of need	Needs established on the basis of general assumptions about what people in certain occupations should know and be able to do, for example, managers need to learn about leadership.	The needs can be readily defined, especially if they are related to common requirements such as leadership, teamworking, communicating and business awareness.	No evidence of what the real needs are for particular occupations. The result could be a generalized programme that satisfies no one.
Gap analysis	The gap between what people know and can do and what they should know and be able to do is identified so that the learning needs to fill the gap can be described. Information on the nature of the gap may be obtained by one or more of the methods described below.	Specifies what needs to be learnt so that deficiencies can be remedied by tailored training programmes.	This 'deficiency model' of training – only putting things right that have gone wrong – is limited. Learning is much more positive than that. It should be concerned with identifying and satisfying development needs – fitting people to take on extra responsibilities or acquire new skills.
Analysis of business and HR plans	Business and HR plans are analysed to indicate in general terms the types of skills and competencies that may be required in the future and the numbers of people with those skills and competencies who will be needed.	Ensures that learning plans and events are rooted firmly in business needs, thus ensuring that they are business-driven. For example, a business model innovation programme may indicate what new skills will be required.	May be too generalized. Leaning events need to be planned to meet specific learning needs. It is not enough for them just to aim to further the business. It is *how* they will do this that matters.
Surveys	Surveys can obtain the views of managers and other employees about what needs to be learnt.	Provide factual information on learning needs as perceived by people in the front line.	The material gathered form a survey may be unspecific and when interviewed people often find it difficult to articulate learning needs.
Performance and development reviews	Assessments are made of development needs and the extent to which the individual meets role requirements. This identifies what sort of development programme is required and what needs to be done to remedy any deficiencies. An overall analysis of performance and development review reports can reveal any common learning needs, which can be satisfied by tailored learning events.		

EXHIBIT 67.1 Continued

Method	Description	Advantages	Disadvantages
Role analysis	Role analysis is the basis for preparing role profiles, which provide a framework for analysing and identifying learning needs. Role profiles define the competencies required to perform the role. This can be used to assess and agree the level of competency displayed and, where necessary, what needs to be done to improve it.	A good method of assessing individual learning needs, which can generate information on common learning needs. This can be related to the organization's competency framework and used to inform the design of competency-based learning events.	The analysis can be time-consuming. It may not always be easy to obtain reliable information.
Skills analysis	Determines the skills required to achieve an acceptable standard of performance. It is mainly used for technical, craft, manual and office jobs to provide the basis for devising learning and training programmes.	If carried out properly it can provide a comprehensive and accurate basis for planned and systematic training.	Needs considerable expertise to be done properly.

Decide on content and delivery

A checklist of the points to be considered when deciding on the overall content of the event, the content of individual sessions and methods of delivery is set out in Exhibit 67.2.

Decide on arrangements

A checklist on points to consider when arranging the event is set out in Exhibit 67.3.

Distribute information on the event

Information in the form of notices, programmes and brochures are distributed to those who are likely to nominate participants for the event. The information should make it clear who should attend and why they should attend, ie the benefits to them and the organization.

Deliver the learning

This should not present too many problems if the planning and preparation for the event have been carried out systematically. However, a flexible approach is desirable because all learning events differ according to the characteristics of the learners, whose learning needs and reactions will vary. Fine tuning will be necessary throughout the programme.

Evaluate

Evaluation can take the form of an immediate assessment of the reactions of participants by getting them to complete an evaluation form (a 'happy sheet'), as illustrated in Exhibit 67.4. A more searching evaluation can be carried out by adding the other three Kirkpatrick levels (see Chapter 23) to the first 'reactions' level and also summing up the extent to which the event met expectations (Exhibit 67.5). A final overall evaluation can be made using the checklist set out in Exhibit 67.6.

EXHIBIT 67.2 Planning learning events checklist

Question	Answer
What are the overall learning objectives of the event?	
How long should the event be? How many sessions per day and what are the specific learning objectives and contents of each session? It is usual for a lecture session to last a maximum of 60 minutes, allowing 30–40 minutes for the presentation (never any more) and time for discussion. A normal day could have three such sessions in the morning and two to three in the afternoon. There is a limit to how much people can absorb in a day and it is often best to have exercises or discussions sessions in the afternoon, especially after lunch (the graveyard shift).	
What are the key learning points in each session?	
How could these be converted into action points?	
What is it expected that participants will do that they could not do at all or very well before they attended the programme?	
What will be done to ensure that the learning is cumulative by building sessions on each other to emphasize that they are related and that each one contributes to achieving the overall learning objectives of the programme?	
What is the policy on the delivery of learning, eg the amount devoted to discussions and exercises rather than lectures? (the more of the former the better)	
What steps will be taken to ensure that learning is transferred to the workplace?	
How will learning be linked to the context of those attending the event?	
How will the specific learning needs of individuals attending the programme be identified and met?	
What learning activities and exercises will be incorporated in the programme to extend and reinforce learning and ensure that active learning takes place?	
Is it certain that participants will be able to absorb and use the volume of material included in the programme?	

EXHIBIT 67.2 Continued

Question	Answer
How will participants be encouraged to put what they have learned into practice?	
How will the interest of participants be maintained throughout the programme?	
How will learning be checked and the pace adjusted to ensure progressive learning?	
How will visual aids be used to support learning?	
What will be done to brief speakers on content, length (no more than 30–40 minutes) and use of visual aids (no more than 15 PowerPoint slides each with no more than six bullet points of six words and simple diagrams).	
What material should participants take away with them after the event?	
How will the immediate reactions of participants be obtained?	
How will the impact of the programme after the event be evaluated?	

EXHIBIT 67.3 Event arrangements checklist

Question	Answer
Who is running the event – in-house or outsourced?	
How many people will be attending?	
Where will the event be held – in-house or at an external location?	
What rooms will be required? For example, a main conference or lecture rooms and smaller (syndicate) rooms for 'breaking out sessions' (groups of participants breaking out from the main session to conduct an exercise or hold a discussion).	
What facilities will be required? For example, projectors, flip charts or any other equipment to be used for training purposes.	
Will there be a technician available to facilitate the use of projectors for PowerPoint presentations?	
What arrangements need to be made for eating (lunch) and refreshments (tea and coffee)?	
What is the budget for the event?	
What is the estimated expenditure?	
Who is to direct or chair the event?	
Who are the speakers/trainers?	
Who will invite them?	
Have the chair and the speakers/trainers been briefed?	
What advance information on the event (notice, programme or brochure) needs to be prepared?	
What material to be used in the event (handouts, discussion or exercise briefs or case studies) needs to be prepared in advance?	

EXHIBIT 67.4 Learning event evaluation form

LEARNING EVENT EVALUATION FORM

Name of event...

Date...

Evaluation of sessions

For each session assess on a scale of 1 to 5 (1 = poor, 5 = excellent):

- the content of the session – how interesting, how useful
- how well the session was presented
- the quality of the visual aids

Session	Rating			Comments
	Content	Presentation	Visual aids	
1				
2				
3				
4				
5				
6				

Evaluation of arrangements

	Rating – 1 to 5	Comments
Joining instructions		
Food and refreshments		
Accommodation		

Overall evaluation of the event

How would you rate the overall value of the event on a scale of 1 to 5?	Comments (please give reasons for your evaluation)

EXHIBIT 67.5 Evaluation levels and return on expectations assessment

Level or type of evaluation	Evaluation
Level 1: Reactions – how those who participated in the training have reacted to it. In a sense, it is a measure of immediate customer satisfaction.	
Level 2: Learning – this level obtains information on the extent to which learning objectives have been attained. It will aim to find how much knowledge was acquired, what skills were developed or improved, and the extent to which attitudes have changed in the desired direction.	
Level 3: Behaviour – this level evaluates the extent to which behaviour has changed as required when people attending the programme have returned to their jobs.	
Level 4: Results – this is the ultimate level of evaluation and provides the basis for assessing the benefits of the training against its costs. The objective is to determine the added value of learning and development programmes – how they contribute to raising organizational performance significantly above its previous level.	
Return on expectation – this is the extent to which the anticipated benefits of any learning investment have been realized. This starts with a definition of expectations – a statement of what the learning event is aiming to achieve at the individual, departmental and, importantly, the organizational level. This would also involve deciding how achievement will be measured – the success criteria. These criteria would be used as the basis for evaluation.	

EXHIBIT 67.6 Overall evaluation of a training event

Questions – to what extent have/are:	Answers
Learning needs been evaluated as a basis for the event?	
Clear objectives been set for the outcomes of the event or programme?	
Success criteria and methods of measuring success been established?	
A blend of learning methods been used that are appropriate for the established needs of those taking part?	
The responsibilities for planning and delivering the event been clarified?	
Those responsible for the learning activity well-qualified in whatever role they are expected to play?	
Adequate resources been allocated to the event?	
Arrangements ensured that the event was implemented effectively as planned, within its budget and in accordance with defined standards?	
Arrangements been made to monitor the planning and delivery of the event to ensure that it meets the defined objectives and standards?	
The achievements of the event been evaluated against the success criteria and swift corrective action taken to deal with any problems?	

68 Performance management toolkit

Purpose of the toolkit

The purpose of this toolkit is to provide practical guidance to those who want to review existing performance management systems and processes or to develop and implement new ones. The toolkit can be used by line managers as a guide to their performance management practices. It can also be the basis for developing understanding and skills through coaching, mentoring, formal training and e-learning.

Structure of the toolkit

The toolkit is divided into the five sections described below and illustrated in Figure 68.1:

1. The analytical and diagnostic toolkit covers the analysis of present arrangements and the diagnosis of the causes of any problems. It provides the basis for the design or modification of a performance management system.
2. The design toolkit covers the development of the constituents of a performance management system – performance planning and agreements, goal setting, feedback, performance analysis and assessment, rating, coaching, and the link to reward and personal development.
3. The implementation toolkit covers the processes of communicating, briefing, training and pilot testing, which must be carried out to ensure the successful operation of performance management.
4. The operations toolkit covers the main performance management activities of completing performance agreements, goal setting, performance review, managing managerial performance and dealing with underperformers.
5. The evaluation toolkit covers methods of evaluating the effectiveness of performance management through checklists and surveys.

Analysis and diagnosis

It is necessary to analyse and understand the strengths and weaknesses of the present arrangements. As far as possible the analysis and diagnosis should involve line managers and employees through surveys, workshops and focus groups, using the checklists in Exhibits 68.1 to 68.3.

Performance management goals

Possible goals for performance management are set out in Exhibit 68.1.

FIGURE 68.1 The performance management design, development, implementation and maintenance pathway

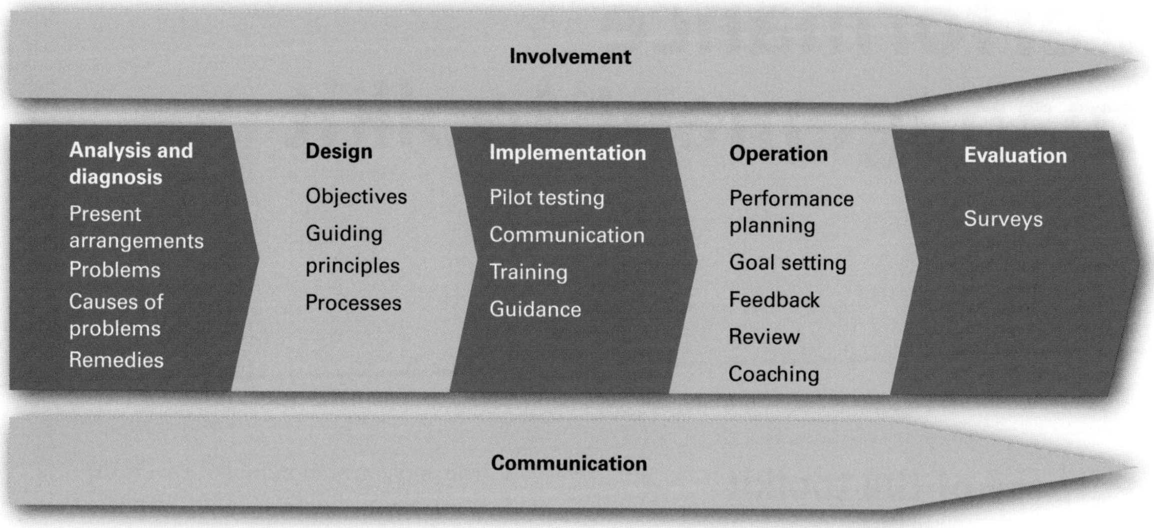

EXHIBIT 68.1 Performance management goals

Possible goals	Importance	Effectiveness
Align individual and organizational objectives		
Improve organizational performance		
Develop a high performance culture		
Improve individual performance		
Provide basis for personal development		
Increase motivation and engagement		
Inform contribution/performance pay decisions		
Measure performance against quantified objectives		
Encourage appropriate behaviours – 'living the values'		
Clarify performance expectations in the role		
Identify potential		
Identify poor performers		

Scale: 10 = high, 1 = low

Performance management gap analysis

The gap analysis shown in Exhibit 68.2 assesses the extent to which desirable characteristics of performance management exist in the organization. It provides the basis for the design and development of performance management systems and processes.

Start gap analysis with senior management, line managers and staff by getting them to complete the grid individually or in groups, by marking with an X the position in which they think the organization is at present and an O where it is believed the organization should be placed. A gap between X and O – between what is and what should be – reveals areas for development. The next step is to get those involved to discuss and agree priorities.

EXHIBIT 68.2 Performance management gap analysis

Desirable characteristics	*X = current situation*				*Undesirable characteristics*
Performance management is perceived by top management as a key process for managing the business					Top management plays lip service to performance management
Line managers are committed to performance management					Line managers see performance management as a waste of time
Line managers have the skills to manage performance effectively					There are serious deficiencies in line managers' skills
Employees believe that performance management operates fairly					Employees do not trust their line managers to review their performance fairly
There is hard evidence that performance management improves business performance					There is no evidence that performance management improves business performance
Performance management is based on agreed definitions of roles in terms of key result areas and competency requirements					Performance management is not related to the reality of what people are expected to do and how they are expected to perform
Clear objectives and performance standards are agreed at the planning stage					Objectives and standards, if agreed at all, are vague or undemanding
Methods of measuring performance and assessing levels of competence are agreed at the performance planning stage					Little or no attempt is made to agree performance or competency indicators
Performance development plans are agreed at the planning stage					Performance development planning is generally neglected
Performance management in the form of review and feedback is practised throughout the year					Performance appraisal takes place, if at all, as a dishonest annual ritual
Line managers provide helpful feedback and support during formal reviews					The quality of feedback and support is generally inadequate
Line managers recognize their responsibility for coaching people and act accordingly					Coaching by line managers is sparse and often inadequate

Analysis of performance review practices

The checklist in Exhibit 68.3 can be used to analyse performance review practices.

EXHIBIT 68.3 Analysis of performance review practices

Review practice	Fully in place	Partly in place	Not in place	Action
1. The content of the performance review is based on a role profile.				
2. Performance expectations are agreed with employees.				
3. Performance objectives are aligned with business goals.				
4. The review is based on evidence in the form of observable job behaviours.				
5. The review process is clearly defined for everyone involved.				
6. Employees participate fully in the review process.				
7. Reviewers are capable of making fair and consistent assessments.				
8. The review focuses on development and improvement needs.				
9. A higher authority checks and comments on reviews.				
10. Reviewers are trained in feedback and assessment techniques.				

Diagnosis

Following the analysis of any problems, their causes and possible remedies should be identified. Exhibit 68.4 shows how they can be summarized.

EXHIBIT 68.4 Diagnostic summary

List any significant problems identified by the analysis and indicate the likely causes of the problems and their possible remedies.

Problem	Likely cause	Possible remedy

Design toolkit

The design should be based on the initial analysis and diagnosis and should involve stakeholders, ie senior management, line managers, employees and their representatives. It is advisable to build on existing practices in order to promote acceptance and assimilation. The steps in the design programme are illustrated in Figure 68.2.

FIGURE 68.2 Steps in the design programme

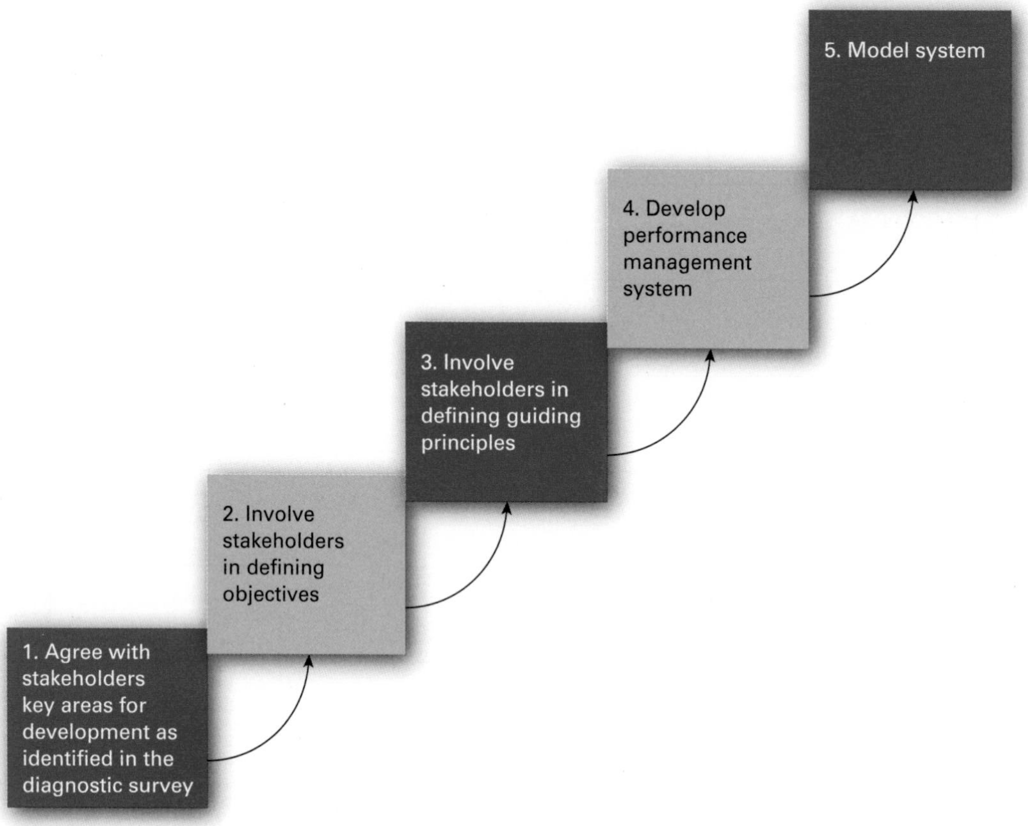

Areas for development

The areas for development will have been identified if a diagnostic survey has been undertaken. They can be summarized under the headings shown in Exhibit 68.5.

EXHIBIT 68.5 Areas for development

Area	What needs to be done	How it can be done
Performance planning and agreement		
Goal setting		
Providing feedback		
Conducting performance reviews		
Assessment and rating		
Coaching		
Documentation		
Use of computers		
Increasing the commitment of line managers to performance management		
Developing performance management skills of line managers		
Educating employees generally on the purpose of performance management, how it works, how it affects them and what part they play		

Analysis of possible objectives and success criteria

It is essential that everyone involved is clear about the objectives of performance management and the criteria that will be used to evaluate the extent to which the objectives have been successfully achieved. Managers and employees should be involved in setting objectives and success criteria. They should consider not only what performance management will do for the organization but also what they hope it will do for them. It is advisable, however, not to try to attempt too much, especially when this is a new development. Some prioritization of objectives may therefore be required. A framework for analysis is given in Exhibit 68.6.

EXHIBIT 68.6 Analysis of possible objectives

Possible objectives	For the organization	For line managers	For employees	Possible success criteria
	Rate the possible objective on a scale of 1–5 where: 1 = crucial, 2 = important, 3 = not sure, 4 = not very important, 5 = irrelevant			
Improve performance	1 2 3 4 5	1 2 3 4 5	1 2 3 4 5	
Develop a performance culture	1 2 3 4 5	1 2 3 4 5	1 2 3 4 5	
Identify people with high potential	1 2 3 4 5	1 2 3 4 5	1 2 3 4 5	
Identify under-performers	1 2 3 4 5	1 2 3 4 5	1 2 3 4 5	
Align individual and organizational objectives	1 2 3 4 5	1 2 3 4 5	1 2 3 4 5	
Provide the basis for personal development	1 2 3 4 5	1 2 3 4 5	1 2 3 4 5	
Enable people to know where they stand	1 2 3 4 5	1 2 3 4 5	1 2 3 4 5	
Provide the basis for performance pay decisions	1 2 3 4 5	1 2 3 4 5	1 2 3 4 5	
Other	1 2 3 4 5	1 2 3 4 5	1 2 3 4 5	

Development of a performance management system

The development of a performance management system involves selecting and describing the components of the system; see Exhibit 68.7.

EXHIBIT 68.7 Analysis of the components of the performance management system

Component	Contents	Considerations
Performance planning and agreement	• Agreeing role profiles • Agreeing objectives (see also goal setting) • Agreeing performance measures • Agreeing development needs (see also personal development planning) • Agreeing areas for performance improvement • Recording decisions in an agreement	• Format of role profiles • Methods of preparing and updating role profiles • Choice of measures • Format of agreement
Goal setting	• Identifying key result areas • Identifying key performance indicators • Agreeing targets and standards of performance	• Methods of goal setting • Ensuring 'SMART' goals are agreed • Selecting appropriate measures
Personal development planning	• Deciding areas for development • Planning methods of development	• Format of development plan • Approaches to development • Emphasis on self-directed development
Feedback	• Provision during year • Provision during formal review	• Developing feedback skills • Use of informal and formal feedback
Performance reviews	• Purpose • Content • Timing	• Use of informal reviews throughout year • Preparation for formal reviews • Conduct of formal reviews
Performance analysis	• Methodology • Use of metrics	• Performance analysis skills • Data collection and analysis
Performance assessment and rating	• Use of overall assessment • Use of rating • Use of forced distribution rating	• Provision of guidelines for overall assessments • Arguments for and against rating • Decisions on type of rating to be used, if at all • Developing assessment/rating skills • Providing rating guidelines, if appropriate • Arguments for and against forced distribution
Link to performance pay	• How assessment/ratings will inform performance pay decisions • The timing of pay reviews and performance reviews	• Arguments for and against performance pay
Coaching	• Methods • Responsibility of line managers for	• Developing coaching skills
Administration	• Documentation • Use of computers	• Design of documentation • Design of computer system • Decision on extent to which a standard approach to performance management should be used

Implementation toolkit

The implementation programme, as illustrated in Figure 68.3, should start with a pilot test of the performance management process and approaches to communication and training that can inform full communication and training programmes and, subject to any modifications required, the launch of the system.

FIGURE 68.3 Implementation programme

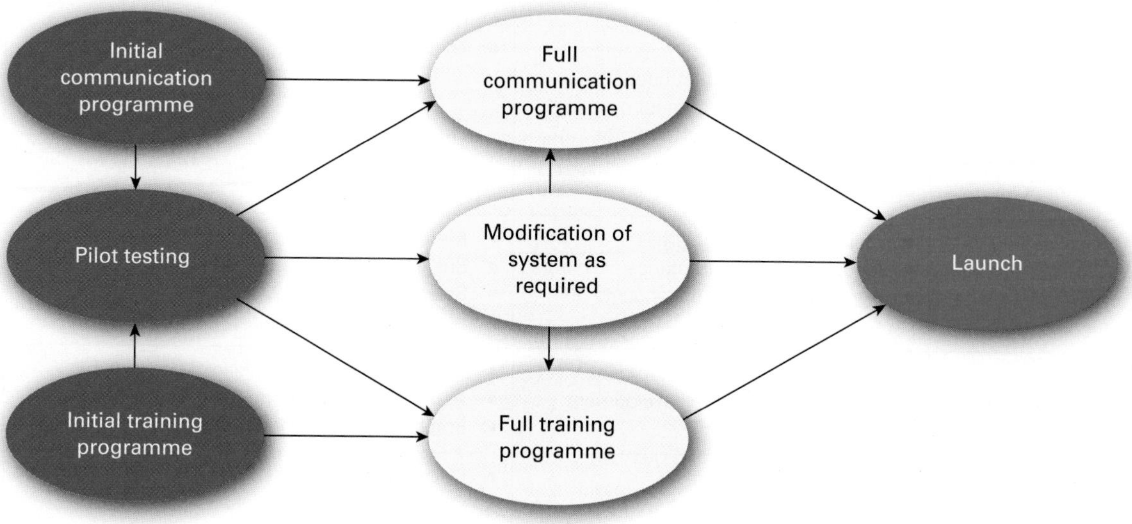

Pilot testing

Before embarking on full implementation it is essential to pilot test the process. This should be done in two or three departments where the managers are sympathetic to performance management and will therefore give it their backing. The test should be preceded by a briefing and training for participants in the processes and skills they should use. Ideally, it should extend over the whole of the performance management cycle, ie 12 months, but a period of between 6 and 12 months will provide an adequate test. The purpose of the test, which should be explained to those taking part, is to ensure that an appropriate and acceptable form of performance management is introduced. Another way of testing is to do it top-down – get senior managers to try it out first so that they know all the wrinkles before cascading it throughout the organization.

The rating questionnaires shown in Exhibits 68.8 and 68.9 can be used to evaluate the test.

EXHIBIT 68.8 Pilot test questionnaire for managers

Rate the following statements on a scale of 1–5 where: 1 = fully agree, 2 = agree, 3 = not sure, 4 = disagree, 5 = strongly disagree	
1. The objectives and processes of performance management were described clearly to me.	1 2 3 4 5
2. I received good training in performance management skills.	1 2 3 4 5
3. I had no difficulty in agreeing role profiles.	1 2 3 4 5
4. I had no difficulty in agreeing objectives.	1 2 3 4 5
5. I had no difficulty in agreeing performance and development plans.	1 2 3 4 5
6. I was able to monitor performance well, providing feedback and coaching as required.	1 2 3 4 5
7. The performance review meeting went very well.	1 2 3 4 5
8. I was able to assess performance accurately and fairly.	1 2 3 4 5
9. I believe that performance management will enable me to do my job better as a manager.	1 2 3 4 5
10. I believe that performance management is a waste of time.	1 2 3 4 5

EXHIBIT 68.9 Pilot test questionnaire for employees

Rate the following statements on a scale of 1–5 where: 1 = fully agree, 2 = agree, 3 = not sure, 4 = disagree, 5 = strongly disagree	
1. The objectives and processes of performance management were described clearly to me.	1 2 3 4 5
2. I received good training in performance management skills.	1 2 3 4 5
3. I had no difficulty in agreeing role profiles.	1 2 3 4 5
4. I had no difficulty in agreeing objectives.	1 2 3 4 5
5. I had no difficulty in agreeing performance and development plans.	1 2 3 4 5
6. I was able to monitor performance well, providing feedback and coaching as required.	1 2 3 4 5
7. The performance review meeting went very well.	1 2 3 4 5
8. I was able to assess performance accurately and fairly.	1 2 3 4 5
9. I believe that performance management will enable me to do my job better as a manager.	1 2 3 4 5
10. I believe that performance management is a waste of time.	1 2 3 4 5

Performance management operations toolkit

The operations toolkit is concerned with the major performance management process of agreeing performance and development plans, goal setting, providing feedback, preparing for and conducting performance reviews, coaching and dealing with underperformers. A summary of performance management activities over the year is given in Exhibit 68.10.

EXHIBIT 68.10 Summary of performance management activities over the year

Start of year ↓	Performance and development agreement	• Define role profiles, updating as necessary. • Ensure that role profiles set out updated key result areas and competency requirements. • Define goals and standards of performance. • Identify and define key performance indicators. • Draw up performance development plans. • Draw up personal development plans.
Continuing dialogue	Managing performance throughout the year	• Monitor progress and review evidence of achievement. • Provide informal feedback as required. • Provide coaching as required. • Update role profiles and objectives as necessary.
End of year	Performance review	• Prepare for performance review by analysing achievements (work and learning) against objectives. • Identify specific strengths and weaknesses on the basis of evidence. • Assess overall performance. • Provide feedback. • Use conclusions of performance review as the basis for next year's performance and development agreement.

The evaluation toolkit

It is essential to evaluate the effectiveness of performance management in meeting its objectives.

Evaluation against success criteria

The performance management activities need to be evaluated against success criteria, as shown in Exhibit 68.11. Unless such evaluation takes place regularly and leads to any remedial action required, the system is likely to decline.

EXHIBIT 68.11 Evaluation of performance management against success criteria

Evaluate effectiveness as follows: 1 = high level of achievement, 2 = acceptable level of achievement, 3 = poor level of achievement	
Measures of improved performance by reference to key performance indicators in such terms as output, productivity, sales, quality, customer satisfaction, return on investment.	1 2 3
Achievement of defined and agreed objectives for performance management.	1 2 3
Measures of employee engagement before and after the introduction of performance management and then at regular intervals.	1 2 3
Assessments of reactions of managers and employees to performance management.	1 2 3
Assessment of the extent to which managers and employees have reached agreement on goals and performance development plans.	1 2 3
Performance development plans agreed and implemented.	1 2 3
Personal development plans agreed and implemented.	1 2 3

69 Strategic reward toolkit

Purpose of the toolkit

Strategic reward means using a systematic approach to ensuring that reward policy and practice support the achievement of business goals and provide fair and equitable pay for employees. This is achieved by analysing the context and needs, assessing the alternatives available, and developing and implementing reward strategies. This toolkit aims to provide the framework and means for making such an approach.

The reward strategy development framework

A framework for developing reward strategy is shown in Figure 69.1.

FIGURE 69.1 The reward strategy development framework

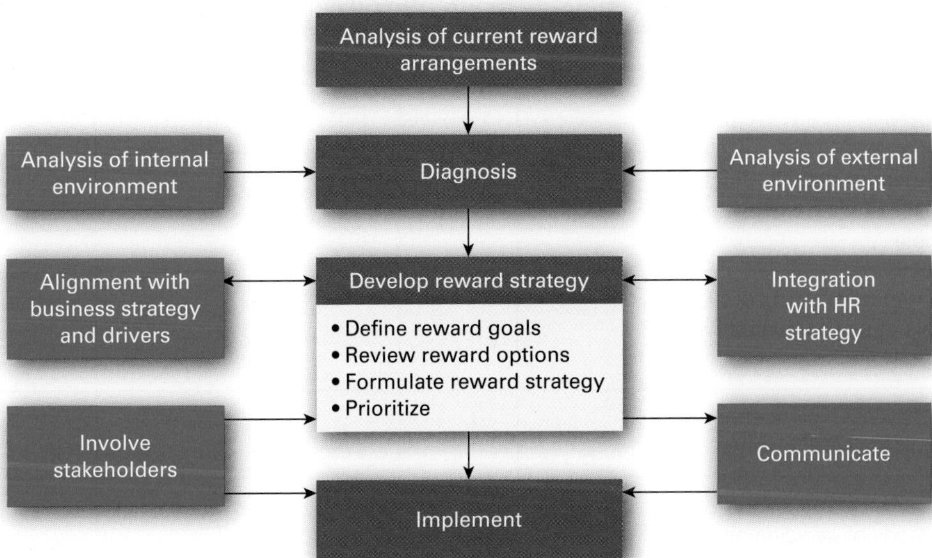

Analysis of reward strategy and practice

The analysis of current reward strategy and practice is the starting point. It can be conducted using the following tools:

- Exhibit 69.1: Analysis of reward strategy
- Exhibit 69.2: Analysis of current reward practices
- Exhibit 69.3: Reward attitude survey

EXHIBIT 69.1 Analysis of reward strategy

The reward strategy:	In full	Mostly	Partly	Not at all
Is aligned to business strategy.				
Has clearly defined goals based on business objectives.				
Well-articulated guiding principles exist.				
Provides a framework for reward decisions.				
Is long term.				
Is flexible enough to change when circumstances require.				

EXHIBIT 69.2 Analysis of current reward practices

Statement	Fully agree	Partly agree	Partly disagree	Fully disagree	Comments
1. We have well-defined and understood reward guiding principles.					
2. Our reward system effectively enhances the engagement of people.					
3. We implement our policy on levels of pay compared with market rates.					
4. We pay insufficient attention to non-financial rewards.					
5. We are satisfied with our methods of deciding on internal relativities.					

EXHIBIT 69.2 *Continued*

Statement	Fully agree	Partly agree	Partly disagree	Fully disagree	Comments
6. There is an unacceptable incidence of grade drift (unjustified upgradings).					
7. We are vulnerable to an equal pay claim.					
8. Our rates of pay are uncompetitive.					
9. We do not have adequate data on market rates.					
10. We have too many grades in our pay structure.					
11. Our grade structure is too complex.					
12. People are fairly rewarded according to their contribution.					
13. Our reward system does not succeed in motivating people.					
14. Our reward system helps to attract and retain high-quality people.					
15. We get value for money from our reward system.					
16. Our performance management processes work well.					
17. We have an excellent and competitive range of employee benefits.					
18. There is room for more choice by employees on benefits.					
19. We spend too much on employee benefits.					
20. Our pension scheme is too expensive.					

EXHIBIT 69.3 Reward attitude survey

Please state the extent to which you agree or disagree with the following statements by placing a circle around the number that most closely matches your opinion.

	Strongly agree	Agree	Disagree	Strongly disagree
1. My contribution is adequately rewarded.	1	2	3	4
2. Pay increases are handled fairly.	1	2	3	4
3. I feel that my pay does not reflect my performance.	1	2	3	4
4. My pay compares favourably with what I could get elsewhere.	1	2	3	4
5. I am not paid fairly in comparison with other people doing similar work in the organization.	1	2	3	4
6. I think the organization's pay policy is overdue for a review.	1	2	3	4
7. Grading decisions are made fairly.	1	2	3	4
8. I am not clear how decisions about my pay are made.	1	2	3	4
9. I understand how my job has been graded.	1	2	3	4
10. I get good feedback on my performance.	1	2	3	4
11. I am clear about what I am expected to achieve.	1	2	3	4
12. I like my job.	1	2	3	4
13. The performance pay scheme encourages better performance.	1	2	3	4
14. I am proud to work for the organization.	1	2	3	4
15. I understand how my pay can progress.	1	2	3	4
16. The job evaluation scheme works fairly.	1	2	3	4
17. The benefits package compares well with those in other organizations.	1	2	3	4
18. I would like more choice about the benefits I receive.	1	2	3	4
19. I feel motivated after my performance review meeting.	1	2	3	4
20. I do not understand the pay policies of the organization.	1	2	3	4

Developing and implementing reward strategy

The formulation of reward strategy can be described as a process for developing a sense of direction and making the best use of resources. The steps required to develop it are:

1. Ensure that the reward strategy supports the achievement of the business and HR strategies by considering the implications of the business strategy and how integration can be achieved (Exhibits 69.4 and 69.5).
2. Define reward goals (Exhibit 69.6).
3. Review reward options in relation to reward goals and practicality (Exhibit 69.7).
4. Formulate strategy with reference to guidelines (Exhibit 69.8).
5. Implement (Exhibit 69.9).

EXHIBIT 69.4 Implications for reward of business strategy

	Possible elements	Actual elements	Implications for reward strategy
Business strategy	• Growth – revenue/profit • Maximize shareholder value • Growth through acquisitions/mergers • Growth in production/servicing facilities • Product development • Market development • Price/cost leadership		
Business drivers	• Innovation • Maximize added value • Productivity • Customer service • Quality • Satisfy stakeholders – investors, employees, elected representatives • Price/cost leadership		

EXHIBIT 69.5 Integration of HR and reward strategies

HR strategy area	Possible reward strategy contribution	Proposed action
Resourcing	• Total reward approaches that help to make the organization a great place in which to work. • Competitive pay structures that help to attract and retain high-quality people.	
Performance management	• Contingent pay schemes that contribute to the motivation and engagement of people. • Performance management processes that promote continuous improvement and encourage people to uphold core values.	
Talent management	• Non-financial rewards such as recognition and opportunities for growth and development. • Policies that recognize talented people for their contribution. • Career-linked grade and pay structure, for example a career family structure.	
Learning and development	• Performance management processes that identify learning needs and how they can be satisfied. • Career family structures that define career ladders in terms of knowledge and skill requirements.	
Work environment	• Total reward approaches that emphasize the importance of enhancing the work environment. • Work–life balance policies.	

EXHIBIT 69.6 Rating framework for reward strategy goals

Goals	Importance*	Effectiveness*
Reinforce the achievement of organizational goals.		
Recruit and retain staff of the required calibre.		
Facilitate staff mobility.		
Strong relationship between pay and performance.		
Reinforce organizational values.		
Motivating for employees.		
Cost-effective.		
Well communicated and understood by employees.		
Managed effectively in practice by line managers.		
Efficient to operate/maintain.		
Flexible, to react to change.		
Others (list).		

* Scale: 10 = high; 1 = low

EXHIBIT 69.7 Review reward options in relation to reward goals and practicality

Strategy area		Examples of possible solutions	Yes √	No √	Modify
Financial	Total reward	Introduce total reward approach			
	Job evaluation	Develop new analytical scheme			
		Develop new non-analytical scheme			
		Modify existing scheme			
		Rely on analytical matching			
	Grade and pay structure	Reduce number of grades considerably (broad-grading)			
		Introduce broad-banding			
		Develop job or career family structure			
		Replace pay spine			
	Contingent pay	Introduce performance-related pay (not pay spine)			
		Introduce contribution-related pay (not pay spine)			
		Introduce variable pay (bonus) scheme			
	Employee benefits	Revise benefits provision			
		Introduce flexible benefits			
	Pensions	Change to defined contribution scheme			
Non-financial	Recognition	Introduce formal recognition scheme			
	Scope for development and growth	Improve learning and development programmes			
	Autonomy	Encourage, guide and train line managers to increase autonomy			
	Working environment	Develop 'great place to work' policies			
	Work–life balance	Introduce more comprehensive work–life balance policies			

EXHIBIT 69.8 Guidelines for formulating reward strategies

To what extent does the reward strategy:	Answer
Support the business strategy?	
Support the HR strategy?	
Have clearly defined goals, success criteria and deliverables?	
Provide a clear basis for future action?	
Demonstrate that it can readily be implemented?	

EXHIBIT 69.9 Implementation checklist

Have you:

- Specified the objectives of the project, its success criteria and its deliverables?
- Defined who is to be responsible for directing and managing the project and the degree of authority they have?
- Set out what should be done (activities), who does what, and when it will be done?
- Involved senior managers/heads of department as sponsors, to provide comment, guidance, support and encouragement?
- Involved line managers and staff in the strategy development, planning and implementation programme?
- Communicated to all concerned the objectives of the programme, how it will take place and how they will be affected?
- Broken down the project into stages with defined starting and completion dates to produce the programme?
- Clarified inter-dependencies?
- Defined resource requirements – people, outside advisers, finance?
- Defined methods of control and risk management, eg progress reports, meetings?
- Ensured that everyone knows what is expected of them and has the briefing, guidance and resources required?
- Seen that progress is monitored continuously against the plan as well as at formal meetings?
- Ensured that corrective action is taken as required; for example, amending timings, reallocating resources?
- Evaluated progress and the end result against objectives, success criteria and deliverables?

70 Total rewards toolkit

Purpose of the toolkit

Total rewards is an approach to reward management that emphasizes the need to consider all aspects of the work experience of value to employees, not just a few such as pay and employee benefits. It aims to blend the financial and non-financial elements of reward into a cohesive whole.

The purpose of the toolkit is to describe how the abstract but compelling concept of total reward can be put into effect. This is not easy. It is not just a matter of introducing a recognition scheme in addition to conventional merit pay systems. And it means going beyond simply tacking on to existing pay and employee benefit practices a number of established HR policies and processes – learning and development, job design, employee well-being and the like. What it should involve – and what this toolkit describes – is ensuring that a cohesive approach is made to integrating the various approaches that are available to increase engagement.

Introducing total rewards

The steps required to introduce total rewards are set out in Figure 70.1. These steps are described below.

FIGURE 70.1 Introducing total rewards

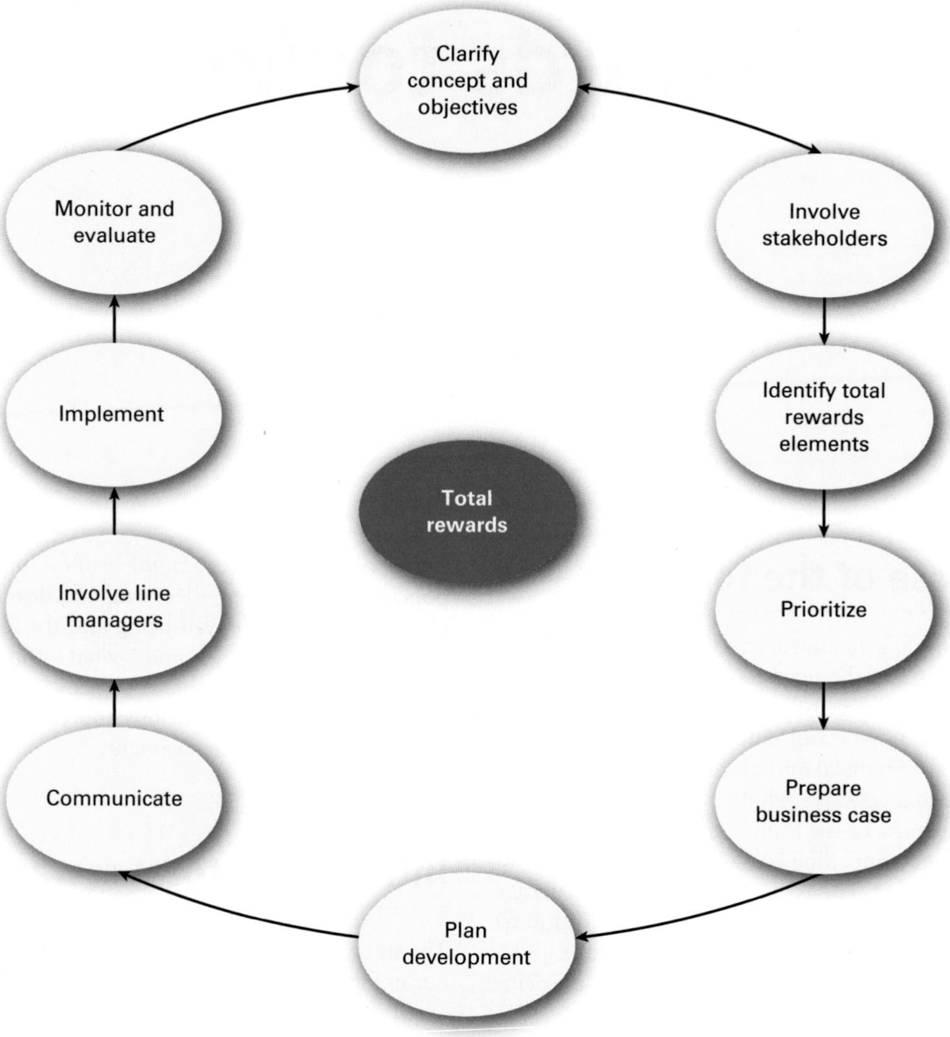

Clarify the concept and objectives of total rewards

A programme for developing total rewards should start with a clarification of the meaning of the concept and its purposes in which stakeholders (senior management, line managers, employees and their representatives) should be involved. Statements of meaning and purpose provide the basis for further discussions with stakeholders, decisions on the elements of a total rewards programme and the preparation of a business case.

It is useful to generate discussions with management and employees about the meaning and purpose of total rewards before considering how the concept might be developed in detail. A forced choice questionnaire can be used, as set out in Exhibit 70.1.

EXHIBIT 70.1 Total rewards forced choice questionnaire

Which of the following statements best describes the concept of total rewards?

a) A combination of base pay and performance pay.

b) A combination of financial and non-financial rewards.

c) A combination of base pay, performance pay and employee benefits.

d) A combination of performance pay and a recognition scheme.

The concept of total reward is:

a) about issuing statements to employees setting out the total value of the pay and benefits they receive;

b) synonymous with the concept of total remuneration;

c) about ensuring that the provision of rewards takes account of all the factors that affect engagement and motivation;

d) about ensuring that individuals are rewarded for their total contribution.

The concept of total rewards provides:

a) a way of thinking about reward strategy;

b) a means of achieving the integration of different financial reward practices;

c) a means of ensuring that all aspects of reward are catered for;

d) a method of conducting base pay management.

The purpose of a total rewards approach is to:

a) ensure that value for money is obtained from the organization's reward practices;

b) contribute to winning the full engagement of employees;

c) help in the design of efficient reward systems;

d) ensure that employees fully understand and appreciate the reward opportunities available to them.

A total rewards approach will:

a) provide the flexibility required to cater for the fact that individuals have different wants and needs that affect their engagement and motivation;

b) ensure that attention is given to the introduction of a recognition scheme;

c) achieve a proper balance between financial and non-financial rewards;

d) guarantee that employees will be more highly motivated.

Identify total reward elements

Basic approach

In its basic form, a total rewards approach means simply getting the financial reward elements right and consciously doing whatever is possible progressively to enhance the elements in the form of various HR practices that contribute to non-financial rewards.

Choice of elements

The core of any total rewards model will be pay and benefits but there is a choice on what other non-financial elements should be included. An analysis of the non-financial elements contained in the various models listed earlier shows that there are plenty to choose from. The choice is made more difficult because while some elements such as recognition, performance management, work–life balance and learning and development are clear-cut, others such as the work environment are more diffuse.

A method of analysing the total rewards strategy in an organization is shown in Exhibit 70.2. This is derived from the Towers Perrin model described in Chapter 26 (Figure 26.3).

EXHIBIT 70.2
Total rewards analysis grid

PAY	BENEFITS
• Now • Future	• Now • Future
LEARNING	**ENVIRONMENT**
• Now • Future	• Now • Future

Groups of managers and/or staff can be asked to describe the current total rewards provision using this grid. They can then be asked to describe the improvements and changes in content and emphases they would like to see to better support the business of the organization, and make it a more rewarding and motivating place to work.

Prioritize

It is best not to be too ambitious in introducing total rewards. Start by identifying 'win-win' initiatives – those that are likely to have a notable effect on employee engagement and can be developed without too much difficulty. If a comprehensive approach is envisaged, priorities will need to be established and the introduction of the less immediate elements phased. Examples of possible developments are given below:

- Revise grade and pay structure, possibly instituting a career family structure that defines career paths.
- Revise contingent pay scheme or develop new one. Include leadership and upholding core values as important factors in a contribution-related pay scheme.
- Introduce flexible benefits scheme.
- Issue total reward statements that spell out to employees the value of all the benefits they receive in addition to pay.
- Introduce a non-financial recognition scheme.
- Improve performance management system, including leadership and upholding core values as important factors.
- Enhance learning and development, talent management and career development programmes.
- Focus management development programmes on improving the ability of line managers to play a major part in providing relational rewards.
- Take steps to improve work–life balance.
- Educate line managers in the principles of job design and provide guidance to them on developing roles that provide for intrinsic motivation.

There is much to be said for involving stakeholders in considering priorities and this can be done by means of an exercise based on Exhibit 70.3.

EXHIBIT 70.3 Total reward priorities

Aspect of employment	Assuming there are 100 points to distribute between the following aspects of your total reward package, distribute these points in terms of how important they are to you. You can allocate points to as many items as you like (up to a maximum of...), eg if basic salary is the only aspect of reward that is important to you, allocate all 100 points to this.
A competitive base salary	
Pension	
Car allowance	
Health benefits	
Death in service cover	
Permanent health insurance (prolonged disability cover)	
Flexibility of working hours	
Holidays	
Identity with organization values	
The leadership of the organization	
Staff discounts	
Stimulating and challenging work	
Flexibility to deal with caring responsibilities	
Working for an organization with a distinct and high profile	
Access to fitness facilities	
Learning and development opportunities	
Encouraging a healthy lifestyle	
Personal recognition (non-monetary)	
Opportunities for career advancement	
Other (please specify)	

Implement

Planning a total rewards programme may be hard; implementing it can be even more difficult. It is an exercise in change management: for employees generally when new reward practices are being introduced and for line managers in particular if they are expected to change their behaviour. Continuing communications and involvement of stakeholders are essential.

Monitor and evaluate

It is essential to monitor the implementation of total rewards carefully and then to evaluate how well each element has worked against the objectives set for it. This can lead to a reclarification of the concept and amendments to reward practices as required.

71
Job evaluation toolkit

Purpose and contents of the toolkit

The toolkit deals with the steps required to develop the most popular form of job evaluation, ie point-factor rating. However, it also refers to the design of analytical matching schemes, which can function independently but are often associated with a point-factor scheme. A typical method is to design and test a point-factor scheme and then use the factors included in that scheme as the basis for analytical matching. Point-factor and analytical matching schemes are described in Chapter 27.

The job evaluation review and development sequence

The following sequence of actions described below is required to develop a point-factor scheme with an associated analytical matching process:

1. Analyse present job evaluation arrangements.
2. Decide approach to job evaluation in principle.
3. Decide on features of new scheme.
4. Prepare project programme.
5. Develop basic factor plan.
6. Test basic factor plan.
7. Amend basic factor plan as necessary.
8. Decide on weighting.
9. Produce full factor plan.
10. Consider use of computer-aided evaluation.
11. Apply scheme to benchmark jobs.
12. Develop analytical matching approach.

These steps are described below.

Analyse present job evaluation arrangements

A preliminary assessment using the questionnaire shown in Exhibit 71.1 can be made of whether or not the present arrangements for job evaluation should be replaced or whether to introduce formal job evaluation.

EXHIBIT 71.1 Analysis of current job evaluation scheme

Statement	Fully agree	Partly agree	Partly disagree	Fully disagree
1. The present arrangements for valuing and grading jobs are quite satisfactory.				
2. Our scheme ensures that there are no grading problems.				
3. The factors in our scheme are no longer appropriate.				
4. Our scheme has decayed.				
5. Our scheme prevents grade drift.				
6. Our scheme would provide a good defence in an equal pay case.				
7. The weightings of factors in the scheme are inappropriate.				
8. There is no gender bias in the scheme's factors and weightings.				
9. The scheme is bureaucratic, paper intensive and time-wasting.				
10. People generally understand how the scheme works.				

Decide approach to job evaluation in principle

The choices available and the factors to be taken into account in making them are set out in Exhibit 71.2.

EXHIBIT 71.2 Choice of approach to job evaluation

Choice	Factors to be taken into account	Decision
Make no change	• Extent to which present arrangements are satisfactory. • Need to avoid disruption. • Cost considerations.	
Introduce new point-factor scheme or substantially amend existing one	• Advantages – analytical, provide equal pay claim defence. • Disadvantages – time-consuming, bureaucratic. • The fact that this is by far the most popular approach.	
Introduce analytical matching	• Advantages – analytical, much less time-consuming than point-factor rating. • Disadvantages – may not resolve equity problems, not a guaranteed defence in an equal pay case, need to be underpinned by point-factor evaluation.	
Introduce combined scheme, ie an underpinning point-factor scheme used to develop grade structure and as back-up and an analytical matching scheme for ongoing evaluations	• Provides support to analytical matching. • Reduces time for ongoing evaluations. • Provides defence in equal pay case. • Can be complex and difficult to understand.	
Purchase 'ready-made' scheme from consultant	• Scheme well-established. • Consultants experienced in implementation. • Linked to market rate database. • May not fit culture and circumstances of organization. • Could be expensive.	
Develop own 'tailor-made' scheme	• Scheme should fit. • Those involved in development should 'own' scheme. • But, untried and could be time-consuming and expensive to develop in terms of the human resources required.	

Decide on features of new scheme

The options are listed in Exhibit 71.3. The decisions made at this stage are interim and could be amended later.

EXHIBIT 71.3 Choice of features

Design area	Options	Interim decision
Job evaluation factors	There will be a choice on the number and types of factors. The number of factors can range from 3 to 14 and the average is 6.	
Factor levels	There will be choice on the number of levels and whether or not there should be the same number of levels in each factor. Typically, there are five or six levels.	
Scoring progression	Scoring intervals between levels can be either arithmetic or geometrical.	
Weighting	Schemes can be unweighted, or if they are weighted, this can be explicit or implicit.	

Prepare project programme

A project programme should be prepared in as much detail as possible. This will provide the basis for managing the project. A programme set out as a bar chart is illustrated in Exhibit 71.4.

EXHIBIT 71.4 Project plan bar chart

Activities
Months
1 2 3 4 5 6 7 8 9 10 11 12 13 14 15 16 17 18 19 20 21 22 23 24
1. Agree deliverables
2. Design and test scheme
3. Evaluate benchmark jobs
4. Design grade structure
5. Evaluate remaining jobs
6. Conduct market survey
7. Design the pay structure
8. Implement

Develop basic factor plan

A factor plan is the key component in a point-factor job evaluation. Its purpose is to provide an analytical framework that will guide evaluators in making decisions on the relative value of jobs. The process of developing a basic factor plan is described below.

Identify and define factors

Guidelines for selecting factors and avoiding gender bias are given in Exhibit 71.5.

Examples of factor definitions are given in Exhibit 71.6.

EXHIBIT 71.5 Guidelines for selecting factors

1. The factors must be capable of identifying relevant and important differences between jobs that will support the creation of a rank order of the jobs to be covered by the scheme.
2. The factors should between them measure all significant job features and should be of broadly comparable scope.
3. The factors should reflect the values of the organization.
4. They should apply equally well to different types of work including specialists and generalists, lower level and higher level jobs, and not be biased in favour of one gender or group.
5. The whole range of jobs to be evaluated at all levels should be covered without favouring men or women, people belonging to a particular racial group, different age groups or any particular job or occupation.
6. The scheme should fairly measure features of female-dominated jobs as well as male-dominated jobs.
7. The choice should not lead to discrimination on the grounds of gender, race, disability, religion, age or for any other reason. Experience should not be included as a factor because it could be discriminatory either on the grounds of gender or age. The same principle applies to education or qualifications as stand alone factors.
8. Job features frequently found in jobs carried out mainly by one gender should not be omitted, for example, manual dexterity, interpersonal skills and 'caring' responsibilities. However, if such features are included, it is important that the scheme captures the range of skills across all jobs, including those that might be dominated by another gender.
9. Double counting should be avoided, ie each factor must be independent of every other factor – the more factors (or sub-factors) in the plan, the higher the probability that double counting will take place.
10. Elision or compression of more than one significant job feature under a single factor heading should be avoided. If important factors are compressed with others it means that they could be undervalued.
11. The factor definitions should be clear, relevant and understandable and written in a way that is meaningful to those who will use the scheme.
12. The factors should be acceptable to those who will be covered by the scheme.

EXHIBIT 71.6 Examples of factor definitions

Factor	Definition
1. Knowledge and skills	The levels of professional, specialist, technical, administrative or operational knowledge and skills required to carry out the role effectively.
2. Contribution	The contribution made to achieving the objectives of the team, department or organization.
3. Communicating	The requirement to communicate orally and in writing to individuals and groups of people inside and outside the organization and to external bodies.
4. Interpersonal skills	The level of skill required to work well with others, to exercise leadership, to respond to people's requests, to handle difficult cases, to argue a case, to negotiate and to exert influence.
5. Planning and organizing	The requirement to plan, schedule and coordinate work, to allocate priorities and to meet deadlines.
6. Judgement and decision-making	The requirement to exercise judgement in making decisions and solving problems, including the degree to which the work involves choice of action and/or creativity.
7. Freedom to act	The degree to which independent action has to be taken, bearing in mind the level of control or guidance provided and the extent to which the work is supervised.
8. Complexity	The variety and diversity of the work carried out, the decisions to be made and the knowledge and skills used.
9. Responsibility for resources	The size of the resources controlled in terms of people, money, equipment, facilities, etc.
10. Demands on the role holder	The demands made by the role on the role holder because of work pressures (including those arising from handling emotional situations), non-social hours or a considerable amount of travelling.

Define factor levels

There are typically five or six levels. It is usual to have the same number of levels for each factor although more levels may be assigned to one or two factors, in which case the plan is said to be implicitly weighted because more points are available in the factors with extra levels. Guidelines on defining levels are given in Exhibit 71.7.

EXHIBIT 71.7 Guidelines on defining factor levels

1. Consider the number of levels (often four, five, six or seven) that may be needed to reflect the range of responsibilities and demands in the jobs covered by the scheme.
2. Analyse what would characterize the highest or lowest level for each factor and how these should be described.
3. Decide provisionally on the number of levels (say three) between the highest and lowest level so that the level structure reflects the graduation in responsibilities or demands. (This decision could be amended following the process of defining levels, which might reveal that more or fewer levels are required.)
4. Define each level as clearly as possible to help evaluators make 'best fit' decisions when they compare role data with level definitions.
5. Ensure that the levels should cover the whole range of demands in this factor that are likely to arise in the jobs with which the evaluation scheme is concerned.
6. Relate the content of level definitions to the definition of the factor concerned and ensure that it does not overlap with other factors.
7. Ensure that the factor levels represent clear and recognizable steps in demand.
8. Provide for uniform progression in the definitions level by level from the lowest to the highest level. There should be no gaps or undefined intermediate levels that might lead to evaluators finding it difficult to be confident about the allocation of a level of demand.
9. Define levels in absolute, not relative terms. So far as possible any dimensions should be defined. They should not rely upon a succession of undefined comparatives, eg small, medium, large.
10. Ensure that each level definition stands on its own. Level definitions should not be defined by reference to a lower or higher level, ie it is insufficient to define a level in words to the effect that it is a higher (or lower) version of an adjacent level.

Develop the scoring model

The next step is to decide on the scoring model. Each level in the factor plan has to be allocated a points value so that there is a scoring progression from the lowest to the highest level. A decision needs to be made on how to set the scoring progression within each factor.

There are two methods. First, the arithmetic or linear approach assumes that there are consistent step differences between factor levels – eg a five-level factor might be scored 10, 20, 30, 40 and 50. Alternatively, geometric scoring assumes that there are larger score differences at each successive level in the hierarchy to reflect progressive increases in responsibility. Thus the levels may be scored 10, 20, 35, 55 and 80, rather than 10, 20, 30, 40 and 50. This increases the scoring differentiation between higher-level jobs.

Test basic factor plan

The basic scored but not explicitly weighted factor plan needs to be tested on a representative sample of jobs (sometimes called 'benchmark jobs' although the term 'test jobs' is more accurate). The sample should include jobs from each of the main levels in the major functions. It is unlikely to be less than 20 per cent of the distinct jobs in the organization and in complex situations could be much more. The test jobs should be analysed to provide information on the key activities and a brief description of the requirements or demands of the job under each of the factor headings. Sufficient detail should be included to enable a job evaluation panel to match a job's characteristics for a factor with the most appropriate level in that factor.

Aim

The aim of this initial test is to check on the extent to which:

- the factors are appropriate;
- level definitions are worded clearly and graduated properly;
- level definitions provide good guidance on the allocation of factor levels to evaluators and thus enable consistent evaluations to be made;
- as far as can be judged, the evaluation produces a valid result.

There is no single, simple test that will establish the validity of a factor plan. The methods available are as follows:

- *Reference ranking* – the team compares the ranking produced by the job evaluation with the rank order produced by a ranking exercise. The technique of paired comparison may be used to guide the ranking process.
- *Hierarchy comparisons* – the rank order produced by the test is compared with the existing organizational hierarchy and any obvious discrepancies are investigated. However, care must be taken not to assume that the existing hierarchy is the correct one.
- *External market test* – compare the internal rank order with that existing in comparable jobs elsewhere. But this may reflect pay differentials between job families rather than internal measures of job worth. It may also replicate existing inequities between male and female jobs.
- *The 'felt fair test'* – the rank order produced by the test is compared with what the job evaluation panel 'feels' is the fair and, therefore, appropriate ranking and discrepancies are identified. This is dangerous because it is liable simply to reproduce existing prejudices.

A common practice is to start with reference ranking and use one or more of the other methods to check on the ranking outcome.

If the rankings produced by job evaluation are not acceptable it is necessary to establish why. There are three basic possible reasons:

1. Inadequacies in the factor plan in terms of the choice of factors, the number of levels, the definition of levels or the scoring system, in which case it will need to be amended.
2. Misjudgements by the panel, in which case consideration will need to be given to revisiting evaluations, especially if only a few jobs stick out like a sore thumb as being wrongly evaluated (this process is called 'sore-thumbing').
3. The possibility that some factors are more important than others and have not been given sufficient weight, in which case a decision may be made to provide for explicit weighting.

Amend basic factor plan as necessary

The initial test will almost certainly reveal the need to amend factor level definitions and it may indicate that more radical changes to the factor plan are required, for example in the choice of factors or the number of levels. Following any amendments it is desirable to retest the basic plan. This is time-consuming, which is why a job evaluation exercise can be a lengthy process. But this is the time to get it right.

Decide on weighting

Weighting recognizes that there are differences in the importance of factors by allocating more or less points to them. The choice is first between weighting and not weighting factors. If weighting is considered desirable, possibly on the basis of the initial test of the basic factor plan, there is a choice between explicit and implicit weighting. Explicit weighting means increasing the maximum points available for what were regarded as more important factors. Implicit weighting means allocating more levels and therefore points to some factors than others.

The most common but highly judgemental approach is for the project team to discuss and agree subjective views on which factors are more important and allocate additional points or extra levels accordingly. Another method of deciding on explicit weighting, ie extra points, is to get each member of the team to distribute 100 points amongst the factors, which are then revealed to the whole team, which reaches an agreement on the most acceptable distribution. This discussion may be expected to take account of guiding principles such as that no factor will have a weighting of less than 5 per cent or more than 30 per cent.

The weighted plan should be retested on the test jobs to ensure that it produces valid results.

Produce full factor plan

The basic factor plan (the range of factors and level definitions) produced after the initial test will be finalized, taking into account decisions on weighting.

Consider use of computer-aided evaluation

Consideration at this stage can be given to the possibility of introducing computer-aided evaluation. The advantages and disadvantages of computer-aided evaluation are set out in Exhibit 71.8.

EXHIBIT 71.8 Advantages and disadvantages of computer-aided job evaluation

Advantages	Disadvantages
• Greater consistency may be achieved – the same input information gives the same output result. • The speed of evaluations can be increased. • Facilities are provided for sorting, analysing, reporting on the input information and system outputs and for record keeping on a database. • The resources required are reduced.	• May be expensive. • May be elaborate or have the feel of a 'black box'. • May lack transparency. • Means abandoning the involvement of employees and their representatives in the traditional panel approach.

A computer-aided system is usually based on the paper-based system's factor plan. So it needs to be tested on the same jobs used for testing the paper-based system to ensure that it replicates the paper scheme's results.

Apply scheme to benchmark jobs

The final paper or computer-aided scheme is used to evaluate benchmark jobs (except in a small organization where all jobs may be evaluated). These are typical jobs that represent the different occupations and levels of work in an organization and are used as points of reference with which other jobs can be compared and evaluated. The evaluated benchmark jobs provide the basis for designing a grade structure and are used in analytical matching, as described below. They will include the test jobs but it may be necessary to select additional ones to provide a sufficient number for designing a grade structure.

Develop analytical matching approach

Analytical matching involves matching jobs to be evaluated on a factor by factor basis either with analytical grade definitions (grade profiles) or analytical job descriptions for benchmark posts (role profiles). The development sequence is illustrated in Figure 71.1.

FIGURE 71.1 Analytical matching job evaluation scheme development sequence

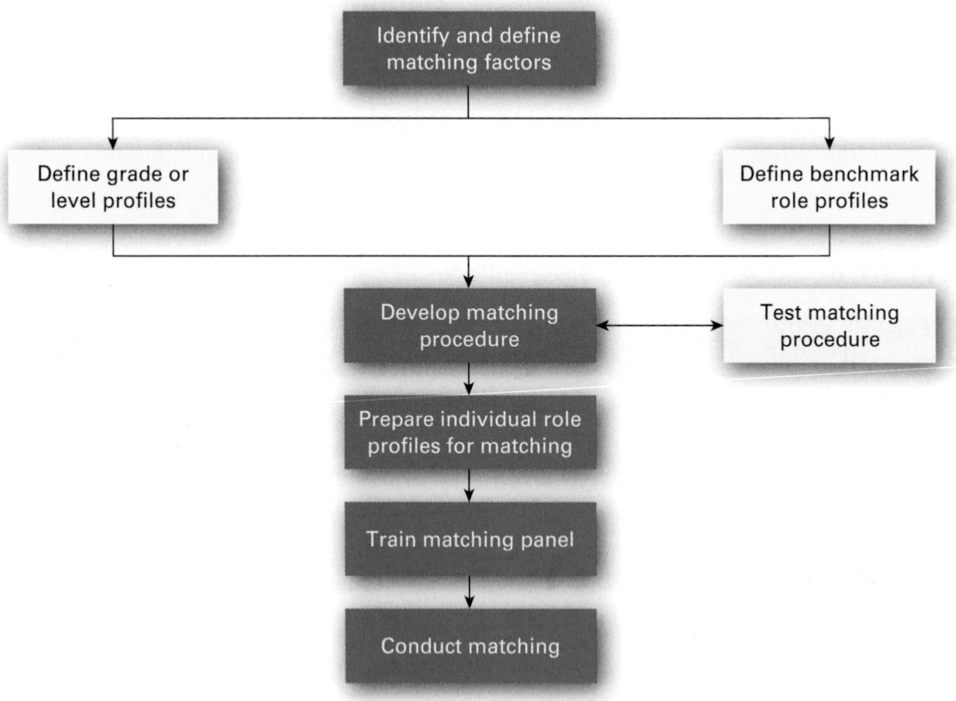

Where analytical matching is developed to support a point factor scheme, the first two steps will involve looking at the pattern of evaluation results for each grade and developing grade/level profiles that reflect the typical pattern of results, factor by factor.

Matching procedure

The matching procedure may be defined as a formal protocol that specifies:

- what constitutes a perfect match, ie where all the elements in the role profile match all the elements in the grade or benchmark role profile;
- the number of matches required of individual elements to indicate that a profile match is justified, for example six out of ten; but it is usual to restrict the mismatches allowed to fairly small variations – if there are any large ones, the match would be invalidated;
- any elements that must match for there to be a profile match, for example it may be decided that there must be a match for an element covering knowledge and skills;
- the procedure for grading if there has been a mismatch; this may specify a full evaluation of the role if the matching process is underpinned by a point-factor or proprietary analytical scheme.

72 Grade and pay structure design toolkit

Purpose of the toolkit

Graded pay structures are a fundamental aspect of base pay management. This toolkit focuses on the design of the most common form of grade and pay structures, namely: broad graded, career family and job family.

The grade and pay structure design sequence

The process of grade and pay structure design is shown in Figure 72.1.

FIGURE 72.1 The grade and pay structure design sequence

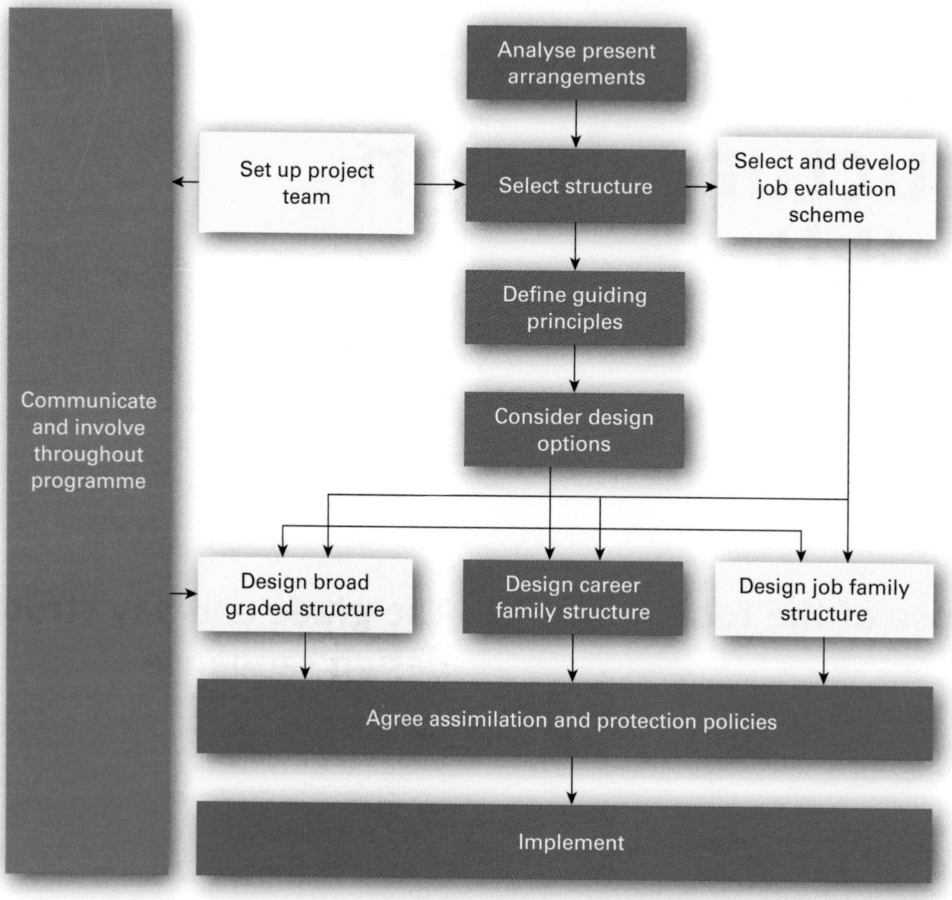

Analysis of present arrangements

Line managers, staff and staff representatives should be involved in an analysis of the present arrangement to indicate where changes may have to be made. The analysis could be based on the questionnaire set out in Exhibit 72.1. Use could be made of surveys, special workshops or focus groups, or it could be discussed in a consultative committee.

EXHIBIT 72.1 Analysis of present grade and pay structure arrangements

Statement	Fully agree	Partly agree	Partly disagree	Fully disagree
1. The present grade and pay structure is quite satisfactory.				
2. We have no problems in grading jobs within the structure.				
3. There are too many anomalies (under or over graded jobs).				
4. The structure no longer fits the way work is organized.				
5. Pay levels are competitive.				
6. The structure is easy to manage and control.				
7. The structure provides adequate scope for pay progression.				
8. The structure does not contribute to the creation of a gender gap.				
9. The structure is inflexible.				
10. People generally understand and accept how their jobs are graded.				

Choice of structure

Assuming that the analysis indicates that radical action is required, a choice needs to be made on which type of structure is appropriate. The choice can be based on an analysis of the features and advantages and disadvantages of different structures, as summarized in Exhibit 72.2 and an assessment of the criteria that can be used to determine the extent to which they are appropriate (Exhibit 72.3).

EXHIBIT 72.2 Summary description of most common grade and pay structures

Type of structure	Features	Advantages	Disadvantages
Broad-graded	• A sequence of between 6 and 9 grades • Fairly broad pay ranges, eg 40%–50% • Progression linked to contribution and may be controlled by thresholds or zones	As for narrow-graded structures but, in addition: • the broader grades can be defined more clearly • better control can be exercised over grade drift	• Too much scope for pay progression • Control mechanisms can be provided but they can be difficult to manage • May be costly
Career family	• Career families identified and defined • Career paths defined for each family in terms of key activities and competence requirements • Same grade and pay structure for each family	• Clarify career paths within and between families • Facilitate the achievement of equity between families and therefore equal pay • Facilitate level definitions	• Could be difficult to manage • May *appear* to be divisive if 'silos' emerge
Job family	• Separate grade and pay structures for job families containing similar jobs • Progression linked to competence and/or contribution	• May inhibit lateral career development • May be difficult to maintain internal equity between job families unless underpinned by job evaluation	• Facilitate pay differentiation between market groups • Define career paths against clear criteria • Can appear to be divisive

EXHIBIT 72.3 Criteria for assessing the extent to which a structure is appropriate

Type of structure	The structure is more likely to be appropriate when:
Broad-graded	• It is believed that if there is a relatively limited number of grades it will be possible to define and therefore differentiate them more accurately as an aid to better precision when grading jobs. • An existing narrow-graded structure is the main cause of grade drift because the structure cannot accommodate market factors. • A broad-banded structure has led to pay drift due to lack of management control. • It is considered that pay progression through grades can be related to contribution and that it is possible to introduce effective control mechanisms.
Career family	• There are distinct families, and different career paths within and between families can be identified and defined. • There is a strong emphasis on career development in the organization. • Robust methods of defining professional, specialist and technical competencies exist. • It is believed to be inappropriate to vary pay structures between families.
Job family	As for career families plus: • There are distinct market groups that need to be rewarded differently. • The range of responsibility and the basis upon which levels exist vary between families.

Definition of guiding principles

Guiding principles for the design of the grade and pay structure need to be defined at this stage. An example of a set of guiding principles is given in Exhibit 72.4.

EXHIBIT 72.4 Example of grade and pay structure guiding principles

Grade and pay structures should:

- be appropriate to the culture, characteristics and needs of the organization and its employees;
- facilitate the management of relativities and the achievement of equity, fairness, consistency and transparency in managing gradings and pay;
- be capable of adapting to pressures arising from market rate changes and skill shortages;
- facilitate operational flexibility and continuous development;
- provide scope as required for rewarding performance, contribution and increases in skill and competence;
- clarify reward, lateral development and career opportunities;
- be constructed logically and clearly so that the basis upon which they operate can readily be communicated to employees;
- enable the organization to exercise control over the implementation of pay policies and budgets.

Design options

Whichever structure is selected, there will be a number of design options as summarized in Exhibit 72.5.

EXHIBIT 72.5 Grade and pay structure design options

Design feature	Design considerations
Number of grades, levels or bands	• The range and types of roles to be covered by the structure. • The range of pay and job evaluation points scores to be accommodated. • The number of levels in the organizational hierarchy (this will be an important factor in a broad-banded structure). • Decisions on where grade boundaries should be placed following a job evaluation exercise that has produced a ranked order of jobs – this might identify the existence of clearly defined clusters of jobs at the various levels in the hierarchy between which there are significant differences in job size. • The potential for 'grade drift' (unjustified upgradings in response to pressure, lack of promotion opportunities or because job evaluation has been applied laxly), which can be increased if there are too many narrow grades.
Pay range spans	• Views on the scope that should be allowed for performance, contribution or career progression within grade. • Equal pay considerations – wide spans, especially extended incremental scales, are a major cause of pay gaps between men and women because women, who are more likely to have career breaks than men, may not have the same opportunity as men to progress to the upper regions of the range. • In a broad-banded structure, the range of market rates and job evaluation scores covering the jobs allocated to the band.
Differentials between pay ranges	• Differentials between pay ranges should provide scope to recognize increases in job size between successive grades. • If differentials are too close – less than 10 per cent – many jobs become borderline cases, which can result in a proliferation of appeals and arguments about grading. • Large differentials below senior management level of more than 25 per cent can create problems for marginal or borderline cases because of the amount at stake. • In most organizations with conventional grade structures a differential of between 15 and 20 per cent is appropriate except, perhaps, at the highest levels.
Pay range overlap	• There is a choice on whether or not pay ranges should overlap and, if so, by how much. • Large overlaps can create equal pay problems if men are clustered at the top of their grades and women are at the lower end.
Pay progression	• There is a choice of methods of pay progression between the various forms of contingent pay, namely performance, competence or contribution-related and the fixed service-related increments common in the public sector.

Graded pay structure design

A graded pay structure involves first designing the grade structure and then deciding on the pay ranges that should be attached to it.

The two approaches to design the grade structure are: 1) *the derived method* in which decisions on the grade structure are led by point-factor job evaluation; and 2) *the pre-emptive method* in which the number of grades is determined first and each grade is then defined as a basis for analytical matching or market pricing.

The derived method (use of point-factor job evaluation)

The derived method consists of the following steps:

1. Use point-factor job evaluation to produce a rank order of jobs according to their job evaluation scores.
2. Either: a) take a preliminary view on the preferred number of grades; or b) analyse the rank order to establish by inspection where jobs might be grouped into grades and how many grades emerge from this procedure.
3. Decide where the boundaries that will define grades should be placed in the rank order by analysing the rank order to identify any significant gaps in the points scores between adjacent jobs. These natural breaks in points scores will then constitute the boundaries between clusters of jobs, which can be allocated to adjacent grades. This is the preferred approach but in many cases there will be no significant gaps. If so, the following method can be used:
   - Jobs with common features as indicated by the job evaluation factors are grouped together so that a distinction can be made between the characteristics of the jobs in different grades – it should be possible to demonstrate that the jobs grouped into one grade resemble each other more than they resemble jobs placed in adjacent grades; all the jobs placed in a grade should be clearly smaller than the jobs in the next higher grade and larger than the jobs placed in the next lower grade.
   - The grade hierarchy should take account of the organizational hierarchy, ie jobs in which the job holder reports to a higher level job holder should be placed in a lower grade, although this principle should not be followed slavishly when an organization is over-hierarchical with, perhaps, a series of one-over-one reporting relationships.
   - There would need to be good justification for placing any boundaries between jobs mainly carried out by men and jobs mainly carried out by women.
   - Caution should be exercised in placing any boundaries immediately above jobs in which large numbers of people are employed because this may result in a large number of appeals against the grading.
4. The grade width in terms of job evaluation points should represent a significant step in demands on job holders as indicated by the job evaluation scheme.

The grades in a structure established in this manner can be defined in the form of grade profiles using the job evaluation factors as the headings for each profile. These can form the basis for analytical matching as described in Chapter 27.

Pre-emptive method

The pre-emptive method takes place in the following steps:

1. *Assume number of grades.* The assumption on how many grades are required is based on an analysis of the existing hierarchy of roles and a judgement on how many levels are needed to produce a logical grouping of those roles, level by level. A logical grouping is one in which each grade contains roles whose levels are broadly comparable in terms of responsibility and decision-making and there is a step difference in the degree of responsibility between each level.
2. *Define grades.* There is choice between a simple non-analytical or semi-analytical job classification approach and a full analytical approach. A non-analytical job classification

approach involves preparing an overall definition of the grade to enable 'job slotting' to take place. This means slotting 'whole jobs' – ie ones that have not been analysed under job evaluation factor headings to grades by comparing the whole job description with the grade. A full analytical approach involves the preparation of grade profiles. These use job evaluation factors as the headings for the profile of each grade, which can be compared with role profiles set out under the same headings so that analytical matching can take place.

3 *Revise initial assumption as necessary.* The process of definition may reveal that the number of grades assumed to be required initially was either too many (the distinctions between them could not be made with sufficient clarity) or too few (it becomes apparent that the range of roles to be fitted into the structure was too great to be accommodated in the number of grades available). If this is the case, the number of grades would have to be adjusted iteratively until a satisfactory result is obtained.

4 *Match benchmark roles.* The benchmark roles are matched to grades in accordance with a predetermined analytical matching protocol, as described in the job evaluation toolkit. When matched, the information on the benchmark roles may suggest changes to the grade profiles.

5 *Match remaining roles.* The remaining roles can be matched to the grade profiles using the protocol. A confirmation of the match can be obtained by comparing them with the graded benchmark roles.

Pay range design

The steps required to determine pay ranges are:

1 Obtain information on the market rates for benchmark jobs where available. If possible this should indicate the median rate and the upper and lower quartiles. Remember that there may be some key jobs for which market-rate data is not available.

2 List the jobs placed within each grade on the basis of job evaluation (these might be limited to benchmark jobs that have been evaluated but there must be an adequate number of them if a proper basis for the design is to be provided).

3 Establish the actual rates of pay of the job holders.

4 For each grade set out the range of pay for job holders and calculate their average or median rate of pay (the pay practice point). It is helpful to plot this pay practice data as illustrated in Figure 72.2, which shows pay in each grade against job evaluation scores and includes a pay practice trend line.

5 Agree policy on how the organization's pay levels should relate to market rates – its 'market stance'. This could be at the median, or above the median if it is believed that pay levels should be more competitive.

6 Calculate the average market rates for the benchmark jobs in each grade according to pay stance policy, eg the median rates. This produces the range market reference point.

7 Compare the practice and market reference points in each range and decide on the range reference point. This usually becomes the mid-point of the pay range for the grade and is regarded as the competitive rate for a fully competent job holder in that grade. This is a judgemental process that takes into account the difference between the practice and policy points, the perceived need to be more competitive if policy rates are higher, and the likely costs of increasing rates.

8 Examine the pay differentials between reference points in adjacent grades. These should provide scope to recognize increases in job size and, so far as possible, variations between differentials should be kept to a minimum. If differentials are too close – less than 10 per cent – many jobs become borderline cases, which can result in a proliferation of appeals and arguments about grading. Large differentials below senior management level of more than 25 per cent can create problems for marginal or borderline cases because of the amount at stake. Experience has shown that in most

FIGURE 72.2 Scattergram of evaluations and pay

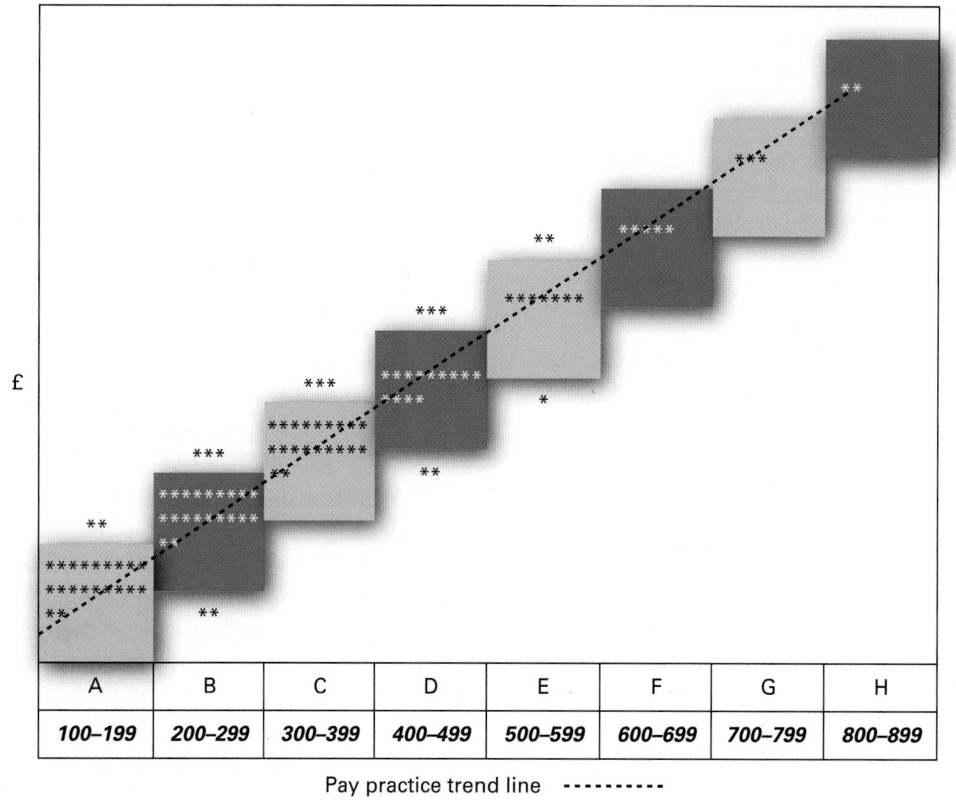

organizations with conventional grade structures a differential of between 15 and 20 per cent is appropriate except, perhaps, at the highest levels.

9 Decide on the range of pay around the reference point, eg 20 per cent on either side of the reference point. Thus, if that point is 100 per cent, the range is from 80 per cent to 120 per cent. The range will, however, vary in accordance with policy on the scope for progression and, if a given range of pay has to be covered by the structure, the fewer the grades the wider the ranges.

10 Decide on the extent, if any, to which pay ranges should overlap. Overlap recognizes that an experienced job holder at the top of a range may be making a greater contribution than an inexperienced job holder at the lower end of the range above. Large overlaps can create equity issues between jobs that have the same salary but are in different grades. This is particularly pronounced if it means that individuals with the same pay could fit within more than two grades.

11 Review the impact of the above pay range decisions on the pay of existing staff in order to calculate implementation costs. Establish the number of staff whose present rate of pay is above or below the pay range for the grade into which their jobs have been placed and the extent of the difference between the rate of pay of those below the minimum and the lowest point of that pay range. Calculate the costs of bringing them up to the minimum. Pay modelling software or Excel spreadsheets can be used for this purpose.

12 When the above steps have been completed it may be necessary to review the decisions made on the grade structure and pay

reference points and ranges, especially when the costs calculated in stage 11 are too high. Iteration is almost always necessary to obtain a satisfactory result that conforms to the criteria for grade and pay structures mentioned earlier and minimizes the cost of implementation. Alternatives can be modelled using the software mentioned above.

Career family structure design

The steps required to design a career family structure are described below:

1. *Select and define career families.* Decide on what career families are required. Typically, not more than four or five families are identified. The choice of families is between functions (eg marketing, finance) or activities (eg administration, support staff) or a combination of functions and activities.
2. *Decide on number of levels in the career family structure and define them with level profiles. Level profiles* are required that apply to all the families in the structure, bearing in mind that the defining characteristic of a career family is that the levels and the pay ranges attached to them are common to all the families in the structure (as distinct from job family structures in which levels and ranges differ between some or all of the families).
3. *Identify, define and match benchmark roles.* A representative sample of benchmark roles are identified, defined as role profiles and matched with the level profiles as described above for a graded structure.
4. *Conduct analytical matching.* Analytical matching procedures are used to allocate the remaining roles to levels. It is advisable to test the process first in one family – this will not only test the procedure but will also enable model career family structures to be used when dealing with the other career families.
5. *Attach pay ranges to levels.* Pay ranges are established for each level, as described above for graded structures.
6. *Validate relativities between career families.* The allocation of jobs to levels through matching across the career families is validated by reference to job evaluation scores to ensure that the relativities between them look reasonable. Some adjustment may need to be made as a result of this cross-check if it exposes inequities between families.

Job family structure design

The process of designing job family structures is essentially the same as that used for career family structures. The difference is that, because some individual families will have their own pay and level structure, the analysis of market rates and the organization of work in families will have a stronger influence on the design.

Assimilation policy

It is necessary to have a policy on where in the new structure the staff will be assimilated. This is usually at their existing salary or, in the case of a revised pay spine, on the nearest point in a new incremental scale above their existing salary.

Protection policy

Protection policy limits any loss in pay arising from the introduction of a new graded pay structure. 'Indefinite protection' – that is, maintaining the difference between current pay and range maximum for as long as the employee remains in the job – is highly undesirable, first because it will create permanent anomalies and, second, because, if there are a lot of men in this situation it will perpetuate unacceptable gender gaps.

Because of these considerations, the most common approach is now to protect pay for a period of between two to four years. During this time the employees will 'mark time' (ie receive no pay increases until their rate of pay falls within the new scale for their job. They will then be entitled to the same increases as any other staff in their grade up to the grade maximum. Alternatively, during the protection period affected employees may receive a general increase/cost of living rise, but where this is the case it is less likely that an individual's pay will fall back within the new pay range during the protection period.

Where there is an incremental pay structure staff may continue to earn increments to which they are entitled under existing arrangements, up to the maximum of their present scale, until the pay protection period ends or their entitlement is bought out.

If a red-circled individual concerned leaves the job, the scale of pay for the job reverts to the standard range as set up following job evaluation.

Implementing new grade and pay structures

Implementation can be challenging and must be planned. The steps required are:

1. Decide at the planning stage the overall change/transition strategy and timing.
2. Model the transition into the new structure and develop policies to manage this transition.
3. Develop detailed operating responsibilities and guidelines for the new structure, including the procedures for grading or regrading jobs and managing pay progression. The authority to make pay and grading decisions and methods of budgetary control should also be covered.
4. Negotiate the introduction of the new arrangements with staff representatives and trade unions, if appropriate. They should have been involved throughout the process, but the detailed 'nitty-gritty' of actual pay levels and assimilation policies and procedures needs to be thrashed out now.
5. Produce and distribute communications about the new structure – how it works, who will be involved in managing it and how people will be affected.
6. Design and run training workshops for managers, and possibly all staff.
7. Run a pilot or simulation exercise if feasible, operating the new approach in parts of the organization, to test its workability and robustness.
8. Full implementation and rollout. This will include giving every person information on how the new structure affects them and on their right to ask for a review of their grading if they are dissatisfied.

73 Attitude surveys toolkit

Introduction

Attitude surveys are being used increasingly by organizations to measure engagement and obtain the views of employees about particular HR policies and practices. This toolkit provides a practical guide to the development and use of such surveys. An example of an attitude survey is provided in Appendix 1.

Developing and conducting an attitude survey

The steps required to develop and conduct an attitude survey are as follows.

Set up survey team

One individual should be given the overall responsibility for planning and conducting the survey, but it is useful to appoint two or three other people to form a survey team that can discuss how the survey can be developed and share in its management.

Define objectives and scope

It is essential to be clear about what the survey is expected to achieve. In general terms it could be any of the reasons mentioned above. In particular, the objectives can be specified in terms of the area they are intended to cover, for example:

- To assess levels of engagement in order to identify any areas in which improvements could be made to people management processes with a view to increasing those levels.
- To measure trends in engagement levels and benchmark the levels against those achieved in comparable organizations.
- To evaluate the impact of the new performance management system.
- To obtain the views of employees about the reward system.
- To evaluate the effectiveness of e-learning.
- To obtain the views of employees about their benefits package as a basis for introducing a flexible benefits system.

The scope of the survey could be a census of all employees or cover a representative sample. A census has the advantage of giving everyone an opportunity to participate and, subject to response rates, information from a larger proportion of employees. A sample survey may be easier to manage in large organizations, but selecting a representative sample may be difficult and some important information may be missed. The scope of a survey may be limited to a category of staff such as senior managers or sales representatives and, again, can be conducted on either a census or a sample basis.

When defining the scope, an estimate should be made of the number of people who will be contacted so that the scale of the survey can be calculated.

In-house, with external support or outsourced

There is a choice at the extremes between planning and administering the survey entirely in-house or entirely outsourced to consultants. In between there is a choice of activities that can be carried out in-house, possibly with outside advice. If a decision is made to outsource, wholly or partly, care has to be taken in selecting an external provider.

Choice between in-house and outsourcing

The factors to be considered when making a choice between in-house and outsourcing to external consultants are set out in Exhibit 73.1, which suggests that, apart from cost considerations, the advantages of using external help for all or part of the survey outweigh the disadvantages.

EXHIBIT 73.1 Advantages and disadvantages of planning and conducting surveys in-house or outsourcing

In-house		Outsourced	
Advantages	*Disadvantages*	*Advantages*	*Disadvantages*
Save costs	Time and trouble taken in planning and administering survey	Resources available to plan and administer survey; relieve organization of time and trouble	Cost
Complete control of survey	Lack of internal expertise	Expertise	Less control
Management visibly involved	Employees may suspect confidentiality	Confidentiality	
		Database available for benchmarking	

Choice of responsibility for activities

The choice for each of the main activities involved in planning and conducting a survey is between carrying it out entirely in-house, carrying it out in-house with advice and possibly some support from an external provider, and outsourcing the whole activity to an external provider. The choices can be mapped out with the help of Exhibit 73.2.

EXHIBIT 73.2 Choice of responsibility for activities

Activity	Wholly in-house	In-house with external advice/support	Wholly external
Decide on objectives and scope			
Decide on content			
Draft survey items			
Draw up survey			
Plan and administer online survey, and/or distribute survey questionnaire			
Follow up to increase level of response			
Analyse responses			
Prepare report			
Issue and discuss report with employees			
Plan and implement action			

Criteria for external adviser

A checklist of the points to consider when choosing an external adviser is set out in Exhibit 73.3. A list of survey providers is given in the appendix at the end of this chapter.

EXHIBIT 73.3 Criteria for selecting an external adviser

Criteria	Comments
Relevant experience in the planning, advisory and administration activities the adviser is to carry out.	
Adequate resources available to carry out the work.	
Qualified, skilled and experienced staff who will conduct the work under proper supervision.	
References from satisfied clients.	
Estimated time to complete work.	
Ability to deliver on time.	
Fee structure and total cost of fees and expenses.	
Acceptability to management and employees and ability to fit in with the organization's culture.	

Identify survey content

It is necessary to decide what subject matter should be covered by the survey in order to achieve its objectives. The areas covered by a specialist survey are usually fairly obvious. But more care is necessary in deciding on what should be included in a more general engagement or attitude survey. The views of senior management and employees should be sought.

The outcome can be a checklist, as illustrated in Exhibit 73.4, which is used as the basis for interviews and focus group discussions, leading to the production of an outline list of survey topics.

EXHIBIT 73.4 Issues checklist

Possible survey issue	Very important – should be covered	Not so important – might be covered	Unimportant
Commitment to the organization			
Leadership			
Line manager effectiveness			
Communications			
Job content and clarity			
Autonomy			
The work environment			
Resources and equipment			
Use of skills and capabilities			
Opportunities for advancement and development			
Job security			
Pay and benefits			
Recognition			
Quality of feedback and guidance available			
Opportunities for involvement and participation			
Teamwork			
Cooperation and relationships with co-workers			
Fair treatment			
Discrimination, harassment and bullying			
Other			

Survey topics

An outline list of survey topics can be prepared by reference to the outcomes of the interviews and focus group findings. This list provides the basis for drawing up questions and constructing the survey.

Draft survey items

Format

The most commonly used format for survey items is a request to respondents to indicate the extent to which they agree or disagree with a statement, for example: 'My work is very satisfying.' The response can be on a five-point scale: 'Strongly agree', 'Inclined to agree', 'Neither agree nor disagree', 'Inclined to disagree' and 'Strongly disagree'. This is the most common approach but there is some support for using a four-point scale, leaving out the middle 'Neither agree nor disagree' on the grounds that respondents may be too inclined to select the central choice, which is not really an expression of opinion.

Scoring

Whichever scale is adopted, the responses can be scored: 5 or 4 for the most positive option; 1 for the most negative option. Adding these item scores can produce an overall score for, say, engagement, which can be used to assess trends as measured by successive surveys.

Positive or negative statements

A decision has to be made on the use of positive or negative statements. For example, a positive statement could be: 'My work is very satisfying', while a negative one would be: 'I get very little satisfaction from my work' (the latter are reverse-scored, ie a 'fully disagree' gets the maximum points and a 'fully agree' gets the minimum).

The argument for including negative as well as positive statements (sometimes called a 'balanced-scale approach') is that it makes people think about their responses, forces them to read the items more carefully and use both ends of the response scale, and prevents them from agreeing or disagreeing with items indiscriminately. The counter-argument is that mixing positive and negative statements can confuse people, and there is no evidence that it does make them think harder about their response. A negative response to a negatively worded item may not be equivalent to a positive response to a positive item. It is best to stick to positive statements.

Guidelines for wording items

The following are the guidelines for wording items:

- *Ask what you want to know* – be certain that the item will convey information relevant to the purpose of the survey and the issues raised in the content analysis.
- *Keep items simple and short* – the aim is to encourage responses and this will not happen if the items are complex or lengthy. Avoid compound sentences and subsidiary clauses. As a rule of thumb, an item should not be longer than 20 words.
- *Cover only one topic per item* – double-barrelled statements confuse respondents who do not know which one of them they are agreeing or disagreeing with.
- *Avoid ambiguous statements* – the aim is to ensure that as far as possible all respondents interpret the item in the same way. Define terms where necessary.
- *Be specific* – the test of a good item is to answer the question: 'If we get a poor rating on this item, will we be clear what needs to be done about it?' A general item such as: 'Our performance management scheme is very effective' may possibly be useful as a broad indicator of satisfaction or dissatisfaction, but it needs to be followed up by more specific items on such aspects of performance management as the quality of feedback, the fairness of performance ratings, or how well managers conduct performance review meetings.
- *Use appropriate, everyday language* – avoid words that may be unfamiliar to respondents. Item compilers should subject each item to a readability analysis.

Open-ended items

Open-ended or unstructured items are invitations to respondents to provide comments or opinions in their own words, for example: 'Please provide any ideas you have on how the performance management system could be improved.' They can be used to produce in-depth information that would not be available from the prescribed survey items and enable people to vent their feelings on emotion-laden topics such as the operation of a performance-related pay scheme. Respondents can be asked to list the three best or worst things associated with an issue such as the quality of communications.

Quotes from open-ended responses can liven up a report by providing an insight into real feelings. The disadvantage is that they are more difficult to process and analyse. They can serve a useful purpose in a survey but their use should be limited. It is, however, a good idea to at least include an item at the end of the survey asking for general comments such as: 'Please provide any other comments you would like to make on the issues covered by this survey.'

Construct the survey

The main areas for consideration when constructing a survey are the length of the survey, the order of items, the demographic information required and the introduction and explanatory notes to the survey.

Length of the survey

Clearly, the length of a survey will vary according to the breadth of issues it deals with. But it is advisable to limit the number of items in order to encourage a good response by not putting off or confusing participants and by reducing the amount of time they take to complete it. An excessive number of items will increase the problems of analysing the outcome of the survey.

It is probably best not to have more than 50 items and to ensure that the survey can be completed within 30 minutes; a trial run can be used to check this.

The order of items

There is a choice in ordering the items in a survey between positioning them at random and clustering (grouping related items together). The argument for random ordering is that biases are better controlled if the topic areas covered are not too obvious.

The arguments for clustering are stronger. If the survey items are placed randomly, this may seem illogical to respondents who could find it difficult to follow and become annoyed or frustrated or even fail to complete the survey. Respondents find it easier to follow a survey where items are clustered. A typical approach when clustering items such as views about the job is to start with questions dealing with particular characteristics, followed by items concerned with general characteristics of the job, followed by an overall assessment of the job.

Demographics

Some information on the demographics of survey respondents is required to enable more detailed analysis. But the information should not be so specific as to threaten the survey's anonymity. The starting point is to consider what forms of analysis are required.

Demographic data should only be sought if it is believed that it will produce useful analyses. Results are typically analysed by occupation (usually expressed in broad categories, eg manager, team leader, administrator), function or department, gender and length of service.

Introduction

The introduction to the survey should cover the following points:

- the purpose of the survey;
- how the survey will be conducted;
- how the results of the survey will be communicated (full disclosure of the analysis should be promised);
- the benefits of the survey to the organization and its employees;
- how anonymity will be preserved (this will be more convincing if the survey is conducted by a third party who carries out the analysis away from the organization);
- contact details for queries about the survey or help in completing it;
- confirmation that the survey can be completed during working hours;
- the date by which the survey should be completed.

Instructions for completing the survey

Clear instructions should be given on how to complete the survey. If care has been taken to adopt a simple and consistent approach (eg a five-point scale to indicate the extent to which a respondent agrees or disagrees with a statement) these instructions need not be too complex. But they should be pilot tested to ensure that they are understood.

Plan survey

The steps required to prepare for a survey are:

1. Plan an initial communications programme for employees.
2. Decide on how results will be analysed and the format of the report.
3. Decide on the use of online technology.

Communicate to employees

It is essential to convey to employees that a survey is to be carried out, its purpose, and how the organization and they will benefit. Details of how the survey will be conducted need to be explained; this should cover the role of the external provider if one is engaged. Employees should be informed that the survey can be completed in working hours and that help will be available in completing the survey if required. Employees need to be assured that their completed surveys will be anonymous and that the survey will therefore be completely confidential. If an outside provider is to be used, assurances can be given that confidentiality will be maintained. The impact of the survey can be enhanced by giving it an identity, such as 'Have your say'.

Analysis

The demographic categories for analysis should have been considered when designing the survey. At this stage, further consideration can be given to the detailed analysis and how the results will be presented in the report – tabulations, graphics, trend analysis, etc. Decisions can also be made on the need for any cross-analyses, for example how responses to an item dealing with career prospects varied between men and women, or between managers and support staff or, more elaborately, how responses varied between male and female managers and male and female support staff.

Use of online technology

Most surveys are conducted online, especially in larger organizations. Web-based software is used. Online surveys are typically operated by external providers. Respondents access the online questionnaire by following an e-mail link, which takes them directly to the provider's site. Some suppliers can set up the survey on the organization's intranet site rather than hosting it remotely. Instructions are given on how to respond to survey items.

Respondents are usually given one practice item. The software may present only one item at a time together with the alternative responses. When an item is completed the next item is displayed.

The software is used to collect completed surveys, analyse responses and prepare reports. External providers can produce elegant reports, complete with graphics.

Online surveys save time and trouble and enable more sophisticated analyses and reports to be produced. When they are conducted by an external provider they can convince employees that their responses will be confidential. They are also easier to complete than paper-based surveys (even the minority of people unfamiliar with computers seldom have any difficulty, and help can be provided if necessary). The only problem is where employees do not have immediate access to a computer. Some companies have overcome this by installing special computer stations with staff available to give advice. Alternatively, a paper-based survey can be carried out.

Pilot testing

It is essential to pilot test the survey to evaluate its content and to assess the administration time. The purposes of the pilot test would be to:

- obtain initial reactions from employees on the proposed survey and its content;
- find out generally if members of the test group have any problems with completing the survey;
- identify specific weaknesses in the draft survey, eg ambiguous or badly worded survey items, inadequate instructions on how to complete the survey, illogical sequence of items, complexity, too many items;
- identify any unnecessary items or any additions that need to be made;
- check on the time taken to complete the survey and identify any need to shorten it.

The pilot test can usefully be conducted with a group of eight to 12 people consisting of a balanced sample of employees (or more groups in large or complex organizations). The individuals in the group complete the draft survey under broadly the same conditions as they would experience in an actual survey. Their opinions under the headings listed above would be obtained by the survey team, who would make any necessary changes to the survey.

Conduct survey

Conducting a survey is simply a matter of implementing the plan. The steps required are:

1. Use the outcomes of the pilot test to make final amendments to the survey document and prepare the software or the paper survey.
2. Inform employees that the survey is to be carried out and remind them of its purpose, how it will be conducted and the arrangements to ensure confidentiality. This will confirm advance communications about the survey.
3. Make arrangements to deal with queries and, if necessary, provide computers and support.
4. Issue the survey online or on paper.
5. Maximize the response rate (the percentage of people who complete and submit a survey). Aim for a minimum of 70 per cent by contacting non-respondents two or three times to remind them to submit the survey.

Analyse responses

The initial analysis should describe the population of respondents. The basic analysis then describes the number and percentage of people who chose each response for each item. To simplify the findings, some analysts combine 'strongly agree' and 'inclined to agree' into one category called 'agree', and 'inclined to disagree' and 'disagree' into one category called 'disagree'.

If the choices are scored from, say, 1 to 5 in increasing order of agreement, an average score for each item and the survey as a whole can be calculated. This provides an index that can be used to assess trends in successive surveys, as long as the score relates to the same items. Cross-analyses can be carried out in addition to the basic analysis to describe results in more detail by identifying variations in the responses between different groups, for example managers and support workers.

More sophisticated analysis can be used to test statistical significance, analyse variance, test the relationship between sub-groups (chi-square test) and assess reliability (internal consistency reliability).

Assessing results

It is an interesting fact that when people are asked directly if they are satisfied with their job, most of them will probably say that they are. This is regardless of the work being done and often in spite of strongly held grievances. A possible reason for this phenomenon is that while most people are willing to admit to having grievances – in fact, if invited to complain, they will complain – they may be reluctant to admit, even to themselves, to being dissatisfied with a job they have no immediate intention of leaving. Many employees have become reconciled to their work, even if they do not like some aspects of it, and have no real desire to do anything else. So they are, in a sense, satisfied enough to continue, even if they have complaints. Finally, many people are satisfied with their job overall, although they grumble about some aspects of it.

Overall measures of satisfaction do not, therefore, always reveal anything interesting. It is more important to look at particular aspects of satisfaction or dissatisfaction to decide whether or not anything needs to be done. In these circumstances, a survey will only indicate a line to be followed up. It will not provide the answers. Hence the advantage of individual meetings or focus group discussions to explore in depth any issue raised.

Post-survey activities

The three essential post-survey activities are:

1. Feed back summaries of the results, including negative views, to all employees.
2. Hold discussions with employees in focus groups and workshops to obtain views on what needs to be done about any of the negative outcomes of the survey.
3. Plan and implement action to deal with problem areas, involving employees as far as possible and keeping everyone informed of what has been accomplished as a result of the survey.

APPENDIX 1
Example of attitude survey

	Strongly agree	Agree	Disagree	Strongly disagree
The organization				
I am proud to work for this organization	1	2	3	4
I would not encourage anyone else to work here	1	2	3	4
I want to go on working for this organization	1	2	3	4
Your job				
I like my job	1	2	3	4
I am not clear about what I am expected to achieve	1	2	3	4
I have plenty of scope to decide how to do my work	1	2	3	4
I have to work too hard to achieve the results expected of me	1	2	3	4
I am well motivated to do a good job	1	2	3	4
The balance between my work and domestic life is unsatisfactory	1	2	3	4
Your boss				
My boss does a very good job	1	2	3	4
My boss gives me clear direction	1	2	3	4
My boss lets me know how I am getting on	1	2	3	4
My boss does not support me very well	1	2	3	4
My boss helps me to improve my performance	1	2	3	4
My boss treats everyone fairly	1	2	3	4
Learning and development				
I have been given every opportunity to develop my knowledge and skills	1	2	3	4
I am satisfied with the career opportunities provided by the organization	1	2	3	4
I am not given much opportunity to discuss my development needs with my boss	1	2	3	4

	Strongly agree	Agree	Disagree	Strongly disagree
Your pay				
I am fairly paid for the work I do	1	2	3	4
I feel that my pay does not reflect my contribution	1	2	3	4
My pay compares favourably with what I could get elsewhere	1	2	3	4
Communication				
I do not feel that I am fully informed about what the organization is setting out to do	1	2	3	4
I am told about the plans for my department/group	1	2	3	4
Teamwork and colleagues				
The members of my team work very effectively together	1	2	3	4
I get on well with my colleagues	1	2	3	4

APPENDIX 2
Survey providers

AF Associates, **afassociates.co.uk**

Alexandria Surveys, **Alexandriasurvey.com**

BDI Surveys, **bdisurveys.com**

Direct Data Analysis, **direct-data-analysis.co.uk**

Electoral Reform Services, **electoralreform.co.uk**

Fargus Consulting Partnership, **fargus.co.uk**

Gallup Inc, **gallup.com**

Ipsos MORI, **ipsos-mori.com**

ORC International, **orc.co.uk**

People in Business, **pib.co.uk**

TNS, **tnsglobal.com**

ABOUT THE AUTHORS

Michael Armstrong is Managing Partner of e-reward. He spent 25 years as an HR practitioner including 12 years as HR director of a publishing company. He headed up the HR consultancy of Coopers and Lybrand (now PLC) for 10 years and is a former chief examiner of the Chartered Institute of Personnel and Development. He is the author of a suite of several best-selling HR books.

Stephen Taylor is a senior lecturer in Human Resource Management at the University of Exeter Business School and a chief examiner for the CIPD. Before his academic career he worked in a variety of management roles in the hotel industry and in the NHS. He is also a widely published author.

AUTHOR INDEX

SUBJECT INDEX

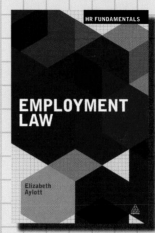